Philosophical Problems

Philosophical Problems
An Annotated Anthology

Laurence BonJour
University of Washington

Ann Baker
University of Washington

PEARSON
Longman

New York   San Francisco   Boston
London   Toronto   Sydney   Tokyo   Singapore   Madrid
Mexico City   Munich   Paris   Cape Town   Hong Kong   Montreal

Publisher:	Priscilla McGeehon
Development Editor:	Marion B. Castellucci
Executive Marketing Manager:	Ann Stypuloski
Media and Supplements Editor:	Kristi Olson
Production Manager:	Denise Phillip
Project Coordination, Text Design, and Electronic Page Makeup:	WestWords, Inc.
Senior Designer/Manager:	Nancy Danahy
Cover Illustration/Photo:	© ImageBank/Getty Inc.
Senior Manufacturing Buyer:	Dennis J. Para
Printer and Binder:	Hamilton Printing
Cover Printer:	Coral Graphic Services

For permission to use copyrighted material, grateful acknowledgement is made to the copyright holders on pp. 873–876, which are hereby made part of this copyright page.

Library of Congress Cataloging-in-Publication Data

Philosophical problems : an annotated anthology / [edited by] Laurence BonJour, Ann Baker.
    p. cm.
 Includes bibliographical references.
 ISBN 0-321-23659-9 (pbk.)
 1. Philosophy. 2. Readers—Philosophy. 3. Philosophy—Authorship. I. BonJour, Laurence, 1943– II. Baker, Ann, 1953–
B72.P47 2004
100–dc22

                           2004016587

Please visit our website at http://www.ablongman.com

ISBN 0–321-23659-9

1 2 3 4 5 6 7 8 9 10—HT—07 06 05 04

For Jen and David

Contents

Preface   xi

(CHAPTER 1) **WHAT IS PHILOSOPHY?**   1

Ann Baker: *Philosophical Thinking*   3
Plato: *Euthyphro*   14
Plato: *Apology*   24
Bertrand Russell: *The Value of Philosophy*   35

(CHAPTER 2) **GOD AND FAITH**   41

Does God Exist?   43
The Cosmological Argument
St. Thomas Aquinas: *The Five Ways, from* Summa Theologica   43
Samuel Clarke: *The Cosmological Argument, from* A Demonstration of the Being and Attributes of God   47
David Hume: *Problems with the Cosmological Argument, from* Dialogues Concerning Natural Religion   51
The Argument from Design
William Paley: *The Argument from Design, from* Natural Theology   55
Stephen Jay Gould: *The Panda's Thumb*   65
David Hume: *Problems with the Argument from Design, from* Dialogues Concerning Natural Religion   69
Antony Flew: *Critique of the Global Argument from Design, from* God: A Critical Inquiry   86
The Ontological Argument
René Descartes: *The Ontological Argument*   90
Immanuel Kant: *The Impossibility of an Ontological Proof of the Existence of God*   93
An Argument Against the Existence of God: The Problem of Evil   97
Fyodor Dostoevsky: *Rebellion, from* The Brothers Karamozov   97
David Hume: *The Problem of Evil, from* Dialogues Concerning Natural Religion   103
J. L. Mackie: *Evil and Omnipotence*   114
John Hick: *The Problem of Evil, from* Philosophy of Religion   122
Must We Have Reasons to Believe in God?   127
Walter Kaufmann: *Pascal's Wager, from* Critique of Religion and Philosophy   127
W. K. Clifford: *The Ethics of Belief*   129
William James: *The Will to Believe*   134

(CHAPTER 3) KNOWLEDGE AND SKEPTICISM **145**

Do We Have Knowledge of the External World?   149
René Descartes: *From* Meditations on First Philosophy   *149*
John Locke: *From* An Essay Concerning Human Understanding   *174*
George Berkeley: *From* Three Dialogues Between Hylas and Philonous   *192*
Thomas Reid: *Direct Realism, from* Essays on the Intellectual
    Powers of Man   *222*
Laurence BonJour: *Knowledge of the External World, from* Epistemology:
    Classic Problems and Contemporary Responses   *239*
Are All Reasons Based on Experience?   258
Immanuel Kant: *Is All Knowledge Based on Experience or Is Some
    Knowledge A Priori?, from* The Critique of Pure Reason   *258*
A. J. Ayer: *The A Priori, from* Language, Truth and Logic   *267*
A. C. Ewing: *The "A Priori" and the Empirical, from* The Fundamental
    Questions of Philosophy   *275*
Is Induction Justified?   284
David Hume: *Skeptical Doubts Concerning the Operations of the
    Understanding, from* An Enquiry Concerning Human Understanding   *284*
Wesley Salmon: *The Problem of Induction, from* The Foundations of
    Scientific Inference   *291*

(CHAPTER 4) MINDS AND BODIES   **307**

Are Minds and Mental States Distinct from Bodies and Material States?   315
Keith Campbell: *How the Mind-Body Problem Arises   315*
John Foster: *A Defense of Dualism   327*
J. J. C. Smart: *Sensations and Brain Processes   334*
Are Mental States Analogous to the States of a Computer?   341
Jerry Fodor: *The Mind-Body Problem   341*
A. M. Turing: *Computing Machinery and Intelligence   354*
John R. Searle: *Is the Brain's Mind a Computer Program?   366*
Jerry Fodor: *Searle on What Only Brains Can Do   375*
John R. Searle: *Author's Response   379*
Can Materialism Account for Qualitative Consciousness?   381
Thomas Nagel: *What Is It Like to Be a Bat?   381*
Frank Jackson: *What Mary Didn't Know   391*
Laurence BonJour: *What Is It Like to Be a Human (Instead of a Bat)?   396*
David Lewis: *Knowing What It's Like   405*
David J. Chalmers: *The Puzzle of Conscious Experience   407*
What is Required for Personal Identity?   415
John Locke: *Personal Identity   415*
Thomas Reid: *Of Mr. Locke's Account of Personal Identity   423*
Bernard Williams: *The Self and the Future   426*
Derek Parfit: *Personal Identity   437*

CHAPTER 5 FREE WILL AND MORAL RESPONSIBILITY   453

Are Human Actions Genuinely Free?   453
Hard Determinism
Miles Corwin: *The Case of Robert Harris   456*
Robert Blatchford: *A Defense of Hard Determinism, from* Not Guilty: A Defense of the Bottom Dog   *460*
Compatibilism
David Hume: *Of Liberty and Necessity   472*
W. T. Stace: *A Compatibalist Account of Free Will, from* Religion and the Modern Mind   *481*
Paul Edwards: *Hard and Soft Determinism   487*
John Hospers: *What Means This Freedom?   492*
Libertarianism
Roderick M. Chisholm: *Responsibility and Avoidability   502*
C. A. Campbell: *In Defense of Free Will   504*
Robert Nozick: *Choice and Indeterminism, from* Philosophical Explanations   *512*
Is Freedom Required for Moral Responsibility?   519
Galen Strawson: *Free Will   519*
Susan Wolf: *Sanity and the Metaphysics of Responsiblility   529*

CHAPTER 6 MORALITY AND MORAL PROBLEMS   541

Is Morality Relative? Are We Motivated Only by Self-Interest?   546
James Rachels: *The Challenge of Cultural Relativism   546*
James Rachels: *Subjectivism in Ethics   554*
Plato: *Are We Better Off Behaving Morally or Immorally?   562*
Joel Feinberg: *Psychological Egoism   571*
What Is the Best Theory of Morality?   578
Utilitarianism: Morality Depends on Consequences
Jeremy Bentham: *From* An Introduction to Principles of Morals and Legislation   *578*
John Stuart Mill: *From* Utilitarianism   *587*
J. J. C. Smart: *Extreme and Restricted Utilitarianism   596*
Bernard Williams: *A Critique of Utilitarianism   603*
Deontological Views: Morality Depends on Duties and Rights
Immanuel Kant: *From* Foundations of the Metaphysics of Morals   *611*
Onora O'Neill: *The Moral Perplexities of Famine Relief   624*
David T. Ozar: *Rights: What They Are and Where They Come From   640*
Virtue Ethics: Morality Depends on Character Traits
Aristotle: *From* The Nichomachean Ethics   *655*
Rosalind Hursthouse: *Normative Virtue Ethics   674*
How Do General Moral Concepts Apply to Concrete Issues?   684
Judith Jarvis Thomson: *A Defense of Abortion   684*
Philippa Foot: *Euthanasia   696*

Thomas Nagel: *War and Massacre* *711*
Tom Regan: *The Case for Animal Rights* *725*

CHAPTER 7 THE LEGITIMACY OF GOVERNMENT AND THE NATURE OF JUSTICE 735

What Is the Justification for Government? **737**
Thomas Hobbes: *The Social Contract, from* Leviathan *737*
John Locke: *The Social Contract, from* Second Treatise of Government *749*
David Hume: *Of the Original Contract* *765*
What Is Social Justice? **772**
Robert Nozick: *The Entitlement Theory of Justice, from* Anarchy, State, and Utopia *772*
John Rawls: *Justice as Fairness, from* A Theory of Justice *782*
Robert Nozick: *A Critique of Rawls, from* Anarchy, State, and Utopia *796*
Thomas M. Scanlon: *Nozick on Rights, Liberty, and Property* *803*

CHAPTER 8 PHILOSOPHY AND THE GOOD LIFE 813

Robert Nozick: *The Experience Machine* *814*
Epictetus: *from the* Manual *817*
Thomas Nagel: *The Absurd* *825*
Susan Wolf: *Happiness and Meaning: Two Aspects of the Good Life* *834*

Appendix: Writing a Philosophical Essay 849
Glossary 857
Credits 873

Preface

This book grew out of our dissatisfaction and even frustration with the sorts of books that are typically available for a standard, topically organized introductory course in philosophy. As we will elaborate further below, we think that single-author textbooks give students too little exposure to original philosophical sources and also fail to adequately convey to students the inherently controversial, dialectical character of philosophy; while anthologies, even with the sorts of aids to understanding that are usually provided, are simply too difficult for many students to adequately comprehend. What we offer instead is still an anthology, but one that gives students far more help than traditional anthologies in understanding the reading selections and making sense of the overall structure of the philosophical issues being discussed.

THE MAIN CONCEPTION OF *PHILOSOPHICAL PROBLEMS:*
AN ANNOTATED ANTHOLOGY

What introductory students really need, we think, is not more help of the same kinds that have standardly been provided, but rather a fundamentally different kind of help. What they need most fundamentally is something like a road map to the specific reading selections and especially to their argumentative and dialectical *structure:* a reader's guide that will help them find their way through, seeing how the various points fit together, why a particular objection is appropriate in a particular place, when an author is expounding his own view and when he is replying to an imagined critic, and so on. We have tried to provide help of this sort: to some extent in the introductions to the chapters and to the individual readings, but the most crucial and novel element in the book is the detailed annotations that we have inserted into each text, together with the closely related discussion questions that follow. Our main thought in writing these annotations was to ask what sort of help or guidance a typical student would need at that specific point in the text: an explanation of a concept, a reference to an issue discussed elsewhere (either in that selection or another one), a critical question to think about, or perhaps just a clearer restatement of what the philosopher is doing at that point and why.

In addition, we have tried to edit the selections so as to bring out the main lines of arguments, excising material that, while interesting in itself, is in one way or another too tangential or remote or inaccessible for introductory students. Unlike some editors, we see no real virtue at the introductory level in presenting students with "complete" philosophical texts, when this means that the parts they can realistically be expected to understand are obscured by others that are, in one way or another, difficult to see the point of and not really worth explaining in the limited time available in an introductory course. We have also tried to choose and arrange the readings in a way that reflects as clearly as possible the ways in which the issues develop and the different authors can be seen as speaking to each other. (The most extreme example of this occurs in Chapter 2, where we have chosen to divide the material from Hume's *Dialogues Concerning Natural Religion* into three separate selections that correspond to the three main topics that Hume discusses, placing these in the corresponding subsections with other selections addressing those same topics, rather than expecting the student or the instructor to sort them out.)

Our ultimate goal is to enable students to think along *with* Plato, or Locke, or Searle, or whoever is assigned: engaging their ideas and arguing with them as they read, instead of just trying to passively absorb they know not what. The result, we believe, is an anthology with some of the virtues of a textbook, one that encourages students to grapple with original sources by giving them more specific help in doing so, and by highlighting the distinctively philosophical attitudes and habits of mind that are reflected in the readings and which they need to acquire for themselves. Rather than just presenting students with an outline of the philosophical dialectic in the way that both textbooks and anthology introductions standardly do, we attempt to show them how that dialectic is actually discernible in the readings.

In Chapter 1, the introductory piece entitled "Introduction to Philosophical Thinking" explains the pretty old-fashioned conception of philosophy that is reflected in the rest of the book. This conception is self-consciously critical and analytic, focusing on arguments, objections, distinctions, counter-examples, definitions, and so on. We believe that it is an accurate account of the best philosophical thinking, but also is especially good for an introduction to philosophy. In addition to outlining a way of thinking that makes good sense of the classical philosophical issues and introducing students to the intellectual skills that will help them understand what is going on in the reading selections, it also provides students with some concrete guidelines for their own positive contributions to the work of the course, whether they are thinking *actively* about the issues and ideas, discussing them in or outside of class, responding to exam questions, or writing an essay. The course objective is no longer merely to:

> learn philosophy (whatever *that* is),

but instead to:

> learn how to read, write, and discuss philosophical topics by evaluating arguments, responding to objections, and explicating the relations between different views, each of which purport to answer the philosophical question of the day.

FEATURES OF THE BOOK

- In Chapter 1 we start with **"Introduction to Philosophical Thinking,"** a general introduction elaborating a very traditional conception of philosophy, one that emphasizes basic strategies of argumentation. This essay introduces the students to the fundamental elements of philosophical thinking that will, if they work at it, become second nature to them.
- The **introduction to each chapter** describes the main issue or issues discussed in the chapter and provides an outline of the main dialectical structure reflected in the selections that follow. Since the student is not yet in a position to understand the issues in much detail, we have tried to keep these introductions fairly brief— though how much brevity is possible varies with the length and complexity of the chapter. Our expectation is that students will be able to derive an initial overview

from these introductions, but that they will often be able to understand them fully only *after* they have worked through the chapter—at which point they will constitute a useful summary.

- The core of the book is a fairly **standard collection of philosophical readings,** both historical and contemporary. These have been carefully chosen and edited in an attempt to focus on the main issues and lines of argument.

- The **introduction to each selection** briefly describes the author's background and explains what he or she is mainly doing in that selection. These introductions also anticipate particular issues or problems with which students might need advance help.

- The **annotations** that are embedded in each selection are primarily designed to aid the student in coming to see and appreciate the detailed structure of the reading itself: its arguments, its transitions, its nuances.

- Each selection is followed by a set of **discussion questions,** often very detailed, that are designed to stimulate the student to think further about various issues that grow out of that selection, including those that relate to other selections. (These often develop more fully questions or issues first raised in the annotations.)

- The appendix entitled **"Writing a Philosophical Essay"** is devoted to teaching students how to write very elementary philosophy papers, papers that reflect the habits of mind and the argumentative and dialectical structures they have been learning.

- The **glossary** at the end of the book provides further elaboration concerning terms and concepts explained elsewhere and also provides a useful summary of the main concepts and positions discussed in the book. Boldfacing in the text indicates items that are in the glossary (sometimes in variant grammatical forms).

In addition, an **Instructor's Manual** provides chapter overviews, questions for discussion, and additional resources. The **Companion Website** (http://www.ablongman.com/bonjour) includes a wealth of resources for students using *Philosophical Problems,* with unique philosophy tools, interactive practice test questions, and web links for each chapter.

MORE ABOUT THE MOTIVATION FOR THIS CONCEPTION

As already mentioned, the books that have been available up to now for a topically organized introductory philosophy course fall into two main classes. On the one hand, there are textbooks written by a single author (or, sometimes, by two or more authors working together). These have the virtue of presenting an account of the philosophical issues that is cohesive, deliberately oriented to introductory students, and couched in modern language and terminology. But they also have two glaring defects. First, a course that employs a textbook gives students little experience in working through and coming to grips with original philosophical sources, both historical and contemporary. Some items of this sort may be added as a kind of supplement, perhaps even included in the textbook itself. But the main focus is inevitably on the account of the issues and arguments offered by the textbook itself. Second, and even more importantly, a textbook tends for the most part to describe philosophical positions and arguments from the outside, at second hand, rather than actually participating in the to and fro of philosophical discussion. Thus students get little sense of the distinctive flavor of philosophical controversy or of the ways in which philosophers actually think and argue—little sense of the essentially *dialectical* character of philosophy. And a further consequence is that the students' opportunity to begin to participate in philosophical discussion and to develop philosophical habits of mind for themselves is severely limited because they aren't really exposed to examples of philosophical debate in the flesh: cases of real philosophers actually arguing with and criticizing each other.

The alternative is of course an anthology composed of a smorgasbord of selections from actual philosophical works, both historical and contemporary, together with editorial introductions and perhaps aids such as study questions or a glossary. Here students are exposed to original philosophical sources with a vengeance, and the argumentative, dialectical character of philosophy is plainly represented—for those who are able to discern it. But just there lies the problem. Actual philosophical writing is notoriously very difficult for introductory students. It is aimed at other philosophers rather than at novices, employs technical terminology that can be very thorny, and often comes from earlier periods in which language and style were very different. Thus many or even most of the selections in a standard anthology are pieces that an introductory student simply cannot read in a useful way without very substantial help. Some help is usually provided in the anthology itself, but it is almost always inadequate for many if not most students. General introductions to philosophical issues and method and also to specific sets of readings are fine as far as they go, but they are not enough, in our experience, to enable typical students to actually read and understand representative pieces of philosophical writing in a way that puts them in a position to think about and evaluate them.

There are two sides to this problem. First, students need more help with the specific details of a selection, most importantly with its structure. They need to be able to see how the specific issues and arguments that the selection discusses connect to each other and to the more general issue that is its ultimate concern. Too often students who at least roughly understand the main point that a selection is supposed to be making are entirely unable to see why *this* specific point is made in *this* specific place or why *this* other specific point immediately follows. The structural signposts that the author provides are often either too subtle or couched in ways that the student is unable to grasp. (A collateral problem is that many philosophical writings, especially those that are largely unedited, include many digressions of various sorts that an introductory student cannot hope to understand, including references to unfamiliar works or authors.) Second, most students need specific help in understanding the *point* of much philosophical discussion. There are certain ways of thinking that philosophers take for granted, habits of mind that are not at all obvious to most first-year students. In particular, the critical stance that most philosophers take even to their own ideas, the constant search for arguments, objections, and responses, is unfamiliar to most students and quite unnatural for many of them.

When these two problems are combined, the result of reading philosophical texts is too often bafflement and frustration, rather than enlightenment. One of the most common complaints we've heard is: "I do all the reading, but I have no idea what I'm looking for." Students can sometimes get intimidated by philosophy, thinking that it is too "deep" or profound, and such fears are confirmed when the readings seem opaque, when the student can't see the intellectual point of what the different authors are saying or how they are engaging each other. Other students become convinced that philosophy is trivial or irrelevant, and again such a view often has the same source as the previous view: the initial opacity of the reading, an opacity which is the direct result of the difficulty of the material, together with the student's lack of understanding of argumentative and dialectical structure and inexperience with the habits of mind typical of philosophers. While most students will continue to try to do the assignments, few will continue to read in a serious, reflective, thoughtful way under such conditions; instead the perceived fruitlessness of their efforts will lead to a kind of passive, disengaged approach to the reading that is ultimately futile.

A good instructor can of course help to solve these problems. But even the best instructor will have great difficulty explaining a piece of philosophical writing to students who have been unable to read it well enough on their own to be able to grasp the specific points and issues that the instructor refers to. What is often really needed is something like this: the instructor first carefully introduces a given selection, then has the students read it, then talks about it some more, then has them read it again, and finally discusses it in a way that presupposes that they have understood it relatively fully. But there is simply not enough time in an introductory course, at least not one that covers any reasonable amount of ground, to do something like this very often, even though anything less is unlikely to succeed for many of the students. Moreover, and this is really the main point, the instructor's job should not be this difficult because the anthology itself should give the students more help. This is what we have tried to do.

THE VALUE OF STUDYING PHILOSOPHY

Our conviction is that teaching students how to do philosophy in the way encouraged by this book can also help them to develop more general abilities. Even the student who fails to be engaged by the content of philosophy will come away with some powerful, extremely valuable skills: broad-gauged capacities for critical, creative, and reflective thinking. These skills will provide an excellent basis from which a student can go on to think critically about any number of topics—including even this approach to philosophy itself.

So our book is based on the assumption that there are basic modes of philosophical thinking, philosophical habits of mind, that these habits can be taught, but, as with all habits, not by just telling the students what they are. These habits of mind need to be exercised on philosophical texts. Our book provides the readings and the accompanying pedagogical tools on which students can exercise and thus acquire these philosophical habits of mind.

When we each started teaching philosophy as enthusiastic graduate students long ago, we were each quite sure that all that had to be done was to find a way to open a student's eyes to philosophy. Once that was done, any student would see that philosophy is deeply fascinating. While we no longer believe that every student will find philosophy fascinating (we have read too many student evaluations to continue to believe that), we do still believe that any student can reap important benefits from taking an introductory philosophy course. According to reports from many students, studying philosophy has taught them that the most important learning does *not* consist solely in memorizing lots of facts, that instead the ability to think clearly with an appreciation for subtlety and nuance is central to real intellectual accomplishment, and that the skill to navigate through areas of gray, instead of insisting that all disputes must be categorized in clear black and white terms, has made philosophy one of the most valuable and relevant subjects of their whole college career—for, as they recognize, the very most important decisions one makes in life often require exactly that kind of subtlety of thought.

ACKNOWLEDGMENTS

With respect to the conception of the book, we owe the greatest debt of gratitude to our many students over the years: at the University of Texas at Austin, the State University of New York at Stony Brook, Illinois Wesleyan University, and the University of Washington. Without their sometimes eager, often puzzled, but usually conscientious efforts to grapple seriously with the contents of various anthologies, we would never have been motivated to think of this alternative approach. We are grateful to our colleagues in the philosophy department at the University of Washington, especially Ken Clatterbaugh, David Keyt, Charles Marks, Angela Smith, and Bill Talbott, for their support, advice, and feedback during the process of preparing this book (and for earlier input on a distant ancestor of it).

With respect to both the development and refinement of the conception and the actual work of creating the book, we owe a tremendous debt of gratitude to Marion Castellucci, our developmental editor: she courageously and tirelessly read through all the reading selections and their associated annotations and discussion questions—in addition to the introductions, glossary, appendix, and preface—and gave us indispensable feedback on every aspect of the book, together with valuable and much appreciated moral support along the way. Without her input, the book would have been very different, if indeed it would have been completed at all. Priscilla McGeehon, our publisher at Longman, also provided valuable help and encouragement: through her unwavering and enthusiastic confidence in the project, through her firm but flexible handling of deadlines, and by providing material support of many kinds.

In addition, we would like to thank all of those who reviewed the project and the manuscript at various stages and offered many helpful comments and suggestions (not all of which we were able to take advantage of in this edition): David Benfield, Montclair State University; Andrei A. Buckareff, University of Rochester; Todd Buras, Baylor University; Susanne D. Claxton, Oklahoma State University; Matti Eklund, University of Colorado at Boulder; Todd S. Ganson, Oberlin College; Philip Goldstein, University of Delaware; Richard V. Greene, Weber State University; Peter Hutcheson, Texas State University; Jason Kawall, University of Tennessee at Chattanooga; Glenn Kuehn, Mississippi State University; David Lefkowitz, University of Maryland; Dorothea Lotter, Wake Forest University; Marc Moffett, University of Wyoming; Hilde L. Nelson, Michigan State University; Walter Ott, East Tennessee State University; William Richards, University of Dayton; Teresa J. Robertson, University of Kansas; Peter Ross, California State Polytechnic University-Pomona; Samuel Ruhmkorff, Simon's Rock College; Edward L. Schoen, Western Kentucky University; Renée Smith, Coastal Carolina University; John Uglietta, Grand Valley State University; David Weberman, Georgia State University; Chase B. Wrenn, University of Alabama; David J. Yount, Mesa Community College; and John Zeis, Canisius College.

Laurence BonJour
Ann Baker

CHAPTER 1

What Is Philosophy?

There are many different views about the nature of philosophy, but probably no very simple definition of the subject. This reflects the fact that the nature of philosophy is itself an important subject of philosophical disagreement, one for which there is a long history of competing views. Our view, which many share, is that in the end a person can obtain a really clear idea of what philosophy is only by actually studying the subject in some detail.

Fortunately, however, there are some modest points that are widely enough agreed upon to provide a reasonable starting point. First, the word "philosophy" literally means the love of wisdom, and from the beginning of its long history, philosophers have asked and tried to answer very tough questions about the issues that seemed most important to humankind, thereby searching for wisdom.

Second, since knowledge seems important, even if not sufficient for wisdom, one might ask what kind of *knowledge* the study of philosophy yields. A traditional answer is that philosophers discover the essential nature of various abstract things: truth, knowledge, thought, freedom, duty, justice, beauty, and even reality itself. A more contemporary and perhaps more modest version of this claim is that philosophers discover the content or correct analysis of the concepts we use when thinking about truth, knowledge, etc.—or perhaps the meanings of the corresponding words.

Third, everyone agrees that many areas of investigation that started as parts of philosophy have since turned into branches of science. This happens roughly when the issues involved become clearly enough defined to make it possible to investigate them scientifically through empirical observation and empirically based theorizing. Thus while virtually every sort of knowledge was part of philosophy for the ancient Greek philosopher Aristotle, physics and biology have been distinct from philosophy for a long time, with other areas following along this path more recently. (For example, psychology was still viewed as part of philosophy until the late nineteenth century.) This suggests that philosophy can be

1

viewed as the home of those issues that people have not yet learned to investigate scientifically. This includes some issues where it is hard to imagine this ever happening because they are so general, so difficult, and possibly so fundamental.

Fourth, almost all philosophers agree that the history of philosophy is important to the very nature of philosophy and to ongoing philosophical investigation in a way that the histories of other disciplines are not equally important to them. This is reflected in the rather large proportion of historical selections in the present book. But philosophers also disagree about how important history of philosophy is—and also about *why* it is important.

An account of philosophy offered by the twentieth-century American philosopher Wilfrid Sellars may help to summarize some of the foregoing ideas and also to give a bit more of the flavor of the subject:

> The aim of philosophy, abstractly formulated, is to understand how things in the broadest possible sense of the term hang together in the broadest possible sense of the term. Under 'things in the broadest possible sense' I include such radically different items as not only 'cabbages and kings', but numbers and duties, possibilities and finger snaps, aesthetic experience and death. To achieve success in philosophy would be, to use a contemporary turn of phrase, to 'know one's way around' with respect to all these things, not in that unreflective way in which the centipede of the story knew its way around before it faced the question, 'how do I walk?', but in that reflective way which means that no intellectual holds are barred.[1]

As this suggests, nothing is really beyond the purview of philosophy. Putting the point only slightly differently, philosophy seeks to understand in a fully reflective way how everything relates to and connects with and differs from everything else.

This is a grandiose conception, to say the least, and there are people who think that the only way to learn philosophy is just to start reading some philosophical texts, trying to figure out what is going on and what the point is, without any additional help or guidance. This view is reflected in an old instructor's adage: throw them in and see who can swim! On the other hand, some people think that an initial orientation to philosophy, even if necessarily one that is only approximate and partial, can be very helpful. Since we believe the latter view is right, we start this chapter with an essay by Ann Baker about the nature of philosophy and especially about the elements of philosophical thinking.

One of the central philosophical activities, reflected in the project of understanding the essential nature of things (or concepts) is *clarification*. Philosophers are constantly asking questions about what various kinds of things really amount to (or what the words in question really mean). Many of Plato's dialogues take the form of asking questions of this sort, especially ones focused on moral or evaluative notions: "what is courage?", "what is justice?", "what is knowledge?", etc. In his dialogue *Euthyphro,* Plato asks the question: "What is piety?", which was approximately the same question for the Greeks as "what is moral rightness?". We learn in the *Euthyphro* that Socrates has been charged with corrupting the youth of Athens; and in Plato's *Apology,* we have an account of his trial (in which he was convicted and condemned to death), thus becoming in effect a martyr for philosophy. In the *Apology,* in explaining why he cannot avoid his punishment by giving up philosophical inquiry, Socrates makes the famous claim that the unexamined life is not worth living.

---

[1]Wilfrid Sellars, "Philosophy and the Scientific Image of Man," reprinted in his *Science, Perception and Reality* (London: Routledge & Kegan Paul, 1963), p. 1.

While many people believe that philosophy is obviously important and valuable, there are those who dismiss philosophical thinking as irrelevant, nit-picking, hair-splitting mental play. Bertrand Russell argues that philosophy is valuable even if it turns out to yield little or no secure knowledge. Thus, more than 2000 years after Plato wrote the *Euthyphro* and the *Apology,* Russell defended the study and practice of philosophy as essential to the best sort of life.

Ann Baker

Ann Baker (1953–) teaches philosophy at the University of Washington in Seattle, and is one of the coeditors of this book. In this selection, she explains what philosophy is, introduces its main branches or subareas, and explains the basic elements of philosophical thinking.

Introduction to Philosophical Thinking

So you have decided to study philosophy. You may have a fairly clear idea of what studying philosophy involves, or you may have only a vague idea, or even no idea at all.①

> ① What do you think philosophy is? Have you read anything that you would call philosophical? Have you had any discussions that you would regard as philosophical? Is there anyone in your family who is especially philosophical?

Since there are some interestingly different conceptions of philosophy (philosophers philosophize even about philosophy!) and since we need a single conception of philosophy to guide our work, we will begin our study of philosophy by first developing a fairly specific conception of philosophy. While we will rely on this conception of philosophy throughout the book, it is your responsibility (as a philosopher) to think carefully about it and have an opinion about its merits by the time you have finished the course. By then you may think that there should be changes or qualifications, small or even large, in the conception of philosophy that we have been using.

Let's start building our conception of philosophy by distinguishing between the distinctive content involved in the discipline of philosophy and the distinctive method of philosophical thinking. The content concerns (obviously) what philosophers think about. For example, philosophers typically think about questions like these: What is knowledge? What is truth? Does God exist? What are minds? What is consciousness? Are we genuinely free? Does being morally responsible require being free? Are we, by our very natures, selfish? Is there a genuine difference between right and wrong or good and evil? What is justice? And even, as we have already seen, what is philosophy? In attempting to answer these questions, philosophers think about **claims** (specific, focused assertions that are put forth as being true or false), and also about more comprehensive views or positions (composed of many related claims) that purport to answer questions like the ones listed above.

To generalize from these examples, it would be reasonable to say that the content of philosophy concerns:

1. the fundamental nature of reality—the nature of space and time, of properties and universals, and especially but obviously not exclusively the part of reality that consists of **persons** (the branch of philosophy called **metaphysics**);

2. the fundamental nature of the cognitive relations between persons and other parts of reality—the relations of thinking about, knowing, and so on, (the branch of philosophy called **epistemology**); and

3. the fundamental nature of values, especially values pertaining to ethical or social relations between persons and between persons and other parts of reality, such as non-human animals, the environment, and so on (the branch of philosophy called **axiology,** which includes the more specific fields of *ethics, political philosophy,* and *aesthetics*).②

---

② Place each of the questions in the previous paragraph into one of these three general categories.

We will forego for now any further explanation of the *content* of philosophy, since that is the main job of the rest of the book. But there are some implicit assumptions made by philosophers, and the clarification of these will require an explanation of the *method* of philosophical thinking.

The method of philosophical thinking requires a set of skills and some intellectual habits, what we call distinctively philosophical habits of mind. We will explain some of these skills and habits in this introductory essay, but the full appreciation of them requires exercising them on the philosophical views and arguments developed in the rest of the book. Two of the most basic skills involved in philosophical thinking are clarifying and justifying claims: as philosophers we are in the business of doing two main kinds of things, clarifying and justifying, in relation to a specific kind of object, a claim. What do we mean by clarifying and justifying claims? Let's break this phrase down.

First, what is a claim? As we have already seen briefly above, a claim is an assertion, something that is said with the intention of saying something that is either true or false. Here are some examples: there are cherry trees in the quad; Chicago is west of Washington, D.C.; 7 + 5 = 12; grass is red; no dog has ever been lost; politicians are uniformly honest. Notice that claims can be false as well as true. Not everything that you say is a claim, since your intention is not always to state truths. For example, a question is not a claim, nor is an exclamation or a command.

Second, what is meant by clarification? When a philosopher *clarifies* a claim, he or she explains or spells out in detail the meaning of the claim. Clarification is often valuable or even urgently required, because the meaning of a claim as it is initially formulated can be seriously unclear in ways that make it difficult to discuss or evaluate it. Consider, for example, the claim that God is love. Presumably, the person who says that God is love intends to say something that is true, but some people find that claim very confusing. Does it mean merely that God is a loving person? No—it seems intended to mean something much more significant than that. But what? Since love is a kind of emotion, the literal meaning of the claim doesn't make clear sense (since God is surely not any kind of emotion). So perhaps the claim is metaphorical instead of literal. It is much easier to clarify literal claims than it is to clarify metaphorical claims. But some important clarifying work is done even by saying that the claim is metaphorical.

Obviously, some claims need more clarification than others. Consider the following claims:

(a) Money can't buy happiness.
(b) God is love.
(c) No bachelor is happy.
(d) If a person is a mother, then that person is female.
(e) Collies are dogs.
(f) Studying philosophy is valuable.

These claims are not all equally clear. Which claim most clearly needs clarification? Claims (a) and (b) are both metaphorical, but one can more easily imagine explaining the metaphorical meaning of (a). Of course you cannot literally buy happiness, since it doesn't show up in any of the stores you go to. But that is not the real point of the claim. Suppose, for example, that you were advising your younger sister against making what seemed to you to be a very bad marriage. The only good thing you can see about her prospective husband is that he is very wealthy. It would be very natural to say to her that money can't buy happiness, meaning that one can have lots of money and still be very unhappy. You would, of course, be assuming that she wants to be happy.

You can clarify a claim without thereby giving any reason to think that the claim is true. Think of how you might clarify claim (c), that no bachelor is happy. This is surely a false claim, but someone might still wonder about "happy." Before you think very hard about it, you might think that you surely understand what happiness is. But as soon as you try to clearly define it, all kinds of problems come up (see

Chapters 6 and 8). Clarification sometimes requires explaining only one of the terms in the claim (as with (c)), while at other times it requires explaining the meaning of several of the terms (as with (f)). Sometimes a claim just needs to be made more precise. For example, someone might wonder if all collies are dogs, or just most collies are dogs, or only some collies are dogs. How much clarification a claim really needs might depend on the context.

Third, what is meant by **justification?** When philosophers justify a claim, they give reasons to believe the claim, and what better reason is there to believe a claim than a reason to think that it is true? Our conception of philosophy assumes that a reason to think that a claim is true is a good reason to believe it. Moreover, such a reason seems at first glance to be the *only* kind of good reason to believe a claim—since to accept the claim is after all to accept it *as true.* In other words, if you don't have a reason to think that a claim is true, then you apparently have no reason at all to believe the claim. (Whether there might be some acceptable basis for believing a claim other than a reason to think that it is true is a question raised explicitly in Chapter 2.)

Let's suppose for the rest of this discussion that a reason for a claim will always be a reason for the truth of the claim. Another supposition that we'll make in explaining what is meant by justification is that the reasons advanced for the truth of a claim will themselves always be claims, assertions made in the attempt to say something true. And the assumption in treating these claims as reasons is that the truth of the reasons provides evidence or warrant of some sort for the truth of the claim in question (the claim that we are trying to justify).

To put forth other claims in support of a claim you are defending is to give an **argument.** Thus, according to our account of justification, when a philosopher justifies a claim, he or she usually gives an argument. In philosophy, an argument is not a disagreement or a fight. According to the standard philosophical definition, an argument is a set of claims, one of which is the conclusion and the others of which are **premises** that are offered to support the conclusion: premises that are alleged by the person putting forth the argument to make it very likely or even guarantee that the conclusion is true. One of the first things you will learn when using the skills that are important to the philosophical

method is to become very sensitive to the difference between a claim being asserted by a philosopher and the premises or reasons that he or she offers in support of that claim, which is the conclusion of an argument (one of the distinctively philosophical habits of mind).

One question that can be asked about the premises of an argument is whether they are true—or at least whether it is reasonable to think they are true. But while the question of whether the premises are true is crucial to the strength of the argument, that shouldn't be the first question you ask when making an argument. Before you worry about whether the claims offered as reasons are true, you should ask yourself whether, *if true,* they would genuinely support the claim. Reasons can support a claim more or less successfully, and when you ask how good the reasons offered for the claim are (assuming that they are true), you are asking about the strength of the relation of support, the evidential relation, between the premises and the conclusion. So the core idea of a philosophical argument is the idea of giving reasons for the truth of a claim: premises offered for the purpose of showing that the conclusion is true.

Some arguments are valid **deductive arguments:** arguments whose premises, if true, *guarantee* the truth of the conclusion. Consider the following argument for the claim that Mary took the car: either John took the car or Mary took the car, and I know that John didn't take the car, so Mary must have taken it. You can assess the strength of the relation of support of this argument without knowing John or Mary or knowing anything about the car. You just ask yourself whether the premises, if true, do support the conclusion. They do. If the premises of this argument are true, then the conclusion must be true.

But some arguments that are intended as deductive are **invalid:** it is possible for the premises to be true while the conclusion is false. Consider the following argument for the claim that Mary took the car: if Mary took the car, then John didn't take it; and I know that John didn't take it; so Mary must have taken it. Suppose that all of the premises are true. Does the truth of those premises guarantee (or even support at all) the truth of the conclusion? No, because this argument commits the *fallacy of affirming the consequent* (a fallacy is a mistake in reasoning). It will be useful to digress just a bit to see clearly what this fallacy is, and why it is a mistake to reason this way.

As you will see, many philosophical arguments include **conditional statements:** statements of the form if *A,* then *B.* For example, if *Mary took the car,* then *John didn't take it.* The first part of the conditional, the *A* part, is called the **antecedent,** and the second part, the *B* part, is called the **consequent.** (A conditional statement can be confusing at first, before one thinks carefully about what exactly it is saying. Consider the claim that if George Washington was an octopus, then George Washington had eight legs. Is that claim true or false? Some students initially say that the claim is false, but once they look again, they see clearly that the claim is true.) The truth of a conditional statement does *not* require the truth of the antecedent (the claim that Mary took the car), because the conditional is claiming only that *if* Mary took the car, then John didn't take it. The *truth* of the conditional requires only that if the antecedent is true, then the consequent must be true (it cannot be false); in other words, if the consequent is false, then the antecedent must be false for the whole conditional statement to be true. Whereas if Mary and John both took the car, (in which case the antecedent is true and the consequent is false) then the conditional statement, *if* Mary took the car, then John didn't, is false. So if a conditional statement is true, and the antecedent is true, then you know that the consequent must also be true; and if a conditional statement is true and the consequent is false, then you know that the antecedent must also be false. But *nothing* follows from the truth of a conditional and the truth of the consequent, and thus arguments that *claim* to draw a conclusion about the truth of the antecedent on the basis of the truth of the conditional and the truth of the consequent are making the mistake in reasoning called the fallacy of affirming the consequent.③

③ There is another fallacy called *denying the antecedent.* You should be able to figure out what that mistake is and why it is a mistake, given this line of argument explaining the fallacy of affirming the consequent.

Since these premises don't actually support the conclusion at all, you might be tempted to say that this is no argument at all. But it doesn't seem right to say flatly that this isn't an argument: it seems clearer to say that it is a *bad* argument, and better still to say exactly what is bad about it. (When faced with an invalid argument, you need not worry about whether its premises are true, since even if they are, they don't provide even minimal support for the conclusion.)

There are other kinds of arguments whose premises provide good but not conclusive grounds for the truth of the conclusion: arguments that offer genuine support for their conclusions but where it is still possible, though unlikely, that the conclusion is false even though the premises are true. The arguments most standardly referred to as **inductive arguments** (or, more explicitly, enumerative inductive arguments) are like this, and many scientific arguments are of this kind. When, for example, someone reasons that all swans are white on the basis of many different observations of white swans, he or she is giving a very simple example of an inductive argument. You cannot reasonably conclude that all swans are white on the basis of one observation of a white swan, or even two or twenty, but if there are enough observations in sufficiently varied locations and circumstances, then you can reasonably conclude that *all* swans (and not just the ones you've observed so far) are white. When you reason that the sun will rise tomorrow on the basis of the claim that it has risen every morning so far for thousands of years, you are giving an inductive argument. Philosophers don't call good inductive arguments valid, because the definition of validity is that it is impossible for the conclusion to be false while the premises are true. Inductive arguments, by definition, have conclusions which might be false even though the premises are true. But the better the inductive argument, the more unlikely or improbable it is that the conclusion is false while the premises are true. Good inductive arguments, ones where the evidential or support relation between the premises and the conclusion is compelling, are usually described as strong. In such an argument, the truth of the premises provides a good reason to think that the conclusion is true.

A different kind of argument whose premises provide good but not conclusive reasons for the truth of its conclusion is what is referred to as an **explanatory argument** (also called an *inference to the best explanation* or an **abductive argument**—sometimes the term "induction" is used more broadly so as to also include arguments of this sort). The idea of an explanatory argument is that there is an alleged fact of some sort to be explained, other considerations that are relevant to the explanation of this fact, and some explanation that is claimed to be the best one in light of those considerations. Thus the premises of such an argument include both a statement of the alleged fact to be explained and statements of these other relevant considerations, and the conclusion is a statement of the explanation alleged to be best. And such an argument will be *strong* (never valid) if the explanation offered really is the best one, assuming that the fact in question really is a fact and the other supposedly relevant considerations are also true.

Here is a simple example. Suppose that the police call you at work to tell you that your car has been in an accident, and that the driver of the car left the scene. The question is how to explain the fact that your car has been in an accident (rather than still parked in the driveway where it was when you left to take the bus to work this morning). The following further considerations seem relevant: that only you and your sister Mary ever drive the car, even though she has recently been forbidden by you to drive it because of the many speeding tickets she has received; that there is only one key to this car (kept hanging on a hook by the back door); that Mary is the only person (other than you) with easy access to this key; and that the police found the car with the key still in it. Thus, it might be claimed, the most likely explanation of the fact that your car was in the accident, instead of still sitting in the driveway where you thought it was, is that Mary drove it (in spite of being forbidden to do so). Obviously you'll have even better evidence once you talk to her or find out from eyewitness reports what the driver of the car looked like, but don't you right now have a pretty good reason for the conclusion that Mary took the car? Your reason is not conclusive—the conclusion is not guaranteed to be true—because there are other possible explanations of the fact that your car is at the scene of an accident that might turn out to be better ones after all (maybe someone broke into your house, took the key, and drove the car away). We use explanatory arguments of this sort in everyday life, and scientists use explanatory arguments to draw conclusions about laws and theoretical entities. Such arguments also often play an important role in philosophical discussions.

Summing up, according to the standard definition of an argument that we started with, if premises are offered for the purpose of supporting the truth of a conclusion, then the set of claims consisting of those premises and the conclusion constitute an argument. The argument is **deductive** if the truth of the premises

is intended to guarantee the truth of the conclusion, and **inductive** or explanatory if the truth of the premises is merely intended to make the truth of the conclusion very likely or probable, but not guaranteed. A deductive argument whose premises are related to its conclusion in the right way to accomplish its purpose is valid, while good inductive or explanatory arguments can only be strong. A further issue about any argument is whether the premises themselves are true.4️⃣

4️⃣ You should now be able to state clearly the difference between an inductive and a deductive argument. Can you?

AN ILLUSTRATION OF THE METHOD OF PHILOSOPHY

We have just thought through an initial explanation of two of the important skills involved in the method of philosophy: clarification and justification;5️⃣ let's now consider an illustration of those skills. Let's clarify and justify the claim that studying philosophy is valuable.

5️⃣ You should be able to clearly distinguish between clarifying and justifying a claim. Can you?

Clarification: Defining What We Mean

Let's first clarify the claim that studying philosophy is valuable. You reasonably wonder about the meaning of both parts of the claim: what is meant by "studying philosophy" and what is meant by "valuable"? Suppose that someone read Bertrand Russell's book *The Problems of Philosophy* one night—is that enough to have "studied philosophy"? Not according to what we mean when we make the claim. You have to do more than read one philosophy book to have studied philosophy. It takes more than one night to study philosophy. But there is no exact amount of study that can be said to be the precise meaning of "studying philosophy." Sometimes what is needed to make an issue clear enough to be reasonably discussed is to replace the original claim with one that is clear and more precise, while still saying approximately the same thing. Thus, somewhat arbitrarily, we will take "studying philosophy" to mean taking and passing at least four philosophy classes or doing something reasonably similar. (You could probably do the equivalent of taking and passing four philosophy courses on your own, if you were sufficiently motivated and had some resources for checking your understanding.)

Now what do we mean by the second part of the claim, "valuable"? All we mean by "valuable" here is that it is good for you, that you will be significantly better off for having done it. You might doubt that our claim is true, but you now have a pretty good sense of what we mean by it. We have clarified (though perhaps not yet enough) our claim that studying philosophy is valuable.

We might make one more clarification. Someone might wonder whether the claim is that studying philosophy is *always* valuable no matter who does it or just that it is *usually* valuable. For example, think about the following claims that have the form *doing A is B:*

Running a marathon is demanding.
Giving birth is done by females.
Watching TV is fun.
Regular exercise is important.
Getting a college degree is worthwhile.

The context, together sometimes with the content of the claim, usually determines whether someone who asserts one of these claims means "always" or "most of the time"—though this may sometimes be unclear. What we mean when we say that studying philosophy is valuable is that it is *always* valuable. So we now have a pretty good restatement of the original claim resulting from this initial effort at clarification: our claim that studying philosophy is valuable means that anyone who does the equivalent of taking and passing at least four philosophy courses will benefit significantly from it. One of the distinctively philosophical habits of mind is that of noticing when claims are more or less clear.

Justification: Giving an Argument

Now let's move from clarification to justification, and remember that philosophical justification typically takes the form of an argument. Here is an argument for the claim we have just clarified:

Studying philosophy always makes you think more
   clearly.
Thinking more clearly is valuable.
Therefore, studying philosophy is (always) valuable.

What makes this an argument? It is a set of claims, one of which is the conclusion and the others of which are premises that are put forward to support the conclusion. (When you give an argument for a claim, the claim is the conclusion of the argument.) So the first two sentences are the premises and the third sentence is the conclusion. Just pretend for a moment that the premises are true. If they are true, does the conclusion follow? In other words, does the truth of the premises make the conclusion likely to be true? For this argument, as for many other arguments, you need to think about the premises and the conclusion in order to answer that question (the answer to that question is not the result of a clear mechanical test). As you acquire the intellectual habit of assessing arguments, you will get better and better at distinguishing the good ones from the bad ones. What you should do is suppose that the premises are true and then try to imagine whether it would be possible for the conclusion to be false, even given the truth of the premises. We suggest that the truth of the premises (if they are true) provides a very good reason to think that the conclusion is true, and that this argument therefore provides a good example of the relationship of *providing a good reason,* which is the core element of an argument.

In the argument above, if the premises are true, then the conclusion is very likely to be true. But we obviously can't just assume that the premises are true. And since the conclusion of the argument has been justified only if the premises are true, our job of justifying the original claim is not finished until we have at least defended the premises (given reasons to think that the premises are true). Furthermore, we should also consider and respond to the most obvious objections, if there are any.

Giving Reasons for the Truth of the Premises

Let's begin with the first premise: studying philosophy always makes you think more clearly. In anticipation, think about what will be involved in studying philosophy: you will read many different philosophical texts from many different periods of history, learning what different philosophers have said about many different topics. Moreover, since the authors are philosophers, they will typically be arguing for their views, so you need to understand and critically evaluate those views and those arguments, in an attempt to figure out what you think about the philosophical topic at issue. In addition, since philosophers have to discuss many other sorts of things in explaining and clarifying their views, presenting arguments, and considering objections to other views (and, as we will see, even to their own), a philosophical work is usually quite complicated, with all of these parts needing to be clearly sorted out. Studying philosophy involves carefully doing all these things.

What then is thinking clearly? Thinking clearly involves being logical. Thinking clearly obviously involves being able to clarify various ideas and views that you encounter. But it also involves considering and sometimes discovering reasons for those views, together with being able to successfully evaluate when those reasons are good ones and when they aren't. One clear-thinking skill is the ability to juggle complicated combinations of ideas, keeping track of the different relations between the ideas, and like any skill, it takes time and practice to become good at it. You obviously need to think clearly in order even to understand philosophers, and you surely need to be able to think clearly in order to evaluate philosophical views. (When you evaluate a view, you decide whether it is a good view (likely to be true) or a bad view (likely to be false), and as a philosopher, you must have reasons for making that evaluation.) Therefore, someone who has studied philosophy (given how we have clarified that idea) has either learned to think really clearly for the first time, or else already knew how to think clearly to some extent but has now had lots of additional practice at it, and so presumably thinks even more clearly. There is a defense of the first premise: a reason to think that the first premise is true.

Now consider a defense for the second premise, that thinking more clearly is valuable. Surely we can all agree that doing something that helps you get what you want is valuable, that you benefit significantly from doing something that enhances your ability to get what you want (unless, of course, what you want is not good for you). We contend that clear thinking does that. Suppose that two people, call them Joe and Doug, each want to finish college as efficiently as possible, and suppose further that Joe thinks much more clearly than Doug. Suppose that Doug never quite thinks hard enough to keep the requirements straight or even realize that some of the requirements exist. Suppose that when an advisor suggests to Doug that he take a particular class, Doug never asks why or how that class will fit into his overall program. Doug probably doesn't even have a clear plan, but he does have the desire to finish college as efficiently as possible. Suppose that Joe is constantly honing his thinking skills: he al-

ways asks the advisor to clarify her advice, always asks why this is a good class to take. It is reasonable to assert that because of Joe's ability to think more clearly than Doug, Joe is more likely to realize his goal than Doug is—and this is not even the best example, is it? You don't have to think really clearly to realize the goal of finishing college as efficiently as possible. Imagine how clearly you have to think to be a responsible citizen or a loving friend or a terrific parent. Being able to distinguish between believing something on the basis of wishful thinking as opposed to believing something on the basis of good evidence might make the difference between doing a good job and an inadequate job in many areas of human relations. So thinking clearly is valuable because it helps you get what you want, whether you want to be a law clerk, a good parent, or a couch potato.

At this point, we have given reasons to think that both premises are true, and it is clear that if the premises are true, then the conclusion is likely to be true. So we have presented and defended an argument, but does that suffice to justify the claim? It surely is a justification, but it isn't yet the strongest justification we could give. An even better justification for a claim also includes considering and responding to objections to our own argument.

Objections: Considering Reasons Against the Truth of the Premises

Some students are reluctant to consider **objections** to an argument they are trying to defend, because it seems to them that they are weakening their own position. But an argument that considers and responds to objections is much stronger than an argument that considers no objections at all. Imagine that you are reading two editorials in the newspaper, one of which expresses your own political views, while the other expresses views contrary to yours. Suppose that each piece argues for its position without considering any alternative points of view that might lead to objections. When you read the one you agree with, it is—unfortunately—all too easy just to go along with the argument (you do, after all, already agree with the conclusion). But when you read the one you disagree with, you are probably thinking of objections along the way, and so perhaps you don't feel challenged in your own view because you think that you have good objections to the reasons given for the conclusion. But imagine that the editorial you disagree with proceeded to consider objections similar to the ones you are thinking of as you read it, and imagine further that the responses it gives to those objections are pretty compelling. Wouldn't you feel more uncomfortable shrugging off the view defended in that case? Wouldn't the challenge to your own view seem more serious? Analogously, wouldn't the piece arguing for the view you agree with be even stronger if it also considered and responded to objections? Any view argued from just one side, without considering alternative perspectives and the resulting objections, is not as compelling as a view that has considered the strongest objections and has also shown how those objections, however strong they seem, need not be taken seriously. This is an especially important philosophical habit of mind: see many sides of an issue—don't be satisfied with just one perspective.

We want to consider and respond to objections for the purpose of strengthening our argument, but presumably we find the argument pretty convincing (since we devised it), so how does one go about finding good objections? This is another one of the skills that you'll acquire as you develop philosophical habits of mind: you will need to be able to take up a critical attitude, criticizing the arguments of other philosophers. You can also take that same point of view in relation to your own argument, pretending that you hold the other point of view and looking for weaknesses in your original argument.

You might think at first that the way to object to an argument is to object to its conclusion—find reasons for thinking that the conclusion is false. But in fact this doesn't really work very well if you are trying to criticize the original argument. For if you offer reasons to think that the conclusion is false, then you have simply produced another argument for the opposite conclusion. You now have two opposed arguments, leading to opposed results, but not really engaging each other in any more substantial way. They can't both be strong or valid arguments with true premises, but the mere conflict between them in itself gives no insight into which one is mistaken or—even more importantly—how it is mistaken. Thus what makes more sense, if the goal is to evaluate, criticize, or strengthen the original argument, is to consider objections to its premises or to the reasoning from the premises to the conclusion, rather than reasons to reject the conclusion. If there are good reasons to think

that the premises of an argument are false or that the reasoning from the premises to the conclusion is faulty, then the argument fails to support its conclusion; but if those objections can be answered, then the overall case for the conclusion is strengthened.

Let's first consider an objection to each premise of our sample argument. An objection to a premise is a reason to think that the premise is false. Consider the first premise: studying philosophy makes you think more clearly. Someone might object by saying that studying philosophy is very confusing. To study philosophy, you have to read many different authors on many different questions, and many of the authors lived a long time ago, so their writing style is very different from ours and often hard to understand. Philosophical questions are hard to understand in the first place because they are so abstract. Thus many people who study philosophy just end up very confused, and surely someone who is very confused is not someone who thinks clearly. Therefore studying philosophy does not make one think more clearly.

What about the second premise: thinking more clearly is valuable? Someone might object to this premise by pointing out that the more clearly one thinks, the more clearly one sees how vulnerable we puny humans are. We have many grand desires, but our ability to "get what we want" is largely dependent upon conditions beyond our control, and thus all our planning and scheming is in the end just pathetic. The more clearly we think, the more clearly we realize this and the more paralyzed we become. We obviously do not benefit from being so paralyzed. On the contrary, ignorance and murky thinking are bliss. Therefore, thinking clearly is not valuable.

Objections can also be made to the *reasoning* involved in arguing that the conclusion is likely to be true, given the truth of the premises. Consider the following objection to the reasoning of the sample argument. Suppose that someone grants the truth of both of the premises but argues that there are other, indeed much easier ways to learn to think more clearly than by studying philosophy. If the conclusion, that studying philosophy is always valuable, means that anyone should, all things considered, study philosophy, then that conclusion might very well be false. Suppose that you are a math major; and suppose also that studying math teaches you to think more clearly; and suppose further that given your talents and interests, taking the time to study philosophy would take time away from other things that you enjoy without adding very much of benefit (since you are already learning to think clearly by studying math). So you could argue that even if it is true that studying philosophy would teach you to think more clearly and that thinking more clearly is valuable, it is false that studying philosophy is valuable for you. It is false that you, given all of what is true about your life, should study philosophy. This objection challenges the reasoning involved in drawing the conclusion from the premises instead of challenging one of the premises.

At this point, we have formulated an objection to each of our premises and an objection to the reasoning of the argument, all with the ultimate goal of strengthening our case for the claim that studying philosophy is valuable by answering these objections.⑥

⑥ Can you think of any other objections to this argument?

Responses: Showing Why the Objections Fail

Obviously we need to *respond* to these objections: we need to show why these objections need not be taken seriously. In responding to objections, you will sometimes show that the reasoning of the objections is faulty, while other times you may respond by showing that the original statement of the premise or the reasoning needs to be qualified in order to accommodate the objection (while still being able to make the case for the claim you are defending).

The first objection claims that studying philosophy is confusing. While some people find it confusing at first, that sense of confusion goes away once one works at it a bit harder. It is really not very easy to pass four philosophy classes without acquiring the thinking skills that clear up the confusion. This objection might have had serious weight if we had specified the idea of studying philosophy as meaning passing only one philosophy course, but it has no weight against the idea that studying philosophy is the kind of thing that requires one to have passed four philosophy courses.

The second objection claims that we are virtually powerless to get what we want no matter how carefully we plan and anticipate. But what evidence can be offered for such a claim? What reason can this objector offer for the view that our planning and careful think-

ing make no difference (or so little difference as to be irrelevant) to the outcome of our efforts? Suppose that you point out that you know of many examples of people who have often succeeded in getting what they want when they've planned carefully, and of other people who don't plan carefully and fail to get what they want. These examples are **counter-examples**⑦ to the objector's view: examples which give some reason to think that the view is false. Of course no one would claim that careful planning guarantees good results. The defense for the premise under consideration need only claim that careful, clear thinking makes getting what you want more likely. So the objector needs to give some reason to think that it is false that careful, clear thinking makes it more likely that you will get what you want.

⑦ Another important philosophical skill is giving counter-examples to philosophical claims or theories. To create a counter-example, you need to first figure out just exactly what the claim or view says and then think carefully about how it applies to many situations, looking for examples that show that it is wrong.

The defender of the objection might respond that all of those people who planned carefully were just lucky, and the people who didn't plan well were just unlucky. Suppose that the objector continues to say the same thing (planners are just lucky) no matter how detailed your examples are and no matter how many examples you come up with. There is nothing that anyone can say that would conclusively prove that we have more control than the objection says we do, and so the objector's view cannot be shown conclusively to be wrong. Is the objector's insistence on the view thereby legitimate? Is it intellectually respectable to insist on a view despite possible counter-examples, just because the view hasn't been conclusively proven to be false?

Our main response to this objection, then, is that the objection relies on a very controversial, ill-defended assumption, one that seems to us to be clearly wrong. Therefore, the objection need not be taken seriously.

What about the objection to the reasoning of the argument? The main response to that objection is that the objection misunderstood the content of the conclusion. The point of the argument was not to argue that everyone ought to study philosophy, even though it was not completely unreasonable for the objector to interpret the conclusion that way. One way to understand the claim that studying philosophy is always valuable is to think that studying philosophy will be valuable for *anyone*. And that strongly suggests that anyone ought to do it. But we could argue that the conclusion of the argument does not mean that anyone, no matter what else is true of him or her, ought to find some time to study philosophy. The conclusion instead just means that *if* you study philosophy, then that study will be valuable for you in the sense that you will benefit from it. This conclusion is completely consistent with the claim that for any particular person, he or she ought not to study philosophy because the study of philosophy, in spite of the benefits that it produces, would not be valuable, all things considered, given what would have to be sacrificed to engage in it. (Here you can see how considering objections also can help to clarify a position.)

Summary

We have clarified and justified the claim that studying philosophy is valuable. We have thereby illustrated many of the skills and philosophical habits of mind required by the method of philosophy. Can you see how the claim is clarified further in the process of justification? Can you see how much stronger the justification is because we have considered and responded to objections?

As you can see now, one of the first challenges of doing philosophy is to learn how to tell when a philosopher (whether it is you or someone you are reading or listening to) is arguing for a view, objecting to it, or responding to objections. As you practice thinking philosophically, you will get better at recognizing these different activities, and you will get better at clarifying claims, drawing distinctions, and making arguments, objections, and responses.

READING PHILOSOPHY AND THINKING PHILOSOPHICALLY

With a little work, anyone can learn to think philosophically. But you might wonder what you need to do to work at it. The first, most valuable resource on which you should practice thinking philosophically is the set of reading selections in this book (and any other philosophical texts you read). But we've learned that students often find reading philosophy very difficult at first, and so we've included some advice about reading philosophy. And while the advice is directed primarily at reading philosophy, the main points apply to listening to a lecture or participating in a discussion.

Philosophical material is primarily argumentative and critical, almost never merely expository. You don't read philosophy in order to gather lots of facts that you will then memorize. You should read philosophy as if you were thinking with the author of the text, as if you were having a conversation with him or her. Philosophers are arguing for a view or position. Think of the author (or lecturer or discussant) as saying: "Look—this is *what* I think, and this is *why* I think it. What do you think?" Thus you should always keep two questions in mind while reading (or listening to lectures, or engaging in discussion with another philosopher): (1) What view or position is the philosopher advocating? The answer to this question may differ at different places in an article: an article may make more than one point, and you should ask how these points connect with each other. Notice also that what is being advocated at a particular point may be very simple and general (e.g., the claim that God exists) or very complicated and specific (e.g., the claim that a particular objection to a particular argument that God exists is mistaken). (2) The second question to ask is what reasons or arguments are being offered in support of the view being advocated. Try to sketch the answers to these two questions as you read—either in your head or, even better, on paper. You will then be in a good position to ask the next question: how strong are the reasons offered, and can they be objected to? It is virtually impossible to do this while relaxing in a passive frame of mind. Successfully reading philosophy requires an active, critical, imaginative mind-set (one of the distinctively philosophical habits of mind that you need to cultivate in order to learn to think philosophically).

There is one major source of confusion to watch out for. Because philosophy is essentially reflective and critical, a philosopher will typically discuss other positions and arguments besides the one defended in a particular article. These may include any of the following: (1) positions opposed to the one defended; (2) positions similar to, but still significantly different in some respect, from the one defended (where the difference helps to clarify the view); (3) arguments in favor of positions opposed to the one defended, which will be criticized; (4) objections to his own position, which will be responded to; and (5) sometimes even arguments for the view defended that the philosopher does *not* accept and wants to distinguish from ones that he does accept. It is obviously important to distinguish all of these from the philosopher's own positive views and arguments, and this is relatively easy to do if you are alert. (For example, arguments and positions other than his own will often be introduced by noncommittal phrases like "it might be claimed that . . ." or "some writers argue that . . ." or perhaps by a reference to a particular person who holds the view or argument in question.)

It is usually a good idea first to look rather quickly through a reading to get an idea of the general "lay of the land" and then to read it again more carefully and critically. Otherwise it is too easy to lose sight of its main point as one works through the detailed arguments. Remember also that considerable rereading will certainly be necessary, especially but not only when reading a later selection that disagrees with an earlier one. Almost no one (including professional philosophers) is capable of adequately grasping a complicated argument in a single reading. And the most important piece of advice: don't give up! The more you work at these skills and habits, the better you will become at them, and the more you will also come to see the point of philosophy. In this way, intellectual tenacity is one of the most essential philosophical habits of mind.

Discussion Questions

1. Why do we need a single conception of philosophy for the purposes of this course? What if someone said, "We don't need a single conception of philosophy. We can work together, doing philosophy, even if we each have different conceptions of philosophy." Does that sound reasonable? Why or why not?

2. The area of philosophy called metaphysics studies the nature of reality. What do you think about reality? Is it clear what things are real and what things are not real? List seven things that are real; list five things that are not real. Does science study the nature of reality? What do you think is the difference between science and philosophy?

3. We claim that how much clarification a claim needs varies depending on the context. Consider, for example, the claim that there are trees in the quad. Now imagine the following context where the claim needs no clarification: suppose a landscaping firm has been hired to fertilize all the trees on campus, and they want to know if they need to go to the quad. You tell them that there are trees in the quad, and your claim is sufficiently clear and precise for the purposes at hand. But suppose there is another context: a landscaping firm has been hired to fertilize all the cherry trees on campus, and they want to know if they need to go to the quad. Now the claim that there are trees in the quad needs to be clarified, in this case made more precise: they need to be told whether there are *cherry* trees in the quad. Now you think of an example of a claim and two contexts, in one of which the claim needs clarification, and in the other of which the claim needs no clarification.

4. We claim that reasons for believing a claim should be reasons for thinking that the claim is true. Does that sound right? What other kinds of reasons might someone think are good ones for believing a claim? Suppose your best friend says that she believes she has won a $10 million lottery. Should you believe her? Suppose that she offers no real reason for thinking that her claim is true, but wants you to believe her anyway (maybe she wants to celebrate). Is that a good reason to believe a claim (that someone *wants* you to believe it)? What about the claim that God exists? On what basis should someone believe that claim? Should you have some reason to think that the claim is true? Suppose that it makes you happy to believe that God exists. Is that a good reason to believe the claim? Think of three examples of claims that you think someone ought not to believe unless there is a good reason to think that they are true, and three examples of claims that you think can *perhaps* be believed on other grounds. You might have to explain the context of the latter examples.

5. Try explaining the argument for the conclusion that studying philosophy is valuable to a friend. What kinds of clarifications did you have to make? Did your friend have any objections? Was your friend convinced?

Plato

Plato (469–399 B.C.) (along with Aristotle) was one of the two major Ancient Greek philosophers and is universally recognized as one of the most important philosophers in the entire history of philosophy. (The twentieth-century British logician and metaphysician Alfred North Whitehead once remarked that the history of Western philosophy "consists of a series of footnotes to Plato"—a mild but pardonable exaggeration.) Plato's writings consist of dialogues in which the leading figure is his teacher Socrates. It is usually thought that the earlier dialogues, of which the present selection is one, more accurately report the actual views of the historical Socrates, with the later ones developing Plato's own views, which he no doubt saw as developing out of his teacher's. This dialogue is set on the court steps of Athens, where Socrates stops to talk to Euthyphro about the business that each has with the court. The background of the dialogue is real: Socrates was accused of corrupting the youth of Athens. (The following selection is an account of the trial itself.)

In this dialogue, we see an example of conceptual clarification: Socrates questions Euthyphro in an attempt to clarify the idea of piety. While there are religious connotations to the idea of piety, there is also broader meaning more appropriate to the arguments in this dialogue: piety is approximately equivalent to moral rightness or correctness. But then the idea of a morally right action itself needs clarification, and that is what the dialogue is really about. Euthyphro is confident that he understands what it is for an action to be pious in this sense and attempts to explain it to Socrates.

Euthyphro

Euthyphro:* What's new, Socrates, to make you leave your usual haunts in the Lyceum and spend your time here by the king-archon's court? Surely you are not prosecuting anyone before the king-archon as I am?

Socrates: The Athenians do not call this a prosecution but an indictment, Euthyphro.

E: What is this you say? Someone must have indicted you, for you are not going to tell me that you have indicted someone else.

S: No indeed.

E: But someone else has indicted you?

S: Quite so.

E: Who is he?

S: I do not really know him myself, Euthyphro. He is apparently young and unknown. They call him

---

From Five Dialogues, *translated by G.M.A. Grube (Indianapolis: Hackett Publishing Company, 1981).*

---

*We know nothing about Euthyphro except what we can gather from this dialogue. He is obviously a professional priest who considers himself an expert on ritual and on piety generally, and, it seems, is generally so considered.

Meletus, I believe. He belongs to the Pitthean deme, if you know anyone from that deme called Meletus, with long hair, not much of a beard, and a rather aquiline nose.

E: I don't know him, Socrates. What charge does he bring against you?

S: What charge? A not ignoble one I think, for it is no small thing for a young man to have knowledge of such an important subject. He says he knows how our young men are corrupted and who corrupts them. He is likely to be wise, and when he sees my ignorance corrupting his contemporaries, he proceeds to accuse me to the city as to their mother. I think he is the only one of our public men to start out the right way, for it is right to care first that the young should be as good as possible, just as a good farmer is likely to take care of the young plants first, and of the others later. So, too, Meletus first gets rid of us who corrupt the young shoots, as he says, and then afterwards he will obviously take care of the older ones and become a source of great blessings for the city, as seems likely to happen to one who started out this way.

E: I could wish this were true, Socrates, but I fear the opposite may happen. He seems to me to start out by harming the very heart of the city by attempting to wrong you. Tell me, what does he say you do to corrupt the young?

S: Strange things, to hear him tell it, for he says that I am a maker of gods, and on the ground that I create new gods while not believing in the old gods, he has indicted me for their sake, as he puts it.

E: I understand, Socrates. This is because you say that the divine sign keeps coming to you.① So he has written this indictment against you as one who makes innovations in religious matters, and he comes to court to slander you, knowing that such things are easily misrepresented to the crowd. The same is true in my case. Whenever I speak of divine matters in the assembly and foretell the future, they laugh me down as if I

---

① As will be explained in the Apology (p. 30), Socrates believes that he has for years heard a voice that he calls the divine sign. This voice typically tells him *not* to do things of which the gods would disapprove. (It is hard to say how literally this should be taken.)

---

were crazy; and yet I have foretold nothing that did not happen. Nevertheless, they envy all of us who do this. One need not worry about them, but meet them head-on.

S: My dear Euthyphro, to be laughed at does not matter perhaps, for the Athenians do not mind anyone they think clever, as long as he does not teach his own wisdom, but if they think that he makes others to be like himself they get angry, whether through envy, as you say, or for some other reason.

E: I have certainly no desire to test their feelings towards me in this matter.

S: Perhaps you seem to make yourself but rarely available, and not to be willing to teach your own wisdom, but I'm afraid that my liking for people makes them think that I pour out to anybody anything I have to say, not only without charging a fee but even glad to reward anyone who is willing to listen. If then they were intending to laugh at me, as you say they laugh at you, there would be nothing unpleasant in their spending their time in court laughing and jesting, but if they are going to be serious, the outcome is not clear except to you prophets.

E: Perhaps it will come to nothing, Socrates, and you will fight your case as you think best, as I think I will mine.

S: What is your case, Euthyphro? Are you the defendant or the prosecutor?

E: The prosecutor.

S: Whom do you prosecute?

E: One whom I am thought crazy to prosecute.

S: Are you pursuing someone who will easily escape you?

E: Far from it, for he is quite old.

S: Who is it?

E: My father.

S: My dear sir! Your own father?

E: Certainly.

S: What is the charge? What is the case about?

E: Murder, Socrates.

S: Good heavens! Certainly, Euthyphro, most men would not know how they could do this and be right. It is not the part of anyone to do this, but of one who is far advanced in wisdom. ②

② Socrates at least pretends to assume that Euthyphro must be very sure that he knows what is the pious or right thing and what is not, since he is willing to do something as initially questionable as prosecuting his own father.

E: Yes, by Zeus, Socrates, that is so.

S: Is then the man your father killed one of your relatives? Or is that obvious, for you would not prosecute your father for the murder of a stranger.

E: It is ridiculous, Socrates, for you to think that it makes any difference whether the victim is a stranger or a relative. One should only watch whether the killer acted justly or not; if he acted justly, let him go, but if not, one should prosecute, even if the killer shares your hearth and table. The pollution is the same if you knowingly keep company with such a man and do not cleanse yourself and him by bringing him to justice. The victim was a dependent of mine, and when we were farming in Naxos he was a servant of ours. He killed one of our household slaves in drunken anger, so my father bound him hand and foot and threw him in a ditch, then sent a man here to enquire from the priest what should be done. During that time he gave no thought or care to the bound man, as being a killer, and it was no matter if he died, which he did. Hunger and cold and his bonds caused his death before the messenger came back from the seer. Both my father and my other relatives are angry that I am prosecuting my father for murder on behalf of a murderer when he hadn't even killed him, they say, and even

③ Euthyphro claims that his family does not know what piety is, because assuming that family ties are relevant to what is right and wrong is a mistake. What do you think about that assumption?

if he had, the dead man does not deserve a thought, since he was a killer. For, they say, it is impious for a son to prosecute his father for murder. But their ideas of the divine attitude to piety and impiety are wrong, Socrates. ③

S: Whereas, by Zeus, Euthyphro, you think that your knowledge of the divine, and of piety and impiety, is so accurate that, when those things happened as you say, you have no fear of having acted impiously in bringing your father to trial?

E: I should be of no use, Socrates, and Euthyphro would not be superior to the majority of men, if I did not have accurate knowledge of all such things.

S: It is indeed most important, my admirable Euthyphro, that I should become your pupil, and as regards this indictment challenge Meletus about these very things and say to him: that in the past too I considered knowledge about the divine to be most important, and that now that he says that I am guilty of improvising and innovating about the gods I have become your pupil. I would say to him: "If, Meletus, you agree that Euthyphro is wise in these matters, consider me, too, to have the right beliefs and do not bring me to trial. If you do not think so, then prosecute that teacher of mine, not me, for corrupting the older men, me and his own father, by teaching me and by exhorting and punishing him. If he is not convinced, and does not discharge me or indict you instead of me, I shall repeat the same challenge in court.

E: Yes, by Zeus, Socrates, and, if he should try to indict me, I think I would find his weak spots and the talk in court would be about him rather than about me.

S: It is because I realize this that I am eager to become your pupil, my dear friend. I know that other people as well as this Meletus do not even seem to notice you, whereas he sees me so sharply and clearly that he indicts me for ungodliness. So tell me now, by Zeus, what you just now maintained you clearly knew: what kind of thing do you say that godliness and ungodliness are, both as regards murder and other things; or is the pious not the same and alike in every action, and the impious the opposite of all that is pious and like itself, and everything that is to be impious presents us with one form or appearance in so far as it is impious? ④

④ Socrates specifically asks Euthyphro to tell him what piety is, since Euthyphro claims to know what it is. By asking for *the form* of piety, Socrates is asking for a definition or account of piety itself: of what it is that all pious things or actions have in common by virtue of which they are pious.

E: Most certainly, Socrates.

S: Tell me then, what is the pious, and what the impious, do you say?

E: I say that the pious is to do what I am doing now, to prosecute the wrongdoer, be it about murder or temple robbery or anything else, whether the wrongdoer is your father or your mother or anyone else; not to prosecute is impious.⑤ And observe, Socrates, that I can quote the law as a great proof that this is so. I have already said to others that such actions are right, not to favour the ungodly, whoever they are. These people themselves believe that Zeus is the best and most just of the gods, yet they agree that he bound his father because he unjustly swallowed his sons, and that he in turn castrated his father for similar reasons. But they are angry with me because I am prosecuting my father for his wrongdoing. They contradict themselves in what they say about the gods and about me.⑥

S: Indeed, Euthyphro, this is the reason why I am a defendant in the case, because I find it hard to accept things like that being said about the gods, and it is likely to be the reason why I shall be told I do wrong. Now, however, if you, who have full knowledge of such things, share their opinions, then we must agree with them too, it would seem. For what are we to say, we who agree that we ourselves have no knowledge of them? Tell me, by the god of friendship, do you really believe these things are true?

E: Yes, Socrates, and so are even more surprising things, of which the majority has no knowledge.

S: And do you believe that there really is war among the gods, and terrible enmities and battles, and other such things as are told by the poets, and other sacred stories such as are embroidered by good writers and by representations of which the robe of the goddess is adorned when it is carried up to the Acropolis? Are we to say these things are true, Euthyphro?

⑤ Here is Euthyphro's first attempt to respond to Socrates's request for clarification: piety is what Euthyphro is doing now by prosecuting his father. Does this attempt succeed in *clarifying the general form or idea* of piety?

⑥ Because Euthyphro is doing something very much like what Zeus did, anyone who says that he is doing something impious must be wrong, since surely Zeus never did anything impious. (Socrates is not impressed by this line of argument.)

E: Not only these, Socrates, but, as I was saying just now, I will, if you wish, relate many other things about the gods which I know will amaze you.

S: I should not be surprised, but you will tell me these at leisure some other time. For now, try to tell me more clearly what I was asking just now, for, my friend, you did not teach me adequately when I asked you what the pious was, but you told me that what you are doing now, prosecuting your father for murder, is pious.

E: And I told the truth, Socrates.

S: Perhaps. You agree, however, that there are many other pious actions.

E: There are.

S: Bear in mind then that I did not bid you tell me one or two of the many pious actions but that form itself that makes all pious actions pious, for you agreed that all impious actions are impious and all pious actions pious through one form, or don't you remember?⑦

E: I do.

S: Tell me then what this form itself is, so that I may look upon it, and using it as a model, say that any action of yours or another's that is of that kind is pious, and if it is not that it is not.

⑦ Giving an example of something fails to clarify the general idea or form, since you may not know why the thing given as an example is the kind of thing in question. Socrates is looking for a general account or definition of piety, not just examples of specific things that are pious. (See Discussion Question 1.)

E: If that is how you want it, Socrates, that is how I will tell you.

S: That is what I want.

E: Well then, what is dear to the gods is pious, what is not is impious.

S: Splendid, Euthyphro! You have now answered in the way I wanted. Whether your answer is true I do not know yet, but you will obviously show me that what you say is true.

E: Certainly.

S: Come then, let us examine what we mean. An action or a man dear to the gods is pious, but an action or a man hated by the gods is impious. They are not the same, but quite opposite, the pious and the impious. Is that not so?⑧

---

⑧ Here is Euthyphro's second attempt to respond to Socrates: piety is what is dear to the gods, where it becomes clear in what follows that this means dear to any of the gods.

E: It is indeed.

S: And that seems to be a good statement?

E: I think so, Socrates.

S: We have also stated that the gods are in a state of discord, that they are at odds with each other, Euthyphro, and that they are at enmity with each other. Has that, too, been said?

E: It has.

S: What are the subjects of difference that cause hatred and anger? Let us look at it this way. If you and I were to differ about numbers as to which is the greater, would this difference make us enemies and angry with each other, or would we proceed to count and soon resolve our difference about this?

E: We would certainly do so.

S: Again, if we differed about the larger and the smaller, we would turn to measurement and soon cease to differ.

E: That is so.

S: And about the heavier and the lighter, we would resort to weighing and be reconciled.

E: Of course.

S: What subject of difference would make us angry and hostile to each other if we were unable to come to a decision? Perhaps you do not have an answer ready, but examine as I tell you whether these subjects are the just and the unjust, the beautiful and the ugly, the good and the bad. Are these not the subjects of difference about which, when we are unable to come to a satisfactory decision, you and I and other men become hostile to each other whenever we do?

E: That is the difference, Socrates, about those subjects.

S: What about the gods, Euthyphro? If indeed they have differences, will it not be about these same subjects?

E: It certainly must be so.

S: Then according to your argument, my good Euthyphro, different gods consider different things to be just, beautiful, ugly, good, and bad, for they would not be at odds with one another unless they differed about these subjects, would they?

E: You are right.

S: And they like what each of them considers beautiful, good, and just, and hate the opposites of these?

E: Certainly.

S: But you say that the same things are considered just by some gods and unjust by others, and as they dispute about these things they are at odds and at war with each other. Is that not so?

E: It is.

S: The same things then are loved by the gods and hated by the gods, and would be both god-loved and god-hated.

E: It seems likely.

S: And the same things would be both pious and impious, according to this argument?

E: I'm afraid so.

S: So you did not answer my question, you surprising man.⑨ I did not ask you what same thing is both pious and impious, and it appears that what is loved by the gods is also hated by them. So it is in no way surprising if your present action, namely punishing your father, may be pleasing to Zeus but displeasing to Kronos and Ouranos, pleasing to Hephaestus but displeasing to Hera, and so with any other gods who differ from each other on this subject.

---

⑨ So Euthyphro's second attempt at a general account of piety is a failure. Think about the problem with it and try to see how this might be fixed.

E: I think, Socrates, that on this subject no gods would differ from one another, that whoever has killed anyone unjustly should pay the penalty.

. . .

S: Come now, my dear Euthyphro, tell me, too, that I may become wiser, what proof you have that all the gods consider that man to have been killed unjustly who became a murderer while in your service, was bound by the master of his victim, and died in his bonds before the one who bound him found out from the seers what was to be done with him, and that it is right for a son to denounce and to prosecute his father on behalf of such a man. Come, try to show me a clear sign that all the gods definitely believe this action to be right. If you can give me adequate proof of this, I shall never cease to extol your wisdom.

E: This is perhaps no light task, Socrates, though I could show you very clearly.

S: I understand that you think me more dull-witted than the jury, as you will obviously show them that these actions were unjust and that all the gods hate such actions.

E: I will show it to them clearly, Socrates, if only they will listen to me.

S: They will listen if they think you show them well. But this thought came to me as you were speaking, and I am examining it, saying to myself: "If Euthyphro shows me conclusively that all the gods consider such a death unjust, to what greater extent have I learned from him the nature of piety and impiety? This action would then, it seems, be hated by the gods, but the pious and the impious were not now defined, for what is hated by the gods has also been shown to be loved by them." So I will not insist on this point; let us assume, if you wish, that all the gods consider this unjust and that they all hate it. However, is this the correction we are making in our discussion, that what all the gods hate is impious, and what they all love is pious, and that what some gods love and others hate is neither or both? Is that how you now wish us to define piety and impiety?

E: What prevents us from doing so, Socrates?

S: For my part nothing, Euthyphro, but you look whether on your part this proposal will enable you to teach me most easily what you promised.

[10] Here is Euthyphro's third attempt, a modification or correction of the second, as suggested by Socrates. Notice how it differs from the second attempt in just the way it needs to in order to avoid the objection that was raised against that attempt.

E: I would certainly say that the pious is what all the gods love, and the opposite, what all the gods hate, is the impious. [10]

S: Then let us again examine whether that is a sound statement, or do we let it pass, and if one of us, or someone else, merely says

that something is so, do we accept that it is so? Or should we examine what the speaker means?

E: We must examine it, but I certainly think that this is now a fine statement.

S: We shall soon know better whether it is. Consider this: Is the pious loved by the gods because it is pious, or is it pious because it is loved by the gods? [11]

E: I don't know what you mean, Socrates.

S: I shall try to explain more clearly: we speak of something being carried and something carrying, of something being led and some-

[11] Socrates's objection to Euthyphro's third attempt is more complicated than any of the others. Think carefully about the question: does the piety of something *explain* why the gods love it—or does the fact that the gods love it explain why it is pious? If one thing A explains another thing B, then A is explanatorily prior to B (and B therefore cannot also explain A, at least not in the same way).

thing leading, of something being seen and something seeing, and you understand that these things are all different from one another and how they differ?

E: I think I do.

S: So there is something being loved and something loving, and the loving is a different thing.

E: Of course.

S: Tell me then whether that which is being carried is being carried because someone carries it or for some other reason.

E: No, that is the reason.

S: And that which is being led is so because someone leads it, and that which is being seen because someone sees it?

E: Certainly.

S: It is not seen by someone because it is being seen but on the contrary it is being seen because someone sees it, nor is it because it is being led that someone leads it but because someone leads it that it is being led; nor does someone carry an object because it is being carried, but it is being carried because someone carries it. Is what I want to say clear, Euthyphro? I want to say this, namely, that if anything comes to be, or is affected, it does not come to be because it is coming to be, but it is coming to be because it comes to be; nor is it affected because it is being affected but because something affects it. Or do you not agree? ⑫

E: I do.

S: What is being loved is either something that comes to be or something that is affected by something?

E: Certainly.

S: So it is in the same case as the things just mentioned; it is not loved by those who love it because it is being loved, but it is being loved because they love it? ⑬

E: Necessarily.

S: What then do we say about the pious, Euthyphro? Surely that it is loved by all the gods, according to what you say?

E: Yes.

S: Is it loved because it is pious, or for some other reason?

E: For no other reason.

S: It is loved then because it is pious, but it is not pious because it is loved?

E: Apparently.

S: And because it is loved by the gods it is being loved and is dear to the gods?

E: Of course.

S: The god-beloved is then not the same as the pious, Euthyphro, nor the pious the same as the god-beloved, as you say it is, but one differs from the other. ⑭

E: How so, Socrates?

S: Because we agree that the pious is beloved for the reason that it is pious, but it is not pious because it is loved. Is that not so?

E: Yes.

S: And that the god-beloved, on the other hand, is so because it is loved by the gods, by the very fact of being loved, but it is not loved because it is god-beloved. ⑮

E: True.

S: But if the god-beloved and the pious were the same, my dear Euthyphro, and the pious were loved because it was pious, then the god-beloved would be loved because it was god-beloved, and if the god-beloved was god-beloved because it was loved by the gods, then the pious would also be pious because it was loved by the gods; but now you see that they are in opposite cases as being altogether different from each other: the one is of a nature to be loved because it is loved, the other is loved because it is of a nature to be loved. ⑯ I'm afraid, Euthyphro, that when you were asked what piety is, you did not wish to make its nature clear to me, but you told me an affect or quality of it, that the pious has the quality of being loved by all the gods, but you have not yet told me what the pious is. Now, if you will, do not hide things from me but tell me again from the beginning what piety is, whether loved by the gods or having some other quality—we shall not quarrel about that—but be keen to tell me what the pious and the impious are. ⑰

E: But Socrates, I have no way of telling you what I have in mind, for

---

⑫ You might have to read this paragraph slowly and more than once. Socrates attempts to illuminate what it means for one thing to be prior to another, in this important sense, by thinking about many different examples. Which thing *explains* the other thing in each of these examples?

---

⑬ The assumption here is that there is some *other* reason that something is loved by someone, and *once* it is loved by that someone, then it becomes something loved. But (assuming that love is not just arbitrary) the thing had to first have some particular characteristic that made that someone love it. That characteristic is then explanatorily prior to being loved: it explains why the thing is loved.

---

⑭ If piety explains why the gods love something, then piety cannot be *the same thing* as the gods loving that thing (the same thing as its being "god-beloved"). (As a rough analogy: if the window breaks *because* I throw a rock through it, then my throwing a rock through the window cannot be the very same thing as the window breaking.)

---

⑮ Here is a case where the fact of being loved by the gods *is* the prior fact, since it explains why something is god-beloved.

---

⑯ So the gods love something because it is pious, and it becomes god-beloved because they love it—making it clear that being god-beloved cannot be the same thing as being pious, since they stand in different relations to the gods actually loving something. (Another way to put the point is to say that piety is in fact *two* explanatory steps prior to being god-beloved, and so obviously cannot be identical to it.)

---

⑰ So Euthyphro has failed again—this time because he has merely specified an effect of piety (it makes gods love things), but he hasn't yet said what piety is—he has yet to clarify the general form or idea of piety.

whatever proposition we put forward goes around and refuses to stay put where we establish it.

S: Your statements, Euthyphro, seem to belong to my ancestor, Daedalus. If I were stating them and putting them forward, you would perhaps be making fun of me and say that because of my kinship with him my conclusions in discussion run away and will not stay where one puts them. As these propositions are yours, however, we need some other jest, for they will not stay put for you, as you say yourself.

E: I think the same jest will do for our discussion, Socrates, for I am not the one who makes them go round and not remain in the same place; it is you who are the Daedalus; for as far as I am concerned they would remain as they were.

S: It looks as if I was cleverer than Daedalus in using my skill, my friend, in so far as he could only cause to move the things he made himself, but I can make other people's move as well as my own. And the smartest part of my skill is that I am clever without wanting to be, for I would rather have your statements to me remain unmoved than possess the wealth of Tantalus as well as the cleverness of Daedalus. But enough of this. Since I think you are making unnecessary difficulties, I am as eager as you are to find a way to teach me about piety, and do not give up before you do. See whether you think all that is pious is of necessity just.

E: I think so.

S: And is then all that is just pious? Or is all that is pious just, but not all that is just pious, but some of it is and some is not?

E: I do not follow what you are saying, Socrates.

S: Yet you are younger than I by as much as you are wiser. As I say, you are making difficulties because of your wealth of wisdom. Pull yourself together, my dear sir, what I am saying is not difficult to grasp. I am saying the opposite of what the poet said who wrote:

> You do not wish to name Zeus, who had done it,
> and who made all things grow, for where there is
> fear there is also shame.

I disagree with the poet. Shall I tell you why?

E: Please do.

S: I do not think that "where there is fear there is also shame," for I think that many people who fear disease and poverty and many other such things feel fear, but are not ashamed of the things they fear. Do you not think so?

E: I do indeed.

S: But where there is shame, there is also fear. For is there anyone who, in feeling shame and embarrassment at anything, does not also at the same time fear and dread a reputation for wickedness?

E: He is certainly afraid.

S: It is then not right to say "where there is fear there is also shame," but that where there is shame there is also fear, for fear covers a larger area than shame. Shame is a part of fear just as odd is a part of number, with the result that it is not true that where there is number there is also oddness, but that where there is oddness there is also number. Do you follow me now?

E: Surely.

S: This is the kind of thing I was asking before, whether where there is piety there is also justice, but where there is justice there is not always piety, for the pious is a part of justice. Shall we say that, or do you think otherwise?

E: No, but like that, for what you say appears to be right.

S: See what comes next: if the pious is a part of the just, we must, it seems, find out what part of the just it is. Now if you asked me something of what we mentioned just now, such as what part of number is the even, and what number that is, I would say it is the number that is divisible into two equal, not unequal, parts. Or do you not think so?

E: I do.

S: Try in this way to tell me what part of the just the pious is, in order to tell Meletus not to wrong us any more and not to indict me for ungodliness, since I have learned from you sufficiently what is godly and pious and what is not.

E: I think, Socrates, that the godly and pious is the part of the just that is concerned with the care of the gods, while that concerned with the care of men is the remaining part of justice.⒅

⒅ Here is Euthyphro's last attempt to explain what piety is. Try to figure out what is wrong with it.

S: You seem to me to put that very well, but I still need a bit of information. I do not know yet what you mean by care, for you do not mean the care of the gods in the same sense as the care of other things, as, for example, we say, don't we, that not everyone knows how to care for horses, but the horse breeder does.

E: Yes, I do mean it that way.

S: So horse breeding is the care of horses.

E: Yes.

S: Nor does everyone know how to care for dogs, but the hunter does.

E: That is so.

S: So hunting is the care of dogs.

E: Yes.

S: And cattle raising is the care of cattle.

E: Quite so.

S: While piety and godliness is the care of the gods, Euthyphro. Is that what you mean?

E: It is.

S: Now care in each case has the same effect; it aims at the good and the benefit of the object cared for, as you can see that horses cared for by horse breeders are benefited and become better. Or do you not think so?

E: I do.

S: So dogs are benefited by dog breeding, cattle by cattle raising, and so with all the others. Or do you think that care aims to harm the object of its care?

E: By Zeus, no.

S: It aims to benefit the object of its care?

E: Of course.

S: Is piety then, which is the care of the gods, also to benefit the gods and make them better? Would you agree that when you do something pious you make some one of the gods better?

E: By Zeus, no.

S: Nor do I think that this is what you mean—far from it—but that is why I asked you what you meant by the care of gods, because I did not be-

lieve you meant this kind of care.⒆

⒆ One meaning of "care of the gods" is inapplicable, since the gods do not need benefits from human beings.

E: Quite right, Socrates, that is not the kind of care I mean.

S: Very well, but what kind of care of the gods would piety be?

E: The kind of care, Socrates, that slaves take of their masters.

S: I understand. It is likely to be a kind of service of the gods.

E: Quite so.

S: Could you tell me to the achievement of what goal service to doctors tends? Is it not, do you think, to achieving health?

E: I think so.

S: What about service to shipbuilders? To what achievement is it directed?

E: Clearly, Socrates, to the building of a ship.

S: And service to housebuilders to the building of a house?

E: Yes.

S: Tell me then, my good sir, to the achievement of what aim does service to the gods tend? You obviously know since you say that you, of all men, have the best knowledge of the divine.

E: And I am telling the truth, Socrates.

S: Tell me then, by Zeus, what is that excellent aim that the gods achieve, using us as their servants?

E: Many fine things, Socrates.

S: So do generals, my friend. Nevertheless you could easily tell me their main concern, which is to achieve victory in war, is it not?

E: Of course.

S: The farmers too, I think, achieve many fine things, but the main point of their efforts is to produce food from the earth.

E: Quite so.

S: Well then, how would you sum up the many fine things that the gods achieve?

E: I told you a short while ago, Socrates, that it is a considerable task to acquire any precise knowledge of these things, but, to put it simply, I say that if a man knows how to say and do what is pleasing to the gods at prayer and sacrifice, those are pious actions such as preserve both private houses and public affairs of state. The opposite of these pleasing actions are impious and overturn and destroy everything.

S: You could tell me in far fewer words, if you were willing, the sum of what I asked, Euthyphro, but you are not keen to teach me, that is clear. You were on the point of doing so, but you turned away. If you had given that answer, I should now have acquired from you sufficient knowledge of the nature of piety. As it is, the lover of inquiry must follow his beloved wherever it may lead him. Once more then, what do you say that piety and the pious are? Are they a knowledge of how to sacrifice and pray?

E: They are.

S: To sacrifice is to make a gift to the gods, whereas to pray is to beg from the gods?

E: Definitely, Socrates.

S: It would follow from this statement that piety would be a knowledge of how to give to, and beg from, the gods.

E: You understood what I said very well, Socrates.

S: That is because I am so desirous of your wisdom, and I concentrate my mind on it, so that no word of yours may fall to the ground. But tell me, what is this service to the gods? You say it is to beg from them and to give to them?

E: I do.

S: And to beg correctly would be to ask from them things that we need?

E: What else?

S: And to give correctly is to give them what they need from us, for it would not be skillful to bring gifts to anyone that are in no way needed.

E: True, Socrates.

S: Piety would then be a sort of trading skill between gods and men?

E: Trading yes, if you prefer to call it that.

S: I prefer nothing, unless it is true. But tell me, what benefit do the gods derive from the gifts they receive from us? What they give us is obvious to all. There is for us no good that we do not receive from them, but how are they benefited by what they receive from us? Or do we have such an advantage over them in the trade that we receive all our blessings from them and they receive nothing from us?

E: Do you suppose, Socrates, that the gods are benefited by what they receive from us?

S: What could those gifts from us to the gods be, Euthyphro?

E: What else, do you think, than honour, reverence, and what I mentioned just now, gratitude?

S: The pious is then, Euthyphro, pleasing to the gods, but not beneficial or dear to them?

E: I think it is of all things most dear to them.

S: So the pious is once again what is dear to the gods.

E: Most certainly.

S: When you say this, will you be surprised if your arguments seem to move about instead of staying put? And will you accuse me of being Daedalus who makes them move, though you are yourself much more skillful than Daedalus and make them go round in a circle? Or do you not realize that our argument has moved around and come again to the same place? You surely remember that earlier the pious and the god-beloved were shown not to be the same but different from each other. Or do you not remember?

E: I do.

S: Do you then not realize now that you are saying that what is dear to the gods is the pious? Is this not the same as the god-beloved?[20] Or is it not?

> [20] The alternative account of "care of the gods" turns out to be the same as the account already refuted.

E: It certainly is.

S: Either we were wrong when we agreed before, or, if we were right then, we are wrong now.

E: That seems to be so.

S: So we must investigate again from the beginning what piety is, as I shall not willingly give up before I learn this. Do not think me unworthy, but concentrate your attention and tell the truth. For you know it, if any man does, and I must not let you go, like Proteus, before you tell me. If you had no clear knowledge of piety and impiety you would never have ventured to prosecute your old father for murder on behalf of a servant. For fear of the gods you would have been afraid to take the risk lest you should not be acting rightly, and would have been ashamed before men, but now I know well that you believe you have clear knowledge of piety and impiety. So tell me, my good Euthyphro, and do not hide what you think it is.

E: Some other time, Socrates, for I am in a hurry now, and it is time for me to go.

S: What a thing to do, my friend! By going you have cast me down from a great hope I had, that I would learn from you the nature of the pious and the impious and so escape Meletus' indictment by showing him that I had acquired wisdom in divine matters from Euthyphro, and my ignorance would no longer cause me to be careless and inventive about such things, and that I would be better for the rest of my life.

Discussion Questions

1. Suppose that someone asks you to explain some particular term. Why is giving an example of something an inadequate response? For example, suppose someone asked you to explain rap music—suppose they said, "What does it mean for a piece of music to be rap music?" If you gave them *an example* of rap music, would that explain it to them? What should you do instead? How would you clarify the idea of moral rightness?

2. Many people think that the source of morality derives from God's commands or laws. Some such assumption lies behind Dostoevsky's remark: "If God is dead, then everything is permitted." As natural as that may seem, there is a serious problem with it, one that has come to be called the Euthyphro problem. Does God say that something is right or command that we do it *because* it is right, or does it become right because God says so? There is again an issue of explanatory priority: is God merely a good judge of what is independently right (so that its being right explains his command) or does God's command make something right? What must someone who wants to defend the idea that God is the source of morality say in answer to this question? What is the objection to saying that? (Could God have commanded anything at all—even murder or genocide—and would it then have been right?)

Plato

While this work is still referred to as a dialogue, Plato in fact lets Socrates do almost all of the talking. Socrates is addressing a very large jury, one that will decide whether he is to be convicted of the charge of corrupting the youth of Athens; and if convicted, what his sentence will be. (The procedure after conviction was for both the prosecution and the defense to propose punishments, with the jury then deciding between the two.) Socrates argues that he is innocent of the charge. (The title of the dialogue comes from the Greek word for defense: Socrates's speech is clearly not an apology in the ordinary sense, but neither is there any irony reflected the title, as one might be tempted to think.)

Apology

I do not know, men of Athens, how my accusers affected you; as for me, I was almost carried away in spite of myself, so persuasively did they speak. And yet, hardly anything of what they said is true. Of the many lies they told, one in particular surprised me, namely that you should be careful not to be deceived by an accomplished speaker like me. That they were not ashamed to be immediately proved wrong by the facts, when I show myself not to be an accomplished speaker at all, that I thought was most shameless on their part—unless indeed they call an accomplished speaker the man who speaks the truth. If they mean that, I would agree that I am an orator, but not after their manner, for indeed, as I say, practically nothing they said was true. From me you will hear the whole truth, though not, by Zeus, gentlemen, expressed in embroidered and stylized phrases like theirs, but things spoken at random and expressed in the first words that come to mind, for I put my trust in the justice of what I say, and let none of you expect anything else. It would not be fitting at my age, as it might be for a young man, to toy with words when I appear before you.

One thing I do ask and beg of you, gentlemen: if you hear me making my defence in the same kind of language as I am accustomed to use in the market place . . . where many of you have heard me, and elsewhere, do not be surprised or create a disturbance on that account. The position is this: this is my first appearance in a lawcourt, at the age of seventy; I am therefore simply a stranger to the manner of speaking here. Just as if I were really a stranger, you would certainly excuse me if I spoke in that dialect and manner in which I had been brought up, so too my present request seems a just one, for you to pay no attention to my manner of speech—be it better or worse—but to concentrate your attention on whether what I say is just or not, for the excellence of a judge lies in this, as that of a speaker lies in telling the truth.

It is right for me, gentlemen, to defend myself first against the first lying accusations made against me and my first accusers, and then against the later accusations and the later accusers. There have been many who have accused me to you for many years now, and none of their accusations are true. These I fear much more than I fear Anytus and his friends, though they too are formidable. These earlier ones, however, are more so, gentlemen; they got hold of most of you from childhood, persuaded you and accused me quite falsely, saying that there is a man called Socrates, a wise man, a student of all things in the sky and below the earth, who makes the worse argument the stronger. Those who spread that rumour, gentlemen, are my dangerous accusers, for their hearers believe that those who study these things do not even believe in the gods. Moreover, these accusers are numerous, and have been at it a long time; also, they spoke to you at an age when you would most readily believe them, some of you being children and adolescents, and they won their case by default, as there was no defence.

What is most absurd in all this is that one cannot even know or mention their names unless one of them is a writer of comedies.* Those who maliciously and slanderously persuaded you—who also, when persuaded themselves then persuaded others—all those are most difficult to deal with: one cannot bring one of them into court or refute him; one must simply fight with shadows, as it were, in making one's defence, and cross-examine when no one answers. I want you to realize too that my accusers are of two kinds: those who have accused me recently, and the old ones I mention; and to think that I must first defend myself against the latter, for you have also heard their accusations first, and to a much greater extent than the more recent.

. . .

Let us then take up the case from its beginning. What is the accusation from which arose the slander

From Five Dialogues, *translated by G.M.A. Grube* (Indianapolis: Hackett Publishing Company, 1981).

---

*This refers in particular to Aristophanes, whose comedy, *The Clouds,* produced in 423 B.C., ridiculed the (imaginary) school of Socrates.

in which Meletus trusted when he wrote out the charge against me? What did they say when they slandered me? I must, as if they were my actual prosecutors, read the affidavit they would have sworn. It goes something like this: Socrates is guilty of wrongdoing in that he busies himself studying things in the sky and below the earth; he makes the worse into the stronger argument, and he teaches these same things to others. You have seen this yourselves in the comedy of Aristophanes, a Socrates swinging about there, saying he was walking on air and talking a lot of other nonsense about things of which I know nothing at all. I do not speak in contempt of such knowledge, if someone is wise in these things—lest Meletus bring more cases against me—but, gentlemen, I have no part in it, and on this point I call upon the majority of you as witnesses. I think it right that all those of you who have heard me conversing, and many of you have, should tell each other if anyone of you has ever heard me discussing such subjects to any extent at all. From this you will learn that the other things said about me by the majority are of the same kind.

Not one of them is true. And if you have heard from anyone that I undertake to teach people and charge a fee for it, that is not true either. Yet I think it a fine thing to be able to teach people as Gorgias of Leontini does, and Prodicus of Ceos, and Hippias of Elis.* Each of these men can go to any city and persuade the young, who can keep company with anyone of their own fellow-citizens they want, without paying, to leave the company of these, to join with themselves, pay them a fee, and be grateful to them besides. . . . Certainly I would pride and preen myself if I had this knowledge, but I do not have it, gentlemen.

One of you might perhaps interrupt me and say: "But Socrates, what is your occupation? From where have these slanders come? For surely if you did not busy yourself with something out of the common, all these rumours and talk would not have arisen unless you did something other than most people. Tell us what it is, that we may not speak inadvisedly about you." Anyone who says that seems to be right, and I will try to show you what has caused this reputation and slander. Listen then. Perhaps some of you will

think I am jesting, but be sure that all that I shall say is true. What has caused my reputation is none other than a certain kind of wisdom. What kind of wisdom? Human wisdom, perhaps. It may be that I really possess this, while those whom I mentioned just now are wise with a wisdom more than human; else I cannot explain it, for I certainly do not possess it, and whoever says I do is lying and speaks to slander me. Do not create a disturbance, gentlemen, even if you think I am boasting, for the story I shall tell does not originate with me, but I will refer you to a trustworthy source. I shall call upon the god at Delphi as witness to the existence and nature of my wisdom, if it be such. You know Chairephon. He was my friend from youth, and the friend of most of you, as he shared your exile and your return. You surely know the kind of man he was, how impulsive in any course of action. He went to Delphi at one time and ventured to ask the oracle—as I say, gentlemen, do not create a disturbance—he asked if any man was wiser than I, and the Pythian replied that no one was wiser.① Chairephon is dead, but his brother will testify to you about this.

① The Greeks believed that ordinary people could communicate with the gods by asking questions of the priests at particular temples. One of the most respected of these temples, Apollo's temple, was in a small village named Delphi.

Consider that I tell you this because I would inform you about the origin of the slander. When I heard of this reply I asked myself: "Whatever does the god mean? What is his riddle? I am very conscious that I am not wise at all; what then does he mean by saying that I am the wisest? For surely he does not lie; it is not legitimate for him to do so." For a long time I was at a loss as to his meaning; then I very reluctantly turned to some such investigation as this: I went to one of those reputed wise, thinking that there, if anywhere, I could refute the oracle and say to it: "This man is wiser than I, but you said I was." Then, when I examined this man—there is no need for me to tell you his name, he was one of our public men—my experience was something like this: I thought that he appeared wise to many people and especially to himself, but he was not. I then tried to show him that he thought himself wise, but that he was not. As a result

---

*These were all well-known Sophists. . . .

he came to dislike me, and so did many of the by-standers. So I withdrew and thought to myself: "I am wiser than this man; it is likely that neither of us knows anything worthwhile, but he thinks he knows something when he does not, whereas when I do not know, neither do I think I know; so I am likely to be wiser than he to this small extent, that I do not think I know what I do not know."② After this I approached another man, one of those thought to be wiser than he, and I thought the same thing, and so I came to be disliked both by him and by many others.

---

② What do you think about this claim that someone who knows that he doesn't know something or indeed that he knows nothing worthwhile is nonetheless wiser than someone who mistakenly thinks that he knows something?

After that I proceeded systematically. I realized, to my sorrow and alarm, that I was getting unpopular, but I thought that I must attach the greatest importance to the god's oracle, so I must go to all those who had any reputation for knowledge to examine its meaning. And . . . gentlemen of the jury—for I must tell you the truth—I experienced something like this: in my investigation in the service of the god I found that those who had the highest reputation were nearly the most deficient, while those who were thought to be inferior were more knowledgeable. I must give you an account of my journeyings as if they were labours I had undertaken to prove the oracle irrefutable. After the politicians, I went to the poets, the writers of tragedies and dithyrambs and the others, intending in their case to catch myself being more ignorant then they. So I took up those poems with which they seemed to have taken most trouble and asked them what they meant, in order that I might at the same time learn something from them. I am ashamed to tell you the truth, gentlemen, but I must. Almost all the bystanders might have explained the poems better than their authors could. I soon realized that poets do not compose their poems with knowledge, but by some inborn talent and by inspiration, like seers and prophets who also say many fine things without any understanding of what they say. The poets seemed to me to have had a similar experience. At the same time I saw that, because of their poetry, they thought themselves very wise men in other respects, which they were not. So there again I withdrew, thinking that I

had the same advantage over them as I had over the politicians.

Finally I went to the craftsmen, for I was conscious of knowing practically nothing, and I knew that I would find that they had knowledge of many fine things. In this I was not mistaken; they knew things I did not know, and to that extent they were wiser than I. But, gentlemen of the jury, the good craftsmen seemed to me to have the same fault as the poets: each of them, because of his success at his craft, thought himself very wise in other most important pursuits, and this error of theirs overshadowed the wisdom they had, so that I asked myself, on behalf of the oracle, whether I should prefer to be as I am, with neither their wisdom nor their ignorance, or to have both. The answer I gave myself and the oracle was that it was to my advantage to be as I am.

As a result of this investigation, gentlemen of the jury, I acquired much unpopularity, of a kind that is hard to deal with and is a heavy burden; many slanders came from these people and a reputation for wisdom, for in each case the bystanders thought that I myself possessed the wisdom that I proved that my interlocutor did not have. What is probable, gentlemen, is that in fact the god is wise and that his oracular response meant that human wisdom is worth little or nothing, and that when he says this man, Socrates, he is using my name as an example, as if he said: "This man among you, mortals, is wisest who, like Socrates, understands that his wisdom is worthless." So even now I continue this investigation as the god bade me—and I go around seeking out anyone, citizen or stranger, whom I think wise. Then if I do not think he is, I come to the assistance of the god and show him that he is not wise. Because of this occupation, I do not have the leisure to engage in public affairs to any extent, nor indeed to look after my own, but I live in great poverty because of my service to the god.

Furthermore, the young men who follow me around of their own free will, those who have most leisure, the sons of the very rich, take pleasure in hearing people questioned; they themselves often imitate me and try to question others. I think they find an abundance of men who believe they have some knowledge but know little or nothing. The result is that those whom they question are angry, not with themselves but with me. They say: "That man Socrates is a pestilential fellow who corrupts the young." If one asks them what he does and what he teaches to corrupt them, they are silent, as they do not know, but, so as not to appear at a loss, they mention those accusations that are available against all philosophers, about "things in the sky and things below the earth," about "not believing in the gods" and "making the worse the stronger argument;" they would not want to tell the truth, I'm sure, that they have been proved to lay claim to knowledge when they know nothing. These people are ambitious, violent and numerous; they are continually and convincingly talking about me; they have been filling your ears for a long time with vehement slanders against me. . . . That, gentlemen of the jury, is the truth for you. I have hidden or disguised nothing. I know well enough that this very conduct makes me unpopular, and this is proof that what I say is true, that such is the slander against me, and that such are its causes. If you look into this either now or later, this is what you will find.

Let this suffice as a defence against the charges of my earlier accusers. After this I shall try to defend myself against Meletus, that good and patriotic man, as he says he is, and my later accusers. As these are a different lot of accusers, let us again take up their sworn deposition. It goes something like this: Socrates is guilty of corrupting the young and of not believing in the gods in whom the city believes, but in other new divinities. Such is their charge. Let us examine it point by point.

He says that I am guilty of corrupting the young, but I say that Meletus is guilty of dealing frivolously with serious matters, of irresponsibly bringing people into court, and of professing to be seriously concerned with things about none of which he has ever cared, and I shall try to prove that this is so. Come here and tell me, Meletus. Surely you consider it of the greatest importance that our young men be as good as possible?— Indeed I do.

Come then, tell the jury who improves them. You obviously know, in view of your concern. You say you have discovered the one who corrupts them, namely me, and you bring me here and accuse me to the jury. Come, inform the jury and tell them who it is. You see, Meletus, that you are silent and know not what to say. Does this not seem shameful to you and a sufficient proof of what I say, that you have not been concerned with any of this? Tell me, my good sir, who improves our young men?—The laws.

That is not what I am asking, but what person who has knowledge of the laws to begin with?— These jurymen, Socrates.

How do you mean, Meletus? Are these able to educate the young and improve them?—Certainly.

All of them, or some but not others?—All of them.

Very good, by Hera. You mention a great abundance of benefactors. But what about the audience? Do they improve the young or not?—They do, too.

What about the members of Council?—The Councillors, also.

But, Meletus, what about the assembly? Do members of the assembly corrupt the young, or do they all improve them?—They improve them.

All the Athenians, it seems, make the young into fine good men, except me, and I alone corrupt them. Is that what you mean?—That is most definitely what I mean.

You condemn me to a great misfortune. Tell me: does this also apply to horses do you think? That all men improve them and one individual corrupts them? Or is quite the contrary true, one individual is able to improve them, or very few, namely the horse breeders, whereas the majority, if they have horses and use them, corrupt them? Is that not the case, Meletus, both with horses and all other animals? Of course it is, whether you and Anytus say so or not. It would be a very happy state of affairs if only one person corrupted our youth, while the others improved them.

You have made it sufficiently obvious, Meletus, that you have never had any concern for our youth; you show your indifference clearly; that you have given no thought to the subjects about which you bring me to trial.

And by Zeus, Meletus, tell us also whether it is better for a man to live among good or wicked fellow-citizens. Answer, my good man, for I am not asking a difficult question. Do not the wicked do some harm to those who are ever closest to them, whereas good people benefit them?—Certainly.

And does the man exist who would rather be harmed than benefited by his associates? Answer, my good sir, for the law orders you to answer. Is there any man who wants to be harmed?—Of course not.

Come now, do you accuse me here of corrupting the young and making them worse deliberately or unwillingly?—Deliberately.

What follows, Meletus? Are you so much wiser at your age than I am at mine that you understand that wicked people always do some harm to their closest neighbours while good people do them good, but I have reached such a pitch of ignorance that I do not realize this, namely that if I make one of my associates wicked I run the risk of being harmed by him so that I do such a great evil deliberately, as you say? I do not believe you, Meletus, and I do not think anyone else will.③ Either I do not corrupt the young or, if I do, it is unwillingly, and you are lying in either case. Now if I corrupt them unwillingly, the law does not require you to bring people to court for such unwilling wrongdoings, but to get hold of them privately, to instruct them and exhort them; for clearly, if I learn better, I shall cease to do what I am doing unwillingly. You, however, have avoided my company and were unwilling to instruct me, but you bring me here, where the law requires one to bring those who are in need of punishment, not of instruction.

③ The underlying assumption is that no one deliberately harms himself. Does that seem right?

And so, gentlemen of the jury, what I said is clearly true: Meletus has never been at all concerned with these matters.

I do not think, gentlemen of the jury, that it requires a prolonged defence to prove that I am not guilty of the charges in Meletus' deposition, but this is sufficient. On the other hand, you know that what I said earlier is true, that I am very unpopular with many people. This will be my undoing, if I am undone, not Meletus or Anytus but the slanders and envy of many people. This has destroyed many other good men and will, I think, continue to do so. There is no danger that it will stop at me.

Someone might say: "Are you not ashamed, Socrates, to have followed the kind of occupation that has led to your being now in danger of death?" However, I should be right to reply to him: "You are wrong, sir, if you think that a man who is any good at all should take into account the risk of life or death; he should look to this only in his actions, whether what he does is right or wrong, whether he is acting like a good or a bad man." . . .

This is the truth of the matter, gentlemen of the jury: wherever a man has taken a position that he believes to be best, or has been placed by his commander, there he must I think remain and face danger, without a thought for death or anything else, rather than disgrace. It would have been a dreadful way to behave, gentlemen of the jury, if . . . when the god ordered me, as I thought and believed, to live the life of a philosopher, to examine myself and others, I had abandoned my post for fear of death or anything else. That would have been a dreadful thing, and then I might truly have justly been brought here for not believing that there are gods, disobeying the oracle, fearing death, and thinking I was wise when I was not. To fear death, gentlemen, is no other than to think oneself wise when one is not, to think one knows what one does not know. No one knows whether death may not be the greatest of all blessings for a man, yet men fear it as if they knew that it is the greatest of evils. And surely it is the most blameworthy ignorance to believe that one knows what one does not know. It is perhaps on this point and in this respect, gentlemen, that I differ from the majority of men, and if I were to claim that I am wiser than anyone in anything, it would be in this, that, as I have no adequate knowledge of things in the underworld, so I do not think I have. I do know, however, that it is wicked and shameful to do wrong, to disobey one's superior, be he god or man. I shall never fear or avoid things of which I do not know, whether they may not be good rather than things that I know to be bad. Even if you acquitted me now and did not believe Anytus, . . . if you said to me in this regard: "Socrates, we do not believe Anytus now; we acquit you, but only on condition that you spend no more time on this investigation and do not practise philosophy, and if you are caught doing so you will die;" if, as I say, you were to acquit me on those terms, I would say to you: "Gentlemen of the jury, I am grateful and I am your friend, but I will obey the god rather than you, and as long as I draw breath and am able, I shall not cease to practise philosophy, to exhort you and in my usual way to point out to any one of you whom I happen to meet: Good Sir, you are an Athenian, a citizen of the greatest city with the greatest reputation for both wisdom and power; are you not ashamed of your eagerness to possess as much wealth, reputation and honours as possible, while you do not care for nor give thought to wisdom or truth, or the best possible state of your soul?" Then, if one of you disputes this and says he does care, I shall not let him go at once or leave him, but I shall question him, examine him and test him, and if I do not think he has attained the goodness that he says he has, I shall reproach him because he attaches little importance to the most important things and greater importance to inferior things. ④ I shall treat in this way anyone I happen to meet, young and old, citizen and stranger, and more so the citizens because you are more kindred to me. Be sure that this is what the god orders me to do, and I think there is no greater blessing for the city than my service to the god. . . .

④ Here is an account of what Socrates believes his job as a philosopher to be: to examine himself and others about claims to knowledge, to challenge himself and others to attain goodness, and to reproach those who attach importance to the wrong things.

Now if by saying this I corrupt the young, this advice must be harmful, but if anyone says that I give different advice, he is talking nonsense. On this point I would say to you, gentlemen of the jury: "Whether you believe Anytus or not, whether you acquit me or not, do so on the understanding that this is my course of action, even if I am to face death many times." Do not create a disturbance, gentlemen, but abide by my request not to cry out at what I say but to listen, for I think it will be to your advantage to listen, and I am about to say other things at which you will perhaps cry out. By no means do this. Be sure that if you kill the sort of man I say I am, you will not harm me more than yourselves. Neither Meletus nor Anytus can harm me in any way; he could not harm me, for I do not think it is permitted that a better man be harmed by a worse; certainly he might kill me, or perhaps banish or disfranchise me, which he and maybe others think to be great harm, but I do not think so. I think he is doing himself much greater harm doing what he is doing now, attempting to have a man executed unjustly. Indeed, gentlemen of the jury, I am far from making a defence now on my own behalf, as might be thought, but on yours, to prevent you from wrongdoing by mistreating the god's gift to you by condemning me; for if you kill me you will not easily find another like me. I was attached to this city by the god—though it seems a ridiculous thing to say— as upon a great and noble horse which was somewhat sluggish because of its size and needed to be stirred up by a kind of gadfly.⑤ It is to fulfill some such func-

⑤ A gadfly is a horsefly, the kind of fly that bites and irritates horses and cattle. The metaphorical meaning of a gadfly as a persistent, irritating critic originates in this dialogue.

tion that I believe the god has placed me in the city. I never cease to rouse each and every one of you, to persuade and reproach you all day long and everywhere I find myself in your company.

Another such man will not easily come to be among you, gentlemen, and if you believe me you will spare me. You might easily be annoyed with me as people are when they are aroused from a doze, and strike out at me; if convinced by Anytus you could easily kill me, and then you could sleep on for the rest of your days, unless the god, in his care for you, sent you someone else. That I am the kind of person to be a gift of the god to the city you might realize from the fact that it does not seem like human nature for me to have neglected all my own affairs and to have tolerated this neglect now for so many years while I was always concerned with you, approaching each one of you like a father or an elder brother to persuade you to care for virtue. Now if I profited from this by charging a fee for my advice, there would be some sense to it, but you can see for yourselves that, for all their shameless accusations, my accusers have not been able in their impudence to bring forward a witness to say that I have ever received a fee or ever asked for one. I, on the other hand, have a convincing witness that I speak the truth, my poverty.

It may seem strange that while I go around and give this advice privately and interfere in private affairs, I do not venture to go to the assembly and there advise the city. You have heard me give the reason for this in many places. I have a divine sign from the god which Meletus has ridiculed in his deposition. This began when I was a child. It is a voice, and whenever it speaks it turns me away from something I am about to do, but it never encourages me to do anything. This is what has prevented me from taking part in public affairs, and I think it was quite right to prevent me. Be sure, gentlemen of the jury, that if I had long ago attempted to take part in politics, I should have died long ago, and benefited neither you nor myself. Do not be angry with me for speaking the truth; no man will survive who genuinely opposes you or any other crowd and prevents the occurrence of many unjust and illegal happenings in the city. A man who really fights for justice must lead a private, not a public, life if he is to survive for even a short time. . . .

Do you think I would have survived all these years if I were engaged in public affairs and, acting as a good man must, came to the help of justice and considered this the most important thing? Far from it, gentlemen of the jury, nor would any other man. Throughout my life, in any public activity I may have engaged in, I am the same man as I am in private life. I have never come to an agreement with anyone to act unjustly, neither with anyone else nor with any one of those who they slanderously say are my pupils. I have never been anyone's teacher. If anyone, young or old, desires to listen to me when I am talking and dealing with my own concerns, I have never begrudged this to anyone, but I do not converse when I receive a fee and not when I do not. I am equally ready to question the rich and the poor if anyone is willing to answer my questions and listen to what I say. And I cannot justly be held responsible for the good or bad conduct of these people, as I never promised to teach them anything and have not done so. If anyone says that he has learned anything from me, or that he heard anything privately that the others did not hear, be assured that he is not telling the truth.

Why then do some people enjoy spending considerable time in my company? You have heard why, gentlemen of the jury, I have told you the whole truth. They enjoy hearing those being questioned who think they are wise, but are not. And this is not unpleasant. To do this has, as I say, been enjoined upon me by the god, by means of oracles and dreams, and in every other way that a divine manifestation has ever ordered a man to do anything. This is true, gentlemen, and can easily be established.

If I corrupt some young men and have corrupted others, then surely some of them who have grown older and realized that I gave them bad advice when they were young should now themselves come up here to accuse me and avenge themselves. If they were unwilling to do so themselves, then some of their kindred, their fathers or brothers or other relations should recall it now if their family had been harmed by me. I see many of these present here, first Crito, my contemporary and fellow demesman . . . ; next Lysanias of Sphettus . . . ; also Antiphon the Cephisian . . . ; Nicostratus . . . , brother of Theodotus, and Theodotus has died so he could not influence him; . . . there is Adeimantus . . . , brother of Plato here; Acantidorus, brother of Apollodorus here.

I could mention many others, some one of whom surely Meletus should have brought in as witness in his own speech. If he forgot to do so, then let him do it now; I will yield time if he has anything of the kind to say. You will find quite the contrary, gentlemen. These men are all ready to come to the help of the corruptor, the man who has harmed their kindred, as Meletus and Anytus say. Now those who were corrupted might well have reason to help me, but the uncorrupted, their kindred who are older men, have no reason to help me except the right and proper one, that they know that Meletus is lying and that I am telling the truth.

Very well, gentlemen of the jury. This, and maybe other similar things, is what I have to say in my defence. Perhaps one of you might be angry as he recalls that when he himself stood trial on a less dangerous charge, he begged and implored the jury with many tears, that he brought his children and many of his friends and family into court to arouse as much pity as he could, but that I do none of these things, even though I may seem to be running the ultimate risk. Thinking of this, he might feel resentful toward me and, angry about this, cast his vote in anger. If there is such a one among you—I do not deem there is, but if there is—I think it would be right to say in reply: My good sir, I too have a . . . family, indeed three sons, gentlemen of the jury, of whom one is an adolescent while two are children. Nevertheless, I will not beg you to acquit me by bringing them here. Why do I do none of these things? Not through arrogance, gentlemen, nor through lack of respect for you. Whether I am brave in the face of death is another matter, but with regard to my reputation and yours and that of the whole city, it does not seem right to me to do these things, especially at my age and with my reputation. For it is generally believed, whether it be true or false, that in certain respects Socrates is superior to the majority of men. Now if those of you who are considered superior, be it in wisdom or courage or whatever other virtue makes them so, are seen behaving like that, it would be a disgrace. Yet I have often seen them do this sort of thing when standing trial, men who are thought to be somebody, doing amazing things as if they thought it a terrible thing to die, and as if they were to be immortal if you did not execute them. I think these men bring shame upon the city so that a stranger, too, would assume that those who are outstanding in virtue among the Athenians, whom they themselves select from themselves to fill offices of state and receive other honours, are in no way better than women. You should not act like that, gentlemen of the jury, those of you who have any reputation at all, and if we do, you should not allow it. You should make it very clear that you will more readily convict a man who performs these pitiful dramatics in court and so makes the city a laughingstock, than a man who keeps quiet.

Quite apart from the question of reputation, gentlemen, I do not think it right to supplicate the jury and to be acquitted because of this, but to teach and persuade them. It is not the purpose of a juryman's office to give justice as a favour to whoever seems good to him, but to judge according to law, and this he has sworn to do. We should not accustom you to perjure yourselves, nor should you make a habit of it. This is irreverent conduct for either of us.

Do not deem it right for me, gentlemen of the jury, that I should act towards you in a way that I do not consider to be good or just or pious, especially, by Zeus, as I am being prosecuted by Meletus here for impiety; clearly, if I convinced you by my supplication to do violence to your oath of office, I would be teaching you not to believe that there are gods, and my defence would convict me of not believing in them. This is far from being the case, gentlemen, for I do believe in them as none of my accusers do. I leave it to you and the god to judge me in the way that will be best for me and for you.

[The jury now gives its verdict of guilty, and Meletus asks for the penalty of death.]

There are many other reasons for my not being angry with you for convicting me, gentlemen of the jury, and what happened was not unexpected. I am much more surprised at the number of votes cast on each side, for I did not think the decision would be by so few votes but by a great many. As it is, a switch of only thirty votes would have acquitted me. I think myself that I have been cleared on Meletus' charges, and not only this, but it is clear to all that, if Anytus and Lycon had not joined him in accusing me, he would have been fined a thousand drachmas for not receiving a fifth of the votes.

He assesses the penalty at death. So be it. What counter-assessment should I propose to you, gentle-men of the jury? Clearly it should be a penalty I deserve, and what do I deserve to suffer or to pay because I have deliberately not led a quiet life but have neglected what occupies most people: wealth, household affairs, the position of general or public orator or the other offices, the political clubs and factions that exist in the city? I thought myself too honest to survive if I occupied myself with those things. I did not follow that path that would have made me of no use either to you or to myself, but I went to each of you privately and conferred upon him what I say is the greatest benefit, by trying to persuade him not to care for any of his belongings before caring that he himself should be as good and as wise as possible, not to care for the city's possessions more than for the city itself, and to care for other things in the same way. What do I deserve for being such a man? Some good, gentlemen of the jury, if I must truly make an assessment according to my deserts, and something suitable. What is suitable for a poor benefactor who needs leisure to exhort you? Nothing is more suitable, gentlemen, than for such a man to be fed in the Prytaneum,* much more suitable for him than for any one of you who has won a victory at Olympia with a pair or a team of horses. The Olympian victor makes you think yourself happy; I make you be happy. Besides, he does not need food, but I do. So if I must make a just assessment of what I deserve, I assess it at this: free meals in the Prytaneum.

When I say this you may think, as when I spoke of appeals to pity and entreaties, that I speak arrogantly, but that is not the case, gentlemen of the jury; rather it is like this: I am convinced that I never willingly wrong anyone, but I am not convincing you of this, for we have talked together but a short time. If it were the law with us, as it is elsewhere, that a trial for life should not last one but many days, you would be convinced, but now it is not easy to dispel great slanders in a short time. Since I am convinced that I wrong no one, I am not likely to wrong myself, to say that I deserve some evil and to make some such assessment against myself. What should I fear? That I should suffer the penalty Meletus has assessed against me, of which I say I do not know whether it is good or bad? Am I then to choose in preference to this some-

---

*The Prytaneum was the magistrates' hall or town hall of Athens in which public entertainments were given, particularly to Olympian victors on their return home.

thing that I know very well to be an evil and assess the penalty at that? Imprisonment? Why should I live in prison, always subjected to the ruling magistrates the Eleven? A fine, and imprisonment until I pay it? That would be the same thing for me, as I have no money. Exile? for perhaps you might accept that assessment.

I should have to be inordinately fond of life, gentlemen of the jury, to be so unreasonable as to suppose that other men will easily tolerate my company and conversation when you, my fellow citizens, have been unable to endure them, but found them a burden and resented them so that you are now seeking to get rid of them. Far from it, gentlemen. It would be a fine life at my age to be driven out of one city after another, for I know very well that wherever I go the young men will listen to my talk as they do here. If I drive them away, they will themselves persuade their elders to drive me out; if I do not drive them away, their fathers and relations will drive me out on their behalf.

Perhaps someone might say: But Socrates, if you leave us will you not be able to live quietly, without talking? Now this is the most difficult point on which to convince some of you. If I say that it is impossible for me to keep quiet because that means disobeying the god, you will not believe me and will think I am being ironical. On the other hand, if I say that it is the greatest good for a man to discuss virtue every day and those

> **6** Here is the famous Socratic saying that the unexamined life is not worth living. It has a rather more literal meaning in this context than it usually does.

other things about which you hear me conversing and testing myself and others, for the unexamined life is not worth living for man, you will believe me even less.**6**

What I say is true, gentlemen, but it is not easy to convince you. At the same time, I am not accustomed to think that I deserve any penalty. If I had money, I would assess the penalty at the amount I could pay, for that would not hurt me, but I have none, unless you are willing to set the penalty at the amount I can pay, and perhaps I could pay you one mina of silver.* So that is my assessment.

Plato here, gentlemen of the jury, and Crito and Critoboulus and Apollodorus bid me put the penalty at

thirty minae, and they will stand surety for the money. Well then, that is my assessment, and they will be sufficient guarantee of payment.

[The jury now votes again and sentences Socrates to death.]

It is for the sake of a short time, gentlemen of the jury, that you will acquire the reputation and the guilt, in the eyes of those who want to denigrate the city, of having killed Socrates, a wise man, for they who want to revile you will say that I am wise even if I am not. If you had waited but a little while, this would have happened of its own accord. You see my age, that I am already advanced in years and close to death. I am saying this not to all of you but to those who condemned me to death, and to these same jurors I say: Perhaps you think that I was convicted for lack of such words as might have convinced you, if I thought I should say or do all I could to avoid my sentence. Far from it. I was convicted because I lacked not words but boldness and shamelessness and the willingness to say to you what you would most gladly have heard from me, lamentations and tears and my saying and doing many things that I say are unworthy of me but that you are accustomed to hear from others. I did not think then that the danger I ran should make me do anything mean, nor do I now regret the nature of my defence. I would much rather die after this kind of defence than live after making the other kind. Neither I nor any other man should, on trial or in war, contrive to avoid death at any cost. Indeed it is often obvious in battle that one could escape death by throwing away one's weapons and by turning to supplicate one's pursuers, and there are many ways to avoid death in every kind of danger if one will venture to do or say anything to avoid it. It is not difficult to avoid death, gentlemen of the jury, it is much more difficult to avoid wickedness, for it runs faster than death. Slow and elderly as I am, I have been caught by the slower pursuer, whereas my accusers, being clever and sharp, have been caught by the quicker, wickedness. I leave you now, condemned to death by you, but they are condemned by truth to wickedness and injustice. So I maintain my assessment, and they maintain theirs. This perhaps had to happen, and I think it is as it should be.

---

*One mina was 100 drachmas, equivalent to, say, twenty-five dollars, though in purchasing power probably five times greater. In any case, a ridiculously small sum under the circumstances.

Now I want to prophesy to those who convicted me, for I am at the point when men prophesy most, when they are about to die. I say gentlemen, to those who voted to kill me, that vengeance will come upon you immediately after my death, a vengeance much harder to bear than that which you took in killing me. You did this in the belief that you would avoid giving an account of your life, but I maintain that quite the opposite will happen to you. There will be more people to test you, whom I now held back, but you did not notice it. They will be more difficult to deal with as they will be younger and you will resent them more. You are wrong if you believe that by killing people you will prevent anyone from reproaching you for not living in the right way. To escape such tests is neither possible nor good, but it is best and easiest not to discredit others but to prepare oneself to be as good as possible. With this prophecy to you who convicted me, I part from you.

I should be glad to discuss what has happened with those who voted for my acquittal during the time that the officers of the court are busy and I do not yet have to depart to my death. So, gentlemen, stay with me awhile, for nothing prevents us from talking to each other while it is allowed. To you, as being my friends, I want to show the meaning of what has occurred. A surprising thing has happened to me, judges—you I would rightly call judges. At all previous times my usual mantic sign frequently opposed me, even in small matters, when I was about to do something wrong, but now that, as you can see for yourselves, I was faced with what one might think, and what is generally thought to be, the worst of evils, my divine sign has not opposed me, either when I left home at dawn, or when I came into court, or at any time that I was about to say something during my speech. Yet in other talks it often held me back in the middle of my speaking, but now it has opposed no word or deed of mine. What do I think is the reason for this? I will tell you. What has happened to me may well be a good thing, and those of us who believe death to be an evil are certainly mistaken. I have convincing proof of this, for it is impossible that my customary sign did not oppose me if I was not about to do what was right.

Let us reflect in this way, too, that there is good hope that death is a blessing, for it is one of two things: either the dead are nothing and have no perception of anything, or it is, as we are told, a change and a relocating for the soul from here to another place. [7] If it is complete lack of perception, like a dreamless sleep, then death would be a great advantage. For I think that if one had to pick out that night during which a man slept soundly and did not dream, put beside it the other nights and days of his life, and then see how many days and nights had been better and more pleasant than that night, not only a private person but the great king would find them easy to count compared with the other days and nights. If death is like this I say it is an advantage, for all eternity would then seem to be no more than a single night. If, on the other hand, death is a change from here to another place, and what we are told is true and all who have died are there, what greater blessing could there be, gentlemen of the jury? If anyone arriving in Hades will have escaped from those who call themselves judges here, and will find those true judges who are said to sit in judgement there, Minos and Radamanthus and Aeacus and Triptolemus and the other demi-gods who have been upright in their own life, would that be a poor kind of change? Again, what would one of you give to keep company with Orpheus and Musaeus, Hesiod and Homer? I am willing to die many times if that is true. It would be a wonderful way for me to spend my time whenever I met Palamedes and Ajax, the son of Telamon, and any other of the men of old who died through an unjust conviction, to compare my experience with theirs. I think it would be pleasant. Most important, I could spend my time testing and examining people there, as I do here, as to who among them is wise, and who thinks he is, but is not.

What would one not give, gentlemen of the jury, for the opportunity to examine the man who led the great expedition against Troy, or Odysseus, or Sisyphus, and innumerable other men and women one could mention. It would be an extraordinary happiness to talk with them, to keep company with them and examine them. In any case, they would certainly not put one to death for doing so. They are happier there than we are here in other respects, and for the rest of time they are deathless, if indeed what we are told is true.

> [7] Suppose that Socrates is right that when you die one of two things happens: either you cease to exist altogether or your body dies but you continue on to a better place. If he is right about that, is death then a blessing (no matter which of the two possibilities is true)?

You too must be of good hope as regards death, gentlemen of the jury, and keep this one truth in mind, that a good man cannot be harmed either in life or in death, and that his affairs are not neglected by the gods. What has happened to me now has not happened of itself, but it is clear to me that it was better for me to die now and to escape from trouble. That is why my divine sign did not oppose me at any point. So I am certainly not angry with those who convicted me, or with my accusers. Of course that was not their purpose when they accused and convicted me, but they thought they were hurting me, and for this they deserve blame.

This much I ask from them: when my sons grow up, avenge yourselves by causing them the same kind of grief that I caused you, if you think they care for money or anything else more than they care for virtue, or if they think they are somebody when they are nobody. Reproach them as I reproach you, that they do not care for the right things and think they are worthy when they are not worthy of anything. If you do this, I shall have been justly treated by you, and my sons also.

Now the hour to part has come. I go to die, you go to live. Which of us goes to the better lot is known to no one, except the god.

Discussion Questions

1. What do you think about the famous Socratic saying that the unexamined life is not worth living? Contrast that with the saying that ignorance is bliss. What assumptions would someone make about the value and importance of human life to defend each one of these very different philosophies of life? Which one strikes you as one you might want to live by? Why? What is wrong with the other one?

2. Do you think that Socrates performed an important function for his society? Do we have any people in our public life who function as gadflies? Do you know anyone personally who functions as a gadfly? Do you think that Socrates should have been put to death? Should someone be punished for being a gadfly?

Bertrand Russell

Bertrand Russell (1872–1970) was a British philosopher who made important contributions to the foundations of mathematics, logic, epistemology, and many other areas of philosophy. Russell was also very active politically (he spent time in prison because of his antiwar activities). He won the Nobel Prize for Literature in 1950.

This selection is the last chapter of one of Russell's most famous books, *The Problems of Philosophy*. In this chapter, Russell explains what he thinks is valuable about philosophy, given his view that there is probably little or no genuine philosophical knowledge.

The Value of Philosophy

Having now come to the end of our brief and very incomplete review of the problems of philosophy, it will be well to consider, in conclusion, what is the value of philosophy and why it ought to be studied. It is the more necessary to consider this question, in view of the fact that many men, under the influence of science or of practical affairs, are inclined to doubt whether philosophy is anything better than innocent

From The Problems of Philosophy *(New York: Oxford University Press, 1959).*

but useless trifling, hair-splitting distinctions, and controversies on matters concerning which knowledge is impossible.

This view of philosophy appears to result, partly from a wrong conception of the ends of life, partly from a wrong conception of the kind of goods which philosophy strives to achieve. Physical science, through the medium of inventions, is useful to innumerable people who are wholly ignorant of it; thus the study of physical science is to be recommended, not only, or primarily, because of the effect on the student, but rather because of the effect on mankind in general. Thus utility does not belong to philosophy. If the study of philosophy has any value at all for others than students of philosophy, it must be only indirectly, through its effects upon the lives of those who study it. It is in these effects, therefore, if anywhere, that the value of philosophy must be primarily sought.

But further, if we are not to fail in our endeavour to determine the value of philosophy, we must first free our minds from the prejudices of what are wrongly called 'practical' men. The 'practical' man, as this word is often used, is one who recognizes only material needs, who realizes that men must have food for the body, but is oblivious of the necessity of providing food for the mind.①

① Think of some examples of things that are "food for the mind." (Do you know anyone who is what Russell calls a "practical man" (or woman)?)

If all men were well off, if poverty and disease had been reduced to their lowest possible point, there would still remain much to be done to produce a valuable society; and even in the existing world the goods of the mind are at least as important as the goods of the body. It is exclusively among the goods of the mind that the value of philosophy is to be found; and only those who are not indifferent to these goods can be persuaded that the study of philosophy is not a waste of time.

Philosophy, like all other studies, aims primarily at knowledge. The knowledge it aims at is the kind of knowledge which gives unity and system to the body of the sciences, and the kind which results from a critical examination of the grounds of our convictions, prejudices, and beliefs. But it cannot be maintained that philosophy has had any very great measure of success in its attempts to provide definite answers to its questions. If you ask a mathematician, a mineralogist, a historian, or any other man of learning, what definite body of truths has been ascertained by his science, his answer will last as long as you are willing to listen. But if you put the same question to a philosopher, he will, if he is candid, have to confess that his study has not achieved positive results such as have been achieved by other sciences.② It is true that this is partly accounted for by the fact that, as soon as definite knowledge concerning any subject becomes possible, this subject ceases to be called philosophy, and becomes a separate science.

② One could agree with this assessment, while still thinking that philosophy itself has generated *some* body of knowledge that is genuine, even if not to the same extent as the sciences. But Russell suggests that there is probably little or no distinctively philosophical knowledge at all.

The whole study of the heavens, which now belongs to astronomy, was once included in philosophy; Newton's great work was called 'the mathematical principles of natural philosophy'. Similarly, the study of the human mind, which was a part of philosophy, has now been separated from philosophy and has become the science of psychology. Thus, to a great extent, the uncertainty of philosophy is more apparent than real: those questions which are already capable of definite answers are placed in the sciences, while those only to which, at present, no definite answer can be given, remain to form the residue which is called philosophy.③

③ This is an important point: when we learn how to investigate a set of issues in a way that yields clear and firmly established results, those issues stop being part of philosophy, and instead become a new area of science (including social science). The questions that we do not yet know how to deal with in this way are the ones that remain in the province of philosophy, including some—as Russell goes on to suggest—that are unlikely ever to be settled in a scientific way.

This is, however, only a part of the truth concerning the uncertainty of philosophy. There are many questions—and among them those that are of the profoundest interest to our spiritual life—which, so far as we can see, must remain insoluble to the human intellect unless its powers become of quite a different order from what they are now. Has the universe any unity of plan or purpose, or is it a fortuitous concourse of atoms? Is consciousness a permanent part of the universe, giving hope of indefinite growth in wisdom, or is it a transitory accident on a small planet on which life must ultimately become impossible? Are good and evil of importance to the universe or only to man? Such questions are asked by philosophy, and variously answered by various philosophers. But it would seem that, whether answers be otherwise discoverable or not, the answers suggested by philosophy are none of them demonstrably true. Yet, however slight may be the hope of discovering an answer, it is part of the business of philosophy to continue the consideration of such questions, to make us aware of their importance, to examine all the approaches to them, and to keep alive that speculative interest in the universe which is apt to be killed by confining ourselves to definitely ascertainable knowledge.④

④ If you insisted that you would think about only those questions that had clear, ascertainable black or white answers, then you would have to refuse to think about many of the most important questions concerning the human condition.

Many philosophers, it is true, have held that philosophy could establish the truth of certain answers to such fundamental questions. They have supposed that what is of most importance in religious beliefs could be proved by strict demonstration to be true.⑤ In order to judge of such attempts, it is necessary to take a survey of human knowledge, and to form an opinion as to its methods and its limitations. On such a subject it would be unwise to pronounce dogmatically; but if the investigations of our previous chapters have not led us astray, we shall be compelled to renounce the hope of finding philosophical proofs of religious beliefs. We cannot, therefore, include as part of the value of philosophy any definite set of answers to such questions. Hence, once more, the value of philosophy must not depend upon any supposed

⑤ For example, many of the authors in Chapter 2 of this book think that one can establish the existence of God through something approaching a demonstrative proof. (But even if Russell is right that such attempts at proofs are very unlikely to succeed, isn't that in itself something worth knowing?)

body of definitely ascertainable knowledge to be acquired by those who study it.

The value of philosophy is, in fact, to be sought largely in its very uncertainty. The man who has no tincture of philosophy goes through life imprisoned in the prejudices derived from common sense, from the habitual beliefs of his age or his nation, and from convictions which have grown up in his mind without the co-operation or consent of his deliberate reason. To such a man the world tends to become definite, finite, obvious; common objects rouse no questions, and unfamiliar possibilities are contemptuously rejected. As soon as we begin to philosophize, on the contrary, we find, as we saw in our opening chapters, that even the most everyday things lead to problems to which only very incomplete answers can be given. Philosophy, though unable to tell us with certainty what is the true answer to the doubts which it raises, is able to suggest many possibilities which enlarge our thoughts and free them from the tyranny of custom.⑥ Thus, while diminishing our feeling of certainty as to what things are, it greatly increases our knowledge as to what they may be; it removes the somewhat arrogant dogmatism of those who have never travelled into the region of liberating doubt, and it keeps alive our sense of wonder by showing familiar things in an unfamiliar aspect.

⑥ Think carefully about what Russell means by the "tyranny of custom." There was a time when the "customary" belief was that the Earth was flat. If custom ruled in a tyrannical fashion, then might we not still believe that the Earth is flat? (Russell's point here is at least similar to the one that Socrates made by saying that "the unexamined life is not worth living"—a life ruled by custom and common-sense prejudice is not really an examined one.)

Apart from its utility in showing unsuspected possibilities, philosophy has a value—perhaps its chief value—through the greatness of the objects which it contemplates, and the freedom from narrow and personal aims resulting from this contemplation. The life of the instinctive man is shut up within the circle of his private interests: family and friends may be included, but the outer world is not regarded except as it may help or hinder what comes within the circle of instinctive wishes. In such a life there is something feverish and confined, in comparison with which the philosophic life is calm and free.[7] The private world of instinctive interests is a small one, set in the midst of a great and powerful world which must, sooner or later, lay our private world in ruins. Unless we can so enlarge our interests as to include the whole outer world, we remain like a garrison in a beleaguered fortress, knowing that the enemy prevents escape and that ultimate surrender is inevitable. In such a life there is no peace, but a constant strife between the insistence of desire and the powerlessness of will. In one way or another, if our life is to be great and free, we must escape this prison and this strife.

One way of escape is by philosophic contemplation. Philosophic contemplation does not, in its widest survey, divide the universe into two hostile camps—friends and foes, helpful and hostile, good and bad—it views the whole impartially. Philosophic contemplation, when it is unalloyed, does not aim at proving that the rest of the universe is akin to man. All acquisition of knowledge is an enlargement of the Self, but this enlargement is best attained when it is not directly sought. It is obtained when the desire for knowledge is alone operative, by a study which does not wish in advance that its objects should have this or that character, but adapts the Self to the characters which it finds in its objects.[8] This enlargement of Self is not obtained when, taking the Self as it is, we try to show that the world is so similar to this Self that knowledge of it is possible without any admission of what seems alien. The desire to prove

this is a form of self-assertion and, like all self-assertion, it is an obstacle to the growth of Self which it desires, and of which the Self knows that it is capable. Self-assertion, in philosophic speculation as elsewhere, views the world as a means to its own ends; thus it makes the world of less account than Self, and the Self sets bounds to the greatness of its goods. In contemplation, on the contrary, we start from the not-Self, and through its greatness the boundaries of Self are enlarged; through the infinity of the universe the mind which contemplates it achieves some share in infinity.[9]

For this reason greatness of soul is not fostered by those philosophies which assimilate the universe to Man. Knowledge is a form of union of Self and not-Self; like all union, it is impaired by dominion, and therefore by any attempt to force the universe into conformity with what we find in ourselves. There is a widespread philosophical tendency towards the view which tells us that Man is the measure of all things, that truth is man-made, that space and time and the world of universals are properties of the mind, and that, if there be anything not created by the mind, it is unknowable and of no account for us. This view, if our previous discussions were correct, is untrue; but in addition to being untrue, it has the effect of robbing philosophic contemplation of all that gives it value, since it fetters contemplation to Self. What it calls knowledge is not a union with the not-Self, but a set of prejudices, habits, and desires, making an impenetrable veil between us and the world beyond. The man who finds pleasure in such a theory of knowledge is like the man who never leaves the domestic circle for fear his word might not be law.[10]

The true philosophic contemplation, on the contrary, finds its satisfaction

[7] If Russell is right about the contrast between the philosophic life and the life of "the instinctive man," then the philosophic life seems clearly better. Do you agree with his assessment? (He proceeds to offer further reasons in what follows.)

[8] How is the acquisition of knowledge supposed to result in an "enlargement" of the self? At least part of the idea is that because philosophical contemplation has the goal of understanding something as it is in itself and not just as it appears to us, philosophical contemplation will rarely just confirm previous prejudices in a way that would promote intellectual stagnation. (In another work, *A History of Western Philosophy*, Russell describes the true philosopher as one who "follows the argument where it leads," meaning that such a person does not shy away from a conclusion just because it does not agree with his own previous views—again we can see here an echo of Socrates.)

[9] The metaphor of the self enlarging, ultimately, to some sort of infinity is hard to make sense of in a clear way. (See Discussion Question 3). But whatever it means, it will be the result of philosophical contemplation only if there is more to reality than what we, in our practical modes, think there is.

[10] To say that humans are the measure of all things is to reject the claim that there are aspects of reality that transcend humans. Russell has argued in previous chapters of this book for a kind of **realism** which insists that there are aspects of reality that go beyond humans.

in every enlargement of the not-Self, in everything that magnifies the objects contemplated, and thereby the subject contemplating. Everything, in contemplation, that is personal or private, everything that depends upon habit, self-interest, or desire, distorts the object, and hence impairs the union which the intellect seeks. By thus making a barrier between subject and object, such personal and private things become a prison to the intellect. The free intellect will see as God might see, without a *here* and *now,* without hopes and fears, without the trammels of customary beliefs and traditional prejudices, calmly, dispassionately, in the sole and exclusive desire of knowledge—knowledge as impersonal, as purely contemplative, as it is possible for man to attain. ⑪ Hence also the free intellect will value more the abstract and universal knowledge into which the accidents of private history do not enter, than the knowledge brought by the senses, and dependent, as such knowledge must be, upon an exclusive and personal point of view and a body whose sense-organs distort as much as they reveal.

⑪ Some philosophers call this the God's eye point of view. You will see it referred to as *sub specie aeternitatis:* from the perspective of eternity. From this perspective, one's own concerns or views are given the proper significance, whereas from the subjective perspective, those same concerns might seem much more important than they really are.

The mind which has become accustomed to the freedom and impartiality of philosophic contemplation will preserve something of the same freedom and impartiality in the world of action and emotion. It will view its purposes and desires as parts of the whole, with the absence of insistence that results from seeing them as infinitesimal fragments in a world of which all the rest is unaffected by any one man's deeds. The impartiality which, in contemplation, is the unalloyed desire for truth, is the very same quality of mind which, in action, is justice, and in emotion is that universal love which can be given to all, and not only to those who are judged useful or admirable. Thus contemplation enlarges not only the objects of our thoughts, but also the objects of our actions and our affections: it makes us citizens of the universe, not only of one walled city at war with all the rest. In this citizenship of the universe consists man's true freedom, and his liberation from the thraldom of narrow hopes and fears.

Thus, to sum up our discussion of the value of philosophy; Philosophy is to be studied, not for the sake of any definite answers to its questions since no definite answers can, as a rule, be known to be true, but rather for the sake of the questions, themselves; because these questions enlarge our conception of what is possible, enrich our intellectual imagination and diminish the dogmatic assurance which closes the mind against speculation; but above all because, through the greatness of the universe which philosophy contemplates, the mind also is rendered great, and becomes capable of that union with the universe which constitutes its highest good.

Discussion Questions

1. A dogmatic belief is a belief firmly held without any basis or reason. Dogmatic beliefs are typically resistant to change. Do you think it is ever appropriate to be dogmatic? Might one argue that there are some arenas in which asking for reasons makes no sense? Think about religion and politics. Some people think that you should never talk about religion or politics with friends or family, because the arguments will just get ugly. How might a philosophically minded person (someone who thinks that you should always look for reasons) respond to such a view?

2. Russell thinks that philosophy can protect you from the "tyranny of custom." Think of some examples of periods of history when the custom dictated that things should be a way that we now disagree with. How could a philosophical attitude protect the people then from the tyranny of custom? What kinds of questions should a philosopher ask now to be protected from the tyranny of custom? Do you think that such protection is the only value philosophy has?

3. Let's try to clarify Russell's metaphor of a self enlarging, achieving some sense of the infinity of the universe by contemplating it philosophically. Contrast is essential to the metaphor, and while it surely applies to the contrast between two people, it also applies to the

contrast between one person before and after engaging in philosophical contemplation. Let's think of the one person case. Suppose that John had never thought about anything philosophical before he went to college in 1969, but 35 years later, he is a very philosophical man, often engaging in philosophical contemplation. What exactly is different about John, if Russell is right that his self is enlarged, that it has achieved some kind of infinity? When John thinks about some important issue now, he can conceive of many more possibilities than he could 35 years ago. Then he was much more willing to merely accept the standard answer endorsed by his government or accepted by his peers. But now he insists on thinking about different possibilities, recognizing that the standard answers, on either side, may not be right. His intellectual imagination now is much richer than it was then, which is one of the reasons why he can conceive of so many more possibilities when he thinks about important issues. He asks many more questions now than he did then, both of himself, but also of others, asking them to clarify and justify their views. There is a sense in which we might call the younger John "small-minded." Is this what Russell is getting at when he talks about the self enlarging? Is such enlargement valuable for anyone or only for those who are inclined in that direction? Should everyone study philosophy?

CHAPTER 2

God and Faith

The selections in this chapter are concerned with two of the main topics in the general area of philosophy known as the philosophy of religion: first, arguments for and against the existence of God; and, second, the question of whether belief in God can be rationally acceptable on some basis other than rational arguments that establish the existence of such a being. Throughout this discussion, the idea of God is to be understood in the way that is more or less standard in the three great monotheistic religions: Judaism, Christianity, and Islam. As formulated by philosophers, this means that God is (a) a *personal* being who is (b) *omnipotent,* (c) *omniscient,* (d) *perfectly good, benevolent, merciful, and just,* and (e) the creator of the universe. (Attributes (b), (c), and (d) in this list are often explained by using the idea of infinity: God is viewed as having infinite power, infinite knowledge, and infinite goodness, benevolence, mercy, and justice.) There are, of course, other possible conceptions of God, but this is the one that has received an overwhelming proportion of attention in the Western philosophical tradition and about which the most interesting philosophical issues have been raised. (Some attention is also given in these readings to the possibility of a being conceived in a parallel but weaker way: one whose attributes fall short of infinity.)

DOES GOD EXIST?

Arguments in Favor of the Existence of God

What reasons are there to believe that such a being actually exists? The first two of the following sections focus on the two arguments that have both been widely discussed by philosophers and also have a good deal of appeal to common sense: the cosmological argument and the argument from design. The third selection is concerned with an argument that has fascinated philosophers (though few have actually accepted it), but which is most unlikely to occur to anyone but a philosopher: the so-called ontological argument.

41

The Cosmological Argument. The cosmological argument starts with the simple and undeniable empirical premise that things exist, that the world is not empty. It is ordinary material objects and processes that are usually cited to support this premise, but in principle any sort of nondivine existence would do. The argument then asks *why* these things exist, demanding a cause or reason or explanation (with the emphasis varying in different versions of the argument). Insisting that there must be an answer to this question is an appeal to the **principle of sufficient reason** (often abbreviated as PSR). Some existing things (other than God) may be explainable by appeal to other such things, but it is argued in various ways that a complete explanation of everything that exists or perhaps of the fact that there is anything at all (rather than nothing) requires the existence of a *necessary* or *self-existent* being, one that could not have failed to exist. This necessary being is then claimed to be in fact identical to God, as standardly conceived—though this last, crucial step often receives relatively little attention. Versions of this argument are discussed by St. Thomas Aquinas, Samuel Clarke, and David Hume.

The Argument from Design. The argument from design also starts from a basic empirical fact and demands an explanation of that fact. This time, however, the fact is vastly more complicated: the appearance of order, (apparent) design, or (apparent) purpose in the world (with the first of these specifications being the least likely to **beg the question**). There are two importantly different versions of this argument, depending on the scope of the order for which an explanation is sought: a *global* version that asks for the explanation of the presence of order in the world taken as a whole; and various *local* versions that ask for the explanation of a particular kind or example of order, most commonly the order reflected in living things and their components—in William Paley's version here, the eye and similar organic structures. The main importance of this distinction, as we will see, is that while the theory of evolution and other relatively limited explanations of the same sort offer alternative, nontheistic explanations of many of the specific features to which local versions of the argument appeal, such alternative explanations turn out to themselves presuppose a more general background of order—and so cannot in principle explain *all* of the order in the world or why there is any order at all. In either case, the claim advanced in the argument is that the features in question can only be adequately explained by supposing that either the world as a whole or the specific aspect in question was deliberately shaped by an intelligent and powerful designer. This falls short of the full standard conception of God, mainly in that a finite world does not demand infinite attributes, but still obviously represents a major step in that direction. Versions of this argument are discussed by Paley, Hume, and Antony Flew.

The Ontological Argument. Unlike the previous two arguments, the ontological argument makes no appeal to any empirical fact, however minimal, but is instead entirely **a priori** in character. The central idea is that God exists, indeed must **necessarily** exist, not as an explanation of something else (as in the other two main arguments), but simply because of the very **concept** of such a being. This is a striking but also rather paradoxical claim: normally the issue of what the concept of a certain kind of thing includes (or what we have in mind in thinking such a thing) is quite distinct from (and logically prior to) the issue of whether any things of that kind actually exist. The claim of the ontological argument is in effect that in the case of God, these two questions are not distinct, but instead that the correct answer to the first question determines the correct answer to the second. René Descartes presents a version of this argument, while Immanuel Kant offers two related objections to it.

An Argument Against the Existence of God: the Problem of Evil

By far the most important argument against the existence of God is in effect the reverse of the argument from design. The problem of evil (which might be better labeled the argument from evil against the existence of God) asks why, if the world was created by a being having the attributes specified by the standard conception of God, there is so much evil (mainly pain and suffering) to be found. For those who are already committed to belief in such a God on other grounds, this is a *problem*—but for those to whom the issue is reasonably open, it may well constitute a pretty compelling argument *against* the existence of such a being. The question is whether this argument can be answered by offering an explanation (such explanations are standardly referred to as **theodicies**) as to why God would permit evil to exist. In discussing such attempts, it is often valuable to distinguish two main classes of evil: **physical** or **natural** **evil,** that caused by natural processes that are beyond human control; and **moral** **evil,** that which results from voluntary human actions. The problem of evil is discussed by Fyodor Dostoevsky, Hume, J. L. Mackie, and John Hick.

Must We Have Reasons in Order to Believe?

Instead of appealing to arguments in favor of God's existence (and responses to arguments against), might there be an alternative basis for belief in God, one that still makes such belief rationally acceptable? Walter Kaufmann explores the idea, deriving from Blaise Pascal, that belief in God might be the best wager in a situation of uncertainty. William James and W. K. Clifford debate the issue of whether it is rational to believe in God on the basis of *faith,* rather than arguments or evidence.

Does God Exist?

The Cosmological Argument

St. Thomas Aquinas

St. Thomas Aquinas (1225–1274) was an Italian philosopher and theologian (though he did most of his teaching and writing in Paris). A monk in the Dominican order (which is devoted to scholarship and education), Aquinas was arguably the most influential thinker of the Middle Ages. Aquinas based much of his philosophical thinking on the works of Aristotle and was primarily responsible for the dominant position that Aristotle came to hold in medieval thought. Aristotle's ideas are reflected at several points in the following arguments.

The *Summa Theologica* has an explicitly **dialectical** structure. It is divided into articles, each of which begins with a question. This is followed by objections that argue for the contrary of the view that Aquinas will defend, then by a statement of Aquinas's own view and his reasons. Finally, the article concludes with explicit responses to the earlier objections. In the following selection, the question is whether God exists, and Aquinas offers five famous, though somewhat obscure, arguments for an affirmative answer. The first three are different versions of the cosmological argument, the fourth (and most obscure) an argument unique to Aquinas, and the last a version of the argument from design.

The Five Ways, from *Summa Theologica*

THIRD ARTICLE: WHETHER GOD EXISTS?

We proceed thus to the Third Article:—

Objection 1. It seems that God does not exist; because if one of two contraries be infinite, the other would be altogether destroyed. But the name *God* means that He is infinite goodness. If, therefore, God existed, there would be no evil discoverable; but there is evil in the world. Therefore God does not exist. ①

Obj. 2. Further, it is superfluous to suppose that what can be accounted for by a few principles has been produced by many. But it seems that everything we see in the world can be accounted for by other principles, supposing God did not exist. For all natural things can be reduced to one principle, which is nature; and all voluntary things can be reduced to one principle, which is human reason, or will. Therefore there is no need to suppose God's existence. ②

On the contrary, It is said in the person of God: *I am Who am* (*Exod.* iii 14).

I answer that, The existence of God can be proved in five ways.

The first and more manifest way is the argument from motion. It is certain, and evident to our senses, that in the world some things are in motion. ③ Now whatever is moved is moved by another, for nothing can be moved except it is in potentiality to that towards which it is moved; whereas a thing moves inasmuch as it is in act. For motion is nothing else than the reduction of something from potentiality to actuality. But nothing can be reduced from potentiality to actuality, except by something in a state of actuality. ④ Thus that which is actually hot, as fire, makes wood, which is potentially hot, to be actually hot, and thereby moves and changes it. Now it is not possible that the same thing should be at once in actuality and potentiality in the same respect, but only in different respects. For what is actually hot cannot simultaneously be potentially hot; but it is simultaneously potentially cold. It is therefore impossible that in the same respect and in the same way a thing should be both mover and moved, *i.e.,* that it should move itself. ⑤ Therefore, whatever is moved must be moved by another. If that by which it is moved be itself moved, then this also must needs be moved by another, and that by another again. But this cannot go on to infinity, because then there would be no first mover, ⑥ and,

① The first objection is in effect the problem of evil, discussed later in this chapter. In this version, the allegedly infinite character of God's attributes plays a crucial role.

② The second objection claims that God is unnecessary for the purpose of explaining what goes on in the world.

③ The meaning of this initial premise is broader than it might seem (as we can see from the example of heat and cold below): "motion" includes not just movement, but any sort of change or activity.

④ Aquinas appeals here to some of the central ideas of Aristotelian metaphysics. Any sort of change (ordinary movement will do for an example) involves a transition from the potential for some property or quality to its actual realization. Such a transition must be produced by the activity of something else (to explain why the transition takes place when it does and why the thing "moves" in the direction that it does). Thus something that is potentially hot (and also potentially colder than it is) is moved to become actually hot (rather than colder) by something else that is already actually hot.

⑤ Thus it follows that something cannot "move" itself, for to do so it would have to merely potentially have the relevant feature and also actually have it. (Does this seem right?)

⑥ Aquinas argues that there cannot be an infinite series of "movers" (extending back into time), each "moved" by the one before it. His reason seems to be that there would then be no explanation why any of them is "moved." (Is he right about this?)

From St. Thomas Aquinas, Summa Theologica, *in* Anton C. Pegis, ed., Introduction to St. Thomas Aquinas *(New York: Random House, 1945, 1948).*

consequently, no other mover, seeing that subsequent movers move only inasmuch as they are moved by the first mover; as the staff moves only because it is moved by the hand. Therefore it is necessary to arrive at a first mover, moved by no other; and this everyone understands to be God.⑦

> ⑦ The first "mover" cannot be moved by another thing, nor can it "move" itself. Thus it must not itself be "moved," but must nonetheless still somehow be capable of "moving" other things—how can this be? Another obvious problem is why such a first "mover" should be identified with God.

The second way is from the nature of efficient cause. In the world of sensible things we find there is an order of efficient causes.⑧ There is no case known (neither is it, indeed, possible) in which a thing is found to be the efficient cause of itself; for so it would be prior to itself, which is impossible. Now in efficient causes it is not possible to go on to infinity, because in all efficient causes following in order, the first is the cause of the intermediate cause, and the intermediate is the cause of the ultimate cause, whether the intermediate cause be several, or one only. Now to take away the cause is to take away the effect. Therefore, if there be no first cause among efficient causes, there will be no ultimate, nor any intermediate, cause. But if in efficient causes it is possible to go on to infinity, there will be no first efficient cause, neither will there be an ultimate effect, nor any intermediate efficient causes; all of which is plainly false. Therefore it is necessary to admit a first efficient cause, to which everyone gives the name of God.⑨

> ⑧ "Efficient" causation means more or less causation in the ordinary sense, in which an earlier occurrence (throwing a rock) causes a later occurrence (a splash in a pond)—except that Aquinas thinks of the items in question as things or objects rather than occurrences. It is thus immediately obvious that nothing can cause itself in this sense (because to do so, it would have to precede itself).

> ⑨ Here again the crucial claim is the denial that an infinite sequence of causes (backwards into time) is possible, and again the rationale seems to be that if this were so, it would be impossible to explain why any of the things in the sequence exist. Again, the rationale for identifying the first efficient cause with God is less than clear.

The third way is taken from possibility and necessity, and runs thus. We find in nature things that are possible to be and not to be, since they are found to be generated, and to be corrupted, and consequently, it is possible for them to be and not to be.⑩ But it is impossible for these always to exist, for that which can not-be at some time is not. Therefore, if everything can not-be, then at one time there was nothing in existence.⑪ Now if this were true, even now there would be nothing in existence, because that which does not exist begins to exist only through something already existing. Therefore, if at one time nothing was in existence, it would have been impossible for anything to have begun to exist; and thus even now nothing would be in existence—which is absurd.⑫ Therefore, not all beings are merely possible, but there must exist something the existence of which is necessary. But every necessary thing either has its necessity caused by another, or not.⑬ Now it is impossible to go on to infinity in necessary things which have their necessity caused by another, as has been already proved in regard to efficient causes. Therefore we cannot but admit the existence of some being having of itself its own necessity, and not receiving it from another,

> ⑩ Anything that can come into being from a prior state of nonexistence or pass out of being from a prior state of existence would be an example. Can you think of anything in the world that does not fit this characterization?

> ⑪ Neither this claim nor the preceding one follows in any obvious way. Why must something for which non-being is *possible* actually fail to exist at some time? More important, even if all things for which non-being is possible do fail to exist at some time, why couldn't their existences overlap so that there is never a time when nothing exists?

> ⑫ The underlying assumption is that something cannot come from nothing, that if there is a moment when nothing exists, then it is impossible for anything to subsequently come into existence.

> ⑬ Aquinas concludes that there must be some things that are necessary: that could not fail to exist. He thinks these fall into two kinds: those whose necessity is caused by something else (would such a thing really be necessary?) and those whose necessity is caused, not by anything other than themselves, but instead by their own nature.

but rather causing in others their necessity. This all men speak of as God. [14]

[14] In a way parallel to the first two arguments, the possibility of an infinite series of beings whose necessity is derivative is rejected, leading to the conclusion that there is a being whose necessity derives only from its own nature. (Might there be more than one such being?) Here there is a bit more rationale for the identification with God, since a being that is necessary by virtue of its own nature and thus somehow explains its own existence is at least very different from ordinary things in the world.

[15] It is hard to make very much of this argument. One question is why the standard to which other things are compared must actually exist. Another is why it should be thought to cause the lesser instances. Still another is why the maximums of all these various qualities must be the same being.

The fourth way is taken from the gradation to be found in things. Among beings there are some *more* and some *less* good, true, noble, and the like. But more and less are predicted of different things according as they resemble in their different ways something which is the maximum, as a thing is said to be hotter according as it more nearly resembles that which is hottest; so that there is something which is truest, something best, something noblest, and, consequently, something which is most being, for those things that are greatest in truth are greatest in being, as it is written in *Metaph.* ii.* Now the maximum in any genus is the cause of all in that genus, as fire, which is the maximum of heat, is the cause of all hot things, as is said in the same book.† Therefore there must also be something which is to all beings the cause of their being, goodness, and every other perfection; and this we call God. [15]

The fifth way is taken from the governance of the world. We see that things which lack knowledge, such as natural bodies, act for an end, and this is evident from their acting always, or nearly always, in the same way, so as to obtain the best result. Hence it is plain that they achieve their end, not fortuitously, but designedly. [16] Now whatever lacks knowledge cannot move towards an end, unless it be directed by some being endowed with knowledge and intelligence; as the arrow is directed by the archer. Therefore some intelligent being exists by whom all natural things are directed to their end; and this being we call God. [17]

Reply Obj. 1. As Augustine says: *Since God is the highest good, He would not allow any evil to exist in His works, unless His omnipotence and goodness were such as to bring good even out of evil.*‡ This is part of the infinite goodness of God, that He should allow evil to exist, and out of it produce good. [18]

Reply Obj. 2. Since nature works for a determinate end under the direction of a higher agent, whatever is done by nature must be traced back to God as to its first cause. So likewise whatever is done voluntarily must be traced back to some higher cause other than human reason and will, since these can change and fail; for all things that are changeable and capable of defect must be traced back to an immovable and self-necessary first principle, as has been shown. [19]

[16] The appeal here seems to be to the regular order in the world: things that conform to such an order cannot be acting at random ("fortuitously"), and Aquinas sees no other explanation besides intelligent design. (Can you think of a third possibility here?)

[17] Why must there be only one such intelligence?—couldn't different natural things be directed by different intelligences? Here again, the identification of this allegedly unique director with God is more plausible, though such a being would not have to have the infinite power that God is standardly credited with.

[18] Aquinas's reply to the problem of evil is in effect that God can bring good out of evil, so that the world is somehow better for containing evil. How plausible do you think this is?

[19] The answer to the second objection is straightforward if the arguments are accepted: all explanation ultimately can be traced back to God.

Metaph. Ia, I (993b 30).

†*Ibid.* (993b 25).

‡*Enchir.,* XI (PL 40, 236).

Discussion Questions

1. A key claim in the first argument is that the cause of a change ("movement") must always come from outside the thing that changes. Does it seem obvious that things always work this way? Might not a change originate from within a thing? Can you think of an example? How might Aquinas reply?

2. Think about the claim that there cannot be an infinite series of efficient causes backwards into time (and the analogous claims for the series of "movers" and the series of necessary beings whose necessity is caused by another). Is there a clear objection to such a view? Aquinas seems to be saying that there would be no explanation of how the series ever got started, but the reply might be that it didn't get *started* because it extends infinitely backwards. Which view is right?

3. A crucial ingredient of the third argument is the idea of a *necessary being:* one that cannot fail to exist. Do we really understand this idea? What would make the existence of such a being necessary—that is, would make it impossible for it not to exist? Can you think of any other examples of necessary beings? What about a number, say the number seven (the number itself, not the numeral that stands for it): could it have failed to exist? Even if we can make sense of necessary existence for an **abstract** object like a number, does it make sense for a **concrete** object like God? (See the subsection on the Ontological argument for further discussion of this issue.)

Samuel Clarke

Samuel Clarke (1675–1729) was an English philosopher, theologian, and preacher, who wrote extensively on philosophical and theological issues, including the existence of God, the nature of space and time, free will, and the nature of morality. He is now best known for his extended correspondence with the great German philosopher Gottfried Wilhelm Leibniz, in which many of these topics are discussed.

Like Aquinas's Third Way but even more explicitly, Clarke's version of the cosmological argument relies on the principle of sufficient reason (PSR): the principle that there must be a reason or cause or explanation for everything that exists. The portion of the argument included here does not purport to prove that God exists but only that "from eternity some one unchangeable and independent being" exists, a result from which Clarke thinks he can go on to prove the existence of the full Judeo-Christian God. (This is a very dense passage, and to understand it, you may have to read it more than once.)

The Cosmological Argument, from
A Demonstration of the Being and Attributes of God

I

First, then, it is absolutely and undeniably certain that *something has existed from all eternity.* This is so evident and undeniable a proposition, that no atheist in any age has ever presumed to assert the contrary, and therefore there is little need of being particular in the proof of it. For, since something now is, it is evident that something always was, otherwise the things

From Samuel Clarke, A Demonstration of the Being and Attributes of God *(1705).*

that now are must have been produced out of nothing, absolutely and without a cause, which is a plain contradiction in terms. For, to say a thing is produced and yet that there is no cause at all for that production, is to say that something is effected when it is effected by nothing, that is, at the same time when it is not effected at all. Whatever exists has a cause, a reason, a ground of its existence, a foundation on which its existence relies, a ground or reason why it does exist rather than not exist, either in the necessity of its own nature (and then it must have been of itself eternal), or in the will of some other being (and then that other being must, at least in the order of nature and causality, have existed before it).①

. . .

II

*There has existed from eternity some one unchangeable and independent being.*② For, since something must needs have been from eternity, as has been already proved and is granted on all hands, either there has always existed some one unchangeable and independent being from which all other beings that are or ever were in the universe have received their original, or else there has been an infinite succession of changeable and dependent beings produced one from another in an endless progression without any original cause at all.③ Now this latter supposition is so very absurd that, though all atheism must in its accounts of most things (as shall be shown hereafter) terminate in it, yet I think very few atheists ever were so weak as openly and directly to defend it. For it is plainly impossible and contradictory to itself.④ I shall not argue against it from the supposed impossibility of infinite succession, barely and absolutely considered in itself, for a reason which shall be mentioned hereafter. But, if we consider such an infinite progression as one entire endless series of dependent beings,⑤ it is plain this whole series of beings can have no cause from without of its existence because in it are supposed to be included all things that are, or ever were, in the universe. And it is plain it can have no reason within itself for its existence because no one being in this infinite succession is supposed to be self-existent or necessary (which is the only ground or reason of existence of anything that can be imagined within the thing itself, as will presently more fully appear),⑥ but every one dependent on the foregoing. And, where no part is necessary, it is manifest the whole cannot be necessary—absolute necessity of existence not being an extrinsic, relative, and accidental denomination but an inward and essential property of the nature of the thing which so exists.⑦

An infinite succession, therefore, of merely dependent beings without any original independent cause is a series of beings that has neither necessity, nor cause, nor any reason or ground at all of its existence either within itself or from without. That is, it is an express contradiction and impossibility. It is a sup-

---

① Clarke's argument here assumes that everything must have a cause or reason (the PSR), and then argues that something that comes to be out of nothing can only be caused by nothing, which is a contradiction: it has a cause (nothing), but to have nothing as a cause is not to have a cause at all.

② This is the conclusion of the main argument, for which Clarke will proceed to give reasons. An *independent being* is a being whose existence does not depend on anything outside itself, whereas a dependent being is one whose existence does depend on something outside itself. (The claim that the independent being is unchangeable is not explained and plays no real role in the argument.)

③ Clarke poses two main alternatives: either there is one independent being (whose existence causes the existence of any dependent beings that exist) or there is nothing but a series of dependent beings, each caused by the previous one. (Can you think of a third possibility?)

④ Clarke claims that the second of these alternatives is impossible and self-contradictory, though without yet explaining how. If this alternative were eliminated, the other one would have to be true.

⑤ Here is the main novelty in Clarke's version of the cosmological argument (and one main difference from Aquinas's Third Way): he proposes to treat the whole series of dependent beings as one entity and asks what explains it (thereby invoking the PSR). Clarke proceeds to pose two alternatives as to the explanation, one of which is easily ruled out.

⑥ Here is an alternative characterization of an *independent* being: a being that is *necessary* or *self-existent*—one that contains within itself the reason for its existence. (This is discussed further later on.)

⑦ The claim is that there is nothing about the inner nature of the series of dependent beings that would explain why the series as a whole exists.

posing something to be caused (because it is granted in every one of its stages of succession not to be necessarily and of itself), and yet that, in the whole, it is caused absolutely by nothing,[8] which every man knows is a contradiction to imagine done in time; and because duration in this case makes no difference, it is equally a contradiction to suppose it done from eternity. And consequently there must, on the contrary, of necessity have existed from eternity some one immutable and independent being.

> [8] Here we finally have an explanation of why the supposition that there is nothing but a series of dependent beings is supposed to result in a contradiction. What is the contradiction? How does it follow from the foregoing discussion?

To suppose an infinite succession of changeable and dependent beings produced one from another in an endless progression without any original cause at all is only a driving back from one step to another and, as it were, removing out of sight the question concerning the ground or reason of the existence of things.*[9] . . .

> [9] Think of the analogy in the footnote. How good is it?

Otherwise, thus: either there has always existed some unchangeable and independent being from which all other beings have received their original, or else there has been an infinite succession of changeable and dependent beings, produced one from another in an endless progression without any original cause at all. According to this latter supposition, there is nothing in the universe self-existent or necessarily existing. And if so, then it was originally equally possible that from eternity there should never have existed anything at all, as that there should from eternity have existed a succession of changeable and dependent beings. Which being supposed, then, what is it that has from eternity determined such a succession of beings to exist, rather than that from eternity there should never have existed anything at all? Necessity it was not because it was equally possible, in this supposition, that they should not have existed at all. Chance is nothing but a mere word, without any signification. And other being it is supposed there was none, to determine the existence of these. Their existence, therefore, was determined by nothing; neither by any necessity in the nature of the things themselves, because it is supposed that none of them are self-existent, nor by any other being, because no other is supposed to exist. That is to say, of two equally possible things, viz., whether anything or nothing should from eternity have existed, the one is determined rather than the other absolutely by nothing, which is an express contradiction.[10] And consequently, as before, there must on the contrary of necessity have existed from eternity some one immutable and independent being. Which, what it is, remains in the next place to be inquired.

> [10] Clarke focuses more clearly on the issue of why this specific series exists, rather than nothing (or rather than some other possible series?). What is the "express contradiction" to which he refers? (See Annotation 1.)

III

That unchangeable and independent being which has existed from eternity, without any external cause of its existence, must be self-existent, that is, necessarily existing. For whatever exists must either have

---

*This matter has been well illustrated by a late able writer: "Suppose a chain hung down out of the heavens from an unknown height, and though every link of it gravitated toward the Earth and what it hung upon was not visible, yet it did not descend but kept its situation; and [suppose] upon this a question should arise, what supported or kept up this chain? Would it be a sufficient answer to say that the first or lowest link hung upon the second, or that next above it, [and] the first, or rather the first and the second together, upon the third, and so on *in infinitum?* For what holds up the *whole?* A chain of ten links would fall down unless something able to bear it hindered. One of twenty, if not staid by something of a yet greater strength, [would fall] in proportion to the increase of weight, and therefore one of infinite links, certainly, if not sustained by something infinitely strong and capable to bear up on infinite weight. And thus it is in a chain of causes and effects tending or, as it were, gravitating towards some end. The last or lowest depends or, as one may say, is suspended upon the cause above it. This again, if it be not the first cause, is suspended as an effect upon something above it, etc. And if they should be infinite, unless agreeably to what has been said there is some cause upon which all hang or depend, they would be but an infinite effect without an efficient. And so to assert there is any such thing would be as great an absurdity as to say that a finite or little weight wants something to sustain it, but an infinite one, or the greatest, does not." W. Wollaston, *The Religion of Nature Delineated* (London, Samuel Palmer, 1724; reprint New York, Garland Publishing Co., 1978), p. 67.

come into being out of nothing, absolutely without cause, or it must have been produced by some external cause, or it must be self-existent. Now to arise out of nothing absolutely without any cause has been already shown to be a plain contradiction. To have been produced by some external cause cannot possibly be true of every thing, but something must have existed eternally and independently, as has likewise been shown already. Which remains, therefore, [is] that that being which has existed independently from eternity must of necessity be self-existent. Now to be self-existent is not to be produced by itself, for that is an express contradiction, but it is (which is the only idea we can frame of self-existence, and without which the word seems to have no signification at all)—it is, I say, to exist by an absolute necessity originally in the nature of the thing itself. And this necessity must be antecedent, not indeed in time, to the existence of the being itself (because that is eternal), but it must be antecedent in the natural order of our ideas to our supposition of its being. That is, this necessity must not barely be consequent upon our supposition of the existence of such a being (for then it would not be a necessity absolutely such in itself, nor be the ground or foundation of the existence of anything, being on the contrary only a consequent of it), but it must antecedently force itself upon us whether we will or no, even when we are endeavoring to suppose that no such being exists.

. . .

From this third proposition it follows, . . . that the only true idea of a self-existent or necessarily existing being is the idea of a being the supposition of whose not-existing is an express contradiction. For, since it is absolutely impossible but there must be somewhat self-existing, that is, [something] which exists by the necessity of its own nature, it is plain that that necessity cannot be a necessity consequent upon any foregoing supposition (because nothing can be antecedent to that which is self-existent, no not its own will, so as to be the cause or ground of its own existence), but it must be a necessity absolutely such in its own nature. Now a necessity not relatively or consequentially, but absolutely such in its own nature, is nothing else but its being a plain impossibility or implying a contradiction to suppose the contrary. [11]

. . . from hence it follows that the material world cannot possibly be the first and original being, uncreated, independent, and of itself eternal. For, since it has been already demonstrated that whatever being has existed from eternity, independent, and without an external cause of its existence, must be self-existent, and that whatever is self-existent must exist necessarily by an absolute necessity in the nature of the thing itself, it follows evidently that unless the material world exists necessarily by an absolute necessity in its own nature, so as that it must be an express contradiction to suppose it not to exist, it cannot be independent and of itself eternal. Now that the material world does not exist thus necessarily is very evident. For absolute necessity of existing and a possibility of not existing being contradictory ideas, it is manifest the material world cannot exist necessarily, if without a contradiction we can conceive it either not to be or to be in any respect otherwise than it now is. Than which nothing is more easy. For whether we consider the form of the world with the disposition and motion of its parts, or whether we consider the matter of it as such, without respect to its present form, every thing in it, both the whole and every one of its parts, their situation and motion, the form and also the matter, are the most arbitrary and dependent things and the farthest removed from necessity that can possibly be imagined. A necessity indeed of fitness, that is, a necessity that things should be as they are in order to the well-being of the whole, there may be in all these things; but an absolute necessity of nature in any of them (which is what the atheist must maintain), there is not the last appearance of. If any man will say in this sense (as every atheist must do) either that the form of the world, or at least the matter and motion of it, is necessary, nothing can possibly be invented more absurd. [12]

. . .

[11] Here is a further explanation of the idea of a necessary or self-existent being: it is one whose existence it is, by virtue of its own nature, **contradictory** to deny. (Can you think of any way in which this might be so?)

[12] In the next selection, David Hume raises the issue of whether the material world itself might be the necessary or self-existent being. Here is Clarke's response. How convincing is it?

Discussion Questions

1. Clarke's argument depends on treating the whole series of dependent beings as one entity and asking what explains the existence of that entity. But think of one of the dependent beings in the series. Is its existence adequately explained by its being caused by the previous being in the series? (Does Clarke offer any reason for a negative answer to this question?) But if the existence of each individual dependent being is adequately explained, does the whole series of such beings require any further explanation? Why or why not? (Suppose you meet several friends at a café, and that you can explain why each of them is there: one works there, one was invited by you, one often hangs out at that café, and so on. Does the fact that all of them are there as a group require a further explanation?)

2. Clarke argues that an independent being must also be a necessary (or self-existent) being. Think carefully about what an independent being is: is it by its very nature necessary? If it is necessary, then must it be eternal? As Clarke's own discussion illustrates, one way to argue for a claim is to infer consequences from its denial and show that they lead to a contradiction, thereby showing that the denial must be false, and thus that the original claim is true (this is called a reduction to absurdity—*reductio ad absurdum*). Suppose, for the sake of the argument, that an independent being is not necessary. Explain the content of such a supposition by clarifying the ideas of independence and necessity. Is there a *reductio ad absurdum* argument for the claim that an independent being must be necessary? If so, explain it as clearly as you can.

David Hume

David Hume (1711–1776), a Scottish philosopher and historian, is usually regarded as one of the most important and influential philosophers of all time. He did very important work in epistemology, metaphysics, ethics, and the philosophy of religion, producing a comprehensive philosophical position that is most distinctive for its skeptical tendencies.

Hume's *Dialogues Concerning Natural Religion* (from which two other selections in this chapter are also drawn) offers a comprehensive discussion of the cosmological argument, the argument from design, the problem of evil, and the related issue of whether God's attributes are knowable by finite human minds. This is presented through an engaging use of dialogue form, rivaled for its combination of naturalness and philosophical cogency only by Plato's dialogues and Berkeley's *Three Dialogues Between Hylas and Philonous*. There are three characters in the dialogue: (1) Cleanthes, who advocates the argument from design and the view that God's attributes are knowable through analogy with human attributes; (2) Demea, who advocates the cosmological argument and the view that God's attributes are beyond human comprehension; and (3) Philo, usually regarded as a spokesman for Hume's own views, who is a subtle advocate of atheism (or at least a very strong agnosticism), but who pretends for most of the dialogue to side with Demea. This short section on the cosmological argument occurs fairly late in the dialogue (after the main discussion of the argument from design).

Problems with the Cosmological Argument, from *Dialogues Concerning Natural Religion*

But if so many difficulties attend the argument *a posteriori,* said Demea; had we not better adhere to that simple and sublime argument a priori, ①

① Demea describes the cosmological argument as a priori, meaning that it does not depend on experience in the extensive way that the argument from design ("the argument *a posteriori*") does. But it is not a purely a priori argument, since it does depend on the premise, known through experience, that a world of some sort exists.

which, by offering to us infallible demonstration, cuts off at once all doubt and difficulty? By this argument, too, we may prove the *infinity* of the divine attributes, which, I am afraid, can never be ascertained with certainty from any other topic. For how can an effect, which either is finite, or, for aught we know, may be so; how can such an effect, I say, prove an infinite cause? The unity too of the Divine Nature, it is very difficult, if not absolutely impossible, to deduce merely from contemplating the works of nature; nor will the uniformity alone of the plan, even were it allowed, give us any assurance of that attribute. Whereas the argument a priori. . . .

You seem to reason, Demea, interposed Cleanthes, as if those advantages and conveniences in the abstract argument were full proofs of its solidity. But it is first proper, in my opinion, to determine what argument of this nature you choose to insist on; and we shall afterwards, from itself, better than from its useful consequences, endeavor to determine what value we ought to put upon it.

② The first part of this sentence is a version of the principle of sufficient reason. The latter part might seem to rule out the very conclusion that Demea is aiming for, but he does not in fact say that a being cannot be such as to *explain* its own existence.

The argument, replied Demea, which I would insist on is the common one. Whatever exists must have a cause or reason of its existence; it being absolutely impossible for anything to produce itself, or be the cause of its own existence. ② In mounting up;

therefore, from effects to causes, we must either go on in tracing an infinite succession, without any ultimate cause at all; or must at last have recourse to some ultimate cause, that is *necessarily* existent. Now that the first supposition is absurd may be thus proved. In the infinite chain or succession of causes and effects, each single effect is determined to exist by the power and efficacy of that cause, which immediately preceded; but the whole eternal chain or succession, taken together, is not determined or caused by anything: and yet it is evident that it requires a cause or reason, as much as any particular object, which begins to exist in time. The question is still reasonable, why this particular succession of causes existed from eternity, and not any other succession, or no succession at all. If there be no necessarily existent being, any supposition, which can be formed, is equally possible; nor is there any more absurdity in *nothing's* having existed from eternity, than there is in that succession of causes, which constitutes the universe. What was it then, which determined something to exist rather than nothing, and bestowed being on a particular possibility, exclusive of the rest? ③ *External causes,* there are supposed to be none. *Chance* is a word without a meaning. Was it *nothing?* But that can never produce anything. We must, therefore, have recourse to a necessarily existent Being, who carries the reason of his existence in himself; and who cannot be supposed not to exist without an express contradiction. ④ There is consequently such a Being, that is, there is a Deity.

③ Demea, like Clarke, appeals to the idea that the whole series of causes and effects is an entity that requires a cause or reason (that is, an explanation). But he develops this point a bit further: the issue is why this series (the one in the actual world) exists, rather than some other series or nothing at all.

④ The answer to the foregoing question is again the idea of a necessarily existent being, here explained further as one whose very nature makes it a contradiction to deny its existence.

I shall not leave it to Philo, said Cleanthes (though I know that the starting objections is his chief delight), to point out the weak-

From David Hume, Dialogues Concerning Natural Religion *(1779).*

ness of this metaphysical reasoning. It seems to me so obviously ill-grounded, and at the same time of so little consequence to the cause of true piety and religion, that I shall myself venture to show the fallacy of it.

I shall begin with observing, that there is an evident absurdity in pretending to demonstrate a matter of fact, or to prove it by any arguments a priori. Nothing is demonstrable, unless the contrary implies a contradiction. Nothing, that is distinctly conceivable, implies a contradiction. Whatever we conceive as existent, we can also conceive as non-existent. There is no being, therefore, whose non-existence implies a contradiction. Consequently there is no being, whose existence is demonstrable.⑤ I propose this argument as entirely decisive, and am willing to rest the whole controversy upon it.

> ⑤ Cleanthes rejects the very idea that the denial that a specified being exists could be self-contradictory. His reason, in the following passage, is that such a denial is always intelligibly conceivable. (Notice that if the denial of God's existence were self-contradictory, this would seemingly yield a much simpler argument for the existence of God. See Discussion Question 1.)

It is pretended that the Deity is a necessarily existent being; and this necessity of his existence is attempted to be explained by asserting, that, if we knew his whole essence or nature, we should perceive it to be as impossible for him not to exist as for twice two not to be four. But it is evident, that this can never happen, while our faculties remain the same as at present. It will still be possible for us, at any time, to conceive the non-existence of what we formerly conceived to exist; nor can the mind ever lie under a necessity of supposing any object to remain always in being; in the same manner as we lie under a necessity of always conceiving twice two to be four. The words, therefore, *necessary existence,* have no meaning; or, which is the same thing, none that is consistent.

But farther; why may not the material universe be the necessarily existent Being, according to this pretended explication of necessity?⑥ We dare not affirm that we know all the qualities of matter; and for aught we can determine, it may contain some qualities, which, were they known, would make its non-existence appear as great a contradiction as that twice two is five. I find only one argument employed to prove, that the material world is not the necessarily existent Being; and this argument is derived from the contingency both of the matter and the form of the world. 'Any particle of matter,' 'tis said,* 'may be *conceived* to be annihilated; and any form may be *conceived* to be altered. Such an annihilation or alteration, therefore, is not impossible.'⑦ But it seems a great partiality not to perceive, that the same argument extends equally to the Deity, so far as we have any conception of him; and that the mind can at least imagine him to be non-existent, or his attributes to be altered. It must be some unknown, inconceivable qualities, which can make his non-existence appear impossible, or his attributes inalterable. And no reason can be assigned, why these qualities may not belong to matter. As they are altogether unknown and inconceivable, they can never be proved incompatible with it.

Add to this, that in tracing an eternal succession of objects, it seems absurd to inquire for a general cause or first author. How can anything, that exists from eternity, have a cause, since that relation implies a priority in time and a beginning of existence?⑧

In such a chain too, or succession of objects, each part is caused by that which preceded it, and causes that which succeeds it. Where then is the difficulty? But the *whole,* you say, wants a cause. I answer, that the uniting of these parts into a whole, like the uniting of several distinct counties into one

> ⑥ If the idea of necessary existence did make sense, Cleanthes is saying, we have no clear understanding of why something would have this property. Hence it might just as well be the material universe rather than God that exists necessarily.

> ⑦ Clarke's response is that particles of matter can be conceived to be annihilated, but God cannot. But is it enough if God can be conceived not to exist in the first place? Is this possible?

> ⑧ If God causes the eternal universe, it is not by existing prior to it. Does the idea that God causes the material universe require that he (or she or it) exists prior to it? Or is there some other way of understanding God's causation?

*Dr. Clarke.

kingdom, or several distinct members into one body, is performed merely by an arbitrary act of the mind, and has no influence on the nature of things. Did I show you the particular causes of each individual in a collection of twenty particles of matter, I should think it very unreasonable, should you afterwards ask me, what was the cause of the whole twenty. This is sufficiently explained in explaining the cause of the parts. ⑨

⑨ Cleanthes offers a response to the idea that the whole series of causes and effects is an entity that requires explanation, claiming that if each part is explained, then the whole is explained. But does this answer the question of why that specific series exists (rather than some other series or nothing)?

Though the reasonings, which you have urged, Cleanthes, may well excuse me, said Philo, from starting any farther difficulties; yet I cannot forbear insisting still upon another topic. 'Tis observed by arithmeticians, that the products of 9 compose always either 9 or some lesser product of 9; if you add together all the characters, of which any of the former products is composed. Thus, of 18, 27, 36, which are products of 9, you make 9 by adding 1 to 8, 2 to 7, 3 to 6. Thus, 369 is a product also of 9; and if you add 3, 6, and 9, you make 18, a lesser product of 9. To a superficial observer, so wonderful a regularity may be admired as the effect either of chance or design: but a skillful algebraist immediately concludes it to be the work of necessity, and demonstrates, that it must forever result from the nature of these numbers. Is it not probable, I ask, that the whole

economy of the universe is conducted by a like necessity, though no human algebra can furnish a key, which solves the difficulty? And instead of admiring the order of natural beings, may it not happen, that, could we penetrate into the intimate nature of bodies, we should clearly see why it was absolutely impossible, they could ever admit of any other disposition? ⑩ So dangerous is it to introduce this idea of necessity into the present question! And so naturally does it afford an inference directly opposite to the religious hypothesis!

⑩ Philo suggests that it is possible that if we understood the material universe well enough, we would see why it had to be the specific way it is (and why it exists rather than nothing?). Does this seem like a genuine possibility?

But dropping all these abstractions, continued Philo; and confining ourselves to more familiar topics; I shall venture to add an observation, that the argument a priori has seldom been found very convincing, except to people of a metaphysical head, who have accustomed themselves to abstract reasoning, and who finding from mathematics, that the understanding frequently leads to truth, through obscurity, and contrary to first appearances, have transferred the same habit of thinking to subjects, where it would not seem to have place. Other people, even of good sense and the best inclined to religion, feel always some deficiency in such arguments, though they are not perhaps able to explain distinctly where it lies. A certain proof, that men ever did, and ever will derive their religion from other sources than from this species of reasoning.

Discussion Questions

1. How could it be that the denial of God's existence leads to a contradiction (which Cleanthes suggests to be the only possible account of how God could be a necessary or self-existent being)? One answer, perhaps the only one, to this question would be that the idea of existence is included in the very concept of God. Suppose that God is defined as an omnipotent, omniscient, perfectly good being who created the universe and who exists. Does it follow that such a being does actually exist? Why or why not? (See the subsection on the ontological argument for more discussion of this issue.)

2. Perhaps the most fundamental version of the cosmological argument starts from the question of why something exists rather than nothing:

   (1) Something exists (rather than nothing).
   (2) There must be a reason or explanation for any positive fact.
   (3) If all things that exist are contingent (not necessary or self existent), there will be no reason or explanation for (1).

   Therefore, there must exist a necessary or self-existent being, namely God.

   What evaluation should be made of this argument? (a) Premise (2) is a version of the principle of sufficient reason, but a more demanding one than those we have seen so far, in that it demands not just explanations for the existence of things, but for any positive fact. How plausible is this premise? (b) Is premise (3) correct? Try to carefully spell out the reasons for this premise. (c) Is the first part of the conclusion really intelligible? (d) Is there any reason for thinking that the necessary or self-existent being must have the characteristics of God, as standardly conceived?

The Argument from Design

William Paley

William Paley (1743–1805) was an English philosopher and also a noted theologian. He wrote widely on the existence and nature of God, and was also one of the early proponents of **utilitarianism** in ethics.

In this selection, Paley offers a local version of the argument from design (as explained in the introduction to this chapter), resting on an analogy between a watch found lying on a heath and the eye of a living creature (though it takes a while for the eye to appear and then the immediate comparison is between an eye and a telescope rather than between an eye and the watch). His basic claim is that just as it is clear that the watch must have been designed by some intelligent designer, the same thing is true of the eye.

The Argument from Design, from *Natural Theology*

CHAPTER ONE: STATE OF THE ARGUMENT

In crossing a heath, suppose I pitched my foot against a *stone* and were asked how the stone came to be there, I might possibly answer that for anything I knew to the contrary it had lain there forever; nor would it, perhaps, be very easy to show the absurdity of this answer. But suppose I had found a *watch* upon the ground, and it should be inquired how the watch happened to be in that place, I should hardly think of the answer which I had before given, that for anything I knew the watch might have always been there. Yet why should not this answer serve for the watch as well as for the stone; why is it not as admissible in the second case as in the first?① For this reason, and for no other, namely, that when we come to inspect the watch, we perceive—what we could not discover in the stone— that its several parts are framed and put together for a purpose, e.g., that they are so formed and adjusted as to produce motion, and that motion so regulated as to point out the hour of the day; that if the different parts had been differently shaped from what they are, or placed after any other manner or in any other order than that in which they are placed, either no motion at all would have been carried on in the machine, or none which would have answered the

① The initial comparison is between the watch and a stone: the former, Paley argues, demands an explanation in a way that the latter does not. Before reading further, stop and ask yourself what the differences are between the two cases (there are several), and try to figure out which of them are responsible for the different need for explanation.

From William Paley, Natural Theology (1802).

use that is now served by it.② To reckon up a few of the plainest of these parts and of their offices, all tending to one result: we see a cylindrical box containing a coiled elastic spring, which, by its endeavor to relax itself, turns round the box. We next observe a flexible chain—artificially wrought for the sake of flexure—communicating the action of the spring from the box to the fusee. We then find a series of wheels, the teeth of which catch in and apply to each other, conducting the motion from the fusee to the balance and from the balance to the pointer, and at the same time, by the size and shape of those wheels, so regulating that motion as to terminate in causing an index, by an equable and measured progression, to pass over a given space in a given time. We take notice that the wheels are made of brass, in order to keep them from rust; the springs of steel, no other metal being so elastic; that over the face of the watch there is placed a glass, a material employed in no other part of the work, but in the room of which, if there had been any other than a transparent substance, the hour could not be seen without opening the case. This mechanism being observed—it requires indeed an examination of the instrument, and perhaps some previous knowledge of the subject, to perceive and understand it; but being once, as we have said, observed and understood—the inference we think is inevitable, that the watch must have had a maker—that there must have existed, at some time and at some place or other, an artificer or artificers who formed it for the purpose which we find it actually to answer, who completely comprehended its construction and designed its use.③

② Here is Paley's answer to the foregoing question: the watch demands an explanation because of the way in which its parts are shaped so as to work together to produce a specific result that would not have been achieved otherwise. (To put this in terms of purpose risks begging the question, since that seems to presuppose an intelligent being.)

③ Here is Paley's explanation for the watch, which he claims to be obvious and compelling. Can you think of any alternative explanation in this case?

I. Nor would it, I apprehend, weaken the conclusion, that we had never seen a watch made—that we had never known an artist capable of making one—that we were altogether incapable of executing such a piece of workmanship ourselves, or of understanding in what manner it was performed; all this being no more than what is true of some exquisite remains of ancient art, of some lost arts, and, to the generality of mankind, of the more curious productions of modern manufacture. Does one man in a million know how oval frames are turned? Ignorance of this kind exalts our opinion of the unseen and unknown artist's skill, if he be unseen and unknown, but raises no doubt in our minds of the existence and agency of such an artist, at some former time and in some place or other.④ Nor can I perceive that it varies at all the inference, whether the question arise concerning a human agent or concerning an agent of a different species, or an agent possessing in some respects a different nature.

④ Paley seems to be right that we do not need to know how watches are made in order to conclude that they are deliberately designed. But do we need to know that a watch contains elements (machined metal, shaped glass, wheels, and springs) that we know to be man-made and not naturally occurring things?

II. Neither, secondly, would it invalidate our conclusion, that the watch sometimes went wrong or that it seldom went exactly right. The purpose of the machinery, the design, and the designer might be evident, and in the case supposed, would be evident, in whatever way we accounted for the irregularity of the movement, or whether we could account for it or not. It is not necessary that a machine be perfect in order to show with what design it was made: still less necessary, where the only question is whether it were made with any design at all.

III. Nor, thirdly, would it bring any uncertainty into the argument, if there were a few parts of the watch, concerning which we could not discover or had not yet discovered in what manner they conduced to the general effect; or even some parts, concerning which we could not ascertain whether they conduced to that effect in any manner whatever. For, as to the first branch of the case, if by the loss, or disorder, or decay of the parts in question, the movement of the watch were found in fact to be stopped, or disturbed, or retarded, no doubt would remain in our minds as to the utility or intention of these parts, although we should be unable to investigate the manner according to which, or the connection by which, the ultimate effect depended upon their action or assistance; and the more complex the machine, the more likely is this obscurity to arise. Then, as to the second thing supposed, namely, that there were parts which might be spared without prejudice to the movement of the watch, and that we had proved this by experiment, these superfluous parts, even if we were completely assured that they were such, would not vacate the reasoning which we had instituted concerning other parts. The indication of contrivance remained, with respect to them, nearly as it was before.⑤

⑤ Is Paley right that these suppositions make no serious difference to the cogency of the argument?

IV. Nor, fourthly, would any man in his senses think the existence of the watch with its various machinery accounted for, by being told that it was one out of possible combinations of material forms; that whatever he had found in the place where he found the watch, must have contained some internal configuration or other; and that this configuration might be the structure now exhibited, namely, of the works of a watch, as well as a different structure.⑥

⑥ This suggestion seems to amount to saying that the watch just occurred at random, that nothing brought about that particular configuration of materials and components. Do you agree with Paley that this is very implausible?

V. Nor, fifthly, would it yield his inquiry more satisfaction, to be answered that there existed in things a principle of order, which had disposed the parts of the watch into their present form and situation. He never knew a watch made by the principle of order; nor can he even form to himself an idea of what is meant by a principle of order distinct from the intelligence of the watchmaker.

VI. Sixthly, he would be surprised to hear that the mechanism of the watch was no proof of contrivance, only a motive to induce the mind to think so:

VII. And not less surprised to be informed that the watch in his hand was nothing more than the result of the laws of *metallic* nature. It is a perversion of language to assign any law as the efficient, operative cause of any thing. A law presupposes an agent, for it is only the mode according to which an agent proceeds: it implies a power, for it is the order according to which that power acts.⑦ Without this agent, without this power, which are both distinct from itself, the *law* does nothing, is nothing. The expression, "the law of metallic nature," may sound strange and harsh to a philosophic ear; but it seems quite as justifiable as some others which are more familiar to him, such as "the law of vegetable nature," "the law of animal nature," or, indeed, as "the law of nature" in general, when assigned as the cause of phenomena, in exclusion of agency and power, or when it is substituted into the place of these.⑧

⑦ Why does Paley think that "a law presupposes an agent"? This is true of the kind of law that is laid down by human beings to govern the behavior of other human beings, such as a traffic law. But is there any reason (without begging the question) to think that laws of nature (that merely describe how things naturally behave) presuppose agents?

⑧ This is a slightly more serious alternative to the hypothesis of a designer: that it is the nature of metal or glass to take these specific forms. How would you reply to this?

VIII. Neither, lastly, would our observer be driven out of his conclusion or from his confidence in its truth by being told that he knew nothing at all about the matter. He knows enough for his argument; he knows the utility of the end; he knows the subserviency and adaptation of the means to the end. These points being known, his ignorance of other points, his doubts concerning other points affect not the certainty of his reasoning. The consciousness of knowing little need not beget a distrust of that which he does know.

CHAPTER TWO: STATE OF THE ARGUMENT CONTINUED

Suppose, in the next place, that the person who found the watch should after some time discover that, in addition to all the properties which he had hitherto observed in it, it possessed the unexpected property of producing in the course of its movement another watch like itself—the thing is conceivable; that it contained within it a mechanism, a system of parts—a mold, for instance, or a complex adjustment of lathes, files, and other tools—evidently and separately calculated for this purpose; let us inquire what effect ought such a discovery to have upon his former conclusion. 9

9 Paley proposes a modification of the case, in order to make it more parallel to living things (since his ultimate aim is to draw an analogy between the watch and living organisms).

I. The first effect would be to increase his admiration of the contrivance, and his conviction of the consummate skill of the contriver. Whether he regarded the object of the contrivance, the distinct apparatus, the intricate, yet in many parts intelligible mechanism by which it was carried on, he would perceive in this new observation nothing but an additional reason for doing what he had already done—for referring the construction of the watch to design and to supreme art. If that construction *without* this property, or, which is the same thing, before this property had been noticed, proved intention and art to have been employed about it, still more strong would the proof appear when he came to the knowledge of this further property, the crown and perfection of all the rest.

II. He would reflect that, though the watch before him were *in some sense* the maker of the watch which was fabricated in the course of its movements, yet it was in a very different sense from that in which a carpenter, for instance, is the maker of a chair—the author of its contrivance, the cause of the relation of its parts to their use. With respect to these, the first watch was no cause at all to the second; in no such sense as this was it the author of the constitution and order, either of the parts which the new watch contained, or of the parts by the aid and instrumentality of which it was produced. We might possibly say, but with great latitude of expression, that a stream of water ground corn; but no latitude of expression would allow us to say, no stretch of conjecture could lead us to think that the stream of water built the mill, though it were too ancient for us to know who the builder was. What the stream of water does in the affair is neither more nor less than this: by the application of an unintelligent impulse to a mechanism previously arranged, arranged independently of it and arranged by intelligence, an effect is produced, namely, the corn is ground. But the effect results from the arrangement. The force of the stream cannot be said to be the cause or the author of the effect, still less of the arrangement. Understanding and plan in the formation of the

mill were not the less necessary for any share which the water has in grinding the corn; yet is this share the same as that which the watch would have contributed to the production of the new watch, upon the supposition assumed in the last section. Therefore,

III. Though it be now no longer probable that the individual watch which our observer had found was made immediately by the hand of an artificer, yet this alteration does not in anywise affect the inference that an artificer had been originally employed and concerned in the production. The argument from design remains as it was. Marks of design and contrivance are no more accounted for now than they were before. In the same thing, we may ask for the cause of different properties. We may ask for the cause of the color of a body, of its hardness, of its heat; and these causes may be all different. We are now asking for the cause of that subserviency to a use, that relation to an end, which we have remarked in the watch before us. No answer is given to this question by telling us that a preceding watch produced it. There cannot be design without a designer; contrivance without a contriver; order without choice; arrangement without anything capable of arranging; subserviency and relation to a purpose without that which could intend a purpose; means suitable to an end, and executing their office in accomplishing that end, without the end ever having been contemplated or the means accommodated to it. Arrangement, disposition of parts, subserviency of means to an end, relation of instruments to a use imply the presence of intelligence and mind. 10 No one, therefore, can rationally believe that the insensible, inanimate watch, from which the watch before us issued, was the proper cause of the mechanism we so much admire in it—could be truly said to have constructed the instrument, disposed its parts, assigned their office, determined their order, action, and mutual dependency, combined their several motions into one result, and that also a result

10 This and the previous sentence express the general conclusions that the watch example is supposed to support. Paley sometimes sounds as though he thinks that these general claims are obvious or **self-evident**, so that he can appeal to them in arguing about the watch (rather than concluding to them on the basis of that argument). But if that were so, he could just apply them to the eye directly, without worrying about the watch.

connected with the utilities of other beings. All these properties, therefore, are as much unaccounted for as they were before.

IV. Nor is anything gained by running the difficulty farther back, that is, by supposing the watch before us to have been produced from another watch, that from a former, and so on indefinitely. Our going back ever so far brings us no nearer to the least degree of satisfaction upon the subject. Contrivance is still unaccounted for. We still want a contriver. A designing mind is neither supplied by this supposition nor dispensed with. If the difficulty were diminished the farther we went back, by going back indefinitely we might exhaust it. And this is the only case to which this sort of reasoning applies. Where there is a tendency, or, as we increase the number of terms, a continual approach toward a limit, *there,* by supposing the number of terms to be what is called infinite, we may conceive the limit to be attained; but where there is no such tendency or approach, nothing is effected by lengthening the series.[11] There is no difference as to the point in question, whatever there may be as to many points, between one series and another—between a series which is finite and a series which is infinite. A chain composed of an infinite number of links can no more support itself than a chain composed of a finite number of links. And of this we are assured, though we never *can* have tried the experiment; because, by increasing the number of links, from ten, for instance, to a hundred, from a hundred to a thousand, etc., we make not the smallest approach, we observe not the smallest tendency toward self-support. There is no difference in this respect—yet there may be a great difference in several respects—between a chain of a greater or less length, between one chain and another, between one that is finite and one that is infinite. This very much resembles the case before us. The machine which we are inspecting demonstrates, by its construction, contrivance and design. Contrivance must have had a contriver, design a designer, whether the machine immediately proceeded from another machine or not. That circumstance alters not the case. That other machine may, in like manner, have proceeded from a former machine: nor does that alter the case; the contrivance must have had a contriver. That former one from one preceding it: no alteration still; a contriver is still necessary. No tendency is perceived, no approach toward a diminution of this necessity. It is the same with any and every succession of these machines—a succession of ten, of a hundred, of a thousand; with one series, as with another—a series which is finite, as with a series which is infinite. In whatever other respects they may differ, in this they do not. In all equally, contrivance and design are unaccounted for.

The question is not simply, how came the first watch into existence?—which question, it may be pretended, is done away by supposing the series of watches thus produced from one another to have been infinite, and consequently to have had no such *first* for which it was necessary to provide a cause. This, perhaps, would have been nearly the state of the question, if nothing had been before us but an unorganized, unmechanized substance, without mark or indication of contrivance. It might be difficult to show that such substance could not have existed from eternity, either in succession—if it were possible, which I think it is not, for unorganized bodies to spring from one another—or by individual perpetuity. But that is not the question now. To suppose it to be so is to suppose that it made no difference whether he had found a watch or a stone. As it is, the metaphysics of that question have no place; for, in the watch which we are examining are seen contrivance, design, an end, a purpose, means for the end, adaptation to the purpose. And the question which irresistibly presses upon our thoughts is, whence this contrivance and design? The thing required is the intending mind, the adapted hand, the intelligence by which that hand was directed. This question, this demand is not shaken off by increasing a number or succession of substances destitute of these properties; nor the more, by increasing that number to infinity. If it be said that, upon the supposition of one watch being produced from another in the course of that other's movements and by means of the mechanism within it, we have a cause for the watch in my hand, namely, the watch from which it proceeded; I deny that for the design, the contrivance,

[11] Think carefully about this point: the claim is that each watch in the series raises the very same issue of explanation, the force of which is thus not reduced by even an infinite series.

the suitableness of means to an end, the adaptation of instruments to a use, all of which we discover in the watch, we have any cause whatever. It is in vain, therefore, to assign a series of such causes or to allege that a series may be carried back to infinity; for I do not admit that we have yet any cause at all for the phenomena, still less any series of causes either finite or infinite. Here is contrivance but no contriver; proofs of design, but no designer. 12

12 Again Paley seems to assume that a contriver is required. But he hasn't shown that this is so until he has shown that the infinite series of watches cannot satisfactorily explain itself—which means that he cannot use the need for a contriver as the reason why the infinite series cannot do this.

V. Our observer would further also reflect that the maker of the watch before him was in truth and reality the maker of every watch produced from it: there being no difference, except that the latter manifests a more exquisite skill, between the making of another watch with his own hands, by the mediation of files, lathes, chisels, etc., and the disposing, fixing, and inserting of these instruments, or of others equivalent to them, in the body of the watch already made, in such a manner as to form a new watch in the course of the movements which he had given to the old one. It is only working by one set of tools instead of another.

The conclusion which the *first* examination of the watch, of its works, construction, and movement, suggested, was that it must have had, for cause and author of that construction, an artificer who understood its mechanism and designed its use. This conclusion is invincible. A *second* examination presents us with a new discovery. The watch is found, in the course of its movement, to produce another watch similar to itself; and not only so, but we perceive in it a system or organization separately calculated for that purpose. What effect would this discovery have or ought it to have upon our former inference? What, as has already been said, but to increase beyond measure our admiration of the skill which had been employed in the formation of such a machine? Or shall it, instead of this, all at once turn us round to an opposite conclusion, namely, that no art or skill whatever has been concerned in the business, although all other evidences of art and skill remain as

they were, and this last and supreme piece of art be now added to the rest? Can this be maintained without absurdity? 13 Yet this is atheism.

13 Paley is saying that if the original watch must be explained by a designer, this is even more clearly so for watches that can create further watches.

CHAPTER THREE: APPLICATION OF THE ARGUMENT

This is atheism; for every indication of contrivance, every manifestation of design which existed in the watch, exists in the works of nature, with the difference on the side of nature of being greater and more, and that in a degree which exceeds all computation. I mean that the contrivances of nature surpass the contrivances of art in the complexity, subtlety, and curiosity of the mechanism; and still more, if possible, do they go beyond them in number and variety; yet, in a multitude of cases, are not less evidently mechanical, not less evidently contrivances, not less evidently accommodated to their end or suited to their office than are the most perfect productions of human ingenuity.

I know no better method of introducing so large a subject than that of comparing a single thing with a single thing: an eye, for example, with a telescope. 14 As far as the examination of the instrument goes, there is precisely the same proof that the eye was made for vision as there is that the telescope was made for assisting it. They are made upon the same principles, both being adjusted to the laws by which the transmission and refraction of rays of light are regulated. I speak not of the origin of the laws themselves; but such laws being fixed, the construction in both cases is adapted to them. For instance, these laws require, in order to produce the same effect, that rays of light in passing from water into the eye should be refracted by a more convex surface than when it passes out of air into the eye. Accordingly, we find that the eye of a fish, in that part of it called the crystalline lens, is much rounder than

14 Finally the eye appears, though the initial comparison is with a telescope (a more similar manufactured object). In some ways the argument would have been simpler had Paley started with the telescope instead of the watch.

the eye of terrestrial animals. What plainer manifestation of design can there be than this difference? What could a mathematical instrument maker have done more to show his knowledge of his principle, his application of that knowledge, his suiting of his means to his end—I will not say to display the compass or excellence of his skill and art, for in these all comparison is indecorous, but to testify counsel, choice, consideration, purpose?

To some it may appear a difference sufficient to destroy all similitude between the eye and the telescope, that the one is a perceiving organ, the other an unperceiving instrument. The fact is that they are both instruments. And as to the mechanism, at least as to the mechanism being employed, and even as to the kind of it, this circumstance varies not the analogy at all.

. . .

In the example before us it is a matter of certainty, because it is a matter which experience and observation demonstrate, that the formation of an image at the bottom of the eye is necessary to perfect vision. The formation then of such an image being necessary—no matter how—to the sense of sight and to the exercise of that sense, the apparatus by which it is formed is constructed and put together not only with infinitely more art, but upon the selfsame principles of art as in the telescope or the camera obscura. The perception arising from the image may be laid out of the question; for the production of the image, these are instruments of the same kind. The end is the same, the means are the same. The purpose in both is alike, the contrivance for accomplishing that purpose is in both alike. The lenses of the telescopes and humors of the eye bear a complete resemblance to one another, in their figure, their position, and in their power over the rays of light, namely, in bringing each pencil to a point at the right distance from the lens; namely, in the eye, at the exact place where the membrane is spread to receive it. How is it possible, under circumstances of such close affinity, and under the operation of equal evidence, to exclude contrivance from the one, yet to acknowledge the proof of contrivance having been employed, as the plainest and clearest of all propositions, in the other? ⑮

The resemblance between the two cases is still more accurate, and obtains in more points than we have yet represented, or than we are, on the first view of the subject, aware of. In dioptric telescopes there is an imperfection of this nature. Pencils of light in passing through glass lenses are separated into different colors, thereby tinging the object, especially the edges of it, as if it were viewed through a prism. To correct this inconvenience had been long a desideratum in the art. At last it came into the mind of a sagacious optician to inquire how this matter was managed in the eye, in which there was exactly the same difficulty to contend with as in the telescope. His observation taught him that in the eye the evil was cured by combining lenses composed of different substances, that is, of substances which possessed different refracting powers. Our artist borrowed thence his hint and produced a correction of the defect by imitating, in glasses made from different materials, the effects of the different humors through which the rays of light pass before they reach the bottom of the eye. Could this be in the eye without purpose, which suggested to the optician the only effectual means of attaining that purpose?

. . .

⑮ The similarities between the telescope and the eye are very great (as elaborated still further in the following paragraph). The telescope is clearly a product of intelligent design (and could be known to be so even if we knew nothing about the specific manufacture of telescopes). By analogy, Paley claims, the same is (probably) true of the eye.

CHAPTER FIVE: APPLICATION OF THE ARGUMENT CONTINUED

Every observation which was made in our first chapter concerning the watch may be repeated with strict propriety concerning the eye, concerning animals, concerning plants, concerning, indeed, all the organized parts of the works of nature. ⑯ As,

I. When we are inquiring simply after the

⑯ Finally the comparison between the watch and the eye (and similar organic things) is drawn explicitly.

existence of an intelligent Creator, imperfection, inaccuracy, liability to disorder, occasional irregularities may subsist in a considerable degree without inducing any doubt into the question; just as a watch may frequently go wrong, seldom perhaps exactly right, may be faulty in some parts, defective in some, without the smallest ground of suspicion from thence arising that it was not a watch, not made, or not made for the purpose ascribed to it. When faults are pointed out, and when a question is started concerning the skill of the artist or the dexterity with which the work is executed, then, indeed, in order to defend these qualities from accusation, we must be able either to expose some intractableness and imperfection in the materials or point out some invincible difficulty in the execution, into which imperfection and difficulty the matter of complaint may be resolved; or, if we cannot do this, we must adduce such specimens of consummate art and contrivance proceeding from the same hand as may convince the inquirer of the existence, in the case before him, of impediments like those which we have mentioned, although, what from the nature of the case is very likely to happen, they be unknown and unperceived by him. This we must do in order to vindicate the artist's skill, or at least the perfection of it; as we must also judge of his intention and of the provisions employed in fulfilling that intention, not from an instance in which they fail but from the great plurality of instances in which they succeed. But, after all, these are different questions from the question of the artist's existence; or, which is the same, whether the thing before us be a work of art or not; and the questions ought always to be kept separate in the mind. [17] So likewise it is in the works of nature. Irregularities and imperfections are of little or no weight in the consideration when that consideration relates simply to the existence of a Creator. When the argument respects his attributes, they are of weight; but are then to be taken in conjunction—the attention

[17] One issue is whether something can only be adequately explained by appeal to an intelligent designer. A second question is how much intelligence and skill must be ascribed to the designer for the explanation to be adequate. The second issue points to a weakness in this version of the argument from design if it is claimed to establish the existence of a God fitting the standard conception. Paley here tries to deal with that weakness.

is not to rest upon them, but they are to be taken in conjunction with the unexceptional evidences which we possess of skill, power, and benevolence displayed in other instances; which evidences may, in strength, number, and variety, be such and may so overpower apparent blemishes as to induce us, upon the most reasonable ground, to believe that these last ought to be referred to some cause, though we be ignorant of it, other than defect of knowledge or of benevolence in the author.

. . .

III. One atheistic way of replying to our observations upon the works of nature, and to the proofs of a Deity which we think that we perceive in them, is to tell us that all which we see must necessarily have had some form, and that it might as well be its present form as any other. Let us now apply this answer to the eye, as we did before to the watch. Something or other must have occupied that place in the animal's head, must have filled up, as we say, that socket; we will say, also, that it must have been of that sort of substance which we call animal substance, as flesh, bone, membrane, or cartilage, etc. But that it should have been an *eye,* knowing as we do what an eye comprehends, namely, that it should have consisted, first, of a series of transparent lenses—very different, by the by, even in their substance, from the opaque materials of which the rest of the body is, in general at least, composed, and with which the whole of its surface, this single portion of it excepted, is covered; secondly, of a black cloth or canvas—the only membrane in the body which is black—spread out behind these lenses, so as to receive the image formed by pencils of light transmitted through them, and at which alone a distinct image could be formed, namely, at the concourse of the refracted rays; thirdly, of a large nerve communicating between this membrane and the brain, without which the action of light upon the membrane, however modified by the organ, would be lost to the purposes of sensation; that this fortunate conformation of parts should have been the lot not of one individual out of many thousand individuals, like the great prize in a lottery or like some singularity in nature, but the happy chance of a whole species; nor of one species out of many thousand species with which we are acquainted, but of by far the greatest number of all that exist, and that under varieties not casual or capricious, but bearing marks of being suited to their respective exigencies; that all this should have taken place merely because something must have occupied these points on every animal's forehead, or that all this should be thought to be accounted for by the short answer that "whatever was there must have had some form or other" is too absurd to be made more so by any argumentation.[18] We are not contented with this answer; we find no satisfaction in it, by way of accounting for appearances of organization far short of those of the eye, such as we observe in fossil shells, petrified bones, or other substances which bear the vestiges of animal or vegetable recrements, but which, either in respect to utility or of the situation in which they are discovered, may seem accidental enough. It is no way of accounting even for these things, to say that the stone, for instance, which is shown to us—supposing the question to be concerning a petrifaction—must have contained some internal conformation or other.

. . .

IV. There is another answer which has the same effect as the resolving of things into chance, which answer would persuade us to believe that the eye, the animal to which it belongs, every other animal, every plant, indeed every organized body which we see are only so many out of the possible varieties and combinations of being which the lapse of infinite ages has brought into existence; that the present world is the relic of that variety; millions of other bodily forms and other species having perished, being, by the defect of their constitution, incapable of preservation, or of continuance by generation. Now there is no foundation whatever for this conjecture in any thing which we observe in the works of nature; no such experiments are going on at present—no such energy operates as that which is here supposed, and which should be constantly pushing into existence new varieties of beings. Nor are there any appearances to support an opinion that every possible combination of vegetable or animal structure has formerly been tried. Multitudes of conformation, both of vegetables and animals, may be conceived capable of existence and succession, which yet do not exist. Perhaps almost as many forms of plants might have been found in the fields as figures of plants can be delineated upon paper. A countless variety of animals might have existed which do not exist. Upon the supposition here stated, we should see unicorns and mermaids, sylphs and centaurs, the fancies of painters and the fables of poets, realized by examples. Or, if it be alleged that these may transgress the bounds of possible life and propagation, we might at least have nations of human beings without nails upon their fingers, with more or fewer fingers and toes than ten, some with one eye, others with one ear, with one nostril, or without the sense of smelling at all. All these and a thousand other imaginable varieties might live and propagate. We may modify any one species many different ways, all consistent with life, and with the actions necessary to preservation, although affording different degrees of conveniency and enjoyment to the animal. And if we carry these modifications through the different species which are known to subsist, their number would be incalculable. No reason can be given why, if these [lost species] ever existed, they have now disappeared. Yet, if all possible existences have been tried, they must have formed part of the catalogue.[19]

. . .

The hypothesis, indeed, is hardly deserving of the consideration which we have given it. What should we think of a man who, because we had never ourselves seen watches, telescopes, stocking mills, steam engines, etc., made, knew not how they were made, nor could prove by testimony when they were made, or by whom, would have us believe that these machines, instead of deriving their curious structures from the thought and design of their inventors and contrivers, in truth derive them from no other origin than this: namely, that a mass of metals and other materials having run, when melted, into all possible figures, and combined themselves in all possible forms and shapes and proportions, these things which we see are what were left from the incident, as best worth preserving, and as such are become the remaining stock of a magazine which, at

---

[18] Again the idea behind the atheistic reply seems to be that eyes might just have occurred at random, as one out of many possibilities.

[19] Here we have a crude anticipation of something like the idea of evolution. But with no account of how some variations rather than others might have been produced and selected, there is no explanation of why so few possibilities seem to actually be realized.

one time or other, has by this means contained every mechanism, useful and useless, convenient and inconvenient, into which such like materials could be thrown? I cannot distinguish the hypothesis, as applied to the works of nature, from this solution, which no one would accept as applied to a collection of machines.

. . .

VI. Others have chosen to refer every thing to a *principle of order* in nature. A principle of order is the word; but what is meant by a principle of order as different from an intelligent Creator has not been explained either by definition or example; and without such explanation it should seem to be a mere substitution of words for reasons, names for causes. Order itself is only the adaptation of means to an end: a principle of order, therefore, can only signify the mind and intention which so adapts them.[20] Or, were it capable of being explained in any other sense, is there

[20] Paley seems to argue here that *any* sort of order presupposes a mind that creates it. Does he have any argument for this claim? Do you see any problem with it?

any experience, any analogy, to sustain it? Was a watch ever produced by a principle of order; and why might not a watch be so produced as well as an eye?

Furthermore, a principle of order, acting blindly and without choice, is negatived by the observation that order is not universal, which it would be if it issued from a constant and necessary principle, nor indiscriminate, which it would be if it issued from an unintelligent principle.[21] Where order is wanted, there we find it; where order is not wanted, that is, where if it prevailed, it would be useless, there we do not find it. In the structure of the eye—for we adhere to our example—in the figure and position of its several parts, the most exact order is maintained. In the forms of rocks and mountains, in the lines which bound the coasts of continents and islands, in the shape of bays and promontories, no order whatever is perceived, because it would have been superfluous.

[21] Here is a different response to the claim that nature itself is orderly in a way that explains the eye: eyes are very rare in comparison to the sorts of materials of which they are composed, so it isn't plausible to think that they are generated by a pervasive natural order. Is this a better answer?

Discussion Questions

1. One difference between the watch and the stone is that we know independently that stones naturally occur in heaths and watches don't. Another is that the watch has features that are known to be present in manufactured items and not in naturally occurring items (see Annotation 4). These features do not pertain to the eye, and they at least weaken the analogy between the watch and the eye upon which Paley ultimately relies (or that between the telescope and the eye). How much does this affect his argument?

2. Is it self-evident that the watch (even the infinite series of self-replicating watches) requires a further explanation? Is it similarly self-evident that it must be explained by appeal to an intelligent designer? Would this be so even if the watch did not resemble any familiar sort of manufactured object, even if it seemed to be an organically produced structure? Why or why not? Is the same thing true of the eye?

3. Suppose that everything about Paley's argument were acceptable. What conception of the designer's attributes would it support? How close would they be to the attributes of God under the standard conception? How important is the fact that some of the allegedly designed features are imperfect (see Annotation 16)?

4. Think carefully about the premise of the argument from design. What is the correct characterization of the facts that allegedly require a designer? Think first about the watch. What exactly is it about the watch that convinces us that it must have had a designer? Not that the watch has a design, for that would beg the question. Paley says that "its parts are framed and put together for a purpose," but that also seems question begging. Try to formulate a description of the watch and an analogous description of the eye that are not question-begging and yet still support the conclusion of the argument.

Stephen Jay Gould

Stephen Jay Gould (1941–2002) was a paleontologist and evolutionary biologist who taught at Harvard. Though his writings are voluminous, he is perhaps best known for his short essays in the periodical *Natural History,* collected in many volumes, which explain and discuss various topics in and around the theory of evolution.

The following selection is one of those essays. In it, Gould argues in favor of the theory of evolution, and so against the hypothesis of divine creation, as an explanation of specific examples of apparent design of the sort to which Paley appeals. The main premise of the argument is that the details of many such examples involve structures existing in other animals that are very imperfectly adapted for a particular use in the case in question. According to Gould, this makes very good sense from an evolutionary perspective, but does not fit well with the idea that intelligent design by an all-powerful creator was at work.

It is important to emphasize that while the appeal to evolution may be a good response to the local version of the argument from design, it does not in itself answer the global version that demands an explanation for the presence of order of any sort in the universe (see the introduction to this chapter). This is so because the details of the evolutionary account presuppose a background of order that is itself left unexplained: in the case of evolution, the order required for genetic inheritance, mixing of genes from different individuals, production of mutations, etc. Other scientific explanations of specific features of the world, for example the explanation of mountains provided by geology, work in the same way: they account for specific, narrowly focused cases of order by appeal to more general background principles of order. Thus explanations of this sort are incapable of providing a complete answer to the global version of the argument.

The Panda's Thumb

Few heroes lower their sights in the prime of their lives; triumph leads inexorably on, often to destruction. Alexander wept because he had no new worlds to conquer; Napoleon, overextended, sealed his doom in the depth of a Russian winter. But Charles Darwin did not follow the *Origin of Species* (1859) with a general defense of natural selection or

with its evident extension to human evolution (he waited until 1871 to publish *The Descent of Man*). Instead, he wrote his most obscure work, a book entitled: *On the Various Contrivances by Which British and Foreign Orchids Are Fertilized by Insects* (1862).

Darwin's many excursions into the minutiae of natural history—he wrote a taxonomy of barnacles, a book on climbing plants, and a treatise on the formation of vegetable mold by earthworms—won him an undeserved reputation as an old-fashioned, somewhat doddering describer of curious plants and animals, a man who had one lucky insight at the right time. A

From Stephen Jay Gould, The Panda's Thumb: More Reflections in Natural History *(New York: W. W. Norton, 1980).*

rash of Darwinian scholarship has laid this myth firmly to rest during the past twenty years. Before then, one prominent scholar spoke for many ill-informed colleagues when he judged Darwin as a "poor joiner of ideas . . . a man who does not belong with the great thinkers."

In fact, each of Darwin's books played its part in the grand and coherent scheme of his life's work demonstrating the fact of evolution and defending natural selection as its primary mechanism.① Darwin did not study orchids solely for their own sake. Michael Ghiselin, a California biologist who finally took the trouble to read all of Darwin's books (see his *Triumph of the Darwinian Method*), has correctly identified the treatise on orchids as an important episode in Darwin's campaign for evolution.

Darwin begins his orchid book with an important evolutionary premise: continued self-fertilization is a poor strategy for long-term survival, since offspring carry only the genes of their single parent, and populations do not maintain enough variation for evolutionary flexibility in the face of environmental change. Thus, plants bearing flowers with both male and female parts usually evolve mechanisms to ensure cross-pollination.② Orchids have formed an alliance with insects. They have evolved an astonishing variety of "contrivances" to attract insects, guarantee that sticky pollen adheres to their visitor, and ensure that the attached pollen comes in contact with female parts of the next orchid visited by the insect.

Darwin's book is a compendium of these contrivances, the botanical equivalent of a bestiary. And, like the medieval bestiaries, it is designed to instruct. The message is paradoxical but profound. Orchids manufacture their intricate devices from the common components of ordinary flowers, parts usually fitted for very different functions. If God had designed a beautiful machine to reflect his wisdom and power, surely he would not have used a collection of parts generally fashioned for other purposes. Orchids were not made by an ideal engineer; they are jury-rigged from a limited set of available components. Thus, they must have evolved from ordinary flowers.③

Thus, the paradox, and the common theme of this trilogy of essays: Our textbooks like to illustrate evolution with examples of optimal design—nearly perfect mimicry of a dead leaf by a butterfly or of a poisonous species by a palatable relative. But ideal design is a lousy argument for evolution, for it mimics the postulated action of an omnipotent creator. Odd arrangements and funny solutions are the proof of evolution—paths that a sensible God would never tread but that a natural process, constrained by history, follows perforce. No one understood this better than Darwin. Ernst Mayr has shown how Darwin, in defending evolution, consistently turned to organic parts and geographic distributions that make the least sense.④ Which brings me to the giant panda and its "thumb."

Giant pandas are peculiar bears, members of the order Carnivora. Conventional bears are the most omnivorous representatives of their order, but pandas have restricted this catholicity of taste in the other direction—they belie the name of their order by subsisting almost entirely on bamboo. They live in dense forests of bamboo at high elevations in the mountains of western China. There they sit, largely unthreatened by predators, munching bamboo ten to twelve hours each day.

As a childhood fan of Andy Panda, and former owner of a stuffed toy won by some fluke when all the

① *Evolution* is the change and development of plants and animals over time, resulting in the emergence of new species (and usually the disappearance of older ones). Natural selection is the hypothesis that this takes place because (a) individuals with varied characteristics occur (through genetic recombination and mutation), and (b) those whose characteristics improve their capacity to survive (in the specific environment in question) are more likely to reproduce, thus passing their characteristics to their offspring ("survival of the fittest").

② The mixing of genes from different parents is one way in which individuals with varied characteristics are produced, so that natural selection can operate. (Another such way is mutation.)

③ This point is elaborated and illustrated toward the end of the selection.

④ The idea is that an intelligent, all-powerful designer would have created features that are perfectly designed for their function, whereas evolution, having to select among only those features that actually occur via genetic combination and mutation, may well end up with features that function adequately but are far short of optimum.

milk bottles actually tumbled at the county fair, I was delighted when the first fruits of our thaw with China went beyond ping pong to the shipment of two pandas to the Washington zoo. I went and watched in appropriate awe. They yawned, stretched, and ambled a bit, but they spent nearly all their time feeding on their beloved bamboo. They sat upright and manipulated the stalks with their forepaws, shedding the leaves and consuming only the shoots.

I was amazed by their dexterity and wondered how the scion of a stock adapted for running could use its hands so adroitly. They held the stalks of bamboo in their paws and stripped off the leaves by passing the stalks between an apparently flexible thumb and the remaining fingers. This puzzled me. I had learned that a dexterous, opposable thumb stood among the hallmarks of human success. We had maintained, even exaggerated, this important flexibility of our primate forebears, while most mammals had sacrificed it in specializing their digits. Carnivores run, stab, and scratch. My cat may manipulate me psychologically, but he'll never type or play the piano.

So I counted the panda's other digits and received an even greater surprise; there were five, not four. Was the "thumb" a separately evolved sixth finger? Fortunately, the giant panda has its bible, a monograph by D. Dwight Davis, late curator of vertebrate anatomy at Chicago's Field Museum of Natural History. It is probably the greatest work of modern evolutionary comparative anatomy, and it contains more than anyone would ever want to know about pandas. Davis had the answer, of course.

The panda's "thumb" is not, anatomically, a finger at all. It is constructed from a bone called the radial sesamoid, normally a small component of the wrist. In pandas, the radial sesamoid is greatly enlarged and elongated until it almost equals the metapodial bones of the true digits in length. The radial sesamoid underlies a pad on the panda's forepaw; the five digits form the framework of another pad, the palmar. A shallow furrow separates the two pads and serves as a channelway for bamboo stalks.

The panda's thumb comes equipped not only with a bone to give it strength but also with muscles to sustain its agility. These muscles, like the radial sesamoid bone itself, did not arise *de novo*. Like the parts of Darwin's orchids, they are familiar bits of anatomy remod-

eled for a new function. The abductor of the radial sesamoid (the muscle that pulls it away from the true digits) bears the formidable name *abductor pollicis longus* ("the long abductor of the thumb"—*pollicis* is the genitive of *pollex,* Latin for "thumb"). Its name is a giveaway. In other carnivores, this muscle attaches to the first digit, or true thumb. Two shorter muscles run between the radial sesamoid and the pollex. They pull the sesamoid "thumb" towards the true digits.

Does the anatomy of other carnivores give us any clue to the origin of this odd arrangement in pandas? Davis points out that ordinary bears and raccoons, the closest relatives of giant pandas, far surpass all other carnivores in using their forelegs for manipulating objects in feeding. Pardon the backward metaphor, but pandas, thanks to their ancestry, began with a leg up for evolving greater dexterity in feeding. Moreover, ordinary bears already have a slightly enlarged radial sesamoid.⑤

In most carnivores, the same muscles that move the radial sesamoid in pandas attach exclusively to the base of the pollex, or true thumb. But in ordinary bears, the long abductor muscle ends in two tendons: one inserts into the base of the thumb as in most carnivores, but the other attaches to the radial sesamoid. The two shorter muscles also attach, in part, to the radial sesamoid in bears. "Thus," Davis concludes, "the musculature for operating this remarkable new mechanism—functionally a new digit—required no intrinsic change from conditions already present in the panda's closest relatives, the bears. Furthermore, it appears that the whole sequence of events in the musculature follows automatically from simple hypertrophy of the sesamoid bone."

The sesamoid thumb of pandas is a complex structure formed by marked enlargement of a bone and an extensive rearrangement of musculature. Yet Davis argues that the entire apparatus arose as a mechanical response to growth of the radial sesamoid

⑤ Thus the panda's "thumb" is not a true thumb at all, but rather a structure involving a bone and muscles that take quite different forms in the panda's relatives. Though it works well enough in eating bamboo, Gould's point is that an all-powerful intelligent designer would have designed a specific structure for this purpose rather than adapting pre-existing parts in a serviceable but still somewhat clumsy way.

itself. Muscles shifted because the enlarged bone

⑥ The claim is that evolution provides a better explanation of the panda's thumb than divine creation (see Annotation 5). If Davis is right, a single mutation could have produced the whole structure (which then would have been favored by natural selection because of its advantage for feeding).

blocked them short of their original sites. Moreover, Davis postulates that the enlarged radial sesamoid may have been fashioned by a simple genetic change, perhaps a single mutation affecting the timing and rate of growth.⑥

In a panda's foot, the counterpart of the radial sesamoid, called the tibial sesamoid, is also enlarged, although not so much as the radial sesamoid. Yet the tibial sesamoid supports no new digit, and its increased size confers no advantage, so far as we know. Davis argues that the coordinated increase of both bones, in response to natural selection upon one alone, probably reflects a simple kind of genetic change. Repeated parts of the body are not fashioned by the action of individual genes—there is no gene "for" your thumb, another for your big toe, or a third for your pinky. Repeated parts are coordinated in development; selection for a change in one element causes a corresponding modification in others. It may be genetically more complex to enlarge a thumb and *not* to modify a big toe, than to increase both together. (In the first case, a general coordination

⑦ This hypothesis is supported by the similar change in the panda's foot—which in itself yields no survival value and so presumably would not have been designed by an intelligent designer.

must be broken, the thumb favored separately, and correlated increase of related structures suppressed. In the second, a single gene may increase the rate of growth in a field regulating the development of corresponding digits.) ⑦

The panda's thumb provides an elegant zoological counterpart to Darwin's orchids. An engineer's best solution is debarred by history. The panda's true thumb is committed to another role, too specialized for a different function to become an opposable, manipulating digit. So the panda must use parts on hand and settle for an enlarged wrist bone and a somewhat clumsy, but quite workable, solution. The sesamoid thumb wins no prize in an engineer's derby. It is, to

use Michael Ghiselin's phrase, a contraption, not a lovely contrivance. But it does its job and excites our imagination all the more because it builds on such improbable foundations.

Darwin's orchid book is filled with similar illustrations. The marsh Epipactus, for example, uses its labellum—an enlarged petal—as a trap. The labellum is divided into two parts. One, near the flower's base, forms a large cup filled with nectar—the object of an insect's visit. The other, near the flower's edge, forms a sort of landing stage. An insect alighting on this runway depresses it and thus gains entrance to the nectar cup beyond. It enters the cup, but the runway is so elastic that it instantly springs up, trapping the insect within the nectar cup. The insect must then back out through the only available exit—a path that forces it to brush against the pollen masses. A remarkable machine but all developed from a conventional petal, a part readily available in an orchid's ancestor.

Darwin then shows how the same labellum in other orchids evolves into a series of ingenious devices to ensure cross-fertilization. It may develop a complex fold that forces an insect to detour its proboscis around and past the pollen masses in order to reach nectar. It may contain deep channels or guiding ridges that lead insects both to nectar and pollen. The channels sometimes form a tunnel, producing a tubular flower. All these adaptations have been built from a part that began as a conventional petal in some ancestral form. Yet nature can do so much with so little that it displays, in Darwin's words, "a prodigality of resources for gaining the very same end, namely, the fertilization of one flower by pollen from another plant."

Darwin's metaphor for organic form reflects his sense of wonder that evolution can fashion such a world of diversity and adequate design with such limited raw material:

> Although an organ may not have been originally formed for some special purpose, if it now serves for this end we are justified in saying that it is specially contrived for it. On the same principle, if a man were to make a machine for some special purpose, but were to use old wheels, springs, and pulleys, only slightly altered, the whole machine, with all its parts, might be said to be specially contrived for that purpose. Thus throughout nature almost

every part of each living being has probably served, in a slightly modified condition, for diverse purposes, and has acted in the living machinery of many ancient and distinct specific forms.

We may not be flattered by the metaphor of refurbished wheels and pulleys, but consider how well we work. Nature is, in biologist François Jacob's words, an excellent tinkerer, not a divine artificer. And who shall sit in judgment between these exemplary skills?

Discussion Questions

1. Why does Gould's example of the panda's thumb constitute an objection to the argument from design? How good is that objection? Since the panda's thumb works quite well, is there any reason why an intelligent designer could not have created it for that purpose? Is there a way in which the evolutionary explanation is *better* than the appeal to God, even though both are possible explanations? Gould also might seem to suggest that for optimum organic structures, intelligent design is just as good an explanation (or even a better one?). Is he right about this?

2. How might a creationist respond to Gould's objection shifting from the local to the global version of the argument from design? Why can't someone appeal to evolutionary theory to explain the order of the universe as a whole? Does the order of the universe as a whole genuinely need an explanation? Why or why not?

David Hume

The longest portion of Hume's *Dialogues* is devoted to the argument from design, with Cleanthes presenting his version of the argument and Philo criticizing it at great length. Though both the local and the global versions of the argument (see the introduction to this chapter) are reflected in the discussion, the main focus is on the global version. Thus the issue is how the overall order of the world (really the universe) is to be explained. See the introduction to the selection from the *Dialogues* on p. 51 for information about Hume, together with a description of the characters in the dialogue (this selection actually comes immediately before that one in the original book itself).

Problems with the Argument from Design, from *Dialogues Concerning Natural Religion*

. . .

Not to lose any time in circumlocutions, said Cleanthes, addressing himself to Demea, . . . ; I shall briefly explain how I conceive this matter. Look round the world: contemplate the whole and every part of it: you will find it to be nothing but one great machine, subdivided into an infinite number of lesser machines, which again admit of subdivisions, to a degree beyond what human senses and faculties can trace and explain.

From David Hume, Dialogues Concerning Natural Religion *(1779).*

All these various machines, and even their most minute parts, are adjusted to each other with an accuracy, which ravishes into admiration all men, who have ever contemplated them. The curious adapting of means to ends, throughout all nature, resembles exactly, though it much exceeds, the productions of human contrivance; of human design, thought, wisdom, and intelligence. Since therefore the effects resemble each other, we are led to infer, by all the rules of analogy, that the causes also resemble; and that the Author of Nature is somewhat similar to the mind of men; though possessed of much larger faculties, proportioned to the grandeur of the work, which he has executed. By this argument *a posteriori,* and by this argument alone, do we prove at once the existence of a Deity, and his similarity to human mind and intelligence.①

> ① Though both versions are discernible, the main emphasis here is on what we have called the global version of the argument from design (see chapter introduction).

I shall be so free, Cleanthes, said Demea, as to tell you, that from the beginning, I could not approve of your conclusion concerning the similarity of the Deity to men; still less can I approve of the mediums, by which you endeavor to establish it. What! No demonstration of the being of a God! No abstract arguments! No proofs a priori!② Are these, which have hitherto been so much insisted on by philosophers, all fallacy, all sophism? Can we reach no farther in this subject than experience and probability? I will not say, that this is betraying the cause of a deity: but surely, by this affected candor, you give advantage to atheists, which they never could obtain, by the mere dint of argument and reasoning.

> ② By an "a priori proof," Demea has the cosmological argument in mind (even though it is not strictly a priori because it relies on the experience that the world exists).

What I chiefly scruple in this subject, said Philo, is not so much, that all religious arguments are by Cleanthes reduced to experience, as that they appear not to be even the most certain and irrefragable of that inferior kind. That a stone will fall, that fire will burn, that the earth has solidity, we have observed a thousand and a thousand times; and when any new instance of this nature is presented, we draw without hesitation the accustomed inference. The exact similarity of the cases gives us a perfect assurance of a similar event; and a stronger evidence is never desired nor sought after. But wherever you depart, in the least, from the similarity of the cases, you diminish proportionably the evidence; and may at last bring it to a very weak *analogy,* which is confessedly liable to error and uncertainty. After having experienced the circulation of the blood in human creatures, we make no doubt that it takes place in Titius and Maevius: but from its circulation in frogs and fishes, it is only a presumption, though a strong one, from analogy, that it takes place in men and other animals. The analogical reasoning is much weaker, when we infer the circulation of the sap in vegetables from our experience, that the blood circulates in animals; and those, who hastily followed that imperfect analogy, are found, by more accurate experiments, to have been mistaken.③

> ③ Many versions of the argument from design, such as Paley's, are arguments by analogy. Philo makes the point that the strength of such an argument depends heavily on the degree of similarity between the cases that are being compared.

If we see a house, Cleanthes, we conclude, with the greatest certainty, that it had an architect or builder; because this is precisely that species of effect, which we have experienced to proceed from that species of cause. But surely you will not affirm, that the universe bears such a resemblance to a house, that we can with the same certainty infer a similar cause, or that the analogy is here entire and perfect. The dissimilitude is so striking, that the utmost you can here pretend to is a guess, a conjecture, a presumption concerning a similar cause; and how that pretension will be received in the world, I leave you to consider.

It would surely be very ill received, replied Cleanthes; and I should be deservedly blamed and detested, did I allow, that the proofs of a Deity amounted to no more than a guess or conjecture. But is the whole adjustment of means to ends in a house and in the universe so slight a resemblance? The economy of final causes? The order, proportion, and arrangement of every part? Steps of a stair are plainly contrived, that human legs may use them in mounting; and this inference is certain and infallible. Human legs are also contrived for walking and mounting; and this inference, I allow, is not altogether so certain, because of the dissimilarity which you remark; but does it, therefore, deserve the name only of presumption or conjecture?

Good God! cried Demea, interrupting him, where are we? Zealous defenders of religion allow, that the proofs of a Deity fall short of perfect evidence! And you, Philo, on whose assistance I depended, in proving the adorable mysteriousness of the Divine Nature, do you assent to all these extravagant opinions of Cleanthes? For what other name can I give them? . . .

You seem not to apprehend, replied Philo, that I argue with Cleanthes in his own way; and by showing him the dangerous consequences of his tenets, hope at last to reduce him to our opinion. But what sticks most with you, I observe, is the representation which Cleanthes has made of the argument *a posteriori;* and finding, that that argument is likely to escape your hold and vanish into air, you think it so disguised, that you can scarcely believe it to be set in its true light. Now, however much I may dissent, in other respects, from the dangerous principles of Cleanthes, I must allow, that he has fairly represented that argument; and I shall endeavor so to state the matter to you, that you will entertain no farther scruples with regard to it.

Were a man to abstract from everything which he knows or has seen, he would be altogether incapable, merely from his own ideas, to determine what kind of scene the universe must be, or to give the preference to one state or situation of things above another. For as nothing which he clearly conceives, could be esteemed impossible or implying a contradiction, every chimera of his fancy would be upon an equal footing; nor could he assign any just reason, why he adheres to one idea or system, and rejects the others, which are equally possible.

Again; after he opens his eyes, and contemplates the world, as it really is, it would be impossible for him, at first, to assign the cause of any one event; much less, of the whole of things or of the universe. He might set his fancy a rambling; and she

might bring him in an infinite variety of reports and representations. These would all be possible; but being all equally possible, he would never, of himself, give a satisfactory account for his preferring one of them to the rest. Experience alone can point out to him the true cause of any phenomenon.④

Now, according to this method of reasoning, Demea, it follows (and is, indeed, tacitly allowed by Cleanthes himself) that order, arrangement, or the adjustment of final causes is not, of itself, any proof of design; but only so far as it has been experienced to proceed from that principle. For aught, we can know a priori, matter may contain the source or spring of order originally, within itself, as well as mind does; and there is no more difficulty in conceiving, that the several elements, from an internal unknown cause, may fall into the most exquisite arrangement, than to conceive that their ideas, in the great, universal mind, from a like internal, unknown cause, fall into that arrangement. The equal possibility of both these suppositions is allowed.⑤ But by experience we find (according to Cleanthes), that there is a difference between them. Throw several pieces of steel together, without shape or form; they will never arrange themselves so as to compose a watch: stone, and mortar, and wood, without an architect, never erect a house. But the ideas in a human mind, we see, by an unknown, inexplicable economy, arrange themselves so as to form the plan of a watch or house. Experience, therefore, proves, that there is an original principle of order in mind, not in matter. From similar effects we infer similar causes. The adjustment of means to ends is alike in the universe, as in a machine of

④ This claim reflects the general **epistemological** view known as **empiricism:** the view that knowledge, especially knowledge of facts about the world, depends essentially on *experience.*

⑤ From an empiricist point of view, the fact that something is orderly is no reason, by itself, to conclude that it was produced by a designer. The only way to know that order (either of any particular sort or order in general) is probably produced by an intelligent designer is by having experiences of it actually being produced in that way.

human contrivance. The causes, therefore, must be resembling.⑥

⑥ The alternative to order being produced by an intelligent designer is order that is natural or intrinsic to the thing in question. That Paley's watch does not result in this way from intrinsic or natural order is shown by both (a) experiences of things of that general kind actually being produced by a designer and (b) also experiences of the sort of material in question failing to have that sort of order when a designer is not present. Ideas in a mind, in contrast, are plausibly regarded as intrinsically or naturally ordered, since neither of these sorts of experience—(a) and (b)—are realized in relation to them. (Note that this is Philo's restatement of Cleanthes's view, not something he accepts.)

I was from the beginning scandalized, I must own, with this resemblance, which is asserted, between the Deity and human creatures; and must conceive it to imply such a degradation of the Supreme Being as no sound theist could endure. With your assistance, therefore, Demea, I shall endeavor to defend what you justly called the adorable mysteriousness of the Divine Nature, and shall refute this reasoning of Cleanthes, provided he allows, that I have made a fair representation of it.

When Cleanthes had assented, Philo, after a short pause, proceeded in the following manner.

That all inferences, Cleanthes, concerning fact, are founded on experience, and that all experimental reasonings are founded on the supposition, that similar causes prove similar effects, and similar effects similar causes; I shall not, at present, much dispute with you. But observe, I entreat you, with what extreme caution all just reasoners proceed in the transferring of experiments to similar cases. Unless the cases be exactly similar, they repose no perfect confidence in applying their past observation to any particular phenomenon. Every alteration of circumstances occasions a doubt concerning the event; and it requires new experiments to prove certainly, that the new circumstances are of no moment or importance. A change in bulk, situation, arrangement, age, disposition of the air, or surrounding bodies; any of these particulars may be attended with the most unexpected consequences: and unless the objects be quite familiar to us, it is the highest temerity to expect with assurance, after any of these changes, an event similar to that which before fell under our observation. The slow and deliberate steps of philoso-

phers, here, if anywhere, are distinguished from the precipitate march of the vulgar, who, hurried on by the smallest similitudes, are incapable of all discernment or consideration.

But can you think, Cleanthes, that your usual phlegm and philosophy have been preserved in so wide a step as you have taken, when you compared to the universe, houses, ships, furniture, machines; and from their similarity in some circumstances inferred a similarity in their causes? Thought, design, intelligence, such as we discover in men and other animals, is no more than one of the springs and principles of the universe, as well as heat or cold, attraction or repulsion, and a hundred others, which fall under daily observation. It is an active cause, by which some particular parts of nature, we find, produce alterations on other parts. But can a conclusion, with any propriety, be transferred from parts to the whole? Does not the great disproportion bar all comparison and inference? From observing the growth of a hair, can we learn anything concerning the generation of a man? Would the manner of a leaf's blowing, even though perfectly known, afford us any instruction concerning the vegetation of a tree?

But allowing that we were to take the *operations* of one part of nature upon another for the foundation of our judgment concerning the *origin* of the whole (which never can be admitted), yet why select so minute, so weak, so bounded a principle as the reason and design of animals is found to be upon this planet? What peculiar privilege has this little agitation of the brain which we call *thought,* that we must thus make it the model of the whole universe? Our partiality in our own favor does indeed present it on all occasions; but sound philosophy ought carefully to guard against so natural an illusion.

So far from admitting, continued Philo, that the operations of a part can afford us any just conclusion concerning the origin of the whole, I will not allow any one part to form a rule for another part, if the latter be very remote from the former.

. . .

Nature, we find, even from our limited experience, possesses an infinite number of springs and principles, which incessantly discover themselves on every change of her position and situation. And what new and unknown principles would actuate her in so new and unknown a situation as that of the formation of a universe, we cannot, without the utmost temerity, pretend to determine.

A very small part of this great system, during a very short time, is very imperfectly discovered to us: and do we thence pronounce decisively concerning the origin of the whole?

Admirable conclusion! Stone, wood, brick, iron, brass, have not, at this time, in this minute globe of earth, an order or arrangement without human art and contrivance: therefore the universe could not originally attain its order and arrangement, without something similar to human art. But is a part of nature a rule for another part very wide of the former? Is it a rule for the whole? Is a very small part a rule for the universe? Is nature in one situation, a certain rule for nature in another situation, vastly different from the former?⑦

> ⑦ Philo points out that the analogy between the universe as a whole and various things that are known in the way just discussed to result from design is relatively weak—and also that there are many other kinds of causes, or apparent causes, to be found in the universe, raising the issue of why design should be singled out as the cause of the whole, rather than one of these others or some combination of them.

... When two species of objects have always been observed to be conjoined together, I can infer, by custom, the existence of one wherever I see the existence of the other: and this I call an argument from experience. But how this argument can have place, where the objects, as in the present case, are single, individual, without parallel, or specific resemblance, may be difficult to explain. And will any man tell me with a serious countenance, that an orderly universe must arise from some thought and art, like the human; because we have experience of it? To ascertain this reasoning, it were requisite, that we had experience of the origin of worlds;⑧ and it is not sufficient surely, that we have seen ships and cities arise from human art and contrivance....

> ⑧ This is a crucial point in relation to the global version of the argument: we do not have experiences of whole orderly universes arising from intelligent design—and so cannot know through experience that the order of a universe must be produced in that way (and cannot be intrinsic). (See the following selection by Flew for more discussion of this point.)

Philo was proceeding in this vehement manner, somewhat between jest and earnest, as it appeared to me; when he observed some signs of impatience in Cleanthes, and then immediately stopped short. What I had to suggest, said Cleanthes, is only that you would not abuse terms, or make use of popular expressions to subvert philosophical reasonings. You know, that the vulgar often distinguish reason from experience, even where the question relates only to matter of fact and existence; though it is found, where that reason is properly analyzed, that it is nothing but a species of experience. To prove by experience the origin of the universe from mind is not more contrary to common speech than to prove the motion of the earth from the same principle. And a caviler might raise all the same objections to the Copernican system, which you have urged against my reasonings. Have you other earths, might he say, which you have seen to move? Have....

Yes! cried Philo, interrupting him, we have other earths. Is not the moon another earth, which we see to turn round its center? Is not Venus another earth, where we observe the same phenomenon? Are not the revolutions of the sun also a confirmation, from analogy, of the same theory? All the planets, are they not earths, which revolve about the sun? Are not the satellites moons, which move round Jupiter and Saturn, and along with these primary planets, round the sun? These analogies and resemblances, with others, which I have not mentioned, are the sole proofs of the Copernican system: and to you it belongs to consider, whether you have any analogies of the same kind to support your theory.

In reality, Cleanthes, continued he, the modern system of astronomy is now so much received by all inquirers, and has become so essential a part even of our earliest education, that we are not commonly very scrupulous in examining the reasons upon which it is founded. It is now become a matter of mere curiosity to study the first writers on that subject, who had the full force of prejudice to encounter, and were obliged to turn their arguments on every side, in order to render them popular and convincing....

In this cautious proceeding of the astronomers, you may read your own condemnation, Cleanthes; or rather may see, that the subject in which you are engaged exceeds all human reason and inquiry. Can you pretend to show any such similarity between the fabric of a house, and the generation of a universe? Have you ever seen nature in any such situation as resembles the first arrangement of the elements? Have worlds ever been formed under your eye? and have you had leisure to observe the whole progress of the phenomenon, from the first appearance of order to its final consummation? If you have, then cite your experience, and deliver your theory.

. . .

How the most absurd argument, replied Cleanthes, in the hands of a man of ingenuity and invention, may acquire an air of probability! Are you not aware, Philo, that it became necessary for Copernicus and his first disciples to prove the similarity of the terrestrial and celestial matter; because several philosophers, blinded by old systems, and supported by some sensible appearances, had denied this similarity? But that it is by no means necessary, that theists should prove the similarity of the works of nature to those of art; because this similarity is self-evident and undeniable? The same matter, a like form: what more is requisite to show an analogy between their causes, and to ascertain the origin of all things from a divine purpose and intention? Your objections, I must freely tell you, are no better than the abstruse cavils of those philosophers who denied motion: and ought to be refuted in the same manner, by illustrations, examples, and instances, rather than by serious argument and philosophy.

Suppose, therefore, that an articulate voice were heard in the clouds, much louder and more melodious than any which human art could ever reach: suppose, that this voice were extended in the same instant over all nations, and spoke to each nation in its own language and dialect: suppose, that the words delivered not only contain a just sense and meaning, but convey some instruction altogether worthy of a benevolent being, superior to mankind: could you possibly hesitate a moment concerning the cause of this voice? and must you not instantly ascribe it to some design or purpose? ⑨

⑨ This example is supposed to show that the general principles underlying Philo's objections are unsound. It is clear, Cleanthes is claiming, that the voice in the clouds would have to be explained by intelligent design or purpose. But the same kind of objections could be applied to it too—or to the natural book case that appears further on. (Is there any important difference, from the standpoint of Philo's objections, between these cases and the one Cleanthes is mainly concerned with?)

Yet I cannot see but all the same objections (if they merit that appellation) which lie against the system of theism, may also be produced against this inference.

Might you not say, that all conclusions concerning fact were founded on experience: that when we hear an articulate voice in the dark, and thence infer a man, it is only the resemblance of the effects, which leads us to conclude that there is a like resemblance in the cause: but that this extraordinary voice, by its loudness, extent, and flexibility to all languages bears so little analogy to any human voice, that we have no reason to suppose any analogy in their causes: and consequently, that a rational, wise, coherent speech proceeded, you knew not whence, from some accidental whistling of the winds, not from any divine reason or intelligence? You see clearly your own objections in these cavils: and I hope too, you see clearly, that they cannot possibly have more force in the one case than in the other.

But to bring the case still nearer the present one of the universe, I shall make two suppositions, which imply not any absurdity or impossibility. Suppose, that there is a natural, universal, invariable language, common to every individual of human race, and that books are natural productions, which perpetuate themselves in the same manner with animals and vegetables, by descent and propagation. Several expressions of our passions contain a universal language: all brute animals have a natural speech, which, however limited, is very intelligible to their own species. And as there are infinitely fewer parts and less contrivance in the finest composition of eloquence, than in the coarsest organized body, the propagation of an *Iliad* or *Aeneid* is an easier supposition than that of any plant or animal.

Suppose, therefore, that you enter into your library, thus peopled by natural volumes, containing the most refined reason and most exquisite beauty: could you possibly open one of them, and doubt, that its original cause bore the strongest analogy to mind and intelligence? When it reasons and discourses; when it expostulates, argues, and enforces its views and topics; when it applies sometimes to the pure intellect, sometimes to the affections; when it collects, disposes, and adorns every consideration suited to the subject: could you persist in asserting, that all this, at the bottom, had really no meaning, and that the first formation of this volume in the loins of its original parent proceeded not from thought and design? Your obstinacy, I know, reaches not that degree of firmness: even your sceptical play and wantonness would be abashed at so glaring an absurdity.

But if there be any difference, Philo, between this supposed case and the real one of the universe, it is all to the advantage of the latter. The anatomy of an animal affords many stronger instances of design than the perusal of Livy or Tacitus: and any objection which you start in the former case, by carrying me back to so unusual and extraordinary a scene as the first formation of worlds, the same objection has place on the supposition of our vegetating library. Choose, then, your party, Philo, without ambiguity or evasion; assert either that a rational volume is no proof of a rational cause, or admit of a similar cause to all the works of nature. ⑩

> 10 Is Cleanthes right that the anatomy of an animal is more clearly a result of design than would be the natural books? Can you think of an argument for the contrary view?

. . .

It seems strange to me, said Cleanthes, that you, Demea, who are so sincere in the cause of religion, should still maintain the mysterious, incomprehensible nature of the Deity, and should insist so strenuously, that he has no manner of likeness or resemblance to human creatures. The Deity, I can readily allow, possesses many powers and attributes, of which we can have no comprehension: but if our ideas, so far as they go, be not just as adequate, and correspondent to his real nature, I know not what there is in this subject worth insisting on. Is the name, without any meaning, of such mighty importance? Or how do you mystics, who maintain the absolute incomprehensibility of the Deity, differ from skeptics or atheists, who assert, that the first cause of all is unknown and unintelligible? Their temerity must be very great, if, after rejecting the production by a mind; I mean, a mind resembling the human (for I know of no other), they pretend to assign, with certainty, any other specific, intelligible cause: and their conscience must be very scrupulous indeed, if they refuse to call the universal, unknown cause a God or Deity; and to bestow on him as many sublime eulogies and unmeaning epithets, as you shall please to require of them.

[Philo replies:] . . . I shall endeavor to show you, a little more distinctly, the inconveniences of that anthropomorphism which you have embraced; and I shall prove, that there is no ground to suppose a plan of the world to be formed in the divine mind, consisting of distinct ideas, differently arranged; in the same manner as an architect forms in his head the plan of a house which he intends to execute.

It is not easy, I own, to see, what is gained by this supposition, whether we judge of the matter by *reason* or by *experience*. We are still obliged to mount higher, in order to find the cause of this cause, which you had assigned as satisfactory and conclusive.

If *reason* (I mean abstract reason, derived from inquiries a priori) be not alike mute with regard to all questions concerning cause and effect; this sentence at least it will venture to pronounce, that a mental world, or universe of ideas, requires a cause as much, as does a material world, or universe of objects; and if similar in its arrangement must require a similar cause. For what is there in this subject, which should occasion a different conclusion or inference? In an abstract view, they are entirely alike; and no difficulty attends the one supposition, which is not common to both of them.

Again, when we will needs force *experience* to pronounce some sentence, even on these subjects, which lie beyond her sphere; neither can she perceive any material difference in this particular, between these two kinds of worlds, but finds them to be governed by similar principles, and to depend upon an equal variety of causes in their operations. We have specimens in miniature of both of them. Our own mind resembles the one: a vegetable or animal body the other. Let experience, therefore, judge from these samples. Nothing seems more delicate with regard to its causes than thought; and as these causes never operate in two persons after the same manner, so we never find two persons, who think exactly alike. Nor indeed does the same person think exactly alike at any two different periods of time. A difference of age, of the disposition of his body, of weather, of food, of company, of books, of passions; any of these particulars, or others more minute, are sufficient to alter the curious machinery of thought, and communicate to it very different movements and operations. As far as we can judge, vegetables and animal bodies are not more delicate in their motions, nor depend upon a greater variety or more curious adjustment of springs and principles.

How therefore shall we satisfy ourselves concerning the cause of that Being, whom you suppose the Author of Nature, or, according to your system of anthropomorphism, the ideal world, into which you trace the material? Have we not the same reason to trace that ideal world into another ideal world, or new intelligent principle? But if we stop, and go no farther; why go so far? Why not stop at the material world? How can we satisfy ourselves without going on *in infinitum?* And after all, what satisfaction is there in that infinite progression? Let us remember the story of the Indian philosopher and his elephant. It was never more applicable than to the present subject. If the material world rests upon a similar ideal world, this ideal world must rest upon some other; and so on, without end. It were better, therefore, never to look beyond the present material world. By supposing it to contain the principle of its order within itself, we really assert it to be God; and the sooner we arrive at that Divine Being, so much the better. When you go one step beyond the mundane system, you only excite an inquisitive humor, which it is impossible ever to satisfy.⑪

⑪ Philo now takes a different tack, demanding an explanation for the order involved in God's intelligence itself. The underlying point is that not every instance of order can be explained by a further instance of order (since this would lead to an infinite regress). Thus some cases of order must eventually be accepted as intrinsic or natural. Why should this stopping point be reached with God, but not with the material universe?

To say, that the different ideas, which compose the reason of the Supreme Being, fall into order, of themselves, and by their own nature, is really to talk without any precise meaning. If it has a meaning, I would fain know, why it is not as good sense to say, that the parts of the material world fall into order, of themselves, and by their own nature. Can the one opinion be intelligible, while the other is not so?

We have, indeed, experience of ideas, which fall into order, of themselves, and without any *known* cause; but, I am sure, we have a much larger experience of matter, which does the same; as, in all instances of generation and vegetation, where the accurate analysis of the cause exceeds all human comprehension. We have also experience of particular systems of thought and of matter, which have no order; of the first, in madness; of the second, in corruption. Why then should we think, that order is more essential to one than the other? And if it requires a cause in both, what do we gain by your system, in tracing the universe of objects into a similar universe of ideas? The first step, which we make, leads us on forever. It were, therefore, wise in us, to limit all our inquiries to the present world, without looking farther. No satisfaction can ever be attained by these speculations, which so far exceed the narrow bounds of human understanding.

. . . when it is asked, what cause produces order in the ideas of the Supreme Being, can any other reason be assigned to you, Anthropomorphites, than that it is a *rational* faculty, and that such is the nature of the Deity? But why a similar answer will not be equally satisfactory in accounting for the order of the world, without having recourse to any such intelligent creator, as you insist on, may be difficult to determine. It is only to say, that such is the nature of material objects, and that they are all originally possessed of a *faculty* of order and proportion. These are only more learned and elaborate ways of confessing our ignorance; nor has the one hypothesis any real advantage above the other, except in its greater conformity to vulgar prejudices.⑫

⑫ Is there any basis for preferring the hypothesis of intrinsic mental order to that of intrinsic material order? Philo claims that experience does not favor one over the other.

You have displayed this argument with great emphasis, replied Cleanthes: you seem not sensible, how easy it is to answer it. Even in common life, if I assign a cause for any event; is it any objection, Philo, that I cannot assign the cause of that cause, and answer every new question, which may incessantly be started? And what philosophers could possibly submit to so rigid a rule? Philosophers, who confess ultimate causes to be totally unknown, and are sensible, that the most refined principles, into which they trace the phenomena, are still to them as inexplicable as these phenomena themselves are to the vulgar. The order and arrangement of nature, the curious adjustment of final causes, the plain use and intention of every part and organ; all these bespeak in the clearest language an intelligent cause or author. The heavens and the earth join in the same testimony: the whole chorus of

Nature raises one hymn to the praises of its creator: you alone, or almost alone, disturb this general harmony. You start abstruse doubts, cavils, and objections: you ask me, what is the cause of this cause? I know not; I care not; that concerns not me. I have found a Deity; and here I stop my inquiry. Let those go farther, who are wiser or more enterprising.

I pretend to be neither, replied Philo: and for that very reason, I should never perhaps have attempted to go so far; especially when I am sensible, that I must at last be contented to sit down with the same answer, which, without farther trouble, might have satisfied me from the beginning. If I am still to remain in utter ignorance of causes, and can absolutely give an explication of nothing, I shall never esteem it any advantage to shove off for a moment a difficulty, which, you acknowledge, must immediately, in its full force, recur upon me. Naturalists indeed very justly explain particular effects by more general causes, though these general causes themselves should remain in the end totally inexplicable: but they never surely thought it satisfactory to explain a particular effect by a particular cause, which was no more to be accounted for than the effect itself. An ideal system, arranged of itself, without a precedent design, is not a whit more explicable than a material one, which attains its order in a like manner; nor is there any more difficulty in the latter supposition than in the former. [13]

[13] Cleanthes responds that the fact that the search for explanations must stop somewhere is no reason not to accept any particular causal explanation. If the divine explanation of the order of the material universe is compelling in the way that he claims, then it is no objection to it that it raises a further issue of explanation that we may be unable to answer. But this misses Philo's main point, which is that the appeal to intrinsic order works equally well whether you say that God or the material universe has intrinsic order.

. . .

But to show you still more inconveniences, continued Philo, in your anthropomorphism; please to take a new survey of your principles. *Like effects prove like causes.* This is the experimental argument; and this, you say too, is the sole theological argument. Now it is certain, that the liker the effects are, which are seen, and the liker the causes, which are inferred, the stronger is the argument. Every departure on ei-

ther side diminishes the probability, and renders the experiment less conclusive. You cannot doubt of the principle: neither ought you to reject its consequences.

. . .

Now, Cleanthes, said Philo, with an air of alacrity and triumph, mark the consequences. *First,* By this method of reasoning, you renounce all claim to infinity in any of the attributes of the Deity. For as the cause ought only to be proportioned to the effect, and the effect, so far as it falls under our cognizance, is not infinite; what pretensions have we, upon your suppositions, to ascribe that attribute to the Divine Being? You will still insist, that, by removing him so much from all similarity to human creatures, we give in to the most arbitrary hypothesis, and at the same time weaken all proofs of his existence.

Secondly, You have no reason, on your theory, for ascribing perfection to the Deity, even in his finite capacity; or for supposing him free from every error, mistake, or incoherence in his undertakings. There are many inexplicable difficulties in the works of nature, which, if we allow a perfect author to be proved a priori, are easily solved, and become only seeming difficulties, from the narrow capacity of man, who cannot trace infinite relations. But according to your method of reasoning, these difficulties become all real; and perhaps will be insisted on, as new instances of likeness to human art and contrivance. At least, you must acknowledge, that it is impossible for us to tell, from our limited views, whether this system contains any great faults, or deserves any considerable praise, if compared to other possible, and even real systems.

. . .

But were this world ever so perfect a production, it must still remain uncertain, whether all the excellences of the work can justly be ascribed to the workman. If we survey a ship, what an exalted idea must we form of the ingenuity of the carpenter, who framed so complicated, useful, and beautiful a machine? And what surprise must we feel, when we find him a stupid mechanic, who imitated others, and copied an art, which, through a long succession of ages, after multiplied trials, mistakes, corrections, deliberations, and controversies, had been gradually improving? Many worlds might have been botched and bungled, throughout an eternity, ere this system was struck out: much labor lost: many fruitless trials made: and a slow, but continued improvement carried on during infinite ages in the art of world-making. In such subjects, who can determine, where the truth; nay, who can conjecture where the probability lies; amidst a great number of hypotheses which may be proposed, and a still greater number which may be imagined? [14]

> [14] The ever-inventive Philo raises yet another objection: the characteristics ascribed to the designer on the basis of this argument cannot be greater than those required to explain the actual effect. This does not require infinite powers or even relatively perfect finite powers.

And what shadow of an argument, continued Philo, can you produce, from your hypothesis, to prove the unity of the Deity? A great number of men join in building a house or ship, in rearing a city, in framing a commonwealth: why may not several deities combine in contriving and framing a world? This is only so much greater similarity to human affairs? By sharing the work among several, we may so much further limit the attributes of each, and get rid of that extensive power and knowledge, which must be supposed in one deity, and which, according to you, can only serve to weaken the proof of his existence. And if such foolish, such vicious creatures as man can yet often unite in framing and executing one plan; how much more those deities or demons, whom we may suppose several degrees more perfect?

To multiply causes, without necessity, is indeed contrary to true philosophy: but this principle applies not to the present case. Were one deity antecedently proved by your theory, who were possessed of every attribute, requisite to the production of the universe; it would be needless, I own (though not absurd) to suppose any other deity existent. But while it is still a question, whether all these attributes are united in one subject, or dispersed among several independent beings: by what phenomena in nature can we pretend to decide the controversy? Where we see a body raised in a scale, we are sure that there is in the opposite scale, however concealed from sight, some counterpoising weight equal to it: but it is still allowed to doubt, whether that weight be an aggregate of several distinct bodies, or one uniform united mass. And if the weight requisite very much exceeds anything which we have ever seen conjoined in any single body, the former supposition becomes still more probable and natural. An intelligent being of such vast power and capacity, as is necessary to produce the universe, or, to speak in the language of ancient philosophy, so prodigious an animal, exceeds all analogy, and even comprehension.

But farther, Cleanthes; men are mortal, and renew their species by generation; and this is common to all living creatures. The two great sexes of male and female, says Milton, animate the world. Why must this circumstance, so universal, so essential, be excluded from those numerous and limited deities? Behold then the theogony of ancient times brought back upon us.

And why not become a perfect anthropomorphite? Why not assert the deity or deities to be corporeal, and to have eyes, a nose, mouth, ears, etc? Epicurus maintained, that no man had ever seen reason but in a human figure; therefore the gods must have a human figure. And this argument, which is deservedly so much ridiculed by Cicero, becomes, according to you, solid and philosophical. [15]

> [15] Nor does it require one designer. And the analogy between God and human designers suggests other human characteristics as well.

In a word, Cleanthes, a man, who follows your hypothesis, is able, perhaps, to assert, or conjecture, that the universe, sometime, arose from something like design: but beyond that position he cannot ascertain one single circumstance, and is left afterwards to fix every point of his theology, by the utmost license of fancy and hypothesis. This world, for aught he knows, is very faulty and imperfect compared to a superior standard; and was only the first rude essay of some infant deity, who afterwards abandoned it, ashamed of his lame performance; it is the work only of some dependent, inferior deity; and is the object of derision to his superiors: it is the production of old age and dotage in some superannuated deity; and ever since his death, has run on at adventures, from the first impulse and active force, which it received from him. You justly give signs of horror, Demea, at these strange suppositions: but these, and a thousand more of the same kind, are Cleanthes's suppositions, not mine. From the moment the attributes of the Deity are supposed finite, all these have place. And I cannot, for my part, think, that so wild and unsettled a system of theology is, in any respect, preferable to none at all.

These suppositions I absolutely disown, cried Cleanthes: they strike me, however, with no horror; especially, when proposed in that rambling way in which they drop from you. On the contrary, they give me pleasure, when I see, that, by the utmost indulgence of your imagination, you never get rid of the hypothesis of design in the universe; but are obliged, at every turn, to have recourse to it. To this concession I adhere steadily; and this I regard as a sufficient foundation for religion. [16]

16 Cleanthes retreats to the general hypothesis of design, which he claims is common to all of Philo's various suggestions. (But this ignores the earlier point about the possibility that the universe is intrinsically orderly.) In the following paragraph, Demea suggests that this is too weak for any serious religion.

. . .

It must be a slight fabric, indeed, said Demea, which can be erected on so tottering a foundation. While we are uncertain, whether there is one deity or many; whether the deity or deities, to whom we owe our existence, be perfect or imperfect, subordinate or supreme, dead or alive; what trust or confidence can we repose in them? What devotion or worship address to them? What veneration or obedience pay them? To all the purposes of life, the theory of religion becomes altogether useless: and even with regard to speculative consequences, its uncertainty, according to you, must render it totally precarious and unsatisfactory.

To render it still more unsatisfactory, said Philo, there occurs to me another hypothesis, which must acquire an air of probability from the method of reasoning so much insisted on by Cleanthes. That like effects arise from like causes: this principle he supposes the foundation of all religion. But there is another principle of the same kind, no less certain, and derived from the same source of experience: that where several known circumstances are *observed* to be similar, the unknown will also be *found* similar. Thus, if we see the limbs of a human body, we conclude, that it is also attended with a human head, though hid from us. Thus, if we see, through a chink in a wall, a small part of the sun, we conclude that, were the wall removed, we should see the whole body. In short, this method of reasoning is so obvious and familiar, that no scruple can ever be made with regard to its solidity.

Now if we survey the universe, so far as it falls under our knowledge, it bears a great resemblance to an animal or organized body, and seems actuated with a like principle of life and motion. A continual circulation of matter in it produces no disorder: a continual waste in every part is incessantly repaired; the closest sympathy is perceived throughout the entire system: and each part or member, in performing its proper offices, operates both to its own preservation and to that of the whole. The world, therefore, I infer, is an animal, and the Deity is the *soul* of the world, actuating it, and actuated by it.

You have too much learning, Cleanthes, to be at all surprised at this opinion, which, you know, was maintained by almost all the theists of antiquity, and chiefly prevails in their discourses and reasonings. For though sometimes the ancient philosophers reason from final causes, as if they thought the world the workmanship of God; yet it appears rather their favorite notion to consider it as his body, whose organization renders it subservient to him. And it must be confessed, that as the universe resembles more a human body than it does the works of human art and contrivance; if our limited analogy could ever, with any propriety, be extended to the whole of nature, the inference seems juster in favor of the ancient than the modern theory.

There are many other advantages too, in the former theory, which recommend it to the ancient theologians. Nothing more repugnant to all their notions, because nothing more repugnant to common experience than mind without body; a mere spiritual substance, which fell not under their senses nor comprehension, and of which they had not observed one single instance throughout all nature. Mind and body they knew, because they felt both: an order, arrangement, organization, or internal machinery in both they likewise knew, after the same manner; and it could not but seem reasonable to transfer this experience to the universe, and to suppose the divine mind and body to be also coeval, and to have, both of them, order and arrangement naturally inherent in them, and inseparable from them.

Here therefore is a new species of anthropomorphism, Cleanthes, on which you may deliberate; and a theory which seems not liable to any considerable difficulties. You are too much superior surely to systematical prejudices, to find any more difficulty in supposing an animal body to be, originally, of itself, or from unknown causes, possessed of order and organization, than in supposing a similar order to belong to mind. But the vulgar prejudice, that body and mind ought always to accompany each other, ought not, one should think, to be entirely neglected; since it is founded on vulgar experience, the only guide which you profess to follow in all these theological inquiries. And if you

---

17 Philo suggests another hypothesis, supported by the same general appeal to analogy: the universe as the body of an animal, of which God is the soul.

---

assert, that our limited experience is an unequal standard, by which to judge of the unlimited extent of nature; you entirely abandon your own hypothesis, and must thenceforward adopt our mysticism, as you call

it, and admit of the absolute incomprehensibility of the Divine Nature. 17

This theory, I own, replied Cleanthes, has never before occurred to me, though a pretty natural one; and I cannot readily, upon so short an examination and reflection, deliver any opinion with regard to it. You are very scrupulous, indeed, said Philo; were I to examine any system of yours, I should not have acted with half that caution and reserve, in stating objections and difficulties to it. However, if anything occur to you, you will oblige us by proposing it.

Why then, replied Cleanthes, it seems to me that, though the world does, in many circumstances, resemble an animal body; yet is the analogy also defective in many circumstances, the most material: no organs of sense; no seat of thought or reason; no one precise origin of motion and action. In short, it seems to bear a stronger resemblance to a vegetable than to an animal, and your inference would be so far inconclusive in favor of the soul of the world.

But, in the next place, your theory seems to imply the eternity of the world; and that is a principle which, I think, can be refuted by the strongest reasons and probabilities. I shall suggest an argument to this purpose, which, I believe, has not been insisted on by any writer. . . . Lucullus was the first that brought cherry-trees from Asia to Europe; though that tree thrives so well in many European climates, that it grows in the woods without any culture. Is it possible, that, throughout a whole eternity, no European had ever passed into Asia, and thought of transplanting so delicious a fruit into his own country? Or if the tree was

once transplanted and propagated, how could it ever afterwards perish? Empires may rise and fall; liberty and slavery succeed alternately; ignorance and knowledge give place to each other; but the cherry-tree will still remain in the woods of Greece, Spain and Italy, and will never be affected by the revolutions of human society.

It is not two thousand years since vines were transplanted into France; though there is no climate in the world more favorable to them. It is not three centuries since horses, cows, sheep, swine, dogs, corn, were known in America. Is it possible, that, during the revolutions of a whole eternity, there never arose a Columbus, who might open the communication between Europe and that continent? . . . All these seem convincing proofs of the youth, or rather infancy, of the world; as being founded on the operation of principles more constant and steady, than those by which human society is governed and directed. Nothing less than a total convulsion of the elements will ever destroy all the European animals and vegetables, which are now to be found in the Western world.

And what argument have you against such convulsions? replied Philo. Strong and almost incontestable proofs may be traced over the whole earth, that every part of this globe has continued for many ages entirely covered with water. And though order were supposed inseparable from matter, and inherent in it; yet may matter be susceptible of many and great revolutions, through the endless periods of eternal duration. The incessant changes, to which every part of it is subject, seem to intimate some such general transformations; though at the same time, it is observable, that all the changes and corruptions, of which we have ever had experience, are but passages from one state of order to another; nor can matter ever rest in total deformity and confusion. What we see in the parts, we may infer in the whole; at least, that is the method of reasoning on which you rest your whole theory. And were I obliged to defend any particular system of this nature (which I never willingly should do), I esteem none more plausible than that which ascribes an eternal, inherent principle of order to the world; though attended with great and continual revolutions and alterations. This at once solves all difficulties; and if the solution, by being so general, is not entirely complete and satisfactory, it is, at least, a theory, that we must, sooner or later, have recourse to, whatever system we embrace. How could things have been as they are, were there not an original, inherent principle of order somewhere, in thought or in matter? And it is very indifferent to which of these we give the preference. Chance has no place, on any hypothesis, sceptical or religious. Everything is surely governed by steady, inviolable laws. And were the inmost essence of things laid open to us, we should then discover a scene, of which, at present, we can have no idea. Instead of admiring the order of natural beings, we should clearly see that it was absolutely impossible for them, in the smallest article, ever to admit of any other disposition. [18]

[18] After a skirmish over the issue of whether the world is eternal (as the foregoing hypothesis would require), Philo returns to the idea that the order of the material world is intrinsic to it, rather than being produced by an external designer. (This is the main alternative to intelligent design in relation to the global version of the argument—see Flew.)

. . .

But here, continued Philo, in examining the ancient system of the soul of the world, there strikes me, all on a sudden, a new idea, which, if just, must go near to subvert all your reasoning, and destroy even your first inferences, on which you repose such confidence. If the universe bears a greater likeness to animal bodies and to vegetables, than to the works of human art, it is more probable that its cause resembles the cause of the former than that of the latter, and its origin ought rather to be ascribed to generation or vegetation than to reason or design. Your conclusion, even according to your own principles, is therefore lame and defective.

Pray open up this argument a little farther, said Demea. For I do not rightly apprehend it, in that concise manner, in which you have expressed it.

Our friend, Cleanthes, replied Philo, as you have heard, asserts, that since no question of fact can be proved otherwise than by experience, the existence of a Deity admits not of proof from any other medium. The world, says he, resembles the works of human contrivance: therefore its cause must also resemble that of the other. Here we may remark, that the operation of one very small part of nature, to wit man, upon another very small part, to wit that inanimate matter lying within his reach, is the rule, by which Cleanthes

judges of the origin of the whole; and he measures objects, so widely disproportioned, by the same individual standard. But to waive all objections drawn from this topic; I affirm, that there are other parts of the universe (besides the machines of human invention) which bear still a greater resemblance to the fabric of the world, and which therefore afford a better conjecture concerning the universal origin of this system. These parts are animals and vegetables. The world plainly resembles more an animal or a vegetable, than it does a watch or a knitting-loom. Its cause, therefore, it is more probable, resembles the cause of the former. The cause of the former is generation or vegetation. The cause, therefore, of the world, we may infer to be some thing similar or analogous to generation or vegetation. [19]

[19] Inspired by the world-soul hypothesis, Philo proposes yet another one: the world is an animal or a vegetable and is caused in the way that pertains to things of those kinds (without the need for a world-soul).

. . . I understand you, says Demea: but what wild, arbitrary suppositions are these? What *data* have you for such extraordinary conclusions? And is the slight, imaginary resemblance of the world to a vegetable or an animal sufficient to establish the same inference with regard to both? Objects, which are in general so widely different; ought they to be a standard for each other?

Right, cries Philo: this is the topic on which I have all along insisted. I have still asserted, that we have no *data* to establish any system of cosmogony. Our experience, so imperfect in itself, and so limited both in extent and duration, can afford us no probable conjecture concerning the whole of things. But if we must needs fix on some hypothesis; by what rule, pray ought we to determine our choice? Is there any other rule than the greater similarity of the objects compared? And does not a plant or an animal, which springs from vegetation or generation, bear a stronger resemblance to the world, than does any artificial machine, which arises from reason and design?

But what is this vegetation and generation of which you talk? said Demea. Can you explain their operations, and anatomize that fine internal structure, on which they depend?

As much, at least, replied Philo, as Cleanthes can explain the operations of reason, or anatomize that internal structure, on which *it* depends. But without any such elaborate disquisitions, when I see an animal, I infer, that it sprang from generation; and that with as great certainty as you conclude a house to have been reared by design. These words, *generation, reason,* mark only certain powers and energies in nature, whose effects are known, but whose essence is incomprehensible; and one of these principles, more than the other, has no privilege for being made a standard to the whole of nature.

In reality, Demea, it may reasonably be expected, that the larger the views are which we take of things, the better will they conduct us in our conclusions concerning such extraordinary and such magnificent subjects. In this little corner of the world alone, there are four principles, *reason, instinct, generation, vegetation,* which are similar to each other, and are the causes of similar effects. What a number of other principles may we naturally suppose in the immense extent and variety of the universe, could we travel from planet to planet and from system to system, in order to examine each part of this mighty fabric? Any one of these four principles above mentioned (and a hundred others which lie open to our conjecture) may afford us a theory, by which to judge of the origin of the world; and it is a palpable and egregious partiality, to confine our view entirely to that principle, by which our own minds operate. Were this principle more intelligent on that account, such a partiality might be somewhat excusable. But reason, in its internal fabric and structure, is really as little known to us as instinct or vegetation; and perhaps even that vague, undeterminate word, *Nature,* to which the vulgar refer everything, is not at the bottom more inexplicable. The effects of these principles are all known to us from experience: but the principles themselves, and their manner of operation, are totally unknown: nor is it less intelligible, or less conformable to experience to say, that the world arose by vegetation from a seed shed by another world, than to say that it arose from a divine reason or contrivance, according to the sense in which Cleanthes understands it. [20]

[20] Demea objects that there is no real data supporting such an hypothesis, to which Philo responds that there is no data supporting any of the hypotheses in question, including intelligent design.

But methinks, said Demea, if the world had a vegetative quality, and could sow the seeds of new worlds into the infinite chaos, this power would be still an additional argument for design in its author. For whence could arise so wonderful a faculty but from design? Or how can order spring from anything, which perceives not that order which it bestows?

You need only look around you, replied Philo, to satisfy yourself with regard to this question. A tree bestows order and organization on that tree, which springs from it, without knowing the order: an animal, in the same manner, on its offspring: a bird, on its nest: and instances of this kind are even more frequent in the world, than those of order, which arise from reason and contrivance. To say, that all this order in animals and vegetables proceeds ultimately from design, is begging the question; nor can that great point be ascertained otherwise than by proving a priori, both that order is, from its nature, inseparably attached to thought, and that it can never, of itself, or from original unknown principles, belong to matter. [21]

[21] Demea, now alarmed at the way the argument is going, tries to support Cleanthes's hypothesis by arguing from the order that the universe would possess if it were either an animal or a vegetable to the hypothesis of design. But Philo responds that this begs the question by assuming that these sorts of order cannot be intrinsic.

But farther, Demea; this objection, which you urge, can never be made use of by Cleanthes, without renouncing a defense, which he has already made against one of my objections. When I inquired concerning the cause of that supreme reason and intelligence, into which he resolves everything; he told me, that the impossibility of satisfying such inquiries could never be admitted as an objection in any species of philosophy. *We must stop somewhere,* says he; *nor is it ever within the reach of human capacity to explain ultimate causes, or show the last connections of any objects. It is sufficient, if our steps, so far as we go, are supported by experience and observation.* Now, that vegetation and generation, as well as reason, are experienced to be principles of order in nature, is undeniable. If I rest my system of cosmogony on the former, preferably to the latter, 'tis at my choice. The matter seems entirely arbitrary. And when Cleanthes asks me what is the cause of my great vegetative or generative faculty, I am equally entitled to ask him the cause of his great reasoning principle. These questions we have agreed to forebear on both sides; and it is chiefly his interest on the present occasion to stick to this agreement. Judging by our limited and imperfect experience, generation has some privileges above reason: for we see every day the latter arise from the former, never the former from the latter.

Compare, I beseech you, the consequences on both sides. The world, say I, resembles an animal, therefore it is an animal, therefore it arose from generations. The steps, I confess, are wide; yet there is some small appearance of analogy in each step. The world, says Cleanthes, resembles a machine, therefore it is a machine, therefore it arose from design. The steps are here equally wide, and the analogy less striking. And if he pretends to carry on *my* hypothesis a step farther, and to infer design or reason from the great principle of generation, on which I insist; I may, with better authority, use the same freedom to push farther *his* hypothesis, and infer a divine generation or theogony from his principle of reason. I have at least some faint shadow of experience, which is the utmost that can ever be attained in the present subject. Reason, in innumerable instances, is observed to arise from the principle of generation, and never to arise from any other principle. [22]

⸱ ⸱ ⸱

I must confess, Philo, replied Cleanthes, that of all men living, the task which you have undertaken, of raising doubts and objections, suits you best, and seems, in a manner, natural and unavoidable to you. So great is your fertility of invention, that I am not ashamed to acknowledge myself unable, on a sudden, to solve regularly such out-of-the-way difficulties as you incessantly start upon me: though I clearly see, in general, their fallacy and error. And I question not, but you are yourself, at present, in the same case, and have not the solution so ready as the objection; while you must be sensible, that common sense and reason are entirely against you, and that such whimsies as you have delivered, may puzzle, but never can convince us.

⸱ ⸱ ⸱

What you ascribe to the fertility of my invention, replied Philo, is entirely owing to the nature of the subject. In subjects, adapted to the narrow compass of human reason, there is commonly but one determination, which carries probability or conviction with it; and to a man of sound judgment, all other suppositions, but that one, appear entirely absurd and chimerical. But in such questions, as the present, a hundred contradictory views may preserve a kind of imperfect analogy; and invention has here full scope to exert itself. Without any great effort of thought, I believe that I could, in an instant, propose other systems of cosmogony, which would have some faint appearance of truth; though it is a thousand, a million to one, if either yours or any one of mine be the true system.

For instance; what if I should revive the old Epicurean hypothesis? This is commonly, and I believe, justly, esteemed the most absurd system, that has yet been proposed; yet, I know not, whether, with a few alterations, it might not be brought to bear a faint appearance of probability. Instead of supposing matter infinite, as Epicurus did; let us suppose it finite. A finite number of particles is only susceptible of finite transpositions: and it must happen, in an eternal duration, that every possible order or position must be tried an infinite number of times. This world, therefore, with all its events, even the most minute, has before been produced and destroyed, and will again be produced and destroyed, without any bounds and limitations. No one, who has a conception of the powers of infinite, in comparison of finite, will ever scruple this determination. [23]

But this supposes, said Demea, that matter can acquire motion, without any voluntary agent or first mover.

And where is the difficulty, replied Philo, of that supposition? Every event, before experience, is equally difficult and incomprehensible; and every event, after experience, is equally easy and intelligible. Motion, in many instances, from gravity, from elasticity, from electricity, begins in matter, without any known voluntary agent; and to suppose always, in these cases, an unknown voluntary agent, is mere hypothesis; and

[22] Since not all order can be explained (see Annotations 11–13), some order must be intrinsic. Between the two explanations of intelligent creation and generation (or vegetation), Philo argues that it is more plausible to take the order of the latter to be intrinsic (since we have experience of intelligence produced by generation, but not of generation produced by intelligent design).

[23] Here is yet another hypothesis, one considered by Paley: order results from random reshufflings of the basic particles that make up the universe.

hypothesis attended with no advantages. The beginning of motion in matter itself is as conceivable a priori as its communication from mind and intelligence.

Besides; why may not motion have been propagated by impulse through all eternity, and the same stock of it, or nearly the same, be still upheld in the universe? As much as is lost by the composition of motion, as much is gained by its resolution. And whatever the causes are, the fact is certain, that matter is, and always has been in continual agitation, as far as human experience or tradition reaches. There is not probably, at present, in the whole universe, one particle of matter at absolute rest.

And this very consideration too, continued Philo, which we have stumbled on in the course of argument, suggests a new hypothesis of cosmogony, that is not absolutely absurd and improbable. Is there a system, an order, an economy of things, by which matter can preserve that perpetual agitation, which seems essential to it, and yet maintain a constancy in the forms, which it produces? There certainly is such an economy: for this is actually the case with the present world. The continual motion of matter, therefore, in less than infinite transpositions, must produce this economy or order; and by its very nature, that order, when once established, supports itself, for many ages, if not to eternity. But wherever matter is so poised, arranged, and adjusted as to continue in perpetual motion, and yet preserve a constancy in the forms, its situation must, of necessity, have all the same appearance of art and contrivance, which we observe at present. All the parts of each form must have a relation to each other, and to the whole: and the whole itself must have a relation to the other parts of the universe; to the element, in which the form subsists; to the materials, with which it repairs its waste and decay; and to every other form, which is hostile or friendly. A defect in any of these particulars destroys the form; and the matter, of which it is composed, is again set loose, and is thrown into irregular motions and fermentations, till it unite itself to some other regular form. If no such form be prepared to receive it, and if there be a great quantity of this corrupted matter in the universe, the universe itself is entirely disordered; whether it be the feeble embryo of a world in its first beginnings, that is thus destroyed, or the rotten carcass of one, languishing in old age and infirmity. In either case, a chaos ensues; till finite, though innumerable revolutions produce at last some forms, whose parts and organs are so adjusted as to support the forms amidst a continued succession of matter.

Suppose (for we shall endeavor to vary the expression), that matter were thrown into any position, by a blind, unguided force; it is evident that this first position must in all probability be the most confused and most disorderly imaginable, without any resemblance to those works of human contrivance, which, along with a symmetry of parts, discover an adjustment of means to ends and a tendency to self-preservation. If the actuating force cease after this operation, matter must remain forever in disorder, and continue an immense chaos, without any proportion or activity. But suppose, that the actuating force, whatever it be, still continues in matter, this first position will immediately give place to a second, which will likewise in all probability be as disorderly as the first, and so on, through many successions of changes and revolutions. No particular order or position ever continues a moment unaltered. The original force, still remaining in activity, gives a perpetual restlessness to matter. Every possible situation is produced, and instantly destroyed. If a glimpse or dawn of order appears for a moment, it is instantly hurried away, and confounded, by that never-ceasing force, which actuates every part of matter.

Thus the universe goes on for many ages in a continued succession of chaos and disorder. But is it not possible that it may settle at last, so as not to lose its motion and active force (for that we have supposed inherent in it) yet so as to preserve an uniformity of appearance, amidst the continual motion and fluctuation of its parts? This we find to be the case with the universe at present. Every individual is perpetually changing, and every part of every individual, and yet the whole remains, in appearance, the same. May we not hope for such a position, or rather be assured of it, from the eternal revolutions of unguided matter, and may not this account for all the appearing wisdom and contrivance, which is in the universe? Let us contemplate the subject a little, and we shall find, that this adjustment, if attained by matter, of a seeming stability in the forms, with a real and perpetual revolution or motion of parts, affords a plausible, if not a true solution of the difficulty. [24]

It is in vain, therefore, to insist upon the uses of the parts in animals or vegetables and their curious adjustment to each other. I would fain know how an animal could subsist, unless its parts were so adjusted? Do we not find, that it immediately perishes whenever this adjustment ceases, and that its matter corrupting tries some new form. It happens, indeed, that the parts of the world are so well adjusted, that some regular form immediately lays claim to this corrupted matter: and if it were not so, could the world subsist? Must it not dissolve as well as the animal, and pass through new positions and situations; till in a great, but finite succession, it fall at last into the present or some such order?

> [24] Philo proposes an interesting refinement of the previous hypothesis: once orderly forms of matter are produced (by chance), this order tends to perpetuate itself. (Notice that this seems to presuppose an underlying order pertaining at least to the particles themselves.)

It is well, replied Cleanthes, you told us, that this hypothesis was suggested on a sudden, in the course of the argument. Had you had leisure to examine it, you would soon have perceived the insuperable objections, to which it is exposed. No form, you say, can subsist, unless it possess those powers and organs, requisite for its subsistence: some new order or economy must be tried, and so on, without intermission; till at last some order, which can support and maintain itself, is fallen upon. But according to this hypothesis, whence arise the many conveniences and advantages which men and all animals possess? Two eyes, two ears, are not absolutely necessary for the subsistence of the species. Human race might have been propagated and preserved, without horses, dogs, cows, sheep and those innumerable fruits and products which serve to our satisfaction and enjoyment. If no camels had been created for the use of man in the sandy deserts of Africa and Arabia, would the world have been dissolved? If no loadstone had been framed to give that wonderful and useful direction to the needle, would human society and the human kind have been immediately extinguished? Though the maxims of Nature be in general very frugal, yet instances of this kind are far from being rare; and any one of them is a sufficient proof of design, and of a benevolent design, which gave rise to the order and arrangement of the universe. [25]

At least, you may safely infer, said Philo, that the foregoing hypothesis is so far incomplete and imperfect; which I shall not scruple to allow. But can we ever reasonably expect greater success in any attempts of this nature? Or can we ever hope to erect a system of cosmogony, that will be liable to no exceptions, and will contain no circumstance repugnant to our limited and imperfect experience of the analogy of nature? Your theory itself cannot surely pretend to any such advantage; even though you have run into anthropomorphism, the better to preserve a conformity to common experience. Let us once more put it to trial. In all instances which we have ever seen, ideas are copied from real objects, and are ectypal, not archetypal, to express myself in learned terms: you reverse this order, and give thought the precedence. In all instances which we have ever seen, thought has no influence upon matter, except where that matter is so conjoined with it, as to have an equal reciprocal influence upon it. No animal can move immediately anything but the members of its own body; and indeed, the equality of action and reaction seems to be an universal law of nature: but your theory implies a contradiction to this experience. [26] These instances, with many more, which it were easy to collect (particularly the supposition of a mind or system of thought that is eternal, or in other words, an animal ingenerable and immortal), these instances, I say, may teach, all of us, sobriety in condemning each other; and let us see, that as no system of this kind ought ever to be received from a slight analogy, so neither ought any to be rejected on account of a small incongruity. For that is an inconvenience, from which we can justly pronounce no one to be exempted.

All religious systems, it is confessed, are subject to great and insuperable difficulties. Each disputant triumphs in his turn; while he carries on an offensive war,

> [25] Cleanthes objects that this would not account for the "conveniences and advantages" that the world contains. Is this as clear as he claims? (Note that evolution might be invoked here as a further explanation, resting on the underlying order.)

> [26] Philo raises one further objection: within our experience ideas are caused by objects, not the other way around. The only exception is where an idea is "conjoined" with matter: if an idea is conjoined with the body of a person who has the idea and that person then proceeds to build something that conforms to the idea, then the idea can be said to cause the resulting object. But God is not supposed to have a body.

and exposes the absurdities, barbarities, and pernicious tenets of his antagonist. But all of them, on the whole, prepare a complete triumph for the sceptic; who tells them, that no system ought ever to be embraced with regard to such subjects: for this plain reason, that no absurdity ought ever to be assented to with regard to any subject. A total suspense of judgment is here our only reasonable resource. And if every attack, as is commonly observed, and no defense, among theologians, is successful; how complete must be *his* victory, who remains always, with all mankind, on the offensive, and has himself no fixed station or abiding city, which he is ever, on any occasion, obliged to defend?

. . .

Discussion Questions

1. Suppose that Hume is right that not all order can be explained, so that some must be intrinsic. Is there any reason for preferring the view that mind (or at least God's mind) is intrinsically orderly to the view that the material universe is intrinsically orderly?

2. Make a list of the different explanations of the order of the universe that are proposed by Philo, in addition to the one proposed by Cleanthes. Are all these explanations equally plausible (which would mean that none is very plausible), or are some better than others? Why?

3. Philo's claim (that you can postulate the existence of a cause only if you've experienced such a cause) provokes impatience in Cleanthes (p. 73). What exactly is Cleanthes's objection to that claim (in relation to the example of the Copernican System)? What is Philo's response to that objection, and how does Cleanthes reply? Surely Cleanthes is right that judgments of dissimilarity (and similarity) are sometimes "blinded by old systems." And clearly judgments of similarity and dissimilarity are essential to drawing conclusions from "like effects prove like causes." What point is Cleanthes attempting to make with the voice in the clouds and natural books examples? Whose position is stronger on this point: Philo's or Cleanthes's?

Antony Flew

Antony Flew (1923–) is an English philosopher, who taught mainly at the Universities of Keele and Reading. He has written widely on many philosophical topics, but is best known for his work in the philosophy of religion and on Hume. In the following selection, he sets forth a fundamental objection to the global version of the argument from design.

Critique of the Global Argument from Design, from *God: A Critical Inquiry*

3.17 The movement of thought desired is from the universe to something other than the universe, although this other has to be not nothing but a supreme individual. For this the most promising line is that illustrated by the second formulation quoted from Aquinas.* Here the argument proposed would proceed to the Orderer from the order of the universe as a

From Antony Flew, God: A Critical Inquiry *(LaSalle, IL.: Open Court, 1966).*

whole. . . . A contemporary attempting such a line would most likely wish to refer explicitly to science and the uniformity of nature. He might even speak of the latter, possibly dignified with initial capitals, as a presupposition of the former; perhaps going on to assert that God is the ultimate presupposition of both. . . . The philosophical question for us now is simply: Does order in nature itself presuppose an Orderer?①

> ① This is the basic issue pertaining to the global version of the argument from design: does any sort of order presuppose an external designer, with the alternative being, as we have already seen in Hume, that some order might be intrinsic—in this case intrinsic to the material universe?

3.18 Some over-sophisticated people may wish to challenge the premise. . . . [Nothing] is gained by suggesting—with allusions perhaps to human affairs or perhaps to quantum mechanics—that the order is maybe not in fact completely uniform and all-embracing. Those spokesmen for the argument who were also believers in the occurrence of miracles have not usually asserted that it is. Aquinas indeed was remarkably reserved: "things of diverse natures come together under one order, and this . . . always or for the most part". The crux in his view, and in that of the whole Thomist tradition, is not so much the amount of order, nor even that it may appear to be for the best, but that there is order at all. It is order as such which is believed to demonstrate an Orderer.②

> ② If the degree or amount of order mattered, then the proponent of the global argument would be in effect saying that some degree of order might be accepted as intrinsic, while a greater degree could not. But if some order can be intrinsic, what would be the basis for such a limit?

3.19 This is the heart of the matter. It is against this that the attack should and shall be launched. As so often in philosophy, once the protracted preliminary manœuvres have located and isolated the key position, the final operation can be short and its tactics simple. Let us recapitulate the logical situation, for a clear grasp of this is a good guide to the understanding of many similar confrontations between theist and naturalist. It is common ground that there is a deal of regularity in things. It is put by the theist that this presupposes an Orderer; and that this must be, as he requires, other than the universe. The aim of the offensive is to show that order presupposes nothing of the kind, and that it belongs to the universe itself.③ . . .

> ③ That is, is intrinsic to the nature of the universe (or the material of which it is composed).

3.20 The picture given in the last paragraph is in one respect misleading. For it suggests that it is a matter of trying to drive the theist from a position already firmly established. In a psychological sense this may be true. Nevertheless it would be a mistake to infer that in logic the onus of proof rests on the naturalist. Quite the reverse: the presumption, defeasible of course by adverse argument, must be that all qualities observed in things are qualities belonging by natural right to those things themselves; and hence that whatever characteristics we think ourselves able to discern in the universe as a whole are the underivative characteristics of the universe itself.④ . . . The present presumption was ap-

> ④ This amounts to saying that a reason is needed for not taking the observed condition of something to be its natural state—that the burden of proof lies on the view that the observed qualities are not intrinsic.

parently first clearly formulated as such by Strato, next but one in succession to Aristotle as head of the Lyceum. It can be seen as the fulfilment of the naturalistic tendency in the founder's own thinking. It was this "Stratonician atheism" which was received by the young Hume as an emancipating revelation: we shall, in piety, follow Bayle and Hume in using the awkward form *Stratonician* as the adjective.

3.21 How then is this presumption to be defeated? Why should it be thought that order presupposes an Orderer? One bad reply would be to say that the two ideas are necessarily connected. This is no good, first and less significantly, because it is surely just not true that, in the ordinary senses of the words, to say there is order and to deny that it is the work of an Orderer is to contradict yourself. Whereas design does presuppose a designer, order does not similarly, as a matter of logic, require an Orderer: that is why the argument here is *to* design but *from* order. Second, it is no good for the more fundamental reason that, even

---

*The reference is to the fifth of the Five Ways, p. 46.

supposing either that the present usage and senses of *order,* or new ones specially introduced, did warrant the deduction of an Orderer from order, this still could advance us no nearer to the desired conclusion. Suppose you do introduce this new sense. A verbal adjustment cannot transform the physical situation. It can affect only the ways in which it is proper to speak about it. In the former sense of *order* we were agreed that there is order and at issue whether there must also be an Orderer. Now the altogether unchanged situation is represented as one in which we are agreed that, if there is order in the new sense of *order,* then there must also be an Orderer. The issue which divides us is whether, in that new sense, there is actually order. This futile exercise provides a pure textbook example of the hopelessness of trying to establish a substantial conclusion by a manœuvre with a definition. . . . ⑤

⑤ Thus the premise of the argument should be that the universe is orderly in a sense that is simply a matter of observation and which both sides can therefore accept, with the issue between them being whether order in that sense requires a designer. It does no good to take as the premise an assertion of design or of a kind of order that by definition requires a designer, for then this starting point will be acceptable only to someone who already accepts the conclusion, and the argument itself will have no point.

3.22 A better sort of reply is to urge that regularities cannot come about by chance, they require explanation, and the only satisfactory explanation is in terms of purpose and design. This is much more complicated, and to make even the main points takes longer. Thomas' version stresses the claim that the order of the universe is of a sort involving coordination: "When diverse things are coordinated the scheme depends on their directed unification, as the order of battle of a whole army hangs on the plan of the Commander-in-Chief. The arrangement of diverse things cannot be dictated by their own private and divergent natures; of themselves they are diverse and exhibit no tendency to form a pattern. It follows that the order of many among themselves is either a matter of chance or must be attributed to one first planner who has a purpose in mind.

What comes about always, or in the great majority of cases, is not the result of accident."* And there we are.

3.23 This sounds fine. Suppose, for instance, we saw a large number of university teachers working energetically and harmoniously towards a common objective; then it would indeed be reasonable—if we could bring ourselves to believe our eyes—to look for some more than human coordinator, a Vice-Chancellor of genius. The phenomenon would cry out for explanation. For everything, or almost everything, we have seen of university teachers has taught us that we are cantankerous and individualistic creatures: creatures having very much "their own private and divergent natures", diverse, and exhibiting no tendency to form a pattern. Therefore, the Thomist will urge, by parity of reasoning, you must concede that our Argument to Design is sound. . . .

3.24 Well now, is there a parity of reasoning? Are the two cases comparable? Remember what they are. In the familiar and accepted one we have, or could have, independent knowledge of the elements now so unbelievably coordinated.⑥ We could also test an hypothesis about control by a supreme Vice-Chancellor: we conceivably might, and would wish to, meet him on his own apart from the colleagues he guides so superlatively well. Now consider the other case. Here both the key terms refer, or are supposed to refer, to things essentially and multiply unique. The universe is, as an immediate consequence of the definition, unique: for in as much as it includes everything there is there can be no possibility of another; if there were a second there would not be a second but only two parts of the one. God would be both unique by definition and endowed with a series of attributes all of which are also unique by definition. These differences make the decisive gap between the two cases.

⑥ Can we have independent knowledge of the constituents of the universe that parallels the knowledge that Flew supposes us to have about university teachers? How?

3.25 For instance, Thomas states that the elements of the universe which he sees as coordinated are "of themselves . . . diverse and exhibit no ten-

---

*Aquinas, *Summa contra Gentiles,* I 42.

dency to form a pattern". How is he, or anyone else, supposed to know this? That they are diverse is obvious to observation. But to know what tendencies they possessed "in themselves", as opposed to knowing what they do and will do under various universal conditions, you would presumably have to be able to study them: either separated from the universe, which is manifestly senseless; and/or without any Divine control, which is a notion which the theist himself would want to rule out.⑦ Look at the same fundamental Stratonician point in another way. All our knowledge of things, of their natures and tendencies, has to be founded upon and checked against the ways those things in fact behave, under whatever conditions they can be available for our study. Yet, if that is so, is it not topsy-turvy to insist that those things cannot naturally do what is, in our experience, precisely what they do do? Ideas about the natures of things, unless they are to be grounded merely upon our definitions of words, can be justified only by reference to what we are able to discover about how those things actually do behave.

⑦ There is, in principle, no way to know *by observation* that the constituents of the universe would behave by themselves in disorderly ways.

3.26 Once this is granted it surely follows that it will be quite unwarranted to proceed, from the perverse premise that what seems to happen naturally nevertheless cannot, on to the gratuitous conclusion that these effects could only occur through—and therefore demonstrate—the agency of something wholly other. The nerve of this argument is both extraordinary and commonplace. It is extraordinary in that it starts by asserting, as if this were obvious, that things or the sum of things cannot be expressing their own inherent tendencies; notwithstanding that they actually are, to all appearances, doing exactly what comes naturally.⑧ A supposed explanation is then introduced for this factitious phenomenon; in terms of something which is, in a sense at once both unusually literal and yet not literal at all,

⑧ Thus the only observation we have of these constituents supports the idea of intrinsic order (given the Stratonician presumption). Is there any other way of defending the contrary view, one that does not appeal to observation?

out of this world. The form of argument is commonplace in that it crops up continually in and around natural theology. It is, for example, frequently maintained that living organisms could not have developed naturally out of matter itself lifeless; or that consciousness and intelligence cannot be the attributes of purely material things; and so on. Yet, in fact, however great the present mystery of the mechanisms involved, all the evidence we have indicates that the only life we know did originate in just this way. It is the same again with intelligence, consciousness, and the like. So far from there being a certainty that these cannot appertain to material things, the question is whether they could significantly be attributed to anything else.

. . .

3.28 "Come come now", someone will say, "surely it is not being seriously and honestly contended that it is to mere chance that we owe the majestic processions of the stars, the fabulous integrative complexity of the human eye?" No. No; of course explanations must be sought. Is not this the quest advanced by the genius of Newton and Darwin; and, in our own time, by all those who made and exploit the great breakthrough into molecular biology? Or are explanations of this sort . . . somehow not what is wanted? Again, no. What is wanted is some sort of explanation of the orderliness, however much or little there be, of the universe as a whole.⑨ However fundamental and inclusive the laws discovered by the physics of the future, the

⑨ Thus smaller-scale explanations (such as evolution) cannot answer the global question.

claim is that the universe itself could not come about by chance; hence—taking at least two steps in one— there must be Design.

3.29 Once more it is the necessary uniqueness of the universe which makes the crux; even before the questions begin to arise from the uniquenesses of the postulated Designer. In this most peculiar context the basis for the usual contrasts between chance and its opposites disappears, and the familiar questions lose their familiar force and application. It is put that it must be immeasurably improbable that there could be so much order without Design. A hearer who failed to catch the sound of the capital

'D' might fairly and truly reply: "Well, fancy that! And yet, of course, we know that nearly all order *is* without design." But we, alerted to the context by that capital, ask: "How does he know what is probable or improbable about universes?" For his question, like the earlier overweening assertion about the tendencies which things possess or lack "of themselves" (3.22), presupposes that he knows something which not merely does he not know, but which neither he nor anyone else conceivably ever could know. No one could acquire an experience of universes to give him the necessary basis for this sort of judgement of probability or improbability; for the decisive reason that there could not be universes to have experience of.[10] Indeed the whole idea of contrasting, on the one hand, chance as randomness with, on the other hand, what seems to demand explanation breaks down in this limiting case. Yet if this fundamental antithesis ceases to apply, how much more inapplicable the relatively sophisticated antithesis between chance as the absence of purpose, and what calls for that rather special sort of explanation which involves planners and plans. It is, therefore, not a matter here of having to choose between the prongs of either fork. Instead the difficulty is to appreciate that and why neither choice can arise. "Universes", as C. S. Peirce remarked, "are not as plentiful as blackberries."

3.30 So we conclude that order in the universe by itself provides no warrant whatsoever for trying to identify an Orderer. Unless and until some strong reason is found elsewhere, and unless the required separate indentification can be achieved, the presumption of the Stratonician atheism stands undefeated. . . .

---

[10] Again, the immediate point is that he could not acquire such knowledge through observation or experience. Is there any other possibility available?

Discussion Questions

1. Is Flew right about the "Stratonician presumption"? Could someone ever be justified, in the absence of further information, in assuming that the way in which things were observed to behave was *not* the natural mode of behavior that reflected their intrinsic character?
2. Think of all the different sorts of order to be found in the universe. Some of them can be explained by appeal to others, in the way that the theory of evolution explains the order of organic structures like the eye or the geological theory of plate tectonics explains things like the occurrence and behavior of volcanoes. Others, if the Stratonician presumption is correct, should be regarded as intrinsic to the basic material constituents of the universe. Can all of the order plausibly be accounted for in one of these two ways?

The Ontological Argument

René Descartes

René Descartes (1596–1650), a French philosopher and mathematician, was one of the most important and influential philosophers of all time. In the following selection from his *Meditations* (much of the rest of which is included in Chapter 2), Descartes presents a version of the ontological argument. The basic idea is that God is, by definition, a being who has all perfections; and since the property of existence is such a perfection, it follows that God must have this property too, and thus must exist.

The Ontological Argument

What I believe must be considered above all . . . is the fact that I find within me countless ideas of certain things, that, even if perhaps they do not exist anywhere outside me, still cannot be said to be nothing. And although, in a sense, I think them at will, nevertheless they are not something I have fabricated; rather they have their own true and immutable natures. For example, when I imagine a triangle, even if perhaps no such figure exists outside my thought anywhere in the world and never has, the triangle still has a certain determinate nature, essence, or form which is unchangeable and eternal, which I did not fabricate, and which does not depend on my mind. This is evident from the fact that various properties can be demonstrated regarding this triangle: namely, that its three angles are equal to two right angles, that its longest side is opposite its largest angle, and so on. These are properties I now clearly acknowledge, whether I want to or not, even if I previously had given them no thought whatever when I imagined the triangle. For this reason, then, they were not fabricated by me.①

> ① Descartes's claim is that merely by thinking of the concept (or **idea**) of a triangle, we can see that certain properties are necessarily true of such a figure, because they are included in its "nature, essence, or form:" such things as having angles equal to two right angles (180 degrees) or having its largest side opposite its largest angle.

It is irrelevant for me to say that perhaps the idea of a triangle came to me from external things through the sense organs because of course I have on occasion seen triangle-shaped bodies. For I can think of countless other figures, concerning which there can be no suspicion of their ever having entered me through the senses, and yet I can demonstrate various properties of these figures, no less than I can those of the triangle. All these properties are patently true because I know them clearly, and thus they are something and not merely nothing. For it is obvious that whatever is true is something, and I have already demonstrated at some length that all that I know clearly is true. And even if I had not demonstrated this, certainly the nature of my mind is such that nevertheless I cannot refrain from assenting to these things, at least while I perceive them clearly. And I recall that even before now, when I used to keep my attention glued to the objects of the senses, I always took the truths I clearly recognized regarding figures, numbers, or other things pertaining to arithmetic, geometry or, in general, to pure and abstract mathematics to be the most certain of all.

But if, from the mere fact that I can bring forth from my thought the idea of something, it follows that all that I clearly and distinctly perceive to belong to that thing really does belong to it, then cannot this too be a basis for an argument proving the existence of God? Clearly the idea of God, that is, the idea of a supremely perfect being, is one I discover to be no less within me than the idea of any figure or number.② And that it belongs to God's nature that he always exists is something I understand no less clearly and distinctly than is the case when I demonstrate in regard to some figure or number that something also belongs to the nature of that figure or number.③ Thus, even if not everything that I have meditated upon during these last few days were true, still the existence of God ought to have for me at least the same degree of certainty that truths of mathematics had until now.

> ② Is it as clear as Descartes thinks that the idea of God (or a supremely perfect being) is present in his mind (or our minds) in the same simple and unproblematic way as the ideas of figures (like a triangle) or numbers are? Part of the issue is whether the idea of God is as clear and well-defined as these other ideas. (See Discussion Question 1.)

> ③ Descartes claims (without yet explaining why) that existence, indeed eternal existence, is part of the nature of God in the same way that having angles equal to two right angles is part of the nature of a triangle.

However, this point is not wholly obvious at first glance, but has a certain look of a sophism about it. Since in all other matters I have become accustomed to

From Meditations on First Philosophy, *3rd ed., translated by Donald A. Cress (Indianapolis: Hackett Publishing Company, 1993).*

distinguishing existence from essence, I easily convince myself that it can even be separated from God's essence, and hence that God can be thought of as not existing. But nevertheless, it is obvious to anyone who pays close attention that existence can no more be separated from God's essence than its having three angles equal to two right angles can be separated from the essence of a triangle, or than that the idea of a valley can be separated from the idea of a mountain. Thus it is no less contradictory to think of God (that is, a supremely perfect being) lacking existence (that is, lacking some perfection) than it is to think of a mountain without a valley.④

---

④ Thus, Descartes suggests (though still without explaining fully), it is **contradictory** to deny the existence of God in exactly the same way that it would be contradictory to say that something is a triangle but does not have one of the essential properties of a triangle.

But granted I can no more think of God as not existing than I can think of a mountain without a valley, nevertheless it surely does not follow from the fact that I think of a mountain without a valley that a mountain exists in the world. Likewise, from the fact that I think of God as existing, it does not seem to follow that God exists, for my thought imposes no necessity on things. And just as one may imagine a winged horse, without there being a horse that has wings, in the same way perhaps I can attach existence to God, even though no God exists.⑤

---

⑤ Descartes considers an objection that is essentially the same as one that will be raised in the following selection from Kant: Even if existence is part of the nature or essence of God, it does not follow that there actually is such a being that has this property (any more than the fact that being next to a valley is essential to the nature of a mountain, it follows that either mountains or valleys actually exist).

But there is a sophism lurking here. From the fact that I am unable to think of a mountain without a valley, it does not follow that a mountain or a valley exists anywhere, but only that, whether they exist or not, a mountain and a valley are inseparable from one another. But from the fact that I cannot think of God except as existing, it follows that existence is inseparable from God, and that for this reason he really exists. Not that my thought brings this about or imposes any necessity on anything; but rather the necessity of the thing itself, namely of the existence of God, forces me to think this. For I am not free to think of God without existence, that is, a supremely perfect being without a supreme perfection, as I am to imagine a horse with or without wings.⑥

Further, it should not be said here that even though I surely need to assent to the existence of God once I have asserted that God has all perfections and that existence is one of these perfections, nevertheless that earlier assertion need not have been made. Likewise, I need not believe that all four-sided figures can be inscribed in a circle; but given that I posit this, it would then be necessary for me to admit that a rhombus can be inscribed in a circle. Yet this is obviously false. For although it is not necessary that I should ever happen upon any thought of God, nevertheless whenever I am of a mind to think of a being that is first and supreme, and bring forth the idea of God as it were from the storehouse of my mind, I must of necessity ascribe all perfections to him, even if I do not at that time enumerate them all or take notice of each one individually. This necessity plainly suffices so that afterwards, when I realize that existence is a perfection, I rightly conclude that a first and supreme being exists.⑦ In the same way, there is no necessity for me ever to imagine a triangle, but whenever I do wish to consider a rectilinear figure having but three angles, I must ascribe to it those properties on the basis of which one rightly infers that the three angles of this figure are no greater than two right angles, even though I do not take note of this at the time. But when I inquire as to the figures that may be inscribed in a circle, there is absolutely no need whatever for my thinking that all four-sided figures are of this sort; for that matter, I cannot even fabricate such a thing, so long as I am of a mind to admit only what I clearly and distinctly under-

---

⑥ But this objection, he claims, is mistaken. If a mountain is inseparable from a valley, it does not follow that either exists (but only that if one does, then the other must). But if existence is inseparable from God, then one cannot think of God without existence, from which it follows that God must exist. (This is so because it is existence, not something else, that is the essential property in question.)

---

⑦ Here (finally!) Descartes explains why existence is included in the nature or essence of God: God, by definition, has all perfections (all good qualities), and existence is one of these perfections.

---

stand. Consequently, there is a great difference between false assumptions of this sort and the true ideas that are inborn in me, the first and chief of which is the idea of God. For there are a great many ways in which I understand that this idea is not an invention that is dependent upon my thought, but is an image of a true and immutable nature. First, I cannot think of anything aside from God alone to whose essence existence belongs. Next, I cannot understand how there could be two or more Gods of this kind. Again, once I have asserted that one God now exists, I plainly see that it is necessary that he has existed from eternity and will endure for eternity. Finally, I perceive many other features in God, none of which I can remove or change.

But, whatever type of argument I use, it always comes down to the fact that the only things that fully convince me are those that I clearly and distinctly perceive. And although some of these things I thus perceive are obvious to everyone, while others are discovered only by those who look more closely and inquire carefully, nevertheless, once they have been discovered, they are considered no less certain than the others. For example, in the case of a right triangle, although it is not so readily apparent that the square of the hypotenuse is equal to the sum of the squares of the other two sides as it is that the hypotenuse is opposite the largest angle, nevertheless, once the former has been ascertained, it is no less believed. However, as far as God is concerned, if I were not overwhelmed by prejudices and if the images of sensible things were not besieging my thought from all directions, I would certainly acknowledge nothing sooner or more easily than him. For what, in and of itself, is more manifest than that a supreme being exists, that is, that God, to whose essence alone existence belongs, exists?

Discussion Questions

1. How clear is the concept of God, especially the version that Descartes focuses on: a being with all perfections? Is it clear enough to make possible confident *and justified* claims about what it does or does not include?

2. Is existence, as Descartes claims, a *perfection:* a good quality that a perfect being would have to have? It seems reasonable to assume that having a perfection always makes something better than it would be without it, but is this true of existence? Can you think of examples of things whose existence does not make them better?

3. Suppose that I would like to have a new car, indeed a *perfect* new car. I form a conception of such an entity, including all of the good features that a car might have. Is existence one of these? If it is, does it follow that my perfect new car actually exists, (and if so, where is it?)? Does this example show that something is wrong with Descartes's reasoning? Why or why not?

Immanuel Kant

The German philosopher Immanuel Kant (1724–1804) was among the most important and influential philosophers of all time, making major contributions to epistemology, metaphysics, ethics, aesthetics, and the philosophy of religion. In the following selection from his most important work, *The Critique of Pure Reason,* Kant offers two objections to the ontological argument. (It is clear that he has Descartes's version explicitly in mind.) The first of these is the one briefly considered by Descartes himself: that even if the property of existence is included in the concept of God, it still does not follow that God exists, since one can still reject the application of this concept to anything and existence along with it.

The second, more famous, objection is that "existence is not a predicate," that is, not the sort of property that can be included in the essential nature or definition of a thing—in which case, the concept of God, as Descartes understands it, is not a legitimate concept.

The Impossibility of an Ontological
Proof of the Existence of God

In all ages men have spoken of an *absolutely necessary* being, and in so doing have endeavoured, not so much to understand whether and how a thing of this kind allows even of being thought, but rather to prove its existence. There is, of course, no difficulty in giving a verbal definition of the concept, namely, that it is something the non-existence of which is impossible. But this yields no insight into the conditions which make it necessary to regard the non-existence of a thing as absolutely unthinkable.① It is precisely these conditions that we desire to know, in order that we may determine whether or not, in resorting to this concept, we are thinking anything at all. . . .

> ① Merely defining God as a necessary being accomplishes nothing without some account of how and why such a being is supposed to be necessary (that is, to exist necessarily).

. . . this concept, at first ventured upon blindly, and now become so completely familiar, has been supposed to have its meaning exhibited in a number of examples; and on this account all further enquiry into its intelligibility has seemed to be quite needless. Thus the fact that every geometrical proposition, as, for instance, that a triangle has three angles, is absolutely necessary, has been taken as justifying us in speaking of an object which lies entirely outside the sphere of our understanding as if we understood perfectly what it is that we intend to convey by the concept of that object.②

> ② As we saw in the previous selection, Descartes tries to explain how the existence of God can be both necessary and knowable a priori by analogy with claims about the essential properties of figures like triangles.

All the alleged examples are, without exception, taken from *judgments,* not from *things* and their existence. But the unconditioned necessity of judgments is not the same as an absolute necessity of things. The absolute necessity of the judgments is only a conditioned necessity of the thing, or of the predicate in the judgment. The above proposition does not declare that three angles are absolutely necessary, but that, under the condition that there is a triangle (that is, that a triangle is given), three angles will necessarily be found in it.③ So great, indeed, is the deluding influence exercised by this logical necessity that, by the simple device of forming an a priori concept of a thing in such a manner as to include existence within the scope of its meaning, we have supposed ourselves to have justified the conclusion that because existence necessarily belongs to the object of this concept—always under the condition that we posit the thing as given (as existing)—we are also of necessity, in accordance with the law of identity, required to posit the existence of its object, and that this being is therefore itself absolutely necessary—and this, to repeat, for the reason that the existence of this being has already been thought in a concept which is assumed arbitrarily and on condition that we posit its object.④

> ③ Kant argues that the necessary truth of judgments like *all triangles have three angles* (or Descartes's example *all triangles have angles equal to two right angles*) cannot be used to explain how necessary existence is possible. His point is that in the case of a judgment, the necessity is always in effect hypothetical: if we posit that there is a triangle, then that entity necessarily has three angles.

> ④ Similarly, granting for the moment Descartes's account of the concept of God, if we posit that something is a being with all perfections, then that being also necessarily exists.

If, in an identical proposition, I reject the predicate while retaining the subject, contradiction results; and I therefore say that the former belongs necessarily to the latter. But if we reject subject and predicate alike, there is no contradiction; for nothing

From The Critique of Pure Reason, *translated by Norman Kemp Smith (London: Macmillan, 1950).*

is then left that can be contradicted. To posit a triangle, and yet to reject its three angles, is self-contradictory; but there is no contradiction in rejecting the triangle together with its three angles. The same holds true of the concept of an absolutely necessary being. If its existence is rejected, we reject the thing itself with all its predicates; and no question of contradiction can then arise. There is nothing outside it that would then be contradicted, since the necessity of the thing is not supposed to be derived from anything external; nor is there anything internal that would be contradicted, since in rejecting the thing itself we have at the same time rejected all its internal properties.⑤ 'God is omnipotent' is a necessary judgment. The omnipotence cannot be rejected if we posit a Deity, that is, an infinite being; for the two concepts are identical. But if we say, 'There is no God',

⑤ But just as if we reject a triangle (that is, deny that there is any such thing), we can also consistently reject the existence of anything with three sides; so also if we reject a being with all perfections, we can also consistently reject the existence of such a being. All that follows from Descartes's conception of God, Kant is saying, is that if there were such a being, then it would necessarily exist—but not that there actually is one.

neither the omnipotence nor any other of its predicates is given; they are one and all rejected together with the subject, and there is therefore not the least contradiction in such a judgment.

We have thus seen that if the predicate of a judgment is rejected together with the subject, no internal contradiction can result, and that this holds no matter what the predicate may be. The only way of evading this conclusion is to argue that there are subjects which cannot be removed, and must always remain. That, however, would only be another way of saying that there are absolutely necessary subjects; and that is the very assumption which I have called in question, and the possibility of which the above argument professes to establish.⑥ For I cannot form the least concept of a thing which, should it be rejected with all its predicates, leaves behind a contradiction; and in the absence of contradiction I have, through pure a priori concepts alone, no criterion of impossibility.

⑥ And to assume that God's existence cannot be rejected in this way is to assume that such a being necessarily exists—thus **begging the question.**

. . .

I should have hoped to put an end to these idle and fruitless disputations in a direct manner, by an accurate determination of the concept of existence, had I not found that the illusion which is caused by the confusion of a logical with a real predicate (that is, with a predicate which determines a thing) is almost beyond correction. Anything we please can be made to serve as a logical predicate; the subject can even be predicated of itself; for logic abstracts from all content. But a *determining* predicate is a predicate which is added to the concept of the subject and enlarges it. Consequently, it must not be already contained in the concept.

'Being' is obviously not a real predicate; that is, it is not a concept of something which could be added to the concept of a thing.⑦ It is merely the positing of a thing, or of certain determinations, as existing in themselves. Logically, it is merely the copula of a judgment. The proposition, 'God is omnipotent', contains two concepts, each of which has its object— God and omnipotence. The small word 'is' adds no new predicate, but only serves to posit the predicate *in its relation* to the subject. If, now, we take the subject (God) with all its predicates (among which is omnipotence), and say 'God is', or 'There is a God', we attach no new predicate to the concept of God, but only posit the subject in itself with all its predicates, and indeed posit it as being an *object* that stands in relation to my *concept*. The content of both must be one and the same; nothing can have been added to the concept, which expresses merely what is possible, by my thinking its object (through the expression 'it is') as given absolutely.⑧

⑦ Kant now raises a second, deeper (but also perhaps less clearly correct) objection: while existence is obviously a *logical predicate* (that is, something that can appear as the predicate of a judgment, as when we judge that something exists), it is not a *real predicate* (that is, a property that can be part of the concept of a thing of a certain sort). If this is right, then Descartes's account of the concept of God as including existence must be mistaken.

⑧ Kant argues for the claim that existence is not a real predicate by pointing out that in ordinary cases, saying that something exists (or just that it is) does not further describe it, but only says that something satisfies the concept already understood.

Otherwise stated, the real contains no more than the merely possible. A hundred real thalers do not contain the least coin more than a hundred possible thalers. For as the latter signify the concept, and the former the object and the positing of the object, should the former contain more than the latter, my concept would not, in that case, express the whole object, and would not therefore be an adequate concept of it. My financial position is, however, affected very differently by a hundred real thalers than it is by the mere concept of them (that is, of their possibility). For the object, as it actually exists, is not analytically contained in my concept, but is added to my concept (which is a determination of my state) synthetically; and yet the conceived hundred thalers are not themselves in the least increased through thus acquiring existence outside my concept.⑨

⑨ Similarly, while there is an important difference between a hundred thalers (a unit of money, from which the word "dollar" is derived) that are merely possible or conceived and a hundred thalers that really exist, this difference is not in the concept of a hundred thalers that is involved in each case (which is exactly the same).

By whatever and by however many predicates we may think a thing—even if we completely determine it—we do not make the least addition to the thing when we further declare that this thing *is*. Otherwise, it would not be exactly the same thing that exists, but something more than we had thought in the concept; and we could not, therefore, say that the exact object of my concept exists. . . . When, therefore, I think a being as the supreme reality, . . . the question still remains whether it exists or not. . . .

Whatever, therefore, and however much, our concept of an object may contain, we must go outside it, if we are to ascribe existence to the object. In the case of objects of the senses, this takes place through their connection with some one of our perceptions, in accordance with empirical laws. But in dealing with objects of pure thought, we have no means whatsoever of knowing their existence, since it would have to be known in a *completely a priori manner*. Our consciousness of all existence (whether immediately through perception, or mediately through inferences which connect something with perception) belongs exclusively to the unity of experience; any [alleged] existence outside this field, while not indeed such as we can declare to be absolutely impossible, is of the nature of an assumption which we can never be in a position to justify.⑩ . . .

⑩ Kant's more general view, elaborated in the work from which this selection comes, is that the existence of anything can never be determined on an a priori basis, but must instead involve some appeal, directly or indirectly, to sense experience. Things may possibly exist that we cannot experience, but we can never have any knowledge of them.

The attempt to establish the existence of a supreme being by means of the famous ontological argument of Descartes is therefore merely so much labour and effort lost; we can no more extend our stock of [theoretical] insight by mere ideas, than a merchant can better his position by adding a few noughts to his cash account.

Discussion Questions

1. Look again at Descartes's anticipatory reply to Kant's first objection (see Annotation 5 to the previous selection and the corresponding text). Who is right here? If existence really is part of the concept of God, why isn't it contradictory to deny that God exists? Does this show (as Descartes thinks) that God must exist, or does it perhaps only show that we cannot correctly use the concept of God (or the term "God") to refer to something that does not exist?—though we could still apparently say that there is no real thing that has all of the properties standardly ascribed to God.

2. Is Kant right that "existence is not a real predicate"—that is, not the sort of property that can legitimately be contained in a concept? His examples show that existence is not part of the ordinary concepts that we employ, but do they show that it could never be part of

any concept? The idea of existence isn't somehow empty or meaningless, so why couldn't we define a concept that includes it? Does Kant give any clear argument that this is impossible? If it is possible, what (if anything) follows about the existence of something satisfying such a concept?

AN ARGUMENT AGAINST THE EXISTENCE OF GOD: THE PROBLEM OF EVIL

Fyodor Dostoevsky

Fyodor Dostoevsky (1821–1881) was one of the greatest Russian novelists. His works include *Crime and Punishment, The Brothers Karamozov* (from which the present selection is taken), and many others.

Dostoevsky develops a version of the problem of evil in the form of a conversation between two of the brothers, the skeptical and atheistically inclined Ivan and the saintly and religious Alyosha. Their discussion focuses on a specific case of moral evil: the horrible ways in which children suffer as a result of the cruelty or indifference of their parents and others. The main concern is whether any divine purpose or subsequent state of "harmony" could genuinely justify or atone for these sufferings.

Rebellion, from *The Brothers Karamazov*

"I must make you one confession," Ivan began. "I could never understand how one can love one's neighbors. It's just one's neighbors, to my mind, that one can't love, though one might love those at a distance. I once read somewhere of John the Merciful, a saint, that when a hungry, frozen beggar came to him, he took him into his bed, held him in his arms, and began breathing into his mouth, which was putrid and loathsome from some awful disease. I am convinced that he did that from 'self-laceration,' from the self-laceration of falsity, for the sake of the charity imposed by duty, as a penance laid on him. For any one to love a man, he must be hidden, for as soon as he shows his face, love is gone."

From Fyodor Dostoevsky, The Brothers Karamazov, *translated by C. Garnett (New York: Modern Library, 1950).*

"Father Zossima has talked of that more than once," observed Alyosha, "he, too, said that the face of a man often hinders many people not practiced in love, from loving him. But yet there's a great deal of love in mankind, and almost Christ-like love. I know that myself, Ivan."

"Well, I know nothing of it so far, and can't understand it, and the innumerable mass of mankind are with me there. The question is, whether that's due to men's bad qualities or whether it's inherent in their nature. To my thinking, Christ-like love for men is a miracle impossible on earth. He was God. But we are not gods. Suppose I, for instance, suffer intensely. Another can never know how much I suffer, because he is another and not I. And what's more, a man is rarely ready to admit another's suffering (as though it were a distinction). Why won't he admit it, do you think? Because I smell unpleasant, because I have a stupid face, because I once trod on his foot. Besides there is suffering and suffering; degrading, humiliating suffering such as humbles me—hunger, for instance—my benefactor will perhaps allow me; but when you come to higher suffering—for an idea, for instance—he will very rarely admit that, perhaps because my face strikes him as not at all what he fancies a man should have who suffers for an idea. And so he deprives me instantly of his favor, and not at all from badness of heart. Beggars, especially genteel beggars, ought never to show themselves, but to ask for charity through the newspapers. One can love one's neighbors in the abstract, or even at a distance, but at close quarters it's almost impossible. If it were as on the stage, in the ballet, where if beggars come in they wear silken rags and tattered lace and beg for alms dancing gracefully, then one might like looking at them. But even then we should not love them. But enough of that. I simply wanted to show you my point of view. I meant to speak of the suffering of mankind generally, but we had better confine ourselves to the sufferings of the children. That reduces the scope of my argument to the tenth of what it would be. Still we'd better keep to the children, though it does weaken my case. But, in the first place, children can be loved even at close quarters, even when they are dirty, even when they are ugly (I fancy, though, children never are ugly). The second reason why I won't speak of grown-up people is that, besides being disgusting and unworthy of love, they have a compensation—they've eaten the apple and know good and evil, and they have become 'like god.' They go on eating it still. But the children haven't eaten anything, and are so far innocent. Are you fond of children, Alyosha? I know you are, and you will understand why I prefer to speak of them. If they, too, suffer horribly on earth, they must suffer for their fathers' sins, they must be punished for their fathers, who have eaten the apple; but that reasoning is of the other world and is incomprehensible for the heart of man here on earth. The innocent must not suffer for another's sins, and especially such innocents![1] You may be surprised at me, Alyosha, but I am awfully fond of children, too. And observe, cruel people, the violent, the rapacious,

[1] It is fairly common, in both Christianity and other religions, to justify the sufferings of some people by citing the crimes or mistakes of their parents or ancestors. Ivan's point is that this is morally incomprehensible.

the Karamazovs are sometimes very fond of children. Children while they are quite little—up to seven, for instance—are so remote from grown-up people; they are different creatures, as it were, of a different species. I knew a criminal in prison who had, in the course of his career as a burglar, murdered whole families, including several children. But when he was in prison, he had a strange affection for them. He spent all his time at his window, watching the children playing in the prison yard. He trained one little boy to come up to his window and made great friends with him . . . You don't know why I am telling you all this, Alyosha? My head aches and I am sad."

"You speak with a strange air," observed Alyosha uneasily, "as though you were not quite yourself."

"By the way, a Bulgarian I met lately in Moscow," Ivan went on, seeming not to hear his brother's words, "told me about the crimes committed by Turks and Circassians in all parts of Bulgaria through fear of a general rising of the Slavs. They burn villages, murder, outrage women and children, they nail their prisoners by the ears to the fences, leave them so till morning, and in the morning they hang them—all sorts of things you can't imagine. People talk sometimes of bestial cruelty, but that's a great injustice and insult to the beasts; a beast can never be so cruel as a man, so artistically cruel. The tiger only tears and gnaws, that's all he can do. He would never think of nailing people by the ears, even if he were able to do it. These Turks took a pleasure in torturing children, too; cutting the unborn child from the mother's womb, and tossing babies up in the air and catching them on the points of their bayonets before their mother's eyes. Doing it before the mother's eyes was what gave zest to the amusement. Here is another scene that I thought very interesting. Imagine a trembling mother with her baby in her arms, a circle of invading Turks around her. They've planned a diversion; they pet the baby, laugh to make it laugh. They succeed, the baby laughs. At that moment a Turk points a pistol four inches from the baby's face. The baby laughs with glee, holds out its little hands to the pistol, and he pulls the trigger in the baby's face and blows out its brains. Artistic, wasn't it? By the way, Turks are particularly fond of sweet things, they say."

"Brother, what are you driving at?" asked Alyosha.

"I think if the devil doesn't exist, but man has created him, he has created him in his own image and likeness."

"Just as he did God, then?" observed Alyosha.

"'It's wonderful how you can turn words,' as Polonius says in *Hamlet,*" laughed Ivan. "You turn my words against me. Well, I am glad. Yours must be a fine God, if man created Him in His image and likeness. You asked just now what I was driving at. You see, I am fond of collecting certain facts, and, would you believe, I even copy anecdotes of a certain sort from newspapers and books, and I've already got a fine collection. The Turks, of course, have gone into it, but they are foreigners. I have specimens from home that are even better than the Turks. You know we prefer beating—rods and scourges—that's our national institution. Nailing ears is unthinkable for us, for we are, after all, Europeans. But the rod and scourge we have always with us and they cannot be taken from us. Abroad now they scarcely do any beating. Manners are more humane, or laws have been passed, so that they don't dare to flog men now. But they make up for it in another way just as national as ours. And so national that it would be practically impossible among us, though I believe we are being inoculated with it, since the religious movement began in our aristocracy. I have a charming pamphlet, translated from the French, describing how, quite recently, five years ago, a murderer, Richard, was executed—a young man, I believe, of three and twenty, who repented and was converted to the Christian faith at the very scaffold. This Richard was an illegitimate child who was given as a child of six by his parents to some shepherds on the Swiss mountains. They brought him up to work for them. He grew up like a little wild beast among them. The shepherds taught him nothing, and scarcely fed or clothed him, but sent him out at seven to herd the flock in cold and wet, and no one hesitated or scrupled to treat him so. Quite the contrary, they thought they had every right, for Richard had been given to them as a chattel, and they did not even see the necessity of feeding him. Richard himself describes how in those years, like the Prodigal Son in the Gospel, he longed to eat of the mash given to the pigs, which were fattened for sale. But they wouldn't even give him that, and beat him when he stole from the pigs. And that was how he spent all his childhood and his youth, till he grew up and was strong enough to go

away and be a thief. The savage began to earn his living as a day laborer in Geneva. He drank what he earned, he lived like a brute, and finished by killing and robbing an old man. He was caught, tried, and condemned to death. They are no sentimentalists there. And in prison he was immediately surrounded by pastors, members of Christian brotherhoods, philanthropic ladies, and the like. They taught him to read and write in prison, and expounded the Gospel to him. They exhorted him, worked upon him, drummed at him incessantly, till at last he confessed his crime. He was converted. He wrote to the court himself that he was a monster, but that in the end God had vouchsafed him light and shown grace. All Geneva was in excitement about him—all philanthropic and religious Geneva. All the aristocratic and well-bred society of the town rushed to the prison, kissed Richard and embraced him: 'You are our brother, you have found grace.' And Richard does nothing but weep with emotion, "Yes, I've found grace! All my youth and childhood I was glad to have pigs' food, but now even I have found grace. I am dying in the Lord.' 'Yes, Richard, die in the Lord; you have shed blood and must die. Though it's not your fault that you knew not the Lord, when you coveted the pigs' food and were beaten for stealing it (which was very wrong of you, for stealing is forbidden); but you've shed blood and you must die.' And on the last day, Richard, perfectly limp, did nothing but cry and repeat every minute: 'This is my happiest day. I am going to the Lord.' 'Yes,' cry the pastors and the judges and philanthropic ladies. 'This is the happiest day of your life, for you are going to the Lord!' They all walk or drive to the scaffold in procession behind the prison van. At the scaffold they call to Richard: 'Die, brother, die in the Lord, for even thou hast found grace!' And so, covered with his brothers' kisses, Richard is dragged onto the scaffold, and led to the guillotine. And they chopped off his head in brotherly fashion, because he had found grace. Yes, that's characteristic. That pamphlet is translated into Russian by some Russian philanthropists of aristocratic rank and evangelical aspirations, and has been distributed gratis for the enlightenment of the people. The case of Richard is interesting because it's national. Though to us it's absurd to cut off a man's head, because he has become our brother and has found grace, yet we have our own specialty, which is all but worse. Our historical pastime is the direct satisfaction of inflicting pain. There are lines in Nekrassov describing how a peasant lashes a horse on the eyes, 'on its meek eyes'; everyone must have seen it. It's peculiarly Russian. He describes how a feeble little nag had foundered under too heavy a load and cannot move. The peasant beats it, beats it savagely, beats it at last not knowing what he is doing in the intoxication of cruelty, thrashes it mercilessly over and over again. 'However weak you are, you must pull, if you die for it.' The nag strains, and he begins lashing the poor defenseless creature on its weeping, on its 'meek eyes.' The frantic beast tugs and draws the load, trembling all over, gasping for breath, moving sideways, with a sort of unnatural spasmodic action—it's awful in Nekrassov. But that's only a horse, and God has given horses to be beaten. So the Tatars have taught us, and they left us the knout as a remembrance of it. But men, too, can be beaten. A well-educated, cultured gentleman and his wife beat their own child with a birchrod, a girl of seven. I have an exact account of it. The papa was glad that the birch was covered with twigs. 'It stings more,' said he, and so he began stinging his daughter. I know for a fact there are people who at every blow are worked up to sensuality, to literal sensuality, which increases progressively at every blow they inflict. They beat for a minute, for five minutes, for ten minutes, more often and more savagely. The child screams. At last the child cannot scream, it gasps, 'Daddy! daddy!' By some diabolical unseemly chance the case was brought into court. A counsel was engaged. The Russian people have long called a barrister 'a conscience for hire.' The counsel protests in his client's defense. 'It's such a simple thing,' he says, 'an everyday domestic event. A father corrects his child. To our shame be it said, it is brought into court.' The jury, convinced by him, gives a favorable verdict. The public roars with delight that the torturer is acquitted. Ah, pity I wasn't there! I would have proposed to raise a subscription in his honor! . . . Charming pictures.

"But I've still better things about children. I've collected a great, great deal about Russian children, Alyosha. There was a little girl of five who was hated by her father and mother, 'most worthy and respectable people, of good education and breeding.' You see, I must repeat again, it is a peculiar characteristic of many people, this love of torturing children,

and children only. To all other types of humanity these torturers behave mildly and benevolently like cultivated and humane Europeans; but they are very fond of tormenting children, even fond of children themselves in that sense. It's just their defenselessness that tempts the tormentor, just the angelic confidence of the child who has no refuge and no appeal that sets his vile blood on fire. In every man, of course, a demon lies hidden—the demon of rage, the demon of lustful heat at the screams of the tortured victim, the demon of lawlessness let off the chain, the demon of diseases that follow on vice, gout, kidney disease, and so on.

"This poor child of five was subjected to every possible torture by those cultivated parents. They beat her, thrashed her, kicked her for no reason till her body was one bruise. Then, they went to greater refinements of cruelty—shut her up all night in the cold and frost in a privy, and because she didn't ask to be taken up at night (as though a child of five sleeping its angelic, sound sleep could be trained to wake and ask), they smeared her face and filled her mouth with excrement, and it was her mother, her mother did this. And that mother could sleep, hearing the poor child's groans! Can you understand why a little creature, who can't even understand what's done to her, should beat her little aching heart with her tiny fist in the dark and the cold, and weep her meek unresentful tears to dear, kind God to protect her? Do you understand that, friend and brother, you pious and humble novice? Do you understand why this infamy must be and is permitted? Without it, I am told, man could not have existed on earth, for he could not have known good and evil. Why should he know that diabolical good and evil when it costs so much?[2] Why, the whole world of knowledge is not worth that child's prayer to 'dear, kind God'! I say nothing of the sufferings of grown-up people, they have eaten the apple, damn them, and the devil take them all! But these little ones! I am making you suffer, Alyosha, you are not yourself. I'll leave off it if you like."

> [2] Dostoevsky seems to have in mind the attempted solution to the problem of evil (mentioned by Mackie later in this section) that says that evil is necessary in order for human beings to understand and appreciate good. His response is to question whether the knowledge in question is worth the price.

"Never mind. I want to suffer too," muttered Alyosha.

"One picture, only one more, because it's so curious, so characteristic, and I have only just read it in some collection of Russian antiquities. I've forgotten the name. I must look it up. It was in the darkest days of serfdom at the beginning of the century, and long live the Liberator of the People! There was in those days a general of aristocratic connections, the owner of great estates, one of those men—somewhat exceptional, I believe, even then—who, retiring from the service into a life of leisure, are convinced that they've earned absolute power over the lives of the subjects. There were such men then. So our general, settled on his property of two thousand souls, lives in pomp, and domineers over his poor neighbors as though they were dependents and buffoons. He has kennels of hundreds of hounds and nearly a hundred dog-boys—all mounted, and in uniform. One day a serf boy, a little child of eight, threw a stone in play and hurt the paw of the general's favorite hound. 'Why is my favorite dog lame?' He is told that the boy threw a stone that hurt the dog's paw. 'So you did it.' The general looked the child up and down. 'Take him.' He was taken—taken from his mother and kept shut up all night. Early that morning the general comes out on horseback, with the hounds, his dependents, dog-boys, and huntsmen, all mounted around him in full hunting parade. The servants are summoned for their edification, and in front of them all stands the mother of the child. The child is brought from the lockup. It's a gloomy, cold, foggy autumn day, a capital day for hunting. The general orders the child to be undressed; the child is stripped naked. He shivers, numb with terror, not daring to cry . . . 'Make him run,' commands the general. 'Run! run!' shout the dog-boys. The boy runs . . . 'At him!' yells the general, and he sets the whole pack of hounds on the child. The hounds catch him, and tear him to pieces before his mother's eyes! . . . I believe the general was afterwards declared incapable of administering his estates. Well—what did he deserve? To be shot? To be shot for the satisfaction of our moral feelings? Speak, Alyosha!"

"To be shot," murmured Alyosha, lifting his eyes to Ivan with a pale, twisted smile.

"Bravo!" cried Ivan delighted. "If even you say so . . . You're a pretty monk! So there is a little devil sitting in your heart, Alyosha Karamazov!"

"What I said was absurd, but—"

"That's just the point, that 'but'!" cried Ivan. "Let me tell you, novice, that the absurd is only too necessary on earth. The world stands on absurdities, and perhaps nothing would have come to pass in it without them. We know what we know!"

"What do you know?"

"I understand nothing," Ivan went on, as though in delirium. "I don't want to understand anything now. I want to stick to the fact. I made up my mind long ago not to understand. If I try to understand anything, I shall be false to the fact and I have determined to stick to the fact."

"Why are you trying me?" Alyosha cried, with sudden distress. "Will you say what you mean at last?"

"Of course, I will; that's what I've been leading up to. You are dear to me, I don't want to let you go, and I won't give you up to your Zossima [priest, Father]."

Ivan for a minute was silent, his face became all at once very sad.

"Listen! I took the case of children only to make my case clearer. Of the other tears of humanity with which the earth is soaked from its crust to its center, I will say nothing. I have narrowed my subject on purpose, I am a bug, and I recognize in all humility that I cannot understand why the world is arranged as it is. Men are themselves to blame, I suppose; they were given paradise, they wanted freedom, and stole fire from heaven, though they knew they would become unhappy, so there is no need to pity them. With my pitiful, earthly, Euclidean understanding, all I know is that there is suffering and that there are none guilty; that cause follows effect, simply and directly; that everything flows and finds its level—but that's only Euclidean nonsense, I know that, and I can't consent to live by it! What comfort is to me that there are none guilty and that cause follows effect simply and directly, and that I know it—I must have justice, or I will destroy myself. And not justice in some remote infinite time and space, but here on earth, and that I could see myself. I have believed in it. I want to see it, and if I am dead by then, let me rise again, for if it all happens without me, it will be too unfair. Surely I haven't suffered, simply that I, my crimes and my sufferings, may manure the soil of the future harmony for somebody else. I want to see with my own eyes the hind lie down with the lion and the victim rise up and embrace his murderer. I want to be there when everyone suddenly understands what it has all been for. All the religions of the world are built on this longing, and I am a believer. But there are the children, and what am I to do about them? That's a question I can't answer. For the hundredth time I repeat, there are numbers of questions, but I've only taken the children, because in their case what I mean is so unanswerably clear. Listen! If all must suffer to pay for the eternal harmony, what have children to do with it, tell me, please? It's beyond all comprehension why they should suffer, and why they should pay for the harmony. Why should they, too, furnish material to enrich the soil for the harmony of the future? I understand solidarity in sin among men. I understand solidarity in retribution, too; but there can be no such solidarity with children. And if it is really true that they must share responsibility for all their father's crimes, such a truth is not of this world and is beyond my comprehension. Some jester will say, perhaps, that the child would have grown up and have sinned, but you see he didn't grow up, he was torn to pieces by the dogs, at eight years old. Oh, Alyosha, I am not blaspheming! I understand, of course, what an upheaval of the universe it will be, when everything in heaven and earth blends in one hymn of praise and everything that lives and has lived cries aloud: 'Thou art just, O Lord, for Thy ways are revealed.' When the mother embraces the fiend who threw her child to the dogs, and all three cry aloud with tears, 'Thou are just, O Lord!' then, of course, the crown of knowledge will be reached and all will be made clear. But what pulls me up here is that I can't accept that harmony. And while I am on earth, I make haste to take my own measures. You see, Alyosha, perhaps it really may happen that if I live to that moment, or rise again to see it, I, too, perhaps, may cry aloud with the rest, looking at the mother embracing the child's torturer, 'Thou are just, O Lord!' but I don't want to cry aloud then. While there is still time, I hasten to protect myself and so I renounce the higher harmony altogether.

It's not worth the tears of that one tortured child who beat itself on the breast with its little fist and prayed in its stinking outhouse with an unexpiated tear to 'dear, kind God'! It's not worth it, because those tears are unatoned for. They must be atoned for, or there can be no harmony. But how? How are you going to atone for them?③ Is it possible? By their being avenged? But what do I care for avenging them? What do I care for a hell for oppressors? What good can hell do, since those children have already been tortured? And what becomes of harmony, if there is hell? I want to forgive. I want to embrace. I don't want more suffering. And if the sufferings of children go to swell the sum of sufferings which was necessary to pay for truth, then I protest that the truth is not worth such a price. I don't want the mother to embrace the oppressor who threw her son to the dogs! She dare not forgive him! Let her forgive him for herself, if she will, let her forgive the torturer for the immeasurable suffering of her mother's heart. But the sufferings of her tortured child she has no right to forgive; she dare not forgive the torturer, even if the child were to forgive him! And if that is so, if they dare not forgive, what becomes of harmony? Is there in the whole world a being who would have the right to forgive and could forgive? I don't want harmony. From love for humanity I don't want it. I would rather be left with the unavenged suffering. I would rather remain with my unavenged suffering and unsatisfied indignation, *even if I were wrong*. Besides, too high a price is asked for harmony; it's beyond our means to pay so much to enter on it. And so I hasten to give back my entrance ticket, and if I am an honest man I am bound to give it back as soon as possible. And that I am doing. It's not God that I don't accept, Alyosha, only I most respectfully return Him the ticket."

"That's rebellion," murmured Alyosha, looking down.

"Rebellion? I am sorry you call it that," said Ivan earnestly. "One can hardly live in rebellion, and I want to live. Tell me yourself, I challenge you—answer. Imagine that you are creating a fabric of human des-

③ Ivan's claim is that no subsequent state of "harmony" (or heaven), however great or wonderful, can really atone for the child's suffering in a way that makes it just.

tiny with the object of making men happy in the end, giving them peace and rest at last, but that it was essential and inevitable to torture to death only one tiny creature—that baby beating its breast with its fist, for

instance—and to found that edifice on its unavenged tears, would you consent to be the architect on those conditions? Tell me, and tell the truth."

"No, I wouldn't consent," said Alyosha softly. . . .

Discussion Question

1. Consider the issue posed in the next-to-last paragraph of the selection. What would you do? Does it matter whether or not the baby will share in the eventual happiness? Would the result be different if someone voluntarily agreed to be tortured in order to achieve this purpose?

David Hume

Following the relatively brief discussion of the cosmological argument, Hume's *Dialogues* turns to a development of the problem of evil, with Philo doing most of the work after an initial (and, from his standpoint, misguided) opening provided by Demea. (For information about Hume, together with a description of the characters in the Dialogues, see p. 51; this selection actually comes immediately after that one in the book itself.)

Unlike Dostoevsky, Hume's main concern is with physical evil, with only brief mentions of moral evil. He is also not inclined to insist on the problem of evil as a refutation of the claim that God exists, emphasizing instead the way in which it undercuts the sort of positive argument for God's existence that the argument from design attempts to provide. (Mackie, in the following selection, refers to this as a "rather half-hearted presentation of the problem.")

The Problem of Evil, from *Dialogues Concerning Natural Religion*

It is my opinion, I own, replied Demea, that each man feels, in a manner, the truth of religion within his own breast; and from a consciousness of his imbecility and misery, rather than from any reasoning, is led to seek protection from that Being, on whom he

From David Hume, Dialogues Concerning Natural Religion *(1779).*

and all nature is dependent. So anxious or so tedious are even the best scenes of life, that futurity is still the object of all our hopes and fears. We incessantly look forward, and endeavor, by prayers, adoration, and sacrifice, to appease those unknown powers, whom we find, by experience, so able to afflict and oppress us. Wretched creatures that we are! what resource for us amidst the innumerable ills of life, did not religion suggest some methods of atonement, and appease those terrors, with which we are incessantly agitated and tormented? ①

I am indeed persuaded, said Philo, that the best and indeed the only method of bringing everyone to a due sense of religion, is by just representations of the misery and wickedness of men. And for that purpose a talent of eloquence and strong imagery is more requisite than that of reasoning and argument. For is it necessary to prove, what everyone feels within himself? 'Tis only necessary to make us feel it, if possible, more intimately and sensibly.

> ① Demea opens the door to Philo by suggesting that suffering and misery provide the strongest motive for religion, with the main idea being that the wretchedness of earthly life makes people hope and long for the sort of happy afterlife ("futurity") that religion promises. There is little doubt that this has indeed been one strong motivation behind religious belief—though reflection on the upshot of the following discussion seems to call into question the rationality of any such expectation.

The people, indeed, replied Demea, are sufficiently convinced of this great and melancholy truth. The miseries of life, the unhappiness of men, the general corruptions of our nature, the unsatisfactory enjoyment of pleasures, riches, honors; these phrases have become almost proverbial in all languages. And who can doubt of what all men declare from their own immediate feeling and experience?

In this point, said Philo, the learned are perfectly agreed with the vulgar; and in all letters, sacred and profane, the topic of human misery has been insisted on with the most pathetic eloquence that sorrow and melancholy could inspire. The poets, who speak from sentiment, without a system, and whose testimony has therefore the more authority, abound in images of this nature. From Homer down to Dr. Young, the whole inspired tribe have ever been sensible, that no other representation of things would suit the feeling and observation of each individual.

As to authorities, replied Demea, you need not seek them. Look round this library of Cleanthes. I shall venture to affirm, that, except authors of particular sciences, such as chemistry or botany, who have no occasion to treat of human life, there scarce is one of those innumerable writers, from whom the sense of human misery has not, in some passage or other, extorted a complaint and confession of it. At least,

the chance is entirely on that side; and no one author has ever, so far as I can recollect, been so extravagant as to deny it.

There you must excuse me, said Philo: Leibnitz has denied it; and is perhaps the first, who ventured upon so bold and paradoxical an opinion; at least, the first, who made it essential to his philosophical system. ②

> ② The fact of widespread human suffering and misery would be conceded by almost everyone. But Leibniz (Hume spells the name "Leibnitz") might seem to deny this by claiming that this is the "best of all possible worlds."

And by being the first, replied Demea, might he not have been sensible of his error? For is this a subject, in which philosophers can propose to make discoveries, especially in so late an age? And can any man hope by a simple denial (for the subject scarcely admits of reasoning) to bear down the united testimony of mankind, founded on sense and consciousness?

And why should man, added he, pretend to an exemption from the lot of all other animals? The whole earth, believe me, Philo, is cursed and polluted. A perpetual war is kindled amongst all living creatures. Necessity, hunger, want, stimulate the strong and courageous: fear, anxiety, terror, agitate the weak and infirm. The first entrance into life gives anguish to the new-born infant and to its wretched parent: weakness, impotence, distress, attend each stage of that life: and 'tis at last finished in agony and horror.

Observe too, says Philo, the curious artifices of nature, in order to embitter the life of every living being. The stronger prey upon the weaker, and keep them in perpetual terror and anxiety. The weaker too, in their turn, often prey upon the stronger, and vex and molest them without relaxation. Consider that innumerable race of insects, which either are bred on the body of each animal, or flying about infix their stings in him. These insects have others still less than themselves, which torment them. And thus on each hand, before and behind, above and below, every animal is surrounded with enemies, which incessantly seek his misery and destruction. ③

> ③ Another dimension of the problem of evil, one often regarded as particularly difficult, is the problem of animal suffering—keep this in mind in considering the theodicies (attempted solutions to the problem) discussed by Mackie and Hick in the following selections.

Man alone, said Demea, seems to be, in part, an exception to this rule. For by combination in society, he can easily master lions, tigers, and bears, whose greater strength and agility naturally enable them to prey upon him.

On the contrary, it is here chiefly, cried Philo, that the uniform and equal maxims of nature are most apparent. Man, it is true, can, by combination, surmount all his *real* enemies, and become master of the whole animal creation: but does he not immediately raise up to himself *imaginary* enemies, the demons of his fancy, who haunt him with superstitious terrors, and blast every enjoyment of life? His pleasure, as he imagines, becomes, in their eyes, a crime: his food and repose give them umbrage and offense: his very sleep and dreams furnish new materials to anxious fear: and even death, his refuge from every other ill, presents only the dread of endless and innumerable woes. Nor does the wolf molest more the timid flock, than superstition does the anxious breast of wretched mortals.

Besides, consider, Demea; this very society, by which we surmount those wild beasts, our natural enemies; what new enemies does it not raise to us? What woe and misery does it not occasion? Man is the greatest enemy of man. Oppression, injustice, contempt, contumely, violence, sedition, war, calumny, treachery, fraud; by these they mutually torment each other: and they would soon dissolve that society which they had formed, were it not for the dread of still greater ills, which must attend their separation. ④

④ Here we have examples of moral evil.

But though these external insults, said Demea, from animals, from men, from all the elements, which assault us, form a frightful catalogue of woes, they are nothing in comparison of those, which arise within ourselves, from the distempered condition of our mind and body. How many lie under the lingering torment of diseases? ⑤

⑤ Disease is one part of the problem of natural evil (at least as long as the diseases are not caused by human actions).

. . .

The disorders of the mind, continued Demea, though more secret, are not perhaps less dismal and vexatious. Remorse, shame, anguish, rage, disappointment, anxiety, fear, dejection, despair; who has

ever passed through life without cruel inroads from these tormentors? How many have scarcely ever felt any better sensations? Labor and poverty, so abhorred by everyone, are the certain lot of the far greater number; and those few privileged persons, who enjoy ease and opulence, never reach contentment or true felicity. All the goods of life united would not make a very happy man: but all the ills united would make a wretch indeed; and anyone of them almost (and who can be free from everyone), nay often the absence of one good (and who can possess all), is sufficient to render life ineligible.

. . .

And is it possible, Cleanthes, said Philo, that after all these reflections, and infinitely more, which might be suggested, you can still persevere in your anthropomorphism, and assert the moral attributes of the Deity, his justice, benevolence, mercy, and rectitude, to be of the same nature with these virtues in human creatures? His power we allow infinite: whatever he wills is executed: but neither man nor any other animal is happy: therefore he does not will their happiness. His wisdom is infinite: he is never mistaken in choosing the means to any end: but the course of nature tends not to human or animal felicity: therefore it is not established for that purpose. Through the whole compass of human knowledge, there are no inferences more certain and infallible than these. In what respect, then, do his benevolence and mercy resemble the benevolence and mercy of men? ⑥

⑥ The issue is raised as to whether God's goodness (mercy and benevolence—and also perhaps justice) are the same qualities ascribed as virtues to human beings. But if not, what would be the point or justification of using those terms to describe God?

Epicurus's old questions are yet unanswered.

Is he willing to prevent evil, but not able? then is he impotent. Is he able, but not willing? then is he malevolent. Is he both able and willing? whence then is evil? ⑦

⑦ Here is the nub of the problem, which can be reformulated as an argument for the conclusion that God (understood according to the standard conception) does not exist.

You ascribe, Cleanthes, (and I believe justly) a purpose and intention to nature. But what, I beseech you, is the object of that curious artifice and machinery, which she has displayed in all animals? The preservation alone of individuals and propagation of the species. It seems enough for her purpose, if such a rank be barely upheld in the universe, without any care or concern for the happiness of the members that compose it. No resource for this purpose: no machinery, in order merely to give pleasure or ease: no fund of pure joy and contentment: no indulgence without some want or necessity accompanying it. At least, the few phenomena of this nature are overbalanced by opposite phenomena of still greater importance.

Our sense of music, harmony, and indeed beauty of all kinds, gives satisfaction, without being absolutely necessary to the preservation and propagation of the species. But what racking pains, on the other hand, arise from gouts, gravels, megrims, toothaches, rheumatisms; where the injury to the animal-machinery is either small or incurable? Mirth, laughter, play, frolic, seem gratuitous satisfactions, which have no farther tendency: spleen, melancholy, discontent, superstition, are pains of the same nature. How then does the divine benevolence display itself, in the sense of you anthropomorphites? None but we mystics, as you were pleased to call us, can account for this strange mixture of phenomena, by deriving it from attributes, infinitely perfect, but incomprehensible.⑧

⑧ Philo alludes to Demea's view that God's attributes are incapable of being understood by human beings, in which case it would be impossible to argue that a being with those attributes would prevent evil. (But if we have no understanding at all of the sort of being in question, then the standard conception and indeed the very claim that God exists cease to have any meaningful content.)

And have you at last, said Cleanthes smiling, betrayed your intentions, Philo? Your long agreement with Demea did indeed a little surprise me; but I find you were all the while erecting a concealed battery against me. And I must confess, that you have now fallen upon a subject, worthy of your noble spirit of opposition and controversy. If you can make out the present point, and prove mankind to be unhappy or corrupted, there is an end at once of all religion. For to what purpose establish the natural attributes of the Deity, while the moral are still doubtful and uncertain?

You take umbrage very easily, replied Demea, at opinions the most innocent, and the most generally re-

ceived even amongst the religious and devout themselves: and nothing can be more surprising than to find a topic like this, concerning the wickedness and misery of man, charged with no less than atheism and profaneness. Have not all pious divines and preachers, who have indulged their rhetoric on so fertile a subject: have they not easily, I say, given a solution of any difficulties, which may attend it? This world is but a point in comparison of the universe; this life but a moment in comparison of eternity. The present evil phenomena, therefore, are rectified in other regions, and in some future period of existence. And the eyes of men, being then opened to larger views of things, see the whole connection of general laws;

⑨ This is the sort of solution to the problem that is discussed by Dostoevsky in the previous selection. Could evils of the sorts that Hume is discussing and especially of the sort that Dostoevsky focuses on be genuinely "rectified in other regions"?

and trace, with adoration, the benevolence and rectitude of the Deity, through all the mazes and intricacies of his providence.⑨

No! replied Cleanthes, No! These arbitrary suppositions can never be admitted, contrary to matter of fact, visible and uncontroverted. Whence can any cause be known but from its known effects? Whence can any hypothesis be proved but from the apparent phenomena? To establish one hypothesis upon another, is building entirely in the air; and the utmost we ever attain, by these conjectures and fictions, is to ascertain the bare possibility of our opinion; but never can we, upon such terms, establish its reality.

The only method of supporting divine benevolence (and it is what I willingly embrace) is to deny absolutely the misery and wickedness of man. Your representations are exaggerated: your melancholy views mostly fictitious: your inferences contrary to fact and experience. Health is more common than sickness: pleasure than pain: happiness than misery. And for one vexation, which we meet with, we attain, upon computation, a hundred enjoyments.⑩

Admitting your position, replied Philo, which yet is extremely doubtful, you must, at the same time, allow, that, if pain be less frequent than pleasure, it is infinitely more violent and durable. One hour of it is often able to outweigh a day, a week, a month of our common insipid enjoyments. And how many days, weeks, and months are passed by several in the most acute torments? Pleasure, scarcely in one instance, is ever able to reach ecstasy and rapture: and in no one instance can it continue for any time at its highest pitch and altitude. The spirits evaporate; the nerves relax; the fabric is disordered; and the enjoyment quickly degenerates into fatigue and uneasiness. But pain often, good God, how often! rises to torture and agony; and the longer it continues, it becomes still more genuine agony and torture. Patience is exhausted; courage languishes; melancholy seizes us; and nothing terminates our misery but the removal of its cause, or another event, which is the sole cure of all evil, but which, from our natural folly, we regard with still greater horror and consternation.

> 10 Dostoevsky's response to this suggestion was the denial that such rectification is possible, that any future state of harmony or bliss could genuinely "rectify" suffering like that of the innocent children. Cleanthes makes the different point that if we have only our earthly situation to go on and if it is really as bad as Philo claims, then there is no reason to expect that a state of this very different sort, even if possible, will actually occur. Thus the theist must deny that Philo's description is correct, arguing that the evils have been exaggerated.

But not to insist upon these topics, continued Philo, though most obvious, certain, and important; I must use the freedom to admonish you, Cleanthes, that you have put this controversy upon a most dangerous issue, and are unawares introducing a total scepticism, into the most essential articles of natural and revealed theology. What! no method of fixing a just foundation for religion, unless we allow the happiness of human life, and maintain a continued existence even in this world, with all our present pains, infirmities, vexations, and follies, to be eligible and desirable! But this is contrary to everyone's feeling and experience: it is contrary to an authority so established as nothing can subvert: no decisive proofs can ever be produced against this authority; nor is it possible for you to compute, estimate, and compare all the pains and all the pleasures in the lives of all men and of all animals: and thus by your resting the whole system of religion on a point, which, from its very nature, must forever be uncertain, you tacitly confess, that that system is equally uncertain.

But allowing you, what never will be believed; at least, what you never possibly can prove, that animal, or at least, human happiness, in this life, exceeds its misery; you have yet done nothing: for this is not, by any means, what we expect from infinite power, infinite wisdom, and infinite goodness. Why is there any misery at all in the world? 11 Not by chance surely. From some cause then. Is it from the intention of the Deity? But he is perfectly benevolent. Is it contrary to his intention? But he is almighty. Nothing can shake the solidity of this reasoning, so short, so clear, so decisive; except we assert, that these subjects exceed all human capacity, and that our common measures of truth and falsehood are not applicable to them; a topic, which I have all along insisted on, but which you have, from the beginning, rejected with scorn and indignation. 12

> 11 But Philo responds that this does no good, since infinite power and goodness would eliminate *all* evil.

> 12 Is there any possible way for a theist to respond to this very simple argument, other than by retreating to the claim that human beings cannot ever really understand such issues?

But I will be contented to retire still from this intrenchment: for I deny that you can ever force me in it: I will allow, that pain or misery in man is *compatible* with infinite power and goodness in the Deity, even in your sense of these attributes: what are you advanced by all these concessions? A mere possible compatibility is not sufficient. You must *prove* these pure, unmixed, and uncontrollable attributes from the present mixed and confused phenomena, and from these alone. A hopeful undertaking! Were the phenomena ever so pure and unmixed, yet being finite, they would be insufficient for that purpose. How much more, where they are also so jarring and discordant!

Here, Cleanthes, I find myself at ease in my argument. Here I triumph. Formerly, when we argued concerning the natural attributes of intelligence and design, I needed all my sceptical and metaphysical subtilty to elude your grasp. In many views of the universe, and of its parts, particularly the latter, the beauty and fitness of final causes strikes us with such irresistible force, that all objections appear (what I believe they really are) mere cavils and sophisms; nor can we then imagine how it was ever possible for us to repose any weight on them. But there is no view of human life or of the condition of mankind, from which, without the greatest violence, we can infer the moral attributes, or learn that infinite benevolence, conjoined with infinite power and infinite wisdom, which we must discover by the eyes of faith alone. It is your turn now to tug the laboring oar, and to support your philosophical subtilties against the dictates of plain reason and experience.⑬

⑬ And even if the foregoing point were wrong, even if evil were not simply incompatible with the existence of such a being (which Philo does not actually concede), Cleanthes's attempt to infer (via the argument from design) to a God satisfying the standard conception is, Philo argues, fatally undermined as far as the moral attributes are concerned.

. . .

I scruple not to allow, said Cleanthes, that I have been apt to suspect the frequent repetition of the word, *infinite,* which we meet with in all theological writers, to savor more of panegyric than of philosophy, and that any purposes of reasoning, and even of religion, would be better served, were we to rest contented with more accurate and more moderate expressions. The terms, *admirable, excellent, superlatively great, wise,* and *holy;* these sufficiently fill the imaginations of men; and anything beyond, besides that it leads into absurdities, has no influence on your affections or sentiments. Thus, in the present subject, if we abandon all human analogy, as seems your intention, Demea, I am afraid we abandon all religion, and retain no conception of the great object of our adoration. If we preserve human analogy, we must forever find it impossible to reconcile any mixture of evil in the universe with infinite attributes; much less can we ever prove the latter from the former. But supposing the Author of Nature to be finitely perfect, though far exceeding mankind; a satisfactory account may then be given of natural and moral evil, and every untoward phenomenon be explained and adjusted. A less evil may then be chosen, in order to avoid a greater; inconveniences be submitted to, in order to reach a desirable end: and in a word, benevolence, regulated by wisdom, and limited by necessity, may produce just such a world as the present.⑭ You,

⑭ Cleanthes considers the possibility of a God with more limited powers, thereby allowing evil to be explained by the recalcitrant nature of the material with which God has to work. This is perhaps the response to the problem of evil that requires the least modification of the traditional theistic position. (The opposite possibility of a God with infinite power but limited goodness is rarely considered.)

Philo, who are so prompt at starting views, and reflections, and analogies, I would gladly hear, at length, without interruption, your opinion of this new theory; and if it deserve our attention, we may afterwards, at more leisure, reduce it into form.

My sentiments, replied Philo, are not worth being made a mystery of; and therefore, without any ceremony, I shall deliver what occurs to me with regard to the present subject. It must, I think, be allowed, that, if a very limited intelligence, whom we shall suppose utterly unacquainted with the universe, were assured, that it were the production of a very good, wise, and powerful being, however finite, he would, from his conjectures, form *beforehand* a different notion of it from what we find it to be by *experience;* nor would he ever imagine, merely from these attributes of the cause, of which he is informed, that the effect could be so full of vice and misery and disorder, as it appears in his life. Supposing now, that this person were brought into the world, still assured, that it was the workmanship of such a sublime and benevolent Being; he might, perhaps, be surprised at the disappointment; but would never retract his former belief, if founded on any very solid argument; since such a limited intelligence must be sensible of his own blindness and ignorance, and must allow, that there may be many solutions of those phenomena, which will forever escape his comprehension. But supposing, which is the real case with regard to man, that this creature is not antecedently convinced of a supreme intelligence, benevolent, and powerful, but is left to gather such a belief from the appearance of things; this entirely alters the case, nor will he ever find any reason for such a conclusion. He may be fully convinced of the narrow limits of his understanding; but this will not help him in forming an inference concerning the goodness of superior powers, since he must form that inference from what he knows, not from what he is ignorant of. The more you exaggerate his weakness and ignorance, the more diffident you render him, and give him the greater suspicion, that such subjects are beyond the reach of his faculties. You are obliged, therefore, to reason with him merely from the known phenomena, and to drop every arbitrary supposition or conjecture.

Did I show you a house or palace, where there was not one apartment convenient or agreeable; where the windows, doors, fires, passages, stairs, and the whole economy of the building were the source of noise, confusion, fatigue, darkness, and extremes of heat and cold; you would certainly blame the contrivance, without any farther examination. The architect would in vain display his subtilty, and prove to you, that if this door or that window were altered, greater ills would ensue. What he says, may be strictly true: the alteration of one particular, while the other parts of the building remain, may only augment the inconveniences. But still you would assert in general, that, if the architect had had skill and good intentions, he might have formed such a plan of the whole, and might have adjusted the parts in such a manner, as would have remedied all or most of these inconveniences. His ignorance, or even your own ignorance of such a plan, will never convince you of the impossibility of it. If you find many inconveniences and deformities in the building, you will always, without entering into any detail, condemn the architect.

In short, I repeat the question: is the world considered in general, and as it appears to us in this life, different from what a man or such a limited being would, beforehand, expect from a very powerful, wise, and benevolent Deity? It must be strange prejudice to assert the contrary. And from thence I conclude, that, however consistent the world may be, allowing certain suppositions and conjectures, with the idea of such a Deity, it can never afford us an inference concerning his existence. The consistency is not absolutely denied, only the inference. Conjectures, especially where infinity is excluded from the Divine attributes, may perhaps be sufficient to prove a consistency; but can never be foundations for any inference. ⑮

There seem to be four circumstances, on which depend all, or the greatest parts of the ills, that molest sensible creatures; and it is not impossible but all these circumstances may be necessary and unavoidable. We know so little beyond common life, or even of common life, that, with regard to the economy of a universe, there is no conjecture, however wild, which may not be just; nor any one, however plausible, which may not be erroneous. All that belongs to human understanding, in this deep ignorance and obscurity, is to be sceptical, or at least cautious; and not to admit of any hypothesis, whatever; much less, of any which is supported by no appearance of probability. Now this I assert to be the case with regard to all the causes of evil, and the circumstances, on which it depends. None of them appear to human reason, in the least degree, necessary or unavoidable; nor can we suppose them such, without the utmost license of imagination.

The *first* circumstance which introduces evil, is that contrivance or economy of the animal creation, by which pains, as well as pleasures, are employed to excite all creatures to action, and make them vigilant in the great work of self-preservation. Now pleasure alone, in its various degrees, seems to human understanding sufficient for this purpose. All animals might be constantly in a state of enjoyment; but when urged by any of the necessities of nature, such as thirst, hunger, weariness; instead of pain, they might feel a diminution of pleasure, by which they might be prompted to seek that object, which is necessary to their subsistence. Men pursue pleasure as eagerly as they avoid pain; at least, might have been so constituted. It seems, therefore, plainly possible to carry on the business of life without any pain. Why then is any animal ever rendered susceptible of such a sensation? If animals can be free from it an hour, they might enjoy a perpetual exemption from it; and it required as particular a contrivance of their organs to produce that feeling, as to endow them with sight, hearing, or any of the senses. Shall we conjecture, that such a contrivance was necessary, without any appearance of reason? and shall we build on that conjecture as on the most certain truth?

But a capacity of pain would not alone produce pain, were it not for the *second* circumstance, viz., the conducting of the world by general laws; and this seems nowise necessary to a very perfect being. It is true; if everything were conducted by particular volitions, the course of nature would be perpetually broken, and no man could employ his reason in the conduct of life. But might not other particular volitions remedy this inconvenience? In short, might not the Deity exterminate all ill, wherever it were to be found; and produce all good, without any preparation or long progress of causes and effects?

⑮ Philo responds that the world we actually find is not what we would expect even a limited God to produce—again the suggestion is that while it may be compatible with the existence of such a being, it can provide no positive argument for its existence. Philo proceeds to enumerate four main circumstances that result in evil and suffering of various kinds, claiming that none of them is plausibly thought to be necessary and unavoidable even for a limited God. Think carefully about each of these.

Besides, we must consider, that, according to the present economy of the world, the course of nature, though supposed exactly regular, yet to us appears not so, and many events are uncertain, and many disappoint our expectations. Health and sickness, calm and tempest, with an infinite number of other accidents, whose causes are unknown and variable, have a great influence both on the fortunes of particular persons and on the prosperity of public societies: and indeed all human life, in a manner, depends on such accidents. A being, therefore, who knows the secret springs of the universe, might easily, by particular volitions, turn all these accidents to the good of mankind, and render the whole world happy, without discovering himself in any operation. A fleet, whose purposes were salutary to society, might always meet with a fair wind: good princes enjoy sound health and long life: persons, born to power and authority, be framed with good tempers and virtuous dispositions. A few such events as these, regularly and wisely conducted, would change the face of the world; and yet would no more seem to disturb the course of nature or confound human conduct, than the present economy of things, where the causes are secret, and variable, and compounded. . . . There may, for aught we know, be good reasons, why Providence interposes not in this manner; but they are unknown to us: and though the mere supposition, that such reasons exist, may be sufficient to *save* the conclusion concerning the divine attributes, yet surely it can never be sufficient to *establish* that conclusion. [16]

[16] One question often asked, about both natural and moral evil, is why God does not intervene (perhaps in a very subtle and unobvious way) when really horrific disasters or crimes are about to occur. Perhaps there is value in a world governed by regular laws (or, to anticipate discussions in later selections, one containing free will). But is the value so great and the harm done to it by even occasional and inconspicuous interventions so serious that it is better not to intervene even when disaster threatens?

If everything in the universe be conducted by general laws, and if animals be rendered susceptible of pain, it scarcely seems possible but some ill must arise in the various shocks of matter, and the various concurrence and opposition of general laws. But this ill would be very rare, were it not for the *third* circumstance, which I proposed to mention, viz., the great frugality with which all powers and faculties are distributed to every particular being. So well adjusted are the organs and capacities of all animals, and so well fitted to their preservation, that, as far as history or tradition reaches, there appears not to be any single species, which has yet been extinguished in the universe. [17] Every animal has the requisite endowments; but these endowments are bestowed with so scrupulous an economy, that any considerable diminution must entirely destroy the creature. Wherever one power is increased, there is a proportional abatement in the others. Animals, which excel in swiftness, are commonly defective in force. Those, which possess both, are either imperfect in some of their senses, or are oppressed with the most craving wants. The human species, whose chief excellency is reason and sagacity, is of all others the most necessitous, and the most deficient in bodily advantages; without clothes, without arms, without food, without lodging, without any convenience of life, except what they owe to their own skill and industry. In short, nature seems to have formed an exact calculation of the necessities of her creatures; and like a *rigid master,* has afforded them little more powers or endowments, than what are strictly sufficient to supply those necessities. An *indulgent parent* would have bestowed a large stock, in order to guard against accidents, and secure the happiness and welfare of the creature, in the most unfortunate concurrence of circumstances. Every course of life would not have been so surrounded with precipices, that the least departure from the true path, by mistake or necessity, must involve us in misery and ruin. Some reserve, some fund would have been provided to ensure happiness; nor would the powers and the necessities have been adjusted with so rigid an economy. The Author of Nature is inconceivably powerful: his force is supposed great, if not altogether inexhaustible: nor is there any reason, as far as we can judge, to make him observe this strict frugality in his dealings with his creatures. It would have been better, were his power extremely limited, to have created fewer animals, and to have endowed these with more faculties for their happiness and preservation. A builder is never esteemed prudent, who undertakes a plan, beyond what his stock will enable him to finish.

[17] We now know, of course, that there are species that have been extinguished. How important to Philo's argument is this claim?

In order to cure most of the ills of human life, I require not that man should have the wings of the eagle, the swiftness of the stag, the force of the ox, the arms of the lion, the scales of the crocodile or rhinoceros; much less do I demand the sagacity of an angel or cherub. I am contented to take an increase in one single power or faculty of his soul. Let him be endowed with a greater propensity to industry and labor; a more vigorous spring and activity of mind; a more constant bent to business and application. Let the whole species possess naturally an equal diligence with that which many individuals are able to attain by habit and reflection; and the most beneficial consequences, without any alloy of ill, is the immediate and necessary result of this endowment. Almost all the moral, as well as natural evils of human life arise from idleness; and were our species, by the original constitution of their frame, exempt from this vice or infirmity, the perfect cultivation of land, the improvement of arts and manufactures, the exact execution of every office and duty, immediately follow; and men at once may fully reach that state of society, which is so imperfectly attained by the best-regulated government. But as industry is a power, and the most valuable of any, nature seems determined, suitably to her usual maxims, to bestow it on men with a very sparing hand; and rather to punish him severely for his deficiency in it, than to reward him for his attainments. She has so contrived his frame, that nothing but the most violent necessity can oblige him to labor; and she employs all his other wants to overcome, at least in part, the want of diligence, and to endow him with some share of a faculty, of which she has thought fit naturally to bereave him. Here our demands may be allowed very humble, and therefore the more reasonable. If we required the endowments of superior penetration and judgment, of a more delicate taste of beauty, of a nicer sensibility to benevolence and friendship; we might be told, that we impiously pretend to break the order of nature, that we want to exalt ourselves into a higher rank of being, that the presents which we require, not being suitable to our state and condition, would only be pernicious to us. But it is hard; I dare to repeat it, it is hard, that being placed in a world so full of wants and necessities; where almost every being and element is either our foe or refuses us their assistance, we should also have our own temper to struggle with, and should be deprived of that faculty, which can alone fence against these multiplied evils.

The *fourth* circumstance, whence arises the misery and ill of the universe, is the inaccurate workmanship of all the springs and principles of the great machine of nature. It must be acknowledged, that there are few parts of the universe, which seem not to serve some purpose, and whose removal would not produce a visible defect and disorder in the whole. The parts hang all together; nor can one be touched without affecting the rest in a greater or less degree. But at the same time, it must be observed, that none of these parts or principles, however useful, are so accurately adjusted, as to keep precisely within those bounds, in which their utility consists; but they are, all of them, apt, on every occasion, to run into the one extreme or the other. One would imagine, that this grand production had not received the last hand of the maker; so little finished in every part, and so coarse are the strokes, with which it is executed. Thus, the winds are requisite to convey the vapors along the surface of the globe, and to assist men in navigation: but how oft, rising up to tempests and hurricanes, do they become pernicious? Rains are necessary to nourish all the plants and animals of the earth: but how often are they defective? how often excessive? Heat is requisite to all life and vegetation; but is not always found in the due proportion. [18] On the mixture and secretion of the humors and juices

> [18] This is a quick gesture at the suffering that results from various kinds of natural disasters.

of the body depend the health and prosperity of the animal: but the parts perform not regularly their proper function. What more useful than all the passions of the mind, ambition, vanity, love, anger? But how oft do they break their bounds, and cause the greatest convulsions in society? There is nothing so advantageous in the universe, but what frequently becomes pernicious, by its excess or defect; nor has nature guarded, with the requisite accuracy, against all disorder or confusion. The irregularity is never, perhaps, so great as to destroy any species; but is often sufficient to involve the individuals in ruin and misery.

On the concurrence, then, of these four circumstances does all, or the greatest part of natural evil depend. Were all living creatures incapable of pain, or were the world administered by particular volitions, evil never could have found access into the universe:

and were animals endowed with a large stock of powers and faculties, beyond what strict necessity requires; or were the several springs and principles of the universe so accurately framed as to preserve always the just temperament and medium; there must have been very little ill in comparison of what we feel at present. What then shall we pronounce on this occasion? Shall we say, that these circumstances are not necessary, and that they might easily have been altered in the contrivance of the universe? This decision seems too presumptuous for creatures, so blind and ignorant. Let us be more modest in our conclusions.

[19] Again Hume's rather cautious point is not that we can know for sure that a God who satisfied the standard conception would modify these various features of the world, but only that since we can see no reason why such modification is not possible (without greater costs of some sort), we have no good reason to accept the existence of such a God on the basis of the world as we find it.

Let us allow, that, if the goodness of the Deity (I mean a goodness like the human)[19] could be established on any tolerable reasons a priori, these phenomena, however untoward, would not be sufficient to subvert that principle; but might easily, in some unknown manner, be reconcilable to it. But let us still assert, that as this goodness is not antecedently established, but must be inferred from the phenomena, there can be no grounds for such an inference, while there are so many ills in the universe, and while these ills might so easily have been remedied, as far as human understanding can be allowed to judge on such a subject. I am sceptic enough to allow, that the bad appearances, notwithstanding all my reasonings, may be compatible with such attributes as you suppose: but surely they can never prove these attributes. Such a conclusion cannot result from scepticism; but must arise from the phenomena, and from our confidence in the reasonings, which we deduce from these phenomena.

Look round this universe. What an immense profusion of beings, animated and organized, sensible and active! You admire this prodigious variety and fecundity. But inspect a little more narrowly these living existences, the only beings worth regarding. How hostile and destructive to each other! How insufficient all of them for their own happiness! How contemptible or odious to the spectator! The whole presents nothing but the idea of a blind nature, impregnated by a great vivifying principle, and pouring forth from her lap, without discernment or parental care, her maimed and abortive children!

Here the Manichaean system occurs as a proper hypothesis to solve the difficulty[20]: and no doubt, in some respects, it is very specious, and has more probability than the common hypothesis, by giving a plausible account of the strange mixture of good and ill, which appears in life. But if we consider, on the other hand, the perfect uniformity and agreement of the parts of the universe, we shall not discover in it any marks of the combat of a malevolent with a benevolent being. There is indeed an opposition of pains and pleasures in the feelings of sensible creatures: but are not all the operations of nature carried on by an opposition of principles, of hot and cold, moist and dry, light and heavy? The true conclusion is, that the original source of all things is entirely indifferent to all these principles, and has no more regard to good above ill than to heat above cold, or to drought above moisture, or to light above heavy.

[20] The Manichean system has two opposed gods or forces, one good and one evil, who struggle for control.

There may four hypotheses be framed concerning the first causes of the universe: that they are endowed with perfect goodness, that they have perfect malice, that they are opposite and have both goodness and malice, that they have neither goodness nor malice. Mixed phenomena can never prove the two former unmixed principles. And the uniformity and steadiness of general laws seem to oppose the third. The fourth, therefore, seems by far the most probable.[21]

[21] Think carefully about the reason given here for rejecting the Manichean possibility. What would a Manichean world look like? Is Hume right that it would be very different from the one we find?

What I have said concerning natural evil will apply to moral, with little or no variation; and we have no more reason to infer, that the rectitude of the Supreme Being resembles human rectitude than that his benevolence resembles the human. Nay, it will be thought, that we have still greater cause to exclude from him moral sentiments, such as we feel them; since moral evil, in the opinion of many, is much more predominant above moral good than natural evil above natural good.

But even though this should not be allowed, and though the virtue, which is in mankind, should be acknowledged much superior to the vice; yet so long as there is any vice at all in the universe, it will very much puzzle you anthropomorphites, how to account for it. You must assign a cause for it, without having recourse to the first cause. But as every effect must have a cause, and that cause another; you must either carry on the progression *in infinitum,* or rest on that original principle, who is the ultimate cause of all things . . . 22⃝

> 22⃝ Hume extends his conclusion to moral evil as well, though without much discussion (and no consideration of the free will theodicy).

Hold! hold! cried Demea: Whither does your imagination hurry you? I joined in alliance with you, in order to prove the incomprehensible nature of the Divine Being, and refute the principles of Cleanthes, who would measure everything by a human rule and standard. But I now find you running into all the topics of the greatest libertines and infidels; and betraying that holy cause, which you seemingly espoused. Are you secretly, then, a more dangerous enemy than Cleanthes himself?

And are you so late in perceiving it? replied Cleanthes. Believe me, Demea; your friend Philo, from the beginning, has been amusing himself at both our expense; and it must be confessed, that the injudicious reasoning of our vulgar theology has given him but too just a handle of ridicule. The total infirmity of human reason, the absolute incomprehensibility of the Divine Nature, the great and universal misery and still greater wickedness of men; these are strange topics

surely to be so fondly cherished by orthodox divines and doctors. In ages of stupidity and ignorance, indeed, these principles may safely be espoused; and perhaps, no views of things are more proper to promote superstition, than such as encourage the blind amazement, the diffidence, and melancholy of mankind. But at present . . .

Blame not so much, interposed Philo, the ignorance of these reverend gentlemen. They know how to change their style with the times. Formerly it was a most popular theological topic to maintain, that human life was vanity and misery, and to exaggerate all the ills and pains, which are incident to men. But of late years, divines, we find, begin to retract this position, and maintain, though still with some hesitation, that there are more goods than evils, more pleasures than pains, even in this life. When religion stood entirely upon temper and education, it was thought proper to encourage melancholy; as indeed, mankind never have recourse to superior powers so readily as in that disposition. But as men have now learned to form principles, and to draw consequences, it is necessary to change the batteries, and to make use of such arguments as will endure, at least some scrutiny and examination. This variation is the same (and from the same causes) with that which I formerly remarked with regard to scepticism.

Thus Philo continued to the last his spirit of opposition, and his censure of established opinions. But I could observe, that Demea did not at all relish the latter part of the discourse; and he took occasion soon after on some pretense or other, to leave the company.

Discussion Questions

1. Formulate the problem of evil as an explicit argument for the conclusion that God (understood in the standard way) does not exist (see Annotation 7). This can be done in a way that makes the argument logically valid, so that either the conclusion must be true or one of the premises must be false. What is the best response that a theist can give to such an argument—that is, which premise should the theist deny, and how might he defend such a denial?

2. Consider the possibility of a more limited God (see Annotation 14), who is either unable or unwilling to eradicate evil. (The Manichean view (see Annotation 20) is in fact one version

of this, with the good god being the relevant one and the evil god being the force that prevents the eradication of evil.) Are views of this sort more defensible than those that advocate a God who satisfies the standard conception, and if so, how much more defensible? (Consider Hume's responses.) How satisfactory is a limited God from the standpoint of religion?

3. Presumably even a limited God could often intervene when natural disasters of various sorts are about to occur, reducing their severity even if not eliminating them entirely. Is there any compelling reason why God (on either the standard or limited view) should not do this because the cost would be greater than the gain?

J. L. Mackie

J. L. Mackie (1917–1981) was an Australian philosopher, who taught in both New Zealand and Australia and later at Oxford. His wide-ranging work includes influential discussions of the nature of causation, the nature of morality, and various issues in the philosophy of religion, as well as work on Locke and Hume. In this selection, Mackie offers a careful statement of the problem of evil, together with a presentation and evaluation of possible solutions.

Evil and Omnipotence

The traditional arguments for the existence of God have been fairly thoroughly criticized by philosophers. But the theologian can, if he wishes, accept this criticism. He can admit that no rational proof of God's existence is possible. And he can still retain all that is essential to his position, by holding that God's existence is known in some other, nonrational way. I think, however, that a more telling criticism can be made by way of the traditional problem of evil. Here it can be shown, not that religious beliefs lack rational support, but that they are positively irrational, that the several parts of the essential theological doctrine are inconsistent with one another, so that the theologian can maintain his position as a whole only by a much more extreme rejection of reason than in the former case. He must now be prepared to believe, not merely what cannot be proved, but what can be *disproved* from other beliefs that he also holds.

The problem of evil, in the sense in which I shall be using the phrase, is a problem only for someone who believes that there is a God who is both omnipotent and wholly good. And it is a logical problem, the problem of clarifying and reconciling a number of beliefs: it is not a scientific problem that might be solved by further observations, or a practical problem that might be solved by a decision or an action. These points are obvious; I mention them only because they

are sometimes ignored by theologians, who sometimes parry a statement of the problem with such remarks as "Well, can you solve the problem yourself?" or "This is a mystery which may be revealed to us later" or "Evil is something to be faced and overcome, not to be merely discussed."

In its simplest form the problem is this: God is omnipotent; God is wholly good; and yet evil exists. There seems to be some contradiction between these three propositions, so that if any two of them were true the third would be false. But at the same time all three are essential parts of most theological positions: the theologian, it seems, at once *must* adhere and *cannot consistently* adhere to all three. (The problem does not arise only for theists, but I shall discuss it in the form in which it presents itself for ordinary theism.)

However, the contradiction does not arise immediately; to show it we need some additional premises, or perhaps some quasi-logical rules connecting the terms "good," "evil," and "omnipotent." These additional principles are that good is opposed to evil, in such a way that a good thing always eliminates evil as far as it can, and that there are no limits to what an omnipotent thing can do. From these it follows that a good omnipotent thing eliminates evil completely, and then the propositions that a good omnipotent thing exists, and that evil exists, are incompatible. [1]

> [1] Mackie's claim is that with these additional assumptions ("quasi-logical rules"), the existence of a God satisfying the standard conception is logically incompatible with the existence of evil, so that it would be contradictory to assert both.

From J. L. Mackie, "Evil and Omnipotence," Mind, Vol. LXIV (1955).

ADEQUATE SOLUTIONS

Now once the problem is fully stated it is clear that it can be solved, in the sense that the problem will not arise if one gives up at least one of the propositions that constitute it. If you are prepared to say that God is not wholly good, or not quite omnipotent, or that evil does not exist, or that good is not opposed to the kind of evil that exists, or that there are limits to what an omnipotent thing can do, then the problem of evil will not arise for you. ②

> ② What Mackie means by an "adequate solution" is one that is logically adequate to avoid the alleged contradiction, not one that is adequate as a defense of the existence of God.

There are, then, quite a number of adequate solutions of the problem of evil, and some of these have been adopted, or almost adopted, by various thinkers. For example, a few have been prepared to deny God's omnipotence, and rather more have been prepared to keep the term "omnipotence" but severely to restrict its meaning, recording quite a number of things that an omnipotent being cannot do. Some have said that evil is an illusion, perhaps because they held that the whole world of temporal, changing things is an illusion, and that what we call evil belongs only to this world, or perhaps because they held that although temporal things *are* much as we see them, those that we call evil are not really evil. Some have said that what we call evil is merely the privation of good, that evil in a positive sense, evil that would really be opposed to good, does not exist. Many have agreed with Pope that disorder is harmony not understood, and that partial evil is universal good. Whether any of these views is *true* is, of course, another question. ③ But each of them gives an adequate solution of the problem of evil in the sense that if you accept it this problem does not arise for you, though you may, of course, have *other* problems to face.

> ③ Mackie mentions several possibilities here, without really elaborating any of them. Think about whether any of these can be developed in a plausible way.

But often enough these adequate solutions are only *almost* adopted. The thinkers who restrict God's power, but keep the term "omnipotence," may reasonably be suspected of thinking, in other contexts, that his power is really unlimited. Those who say that evil is an illusion may also be thinking, inconsistently, that this illusion is itself an evil. Those who say that "evil" is merely privation of good may also be thinking, inconsistently, that privation of good is an evil. . . . If Pope meant what he said in the last line of his couplet, that "disorder" is only harmony not understood, the "partial evil" of the second line must, for consistency, mean "that which, taken in isolation, falsely appears to be evil," but it would more naturally mean "that which, in isolation, really is evil." The second line, in fact, hesitates between two views, that "partial evil" isn't really evil, since only the universal quality is real, and that "partial evil" is really an evil, but only a little one.

In addition, therefore, to adequate solutions, we must recognize unsatisfactory inconsistent solutions, in which there is only a half-hearted or temporary rejection of one of the propositions which together constitute the problem. In these, one of the constituent propositions is explicitly rejected, but it is covertly reasserted or assumed elsewhere in the system.

FALLACIOUS SOLUTIONS

Besides these half-hearted solutions, which explicitly reject but implicitly assert one of the constituent propositions, there are definitely fallacious solutions which explicitly maintain all the constituent propositions, but implicitly reject at least one of them in the course of the argument that explains away the problem of evil.

There are, in fact, many so-called solutions which purport to remove the contradiction without abandoning any of its constituent propositions. These must be fallacious, as we can see from the very statement of the problem, but it is not so easy to see in each case precisely where the fallacy lies. I suggest that in all cases the fallacy has the general form suggested above: in order to solve the problem one (or perhaps more) of its constituent propositions is given up, but in such a way that it appears to have been retained, and can therefore be asserted without qualification in other contexts. Sometimes there is a further complication: the supposed solution moves to and fro between, say, two of the constituent propositions, at one point asserting the first of these but covertly abandoning the second, at another point asserting the second but covertly abandoning the first. These fallacious solutions often turn upon some equivocation with the words "good" and "evil," or upon some vagueness about the way in which good and evil are opposed to one another, or about how much is meant by "omnipotence." I propose to examine some of these so-called solutions, and to exhibit their fallacies in detail. Incidentally, I shall also be considering whether an adequate solution could be reached by a minor modification of one or more of the constituent propositions, which would, however, still satisfy all the essential requirements of ordinary theism.

1. "Good cannot exist without evil" or "Evil is necessary as a counterpart to good."

It is sometimes suggested that evil is necessary as a counterpart to good, that if there were no evil there could be no good either, and that this solves the problem of evil. It is true that it points to an answer to the question "Why should there be evil?" But it does so only by qualifying some of the propositions that constitute the problem.

First, it sets a limit to what God can do, saying that God *cannot* create good without simultaneously creating evil, and this means either that God is not omnipotent or that there are *some* limits to what an omnipotent thing can do. It may be replied that these limits are always presupposed, that omnipotence has never meant the power to do what is logically impossible, and on the present view the existence of good without evil would be a logical impossibility.④ This interpretation of omnipotence may, indeed, be accepted as a modification of our original account which does not reject anything that is essential to theism, and I shall in general assume it in the subsequent discussion. It is, perhaps, the most common theistic view, but I think that some theists at least have maintained that God can do what is logically impossible. Many theists, at any rate, have held that logic itself is created or laid down by God, that logic is the way in which God arbitrarily chooses to think. (This is, of course, parallel to the ethical view that morally right actions are those which God arbitrarily chooses to command,

④ Think about this conception of (or limitation on) God's omnipotence. Should God also be able to do the logically impossible, or does that really make any sense? Can God create a round square? Can God make a contradiction true?

and the two views encounter similar difficulties.) And *this* account of logic is clearly inconsistent with the view that God is bound by logical necessities—unless it is possible for an omnipotent being to bind himself, an issue which we shall consider later, when we come to the Paradox of Omnipotence. This solution of the problem of evil cannot, therefore, be consistently adopted along with the view that logic is itself created by God.

But, secondly, this solution denies that evil is opposed to good in our original sense. If good and evil are counterparts, a good thing will not "eliminate evil as far as it can." Indeed, this view suggests that good and evil are not strictly qualities of things at all. Perhaps the suggestion is that good and evil are related in much the same way as great and small. Certainly, when the term "great" is used relatively as a condensation of "greater than so-and-so," and "small" is used correspondingly, greatness and smallness are counterparts and cannot exist without each other. But in this sense greatness is not a quality, not an intrinsic feature of anything; and it would be absurd to think of a movement in favor of greatness and against smallness in this sense. Such a movement would be self-defeating, since relative greatness can be promoted only by a simultaneous promotion of relative smallness. I feel sure that no theists would be content to regard God's goodness as analogous to this—as if what he supports were not the *good* but the *better,* and as if he had the paradoxical aim that all things should be better than other things.⑤

⑤ On this relative conception, evil things (that is, less good things) would have to exist—unless everything was equal in goodness. Would that account in a plausible way for the actual evils that the world contains?

This point is obscured by the fact that "great" and "small" seem to have an absolute as well as a relative sense. I cannot discuss here whether there is absolute magnitude or not, but if there is, there could be an absolute sense for "great," it could mean of at least a certain size, and it would make sense to speak of all things getting bigger, of a universe that was expanding all over, and therefore it would make sense to speak of promoting greatness. But in *this* sense great and small are not logically necessary counterparts: either quality could exist without the other. There would be no logical impossibility in everything's being small or in everything's being great.⑥

Neither in the absolute nor in the relative sense, then, of "great" and "small" do these terms provide an analogy of the sort that would be needed to support this solution of the problem of evil. In neither case are greatness and smallness *both* necessary counterparts *and* mutually opposed forces or possible objects for support and attack.

> ⑥ If "good" and "evil" are understood in this second, absolute way, is there any reason why the world must contain evil if it is to contain good?

It may be replied that good and evil are necessary counterparts in the same way as any quality and its logical opposite: redness can occur, it is suggested, only if nonredness also occurs. But unless evil is merely the privation of good, they are not logical opposites, and some further argument would be needed to show that they are counterparts in the same way as genuine logical opposites. Let us assume that this could be given. There is still doubt of the correctness of the metaphysical principle that a quality must have a real opposite: I suggest that it is not really impossible that everything should be, say, red, that the truth is merely that if everything were red we should not notice redness, and we should have no word "red"; we observe and give names to qualities only if they have real opposites. If so, the principle that a term must have an opposite would belong only to our language or to our thought, and would not be an ontological principle, and, correspondingly, the rule that good cannot exist without evil would not state a logical necessity of a sort that God would just have to put up with. God might have made everything good, though *we* should not have noticed it if he had.⑦

> ⑦ Is the fact that we would not otherwise have noticed good a compelling reason for God to permit evil? Is it a compelling reason for permitting the kinds and quantity of evil that actually exist? (An "ontological principle" is one that pertains to the existence of things, rather than to our language or concepts.)

But, finally, even if we concede that this *is* an ontological principle, it will provide a solution for the problem of evil only if one is prepared to say, "Evil exists, but only just enough evil to serve as the counterpart of good." I doubt whether any theist will accept this. After all, the *ontological* requirement that nonredness should occur would be satisfied even if all the universe, except for a minute speck, were red, and, if there were a corresponding requirement for evil as a counterpart to good, a minute dose of evil would presumably do. But theists are not usually willing to say, in all contexts, that all the evil that occurs is a minute and necessary dose.⑧

> ⑧ Would such a claim have any real plausibility?

2. "Evil is necessary as a means to good."

It is sometimes suggested that evil is necessary for good not as a counterpart but as a means. In its simple form this has little plausibility as a solution of the problem of evil, since it obviously implies a severe restriction of God's power. It would be a *causal* law that you cannot have a certain end without a certain means, so that if God has to introduce evil as a means to good, he must be subject to at least some causal laws. This certainly conflicts with what a theist normally means by omnipotence. This view of God as limited by causal laws also conflicts with the view that causal laws are themselves made by God, which is more widely held than the corresponding view about the laws of logic. This conflict would, indeed, be resolved if it were possible for an omnipotent being to bind himself, and this possibility has still to be considered. Unless a favorable answer can be given to this question, the suggestion that evil is necessary as a means to good solves the problem of evil only by denying one of its constituent propositions, either that God is omnipotent or that "omnipotent" means what it says.⑨

> ⑨ Implicit here is a criterion of omnipotence: an omnipotent being is one that does not need means to his (or her or its) ends, but rather can simply produce them directly.

3. "The universe is better with some evil in it than it could be if there were no evil."

Much more important is a solution which at first seems to be a mere variant of the previous one, that evil may contribute to the goodness of a whole in which it is found, so that the universe as a whole is better as it is, with some evil in it, than it would be if there were no evil. This solution may be developed in either of two ways. It may be supported by an aesthetic analogy, by the fact that contrasts heighten beauty, that in a musical work, for example, there may occur discords which somehow add to the beauty of the work as a whole. Alternatively, it may be worked out in connection with the notion of progress, that the best possible organization of the universe will not be static, but progressive, that the gradual overcoming of evil by good is really a finer thing than would be the eternal unchallenged supremacy of good. [10]

In either case, this solution usually starts from the assumption that the evil whose existence gives rise to the problem of evil is primarily what is called physical evil, that is to say, pain. In Hume's rather half-hearted presentation of the problem of evil, the evils that he stresses are pain and disease, and those who reply to him argue that the existence of pain and disease makes possible the existence of sympathy, benevolence, heroism, and the gradually successful struggle of doctors and reformers to overcome these evils. In fact, theists often seize the opportunity to accuse those who stress the problem of evil of taking a low, materialistic view of good and evil, equating these with pleasure and pain, and of ignoring the more spiritual goods which can arise in the struggle against evils.

But let us see exactly what is being done here. Let us call pain and misery "first order evil" or "evil (1)." What contrasts with this, namely, pleasure and happiness, will be called "first order good" or "good (1)." Distinct from this is "second order good" or "good (2)" which somehow emerges in a complex situation in which evil (1) is a necessary component—logically, not merely causally, necessary. (Exactly *how* it emerges does not matter: in the crudest version of this solution good (2) is simply the heightening of happiness by the contrast with misery, in other versions it includes sympathy with suffering, heroism in facing danger, and the gradual decrease of first order evil and increase of first order good.) It is also being assumed that second order good is more important than first order good or evil, in particular that it more than outweighs the first order evil it involves. [11]

[10] The suggestion is that something that is evil when taken by itself can contribute to a larger whole that is better than could exist without that evil—not because the evil is an essential *means* to the end of good, but because it is an essential *constituent* of the good state. Mackie proceeds to develop one version of this idea. (Can you think of any others?)

Now this is a particularly subtle attempt to solve the problem of evil. It defends God's goodness and omnipotence on the ground that (on a sufficiently long view) this is the best of all logically possible worlds because it includes the important second order goods, and yet it admits that real evils, namely first order evils, exist. But does it still hold that good and evil are opposed? Not, clearly, in the sense that we set out originally: good does not tend to eliminate evil in general. Instead, we have a modified, a more complex pattern. First order good (e.g., happiness) *contrasts with* first order evil (e.g., misery): these two are opposed in a fairly mechanical way; some second order goods (e.g., benevolence) try to maximize first order good and minimize first order evil; but God's goodness is not this, it is rather the will to maximize *second* order good. We might, therefore, call God's goodness an example of a third order goodness, or good (3). While this account is different from our original one, it might well be held to be an improvement on it, to give a more accurate description of the way in which good is opposed to evil, and to be consistent with the essential theist position.

There might, however, be several objections to this solution.

First, some might argue that such qualities as benevolence—and *a fortiori* the third order goodness which promotes benevolence—have a merely derivative value, that they are not higher sorts of good, but merely means to good (1), that is, to happiness, so that it would be absurd for God to keep misery in existence in order to make possible the virtues of benevolence, heroism, etc. The theist who adopts the present solution must, of course, deny this, but he can do so with some plausibility, so I should not press this objection. [12]

Secondly, it follows from this solution that God is not in our sense benevolent or sympathetic: he is not concerned to minimize evil (1), but only to promote

[11] This last assumption is crucial: at least in general, the value of the second-order goods must outweigh the value of the corresponding first-order evils, or else the problem has not really been solved. Notice also Mackie's insistence that the evil is logically required for the good, not just a means to it. Think about how this might be so.

[12] How plausible is the theistic claim on this point? (See Discussion Question 1.)

good (2); and this might be a disturbing conclusion for some theists.

But, thirdly, the fatal objection is this. Our analysis shows clearly the possibility of the existence of a *second* order evil, an evil (2) contrasting with good (2) as evil (1) contrasts with good (1). This would include malevolence, cruelty, callousness, cowardice, and states in which good (1) is decreasing and evil (1) increasing. And just as good (2) is held to be the important kind of good, the kind that God is concerned to promote, so evil (2) will, by analogy, be the important kind of evil, the kind which God, if he were wholly good and omnipotent, would eliminate. And yet evil (2) plainly exists, and indeed most theists (in other contexts) stress its existence more than that of evil (1). We should, therefore, state the problem of evil in terms of second order evil, and against this form of the problem the present solution is useless.[13]

13 Think carefully about why this is supposed to be so. Can you think of any way the theist might reply?

An attempt might be made to use this solution again, at a higher level, to explain the occurrence of evil (2): indeed the next main solution that we shall examine does just this, with the help of some new notions. Without any fresh notions, such a solution would have little plausibility: for example, we could hardly say that the really important good was a good (3), such as the increase of benevolence in proportion to cruelty, which logically required for its occurrence the occurrence of some second order evil. But even if evil (2) could be explained in this way, it is fairly clear that there would be third order evils contrasting with this third order good: and we should be well on the way to an infinite regress, where the solution of a problem of evil, stated in terms of evil (*n*), indicated the existence of an evil (*n* + 1), and a further problem to be solved.

4. "Evil is due to human free will."

Perhaps the most important proposed solution of the problem of evil is that evil is not to be ascribed to God at all, but to the independent actions of human beings, supposed to have been endowed by God with freedom of the will. This solution may be combined with the preceding one: first order evil (e.g., pain) may be justified as a logically necessary component in

second order good (e.g., sympathy) while second order evil (e.g., cruelty) is not *justified,* but is so ascribed to human beings that God cannot be held responsible for it. This combination evades my third criticism of the preceding solution.[14]

14 Thus the suggestion is essentially that natural evil is explained by appeal to the second-order goods of which it is an essential component, and moral evil is explained by appeal to human free will. (This is very similar to Hick's appeal to the combination of free will and "soul-making" in the following selection.)

The free-will solution also involves the preceding solution at a higher level. To explain why a wholly good God gave men free will although it would lead to some important evils, it must be argued that it is better on the whole that men should act freely, and sometimes err, than that they should be innocent automata, acting rightly in a wholly determined way. Freedom, that is to say, is now treated as a third order good, and as being more valuable than second order goods (such as sympathy and heroism) would be if they were deterministically produced, and it is being assumed that second order evils, such as cruelty, are logically necessary accompaniments of freedom, just as pain is a logically necessary pre-condition of sympathy.[15]

15 Again, the claim has to be that a world containing free will and the moral evil (and also moral good) that it makes possible is better than one that contains none of these things. Does this seem plausible?

I think that this solution is unsatisfactory primarily because of the incoherence of the notion of freedom of the will:[16] but I cannot discuss this topic adequately here, although some of my criticisms will touch upon it.

16 See Chapter 5 for more discussion of the problems associated with the idea of free will.

First I should query the assumption that second order evils are logically necessary accompaniments of freedom. I should ask this: if God has made men such that in their free choices they sometimes prefer what is good and sometimes what is evil, why could he not have made men such that they always freely choose the good? If there is no logical impossibility in a man's freely choosing the good on one, or on several occasions, there cannot be a logical impossibility in his freely choosing the good on every occasion. God was not, then, faced with a choice between making innocent automata and making beings who, in acting freely, would sometimes go wrong: there was open to him the obviously better possibility of making beings who would act freely but always go right.[17] Clearly, his failure to avail himself of this possibility is inconsistent with his being both omnipotent and wholly good.

[17] Could God really do this? Could he create beings who always do the right thing while leaving them genuinely free?

If it is replied that this objection is absurd, that the making of some wrong choices is logically necessary for freedom, it would seem that "freedom" must here mean complete randomness or indeterminacy, including randomness with regard to the alternatives good and evil, in other words that men's choices and consequent actions can be "free" only if they are not determined by their characters. Only on this assumption can God escape the responsibility for men's actions; for if he made them as they are, but did not determine their wrong choices, this can only be because the wrong choices are not determined by men as they are. But then if freedom is randomness, how can it be a characteristic of *will?* And, still more, how can it be the most important good? What value or merit would there be in free choices if these were random actions which were not determined by the nature of the agent?[18]

[18] One issue about free will (see Chapter 5) is whether it is only having one's actions causally determined in the right way (by one's own choices—the *compatibilist* or *soft determinist* view) or whether free will is incompatible with any sort of causal determination (the *libertarian* view). Mackie raises a standard objection to libertarianism: that if actions (or choices) are not determined, then they are random (where this would mean either that the libertarian is wrong about what freedom requires or else that freedom has no real value). On a compatibilist view of free will, God could apparently bring it about that people always do the right thing by controlling their choices, while still leaving them free.

I conclude that to make this solution plausible two different senses of "freedom" must be confused, one sense which will justify the view that freedom is a third order good, more valuable than other goods would be without it, and another sense, sheer randomness, to prevent us from ascribing to God a decision to make men such that they sometimes go wrong when he might have made them such that they would always freely go right.

This criticism is sufficient to dispose of this solution. But besides this there is a fundamental difficulty in the notion of an omnipotent God creating men with free will, for if men's wills are really free this must mean that even God cannot control them, that is, that God is no longer omnipotent.[19] It may be objected that God's gift of freedom to men does not mean that he *cannot* control their wills, but that he always *refrains* from controlling their wills. But why, we may ask, should God refrain from controlling evil wills? Why should he not leave men free to will rightly, but intervene when he sees them beginning to will wrongly? If God could do this, but does not, and if he is wholly good, the only explanation could be that even a wrong free act of will is not really evil, that its freedom is a value which outweighs its wrongness, so that there would be a loss of value if God took away the wrongness and the freedom together.[20] But this is utterly opposed to what theists say about sin in other contexts. The present solution of the problem of evil, then, can be maintained only in the form that God has made men so free that he *cannot* control their wills.

[19] Is this the right understanding of what it means for God to give human beings "the gift of freedom"?

[20] The proponent of the free will **theodicy** will apparently have to say that *any* intervention by God, any restriction or limitation on human free will, would make the world less good than it would otherwise have been.

This leads us to what I call the Paradox of Omnipotence: can an omnipotent being make things which he cannot subsequently control? Or, what is practically equivalent to this, can an omnipotent being make rules which then bind himself? (These are practically equivalent because any such rules could be regarded as setting certain things beyond his control, and *vice versa.*) The second of these formulations is relevant to the suggestions that we have already met, that an omnipotent God creates the rules of logic or causal laws, and is then bound by them.

It is clear that this is a paradox: the questions cannot be answered satisfactorily either in the affirmative or in the negative. If we answer "Yes," it follows that if

God actually makes things which he cannot control, or makes rules which bind himself, he is not omnipotent once he has made them: there are *then* things which he cannot do. But if we answer "No," we are immediately asserting that there are things which he cannot do, that is to say that he is already not omnipotent. [21]

It cannot be replied that the question which sets this paradox is not a proper question. It would make perfectly good sense to say that a human mechanic has made a machine which he cannot control: if there is any difficulty about the question it lies in the notion of omnipotence itself.

This, incidentally, shows that although we have approached this paradox from the free-will theory, it is equally a problem for a theological determinist. No one thinks that machines have free will, yet they may well be beyond the control of their makers. The determinist might reply that anyone who makes anything determines its ways of acting, and so determines its subsequent behavior: even the human mechanic does this by his *choice* of materials and structure for his machine, though he does not know all about either of these: the mechanic thus determines, though he may not foresee, his machine's actions. And since God is omniscient, and since his creation of things is total, he both determines and foresees the ways in which his creatures will act. We may grant this, but it is beside the point. The question is not whether God *originally* determined the future actions of his creatures, but whether he can *subsequently* control their actions, or whether he was able in his original creation to put things beyond his subsequent control. Even on determinist principles the answers "Yes" and "No" are equally irreconcilable with God's omnipotence.

Before suggesting a solution of this paradox, I would point out that there is a parallel Paradox of Sovereignty. Can a legal sovereign make a law restricting its own future legislative power? For example, could the British parliament make a law forbidding any future parliament to socialize banking, and also forbidding the future repeal of this law itself? Or could the British parliament, which was legally sovereign in Australia in, say, 1899, pass a valid law, or series of laws, which made it no longer sovereign in 1933?

Again, neither the affirmative nor the negative answer is really satisfactory. If we were to answer "Yes," we should be admitting the validity of a law which, if it were actually made, would mean that parliament was no longer sovereign. If we were to answer "No," we should be admitting that there is a law, not logically absurd, which parliament cannot validly make, that is, that parliament is not now a legal sovereign. This paradox can be solved in the following way. We should distinguish between first order laws, that is, laws governing the actions of individuals and bodies other than the legislature, and second order laws, that is, laws about laws, laws governing the actions of the legislature itself. Correspondingly, we should distinguish two orders of sovereignty, first order sovereignty (sovereignty [1]) which is unlimited authority to make first order laws, and second order sovereignty (sovereignty [2]) which is unlimited authority to make second order laws. If we say that parliament is sovereign we might mean that any parliament at any time has sovereignty (1), or we might mean that parliament has both sovereignty (1) and sovereignty (2) at present, but we cannot without contradiction mean both that the present parliament has sovereignty (2) and that every parliament at every time has sovereignty (1), for if the present parliament has sovereignty (2) it may use it to take away the sovereignty (1) of later parliaments. What the paradox shows is that we cannot ascribe to any continuing institution legal sovereignty in an inclusive sense.

The analogy between omnipotence and sovereignty shows that the paradox of omnipotence can be solved in a similar way. We must distinguish between first order omnipotence (omnipotence [1]), that is, unlimited power to act, and second order omnipotence (omnipotence [2]), that is, unlimited power to determine what powers to act things shall have. Then we could consistently say that God all the time has omnipotence (1), but if so no beings at any time have powers to act independently of God. Or we could say that God at one time had omnipotence (2), and used it to assign independent powers to act to certain things, so that God thereafter did not have omnipotence (1). But what the paradox shows is that we cannot consistently ascribe to any continuing being omnipotence in an inclusive sense.

An alternative solution of this paradox would be simply to deny that God is a continuing being, that any times can be assigned to his actions at all. But on this assumption (which also has difficulties of its own) no meaning can be given to the assertion that God made men with wills so free that he could not control them. The paradox of omnipotence can be avoided by putting God outside time, but the free-will solution of the problem of evil cannot be saved in this way, and equally it remains impossible to hold that an omnipotent God *binds himself* by causal or logical laws.

CONCLUSION

Of the proposed solutions of the problem of evil which we have examined, none has stood up to criticism. There may be other solutions which require examination, but this study strongly suggests that there is no valid solution of the problem which does not modify at least one of the constituent propositions in a way which would seriously affect the essential core of the theistic position.

Quite apart from the problem of evil, the paradox of omnipotence has shown that God's omnipotence must in any case be restricted in one way or another, that unqualified omnipotence cannot be ascribed to any being that continues through time. And if God and his actions are not in time, can omnipotence, or power of any sort, be meaningfully ascribed to him?

Discussion Questions

1. Are things like benevolence, heroism, compassion, etc., *intrinsically* valuable (so that the world is better for containing them along with the evils to which they are a response), or are they only *instrumentally* valuable (because the world happens in fact to contain those evils, though things would be better if neither the evils nor the corresponding second-order qualities existed)? If people were too successful at eradicating evils of various sorts (diseases, natural disasters, etc.), would it be preferable to reintroduce them so as not to lose the second-order goods?

2. One question about the free will theodicy is why God doesn't intervene, perhaps only very selectively, to prevent at least the most extreme sorts of evil actions from occurring: such actions as the murder of 6 million Jews during World War II. Perhaps God might have influenced Hitler in such a way that he ordered the Jews to be deported rather than murdered. If free will does indeed have significant positive value, this would involve some cost: the loss of a bit of Hitler's freedom plus a qualification on God's "gift of freedom" generally. But the gain would be a saving of many lives and the elimination of a lot of suffering—plus lots of free choices by those whose lives were saved. Is it at all plausible that the overall result of such a divine intervention would have made the world worse? Is there any other response that the theist can make to this point?

John Hick

John Hick (1922–) is an English philosopher and theologian who has taught at Cornell University, Princeton Theological Seminary, the Claremont Graduate School, and the University of Birmingham (England). He is a major contributor to contemporary philosophy of religion. In this selection, Hick offers two main responses to the problem of evil: the free will theodicy (as a solution to the problem of moral evil) and what might be described as the soul-making theodicy (as a solution to the problem of natural evil, which he refers to as the problem of suffering).

The Problem of Evil, from *Philosophy of Religion*

To many, the most powerful positive objection to belief in God is the fact of evil. Probably for most agnostics it is the appalling depth and extent of human suffering, more than anything else, that makes the idea of a loving Creator seem so implausible and disposes them toward one or another of the various naturalistic theories of religion.

As a challenge to theism, the problem of evil has traditionally been posed in the form of a dilemma: if God is perfectly loving, he must wish to abolish evil; and if he is all-powerful, he must be able to abolish evil. But evil exists; therefore God cannot be both omnipotent and perfectly loving.

Certain solutions, which at once suggest themselves, have to be ruled out so far as the Judaic-Christian faith is concerned.

To say, for example (with contemporary Christian Science), that evil is an illusion of the human mind, is impossible within a religion based upon the stark realism of the Bible. Its pages faithfully reflect the characteristic mixture of good and evil in human experience. They record every kind of sorrow and suffering, every mode of man's inhumanity to man and of his painfully insecure existence in the world. There is no attempt to regard evil as anything but dark, menacingly ugly, heart-rending, and crushing. In the Christian scriptures, the climax of this history of evil is the crucifixion of Jesus, which is presented not only as a case of utterly unjust suffering, but as the violent and murderous rejection of God's Messiah. There can be no doubt, then, that for biblical faith evil is unambiguously evil and stands in direct opposition to God's will.

Again, to solve the problem of evil by means of the theory . . . of a finite deity who does the best he can with a material, intractable, and coeternal with himself, is to have abandoned that basic premise of Hebrew-Christian monotheism; for the theory amounts to rejecting belief in the infinity and sovereignty of God.

Indeed, any theory that would avoid the problem of the origin of evil by depicting it as an ultimate con-

From John Hick, Philosophy of Religion, *2nd ed. (Englewood Cliffs, N.J.: Prentice Hall, 1973).*

stituent of the universe, co-ordinate with good, has been repudiated in advance by the classic Christian teaching, first developed by Augustine, that evil represents the going wrong of something that in itself is good. Augustine holds firmly to the Hebrew-Christian conviction that the universe is *good*—that is to say, it is the creation of a good God for a good purpose. He completely rejects the ancient prejudice that matter is evil. There is, according to Augustine, higher and lower, greater and lesser goods in immense abundance and variety; but everything that has being is good in its own way and degree, except in so far as it may have become spoiled or corrupted. Evil—whether it be an evil will, an instance of pain, or some disorder or decay in nature—has not been set there by God, but represents the distortion of something that is inherently valuable. Whatever exists is, as such, and in its proper place, good; evil is essentially parasitic upon good, being disorder and perversion in a fundamentally good creation. This understanding of evil as something negative means that it is not willed and created by God; but it does not mean (as some have supposed) that evil is unreal and can be disregarded. On the contrary, the first effect of this doctrine is to accentuate even more the question of the origin of evil.[1]

> **1** Even if God does not will evil, the question is why he (or she or it) permits evil to exist.

Theodicy, as many modern Christian thinkers see it, is a modest enterprise, negative rather than positive in its conclusions. It does not claim to explain, nor to explain away, every instance of evil in human experience, but only to point to certain considerations that prevent the fact of evil (largely incomprehensible though it remains) from constituting a final and insuperable bar to rational belief in God.[2]

In indicating these considerations it will be useful to follow the traditional division of the subject. There is the problem of *moral evil* or wickedness: why does an all-good and all-powerful God permit

> **2** Hick uses the term "theodicy" to refer to the intellectual task of solving or at least defusing the problem of evil. To achieve even the relatively modest goal that he specifies, the contradiction that Mackie alleged to exist would have to be avoided.

this? And there is the problem of the *nonmoral evil* of suffering or pain, both physical and mental: why has an all-good and all-powerful God created a world in which this occurs?

Christian thought has always considered moral evil in its relation to human freedom and responsibility. To be a person is to be a finite center of freedom, a (relatively) free and self-directing agent responsible for one's own decisions. This involves being free to act wrongly as well as to act rightly. The idea of a person who can be infallibly guaranteed always to act rightly is self-contradictory. There can be no certainty in advance that a genuinely free moral agent will never choose amiss. Consequently, the possibility of wrongdoing or sin is logically inseparable from the creation of finite persons, and to say that God should not have created beings who might sin amounts to saying that he should not have created people.

This thesis has been challenged in some recent philosophical discussions of the problem of evil, in which it is claimed that no contradiction is involved in saying that God might have made people who would be genuinely free but who could at the same time be guaranteed always to act rightly. A quote from one of these discussions follows:

> If there is no logical impossibility in a man's freely choosing the good on one, or on several occasions, there cannot be a logical impossibility in his freely choosing the good on every occasion. God was not, then, faced with a choice between making innocent automata and making beings who, in acting freely, would sometimes go wrong: there was open to him the obviously better possibility of making beings who would act freely but always go right. Clearly, his failure to avail himself of this possibility is inconsistent with his being both omnipotent and wholly good.*

A reply to this argument is indirectly suggested in another recent contribution to the discussion. If by a free action we mean an action that is not externally compelled but that flows from the nature of the agent as he reacts to the circumstances in which he finds himself, there is indeed no contradiction between our being free and our actions being "caused" (by our own nature) and therefore being in principle predictable.③

There is a contradiction, however, in saying that God is the cause of our acting as we do but that we are free beings *in relation to God.* There is, in other words, a contradiction in saying that God has made us so that we shall of necessity act in a certain way, and that we are genuinely independent persons in relation to him. If all our thoughts and actions are divinely predestined, however free and morally responsible we may seem to be to ourselves, we cannot be free and morally responsible in the sight of God, but must instead be his helpless puppets. Such "freedom" is like that of a patient acting out a series of posthypnotic suggestions: he appears, even to himself, to be free, but his volitions have actually been predetermined by another will, that of the hypnotist, in relation to whom the patient is not a free agent.④

③ This would be a compatibilist conception of freedom. See Annotation 18 in the previous selection and Chapter 5.

④ Hick responds that a person's being shaped by God so as to act in specific ways, would not be genuine freedom, even if the person's actions were still caused by his (or her) nature.

A different objector might raise the question of whether or not we deny God's omnipotence if we admit that he is unable to create persons who are free from the risks inherent in personal freedom. The answer that has always been given is that to create such beings is logically impossible. It is no limitation upon God's power that he cannot accomplish the logically impossible, since there is nothing here to accomplish, but only a meaningless conjunction of words—in this case "person who is not a person." God is able to create beings of any and every conceivable kind; but creatures who lack moral freedom, however superior they might be to human beings in other respects, would not be what we mean by persons. They would constitute a different form of life that God might have brought into existence instead of persons. When we ask why God did not create such beings in place of persons the traditional answer is that only persons could, in any meaningful sense, become "children of God," capable of entering into a personal relationship with their Creator by a free and uncompelled response to his love.⑤

---

*J. L. Mackie, "Evil and Omnipotence," pp. 119–120 of this book.

When we turn from the possibility of moral evil as a correlate of man's personal freedom to its actuality, we face something that

> **5** Here the claim has to be that the value of having genuine persons with free will is greater than that of having person-like beings who lack freedom, even allowing for the negative value of the evil that results (and also better than having a freedom that is limited by occasional divine interventions— see Discussion Question 2 to the Mackie selection on p. 122).

must remain inexplicable even when it can be seen to be possible. For we can never provide a complete causal explanation of a free act; if we could, it would not be a free act. The origin of moral evil lies forever concealed within the mystery of human freedom.

The necessary connection between moral freedom and the possibility, now actualized, of sin throws light upon a great deal of the suffering that afflicts mankind. For an enormous amount of human pain arises either from the inhumanity or the culpable incompetence of mankind. This includes such major scourges as poverty, oppression and persecution, war, and all the injustice, indignity, and inequity that occur even in the most advanced societies. These evils are manifestations of human sin. Even disease is fostered to an extent, the limits of which have not yet been determined by psychosomatic medicine, by emotional and moral factors seated both in the individual and in his social environment. To the extent that all of these evils stem from human failures and wrong decisions, their possibility is inherent in the creation of free persons inhabiting a world that presents them with real choices followed by real consequences.

We may now turn more directly to the problem of suffering. Even though the major bulk of actual human pain is traceable to man's misused freedom as a sole or part cause, there remain other sources of pain that are entirely independent of the human will, for example, earthquake, hurricane, storm, flood, drought, and

> **6** The problem of suffering is thus essentially the same as the problem of natural or physical evil.

blight.**6** In practice, it is often impossible to trace a boundary between the suffering that results from human wickedness and folly and that which falls upon mankind from without; both kinds of suffering are inextricably mingled together in human experience. For our present purpose, however, it is important to note that the latter category

does exist and that it seems to be built into the very structure of our world. In response to it, theodicy, if it is wisely conducted, follows a negative path. It is not possible to show positively that each item of human pain serves a divine purpose of good; but, on the other hand, it does seem possible to show that the divine purpose as it is understood in Judaism and Christianity could not be forwarded in a world that was designed as a permanent hedonistic paradise.

An essential premise of this argument concerns the nature of the divine purpose in creating the world. The sceptic's assumption is that man is to be viewed as a completed creation and that God's purpose in making the world was to provide a suitable dwelling-place for this fully formed creature. Since God is good and loving, the environment that he has created for human life to inhabit will naturally be as pleasant and comfortable as possible. The problem is essentially similar to that of a man who builds a cage for some pet animal. Since our world, in fact, contains sources of hardship, inconvenience, and danger of innumerable kinds, the conclusion follows that this world cannot have been created by a perfectly benevolent and all-powerful deity.

Christianity, however, has never supposed that God's purpose in the creation of the world was to construct a paradise whose inhabitants would experience a maximum of pleasure and a minimum of pain. The world is seen, instead, as a place of "soul making" or person making in which free beings, grappling with the tasks and challenges of their existence in a common environment, may become "children of God" and "heirs of eternal life." A way of thinking theologically of God's continuing creative purpose for man was suggested by some of the early Hellenistic Fathers of the Christian Church, especially Irenaeus. Following hints from Saint Paul, Irenaeus taught that man has been made as a person in the image of God but has not yet been brought as a free and responsible agent into the finite likeness of God, which is revealed in Christ. Our world, with all its rough edges, is the sphere in which this second and harder stage of the creative process is taking place.**7**

> **7** Since God is supposedly omnipotent, it cannot be that he needs the hardships of the world as a means for "making souls" (see the discussion in Mackie). Thus the claim has to be that the *process* of making souls in this way is itself valuable enough to outweigh the cost.

This conception of the world (whether or not set in Irenaeus's theological framework) can be supported by the method of negative theodicy. Suppose, contrary to fact, that this world were a paradise from which all possibility of pain and suffering were excluded. The consequences would be very far-reaching. For example, no one could ever injure anyone else: the murderer's knife would turn to paper or his bullets to thin air; the bank safe, robbed of a million dollars, would miraculously become filled with another million dollars (without this device, on however large a scale, proving inflationary); fraud, deceit, conspiracy, and treason would somehow always leave the fabric of society undamaged. Again, no one would ever be injured by accident: the mountain climber, steeplejack, or playing child falling from a height would float unharmed to the ground; the reckless driver would never meet with disaster. There would be no need to work, since no harm could result from avoiding work; there would be no call to be concerned for others in time of need or danger, for in such a world there could be no real needs or dangers.

To make possible this continual series of individual adjustments, nature would have to work by "special providences" instead of running according to general laws that men must learn to respect on penalty of pain or death. The laws of nature would have to be extremely flexible: sometimes gravity would operate, sometimes not; sometimes an object would be hard and solid, sometimes soft. There could be no sciences, for there would be no enduring world structure to investigate. In eliminating the problems and hardships of an objective environment, with its own laws, life would become like a dream in which, delightfully but aimlessly, we would float and drift at ease.⁸

⸻
8 Obviously there are intermediate alternatives between this one and the actual world, worlds with some hazards but fewer or less extreme ones. A complete defense of the soul-making theodicy will have to claim that all of these alternative worlds are also unsatisfactory for the purpose of soul making.
⸻

One can at least begin to imagine such a world. It is evident that our present ethical concepts would have no meaning in it. If, for example, the notion of harming someone is an essential element in the concept of a wrong action, in our hedonistic paradise there could be no wrong actions—nor any right actions in distinction from wrong. Courage and fortitude would have no point in an environment in which there is, by definition, no danger or difficulty. Generosity, kindness, the *agape* aspect of love, prudence, unselfishness, and all other ethical notions which presuppose life in an objective environment could not even be formed. Consequently, such a world, however well it might promote pleasure, would be very ill adapted for the development of the moral qualities of human personality. In relation to this purpose it might be the worst of all possible worlds!

It would seem, then, that an environment intended to make possible the growth in free beings of the finest characteristics of personal life must have a good deal in common with our present world. It must operate according to general and dependable laws; and it must involve real dangers, difficulties, problems, obstacles, and possibilities of pain, failure, sorrow, frustration, and defeat. If it did not contain the particular trials and perils that—subtracting man's own very considerable contribution—our world contains, it would have to contain others instead.

To realize this is not, by any means, to be in possession of a detailed theodicy. It is to understand that this world, with all its "heartaches and the thousand natural shocks that flesh is heir to," an environment so manifestly not designed for the maximization of human pleasure and the minimization of human pain, may nevertheless be rather well adapted to the quite different purpose of "soul making."⁹

⸻
9 How much like our actual world would such a world have to be? (See Discussion Question 1.)
⸻

These considerations are related to theism as such. Specifically Christian theism goes further in the light of the death of Christ, which is seen paradoxically both (as the murder of the divine Son) as the worst thing that has ever happened and (as the occasion of man's salvation) as the best thing that has ever happened. As the supreme evil turned to supreme good, it provides the paradigm for the distinctively Christian reaction to evil. Viewed from the standpoint of Christian faith, evils do not cease to be evils; and certainly, in view of Christ's healing work, they cannot be said to have been sent by God. Yet, it has been the persistent claim of those seriously and wholeheartedly committed to Christian discipleship that tragedy, though truly tragic, may nevertheless be turned, through a man's reaction to it, from a cause of despair and alienation from God to a stage in the fulfillment of God's loving purpose for that individual. As the greatest of all evils, the crucifixion of Christ was made the occasion of man's redemption, so good can be won from other evils. As Jesus saw his execution by the Romans as an experience which God desired him to accept, an experience which was to be brought within the sphere of the divine purpose and made to serve the divine ends, so the Christian response to calamity is to accept the adversities, pains, and afflictions which life brings, in order that they can be turned to a positive spiritual use.

At this point, theodicy points forward in two ways to the subject of life after death. . . .

First, although there are many striking instances of good being triumphantly brought out of evil through a man's or a woman's reaction to it, there are many other cases in which the opposite has happened. Sometimes obstacles breed strength of character, dangers evoke courage and unselfishness, and calamities produce patience and moral steadfastness. But sometimes they lead, instead, to resentment, fear, grasping selfishness, and disintegration of character. Therefore, it would seem that any divine purpose of soul making that is at work in earthly history must continue beyond this life if it is ever to achieve more than a very partial and fragmentary success.

Second, if we ask whether the business of soul making is worth all the toil and sorrow of human life, the Christian answer must be in terms of a future good great enough to justify all that has happened on the way to it. [10]

> [10] Hick seems to be conceding here that the soul making would not have enough value to outweigh the cost without an afterlife that the developed souls will eventually experience.

Discussion Questions

1. How plausible is it that a world created for the purpose of soul making would contain the kinds and degrees of natural evil that are to be found in the actual world? In thinking about this question, it may help to consider an analogy: Suppose that you are developing an environment for the purpose of building the character of children—and that you also care strongly about the well-being of those children. What sorts of obstacles and challenges would you put into the designed environment, and what sorts would you exclude?

2. Suppose that we grant that (contrary to Mackie's claim) God could not give people free will and still control their choices so that they always do the right thing. Suppose that it is also granted that unlimited free will is so great a value that God would be wrong to engage in occasional intervention. A question that remains is whether free will must bring with it the possibility of choices as horrendous as Hitler's decision to bring about the murder of the 6 million Jews. Is any person who has free will automatically capable of doing things as evil as that? Or is there still a limit in at least many normal free people as to how much evil they are capable of? If the latter of these possibilities is the case, why didn't God make all people good enough that at least really extreme evils would be ruled out?

MUST WE HAVE REASONS TO BELIEVE IN GOD?

Walter Kaufmann

Walter Kaufmann (1921–1980) taught philosophy at Princeton University. He is best known for his discussions and translations of Friedrich Nietzsche (a nineteenth-century German philosopher and poet) and his work in the philosophy of religion. This selection discusses a version of Pascal's argument that belief in God is the best wager in a situation of uncertainty. As Kaufmann notes, his version is more complete and explicit than Pascal's own.

Pascal's Wager, from *Critique of Religion and Philosophy*

Pascal, mathematician, physicist, polemicist, and mystic, sewed into the lining of his coat a piece of parchment dating from the day of his great mystical experience, to remind himself that the God of Abraham, Isaac, and Jacob is not the God of the philosophers and theologians. He saw the weaknesses of the old proofs of God's existence and had some intimations that faith is related somehow to commitment. His attempt to spell out this commitment in his posthumously published *Pensées* is, however, weirder still than any of the proofs of the philosophers and theologians.

"Either God exists, or he does not exist," argues Pascal; and neither proposition can be proved. So we must wager: this strange word is Pascal's own; and with a desperate concern, he proceeds to figure out the odds. If we wager that God exists and we are right, we win everything; if we are wrong we lose nothing. If you passed this up, "you would be imprudent." What more could you ask?

Pascal stops with these two possibilities; but we might as well complete the picture and spell out all four possibilities.

	God Does Exist	**God Does Not Exist**
We wager, God exists:	We win everything; we hit the jackpot; up we go.	We lose nothing.
We wager, He does not:	We lose everything; we have had it; down we go.	We win nothing.

Clearly, this is the opportunity of a lifetime. Anybody who is not out of his mind will bet that God exists. This looks much better than the proofs of Anselm and Aquinas. Or has Pascal, too, overlooked something?

The first objection of which people usually think is ill advised. They say that we cannot induce belief merely by representing to ourselves the great ad-

vantage of belief.[1] But it is Pascal's *logic* that is at fault, not his psychology.

"Follow the way by which they began; by acting as if they believe, taking the holy water, having masses said, etc. Even this will naturally make you believe, and deaden your acuteness." Pascal's psychology is corroborated by millions of examples in totalitarian countries: once people realize the dreadful risks of nonbelief and the rewards for the acceptance of beliefs, it takes most men at most a few years to believe quite firmly. First, one makes believe that one believes, and soon one does believe.

That is the origin of most religious faith: the child begins by acting like the grownups who believe, and soon believes himself. The proofs come later, if at all. *Religious belief generally starts as make-believe.*

What Pascal overlooked was the hair-raising possibility that God might out-Luther Luther. A special area in hell might be reserved for those who go to mass. Or God might punish those whose faith is prompted by prudence. Perhaps God prefers the abstinent to those who whore around with some denomination he despises. Perhaps he reserves special rewards for those who deny themselves the comfort of belief. Perhaps the intellectual ascetic will win all while those who compromised their intellectual integrity lose everything.[2]

There are many other possibilities. There might be many gods, including one who favors people like Pascal; but the other gods might overpower or outvote him, à la Homer. Nietzsche might well have applied to Pascal his cutting remark about Kant: when he wagered on God, the great mathematician "became an idiot."

[1] The point of the objection is that a person cannot just choose to believe something—because belief is not within voluntary control.

[2] The general point in this and the following paragraph is that there are many, probably indefinitely many, possible gods or god-like beings, so that a full assessment of the wager would have to take account of the results if any of these should turn out to exist instead of the God that Pascal has in mind.

From Walter Kaufmann, Critique of Religion and Philosophy *(New York: Harper, 1958).*

Even an astounding competence in mathematics provides no safeguard against pathetic pitfalls when it comes to arguments about religion. Some people think that the existence of some scientists, especially atomic physicists, who hold traditional beliefs creates a strong presumption that these beliefs must be true. Clearly, it does not.

Arguments based on the realities of this world can prove at best the existence of such morally revolt-ing functionaries as Kafka portrays in his two great novels, and the God of Pascal's wager who saves those who shun imprudent risks is not the God of Abraham. When God said to Abraham, "Go from your land, and from your kindred, and from your father's house to the land that I will show you," Abraham could not have wagered that he stood to win all without risking anything. The God of Abraham, Isaac, and Jacob asks men to risk everything.

Discussion Questions

1. As Kaufmann reports (see Annotation 1), one objection often made to Pascal is that we cannot just choose to believe something because it would be advantageous to do so—where the underlying reason is that belief is not within our voluntary control. Do you think it is possible to simply adopt a belief because for some reason you want to or think that it would be good to do so? (Think of some examples.) Now consider Kaufmann's response in the following paragraph. Is he right that belief can be arrived at in the way he suggests? Does this show that belief is voluntary after all?

2. In Kaufmann's version (which follows Pascal), the value of the possibility where a person believes (and acts accordingly), but God does not exist, is said to be that nothing is lost. Does this seem like the right assessment? Or are there significant losses or gains in this sit-uation as well? Does this make any difference to the overall argument?

3. Pascal clearly has in mind more or less the standard conception of God, as discussed in the introduction to this chapter. Do you think he is right about how a God of that sort would respond to one who believed in him (or her or it) on pragmatic grounds of this sort? Is the result as clear as Pascal thinks even if other possible gods and god-like beings are, for some reason, not considered?

4. If all other possible gods and god-like beings are brought into the picture, the matrix of possible choices and results becomes vastly more complicated, with many different possibilities for belief and many different possible results. Does any definite choice of belief or nonbelief emerge as rationally preferred? Why or why not?

W. K. Clifford

William Kingdon Clifford (1845–1879) was an English mathematician and philosopher, who taught at Cambridge University and the University of London. He is best known for the essay presented here, in which he argues for a strong moral obligation never to believe anything except on the basis of sufficient evidence, evidence that has stood up under careful scrutiny. Though religion is not specifically mentioned until the end of the essay, it is religious belief and belief in God that Clifford has primarily in mind, and he is thus rejecting belief on the basis of faith. (In his own case, this led Clifford to reject his previously held Catholic beliefs in favor of **agnosticism**.)

The Ethics of Belief

A shipowner was about to send to sea an emigrant-ship. He knew that she was old, and not over-well built at the first; that she had seen many seas and climes, and often had needed repairs. Doubts had been suggested to him that possibly she was not seaworthy. These doubts preyed upon his mind and made him unhappy; he thought that perhaps he ought to have her thoroughly overhauled and refitted, even though this should put him to great expense. Before the ship sailed, however, he succeeded in overcoming these melancholy reflections. He said to himself that she had gone safely through so many voyages and weathered so many storms that it was idle to suppose she would not come safely home from this trip also. He would put his trust in Providence, which could hardly fail to protect all these unhappy families that were leaving their fatherland to seek for better times elsewhere. He would dismiss from his mind all ungenerous suspicions about the honesty of builders and contractors. In such ways he acquired a sincere and comfortable conviction that his vessel was thoroughly safe and seaworthy; he watched her departure with a light heart, and benevolent wishes for the success of the exiles in their strange new home that was to be; and he got his insurance-money when she went down in mid-ocean and told no tales.

What shall we say of him? Surely this, that he was verily guilty of the death of those men. It is admitted that he did sincerely believe in the soundness of his ship; but the sincerity of his conviction can in no wise help him, because *he had no right to believe on such evidence as was before him.* He had acquired his belief not by honestly earning it in patient investigation, but by stifling his doubts. And although in the end he may have felt so sure about it that he could not think otherwise, yet inasmuch as he had knowingly and willingly worked himself into that frame of mind, he must be held responsible for it.①

Let us alter the case a little, and suppose that the ship was not unsound after all; that she made her voyage safely, and many others after it. Will that diminish the guilt of her owner? Not one jot. When an action is once done, it is right or wrong for ever; no accidental failure of its good or evil fruits can possibly alter that. The man would not have been innocent, he would only have been not found out. The question of right or wrong has to do with the origin of his belief, not the matter of it; not what it was, but how he got it; not whether it turned out to be true or false, but whether he had a right to believe on such evidence as was before him.②

There was once an island in which some of the inhabitants professed a religion teaching neither the doctrine of original sin nor that of eternal punishment. A suspicion got abroad that the professors of this religion had made use of unfair means to get their doctrines taught to children. They were accused of wresting the laws of their country in such a way as to remove children from the care of their natural and legal guardians; and even of stealing them away and keeping them concealed from their friends and relations. A certain number of men formed themselves into a society for the purpose of agitating the public about this matter. They published grave accusations against individual citizens of the highest position and character, and did all in their power to injure these citizens in the exercise of their professions. So great was the noise they made, that a Commission was appointed to investigate the facts; but after the Commission had carefully inquired into the evidence that could be got, it appeared that the accused were innocent. Not only had they been accused on insufficient evidence, but the evidence of their innocence was such as the agitators might easily have obtained, if they had attempted a fair inquiry. After these disclosures the inhabitants of the country looked upon the members of the agitating society, not only as person whose judgment was to be distrusted, but also as no longer to be counted hon-

> ① It is clear in this case, first, that the shipowner has no very good reason or evidence for his belief in the soundness of the ship; and, second, that he is acting in an irresponsible and negligent fashion in allowing the voyage to proceed without making reasonably sure that the ship is safe. Clifford is claiming further that his very holding of the belief that the ship is sound is immoral, that he has no (moral) right to believe in this way.

> ② Clifford claims further that if it turned out to be true that the ship was safe, this would make no difference to this last point (nor to the others).

From W. K. Clifford, Lectures and Essays *(1879).*

ourable men. For although they had sincerely and conscientiously believe in the charges they had made, yet *they had no right to believe on such evidence as was before them.* Their sincere convictions, instead of being honestly earned by patient inquiring, were stolen by listening to the voice of prejudice and passion.③

③ Again, the claim is not just that the beliefs in question were irrational and unjustified, nor merely that the people in question were wrong to act on them in the ways that they did, but that the holding of the beliefs was itself immoral.

Let us vary this case also, and suppose, other things remaining as before, that a still more accurate investigation proved the accused to have been really guilty. Would this make any difference in the guilt of the accusers? Clearly not; the question is not whether their belief was true or false, but whether they entertained it on wrong grounds. They would no doubt say "Now you see that we were right after all; next time perhaps you will believe us." And they might be believed, but they would not thereby become honourable men. They would not be innocent, they would only be not found out. Every one of them, if he chose to examine himself *in foro conscientiae,* would know that he had acquired and nourished a belief, when he had no right to believe on such evidence as was before him; and therein he would know that he had done a wrong thing.④

④ And again the truth of the belief would make no difference.

It may be said, however, that in both of these supposed cases it is not the belief which is judged to be wrong, but the action following upon it. The shipowner might say, "I am perfectly certain that my ship is sound, but still I feel it my duty to have her examined, before trusting the lives of so many people to her." And it might be said to the agitator, "However convinced you were of the justice of your cause and the truth of your convictions, you ought not to have made a public attack upon any man's character until you had examined the evidence on both sides with the utmost patience and care."

In the first place, let us admit that, so far as it goes, this view of the case is right and necessary; right, because even when a man's belief is so fixed that he cannot think otherwise, he still has a choice in regard to the action suggested by it, and so cannot escape the duty of investigating on the ground of the strength of his convictions; and necessary, because those who are not yet capable of controlling their feelings and thoughts must have a plain rule dealing with overt acts.

But this being premised as necessary, it becomes clear that it is not sufficient, and that our previous judgment is required to supplement it. For it is not possible so to sever the belief from the action it suggests as to condemn the one without condemning the other. No man holding a strong belief on one side of a question, or even wishing to hold a belief on one side, can investigate it with such fairness and completeness as if he were really in doubt and unbiased; so that the existence of a belief not founded on fair inquiry unfits a man for the performance of this necessary duty.⑤

⑤ Here is one response to the suggestion that it is only action on unfounded belief and not the belief itself that is immoral. This point is debatable, however: is a person who holds a belief, even one who is thoroughly convinced, really *incapable* of investigating the issue further in a fair and unbiased manner?

Nor is that truly a belief at all which has not some influence upon the actions of him who holds it. He who truly believes that which prompts him to an action has looked upon the action to lust after it, he has committed it already in his heart. If a belief is not realized immediately in open deeds, it is stored up for the guidance of the future. It goes to make a part of that aggregate of beliefs which is the link between sensation and action at every moment of all our lives, and which is so organized and compacted together that no part of it can be isolated from the rest, but every new addition modifies the structure of the whole. No real belief, however trifling and fragmentary it may seem, is ever truly insignificant; it prepares us to receive more of its like, confirms those which resembled it before, and weakens others; and so gradually it lays a stealthy train in our inmost thoughts, which may some day explode into overt action, and leave its stamp upon our character for ever.⑥

⑥ Another problem with the foregoing suggestion is that even if a person does not act on a poorly grounded belief in the short run, it is much more difficult to keep it from influencing other beliefs and eventually action in the long run.

And no one man's belief is in any case a private matter which concerns himself alone. Our lives are guided by that general conception of the course of things which has been created by society for social purposes. Our words, our phrases, our forms and processes and modes of thought, are common property, fashioned and perfected from age to age; an heirloom which every succeeding generation inherits as a precious deposit and a sacred trust to be handed on to the next one, not unchanged but enlarged and purified, with some clear marks of its proper handiwork. Into this, for good or ill, is woven every belief of every man who has speech of his fellows. An awful privilege, and an awful responsibility, that we should help to create the world in which posterity will live.

In the two supposed cases which have been considered, it has been judged wrong to believe on insufficient evidence, or to nourish belief by suppressing doubts and avoiding investigation. The reason of this judgment is not far to seek: it is that in both these cases the belief held by one man was of great importance to other men. But forasmuch as no belief held by one man, however seemingly trivial the belief, and however obscure the believer, is ever actually insignificant or without its effect on the fate of mankind, we have no choice but to extend our judgment to all cases of belief whatever. Belief, that sacred faculty which prompts the decisions of our will, and knits into harmonious working all the compacted energies of our being, is ours not for ourselves, but for humanity. It is rightly used on truths which have been established by long experience and waiting toil, and which have stood in the fierce light of free and fearless questioning. Then it helps to bind men together, and to strengthen and direct their common action. It is desecrated when given to unproved and unquestioned statements, for the solace and private pleasure: of the believer; to add a tinsel splendour to the plain straight road of our life and display a bright mirage beyond it; or even to drown the common sorrows of our kind by a self-deception which allows them not only to cast down, but also to degrade us. Whoso would deserve well of his fellows in this matter will guard the purity of his belief with a very fanaticism of jealous care, lest at any time it should rest on an unworthy object, and catch a stain which can never be wiped away.

It is not only the leader of men, statesman, philosopher, or poet, that owes this bounden duty to mankind. Every rustic who delivers in the village alehouse his slow, infrequent sentences, may help to kill or keep alive the fatal superstitions which clog his race. Every hard-worked wife of an artisan may transmit to her children beliefs which shall knit society together, or rend it in pieces. No simplicity of mind, no obscurity of station, can escape the universal duty of questioning all that we believe.[7]

> [7] Clifford points to another way in which even a poorly grounded belief that is not acted on can have a larger influence: by its influence on other people and on the culture at large, both with regard to the specific issue in question and related issues and with regard to the general practice of inquiry. Are these points enough to establish the "universal duty" of which he speaks?

It is true that this duty is a hard one, and the doubt which comes out of it is often a very bitter thing. It leaves us bare and powerless where we thought that we were safe and strong. To know all about anything is to know how to deal with it under all circumstances. We feel much happier and more secure when we think we know precisely what to do, no matter what happens, than when we have lost our way and do not know where to turn. And if we have supposed ourselves to know all about anything, and to be capable of doing what is fit in regard to it, we naturally do not like to find that we are really ignorant and powerless, that we have to begin again at the beginning, and try to learn what the thing is and how it is to be dealt with—if indeed anything can be learnt about it. It is the sense of power attached to a sense of knowledge that makes men desirous of believing, and afraid of doubting.

This sense of power is the highest and best of pleasures when the belief on which it is founded is a true belief, and has been fairly earned by investigation. For then we may justly feel that it is common property, and hold good for others as well as for ourselves. Then we may be glad, not that *I* have learned secrets by which I am safer and stronger, but that *we men* have got mastery over more of the world; and we shall be strong, not for ourselves, but in the name of Man and in his strength. But if the belief has been accepted on insufficient evidence, the pleasure is a stolen one. Not only does it deceive ourselves by giving us a sense of power which we do not really possess, but it is sinful, because it is stolen in defiance of our duty to mankind. That duty is to guard ourselves from such beliefs as from a pestilence, which may shortly master our own body and then spread to the rest of the town. What would be thought of one who, for the sake of a sweet fruit, should deliberately run the risk of bringing a plague upon his family and his neighbours?

And, as in other such cases, it is not the risk only which has to be considered; for a bad action is always bad at the time when it is done, no matter what happens afterwards. Every time we let ourselves believe for unworthy reasons, we weaken our powers of self-control, of doubting, of judicially and fairly weighing evidence. We all suffer severely enough from the maintenance and support of false beliefs and the fatally wrong actions which they lead to, and the evil born when one such belief is entertained is great and wide. But a greater and wider evil arises when the credulous character is maintained and supported, when a habit of believing for unworthy reasons is fostered and made permanent. If I steal money from any person, there may be no harm done by the mere transfer of possession; he may not feel the loss, or it may prevent him from using the money badly. But I cannot help doing this great wrong towards Man, that I make myself dishonest. What hurts society is not that it should lose its property, but that it should become a den of thieves; for then it must cease to be society. This is why we ought not to do evil that good may come; for at any rate this great evil has come, that we have done evil and are made wicked thereby. In like manner, if I let myself believe anything on insufficient evidence, there may be no great harm done by the mere belief; it may be true after all, or I may never have occasion to exhibit it in outward acts. But I cannot help doing this great wrong towards Man, that I make myself credulous. The danger to society is not merely that it should believe wrong things, though that is great enough; but that it should become credulous, and lose the habit of testing things and inquiring into them; for then it must sink back into savagery.

The harm which is done by credulity in a man is not confined to the fostering of a credulous character in others, and consequent support of false beliefs. Habitual want of care about what I believe leads to habitual want of care in others about the truth of what is told to me. Men speak the truth to one another when each reveres the truth in his own mind and in the other's mind; but how shall my friend revere the truth in my mind when I myself am careless about it, when I believe things because I want to believe them, and because they are comforting and pleasant? Will he not learn to cry, "Peace," to me, when there is no peace? By such a course I shall surround myself with a thick atmosphere of falsehood and fraud, and in that I must live. It may matter little to me, in my cloud-castle of sweet illusions and darling lies; but it matters much to Man that I have made my neighbours ready to deceive. The credulous man is father to the liar and the cheat; he lives in the bosom of this his family, and it is no marvel if he should become even as they are. So closely are our duties knit together, that whoso shall keep the whole law, and yet offend in one point, he is guilty of all.

To sum up: it is wrong always, everywhere, and for anyone, to believe anything upon insufficient evidence.[8]

> [8] And, he might have added, without adequate critical scrutiny.

If a man, holding a belief which he was taught in childhood or persuaded of afterwards, keeps down and pushes away any doubts which arise about it in his mind, purposely avoids the reading of books and the company of men that call in question or discuss it, and regards as impious those question which cannot easily be asked without disturbing it—the life of that man one long sin against mankind.

If this judgment seems harsh when applied to those simple souls who have never known better, who have been brought up from the cradle with a horror of doubt, and taught that their eternal welfare depends on *what* they believe then it leads to the very serious question, *Who hath made Israel to sin?*

It may be permitted me to fortify this judgment with the sentence of Milton—

> A man may be a heretic in the truth; and if he believe things only because his pastor says so, or the assembly so determine, without knowing other reason, though his belief be true, yet the very truth he holds becomes his heresy.

And with this famous aphorism of Coleridge—

> He who begins by loving Christianity better than Truth, will proceed by loving his own sect or Church better than Christianity, and end in loving himself better than all.

Inquiry into the evidence of a doctrine is not to be made once for all, and then taken as finally settled. It is never lawful to stifle a doubt; for either it can be honestly answered by means of the inquiry already made, or else it proves that the inquiry was not complete.

"But," says one, "I am a busy man; I have no time for the long course of study which would be necessary to make me in any degree a competent judge of certain questions, or even able to understand the nature of the arguments." Then he should have no time to believe.⑨

⑨ Here is one problem with Clifford's view: what if there are issues that make an essential practical difference to how we act, but which we have no time (or perhaps no capacity) to investigate in the way that Clifford's principle requires?

Discussion Questions

1. What is the basis for the moral principle about belief that Clifford eventually formulates? It is quite plausible that accepting beliefs uncritically and without adequate evidence can have bad consequences, both in the short run and the long run, in the ways that Clifford describes. But is this enough to show that there is a duty never to believe in this way? Do we have a duty never to do anything that might lead to bad consequences? Is there any way to strengthen Clifford's argument here?

2. It is fairly common for there to be practical situations (a) in which one cannot avoid acting (often these are ones where inaction is itself a significant action), but (b) where the correct choice of action depends on issues that there is not enough time to settle in the way that Clifford's principle would require—or where adequate and relevant evidence is simply not available, given the available methods of inquiry. As an example, consider a desperately ill or injured person, who will surely die if nothing is done, but where there is insufficient evidence to decide which of the available treatments is best. What would Clifford say about such a case?

William James

William James (1842–1910) was an American philosopher and psychologist, who taught at Harvard. He was one of the founders of the pragmatist movement in philosophy, and made important contributions to epistemology, metaphysics, and the philosophy of religion. A characteristic Jamesian view is that truth is to be measured by practical success ("the truth is what works"). In this selection, James argues for the rational permissibility of religious belief based on voluntary commitment or faith rather than evidence.

The Will To Believe

In the recently published Life by Leslie Stephen of his brother, Fitz-James, there is an account of a school to which the latter went when he was a boy. The teacher, a certain Mr. Guest, used to converse with his pupils in this wise: "Gurney, what is the difference between justification and sanctification?—Stephen, prove the omnipotence of God!" etc. In the midst of our Harvard freethinking and indifference we are prone to imagine

From an address to the Philosophical Clubs of Yale and Brown Universities, first published in 1896.

that here at your good old orthodox College conversation continues to be somewhat upon this order; and to show you that we at Harvard have not lost all interest in these vital subjects, I have brought with me to-night something like a sermon on justification by faith to read to you—I mean an essay in justification *of* faith, a defence of our right to adopt a believing attitude in religious matters, in spite of the fact that our merely logical intellect may not have been coerced. "The Will to Believe," accordingly, is the title of my paper.

I have long defended to my own students the lawfulness of voluntarily adopted faith; but as soon as they have got well imbued with the logical spirit, they have as a rule refused to admit my contention to be lawful philosophically,① even though in point of fact they were personally all the time chock-full of some faith or other themselves. I am all the while, however, so profoundly convinced that my own position is correct, that your invitation has seemed to me a good occasion to make my statements more clear. Perhaps your minds will be more open than those with which I have hitherto had to deal. I will be as little technical as I can, though I must begin by setting up some technical distinctions that will help us in the end.

> ① By "lawful philosophically," James seems to mean that voluntarily adopted faith is rationally permissible or acceptable. (As he makes clear later, he does not think it is always mandatory.)

I

Let us give the name of *hypothesis* to anything that may be proposed to our belief; and just as the electricians speak of live and dead wires, let us speak of any hypothesis as either *live* or *dead.* A live hypothesis is one which appeals as a real possibility to him to whom it is proposed. If I ask you to believe in the Mahdi, the notion makes no electric connection with your nature—it refuses to scintillate with any credibility at all. As an hypothesis it is completely dead.② To an Arab, however (even if he

> ② The Mahdi was a Sudanese religious and military leader in the latter part of the nineteenth century who claimed to be the successor of Mohammed. By "willingness to act" in the following passage, James means willingness to act as though the hypothesis were true.

be not one of the Mahdi's followers), the hypothesis is among the mind's possibilities: it is alive. This shows that deadness and liveness in an hypothesis are not intrinsic properties, but relations to the individual thinker. They are measured by his willingness to act. The maximum of liveness in an hypothesis means willingness to act irrevocably. Practically, that means belief; but there is some believing tendency wherever there is willingness to act at all.

Next, let us call the decision between two hypotheses an *option.* Options may be of several kinds. They may be—1, *living* or *dead;* 2, *forced* or *avoidable;* 3, *momentous* or *trivial;* and for our purposes we may call an option a *genuine* option when it is of the forced, living, and momentous kind.

1. A living option is one in which both hypotheses are live ones. If I say to you: "Be a theosophist or be a Mohammedan," it is probably a dead option, because for you neither hypothesis is likely to be alive. But if I say: "Be an agnostic or be a Christian," it is otherwise: trained as you are, each hypothesis makes some appeal, however small, to your belief.

2. Next, if I say to you: "Choose between going out with your umbrella or without it," I do not offer you a genuine option, for it is not forced. You can easily avoid it by not going out at all. Similarly, if I say, "Either love me or hate me," "Either call my theory true or call it false," your option is avoidable. You may remain indifferent to me, neither loving nor hating, and you may decline to offer any judgment as to my theory. But if I say, "Either accept this truth or go without it," I put on you a forced option, for there is no standing place outside of the alternative. Every dilemma based on a complete logical disjunction, with no possibility of not choosing, is an option of this forced kind.③

> ③ It seems to follow that any claim can be made to present a "forced option," simply by contrasting it with its logical contradictory.

3. Finally, if I were Dr. Nansen and proposed to you to join my North Pole expedition, your option would be momentous; for this would probably be your only similar opportunity, and your choice now would either exclude you from the North Pole sort of immortality altogether or put at least the chance of it into your hands. He who refuses to embrace a unique opportunity loses the prize as surely as if he tried and failed. *Per contra,* the option is trivial when the

opportunity is not unique, when the stake is insignificant, or when the decision is reversible if it later prove unwise. Such trivial options abound in the scientific life. A chemist finds an hypothesis live enough to spend a year in its verification: he believes in it to that extent. But if his experiments prove inconclusive either way, he is quit for his loss of time, no vital harm being done.

It will facilitate our discussion if we keep all these distinctions well in mind.

II

The next matter to consider is the actual psychology of human opinion. When we look at certain facts, it seems as if our passional and volitional nature lay at the root of all our convictions. When we look at others, it seems as if they could do nothing when the intellect had once said its say. Let us take the latter facts up first.

4 One possible objection to James's view, as to Pascal's wager, is that genuine belief is not voluntary. James agrees that a person can't voluntarily believe just anything, as these examples show.

Does it not seem preposterous on the very face of it to talk of our opinions being modifiable at will? Can our will either help or hinder our intellect in its perceptions of truth?[4] Can we, by just willing it, believe that Abraham Lincoln's existence is a myth, and that the portraits of him in McClure's Magazine are all of some one else? Can we, by any effort of our will, or by any strength of wish that it were true, believe ourselves well and about when we are roaring with rheumatism in bed, or feel certain that the sum of the two one-dollar bills in our pocket must be a hundred dollars? We can *say* any of these things, but we are absolutely impotent to believe them; and of just such things is the whole fabric of the truths that we do believe in made up,—matters of fact, immediate or remote, as Hume said, and relations between ideas, which are either there or not there for us if we see them so, and which if not there cannot be put there by any action of our own.

In Pascal's *Thoughts* there is a celebrated passage known in literature as Pascal's wager.[5] In it he tries to force us into Christianity by reasoning as if our concern with

5 See the previous selection, by Kaufmann, for a discussion of Pascal's wager.

truth resembled our concern with the stakes in a game of chance. Translated freely his words are these: You must either believe or not believe that God is—which will you do? Your human reason cannot say. A game is going on between you and the nature of things which at the day of judgment will bring out either heads or tails. Weigh what your gains and your losses would be if you should stake all you have on heads, or God's existence: if you win in such case, you gain eternal beatitude; if you lose, you lose nothing at all. If there were an infinity of chances, and only one for God in this wager, still you ought to stake your all on God; for though you surely risk a finite loss by this procedure, any finite loss is reasonable, even a certain one is reasonable, if there is but the possibility of infinite gain. Go, then, and take holy water, and have masses said; belief will come and stupefy your scruples. . . . Why should you not? At bottom, what have you to lose?

You probably feel that when religious faith expresses itself thus, in the language of the gaming-table, it is put to its last trumps. Surely Pascal's own personal belief in masses and holy water had far other springs; and this celebrated page of his is but an argument for others, a last desperate snatch at a weapon against the hardness of the unbelieving heart. We feel that a faith in masses and holy water adopted wilfully after such a mechanical calculation would lack the inner soul of faith's reality; and if we were ourselves in the place of the Deity, we should probably take particular pleasure in cutting off believers of this pattern from their infinite reward. It is evident that unless there be some pre-existing tendency to believe in masses and holy water, the option offered to the will by Pascal is not a living option. Certainly no Turk ever took to masses and holy water on its account; and even to us Protestants these means of salvation seem such foregone impossibilities that Pascal's logic, invoked for them specifically, leaves us unmoved. As well might the Mahdi write to us, saying, "I am the Expected One whom God has created in his effulgence. You shall be infinitely happy if you confess me; otherwise you shall be cut off from the light of the sun. Weigh, then, your infinite gain if I am genuine against your finite sacrifice if I am not!" His logic would be that of Pascal; but he would vainly use it on us, for the hypothesis he offers us is dead. No tendency to act on it exists in us to any degree.

The talk of believing by our volition seems, then, from one point of view, simply silly. From another point of view it is worse than silly, it is vile.⑥ When one turns to the magnificent edifice of the physical sciences, and sees how it was reared; what thousands of disinterested moral lives of men lie buried in its mere foundations;

⑥ A second objection is that believing by choice (rather than as a result of evidence), even if it were possible, would be "vile," morally unacceptable—this is basically Clifford's view.

what patience and postponement, what choking down of preference, what submission to the icy laws of outer fact are wrought into its very stones and mortar; how absolutely impersonal it stands in its vast augustness—then how besotted and contemptible seems every little sentimentalist who comes blowing his voluntary smoke-wreaths, and pretending to decide things from out of his private dream! Can we wonder if those bred in the rugged and manly school of science should feel like spewing such subjectivism out of their mouths? The whole system of loyalties which grow up in the schools of science go dead against its toleration; so that it is only natural that those who have caught the scientific fever should pass over to the opposite extreme, and write sometimes as if the incorruptibly truthful intellect ought positively to prefer bitterness and unacceptableness to the heart in its cup.

It fortifies my soul to know
That, though I perish, Truth is so—

sings Clough, while Huxley exclaims: "My only consolation lies in the reflection that, however bad our posterity may become, so far as they hold by the plain rule of not pretending to believe what they have no reason to believe, because it may be to their advantage so to pretend [the word 'pretend' is surely here redundant], they will not have reached the lowest depth of immortality." And that delicious *enfant terrible* Clifford writes: "Belief is desecrated when given to unproved and unquestioned statements for the solace and private pleasure of the believer.... Whoso would deserve well of his fellows in this matter will guard the purity of his belief with a very fanaticism of jealous care, lest at any time it should rest on an unworthy object, and catch a stain which can never be wiped away.... If [a] belief has been accepted on insufficient evidence [even though the belief be true, as Clifford on the same page explains] the pleasure is a stolen one.... It is sinful because it is stolen in defiance of our duty to mankind. That duty is to guard ourselves from such beliefs as from a pestilence which may shortly master our own body and then spread to the rest of the town.... It is wrong always, everywhere, and for every one, to believe anything upon insufficient evidence."

III

All this strikes one as healthy, even when expressed, as by Clifford, with somewhat too much of robustious pathos in the voice. Free-will and simple wishing do seem, in the matter of our credences, to be only fifth wheels to the coach. Yet if any one should thereupon assume that intellectual insight is what remains after wish and will and sentimental preference have taken wing, or that pure reason is what then settles our opinions, he would fly quite as directly in the teeth of the facts.

It is only our already dead hypotheses that our willing nature is unable to bring to life again. But what has made them dead for us is for the most part a previous action of our willing nature of an antagonistic kind. When I say "willing nature," I do not mean only such deliberate volitions as may have set up habits of belief that we cannot now escape from—I mean all such factors of belief as fear and hope, prejudice and passion, imitation and partisanship, the circumpressure of our caste and set. As a matter of fact we find ourselves believing, we hardly know how or why. Mr. Balfour gives the name of "authority" to all those influences, born of the intellectual climate, that make hypotheses possible or impossible for us, alive or dead. Here in this room, we all of us believe in molecules and the conservation of energy, in democracy and necessary progress, in Protestant Christianity and the duty of fighting for "the doctrine of the immortal Monroe," all for no reasons worthy of the name. We see into these matters with no more inner clearness, and probably with much less, than any disbeliever in them might possess. His unconventionality would probably have some grounds to show for its conclusions; but for us, not insight, but the *prestige* of the opinions, is what makes the spark shoot from them and light up our sleeping magazines of faith. Our reason is quite satisfied, in nine hundred and ninety-nine cases out of every thousand of us, if it can find a few arguments that will do to recite in case our credulity is criticised by some one else. Our faith is faith in some one else's faith, and in the greatest matters this is most the case.⑦

⑦ James responds that almost all our beliefs result from our "willing nature," in which he includes all factors other than evidence that produce belief: fear, hope, prejudice, social pressures and influences (especially prestige), etc. The suggestion seems to be that belief on this sort of basis is simply unavoidable. (Would this mean that it can't be wrong in the way that Clifford claims?)

Our belief in truth itself, for instance, that there is a truth, and that our minds and it are made for each other—what is it but a passionate affirmation of desire, in which our social system backs us up? We want to have a truth; we want to believe that our experiments and studies and discussions must put us in a continually better and better position towards it; and on this line we agree to fight out our thinking lives. But if a pyrrhonistic sceptic asks us *how we know* all this, can our logic find a reply? No! certainly it cannot. It is just one volition against another—we

⑧ Is the nonexistence of truth itself an intelligible possibility? What would it mean for there to simply be no truth at all? (Would that claim itself be true?) What about the possibility that there is truth, but that our minds are somehow incapable of comprehending it?

willing to go in for life upon a trust or assumption which he, for his part, does not care to make.⑧

As a rule we disbelieve all facts and theories for which we have no use. Clifford's cosmic emotions find no use for Christian feelings. Huxley belabors the bishops because there is no use for sacerdotalism in his scheme of life. Newman, on the contrary, goes over to Romanism, and finds all sorts of reasons good for staying there, because a priestly system is for him an organic need and delight. Why do so few "scientists" even look at the evidence for telepathy, so called? Because they think, as a leading biologist, now dead, once said to me, that even if such a thing were true, scientists ought to band together to keep it suppressed and concealed. It would undo the uniformity of Nature and all sorts of other things without which scientists cannot carry on their pursuits. But if this very man had been shown something which as a scientist he might *do* with telepathy, he might not only have examined the evidence, but even have found it good enough. This very law which the logicians would impose upon us—

if I may give the name of logicians to those who would rule out our willing nature here—is based on nothing but their own natural wish to exclude all elements for which they, in their professional quality of logicians, can find no use.

Evidently, then, our non-intellectual nature does influence our convictions. There are passional tendencies and volitions which run before and others which come after belief, and it is only the latter that are too late for the fair, and they are not too late when the previous passional work has been already in their own direction.⑨ Pascal's argument, instead of being powerless, then seems a regular clincher, and is the last stroke needed to make our faith in masses and holy water complete. The state of things is evidently far from simple; and pure insight and logic, whatever they might do ideally, are not the only things that really do produce our creeds.

⑨ James seems to reject the claim that belief is never voluntary, suggesting that it is only claims that are not "live" that cannot be accepted in this way. But he seems to be running together genuinely voluntary belief with belief that results from "passional" factors. Couldn't a passional belief still be involuntary? Indeed, isn't that the most likely situation?

IV

Our next duty, having recognized this mixed-up state of affairs, is to ask whether it be simply reprehensible and pathological, or whether, on the contrary, we must treat it as a normal element in making up our minds. The thesis I defend is, briefly stated, this: *Our passional nature not only lawfully may, but must, decide an option between propositions, whenever it is a genuine option that cannot by its nature be decided on intellectual grounds; for to say, under such circumstances, "Do not decide, but leave the question open," is itself a passional decision—just like deciding yes or no—and is attended with the same risk of losing the truth.*⑩ The thesis thus abstractly expressed will, I trust, soon become quite clear. But I must first indulge in a bit more of preliminary work.

⑩ Think carefully about the content of this principle, relating it back to the previous discussions of the various elements, especially the idea of a "genuine" option.

. . .

VII

One more point, small but important, and our preliminaries are done. There are two ways of looking at our duty in the matter of opinion—ways entirely different, and yet ways about whose difference the theory of knowledge seems hitherto to have shown very little concern. *We must know the truth;* and *we must avoid error*—these are our first and great commandments as would-be knowers; but they are not two ways of stating an identical commandment, they are two separable laws. Although it may indeed happen that when we believe the truth *A,* we escape as an incidental consequence from believing the falsehood *B,* it hardly ever happens that by merely disbelieving *B* we necessarily believe *A.* We may in escaping *B* fall into believing other falsehoods, *C* or *D,* just as bad as *B;* or we may escape *B* by not believing anything at all, not even *A.*

Believe truth! Shun error!—these, we see, are two materially different laws; and by choosing between them we may end by coloring differently our whole intellectual life. We may regard the chase for truth as paramount, and the avoidance of error as secondary; or we may, on the other hand, treat the avoidance of error as more imperative, and let truth take its chance.[11] Clifford, in the instructive passage which I have quoted, exhorts us to the latter course. Believe nothing, he tells us, keep your mind in suspense forever, rather than by closing it on insufficient evidence incur the awful risk of believing lies. You, on the other hand, may think that the risk of being in error is a very small matter when compared with the blessings of real knowledge, and be ready to be duped many times in your investigation rather than postpone indefinitely the chance of guessing true. I myself find it impossible to go with Clifford. We must remember that these feelings of our duty about either truth or error are in any case only expressions of our passional life. Biologically considered, our minds are as ready to grind out

[11] James's point here is that it would be easy to avoid error if one gave no weight to also finding truth, and almost as easy to find truth if there were no concern to avoid error—think how a person could do each of these things. What is hard is to do both, thus raising the question of how much weight to give each of these goals.

falsehood as veracity, and he who says, "Better go without belief forever than believe a lie!" merely shows his own preponderant private horror of becoming a dupe. He may be critical of many of his desires and fears, but this fear he slavishly obeys. He cannot imagine any one questioning its binding force. For my own part, I have also a horror of being duped; but I can believe that worse things than being duped may happen to a man in this world: so Clifford's exhortation has to my ears a thoroughly fantastic sound. It is like a general informing his soldiers that it is better to keep out of battle forever than to risk a single wound. Not so are victories either over enemies or over nature gained. Our errors are surely not such awfully solemn things. In a world where we are so certain to incur them in spite of all our caution, a certain lightness of heart seems healthier than this excessive nervousness on their behalf. At any rate it seems the fittest thing for the empiricist philosopher.

VIII

And now, after all this introduction, let us go straight at our question. I have said, and now repeat it, that not only as a matter of fact do we find our passional nature influencing us in our opinions, but that there are some options between opinions in which this influence must be regarded both as an inevitable and as a lawful determinant of our choice.

I fear here that some of you my hearers will begin to scent danger, and lend an inhospitable ear. Two first steps of passion you have indeed had to admit as necessary—we must think so as to avoid dupery, and we must think so as to gain truth; but the surest path to those ideal consummations, you will probably consider, is from now onwards to take no further passional step.

Well, of course, I agree as far as the facts will allow. Wherever the option between losing truth and gaining it is not momentous, we can throw the chance of *gaining truth* away, and at any rate save ourselves from any chance of *believing falsehood,* by not making up our minds at all till objective evidence has come. In scientific questions, this is almost always the case; and even in human affairs in general, the need of acting is seldom so urgent that a false belief to act on is better than no belief at all. Law courts, indeed, have to decide on the best evidence attainable for the moment, because a judge's duty is to make law as well as to ascertain it, and (as a learned judge once said to me) few cases are worth spending much time over: the great thing is to have them decided on *any* acceptable principle, and got out of the way. But in our dealings with objective nature we obviously are recorders, not makers, of the truth; and decisions for the mere sake of deciding promptly and getting on to the next business would be wholly out of place. Throughout the breadth of physical nature facts are what they are quite independently of us, and seldom is there any such hurry about them that the risks of being duped by believing a premature theory need be faced. The questions here are always trivial options, the hypotheses are hardly living (at any rate not living for us spectators), the choice between believing truth or falsehood is seldom forced.⟦12⟧ The attitude of sceptical balance is therefore the absolutely wise one if we would escape mistakes. What difference, indeed, does it make to most of us whether we have or have not a theory of the Röntgen rays, whether we believe or not in mind-stuff, or have a conviction about the causality of conscious states? It makes no difference. Such options are not forced on us. On every account it is better not to make them, but still keep weighing reasons *pro et contra* with an indifferent hand.

⟦12⟧ Think carefully about each of these claims. None of them is as obvious as James seems to think.

. . . Let us agree, however, that wherever there is no forced option, the dispassionately judicial intellect with no pet hypothesis, saving us, as it does, from dupery at any rate, ought to be our ideal.

The question next arises: Are there not somewhere forced options in our speculative questions, and can we (as men who may be interested at least as much in positively gaining truth as in merely escaping dupery) always wait with impunity till the coercive evidence shall have arrived? It seems a priori improbable that the truth should be so nicely adjusted to our needs and powers as that. In the great boarding-house of nature, the cakes and the butter and the syrup seldom come out so even and leave the plates so clean. Indeed, we should view them with scientific suspicion if they did.

IX

Moral questions immediately present themselves as questions whose solution cannot wait for sensible proof. A moral question is a question not of what sensibly exists, but of what is good, or would be good if it did exist. Science can tell us what exists; but to compare the *worths,* both of what exists and of what does not exist, we must consult not science, but what Pascal calls our heart. Science herself consults her heart when she lays it down that the infinite ascertainment of fact and correction of false belief are the supreme goods for man. Challenge the statement, and science can only repeat it oracularly, or else prove it by showing that such ascertainment and correction bring man all sorts of other goods which man's heart in turn declares. The question of having moral beliefs at all or not having them is decided by our will. Are our moral preferences true or false, or are they only odd biological phenomena, making things good or bad for *us,* but in themselves indifferent? How can your pure intellect decide?⟦13⟧ If your heart does not *want* a world of moral reality, your head will assuredly never make you believe in one. Mephistophelian scepticism, indeed, will satisfy the head's play-instincts much better than any rigorous idealism can. Some men (even at the student age) are so naturally cool-hearted that the moralistic hypothesis never has for them any pungent life, and in their supercilious presence the hot young moralist always feels strangely ill at ease. The appearance of knowingness is on their side, of *naïveté* and gullibility on his. Yet, in the inarticulate heart of him, he clings to it that he is not a dupe, and that there is a realm in which (as Emerson says) all their wit and intellectual superiority is no better than the cunning of a fox. Moral scepticism can no more be refuted or proved by logic than intellectual scepticism can. When we stick to it that there *is* truth (be it of either kind), we do so with our whole nature, and resolve to stand or fall by the results. The sceptic with his whole nature adopts the doubting attitude; but which of us is the wiser, Omniscience only knows.

⟦13⟧ There are two questions here. One is whether there are any moral truths at all, and the second is *which* moral claims are true if any are. Can the answer to either of these be settled in a way that would satisfy Clifford?

Turn now from these wide questions of good to a certain class of questions of fact, questions concerning personal relations, states of mind between one man and another. *Do you like me or not?*—for example. Whether you do or not depends, in countless instances, on whether I meet you half-way, am willing to assume that you must like me, and show you trust and expectation. The previous faith on my part in your liking's existence is in such cases what makes your liking come. But if I stand aloof, and refuse to budge an inch until I have objective evidence, until you shall have done something apt, . . . ten to one your liking never comes. How many women's hearts are vanquished by the mere sanguine insistence of some man that they *must* love him! he will not consent to the hypothesis that they cannot. The desire for a certain kind of truth here brings about that special truth's existence; and so it is in innumerable cases of other sorts. Who gains promotions, boons, appointments, but the man in whose life they are seen to play the part of live hypotheses, who discounts them, sacrifices other things for their sake before they have come, and takes risks for them in advance? His faith acts on the powers above him as a claim, and creates its own verification.

A social organism of any sort whatever, large or small, is what it is because each member proceeds to his own duty with a trust that the other members will simultaneously do theirs. Wherever a desired result is achieved by the co-operation of many independent persons, its existence as a fact is a pure consequence of the precursive faith in one another of those immediately concerned. A government, an army, a commercial system, a ship, a college, an athletic team, all exist on this condition, without which not only is nothing achieved, but nothing is even attempted. A whole train of passengers (individually brave enough) will be looted by a few highwaymen, simply because the latter can count on one another, while each passenger fears that if he makes a movement of resistance, he will be shot before any one else backs him up. If we believed that the whole car-full would rise at once with us, we should each severally rise, and train-robbing would never even be attempted. There are, then, cases where a fact cannot come at all unless a preliminary faith exists in its coming. *And where faith in a fact can help create the fact,* that would be an insane logic which should say that faith running ahead of scientific evidence is the "lowest kind of immorality" into which a thinking being can fall. Yet such is the logic by which our scientific absolutists pretend to regulate our lives!

X

In truths dependent on our personal action, then, faith based on desire is certainly a lawful and possibly an indispensable thing.[14]

But now, it will be said, these are all childish human cases, and have nothing to do with great cosmical matters, like the question of religious faith. Let us then pass on to that. Religions differ so much in their accidents that in discussing the religious question we must make it very generic and broad. What then do we now mean by the religious hypothesis? Science says things are; morality says some things are better than other things; and religion says essentially two things.

First, she says that the best things are the more eternal things, the overlapping things, the things in the universe that throw the last stone, so to speak, and say the final word. "Perfection is eternal,"—this phrase of Charles Secrétan seems a good way of putting this first affirmation of religion, a affirmation which obviously cannot yet be verified scientifically at all.

The second affirmation of religion is that we are better off even now if we believe her first affirmation to be true.[15]

Now, let us consider what the logical elements of this situation are *in case the religious hypothesis in both its branches be really true.* (Of course, we must admit that possibility at the outset. If we are to discuss the question at all, it must involve a living option. If for any of you religion be a hypothesis that cannot, by any living possibility be true, then you need go no farther. I speak to the "saving remnant" alone.) So proceeding, we see, first, that religion offers itself as a *momentous* option. We are supposed to gain, ever now, by our belief, and to lose

[14] James should say here both that our actions may affect the truth and that our beliefs affect how we act. This is how belief (faith) in a fact may help to create that very fact.

[15] This is a rather meager conception of what "religion says." Does any actual religion say that merely believing the first claim will make a person significantly better off?

by our non-belief, a certain vital good. Secondly, religion is a *forced* option, so far as that good goes. We cannot escape the issue by remaining sceptical and waiting for more light, because, although we do avoid error in that way *if religion be untrue,* we lose the good, *if it be true,* just as certainly as if we positively chose to disbelieve.⟦16⟧ It is as if a man should hesitate indefinitely to ask a certain woman to marry him because he was not perfectly sure that she would prove an angel after he brought her home. Would he not cut himself off from that particular angel-possibility as decisively as if he went and married some one else? Scepticism, then, is not avoidance of option; it is option of a certain particular kind of risk. *Better risk loss of truth than chance of error*—that is your faith-vetoer's exact position. He is actively playing his stake as much as the believer is; he is backing the field against the religious hypothesis, just as the believer is backing the religious hypothesis against the field. To preach scepticism to us as a duty until "sufficient evidence" for religion be found, is tantamount therefore to telling us, when in presence of the religious hypothesis, that to yield to our fear of its being error is wiser and better than to yield to our hope that it may be true. It is not intellect against all passions, then; it is only intellect with one passion laying down its law. And by what, forsooth, is the supreme wisdom of this passion warranted? Dupery for dupery, what proof is there that dupery through hope is so much worse than dupery through fear? I, for one, can see no proof; and I simply refuse obedience to the scientist's command to imitate his kind of option, in a case where my own stake is important enough to give me the right to choose my own form of risk. If religion be true and the evidence for it be still insufficient, I do not wish, by putting your extinguisher upon my nature (which feels to me as if it had after all some business in this matter), to forfeit

⟦16⟧ Here the idea of a forced option seems to be understood in a somewhat different and stronger way than was explained earlier, one that in effect incorporates the idea that the choice is momentous: any option can be made one side of an exhaustive disjunction (see Annotation 3). But not just any option will be one where a vital good can be achieved only by accepting it, so that the choice is either to accept it or to lose that good.

my sole chance in life of getting upon the winning side—that chance depending, of course, on my willingness to run the risk of acting as if my passional need of taking the world religiously might be prophetic and right.⟦17⟧

All this is on the supposition that it really may be prophetic and right, and that, even to us who are discussing the matter, religion is a live hypothesis which may be true. Now, to most of us religion comes in a still further way that makes a veto on our active faith even more illogical. The more perfect and more eternal aspect of the universe is represented in our religions as having personal form. The universe is no longer a mere *It* to us, but a *Thou,* if we are religious; and any relation that may be possible from person to person might be possible here. For instance, although in one sense we are passive portions of the universe, in another we show a curious autonomy, as if we were small active centres on our own account. We feel, too, as if the appeal of religion to us were made to our own active goodwill, as if evidence might be forever withheld from us unless we met the hypothesis half-way. To take a trivial illustration: just as a man who in a company of gentlemen made no advances, asked a warrant for every concession, and believed no one's word without proof, would cut himself off by such churlishness from all the social rewards that a more trusting spirit would earn—so here, one who should shut himself up in snarling logicality and try to make the gods extort his recognition willy-nilly, or not get it at all, might cut himself off forever from his only opportunity of making the gods' acquaintance.⟦18⟧ This feeling, forced on us we know not whence, that by obstinately believing that there are gods (although not to do so would be so easy both for our

⟦17⟧ This argument depends heavily on there being only two options: accept "religion" (and have a chance of a great good) or refuse to accept it (and lose that chance). This is very close to Pascal's wager and faces the same problem that there are really many more options.

⟦18⟧ Here James tries to connect the issue of religious belief with the earlier discussion of the way in which one's beliefs and resulting actions may affect personal relations. Does the fact that the very existence of the being to whom one might relate is in doubt make a difference to this point?

logic and our life) we are doing the universe the deepest service we can, seems part of the living essence of the religious hypothesis. If the hypothesis *were* true in all its parts, including this one, then pure intellectualism, with its veto on our making willing advances, would be an absurdity; and some participation of our sympathetic nature would be logically required. I, therefore, for one, cannot see my way to accepting the agnostic rules for truth-seeking, or wilfully agree to keep my willing nature out of the game. I cannot do so for this plain reason, that *a rule of thinking which would absolutely prevent me from acknowledging certain kinds of truth if those kinds of truth were really there, would be an irrational rule.* [19] That for me is the long and short of the formal logic of the situation, no matter what the kinds of truth might materially be.

[19] "Acknowledging" is misleading here, since it suggests the situation where the truth in question is apparent or recognizable in some way; it would be better to substitute just "believing."

I confess I do not see how this logic can be escaped. But sad experience makes me fear that some of you may still shrink from radically saying with me, *in abstracto,* that we have the right to believe at our own risk any hypothesis that is live enough to tempt our will. I suspect, however, that if this is so, it is because you have got away from the abstract logical point of view altogether, and are thinking (perhaps without realizing it) of some particular religious hypothesis which for you is dead. The freedom to "believe what we will" you apply to the case of some patent superstition; and the faith you think of is the faith defined by the schoolboy when he said, "Faith is when you believe something that you know ain't true." I can only repeat that this is misapprehension. *In concreto,* the freedom to believe can only cover living options which the intellect of the individual cannot by itself resolve; and living options never seem absurdities to him who has them to consider.

When I look at the religious question as it really puts itself to concrete men, and when I think of all the possibilities which both practically and theoretically it involves, then this command that we shall put a stopper on our heart, instincts, and courage, and *wait*—acting of course meanwhile more or less as if religion were *not* true*—till doomsday, or till such time as our intellect and sense working together may have raked in evidence enough—this command, I say, seems to me the queerest idol ever manufactured in the philosophic cave. Were we scholastic absolutists, there might be more excuse. If we had an infallible intellect with its objective certitudes, we might feel ourselves disloyal to such a perfect organ of knowledge in not trusting to it exclusively, in not waiting for its releasing word. But if we are empiricists, if we believe that no bell in us tolls to let us know for certain when truth is in our grasp, then it seems a piece of idle fantasticality to preach so solemnly our duty of waiting for the bell. Indeed we *may* wait if we will—I hope you do not think that I am denying that—but if we do so, we do so at our peril as much as if we believed. In either case we *act,* taking our life in our hands. No one of us ought to issue vetoes to the other, nor should we bandy words of abuse. We ought, on the contrary, delicately and profoundly to respect one another's mental freedom: then only shall we bring about the intellectual republic; then only shall we have that spirit of inner tolerance without which all our outer tolerance is soulless, and which is empiricism's glory; then only shall we live and let live, in speculative as well as in practical things.

I began by a reference to Fitz-James Stephen; let me end by a quotation from him. "What do you think of yourself? What do you think of the world?" . . . These are questions with which all must deal as it seems good to them. They are riddles of the Sphinx, and in some way or other we must deal with them. . . . In all important transactions of life we have to take a leap in the dark. . . . If we decide to leave the riddles unanswered,

---

*Since belief is measured by action, he who forbids us to believe religion to be true necessarily also forbids us to act as we should if we did believe it to be true. The whole defence of religious faith hinges upon action. If the action required or inspired by the religious hypothesis is in no way different from that dictated by the naturalistic hypothesis then religious faith is a pure superfluity, better pruned away, and controversy about its legitimacy is a piece of idle trifling, unworthy of serious minds. I myself believe, of course that the religious hypothesis gives to the world an expression which specifically determine our reactions, and makes them in a large part unlike what they might be on a purely naturalistic scheme of belief.

that is a choice; if we waver in our answer, that, too, is a choice: but whatever choice we make, we make it at our peril. If a man chooses to turn his back altogether on God and the future, no one can prevent him; no one can show beyond reasonable doubt that he is mistaken. If a man thinks otherwise and acts as he thinks, I do not see that any one can prove that *he* is mistaken. Each must act as he thinks best; and if he is wrong, so much the worse for him. We stand on a mountain pass in the midst of whirling snow and blinding mist, through which we get glimpses now and then of paths which may be deceptive. If we stand still we shall be frozen to death. If we take the wrong road we shall be dashed to pieces. We do not certainly know whether there is any right one. What must we do? 'Be strong and of good courage.' Act for the best, hope for the best and take what comes. . . . If death ends all, we cannot meet death better."*

Discussion Questions

1. To what extent, if any, is it possible to voluntarily believe things? (See Kaufmann's discussion of the analogous point in relation to Pascal on p. 128.) How much does the answer to this question matter for James's position? Would it change his view very much if he spoke only of the rational permissibility of belief resulting from "passional" factors, without claiming that such belief is strictly voluntary?

2. Suppose that an option is not "live" in the sense that James defines. Might it not be still both forced and momentous? Isn't there a risk that a person will lose a great good by being unable to take certain options seriously? And if so, aren't there ways of overcoming this limitation? Couldn't one study accounts of the life of the Mahdi and the background of his views written by believers and perhaps thereby convert belief in the Mahdi into a "live" option? Would this be a rational thing to do in all such cases? Why or why not?

3. In a case where belief (faith) in a fact may help to create that very fact (or belief in an opposite fact may help to create that one) and where one strongly wants one of these facts to be true, is it rational to believe and act in a way that might help to bring about that fact, even though there is not adequate evidence for the belief? Is it morally acceptable to do so?

4. What happens if we consider different religious options (in James's fairly broad understanding of what counts as "religious"): different sorts of gods or religious teachings that cannot all be accepted at the same time? What do you think that James would say about such a case?

Liberty, Equality, Fraternity, p. 353, 2d ed., London, 1874.

3

Knowledge and Skepticism

The selections in this chapter are concerned with three main issues in the general area of philosophy known as the theory of knowledge or **epistemology,** all having to do in one way or another with whether and how knowledge of certain specified kinds is possible, and with the possibility and plausibility of **skepticism** with respect to the kinds of knowledge in question. The largest section of the chapter focuses on one of the most central issues of modern philosophy: the problem of the external world, which asks whether and how beliefs about material objects outside the mind are justified on the basis of sense perception. Two other sections deal with (a) the problem of **a priori** knowledge, which concerns the existence and nature of knowledge that is not based on sensory (or introspective) experience; and (b) the problem of **induction,** which asks whether and why it is justifiable to infer from apparent regularities found in observation to more general conclusions that extend beyond those observations.

Before we discuss these more specific problems, it will be helpful to say something about the concept of knowledge itself. According to a definition often characterized as traditional or standard, knowledge is (1) belief that is (2) true and (3) adequately justified. Problems can be raised about each of these three elements, but it will be adequate for the purposes of this chapter to understand **belief** as the mental acceptance or affirmation of a propositional claim and **truth** as the correspondence or agreement of that claim with whatever it is about. The nature of **justification** in the sense relevant to knowledge has been the subject of widespread debate in recent philosophy, but the authors of all the present selections would have accepted the view that justification is having a good reason or warrant for thinking that the claim in question is true.[1]

---

[1]It has become clear as a result of relatively recent discussion that the traditional definition of knowledge is inadequate in that there are cases in which the three conditions are satisfied but it is intuitively clear that genuine knowledge is not present. Intuitively, these are cases in which the belief is true in an accidental way that does not connect appropriately with the way in which it is justified. The problem has become known as "the Gettier problem," named after the philosopher who first discovered it, and the interested student can easily find discussions of it in philosophical dictionaries and encyclopedias.

One other preliminary remark is perhaps worth making: the issues discussed in this chapter, especially the second of the three discussed, rely heavily on concepts and terminology that are relatively technical and difficult. You will need to work at mastering these, and you should only expect gradual success, especially at first. This also applies to the material in this introduction: we have kept it short so that you can reread it easily, and if you do so, you will find concepts and issues that were initially puzzling gradually becoming clear.

Do We Have Knowledge of the External World?

It seems entirely obvious from the standpoint of both common sense and science that we have a great deal of knowledge of material objects, and of the material world generally, on the basis of sense experience. The basic issue is how this works, and in particular how sense experience provides us with justification of the sort just explained for the beliefs about material objects that we arrive at on the basis of it. One initial question concerns the nature of sense experience itself: When we have the sense experience of, for example, a table, what is it that we are most directly or immediately aware of? Contrary to the apparent view of common sense, most of the philosophers in this section would reply that the *direct* or *immediate* object of awareness in sense experience is *not* the external physical object whose presence the experience seems to reflect, but rather a subjective mental entity: an perceptual *idea,* in the terminology of John Locke and George Berkeley, or a sense-datum (plural: sense-data), in the terminology of more recent philosophers. Both René Descartes and Locke take such a view more or less for granted, as does Laurence BonJour; Berkeley argues for it at considerable length; and Thomas Reid rejects it.

If this view of the nature of sense experience is accepted, then the question becomes how claims about material objects can be justified on the basis of awareness of sensory ideas or sense-data. One alternative here is **representative realism:** the view that perceptual beliefs about material objects can be justified by inference from an awareness of the ideas or sense-data that lead us to have those beliefs and seem in some way to represent the corresponding objects. Descartes, Locke, and BonJour all defend versions of such a view, while Berkeley and Reid reject the possibility of any cogent inference of this sort.

A second, initially less obvious alternative is to say that material objects, rather than existing outside the mind, are in fact themselves nothing more than collections or patterns of sensory ideas or sense-data, including both those that are actually experienced and those that would be experienced under various conditions. All such views are versions of **idealism.** Berkeley defends one specific version of idealism, according to which the ideas that make up real material objects are systematically put into our human minds by God (who is thus the ultimate source of their reality). A more recent version of idealism that dispenses with God and takes the availability of orderly patterns of sense-data to be the most fundamental, not further explainable fact about reality is called **phenomenalism;** this view is explained and criticized by BonJour.

A third alternative, much closer to common sense, is to reject the common denominator of these two views, the idea that the immediate object of awareness in perceptual experience is a sensory idea or sense-datum, and hold instead that we are directly or immediately aware of material objects, with no need for the sort of justifying inference invoked by the representative realists. Once referred to as naïve realism because it was thought to be philosophically untenable, such a view has more recently been referred to simply as **direct realism.** A version of direct realism is defended by Reid, who argues that the acceptability of our sensory beliefs about the material world is a first principle of human thought, one that requires no further defense.

Are All Reasons Based on Experience?: A Priori Justification and Knowledge

The issue of a priori knowledge is structured around three main distinctions, all of them complicated and subtle—and easily confused with one another. First, there is a **metaphysical** distinction between two ways in which a proposition can be true or false. Some propositions, most philosophers agree, are logically or metaphysically **necessary:** true in any world or situation that is logically or metaphysically possible; while others are logically or metaphysically **contingent:** true in some logically or metaphysically possible worlds and not in others. Thus, for example, propositions of logic and mathematics are usually held to be necessary in this sense, while most propositions about things and happenings in the material world are contingent. (Some unfortunate propositions are **necessarily false:** false in every logically or metaphysically possible world; the proposition that $2 + 2 = 5$ is an example.)

Second, there is the **epistemological** distinction between two different ways in which a proposition can be *justified:* two different sorts of reasons for thinking that it is true (and derivatively, assuming that knowledge requires justification, two different kinds of knowledge). While it seems obvious that much of our knowledge depends for its justification on sense experience (and so is justified *a posteriori* or **empirically**), it has seemed equally obvious to most philosophers that there is knowledge that does not depend on sense experience for its justification, but is instead a priori: justified via pure reason or thought alone. Here the most obvious examples are again the claims of logic and mathematics, but there are many other sorts of claims that have been claimed (rightly or wrongly) to be justified a priori: metaphysical claims (for example, the claim that there must be an explanation for everything that happens or that space has only three dimensions); perhaps some **ethical** claims (such as that causing unnecessary suffering is morally wrong or that racial discrimination is unjust); and various claims about common-sense properties and relations (that nothing can be red all over and green all over at the same time or that all cubes have 12 edges). The central issues here are: First, how is such a priori knowledge possible, given that it is not justified by sense experience? Where exactly does the justification for such claims come from? And, second, what specific sorts of things are knowable on an a priori basis? In particular, does a priori knowledge include only essentially trivial (even though perhaps sometimes complicated) matters of definition (such as the claim that all bachelors are unmarried)—claims often referred to as **tautologies** or, more technically, as analytic?

Third, there is a logical or structural distinction between two kinds of propositions, analytic and synthetic. As Kant defines the notion, an **analytic** proposition is one of subject-predicate form whose predicate is included in its subject, either explicitly (all tall men are tall) or implicitly (all bachelors are unmarried). The point of the distinction for Kant is that if a proposition is analytic, then it is easy to see how it can be justified and known a priori: simply by understanding the concepts involved and noticing the relation of containment. What is problematic is how any **synthetic** proposition—one that does *not* have this sort of form, that is, in which the predicate is not contained in the subject—could still be justified and known a priori (something that Kant nonetheless believes to occur). What makes this distinction especially tricky is that some philosophers, such as Ayer, have retained these terms and the basic idea that a certain sort of logical structure can be used to explain a priori justification, while altering Kant's account of what this structural feature is. This raises the issue, often not addressed very explicitly, of whether the new account of analyticity has the same capacity to explain a priori justification that the old one did.

The main positions on the issue of the a priori are versions of **empiricism** and **rationalism.** Empiricism is a general view about human cognition that involves two main theses, each of them having to do with the relation between cognition and sense experience, and each of them reflected in Locke's thought, though one much more clearly and unambiguously than the other. The first thesis, most standardly referred to as **concept empiricism** (but it could also in relation to the following selections be called idea empiricism), is a claim about where and how the human mind acquires the ideas or concepts that it uses to think about the world or indeed about anything. According to the concept empiricist, all concepts are derived from sense experience (construed broadly so as to also include introspective experience). Here the main opposing view is the claim, held by Descartes and his rationalist successors, that at least some ideas or concepts are innate, "programmed" into the mind at birth (with this "programming" usually attributed to God). The issue of whether there are innate ideas (which is not in fact very relevant to the main issue concerning the a priori) is discussed by Descartes, Locke, and A. C. Ewing.

The second main strand of empiricism (the one that is more relevant to the present issue) lacks a completely standard label, but will be referred to here as **justificatory empiricism.** This is a view about the *reasons* or *warrant* for thinking that beliefs or propositional claims are true. According to one version of justificatory empiricism, all justification for claims that are not mere logical or definitional tautologies (not analytic in Kant's sense or perhaps in some other sense of that term) must derive from sense experience (again construed broadly so as to include introspection). Versions of this **moderate empiricist** view are defended by A. J. Ayer and by Wesley Salmon (in the induction section).[2]

The main alternative to moderate empiricism is the **moderate rationalist** view that a priori justification and a priori knowledge include more than mere definitional tautologies or analytic propositions. Instead, it is claimed, the human mind has the capacity for direct a priori insight into certain necessary features of reality. Here the main examples would be the kinds of claims briefly listed above, none of which are, according to the rationalist, mere matters of definition or analytic in any epistemologically helpful sense. (The moderate rationalist does not claim that all justification and knowledge is a priori—a view that very few philosophers since perhaps Plato have ever held.) Such a view is defended by Immanuel Kant (though with major qualifications that are not fully reflected in the present selection) and by Ewing.

IS INDUCTION JUSTIFIED?

The problem of induction concerns the justification for generalizing from regularities observed in experience to more general claims. Thus suppose that a large number of cases of some observable property or category A have been observed (by various observers and under widely varied collateral conditions). Suppose also that all the observed cases of A

---

[2]There is also a more radical version of empiricism that denies the existence of a priori justification or knowledge of any sort; this view is not represented in the present anthology. The main proponent of this more radical version of empiricism is the American philosopher and logician W. V. O. Quine.

have also been cases of some further observable property or category B. (A more general version of the problem would include the possibility that some definite and stable fraction m/n of A's have been B's). Given an observational premise of this sort, inductive reasoning of the most standard sort leads to the conclusion that *all* cases of A (observed or not, past, present, or future) are also cases of B (or in the more general version that approximately m/n of all A's are B's). It is obvious that reasoning of this sort is accepted by common sense and relied upon by science. The question is whether it is rationally justified, and if so, why: that is, why such a conclusion is genuinely likely to be true whenever the corresponding premise is true. Hume considers this issue in the more specific context of a causal claim (with A the supposed cause and B the supposed effect, and observed A's all being followed by B's). Having posed the problem, he argues for the skeptical view that there is no rational justification for an inductive conclusion because there is no cogent reasoning from the observational premise to the inductive conclusion. Salmon recapitulates Hume's account and then surveys a number of different responses, rejecting most of them but arguing that one response is at least promising. Ewing (in the a priori section) briefly defends one of the responses that Salmon rejects: a rationalist solution that holds that inductive reasoning is justified a priori. (As this suggests, there are important connections between the issue of induction and the issue of a priori justification, connections that are reflected at certain points in the reading.)

DO WE HAVE KNOWLEDGE OF THE EXTERNAL WORLD?

René Descartes

René Descartes (1596–1650), a French philosopher and mathematician, was one of the most important and influential philosophers of all time. Descartes is called "the father of modern philosophy" because several of the central problems and themes of modern (post-renaissance) philosophy first appear in his work: most fundamentally, the insistence on beginning with questions about knowledge (epistemological questions) rather than questions about reality (metaphysical questions). Among the more specific philosophical problems that first appear clearly in Descartes are the problem of the external world (concerning how claims about material objects can be justified on the basis of sense experience) and the mind-body problem (see Chapter 4). The *Meditations* is his most important and influential work.

Descartes's fundamental concern for issues of knowledge is reflected in the very first sentence of the *Meditations:* "Several years have now passed since I first realized how numerous were the false opinions that in my youth I had taken to be true, and thus how doubtful were all those that I had subsequently built upon them." Descartes lived in a time of great intellectual ferment, when medieval views were still being replaced by more modern ones and the scientific revolution was just underway. It was clear to him that many of the opinions he had accepted from various sources were false, and the central issue of the *Meditations* is how to correct this situation. Descartes's aim in writing the *Meditations* is to lay bare his process of thought so that the reader can follow along with him, think with him, and thereby come to the same conclusions he does.

Descartes's solution to the problem of how to eliminate erroneous beliefs is to accept only beliefs that are *certain,* in the sense of being incapable of being mistaken. His method for reaching certainty is to systematically doubt whole categories of belief, withholding assent from them on the basis of the mere *possibility* that they are false. He is thus suggesting that genuine knowledge requires certainty in the sense of *conclusive* justification: reasons strong enough to guarantee the truth of the claim. (Thus understood, Descartes agrees with the traditional conception of knowledge with one addition: knowledge is not merely justified true belief, but rather *conclusively* justified true belief.)

By the end of *Meditation One,* Descartes has suspended belief in every opinion that he has considered, first on the basis of the possibility that he might be dreaming and later on the basis of the more radical possibility that he might be deceived by an all-powerful evil genius. But in *Meditation Two,* he finds a belief that cannot be doubted for even the latter of these reasons: the belief that he himself exists as a thinking thing. Later he identifies other beliefs about which he thinks he can be certain on essentially the same basis: beliefs about his various conscious states of mind. And so the project in *Meditations Three* and *Six* is to reclaim as many of the previously suspended beliefs as possible on the basis of the indubitable beliefs identified in *Meditation Two.* In the end, you need to judge whether or not Descartes is successful at securing a foundation on the basis of which his previously held beliefs can be justified.

Meditations on First Philosophy in Which the Existence of God and the Distinction Between the Soul and the Body are Demonstrated

MEDITATION ONE: Concerning Those Things That Can Be Called into Doubt

Several years have now passed since I first realized how numerous were the false opinions that in my youth I had taken to be true, and thus how doubtful were all those that I had subsequently built upon them. ① And thus I realized that once in my life I had to raze everything to the ground and begin again from the original foundations, if I wanted to establish anything firm and lasting in the sciences. But the task seemed enormous, and I was waiting until I reached a point in my life that was so timely that no more suitable time for undertaking these plans of action would come to pass. For this reason, I procrastinated for so long that I would henceforth be at fault, were I to waste the time that remains for carrying out the project by brooding over it. Accordingly, I have today suitably freed my mind of all cares, secured for myself a period of leisurely tranquillity, and am withdrawing into solitude. At last I will apply myself earnestly and unreservedly to this general demolition of my opinions.

Yet to bring this about I will not need to show that

① Can you think of things that you believed when you were younger but no longer believe are true? Might some (or even many) of the things that you now believe turn out to be false in the same way? (Suppose someone asked you for your reasons for being confident about the truth of those beliefs of which you are confident: what would your answer be?)

From Meditations on First Philosophy, *3rd ed., translated by Donald A. Cress (Indianapolis: Hackett Publishing Company, 1993).*

all my opinions are false, which is perhaps something I could never accomplish. But reason now persuades me that I should withhold my assent no less carefully from opinions that are not completely certain and indubitable than I would from those that are patently false. For this reason, it will suffice for the rejection of all of these opinions, if I find in each of them some reason for doubt.② Nor therefore need I survey each opinion individually, a task that would be endless. Rather, because undermining the foundations will cause whatever has been built upon them to crumble of its own accord, I will attack straightaway those principles which supported everything I once believed.③

Surely whatever I had admitted until now as most true I received either from the senses or through the senses. However, I have noticed that the senses are sometimes deceptive; and it is a mark of prudence never to place our complete trust in those who have deceived us even once.

But perhaps, even though the senses do sometimes deceive us when it is a question of very small and distant things, still there are many other matters concerning which one simply cannot doubt, even though they are derived from the very same senses: for example, that I am sitting here next to the fire, wearing my winter dressing gown, that I am holding this sheet of paper in my hands, and the like. But on what grounds could one deny that these hands and this entire body are mine? Unless perhaps I were to liken myself to the insane, whose brains are impaired by such an unrelenting vapor of black bile that they steadfastly insist that they are kings when they are utter paupers, or that they are arrayed in purple robes when they are naked, or that they have heads made of clay, or that they are gourds, or that they are made of glass. But such people are mad, and I would appear no less mad, were I to take their behavior as an example for myself.

This would all be well and good, were I not a man who is accustomed to sleeping at night, and to experiencing in my dreams the very same things, or now and then even less plausible ones, as these insane people do when they are awake. How often does my evening slumber persuade me of such ordinary things as these: that I am here, clothed in my dressing gown, seated next to the fireplace—when in fact I am lying undressed in bed! But right now my eyes are certainly wide awake when I gaze upon this sheet of paper. This head which I am shaking is not heavy with sleep. I extend this hand consciously and deliberately, and I feel it. Such things would not be so distinct for someone who is asleep. As if I did not recall having been deceived on other occasions even by similar thoughts in my dreams! As I consider these matters more carefully, I see so plainly that there are no definitive signs by which to distinguish being awake from being asleep.④ As a result, I am becoming quite dizzy, and this dizziness nearly convinces me that I am asleep.

Let us assume then, for the sake of argument, that we are dreaming and that such particulars as these are not true: that we are opening our eyes, moving our head, and extending our hands. Perhaps we do not even have such hands, or any such body at all. Nevertheless, it surely must be admitted that the things seen during slumber are, as it were, like painted images, which could only have been produced in the likeness of true things, and that therefore at least these general things—eyes, head, hands, and the whole body—are not imaginary things, but are true and exist. For indeed when painters themselves wish to represent sirens and satyrs by means of especially bizarre forms, they surely cannot assign to them utterly new natures. Rather, they simply fuse together the members of various animals. Or if perhaps they concoct

② This is Descartes's famous *method of doubt:* doubt anything that can possibly be false, thereby arriving (if anything is left) at certainty. Notice that he is not seeking merely *psychological* certainty. Many people are convinced of various things (perhaps that God exists), even though they can give no reasons for thinking that they are true, but this is not the kind of certainty that will help to avoid error (since something that is psychologically certain can still be false). Instead he is looking for a kind of certainty that guarantees truth: beliefs for which there is a *conclusive* reason.

③ Rather than scrutinizing beliefs individually, Descartes proposes to examine the *foundations* upon which whole categories of beliefs rest. This is an architectural metaphor, and you should think carefully about how it applies to the issue of knowledge. The first such category, discussed in the following paragraphs, is beliefs justified by sense experience (justified *a posteriori*).

④ This paragraph contains Descartes's reason for doubting this first category of beliefs. Think carefully about what it amounts to and whether it is a good reason.

something so utterly novel that nothing like it has ever been seen before (and thus is something utterly fictitious and false), yet certainly at the very least the colors from which they fashion it ought to be true. And by the same token, although even these general things—eyes, head, hands and the like—could be imaginary, still one has to admit that at least certain other things that are even more simple and universal are true. It is from these components, as if from true colors, that all those images of things that are in our thought are fashioned, be they true or false.⑤

This class of things appears to include corporeal nature in general, together with its extension; the shape of extended things; their quantity, that is, their size and number; as well as the place where they exist; the time through which they endure, and the like.

Thus it is not improper to conclude from this that physics, astronomy, medicine, and all the other disciplines that are dependent upon the consideration of composite things are doubtful, and that, on the other hand, arithmetic, geometry, and other such disciplines, which treat of nothing but the simplest and most general things and which are indifferent as to whether these things do or do not in fact exist, contain something certain and indubitable. For whether I am awake or asleep, two plus three make five, and a square does not have more than four sides. It does not seem possible that such obvious truths should be subject to the suspicion of being false.⑥

Be that as it may, there is fixed in my mind a certain opinion of long standing, namely that there exists a God who is able to do anything and by whom I, such as I am, have been created. How do I know that he did not bring it about that there is no earth at all, no heavens, no extended thing, no shape, no size, no place, and yet bringing it about that all these things appear to me to exist precisely as they do now? Moreover, since I judge that others sometimes make mistakes in matters that they believe they know most perfectly, may I not, in like fashion, be deceived every time I add two and three or count the sides of a square, or perform an even simpler operation, if that can be imagined? But perhaps God has not willed that I be deceived in this way, for he is said to be supremely good. Nonetheless, if it were repugnant to his goodness to have created me such that I be deceived all the time, it would also seem foreign to that same goodness to permit me to be deceived even occasionally. But we cannot make this last assertion.⑦

Perhaps there are some who would rather deny so a powerful a God than believe that everything else is uncertain. Let us not oppose them; rather, let us grant that everything said here about God is fictitious. Now they suppose that I came to be what I am either by fate, or by chance, or by a connected chain of events, or by some other way. But because being deceived and being mistaken appear to be a certain imperfection, the less powerful they take the author of my origin to be, the more probable it will be that I am so imperfect that I am always deceived. I have nothing to say in response to these arguments. But eventually I am forced to admit that there is nothing among the things I once believed to be true which it is not permissible to doubt—and not out of frivolity or lack of forethought, but for valid and considered reasons. Thus I must be no less careful to withhold assent henceforth even from these beliefs than I would from those that are patently false, if I wish to find anything certain.

But it is not enough simply to have realized these things; I must take steps to keep myself mindful of them. For long-standing opinions keep returning, and, almost against my will, they take advantage of my

⑤ The suggestion is that the creativity involved in dreams is limited to the recombination of elements derived in some other way. This means that the dreaming hypothesis does not provide a reason for thinking that everything involved in our experience is mistaken: the basic elements may still be true, even if the ways in which they are combined are mistaken.

⑥ Thus while sciences that deal with complex things are called into question by the dreaming hypothesis, those that deal with these simpler elements are not. The examples Descartes gives at the end of this paragraph suggest that he has in mind at least primarily beliefs justified on a completely different basis than sense experience: a priori beliefs justified by reason or rational thought, rather than sense experience (which could be just a dream).

⑦ Here is a theme that will become important in *Meditation Six*: God, being perfectly good, would seemingly not have made me so that I fall into error all the time. The problem is that God's goodness seems incompatible with my making any errors at all, which I obviously do. (No resolution of the issue is offered at this point.)

credulity, as if it were bound over to them by long use and the claims of intimacy. Nor will I ever get out of the habit of assenting to them and believing in them, so long as I take them to be exactly what they are, namely, in some respects doubtful, as has just now been shown, but nevertheless highly probable, so that it is much more consonant with reason to believe them than to deny them. Hence, it seems to me I would do well to deceive myself by turning my will in completely the opposite direction and pretend for a time that these opinions are wholly false and imaginary, until finally, as if with prejudices weighing down each side equally, no bad habit should turn my judgment any further from the correct perception of things. For indeed I know that meanwhile there is no danger or error in following this procedure, and that it is impossible for me to indulge in too much distrust, since I am now concentrating only on knowledge, not on action.

Accordingly, I will suppose not a supremely good God, the source of truth, but rather an evil genius, supremely powerful and clever, who has directed his entire effort at deceiving me. I will regard the heavens, the air, the earth, colors, shapes, sounds, and all external things as nothing but the bedeviling hoaxes of my dreams, with which he lays snares for my credulity. I will regard myself as not having hands, or eyes, or flesh, or blood, or any senses, but as nevertheless falsely believing that I possess all these things. I will remain resolute and steadfast in this meditation, and even if it is not within my power to know anything true, it certainly is within my power to take care resolutely to withhold my assent to what is false, lest this deceiver, however powerful, however clever he may be, have any effect on me.⑧ But this undertaking is arduous, and a certain laziness brings me back to my customary way of living. I am not unlike a prisoner who enjoyed an imaginary freedom during his sleep, but, when he later begins to suspect that he is dreaming, fears being awakened and nonchalantly conspires with these pleasant illusions. In just the same way,

⑧ Here is Descartes's second and more important reason for doubting whole categories of belief, one that is much more powerful than the one that appeals to the possibility of dreaming because it calls many more beliefs into question, including apparently those (like 2 + 3 = 5) that result from a priori reason. Do any beliefs at all escape this second reason for doubt?

I fall back of my own accord into my old opinions, and dread being awakened, lest the toilsome wakefulness which follows upon a peaceful rest must be spent thenceforward not in the light but among the inextricable shadows of the difficulties now brought forward.⑨

⑨ Descartes suggests here that maintaining the attitude of doubt is "arduous." Is it even possible to doubt all of one's beliefs while one is engaged in the world in the ordinary way? Does this make any difference in relation to the purpose for which the method of doubt is adopted?

MEDITATION TWO: Concerning the Nature of the Human Mind: That It Is Better Known Than the Body

Yesterday's meditation has thrown me into such doubts that I can no longer ignore them, yet I fail to see how they are to be resolved. It is as if I had suddenly fallen into a deep whirlpool; I am so tossed about that I can neither touch bottom with my foot, nor swim up to the top. Nevertheless I will work my way up and will once again attempt the same path I entered upon yesterday. I will accomplish this by putting aside everything that admits of the least doubt, as if I had discovered it to be completely false. I will stay on this course until I know something certain, or, if nothing else, until I at least know for certain that nothing is certain. Archimedes sought but one firm and immovable point in order to move the entire earth from one place to another. Just so, great things are also to be hoped for if I succeed in finding just one thing, however slight, that is certain and unshaken.

Therefore I suppose that everything I see is false. I believe that none of what my deceitful memory represents ever existed. I have no senses whatever. Body, shape, extension, movement, and place are all chimeras. What then will be true? Perhaps just the single fact that nothing is certain.

But how do I know there is not something else, over and above all those things that I have just reviewed, concerning which there is not even the slightest occasion for doubt? Is there not some God, or by whatever name I might call him, who instills these very thoughts in me? But why would I think that, since I myself could perhaps be the author of these thoughts? Am I not then at least something? But I have already denied that I have any senses and any body. Still I hesitate; for what follows from this? Am I so tied to a body and to the senses that I cannot exist without them? But I have persuaded myself that there is absolutely nothing in the world: no sky, no earth, no minds, no bodies. Is it then the case that I too do not exist? But doubtless I did exist, if I persuaded myself of something. But there is some deceiver or other who is supremely powerful and supremely sly and who is always deliberately deceiving me. Then too there is no doubt that I exist, if he is deceiving me. And let him do his best at deception, he will never bring it about that I am nothing so long as I shall think that I am something. Thus, after everything has been most carefully weighed, it must finally be established that this pronouncement "I am, I exist" is necessarily true every time I utter it or conceive it in my mind. 10

10 The insight here is the one that Descartes expresses more succinctly in another work (his *Discourse on Method*) as (in Latin) "*Cogito ergo sum*," "I think, therefore I am"—often referred to just as the Cogito. What exactly is the claim that is supposed to be indubitable? Is Descartes right that even the evil genius is unable to deceive him about the truth of that claim: to make him believe that it is true when it is really false? Is there an argument here or some other sort of insight? (See Discussion Question 1.)

But I do not yet understand sufficiently what I am—I, who now necessarily exist. And so from this point on, I must be careful lest I unwittingly mistake something else for myself, and thus err in that very item of knowledge that I claim to be the most certain and evident of all. Thus, I will meditate once more on what I once believed myself to be, prior to embarking upon these thoughts. For this reason, then, I will set aside whatever can be weakened even to the slightest degree by the arguments brought forward, so that eventually all that remains is precisely nothing but what is certain and unshaken.

What then did I [formerly] think I was? A man, of course. But what is a man? Might I not say a "rational animal"? No, because then I would have to inquire what "animal" and "rational" mean. And thus from one question I would slide into many more difficult ones. Nor do I now have enough free time that I want to waste it on subtleties of this sort. Instead, permit me to focus here on what came spontaneously and naturally into my thinking whenever I pondered what I

was. Now it occurred to me first that I had a face, hands, arms, and this entire mechanism of bodily members: the very same as are discerned in a corpse, and which I referred to by the name "body." It next occurred to me that I took in food, that I walked about, and that I sensed and thought various things; these actions I used to attribute to the soul. But as to what this soul might be, I either did not think about it or else I imagined it a rarified I-know-not-what, like a wind, or a fire, or ether, which had been infused into my coarser parts. But as to the body I was not in any doubt. On the contrary, I was under the impression that I knew its nature distinctly. Were I perhaps tempted to describe this nature such as I conceived it in my mind, I would have described it thus: by "body," I understand all that is capable of being bounded by some shape, of being enclosed in a place, and of filling up a space in such a way as to exclude any other body from it; of being perceived by touch, sight, hearing, taste, or smell; of being moved in several ways, not, of course, by itself, but by whatever else impinges upon it. For it was my view that the power of self-motion, and likewise of sensing or of thinking, in no way belonged to the nature of the body. Indeed I used rather to marvel that such faculties were to be found in certain bodies.

But now what am I, when I suppose that there is some supremely powerful and, if I may be permitted to say so, malicious deceiver who deliberately tries to fool me in any way he can? Can I not affirm that I possess at least a small measure of all those things which I have already said belong to the nature of the body? I focus my attention on them, I think about them, I review them again, but nothing comes to mind. I am tired of repeating this to no purpose. But what about those things I ascribed to the soul? What about being nourished or moving about? Since I now do not have a body, these are surely nothing but fictions. What about sensing? Surely this too does not take place without a body; and I seemed to have sensed in my dreams many things that I later realized I did not sense. What about thinking? Here I make my discovery: thought exists; it alone cannot be separated from me. I am; I exist—this is certain. But for how long? For as long as I am thinking; for perhaps it could also come to pass that if I were to cease all thinking I would then utterly cease to exist. At this time I admit nothing that is not necessarily true. I am therefore precisely nothing but a thinking thing; that is, a mind, or intellect, or understanding, or reason— words of whose meanings I was previously ignorant. Yet I am a true thing and am truly existing; but what kind of thing? I have said it already: a thinking thing.⑪

⑪ Think very carefully about the contrast between what Descartes used to think he was and what he now claims to know that he is.

What else am I? I will set my imagination in motion. I am not that concatenation of members we call the human body. Neither am I even some subtle air infused into these members, nor a wind, nor a fire, nor a vapor, nor a breath, nor anything I devise for myself. For I have supposed these things to be nothing. The assumption still stands; yet nevertheless I am something. But is it perhaps the case that these very things which I take to be nothing, because they are unknown to me, nevertheless are in fact no different from that "me" that I know? This I do not know, and I will not quarrel about it now. I can make a judgment only about things that are known to me. I know that I exist; I ask now who is this "I" whom I know? Most certainly, in the strict sense the knowledge of this "I" does not depend upon things of whose existence I do not yet have knowledge. Therefore it is not dependent upon any of those things that I simulate in my imagination. But this word "simulate" warns me of my error. For I would indeed be simulating were I to "imagine" that I was something, because imagining is merely the contemplating of the shape or image of a corporeal thing. But I now know with certainty that I am and also that all these images—and, generally, everything belonging to the nature of the body— could turn out to be nothing but dreams. Once I have realized this, I would seem to be speaking no less foolishly were I to say: "I will use my imagination in order to recognize more distinctly who I am," than were I to say: "Now I surely am awake, and I see something true; but since I do not yet see it clearly enough, I will deliberately fall asleep so that my dreams might represent it to me more truly and more clearly." Thus I realize that none of what I can grasp by means of the imagination pertains to this knowledge that I have of myself. Moreover, I realize that I must be most diligent about withdrawing my mind from these things so that it can perceive its nature as distinctly as possible.

But what then am I? A thing that thinks. What is that? A thing that doubts, understands, affirms, denies, wills, refuses, and that also imagines and senses.

Indeed it is no small matter if all of these things belong to me. But why should they not belong to me? Is it not the very same "I" who now doubts almost everything, who nevertheless understands something, who affirms that this one thing is true, who denies other things, who desires to know more, who wishes not to be deceived, who imagines many things even against my will, who also notices many things which appear to come from the senses? What is there in all of this that is not every bit as true as the fact that I exist—even if I am always asleep or even if my creator makes every effort to mislead me? Which of these things is distinct from my thought? Which of them can be said to be separate from myself? For it is so obvious that it is I who doubt, I who understand, and I who will, that there is nothing by which it could be explained more clearly. But indeed it is also the same "I" who imagines; for although perhaps, as I supposed before, absolutely nothing that I imagined is true, still the very power of imagining really does exist, and constitutes a part of my thought. Finally, it is this same "I" who senses or who is cognizant of bodily things as if through the senses. For example, I now see a light, I hear a noise, I feel heat. These things are false, since I am asleep. Yet I certainly do seem to see, hear, and feel warmth. This cannot be false. Properly speaking, this is what in me is called "sensing." But this, precisely so taken, is nothing other than thinking.⑫

⑫ Here Descartes is claiming that there are many more beliefs that are beyond doubt in the same way that the belief in his own existence is— thus greatly expanding the foundation of certainty upon which he will eventually try to rebuild his knowledge. What are these further beliefs, and is he right that they are indubitable in the same way, even given the evil genius possibility? (See Discussion Question 2.)

From these considerations I am beginning to know a little better what I am. But it still seems (and I cannot resist believing) that corporeal things—whose images are formed by thought, and which the senses themselves examine—are much more distinctly known than this mysterious "I" which does not fall within the imagination. And yet it would be strange indeed were I to grasp the very things I consider to be doubtful, unknown, and foreign to me more distinctly than what is true, what is known—than, in short, myself. But I see what is happening: my mind loves to wander and does not yet permit itself to be restricted within the confines of truth. So be it then; let us just this once allow it completely free rein, so that, a little while later, when the time has come to pull in the reins, the mind may more readily permit itself to be controlled.

Let us consider those things which are commonly believed to be the most distinctly grasped of all: namely the bodies we touch and see. Not bodies in general, mind you, for these general perceptions are apt to be somewhat more confused, but one body in particular. Let us take, for instance, this piece of wax. It has been taken quite recently from the honeycomb; it has not yet lost all the honey flavor. It retains some of the scent of the flowers from which it was collected. Its color, shape, and size are manifest. It is hard and cold; it is easy to touch. If you rap on it with your knuckle it will emit a sound. In short, everything is present in it that appears needed to enable a body to be known as distinctly as possible. But notice that, as I am speaking, I am bringing it close to the fire. The remaining traces of the honey flavor are disappearing; the scent is vanishing; the color is changing; the original shape is disappearing. Its size is increasing; it is becoming liquid and hot; you can hardly touch it. And now, when you rap on it, it no longer emits any sound. Does the same wax still remain? I must confess that it does; no one denies it; no one thinks otherwise. So what was there in the wax that was so distinctly grasped? Certainly none of the aspects that I reached by means of the senses. For whatever came under the senses of taste, smell, sight, touch or hearing has now changed; and yet the wax remains.

Perhaps the wax was what I now think it is: namely that the wax itself never really was the sweetness of the honey, nor the fragrance of the flowers, nor the whiteness, nor the shape, nor the sound, but instead was a body that a short time ago manifested itself to me in these ways, and now does so in other ways. But just what precisely is this thing that I thus imagine? Let us focus our attention on this and see what remains after we have removed everything that does not belong to the wax: only that it is something extended, flexible, and mutable. But what is it to be

flexible and mutable? Is it what my imagination shows it to be: namely, that this piece of wax can change from a round to a square shape, or from the latter to a triangular shape? Not at all; for I grasp that the wax is capable of innumerable changes of this sort, even though I am incapable of running through these innumerable changes by using my imagination. Therefore this insight is not achieved by the faculty of imagination. What is it to be extended? Is this thing's extension also unknown? For it becomes greater in wax that is beginning to melt, greater in boiling wax, and greater still as the heat is increased. And I would not judge correctly what the wax is if I did not believe that it takes on an even greater variety of dimensions than I could ever grasp with the imagination. It remains then for me to concede that I do not grasp what this wax is through the imagination; rather, I perceive it through the mind alone. The point I am making refers to this particular piece of wax, for the case of wax in general is clearer still. But what is this piece of wax which is perceived only by the mind? Surely it is the same piece of wax that I see, touch, and imagine; in short it is the same piece of wax I took it to be from the very beginning. But I need to realize that the perception of the wax is neither a seeing, nor a touching, nor an imagining. Nor has it ever been, even though it previously seemed so; rather it is an inspection on the part of the mind alone. This inspection can be imperfect and confused, as it was before, or clear and distinct, as it is now, depending on how closely I pay attention to the things in which the piece of wax consists.

But meanwhile I marvel at how prone my mind is to errors. For although I am considering these things within myself silently and without words, nevertheless I seize upon words themselves and I am nearly deceived by the ways in which people commonly speak. For we say that we see the wax itself, if it is present, and not that we judge it to be present from its color or shape. Whence I might conclude straightaway that I know the wax through the vision had by the eye, and not through an inspection on the part of the mind alone. But then were I perchance to look out my window and observe men crossing the square, I would ordinarily say I see the men themselves just as I say I see the wax. But what do I see aside from hats and clothes, which could conceal automata? Yet I judge them to be men. Thus what I thought I had seen with my eyes, I actually grasped solely with the faculty of judgment, which is in my mind.

But a person who seeks to know more than the common crowd ought to be ashamed of himself for looking for doubt in common ways of speaking. Let us then go forward and inquire when it was that I perceived more perfectly and evidently what the piece of wax was. Was it when I first saw it and believed I knew it by the external sense, or at least by the so-called common sense, that is, the power of imagination? Or do I have more perfect knowledge now, when I have diligently examined both what the wax is and how it is known? Surely it is absurd to be in doubt about this matter. For what was there in my initial perception that was distinct? What was there that any animal seemed incapable of possessing? But indeed when I distinguish the wax from its external forms, as if stripping it of its clothing, and look at the wax in its nakedness, then, even though there can be still an error in my judgment, nevertheless I cannot perceive it thus without a human mind.

But what am I to say about this mind, that is, about myself? For as yet I admit nothing else to be in me over and above the mind. What, I ask, am I who seem to perceive this wax so distinctly? Do I not know myself not only much more truly and with greater certainty, but also much more distinctly and evidently? For if I judge that the wax exists from the fact that I see it, certainly from this same fact that I see the wax it follows much more evidently that I myself exist. For it could happen that what I see is not truly wax. It could happen that I have no eyes with which to see anything. But it is utterly impossible that, while I see or think I see (I do not now distinguish these two), I who think am not something. Likewise, if I judge that the wax exists from the fact that I touch it, the same outcome will again obtain, namely that I exist. If I judge that the wax exists from the fact that I imagine it, or for any other reason, plainly the same thing follows. But what I note regarding the wax applies to everything else that is external to me. Furthermore, if my perception of the wax seemed more distinct after it became known to me not only on account of sight or touch, but on account of many reasons, one has to admit how much

more distinctly I am now known to myself. For there is not a single consideration that can aid in my perception of the wax or of any other body that fails to make even more manifest the nature of my mind. But there are still so many other things in the mind itself on the basis of which my knowledge of it can be rendered more distinct that it hardly seems worth enumerating those things which emanate to it from the body.

But lo and behold, I have returned on my own to where I wanted to be. For since I now know that even bodies are not, properly speaking, perceived by the senses or by the faculty of imagination, but by the intellect alone,[13] and that they are not perceived through their being touched or seen, but only through their being understood, I manifestly know that nothing can be perceived more easily and more evidently than my own mind. But since the tendency to hang on to long-held beliefs cannot be put aside so quickly, I want to stop here, so that by the length of my meditation this new knowledge may be more deeply impressed upon my memory.

[13] Descartes uses the wax example and the possibility that men are robots ("automata") to argue for this claim (that bodies themselves are not properly perceived by the senses nor by the faculty of imagination, but by the intellect alone). How much support do they really provide for it?

MEDITATION THREE: Concerning God, That He Exists

I will now shut my eyes, stop up my ears, and withdraw all my senses. I will also blot out from my thoughts all images of corporeal things, or rather, since the latter is hardly possible, I will regard these images as empty, false and worthless. And as I converse with myself alone and look more deeply into myself, I will attempt to render myself gradually better known and more familiar to myself. I am a thing that thinks, that is to say, a thing that doubts, affirms, denies, understands a few things, is ignorant of many things, wills, refrains from willing, and also imagines and senses. For as I observed earlier, even though these things that I sense or imagine may perhaps be nothing at all outside me, nevertheless I am certain that these modes of thinking, which are cases of what

I call sensing and imagining, insofar as they are merely modes of thinking, do exist within me.

⟨14⟩ Here Descartes summarizes the main result of *Meditation Two:* the tiny amount of knowledge that has (allegedly) escaped the doubt resulting from the evil genius possibility. Think carefully about what this includes and what is still subject to doubt. Stated in the first person as is appropriate, I can know that I am thinking and also that I am thinking (experiencing, doubting, wondering) about various things, but not that anything beyond myself and my own conscious states exists.

⟨15⟩ This is Descartes's suggestion for a general rule that captures the way in which his belief about his own existence escapes the doubt. But is he right about this? Is clarity and distinctness the reason that I can't doubt my own existence? In fact, Descartes himself proceeds to show that it is not, since he goes on to question whether this rule can be trusted, even though he never questions his own existence.

In these few words, I have reviewed everything I truly know, or at least what so far I have noticed that I know.⟨14⟩ Now I will ponder more carefully to see whether perhaps there may be other things belonging to me that up until now I have failed to notice. I am certain that I am a thinking thing. But do I not therefore also know what is required for me to be certain of anything? Surely in this first instance of knowledge, there is nothing but a certain clear and distinct perception of what I affirm. Yet this would hardly be enough to render me certain of the truth of a thing, if it could ever happen that something that I perceived so clearly and distinctly were false. And thus I now seem able to posit as a general rule that everything I very clearly and distinctly perceive is true.⟨15⟩

Be that as it may, I have previously admitted many things as wholly certain and evident that nevertheless I later discovered to be doubtful. What sort of things were these? Why, the earth, the sky, the stars, and all the other things I perceived by means of the senses. But what was it about these things that I clearly perceived? Surely the fact that the ideas or thoughts of these things were hovering before my mind. But even now I do not deny that these ideas are in me. Yet there was something else I used to affirm, which, owing to my habitual tendency to believe it, I used to think was something I clearly perceived, even though I actually did not perceive it at all: namely, that certain things existed outside me,

things from which those ideas proceeded and which those ideas completely resembled. But on this point I was mistaken; or rather, if my judgment was a true one, it was not the result of the force of my perception.

But what about when I considered something very simple and easy in the areas of arithmetic or geometry, for example that two plus three make five, and the like? Did I not intuit them at least clearly enough so as to affirm them as true? To be sure, I did decide later on that I must doubt these things, but that was only because it occurred to me that some God could perhaps have given me a nature such that I might be deceived even about matters that seemed most evident. But whenever this preconceived opinion about the supreme power of God occurs to me, I cannot help admitting that, were he to wish it, it would be easy for him to cause me to err even in those matters that I think I intuit as clearly as possible with the eyes of the mind.⟨16⟩ On the other hand, whenever I turn my attention to those very things that I think I perceive with such great clarity, I am so completely persuaded by them that I

⟨16⟩ Since Descartes has already said that God wouldn't deceive us in this way, it is better to take him to be talking about the evil genius here.

spontaneously blurt out these words: "let anyone who can do so deceive me; so long as I think that I am something, he will never bring it about that I am nothing. Nor will he one day make it true that I never existed, for it is true now that I do exist. Nor will he even bring it about that perhaps two plus three might equal more or less than five, or similar items in which I recognize an obvious contradiction." And certainly, because I have no reason for thinking that there is a God who is a deceiver (and of course I do not yet sufficiently know whether there even is a God), the basis for doubting, depending as it does merely on the above hypothesis, is very tenuous and, so to speak, metaphysical. But in order to remove even this basis for doubt, I should at the first opportunity inquire whether there is a God, and, if there is, whether or not he can be a deceiver. For if I am ignorant of this, it appears I am never capable of being completely certain about anything else. ⟨17⟩

However, at this stage good order seems to demand that I first group all my thoughts into certain classes, and ask in which of them truth or falsity properly resides. Some of these thoughts are like images of things; to these alone does the word "idea" properly apply, as when I think of a man, or a chimera, or the sky, or an angel, or God. Again there are other thoughts that take different forms: for example, when I will, or fear, or affirm, or deny, there is always something that I grasp as the subject of my thought, yet I embrace in my thought something more than the likeness of that thing. Some of these thoughts are called volitions or affects, while others are called judgments.

Now as far as ideas are concerned, if they are considered alone and in their own right, without being referred to something else, they cannot, properly speaking, be false. For whether it is a she-goat or a chimera that I am imagining, it is no less true that I imagine the one than the other. Moreover, we need not fear that there is falsity in the will itself or in the affects, for although I can choose evil things or even things that are utterly non-existent, I cannot conclude from this that it is untrue that I do choose these things. Thus there remain only judgments in which I must take care not to be mistaken. Now the principal and most frequent error to be found in judgments consists in the fact that I judge that the ideas which are in me are similar to or in conformity with certain things outside me. Obviously, if I were to consider these ideas merely as certain modes of my thought, and were not to refer them to anything else, they could hardly give me any subject matter for error. [18]

Among these ideas, some appear to me to be innate, some adventitious, and some produced by me. For I understand what a thing is, what truth is, what thought is, and I appear to have derived this exclusively from my very own nature. But say I am now hearing a noise, or looking at the sun, or feeling the fire; up until now I judged that these things proceeded from certain things outside me, and finally, that sirens, hippogriffs, and the like are made by me. Or perhaps I can even think of all these ideas as being adventitious, or as being innate, or as fabrications, for I have not yet clearly ascertained their true origin. [19]

But here I must inquire particularly into those ideas that I believe to be derived from things existing outside me. Just what reason do I have for believing that these ideas resemble those things? Well, I do seem to have been so taught by nature. Moreover, I do know from experience that these ideas do not depend upon my will, nor consequently upon myself, for I often notice them even against my will. Now, for example, whether or not I will it, I feel heat. It is for this reason that I believe this feeling or idea of heat comes to me from something other than myself, namely from the heat of the fire by which I am sitting. Nothing is more obvious than the judgment that this thing is sending its likeness rather than something else into me. [20]

I will now see whether these reasons are powerful enough. When I say here "I have been so taught by nature," all I have in mind is that I am driven by a spontaneous impulse to believe this, and not that some light of nature is showing me that it is true. These are two very different things. For whatever is shown me by this light of nature, for example, that from the fact that I doubt, it follows that I am, and the like, cannot in any way be doubtful. This is owing to the fact that there can be no other faculty that I can trust as much

[17] Here Descartes might seem to be questioning even his own existence and states of mind, but the subsequent discussion shows he is not really doing so. (If he did, he would have nothing to start from in attempting to prove God's existence). Thus the issue seems to be whether he can safely believe things other than his own existence and states of mind that seem "clear and distinct" (things like 2 + 3 = 5). The evil genius could deceive him about such things, so the only way to be sure is to prove the existence of God (and thereby the nonexistence of the evil genius).

[18] So Descartes is worried about whether his thoughts *about the world* are accurate, not about whether his thoughts *about his thoughts* are accurate, for (he claims) he could never be in error about that.

[19] An innate idea is one that is programmed into a person at birth (by God, in Descartes's view). Ideas produced by me are ones that I make up or that are "fictitious." What then is an "adventitious" idea? What is the third alternative besides being innate or being "produced by me"?

[20] Here are two initial reasons for the view that sense experience accurately reflects the nature of external things. Think carefully about each of them. How much force (if any) do they have?

as this light and which could teach that these things are not true.[21] But as far as natural impulses are concerned, in the past I have often judged myself to have been driven by them to make the poorer choice when it was a question of choosing a good; and I fail to see why I should place any greater faith in them than in other matters.

Again, although these ideas do not depend upon my will, it does not follow that they necessarily proceed from things existing outside me. For just as these impulses about which I spoke just now seem to be different from my will, even though they are in me, so too perhaps there is also in me some other faculty, one not yet sufficiently known to me, which produces these ideas, just as it has always seemed up to now that ideas are formed in me without any help from external things when I am asleep.

And finally, even if these ideas did proceed from things other than myself, it does not therefore follow that they must resemble those things. Indeed it seems I have frequently noticed a vast difference in many respects. For example, I find within myself two distinct ideas of the sun. One idea is drawn, as it were, from the senses. Now it is this idea which, of all those that I take to be derived from outside me, is most in need of examination. By means of this idea the sun appears to me to be quite small. But there is another idea, one derived from astronomical reasoning, that is, it is elicited from certain notions that are innate in me, or else is fashioned by me in some other way. Through this idea the sun is shown to be several times larger than the earth. Both ideas surely cannot resemble the same sun existing outside me; and reason convinces me that the idea that seems to have emanated from the sun itself from so close is the very one that least resembles the sun.

All these points demonstrate sufficiently that up to this point it was not a well-founded judgment but

only a blind impulse that formed the basis of my belief that things existing outside me send ideas or images of themselves to me through the sense organs or by some other means.[22]

But still another way occurs to me for inquiring whether some of the things of which there are ideas in me do exist outside me: insofar as these ideas are merely modes of thought, I see no inequality among them; they all seem to proceed from me in the same manner. But insofar as one idea represents one thing and another idea another thing, it is obvious that they do differ very greatly from one another. Unquestionably, those ideas that display substances to me are something more and, if I may say so, contain within themselves more objective reality than those which represent only modes or accidents. Again, the idea that enables me to understand a supreme deity, eternal, infinite, omniscient, omnipotent, and creator of all things other than himself, clearly has more objective reality within it than do those ideas through which finite substances are displayed.[23]

Now it is indeed evident by the light of nature that there must be at least as much [reality] in the efficient and total cause as there is in the effect of that same cause. For whence, I ask, could an effect get its reality, if not from its cause? And how could the cause give that reality to the effect, unless it also possessed that reality? Hence it follows that something cannot come into being out of nothing, and also that what is more perfect (that is, what contains in itself more reality) cannot come into being from what is

---

21 By "the natural light," Descartes seems to mean something like a priori insight into *why* a claim must be true—the sort of insight that is reflected in the claim seeming "clear and distinct." His point is that while I naturally and spontaneously believe what the senses seem to tell me, there is nothing in that case that shows me that the claims in question must be true. (But, as we have seen, the evil genius can apparently deceive me even about things (other than my own existence and states of mind) that seem to be shown by the natural light or that seem clear and distinct (such as 2 + 3 = 5).)

22 Descartes concludes that the two initial reasons (see Annotation 20) have no real force.

23 Another approach is to see whether the claim that some of my ideas correspond to things existing outside my mind can be derived from their *content:* what they seem to represent or depict. Descartes puts this in terms of the obscure (to us, anyway) medieval conception of *objective reality:* reality as an object of thought. (So, for example, Santa Claus would have "objective reality" when anyone has a thought of Santa Claus.) In his view, different ideas contain different degrees of objective reality, corresponding to the degree of perfection of the object of the idea. In these terms, ideas of finite substances (such as the idea of a tree or of a dog) contain more objective reality than ideas of properties (such as the idea of redness or hardness); and the idea of God contains more objective reality than any other idea.

less perfect. But this is manifestly true not merely for those effects whose reality is actual or formal, but also for ideas in which only objective reality is considered. [24] For example, not only can a stone which did not exist previously not now begin to exist unless it is produced by something in which there is, either formally or eminently, everything that is in the stone; nor heat be introduced into a subject which was not already hot unless it is done by something that is of at least as perfect an order as heat—and the same for the rest—but it is also true that there can be in me no idea of heat, or of a stone, unless it is placed in me by some cause that has at least as much reality as I conceive to be in the heat or in the stone. For although this cause conveys none of its actual or formal reality to my idea, it should not be thought for that reason that it must be less real. Rather, the very nature of an idea is such that of itself it needs no formal reality other than what it borrows from my thought, of which it is a mode. But that a particular idea contains this as opposed to that objective reality is surely owing to some cause in which there is at least as much formal reality as there is objective reality contained in the idea. For if we assume that something is found in the idea that was not in its cause, then the idea gets that something from nothing. Yet as imperfect a mode of being as this is by which a thing exists in the intellect objectively through an idea, nevertheless it is plainly not nothing; hence it cannot get its being from nothing.

Moreover, even though the reality that I am considering in my ideas is merely objective reality, I ought not on that account to suspect that there is no need for the same reality to be formally in the causes of these ideas, but that it suffices for it to be in them objectively. For just as the objective mode of being belongs to ideas by their very nature, so the formal mode of being belongs to the causes of ideas, at least to the first and preeminent ones, by their very nature. And although one idea can perhaps issue from another, nevertheless no infinite regress is permitted here; eventually some first idea must be reached whose cause is a sort of archetype that contains formally all the reality that is in the idea merely objectively. [25] Thus it is clear to me by the light of nature that the ideas that are in me are like images that can easily fail to match the perfection of the things from which they have been drawn, but which can contain nothing greater or more perfect.

And the longer and more attentively I examine all these points, the more clearly and distinctly I know they are true. But what am I ultimately to conclude? If the objective reality of any of my ideas is found to be so great that I am certain that the same reality was not in me, either formally or eminently, and that therefore I myself cannot be the cause of the idea, then it necessarily follows that I am not alone in the world, but that something else, which is the cause of this idea, also exists. But if no such idea is found in me, I will have no argument whatsoever to make me certain of the existence of anything other than myself, for I have conscientiously reviewed all these arguments, and so far I have been unable to find any other. [26]

[24] Here is the first of two important metaphysical principles involved in Descartes's argument for the existence of God: the principle that any cause must have at least as much reality (must be at least as perfect as) as its effect. He applies this to both formal or actual reality (reality in the ordinary sense) and objective reality. (The labels "formal" and "objective" strike our contemporary ears as terminologically backwards. "Objective reality," as we have already seen, is reality as an object of thought; "formal reality," on the other hand (and as Descartes does indicate), is what we would call actual reality.)

[25] Here is the second important metaphysical principle involved in Descartes's argument: anything with objective reality must ultimately be caused by something with formal reality. From this, Descartes thinks that it follows, given the previous principle, that something with a specific degree of objective reality must ultimately be caused by something with at least that same degree of formal reality. Is there any plausibility to this claim? (Even more importantly, how does Descartes know that either of these metaphysical principles is true?—look carefully at what he says. Do you see any problem here? See Discussion Question 3.)

[26] Thus the issue becomes whether I have any idea that I myself could not, according to the foregoing principle, be the cause of. If so, I can know on this basis that something outside myself exists; if not, since according to Descartes there are no other arguments that have any force, I will not be able to know this. (You should be already able to figure out where the argument is going.)

Among my ideas, in addition to the one that displays me to myself (about which there can be no difficulty at this point), are others that represent God, corporeal and inanimate things, angels, animals, and finally other men like myself.

As to the ideas that display other men, or animals, or angels, I easily understand that they could be fashioned from the ideas that I have of myself, of corporeal things, and of God—even if no men (except myself), no animals, and no angels existed in the world.

As to the ideas of corporeal things, there is nothing in them that is so great that it seems incapable of having originated from me. For if I investigate them thoroughly and examine each one individually in the way I examined the idea of wax yesterday, I notice that there are only a very few things in them that I perceive clearly and distinctly: namely, size, or extension in length, breadth, and depth; shape, which arises from the limits of this extension; position, which various things possessing shape have in relation to one another; and motion, or alteration in position. To these can be added substance, duration, and number. But as for the remaining items, such as light and colors, sounds, odors, tastes, heat and cold and other tactile qualities, I think of these only in a very confused and obscure manner, to the extent that I do not even know whether they are true or false, that is, whether the ideas I have of them are ideas of things or ideas of non-things. For although a short time ago I noted that falsity properly so called (or "formal" falsity) is to be found only in judgments, nevertheless there is another kind of falsity (called "material" falsity) which is found in ideas whenever they represent a non-thing as if it were a thing. For example, the ideas I have of heat and cold fall so far short of being clear and distinct that I cannot tell from them whether cold is merely the privation of heat or whether heat is the privation of cold, or whether both are real qualities, or whether neither is. And because ideas can only be, as it were, of things, if it is true that cold is merely the absence of heat, then an idea that represents cold to me as something real and positive will not inappropriately be called false. The same holds for other similar ideas.

Assuredly I need not assign to these ideas an author distinct from myself. For if they were false, that is, if they were to represent non-things, I know by the light of nature that they proceed from nothing; that is,

they are in me for no other reason than that something is lacking in my nature, and that my nature is not entirely perfect. If, on the other hand, these ideas are true, then because they exhibit so little reality to me that I cannot distinguish it from a non-thing, I see no reason why they cannot get their being from me.

As for what is clear and distinct in the ideas of corporeal things, it appears I could have borrowed some of these from the idea of myself: namely, substance, duration, number, and whatever else there may be of this type. For instance, I think that a stone is a substance, that is to say, a thing that is suitable for existing in itself; and likewise I think that I too am a substance. Despite the fact that I conceive myself to be a thinking thing and not an extended thing, whereas I conceive of a stone as an extended thing and not a thinking thing, and hence there is the greatest diversity between these two concepts, nevertheless they seem to agree with one another when considered under the rubric of substance. Furthermore, I perceive that I now exist and recall that I have previously existed for some time. And I have various thoughts and know how many of them there are. It is in doing these things that I acquire the ideas of duration and number, which I can then apply to other things. However, none of the other components out of which the ideas of corporeal things are fashioned (namely extension, shape, position, and motion) are contained in me formally, since I am merely a thinking thing. But since these are only certain modes of a substance, whereas I am a substance, it seems possible that they are contained in me eminently.

Thus there remains only the idea of God. I must consider whether there is anything in this idea that could not have originated from me.[27] I understand by the name "God" a certain substance that is infinite, independent, supremely intelligent and supremely powerful, and that created me along with everything else that exists—if anything else exists. Indeed all these are such that, the more carefully I focus my attention on them, the less possible it seems they could have arisen from myself alone. Thus, from what has been said, I must conclude that God necessarily exists.

[27] The crucial idea is, of course, the idea of God: can this idea be caused only by me, given the two principles?

For although the idea of substance is in me by virtue of the fact that I am a substance, that fact is not sufficient to explain my having the idea of an infinite substance, since I am finite, unless this idea proceeded from some substance which really was infinite.

Nor should I think that I do not perceive the infinite by means of a true idea, but only through a negation of the finite, just as I perceive rest and darkness by means of a negation of motion and light. On the contrary, I clearly understand that there is more reality in an infinite substance than there is in a finite

28 One reason for thinking that I cannot be the cause of my idea of God is that it involves the property of infinity and I am only finite. Descartes considers the response that the idea of infinity is only the negation of the idea of the finite and claims that, on the contrary, the idea of infinity or of an infinite being comes first. How plausible is this, especially given the concession at the end of the following paragraph?

one. Thus the perception of the infinite is somehow prior in me to the perception of the finite, that is, my perception of God is prior to my perception of myself. For how would I understand that I doubt and that I desire, that is, that I lack something and that I am not wholly perfect, unless there were some idea in me of a more perfect being, by comparison with which I might recognize my defects? 28

Nor can it be said that this idea of God is perhaps materially false and thus can originate from nothing, as I remarked just now about the ideas of heat and cold, and the like. On the contrary, because it is the most clear and distinct and because it contains more objective reality than any other idea, no idea is in and of itself truer and has less of a basis for being suspected of falsehood. I maintain that this idea of a being that is supremely perfect and infinite is true in the highest degree. For although I could perhaps pretend that such a being does not exist, nevertheless I could not pretend that the idea of such a being discloses to me nothing real, as was the case with the idea of cold which I referred to earlier. It is indeed an idea that is utterly clear and distinct; for whatever I clearly and distinctly perceive to be real and true and to involve some perfection is wholly contained in that idea. It is no objection that I do not comprehend the infinite or that there are countless other things in God that I can in no way either comprehend or perhaps

even touch with my thought. For the nature of the infinite is such that it is not comprehended by a being such as I, who am finite. And it is sufficient that I understand this very point and judge that all those things that I clearly perceive and that I know to contain some perfection—and perhaps even countless other things of which I am ignorant—are in God either formally or eminently. The result is that, of all the ideas that are in me, the idea that I have of God is the most true, the most clear and distinct.

But perhaps I am something greater than I myself understand. Perhaps all these perfections that I am attributing to God are somehow in me potentially, although they do not yet assert themselves and are not yet actualized. For I now observe that my knowledge is gradually being increased, and I see nothing standing in the way of its being increased more and more to infinity. Moreover, I see no reason why, with my knowledge thus increased, I could not acquire all the remaining perfections of God. And, finally, if the potential for these perfections is in me already, I see no reason why this potential would not suffice to produce the idea of these perfections.

Yet none of these things can be the case. First, while it is true that my knowledge is gradually being increased and that there are many things in me potentially that are not yet actual, nevertheless, none of these pertains to the idea of God, in which there is nothing whatever that is potential. Indeed this gradual increase is itself a most certain proof of imperfection. Moreover, although my knowledge may always increase more and more, nevertheless I understand that this knowledge will never by this means be actually infinite, because it will never reach a point where it is incapable of greater increase. On the contrary, I judge God to be actually infinite, so that nothing can be added to his perfection. Finally, I perceive that the objective being of an idea cannot be produced by a merely potential being (which, strictly speaking, is nothing), but only by an actual or formal being.

Indeed there is nothing in all these things that is not manifest by the light of nature to one who is conscientious and attentive. But when I am less attentive, and the images of sensible things blind the mind's eye, I do not so easily recall why the idea of a being more perfect than me necessarily proceeds from a being that really is more perfect. This being the case, it is appropriate to ask further whether I myself who have this idea could exist, if such a being did not exist. [29]

From what source, then, do I derive my existence? Why, from myself, or from my parents, or from whatever other things there are that are less perfect than God. For nothing more perfect than God, or even as perfect as God, can be thought or imagined.

But if I got my being from myself, I would not doubt, nor would I desire, nor would I lack anything at all. For I would have given myself all the perfections of which I have some idea; in so doing, I myself would be God! I must not think that the things I lack could perhaps be more difficult to acquire than the ones I have now. On the contrary, it is obvious that it would have been much more difficult for me (that is, a thing or substance that thinks) to emerge out of nothing than it would be to acquire the knowledge of many things about which I am ignorant (these items of knowledge being merely accidents of that substance). Certainly, if I got this greater thing from myself, I would not have denied myself at least those things that can be had more easily. Nor would I have denied myself any of those other things that I perceive to be contained in the idea of God, for surely none of them seem to me more difficult to bring about. But if any of them were more difficult to bring about, they would certainly also seem more difficult to me, even if the remaining ones that I possess I got from myself, since it would be on account of them that I would experience that my power is limited.

Nor am I avoiding the force of these arguments, if I suppose that perhaps I have always existed as I do now, as if it then followed that no author of my existence need be sought. For because the entire span of one's life can be divided into countless parts, each one wholly independent of the rest, it does not follow from the fact that I existed a short time ago that I must exist now, unless some cause, as it were, creates me all over again at this moment, that is to say, which preserves me. For it is obvious to one who pays close attention to the nature of time that plainly the same force and

action are needed to preserve anything at each individual moment that it lasts as would be required to create that same thing anew, were it not yet in existence. Thus conservation differs from creation solely by virtue of a distinction of reason; this too is one of those things that are manifest by the light of nature.

Therefore I must now ask myself whether I possess some power by which I can bring it about that I myself, who now exist, will also exist a little later on. For since I am nothing but a thinking thing—or at least since I am now dealing simply and precisely with that part of me which is a thinking thing—if such a power were in me, then I would certainly be aware of it. But I observe that there is no such power; and from this very fact I know most clearly that I depend upon some being other than myself.

But perhaps this being is not God, and I have been produced either by my parents or by some other causes less perfect than God. On the contrary, as I said before, it is obvious that there must be at least as much in the cause as there is in the effect. Thus, regardless of what it is that eventually is assigned as my cause, because I am a thinking thing and have within me a certain idea of God, it must be granted that what caused me is also a thinking thing and it too has an idea of all the perfections which I attribute to God. And I can again inquire of this cause whether it got its existence from itself or from another cause. For if it got its existence from itself, it is evident from what has been said that it is itself God, because, having the power of existing in and of itself, it unquestionably also has the power of actually possessing all the perfections of which it has in itself an idea—that is, all the perfections that I conceive to be in God. However, if it got its existence from another cause, I will once again inquire in similar fashion about this other cause: whether it got its existence from itself or from another cause, until finally I arrive at the ultimate cause, which will be God. For it is apparent enough that there can be no infinite regress here, especially since I am not dealing here merely with the cause that once produced me, but also and most especially with the cause that preserves me at the present time.

Nor can one fancy that perhaps several partial causes have concurred in bringing me into being, and that I have taken the ideas of the various perfections I attribute to God from a variety of causes, so that all of these perfections are found somewhere in the uni-

[29] The main argument—that I cannot have caused my idea of God, indeed that nothing but God can have caused it, so that God must exist—is already essentially complete at this point. The discussion of Descartes's own existence that follows is something of a digression.

verse, but not all joined together in a single being—God. On the contrary, the unity, the simplicity, that is, the inseparability of all those features that are in God is one of the chief perfections that I understand to be in him. Certainly the idea of the unity of all his perfections could not have been placed in me by any cause from which I did not also get the ideas of the other perfections; for neither could some cause have made me understand them joined together and inseparable from one another, unless it also caused me to recognize what they were.

Finally, as to my parents, even if everything that I ever believed about them were true, still it is certainly not they who preserve me; nor is it they who in any way brought me into being, insofar as I am a thinking thing. Rather, they merely placed certain dispositions in the matter which I judged to contain me, that is, a mind, which now is the only thing I take myself to be. And thus there can be no difficulty here concerning my parents. Indeed I have no choice but to conclude that the mere fact of my existing and of there being in me an idea of a most perfect being, that is, God, demonstrates most evidently that God too exists. [30]

All that remains for me is to ask how I received this idea of God. For I did not draw it from the senses; it never came upon me unexpectedly, as is usually the case with the ideas of sensible things when these things present themselves (or seem to present themselves) to the external sense organs. Nor was it made by me, for I plainly can neither subtract anything from it nor add anything to it. Thus the only option remaining is that this idea is innate in me, just as the idea of myself is innate in me. [31]

To be sure, it is not astonishing that in creating me, God should have endowed me with this idea, so that it would be like the mark of the craftsman impressed upon his work, although this mark need not be something distinct from the work itself. But the mere fact that God created me makes it highly plausible that I have somehow been made in his image and likeness, and that I perceive this likeness, in which the idea of God is contained, by means of the same faculty by which I perceive myself. That is, when I turn the mind's eye toward myself, I understand not only that I am something incomplete and dependent upon another, something aspiring indefinitely for greater and greater or better things, but also that the being on whom I depend has in himself all those greater things—not merely indefinitely and potentially, but infinitely and actually, and thus that he is God. The whole force of the argument rests on the fact that I recognize that it would be impossible for me to exist, being of such a nature as I am (namely, having in me the idea of God), unless God did in fact exist. God, I say, that same being the idea of whom is in me: a being having all those perfections that I cannot comprehend, but can somehow touch with my thought, and a being subject to no defects whatever. From these considerations it is quite obvious that he cannot be a deceiver, for it is manifest by the light of nature that all fraud and deception depend on some defect.

But before examining this idea more closely and at the same time inquiring into other truths that can be gathered from it, at this point I want to spend some time contemplating this God, to ponder his attributes and, so far as the eye of my darkened mind can take me, to gaze upon, to admire, and to adore the beauty of this immense light. For just as we believe by faith that the greatest felicity of the next life consists solely in this contemplation of the divine majesty, so too we now experience that from the same contemplation, although it is much less perfect, the greatest pleasure of which we are capable in this life can be perceived.

. . .

MEDITATION SIX: Concerning the Existence of Material Things, and the Real Distinction Between Mind and Body

It remains for me to examine whether material things exist. Indeed I now know that they can exist, at least insofar as they are the object of pure mathematics,

[30] The result that is supposed to follow from the ingredients already discussed finally emerges here: only a genuinely existing God could be the cause of Descartes's idea of God. And once Descartes knows that God exists, he can trust that his clear and distinct ideas are true. The rest of *Meditation Three* raises and attempts to answer various objections to his overall argument. But there is a more serious objection that was raised by Descartes's contemporaries. (See Discussion Question 3.)

[31] Here Descartes refers to the three options mentioned at Annotation 19.

since I clearly and distinctly perceive them. For no doubt God is capable of bringing about everything that I am capable of perceiving in this way. And I have never judged that God was incapable of something, except when it was incompatible with my perceiving it distinctly. [32]

Moreover, from the faculty of imagination, which I notice I use while dealing with material things, it seems to follow that they exist. For to anyone paying very close attention to what imagination is, it appears to be simply a certain application of the knowing faculty to a body intimately present to it, and which therefore exists. [33]

To make this clear, I first examine the difference between imagination and pure intellection. So, for example, when I imagine a triangle, I not only understand that it is a figure bounded by three lines, but at the same time I also envisage with the mind's eye those lines as if they were present; and this is what I call "imagining." On the other hand, if I want to think about a chiliagon, I certainly understand that it is a figure consisting of a thousand sides, just as well as I understand that a triangle is a figure consisting of three sides, yet I do not imagine those thousand sides in the same way, or envisage them as if they were present. And although in that case—because of force of habit I always imagine something whenever I think about a corporeal thing—I may perchance represent to myself some figure in a confused fashion, nevertheless this figure is obviously not a chiliagon. For this figure is really no different from the figure I would represent to myself, were I thinking of a myriagon or any other figure with a large number of sides. Nor is this figure of any help in knowing the properties that differentiate a chiliagon from other polygons. But if the figure in question is a pentagon, I surely can understand its figure, just as was the case with the chiliagon, without the help of my imagination. But I can also imagine a pentagon by turning the mind's eye both to its five sides and at the same time to the area bounded by those sides. At this point I am manifestly aware that I am in need of a peculiar sort of effort on the part of the mind in order to

imagine, one that I do not employ in order to understand. This new effort on the part of the mind clearly shows the difference between imagination and pure intellection.

Moreover, I consider that this power of imagining that is in me, insofar as it differs from the power of understanding, is not required for my own essence, that is, the essence of my mind. For were I to be lacking this power, I would nevertheless undoubtedly remain the same entity I am now. Thus it seems to follow that the power of imagining depends upon something distinct from me. [34] And I readily understand that, were a body to exist to which a mind is so joined that it may apply itself in order, as it were, to look at it any time it wishes, it could happen that it is by means of this very body that I imagine corporeal things. As a result, this mode of thinking may differ from pure intellection only in the sense that the mind, when it understands, in a sense turns toward itself and looks at one of the ideas that are in it; whereas when it imagines, it turns toward the body, and intuits in the body something that conforms to an idea either understood by the mind or perceived by sense. To be sure, I easily understand that the imagination can be actualized in this way, provided a body does exist. And since I can think of no other way of explaining imagination that is equally appropriate, I make a probable conjecture from this that a body exists. But this is only a probability. And even though I may examine everything carefully, nevertheless I do not yet see how the distinct idea of corporeal nature that I find in my imagination can enable me to develop an argument which necessarily concludes that some body exists. [35]

But I am in the habit of imagining many other things, over and above that corporeal nature which is

[32] This amounts to the claim that clear and distinct perception is a good criterion for what is at least *possible*. Is there any argument here for this claim?

[33] Descartes eventually retreats from this not very plausible claim.

[34] The point here is that the power of imagining is more than follows from the idea of a thinking thing: a thing might be able to think without being able to imagine (or sense, as emerges later). Does it follow in any clear way that this power must derive from something distinct from the thinking thing—as opposed to just being a further feature that it has (even though it might not have)?

[35] Imagination provides no conclusive argument for the existence of bodies. Does it even make it probable that they exist, as Descartes seems to claim?

the object of pure mathematics, such as colors, sounds, tastes, pain, and the like, though not so distinctly. And I perceive these things better by means of the senses, from which, with the aid of the memory, they seem to have arrived at the imagination. Thus I should pay the same degree of attention to the senses, so that I might deal with them more appropriately. I

[36] We now come to the main issue: does sense experience yield any good reason for thinking that external material bodies exist?

must see whether I can obtain any reliable argument for the existence of corporeal things from those things that are perceived by the mode of thinking that I call "sense." [36]

First of all, to be sure, I will review here all the things I previously believed to be true because I had perceived them by means of the senses and the causes I had for thinking this. Next I will assess the causes why I later called them into doubt. Finally, I will consider what I must now believe about these things.

So first, I sensed that I had a head, hands, feet, and other members that comprised this body which I viewed as part of me, or perhaps even as the whole of me. I sensed that this body was found among many other bodies, by which my body can be affected in various beneficial or harmful ways. I gauged what was opportune by means of a certain sensation of pleasure, and what was inopportune by a sensation of pain. In addition to pain and pleasure, I also sensed within me hunger, thirst, and other such appetites, as well as certain bodily tendencies toward mirth, sadness, anger, and other such affects. And externally, besides the extension, shapes, and motions of bodies, I also sensed their hardness, heat, and other tactile qualities. I also sensed light, colors, odors, tastes, and sounds, on the basis of whose variety I distinguished the sky, the earth, the seas, and the other bodies, one from the other. Now given the ideas of all these qualities that presented themselves to my thought, and which were all that I properly and immediately sensed, still it was surely not without reason that I thought I sensed things that were manifestly different from my thought, namely, the bodies from which these ideas proceeded. For I knew by experience that these ideas came upon me utterly without my consent, to the extent that, wish as I may, I could not sense any object unless it was present to a sense organ. Nor

could I fail to sense it when it was present. And since the ideas perceived by sense were much more vivid and explicit and even, in their own way, more distinct than any of those that I deliberately and knowingly formed through meditation or that I found impressed on my memory, it seemed impossible that they came from myself. Thus the remaining alternative was that they came from other things. Since I had no knowledge of such things except from those same ideas themselves, I could not help entertaining the thought that they were similar to those ideas. [37] Moreover, I also recalled that the use of the senses antedated the use of reason. And since I saw that the ideas that I myself fashioned were not as explicit as those that I per-

[37] This is one of the reasons mentioned earlier at Annotation 20. It is also one of those that Locke appeals to in his attempt to argue, without any appeal to God, for the existence of material objects corresponding to sense experience.

ceived through the faculty of sense, and were for the most part composed of parts of the latter, I easily convinced myself that I had absolutely no idea in the intellect that I did not have beforehand in the sense faculty. Not without reason did I judge that this body, which by a certain special right I called "mine," belongs more to me than did any other. For I could never be separated from it in the same way I could be from other bodies. I sensed all appetites and feelings in and on behalf of it. Finally, I noticed pain and pleasurable excitement in its parts, but not in other bodies external to it. But why should a certain sadness of spirit arise from some sensation or other of pain, and why should a certain elation arise from a sensation of excitement, or why should that peculiar twitching in the stomach, which I call hunger, warn me to have something to eat, or why should dryness in the throat warn me to take something to drink, and so on? I plainly had no explanation other than that I had been taught this way by nature. For there is no affinity whatsoever, at least none I am aware of, between this twitching in the stomach and the will to have something to eat, or between the sensation of something causing pain and the thought of sadness arising from this sensation. But nature also seems to have taught me everything else as well that I judged concerning the objects of the senses, for I had already convinced myself that this was how things were, prior to my assessing any of the arguments that might prove it. ⒊⒏

⒊⒏ This paragraph describes Descartes's previous *faith* in his senses. He has made many assumptions about the existence of bodies and the accuracy of the beliefs based on his sense experiences, but he recognizes that he had no arguments for the correctness of these assumptions. Think about this issue: what reason do you have for thinking that the belief you have right now that there is a physical book in front of you (a belief based on your visual sense experience) is true?

Afterwards, however, many experiences gradually weakened any faith that I had in the senses. Towers that had seemed round from afar occasionally appeared square at close quarters. Very large statues mounted on their pedestals did not seem large to someone looking at them from ground level. And in countless other such instances I determined that judgments in matters of the external senses were in error. And not just the external senses, but the internal senses as well. For what can be more intimate than pain? But I had sometimes heard it said by people whose leg or arm had been amputated that it seemed to them that they still occasionally sensed pain in the very limb they had lost. Thus, even in my own case it did not seem to be entirely certain that some bodily member was causing me pain, even though I did sense pain in it.⒊⒐ To these causes for doubt I recently added two quite general ones. The first was that everything I ever thought I sensed while awake I could believe I also sometimes sensed while asleep, and since I do not believe that what I seem to sense in my dreams comes to me from things external to me, I saw no reason why I should hold this belief about those things I seem to be sensing while awake. The second was that, since I was still ignorant of the author of my origin (or at least pretended to be ignorant of it), I saw nothing to prevent my having been so constituted by nature that I should be mistaken even about what seemed to me most true.⒋⒈ As to the arguments that used to convince me of the truth of sensible things, I

⒊⒐ Think about this example. Is the amputee genuinely in pain, even though the limb is gone? He is wrong about the source of his pain, but is he wrong about being in pain? How exactly does this example provide a basis for doubting?

⒋⒈ This is an allusion to the evil genius.

found no difficulty responding to them. For since I seemed driven by nature toward many things about which reason tried to dissuade me, I did not think that what I was taught by nature deserved much credence. And even though the perceptions of the senses did not depend on my will, I did not think that we must therefore conclude that they came from things distinct from me, since perhaps there is some faculty in me, as yet unknown to me, that produces these perceptions.

But now, having begun to have a better knowledge of myself and the author of my origin, I am of the opinion that I must not rashly admit everything that I seem to derive from the senses; but neither, for that matter, should I call everything into doubt.

First, I know that all the things that I clearly and distinctly understand can be made by God such as I understand them. For this reason, my ability clearly and distinctly to understand one thing without another suffices to make me certain that the one thing is different from the other, since they can be separated from each other, at least by God. The question as to the sort of power that might effect such a separation is not relevant to their being thought to be different. For this reason, from the fact that I know that I exist, and that at the same time I judge that obviously nothing else belongs to my nature or essence except that I am a thinking thing, I rightly conclude that my essence consists entirely in my being a thinking thing. And although perhaps (or rather, as I shall soon say, assuredly) I have a body that is very closely joined to me, nevertheless, because on the one hand I have a clear and distinct idea of myself, insofar as I am merely a thinking thing and not an extended thing, and because on the other hand I have a distinct idea of a body, insofar as it is merely an extended thing and not a thinking thing, it is certain that I am really distinct from my body, and can exist without it. ⒋⒈

⒋⒈ Here is an argument for the conclusion that a person (his or her mind) is distinct from his or her body. What is the reason offered for that conclusion? What underlying principle does it appeal to? Is the argument a good one? (See Discussion Question 4.)

Moreover, I find in myself faculties for certain special modes of thinking, namely the faculties of imagining and sensing. I can clearly and distinctly understand myself in my entirety without these faculties, but not vice versa: I cannot understand them clearly and distinctly without me, that is, without a substance endowed with understanding in which they inhere, for they include an act of understanding in their formal concept. Thus I perceive them to be distinguished from me as modes from a thing. I also acknowledge that there are certain other faculties, such as those of moving from one place to another, of taking on various shapes, and so on, that, like sensing or imagining, cannot be understood apart from some substance in which they inhere, and hence without which they cannot exist. But it is clear that these faculties, if in fact they exist, must be in a corporeal or extended substance, not in a substance endowed with understanding. For some extension is contained in a clear and distinct concept of them, though certainly not any understanding. Now there clearly is in me a passive faculty of sensing, that is, a faculty for receiving and knowing the ideas of sensible things; but I could not use it unless there also existed, either in me or in something else, a certain active faculty of producing or bringing about these ideas. But this faculty surely cannot be in me, since it clearly presupposes no act of understanding, and these ideas are produced without my cooperation and often even against my will. Therefore the only alternative is that it is in some substance different from me, containing either formally or eminently all the reality that exists objectively in the ideas produced by that faculty, as I have just noted above. Hence this substance is either a body, that is, a corporeal nature, which contains formally all that is contained objectively in the ideas, or else it is God, or some other creature more noble than a body, which contains eminently all that is contained objectively in the ideas. But since God is not a deceiver, it is patently obvious that he does not send me these ideas either immediately by himself, or even through the mediation of some creature that contains the objective reality of these ideas not formally but only eminently. For since God has given me no faculty whatsoever for making this determination, but instead has given me a great inclination to believe that these ideas issue from corporeal things, I fail to see how God could be understood not to be a deceiver, if these ideas were to issue from a source other than corporeal things. And consequently corporeal things exist. Nevertheless, perhaps not all bodies exist exactly as I grasp them by sense, since this sensory grasp is in many cases very obscure and confused. But at least they do contain everything I clearly and distinctly understand—that is, everything, considered in a general sense, that is encompassed in the object of pure mathematics. (42)

As far as the remaining matters are concerned, which are either merely particular (for example, that the sun is of such and such a size or shape, and so on) or less clearly understood (for example, light, sound, pain, and the like), even though these matters are very doubtful and uncertain, nevertheless the fact that God is no deceiver (and thus no falsity can be found in my opinions, unless there is also in me a faculty given me by God for the purpose of rectifying this falsity) offers me a definite hope of reaching the truth even in these matters. And surely there is no doubt that all that I am taught by nature has some truth to it; for by "nature," taken generally, I understand nothing other than God himself or the ordered network of created things which was instituted by God. By my own particular nature I understand nothing other than the combination of all the things bestowed upon me by God.

There is nothing that this nature teaches me more explicitly than that I have a body that is ill-disposed when I feel pain, that needs food and drink when I suffer hunger or thirst, and the like. Therefore, I should not doubt that there is some truth in this.

By means of these sensations of pain, hunger, thirst and so on, nature also teaches not merely that I am present to my body in the way a sailor is present in a ship, but that I am most tightly joined and, so to speak, commingled with it, so much so that I and the body constitute one single thing. For if this were not the case, then I, who am only a thinking thing, would not sense pain when the body is injured; rather, I would perceive the wound by means of the

(42) Here finally is Descartes's main reason for thinking that there are external things: My sensory ideas of external things cannot be produced by me, since they are involuntary and the faculty that produces them is not an essential part of my nature as a thinking thing. Therefore they must be produced by something else, and God would be a deceiver if he so arranged things that these ideas were produced by something other than things. But God is not a deceiver (since deception would be an imperfection). Therefore, external things must exist—though not necessarily with all the specific features that I experience. How good is this argument? (See Discussion Question 5.)

pure intellect, just as a sailor perceives by sight whether anything in his ship is broken. And when the body is in need of food or drink, I should understand this explicitly, instead of having confused sensations of hunger and thirst. For clearly these sensations of

[43] Here is Descartes's account of the relation between his mind and his body: they are two distinct things, but still intricately connected with each other.

thirst, hunger, pain, and so on are nothing but certain confused modes of thinking arising from the union and, as it were, the commingling of the mind with the body. [43]

Moreover, I am also taught by nature that various other bodies exist around my body, some of which are to be pursued, while others are to be avoided. And to be sure, from the fact that I sense a wide variety of colors, sounds, odors, tastes, levels of heat, and grades of roughness, and the like, I rightly conclude that in the bodies from which these different perceptions of the senses proceed there are differences corresponding to the different perceptions—though perhaps the latter do not resemble the former. And from the fact that some of these perceptions are pleasant while others are unpleasant, it is plainly certain that my body, or rather my whole self, insofar as I am comprised of a body and a mind, can be affected by various beneficial and harmful bodies in the vicinity.

Granted, there are many other things that I seem to have been taught by nature; nevertheless it was not really nature that taught them to me but a certain habit of making reckless judgments. And thus it could easily happen that these judgments are false: for example, that any space where there is absolutely nothing happening to move my senses is empty; or that there is something in a hot body that bears an exact likeness to the idea of heat that is in me; or that in a white or green body there is the same whiteness or greenness that I sense; or that in a bitter or sweet body

[44] Here Descartes lists various sorts of mistaken judgments that his sensory experiences tempt him to make. Locke and Berkeley will have more to say about these matters.

there is the same taste, and so on; or that stars and towers and any other distant bodies have the same size and shape that they present to my senses, and other things of this sort. [44] But to ensure that my per-

ceptions in this matter are sufficiently distinct, I ought to define more precisely what exactly I mean when I say that I am "taught something by nature." For I am taking "nature" here more narrowly than the combination of everything bestowed on me by God. For this combination embraces many things that belong exclusively to my mind, such as my perceiving that what has been done cannot be undone, and everything else that is known by the light of nature. That is not what I am talking about here. There are also many things that belong exclusively to the body, such as that it tends to move downward, and so on. I am not dealing with these either, but only with what God has bestowed on me insofar as I am composed of mind and body. Accordingly, it is this nature that teaches me to avoid things that produce a sensation of pain and to pursue things that produce a sensation of pleasure, and the like. But it does not appear that nature teaches us to conclude anything, besides these things, from these sense perceptions unless the intellect has first conducted its own inquiry regarding things external to us. For it seems to belong exclusively to the mind, and not to the composite of mind and body, to know the truth in these matters. Thus, although a star affects my eye no more than does the flame from a small torch, still there is no real or positive tendency in my eye toward believing that the star is no larger than the flame. Yet, ever since my youth, I have made this judgment without any reason for doing so. And although I feel heat as I draw closer to the fire, and I also feel pain upon drawing too close to it, there is not a single argument that persuades me that there is something in the fire similar to that heat, any more than to that pain. On the contrary, I am convinced only that there is something in the fire that, regardless of what it finally turns out to be, causes in us those sensations of heat or pain. And although there may be nothing in a given space that moves the senses, it does not therefore follow that there is no body in it. But I see that in these and many other instances I have been in the habit of subverting the order of nature. For admittedly I use the perceptions of the senses (which are properly given by nature only for signifying to the mind what things are useful or harmful to the composite of which it is a part, and to that extent they are clear and distinct enough) as reliable rules for immediately discerning what is the essence of bodies located outside us. Yet they signify nothing about that except quite obscurely and confusedly. ④⑤

④⑤ Descartes's view is that the specific perceptions of the senses should not be taken to reveal the actual nature of external objects, but only as a guide to what things are useful or harmful. Thus the sensation of heat does not describe any property that is actually in the fire, but nonetheless warns us not to get too close to it. Thus the fact that people who do not think carefully about such matters are sometimes misled does not show that God is a deceiver.

I have already examined in sufficient detail how it could happen that my judgments are false, despite the goodness of God. But a new difficulty now arises regarding those very things that nature shows me are either to be sought out or avoided, as well as the internal sensations where I seem to have detected errors, as for example, when someone is deluded by a food's pleasant taste to eat the poison hidden inside it. In this case, however, he is driven by nature only toward desiring the thing in which the pleasurable taste is found, but not toward the poison, of which he obviously is unaware. I can only conclude that this nature is not omniscient. This is not remarkable, since man is a limited thing, and thus only what is of limited perfection befits him.

But we not infrequently err even in those things to which nature impels us. Take, for example, the case of those who are ill and who desire food or drink that will soon afterwards be injurious to them. ④⑥ Perhaps it could be said here that they erred because their nature was corrupt. However, this does not remove our difficulty, for a sick man is no less a creature of God than a healthy one, and thus it seems no less inconsistent that the sick man got a deception-prone nature from God. And a clock made of wheels and counter-weights follows all the laws of nature no less closely when it has been badly constructed and does not tell time accurately than it does when it completely satisfies the wish of its maker. Likewise, I might regard a man's body as a kind of mechanism that is outfitted with and composed of bones, nerves,

④⑥ There is still a problem, however, since our sense experience sometimes misleads us even concerning which things are helpful or harmful.

muscles, veins, blood and skin in such a way that, even if no mind existed in it, the man's body would still exhibit all the same motions that are in it now except for those motions that proceed either from a command of the will or, consequently, from the mind. I easily recognize that it would be natural for this body, were it, say, suffering from dropsy and experiencing dryness in the throat (which typically produces a thirst sensation in the mind), and also so disposed by its nerves and other parts to take something to drink, the result of which would be to exacerbate the illness. This is as natural as for a body without any such illness to be moved by the same dryness in the throat to take something to drink that is useful to it. And given the intended purpose of the clock, I could say that it deviates from its nature when it fails to tell the right time. And similarly, considering the mechanism of the human body in terms of its being equipped for the motions that typically occur in it, I may think that it too is deviating from its nature, if its throat were dry when having something to drink is not beneficial to its conservation. Nevertheless, I am well aware that this last use of "nature" differs greatly from the other. For this latter "nature" is merely a designation dependent on my thought, since it compares a man in poor health and a poorly constructed clock with the ideas of a healthy man and of a well-made clock, a designation extrinsic to the things to which it is applied. But by "nature" taken in the former sense, I understand something that is really in things, and thus is not without some truth.

When we say, then, in the case of the body suffering from dropsy, that its "nature" is corrupt, given the fact that it has a parched throat and yet does not need something to drink, "nature" obviously is merely an extrinsic designation. Nevertheless, in the case of the composite, that is, of a mind joined to such a body, it is not a mere designation, but a true error of nature that this body should be thirsty when having something to drink would be harmful to it. It therefore remains to inquire here how the goodness of God does not prevent "nature," thus considered, from being deceptive.

Now my first observation here is that there is a great difference between a mind and a body in that a body, by its very nature, is always divisible. On the other hand, the mind is utterly indivisible. For when I consider the mind, that is, myself insofar as I am only a thinking thing, I cannot distinguish any parts within me; rather, I understand myself to be manifestly one complete thing. Although the entire mind seems to be united to the entire body, nevertheless, were a foot or an arm or any other bodily part to be amputated, I know that nothing has been taken away from the mind on that account. Nor can the faculties of willing, sensing, understanding, and so on be called "parts" of the mind, since it is one and the same mind that wills, senses, and understands. On the other hand, there is no corporeal or extended thing I can think of that I may not in my thought easily divide into parts; and in this way I understand that it is divisible. This consideration alone would suffice to teach me that the mind is wholly diverse from the body, had I not yet known it well enough in any other way. [47]

47 As a part of his explanation of the fact that our nature is liable to errors of this last sort, Descartes argues again that his mind is distinct from his body, this time appealing to the properties of divisibility and indivisibility. (See Discussion Question 4.)

My second observation is that my mind is not immediately affected by all the parts of the body, but only by the brain, or perhaps even by just one small part of the brain, namely, by that part where the "common" sense is said to reside. Whenever this part of the brain is disposed in the same manner, it presents the same thing to the mind, even if the other parts of the body are able meanwhile to be related in diverse ways. Countless experiments show this, none of which need be reviewed here.

My next observation is that the nature of the body is such that whenever any of its parts can be moved by another part some distance away, it can also be moved in the same manner by any of the parts that lie between them, even if this more distant part is doing nothing. For example, in the cord ABCD, if the final part D is pulled, the first part A would be moved in exactly the same manner as it could be, if one of the intermediate parts B or C were pulled, while the end part D remained immobile. Likewise, when I feel a pain in my foot, physics teaches me that this sensation took place by means of nerves distributed throughout the foot, like stretched cords extending from the foot all the way to the brain. When these nerves are pulled in the foot, they also pull on the inner parts of the brain to which they extend, and produce a certain mo-

tion in them. This motion has been constituted by nature so as to affect the mind with a sensation of pain, as if it occurred in the foot. But because these nerves need to pass through the shin, thigh, loins, back, and neck to get from the foot to the brain, it can happen that even if it is not the part in the foot but merely one of the intermediate parts that is being struck, the very same movement will occur in the brain that would occur were the foot badly injured. The inevitable result will be that the mind feels the same pain. The same opinion should hold for any other sensation.

My final observation is that, since any given motion occurring in that part of the brain immediately affecting the mind produces but one sensation in it, I can think of no better arrangement than that it produces the one sensation that, of all the ones it is able to produce, is most especially and most often conducive to the maintenance of a healthy man. Moreover, experience shows that all the sensations bestowed on us by nature are like this. Hence there is absolutely nothing to be found in them that does not bear witness to God's power and goodness. Thus, for example, when the nerves in the foot are agitated in a violent and unusual manner, this motion of theirs extends through the marrow of the spine to the inner reaches of the brain, where it gives the mind the sign to sense something, namely, the pain as if it is occurring in the foot. This provokes the mind to do its utmost to move away from the cause of the pain, since it is seen as harmful to the foot. But the nature of man could have been so constituted by God that this same motion in the brain might have indicated something else to the mind: for example, either the motion itself as it occurs in the brain, or in the foot, or in some place in between, or something else entirely different. But nothing else would have served so well the maintenance of the body. Similarly, when we need something to drink, a certain dryness arises in the throat that moves the nerves in the throat, and, by means of them, the inner parts of the brain. And this motion affects the mind with a sensation of thirst, because in this entire affair nothing is more useful for us to know than that we need something to drink in order to maintain our health; the same holds in the other cases.

From these considerations it is utterly apparent that, notwithstanding the immense goodness of God, the nature of man, insofar as it is composed of mind and body, cannot help being sometimes mistaken. For if some cause, not in the foot but in some other part through which the nerves extend from the foot to the brain, or perhaps even in the brain itself, were to produce the same motion that would normally be produced by a badly injured foot, the pain will be felt as if it were in the foot, and the senses will naturally be deceived. For since an identical motion in the brain can only bring about an identical sensation in the mind, and it is more frequently the case that this motion is wont to arise on account of a cause that harms the foot than on account of some other thing existing elsewhere, it is reasonable that the motion should always show pain to the mind as something belonging to the foot rather than to some other part. And if dryness in the throat does not arise, as is normal, because taking something to drink contributes to bodily health, but from a contrary cause, as happens in the case of someone with dropsy, then it is far better that it should deceive on that occasion than that it should always be deceptive when the body is in good health. The same holds for the other cases. 48

48 The preceding paragraphs contain Descartes's explanation of why the sorts of mistakes as to what is desirable or harmful that result from various sorts of abnormal conditions do not count against the goodness of God or show that he is a deceiver. Is his account adequate?

This consideration is most helpful, not only for my noticing all the errors to which my nature is liable, but also for enabling me to correct or avoid them without difficulty. To be sure, I know that all the senses set forth what is true more frequently than what is false regarding what concerns the welfare of the body. Moreover, I can nearly always make use of several of them in order to examine the same thing. Furthermore, I can use my memory, which connects current happenings with past ones, and my intellect, which now has examined all the causes of error.

Hence I should no longer fear that those things that are daily shown me by the senses are false. On the contrary, the hyperbolic doubts of the last few days ought to be rejected as ludicrous. This goes especially for the chief reason for doubting, which dealt with my failure to distinguish being asleep from being awake. For I now notice that there is a considerable difference between these two; dreams are never joined by the memory with all the other actions of life, as is the case with those actions that occur when one is awake. For surely, if, while I am awake, someone were suddenly to appear to me and then immediately disappear, as occurs in dreams, so that I see neither where he came from nor where he went, it is not without reason that I would judge him to be a ghost or a phantom conjured up in my brain, rather than a true man. But when these things happen, and I notice distinctly where they come from, where they are now, and when they come to me, and when I connect my perception of them without interruption with the whole rest of my life, I am clearly certain that these perceptions have happened to me not while I was dreaming but while I was awake. 49 Nor ought I have even the least doubt regarding the

49 And here, finally, is a response to the concern about dreaming. How does he think that dreams and waking experience can be distinguished? Is he right about this?

truth of these things, if, having mustered all the senses, in addition to my memory and my intellect, in order to examine them, nothing is passed on to me by one of these sources that conflicts with the others. For from the fact that God is no deceiver, it follows that I am in no way mistaken in these matters. But because the need to get things done does not always permit us the leisure for such a careful inquiry, we must confess that the life of man is apt to commit errors regarding particular things, and we must acknowledge the infirmity of our nature.

Discussion Questions

1. Descartes finally finds something indubitable in *Meditation Two:* his own existence. One question about this is whether Descartes's insight really takes the form of an argument, as the formulation "I think, therefore I am" suggests. On this view, the premise would be the claim (in the first person) "I think," from which the conclusion "I exist" is inferred. There is little doubt about the cogency of this inference, but the obvious question is why the premise is itself justified. Could the evil genius deceive me about the truth of this premise? Why or why not? Or is it perhaps, as some have suggested, a mistake to think of the Cogito as an argument

at all, rather than as just one unitary insight? And what exactly would that insight be?

2. In addition to the claim that he cannot be deceived about his own existence, Descartes also claims that he cannot be deceived about the existence and content of his specific conscious states of mind. (See Annotation 12.) This is a crucial step, since very little could be inferred from his existence alone. Is he right that the evil genius could not deceive him about such things? Why or why not? (In thinking about this, it may be helpful to consider carefully just what form such deception would take: what would the evil genius do if he were trying to deceive me into thinking that I had a state of mind—perhaps a certain sensory experience— that I didn't really have?)

3. In *Meditation Three,* Descartes attempts to prove the existence of God in order to establish that he can safely accept claims that seem to him to be clear and distinct—which seems to amount to the same thing as claims revealed by the "light of nature." (See Annotation 21.) But to do this, he has to appeal to two general metaphysical principles (see Annotations 24 and 25). How does Descartes know that these principles are true? (Look carefully at what he says.) Can he safely accept these principles on this basis *before* he

has proved the existence of God? What does this show about Descartes's main argument in *Meditation Three:* that God exists and therefore that he can trust his clear and distinct ideas?

4. Descartes offers two arguments for the conclusion that his mind and his body are two distinct entities, one in the passage at Annotation 41 and the second in the passage at Annotation 47. Formulate each of these arguments as carefully as you can and then assess their cogency.

5. How compelling is Descartes's main argument for the existence of external things (see Annotation 42)? One question is how essential the first part of the argument is (the argument for the conclusion that my sensory ideas of external things are produced by something other than myself). If sensory ideas were somehow produced by my own self, would that absolve God of the charge of being a deceiver? A second issue is whether this argument really yields the sort of *conclusive* reason for such beliefs that Descartes is seeking. And a third issue is just what specific conclusions about external things can be justified in this way: do we come to know merely that there are things of some sort out there, or can we know more specific facts about the nature and properties of particular things?

John Locke

The English philosopher John Locke (1632–1704) was one of the most influential philosophers of all time, making major contributions to epistemology, metaphysics, and political philosophy. Locke was the founder of the philosophical movement that has come to be called *British Empiricism* (which also includes George Berkeley, David Hume, and John Stuart Mill, among others). The *Essay Concerning Human Understanding* is his major epistemological and metaphysical work and one of the most widely read philosophical books of all time, having attained the status of both a classic work and a wisely used textbook for students almost as soon as it was published. (For more about Locke's rather colorful life, see the introduction to the selection from his *Second Treatise of Government,* in Chapter 7.)

Perhaps the key term of Locke's epistemology is "idea." Ideas are said to be the objects of the understanding when a person thinks, but this must not be taken to mean that we think only *about* ideas and not in some way about various other sorts of things, most of them external to the mind (including material objects). Locke's view is that ideas are the *immediate* objects of consciousness, that which is directly before the mind, but that these ideas *represent* other things and thus allow us to think about them. Thus it might be clearer to describe ideas as the *vehicles* of thinking, the means by which we think about other things. On this view, an idea is essentially the same thing or at least plays the same role as what more recent philosophers refer to with the term "concept": it is something that exists in or is a feature of the mind, and that allows it to think about some specific sort of thing. But Locke also has at least a tendency to think of ideas as something like mental pictures or images, and it is doubtful that images can do the job of accounting for thought in general. (See Discussion Question 1.)

With regard to the acquisition of ideas, Locke is a thoroughgoing proponent of concept empiricism (see the introduction to the chapter). He argues in Book I of the *Essay* that there is no reason to hold that any ideas are innate, and offers in Book II a detailed account of the derivation of various specific ideas from experience. (The way to evaluate his general view is to think carefully about these specific examples.)

With regard to justificatory empiricism, Locke's stance is more equivocal. Though the main work of Book IV of the *Essay* is to give an account of the justification of knowledge that relies heavily on sense experience, Locke also holds (though not in the parts of the book excerpted here) that there are claims that are justified a priori and that not all of these are merely trivial matters of definition (trifling truths, as he calls them). Locke is thus essentially a moderate rationalist, in fact very similar to Descartes, as regards the justification of claims to knowledge, holding that many or most such claims are justified by appeal to experience, but that some are justified a priori. (His being labeled an empiricist reflects the fact that the issue about the acquisition of ideas or concepts was formulated both earlier and initially more clearly than the issue about the nature of justification.)

The main focus of Book IV is on the specific issue of the justification of claims about the external material world. It is fair to say that Locke struggles with this question, first giving a definition of knowledge that seems to leave no room for such knowledge and then gradually altering his position as he proceeds. This part of his discussion culminates in Chapter XI of Book IV, where Locke attempts to argue from certain features of our experience to the probable truth of the claims about material objects that we hold on the basis of that experience. This is a representative realist view similar to Descartes's attempt in *Meditation Six,* but unlike Descartes, Locke does not invoke God as a basis for his solution.

From *An Essay Concerning Human Understanding*

THE EPISTLE TO THE READER

... Were it fit to trouble thee with the history of this *Essay,* I should tell thee that five or six friends, meeting at my chamber and discoursing on a subject very remote from this, found themselves quickly at a stand, by the difficulties that rose on every side. After we had awhile puzzled ourselves, without coming any nearer a resolution of those doubts which perplexed us, it came into my thoughts that we took a

From An Essay Concerning Human Understanding, *1689.*

wrong course; and that before we set ourselves upon inquiries of that nature, it was necessary to examine our own abilities and see what objects our understandings were, or were not, fitted to deal with. . . .

The commonwealth of learning is not at this time without master-builders, whose mighty designs, in advancing the sciences, will leave lasting monuments to the admiration of posterity; but everyone must not hope to be a *Boyle* or a *Sydenham;* and in an age that produces such masters as the great *Huygenius* and the incomparable Mr. *Newton,* with some others of that strain, it is ambition enough to be employed as an under-labourer in clearing ground a little, and removing some of the rubbish that lies in the way to knowledge.① . . .

① In these two passages, we have a fairly standard conception of epistemology and its role: to investigate the nature of human understanding (human cognitive capacities) itself and to remove various sorts of confusions and other mistakes about cognition that impede the quest for more substantive knowledge.

BOOK I: OF INNATE NOTIONS

Chapter I

1. Since it is the *understanding* that sets man above the rest of sensible beings, and gives him all the advantage and dominion which he has over them, it is certainly a subject, even for its nobleness, worth our labour to inquire into. The understanding, like the eye, whilst it makes us see and perceive all other things, takes no notice of itself; and it requires art and pains to set it at a distance and make it its own object. But whatever be the difficulties that lie in the way of this inquiry, whatever it be that keeps us so much in the dark to ourselves, sure I am that all the light we can let in upon our own minds, all the acquaintance we can make with our own understandings, will not only be very pleasant, but bring us great advantage, in directing our thoughts in the search of other things.

2. This, therefore, being my *purpose,* to inquire into the original, certainty, and extent of human knowledge, together with the grounds and degrees of belief, opinion, and assent. . . .

3. It is therefore worth while to search out the *bounds* between opinion and knowledge, and examine by what measures, in things whereof we have no cer-

tain knowledge, we ought to regulate our assent and moderate our persuasions. In order whereunto I shall pursue this following method:

First, I shall inquire into the *original* of those *ideas,* notions, or whatever else you please to call them, which a man observes and is conscious to himself he has in his mind; and the ways whereby the understanding comes to be furnished with them.②

② By "original," Locke means just *origin.*

Secondly, I shall endeavour to show what *knowledge* the understanding hath by those *ideas,* and the certainty, evidence, and extent of it.

. . .

4. If by this inquiry into the nature of the understanding, I can discover the powers thereof: *how far* they reach; to what things they are in any degree proportionate; and where they fail us, I suppose it may be of use to prevail with the busy mind of man to be more cautious in meddling with things exceeding its comprehension; to stop when it is at the utmost extent of its tether; and to sit down in a quiet ignorance of those things which upon examination are found to be beyond the reach of our capacities. . . .

But, before I proceed on to what I have thought on this subject, I must here in the entrance beg pardon of my reader for the frequent use of the word *idea,* which he will find in the following treatise. It being that term which, I think, serves best to stand for whatsoever is the object of the understanding when a man thinks, I have used it to express whatever is meant by *phantasm, notion, species,* or whatever it is which the mind can be employed about in thinking; and I could not avoid frequently using it.③

③ This is Locke's initial attempt to explain the term "idea." It is important to realize that "thinking" here includes any sort of conscious experience, including sense perception. (The terms "phantasm" and "species" are medieval terms that attempt to capture the same general sort of thing.)

I presume it will be easily granted me that there are such *ideas* in men's minds: everyone is conscious of them in himself, and men's words and actions will satisfy him that they are in others.

Our first inquiry then shall be how they come into the mind.

Chapter II: No Innate Principles in the Mind

1. It is an established opinion amongst some men that there are in the *understanding* certain *innate principles,* some primary notions, ... stamped upon the mind of man, which the soul receives in its very first being and brings into the world with it. It would be sufficient to convince unprejudiced readers of the falseness of this supposition, if I should only show (as I hope I shall in the following parts of this discourse) how men, barely by the use of their natural faculties, may attain to all the knowledge they have, without the help of any innate impressions, and may arrive at certainty without any such original notions or principles.④ ...

④ If allegedly innate principles can be accounted for on the basis of experience, Locke is saying, then there is no good reason for regarding them as innate. Among the ideas held to be innate were such ones as identity, substance, causation, and God.

Chapter IV: Other Considerations Concerning Innate Principles, Both Speculative and Practical

1. Had those who would persuade us that there are innate principles not taken them together in gross, but considered separately the parts out of which those propositions are made, they would not, perhaps, have been so forward to believe they were innate: since, if the *ideas* which made up those truths were not, it was impossible that the propositions made up of them should be innate or our knowledge of them be born with us. For if the *ideas* be not *innate,* there was a time when the mind was without those principles; and then they will not be innate, but be derived from some other original. For, where the *ideas* themselves are not, there can be no knowledge, no assent, no mental or verbal propositions about them.

2. If we will attentively consider new-born *children,* we shall have little reason to think that they bring many *ideas* into the world with them. For, bating perhaps some faint *ideas* of hunger, and thirst, and warmth, and some pains which they may *have* felt in the womb, there is *not* the least appearance of any settled *ideas* at all in them, especially of *ideas answering the terms which make up those universal propositions* that are esteemed innate principles. One may perceive how, by degrees, afterwards, *ideas* come into their minds, and that they get no more nor no other than what experience and the observation of things that come in their way furnish them with: which might be enough to satisfy us that they are not original characters stamped on the mind.⑤

...

⑤ Here is Locke's main argument against innate ideas (and against innate principles): he takes innateness to mean that children are born thinking about the things corresponding to the various innate ideas, a view he thinks is obviously false. In fact, the proponents of innateness had something more subtle than this in mind. See the subsequent selection from Kant (in the a priori section).

BOOK II: OF IDEAS

Chapter I: Of Ideas in General, and Their Original

1. Every man being conscious to himself that he thinks, and that which his mind is applied about whilst thinking being the *ideas* that are there, it is past doubt that men have in their minds several *ideas* such as are those expressed by the words *whiteness, hardness, sweetness, thinking, motion, man, elephant, army, drunkenness* and others: it is in the first place then to be inquired, how he comes by them? ...

2. Let us then suppose the mind to be, as we say, white paper void of all characters, without any *ideas.* How comes it to be furnished? Whence comes it by that vast store which the busy and boundless fancy of man has painted on it with an almost endless variety? Whence has it all the materials of reason and knowledge? To this I answer, in one word, from *experience;* in that all our knowledge is founded, and from that it ultimately derives itself. Our observation, employed either about *external sensible objects, or about the internal operations of our minds perceived and reflected on by ourselves, is that which supplies our understandings with all the materials of thinking.* These two are the fountains of knowledge, from whence all the *ideas* we have, or can naturally have, do spring.⑥

⑥ Here is Locke's initial statement of concept empiricism, which he will elaborate in the rest of Book II. The mind is initially "white paper," in Latin a *tabula rasa,* and it is only through experience that it comes to have the capacity to think about any specific thing.

3. First, *our senses,* conversant about particular sensible objects, do *convey into the mind* several distinct *perceptions* of things, according to those various ways wherein those objects do affect them. And thus we come by those *ideas* we have of *yellow, white, heat, cold, soft, hard, bitter, sweet,* and all those which we call sensible qualities; which when I say the senses convey into the mind, I mean, they from external objects convey into the mind what produces there those *perceptions.* This great source of most of the *ideas* we have, depending wholly upon our senses, and derived by them to the understanding, I call SENSATION.

4. Secondly, the other fountain from which experience furnisheth the understanding with *ideas* is the *perception of the operations of our own minds* within us, as it is employed about the *ideas* it has got; which operations, when the soul comes to reflect on and consider, do furnish the understanding with another set of *ideas,* which could not be had from things without. And such are *perception, thinking, doubting, believing, reasoning, knowing, willing,* and all the different actings of our own minds; which we, being conscious of and observing in ourselves, do from these receive into our understandings as distinct *ideas* as we do from bodies affecting our senses. This source of *ideas* every man has wholly in himself; and though it be not sense, as having nothing to do with external objects, yet it is very like it, and might properly enough be called internal sense. But as I call the other *sensation,* so I call this REFLECTION, the *ideas* it affords being such only as the mind gets by reflecting on its own operations within itself. . . . These two, I say, viz. external material things as the objects of SENSATION, and the operations of our own minds within as the objects of REFLECTION, are to me the only originals from whence all our *ideas* take their beginnings. . . .

5. The understanding seems to me not to have the least glimmering of any *ideas* which it doth not receive from one of these two. *External objects furnish the mind with the* ideas *of sensible qualities,* which are all those different perceptions they produce in us; and the *mind furnishes the understanding with* ideas *of its own operations.*

These, when we have taken a full survey of them and their several modes, combinations, and relations, we shall find to contain all our whole stock of *ideas,* and that we have nothing in our minds which did not come in one of these two ways. Let anyone examine his own thoughts and thoroughly search into his understanding and then let him tell me whether all the original *ideas* he has there are any other than of the objects of his *senses,* or of the operations of his mind, considered as objects of his *reflection.* And how great a mass of knowledge soever he imagines to be lodged there, he will, upon taking a strict view, see that he has *not any* idea *in his mind but what one of these two have imprinted,* though perhaps, with infinite variety compounded and enlarged by the understanding, as we shall see hereafter.⑦

⑦ Here is the basic concept empiricist argument: a challenge to the opponent to identify any idea that cannot be accounted for in the empiricist way. (You should attempt to do this, in order to see how plausible Locke's claim is.)

. . .

23. If it shall be demanded then *when a man begins to have any ideas,* I think the true answer is, when he first has any *sensation.* For, since there appear not to be any *ideas* in the mind before the senses have conveyed any in, I conceive that *ideas* in the understanding are coeval with *sensation;* which is such an impression or motion made in some part of the body, as produces some perception in the understanding. It is about these impressions made on our senses by outward objects that the mind seems first to employ itself in such operations as we call *perception, remembering, consideration, reasoning,* etc.

24. In time, the mind comes to reflect on its own *operations* about the *ideas* got by *sensation* and thereby stores itself with a new set of *ideas,* which I call *ideas* of *reflection.* These *impressions* that are made on our *senses* by outward objects that are extrinsical to the mind; and *its own operations,* proceeding from powers intrinsical and proper to itself, which when reflected on by itself become also objects of its contemplation, are, as I have said, *the original of all knowledge.* Thus the first capacity of human intellect is that the mind is fitted to receive the impressions made on it either through the *senses* by outward objects, or by its own operations when it *reflects* on them.⑧ . . .

⑧ Try to think of examples of ideas that derive from each of the two main sources Locke mentions, specifying in each case the experience from which Locke would claim that the idea is derived.

25. In this part the *understanding* is merely *passive;* and whether or no it will have these beginnings and, as it were, materials of knowledge, is not in its own power. For the objects of our senses do, many of them, obtrude their particular *ideas* upon our minds whether we will or no; and the operations of our minds will not let us be without, at least, some obscure notions of them. No man can be wholly ignorant of what he does when he thinks.⑨ . . .

---

⑨ As a *tabula rasa,* the mind is entirely passive in its acquisition of ideas. (Many later philosophers have challenged whether this is so, at least for ideas having much complexity.)

Chapter II: Of Simple Ideas

1. The better to understand the nature, manner, and extent of our knowledge, one thing is carefully to be observed concerning the *ideas* we have, and that is that *some* of them are *simple* and *some complex.*

Though the qualities that affect our senses are, in the things themselves, so united and blended that there is no separation, no distance between them, yet it is plain the *ideas* they produce in the mind enter by the senses simple and unmixed. For, though the sight and touch often take in from the same object, at the same time, different *ideas,* as a man sees at once motion and colour, the hand feels softness and warmth in the same piece of wax: yet the simple *ideas* thus united in the same subject are as perfectly distinct as those that come in by different senses. The coldness and hardness which a man feels in a piece of *ice* being as distinct *ideas* in the mind as the smell and whiteness of a lily, or as the taste of sugar, and smell of a rose; and there is nothing can be plainer to a man than the clear and distinct perception he has of those simple *ideas;* which, being each in itself uncompounded, contains in it nothing but *one uniform appearance* or conception in the mind, and is not distinguishable into different *ideas.* ⑩

---

⑩ Think carefully about this account of what it is for an idea to be *simple.* Note that there are two criteria here, not just one: (a) presenting one uniform appearance (such as the idea of a specific shade of red or a specific musical tone) and (b) not being distinguishable into different ideas (in terms of which it would be definable and so not simple). Do these two always apply to the same things, or might there be ideas that are simple in the second sense (not definable) but not in the first (one uniform appearance)?

---

2. These simple *ideas,* the materials of all our knowledge, are suggested and furnished to the mind only by those two ways above mentioned, viz. *sensation* and *reflection.* When the understanding is once stored with these simple *ideas,* it has the power to repeat, compare, and unite them, even to an almost infinite variety, and so can make at pleasure new complex *ideas.* But it is not in the power of the most exalted wit or enlarged understanding, by any quickness or variety of thought, to *invent or frame one new simple* idea in the mind, not taken in by the ways before mentioned; nor can any force of the understanding *destroy* those that are there. . . .

Chapter III: Of Ideas of One Sense

1. The better to conceive the *ideas* we receive from sensation, it may not be amiss for us to consider them in reference to the different ways whereby they make their approaches to our minds and make themselves perceivable by us.

First, then, There are some which come into our minds *by one sense* only.

Secondly, There are others that convey themselves into the mind *by more senses than one.*

Thirdly, Others that are had from *reflection* only.

Fourthly, There are some that make themselves way and are suggested to the mind *by all the ways of sensation and reflection.*

We shall consider them apart under these several heads.

First, There are *some* ideas *which have admittance only through one sense,* which is peculiarly adapted to receive them. Thus light and colours, as white, red, yellow, blue, with their several degrees or shades and mixtures, as green, scarlet, purple, seagreen, and the rest, come in only by the eyes. All kinds of noises, sounds, and tones, only by the ears. The several tastes and smells, by the nose and palate. And if these organs or the nerves which are the conduits to convey them from without to their audience in the brain, the mind's presence-room (as I may so call it), are any of them so disordered as not to perform their functions, they have no postern to be admitted by, no other way to bring themselves into view and be perceived by the understanding.

The most considerable of those belonging to the touch are heat and cold, and solidity; all the rest—consisting almost wholly in the sensible configuration, as smooth and rough; or else, more or less firm adhesion of the parts, as hard and soft, tough and brittle—are obvious enough.

. . .

Chapter IV: Of Solidity

1. The *idea of solidity* we receive by our touch; and it arises from the resistance which we find in body to the entrance of any other body into the place it possesses, till it has left it. There is no *idea* which we receive more constantly from sensation than *solidity.* Whether we move or rest, in what posture soever we are, we always feel something under us that supports us and hinders our further sinking downwards; and the bodies which we daily handle make us perceive that, whilst they remain between them, they do, by an insurmountable force, hinder the approach of the parts of our hands that press them. That which thus hinders the approach of two bodies, when they are moving one towards another, I call *solidity.* ⑪ . . . but if anyone think it better to call it *impenetrability,* he has my consent. . . .

⑪ The idea of *solidity* plays a central role in Locke's view, since it marks the main difference between empty space and material objects. Is solidity, as Locke claims, a simple idea in both the ways specified earlier?

2. This is the *idea* which belongs to body, whereby we conceive it *to fill space.* The *idea* of which filling of space is that, where we imagine any space taken up by a solid substance, we conceive it so to possess it that it excludes all other solid substances. . . .

5. By this *idea* of solidity is the extension of body distinguished from the extension of space: the extension of body being nothing but the cohesion or continuity of solid, separable, moveable parts; and the extension of space, the continuity of unsolid, inseparable, and immoveable parts. *Upon the solidity of bodies* also *depend their mutual impulse, resistance, and protrusion.* . . .

Chapter V: Of Simple Ideas of Divers Senses

The *ideas* we get by more than one sense are of *space* or *extension, figure, rest,* and *motion.* For these make perceivable impressions, both on the eyes and touch; and we can receive and convey into our minds the *ideas* of the extension, figure, motion, and rest of bodies, both by seeing and feeling. . . .

Chapter VI: Of Simple Ideas of Reflection

1. The mind, receiving the *ideas* mentioned in the foregoing chapters from without, when it turns its view inward upon itself and observes its own actions about those *ideas* it has, takes from thence other *ideas,* which are as capable to be the objects of its contemplation as any of those it received from foreign things.

2. The two great and principal actions of the mind, which are most frequently considered, and which are so frequent that everyone that pleases may take notice of them in himself, are these two:

> *Perception,* or
>   *Thinking;* and
> *Volition,* or *Willing.*

The power of thinking is called the *understanding* and the power of volition is called the *will,* and these two powers or abilities in the mind are denominated *faculties.* ⑫ . . .

⑫ Are the ideas in this chapter and the previous one simple in both of the relevant ways? Does perception, for example, involve "one uniform appearance" in the way that an idea of red does? What about the ones in the following chapter?

Chapter VII: Of Simple Ideas of Both Sensation and Reflection

1. There be other simple *ideas* which convey themselves into the mind by all the ways of sensation and reflection, viz:

> *Pleasure* or *Delight,* and its opposite.
> *Pain,* or *Uneasiness.*
> *Power.*
> *Existence.*
> *Unity.*

. . .

7. *Existence* and *unity* are two other *ideas* that are suggested to the understanding by every object without, and every *idea* within. When *ideas* are in our minds, we consider them as being actually there, as well as we consider things to be actually without us; which is, that they exist or have *existence.* And whatever we can consider as one thing, whether a real being or *idea,* suggests to the understanding the *idea* of *unity.*

8. *Power* also is another of those simple *ideas* which we receive from *sensation* and *reflection.* For,

observing in ourselves that we can at pleasure move several parts of our bodies which were at rest; the effects, also, that natural bodies are able to produce in one another occurring every moment to our senses, we both these ways get the *idea* of *power.*

. . .

Chapter VIII: Some Further Considerations Concerning Our Simple Ideas

1. Concerning the simple *ideas* of sensation, it is to be considered that whatsoever is so constituted in nature as to be able, by affecting our senses, to cause any perception in the mind, doth thereby produce in the understanding a simple *idea;* which, whatever be the external cause of it, when it comes to be taken notice of by our discerning faculty, it is by the mind looked on and considered there to be a real *positive idea* in the understanding, as much as any other whatsoever, though perhaps the cause of it be but a privation in the subject.

2. Thus the *ideas* of heat and cold, light and darkness, white and black, motion and rest, are equally clear and *positive ideas* in the mind, though perhaps some of *the causes* which produce them are barely *privations* in those subjects from whence our senses derive those *ideas.* These the understanding, in its view of them, considers all as distinct positive *ideas,* without taking notice of the causes that produce them: which is an inquiry not belonging to the *idea,* as it is in the understanding, but to the nature of the things existing without us. These are two very different things, and carefully to be distinguished: it being one thing to perceive and know the *idea* of white or black, and quite another to examine what kind of particles they must be and how ranged in the superficies, to make any object appear white or black.

. . .

7. To discover the nature of our *ideas* the better, and to discourse of them intelligibly, it will be convenient to distinguish them as they are *ideas* or perceptions in our minds, and as they are modifications of matter in the bodies that cause such perceptions in us: that so we *may not* think (as perhaps usually is done) that they are exactly the images and *resemblances* of something inherent in the subject: most of those of sensation being in the mind no more

the likeness of something existing without us, than the names that stand for them are the likeness of our *ideas,* which yet upon hearing they are apt to excite in us.

8. Whatsoever the mind perceives in itself, or is the immediate object of perception, thought, or understanding, that I call *idea;* and the power to produce any *idea* in our mind, I call *quality* of the subject wherein that power is. Thus a snowball having the power to produce in us the *ideas* of *white, cold,* and *round,* the powers to produce those *ideas* in us as they are in the snowball I call *qualities;* and as they are sensations or perceptions in our understandings, I call them *ideas;* which *ideas,* if I speak of sometimes as in the things themselves, I would be understood to mean those qualities in the objects which produce them in us. ⑬

> ⑬ An *idea* in the mind is one thing; the corresponding *quality* in an object is something quite different. (At the beginning of section 7, and elsewhere, Locke seems to say that ideas have two kinds of existence: in minds and in objects. But as he clarifies, by speaking of ideas "as they are modifications of matter in the bodies that cause such perceptions," Locke means to refer to whatever in the body causes that idea—without assuming that it fits the content of the idea very closely.)

9. Qualities thus considered in bodies are:

First, such as are utterly inseparable from the body, in what state soever it be; such as in all the alterations and changes it suffers, all the force can be used upon it, it constantly keeps; and such as sense constantly finds in every particle of matter which has bulk enough to be perceived; and the mind finds inseparable from every particle of matter, though less than to make itself singly be perceived by our senses. V.g., take a grain of wheat, divide it into two parts, each part has still *solidity, extension, figure,* and *mobility;* divide it again, and it retains still the same qualities; and so divide it on, till the parts become insensible: they must retain still each of them all those qualities. For division (which is all that a mill or pestle or any other body does upon another in reducing it to insensible parts) can never take away either solidity, extension, figure, or mobility from any body, but only makes two or more distinct separate masses of matter, of that which was but one before; all which distinct masses, reckoned as so many distinct bodies, after division make a certain number. These I call *original* or *primary qualities* of body; which I think we may observe to produce simple *ideas* in us, viz. solidity, extension, figure, motion or rest, and number.

10. Secondly, such *qualities* which in truth are nothing in the objects themselves but powers to produce various sensations in us by their *primary qualities,* i.e. by the bulk, figure, texture, and motion of their insensible parts, as colours, sounds, tastes, etc. These I call *secondary qualities.* ⑭ To these might be added a third sort, which are allowed to be barely powers, though they are as much real qualities in the subject as those which I, to comply with the common way of speaking, call *qualities,* but for distinction, *secondary qualities.* For the power in fire to produce a new colour, or consistency in wax or clay, by its primary qualities, is as much a quality in fire as the power it has to produce in me a new *idea* or sensation of warmth or burning, which I felt not before, by the same primary qualities, viz. the bulk, texture, and motion of its insensible parts. ⑮

11. The next thing to be considered is how *bodies* produce *ideas* in us; and that is manifestly *by impulse,* the only way which we can conceive bodies operate in.

12. If then external objects be not united to our minds when they produce *ideas* in it and yet we perceive *these original qualities* in such of them as singly fall under our senses, it is evident that some motion must be thence continued by our nerves or animal spirits, by some parts of our bodies, to the brains or the seat of sensation, there to *produce in our minds the particular* ideas *we have of them.* And since the extension, figure, number, and motion of bodies of an observable bigness may be perceived at a distance *by* the sight, it is evident some singly imperceptible bodies must come from them to the eyes, and thereby convey to the brain some *motion,* which produces these *ideas* which we have of them in us.

13. After the same manner that the *ideas* of these original qualities are produced in us, we may conceive that the *ideas of secondary qualities* are also *produced,* viz. *by the operation of insensible particles on our senses.* For it being manifest that there are bodies and good store of bodies, each whereof are so small that we cannot by any of our senses discover either their bulk, figure, or motion, as is evident in the particles of the air and water and others extremely smaller than those, perhaps as much smaller than the particles of air or water as the particles of air or water are smaller than peas or hail-stones: let us suppose at present that the different motions and figures, bulk and number, of such particles, affecting the several organs of our senses, produce in us those different sensations which we have from the colours and smells of bodies: v.g. that a violet, by the impulse of such insensible particles of matter, of peculiar figures and bulks, and in different degrees and modifications of their motions, causes the *ideas* of the blue colour and sweet scent of that flower to be produced in our minds. It being no more impossible to conceive that God should annex such *ideas* to such motions, with which they have no similitude, than that he should annex the *idea* of pain to the motion of a piece of steel dividing our flesh, with which that *idea* hath no resemblance.

14. What I have said concerning *colours* and *smells* may be understood also of *tastes* and *sounds, and other the like sensible qualities;* which, whatever reality we by mistake attribute to them, are in truth nothing in the objects themselves but powers to produce various sensations in us, and depend *on those primary qualities,* viz. bulk, figure, texture, and motion of parts, as I have said.

⑭ **Primary qualities** are genuinely in bodies *as the ideas in question represent them,* with the main argument being that bodies are inconceivable without such qualities. (Note here that solidity is the only such quality that is not essentially spatial or geometrical in character.) **Secondary qualities** are powers (causal capacities) in bodies to produce ideas in us; these powers result from the "bulk, figure, texture, and motion" of the "insensible parts" of the bodies—that is, from their primary qualities (compare the list of these here with the original one)—but the quality represented by an idea of a secondary quality does not exist, *as thus represented,* in the object. (Locke offers no argument for this view here. Can you think of one? See Discussion Question 3.)

⑮ A third sort of quality is a causal capacity in the object that is represented as such. Such qualities are again a result of the primary qualities of the insensible parts of the body. (Thus what is odd and misleading about secondary qualities is that while they are, in Locke's view, really no more than powers, they are represented as though they were qualities on a par with primary qualities.)

15. From whence I think it easy to draw this observation: that the *ideas of primary qualities* of bodies *are resemblances* of them, and their patterns do really exist in the bodies themselves; but the *ideas produced* in us *by* these *secondary qualities have no resemblance* of them at all. There is nothing like our *ideas* existing in the bodies themselves. They are, in the bodies we denominate from them, only a power to produce those sensations in us; and what is sweet, blue, or warm in *idea* is but the certain bulk, figure, and motion of the insensible parts in the bodies themselves, which we call so. 16

16 This is a good, rather clearer summary of Locke's view of primary and secondary qualities. But a possible source of trouble is the talk of ideas *resembling* qualities in objects, something Berkeley will strongly object to. Think here of your idea of a certain shape (say, squareness) and an object whose surface has the quality in question. Is *resemblance* the right way to think about the relation between these two?

16. *Flame* is denominated *hot* and *light; snow, white* and *cold;* and *manna, white* and *sweet,* from the *ideas* they produce in us. Which qualities are commonly thought to be the same in those bodies that those *ideas* are in us, the one the perfect resemblance of the other, as they are in a mirror, and it would by most men be judged very extravagant if one should say otherwise. And yet he that will consider that *the same fire* that at one distance *produces* in us the sensation of *warmth* does, at a nearer approach, produce in us the far different sensation of *pain,* ought to bethink himself what reason he has to say that his *idea* of *warmth,* which was produced in him by the fire, is actually *in the fire;* and his *idea* of *pain,* which the same fire produced in him the same way, is *not* in the *fire.* Why are whiteness and coldness in snow, and pain not, when it produces the one and the other *idea* in us; and can do neither, but by the bulk, figure, number, and motion of its solid parts?

17. The particular *bulk, number, figure, and motion of the parts of fire or snow are really in them,* whether anyone's senses perceive them or no; and therefore they may be called *real qualities,* because they really exist in those bodies. But *light, heat, whiteness,* or *coldness are no more really in them than sickness or pain is in* manna. Take away the sensation of them; let not the eyes see light or colours,

nor the ears hear sounds; let the palate not taste, nor the nose smell; and all colours, tastes, odours, and sounds, as they are such particular *ideas,* vanish and cease, and are reduced to their causes, i.e. bulk, figure, and motion of parts.

. . .

21. *Ideas* being thus distinguished and understood, we may be able to give an account how the same water, at the same time, may produce the *idea* of cold by one hand and of heat by the other, whereas it is impossible that the same water, if those *ideas* were really in it, should at the same time be both hot and cold. For if we imagine *warmth* as it is *in our hands* to be *nothing but a certain sort and degree of motion in the minute particles of our nerves, or animal spirits,* we may understand how it is possible that the same water may at the same time produce the sensation of heat in one hand and cold in the other; which yet figure never does, that never producing the *idea* of a square by one hand which has produced the *idea* of a globe by another. But if the sensation of heat and cold be nothing but the increase or diminution of the motion of the minute parts of our bodies, caused by the corpuscles of any other body, it is easy to be understood that, if that motion be greater in one hand than in the other, if a body be applied to the two hands, which has in its minute particles a greater motion than in those of one of the hands, and a less than in those of the other, it will increase the motion of the one hand and lessen it in the other, and so cause the different sensations of heat and cold that depend thereon. 17

17 This example, also used by Berkeley, leads to the **argument from illusion.** To see the point, imagine that one of your hands has previously been in ice water and the other in water as hot as you can stand, while the "same water" in which they are now placed is lukewarm. If the experiences in question were direct apprehensions of actual qualities of the water, the discrepancy between them would be inexplicable. This is taken to show that the directly experienced qualities are only ideas in the mind.

22. I have in what just goes before been engaged in physical inquiries a little further than perhaps I intended. But, it being necessary to make the nature of

sensation a little understood; and to make the *difference between the qualities in bodies, and the* ideas *produced by them in the mind,* to be distinctly conceived. . . .

23. The *qualities,* then, that are in *bodies,* rightly considered, are of *three sorts:*

First, The *bulk, figure, number, situation,* and *motion or rest* of their solid parts. Those are in them, whether we perceive them or no; and when they are of that size that we can discover them, we have by these an *idea* of the thing as it is in itself, as is plain in artificial things. These I call *primary qualities.*

Secondly, The *power* that is in any body, by reason of *its* insensible *primary qualities,* to operate after a peculiar manner on any of our senses, and thereby *produce in us* the *different ideas* of several colours, sounds, smells, tastes, etc. These are usually called sensible qualities.

Thirdly, The *power* that is in any body, *by* reason of the particular constitution of *its primary qualities, to* make such a *change* in the *bulk, figure, texture, and motion of another body,* as to make it operate on our senses differently from what it did before. Thus the sun has a power to make wax white, and fire to make lead fluid. These *are* usually called powers.

The first of these, as has been said, I think may be properly called *real, original,* or *primary qualities,* because they are in the things themselves, whether they are perceived or no; and upon their different modifications it is that the secondary qualities depend.

The other two are only powers to act differently upon other things, which powers result from the different modifications of those primary qualities.

24. But though *these two latter sorts of qualities are powers barely,* and nothing but powers relating to several other bodies and resulting from the different modifications of the original qualities, yet they are generally otherwise thought of. For *the second sort,* viz. the powers to produce several *ideas* in us by our senses, *are looked upon as real qualities in the things* thus affecting us; but *the third sort are called and esteemed barely powers,* v.g. the *idea* of heat or light which we receive by our eyes or touch from the sun are commonly thought *real qualities* existing in the sun and something more than mere powers in it. . . .

Chapter IX: Of Perception

1. Perception, as it is the first faculty of the mind exercised about our *ideas,* so it is the first and simplest *idea* we have from reflection, and is by some called thinking in general. Though thinking, in the propriety of the *English* tongue, signifies that sort of operation in the mind about its *ideas,* wherein the mind is active, where it, with some degree of voluntary attention, considers anything. For in bare naked *perception,* the mind is, for the most part, only passive; and what it perceives, it cannot avoid perceiving.

2. *What perception is,* everyone will know better by reflecting on what he does himself, when he sees, hears, feels, etc., or thinks, than by any discourse of mine. Whoever reflects on what passes in his own mind cannot miss it. And if he does not reflect, all the words in the world cannot make him have any notion of it.⑱

⑱ In Locke's view, anyone who has experience at all *perceives* ideas. (Thus what he refers to as perception is not restricted to sense perception, but really includes any sort of awareness of something.) Does this mean, as he claims, that the rather complicated and subtle idea of perception (or awareness) can be obtained simply by reflecting on what is going on in any situation of experience? Could you explain it to a baby (who is after all aware of things) just by pointing at what he is doing?

. . .

Chapter XI: Of Discerning, and Other Operations of the Mind

1. Another faculty we may take notice of in our minds is that of *discerning* and distinguishing between the several *ideas* it has. It is not enough to have a confused perception of something in general; unless the mind had a distinct perception of different objects and their qualities, it would be capable of very little knowledge, though the bodies that affect us were as busy about us as they are now, and the mind were continually employed in thinking. On this faculty of distinguishing one thing from another depends the *evidence and certainty* of several, even very general, propositions, which have passed for innate truths: because men, overlooking the true cause why those propositions find

universal assent, impute it wholly to native uniform impressions; whereas it in truth *depends upon this clear discerning faculty* of the mind whereby it perceives two *ideas* to be the same, or different.

. . .

4. The COMPARING them one with another, in respect of extent, degrees, time, place, or any other circumstances, is another operation of the mind about its *ideas,* and is that upon which depends all that large tribe of *ideas* comprehended under *relation.* . . .

6. The next operation we may observe in the mind about its *ideas* is COMPOSITION, whereby it puts together several of those simple ones it has received from sensation and reflection, and combines them into complex ones. Under this of composition may be reckoned also that of ENLARGING, wherein, though the composition does not so much appear as in more complex ones, yet it is nevertheless a putting several *ideas* together, though of the same kind. Thus, by adding several units together, we make the *idea* of a dozen; and putting together the repeated *ideas* of several perches, we frame that of furlong. [19]

[19] Here is one sort of complex idea: one composed of repetitions of simple ideas.

. . .

9. The use of words then being to stand as outward marks of our internal *ideas,* and those *ideas* being taken from particular things, if every particular *idea* that we take in should have a dictinct name, names must be endless. To prevent this, the mind makes the particular *ideas* received from particular objects to become general; which is done by considering them as they are in the mind such appearances, separate from all other existences and the circumstances of real existence, as time, place, or any other concomitant *ideas.* This is called ABSTRACTION, whereby *ideas* taken from particular beings become general representatives of all of the same kind; and their names, general names, applicable to whatever exists conformable to such abstract *ideas.* Such precise, naked appearances in the mind, without considering how, whence, or with what others they came there, the understanding lays up (with names commonly annexed to them) as the

standards to rank real existences into sorts, as they agree with these patterns, and to *denominate* them accordingly. Thus the same colour being observed to-day in chalk or snow, which the mind yesterday received from milk, it considers that appearance alone, makes it a representative of all of that kind; and having given it the name *whiteness,* it by that sound signifies the same quality wheresoever to be imagined or met with; and thus universals, whether *ideas* or terms, are made. [20]

. . . the *ideas first* in the mind, it is evident, are those of particular things; from whence, by slow degrees, the understanding proceeds to some few general ones; which, being taken from the ordinary and familiar objects of sense, are settled in the minds with general names to them. Thus particular *ideas* are *first* received and distinguished, and so knowledge got about them; and next to them, the less general or specific, which are next to particular. For abstract *ideas* are not so obvious or easy, to children or the yet unexercised mind, as particular ones. If they seem so to grown men, it is only because by constant and familiar use they are made so. For when we nicely reflect upon them, we shall find that general *ideas* are fictions and contrivances of the mind that carry difficulty with them, and do not so easily offer themselves as we are apt to imagine. For example, does it not require some pains and skill to form the *general idea* of a *triangle* (which is yet none of the most abstract, comprehensive, and difficult), for it must be neither oblique nor rectangle, neither equilateral, equicrural, nor scalenon; but all and none of these at once. In effect, it is something imperfect that cannot exist, an *idea* wherein some parts of several different and inconsistent *ideas* are put together. It is true, the mind in this imperfect state has need of such *ideas,* and makes all the haste to them it can, for the conveniency of communication and enlargement of knowledge, to both which it is naturally very much inclined. But yet one has reason to

[20] It is the alleged capacity of abstraction that allows the mind to think in general or abstract terms. Locke's account of this is that it involves separating one idea (or composite of ideas, since not all abstract ideas are simple) from others it is accompanied by in experience. This works reasonably well for the example discussed here.

suspect such *ideas* are marks of our imperfection: at least, this is enough to show that the most abstract and general *ideas* are not those that the mind is *first* and most easily acquainted with, nor such as its earliest knowledge is conversant about. 21

21 Here we insert a later passage (from Book IV, chapter VII, section 9) in which Locke discusses a different, more difficult, and unfortunately probably more typical example: the abstract idea of a triangle. (This is one of the places where he seems to be thinking of ideas as images. Think what an abstract image of a triangle would be like.)

. . .

Chapter XII: Of Complex Ideas

1. We have hitherto considered those *ideas* in the reception whereof the mind is only passive, which are those simple ones received from *sensation* and *reflection* before mentioned, whereof the mind cannot make one to itself, nor have any *idea* which does not wholly consist of them. But as the mind is wholly passive in the reception of all its simple *ideas,* so it exerts several acts of its own whereby out of its simple *ideas,* as the materials and foundations of the rest, the others are framed. The acts of the mind, wherein it exerts its power over its simple *ideas,* are chiefly these three: (1) Combining several simple *ideas* into one compound one; and thus all complex *ideas* are made.

22 Complex ideas are made by the mind, rather than being directly derived from experience. They are not all complex in the same way. Category (1) is the easiest to understand, and it is in this way that Locke accounts for examples like the idea of a unicorn. (Why couldn't other complex ideas, such as the idea of an automobile, be derived directly from experiences of that sort of object?)

(2) The second is bringing two *ideas,* whether simple or complex, together, and setting them by one another, so as to take a view of them at once, without uniting them into one; by which way it gets all its *ideas* of relations. (3) The third is separating them from all other *ideas* that accompany them in their real existence: this is called *abstraction;* and thus all its general *ideas* are made. 22 . . .

6. . . . the *ideas* of *substances* are such combinations of simple ideas as are taken to represent distinct particular things subsisting by themselves, in which the supposed or confused *idea* of substance, such as it is, is always the first and chief. Thus if to substance be joined the simple *idea* of a certain dull whitish colour, with certain degrees of weight, hardness, ductility, and fusibility, we have the *idea* of *lead;* and a combination of the *ideas* of a certain sort of figure, with the powers of motion, thought, and reasoning, joined to substance, make the ordinary *idea* of *a man.* 23 . . .

23 One particularly important class of complex ideas is ideas of *substances:* concrete kinds of objects. By "the supposed or confused idea of substance," Locke means the underlying idea of a *substratum* in which all the various qualities exist, but which has no qualities in itself. This is a puzzling notion, which Berkeley was quick to attack.

BOOK IV: OF KNOWLEDGE AND OPINION

Chapter I: Of Knowledge in General

1. Since *the mind,* in all its thoughts and reasonings, hath no other immediate object but its own *ideas,* which it alone does or can contemplate, it is evident that our knowledge is only conversant about them.

2. *Knowledge* then seems to me to be nothing but *the perception of the connexion and agreement, or disagreement and repugnancy, of any of our ideas.* In this alone it consists. 24 Where this perception is, there is knowledge; and where it is not, there, though we may fancy, guess, or believe, yet we always come short of knowledge. For when we know that *white is not black,* what do we else but perceive that these two *ideas* do not agree? When we possess ourselves with the utmost security of the demonstration that *the three angles of a triangle are equal to two right ones,* what do we more but perceive that equality to two right ones does necessarily agree to and is inseparable from the three angles of a triangle?

24 Here is Locke's initial definition of knowledge, which follows very naturally from the account of mental operations in the previous paragraph. If all that is immediately before the mind is ideas, then what can knowledge be but the perception of the ways in which they agree or disagree?

3. But to understand a little more distinctly wherein this agreement or disagreement consists, I think we may reduce it all to these four sorts:

1. *Identity,* or *diversity.*
2. *Relation.*
3. *Co-existence,* or *necessary connexion.*
4. *Real existence.*

4. *First,* As to the first sort of agreement or disagreement, viz. *identity* or *diversity.* It is the first act of the mind, when it has any sentiments or *ideas* at all, to perceive its *ideas,* and so far as it perceives them, to know each what it is, and thereby also to perceive their difference and that one is not another. This is so absolutely necessary that without it there could be no knowledge, no reasoning, no imagination, no distinct thoughts at all. . . .

5. *Secondly,* The next sort of agreement or disagreement the mind perceives in any of its *ideas* may, I think, be called *relative,* and is nothing but *the perception of the relation between any two ideas,* of what kind soever, whether substances, modes, or any other . . . .

6. *Thirdly,* The third sort of agreement or disagreement to be found in our *ideas,* which the perception of the mind is employed about, is *co-existence* or *non-co-existence* in the same subject; and this belongs particularly to substances. Thus when we pronounce, concerning *gold,* that it is fixed, our knowledge of this truth amounts to no more but this: that fixedness, or a power to remain in the fire unconsumed, is an *idea* that always accompanies and is joined with that particular sort of yellowness, weight, fusibility, malleableness, and solubility in *aqua regia,* which make our complex *idea* signified by the word *gold.*

7. *Fourthly,* The fourth and last sort is that of *actual real existence* agreeing to any *idea.* [25] Within these four sorts of agreement or disagreement is, I suppose, contained all the knowledge we have or are capable of; for all the inquiries that we can make concerning any of our *ideas,* all that we know or can affirm concerning any of them is that it is or is not the same with some other; that it does or does not always

[25] The immediate problem, however, is how this allows for knowledge of things outside the mind, such as material objects of various sorts. Locke's first attempt is to construe this as a kind of agreement of ideas, one of which is the idea of "actual real existence." But what is it for this idea to agree or disagree with others, and why couldn't it do so even if the thing in question didn't really exist?

co-exist with some other *idea* in the same subject; that it has this or that relation to some other *idea;* or that it has a real existence without the mind. . . .

Chapter II: Of the Degrees of Our Knowledge

1. All our knowledge consisting, as I have said, in the view the mind has of its own *ideas,* which is the utmost light and greatest certainty we, with our faculties and in our way of knowledge, are capable of, it may not be amiss to consider a little the degrees of its evidence. The different clearness of our knowledge seems to me to lie in the different way of perception the mind has of the agreement or disagreement of any of its *ideas.* For if we will reflect on our own ways of thinking, we shall find that sometimes the mind perceives the agreement or disagreement of two *ideas* immediately by themselves, without the intervention of any other; and this I think we may call *intuitive knowledge.* For in this the mind is at no pains of proving or examining but perceives the truth, as the eye doth light, only by being directed toward it. Thus the mind perceives that *white* is not *black,* that a *circle* is not a *triangle,* that *three* are more than *two* and equal to *one* and *two.* Such kind of truths the mind perceives at the first sight of the *ideas* together, by bare *intuition,* without the intervention of any other *idea;* and this kind of knowledge is the clearest and most certain that human frailty is capable of. [26] . . .

[26] *Intuitive knowledge* is the basis, in Locke's view, for knowledge of simple, self-evident truths like the ones enumerated. Later philosophers will describe these as **a priori.**

2. The next degree of knowledge is where the mind perceives the agreement or disagreement of any *ideas,* but not immediately. . . . In this case then, when the mind cannot so bring its *ideas* together as by their immediate comparison and as it were juxtaposition or application one to another, to perceive their agreement or disagreement, it is fain, by the intervention of other *ideas* (one or more, as it happens) to discover the agreement or disagreement which it searches; and this is that which we call *reasoning.* Thus the mind, being willing to know the agreement or disagreement in bigness between the three angles of a triangle and two right ones, cannot by an immediate view and comparing them do it, because the three angles of a triangle cannot be brought at once and be compared with any one or two angles; and so of this the mind has no

immediate, no intuitive knowledge. In this case the mind is fain to find out some other angles to which the

---

27 A second kind of knowledge is *demonstrative knowledge:* knowledge that results from more extended arguments or proofs, in which the individual steps are known intuitively. Where the starting point is known a priori, the result of such a demonstration will also be a priori. (Notice that Locke sometimes writes as though the steps in the argument are individual ideas, rather than claims or propositions composed of ideas—which seems to be a mistake.)

---

three angles of a triangle have an equality, and finding those equal to two right ones, comes to know their equality to two right ones.

3. Those intervening *ideas* which serve to show the agreement of any two others are called *proofs;* and where the agreement or disagreement is by this means plainly and clearly perceived, it is called *demonstration:* it being *shown* to the understanding, and the mind made see that it is so. 27 . . .

14. These two, viz. intuition and demonstration, are the degrees of our knowledge; whatever comes short of one of these, with what assurance soever embraced, is but faith or opinion, but not knowledge, at least in all general truths. There is, indeed, another *perception* of the mind, employed about *the particular existence of finite beings* without us, which, going beyond bare probability and yet not reaching perfectly to either of the foregoing degrees of certainty, passes under the name of knowledge. There can be nothing more certain than that the *idea* we receive from an external object is in our minds: this is intuitive knowledge. But whether there be anything more than barely that *idea* in our minds, whether we can thence certainly infer the existence of anything without us which corresponds to that *idea* is that whereof some men think there may be a question made: because men may have such *ideas* in their minds, when no such thing exists, no such object affects their senses. But yet here I think we are provided with an evidence that puts us past doubting: for I ask anyone whether he be not invincibly conscious to himself of a different perception, when he looks on the sun by day and thinks on it by night, when he actually tastes wormwood or smells a rose or only thinks on that savour or odour? We as plainly find the difference there is between any *idea* revived in our minds by our own memory and actually coming into our minds by our senses, as we do between any two

distinct *ideas*. If anyone say a dream may do the same thing, and all these *ideas* may be produced in us without any external objects, he may please to dream that I make him this answer: (1) That it is no great matter whether I remove his scruple or no: where all is but dream, reasoning and arguments are of no use, truth and knowledge nothing. (2) That I believe he will allow a very manifest difference between dreaming of being in the fire and being actually in it. But yet if he be resolved to appear so sceptical as to maintain that what I call being actually in the fire is nothing but a dream, and that we cannot thereby certainly know that any such thing as fire actually exists without us, I answer: that we certainly finding that pleasure or pain follows upon the application of certain objects to us whose existence we perceive or dream that we perceive by our senses, this certainty is as great as our happiness or misery, beyond which we have no concernment to know or to be. So that, I think, we may add to the two former sorts of *knowledge* this also of the existence of particular external objects, by that perception and consciousness we have of the actual entrance of *ideas* from them, and allow these *three degrees of knowledge,* viz. *intuitive, demonstrative, and sensitive,* in each of which there are different degrees and ways of evidence and certainty. 28

---

28 Here is Locke's second, and rather different, attempt to account for knowledge of external objects. Rather than an appeal to agreement of an idea of the thing in question with the idea of "actual real existence," Locke now seems to be appealing to the distinctive character of the ideas involved in sense perception, as contrasted with other ideas of the same object that are involved in memory or thought. But it is far from clear just what this difference amounts to or why it should be taken to indicate actual existence outside the mind. Locke's nervousness about this issue is shown by the way he attempts to ridicule the skeptic—and also by his saying that cognition of the sort in question "passes under the name of knowledge," which surely raises the issue of whether it really is knowledge.

. . .

Chapter IV: Of the Reality of Knowledge

1. I doubt not but my reader, by this time, may be apt to think that I have been all this while only building a castle in the air and be ready to say to me: To what purpose

all this stir? Knowledge, say you, is only the perception of the agreement or disagreement of our own *ideas;* but who knows what those *ideas* may be? Is there anything so extravagant as the imaginations of men's brains? Where is the head that has no *chimeras* in it? Or if there be a sober and a wise man, what difference will there be by your rules between his knowledge and that of the most extravagant fancy in the world? They both have their *ideas* and perceive their agreement and disagreement one with another. If there be any difference between them, the advantage will be on the warm-headed man's side, as having the more *ideas* and the more lively. And so, by your rules, he will be the more knowing. If it be true that all knowledge lies only in the perception of the agreement or disagreement of our own *ideas,* the visions of an enthusiast and the reasonings of a sober man will be equally certain . . . .

3. It is evident the mind knows not things immediately, but only by the intervention of the *ideas* it has of them. *Our knowledge,* therefore, is *real* only so far as there is a conformity between our *ideas* and the reality of things. But what shall be here the criterion? How shall the mind, when it perceives nothing but its own *ideas,* know that they agree with things themselves?⟨29⟩ . . .

⟨29⟩ Here the problem is realized and stated more clearly: how can we know, via perception of our ideas, that they accurately depict something existing outside our minds in the world?

Chapter XI: Of Our Knowledge of the Existence of Other Things

1. The knowledge of our own being we have by intuition. The existence of a GOD, reason clearly makes known to us. . . .

The *knowledge of the existence* of any other thing we can have only by *sensation:* for, there being no necessary connexion of *real existence* with any *idea* a man hath in his memory, . . . no particular man can know the *existence* of any other being but only when, by actual operating upon him, it makes itself perceived by him. For the having the *idea* of anything in our mind no more proves the existence of that thing, than the picture of a man evidences his being in the world, or the visions of a dream make thereby a true history.

2. It is therefore the actual receiving of *ideas* from without that gives us notice of the *existence* of

other things and makes us know that something doth exist at that time without us which causes that *idea* in us, though perhaps we neither know nor consider how it does it; for it takes not, from the certainty of our senses and the *ideas* we receive by them, that we know not the manner wherein they are produced.⟨30⟩ . . .

⟨30⟩ Here is another take on the issue of how external existence is known: not by agreement with the idea of "actual real existence" and not by the quality of the ideas, but by "the actual receiving" of them "from without." But how, we may ask, is this known?

3. *The notice we have by our senses of the existing of things without us,* though it be not altogether so certain as our intuitive knowledge or the deductions of our reason employed about the clear abstract *ideas* of our own minds, yet it is an assurance that *deserves the name of knowledge.* If we persuade ourselves that our faculties act and inform us right concerning the existence of those objects that affect them, it cannot pass for an ill-grounded confidence: for I think nobody can, in earnest, be so sceptical as to be uncertain of the existence of those things which he sees and feels. At least, he that can doubt so far (whatever he may have with his own thoughts) will never have any controversy with me, since he can never be sure I say anything contrary to his opinion. ⟨31⟩ As to myself, I think GOD has given me assurance enough of the existence of things without me, since, by their different application, I can produce in myself both pleasure and pain, which is one great concernment of my present state. This is certain: the confidence that

⟨31⟩ Again Locke shows his uncertainty about the question (the assurance in question "deserves the name of knowledge") and attempts to refute the skeptic through mockery. Think about the reasons for trusting our senses that are offered in this paragraph. Do any of them have any serious weight?

our faculties do not herein deceive us is the greatest assurance we are capable of concerning the existence of material beings. For we cannot act anything but by our faculties, nor talk of knowledge itself but by the help of those faculties which are fitted to apprehend even what knowledge is. But besides the assurance we have from our senses themselves, that they do not err in the information they give us of the existence of things without us when they are affected by them, we are further confirmed in this assurance by other concurrent reasons.

4. *First,* It is plain those perceptions are produced in us by exterior causes affecting our senses, because *those that want the organs of any sense never can have the* ideas *belonging to that sense* produced in their minds. This is too evident to be doubted, and therefore we cannot but be assured that they come in by the organs of that sense, and no other way. The organs themselves, it is plain, do not produce them: for then the eyes of a man in the dark would produce colours, and his nose smell roses in the winter; but we see nobody gets the relish of a pineapple till he goes to the *Indies,* where it is, and tastes it.

5. *Secondly,* Because *sometimes I find that I cannot avoid the having those* ideas *produced in my mind.* For though, when my eyes are shut, or windows fast, I can at pleasure recall to my mind the *ideas* of *light,* or the *sun,* which former sensations had lodged in my memory: so I can at pleasure lay by that *idea,* and take into my view that of the *smell* of a rose, or *taste* of sugar. But, if I turn my eyes at noon towards the sun, I cannot avoid the *ideas* which the light or sun then produces in me. So that there is a manifest difference between the *ideas* laid up in my memory (over which, if they were there only, I should have constantly the same power to dispose of them and lay them by at pleasure) and those which force themselves upon me and I cannot avoid having. And therefore it must needs be some exterior cause and the brisk acting of some objects without me, whose efficacy I cannot resist, that produces those *ideas* in my mind, whether I will or no. Besides, there is nobody who doth not perceive the difference in himself between contemplating the sun as he hath the *idea* of it in his memory, and actually looking upon it: of which two, his perception is so distinct that few of his *ideas* are more distinguishable one from another, and therefore he hath certain knowledge that they are not both memory or the actions of his mind and fancies only within him, but that actual seeing hath a cause without.

6. *Thirdly,* Add to this, that *many of those* ideas *are produced in us with pain, which afterwards we remember without the least offence.* Thus, the pain of heat or cold, when the *idea* of it is revived in our minds, gives us no disturbance, which when felt was very troublesome, and is again when actually repeated: which is occasioned by the disorder the exter-

nal object causes in our bodies when applied to it; and we remember the pain of *hunger, thirst,* or the *headache* without any pain at all: which would either never disturb us, or else constantly do it as often as we thought of it, were there nothing more but *ideas* floating in our minds and appearances entertaining our fancies, without the real existence of things affecting us from abroad. The same may be said of pleasure accompanying several actual sensations; and though mathematical demonstration depends not upon sense, yet the examining them by diagrams gives great credit to the evidence of our sight and seems to give it a certainty approaching to that of the demonstration itself. For it would be very strange that a man should allow it for an undeniable truth that two angles of a figure, which he measures by lines and angles of a diagram, should be bigger one than the other, and yet doubt of the existence of those lines and angles which, by looking on, he makes use of to measure that by.

7. *Fourthly,* Our *senses* in many cases bear *witness* to the truth of each other's report concerning the existence of sensible things without us. He that sees a *fire* may, if he doubt whether it be anything more than a bare fancy, feel it too and be convinced by putting his hand in it. Which certainly could never be put into such exquisite pain by a bare *idea* or phantom, unless that the pain be a fancy too: which yet he cannot, when the burn is well, by raising the *idea* of it, bring upon himself again. ⫿32⫾

⫿32⫾ These four "concurrent" reasons for thinking that our senses "do not err" are the closest that Locke comes to an argument for the truth of perceptual claims about the external world. Think about them carefully. They are of very unequal weight, and each of them can be considered alone or in combination with some or all of the others. Is there a good argument, or at least the beginnings of one, for the thesis that some of our ideas accurately represent external objects that really exist? (See Discussion Question 5.)

. . .

8. But yet, if after all this anyone will be so sceptical as to distrust his senses and to affirm that all we see and hear, feel and taste, think and do during our whole being is but the series and deluding appearances of a long dream, whereof there is no reality, and therefore will question the existence of all things or our knowledge of anything: I must desire him to con-

sider that, if all be a dream, then he doth but dream that he makes the question, and so it is not much matter that a waking man should answer him. But yet if he pleases he may dream that I make him this answer, that *the certainty of* things existing *in rerum natura,* when we have *the testimony of our senses* for it, is not only *as great* as our frame can attain to, but *as our condition needs.* For our faculties being suited not to the full extent of being, nor to a perfect, clear, comprehensive knowledge of things free from all doubt and scruple, but to the preservation of us in whom they are, and accommodated to the use of life: they serve to our purpose well enough if they will but give us certain notice of those things which are convenient or inconvenient to us. For he that sees a candle burning and hath experimented the force of its flame by putting his finger in it will little doubt that this is something existing without him which does him harm and puts him to great pain: which is assurance enough, when no man requires greater certainty to govern his actions by than what is as certain as his actions themselves. And if our dreamer pleases to try whether the glowing heat of a glass furnace be barely a wandering imagination in a drowsy man's fancy, by putting his hand into it, he may perhaps be wakened into a certainty greater than he could wish that it is something more than bare imagination. So that this evidence is as great as we can desire, being as certain to us as our pleasure or pain, i.e. happiness or misery, beyond which we have no concernment, either of knowing or being. Such an assurance of the existence of things without us is sufficient to direct us in the attaining the good and avoiding the evil which is caused by them, which is the important concernment we have of being made acquainted with them.[33]

[33] Again he resorts to mockery of the skeptic.

9. In fine then, when our senses do actually convey into our understandings any *idea,* we cannot but be satisfied that there doth something at that time really exist without us which doth affect our senses, and by them give notice of itself to our apprehensive faculties, and actually produce that *idea* which we then perceive; and we cannot so far distrust their testimony as to doubt that such collections of simple *ideas,* as we have observed by our senses to be united together, do really exist together. But *this knowledge extends as far as the present testimony of our senses,* employed about particular objects that do then affect them, *and no further.* For if I saw such a collection of simple *ideas* as is wont to be called *man,* existing together one minute since, and am now alone, I cannot be certain that the same man exists now, since there is no necessary connexion of his existence a minute since with his existence now: by a thousand ways he may cease to be since I had the testimony of my senses for his existence. And if I cannot be certain that the man I saw last today is now in being, I can less be certain that he is so who hath been longer removed from my senses and I have not seen since yesterday or since the last year; and much less can I be certain of the existence of men that I never saw. And, therefore, though it be highly probable that millions of men do now exist, yet, whilst I am alone, writing this, I have not that certainty of it which we strictly call knowledge: though the great likelihood of it puts me past doubt, and it be reasonable for me to do several things upon the confidence that there are men (and men also of my acquaintance, with whom I have to do) now in the world; but this is but probability, not knowledge.

10. Whereby yet we may observe how foolish and vain a thing it is for a man of a narrow knowledge who, having reason given him to judge of the different evidence and probability of things and to be swayed accordingly, how *vain,* I say, it is *to expect demonstration* and certainty *in things not capable of it,* and refuse assent to very rational propositions and act contrary to very plain and clear truths because they cannot be made out so evident as to surmount every the least (I will not say reason, but) pretence of doubting. He that, in the ordinary affairs of life, would admit of nothing but direct plain demonstration would be sure of nothing in this world but of perishing quickly. The wholesomeness of his meat or drink would not give him reason to venture on it, and I would fain know what it is he could do upon such grounds as were capable of no doubt, no objection.

11. As, when our senses are actually employed about any object, we do know that it does exist, so *by our memory* we may be assured that heretofore things that affected our senses have existed. And thus *we have knowledge of the past existence* of several things whereof, our senses having informed us, our memories still retain the *ideas;* and of this we are past all doubt, so long as we remember well. But this knowledge also reaches no further than our senses have formerly assured us. . . .

Discussion Questions

1. Locke often seems to be thinking of ideas as mental images. This would in effect mean that to think of things is to have a sequence of images pass through our minds. Is this an adequate view of thought? One specific problem is whether images as such, without anything accompanying them in the way that a caption accompanies a picture in the newspaper, really make claims that could be true or false.

2. How plausible is Locke's account in Book II of how we acquire our various concepts? Think of a range of examples, ask what Locke would say about them, and then evaluate whether his view seems correct. One issue that arises in many cases is whether the experience that Locke would appeal to really contains the idea in question in a clear and easily isolatable form. Remember that the issue is not whether you can find an experience to which the idea applies in some way or that provides an instance of the idea, but rather whether all the content of that idea can be found in explicit form in that experience, whether the experience in itself is rich enough to supply all of that content. (Here are some cases to think about: the idea of the taste of lemon, the idea of a dog (not some particular dog or breed of dog, just dog in general), the idea of reflection (to which Locke appeals), the idea of trump (as it figures in various card games), the idea of a politician, and the idea of an electron.)

3. The distinction between primary and secondary qualities (in Book II, Chapter VIII) is one that Locke inherits from earlier thinkers, including Descartes, and he thinks it is obvious enough not to need argument. Does Locke's thesis here seem plausible to you: for example, do shapes really exist in material objects, while colors as we experience them exist only in our minds, with only the power to produce such an experience being in the object? Can you see any way to argue for this thesis? (Hint: think of what would be required to *explain* our having the experiences of these two qualities.)

4. Do we have abstract ideas? There are certainly abstract terms in our language, and on Locke's theory of meaning (expounded in Book III of the *Essay*), this means there are corresponding abstract ideas that provide the meanings of such terms. But do such ideas actually exist? Think first of the construal of them as images, considering various cases. Does this work? If not, can you think of any alternative to the image view that would still account for abstract thought?

5. Reconsider Locke's four reasons for thinking that our senses "do not err" in Chapter XI of Book IV. One of these is thoroughly question-begging (that is, it assumes the very sort of knowledge that Locke is trying to account for). Another, while perhaps correct, doesn't seem to point to the desired conclusion in any very clear way. The other two, while more suggestive, don't seem to work when taken individually, but may do better when taken together. With these hints, try to sort out these reasons and figure out which two of them, when taken together, do yield an argument for something like the conclusion Locke is aiming at. How strong is this argument? Can you think of any answer to it?

George Berkeley

George Berkeley (1685–1753) was an Irish philosopher who was also an Anglican bishop. Berkeley is the second of the British Empiricists, and was greatly influenced by Locke. He is, however, most famous for his criticisms of Locke and his radically different view of both the objects and nature of human knowledge, especially perceptual knowledge.

While both Locke and Berkeley believe that the direct or immediate objects of our experience, including perceptual experience, are ideas in our minds, Locke nonetheless believes in a commonsensical world of mind-independent material objects and thinks that we can have knowledge of such objects through inference from our sense experience, thus holding a **realist** view. Berkeley, in contrast, thinks that no such inference can be justified, and for this and other reasons holds the **idealist** view that ordinary objects (trees, tables, buildings, and so on) are nothing more than collections of ideas that are caused by God to occur in our minds. (Paradoxical though this may seem, he believes that in advocating this view, he is defending common sense against the threat of skepticism.)

Berkeley first defended idealism in his *Principles of Human Knowledge* (1710). When this book was poorly received, he attempted to restate its arguments in a more popularly accessible form in the *Three Dialogues,* including also an extended defense of the thesis that the direct or immediate object of perceptual experience is always an idea in the mind—something that is not defended very explicitly in either Locke's *Essay* or Berkeley's *Principles*. The two characters in the dialogue are Hylas (the name comes from the Greek word for matter) and Philonous (again from the Greek, meaning lover of mind), who is the spokesman for Berkeley's own views. Hylas begins by defending a roughly commonsensical view, gets driven into a roughly Lockean view, and eventually is forced to accept idealism. (The *Three Dialogues* are usually regarded as one of the most successful philosophical uses of dialogue form, ranking with Plato's dialogues and Hume's *Dialogues Concerning Natural Religion*—see Chapter 2.)

To help you discern the structure of the argument, we have inserted roman numerals in brackets to mark the main divisions.

From *Three Dialogues Between Hylas and Philonous*

THE FIRST DIALOGUE

[I]

Philonous: Good morrow, Hylas: I did not expect to find you abroad so early.

Hylas: It is indeed something unusual; but my thoughts were so taken up with a subject I was discoursing of last night, that finding I could not sleep, I resolved to rise and take a turn in the garden.

Phil. It happened well, to let you see what innocent and agreeable pleasures you lose every morning. Can there be a pleasanter time of the day, or a more delightful season of the year? That purple sky, these wild but sweet notes of birds, the fragrant bloom upon the trees and flowers, the gentle influence of the rising sun, these and a thousand nameless beauties of nature inspire the soul with secret transports; its faculties too being at this time fresh and lively, are fit for those meditations, which the solitude of a garden and tranquillity of the morning naturally dispose us to.① But I am afraid I interrupt your thoughts: for you seemed very intent on something.

① This opening speech is intended to make clear at the outset that Philonous is not denying the existence of ordinary objects, such as those found in nature. Instead, as we will see further, he is offering an interpretation of what that existence amounts to, one that Berkeley at least believes to be in accord with common sense.

From Three Dialogues Between Hylas and Philonous, *1713.*

Hyl. It is true, I was, and shall be obliged to you if you will permit me to go on in the same vein; not that I would by any means deprive myself of your company, for my thoughts always flow more easily in conversation with a friend, than when I am alone; but my request is, that you would suffer me to impart my reflections to you.

Phil. With all my heart, it is what I should have requested myself, if you had not prevented me.

Hyl. I was considering the odd fate of those men who have in all ages, through an affectation of being distinguished from the vulgar, or some unaccountable turn of thought, pretended either to believe nothing at all, or to believe the most extravagant things in the world. This however might be borne, if their paradoxes and scepticism did not draw after them some consequences of general disadvantage to mankind. But the mischief lies here; that when men of less leisure see them who are supposed to have spent their whole time in the pursuits of knowledge, professing an entire ignorance of all things, or advancing such notions as are repugnant to plain and commonly received principles, they will be tempted to entertain suspicions concerning the most important truths, which they had hitherto held sacred and unquestionable.

Phil. I entirely agree with you, as to the ill tendency of the affected doubts of some philosophers, and fantastical conceits of others. I am even so far gone of late in this way of thinking, that I have quitted several of the sublime notions I had got in their schools for vulgar opinions. And I give it you on my word, since this revolt from metaphysical notions to the plain dictates of nature and common sense, I find my understanding strangely enlightened, so that I can now easily comprehend a great many things which before were all mystery and riddle.

Hyl. I am glad to find there was nothing in the accounts I heard of you.

Phil. Pray, what were those?

Hyl. You were represented in last night's conversation, as one who maintained the most extravagant opinion that ever entered into the mind of man, to wit, that there is no such thing as *material substance* in the world.②

Phil. That there is no such thing as what philosophers call *material substance,* I am seriously persuaded: but if I were made to see anything absurd or sceptical in this, I should then have the same reason to renounce this, that I imagine I have now to reject the contrary opinion.

> ② The doctrine of material *substance* is Berkeley's interpretation of Locke's view of material objects, according to which an object consists of a *substance* (an independently existing thing) that has various *qualities* (for Locke, only primary qualities). Thus material substance is the sort of substance that exists outside the mind.

Hyl. What! Can anything be more fantastical, more repugnant to common sense, or a more manifest piece of scepticism, than to believe there is no such thing as *matter?*

Phil. Softly, good Hylas. What if it should prove, that you, who hold there is, are by virtue of that opinion a greater *sceptic,* and maintain more paradoxes and repugnancies to common sense, than I who believe no such thing?

Hyl. You may as soon persuade me, the part is greater than the whole, as that, in order to avoid absurdity and skepticism, I should ever be obliged to give up my opinion in this point.

Phil. Well, then, are you content to admit that opinion for true, which upon examination shall appear most agreeable to common sense, and remote from skepticism?

Hyl. With all my heart. Since you are for raising disputes about the plainest things in nature, I am content for once to hear what you have to say.

Phil. Pray, Hylas, what do you mean by a *sceptic?*

Hyl. I mean what all men mean, one that doubts of everything.

Phil. He then who entertains no doubt concerning some particular point, with regard to that point cannot be thought a *sceptic.*

Hyl. I agree with you.

Phil. Whether does doubting consist in embracing the affirmative or negative side of a question?

Hyl. In neither; for whoever understands English, cannot but know that *doubting* signifies a suspense between both.

Phil.   He then that denies any point, can no more be said to doubt of it, than he who affirms it with the same degree of assurance.

Hyl.   True.

Phil.   And consequently, for such his denial is no more to be esteemed a *sceptic* than the other.

Hyl.   I acknowledge it.

Phil.   How comes it then, Hylas, that you pronounce me a *sceptic,* because I deny what you affirm, to wit, the existence of matter? Since, for aught you can tell, I am as peremptory in my denial, as you in your affirmation.

Hyl.   Hold, Philonous, I have been a little out in my definition; but every false step a man makes in discourse is not to be insisted on. I said indeed, that a *sceptic* was one who doubted of everything; but I should have added, or who denies the reality and truth of things.

Phil.   What things? Do you mean the principles and theorems of sciences? But these you know are universal intellectual notions, and consequently independent of matter; the denial therefore of this doth not imply the denying them.

Hyl.   I grant it. But are there no other things? What think you of distrusting the senses, of denying the real existence of sensible things, or pretending to know nothing of them. Is not this sufficient to denominate a man a *sceptic?*

Phil.   Shall we therefore examine which of us it is that denies the reality of sensible things, or professes the greatest ignorance of them since, if I take you rightly, he is to be esteemed the greatest *sceptic?*

Hyl.   That is what I desire.

[II]

Phil.   What mean you by sensible things?

Hyl.   Those things which are perceived by the senses. Can you imagine that I mean anything else?

Phil.   Pardon me, Hylas, if I am desirous clearly to apprehend your notions, since this may much shorten our inquiry. Suffer me then to ask you this farther question. Are those things only perceived by the senses which are perceived immediately? Or, may those things properly be said to be *sensible,* which are perceived mediately, or not without the intervention of others? ③

Hyl.   I do not sufficiently understand you.

Phil.   In reading a book, what I immediately perceive are the letters, but mediately, or by means of these, are suggested to my mind the notions of God, virtue, truth, &c. Now, that the letters are truly sensible things, or perceived by sense, there is no doubt: but I would know whether you take the things suggested by them to be so too.

Hyl.   No certainly, it were absurd to think *God* or *virtue* sensible things, though they may be signified and suggested to the mind by sensible marks, with which they have an arbitrary connection.

Phil.   It seems then, that by *sensible things* you mean those only which can be perceived immediately by sense.

. . .

Hyl.   . . . I tell you once for all, that by *sensible things* I mean those only which are perceived by sense, and that in truth the senses perceive nothing which they do not perceive immediately: for they make no inferences. The deducing therefore of causes or occasions from effects and appearances, which alone are perceived by sense, entirely relates to reason.

Phil.   This point then is agreed between us, that *sensible things are those only which are immediately perceived by sense.* You will farther inform me, whether we immediately perceive by sight anything beside light, and colors, and figures: or by hearing anything but sounds: by the palate, anything beside tastes: by the smell, beside odors: or by the touch, more than tangible qualities.

Hyl.   We do not.

Phil.   It seems therefore, that if you take away all sensible qualities, there remains nothing sensible.

Hyl.   I grant it.

Phil.   Sensible things therefore are nothing else but so many sensible qualities, or combinations of sensible qualities.

③ Most of the First Dialogue is concerned with the question of just what it is that is *directly* or *immediately* perceived, directly before the mind, in sense perception. (Before reading further, ask yourself what the answer is to this question.)

Hyl. Nothing else.④

④ The initial answer is that it is sensible qualities, qualities like color or shape or sound or taste or odor, that are immediately perceived, and that *sensible things* (things immediately perceived) consist only of these qualities. The question is then what such qualities themselves amount to, and the argument proceeds by considering separately various specific kinds of sensible qualities.

⑤ Berkeley's eventual thesis is that such qualities are only ideas in the mind and exist only by being perceived. Hylas attempts to attribute an independent existence to them, starting with the first example of heat (and cold).

Hyl. It must.

Phil. Tell me, Hylas, is this real existence equally compatible to all degrees of heat, which we perceive: or is there any reason why we should attribute it to some, and deny it to others? And if there be, pray let me know that reason.

Hyl. Whatever degree of heat we perceive by sense, we may be sure the same exists in the object that occasions it.

Phil. What, the greatest as well as the least?

Hyl. I tell you, the reason is plainly the same in respect of both: they are both perceived by sense; nay, the greater degree of heat is more sensibly perceived; and consequently, if there is any difference, we are more certain of its real existence than we can be of the reality of a lesser degree.

[III]

Phil. Heat then is a sensible thing.

Hyl. Certainly.

Phil. Does the reality of sensible things consist in being perceived? Or, is it something distinct from their being perceived, and that bears no relation to the mind?

Hyl. To *exist* is one thing, and to be *perceived* is another.

Phil. I speak with regard to sensible things only: and of these I ask, whether by their real existence you mean a subsistence exterior to the mind, and distinct from their being perceived?

Hyl. I mean a real absolute being, distinct from, and without any relation to, their being perceived.

Phil. Heat therefore, if it be allowed a real being, must exist without the mind.⑤

Phil. But is not the most vehement and intense degree of heat a very great pain?

Hyl. No one can deny it.

Phil. And is any unperceiving thing capable of pain or pleasure?

Hyl. No, certainly.

Phil. Is your material substance a senseless being, or a being endowed with sense and perception?

Hyl. It is senseless, without doubt.

Phil. It cannot therefore be the subject of pain.

Hyl. By no means.

Phil. Nor consequently of the greatest heat perceived by sense, since you acknowledge this to be no small pain.

Hyl. I grant it.

Phil. What shall we say then of your external object; is it a material substance, or no?

Hyl. It is a material substance with the sensible qualities inhering in it.⑥

⑥ If heat exists outside the mind, it must exist in a material substance. (Being a quality or property, it couldn't simply exist on its own—think carefully about this rather deep metaphysical point.)

Phil. How then can a great heat exist in it, since you own it cannot in a material substance? I desire you would clear this point.

Hyl. Hold, Philonous, I fear I was out in yielding intense heat to be a pain. It should seem rather, that pain is something distinct from heat, and the consequence or effect of it.

Phil. Upon putting your hand near the fire, do you perceive one simple uniform sensation, or two distinct sensations?

Hyl. But one simple sensation.

Phil. Is not the heat immediately perceived?

Hyl. It is.

Phil. And the pain?

Hyl. True.

Phil. Seeing therefore they are both immediately perceived at the same time, and the fire affects you only with one simple, or uncompounded idea, it follows that this same simple idea is both the intense heat immediately perceived, and the pain; and consequently, that the intense heat immediately perceived, is nothing distinct from a particular sort of pain.⑦

⑦ Is this claim correct? Is an intense sensation of heat the very same quality as the corresponding sensation of pain, so that there is only one idea and not two?

Hyl. It seems so.

Phil. Again, try in your thoughts, Hylas, if you can conceive a vehement sensation to be without pain, or pleasure.

Hyl. I cannot.

Phil. Or can you frame to yourself an idea of sensible pain or pleasure in general, abstracted from every particular idea of heat, cold, tastes, smells? &c.

Hyl. —I do not find that I can.

Phil. Does it not therefore follow, that sensible pain is nothing distinct from those sensations or ideas, in an intense degree?

Hyl. It is undeniable; and to speak the truth, I begin to suspect a very great heat cannot exist but in a mind perceiving it.

Phil. What! Are you then in that *sceptical* state of suspense, between affirming and denying?

⑧ Having answered affirmatively to the question in the previous annotation, Hylas is forced to admit that heat of this degree cannot exist outside the mind.

Hyl. I think I may be positive in the point. A very violent and painful heat cannot exist without the mind.⑧

Phil. It has not therefore, according to you, any real being.

Hyl. I own it.

Phil. Is it therefore certain, that there is no body in nature really hot?

Hyl. I have not denied there is any real heat in bodies. I only say, there is no such thing as an intense real heat.

Phil. But did you not say before, that all degrees of heat were equally real: or if there was any difference, that the greater were more undoubtedly real than the lesser?

Hyl. True: but it was, because I did not then consider the ground there is for distinguishing between them, which I now plainly see. And it is this: because intense heat is nothing else but a particular kind of painful sensation; and pain cannot exist

but in a perceiving being; it follows that no intense heat can really exist in an unperceiving corporeal substance. But this is no reason why we should deny heat in an inferior degree to exist in such a substance.

Phil. But how shall we be able to discern those degrees of heat which exist only in the mind, from those which exist without it?

Hyl. That is no difficult matter. You know, the least pain cannot exist unperceived; whatever, therefore, degree of heat is a pain, exists only in the mind. But as for all other degrees of heat, nothing obliges us to think the same of them.

Phil. I think you granted before, that no unperceiving being was capable of pleasure, any more than of pain.

Hyl. I did.

Phil. And is not warmth, or a more gentle degree of heat than what causes uneasiness, a pleasure?

Hyl. What then?

Phil. Consequently it cannot exist without the mind in any unperceiving substance, or body.

Hyl. So it seems.

Phil. Since therefore, as well those degrees of heat that are not painful, as those that are, can exist only in a thinking substance; may we not conclude that external bodies are absolutely incapable of any degree of heat whatsoever?

Hyl. On second thoughts, I do not think it so evident that warmth is a pleasure, as that a great degree of heat is a pain.

Phil. I do not pretend that warmth is as great a pleasure as heat is a pain. But if you grant it to be even a small pleasure, it serves to make good my conclusion.

Hyl. I could rather call it an *indolence.* It seems to be nothing more than a privation of both pain and pleasure. And that such a quality or state as this may agree to an unthinking substance, I hope you will not deny.

Phil. If you are resolved to maintain that warmth, or a gentle degree of heat, is no pleasure, I know not how to convince you otherwise than by appealing to your own sense. But what think you of cold?

Hyl. The same that I do of heat. An intense degree of cold is a pain; for to feel a very great cold, is to perceive a great uneasiness: it cannot therefore exist without the mind; but a lesser degree of cold may, as well as a lesser degree of heat.

Phil. Those bodies, therefore, upon whose application to our own, we perceive a moderate degree of heat, must be concluded to have a moderate degree of heat or warmth in them: and those, upon whose application we feel a like degree of cold, must be thought to have cold in them.

⑨ Hylas resists saying that all degrees of heat and cold exist only in the mind, conceding this only for degrees of heat and cold extreme enough to involve pain. (How plausible is the resulting view? Think of starting with a mild degree of heat or cold and gradually increasing it—does it make sense for it to initially be in an external object but at a certain point only in the mind?)

Hyl. They must.⑨

Phil. Can any doctrine be true that necessarily leads a man into an absurdity?

Hyl. Without doubt it cannot.

Phil. Is it not an absurdity to think that the same thing should be at the same time both cold and warm?

Hyl. It is.

Phil. Suppose now one of your hands hot, and the other cold and that they are both at once put into the same vessel of water, in an intermediate state; will not the water seem cold to one hand, and warm to the other?

Hyl. It will.

Phil. Ought we not therefore by your principles to conclude, it is really both cold and warm at the same time, that is, according to your own concession, to believe an absurdity?

⑩ Here is quite a different argument, one usually regarded as substantially more compelling: the **argument from illusion** (or from perceptual relativity). Try to formulate it more explicitly. Philonous argues that it is absurd to say that both of the experienced qualities are in the water, but does it follow (as is eventually concluded) that *neither* of them is? How might Philonous argue more explicitly for this further claim?

Hyl. I confess it seems so.⑩

Phil. Consequently, the principles themselves are false, since you have granted that no true principle leads to an absurdity.

Hyl. But after all, can anything be more absurd than to say, *there is no heat in the fire?*

Phil. To make the point still clearer; tell me, whether in two cases exactly alike, we ought not to make the same judgment?

Hyl. We ought.

Phil. When a pin pricks your finger, does it not rend and divide the fibres of your flesh?

Hyl. It does.

Phil. And when a coal burns your finger, does it any more?

Hyl. It does not.

Phil. Since therefore you neither judge the sensation itself occasioned by the pin, nor anything like it to be in the pin; you should not, conformably to what you have now granted, judge the sensation occasioned by the fire, or anything like it, to be in the fire.

Hyl. Well, since it must be so, I am content to yield this point, and acknowledge, that heat and cold are only sensations existing in our minds: but there still remain qualities enough to secure the reality of external things.

[IV]

Phil. But what will you say, Hylas, if it shall appear that the case is the same with regard to all other sensible qualities, and that they can no more be supposed to exist without the mind, than heat and cold?

Hyl. Then indeed you will have done something to the purpose; but that is what I despair of seeing proved.⑪

⑪ Can the conclusion regarding heat be extended to all other sensible qualities as well? This is the issue in the next several sections.

Phil. Let us examine them in order. What think you of tastes, do they exist without the mind, or no?

Hyl. Can any man in his senses doubt whether sugar is sweet, or wormwood bitter?

Phil. Inform me, Hylas. Is a sweet taste a particular kind of pleasure or pleasant sensation, or is it not?

Hyl. It is.

Phil. And is not bitterness some kind of uneasiness or pain?

Hyl. I grant it.

Phil. If therefore sugar and wormwood are unthinking corporeal substances existing without the mind, how can sweetness and bitterness, that is, pleasure and pain, agree to them?

Hyl. Hold, Philonous, I now see what it was deluded me all this time. You asked whether heat and cold, sweetness and bitterness, were not particular sorts of pleasure and pain; to which I answered simply, that they were. Whereas I should have thus distinguished: those qualities, as perceived by us, are pleasures or pains, but not as existing in the external objects. We must not therefore conclude absolutely, that there is no heat in the fire, or sweetness in the sugar, but only that heat or sweetness, as perceived by us, are not in the fire or sugar. What say you to this?

Phil. I say it is nothing to the purpose. Our discourse proceeded altogether concerning sensible things, which you defined to be the things we *immediately perceived by our senses*. Whatever other qualities therefore you speak of, as distinct from these, I know nothing of them, neither do they at all belong to the point in dispute. You may indeed pretend to have discovered certain qualities which you do not perceive, and assert those insensible qualities exist in fire and sugar. But what use can be made of this to your present purpose, I am at a loss to conceive. Tell me then once more, do you acknowledge that heat and cold, sweetness and bitterness, (meaning those qualities which are perceived by the senses) do not exist without the mind?

> ⑫ Philonous applies to tastes the same sort of argument as the first one for heat, raising again the question of whether the qualities in question are really indistinguishable from the pains or pleasures involved. (Notice the insistence that only immediately perceived qualities are in question.)

Hyl. I see it is to no purpose to hold out, so I give up the cause as to those mentioned qualities. Though I profess it sound oddly, to say that sugar is not sweet.⑫

Phil. But for your farther satisfaction, take this along with you: that which at other times seems sweet, shall to a distempered palate appear bitter. And nothing can be plainer, than that divers persons perceive different tastes in the same food, since that which one man delights in, another abhors. And how could this be, if the taste was something really inherent in the food?

Hyl. I acknowledge I know not how.⑬

Phil. In the next place, odors are to be considered. And, with regard to these, I would fain know whether what has been said of tastes does not exactly agree to them? Are they not so many pleasing or displeasing sensations?

> ⑬ Here is a brief reprisal of the argument from illusion, in application to taste. Think again of how the argument could be spelled out more explicitly, and of the justification for the claim that *none* of the perceived qualities exists in the supposed external object.

Hyl. They are.

Phil. Can you then conceive it possible that they should exist in an unperceiving thing?

Hyl. I cannot.

Phil. Or can you imagine, that filth and ordure affect those brute animals that feed on them out of choice, with the same smells which we perceive in them?

Hyl. By no means.

Phil. May we not therefore conclude of smells, as of the other forementioned qualities, that they cannot exist in any but a perceiving substance or mind?

Hyl. I think so.⑭

Phil. Then as to sounds, what must we think of them: are they accidents really inherent in external bodies, or not?

> ⑭ The pain/pleasure argument is applied to odor, raising the same issue as before. No version of the argument from illusion is offered for qualities of smell, but you should be able to construct one.

Hyl. That they inhere not in the sonorous bodies, is plain from hence; because a bell struck in the exhausted receiver of an air-pump, sends forth no sound. The air therefore must be thought the subject of sound.

Phil. What reason is there for that, Hylas?

Hyl. Because when any motion is raised in the air, we perceive a sound greater or lesser, to the air's motion; but without some motion in the air, we never hear any sound at all.

Phil. And granting that we never hear a sound but when some motion is produced in the air, yet I do not see how you can infer from thence, that the sound itself is in the air.

Hyl. It is this very motion in the external air, that produces in the mind the sensation of *sound.* For, striking on the drum of the ear, it causes a vibration, which by the auditory nerves being communicated to the brain, the soul is thereupon affected with the sensation called *sound.*

Phil. What! Is sound then a sensation?

Hyl. I tell you, as perceived by us, it is a particular sensation in the mind.

Phil. And can any sensation exist without the mind?

Hyl. No certainly.

Phil. How then can sound, being a sensation, exist in the air, if by the *air* you mean a senseless substance existing without the mind?

[15] Hylas does not question that sound *as heard* is a sensation in the mind, but attempts to argue that sound in a different sense exists as a vibration in the air. In the immediately following passage, Philonous insists again that it is only immediately perceived qualities with which the argument is concerned (referring back to the analogous point about taste—see the passage before Annotation 12).

Hyl. You must distinguish, Philonous, between sound as it is perceived by us, and as it is in itself; or (which is the same thing) between the sound we immediately perceive and that which exists without us. The former indeed is a particular kind of sensation, but the latter is merely a vibrative or undulatory motion in the air. [15]

Phil. I thought I had already obviated that distinction by the answer I gave when you were applying it in a like case before. But to say no more of that; are you sure then that sound is really nothing but motion?

Hyl. I am.

Phil. Whatever therefore agrees to real sound, may with truth be attributed to motion.

Hyl. It may.

Phil. It is then good sense to speak of *motion,* as of a thing that is *loud, sweet, acute,* or *grave.*

Hyl. I see you are resolved not to understand me. Is it not evident, those accidents or modes belong only to sensible sound, or *sound* in the common acceptation of the word, but not to *sound* in the real and philosophic sense, which, as I just now

told you, is nothing but a certain motion of the air?

Phil. It seems then there are two sorts of sound, the one vulgar, or that which is heard, the other philosophical and real.

Hyl. Even so.

Phil. And the latter consists in motion.

Hyl. I told you so before.

Phil. Tell me, Hylas, to which of the senses, think you, the idea of motion belongs: to the hearing?

Hyl. No certainly, but to the sight and touch.

Phil. It should follow then, that according to you, real sounds may possibly be *seen* or *felt,* but never *heard.*

Hyl. Look you, Philonous, you may if you please make a jest of my opinion, but that will not alter the truth of things. I own indeed, the inferences you draw me into, sound something oddly; but common language, you know, is framed by, and for the use of, the vulgar: we must not therefore wonder, if expressions adapted to exact philosophic notions, seem uncouth and out of the way.

Phil. Is it come to that? I assure, you, I imagine myself to have gained no small point, since you make so light of departing from common phrases and opinions; it being a main part of our inquiry, to examine whose notions are widest of the common road, and most repugnant to the general sense of the world. But can you think it no more than a philosophical paradox, to say that *real sounds are never heard,* and that the idea of them is obtained by some other sense. And is there nothing in this contrary to nature and the truth of things?

[16] The further argument is offered that sound as a motion is not the sort of thing that could be heard. How compelling is this? (Note that the issue doesn't really matter very much, since the sensible qualities have already been conceded to exist only in the mind. Think how Berkeley might have argued further for this last claim by using arguments of the same sorts as were applied to heat and tastes.)

Hyl. To deal ingenuously, I do not like it. And after the concessions already made, I had as well grant that sounds too have no real being without the mind. [16]

[V]

Phil. And I hope you will make no difficulty to acknowledge the same of colors.

Hyl. Pardon me: the case of colors is very different. Can anything be plainer, than that we see them on the objects?

Phil. The objects you speak of are, I suppose, corporeal substances existing without the mind.

Hyl. They are.

Phil. And have true and real colors inhering in them?

⎾17⏌ The claim that corporeal objects have the color we see in them is at least roughly the common sense view of color.

Hyl. Each visible object has that color which we see in it. ⎾17⏌

Phil. How! Is there anything visible but what we perceive by sight.

Hyl. There is not.

Phil. And do we perceive anything by sense, which we do not perceive immediately?

Hyl. How often must I be obliged to repeat the same thing? I tell you, we do not.

Phil. Have patience, good Hylas; and tell me once more, whether there is anything immediately perceived by the senses, except sensible qualities. I know you asserted there was not: but I would now be informed, whether you still persist in the same opinion.

Hyl. I do.

Phil. Pray, is your corporeal substance either a sensible quality, or made up of sensible qualities?

Hyl. What a question that is! Who ever thought it was?

Phil. My reason for asking was, because in saying, *Each visible object has that color which we see in it,* you make visible objects to be corporeal substances; which implies either that corporeal substances are sensible qualities, or else that there is something beside sensible qualities perceived by sight: but as this point was formerly agreed between us, and is still maintained by you, it is a clear consequence, that your corporeal substance is nothing distinct from sensible qualities. ⎾18⏌

Hyl. You may draw as many absurd consequences as you please, and endeavor to perplex the plainest things; but you shall never persuade me out of my senses. I clearly understand my own meaning.

Phil. I wish you would make me understand it too. But since you are unwilling to have your notion of corporeal substance examined, I shall urge that point no farther. Only be pleased to let me know, whether the same colors which we see, exist in external bodies, or some other.

Hyl. The very same.

Phil. What! Are then the beautiful red and purple we see on yonder clouds, really in them? Or do you imagine they have in themselves any other form, than that of a dark mist or vapor?

⎾18⏌ This is an argument against Locke's conception of substance (see Annotation 23 to the Locke selection): a material or corporeal substance is supposed to be something that *has* sensible qualities like color, but is itself distinct from them; but all we perceive is sensible qualities, so such a substance must be nothing more than sensible qualities—or else something that we do not perceive at all and so arguably have no idea at all of. (Berkeley takes this to be an objection to corporeal substance only, but the same issue can be raised about mental substances: the minds that have various ideas and experiences but are supposed to be distinct from them. See Annotation 47 and Discussion Question 3.)

Hyl. I must own, Philonous, those colors are not really in the clouds as they seem to be at this distance. They are only apparent colors.

Phil. *Apparent* call you them? How shall we distinguish these apparent colors from real?

Hyl. Very easily. Those are to be thought apparent, which appearing only at a distance, vanish upon a nearer approach.

Phil. And those I suppose are to be thought real, which are discovered by the most near and exact survey.

Hyl. Right.

Phil. Is the nearest and exactest survey made by the help of a microscope, or by the naked eye?

Hyl. By a microscope, doubtless.

Phil. But a microscope often discovers colors in an object different from those perceived by the unassisted sight. And in case we had microscopes magnifying to any assigned degree; it is certain, that no object whatsoever, viewed through them, would appear in the same color which it exhibits to the naked eye.

Hyl.   And what will you conclude from all this? You cannot argue that there are really and naturally no colors on objects: because by artificial managements they may be altered, or made to vanish.

Phil.   I think it may evidently be concluded from your own concessions, that all the colors we see with our naked eyes, are only apparent as those on the clouds, since they vanish upon a more close and accurate inspection, which is afforded us by a microscope. Then as to what you say by way of prevention: I ask you, whether the real and natural state of an object is better discovered by a very sharp and piercing sight, or by one which is less sharp?

Hyl.   By the former without doubt.

Phil.   Is it not plain . . . that microscopes make the sight more penetrating, and represent objects as they would appear to the eye in case it were naturally endowed with a most exquisite sharpness?

Hyl.   It is.

Phil.   Consequently the microscopical representation is to be thought that which best sets forth the real nature of the thing, or what it is in itself. The colors, therefore, by it perceived, are more genuine and real, than those perceived otherwise.

Hyl.   I confess there is something in what you say.

. . .

Phil.   The point will be past all doubt, if you consider, that in case colors were real properties or affections inherent in external bodies, they could admit of no alteration, without some change wrought in the very bodies themselves: but is it not evident from what has been said, that upon the use of microscopes, upon a change happening in the humors of the eye, or a variation of distance, without any manner of real alteration in the thing itself, the colors of any object are either changed, or totally disappear? Nay, all other circumstances remaining the same, change but the situation of some objects, and they shall present different colors to the eye. The same thing happens upon viewing an object in various degrees of light. And what is more known, than that the same bodies appear differently colored by candlelight from what they do in the open day? Add to these the experiment of a prism, which separating the heterogeneous rays of light, alters the color of any object; and will cause the whitest to appear of a deep blue or red to the naked eye. And now tell me, whether you are still of opinion that every body has its true real color inhering in it: and if you think it has, I would fain know farther from you, what certain distance and position of the object, what peculiar texture and formation of the eye, what degree or kind of light is necessary for ascertaining that true color, and distinguishing it from apparent ones. [19]

> [19] Here is another version of the argument from illusion, this time applied to colors. This version is more complicated, because the different color qualities are not experienced at the same moment. The additional premise needed is that the changes that yield different color experiences involve no change in the object itself. Here again, you should try to formulate the argument more explicitly—and consider again the issue raised in Annotation 10. (Philonous's remark at the end of this last paragraph may suggest a way of dealing with that issue.)

Hyl.   I own myself entirely satisfied, that they are all equally apparent; and that there is no such thing as color really inhering in external bodies, but that it is altogether in the light. And what confirms me in this opinion is, that in proportion to the light, colors are still more or less vivid; and if there be no light, then are there no colors perceived. Besides, allowing there are colors on external objects, yet how is it possible for us to perceive them? For no external body affects the mind, unless it act first on our organs of sense. But the only action of bodies is motion; and motion cannot be communicated otherwise than by impulse. A distant object therefore cannot act on the eye, nor consequently make itself or its properties perceivable to the soul. Whence it plainly follows, that it is immediately some contiguous substance, which operating on the eye occasions a perception of colors: and such is light.

Phil.   How! Is light then a substance?

Hyl.   I tell you, Philonous, external light is nothing but a thin fluid substance, whose minute particles being agitated with a brisk motion, and in various manners reflected from the different surfaces of outward objects to the eyes, communicate different motions to the optic nerves; which, being propagated to the brain, cause therein various impressions: and these are attended with the sensations of red, blue, yellow, &c.

Phil. It seems then, the light does no more than shake the optic nerves.

Hyl. Nothing else.

Phil. And consequent to each particular motion of the nerves, the mind is affected with a sensation, which is some particular color.

Hyl. Right.

Phil. And these sensations have no existence without the mind.

Hyl. They have not.

Phil. How then do you affirm that colors are in the light, since by *light* you understand a corporeal substance external to the mind?

Hyl. Light and colors, as immediately perceived by us, I grant cannot exist without the mind. But in themselves they are only the motions and configurations of certain insensible particles of matter.

Phil. Colors then, in the vulgar sense, or taken for the immediate objects of sight, cannot agree to any but a perceiving substance.

Hyl. That is what I say.

Phil. Well then, since you give up the point as to those sensible qualities, which are alone thought colors by all mankind beside, you may hold what you please with regard to those invisible ones of the philosophers.[20] It is not my business to dispute about them; only I would advise you to bethink yourself, whether considering the inquiry we are upon, it be prudent for you to affirm, *The red and blue which we see are not real colors, but certain unknown motions and figures which no man ever did or can see are truly so.* Are not these shocking notions and are not they subject to as many ridiculous inferences, as those you were obliged to renounce before in the case of sounds?

20 Hylas accepts the result that color is not in bodies, but suggests that it is in light instead (which would still be something external to the mind). But in trying to explain how color is in light, he is forced to admit that the color sensations we directly experience are in the mind, even if their cause is external.

[VI]

Hyl. I frankly own, Philonous, that it is in vain to stand out any longer. Colors, sounds, tastes, in a word, all those termed *secondary qualities,* have certainly no existence without the mind. But by this acknowledgment I must not be supposed to derogate anything from the reality of matter or external objects, seeing it is no more than several philosophers maintain, who nevertheless are the farthest imaginable from denying matter. For the clearer understanding of this, you must know sensible qualities are by philosophers divided into *primary* and *secondary.* The former are extension, figure, solidity, gravity, motion, and rest. And these they hold exist really in bodies. The latter are those above enumerated; or briefly, all sensible qualities beside the primary, which they assert are only so many sensations or ideas existing nowhere but in the mind. But all this, I doubt not, you are already apprised of. For my part, I have been a long time sensible there was such an opinion current among philosophers, but was never thoroughly convinced of its truth till now.[21]

21 Hylas retreats to the Lockean distinction between primary and secondary qualities, agreeing that secondary qualities exist only in the mind, but claiming that primary qualities exist in external objects. (See Annotation 14 to the Locke selection and the associated text.) Philonous will now argue against that distinction, claiming that the arguments that allegedly show that secondary qualities exist only in the mind also apply to primary qualities.

Phil. You are still then of opinion that extension and figures are inherent in external unthinking substances.

Hyl. I am.

Phil. But what if the same arguments which are brought against secondary qualities, will hold good against these also?

Hyl. Why then I shall be obliged to think, they too exist only in the mind.

Phil. Is it your opinion, the very figure and extension which you perceive by sense, exist in the outward object or material substance?

Hyl. It is.

. . .

Phil. . . . have you not acknowledged that no real inherent property of any object can be changed, without some change in the thing itself?

Hyl. I have.

Phil. But as we approach to or recede from an object, the visible extension varies, being at one distance ten or a hundred times greater than at another. Does it not therefore follow from hence likewise, that it is not really inherent in the object?

Hyl. I own I am at a loss what to think.

Phil. Your judgment will soon be determined, if you will venture to think as freely concerning this quality, as you have done concerning the rest. Was it not admitted as a good argument, that neither heat nor cold was in the water, because it seemed warm to one hand, and cold to the other?

Hyl. It was.

Phil. Is it not the very same reasoning to conclude, there is no extension or figure in an object, because to one eye it shall seem little, smooth, and round, when at the same time it appears to the other, great, uneven, and angular?

Hyl. The very same. But does this latter fact ever happen?

[22] Philonous proceeds to apply the argument from illusion to figure (shape) and extension (size). (In the following paragraph, a different line of argument is suggested, namely that ideas or anything like them cannot exist in an unperceiving substance. This seems to make the mistake of assuming that a quality we have an idea of is itself just an idea or like an idea—which is far from obviously true.)

Phil. You may at any time make the experiment, by looking with one eye bare, and with the other through a microscope.

Hyl. I know not how to maintain it, and yet I am loath to give up *extension,* I see so many odd consequences following upon such a concession.[22]

Phil. Odd, say you? After the concessions already made, I hope you will stick at nothing for its oddness. But on the other hand

should it not seem very odd, if the general reasoning which includes all other sensible qualities did not also include extension? If it be allowed that no idea nor anything like an idea can exist in an unperceiving substance, then surely it follows, that no figure or mode of extension, which we can either perceive or imagine, or have any idea of, can be really inherent in matter; not to mention the peculiar difficulty there must be, in conceiving a material substance, prior to and distinct from extension, to be the *substratum* of extension. Be the sensible quality what it will, figure, or sound, or color; it seems alike impossible it should subsist in that which doth not perceive it.

Hyl. I give up the point for the present, reserving still a right to retract my opinion, in case I shall hereafter discover any false step in my progress to it.

[VII]

Phil. That is a right you cannot be denied. Figures and extension being dispatched, we proceed next to *motion.* Can a real motion in any external body be at the same time both very swift and very slow?

Hyl. It cannot.

Phil. Is not the motion of a body swift in a reciprocal proportion to the time it takes up in describing any given space? Thus a body that describes a mile in an hour, moves three times faster than it would in case it described only a mile in three hours.

Hyl. I agree with you.

Phil. And is not time measured by the succession of ideas in our minds?

Hyl. It is.

Phil. And is it not possible ideas should succeed one another twice as fast in your mind, as they do in mine, or in that of some spirit of another kind.

Hyl. I own it.

Phil. Consequently the same body may to another seem to perform its motion over any space in half the time that it does to you. And the same reasoning will hold as to any other proportion: that is to say, according to your principles (since the motions perceived are both really in the object) it is possible one and the same body shall be really moved the same way at once, both very swift and very slow. How is this consistent either with common sense, or with what you just now granted?

23 Here it is important to realize that what the argument is concerned with is motion as directly experienced, not motion as measured (for example, by a speedometer). The claim that time is measured by the speed with which ideas succeed each other in the mind is not particularly plausible. Can you think of a better argument here? (See Discussion Question 4.)

Hyl. I have nothing to say to it. **23**

Phil. Then as for *solidity;* either you do not mean any sensible quality by that word, and so it is beside our inquiry: or if you do, it must be either hardness or resistance. But both the one and the other are plainly relative to our senses: it being evident, that what seems hard to one animal, may appear soft to another, who hath greater force and firmness of limbs. Nor is it less plain, that the resistance I feel is not in the body.

Hyl. I own the very sensation of resistance, which is all you immediately perceive, is not in the *body;* but the cause of that sensation is.

Phil. But the causes of our sensations are not things immediately perceived, and therefore not sensible. This point I thought had been already determined.

24 Here is a quick gesture at the argument from illusion in application to solidity—you should spell it out more fully. In the following paragraph, Philonous argues further that other primary qualities presuppose extension and so cannot be outside the mind if it is not.

Hyl. I own it was; but you will pardon me if I seem a little embarrassed: I know not how to quit my old notions. **24**

Phil. To help you out, do but consider that if extension be once acknowledged to have no existence without the mind, the same must necessarily be granted of motion, solidity, and gravity, since they all evidently suppose extension. It is therefore superfluous to inquire particularly concerning each of them. In denying extension, you have denied them all to have any real existence.

. . .

Hyl. It is just come into my head, Philonous, that I have somewhere heard of a distinction between absolute and sensible extension. Now though it be acknowledged that *great* and *small,* consisting

merely in the relation which other extended beings have to the parts of our own bodies, do not really inhere in the substances themselves; yet nothing obliges us to hold the same with regard to *absolute extension,* which is something abstracted from *great* and *small,* from this or that particular magnitude or figure. So likewise as to motion, *swift* and *slow* are altogether relative to the succession of ideas in our own minds. But it does not follow, because those modifications of motion exist not without the mind, that therefore absolute motion abstracted from them does not.

Phil. Pray what is it that distinguishes one motion, or one part of extension, from another? Is it not something sensible, as some degree of swiftness or slowness, some certain magnitude or figure peculiar to each?

Hyl. I think so.

. . .

Phil. But I think the point may be speedily decided. Without doubt you can tell, whether you are able to frame this or that idea. Now I am content to put our dispute on this issue. If you can frame in your thoughts a distinct abstract idea of motion or extension, divested of all those sensible modes, as swift and slow, great and small, round and square, and the like, which are acknowledged to exist only in the mind, I will then yield the point you contend for. But if you cannot, it will be unreasonable on your side to insist any longer upon what you have no notion of.

25 Hylas attempts to defend Locke's view of extension and motion as "absolute" qualities that are independent of our experiences of them, but is forced to admit that he has no ideas of such qualities—which seems to mean here no definite *image.*

Hyl. To confess ingenuously, I cannot. **25**

Phil. Can you even separate the ideas of extension and motion, from the ideas of all those qualities which they who make the distinction, term *secondary.*

Hyl. What! Is it not an easy matter, to consider extension and motion by themselves, abstracted from all other sensible qualities? Pray how do the mathematicians treat of them?

Phil. I acknowledge, Hylas, it is not difficult to form general propositions and reasonings about those qualities, without mentioning any other; and in this sense to consider or treat of them abstractedly. But how does it follow that because I can pronounce the word *motion* by itself, I can form the idea of it in my mind exclusive of body? Or because theorems may be made of extension and figures, without any mention of *great* or *small,* or any other sensible mode or quality; that therefore it is possible such an abstract idea of extension, without any particular size or figure, or sensible quality, should be distinctly formed, and apprehended by the mind? Mathematicians treat of quantity, without regarding what other sensible qualities it is attended with, as being altogether indifferent to their demonstrations. But when laying aside the words, they contemplate the bare ideas, I believe you will find, they are not the pure abstracted ideas of extension.

Hyl. But what say you to *pure intellect?* May not abstracted ideas be framed by that faculty?

Phil. Since I cannot frame abstract ideas at all, it is plain, I cannot frame them by the help of *pure intellect,* whatsoever faculty you understand by those words. Besides, not to inquire into the nature of pure intellect and its spiritual objects, as *virtue, reason, God,* or the like; thus much seems manifest, that sensible things are only to be perceived by sense, or represented by the imagination. Figures, therefore, and extension, being originally perceived by sense, do not belong to pure intellect. But for your farther satisfaction, try if you can frame the idea of any figure, abstracted from all particularities of size, or even from other sensible qualities.

Hyl. Let me think a little—I do not find that I can.

Phil. And can you think it possible, that should really exist in nature, which implies a repugnancy in its conception?

Hyl. By no means.

Phil. Since therefore it is impossible even for the mind to disunite the ideas of extension and motion from all other sensible qualities, does it not follow, that where the one exist, there necessarily the other exist likewise?

Hyl. It should seem so.

Phil. Consequently the very same arguments which you admitted, as conclusive against the secondary

qualities, are, without any farther application of force, against the primary too. Besides, if you will trust your senses, is it not plain, all sensible qualities coexist, or, to them, appear as being in the same place? Do they ever represent a motion, or figure, as being divested of all other visible and tangible qualities?

Hyl. You need say no more on this head. I am free to own, if there be no secret error or oversight in our proceedings hitherto, that all sensible qualities are alike to be denied existence without the mind. But my fear is, that I have been too liberal in my former concessions, or overlooked some fallacy or other. In short, I did not take time to think. 26

26 A further argument against the separate existence of primary qualities is that we have no ideas of them in isolation from secondary qualities. Here again, ideas seem to be regarded as *images,* with the point being that any image of, for example, a particular shape must also involve other qualities like color that delineate the shape. At this point, Hylas surrenders and concedes that all sensible qualities exist only in the mind.

Phil. For that matter, Hylas, you may take what time you please in reviewing the progress of our inquiry. You are at liberty to recover any slips you might have made, or offer whatever you have omitted, which makes for your first opinion.

. . .

[VIII]

Hyl. I acknowledge, Philonous, that upon a fair observation of what passes in my mind, I can discover nothing else, but that I am a thinking being, affected with variety of sensations; neither is it possible to conceive how a sensation should exist in an unperceiving substance. But then on the other hand, when I look on sensible things in a different view, considering them as so many modes and qualities, I find it necessary to suppose a material *substratum,* without which they cannot be conceived to exist.

Phil. *Material substratum* call you it? Pray, by which of your senses came you acquainted with that being?

Hyl.   It is not itself sensible; its modes and qualities only being perceived by the senses.

Phil.   I presume then it was by reflection and reason you obtained the idea of it.

㉗ Here is another attack on the Lockean idea of substance, spelling out the argument that was only hinted at in the text corresponding to Annotation 18. Hylas uses the variant term *substratum,* with the idea being that material substance underlies or supports the qualities that *inhere* in it. But since all our ideas are of qualities, he is forced to admit that he has no real idea of material substance itself.

Hyl.   I do not pretend to any proper positive idea of it. However I conclude it exists, because qualities cannot be conceived to exist without a support. ㉗

Phil.   It seems then you have only a relative notion of it, or that you conceive it not otherwise than by conceiving the relation it bears to sensible qualities.

Hyl.   Right.

Phil.   Be pleased therefore to let me know wherein that relation consists.

Hyl.   Is it not sufficiently expressed in the term *substratum,* or *substance?*

Phil.   If so, the word *substratum* should import, that it is spread under the sensible qualities or accidents.

Hyl.   True.

Phil.   And consequently under extension.

Hyl.   I own it.

Phil.   It is therefore somewhat in its own nature entirely distinct from extension.

Hyl.   I tell you, extension is only a mode, and matter is something that supports modes. And is it not evident the thing supported is different from the thing supporting?

Phil.   So that something distinct from, and exclusive of, extension, is supposed to be the *substratum* of extension.

Hyl.   Just so.

Phil.   Answer me, Hylas. Can a thing be spread without extension? Or is not the idea of extension necessarily included in *spreading?*

Hyl.   It is.

Phil.   Whatsoever therefore you suppose spread under anything, must have in itself an extension distinct from the extension of that thing under which it is spread.

Hyl.   It must.

Phil.   Consequently every corporeal substance, being the *substratum* of extension, must have in itself another extension by which it is qualified to be a *substratum:* and so on to infinity. And I ask whether this be not absurd in itself, and repugnant to what you granted just now, to wit, that the *substratum* was something distinct from, and exclusive of, extension.

Hyl.   Aye but, Philonous, you take me wrong. I do not mean that matter is *spread* in a gross literal sense under extension. The word *substratum* is used only to express in general the same thing with *substance.*

Phil.   Well then, let us examine the relation implied in the term *substance.* Is it not that it stands under accidents?

Hyl.   The very same.

Phil.   But that one thing may stand under or support another, must it not be extended?

Hyl.   It must.

Phil.   Is not therefore this supposition liable to the same absurdity with the former?

Hyl.   You still take things in a strict literal sense: that is not fair, Philonous.

Phil.   I am not for imposing any sense on your words: you are at liberty to explain them as you please. Only I beseech you, make me understand something by them. You tell me, matter supports or stands under accidents. How! Is it as your legs support your body?

Hyl.   No; that is the literal sense.

Phil.   Pray let me know any sense, literal or not literal, that you understand it in.—How long must I wait for an answer, Hylas?

Hyl.   I declare I know not what to say. I once thought I understood well enough what was meant by matter's supporting accidents. But now the more I think on it, the less can I comprehend it; in short, I find that I know nothing of it.

Phil.   It seems then you have no idea at all, neither relative nor positive of matter; you know neither what it is in itself, nor what relation it bears to accidents.

Hyl. I acknowledge it. ㉘

Phil. And yet you asserted, that you could not conceive how qualities or accidents should really exist, without conceiving at the same time a material support of them.

> ㉘ Philonous ruthlessly drives home the point that Hylas has no intelligible idea of either substance itself or its relation to qualities.

Hyl. I did.

Phil. That is to say, when you conceive the real existence of qualities, you do withal conceive something which you cannot conceive.

[IX]

Hyl. It was wrong I own. But still I fear there is some fallacy or other. Pray what think you of this? It is just come into my head, that the ground of all our mistake lies in your treating of each quality by itself. Now, I grant that each quality cannot singly subsist without the mind. Color cannot without extension, neither can figure without some other sensible quality. But as the several qualities united or blended together form entire sensible things, nothing hinders why such things may not be supposed to exist without the mind.

Phil. Either, Hylas, you are jesting, or have a very bad memory. Though indeed we went through all the qualities by name one after another; yet my arguments, or rather your concessions, nowhere tended to prove, that the secondary qualities did not subsist each alone by itself; but that they were not *at all* without the mind. Indeed in treating of figure and motion, we concluded they could not exist without the mind, because it was impossible even in thought to separate them from all secondary qualities, so as to conceive them existing by themselves. But then this was not the only argument made use of upon that occasion. But (to pass by all that hath been hitherto said, and reckon it for nothing, if you will have it so) I am content to put the whole upon this issue. If you can conceive it possible for any mixture or combination of qualities, or any sensible object whatever, to exist without the mind, then I will grant it actually to be so.

Hyl. If it comes to that, the point will soon be decided. What more easy than to conceive a tree or house existing by itself, independent of, and unperceived

by, any mind whatsoever? I do at this present time conceive them existing after that manner.

Phil. How say you, Hylas, can you see a thing which is at the same time unseen?

Hyl. No, that were a contradiction.

Phil. Is it not as great a contradiction to talk of *conceiving* a thing which is *unconceived?*

Hyl. It is.

Phil. The tree or house therefore which you think of, is conceived by you.

Hyl. How should it be otherwise?

Phil. And what is conceived is surely in the mind.

Hyl. Without question, that which is conceived is in the mind.

Phil. How then came you to say, you conceived a house or tree existing independent and out of all minds whatsoever?

Hyl. That was I own an oversight; but stay, let me consider what led me into it.—It is a pleasant mistake enough. As I was thinking of a tree in a solitary place, where no one was present to see it, methought that was to conceive a tree as existing unperceived or unthought of, not considering that I myself conceived it all the while. But now I plainly see, that all I can do is to frame ideas in my own mind. I may indeed conceive in my own thoughts the idea of a tree, or a house, or a mountain, but that is all. And this is far from proving, that I can conceive them *existing out of the minds of all spirits.*

> ㉙ According to the realist view that objects exist outside the mind, it would be possible for such an object to exist even though conceived by no one. But if one attempts to conceive of such a situation, it seems to follow that the object is both allegedly unconceived but also conceived, which is seemingly a contradiction. Thus both the possibility in question and the realist view that leads to it appear to be inconceivable, and so apparently impossible. This is one of Berkeley's favorite arguments, one that is unique to him and also very tricky. Can you see any way to reply to it?

Phil. You acknowledge then that you cannot possibly conceive, how any one corporeal sensible thing should exist otherwise than in a mind.

Hyl. I do. ㉙

Phil. And yet you will earnestly contend for

the truth of that which you cannot so much as conceive.

Hyl. I profess I know not what to think, but still there are some scruples remain with me. Is it not certain I see things at a distance? Do we not perceive the stars and moon, for example, to be a great way off? Is not this, I say, manifest to the senses?

Phil. Do you not in a dream too perceive those or the like objects?

Hyl. I do.

Phil. And have they not then the same appearance of being distant?

Hyl. They have.

Phil. But you do not thence conclude the apparitions in a dream to be without the mind?

Hyl. By no means.

Phil. You ought not therefore to conclude that sensible objects are without the mind, from their appearance or manner wherein they are perceived.

Hyl. I acknowledge it. But doth not my sense deceive me in those cases?

. . .

Phil. Good Hylas, do but reflect a little on the point, and then tell me whether there be any more in it than this. From the ideas you actually perceive by sight, you have by experience learned to collect what other ideas you will (according to the standing order of nature) be affected with, after such a certain succession of time and motion.

Hyl. Upon the whole, I take it to be nothing else.

Phil. Now is it not plain, that if we suppose a man born blind was on a sudden made to see, he could at first have no experience of what may be suggested by sight.

Hyl. It is.

Phil. He would not then according to you have any notion of distance annexed to the things he saw; but would take them for a new set of sensations existing only in his mind.

Hyl. It is undeniable.

Phil. But to make it still more plain: is not *distance* a line turned endwise to the eye?

Hyl. It is.

Phil. And can a line so situated be perceived by sight?

Hyl. It cannot.

Phil. Does it not therefore follow that distance is not properly and immediately perceived by sight?

Hyl. It should seem so. [30]

. . .

30 Berkeley here invokes his own theory of vision (developed more fully in his *Essay Towards a New Theory of Vision*). The claim is that distance from the perceiver is not something that is directly or immediately perceived.

Phil. But allowing that distance was truly and immediately perceived by the mind, yet it would not thence follow it existed out of the mind. For whatever is immediately perceived is an idea: and can any *idea* exist out of the mind?

[X]

Hyl. To suppose that, were absurd: but inform me, Philonous, can we perceive or know nothing beside our ideas?

Phil. As for the rational deducing of causes from effects, that is beside our inquiry. And by the senses you can best tell, whether you perceive anything which is not immediately perceived. And I ask you whether the things immediately perceived, are other than your own sensations or ideas? Your have indeed more than once, in the course of this conversation, declared yourself on those points; but you seem by this last question to have departed from what you then thought.

Hyl. To speak the truth, Philonous, I think there are two kinds of objects, the one perceived immediately, which are likewise called *ideas;* the other are real things or external objects perceived by the mediation of ideas, which are their images and representations. Now I own, ideas do not exist without the mind; but the latter sort of objects do. I am sorry I did not think of this distinction sooner; it would probably have cut short your discourse.

Phil. Are those external objects perceived by sense, or by some other faculty?

Hyl. They are perceived by sense.

Phil. How! Is there anything perceived by sense, which is not immediately perceived?

Hyl. Yes, Philonous, in some sort there is. For example, when I look on a picture or statue of Julius Caesar, I may be said after a manner to perceive him (though not immediately) by my senses.

31 At this point, Hylas has finally arrived at Locke's main view: we are immediately or directly aware of ideas in the mind, but these represent objects outside the mind in virtue of the "conformity or resemblance" between the two.

Phil. It seems then, you will have our ideas, which alone are immediately perceived, to be pictures of external things; and that these also are perceived by sense, inasmuch as they have a conformity or resemblance to our ideas. 31

Hyl. That is my meaning.

Phil. And in the same way that Julius Caesar, in himself invisible, is nevertheless perceived by sight; real things, in themselves imperceptible, are perceived by sense.

Hyl. In the very same.

Phil. Tell me, Hylas, when you behold the picture of Julius Caesar, do you see with your eyes any more than some colors and figures, with a certain symmetry and composition of the whole?

Hyl. Nothing else.

Phil. And would not a man, who had never known anything of Julius Caesar, see as much?

Hyl. He would.

Phil. Consequently he hath his sight, and the use of it, in as perfect a degree as you.

Hyl. I agree with you.

Phil. Whence comes it then that your thoughts are directed to the Roman emperor, and his are not? This cannot proceed from the sensations or ideas of sense by you then perceived; since you acknowledge you have no advantage over him in that respect. It should seem therefore to proceed from reason and memory: should it not?

Hyl. It should.

Phil. Consequently it will not follow from that instance, that anything is perceived by sense which is not immediately perceived. Though I grant we may in one acceptation be said to perceive sensible things mediately by sense: that is, when from a frequently perceived connection, the immediate

perception of ideas by one sense suggests to the mind others, perhaps belonging to another sense, which are wont to be connected with them. For instance, when I hear a coach drive along the streets, immediately I perceive only the sound; but from the experience I have had that such a sound is connected with a coach, I am said to hear the coach. It is nevertheless evident, that in truth and strictness, nothing can be *heard* but *sound:* and the coach is not then properly perceived by sense, but suggested from experience. So likewise when we are said to see a red-hot bar of iron; the solidity and heat of the iron are not the objects of sight, but suggested to the imagination by the color and figure, which are properly perceived by that sense. In short, those things alone are actually and strictly perceived by any sense, which would have been perceived, in case that same sense had then been first conferred on us. As for other things, it in plain they are only suggested to the mind by experience grounded on former perceptions. But to return to your comparison of Caesar's picture, it is plain, if you keep to that, you must hold the real things, or archetypes of our ideas, are not perceived by sense, but by some internal faculty of the soul, as reason or memory. I would therefore fair know, what arguments you can draw from reason for the existence of what you call *real things* or *material objects.* Or whether you remember to have seen them formerly as they are in themselves? Or if you have heard or read of any one that did.

Hyl. I see, Philonous, you are disposed to raillery; but that will never convince me.

Phil. My aim is only to learn from you, the way to come at the knowledge of *material beings.* Whatever we perceive, is perceived immediately or mediately: by sense, or by reason and reflection. But as you have excluded sense, pray show me what reason you have to believe their existence; or what *medium* you can possibly make use of, to prove it either to mine or your own understanding.

Hyl. To deal ingenuously, Philonous, now I consider the point, I do not find I can give you any good reason for it. 32 But thus much seem pretty plain, that it is at least possible such things may really exist. And as long as there is no absurdity in supposing them, I am resolved to believe as I did, till you bring good reasons to the contrary.

[32] Philonous raises the same issue that Locke was grappling with in Book IV, chapter XI of the *Essay* (pp. 189–191): what reason is there to believe in the existence of external objects that are never directly perceived or experienced? In the case of the coach and the bar of iron, the claim is that some immediately perceived ideas suggest others previously perceived along with them—but this account will not work for something that is *never* immediately perceived. Hylas has no reply.

Phil.   What! Is it come to this, that you only believe the existence of material objects, and that your belief is founded barely on the possibility of its being true? Then you will have me bring reasons against it: though another would think it reasonable, the proof should lie on him who holds the affirmative. And after all, this very point which you are now resolved to maintain without any reason, is in effect what you have more than once during this discourse seen good reason to give up. But to pass over all this; if I understand you rightly, you say our ideas do not exist without the mind; but that they are copies, images, or representations of certain originals that do.

Hyl.   You take me right.

Phil.   They are then like external things.

Hyl.   They are.

Phil.   Have those things a stable and permanent nature independent of our senses; or are they in a perpetual change, upon our producing any motions in our bodies, suspending, exerting, or altering our faculties or organs of sense.

Hyl.   Real things, it is plain, have a fixed and real nature, which remains the same, not withstanding any change in our senses, or in the posture and motion of our bodies; which indeed may affect the ideas in our minds, but it were absurd to think they had the same effect on things existing without the mind.

Phil.   How then is it possible, that things perpetually fleeting and variable as our ideas, should be copies or images of anything fixed and constant? Or in other words, since all sensible qualities, as size, figure, color, &c., that is, our ideas, are continually changing upon every alteration in the distance, medium, or instruments of sensation; how can any determinate material objects be properly represented or painted forth by several distinct things, each of which is so different from and unlike the rest? Or if you say it resembles some one only of our ideas, how shall we be able to distinguish the true copy from all the false ones?

Hyl.   I profess, Philonous, I am at a loss. I know not what to say to this.

Phil.   But neither is this all. Which are material objects in themselves, perceptible or imperceptible?

Hyl.   Properly and immediately nothing can be perceived but ideas. All material things therefore are in themselves insensible, and to be perceived only by their ideas.

Phil.   Ideas then are sensible, and their archetypes or originals insensible.

Hyl.   Right.

Phil.   But how can that which is sensible be like that which is insensible? Can a real thing in itself *invisible* be like a *color;* or a real thing which is not *audible,* be like a *sound?* In a word, can anything be like a sensation or idea, but another sensation or idea?

Hyl.   I must own, I think not.

Phil.   Is it possible there should be any doubt in the point? Do you not perfectly know your own ideas?

Hyl.   I know them perfectly; since what I do not perceive or know, can be no part of my idea.

Phil.   Consider therefore, and examine them, and then tell me if there be anything in them which can exist without the mind: or if you can conceive anything like them existing without the mind.

Hyl.   Upon inquiry, I find it is impossible for me to conceive or understand how anything but an idea can be like an idea. And it is most evident, that *no idea can exist without the mind.* [33]

Phil.   You are therefore by your principles forced to deny the reality of sensible things, since

[33] Philonous now challenges the claim that ideas *resemble* external objects. One problem is the fluctuating character of experience as contrasted with the stable character of objects. But a deeper problem is that it is hard to see how an insensible, unperceiving thing can literally *resemble* a bit of experience like an idea or sensation. Hylas concedes that he can make no sense of this.

you made it to consist in an absolute existence exterior to the mind. That is to say, you are a downright *sceptic.* So I have gained my point, which was to show your principles led to scepticism.

Hyl. For the present I am, if not entirely convinced, at least silenced.

Phil. I would fain know what more you would require in order to a perfect conviction. Have you not had the liberty of explaining yourself all manner of ways? Were any little slips in discourse laid hold and insisted on? Or were you not allowed to retract or reinforce anything you had offered, as best served your purpose? Has not everything you could say been heard and examined with all the fairness imaginable? In a word, have you not in every point been convinced out of your own mouth? And if you can at present discover any flaw in any of your former concessions, or think of any remaining subterfuge, any new distinction, color, or comment whatsoever, why do you not produce it?

Hyl. A little patience, Philonous. I am at present so amazed to see myself ensnared, and as it were imprisoned in the labyrinths you have drawn me into, that on the sudden it cannot be expected I should find my way out. You must give me time to look about me, and recollect myself.

Phil. Hark; is not this the college bell?

Hyl. It rings for prayers.

Phil. We will go in then if you please, and meet here again tomorrow morning. In the meantime you may employ your thoughts on this morning's discourse, and try if you can find any fallacy in it, or invent any new means to extricate yourself.

Hyl. Agreed.

THE SECOND DIALOGUE

[XI]

Hyl. I beg your pardon, Philonous, for not meeting you sooner. All this morning my head was so filled with our late conversation, that I had not leisure to think of the time of the day, or indeed of anything else.

Phil. I am glad you were so intent upon it, in hopes if there were any mistakes in your concessions, or

fallacies in my reasonings from them, you will now discover them to me.

Hyl. I assure you, I have done nothing ever since I saw you, but search after mistakes and fallacies, and with that view have minutely examined the whole series of yesterday's discourse: but all in vain, for the notions it led me into, upon review, appear still more clear and evident; and the more I consider them, the more irresistibly do they force my assent.

Phil. And is not this, think you, a sign that they are genuine, that they proceed from nature, and are conformable to right reason? Truth and beauty are in this alike, that the strictest survey sets them both off to advantage. While the false lustre of error and disguise cannot endure being reviewed, or too nearly inspected.

Hyl. I own there is a great deal in what you say. Nor can any one be more entirely satisfied of the truth of those odd consequences, so long as I have in view the reasonings that lead to them. . . .

Phil. Well then, are you at length satisfied that no sensible things have a real existence; and that you are in truth an arrant *sceptic?*

Hyl. It is too plain to be denied.

Phil. Look! Are not the fields covered with a delightful verdure? Is there not something in the woods and groves, in the rivers and clear springs, that soothes, that delights, that transports the soul? At the prospect of the wide and deep ocean, or some huge mountain whose top is lost in the clouds, or of an old gloomy forest, are not our minds filled with a pleasing horror? Even in rocks and deserts, is there not an agreeable wildness? How sincere a pleasure is it to behold the natural beauties of the earth! . . . How exquisitely are all things suited, as well to their particular ends, as to constitute apposite parts of the whole! . . . The motion and situation of the planets, are they not admirable for use and order? Were those . . . globes ever known to stray, in their repeated journeys through the pathless void? Do they not measure areas round the sun ever proportioned to the times? So fixed, so immutable are the laws by which the unseen author of nature actuates the universe. How vivid and radiant is the luster of the fixed stars! . . . But neither sense nor imagination are big enough to comprehend the boundless extent with all its glittering furniture. . . . Yet all the vast bodies that compose this mighty frame, how distant and remote soever, are by some secret mechanism, some divine art and force, linked in a mutual dependence and intercourse with each other. . . . Is not the whole system immense, beautiful, glorious beyond expression and beyond thought! What treatment then do those philosophers deserve, who would deprive these noble and delightful scenes of all reality? How should those principles be entertained, that lead us to think all the visible beauty of the creation a false imaginary glare? To be plain, can you expect this scepticism of yours will not be thought extravagantly absurd by all men of sense? 34

34 Having driven Hylas into what Hylas regards as skepticism about the world of ordinary objects, Philonous launches into another oration on the glories of nature, again suggesting that he is not denying the existence of such things.

Hyl. Other men may think as they please: but for your part you have nothing to reproach me with. My comfort is, you are as much a *sceptic* as I am.

Phil. There, Hylas, I must beg leave to differ from you.

Hyl. What! Have you all along agreed to the premises, and do you now deny the conclusion, and leave me to maintain those paradoxes by myself which you led me into? This surely is not fair.

Phil. I deny that I agreed with you in those notions that led to scepticism. You indeed said, the reality of sensible things consisted in an *absolute existence* out of the minds of spirits, or distinct from their being perceived. And pursuant to this notion of reality, you are obliged to deny sensible things any real existence: that is, according to your own definition, you profess yourself a *sceptic.* But I neither said nor thought the reality of sensible things was to be defined after that manner. To me it is evident, for the reasons you allow of, that sensible things cannot exist otherwise than in a mind or spirit. Whence I conclude, not that they have no real existence, but that seeing they depend not on my thought, and have an existence distinct from being perceived by me, *there must be some other mind wherein they*

exist. As sure therefore as the sensible world really exists, so sure is there any infinite omnipresent spirit who contains and supports it. 35

35 Philonous denies that he is a skeptic. Instead, he views himself as merely offering a different and more correct account of what the reality of objects like those in nature (whose existence he does not deny) amounts to: such things exist only as ideas in the mind, and if they have an existence that is independent of *his* mind (and those of others like him), this must be because there is some other mind (God's mind) in which they exist.

Hyl. What! This is no more than I and all Christians hold; nay, and all others too who believe there is a God, and that he knows and comprehends all things.

Phil. Aye, but here lies the difference. Men commonly believe that all things are known or perceived by God, because they believe the being of a God, whereas I, on the other side, immediately and necessarily conclude the being of a God, because all sensible things must be perceived by him.

. . .

. . . Sensible things do really exist: and if they really exist, they are necessarily perceived by an infinite mind: therefore there is an infinite mind, or God. This furnishes you with a direct and immediate demonstration, from a most evident principle, of the *being of a God.* 36 Divines and philosophers had proved beyond all controversy, from the beauty and usefulness of the several parts of the creations that it was the workmanship

36 Here is an outline of one of Berkeley's arguments for the existence of God, the details of which are elaborated in the following passages.

of God. But that setting aside all help of astronomy and natural philosophy, all contemplation of the contrivance, order, and adjustment of things, an infinite mind should be necessarily inferred from the bare existence of the sensible world, is an advantage peculiar to them only who have made this easy reflection: that the sensible world is that which we perceive by our several senses; and that nothing is perceived by the senses beside ideas; and that no idea or archetype of an idea can exist otherwise than in a mind. You may now, without any laborious search into the sciences, without any subtlety of reason, or tedious length of discourse, oppose and baffle the most strenuous advocate for atheism. . . .

Take here in brief my meaning. It is evident that the things I perceive are my own ideas, and that no idea can exist unless it be in a mind. Nor is it less plain that these ideas or things by me perceived, either themselves or their archetypes, exist independently of my mind, since I know myself not to be their author, it being out of my power to determine at pleasure, what particular ideas I shall be affected with upon opening my eyes or ears. [37] They must therefore exist in some other mind, whose will it is they should be exhibited to me. The things, I say, immediately perceived, are ideas or sensations, call them which you will. But how can any idea or sensation exist in, or be produced by, anything but a mind or spirit? This indeed is inconceivable; and to assert that which is inconceivable, is to talk nonsense: is it not?

> [37] Here is a reason for thinking that sensible things exist independently of Philonous's mind (or of any human mind): the ideas that make them up are not within his (or any other human's) voluntary control. How compelling a reason is this? (Compare this with the second of Locke's "four concurrent reasons" in chapter XI of Book IV of the *Essay*.)

Hyl. Without doubt.

Phil. But on the other hand, it is very conceivable that they should exist in, and be produced by, a spirit; since this is no more than I daily experience in myself, inasmuch as I perceive numberless ideas; and by an act of my will can form a great variety of them, and raise them up in my imagination: [38] though it must be confessed, these creatures of the fancy are not altogether so distinct, so strong, vivid, and permanent, as those perceived by my senses, which latter are called *real things*. From all which I conclude, *there is a mind which affects me every moment with all the sensible impressions I perceive*. And from the variety, order, and manner of these, I conclude the author of them to be *wise, powerful, and good, beyond comprehension*. [39] . . . the things by me perceived are known by the understanding, and produced by the will, of an infinite spirit. And is not all this most plain and evident? Is there any more in it, than what a little observation of our own minds, and that which passes in them not only enables us to conceive, but also obliges us to acknowledge?

> [38] Berkeley's view is that the ideas corresponding to real objects (as opposed, for example, to merely imaginary ones) are produced in us by God. He suggests that this can be understood by analogy with our own weaker power to deliberately imagine or think of various things. Is this a good comparison?

> [39] This is an appeal to something like the argument from design (see Chapter 2). It also resembles the fourth of Locke's "four concurrent reasons," though perhaps not as clearly as the earlier point resembled the second of Locke's reasons.

[XII]

Hyl. I think I understand you very clearly; and own the proof you give of a deity seems no less evident, than it is surprising. But allowing that God is the supreme and universal cause of all things, yet may not there be still a third nature besides spirits and ideas? May we not admit a subordinate and limited cause of our ideas? In a word, may there not for all that be *matter*?

Phil. How often must I inculcate the same thing? You allow the things immediately perceived by sense to exist nowhere without the mind: but there is nothing perceived by sense, which is not perceived immediately: therefore there is nothing sensible that exists without the mind. The matter therefore which you still insist on, is something intelligible, I suppose; something that may be discovered by reason, and not by sense.

Hyl. You are in the right.

Phil. Pray let me know what reasoning your belief of matter is grounded on; and what this matter is in your present sense of it.

Hyl. I find myself affected with various ideas, whereof I know I am not the cause; neither are they the cause of themselves, or of one another, or capable of subsisting by themselves, as being altogether inactive, fleeting, dependent beings. They have therefore some cause distinct from me and them: of which I pretend to know no more, than that it is *the cause of my ideas.* And this thing, whatever it be, I call matter.

. . .

Phil. . . . does not *matter,* in the common current acceptation of the word, signify an extended, solid, moveable, unthinking, inactive substance?

Hyl. It does.

Phil. And, has it not been made evident, that no such substance can possibly exist? And though it should be allowed to exist, yet how can that which is *inactive* be a *cause;* or that which is *unthinking* be a *cause of thought?* ⁴⁰ You may indeed, if you please, annex to the word *matter* a contrary meaning to what is vulgarly received; and tell me you understand by it an unextended, thinking, active being, which is the cause of our ideas. But what else is this, than to play with words, and run into that very fault you just now condemned with so much reason? I do by no means find fault with your reasoning, in that you collect a cause from the *phenomena:* but I deny that the cause deducible by reason can properly be termed matter.

Hyl. There is indeed something in what you say. But I am afraid you do not thoroughly comprehend my meaning. I would by no means be thought to deny that God or an infinite spirit is the supreme cause of all things. All I contend for, is, that subordinate to the supreme agent there is a cause of a limited and inferior nature, which concurs in the production of our ideas, not by any act of will or spiritual efficiency, but by that kind of action which belongs to matter, *viz. motion.*

Phil. I find, you are at every turn relapsing into your old exploded conceit, of a moveable and consequently an extended substance existing without

⌐40⌐ Hylas attempts again to justify a belief in matter (material substance or a material substratum) as at least part of the cause of our ideas. Philonous raises two objections: one based on the idea that only an active agent can be a genuine cause; and the second based on the idea that thought cannot be caused by an unthinking thing. Neither of these views now seems very plausible, though the first even less than the second.

the mind. What! Have you already forgot you were convinced, or are you willing I should repeat what has been said on that head? In truth this is not fair dealing in you, still to suppose the being of that which you have so often acknowledged to have no being. . . .

And yet you are loath to part with your old prejudice. But to make you quit it more easily, I desire that, beside what has been hitherto suggested, you will farther consider whether, upon supposition that matter exists, you can possibly conceive how you should be affected by it? Or supposing it did not exist, whether it be not evident you might for all that be affected with the same ideas you now are, and consequently have the very same reasons to believe its existence that you now can have.

Hyl. I acknowledge it is possible we might perceive all things just as we do now, though there was no matter in the world; neither can I conceive, if there be matter, how it should produce any idea in our minds. ⁴¹ . . .

Phil. Pray where do you suppose this unknown matter to exist?

⌐41⌐ But the main objection is that Hylas can give no account of *how* matter would cause ideas (a reference to worries about how minds and bodies can causally interact—see the discussion in Chapter 4); and hence has to admit that he could just as well have the same ideas if there were no matter, in which case there is no reason to believe in it.

Hyl. Oh Philonous! now you think you have entangled me; for if I say it exists in place, then you will infer that it exists in the mind, since it is agreed that place or extension exists only in the mind: but I am not ashamed to own my ignorance. I know not where it exists; only I am sure it exists not in place. There is a negative answer for you: and you must expect no other to all the questions you put for the future about matter.

Phil. Since you will not tell me where it exists, be pleased to inform me after what manner you suppose it to exist, or what you mean by its *existence.*

Hyl. It neither thinks nor acts, neither perceives, nor is perceived.

Phil. But what is there positive in your abstracted notion of its existence?

Hyl. Upon a nice observation, I do not find I have any positive notion or meaning at all. I tell you again I am not ashamed to own my ignorance. I know not what is meant by its *existence,* or how it exists. ㊷

> ㊷ Hylas is forced to concede that he has no positive idea at all of matter or what it would be for it to exist.

. . .

But I am not so thoroughly satisfied that you have proved the impossibility of matter in the last most obscure abstracted and indefinite sense.

Phil. When is a thing shown to be impossible?

Hyl. When a repugnancy is demonstrated between the ideas comprehended in its definition.

Phil. But where there are no ideas, there no repugnancy can be demonstrated between ideas.

Hyl. I agree with you.

Phil. Now in that which you call the obscure indefinite sense of the word *matter,* it is plain, by your own confession, there was included no idea at all, no sense except an unknown sense, which is the same thing as none. You are not therefore to expect I should prove a repugnancy between ideas where there are no ideas; or the impossibility of Matter taken in an *unknown* sense, that is no sense at all. My business was only to show, you meant *nothing;* and this you were brought to own. So that in all your various senses, you have been showed either to mean nothing at all, or if anything, an absurdity. And if this be not sufficient to prove the impossibility of a thing, I desire you will let me know what is.

Hyl. I acknowledge you have proved that matter is impossible; nor do I see what more can be said in defense of it. But at the same time that I give up this, I suspect all my other notions. For surely none could be more seemingly evident than this once was: and yet it now seems as false and absurd as ever it did true before. But I think we have discussed the point sufficiently for the present. The remaining part of the day I would willingly spend, in running over in my thoughts the several heads of this morning's conversation, and tomorrow shall be glad to meet you here again about the same time.

Phil. I will not fail to attend you.

THE THIRD DIALOGUE

[XIII]

Philonous: Tell me, Hylas, what are the fruits of yesterday's meditation? Has it confirmed you in the same mind you were in at parting? Or have you since seen cause to change your opinion?

Hylas: Truly my opinion is, that all our opinions are alike vain and uncertain. What we approve to-day, we condemn tomorrow. We keep a stir about knowledge, and spend our lives in the pursuit of it, when, alas! we know nothing all the while: nor do I think it possible for us ever to know anything in this life. Our faculties are too narrow and too few. Nature certainly never intended us for speculation.

Phil. What! Say you we can know nothing, Hylas?

Hyl. There is not that single thing in the world, whereof we can know the real nature, or what it is in itself.

Phil. Will you tell me I do not really know what fire or water is?

Hyl. You may indeed know that fire appears hot, and water fluid: but this is no more than knowing what sensations are produced in your own mind, upon the application of fire and water to your organs of sense. Their internal constitution, their true and real nature, you are utterly in the dark as to *that.*

Phil. Do I not know this to be a real stone that I stand on, and that which I see before my eyes to be a real tree?

Hyl. *Know?* No, it is impossible you or any man alive should know it. All you know, is, that you have such a certain idea or appearance in your own mind. But what is this to the real tree or stone? I tell you, that color, figure, and hardness, which you perceive, are not the real natures of those things, or in the least like them. The same may be said of all other real things or corporeal substances which compose the world. They have none of them anything in themselves, like those sensible qualities by us perceived. We should not therefore pretend to affirm or know anything of them, as they are in their own nature.

Phil. But surely, Hylas, I can distinguish gold, for example, from iron: and how could this be, if I knew not what either truly was?

Hyl. Believe me, Philonous, you can only distinguish between your own ideas. That yellowness, that weight, and other sensible qualities, think you they are really in the gold? They are only relative to the senses, and have no absolute existence in nature. And in pretending to distinguish the species of real things, by the appearances in your mind, you may perhaps act as wisely as he that should conclude two men were of a different species, because their clothes were not of the same color.

Phil. It seems then we are altogether put off with the appearances of things, and those false ones too. The very meat I eat, and the cloth I wear, have nothing in them like what I see and feel.

Hyl. Even so.

Phil. But is it not strange the whole world should be thus imposed on, and so foolish as to believe their senses? And yet I know not how it is, but men eat, and drink, and sleep, and perform all the offices of life, as comfortably and conveniently, as if they really knew the things they are conversant about.

Hyl. They do so: but you know ordinary practice does not require a nicety of speculative knowledge. Hence the vulgar retain their mistakes, and for all that, make a shift to bustle through the affairs of life. But philosophers know better things.

Phil. You mean, they know that they *know nothing*.

Hyl. That is the very top and perfection of human knowledge.

Phil. But are you all this while in earnest, Hylas; and are you seriously persuaded that you know nothing real in the world? Suppose you are going to write, would you not call for pen, ink, and paper, like another man; and do you not know what it is you call for?

Hyl. How often must I tell you, that I know not the real nature of any one thing in the universe? I may indeed upon occasion make use of pen, ink, and paper. But what any one of them is in its own true nature, I declare positively I know not. And the same is true with regard to every other corporeal thing. And, what is more, we are not only ignorant of the true and real nature of things, but even of their existence. It cannot be denied that we perceive such certain appearances or ideas; but it cannot be concluded from thence that bodies really exist. Nay, now I think on it, I must

agreeably to my former concessions farther declare, that it is impossible any real corporeal thing should exist in nature.

Phil. You amaze me. Was ever anything more wild and extravagant than the notions you now maintain: and is it not evident you are led into all these extravagancies by the belief of *material substance?* 43 This makes you dream of those unknown natures in everything. It is this occasions your

> 43 Hylas again lapses into skepticism, claiming that he knows nothing about the true nature of anything. Philonous suggests that this results from clinging irrationally to the idea of material substance.

distinguishing between the reality and sensible appearances of things. It is to this you are indebted for being ignorant of what everybody else knows perfectly well. Nor is this all: you are not only ignorant of the true nature of everything, but you know not whether anything really exists, or whether there are any true natures at all; forasmuch as you attribute to your material beings an absolute or external existence, wherein you suppose their reality consists. And as you are forced in the end to acknowledge such an existence means either a direct repugnancy, or nothing at all, it follows that you are obliged to pull down your own hypothesis of material substance, and positively to deny the real existence of any part of the universe. And so you are plunged into the deepest and most deplorable *scepticism* that ever man was. Tell me, Hylas, is it not as I say?

[XIV]

Hyl. I agree with you. *Material substance* was no more than an hypothesis, and a false and groundless one too. I will no longer spend my breath in defence of it. But whatever hypothesis you advance, or whatsoever scheme of things you introduce in its stead, I doubt not it will appear every whit as false: let me but be allowed to question you upon it. That is, suffer me to serve you in your own kind, and I warrant it shall conduct you through as many perplexities and contradictions, to the very same state of scepticism that I myself am in at present.

Phil. I assure you, Hylas, I do not pretend to frame any hypothesis at all. I am of a vulgar cast, simple enough to believe my senses, and leave things as I find them. To be plain, it is my opinion, that the real things are those very things I see and feel, and perceive by my senses. These I know, and finding they answer all the necessities and purposes of life, have no reason to be solicitous about any other unknown beings. A piece of sensible bread, for instance, would stay my stomach better than ten thousand times as much of that insensible, unintelligible, real bread you speak of. It is likewise my opinion, that colors and other sensible qualities are on the objects. I cannot for my life help thinking that snow is white, and fire hot. You indeed, who by *snow* and *fire* mean certain external, unperceived, unperceiving substances, are in the right to deny whiteness or heat to be affections inherent in them. But I, who understand by those words the things I see and feel, am obliged to think like other folks. And as I am no sceptic with regard to the nature of things, so neither am I as to their existence. That a thing should be really perceived by my senses, and at the same time not really exist, is to me a plain contradiction; since I cannot prescind or abstract, even in thought, the existence of a sensible thing from its being perceived. Wood, stones, fire, water, flesh, iron, and the like things, which I name and discourse of, are things that I know; . . . And I should not have known them, but that I perceived them by my senses; and things perceived by the senses are immediately perceived; and things immediately perceived are ideas; and ideas cannot exist without the mind; their existence therefore consists in being perceived; when therefore they are actually perceived, there can be no doubt of their existence. Away then with all that scepticism, all those ridiculous philosophical doubts. 44 What a jest is it for a philosopher to question the existence of sensible things, till he has it proved to him from the veracity of God: or to pretend our knowledge in this point falls short of intuition or demonstration? I might as well doubt of my own being, as of the being of those things I actually see and feel.

44 Philonous's contrary view is that for a thing to exist is just for the relevant ideas to exist, and that to know those ideas is to know all there is to know about the nature of such a thing. (The immediately following passage is aimed at Descartes and Locke.)

Hyl. Not so fast, Philonous: you say you cannot conceive how sensible things should exist without the mind. Do you not?

Phil. I do.

Hyl. Supposing you were annihilated, cannot you conceive it possible, that things perceivable by sense may still exist?

Phil. I can; but then it must be in another mind. When I deny sensible things an existence out of the mind, I do not mean my mind in particular, but all minds. Now it is plain they have an existence exterior to my mind, since I find them by experience to be independent of it. There is therefore some other mind wherein they exist, during the intervals between the times of my perceiving them: as likewise they did before my birth, and would do after my supposed annihilation. And as the same is true, with regard to all other finite created spirits; it necessarily follows, there is an *omnipresent eternal mind,* which knows and comprehends all things, and exhibits them to our view in such a manner, and according to such rules as he himself has ordained, and are by us termed the *laws of nature.*

[XV]

Hyl. Answer me, Philonous. Are all our ideas perfectly inert beings? Or have they any agency included in them?

Phil. They are altogether passive and inert.

Hyl. And is not God an agent, a being purely active?

Phil. I acknowledge it.

Hyl. No idea therefore can be like unto, or represent the nature of God.

Phil. It cannot.

Hyl. Since therefore you have no idea of the mind of God, how can you conceive it possible, that things should exist in his mind? Or, if you can conceive the mind of God without having an idea of it, why may not I be allowed to conceive the existence of matter, notwithstanding that I have no idea of it? 45

Phil. As to your first question; I own I have properly no idea, either of God or any other spirit; for these being active, cannot be represented by things perfectly inert, as our ideas are. I do nevertheless know, that I, who am a spirit or thinking substance, exist as certainly, as I know my ideas exist. Farther, I know what I mean by the terms *I* and *myself;* and I know this immediately, or intuitively, though I do not perceive it as I perceive a triangle, a color, or a sound. The mind, spirit, or soul, is that indivisible unextended thing, which thinks, acts, and perceives. I say *indivisible,* because unextended; and *unextended,* because extended, figured, moveable things, are ideas; and that which perceives ideas, which thinks and wills, is plainly itself no idea, nor like an idea. Ideas are things inactive, and perceived: and spirits a sort of beings altogether different from them. I do not therefore say my soul is an idea, or like an idea. However, taking the word *idea* in a large sense, my soul may be said to furnish me with an idea, that is, an image, or likeness of God, though indeed extremely inadequate. For all the notion I have of God, is obtained by reflecting on my own soul, heightening its powers, and removing its imperfections. I have therefore, though not an inactive idea, yet in myself some sort of an active thinking image of the Deity. And though I perceive him not by sense, yet I have a notion of him, or know him by reflection and reasoning. [46] My own mind and my own ideas I have an immediate knowledge of; and by the help of these, do mediately apprehend the possibility of the existence of other spirits and ideas. Farther, from my own being, and from the dependency I find in myself and my ideas, I do, by an act of reason, necessarily infer the existence of a God, and of all created things in the mind of God. So much for your first question. For the second: I suppose by this time you can answer it yourself. For you neither perceive matter objectively, as you do an inactive being or idea, nor know it, as you do yourself, by a reflex act: neither do you mediately apprehend it by similitude of the one or the other: nor yet collect it by reasoning from that which you know immediately. All which makes the case of *matter* widely different from that of the *Deity.*

. . .

Hyl. Notwithstanding all you have said, to me it seems, that according to your own way of thinking, and in consequence of your own principles, it should follow that you are only a system of floating ideas, without any substance to support them. Words are not to be used without a meaning. And as there is no more meaning in spiritual substance than in material substance, the one is to be exploded as well as the other. [47]

Phil. How often must I repeat, that I know or am conscious of my own being; and that I myself am not my ideas, but somewhat else, a thinking active principle that perceives, knows, wills, and operates about ideas. I know that I, one and the same self, perceive both colors and sounds: that a color cannot perceive a sound, nor a sound a color: that I am therefore one individual principle, distinct from color and sound; and, for the same reason, from all other sensible things and inert ideas. But I am not in like manner conscious either of the existence or essence of matter. On the contrary, I know that nothing inconsistent can exist, and that the existence of matter implies an

---

[45] Hylas goes on the attack, questioning how Philonous can have knowledge of God or even think about God. The point is made by pointing to the inertness (inactivity) of ideas, but it could also be put in terms of resemblance: just as an idea cannot *resemble* an external material thing, so also it cannot seemingly resemble an active spirit.

---

[46] Philonous responds by claiming that while he has no *idea* of God, he does have some sort of "image or likeness" or notion of God, via an analogy with his own self. Does this really help, or isn't there just as much of a problem for knowledge of his self? If representation works by resemblance, and an idea cannot resemble anything but other ideas, how can we think about or know anything but ideas?

---

[47] In fact, Locke does not speak of material substance or of spiritual substance, but only of substance in general: that which underlies or supports qualities. Hylas's point is really that the criticisms made earlier of material substance apply to any sort of substance, including the spiritual substances (our minds and God's mind) to which Philonous himself appeals. Philonous's response is weak.

inconsistency. Farther, I know what I mean, when I affirm that there is a spiritual substance or support of ideas, that is, that a spirit knows and perceives ideas. But I do not know what is meant, when it is said, that an unperceiving substance hath inherent in it and supports either ideas or the archetypes of ideas. There is therefore upon the whole no parity of case between spirit and matter.

. . .

[XVI]

Hyl. But according to your notions, what difference is there between real things, and chimeras formed by the imagination, or the visions of a dream, since they are all equally in the mind?

Phil. The ideas formed by the imagination are faint and indistinct; they have, besides, an entire dependence on the will. But the ideas perceived by sense, that is, real things, are more vivid and clear, and being imprinted on the mind by a spirit distinct from us, have not a like dependence on our will. There is therefore no danger of confounding these with the foregoing: and there is as little of confounding them with the visions of a dream, which are dim, irregular, and confused. And though they should happen to be never so lively and natural, yet by their not being connected, and of a piece with the preceding and subsequent transactions of our lives, they might easily be distinguished from realities. In short, by whatever method you distinguish *things* from *chimeras* on your own scheme, the same, it is evident, will hold also upon mine. For it must be, I presume, by some perceived difference, and I am not for depriving you of any one thing that you perceive. **48**

---

48 If the reality of things consists only of ideas in minds, how can we tell the difference between *real things* (those that exist in God's mind and are caused by God to exist in our minds) and various sorts of illusion? Philonous's response is that any criterion for this distinction that appeals to experience, that is to ideas of perception, will be equally available to him.

Hyl. What say you to this? Since, according to you, men judge of the reality of things by their senses, how can a man be mistaken in thinking the moon a plain lucid surface, about a foot in diameter; or a square tower, seen at a distance, round; or an oar, with one end in the water, crooked?

Phil. He is not mistaken with regard to the ideas he actually perceives; but in the inferences he makes from his present perceptions. Thus in the case of the oar, what he immediately perceives by sight is certainly crooked; and so far he is in the right. But if he thence conclude, that upon taking the oar out of the water he shall perceive the same crookedness; or that it would affect his touch, as crooked things are wont to do: in that he is mistaken. In like manner, if he shall conclude from what he perceives in one station, that in case he advances toward the moon or tower, he should still be affected with the like ideas, he is mistaken. But his mistake lies not in what he perceives immediately and at present, (it being a manifest contradiction to suppose he should err in respect of that) but in the wrong judgment he makes concerning the ideas he apprehends to be connected with those immediately perceived: or concerning the ideas that, from what he perceives at present, he imagines would be perceived in other circumstances. The case is the same with regard to the Copernican system. We do not here perceive any motion of the earth: but it were erroneous thence to conclude, that, in case we were placed at as great a distance from that, as we are now from the other planets, we should not then perceive its motion. **49**

---

49 Here is Berkeley's account of perceptual error: the ideas in question are not mistaken in themselves; rather the mistake lies in the inferences we draw from them as to other ideas that are or could be perceived.

. . .

Hyl. . . . Pray are not the objects perceived by the senses of one, likewise perceivable to others present? If there were an hundred more here, they would all see the garden, the trees, and flowers as I see them. But they are not in the same manner affected with the ideas I frame in my imagination. Does not this make a difference between the former sort of objects and the latter?

Phil. I grant it does. Nor have I ever denied a difference between the objects of sense and those of imagination. But what would you infer from thence? You cannot say that sensible objects exist unperceived, because they are perceived by many.

Hyl. I own I can make nothing of that objection: but it hath led me into another. Is it not your opinion that by our senses we perceive only the ideas existing in our minds?

Phil. It is.

Hyl. But the same idea which is in my mind, cannot be in yours, or in any other mind. Doth it not therefore follow from your principles, that no two can see the same thing? And is not this highly absurd?

Phil. If the term *same* be taken in the vulgar acceptation, it is certain, (and not at all repugnant to the principles I maintain) that different persons may perceive the same thing; or the same thing or idea exist in different minds. . . . Let us suppose several men together, all endued with the same faculties, and consequently affected in like sort by their senses, and who had yet never known the use of language; they would without question agree in their perceptions. Though perhaps, when they came to the use of speech, some regarding the uniformness of what was perceived, might call it the *same* thing: others especially regarding the diversity of persons who perceived, might choose the denomination of different things. But who sees not that all the dispute is about a word? to wit, whether what is perceived by different persons, may yet have the term *same* applied to it? . . . Take this farther reflexion with you: that whether matter be allowed to exist or no, the case is exactly the same as to the point in hand. For the materialists themselves acknowledge what we immediately perceive by our senses, to be our own ideas. Your difficulty therefore, that no two see the same thing, makes equally against the materialists and me. 50

Hyl. But they suppose an external archetype, to which referring their several ideas, they may truly be said to perceive the same thing.

Phil. And (not to mention your having discarded those archetypes) so may you suppose an external archetype on my principles; *external,* I mean, to your own mind; though indeed it must be supposed to exist in that mind which comprehends all things; but then this serves all the ends of identity, as well as if it existed out of a mind. And I am sure you yourself will not say, it is less intelligible. 51

. . .

50 Can two people perceive the same thing according to Berkeley's view? They cannot immediately perceive the same ideas, but this is true on Locke's view as well.

51 And just as Locke takes the ideas of different people to reflect one object that they are all perceiving, so Berkeley can take the ideas of different people to reflect one idea in the mind of God that they can all be said to be perceiving. (Does this suggest that the reality of a thing is ultimately to be located in God's idea of it and not in ours?)

Hyl. I have been a long time distrusting my senses; methought I saw things by a dim light, and through false glasses. Now the glasses are removed, and a new light breaks in upon my understanding. I am clearly convinced that I see things in their native forms; and am no longer in pain about their unknown natures or absolute existence. This is the state I find myself in at present: though indeed the course that brought me to it, I do not yet thoroughly comprehend. You set out upon the same principles that Academics, Cartesians, and the like sects, usually do; and for a long time it looked as if you were advancing their philosophical *scepticism;* but in the end your conclusions are directly opposite to theirs.

Phil. You see, Hylas, the water of yonder fountain, how it is forced upwards, in a round column, to a certain height; at which it breaks and falls back into the basin from whence it rose: its ascent as well as descent, proceeding from the same uniform law or principle of *gravitation*. Just so, the same principles which at first view lead to *scepticism,* pursued to a certain point, bring men back to common sense.

Discussion Questions

1. Some of Berkeley's arguments rely on the claim that certain of our sensory ideas are indistinguishable from ideas of pleasure or pain. Is he right about this claim?

2. Spell out the argument from illusion for the case of the two buckets of water and then for the case of colors seen with the naked eye and through a microscope. (Assuming that you cannot look at something simultaneously in both ways, the second argument will have to be more complicated, involving the claim that the object does not change when you shift from one view to the other). In each case, start with an argument for the conclusion that at least one of the perceived qualities is not in the object, and then argue for the claim that none of them is. (See Annotation 19 for a suggestion about this.) How compelling are these arguments? Can you think of an answer to them?

3. Locke invoked the idea of substance because it seemed to him impossible that qualities could simply exist on their own, even in groups, without being qualities of anything. Consider Berkeley's criticisms of this view, centering around the claim that we have no intelligible idea of such an underlying thing. Do these objections also apply to Berkeley's idea of a mind that perceives ideas? Why or why not? If material objects do after all exist outside the mind, must there also be material substance?

4. It is a fairly common experience for a given speed, for example while riding in a car, to seem faster or slower depending on how fast one was traveling just before: 30 mph seems slow after going 60, but fast after sitting still. Can you construct on this basis an argument that is parallel to the other versions of the argument from illusion that Berkeley formulates and that leads to the conclusion that *apparent speed* (speed as directly perceived or experienced) exists only in the mind?

5. Both Locke and Berkeley tend to think of ideas as mental images and of representation of things by ideas as depending on *resemblance* between the two. Are all ideas images? (See Discussion Question 1 for the Locke selection.) Do we have images of our own minds or selves? If a person does have a mental image, is it automatically a representation of any object that the image resembles (assuming that such resemblance makes sense)?

6. Locke and Berkeley both appeal to roughly the same features of our perceptual ideas: their involuntary character and their systematic regularity and order. Locke can be viewed as arguing that these features are best explained by supposing that ideas are systematically caused by a world of external objects; while Berkeley argues that they are best explained by supposing that the ideas are caused in us by an infinite mind or spirit. Whose explanation do you think is better? How would you argue for one as against the other?

Thomas Reid

The Scottish philosopher Thomas Reid (1710–1796) was one of the founders of what became known as the "common sense" school of philosophy. He is best known for his contributions to epistemology, which are mainly focused on defending the common-sense view of our knowledge of the material world against what he sees as the skeptical tendencies to be found in his British predecessors, Locke, Berkeley, and Hume, as well as in Descartes and others.

In the following selection, Reid attacks the Lockean view that we perceive external material objects by perceiving in a more immediate way ideas that represent them. His alternative is an early version of **direct realism,** according to which material objects are themselves the most direct objects of our perceptions. As Reid recognizes, the view that perception is in this way direct does not in itself answer the question of what reason or ground we have for thinking that our direct perceptual judgments are true. Thus he also argues that the claim that the "evidence of the senses" is good evidence for the claims we accept on that basis has the status of an axiom or "first principle": something that is immediately known without any need for further justification.

Direct Realism, from
Essays on the Intellectual Powers of Man

OF PERCEPTION

In speaking of the impressions made on our organs in perception, we build upon facts borrowed from anatomy and physiology, for which we have the testimony of our senses. But being now to speak of perception itself, which is solely an act of the mind, we must appeal to another authority. The operations of our minds are known not by sense, but by consciousness, the authority of which is as certain and as irresistible as that of sense.

In order, however, to our having a distinct notion of any of the operations of our own minds, it is not enough that we be conscious of them, for all men have this consciousness: it is further necessary that we attend to them while they are exerted, and reflect upon them with care, while they are recent and fresh in our memory. It is necessary that, by employing ourselves frequently in this way, we get the habit of this attention and reflection; and therefore, for the proof of facts which I shall have occasion to mention upon this subject, I can only appeal to the reader's own thoughts, whether such facts are not agreeable to what he is conscious of in his own mind.

If, therefore, we attend to that act of our mind which we call the perception of an external object of sense, we shall find in it these three things. *First,* Some conception or notion of the object perceived. *Secondly,* A strong and irresistible conviction and belief of its present existence. And, *thirdly,* That this conviction and belief are immediate, and not the effect of reasoning.[1]

1st, It is impossible to perceive an object without having some notion or conception of that which we perceive. We may indeed conceive an object which we do not perceive; but when we perceive the object, we must have some conception of it at the same time; and we have commonly a more clear and steady notion of the object while we perceive it, than we have from memory or imagination when it is not perceived. Yet, even in perception, the notion which our senses give of the object may be more or less clear, more or less distinct, in all possible degrees.

Thus we see more distinctly an object at a small than at a great distance. An object at a great distance is seen more distinctly in a clear than in a foggy day. An object seen indistinctly with the naked eye, on account of its smallness, may be seen distinctly with a microscope. The objects in this room will be seen by a person in the room less and less distinctly as the light of the day fails; they pass through all the various degrees of distinctness according to the degrees of the light, and at last, in total darkness, they are not seen at all. What has been said of the objects of sight is so easily applied to the objects of the other senses, that the application may be left to the reader.

[1] This is Reid's basic account of what happens when a person perceives an external material object. Notice, however, that it so far says nothing at all about whether and how the resulting belief is *justified,* that is, whether and how the person has a ground or reason for thinking that it is true.

From Essays on the Intellectual Powers of Man *(Cambridge, Mass.: The MIT Press, 1969).*

. . .

2dly, In perception we not only have a notion more or less distinct of the object perceived, but also an irresistible conviction and belief of its existence. This is always the case when we are certain that we perceive it. There may be a perception so faint and indistinct, as to leave us in doubt whether we perceive the object or not. Thus, when a star begins to twinkle as the light of the sun withdraws, one may, for a short time, think he sees it, without being certain, until the perception acquires some strength and steadiness. When a ship just begins to appear in the utmost verge of the horizon, we may at first be dubious whether we perceive it or not: but when the perception is in any degree clear and steady, there remains no doubt of its reality; and when the reality of the perception is ascertained, the existence of the object perceived can no longer be doubted.

By the laws of all nations, in the most solemn judicial trials wherein men's fortunes and lives are at stake, the sentence passes according to the testimony of eye or ear witnesses of good credit. An upright judge will give a fair hearing to every objection that can be made to the integrity of a witness, and allow it to be possible that he may be corrupted; but no judge will ever suppose, that witnesses may be imposed upon by trusting to their eyes and ears: and if a skeptical counsel should plead against the testimony of the witnesses, that they had no other evidence for what they declared, but the testimony of their eyes and ears, and that we ought not to put so much faith in our senses, as to deprive men of life or fortune upon their testimony; surely no upright judge would admit a plea of this kind. I believe no counsel, however skeptical, ever dared to offer such an argument; and if it was offered, it would be rejected with disdain.

Can any stronger proof be given, that it is the universal judgment of mankind that the evidence of sense is a kind of evidence which we may securely rest upon in the most momentous concerns of mankind; that it is a kind of evidence against which we ought not to admit any reasoning; and therefore, that to reason either for or against it, is an insult to common sense? ②

The whole conduct of mankind, in the daily occurrences of life, as well as the solemn procedure of judicatories in the trial of causes, civil and criminal, demonstrates this. I know only of two exceptions that may be offered against this being the universal belief of mankind.

The first exception is that of some lunatics, who have been persuaded of things that seem to contradict the clear testimony of their senses. It is said there have been lunatics and hypochondriacal persons, who seriously believed themselves to be made of glass; and, in consequence of this, lived in continual terror of having their brittle frame shivered into pieces.

. . .

The other exception that may be made to the principle we have laid down, is that of some philosophers who have maintained, that the testimony of sense is fallacious, and therefore ought never to be trusted. Perhaps it might be a sufficient answer to this to say, that there is nothing so absurd which some philosophers have not maintained. It is one thing to profess a doctrine of this kind, another seriously to believe it, and to be governed by it in the conduct of life. It is evident, that a man who did not believe his senses, could not keep out of harm's way an hour of his life; yet, in all the history of philosophy, we never read of any skeptic that ever stepped into fire or water because he did not believe his senses, or that showed, in the conduct of life, less trust in his senses than other men have. This gives us just ground to apprehend, that philosophy was never able to conquer that natural belief which men have in their senses; and that all their subtile reasonings against this belief were never able to persuade themselves.

It appears, therefore, that the clear and distinct testimony of our senses carries irresistible conviction along with it, to every man in his right judgment.

I observed, 3dly, That this conviction is not only irresistible, but it is immediate; that is, it is not by a train of reasoning and argumentation that we come to

② There are two importantly different claims being made here: first, that skeptical doubts about perceptual knowledge should not be taken seriously because they go against "the universal judgment of mankind" (how strong a reason is this?); and, second, that this universal judgment shows that "the evidence of sense" does not depend on or require any sort of reasoning in its support.

be convinced of the existence of what we perceive; we ask no argument for the existence of the object, but that we perceive it; perception commands our belief upon its own authority, and disdains to rest its authority upon any reasoning whatsoever.③

> ③ Reid is clearly right that perceptual judgments are not ordinarily arrived at through an explicit process of reasoning. Does it follow that no reasoning is involved, even implicitly, or that no reasoning is required to show that the resulting belief is indeed likely to be true?

The conviction of a truth may be irresistible, and yet not immediate. Thus, my conviction that the three angles of every plain triangle, are equal to two right angles, is irresistible, but it is not immediate: I am convinced of it by demonstrative reasoning. There are other truths in mathematics of which we have not only an irresistible, but an immediate conviction. Such are the axioms. Our belief of the axioms in mathematics is not grounded upon argument. Arguments are grounded upon them, but their evidence is discerned immediately by the human understanding.

It is, no doubt, one thing to have an immediate conviction of a self evident axiom; it is another thing to have an immediate conviction of the existence of what we see: but the conviction is equally immediate and equally irresistible in both cases. No man thinks of seeking a reason to believe what he sees; and, before we are capable of reasoning, we put no less confidence in our senses than after. The rudest savage is as fully convinced of what he sees, and hears, and feels, as the most expert logician. . . .

OF THE SENTIMENTS OF MR. LOCKE

[Locke] sets out in his Essay with a full conviction, common to him with other philosophers, that ideas in the mind are the objects of all our thoughts in every operation of the understanding. This leads him to use the word *idea* so very frequently, beyond what was usual in the English language, that he thought it necessary in his introduction to make [an] apology. . . .

Speaking of the reality of our knowledge, he says, "It is evident the mind knows not things immediately, but only by the intervention of the ideas it has of them. Our knowledge therefore is real, only so far as there is a conformity between our ideas and the reality of things. But what shall be here the criterion? How shall the mind, when it perceives nothing but its own ideas, know that they agree with things themselves? . . . "

We see that Mr. Locke was aware no less than Des Cartes, that the doctrine of ideas made it necessary, and at the same time difficult, to prove the existence of a material world without us; because the mind, according to that doctrine, perceives nothing but a world of ideas in itself. Not only Des Cartes, but Malebranche, Arnauld, and Norris, had perceived this difficulty, and attempted to remove it with little success. Mr. Locke attempts the same thing; but his arguments are feeble. He even seems to be conscious of this: for he concludes his reasoning with this observation, "That we have evidence sufficient to direct us in attaining the good and avoiding the evil, caused by external objects, and that this is the important concern we have in being made acquainted with them." This indeed is saying no more than will be granted by those who deny the existence of a material world.

As there is no material difference between Locke and Des Cartes with regard to the perception of objects by the senses, there is the less occasion, in this place, to take notice of all their differences in other points. . . .

Although no author has more merit than Mr. Locke in pointing out the ambiguity of words, and resolving by that means many knotty questions, which had tortured the wits of the schoolmen; yet, I apprehend he has been sometimes misled by the ambiguity of the word *idea,* which he uses so often almost in every page of his Essay.

In the explication given of this word, we took notice of two meanings given to it; a popular and a philosophical. In the popular meaning, to have an idea of any thing, signifies nothing more than to think of it.

Although the operations of the mind are most properly and naturally, and indeed most commonly in all vulgar languages, expressed by active verbs, there is another way of expressing them less common, but equally well understood. To think of a thing, and to have a thought of it; to believe a thing, and to have a belief of it; to see a thing, and have a sight of it; to conceive a thing, and to have a conception, notion, or idea of it, are phrases perfectly synonymous. In these, phrases the thought means nothing but the act of thinking; the belief, the act of believing; and the conception, notion, or idea, the act of conceiving. To have a clear and distinct idea, is, in this sense, nothing else but to conceive the thing clearly and distinctly. When the word *idea* is taken in this popular sense, there can be no doubt of our having ideas in our minds. To think without ideas would be to think without thought, which is a manifest contradiction.④

④ Thus in one sense, to have an idea of something is just to think of it, without any implication that the idea is a distinct entity that has to be perceived on its own.

But there is another meaning of the word *idea* peculiar to philosophers, and grounded upon a philosophical theory, which the vulgar never think of. Philosophers, ancient and modern, have maintained, that the operations of the mind, like the tools of an artificer, can only be employed upon objects that are present in the mind, or in the brain, where the mind is supposed to reside. Therefore, objects that are distant, in time or place, must have a representative in the mind, or in the brain; some image or picture of them, which is the object that the mind contemplates.⑤ This representative image was, in the old philosophy, called a *species* or *phantasm*. Since the time of Des Cartes, it has more commonly been called an *idea;* and every thought is conceived to have an idea for its object.

⑤ In contrast to the view in the previous paragraph, the Lockean view treats ideas as mental entities that are perceived on their own and are (somehow) the basis for the perception of things outside the mind.

As this has been a common opinion among philosophers, as far back as we can trace philosophy, it is the less to be wondered at, that they should be apt to confound the operation of the mind in thinking, with the idea or object of thought, which is supposed to be its inseparable concomitant.

If we pay any regard to the common sense of mankind, thought and the object of thought are different things, and ought to be distinguished. It is true, thought cannot be without an object, for every man who thinks must think of something; but the object he thinks of is one thing, his thought of that object is another thing. They are distinguished in all languages even by the vulgar; and many things may

be affirmed of thought, that is, of the operation of the mind in thinking, which cannot without error, and even absurdity, be affirmed of the object of that operation.

From this, I think it is evident, that if the word *idea* in a work where it occurs in every paragraph, be used without any intimation of the ambiguity of the word, sometimes to signify thought, or the operation of the mind in thinking, sometimes to signify those internal objects of thought which philosophers suppose, this must occasion confusion in the thoughts both of the author and of the readers. I take this to be the greatest blemish in the Essay on Human Understanding, I apprehend this is the true source of several paradoxical opinions in that excellent work, which I shall have occasion to take notice of.

Here it is very natural to ask, Whether it was Mr. Locke's opinion, that ideas are the only objects of thought? or, Whether it is not possible for men to think of things which are not ideas in the mind?

To this question it is not easy to give a direct answer. On the one hand, he says often, in distinct and studied expressions, that the term *idea* stands for whatever is the object of the understanding when a man thinks, or whatever it is which the mind can be employed about in thinking: that the mind perceives nothing but its own ideas: that all knowledge consists in the perception of the agreement or disagreement of our ideas: that we can have no knowledge further than we have ideas. These, and many other expressions of the like import, evidently imply, that every object of thought must be an idea, and can be nothing else.

On the other hand, I am persuaded that Mr. Locke would have acknowledged, that we may think of Alexander the Great, or of the planet Jupiter, and of numberless things, which he would have owned are not ideas in the mind, but objects which exist independent of the mind that thinks of them.

How shall we reconcile the two parts of this apparent contradiction? All I am able to say upon Mr. Locke's principles to reconcile them, is this, That we cannot think of Alexander, or of the planet Jupiter, unless we have in our minds an idea, that is, an image or picture of those objects. The idea of Alexander is an image, or picture, or representation of that hero in my mind; and this idea is the immediate object of my thought when I think of Alexander. That this was

Locke's opinion, and that it has been generally the opinion of philosophers, there can be no doubt.⑥

⑥ Notice that Locke is thereby attempting to offer an account of *how* the mind perceives something outside of it (see Annotation 3 to the Locke selection). Reid, in contrast, makes no attempt to offer any such account.

But, instead of giving light to the question proposed, it seems to involve it in greater darkness.

When I think of Alexander, I am told there is an image or idea of Alexander in my mind, which is the immediate object of this thought. The necessary consequence of this seems to be, that there are two objects of this thought; the idea, which is in the mind, and the person represented by that idea; the first, the immediate object of the thought, the last, the object of the same thought, but not the immediate object. This is a hard saying; for it makes every thought of things external to have a double object. Every man is conscious of his thoughts, and yet, upon attentive reflection, he perceives no such duplicity in the object he thinks about. Sometimes men see objects double, but they always know when they do so: and I know of no philosopher who has expressly owned this duplicity in the object of thought, though it follows necessarily from maintaining, that, in the same thought, there is one object that is immediate and in the mind itself; and another object, which is not immediate, and which is not in the mind.⑦

⑦ This suggests at least that the two objects are not perceived in the same way—that in ordinary cases the focus of awareness is on the external object, with the idea (if there is one) serving as the way in which the mind is able to access that external object. Do Reid's remarks contain a clear objection to this sort of view?

Besides this, it seems very hard, or rather impossible, to understand what is meant by an object of thought, that is not an immediate object of thought. . . . There is a sense in which a thing may be said to be perceived by a medium. Thus, any kind of sign may be said to be the medium by which I perceive or understand the thing signified. The sign by custom, or compact, or perhaps by nature, introduces the thought of the thing signified. But here the thing signified, when it is introduced to the thought, is an object of thought no less immediate than the sign was before: and there are here two objects of thought, one succeeding another, which

we have shown is not the case with respect to an idea, and the object it represents.⑧

I apprehend, therefore, that if philosophers will maintain, that ideas in the mind are the only immediate objects of thought, they will be forced to grant that they are the sole objects of thought, and that it is impossible for men to think of any thing else. Yet, surely Mr. Locke believed that we can think of many things that are not ideas in the mind; but he seems not to have perceived, that the maintaining that ideas in the mind are the only immediate objects of thought, must necessarily draw this consequence along with it.

The consequence, however, was seen by bishop Berkeley and Mr. Hume, who rather chose to admit the consequence than to give up the principle from which it follows.⑨

⑧ Signs do sometimes work in this way: they call attention to something that is then thought about on its own, independently of the sign (think of a name tag on a person). But are there not also other cases in which a sign supplies an ongoing way of thinking about the thing signified, so that both are objects of consciousness at the same time, though not in the same way? (Think of reading a story about something: you are able to think about the object of the story through the vehicle of the written words and could not think about it without them.)

⑨ Berkeley's view was, of course, **idealism.** (Hume holds a somewhat similar view.)

. . .

REFLECTIONS ON THE COMMON THEORY OF IDEAS

After so long a detail of the sentiments of philosophers, ancient and modern, concerning ideas, it may seem presumptuous to call in question their existence. But no philosophical opinion, however ancient, however generally received, ought to rest upon authority. There is no presumption in requiring evidence for it, or in regulating our belief by the evidence we can find.

To prevent mistakes, the reader must again be reminded, that if by *ideas* are meant only the acts or operations of our minds in perceiving, remembering, or imagining objects, I am far from calling in question the existence of those acts; we are conscious of them every day, and every hour of life; and I believe no man of a sound mind ever doubted of the real existence of the operations of mind, of which he is conscious. Nor is it to be doubted, that by the faculties which God has given us, we can conceive things that are absent, as well as perceive those that are within the reach of our senses; and that such conceptions may be more or less distinct, and more or less lively and strong. . . . The ideas, of whose existence I require the proof, are not the operations of any mind, but supposed objects of those operations. They are not perception, remembrance, or conception, but things that are said to be perceived, or remembered, or imagined.

Nor do I dispute the existence of what the vulgar call the objects of perception. These, by all who acknowledge their existence, are called *real things,* not *ideas.* But philosophers maintain, that, besides these, there are immediate objects of perception in the mind itself: that, for instance, we do not see the sun immediately, but an idea. . . . This idea is said to be the image, the resemblance, the representative of the sun, if there be a sun. **[10]** It is from the existence of the idea that we must infer the existence of the sun. But the idea being immediately perceived, there can be no doubt, as philosophers think, of its existence.

> **[10]** The most crucial claim here is that ideas *represent* external objects. That they do it by *resembling* them or that they are mental *images* are further claims made in an effort to explain how the relation of representation works. (Thus it would be at least possible to reject these latter claims and the account of representation they embody, while still holding onto the claim of representation itself—though then some other account of representation would be needed.)

. . .

The *first* reflection I would make on this philosophical opinion is, that it is directly contrary to the universal sense of men who have not been instructed in philosophy. When we see the sun or moon, we have no doubt that the very objects which we immediately see, are very far distant from us, and from one another. We have not the least doubt, that this is the sun and moon which God created some thousands of years ago, and which have continued to perform their revolutions in the heavens ever since. But how are we astonished when the philosopher informs us, that we are mistaken in all this; that the sun and moon which we see, are not, as we imagine, many miles distant from us, and from each other, but that they are in our own mind; that they had no existence before we saw them, and will have none when we cease to perceive and to think of them; because the objects we perceive are only ideas in our own minds, which can have no existence a moment longer than we think of them. **[11]**

> **[11]** Here Reid misrepresents the view he is criticizing. Locke does not say that the sun and moon are in our minds or cease to exist when we are not thinking of them. And while Berkeley says the first of these things, he would not agree to the second (think about why).

If a plain man, uninstructed in philosophy, has faith to receive these mysteries, how great must be his astonishment. He is brought into a new world, where every thing he sees, tastes, or touches, is an idea; a fleeting kind of being which he can conjure into existence, or can annihilate in the twinkling of an eye.

After his mind is somewhat composed, it will be natural for him to ask his philosophical instructor, pray, sir, are there then no substantial and permanent beings called the sun and moon, which continue to exist whether we think of them or not?

Here the philosophers differ. Mr. Locke, and those that were before him, will answer to this question, that it is very true, there are substantial and permanent beings called the sun and moon; but they never appear to us in their own person, but by their representatives, the ideas in our own minds, and we know nothing of them but what we can gather from those ideas. **[12]**

Bishop Berkeley and Mr. Hume, would give a different answer to the question proposed. They would assure the querist, that it is a vulgar error, a mere prejudice of the ignorant and unlearned, to think that there are any permanent and substantial beings called the sun and moon; that the heavenly bodies, our own bodies, and all bodies whatsoever, are nothing but ideas in our minds; and that there can be nothing like the ideas of one

> **[12]** This is a more accurate statement of Locke's view. What is Reid's alternative? Do the sun and moon "appear to us in their own person," and if so, *how* do they do this—given that Reid too holds that they exist outside the mind? Can the mind think about something outside it without there being some internal feature—whether or not it is an entity like an idea—that represents the thing in question?

mind, but the ideas of another mind. There is nothing in nature but minds and ideas, says the bishop: nay, says Mr. Hume, there is nothing in nature but ideas only; for what we call a mind, is nothing but a train of ideas connected by certain relations between themselves.

In this representation of the theory of ideas, there is nothing exaggerated or misrepresented, as far as I am able to judge; and surely nothing further is necessary to show, that, to the uninstructed in philosophy, it must appear extravagant and visionary, and most contrary to the dictates of common understanding.

. . .

A *second* reflection upon this subject is, that the authors who have treated of ideas, have generally taken their existence for granted, as a thing that could not be called in question; and such arguments as they have mentioned incidentally, in order to prove it, seem too weak to support the conclusion.

Mr. Locke, in the introduction to his Essay, tells us, that he uses the word *idea* to signify whatever is the immediate object of thought; and then adds, "I presume it will be easily granted me that there are such ideas in men's minds; every one is conscious of them in himself, and men's words and actions will satisfy him that they are in others." I am indeed conscious of perceiving, remembering, imagining; but that the objects of these operations are images in my mind I am not conscious. I am satisfied by men's words and actions, that they often perceive the same objects which I perceive, which could not be, if those objects were ideas in their own minds. 13

13 Locke would not, of course, deny that different people can perceive the same external object, though he would insist that they do so by each of them having their own separate ideas of it. (Again, what is Reid's alternative? *How* do different people perceive the same object?)

. . .

There remains only one other argument that I have been able to find urged against our perceiving external objects immediately. It is proposed by Mr. Hume, who, in the Essay already quoted, after acknowledging that it is an universal and primary opinion of all men, that we perceive external objects immediately, subjoins what follows:

"But this universal and primary opinion of all men is soon destroyed by the slightest philosophy, which teaches us, that nothing can ever be present to the mind but an image or perception; and that the senses are only the inlets through which these images are received, without being ever able to produce any immediate intercourse between the mind and the object. The table, which we see, seems to diminish as we remove further from it; but the real table, which exists independent of us, suffers no alteration. It was therefore nothing but its image which was present to the mind. These are the obvious dictates of reason. . . ." 14

14 Though Reid is focusing on Hume, this is the same basic line of argument, the argument from illusion (or perceptual relativity), that appears many times in Berkeley's *Three Dialogues*.

We have here a remarkable conflict between two contradictory opinions, wherein all mankind are engaged. On the one side, stand all the vulgar, who are unpractised in philosophical researches, and guided by the uncorrupted primary instincts of nature. On the other side, stand all the philosophers ancient and modern; every man without exception who reflects. In this division, to my great humiliation, I find myself classed with the vulgar.

The passage now quoted is all I have found in Mr. Hume's writings upon this point; and indeed there is more reasoning in it than I have found in any other author; I shall therefore examine it minutely. . .
The argument, the only argument follows:

The table, which we see, seems to diminish as we remove further from it; but the real table, which exists independent of us, suffers no alteration. It was therefore nothing but its image which was presented to the mind. These are the obvious dictates of reason.

To judge of the strength of this argument, it is necessary to attend to . . . the distinction between real and apparent magnitude. The real magnitude of a line is measured by some known measure of length, as inches, feet, or miles. . . . This magnitude is an object of touch only, and not of sight; nor could we even have had any conception of it, without the sense of touch. . . .

Apparent magnitude is measured by the angle which an object subtends at the eye. . . . This apparent magnitude is an object of sight, and not of touch. . . .

From what has been said, it is evident that the real magnitude of a body must continue unchanged, while the body is unchanged. This we grant. But is it likewise evident, that the apparent magnitude must continue the same while the body is unchanged? So far otherwise, that every man who knows any thing of mathematics can easily demonstrate, that the same individual object, remaining in the same place, and unchanged, must necessarily vary in its apparent magnitude, according as the point from which it is seen is more or less distant; and that its apparent length or breadth will be nearly in a reciprocal proportion to the distance of the spectator. This is as certain as the principles of geometry.

. . .

If these things be considered, it will appear, that Mr. Hume's argument has no force to support his conclusion, nay, that it leads to a contrary conclusion. The argument is this. The table we see, seems to diminish as we remove further from it; that is, its apparent magnitude is diminished; but the real table suffers no alteration, to wit, in its real magnitude; therefore it is not the real table we see. I admit both the premises in this syllogism, but I deny the conclusion. The syllogism has what the logicians call two middle terms. Apparent magnitude is the middle term in the first premise; real magnitude in the second. Therefore, according to the rules of logic, the conclusion is not justly drawn from the premises; but, laying aside the rules of logic, let us examine it by the light of common sense.

Let us suppose, for a moment, that it is the real table we see. Must not this real table seem to diminish as we remove further from it? It is demonstrable that it must. How then can this apparent diminution be an argument that it is not the real table? When that which must happen to the real table, as we remove further from it, does actually happen to the table we see, it is absurd to conclude from this, that it is not the real table we see. It is evident, therefore, that this ingenious author has imposed upon himself, by confounding real magnitude with apparent magnitude, and that his argument is a mere sophism. [15]

. . .

The *last* reflection I shall make upon this theory is, that the natural and necessary consequences of it furnish a just prejudice against it to every man who pays a due regard to the common sense of mankind.

. . .

It was this theory or means that led Des Cartes, and those that followed him, to think it necessary to prove, by philosophical arguments, the existence of material objects. And who does not see that philosophy must make a very ridiculous figure in the eyes of sensible men, while it is employed in mustering up metaphysical arguments, to prove that there is a sun and a moon, an earth and a sea? Yet we find these truly great men, Des Cartes, Malebranche, Arnauld, and Locke, seriously employing themselves in this argument.

Surely their principles led them to think, that all men, from the beginning of the world, believed the existence of these things upon insufficient grounds, and to think that they would be able to place upon a more rational foundation this universal belief of mankind. But the misfortune is, that all the laboured arguments they have advanced, to prove the existence of those things we see and feel, are mere sophisms. Not one of them will bear examination.

. . .

However, all these consequences of the doctrine of ideas were tolerable, compared with those which came afterward to be discovered by Berkeley and Hume: That there is no material world: No abstract ideas or notions: That the mind is only a train of related impressions and ideas, without any subject on which they may be impressed: That there is neither space nor time, body nor mind, but impressions and ideas only: And, to sum up all, That there is no probability, even in demonstration itself, nor any one proposition more probable than its contrary.

These are the noble fruits which have grown upon this theory of ideas, since it began to be culti-

[15] Is this an adequate response to the argument? What is it for a person to be aware of the apparent magnitude of the table and for that to diminish while the table does not change? Berkeley (and Hume) would say that our awareness of this apparent magnitude involves having something like a mental image that changes (in the sense that the table occupies a smaller part of it) even while the table undergoes no change, so that it is this image (and idea) that we are most immediately aware of. What is Reid's alternative to this view?

vated by skilful hands. It is no wonder that sensible men should be disgusted at philosophy, when such wild and shocking paradoxes pass under its name. However, as these paradoxes have, with great acuteness and ingenuity, been deduced by just reasoning from the theory of ideas, they must at last bring this advantage, that positions so shocking to the common sense of mankind, and so contrary to the decisions of all our intellectual powers, will open men's eyes, and break the force of the prejudice which has held them entangled in that theory.⟦16⟧

⟦16⟧ Is Reid right that the view that the existence of the material world needs to be proved and the skepticism that results from failed attempts to do so results only from the theory of ideas? Does his own view preclude raising essentially the same problem—and if so, why?

. . .

OF SENSATION

Having finished what I intend, with regard to that act of mind which we call the perception of an external object, I proceed to consider another, which, by our constitution, is conjoined with perception, and not with perception only, but with many other acts of our minds; and that is sensation. . . .

Almost all our perceptions have corresponding sensations which constantly accompany them, and, on that account, are very apt to be confounded with them. Neither ought we to expect, that the sensation, and its corresponding perception, should be distinguished in common language, because the purposes of common life do not require it. Language is made to serve the purposes of ordinary conversation; and we have no reason to expect that it should make distinctions that are not of common use. Hence it happens, that a quality perceived, and the sensation corresponding to that perception, often go under the same name.

This makes the names of most of our sensations ambiguous, and this ambiguity has very much perplexed philosophers. It will be necessary to give some instances, to illustrate the distinction between our sensations and the objects of perception.

When I smell a rose, there is in this operation both sensation and perception. The agreeable odour I feel, considered by itself, without relation to any external object, is merely a sensation. It affects the mind in a certain way; and this affection of the mind may be conceived, without a thought of the rose, or any other object. This sensation can be nothing else than it is felt to be. Its very essence consists in being felt; and when it is not felt, it is not. There is no difference between the sensation and the feeling of it; they are one and the same thing. It is for this reason, that we before observed, that, in sensation, there is no object distinct from that act of the mind by which it is felt; and this holds true with regard to all sensations.

Let us next attend to the perception which we have in smelling a rose. Perception has always an external object; and the object of my perception, in this case, is that quality in the rose which I discern by the sense of smell. Observing that the agreeable sensation is raised when the rose is near, and ceases when it is removed, I am led, by my nature, to conclude some quality to be in the rose, which is the cause of this sensation. This quality in the rose is the object perceived; and that act of my mind, by which I have the conviction and belief of this quality, is what in this case I call perception.⟦17⟧

⟦17⟧ Here Reid seems to come perilously close to Locke's view: I am aware of a sensation of smell, which is an "affection of the mind" that by its very nature must be just as I experience it to be. On this basis, I "conclude" (though not through any explicit reasoning) that there is a quality in the rose that causes this sensation. I think about this external quality, but I do not experience it in the same immediate way in which I experience the sensation. (Why couldn't a skeptic challenge whether I have any good reason for believing in the external quality—or in the rose—if everything about it is believed in on this same basis?)

But it is here to be observed, that the sensation I feel, and the quality in the rose which I perceive, are both called by the same name. The smell of a rose is the name given to both: so that this name has two meanings; and the distinguishing its different meanings removes all perplexity, and enables us to give clear and distinct answers to questions, about which philosophers have held much dispute.

Thus, if it is asked, whether the smell be in the rose, or in the mind that feels it? The answer is obvious: that there are two different things signified by the smell of a rose; one of which is in the mind, and can be in nothing but in a sentient being; the other is truly and properly in the rose. The sensation which I feel is in my mind. The mind is the sentient being; and as the rose is insentient, there can be no sensation, nor any thing resembling sensation in it. But this sensation in my mind is occasioned by a certain quality in the rose, which is called by the same name with the sensation, not on account of any similitude, but because of their constant concomitancy.

All the names we have for smells, tastes, sounds, and for the various degrees of heat and cold, have a like ambiguity; and what has been said of the smell of a rose may be applied to them. They signify both a sensation, and a quality perceived by means of that sensation. The first is the sign, the last the thing signified. As both are conjoined by nature, and as the purposes of common life do not require them to be disjoined in our thoughts, they are both expressed by the same name: and this ambiguity is to be found in all languages, because the reason of it extends to all.

. . .

I shall conclude this chapter by observing, that as the confounding our sensations with that perception of external objects, which is constantly conjoined with them, has been the occasion of most of the errors and false theories of philosophers with regard to the senses; so the distinguishing these operations seems to me to be the key that leads to a right understanding of both.

Sensation, taken by itself, implies neither the conception nor belief of any external object. It supposes a sentient being, and a certain manner in which that being is affected; but it supposes no more. Perception implies an immediate conviction and belief of something external; something different both from the mind that perceives, and from the act of perception. Things so different in their nature ought to be distinguished; but by our constitution they are always united. Every different perception is conjoined with a sensation that is proper to it. The one is the sign, the other the thing signified. They coalesce in our imagination. They are signified by one name, and are considered as one simple operation. The purposes of life do not require them to be distinguished.

It is the philosopher alone who has occasion to distinguish them, when he would analyze the operation compounded of them. But he has no suspicion that there is any composition in it; and to discover this requires a degree of reflection which has been too little practised even by philosophers.

. . .

Des Cartes and Locke, attending more to the operations of their own minds, say, that the sensations by which we have notice of secondary qualities, have no resemblance to any thing that pertains to body; but they did not see that this might with equal justice be applied to the primary qualities. Mr. Locke maintains, that the sensations we have from primary qualities are resemblances of those qualities. This shows how grossly the most ingenious men may err with regard to the operations of their minds. It must indeed be acknowledged, that it is much easier to have a distinct notion of the sensations that belong to secondary, than of those that belong to the primary qualities. . . .

But had Mr. Locke attended with sufficient accuracy to the sensations which he was every day and every hour receiving from primary qualities, he would have seen, that they can as little resemble any quality of an inanimated being, as pain can resemble a cube or a circle.

What had escaped this ingenious philosopher was clearly discerned by bishop Berkeley. He had a just notion of sensations, and saw that it was impossible that any thing in an insentient being could resemble them; a thing so evident in itself, that it seems wonderful that it should have been so long unknown.[18]

But let us attend to the consequence of this discovery. Philosophers, as well as the vulgar, had been accustomed to comprehend both sensation and perception under one name, and to consider them as one uncompounded operation. Philosophers, even more than the vulgar, gave the name of sensation to the whole operation of the senses; and all the notions we have of material things were called ideas of sensation. This led bishop Berkeley to take one ingredient of a complex operation for the whole; and having clearly discovered the nature of sensation, taking it for granted, that all that the senses

[18] Here Reid in effect endorses Berkeley's claim that an idea can only resemble another idea. But the real issue is not resemblance, but representation: does the experience of primary qualities present us with an accurate idea of their true nature in a way that the experience of secondary qualities does not? This could be true even if there was no literal resemblance.

present to the mind is sensation, which can have no resemblance to any thing material, he concluded that there is no material world.

If the senses furnished us with no materials of thought but sensations, his conclusion must be just; for no sensation can give us the conception of material things, far less any argument to prove their existence. But if it is true that by our senses we have not only a variety of sensations, but likewise a conception, and an immediate natural conviction of external objects, he reasons from a false supposition, and his arguments fall to the ground. [19]

[19] Reid seems right to distinguish the sensation from the conception and belief that results from it. Thus while for Berkeley there is a problem of how we can even *think* about external objects if they are supposed to be more than patterns of ideas, Reid avoids this problem (though without really explaining where this conception comes from). But doesn't Reid still have essentially the same problem about the justification of the resulting belief (the ground or reason for thinking it to be true), whether this is on the basis of the sensation or in some other way?

. . .

OF THE EVIDENCE OF SENSE, AND OF BELIEF IN GENERAL

The intention of nature in the powers which we call the external senses, is evident. They are intended to give us that information of external objects which the Supreme Being saw to be proper for us in our present state; and they give to all mankind the information necessary for life, without reasoning, without any art or investigation on our part.

The most uninstructed peasant has as distinct a conception, and as firm a belief of the immediate objects of his senses, as the greatest philosopher; and with this he rests satisfied, giving himself no concern how he came by this conception and belief. But the philosopher is impatient to know how his conception of external objects, and his belief of their existence, is produced. This, I am afraid, is hid in impenetrable darkness. But where there is no knowledge, there is the more room for conjecture: and of this philosophers have always been very liberal.

. . .

That we can assign no adequate cause of our first conceptions of things, I think, is now acknowledged by the most enlightened philosophers. We know that such is our constitution, that in certain circumstances we have certain conceptions; but how they are produced, we know no more than how we ourselves were produced.

When we have got the conception of external objects by our senses, we can analyze them in our thought into their simple ingredients; and we can compound those ingredients into various new forms, which the senses never presented. But it is beyond the power of human imagination to form any conception, whose simple ingredients have not been furnished by nature in a manner unaccountable to our understanding.

. . .

If our conception of external objects be unaccountable, the conviction and belief of their existence, which we get by our senses, is no less so.

. . .

That men often believe what there is no just ground to believe, and thereby are led into hurtful errors, is too evident to be denied: and, on the other hand, that there are just grounds of belief, can as little be doubted by any man who is not a perfect skeptic.

We give the name of evidence to whatever is a ground of belief. To believe without evidence is a weakness which every man is concerned to avoid, and which every man wishes to avoid. Nor is it in a man's power to believe any thing longer than he thinks he has evidence. [20]

[20] This last part is highly questionable. But the main point here is that what is *thought* to be good evidence need not actually *be* good evidence.

. . .

The common occasions of life lead us to distinguish evidence into different kinds, to which we give names that are well understood; such as the evidence of sense, the evidence of memory, the evidence of consciousness, the evidence of testimony, the evidence of axioms, the evidence of reasoning. . . .

I confess that, although I have, as I think, a distinct notion of the different kinds of evidence above mentioned, and perhaps of some others, which it is unnecessary here to enumerate, yet I am not able to find any common nature to which they may all be reduced. They seem to me to agree only in this, that they are all fitted by nature to produce belief in the human mind; some of them in the highest degree, which we call certainty, others in various degrees according to circumstances.

I shall take it for granted, that the evidence of sense, when the proper circumstances concur, is good evidence, and a just ground of belief.[21] My intention in this place is only to compare it with the other kinds that have been mentioned, that we may judge whether it be reducible to any of them, or of a nature peculiar to itself.

[21] This is in keeping with Reid's common-sense outlook. But even if it is acceptable to take this for granted, it can still be asked *why* and *how* this is so.

1st, It seems to be quite different from the evidence of reasoning. All good evidence is commonly called reasonable evidence, and very justly, because it ought to govern our belief as reasonable creatures. And, according to this meaning, I think the evidence of sense no less reasonable than that of demonstration. . . .

But when we speak of the evidence of reasoning as a particular kind of evidence, it means the evidence of propositions that are inferred by reasoning, from propositions already known and believed. . . .

That the evidence of sense is of a different kind, needs little proof. No man seeks a reason for believing what he sees or feels; and if he did, it would be difficult to find one. But though he can give no reason for believing his senses, his belief remains as firm as if it were grounded on demonstration.

Many eminent philosophers, thinking it unreasonable to believe, when they could not show a reason, have laboured to furnish us with reasons for believing our senses; but their reasons are very insufficient, and will not bear examination.[22] Other philosophers have shown very clearly the fallacy of these reasons, and have, as they imagine, discovered invincible reasons against this belief; but they have never been able either to shake it in themselves, or to convince others. . . . a man may as soon, by reasoning, pull the moon out of her orbit, as destroy the belief of the objects of sense.

[22] Here Reid has Descartes and Locke mainly in mind.

Shall we say then that the evidence of sense is the same with that of axioms, or self-evident truths? I answer, 1st, that all modern philosophers seem to agree, that the existence of the objects of sense is not self-evident, because some of them have endeavoured to prove it by subtile reasoning, others to refute it. Neither of these can consider it as self-evident.

2dly, I would observe, that the word *axiom* is taken by philosophers in such a sense, as that the existence of the objects of sense cannot, with propriety, be called an axiom. They give the name of axiom only to self-evident truths that are necessary, and are not limited to time and place, but must be true at all times, and in all places. The truths attested by our senses are not of this kind; they are contingent, and limited to time and place.

Thus, that one is the half of two, is an axiom. It is equally true at all times, and in all places. We perceive, by attending to the proposition itself, that it cannot but be true; and therefore it is called an eternal, necessary and immutable truth. That there is at present a chair on my right hand, and another on my left, is a truth attested by my senses; but it is not necessary, nor eternal, nor immutable. It may not be true next minute; and therefore, to call it an axiom, would, I apprehend, be to deviate from the common use of the word.

3dly, If the word *axiom* be put to signify every truth which is known immediately, without being deduced from any antecedent truth, then the existence of the objects of sense may be called an axiom. For my senses give me as immediate conviction of what they testify, as my understanding gives me of what is commonly called an axiom.[23]

[23] There is no doubt that the senses produce immediate *conviction*. But for this to be knowledge seems to require justification: some sort of ground or reason for thinking that the conviction is true. In other sorts of cases (such as mathematics), this may be furnished by self-evidence or the awareness of the necessity of the claims in question, but Reid concedes that this does not apply to the claims of the senses. So how then are such claims justified, according to him?

. . .

When I compare the different kinds of evidence above mentioned, I confess, after all, that the evidence of reasoning, and that of some necessary and self-evident truths, seems to be the least mysterious, and the most perfectly comprehended; and therefore I do not think it strange that philosophers should have endeavoured to reduce all kinds of evidence to these.

. . . when I . . . see an object before my eyes, this commands my belief no less than an axiom. But when, as a philosopher, I reflect upon this belief, and want to trace it to its origin, I am not able to resolve it into necessary and self-evident axioms, or conclusions that are necessarily consequent upon them. I seem to want that evidence which I can best comprehend, and which gives perfect satisfaction to an inquisitive mind; yet it is ridiculous to doubt, and I find it is not in my power. An attempt to throw off this belief, is like an attempt to fly, equally ridiculous and impracticable. 24

> 24 Doubt isn't really the issue. Even if Reid is right that doubt is "ridiculous," a philosopher can (and seemingly should) ask what makes beliefs of this sort acceptable.

To a philosopher, who has been accustomed to think that the treasure of his knowledge is the acquisition of that reasoning power of which he boasts, it is no doubt humiliating to find, that his reason can lay no claim to the greater part of it.

By his reason, he can discover certain abstract and necessary relations of things; but his knowledge of what really exists, or did exist, comes by another channel, which is open to those who cannot reason. He is led to it in the dark, and knows not how he came by it.

It is no wonder that the pride of philosophy should lead some to invent vain theories, in order to account for this knowledge; and others who see this to be impracticable, to spurn at a knowledge they cannot account for, and vainly attempt to throw it off, as a reproach to their understanding. But the wise and the humble will receive it as the gift of Heaven, and endeavour to make the best use of it.

. . .

OF FIRST PRINCIPLES IN GENERAL

One of the most important distinctions of our judgments is, that some of them are intuitive, others grounded on argument.

It is not in our power to judge as we will. The judgment is carried along necessarily by the evidence, real or seeming, which appears to us at the time. But in propositions that are submitted to our judgment, there is this great difference; some are of such a nature that a man of ripe understanding may apprehend them distinctly, and perfectly understand their meaning without finding himself under any necessity of believing them to be true or false, probable or improbable. The judgment remains in suspense, until it is inclined to one side or another by reasons or arguments.

But there are other propositions which are no sooner understood than they are believed. The judgment follows the apprehension of them necessarily, and both are equally the work of nature, and the result of our original powers. There is no searching for evidence; no weighing of arguments; the proposition is not deduced or inferred from another; it has the light of truth in itself, and has no occasion to borrow it from another. 25

> 25 There are two different features indicated here, which should not be run together (as Reid at least sometimes seems to do): first, that the proposition is accepted as soon as it is understood, without any searching for evidence or weighing of arguments; and, second, that there is some sort of ground or basis for thinking that it is true (it has the "light of truth in itself").

Propositions of the last kind, when they are used in matters of science, have commonly been called *axioms;* and on whatever occasion they are used, are called *first principles, principles of common sense, common notions, self-evident truths. . . .*

I take it for granted, that there are self-evident principles. Nobody, I think, denies it. And if any man were so skeptical as to deny that there is any proposition that is self-evident, I see not how it would be possible to convince him by reasoning.

But yet there seems to be great difference of opinions among philosophers about first principles. What one takes to be self-evident, another labours to prove by arguments, and a third denies altogether.

Thus, before the time of Des Cartes, it was taken for a first principle, that there is a sun and a moon, an earth and sea, which really exist, whether we think of them or not. Des Cartes thought that the existence of those things ought to be proved by argument; and in this he has been followed by Malebranche, Arnauld, and Locke. They have all laboured to prove, by very weak reasoning, the existence of external objects of sense; and Berkeley, and Hume, sensible of the weakness of their arguments, have been led to deny their existence altogether.

. . .

THE FIRST PRINCIPLES OF CONTINGENT TRUTHS

"Surely, says bishop Berkeley, it is a work well deserving our pains, to make a strict inquiry concerning the first principles of knowledge; to sift and examine them on all sides." What was said in the last chapter, is intended both to show the importance of this inquiry, and to make it more easy.

But, in order that such an inquiry may be actually made, it is necessary that the first principles of knowledge be distinguished from other truths, and presented to view, that they may be sifted and examined on all sides. In order to this end, I shall attempt a detail of those I take to be such, and of the reasons why I think them entitled to that character.

. . .

The truths that fall within the compass of human knowledge, whether they be self-evident, or deduced from those that are self-evident, may be reduced to two classes. They are either necessary and immutable truths, whose contrary is impossible; or they are contingent and mutable, depending upon some effect of will and power, which had a beginning, and may have an end.

. . .

26 Reid is denying that the existence of anything can be necessary. Is this true for things like numbers (the number six itself, not the numeral that represents it) or properties (redness itself, whether or not there are red things)?

Thus, as the axioms in mathematics are all necessary truths; so are all the conclusions drawn from them; that is, the whole body of that science. But from no mathematical truth can we deduce the existence of any thing; not even of the objects of the science. 26

. . .

As the minds of men are occupied much more about truths that are contingent than about those that are necessary, I shall first endeavour to point out the principles of the former kind.

1st. *First,* Then, I hold, as a first principle, the existence of every thing of which I am conscious.

Consciousness is an operation of the understanding of its own kind, and cannot be logically defined. The objects of it are our present pains, our pleasures, our hopes, our fears, our desires, our doubts, our thoughts of every kind; in a word, all the passions; and all the actions and operations of our own minds, while they are present. We may remember them when they are past; but we are conscious of them only while they are present.

When a man is conscious of pain, he is certain of its existence; when he is conscious that he doubts, or believes, he is certain of the existence of those operations.

But the irresistible conviction he has of the reality of those operations is not the effect of reasoning; it is immediate and intuitive. The existence therefore of those passions and operations of our minds, of which we are conscious, is a first principle, which nature requires us to believe upon her authority.

If I am asked to prove that I cannot be deceived by consciousness, to prove that it is not a fallacious sense; I can find no proof. I cannot find any antecedent truth from which it is deduced, or upon which its evidence depends. It seems to disdain any such derived authority, and to claim my assent in its own right.

If any man could be found so frantic as to deny that he thinks, while he is conscious of it; I may wonder, I may laugh, or I may pity him, but I cannot reason the matter with him. We have no common principles from which we may reason, and therefore can never join issue in an argument. 27

27 Here Reid has in mind consciousness of mental entities and processes, not consciousness of external objects. Is he right that there is no reason or argument that supports the truth of claims resulting from such consciousness? (Look back at the paragraph that begins "When I smell a rose . . ." on page 231, and see Discussion Question 1.)

. . .

3dly, Another first principle I take to be, That those things did really happen which I distinctly remember.

This has one of the surest marks of a first principle; for no man ever pretended to prove it, and yet no man in his wits calls it in question; the testimony of memory, like that of consciousness, is immediate; it claims our assent upon its own authority.

. . .

Indeed the theory concerning ideas, so generally received by philosophers, destroys all the authority of memory, as well as the authority of the senses. Des Cartes, Malebranche, and Locke, were aware that this theory made it necessary for them to find out arguments to prove the existence of external objects, which the vulgar believe upon the bare authority of their senses; but those philosophers were not aware, that this theory made it equally necessary for them to find arguments to prove the existence of things past, which we remember, and to support the authority of memory.

All the arguments they advanced to support the authority of our senses, were easily refuted by bishop Berkeley and Mr. Hume, being indeed very weak and inconclusive. And it would have been as easy to answer every argument they could have brought, consistent with their theory, to support the authority of memory.⟨28⟩

⟨28⟩ Here is Reid's response to another very difficult epistemological issue, one that there is no further consideration of in this book. Reid is suggesting in part that the problem of memory and the problem of perception are parallel, and that the futility of trying to defend perceptual beliefs via argument can be made even more obvious by reflecting on this parallel case. (See Discussion Question 3.)

. . .

⟨29⟩ This is Reid's basic response to the issue of how perceptual beliefs are justified: that the things we perceive (probably?) exist and are as we perceive them to be is a *first principle*. Is this an adequate solution to the problem? (See Discussion Question 2.)

5thly, Another first principle is, That those things do really exist which we distinctly perceive by our senses, and are what we perceive them to be.⟨29⟩

It is too evident to need proof, that all men are by nature led to give implicit faith to the distinct testimony of their senses, long before they are capable of any bias from prejudices of education or of philosophy.

. . .

It is evident we can have no communication, no correspondence or society with any created being, but by means of our senses. And until we rely upon their testimony, we must consider ourselves as being alone in the universe, without any fellow creature, living or inanimate, and be left to converse with our own thoughts.

. . .

All the arguments urged by Berkeley and Hume against the existence of a material world are grounded upon this principle, that we do not perceive external objects themselves, but certain images or ideas in our own minds. But this is no dictate of common sense, but directly contrary to the sense of all who have not been taught it by philosophy.

We have before examined the reasons given by philosophers, to prove that ideas, and not external objects, are the immediate objects of perception, and the instances given to prove the senses fallacious. Without repeating what has before been said upon those points, we shall only here observe, that if external objects be perceived immediately, we have the same reason to believe their existence as philosophers have to believe the existence of ideas, while they hold them to be the immediate objects of perception.⟨30⟩

⟨30⟩ Reid offers a further argument: once it is granted that external objects are perceived immediately, we have as good a reason to accept the perceptual beliefs that result as we would have for beliefs about ideas (if they existed)—or, presumably, as we do in the case of beliefs about states of mind such as sensations. Is he right about this? (See Discussion Question 1.)

. . .

7thly, Another first principle is, that the natural faculties, by which we distinguish truth from error, are not fallacious. If any man should demand a proof of this, it is impossible to satisfy him. For suppose it should be mathematically demonstrated, this would signify nothing in this case; because, to judge of a demonstration, a man must trust his faculties, and take for granted the very thing in question.

If a man's honesty were called in question, it would be ridiculous to refer it to the man's own word, whether he be honest or not. The same absurdity there is in attempting to prove, by any kind of reasoning, probable or demonstrative, that our reason is not fallacious, since the very point in question is, whether reasoning may be trusted.

If a skeptic should build his skepticism upon this foundation, that all our reasoning, and judging powers are fallacious in their nature, or should resolve at least to withhold assent until it be proved that they are not; it would be impossible by argument to beat him out of this strong hold, and he must even be left to enjoy his skepticism.

Des Cartes certainly made a false step in this matter; for having suggested this doubt among others, that whatever evidence he might have from his consciousness, his senses, his memory, or his reason; yet possibly some malignant being had given him those faculties on purpose to impose upon him; and therefore, that they are not to be trusted without a proper voucher: to remove this doubt, he endeavours to prove the being of a Deity who is no deceiver; whence he concludes, that the faculties he had given him are true and worthy to be trusted.

It is strange that so acute a reasoner did not perceive, that in this reasoning there is evidently a begging of the question.③①

> **③①** Here Reid has in mind the power of reasoning and rational thought. He points out, correctly, that there is no way to prove the reliability of this basic capacity, since any proof would rely on the very capacity in question and so would beg the question.

. . .

We may here take notice of a property of the principle under consideration, that seems to be common to it with many other first principles, and which can hardly be found in any principle that is built solely upon reasoning; and that is, that in most men it produces its effect without ever being attended to, or made an object of thought. No man ever thinks of this principle, unless when he considers the grounds of skepticism; yet it invariably governs his opinions. When a man in the common course of life gives credit to the testimony of his senses, his memory, or his reason, he does not put the question to himself, whether these faculties may deceive him; yet the trust he reposes in them supposes an inward conviction, that, in that instance at least, they do not deceive him.

It is another property of this and of many first principles, that they force assent in particular instances, more powerfully than when they are turned into a general proposition. Many skeptics have denied every general principle of science, excepting perhaps the existence of our present thoughts; yet these men reason, and refute, and prove, they assent and dissent in particular cases. They use reasoning to overturn all reasoning, and judge that they ought to have no judgment, and see clearly that they are blind. Many have, in general, maintained that the senses are fallacious, yet there never was found a man so skeptical as not to trust his senses in particular instances when his safety required it; and it may be observed of those who have professed skepticism, that their skepticism lies in generals, while in particulars they are no less dogmatical than others.

. . .

12thly, The last principle of contingent truths I mention, is, That, in the phenomena of nature, what is to be, will probably be like to what has been in similar circumstances.

We must have this conviction as soon as we are capable of learning any thing from experience; for all experience is grounded upon a belief that the future will be like the past. Take away this principle, and the experience of an hundred years makes us no wiser with regard to what is to come.

This is one of those principles, which, when we grow up and observe the course of nature, we can confirm by reasoning. We perceive that nature is governed by fixed laws, and that if it were not so, there could be no such thing as prudence in human conduct; there would be no fitness in any means to promote an end; and what, on one occasion, promoted it, might as probably, on another occasion, obstruct it. ③②

> **③②** Here is one more interesting example of Reid's idea of "first principles." He is claiming here that the principle that underlies inductive reasoning is a first principle, in which case the problem of induction is immediately solved and indeed doesn't really arise in the first place. But is this perhaps too easy a solution to be plausible? (See the induction section.) Does the same worry arise about Reid's other first principles? (See Discussion Question 2.)

. . .

Discussion Questions

1. Consider an introspective belief about one of your own conscious states of mind: the belief that you are experiencing a pain in your wrist, perhaps, or the belief that you are thinking about Reid. What sort of reason or basis do you have for thinking that such beliefs are true? Is this just something that has to be accepted as a "first principle," or is there something more

to be said? In the paragraph that begins "When I smell a rose . . ." on page 231, Reid suggests that the very nature of a sensation consists in being felt, so that it has to be the way it is felt to be. Does this provide a reason for thinking that a belief that it feels that way is true? Why or why not? (If there is a reason of this sort, then the next question is whether anything parallel can be said about perceptual beliefs concerning external objects.)

2. Even if external objects are perceived directly in the sense that there is no intermediate entity that is perceived more immediately, it can still apparently be asked whether the specific belief or conviction that is the content of a perceptual judgment is true (or likely to be true). Is it enough of a response to this question to say, as Reid does, that it is simply a first principle that beliefs of this sort are true— especially if it is admitted, as he does, that such a claim is not self-evident or necessary? Bertrand Russell remarks that the method of postulation "has all the advantages of theft over honest toil," by which he means that simply postulating that something is so is too easy to be satisfying. Does this same objection pertain to Reid's first principles (and if not, why not)?

3. Think about the somewhat analogous problem of how, if at all, memory beliefs can be justified (where we are using the term "memory belief" to refer to beliefs that seem to be memories, whether they are actually so or not). Reid is right that philosophers who discuss perception at great length often say very little about memory, even though very similar issues seem to arise there. Think of how solutions parallel to Locke's and to Berkeley's would apply to the case of memory, and consider the problems that arise in each case. Can memory beliefs be justified in either of these two ways? If not, is a Reidian solution the only one available? And if this is so, does it, by analogy, support Reid's account of perception?

Laurence BonJour

Laurence BonJour (1943–) is an American philosopher who teaches at the University of Washington. He has written or cowritten several books in epistemology (and is the coeditor of this volume). In this selection, BonJour recapitulates the problem of the external world, as it grows out of the work of Descartes, Locke, and Berkeley; then explains and criticizes the phenomenalist response to this problem, growing out of Berkeley's view (and Hume's); and finally offers a tentative solution along very roughly Lockean lines. At the end, he also has a bit to say about direct realist views like the one offered by Reid.

Knowledge of the External World, from *Epistemology: Classic Problems and Contemporary Responses*

We have so far tentatively accepted the conclusion that the *immediate* object of awareness in perceptual experience is never an external material object, but is instead something of a quite different sort: either a sense-datum or else the content of a

From Epistemology: Classic Problems and Contemporary Responses *(Lanham: Rowman & Littlefield, 2002).*

state of sensing or being appeared to (in the latter case there is of course, strictly speaking, no *object* at all).① It will be useful to have a brief label for this dis-

① Sense-data (singular: sense-datum) are roughly the same things that Locke and Berkeley have in mind when they speak of perceptual ideas: entities that have the qualities that are directly or immediately experienced and that exist in the mind. The alternative view mentioned here (sometimes called the "adverbial theory") speaks of states of "being appeared to," also existing in the mind, with the various immediately experienced qualities being construed as different ways of "being appeared to," rather than as qualities of entities. The idea is that being appeared to redly and squarely—that is, in a way that seems to present or depict a red square—need not involve any object or entity that actually has those properties. (This difference makes little difference in the subsequent discussion.)

junctive result, and I will refer to it here as *perceptual subjectivism.* We have not tried to decide in any firm way between these two views, which, I have suggested, are in fact more or less equivalent in their epistemological (though obviously not their metaphysical) implications. In the present chapter, however, it will be convenient, for reasons of simplicity, to couch our discussion mainly in terms of sense-data. . . .

We have now to consider the implications of perceptual subjectivism for the epistemological issue upon which it bears most directly, which is also arguably the most central issue of the modern period of epistemology, which began with Descartes: the issue of whether and, if so, how beliefs concerning the external material world and the objects that it allegedly contains can be justified on the basis of our immediate sensory experience, thus understood. . . . we will first look at the views of Descartes's immediate successors, the so-called British Empiricists Locke, Berkeley, and Hume, whose arguments played a major role in shaping the subsequent discussion. We will then examine the two main alternative accounts of "knowledge of the external world" (on the assumption that perceptual subjectivism or something like it is indeed true) that have subsequently emerged, mainly in the forms that they have taken in the twentieth century: *phenomenalism*

and *representationalism.* Difficulties with these views will then prompt, in the last part of the chapter, a reconsideration of whether rejecting perceptual subjectivism might make available a further, more promising alternative.

LOCKE, BERKELEY, AND HUME ON PERCEPTION AND THE EXTERNAL WORLD

As noted earlier, Locke and Berkeley speak not of sense-data . . . but of "ideas" or "ideas of sense"—with the former term being applied also to contents of thought and indeed apparently to conscious contents of any kind. The way that they use these rather slippery terms suggests in many places something like a sense-datum theory of the immediate objects of sensory experience. For our purposes, however, it will suffice to take the term "idea" merely to refer to conscious contents of any sort, and "ideas of sense" to the distinctive contents of sensory experience, without supposing these terms to indicate any definite metaphysical picture of the nature of such contents.

Locke's view is clearly that our beliefs or opinions about material objects existing outside of our minds are justified by our ideas of sense.* But his discussion of this point is both rather uncertain and quite guarded. He says that our assurance on this basis concerning material objects "deserves the name of knowledge" [p. 189], thus seeming to suggest that it is not knowledge simply and with no qualification. He also questions whether anyone can be genuinely skeptical about the existence of the things that he sees and feels, and speaks rather vaguely of "the assurance we have from our senses themselves, that they do not err in the information they give us" [p. 189].

But the closest that Locke comes to explaining *how* such beliefs are justified by sensory experience is his citing of four "concurrent reasons" that are supposed to further confirm the assurance derived from the senses: First, we can know that sensory ideas are "produced in us by exterior causes" by observing that those lacking a particular sense organ can never have the corresponding sensory ideas [p. 190]. (Thus, for

---

*Locke, *Essay Concerning Human Understanding,* Book IV, ch. XI. Subsequent page references in the text are to the selection in the present book.

example, a blind man can never have immediate sensory experiences of visual qualities such as color.) Second, another reason for thinking that our sensory ideas result from external causes is their *involuntary* character, as contrasted with imagination and, to a lesser extent, memory [p. 190]. (Thus if I have my eyes open and am facing in a particular direction, I have no choice as to what apparent objects or properties I will experience, that is, in Locke's view, what ideas of vision I will experience—as I look out my study window, I cannot help being aware of a mass of variegated green and brown that I take to be a perception of trees, branches, and leaves.) Third, another difference between our immediate sensory experiences and other sorts of ideas, such as those of imagination and memory, is that sensory ideas of certain kinds are accompanied by *pain,* whereas the corresponding ideas of imagination and memory are not [p. 190]. (For example, if I have the immediate sensory experience of apparently hitting my hand with a hammer while attempting to drive a nail, I will usually experience pain along with it; but if I merely imagine or remember such an experience, there is no pain.* Fourth, "our senses, in many cases, bear witness to the truth of each other's report, concerning the existence of sensible things without us" [p. 190]. (For example, my visual experience of the appearance of a fire close to my body is normally accompanied by tactile experiences of heat, apparent smells of burning, the apparent hearing of cracklings or other distinctive firelike sounds, etc.—think here of other examples of your own.) But Locke has little to say as to just *how* these "concurrent reasons" are supposed to show that our beliefs concerning material objects that are arrived on the basis of our immediate sensory experiences are justified by those experiences. Does such a conclusion really follow, and, if so, how and why? . . .

In fact, Locke's supposed reasons are of very unequal weight. The first one is totally worthless, because it begs the very question at issue and also would require a prior solution of another, related epistemological problem. Until the problem of justifying belief in external objects on the basis of his sensory experience has been solved, Locke is obviously not in a position to appeal to supposed facts about other people's sense or-

gans, since sense organs are physical structures and so beliefs about them would have to be justified in just the way that is in question. Moreover, to invoke this first reason, he would also have to have justified beliefs about the mental states of other people, specifically concerning whether they do or do not have sensory ideas of the relevant sort. How this latter sort of knowledge is possible is a serious problem in itself (the "problem of other minds". . .) But it is pretty clear on reflection . . . that knowledge of other people's mental states normally depends on *prior* knowledge of the behavior and condition of their physical bodies, thus again presupposing the very knowledge of the material world that has not yet been accounted for. ② . . .

> ② Think about this problem: how do you know of the existence and specific character of other people's mental states? What reason do you have for thinking that they are not, for example, just cleverly designed robots that have no conscious mental states at all? (See Discussion Question 1.)

Locke's second reason is at least a bit better. The involuntary or spontaneous character of my sensory experience does at least distinguish it from other sorts of mental states and experience (albeit perhaps not in a completely sharp way—aren't many memories and even some imaginings similarly involuntary?). But this fact does not by itself seem to establish that immediate sensory experiences are, as he claims, caused by something external to the person who has them. Why couldn't my involuntary sensory experiences result instead from some subconscious or unconscious faculty of my own mind that is outside my voluntary control? And, even more obviously, that the ideas are involuntary tells us nothing at all about whether the external cause, if there is one, has the specific properties that my sensory experience seems to portray (whether it "resembles my ideas," as Locke would put it). Why couldn't the external cause of my idea of a green tree, again if there is one, neither be green nor have the other properties of a tree? Indeed, why couldn't it, as Berkeley will suggest, be something utterly different from a material object? And the third reason, while again perhaps showing that sensory experiences are importantly different from many other

---

*There may of course be *imagined* or *remembered* pain, but that is obviously not the same thing as really experienced pain.

mental phenomena, also does not support in any clear way a conclusion about what is responsible for this difference.

What about the fourth reason? Surely it is a striking fact that my various sensory experiences fit together in an extremely orderly and coherent fashion to depict an ongoing world that is both extremely complicated and highly regular or law-governed. The information or apparent information derived at a given time from one sense agrees to a very great degree with both that derived at that time from other senses and also with that derived from both the same sense and others at other times—allowing, of course, for the ongoing change and development of the world, which is also something that is reflected in regularities within our sensory experience. Thus if I seem to see a chair, I can normally also have the experience of touching it, given that I also have the experience of moving my body in the right direction and far enough. And the experiences that I have of the furniture and contents of my office before leaving for a class agree very well with the similar experiences that I have after I have apparently returned—allowing, in some cases, for the actions of the janitor or my dog (who is sometimes left there) or my wife (who has a key).③ . . .

> ③ Think of further examples of order and agreement between the perceptions of different senses or between the perceptions of one sense at different times, trying to specify them in detail.

But how exactly is this admittedly striking fact supposed to support Locke's intended conclusion, namely that there is good reason or justification for thinking that the beliefs about the material world that we arrive at on the basis of our immediate sensory experience are likely to be true? On this obviously crucial question, Locke has very little to say. . . .

In fact, if you think carefully about it, the order of my immediate sensory experience and the seeming agreement between experiences apparently produced by different senses would not be striking, or at least not nearly so striking, if those ideas were under my voluntary control—for then I could deliberately imagine an orderly world, in something like the way in which this is done by an artist or novelist. What makes the order so noteworthy is precisely that it is not voluntarily created, but just occurs spontaneously and, in

many of its details, unexpectedly. Thus we see that Locke's fourth "concurrent reason" needs to be supplemented by his second, and that it is these two *together* that might provide at least the beginnings of a real argument. Experience that was involuntary but chaotic would show very little, and neither would experience that was orderly but voluntarily controlled. It is experience that is *both* involuntary and highly orderly that seems to demand some sort of further *explanation:* what is it that produces and sustains the order? Thus it is natural to interpret Locke as arguing, admittedly without formulating the point very clearly or explicitly, that the *best explanation* of his involuntary but orderly experience is that it is systematically caused by a world of independent material objects which it depicts with at least approximate accuracy. (The main way in which the depiction is only approximately accurate is that, according to Locke, material objects have only *primary qualities* like size, shape, and motion, but not *secondary qualities* like color, smell, taste, and temperature (as felt).)

Does this argument really show that our beliefs about the material world that are arrived at on the basis of our involuntary sensory experience are likely to be true and hence justified? It seems reasonable to think that there must be *some* explanation for these features of our sensory ideas, which is just to say that the sort of order that they exhibit is extremely unlikely to result from mere chance. But is Locke's proposed explanation the right one?

Berkeley, while appealing to essentially the same features of our sensory ideas (their being independent of our will and their being orderly and coherent), offers a quite different and in his view superior explanation: that our sensory ideas are produced in our minds by God, who determines and controls their orderly character, so that there is thus no need or justification for supposing that the independent material realm advocated by Locke really exists. Berkeley's God obviously bears a striking resemblance to Descartes's evil genius, with the crucial difference that whereas Descartes assumes that the evil genius would be *deceiving* us, Berkeley's view is in effect that having sensory ideas systematically produced in us by God (presumably reflecting God's ideally complete picture of the world thus depicted) is *just what it is* for a world of ordinary objects to exist. Thus we have at least two competing explanations for the same facts concerning our sensory experience, and the question is how we should decide between such explanations.④

④ Can you think of any way to rationally choose between these two explanations? Can you think of any other possible explanations?

Assuming, that is, that we can rationally decide at all. Hume's response to the problem is to deny that *any* such attempt to explain our experience by appeal to objects or entities existing outside of that experience could ever be justified. An essential ingredient of both Locke's and Berkeley's proposed explanations is the claim that our immediately experienced sensory ideas (or "impressions," as Hume calls them, in order to distinguish them from other kinds of ideas) are *caused* by the external entities that those explanations invoke—by material objects, according to Locke's explanation, and by God, according to Berkeley's. Moreover, it seems obvious that any similar attempt to explain experience by appeal to something existing outside experience (even the person's own unconscious mind) will require a similar causal claim (for how else would the explanation work?). But, argues Hume, causal relations can be known only by *experiencing* the regular sequence of cause and effect, something that is impossible in the case of an alleged causal relation between something outside immediate experience and that experience itself. ⑤ In relation to Locke's explanation specifically, the point is that I cannot immediately experience material bodies causing my sensory ideas because I have no immediate experience of such bodies at all; and the claim that I *indirectly* perceive material bodies presupposes for its justification an explanation relying on the very causal relation in question and so cannot be used to establish that such a causal relation exists.

⑤ For Hume's discussion of this, see the selection in the induction section. Is Hume right that causal relations are always known by repeated experiences of the sequence of cause and effect? Think here of various examples of causal relations that seem to be known. Can you think of any plausible causal claims that don't seem to be known in this way?

Hume's further discussion of the issue of the external world is characteristically muddled by his general tendency to conflate and confuse issues concerning justification with issues having to do with the psychological causation or genesis of the beliefs in question. . . . But it is nonetheless easy to see how a Hume who was clearer about the distinction between psychological explanation and epistemic justification might have argued that the content of our claims about material objects, to the extent that this is justified, must have to do *solely* with features and patterns of our sensory experience, rather than with genuinely mind-transcendent objects.⑥ . . .

⑥ The phenomenalist view is at least similar to Berkeley's view of material objects, though without the reference to God: for both views, material objects exist only as patterns of ideas or experiences or sense-data in minds, and have no existence outside of all minds (that would be "mind-transcendent" existence).

Thus we have initial adumbrations of the two main views that we will now proceed to discuss more systematically. Locke's view, according to which our subjective sensory experience and the beliefs that we adopt on the basis of it constitute a *representation* of the external material world, one that is caused by that world and that we are justified in thinking to be at least approximately accurate, is a version of the more general position known as *representationalism* or *representative realism*. (So also is Descartes's view.) The second main view, which Hume's discussion suggests but never quite arrives at, is that (i) we can have no knowledge (or perhaps even no intelligible conception) of a realm of external causes of our experience, but also (ii) that our beliefs about the material world can still be in general justified and true because their content in fact has to do only with the features and order of our subjective experience. This is the view that has come to be known as *phenomenalism,* a version of idealism. (Contrary to what is often suggested, Berkeley's "idealist" view is not in fact in any clear way an anticipation of phenomenalism, but rather in effect a curious version of representationalism, in which our perceptual ideas constitute partial representations of the much more complete picture of the material world constituted by God's much more complete ideas; to take Berkeley to be a proto-phenomenalist is to ignore the central role of God in his view.) Yet a third possibility would be the essentially skeptical view that we can know that our experiences are externally caused in *some* way, but can know nothing further about the nature of those causes.* Such a skeptical view would, of course not be a *solution* to the problem of the external world, but rather a confession that there is no solution; it is thus a view to be adopted only after the other two possibilities have clearly failed.

Historically, the objections to the representationalism of Descartes and Locke, especially the Humean one discussed above, were widely taken to be decisive, with positions in the direction of phenomenalism being viewed as the main nonskeptical alternative, especially in the first two-thirds or so on the twentieth century. Thus we will begin our more systematic discussion with a consideration of phenomenalism, and then return later to the consideration of representationalism that was begun in the discussion of Locke.

PHENOMENALISM

As just briefly formulated, the phenomenalist view is that the content of propositions about material objects and the material world is *entirely* concerned with features and relations of the immediate objects of our perceptual experience, that is, the features and relations of our sense-data. According to the phenomenalist, to believe that a physical or material object of a certain sort exists just *is* to believe that sense-data of various sorts have been experienced, are being experienced, will be experienced, and/or would be experienced under certain specifiable conditions. Thus, for example, to believe that there is a large brown table in a certain room in the University of Washington Library is to believe, roughly, (i) that the sorts of sense-data that seem from a commonsense standpoint to reflect the presence of such a table either have been, are presently, or will in the future be experienced in the context of other sense-data, themselves experienced concurrently or immediately before or after,

that reflect the location as the room in question; and in addition—or instead, if the table has never in fact been perceived and never in fact will be perceived—(ii) that such sense-data *would* be experienced *if* other sense-data that reflect the perceiver's going to the library and to that room were experienced. (This is quite a complicated specification, and you will have to think very carefully about what it is saying.)†⑦

⑦ Try to spell out the details of this example, and think of others of your own.

In a fairly standard formula, to believe that such a material object exists is, according to the phenomenalist, to believe nothing more than that sense-data of the appropriate sort are actual (in the past, present, or future) and/or possible—where to say that certain sense-data are *possible* is to say, not just that it is logically possible for them to be experienced (which would apparently always be so as long as the description of them is not contradictory), but that they *would* in fact actually be experienced under certain specifiable circumstances (specifiable in sense-datum terms); thus it would be somewhat clearer to speak of actual and *obtainable* sense-data. The British philosopher John Stuart Mill put this point by saying that material objects are nothing but "permanent possibilities of sensation," that is, of sense-data—where, of course, the possibilities in question are only *relatively* permanent, since objects can change or be destroyed. The crucial thing to see is that what Mill and the other phenomenalists are saying is that there are no independently existing objects that are responsible for the possibilities of sensation or the obtainability of sense-data; the actuality and obtainability of sense-data are *all there is* to the physical or material world.

Phenomenalism is in fact one of those occasional (some would say more than occasional) philosophical views that is *so* monumentally bizarre and implausible, at least from anything close to a commonsense

---

*This third possibility bears some resemblance to Immanuel Kant's view (in the *Critique of Pure Reason*), which is, confusingly, also sometimes referred to with the term "phenomenalism."

†This specification and those that follow seem on the surface to suggest that any person who has beliefs about physical objects must be thinking explicitly in terms of sense-data (and so must possess the concept of a sense-datum), something that is extremely implausible (think about it). Phenomenalists have not in fact generally wanted to make such a claim, and have attempted to avoid it by saying that the sense-datum formulation is what the content of the beliefs "really amounts to" or is how it is correctly to be "philosophically analyzed." Whether the ideas involved in such formulations really succeed in solving this apparent problem is an issue that I cannot pursue further here.

standpoint, as to perhaps make it difficult . . . to believe that it really says what it does—and even more difficult to believe that such a view has in fact sometimes been widely advocated and (apparently) believed, indeed that it was arguably the dominant view concerning the problem of the external world for a good portion of the twentieth century. The first and most important thing to say about this situation is that you must not, as sometimes happens, allow it to cause you to fail to understand what the view is saying by trying to make it more reasonable than it is. The phenomenalist really is saying that there is *nothing more* to the material world (including, of course, our own physical bodies! . . .) than our subjective sensory experiences and the possibility, in the sense explained, of further such experiences (though there is, as we will eventually see, a serious problem about the "our").

But why should such an obviously implausible view be taken seriously, even for a moment? We have already in fact encountered the essential ingredients of the main argument for phenomenalism, but it will be helpful to reiterate them in a somewhat more explicit fashion. One main premise of the argument is the Humean thesis that causal relations can be known only via experience of the causal sequence, so that, as already explained, there is no way in which a causal relation between the immediate content of experience and something outside that immediate content could be known, and hence no way to justifiably invoke such external causes as explanations of that experience. This thesis has a good deal of initial plausibility, and can be rebutted only by offering some other account of how causal relations can be known. The other main premise is simply the commonsense conviction that skepticism is false, that we do *obviously* have justified beliefs and knowledge concerning ordinary objects like trees and rocks and buildings and about the material world in which they exist. And the argument is then just that the only way that such justified beliefs and knowledge are possible, given that no causal or

explanatory inference from immediate experience to material objects that are genuinely external to that experience could ever even in principle be justified, is if the content of our beliefs about the material world does not really have to do with objects existing outside our immediate experience, but instead pertains just to the objects of that experience and the order that they manifest.⑧ Most phenomenalists will admit that this seems initially very implausible, but will try to argue that this apparent implausibility is in some way an illusion, one that can be explained away once the phenomenalist view and the considerations in favor of it have been fully understood.*

⑧ This is similar to Berkeley's argument, except that Berkeley claims only that causal relations between experience and external material objects are unknowable. Does Berkeley have any good reasons for thinking that causation of experience by God is more knowable?

OBJECTIONS TO PHENOMENALISM

The foregoing argument, like most arguments for implausible philosophical views that are nonetheless widely held, is a serious argument, one not easily dismissed. Neither premise is easy to rebut, and the conclusion does seem to follow from these premises. But it is, of course, still abundantly obvious that this conclusion cannot be correct, and so that something must have gone wrong. For it is obvious upon even the slightest unbiased reflection that the content of propositions about physical or material objects does pertain, whether justifiably or not, to a realm of entities that, if genuine, exist outside of our minds and experiences in an independent physical realm.

This basic insight seems in fact to constitute by itself a more than adequate reason to reject phenomenalism. But since it nevertheless amounts to little more than a direct, unargued denial of the view, it will be useful to see if we can find further objections and

---

*There is also a second fairly widely advocated argument for phenomenalism, one that starts from the premise that all intelligible ideas or concepts are derived by "abstraction" from immediate experience, so that we arguably could not even *understand* the idea of objects existing outside of that experience. If this were so, and if (as again seems obvious) we do understand the idea or concept of a physical or material object, then it would follow that this idea or concept is not about transexperiential objects, and so apparently can only be about some feature or aspect of experience itself. The problem with this argument is that the initial premise about the derivation of concepts is far less obviously correct than is the claim that we do in fact obviously have ideas or concepts, indeed lots of them, that are about things outside immediate experience, making it far more reasonable to reject the conclusion than to accept the premise.

problems of a more articulated sort pertaining to phenomenalism. (Considering such objections and the responses available to the phenomenalist will also help you to better understand the view.) In fact, there are many such objections and problems that have been advanced. Here we will be content with a few of the most interesting ones.

Consider, first, what is perhaps the most obvious question about the phenomenalist view: *Why,* according to the phenomenalist, are the orderly sense-data in question obtainable or "permanently possible"? What is the *explanation* for the pattern of actual and obtainable sense experiences that allegedly constitutes the existence of a material object or of the material world as a whole, if this is not to be explained by appeal to genuinely external objects? The only possible phenomenalist response to this question is to say that the fact that sensory experience reflects this sort of order is simply the most fundamental fact about reality, not further explainable in terms of anything else. For *any* attempted further explanation, since it would obviously have to appeal to something outside of that experience, would be (for the reasons already discussed) unjustified and unknowable. The phenomenalist will add that it is obvious anyway that not everything can be explained, since each explanation just introduces some further fact for which an explanation might be demanded.

But while this last point seems correct (doesn't it?), it seems quite implausible to suppose that something as large and complicated as the total order of our immediate experience has no explanation at all—and also very obvious that common sense (at least if it accepted perceptual subjectivism) would regard claims about material objects as providing such an explanation, rather than as just a redescription of the experiential order itself (as the phenomenalist claims them to be). Perhaps, for all we have seen so far, the phenomenalist is right that we cannot ever know that any such explanation is correct, but this, if so, is an argument for *skepticism* about the material world, not a justification for perversely reinterpreting the meaning or content of claims about material objects. (Here it is important to be very clear that phenomenalism is *not* supposed to be a skeptical view, but rather an account of how beliefs about material objects are indeed justified and do constitute knowledge—given the phenom-

enalist account of the content of such beliefs.)⑨

A second problem (or rather a set of related problems) has to do with the specification of the *conditions* under which the various sense-data that (according to phenomenalism) are what a material-object proposition is about either are or would be experienced. It is clear that such conditions must be specified to have even a hope of capturing the content of at least most such propositions in sense-datum terms. To recur to our earlier example, to say merely that the sense-data that are characteristic of a brown table are actual or obtainable in some circumstances or other may perhaps capture the content of the claim that the world contains at least one brown table (though even that is doubtful), but surely not of any more specific claim, such as the one about such a table being in a particular room in the University of Washington Library. For that, as we saw briefly, conditions must be specified that say, as it were, that it is in relation to that particular room that the sense-data are or would be experienced. (But remember here that for the phenomenalist, the room does not exist as a mind-external place; talk of a room or of any physical location is to be understood merely as a way of indicating one aspect of the order of immediate experience, namely that the various sense-data that reflect the various features ascribed to the room tend to be experienced together or in close succession, with this whole "cluster" of sense-data standing in similar relations to the further sense-data that pertain to the surrounding area.)

What makes this problem extremely difficult at best is that for phenomenalism to be a viable position, the conditions under which sense-data are experienced or obtainable must themselves (as just in effect indicated) be specifiable in terms of *other sense-data,* not in terms of material objects and structures such as the library or room in question. For the essential claim of phenomenalism is that the content of propositions about material objects can be *entirely* given in terms of sense-data. If in specifying the conditions under which the actual and obtainable sense-data relevant to one material-object proposition would occur, it were necessary to make reference to other material

⑨ The phenomenalist, like Berkeley, means to be giving an account of what the existence of ordinary objects amounts to, *not* to be denying their existence.

objects, then the account of the content of the first proposition would not yet be completely in sense-datum terms. And if in specifying the conditions relevant to claims about those other material objects, still other material objects would have to be mentioned, and so on, then the phenomenalist account would never be complete. If the content of propositions about material objects cannot be given *entirely* in terms of sense-data, if that content involves essential and ineliminable reference to further such objects, then phenomenalism fails.

There are in fact many problems here, but we may continue to focus on the one suggested by the example of the table in the library room. How can the idea that sense-data are or would be observed in a certain location be adequately captured in purely sense-datum terms? The natural response, which was in effect invoked when the example was originally discussed, is to appeal to the idea of a *sensory route:* a series of juxtaposed and often overlapping sense-data that would be experienced in what we think of intuitively as moving to the location in question. (But, to reiterate, there is not supposed to be any real mind-external location or bodily movement; according to the phenomenalist, claims about this sort of experienced movement have to do *only* with sequences of sense-data that are experienced or could be experienced—including those that we think of intuitively as the feelings associated with bodily movements like walking.)

There are at least two serious problems pertaining to this answer, however. One is that there are normally many *different* sensory routes to a given location, depending on where one starts and how one approaches it; and if the starting location is itself determined by a previous sensory route, then a regress threatens, in which the sensory conditions must go further and further back in time without ever reaching a place from which they can begin. A second problem is that it seems clear that we can often understand the claim that a certain material object or set of objects exists at a certain physical location without having any clear idea of the relevant sensory route: for example, I understand the claim that there are penguins at the South Pole, but have no clear idea of the sensory route that I would have to follow to guarantee or even make it likely that I have reached the South Pole. (Note that it is a *guarantee* that is actually required, for otherwise the content of the claim in question as not been fully captured.)*

An alternative possibility† is that the relevant location can be adequately identified in sensory terms by specifying other sense-data that would, as it were, be experienced there, rather than by a sensory route: by those pertaining to the local scenery or landmarks or reflecting locating measurements of some kind. Perhaps there are some locations where this would work (though one must remember such things as movie sets and amusement parks and, before long, virtual reality devices). But we must remember that it is the content of the original material object proposition that is supposed to be reflected in these specifications, and it seems abundantly clear (but this is again something to think about carefully and in detail) that there are many, many propositions about material objects in various locations that I can understand perfectly well without having in mind any adequate way of identifying that location in purely sensory terms— or, to bring in the other possibility, a way of specifying a sensory route from some location that I can thus identify.

And there is also the related, but still much more difficult problem of what the phenomenalist can say about the content of propositions about material objects and events in the *past,* perhaps the very distant past. Consider this one carefully on your own, focusing on the most difficult case: past events that were not observed by anyone at the time in question. Under what sensory conditions would sense-data of a tree have to have been obtainable to make it true that there was a pine tree in the place now occupied by my house in 1000 B.C.? It is thus very doubtful that the sort of specification of conditions that the phenomenalist needs is possible in general.

. . .

---

*See A. J. Ayer, "Phenomenalism," *Proceedings of the Aristotelian Society,* vol. 47 (1946–47), pp. 189–91, for a discussion of this example.

†Suggested by Ayer, *ibid.*

A . . . final objection to phenomenalism, one that is, thankfully, much simpler and more straightforward, concerns what the phenomenalist must apparently say about the knowledge of the mental states of people other than myself (or other than whoever is thinking about the issue—for reasons that will become clear, each of you will have to formulate this issue for yourselves). The whole thrust of the phenomenalist position, as we have seen, is that *any* inference beyond immediate experience is impossible, that claims that might seem to be about things outside of experience must, if they are to be justified and knowable, be understood as pertaining only to features and orderly patterns of that experience. But the mental states of *other* people, their experiences and feelings and conscious thoughts, are surely outside of *my* immediate experience. Indeed, to reach justified conclusions about what people distinct from me are genuinely thinking and experiencing would apparently require *two* inferences: first, an inference from my immediate experience of sense-data pertaining to their physical bodies to conclusions about those bodies; and then, second, an inference from the facts about those bodies thus arrived at to further conclusions about the minds and mental states of the people in question. *Both* of these inferences depend on causal relations that are, according to the phenomenalist, unknowable, because we cannot experience both sides, or in the second case even one side, of the relation; and thus neither inference, construed in that way, is justified according to the basic phenomenalist outlook.

What phenomenalism must apparently say here, in order to be consistent, is (i) that the content of propositions about the conditions and behavior of other people's bodies (like that of all other material object propositions) pertains only to facts about *my* immediate experience; and (ii) that the content of further claims about the mental states associated with those bodies is only a further, more complicated and less direct description of, once again, *my* experience. Though the phenomenalist would perhaps resist putting it this way, the upshot is that *my* mind and mental states, including my immediate experience, is the only

mind and the only collection of mental states that genuinely exist, with claims that are apparently about other minds amounting only to further descriptions of this one mind and its experiences. This is the view known as *solipsism*—which each of you must obviously formulate for yourselves (assuming that any of you are really out there!). It seems clearly to be an absurd consequence, thus yielding a really decisive objection, if one were still needed, to phenomenalism.*

BACK TO REPRESENTATIONALISM

If phenomenalism is indeed untenable, and assuming that we continue to accept perceptual subjectivism, then the only nonskeptical alternative apparently left is *representationalism:* the view, restating it a bit, that our immediately experienced sense-data, together with the further beliefs that we arrive at on the basis of them, constitute a *representation* or depiction of an independent realm of material objects—one that we are in general, according to the representationalist, justified in believing to be true.

Defenses of representationalism have taken a variety of forms, but I will assume here that the best sort of defense for such a view is one along the general lines that we found to be suggested, albeit not very explicitly, in Locke (and indeed also, though even less explicitly, in Descartes). The central idea is, first, that (contrary to the claim of the phenomenalist) some *explanation* is needed for the complicated and intricate order that we find in our involuntarily experienced sense-data . . . ; and, second, that the *best* explanation, that is, the one most likely to be correct, is that those experiences are caused by and, with certain qualifications, systematically reflect the character of a world of genuinely independent material objects, which we accordingly have good reasons for believing to exist.

I have already remarked that representationalism was widely repudiated as untenable during most of the period between Locke and recent times, with the main argument being the one that we found in Hume about the unknowability of any causal relation be-

---

*A woman once allegedly wrote to Bertrand Russell that she found solipsism to be so obviously a correct view that she couldn't understand why it wasn't more widely accepted. (Think about it!)

tween something outside experience and experience itself. We will begin by looking further at that argument and considering in a general way how it might be answered. Having argued that representationalism cannot be simply ruled out as impossible in the way that Hume tries to do, we will then consider the further issue of whether and how the specific explanation of experience that the representationalist proposes can be defended against other alternatives, such as Berkeley's. Finally, we will look at the significant qualification, already briefly mentioned, advocated by Descartes, Locke, and many others with regard to the accuracy with which our experience represents the true character of material objects: the one having to do with the distinction between *primary* and *secondary* qualities.

A RESPONSE TO HUME'S ARGUMENT: THEORETICAL OR EXPLANATORY INFERENCE

To recall, Hume's objection to representationalism rests on the premise that causal relations can be known only by experiencing the regular sequence between cause and effect, which requires experiencing both sides of the causal relation. This, he argues, is impossible for an alleged causal relation between something outside of direct experience and the experience itself, so that the claim that such a causal relation exists can never be justified or known.* And therefore, he concludes, neither can the representationalist's proposed explanation of the order of our experience, since that depends essentially on such an unknowable and unjustifiable causal claim.

If Hume's initial premise is accepted, then the rest of his argument seems to follow. But should that premise be accepted? One way to approach this issue is to consider examples where we seem to reason in ways that conflict with that premise but which still seem intuitively cogent. Here I will consider [one ex-

ample] of this kind, . . . having to do with knowledge concerning unobservable entities and events, such as electrons or quarks or radioactivity, in theoretical physics. In [this case], we seem intuitively to have justified belief and knowledge pertaining to causal relations that could not be arrived at in the way that Hume's premise, if correct, would require. (In considering [this example], we adopt the standpoint of common sense, thus assuming that the problem of the external world has—somehow—been solved.)

. . .

[In the] case of unobservable scientific entities and events[,] . . . we seem to have justified belief and knowledge concerning causal relations among such entities and events and between them and various sorts of observable results, even though the entities and events themselves cannot be experienced in even the indirect sense: knowledge, for example, that radioactivity results from the splitting or decay of various sorts of atoms and that it produces a crackling sound in a Geiger counter. Obviously beliefs concerning relations of these kinds cannot be justified by experiencing both sides of the causal relation in the way that Hume's premise would require.

Notice carefully that the claim so far is *not* that these alleged cases of causal knowledge are genuine, so that Hume's premise would have to be mistaken. It is possible for a proponent of Hume's view to respond by claiming either that we do not really have the causal knowledge in question (or possibly, though this seems even more difficult to defend, that it can in fact be somehow accounted for in a way that is compatible with the Humean claim). Thus defenders of Hume's view have often also been advocates . . . of *fictionalism* (the view that seemingly unobservable scientific entities do not really exist, but only reflect ways of talking that help to systematically describe observations). But [this view seems] desperately implausible, so that if a reasonably plausible general

---

*Notice that Hume's thesis would *not* rule out the experiential justification of claims about a causal relation between two material objects or events, as long as we are assuming that the problem presently under discussion, the problem of the external world, has been somehow solved. For then both of the relevant objects or events could be claimed to be *indirectly* experienced by experiencing the relevant sense-data. But this notion of indirectly experiencing something obviously cannot be invoked in this way where it is exactly the justification of the transition from immediately experienced sense-data to indirectly experienced material objects that is in question.

account can be given of how such causal knowledge can be justifiably arrived at, this would be enough to warrant the rejection of Hume's premise and the argument that results from it. ⑩

The account that has been offered, by a series of philosophers of whom the first was probably the American philosopher Charles Sanders Peirce, holds that knowledge of the sort in question depends on a fundamental and sometimes unrecognized mode of reasoning, one that is quite distinct from both deductive reasoning and . . . inductive reasoning . . . . Peirce called it "abductive reasoning," but it is perhaps more perspicuously characterized as *theoretical* or *explanatory* reasoning. In reasoning of this sort, a hypothesis is advanced to explain some relevant set of data and is justified simply on the basis of being the *best explanation* of the data in question.*⑪ Exactly what makes an explanation the *best* is a difficult and complicated issue, as we will see to some extent below, but the point for the moment is that *if* such an assessment can be defended, then it allegedly becomes justifiable to accept the entire explanatory hypothesis, *including any causal claims that it may involve,* on that basis—without any requirement that there be experiential evidence of the sort that Hume's premise would require for those causal claims by themselves. Thus for example

when the entire physical theory of radioactive isotopes and their decay into other kinds of atoms is justified as the best explanation of a variety of observed phenomena, including the fogging of photographic film, changes in the composition of samples, tracks in cloud chambers, etc., the causal relations between the various kinds of atoms and particles and also between these unobservable entities and processes and their observable manifestations are justified as part of the total package, with accordingly no need for them to be justified separately.

A full defense of the idea of theoretical or explanatory reasoning is obviously not possible [here]. The suggestion for the moment is only that the idea is plausible enough, especially in light of examples like those given, to make it reasonable to reject Hume's thesis about knowledge of causal relations, at least tentatively, thus opening the door to the possibility that the representationalist position on the problem of the external world might be defensible after all. ⑫

THE REPRESENTATIONALIST EXPLANATION

But this only opens the door. We still need to worry about whether the representationalist's proposed explanation of our experience is really the *best* one. And before we can do that, we need to consider in substantially more detail what the rationale for that explanation might be and how it is supposed to work.

The place to start is to ask what it is about the character of our immediate sensory experience that points to or perhaps even seems to demand such an explanation. As we saw earlier, Locke points to two features of our experience in this connection: its involuntary character and its systematic order. But while these features may indeed demand *some* sort of explanation, they do not, at least when described at that level of abstraction, seem to point at all clearly at the specific one that the representationalist favors (which is why the door is seemingly open to

⑩ This is a *counterexample* to Hume's general claim about knowledge of causality: a case where the sort of knowledge that he rejects as impossible seems nonetheless to exist. How clear is it that such knowledge is genuine (and hence that fictionalism is mistaken)?

⑪ Deductive reasoning is reasoning that is logically conclusive and entirely a priori. Inductive reasoning, as BonJour is using the term, is reasoning that involves simple generalization from observed patterns in experience: from the observation of many ravens that are black (and none that are any other color) to the conclusion that all ravens are black. Abductive reasoning also depends on observations, but concludes to an explanation in other terms rather than just a generalization. (Sometimes the term "induction" is used for both of these last sorts of reasoning, but they are nonetheless importantly different.)

⑫ Theoretical or explanatory reasoning is in fact quite common. Try to think of other examples.

---

*Thus the sort of reasoning in question is also sometimes referred to as "inference to the best explanation."

Berkeley's alternative). If anything about experience does this, it will thus have to be, I would suggest, more specific features than any that Locke explicitly mentions.

Here is a question for you to think hard about, preferably before reading beyond this paragraph—one that is both historically and substantively as fundamental as any in the whole field of epistemology. Think as carefully as you can about your immediate sensory experience: your experience of qualities like colors and shapes and apparent spatial relations and apparent sounds and tactile qualities and so on. You are presently experiencing patterns of black and white marks that according to the representationalist are caused by and represent the pages of this book, along with other colors reflecting the immediate surrounding environment; your auditory sensations might be those allegedly reflecting the steps of people in the library or the music that you listen to while you read; you have tactile sensations allegedly reflecting things like the book in your hand, the chair or couch you are sitting on, and so on; perhaps there is an odd smell of some sort as well. What, if anything, about those experienced qualities *taken in themselves* suggests that their source or cause is an independent realm of material objects of the sort that the representationalist advocates? Why, apart from mere familiarity, does such an explanation of experience seem so natural and compelling?

My suggestion is that the answer to this question has two main parts. The first points to the presence in immediate experience of repeatable *sequences* of experienced qualities, qualities that overlap and often shade gradually into one another. Here I have in mind something like the "sensory routes" that are, as discussed earlier, invoked by the phenomenalist. While these "sensory routes" cannot ultimately do the job that the phenomenalist needs them to do, for the reasons given there, they are nonetheless very real and pervasive. Think of the ways in which such "sensory routes" can be experienced in opposite orders (imagine here what common sense would regard as walking from one place to another and then returning to the first place by the same route—perhaps even walking

backwards, so as to make the two sequences as similar as possible). Think of the ways in which such "sensory routes" intersect with each other, thus, for example, allowing one to get from one end to the other without going through the "route" itself, thereby delineating a sensory loop. Think of the resulting structure of a whole set of overlapping and intersecting "sensory routes."*

Here it may be helpful, as a kind of analogy, to think from a commonsense standpoint of how you would go about programming a computer game to simulate a "space" containing "objects" through which the computer character can move. You would program successive "screens" of visually observable colors and shapes in such a way as to mimic the appearance of objects that are gradually approached and passed, perhaps with concomitant sound qualities that get louder and then softer and imaginably even other systematically varying qualities like smells or temperatures. (Perhaps the game is played in an enclosed booth that can be heated or cooled.) You would also include some controllable way in which the character can be made to face in different directions, move at different rates, and stand still. In these terms, my suggestion is that our actual immediate experience has more or less exactly the features that an ideal program of this sort would create. (Again, you will have to ponder this point, "chew on" it, in relation to a range of your own examples, in order to fully understand it.)

The idea is then that at least the most obvious and natural explanation of these features of our experience is that we are located in a spatial realm of objects through which we move and of which we can perceive at any given moment only the limited portion that is close enough to be accessible to our various senses (what this requires differs from sense to sense)—a kind of experiential "tunnel." Our experience reflects both the qualities of these objects and the different perspectives from which they are perceived as we gradually approach them from different directions, at different speeds, under different conditions of perception, etc. Thus the relatively permanent structure of this spatial array of objects is partially reflected in the much more temporary and

---

*For a much more extensive elaboration of this general sort of point, see H. H. Price, *Perception* (London: Methuen, 1932; 2nd ed., 1950).

variable, but broadly repeatable features of our immediate experience. . . . ⑬

⑬ Think carefully about patterns of experience of the sort indicated, making them as detailed as possible. Think about why the hypothesis that the experiences are caused by a stable world of external objects seems to explain those experiences quite well. Can you think of any alternative explanation that doesn't invoke a being like Berkeley's God or a Cartesian evil genius?

The second part of the answer to the question of what it is about the character of immediate experience that points to the representationalist explanation cites the fact, already noticed in our discussion of phenomenalism, that the experiential order just described, though undeniably impressive, is in fact *incomplete* or *fragmentary* in a number of related ways. The easiest way to indicate these is by reference to the sorts of situations that, from a commonsense standpoint, produce and explain them (though the representationalist cannot, of course, assume at this stage, without begging the question, that these things are what is actually going on). Imagine then traversing a "sensory route" of the sort just indicated, but doing so (i) with one's eyes closed (or one's ears plugged, etc.) during some of the time required, or perhaps while asleep during part of the time (traveling in a car or train); or (ii) while the conditions of perception, including those pertaining to the functioning of your sense-organs and to your mental "processing," are changing or being varied (involving such things as changing lighting, including complete darkness; jaundice and similar diseases that affect perception; objects and conditions that temporarily block or interfere with perception; even something as simple as turning one's head in a different direction, blinking, or wiping one's eyes). If you think about it carefully, you will see that interfering factors of these various kinds make the sensory sequences that define the various "routes" far less regular and dependable than they might at first seem. . . . ⑭

⑭ Try to think of specific examples of fragmentary or interrupted order. How common are they?

Thus the basic claim is that the realm of immediate sensory experience, of sense-data . . . , is both *too orderly* not to demand an explanation and *not orderly*

enough for that explanation to be that the sense-data have an intrinsic order of their own. What this strongly suggests, the representationalist will argue, is an independent realm of objects outside our experience, one that has its own patterns of (mainly spatial) order, with the partial and fragmentary order of our experience resulting from our partial and intermittent perceptual contact with that larger and more stable realm.

The discussion so far provides only an initial and highly schematic picture of the representationalist's proposed explanation. It would have to be filled out in a number of ways in order to be even approximately complete. Here I will be content with three further points. First, the main focus of the discussion so far has been on *spatial* properties of material objects and the features of immediate experience that seem to suggest them. Thus the result to this point is at best only a kind of skeletal picture of the material world, one that would have to be "fleshed out" in various ways in order to even approximate the commonsense picture of the world. In fact, it is useful to think of the representationalist explanation as starting with spatial properties as a first and most fundamental stage and then adding further refinements to that starting point.

Second, the main addition to this initial spatial picture of the world would be various sorts of *causal* relations among material objects and between such objects and perceivers, together with the causal and dispositional properties of objects (flammability, solubility, malleability, brittleness, toxicity, etc.) that underlie such relations. These are, from the representationalist standpoint, basically added in order to explain apparent changes in material objects that are reflected in relatively permanent changes in the otherwise stable "sensory routes." Here it is important to note that like the stable spatial order, the causal regularities that pertain to material objects are only intermittently and fragmentarily reflected in immediate experience, partially for the reasons already considered, but also because any given perceiver may simply not be in the right position to observe the beginning or end or some intermediate part of a given causal sequence, even though other parts are experienced. Simple examples would include throwing a rock into the air without seeing or hearing it land, pulling on a string without observing the movement of an object at the other end (or seeing the object move but without observing the movement of part of the intervening string), or planting a seed and returning later to find a well-developed plant.

Third, there is the issue of primary and secondary qualities. As already noted, Locke's view is that material objects have *primary* qualities like size, shape, and motion through space, but not *secondary* qualities like color, smell, taste, and felt temperature, a view with which most other representationalists have tended to agree. Here it will suffice to focus on color, surely the most apparently pervasive and interesting of the secondary qualities.* Clearly to deny that material objects are genuinely colored complicates the representationalist's proposed explanation by making the relation between material objects and our immediate experiences much less straightforward than it would otherwise be: according to such a view, whereas our immediate experiences of spatial properties are caused more or less directly by closely related spatial properties of objects (allowing, importantly, for perspective), our immediate experiences of color properties are caused by utterly different properties of material objects, primarily by how their surfaces differentially reflect wavelengths of light.

Locke offers little real argument for this view, but the argument he seems to have in mind† is that as the causal account of the material world develops, it turns out that ascribing a property like color (construed as the "sensuous" property that is present in immediate visual experience) to material objects is in fact quite useless for explaining our experiences of colors. What colors we experience depend on the properties of the light that strikes our eyes and this in turn, in the most standard cases, depend on how material objects reflect

and absorb light, which yet in turn depends on the structure of their surfaces as constituted by primary and causal properties. I think that this is correct as a matter of science, but the important point for the moment is that *if* it is correct, then the denial that material objects are really colored simply follows from the basic logic of the representationalist position: according to representationalism, the only justification for ascribing *any* property to the material world is that it best explains some aspect of our immediate experience, so that the ascription of properties that do not figure in such explanations is automatically unjustified. ⑮

> ⑮ Is this a good reason for thinking that color is not a genuine feature of external material objects? (See Discussion Question 2.)

ALTERNATIVES TO THE REPRESENTATIONALIST EXPLANATION

The discussion so far has perhaps made a reasonable case, though of course nothing like a conclusive one, first, that the representationalist's proposed explanation of the order of our immediate experience cannot be ruled out on Humean grounds; and, second, that this explanation has a good deal of plausibility in relation to that experience. But this is still not enough to show that it is the *best* explanation and hence the one, even assuming the general acceptability of theoretical reasoning, whose acceptance is thereby justified. Here we are essentially back to the question posed very early on in this chapter: why, if at all, should the explanation of our experience that invokes external, mind-independent material objects be preferred to

---

*There are at least two further related questions lurking in the vicinity, which there is no space to adequately consider here. One concerns the way in which the two groups of qualities are distinguished. Primary qualities are predominantly spatial or geometrical in character. As noted earlier, however, Locke adds *solidity* to the list of primary qualities. What he has in mind by this is not entirely clear, but solidity seems to be *either* the feeling of resistance that a rigid object produces when touched (in which case, it seems to belong with the secondary qualities) or else the causal capacity of preventing other objects from occupying the same space (in which case it is a causal property, what Locke calls a "power," and again not a primary quality on a par with the others, all of which are directly reflected in experience). The other issue concerns Locke's apparent view that all genuine qualities of material objects amount in the end to primary qualities or patterns of primary qualities. This would include all "powers" or causal capacities, including the causal capacities that are responsible for producing experiences of color and other secondary qualities in human perceivers. But this cannot be right if the primary qualities are the merely spatial or geometrical ones: a real object cannot have only properties of these sorts, since it would otherwise be indistinguishable from a geometrically specified region of empty space.

†Originally put forth by his friend Robert Boyle (the discoverer of the law pertaining to the behavior of gases that bears his name).

other possible explanations such as Berkeley's (or the very similar if not identical one that appeals to Descartes's evil genius)?

It should be obvious that Berkeley's explanatory hypothesis is capable of explaining the very same features of immediate experience that the representationalist appeals to. All that is needed, as suggested earlier, is for God to have an ideally complete conception or picture of the representationalist's material world and then to systematically cause experiences in perceivers that reflect their apparent location in and movement through such a world. (This assumes that God can recognize intentions to "move" in various directions and adjust the person's perceptions accordingly; of course, no genuine movement really takes place, nor does the perceiver really have a physical location.*) A different, but essentially parallel explanatory hypothesis, is provided by a science fiction scenario: the perceiver is a disembodied brain floating in a vat of brain nutrients and receiving electrical impulses from a computer that again contains an ideally complete model or representation of a material world and generates the impulses accordingly, taking account of motor impulses received from the brain that reflect the person's intended movements. And further explanatory hypotheses can be generated according to the same basic formula: there must be some sort of a representation or model of a material world together with some sort of mechanism (which need not be mechanical in the ordinary sense) that systematically produces experience in perceivers, allowing for their subjectively intended movements. *Any* pattern of immediate experience that can be explained by the representationalist's explanatory hypothesis can thus automatically be also explained by explanatory hypotheses of this latter sort, probably indefinitely many of them, with no possible experiential basis for deciding between them or between any one of them and the representationalist hypothesis.

If there is to be a reason for favoring the representationalist hypothesis, therefore, it will have to be a *priori* in character, and it is more than a little difficult to see what it might be. Here I will limit myself to one fairly tentative suggestion. . . .

One striking contrast between the representationalist's explanatory hypothesis and the others we have looked at is that under the representationalist view there is a clear intuitive sense in which the qualities of the objects that explain our immediate experience are directly reflected in the character of that experience itself, so that the latter can be said to be, allowing for perspective and perhaps other sorts of distortion, experiences of the former, albeit indirect ones. Once again this applies most straightforwardly to spatial properties: thus, for example, the rectangular or trapezoidal shape that is immediately experienced can be said to be an indirect perception of a rectangular face of the material object that causes that experience. In contrast, the features of the elements in the other explanatory hypotheses that are responsible for the various features of our experience are not directly reflected in that experience. For example, what is responsible in these other hypotheses for the rectangular or trapezoidal shape in my immediate experience is one aspect of God's total picture or conception of a material world, or perhaps one aspect of a representation of such a world stored in a computer. This aspect has in itself no shape of any sort (or at least, in the case of the computer, none that is at all relevant to the shape that I experience); it is merely a *representation* of a related shape, according to some system of representation or coding. Thus its relation to the character of the experience that it is supposed to explain is inherently less direct, more convoluted than in the case of the representationalist's explanation.

My suggestion is that the inherently less direct, more convoluted character of the way that these competing explanatory hypotheses account for the features of our immediate experience may yield a reason for preferring the more direct and thus in an sense simpler representationalist explanatory hypothesis,

---

*Here again a computer game provides a helpful analogy. In playing many such games, you control the "movement" of a computer character through the "world," often in a fairly realistic way, even though there is really no movement of that sort nor any world of that sort in which it might take place. In Berkeley's explanatory hypothesis, God plays the role of the computer.

for regarding it as more likely to be true. But how, exactly?* The idea is that an explanatory hypothesis like Berkeley's, at least as we have construed it, depends for its explanatory success on the truth of two equally essential claims: first, the claim that a material world of the sort postulated by the representationalist *could* account for the features of our experience, for it is precisely by emulating or mimicking the action of such a world that God (or the computer) decides just what experiences to produce in us; and, second, that God (or the computer) can indeed successfully produce the required emulation. But the representationalist view requires only the truth of the first of these two claims. It is thus, I suggest, inherently less vulnerable to problems and challenges and so more likely to be true. And this is an apparent reason for regarding the representationalist's explanatory hypothesis as providing the best of these competing explanations.† . . . 16

---

16 Is this a good reason for favoring the representationalist's explanation over Berkeley's? Can you think of any reason for preferring Berkeley's explanation to the representationalist's?

Is this a successful argument for representationalism? There are at least two questions about it that need to be considered. First, the argument assumes that the competitors to representationalism are all parasitic upon the representationalist explanatory hypothesis in the way indicated, and it is worth asking whether this is really so. Is there an explanation of our immediate experience that does not in this way rely on an emulation of the way in which a material world would produce that experience? It will not do to say simply that God causes our experience without saying how and why it produces the specific results that he does, for that is not really to give a complete explanation. But is there some other way of filling out Berkeley's explanatory hypothesis or one of the parallel ones that does not invoke a conception or model of a material world? Second, even if the argument succeeds to a degree, *how* probable or likely does it make the material world hypothesis in comparison to these others? Is the resulting degree of probability or likelihood high enough to agree approximately with our commonsense convictions in this regard (or to yield knowledge . . .)? I will leave these further difficult questions for you to think about.

IS THERE A BETTER ALTERNATIVE?: DIRECT REALISM

The upshot of our discussion so far is that phenomenalism appears entirely untenable, and that at least a better defense than many have supposed possible can be offered for representationalism. Many recent philosophers, however, have thought that there is a *third* alternative that is superior to either of these: one usually referred to as *direct realism*. The central idea of direct realism is that the view we have called perceptual subjectivism is false, that is, that instead of immediately experiencing . . . sense-data . . . , we instead *directly* experience external material objects, without the mediation of these other sorts of entities or states. And the suggestion often seems to be, though this is usually not explained very fully, that such a view can simply bypass the representationalist's problem of justifying an inference from immediate experience to the material world and do so without having to advocate anything as outlandish as phenomenalism.

---

etimes philosophers appeal in such discussions to a general standard of simplicity, according to which it is just a fundamental principle that npler explanation is more likely to be true. The problem with this is twofold: first, the justification or rationale for the principle in question is ng but clear; and, second, the way in which it would apply to the case with which we are concerned is at least debatable, since Berkeley's exion, for example, might be claimed to be simpler, in a different way from the one just discussed, on the grounds that it invokes only one entity, an extremely complicated one, rather than the many objects that make up a material world.

ome of you will know, it is a fact of probability theory that the probability of the conjunction of two propositions is equal to the product of eparate probabilities, so that where each of them has a separate probability less than one (that is, is not a necessary truth), the probability of njunction is automatically smaller than either of the separate probabilities. I have not formulated the foregoing argument in this form beit could be argued that the second claim, at least the version that pertains to God, is necessary truth. I am not convinced that this is right, but ues involved cannot be discussed here.

For anyone who has struggled with the idea of sense-data . . . and with the difficulties and complexities of representationalism and phenomenalism, the apparent simplicity of direct realism, the way in which it seems to make extremely difficult or even intractable problems simply vanish, may be difficult to resist. We must be cautious, however. What does such a view amount to, and can it really deliver the results that it promises?

We may begin with a point that is often advanced in arguments for direct realism, one that, while correct as far as it goes, turns out in fact to be of much less help than has sometimes been thought in either defending or even explaining the view. Think about an ordinary example of perceptual experience: standing in my back yard, I watch my dogs chasing each other in a large circle around some bushes, weaving in and out of the sunshine and shadows, as a car drives by on the street. The direct realist's claim is that in such a case (assuming that I am in a normal, nonphilosophical frame of mind), the picture that it is easy to find in or read into some representationalists, according to which I *first* have thoughts or occurrent beliefs about the character of my experience (. . . in sense-datum . . . terms) and *then* infer explicitly from these to thoughts or beliefs about material objects is simply and flatly wrong as a description of my actual conscious state. In fact, the only things that I think about at all *directly* and explicitly in such a case are things like dogs and bushes and cars and sunlight, not anything as subtle and abstruse as sense-data. . . . The direct realist need not deny (though some have seemed to) that my sensory experience somehow involves the various qualities, such as complicated patterns of shape and color, that these other views have spoken of, or even that I am in *some* way aware or conscious of these. His point is that whatever may be said about these other matters, from an intuitive standpoint it is material object and nothing else that are "directly before my mind"—and that any view that denies this obvious truth is simply mistaken about the facts.

I have already said that I think that the direct realist is at least mostly right about this. What happens most centrally in perceptual experience is that we have explicit thoughts or "perceptual judgments" about what we are perceiving; and in normal cases (apart from very special artistic or perhaps philosophical contexts), these perceptual judgments are directly and entirely about things (and processes and qualities) in the external material world. Philosophers speak of that which a propositional state of mind is directly about as its *intentional object,* and we can accordingly say that the intentional objects of our basic perceptual judgments are normally alleged or apparent material objects. In this way, the relation of such judgments to material objects is, it might be said, *intentionally* direct. [17]

[17] This does not mean that ideas or sense-data play no role, but only that they are not the object of the perceptual judgment that results. Instead, they might be essential *vehicles* for our perceptual consciousness, essential to explaining *how* we are able to think "directly" of objects outside the mind. (See the introduction to the Locke selection.)

But what bearing, if any, does this intentional directness have on the central epistemological question of what reason or justification we have for thinking that such perceptual judgments about the material world are *true?* Perhaps the sort of direct presence to the mind that is involved in the idea of immediate experience . . . yields the result that one's beliefs or awarenesses concerning the objects of such experience are automatically justified, simply because there is no room for error to creep in. [18] But is there any way in which it follows from the mere fact that perceptual judgments about material objects are *intentionally* direct that they are also *justified?* It still seems obvious that both a perceptual judgment and the total state of mind of which it is a part are quite distinct from the material object, if any, that is its intentionally direct object. This is shown by the fact that in cases like hallucination, the object in question need not exist at all, but it would be clear enough even without such cases—phenomenalist views having been rejected, the material object does not somehow literally enter the mind. Thus even though perceptual judgments are directly about such objects in the intentional sense, the question of whether they represent them *correctly* still arises in exactly the same way that it does for the representationalist. And this question must apparently still be answered, if at all, by appeal to the immediately experienced features involved in the perceiver's state of

[18] Only ideas or sense-data and other states of mind are immediately experienced in this sense.

mind, with the specific character of the sensory experience being the only obvious thing to invoke.

Thus while the idea of intentional directness can be used to present a somewhat more accurate picture of a normal perceiver's state of mind, the view that results is still fundamentally a version of representationalism in that it faces the same essential problem of justifying the transition (whether it is an explicit inference or not) from the character of the person's experience to beliefs or judgments about the material world. If this is all that direct realism amounts to, then it is not a genuinely distinct third alternative with regard to the basic issue of how perceptual beliefs or judgments are justified. [19]

Is there any further way to make sense of the "directness" to which direct realist appeals, one that might yield more interesting epistemological results? It is far from obvious what it would be. Some proponents of this supposed view have tried to deny that we have any awareness of the character of our immediate experience that is both distinct from our judgmental awareness of material objects and of the sort that could provide the basis for the justification of material object claims. Such a challenge raises subtle and difficult issues about different kinds of awareness, but it is hard to see how it could really be correct. Moreover, the correctness of this challenge, while it would surely constitute a serious or perhaps even conclusive objection to representationalism, would not in any way yield a positive direct realist account of how beliefs about the material world are justified, if not in the representationalist way.

My tentative conclusion . . . is that the idea that direct realism represents a further alternative on the present issue is a chimera. Thus, once phenomenalism is rejected as hopeless, the only alternatives with regard to knowledge of the external world appear to be skepticism and some version of representationalism, perhaps one that recognizes and incorporates the view that perceptual judgments about the material world are intentionally direct.

> [19] The claim is that the way in which we are directly aware of external objects (the fact that such objects and not our experiences or ideas or sense-data are what we are thinking about in such experience) really does nothing at all to explain why our perceptual claims are *justified,* why we have good reasons to think that they are true. Our state of mind is still distinct from the object, and so the issue of whether it represents such an object correctly can still be raised—in exactly the same way that it arises for Locke.

Discussion Questions

1. Can you think of a good argument for the existence of mental states other than your own in what appear to be other people? The obvious starting point is the behavior of other bodies. Try to construct such an argument, and evaluate its strength.

2. Think of how a scientific explanation of color experience might go. Are Locke and BonJour right that color as a feature of material objects plays no role in such an explanation? If so, does it follow that we have no reason to believe that such objects are really colored, or is there some other reason (besides a role in explanation) for thinking they are colored?

3. Whose explanation of the patterns of experience is better: the representationalist's or Berkeley's? Why? Can you think of other explanations that are significantly different from either of these? What general standards are the right ones for choosing among such explanations, and why?

4. BonJour offers what is admittedly only a sketch of an argument for the existence of material objects. How hard would it be to fill this out into a complete argument (where a large part of the job would be giving a much fuller description of the relevant features of experience)? Is it plausible to suppose that ordinary people who have beliefs about material objects have this argument or anything like it in mind? If not, does this mean that they have no good reasons to think that their beliefs are true? How implausible is such a result?

ARE ALL REASONS BASED ON EXPERIENCE?

Immanuel Kant

The German philosopher Immanuel Kant (1724–1804) was among the most important and influential philosophers of all time, making major contributions to epistemology, metaphysics, ethics, aesthetics, and the philosophy of religion. In the following selection from his most important work, *The Critique of Pure Reason,* Kant explains the distinctions between a priori and *a posteriori* (empirical) knowledge and between analytic and synthetic judgments. He then argues that there is knowledge that is both a priori and synthetic, and explains why the existence of such knowledge poses a fundamental epistemological puzzle.

One important ingredient of Kant's discussion is what he calls the *principle of contradiction* (also sometimes referred to, somewhat confusingly, as the principle of noncontradiction). This is the principle that a contradiction (or "self-contradiction") cannot be true, where by a contradiction is meant a statement or proposition one part of which denies what another part affirms. "Some unmarried adult males are married" is an *explicit* contradiction, since the predicate ("married") explicitly denies part of what is affirmed in the subject ("unmarried"); "some bachelors are married" is an *implicit* contradiction for essentially the same reason, since "married" denies part of what is affirmed by "bachelor," as can be seen by spelling out the meaning of "bachelor." As will be seen, if a statement or proposition is *analytic* as Kant understands this concept, then its denial will always be a contradiction, whether explicit or implicit. (Pointing out that such a statement must be true because it would be a contradiction to deny it is what Kant means by his talk of "extracting the predicate from the subject via the principle of contradiction.")

Is All Knowledge Based on Experience or Is Some Knowledge A Priori? from *The Critique of Pure Reason*

I. THE DISTINCTION BETWEEN PURE AND EMPIRICAL KNOWLEDGE

There can be no doubt that all our knowledge begins with experience. For how should our faculty of knowledge be awakened into action did not objects affecting our senses partly of themselves produce representations, partly arouse the activity of our understanding to compare these representations, and, by combining or separating them, work up the raw material of the sensible impressions into that knowledge of objects which is entitled experience? In the order of time, therefore, we have no knowledge antecedent to experience, and with experience all our knowledge begins.

But though all our knowledge begins with experience, it does not follow that it all arises out of expe-

From The Critique of Pure Reason, *translated by Norman Kemp Smith (London: Macmillan, 1950).*

rience. For it may well be that even our empirical knowledge is made up of what we receive through impressions and of what our own faculty of knowledge (sensible impressions serving merely as the occasion) supplies from itself. If our faculty of knowledge makes any such addition, it may be that we are not in a position to distinguish it from the raw material, until with long practice of attention we have become skilled in separating it.①

① To say that not all knowledge *arises* from experience is to say that there are elements in knowledge that cannot be derived from the content of experience, even though they might not have yielded any knowledge had not our faculties been "awakened into action" by experience. Innate concepts would be the most obvious example of such elements.

This, then, is a question which at least calls for closer examination, and does not allow of any offhand answer:—whether there is any knowledge that is thus independent of experience and even of all impressions of the senses. Such knowledge is entitled a priori, and distinguished from the *empirical,* which has its sources *a posteriori,* that is, in experience.

The expression 'a priori' does not, however, indicate with sufficient precision the full meaning of our question. For it has been customary to say, even of much knowledge that is derived from empirical sources, that we have it or are capable of having it a priori, meaning thereby that we do not derive it immediately from experience, but from a universal rule—a rule which is itself, however, borrowed by us from experience. Thus we would say of a man who undermined the foundations of his house, that he might have known a priori that it would fall, that is, that he need not have waited for the experience of its actual falling. But still he could not know this completely a priori. For he had first to learn through experience that bodies are heavy, and therefore fall when their supports are withdrawn.②

② Kant is saying that the *justification* of such a claim (the man's reason for thinking it to be true) still derives ultimately from experience—he didn't have to experience this particular house collapsing, but he did have to have experienced analogous cases (either other houses falling or unsupported heavy objects of others sorts falling).

In what follows, therefore, we shall understand by a priori knowledge, not knowledge independent of this or that experience, but knowledge absolutely independent of all experience. Opposed to it is empirical knowledge, which is knowledge possible only *a posteriori,* that is, through experience. A priori modes of knowledge are entitled pure when there is no admixture of anything empirical. Thus, for instance, the proposition, 'every alteration has its cause', while an a priori proposition, is not a pure proposition, because alteration is a concept which can be derived only from experience.③

③ Knowledge is a priori if its *justification* does not depend on experience; it is *pure* a priori when the concepts involved do not derive from experience (and so are innate). (Note that Kant sometimes confusingly uses "pure" as just a synonym of "a priori"—as indeed in the very next sentence.)

II. WE ARE IN POSSESSION OF CERTAIN MODES OF A PRIORI KNOWLEDGE, AND EVEN THE COMMON UNDERSTANDING IS NEVER WITHOUT THEM

What we here require is a criterion by which to distinguish with certainty between pure and empirical knowledge. Experience teaches us that a thing is so and so, but not that it cannot be otherwise. First, then, if we have a proposition which in being thought is thought as *necessary,* it is an a priori judgment; and if, besides, it is not derived from any proposition except one which also has the validity of a necessary judgment, it is an absolutely a priori judgment. Secondly, experience never confers on its judgments true or strict, but only assumed and comparative universality, through induction. We can properly only say, therefore, that, so far as we have hitherto observed, there is no exception to this or that rule. If, then, a judgment is thought with strict universality, that is, in such manner that no exception is allowed as possible, it is not derived from experience, but is valid absolutely a priori. Empirical universality is only an arbitrary extension of a validity holding in most cases to one which holds in all, for instance, in the proposition, 'all bodies are heavy'. When, on the other hand, strict universality is essential to a judgment, this indicates a special source of knowledge, namely, a faculty of a priori knowledge. Necessity and strict universality are thus sure criteria of a priori knowledge, and are inseparable from one another.④ But since in the employment of these criteria the contingency of judgments is sometimes more easily shown than their empirical limitation, or, as sometimes also happens, their unlimited universality can be more convincingly proved than their necessity, it is advisable to use the two criteria separately, each by itself being infallible.

> **④** Is there any real difference between these two criteria? What does "strict universality" mean if not truth in every possible situation, which is the same as necessity?

Now it is easy to show that there actually are in human knowledge judgments which are necessary and in the strictest sense universal, and which are therefore pure a priori judgments. If an example from the sciences be desired, we have only to look to any of the propositions of mathematics; if we seek an example from the understanding in its quite ordinary employment, the proposition, 'every alteration must have a cause', will serve our purpose. In the latter case, indeed, the very concept of a cause so manifestly contains the concept of a necessity of connection with an effect and of the strict universality of the rule, that the concept would be altogether lost if we attempted to derive it, as Hume has done, from a repeated association of that which happens with that which precedes, and from a custom of connecting representations, a custom originating in this repeated association, and constituting therefore a merely subjective necessity.⑤ Even without appealing to such examples, it is possible to show that pure a priori principles are indispensable for the possibility of

> **⑤** This argument appears to be confused, because Kant does not distinguish (as more recent philosophers do) between **causal** or **nomological necessity**, on the one hand, and **logical** or **metaphysical necessity**, on the other. Causal necessity is the sort of necessity that pertains to specific causal relations or the laws that describe them, and Kant does not think that these can be known a priori. Logical necessity is that which pertains to logical and mathematical claims and any others that are "true in every possible world." Only logical or metaphysical necessity is a plausible criterion for a priori knowledge. Kant does think that "every alteration has a cause" is logically or metaphysically necessary, but he gives no good reason for this claim here.

experience, and so to prove their existence a priori. For whence could experience derive its certainty, if all the rules, according to which it proceeds, were always themselves empirical, and therefore contingent? Such rules could hardly be regarded as first principles. At present, however, we may be content to have established the fact that our faculty of knowledge does have a pure employment, and to have shown what are the criteria of such an employment.

Such a priori origin is manifest in certain concepts, no less than in judgments. If we remove from our empirical concept of a body, one by one, every feature in it which is merely empirical, the colour, the hardness or softness, the weight, even the impenetrability, there still remains the space which the body (now entirely vanished) occupied, and this cannot be removed. Again, if we remove from our empirical concept of any object, corporeal or incorporeal, all properties which experience has taught us, we yet cannot take away that property through which the object is thought as substance or as inhering in a substance (although this concept of substance is more determinate than that of an object in general). Owing, therefore, to the necessity with which this concept of substance forces itself upon us, we have no option save to admit that it has its seat in our faculty of a priori knowledge.⑥

> **⑥** Thus Kant would reply to Berkeley's argument that the idea of substance is not to be found in experience by saying that this idea or concept is innate and so need not be one derived from or present in experience. How might he answer Locke's arguments against innateness? (See Discussion Question 1.)

III. PHILOSOPHY STANDS IN NEED OF A SCIENCE WHICH SHALL DETERMINE THE POSSIBILITY, THE PRINCIPLES, AND THE EXTENT OF ALL A PRIORI KNOWLEDGE

But what is still more extraordinary than all the preceding is this, that certain modes of knowledge leave the field of all possible experiences and have the appearance of extending the scope of our judgments beyond all limits of experience, and this by means of concepts to which no corresponding object can ever be given in experience.

It is precisely by means of the latter modes of knowledge, in a realm beyond the world of the senses, where experience can yield neither guidance nor correction, that our reason carries on those enquiries which owing to their importance we consider to be far more excellent, and in their purpose far more lofty, than all that the understanding can learn in the field of appearances. Indeed we prefer to run every risk of error rather than desist from such urgent enquiries, on the ground of their dubious character, or from disdain and indifference. These unavoidable problems set by pure reason itself are *God, freedom,* and *immortality.* The science which, with all its preparations, is in its final intention directed solely to their solution is metaphysics; and its procedure is at first dogmatic, that is, it confidently sets itself to this task without any previous examination of the capacity or incapacity of reason for so great an undertaking. ⑦

> ⑦ Kant's claim is that human beings cannot help but ask questions about such things, even though it is unclear that we have the capacity to have any knowledge about them.

Now it does indeed seem natural that, as soon as we have left the ground of experience, we should, through careful enquiries, assure ourselves as to the foundations of any building that we propose to erect, not making use of any knowledge that we possess without first determining whence it has come, and not trusting to principles without knowing their origin. It is natural, that is to say, that the question should first be considered, how the understanding can arrive at all this knowledge a priori, and what extent, validity, and worth it may have. Nothing, indeed, could be more natural, if by the term 'natural' we signify what fittingly and reasonably ought to happen. But if we mean by 'natural' what ordinarily happens, then on the contrary nothing is more natural and more intelligible than the fact that this enquiry has been so long neglected. For one part of this knowledge, the mathematical, has long been of established reliability, and so gives rise to a favourable presumption as regards the other part, which may yet be of quite different nature. Besides, once we are outside the circle of experience, we can be sure of not being *contradicted* by experience. The charm of extending our knowledge is so great that nothing short of encountering a direct contradiction can suffice to arrest us in our course; and this can be avoided, if we are careful in our fabrications— which none the less will still remain fabrications. Mathematics gives us a shining example of how far, independently of experience, we can progress in a priori knowledge. . . . Misled by such a proof of the power of reason, the demand for the extension of knowledge recognises no limits. The light dove, cleaving the air in her free flight, and feeling its resistance, might imagine that its flight would be still easier in empty space. It was thus that Plato left the world of the senses, as setting too narrow limits to the understanding, and ventured out beyond it on the wings of the ideas, in the empty space of the pure understanding. He did not observe that with all his efforts he made no advance—meeting no resistance that might, as it were, serve as a support upon which he could take a stand, to which he could apply his powers, and so set his understanding in motion. It is, indeed, the common fate of human reason to complete its speculative structures as speedily as may be, and only afterwards to enquire whether the foundations are reliable. All sorts of excuses will then be appealed to, in order to reassure us of their solidity, or rather indeed to enable us to dispense altogether with so late and so dangerous an enquiry. But what keeps us, during the actual building, free from all apprehension and suspicion, and flatters us with a seeming thoroughness, is this other circumstance, namely, that a great, perhaps the greatest, part of the business of our reason consists in analysis of the concepts which we already have of objects. This analysis supplies us with a considerable body of knowledge, which, while nothing but explanation or elucidation of what has already been thought in our concepts, though in a confused manner, is yet prized as being, at least as regards its form, new insight. But so far as the matter or content is concerned, there has been no extension of our previously possessed concepts, but only an analysis of them. Since this procedure yields real knowledge a priori, which progresses in an assured and useful fashion, reason is so far misled as surreptitiously to introduce, without itself being aware of so doing, assertions of an entirely different order, in which it attaches to given concepts others completely foreign to them, and moreover attaches them a priori.⑧ And yet it is not known how reason can be in position to do this. Such a question is never so much as thought of. I shall therefore at once proceed to deal with the difference between these two kinds of knowledge.

⑧ Thus there are two fundamentally different kinds of a priori knowledge: a priori knowledge that derives from analyzing or spelling out the meaning of concepts, which Kant regards as posing no serious problems (this is the way we know that "all bachelors are unmarried" is true); and a priori knowledge that cannot be understood or explained in this way, which he regards as much more difficult to understand. The next section further explicates this contrast.

IV. THE DISTINCTION BETWEEN ANALYTIC AND SYNTHETIC JUDGMENTS

In all judgments in which the relation of a subject to the predicate is thought (I take into consideration affirmative judgments only, the subsequent application to negative judgments being easily made), this relation is possible in two different ways. Either the predicate B belongs to the subject A, as something which is (covertly) contained in this concept A; or B lies outside the concept A, although it does indeed stand in connection with it. In the one case I entitle the judgment analytic, in the other synthetic. Analytic judgments (affirmative) are therefore those in which the connection of the predicate with the subject is thought through identity; those in which this connection is thought without identity should be entitled synthetic. The former, as adding nothing through the predicate to the concept of the subject, but merely breaking it up into those constituent concepts that have all along been thought in it, although confusedly, can also be entitled explicative. The latter, on the other hand, add to the concept of the subject a predicate which has not been in any wise thought in it, and which no analysis could possibly extract from it; and they may therefore be entitled ampliative. If I say, for instance, 'All bodies are extended', this is an analytic judgment. For I do not require to go beyond the concept which I connect with 'body' in order to find extension as bound up with it. To meet with this predicate, I have merely to analyse the concept, that is, to become conscious to myself of the manifold which I always think in that concept. The judgment is therefore analytic.⑨ But when I say, 'All bodies are heavy', the predicate is something quite different from anything that I think in the mere concept of body in general; and the addition of such a predicate therefore yields a synthetic judgment.

Judgments of experience, as such, are one and all synthetic. For it would be absurd to found an analytic judgment on experience. Since, in framing the judgment, I must not go outside my concept, there is no need to appeal to the testimony of experience in its support.⑩ That a body is extended is a proposition that holds a priori and is not empirical. For, before appealing to experience, I have already in the concept of body all the conditions required for my judgment. I have only to extract from it, in accordance with the principle of contradiction, the required predicate, and in so doing can at the same time become conscious of the necessity of the judgment—and that is what experience could never have taught me.⑪ On the other hand, though I do not include in the concept of a body in general the predicate 'weight', none the less this concept indicates an object of experience through one of its parts, and I can add to that part other parts of this same experience, as in this way belonging together with the concept. From the start I can apprehend the concept of body analytically through the characters of extension, impenetrability, figure, etc., all of which are thought in the concept. Now, however, looking

⑨ Kant doesn't actually give the analysis of the concept of a body, but it is presumably something like *extended, solid substance,* from which the predicate *extended* can obviously be derived. A more standard example of an analytic judgment is "all bachelors are unmarried"—think about how the predicate of this judgment is included in its subject.

⑩ Kant overstates just a bit here. There is no need for "the testimony of experience" in the case of an analytic judgment, but experience could still provide evidence for it— think of the example at the end of the previous annotation and how it might be supported by experience.

⑪ But experience can't, according to Kant, show that a judgment is (logically or metaphysically) necessary. Think carefully about what it means to "extract" a predicate from a concept "in accordance with the principle of contradiction" (that is, the principle that a contradiction cannot be true).

back on the experience from which I have derived this concept of body, and finding weight to be invariably connected with the above characters, I attach it as a predicate to the concept; and in doing so I attach it synthetically, and am therefore extending my knowledge. The possibility of the synthesis of the predicate 'weight' with the concept of 'body' thus rests upon experience. While the one concept is not contained in the other, they yet belong to one another, though only contingently, as parts of a whole, namely, of an experience which is itself a synthetic combination of intuitions.

But in a priori synthetic judgments this help is entirely lacking: I do not here have the advantage of looking around in the field of experience. Upon what, then, am I to rely, when I seek to go beyond the concept A, and to know that another concept B is connected with it? Through what is the synthesis made possible? Let us take the proposition, 'Everything which happens has its cause' In the concept of 'something which happens', I do indeed think an existence which is preceded by a time, etc., and from this concept analytic judgments may be obtained. But the concept of a 'cause' lies entirely outside the other concept, and signifies something different from 'that which happens', and is not therefore in any way contained in this latter representation. How come I then to predicate of that which happens something quite different, and to apprehend that the concept of cause, though not contained in it, yet belongs, and indeed necessarily belongs, to it? What is here the unknown = X which gives support to the understanding when it believes that it can discover outside the concept A a predicate B foreign to this concept, which it yet at the same time considers to be connected with it? It cannot be experience, because the suggested principle has connected the second representation with the first, not only with greater universality, but also with the character of necessity, and therefore completely a priori and on the basis of mere concepts. Upon such synthetic, that is, ampliative principles, all our a priori speculative knowledge must ultimately rest; analytic judgments are very important, and indeed nec-

12 Here is the fundamental puzzle about knowledge that is both synthetic and a priori: the claim that the predicate correctly applies to the subject is supported by neither experience nor conceptual analysis—so how then is it supported or justified (which is required for the claim to be knowledge)?

essary, but only for obtaining that clearness in the concepts which is requisite for such a sure and wide synthesis as will lead to a genuinely new addition to all previous knowledge.

V. IN ALL THEORETICAL SCIENCES OF REASON SYNTHETIC A PRIORI JUDGMENTS ARE CONTAINED AS PRINCIPLES

1. All mathematical judgments, without exception, are synthetic. 13 This fact, though incontestably certain and in its consequences very important, has hitherto escaped the notice of those who are engaged in the analysis of human reason, and is, indeed, directly opposed to all their conjectures. For as it was found that all mathematical inferences proceed in accordance with the principle of contradiction (which the nature of all apodeictic certainty requires), it was supposed that the fundamental propositions of the science can themselves be known to be true through that principle. This is an erroneous view. For though a synthetic proposition can indeed be discerned in accordance with the principle of contradiction, this can only be if another synthetic proposition is presupposed, and if it can then be apprehended as following from this other proposition: it can never be so discerned in and by itself.

13 Again, Kant overstates. There is no reason why mathematical concepts cannot be analyzed, so as to yield analytic judgments—as Kant himself recognizes later in this very section. The point is rather that important or significant mathematical judgments do not have this character. ("Apodeictic" in this paragraph just means that the certainty is beyond all possible doubt.)

. . .

We might, indeed, at first suppose that the proposition 7 + 5 = 12 is a merely analytic proposition, and follows by the principle of contradiction from the concept of a sum of 7 and 5. But if we look more closely we find that the concept of the sum of 7 and 5 contains nothing save the union of the two numbers into one, and in this no thought is being taken as to what that single number may be which combines both. The concept of 12 is by no means already thought in merely thinking this union of 7 and 5; and I may analyse my concept of such a possible sum as long as I please, still I shall never find the 12 in it. . . . That 5 should be added to 7, I have indeed already thought in the concept of a sum = 7 + 5, but not that this sum is equivalent to the number 12.⑭ Arithmetical propositions are therefore always synthetic. This is still more evident if we take larger numbers. For it is then obvious that, however we might turn and twist our concepts, we could never, by the mere analysis of them . . . discover what the number is that is the sum.⑮

⑭ Here is one of Kant's key examples and one of the most widely discussed examples of all. Is Kant right that 7 + 5 = 12 is synthetic rather than analytic? (See Discussion Question 2.)

⑮ Here is one way to think about this question. Consider the claim that 18,697 + 23,849 = 42,546. Is the predicate here included in the subject? Kant is assuming that all arithmetical claims have the same status in this respect: either all are analytic or all are synthetic. (See Discussion Question 3.)

Just as little is any fundamental proposition of pure geometry analytic. That the straight line between two points is the shortest, is a synthetic proposition. For my concept of *straight* contains nothing of quantity, but only of quality. The concept of the shortest is wholly an addition, and cannot be derived, through any process of analysis, from the concept of the straight line. . . .

Some few fundamental propositions, presupposed by the geometrician, are, indeed, really analytic, and rest on the principle of contradiction. But, as identical propositions, they serve only as links in the chain of method and not as principles; for instance, $a = a$; the whole is equal to itself; or $(a + b) > a$, that is, the whole is greater than its part. . . .

2.   *Natural science (physics) contains a priori synthetic judgments as principles.* I need cite only two such judgments: that in all changes of the material world the quantity of matter remains unchanged; and that in all communication of motion, action and reaction must always be equal. Both propositions, it is evident, are not only necessary, and therefore in their origin a priori, but also synthetic. For in the concept of matter I do not think its permanence, but only its presence in the space which it occupies. I go outside and beyond the concept of matter, joining to it a priori in thought something which I have not thought *in* it. The proposition is not, therefore, analytic, but synthetic, and yet is thought a priori; and so likewise are the other propositions of the pure part of natural science.⑯

3.   *Metaphysics,* even if we look upon it as having hitherto failed in all its endeavours, is yet, owing to the nature of human reason, a quite indispensable science, and *ought to contain* a priori *synthetic knowledge.* For its business is not merely to analyse concepts which we make for ourselves a priori of things, and thereby to clarify them analytically, but to extend our a priori knowledge. And for this purpose we must employ principles which add to the given concept something that was not contained in it, and through a priori synthetic judgments venture out so far that experience is quite unable to follow us, as, for instance, in the proposition, that the world must have a first beginning, and such like. Thus metaphysics consists, at least *in intention,* entirely of a priori synthetic propositions.⑰

⑯ Many philosophers would deny that judgments like these are synthetic a priori, claiming that all scientific claims are instead empirical. What do you think about this?

⑰ That is, *if* there were metaphysical knowledge, it would have this status.

VI. THE GENERAL PROBLEM OF PURE REASON

Much is already gained if we can bring a number of investigations under the formula of a single problem. For we not only lighten our own task, by defining it accurately, but make it easier for others, who would test our results, to judge whether or not we have succeeded in what we set out to do. Now the proper problem of pure reason is contained in the question: How are a priori synthetic judgments possible?

That metaphysics has hitherto remained in so vacillating a state of uncertainty and contradiction, is entirely due to the fact that this problem, and perhaps even the distinction between analytic and synthetic judgments, has never previously been considered. Upon the solution of this problem, or upon a sufficient proof that the possibility which it desires to have explained does in fact not exist at all, depends the success or failure of metaphysics. Among philosophers, David Hume came nearest to envisaging this problem, but still was very far from conceiving it with sufficient definiteness and universality. He occupied himself exclusively with the synthetic proposition regarding the connection of an effect with its cause (*principium causalitatis*), and he believed himself to have shown that such an a priori proposition is entirely impossible.[18] If we accept his conclusions, then all that we call metaphysics is a mere delusion whereby we fancy ourselves to have rational insight into what, in actual fact, is borrowed solely from experience, and under the influence of custom has taken the illusory semblance of necessity. If he had envisaged our problem in all its universality, he would never have been guilty of this statement, so destructive of all pure philosophy. For he would then have recognised that, according to his own argument, pure mathematics, as certainly containing a priori synthetic propositions, would also not be possible; and from such an assertion his good sense would have saved him.

In the solution of the above problem, we are at the same time deciding as to the possibility of the employment of pure reason in establishing and developing all those sciences which contain a theoretical a priori knowledge of objects, and have therefore to answer the questions:

How is pure mathematics possible?
How is pure science of nature possible?

Since these sciences actually exist, it is quite proper to ask *how* they are possible; for that they must be possible is proved by the fact that they exist.* But the poor progress which has hitherto been made in metaphysics, and the fact that no system yet propounded can, in view of the essential purpose of metaphysics, be said really to exist, leaves everyone sufficient ground for doubting as to its possibility.

Yet, in a certain sense, this *kind of knowledge* is to be looked upon as given; that is to say, metaphysics actually exists, if not as a science, yet still as natural

[18] See the Hume reading in the induction section.

disposition (*metaphysica naturalis*). For human reason, without being moved merely by the idle desire for extent and variety of knowledge, proceeds impetuously, driven on by an inward need, to questions such as cannot be answered by any empirical employment of reason, or by principles thence derived. Thus in all men, as soon as their reason has become ripe for speculation, there has always existed and will always continue to exist some kind of metaphysics. And so we have the question:

How is metaphysics, as natural disposition, possible?

that is, how from the nature of universal human reason do those questions arise which pure reason propounds to itself, and which it is impelled by its own need to answer as best it can?

But since all attempts which have hitherto been made to answer these natural questions—for instance, whether the world has a beginning or is from eternity—have always met with unavoidable contradictions, we cannot rest satisfied with the mere natural disposition to metaphysics, that is, with the pure faculty of reason itself, from which, indeed, some sort of metaphysics (be it what it may) always arises. It must be possible for reason to attain to certainty whether we know or do not know the objects of metaphysics, that is, to come to a decision either in regard to the objects of its enquiries or in regard to the capacity or incapacity of reason to pass any judgment upon them, so that we may either with confidence extend our pure reason or set to it sure and determinate limits. This last question, which arises out of the previous general problem, may, rightly stated, take the form:

How is metaphysics, as science, possible?[19]

Thus the critique of reason, in the end, necessarily leads to scientific knowledge; while its dogmatic employment, on the other hand, lands us in dogmatic assertions to which other

[19] That is, what would be required for it to be possible?

---

*Many may still have doubts as regards pure natural science. We have only, however, to consider the various propositions that are to be found at the beginning of (empirical) physics, properly so called, those, for instance, relating to the permanence in the quantity of matter, to inertia, to the equality of action and reaction, etc., in order to be soon convinced that they constitute a *physica pura,* or *rationalis,* which well deserves, as an independent science, to be separately dealt with in its whole extent, be that narrow or wide.

assertions, equally specious, can always be opposed—that is, in *scepticism*.

This science cannot be of any very formidable prolixity, since it has to deal not with the objects of reason, the variety of which is inexhaustible, but only with itself and the problems which arise entirely from within itself, and which are imposed upon it by its own nature, not by the nature of things which are distinct from it. When once reason has learnt completely to understand its own power in respect of objects which can be presented to it in experience, it should easily be able to determine, with completeness and certainty, the extent and the limits of its attempted employment beyond the bounds of all experience.

We may, then, and indeed we must, regard as abortive all attempts, hitherto made, to establish a metaphysic *dogmatically*. For the analytic part in any such attempted system, namely, the mere analysis of the concepts that inhere in our reason a priori, is by no means the aim of, but only a preparation for, metaphysics proper, that is, the extension of its a priori synthetic knowledge. For such a purpose, the analysis of concepts is useless, since it merely shows what is contained in these concepts, not how we arrive at them a priori. A solution of this latter problem is required, that we may be able to determine the valid employment of such concepts in regard to the objects of all knowledge in general. Nor is much self-denial needed to give up these claims, seeing that the undeniable, and in the dogmatic procedure of reason also unavoidable, contradictions of reason with itself have long since undermined the authority of every metaphysical system yet propounded. Greater firmness will be required if we are not to be deterred by inward difficulties and outward opposition from endeavouring, through application of a method entirely different from any hitherto employed, at last to bring to a prosperous and fruitful growth a science indispensable to human reason—a science whose every branch may be cut away but whose root cannot be destroyed.

. . .

Discussion Questions

1. Kant's view is that concepts like substance and causality (and a priori knowledge pertaining to them) are innate in the human mind, rather than being derived from experience. But he does not think that babies are born thinking about substance or causality, but instead that such thoughts have to be "awakened by experience." Locke would have denied that such a view makes good sense. Who is right here?

2. Is $7 + 5 = 12$ knowable a priori? If so, is it analytic or synthetic, as Kant defines these concepts? Here it is important to get the issue into very clear focus: the issue is not merely whether the claim is one that anyone who understands can see to be true. It is rather whether the way it is seen to be true is by analyzing the concept of $7 + 5$ and finding 12 to be contained in it, in the way in which *unmarried* is contained in *bachelor*. Another way to put this question: is the denial of $7 + 5 = 12$ a contradiction in the way that the claim that some bachelors are married is? It is false and indeed necessarily false, but is it contradictory in itself—without bringing in other mathematical principles or axioms? (This is a hard question.)

3. Is $18,697 + 23,849 = 42,546$ analytic or synthetic? Clearly most people can understand the concept of *the sum of 18,697 and 23,849* without thereby knowing that it has the property of *being equal to 42,546,* in a way that they could not understand the concept of *bachelor* without thereby knowing that the property of *unmarried* is contained in it. Does this show that the claim is synthetic? Why or why not?

4. Consider the claim that nothing can be red all over and green all over at the same time. Is this claim knowable a priori? Is it analytic or synthetic? This claim is not clearly of subject-predicate form as it stands, but here is a somewhat convoluted rewording that is of subject-predicate form and is parallel to "all bachelors are unmarried": all things that are red all over at a given time have the property of not being green all over at that same time. Is the predicate of this claim included in its subject—which amounts to asking whether

not being green is included in red? (One relevant question here: could one understand the concept of red without yet having learned the concept of green?)

5. If there is synthetic a priori knowledge, how is it possible? Kant's view (not expressed in this selection) is that such knowledge applies only to a kind of reality that is somehow constructed by the mind in such a way as to satisfy the various synthetic a priori claims. Thus in his view, 7 + 5 = 12 is true in the "world of appearances," but not true of (because it does not apply to) reality that is independent of the mind. Does it make sense to suppose that there is any sort of reality to which 7 + 5 = 12 does not apply and of which it is not true? Can you see any more straightforward way of explaining such knowledge? (This is an especially hard question.)

A. J. Ayer

Alfred Jules Ayer (1910–1989) was a British philosopher who taught at Oxford University and the University of London. Ayer was one of the first British proponents of **logical positivism,** especially in the book from which the present selection is taken. Ayer made major contributions to epistemology and metaphysics, and also wrote widely on the history of recent philosophy.

In the following selection, Ayer defends what may be described as a moderate empiricist view of a priori justification and knowledge: one that does not deny the existence of the a priori, but holds that claims that are justified a priori are always analytic and so are mere tautologies, thus having no "factual" content. (Thus all "factual" claims require an appeal to sense experience, including here introspective experience of one's own states of mind, if they are to be justified.) Ayer defends this view by putting forward an account of what it is for a claim to be analytic that differs importantly from the one offered by Kant. For Ayer, an analytic proposition is one that is true by virtue of the definitions of the terms it contains, where this amounts to saying that anyone who understands those definitions (and the way in which the terms in question are combined in that proposition) can see on that basis alone that the proposition must be true. (A further defense of moderate empiricism can be found in the Salmon selection in the induction section.)

In assessing Ayer's view on this point, it is important to keep in mind that (as he makes clear at the beginning) the main underlying issue is the epistemological issue of how a priori justification is to be accounted for: does it require the rationalist's idea of insight into the necessary character of reality (see the following selection by Ewing for more on this) or can it be accounted for in some way more acceptable to empiricism? Thus what matters is not whether a priori claims are analytic under *some* definition of that term, but whether they are analytic in a sense that offers a clear and explicit account of how they are justified and so avoids the need for the rationalistic insight. (Kant's conception of analyticity does seem to yield a clear epistemological account: if the predicate of a proposition is really contained in the subject, then the proposition must be true. But it is less obvious that Ayer's alternative account of analyticity does this in the same clear way.)

The A Priori, from *Language, Truth and Logic*

The view of philosophy which we have adopted may, I think, fairly be described as a form of empiricism. For it is characteristic of an empiricist to eschew metaphysics, on the ground that every factual proposition must refer to sense-experience.① . . .

> ① This is not a very clear formulation of the basic empiricist claim. The issue is really whether "factual" propositions must always be *justified* by appeal to sense experience (if they are to be justified at all). And what counts as a "factual" proposition still needs to be explained.

> ② Again, this doesn't make the issue quite clear. The main question is how to account for a priori justification, with (logically or metaphysically) necessary truths being relevant because they can seemingly only be justified in this way.

Having admitted that we are empiricists, we must now deal with the objection that is commonly brought against all forms of empiricism; the objection, namely, that it is impossible on empiricist principles to account for our knowledge of necessary truths.② For, as Hume conclusively showed, no general proposition whose validity is subject to the test of actual experience can ever be logically certain. No matter how often it is verified in practice, there still remains the possibility that it will be confuted on some future occasion. The fact that a law has been substantiated in $n - 1$ cases affords no logical guarantee that it will be substantiated in the nth case also, no matter how large we take n to be. And this means that no general proposition referring to a matter of fact can ever be shown to be necessarily and universally true. It can at best be a probable hypothesis. And this, we shall find, applies not only to general propositions, but to all propositions which have a factual content. They can none of them ever become logically certain. This conclusion, which we shall elaborate later on, is one which must be accepted by every consistent empiricist. It is often thought to involve him in complete scepticism; but this is not the case. For the fact that the validity of a proposition cannot be logically guaranteed in no way entails that it is irrational for us to believe it. On the contrary, what is irrational is to look for a guarantee where none can be forthcoming; to demand certainty where probability is all that is obtainable. . . .

Where the empiricist does encounter difficulty is in connection with the truths of formal logic and mathematics. For whereas a scientific generalisation is readily admitted to be fallible, the truths of mathematics and logic appear to everyone to be necessary and certain. But if empiricism is correct no proposition which has a factual content can be necessary or certain. Accordingly the empiricist must deal with the truths of logic and mathematics in one of the two following ways: he must say either that they are not necessary truths, in which case he must account for the universal conviction that they are; or he must say that they have no factual content, and then he must explain how a proposition which is empty of all factual content can be true and useful and surprising.

If neither of these courses proves satisfactory, we shall be obliged to give way to rationalism. We shall be obliged to admit that there are some truths about the world which we can know independently of experience; that there are some properties which we can ascribe to all objects, even though we cannot conceivably observe that all objects have them. And we shall have to accept it as a mysterious inexplicable fact that our thought has this power to reveal to us authoritatively the nature of objects which we have never observed. . . .

It is vital, therefore, for us to be able to show that one or other of the empiricist accounts of the propositions of logic and mathematics is correct. If we are successful in this, we shall have destroyed the foundations of rationalism. For the fundamental tenet of rationalism is that thought is an independent source of knowledge, and is moreover a more trustworthy source of knowledge than experience; indeed some rationalists have gone so far as to say that thought is the only source of knowledge.③ And the ground for this view is simply that the only necessary truths about the world

> ③ The main issue concerns the first of these rationalist claims: that genuine knowledge can be justified by thinking alone, with no need for an appeal to sense experience.

From Language, Truth and Logic, *2nd ed. (New York: Dover, 1952).*

which are known to us are known through thought and not through experience. So that if we can show either that the truths in question are not necessary or that they are not "truths about the world," we shall be taking away the support on which rationalism rests. We shall be making good the empiricist contention that there are no "truths of reason" which refer to matters of fact.

The course of maintaining that the truths of logic and mathematics are not necessary or certain was adopted by Mill. He maintained that these propositions were inductive generalizations based on an extremely large number of instances. The fact that the number of supporting instances was so very large accounted, in his view, for our believing these generalizations to be necessarily and universally true. The evidence in their favour was so strong that it seemed incredible to us that a contrary instance should ever arise. Nevertheless it was in principle possible for such generalizations to be confuted. They were highly probable, but, being inductive generalizations, they were not certain. The difference between them and the hypotheses of natural science was a difference in degree and not in kind. Experience gave us very good reason to suppose that a "truth" of mathematics or logic was true universally; but we were not possessed of a guarantee. For these "truths" were only empirical hypotheses which had worked particularly well in the past; and, like all empirical hypotheses, they were theoretically fallible.

___

4️⃣ Does this view of mathematical and logical truths have any real plausibility? Think of some specific examples.

___

I do not think that this solution of the empiricist's difficulty with regard to the propositions of logic and mathematics is acceptable. In discussing it, it is necessary to make a distinction which is perhaps already enshrined in Kant's famous dictum that, although there can be no doubt that all our knowledge begins with experience, it does not follow that it all arises out of experience.* When we say that the truths of logics are known independently of experience, we are not of course saying that they are innate, in the sense that we are born knowing them. It is obvious that mathematics and logic have to be learned in the same way as chem-

istry and history have to be learned. Nor are we denying that the first person to discover a given logical or mathematical truth was led to it by an inductive procedure. It is very probable, for example, that the principle of the syllogism was formulated not before but after the validity of syllogistic reasoning had been observed in a number of particular cases. What we are discussing, however, when we say that logical and mathematical truths are known independently of experience, is not a historical question concerning the way in which these truths were originally discovered, nor a psychological question concerning the way in which each of us comes to learn them, but an epistemological question. The contention of Mill's which we reject is that the propositions of logic and mathematics have the same status as empirical hypotheses; that their validity is determined in the same way. We maintain that they are independent of experience in the sense that they do not owe their validity to empirical verification.5️⃣ We may come to discover them through an inductive process; but once we have apprehended them we see that they are necessarily true, that they hold good for every conceivable instance.

___

5️⃣ By "validity," Ayer means *justification* in the sense of having a reason to think that the claim is true. (Recent philosophers reserve the term "validity" for the assessment of arguments, not the justification of individual claims—see the glossary.)

___

And this serves to distinguish them from empirical generalizations. For we know that a proposition whose validity depends upon experience cannot be seen to be necessarily and universally true.

. . .

The best way to substantiate our assertion that the truths of formal logic and pure mathematics are necessarily true is to examine cases in which they might seem to be confuted. It might easily happen, for example, that when I came to count what I had taken to be five pairs of objects, I found that they amounted only to nine. And if I wished to mislead people I might say that on this occasion twice five was not ten. But in that case I should not be using the complex sign "2 × 5 = 10" in the way in which it is ordinarily used. I should

___

Critique of Pure Reason, 2nd ed., Introduction, section i.

be taking it not as the expression of a purely mathematical proposition, but as the expression of an empirical generalization, to the effect that whenever I counted what appeared to me to be five pairs of objects I discovered that they were ten in number. This generalization may very well be false. But if it proved false in a given case, one would not say that the mathematical proposition "2 × 5 = 10" had been confuted. One would say that I was wrong in supposing that there were five pairs of objects to start with, or that one of the objects had been taken away while I was counting, or that two of them had coalesced, or that I had counted wrongly. One would adopt as an explanation whatever empirical hypothesis fitted in best with the accredited facts. The one explanation which would in no circumstances be adopted is that ten is not always the product of two and five.⑥

⑥ Think carefully about this example. Is there any possible experience that would justify concluding that 2 × 5 doesn't equal 10 after all? See Discussion Question 1.

. . .

The same thing applies to the principles of formal logic. We may take an example relating to the so-called law of excluded middle, which states that a proposition must be either true or false, or, in other words, that it is impossible that a proposition and its contradictory should neither of them be true. One might suppose that a proposition of the form "*x* has stopped doing *y*" would in certain cases constitute an exception to this law. For instance, if my friend has never yet written to me, it seems fair to say that it is neither true nor false that he has stopped writing to me. But in fact one would refuse to accept such an instance as an invalidation of the law of excluded middle. One would point out that the proposition "My friend has stopped writing to me" is not a simple proposition, but the conjunction of the two propositions "My friend wrote to me in the past" and "My friend does not write to me now": and, furthermore, that the proposition "My friend has not stopped writing to me" is not, as it appears to be, contradictory to "My friend has stopped writing to me," but only contrary to it. For it means "My friend wrote to me in the past, and he still writes to me." When, therefore, we say that such a proposition as "My friend has stopped writing to me" is sometimes neither true nor false, we are speaking inaccurately. For we seem to be saying that neither it nor its contradictory is true. Whereas what we mean, or anyhow should mean, is that neither it nor its apparent contradictory is true. And its apparent contradictory is really only its contrary. Thus we preserve the law of excluded middle by showing that the negating of a sentence does not always yield the contradictory of the proposition originally expressed.⑦

⑦ A *contrary* of a claim is another claim that cannot be true if the first one is true, but where both claims can be false. The contradictory of the statement that my friend has stopped writing me would be the denial of the whole conjunction Ayer specifies: that my friend wrote to me in the past and does not write to me now. To deny this is logically equivalent to saying that *either* my friend did not write to me in the past *or* else my friend does write to me now. And the "law of the excluded middle" says that either the original claim (that my friend has stopped writing me) or this last either-or statement must be true. (Think about this.)

There is no need to give further examples. Whatever instance we care to take, we shall always find that the situations in which a logical or mathematical principle might appear to be confuted are accounted for in such a way as to leave the principle unassailed. And this indicates that Mill was wrong in supposing that a situation could arise which would overthrow a mathematical truth. The principles of logic and mathematics are true universally simply because we never allow them to be anything else. And the reason for this is that we cannot abandon them without contradicting ourselves, without sinning against the rules which govern the use of language, and so making our utterances self-stultifying. In other words, the truths of logic and mathematics are analytic propositions or tautologies. In saying this we are making what will be held to be an extremely controversial statement, and we must now proceed to make its implications clear.

The most familiar definition of an analytic proposition, or judgement, as he called it, is that given by Kant. He said* that an analytic judgement was one in

---

Critique of Pure Reason, 2nd ed., Introduction, sections iv and v.

which the predicate B belonged to the subject A as something which was covertly contained in the concept of A. He contrasted analytic with synthetic judgements, in which the predicate B lay outside the subject A, although it did stand in connection with it. Analytic judgements, he explains, "add nothing through the predicate to the concept of the subject, but merely break it up into those constituent concepts that have all along been thought in it, although confusedly." Synthetic judgements, on the other hand, "add to the concept of the subject a predicate which has not been in any wise thought in it, and which no analysis could possibly extract from it." Kant gives "all bodies are extended" as an example of an analytic judgement, on the ground that the required predicate can be extracted from the concept of "body," "in accordance with the principle of contradiction"; as an example of a synthetic judgement, he gives "all bodies are heavy." He refers also to "7 + 5 = 12" as a synthetic judgement, on the ground that the concept of twelve is by no means already thought in merely thinking the union of seven and five. And he appears to regard this as tantamount to saying that the judgement does not rest on the principle of contradiction alone. He holds, also, that through analytic judgements our knowledge is not extended as it is through synthetic judgements. For in analytic judgements "the concept which I already have is merely set forth and made intelligible to me."

I think that this is a fair summary of Kant's account of the distinction between analytic and synthetic propositions, but I do not think that it succeeds in making the distinction clear. For even if we pass over the difficulties which arise out of the use of the vague term "concept," and the unwarranted assumption that every judgement, as well as every German or English sentence, can be said to have a subject and a predicate, there remains still this crucial defect. Kant does not give one straightforward criterion for distinguishing between analytic and synthetic propositions; he gives two distinct criteria, which are by no means equivalent. Thus his ground for holding that the proposition "7 + 5 = 12" is synthetic is, as we have seen, that the subjective intension of "7 + 5" does not comprise the subjective intension of "12"; whereas his ground for holding that "all bodies are extended" is an analytic proposition is that it rests on the principle of contradiction alone. That is, he employs a psychological criterion in the first of these examples, and a logical

criterion in the second, and takes their equivalence for granted.[8] But, in fact, a proposition which is synthetic according to the former criterion may very well be analytic according to the latter. For . . . it is possible for symbols to be synonymous without having the same intensional meaning for anyone: and accordingly from the fact that one can think of the sum of seven and five without necessarily thinking of twelve, it by no means follows that the proposition "7 + 5 = 12" can be denied without self-contradiction. From the rest of his argument, it is clear that it is this logical proposition, and not any psychological proposition, that Kant is really anxious to establish. His use of the psychological criterion leads him to think that he has established it, when he has not.

I think that we can preserve the logical import of Kant's distinction between analytic and synthetic propositions, while avoiding the confusions which mar his actual account of it, if we say that a proposition is analytic when its validity depends solely on the definitions of the symbols it contains, and synthetic when its validity is determined by the facts of experience.[9] Thus, the proposition "There are ants which have established a system of slavery" is a synthetic proposition. For we cannot tell whether it is true or false merely by considering the definitions of the symbols which constitute it. We have to resort to actual observation of the behaviour of ants. On the other hand, the proposition "Either some ants are parasitic or none are" is an analytic proposition. For one need not resort to observation to discover that there either are or are not ants which are

[8] "Subjective intension" is what a person must have in mind in order to correctly understand the term in question (not the associations that particular people might happen to have in mind). Does this make Kant's criterion psychological in a way that makes it unacceptable (as Ayer is suggesting)?

[9] Here is Ayer's alternative definition of "analytic": a claim is analytic when its validity (justification) depends only on the definitions of its terms. But his definition of "synthetic" is mistaken, since it assumes the very thing he is trying to establish: that any claim that is not analytic must be justified by sense experience. "Synthetic" should just mean nonanalytic, with it being a further issue whether any nonanalytic claim must be justified by sense experience.

parasitic. If one knows what is the function of the words "either," "or," and "not," then one can see that any proposition of the form "Either p is true or p is not true" is valid, independently of experience. Accordingly, all such propositions are analytic. [10]

It is to be noticed that the proposition "Either some ants are parasitic or none are" provides no information whatsoever about the behaviour of ants, or, indeed, about any matter of fact. And this applies to all analytic propositions. They none of them provide any information about any matter of fact. In other words, they are entirely devoid of factual content. And it is for this reason that no experience can confute them. [11]

When we say that analytic propositions are devoid of factual content, and consequently that they say nothing, we are not suggesting that they are senseless in the way that metaphysical utterances are senseless. For, although they give us no information about any empirical situation, they do enlighten us by illustrating the way in which we use certain symbols. Thus if I say, "Nothing can be coloured in different ways at the same time with respect to the same part of itself," I am not saying anything about the properties of any actual thing; but I am not talking nonsense. I am expressing an analytic proposition, which records our determination to call a colour expanse which differs in quality from a neighbouring colour expanse a different part of a given thing. [12] In other words, I am simply calling attention to the implications of a certain linguistic usage. Similarly, in saying that if all Bretons are Frenchmen, and all Frenchmen Europeans, then all Bretons are Europeans, I am not describing any matter of fact. But I am showing that in the statement that all Bretons are Frenchmen, and all Frenchmen Europeans, the further statement that all Bretons are Europeans is implicitly contained. [13] And I am thereby indicating the convention which governs our usage of the words "if" and "all."

We see, then, that there is a sense in which analytic propositions do give us new knowledge. They call attention to linguistic usages, of which we might otherwise not be conscious, and they reveal unsuspected implications in our assertions and beliefs. But we can see also that there is a sense in which they may be said to add nothing to our knowledge. For they tell us only what we may be said to know already. Thus, if I know that the existence of May Queens is a relic of tree-worship, and I discover that May Queens still exist in England, I can employ the tautology "If p implies q, and p is true, q is true" to show that there still exists a relic of tree-worship in England. But in saying that there are still May Queens in England, and that the existence of May Queens is a relic of tree-worship, I have already asserted the existence in England of a relic of tree-worship. The use of the tautology does, indeed, enable me to make this concealed assertion explicit. [14] But it does not provide me with any new knowledge, in the sense in which empirical evidence that the election of May Queens had been forbidden by law would provide me with new knowledge. If one had to set forth all the information one possessed, with regard to matters of fact, one would not write down any analytical propositions. But one would make use of analytic propositions in compiling one's encyclopaedia, and would thus come to include propositions which one would otherwise have overlooked. And, besides enabling one to make one's list of information complete, the formulation of ana-

---

[10] Here we have a further elaboration of what justification by definitions amounts to: someone who understands the meanings of the terms can see that the claim is justified, without appeal to experience. How, if at all, does this differ from the claim being a priori justified? (See Discussion Question 2.)

[11] What does Ayer mean here by "factual content"? Why doesn't the truth of the proposition about ants provide information about any matter of fact? (See Discussion Question 3.)

[12] Here is Ayer's attempt to deal with examples having to do with color incompatibility. (See Discussion Question 5 to the Kant reading.) Is it successful? (See Discussion Question 4.)

[13] What does Ayer mean here by containment? Is there a clear way in which this last statement is literally *contained* in the other two? Remember that the issue isn't whether the statement that all Bretons are Europeans *follows* somehow from the other two statements (which no one would deny), but whether it does so because of containment, rather than in some other way.

[14] In what sense, if any, is this last assertion "concealed" in the other two? Is it "concealed" in a way that *explains* how a person can know it a priori on the basis of the others?

lytic propositions would enable one to make sure that the synthetic propositions of which the list was composed formed a self-consistent system. By showing which ways of combining propositions resulted in contradictions, they would prevent one from including incompatible propositions and so making the list self-stultifying. But in so far as we had actually used such words as "all" and "or" and "not" without falling into self-contradiction, we might be said already to know what was revealed in the formulation of analytic propositions illustrating the rules which govern our usage of these logical particles. So that here again we are justified in saying that analytical propositions do not increase our knowledge.

. . .

The mathematical propositions which one might most pardonably suppose to be synthetic are the propositions of geometry. For it is natural for us to think, as Kant thought, that geometry is the study of the properties of physical space, and consequently that its propositions have factual content. And if we believe this, and also recognise that the truths of geometry are necessary and certain, then we may be inclined to accept Kant's hypothesis that space is the form of intuition of our outer sense, a form imposed by us on the matter of sensation, as the only possible explanation of our a priori knowledge of these synthetic propositions. [15]
But while the view that pure geometry is concerned with physical space was plausible enough in Kant's day, when the geometry of

[15] This view of space was a part of Kant's attempt to explain how synthetic a priori knowledge is possible.

Euclid was the only geometry known, the subsequent invention of non-Euclidean geometries has shown it to be mistaken. We see now that the axioms of a geometry are simply definitions, and that the theorems of a geometry are simply the logical consequences of these definitions. A geometry is not in itself about physical space; in itself it cannot be said to be "about" anything. But we can use a geometry to reason about physical space. That is to say, once we have given the axioms a physical interpretation, we can proceed to apply the theorems to the objects which satisfy the axioms. Whether a geometry can be applied to the actual physical world or not, is an empirical question which falls outside the scope of the geometry itself. There is

no sense, therefore, in asking which of the various geometries known to us are false and which are true. In so far as they are all free from contradiction, they are all true. What one can ask is which of them is the most useful on any given occasion, which of them can be applied most easily and most fruitfully to an actual empirical situation. But the proposition which states that a certain application of a geometry is possible is not itself a proposition of that geometry. All that the geometry itself tells us is that if anything can be brought under the definitions, it will also satisfy the theorems. It is therefore a purely logical system, and its propositions are purely analytic propositions. [16]

[16] Until the discovery of non-Euclidean geometries, Euclidean geometry was thought to represent a priori knowledge of space itself, which is obviously a feature of the world. But if geometries are merely systems of definitions and their analytic consequences that can be applied to the world only on the basis of experience, then such a claim is mistaken.

. . .

We conclude, then, that the propositions of pure geometry are analytic. And this leads us to reject Kant's hypothesis that geometry deals with the form of intuition of our outer sense. For the ground for this hypothesis was that it alone explained how the propositions of geometry could be both true a priori and synthetic: and we have seen that they are not synthetic. . . . the only argument which can be brought in favour of Kant's theory is that it alone explains certain "facts." And now we have found that the "facts" which it purports to explain are not facts at all. For while it is true that we have a priori knowledge of necessary propositions, it is not true, as Kant supposed, that any of these necessary propositions are synthetic. They are without exception analytic propositions, or, in other words, tautologies.

We have already explained how it is that these analytic propositions are necessary and certain. We saw that the reason why they cannot be confuted in experience is that they do not make any assertion about the empirical world. They simply record our determination to use words in a certain fashion. We cannot deny them without infringing the conventions which are presupposed by our very denial, and so falling into self-contradiction. And this is the sole ground of their necessity. As Wittgenstein puts it, our justification for holding that the world could not conceivably disobey the laws of logic is simply that we could not say of an unlogical world how it would look. And just as the validity of an analytic proposition is independent of the nature of the external world; so is it independent of the nature of our minds. It is perfectly conceivable that we should have employed different linguistic conventions from those which we actually do employ. But whatever these conventions might be, the tautologies in which we recorded them would always be necessary. For any denial of them would be self-stultifying.[17]

We see, then, that there is nothing mysterious about the apodeictic certainty of logic and mathematics. Our knowledge that no observation can ever confute the proposition "7 + 5 = 12" depends simply on the fact that the symbolic expression "7 + 5" is synonymous with "12," just as our knowledge that every oculist is an eye-doctor depends on the fact that the symbol "eye-doctor" is synonymous with "oculist." And the same explanation holds good for every other a priori truth.

What is mysterious at first sight is that these tautologies should on occasion be so surprising, that there should be in mathematics and logic the possibility of invention and discovery. As Poincaré says: "If all the assertions which mathematics puts forward can be derived from one another by formal logic, mathematics cannot amount to anything more than an immense tautology. Logical inference can teach us nothing essentially new, and if everything is to proceed from the principle of identity, everything must be reducible to it. But can we really allow that these theorems which fill so many books serve no other purpose than to say in a round-about fashion 'A = A'?"* Poincaré finds this incredible. His own theory is that the sense of invention and discovery in mathematics belongs to it in virtue of mathematical induction, the principle that what is true for the number 1, and true for $n + 1$ when it is true for n, is true for all numbers. And he claims that this is a synthetic a priori principle. It is, in fact, a

priori, but it is not synthetic. It is a defining principle of the natural numbers, serving to distinguish them from such numbers as the infinite cardinal numbers, to which it cannot be applied. Moreover, we must remember that discoveries can be made, not only in arithmetic, but also in geometry and formal logic, where no use is made of mathematical induction. So that even if Poincaré were right about mathematical induction, he would not have provided a satisfactory explanation of the paradox that a mere body of tautologies can be so interesting and so surprising.

The true explanation is very simple. The power of logic and mathematics to surprise us depends, like their usefulness, on the limitations of our reason. A being whose intellect was infinitely powerful would take no interest in logic and mathematics. For he would be able to see at a glance everything that his definitions implied, and, accordingly, could never learn anything from logical inference which he was not fully conscious of already. But our intellects are not of this order. It is only a minute proportion of the consequences of our definitions that we are able to detect at a glance. Even so simple a tautology as "91 × 79 = 7189" is beyond the scope of our immediate apprehension. To assure ourselves that "7189" is synonymous with "91 × 79" we have to resort to calculation, which is simply a process of tautological transformation—that is, a process by which we change the form of expressions without altering their significance. The multiplication tables are rules for carrying out this process in arithmetic, just as the laws of logic are rules for the tautological transformation of sentences expressed in logical symbolism or in ordinary language. As the process of calculation is carried out more or less mechanically, it is easy for us to make a slip and so unwittingly contradict ourselves. And this accounts for the existence of logical and mathematical "falsehoods," which otherwise might appear paradoxical. Clearly the risk of error in logical reasoning is proportionate to the length and the complexity of the process of calculation. And in the same way, the more complex an analytic proposition is, the more chance it has of interesting and surprising us.

. . .

*La Science et l'Hypothése, Part I, Chapter i.

Having thus shown that there is no inexplicable paradox involved in the view that the truths of logic and mathematics are all of them analytic, we may safely adopt it as the only satisfactory explanation of their a priori necessity. And in adopting it we vindicate the empiricist claim that there can be no a priori knowledge of reality. For we show that the truths of pure reason, the propositions which we know to be valid independently of all experience, are so only in virtue of their lack of factual content. To say that a proposition is true a priori is to say that it is a tautology. And tautologies, though they may serve to guide us in our empirical search for knowledge, do not in themselves contain any information about any matter of fact.

. . .

Discussion Questions

1. Could any experience refute the claim that 2 × 5 = 10? Such an experience would apparently have to be either (a) one in which *at one moment* there are two groups of five things of some sort (or five groups of two things of that sort) but not ten things of that sort; or else (b) one in which there are ten things of some sort that are incapable of being divided *at that moment* into two groups of five or five groups of two. Could there be experiences of either of these sorts?

2. To say that a proposition of the form "either p is true or p is not true" is justifiable a priori is to say that it is justifiable without appeal to sense experience. Think carefully about what would be involved in a person being justified in accepting such a proposition on this basis. Would such a person have to understand the meaning of the proposition and so the relevant definitions? If so, what, if anything, does the claim that such a proposition is analytic in Ayer's sense add to the claim that it is justifiable a priori? (If it adds nothing, then it can hardly explain a priori justification.)

3. What does Ayer mean by "factual content"? One suggestion would be that any claim that is logically or metaphysically *necessary* lacks factual content. Would a rationalist like Kant dispute the claim that his alleged synthetic a priori claims lack factual content in this sense? Does the fact that a claim lacks factual content in this sense help to explain how we are *justified* in thinking that it is true? What is the relevance of this notion of factual content to the main issue that Ayer is discussing?

4. Can Ayer's discussion of color incompatibility (see the text at Annotation 12) account for the a priori justification of the claim that nothing can be red all over and green all over at the same time? If so, explain more fully how the account would go. If not, explain why not.

5. Is "7 + 5" *synonymous* with "12" in the sense that "eye-doctor" is synonymous with "oculist"? (In thinking about this, it is important not to confuse synonymy with sameness of reference—both expressions refer to the same number, but do they pick it out in the same way?)

A. C. Ewing

Alfred Cyril Ewing (1899–1973) was a British philosopher who taught at Cambridge University and made important contributions to ethics and metaphysics. In this selection, he defends a rationalist view of a priori justification, according to which the human mind has a fundamental capacity for insight into necessary truths. Along the way, he replies to many of Ayer's arguments for moderate empiricism (though without mentioning Ayer by name) and also discusses the issues of innate ideas and induction.

The "A Priori" and the Empirical,
from *The Fundamental Questions of Philosophy*

MEANING OF THE DISTINCTION; "A PRIORI" CHARACTER OF MATHEMATICS

In the theory of knowledge, the first point that confronts us is the sharp distinction between two kinds of knowledge which have been called respectively a priori and empirical. Most of our knowledge we obtain by observation of the external world (sense–perception) and of ourselves (introspection). This is called empirical knowledge. But some knowledge we can obtain by simply thinking. That kind of knowledge is called a priori. Its chief exemplifications are to be found in logic and mathematics. In order to see that $5 + 7 = 12$ we do not need to take five things and seven things, put them together, and then count the total number. We can know what the total number will be simply by thinking.

Another important difference between a priori and empirical knowledge is that in the case of the former we do not see merely that something, S, is in fact P, but that it must be P and why it is P.① I can discover that a flower is yellow (or at least produces sensations of yellow) by looking at it, but I cannot thereby see why it is yellow or that it must be yellow. For anything I can tell it might equally well have been a red flower. But with a truth such as that $5 + 7 = 12$ I do not see merely that it is a fact but that it must be a fact. It would be quite absurd to suppose that $5 + 7$ might have been equal to 11 and just happened to be equal to 12, and I can see that the nature of 5 and 7 constitutes a fully adequate and intelligible reason why their sum should be 12 and not some other number. It is indeed conceivable that some of the things which make the two groups of 5 and 7 might, when they were put together, fuse like drops of water, or even vanish, so that there were no longer 12 things; but what is inconceivable is that there could *at the same time* be $5 + 7$ things of a certain kind at once in a certain place

> ① This is an important claim about the apparent character of a priori insight: it seems to reveal not only that the claim in question is true, but also *why* the claim is true and that the claim is *necessary* (in the logical or metaphysical sense)—and also, it might be added, why it is necessary.

and yet less than 12 things of that kind in that place. Before some of the things fused or vanished they would be $5 + 7$ in number and also 12 in number, and after the fusion or disappearance they would be neither $5 + 7$ nor 12.② When I say in this connection that something is inconceivable, I do not mean merely or primarily that we cannot conceive it—this is not a case of a mere psychological inability like the inability to understand higher mathematics. It is a positive insight: we definitely see it to be impossible that certain things could happen. This we do not see in the case of empirical propositions which are false: they are not true but might for anything we know have been true. It is even conceivable, so far as we can see, that the fundamental laws of motion might have been quite different from what they are, but we can see that there could not have been a world which contradicted the laws of arithmetic. This is expressed by saying that empirical propositions are *contingent,* but true a priori propositions *necessary.*③

> ② Ewing, like Ayer, thinks that it is impossible that $7 + 5$ not equal 12. Here, however, the emphasis is on the necessity that this be so, not on any relation to language or definition.

What we see to be necessary is not indeed that arithmetic should apply to the universe. It is conceivable that the universe might have been constituted entirely of a homogeneous fluid, and then, since there would have been no distinction between different things, it is difficult to see how arithmetic could have applied to it. What we do see is that arithmetic must be true of whatever can be numbered at all.

> ③ Could a contingent claim, one that is false in some possible worlds, ever be known a priori to be true in the actual world? Ewing is denying that this could happen.

We must not be misled here by the fact that in order to come to understand arithmetic we originally required examples. Once we have learnt the beginnings of arithmetic in the kindergarten with the help

From The Fundamental Questions of Philosophy *(New York: Collier, 1962).*

of examples, we do not need examples any more to grasp it, and we can see the truth of many arithmetical propositions, e.g. that $3112 + 2467 = 5579$, of which we have never had examples. We have probably never taken 3112 things and 2467 things, put them together and counted the resulting set, but we still know that this is what the result of the counting would be. If it were empirical knowledge, we could not know it without counting. The examples are needed, not to prove anything, but only in order to enable us to come to understand in the first instance what is meant by number.

. . .

THE "A PRIORI" IN LOGIC

Another important field for a priori knowledge is logic. The laws of logic must be known a priori or not at all. They certainly are not a matter for empirical observation, and the function of logical argument is just to give us conclusions which we have not discovered by observation. The argument would be superfluous if we had observed them already. We are able to make inferences because there is sometimes a logical connection between one or more propositions (the premise or premises) and another proposition, the conclusion, such that the latter must be true if the former is. Then, if we know the former, we can assert the latter on the strength of it, thus anticipating any experience. To take an example, there is a story that Mr. X., a man of high reputation and great social standing, had been asked to preside at a big social function. He was late in coming, and so a Roman Catholic priest was asked to make a speech to pass the time till his arrival. The priest told various anecdotes, including one which recorded his embarrassment when as confessor he had to deal with his first penitent and the latter confessed to a particularly atrocious murder. Shortly afterwards Mr. X. arrived, and in his own speech he said: "I see Father_____is here. Now, though he may not recognize me, he is an old friend of mine, in fact I was his first penitent." It is plain that such an episode would enable one to infer that Mr. X. had committed a murder without having observed the crime.[4] . . .

> [4] Think carefully about this example. The claim that Mr. X is a murderer *follows logically* from the two premises indicated. Is it *contained* in them in any sense that would help to explain *why* it follows logically?

OTHER CASES OF THE "A PRIORI"

A priori knowledge, while most prominent in mathematics and logic, is not limited to these subjects. For instance, we can see a priori that the same surface cannot have two different colours all over at the same time, or that a thought cannot have a shape. Philosophers have been divided into rationalists and empiricists according to whether they stressed the a priori or the empirical element more. The possibility of metaphysics depends on a priori knowledge, for our experience is quite inadequate to enable us to make on merely empirical grounds any sweeping generalizations of the kind the metaphysician desires. The term a priori covers both self-evident propositions, i.e. those which are seen to be true in their own right, and those which are derived by inference from propositions themselves self-evident.

THE LINGUISTIC THEORY OF THE "A PRIORI" AND THE DENIAL THAT "A PRIORI" PROPOSITIONS OR INFERENCES CAN GIVE NEW KNOWLEDGE

At the present time even empiricist philosophers recognize the impossibility of explaining away a priori propositions as merely empirical generalizations, but they are inclined to the view that a priori propositions and a priori reasoning are merely concerned with language, and so cannot tell us anything new about the real world. Thus it is said that, when we make an inference, the conclusion is just part of the premises expressed in different language. If so, inference would be of use merely for clarifying our language and would involve no real advance in knowledge. Some inferences are of this type, e.g. A is a father, therefore A is male.[5] But are they all? That would be hard indeed to square with the *prima facie* novelty of many conclusions. Take, for instance, the proposition that the square on the hypotenuse of a right-angled triangle is equal to the sum of the squares on the other two sides. Such a proposition can be inferred from the axioms and postulates of Euclid, but it certainly does not seem to be included in their

> [5] Think about why this claim is analytic in Kant's sense of that term.

meaning.* Otherwise we should know it as soon as we understood the axioms and postulates. The example I gave of the murder discovered by a logical argument seems to be another case of a fact not known at all beforehand by the reasoner which is discovered by his reasoning. Extreme empiricist philosophers contend that this appearance of novelty is really illusory, and that in some sense we knew the conclusion all along; but they have never succeeded in making clear in what sense we did so. It is not enough to say that the conclusion is implicit in the premises. "Implicit" means "implied by," and of course a conclusion is implied by its premises, if the inference is correct at all.† But this admission leaves quite open the question whether or not a proposition can follow from a different one which does not contain it as part of itself; and since we obviously can by deductive inference come to know things which we did not know before in any ordinary sense of "know," we must treat the empiricist's claim as unjustified till he has produced a clearly defined sense of "implicit in" or "contained in" which leaves room for that novelty in inference which we all cannot help really admitting. In any ordinary sense of "know" the conclusion is not in the cases I have mentioned known prior to the inference, and since the premises are and indeed must be known before we know the conclusion, it is therefore in no ordinary sense of "part" part of the premises.⑥

> ⑥ If the claim of containment just means that the conclusion follows from the premises, then it cannot explain why this is so (or how we are able to see that it is).

. . .

Nevertheless, the view that inference cannot yield new conclusions dies hard, and so it will not be superfluous to bring further arguments. (1) "This has shape" admittedly follows logically from "this has size" and vice versa. If the view I am criticizing were true, "this has size" would, therefore, have to include in its meaning "this has shape," and "this has shape" would also have to include in its meaning "this has size." But this would only be possible if the two sentences meant exactly the same thing, which they obviously do not.⑦ (2) Take an argument such as— Montreal is to the north of New York, New York is to the north of Washington, therefore Montreal is to the north of Washington. If the view I am discussing is true, the conclusion is part of the premises. But it is not part of either premise by itself, otherwise both premises would not be needed. So the only way in which it could be part of both together would be if it were divisible into two propositions one of which was part of the first and the other part of the second. I defy anybody to divide it in this way. ⑧ (3) The proposition "Socrates was a philosopher" certainly entails the proposition "if Socrates had measles some philosophers have had measles," but it cannot be that the second proposition is included in the first. For the first proposition certainly does not include the notion of measles.

> ⑦ An analogy: if the membership of group A is contained in that of group B, and vice versa, then the two groups must have exactly the same membership. Thus if all the elements included in the meaning of one claim are included in that of the other and vice versa, the total set of elements must be exactly the same.

> ⑧ Pretty clearly someone like Ayer does not want to say that part of the meaning of "Montreal is to the north of Washington" is contained in "Montreal is to the north of New York" and part in "New York is to the north of Washington." But how can the whole meaning be contained in the other two claims together, if no part of it is contained in either of them separately?

What is really the same view is often expressed by saying that all a priori propositions are "analytic." A distinction has commonly been drawn between *analytic* propositions, in which the predicate is in the notion of the subject already formed before the proposition is asserted, so that the proposition gives no new information, and *synthetic* propositions in which the predicate is not so contained and which are

---

*It is no objection to this illustration that Euclidean geometry has not been proved true of the physical world, for the proposition in question undoubtedly follows from the premises of Euclid and therefore should on the theory we are discussing be included as part of them. What is denied by modern scientists is not that the conclusion follows from the premises, but that the premises and what follows from them are true of the world.

†Similarly, the phrase "is contained in" is sometimes used just to mean "follows from" or "is implied by" and need not connote that the conclusion is actually part of the premises, as would be the case on the literal meaning of "contained."

thus capable of giving new information.* Analytic propositions are essentially verbal, being all true by definition, e.g. all fathers are male. As an example of a synthetic proposition we could take any proposition established by experience such as "I am cold" or "It is snowing," but empiricists often assert that there are no synthetic a priori propositions. That this view cannot be justified may be shown at once. The proposition that there are no synthetic a priori propositions, since it cannot be established by empirical observations, would be, if justified, itself a synthetic a priori proposition, and we cannot affirm it as a synthetic a priori proposition that there are no synthetic a priori propositions.⑨ We may therefore dismiss off-hand any arguments for the theory. Such arguments, whatever they were, would have to involve synthetic a priori propositions. . . .

⑨ Here is another point that you need to consider carefully. Restate the claim in question to make it explicitly of subject-predicate form. (See Discussion Question 1.)

The analytic view seems plausible when we are concerned with the simplest propositions of logic and arithmetic, but we must not assume that a proposition is analytic because it is obvious. Though it may be very difficult to determine precisely where analytic propositions end and synthetic propositions begin, we cannot use this as a ground for denying the latter. It is very difficult to say precisely where blue ends and green begins, since the different shades run into each other imperceptibly, but we cannot therefore argue that all blue is really green. Taking arithmetic, even if there is a good deal of plausibility in saying that 2 + 2 is included in the meaning of "4," there is none in saying $95 - 91$ or $\frac{216}{2} - \frac{287 + 25}{3}$

⑩ Notice that it would also have to be claimed that the meaning of each of these more complicated expressions is included in that of the other—and hence that they also have the same meaning.

are so included. ⑩ Yet, if the analytic view were true, all the infinite numerical combinations which could be seen a priori to be equal to 4 would have to be included in the meaning of "4."

Some empiricists, without committing themselves to the view that all a priori propositions are analytic, still say these are a matter of arbitrary choice or verbal convention. ⑪ . . .

That the truth of a priori propositions does not just depend on the nature of language can be easily seen when we consider that, even if we do not know any Fijian or Hottentot, we can know that also in these languages and not only in the languages we know the propositions 5 + 7 = 12 must be true. It is of course true that by altering the meaning of the words we could make the proposition we expressed by "5 + 7 = 12" false, e.g. if I used "12" in a new sense to mean what other people mean by "11," but then it would be a different proposition. I could play the same trick with empirical propositions and say truly, e.g., that "fire does not burn" or "there is an elephant in this room" if I used "burn" to mean "drown" or "elephant" to mean "table."⑫ This does not in the least impair the obviousness of the contrary propositions established by experience. . . .

⑪ Sometimes an analytic proposition is defined as one that is true by linguistic convention.

⑫ Remember here that a **proposition** is a certain content, not the way in which it happens to be verbally expressed. If the meanings of the symbols "11" and "12" were interchanged (perhaps by a governmental decree), then "7 + 5 = 11" would be true (and would express the same proposition that "7 + 5 = 12" previously expressed, while "7 + 5 = 12" would express a false proposition (the same one that "7 + 5 = 11" formerly expressed).

The views we have been criticizing contain the following elements of truth. (1) A priori propositions can be seen to be true and the conclusions of an inference seem to follow from their premises without any further observation, provided we understand the meaning of the words used. But to say that q follows from p once we understand the meaning of the words is not to say that q is part of the meaning of the words used to express p. "Follow from" and "be part of" are not synonyms. ⑬ (2) If q follows from p you cannot assert p

⑬ See Discussion Question 2 to the Ayer selection.

---

*This definition would have to be amended slightly to suit modern logicians who (I think, rightly) deny that all propositions are of the subject-predicate form, but this would not alter the principle though importing a complication of detail with which we need not deal here.

and deny q without contradicting yourself, but this is only to say that in that case the denial of q implies the denial of p. It is not to say that q is part of what you assert when you assert p, unless we already assume that what is implied is always part of what implies it, i.e. beg the question at issue. (3) An a priori proposition cannot be fully understood without being seen to be true. It may be impossible to understand something fully without understanding something else not included in it at all, so it may still be synthetic.

People have been inclined to deny synthetic a priori propositions because they could not see how one characteristic could necessarily involve another, but that this could not happen would be itself a synthetic a priori metaphysical proposition. People have also thought that it was necessary to give some sort of explanation of a priori knowledge, and could not see how this could be done except in terms of language. To this I should reply that there is no reason to suppose that a priori knowledge requires some special explanation any more than does our ability to attain knowledge empirically by observation. Why not take it as an ultimate fact? Human beings certainly cannot explain everything, whether there is ultimately an explanation for it or not.

. . .

INNATE IDEAS

The question whether a priori knowledge is possible must not be confused with the question whether there are "innate ideas," i.e. ideas born with one. The theory of "innate ideas" was put forward to account for the occurence of ideas which did not seem derivable from sense-experience. The British seventeenth-century philosopher, Locke, criticizes it on the ground that it is absurd to suppose that the new-born babies have ideas of God or of the law of contradiction, but all the advocates of the theory of whom we know have expressly denied that they meant to assert this and have said that all that was innate was a faculty to form the ideas. . . . The theory usually opposed to that of innate ideas asserts that all our ideas were ultimately derived from sense-experience (including observation of ourselves). Obviously it must be admitted that I can have ideas of things which I have never experienced by my senses, e.g. centaurs, but it was contended that such ideas were always formed by combining in some way

ideas thus derived, e.g. in this case the idea of a horse's body and that of a man's head, or at least by comparing such ideas or abstracting elements in them. But there must be at least one idea that is not so derived. Inference is impossible unless we have the idea of logically necessary connection between the premises from which we start in our inference and the conclusion we reach, and this idea is clearly quite different from any which could be given in sense-experience. Other ideas which have been, at least plausibly, supposed not to be derived from sense-experience are God, good, duty, the laws of logic, substance, cause, and the ideas of geometry such as that of a perfect circle or square. . . .

But, if we deny that all ideas are derivable from sense-experience, we still need not hold the doctrine of innate ideas. A third alternative is to say that the ideas are not made by our mind but derived, like empirical ideas, by apprehension of the real, only to add that there are other ways besides sense-experience of apprehending the real. E.g., we may make three alternative suppositions about the idea of cause:

(1) We may suppose that we are innately so constituted that we call up the idea out of our own resources and apply it when we are confronted with experiences, such as that of regular succession, which suggest it. [14] (2) We may suppose that the idea of causation is simply that of regular sequence in time, in which case we could easily explain it by sense-experience, since regular sequence is a relation which can be discovered by the senses easily enough.[15] (3) If we think (as I do) that causation cannot be identified with regular sequence or anything else which could be apprehended by the senses, we may still avoid the innate theory by maintaining that it is a relation in the real which we immediately apprehend by some means other than sense-experience on certain occasions, e.g. when we cause something to happen by an act of will or when we encounter physical resistance. Having acquired the idea of cause in this way, we might then apply it in cases where we do not immediately experience the relation. . . . Similarly, if we accept the idea of substance as not an object of sense-

[14] This is at least roughly what proponents of innate ideas or concepts (such as Kant) seem to have had in mind.

[15] This is Hume's view.

experience, we might explain it either by supposing it innate or by maintaining that each person had an intuition of himself as substance and then applied the idea that gained to other minds and material things. It would not be necessary to hold that we had this immediate apprehension each time the idea of substance or cause was applied, provided we had it occasionally. Again, if we can ever by thinking see two characteristics to be logically connected, this is sufficient to account for the idea of logically necessary connection without supposing it innate. 16

16 Is this a clear alternative to both Locke's view and the innatist view? (See Discussion Question 2.)

We need not suppose either that the fundamental ideas of logic . . . are innate or that they are derivable from sense-experience or ordinary introspection. The fundamental characteristics or relations . . . of logic in thinking logically (i.e. apprehending the validity of inferences and the formal nature of propositions, etc.), and this does not mean that they are or are only characteristics of the experiences . . . of thinking logically. They are characteristics . . . of that about which we think logically.

. . .

INDUCTION

The chief use of a priori knowledge is to enable us to make inferences. Whenever we can make an inference from p to q, we must know, or at least be justified in believing, the hypothetical "if p, then q." For q to follow necessarily from p that hypothetical proposition must be a priori; necessary connection is not a matter of empirical observation. An important distinction is, however, drawn between deduction and induction. Both are inferences, but they differ in that deduction proceeds from the more to the less general, induction from the less to the more general. 17 Induction in all its more characteristic forms is a matter of empirical generalization, i.e. we argue that, because something has proved true in a number of observed cases, it will be likely to prove true in similar cases that have not yet been ob-

17 Though often invoked, this is not a particularly good characterization of the difference between induction and deduction. The following characterization of induction is much better.

served. The conclusion is not (except in very special cases) certain, but it may be highly probable, and all our rational predictions about the future depend on an inference of this kind. Induction has presented very serious problems to logicians and philosophers generally. The inference in induction is certainly not a merely empirical matter: we use it to enable us to forecast the future, but we have not observed the future empirically. The whole use of induction is indeed to enable us to infer what we have never observed. Therefore some a priori principle about the world is required if induction is to be justified. The principle must be of such a nature as to justify us in supposing that what has happened in observed cases is likely to recur in unobserved; but logicians have certainly not hit upon a principle which is both self-evident and adequate to justify inductive inference. The one which has been most commonly put forward as supplying what is needed is the principle that every change has a cause, but it would be much disputed nowadays whether this was either necessary or sufficient to justify induction. The meaning of "cause" itself is also very much a subject on which there are varying views. So the justification of induction is one of the worst problems of logic. The fact that we must use induction if we are to have any science at all is a proof that science cannot be merely empirical (even where it does not use mathematics), but we cannot say that the conclusion of an inductive inference follows from its premises with the same necessity as does the conclusion of a deductive one.

Most of the propositions we call empirical are not justified by mere observation but by that together with induction. This applies to all conclusions of science, for these are never statements of single observed facts but generalizations about what usually happens or inferences from such generalizations. It applies also to all our ordinary judgments about physical objects, for we always read in more than is actually observed and the only justification for what we read in must be found in induction (i.e. we assume that objects will have besides the characteristics we actually observe at the time those characteristics which we observed in the past in similar objects, e.g. that the ice we see is cold though we are not feeling the cold). This does not mean that, whenever we observe, we are consciously making inferences. But we can speak of "implicit inferences," meaning that without making conscious inferences we hold beliefs on the strength of experiences which could be used as premises to justify the beliefs by explicit inferences.

INTUITION

A necessary, though not always recognized, presupposition of inference is intuition. To argue validly—A ∴ B ∴ C—we must see a connection between A and B and a connection between B and C. But how do we know that that connection itself holds? We may be able to interpolate further terms, D and E, and say A, ∴ D, ∴ B, ∴ E, ∴ C; but we obviously cannot go on in this way *ad infinitum.* Sooner or later we must come to a point where we just see immediately that there is a connection, but cannot *prove* this to be so. When we see immediately something to be true otherwise than by observing it empirically, we are said to have an *intuition.* [18] No doubt apparent intuitions are often to be explained as really implicit or suppressed inferences, but the argument I have just given shows that this cannot be so with all cases of intuition. Even when we have made explicit all the omitted steps, the logical point remains that for it to be possible to infer any one proposition from any other we must see the connection between them, and this connection cannot always be proved by interpolating fresh propositions, yet it must be known somehow. The connection may be said to be derived from the fundamental laws of logic, but the laws themselves are known intuitively. Further, before we can see their validity in the abstract, we must have seen their validity in particular cases. All of us have used syllogisms long before we knew anything about the rules of syllogistic inference. That was because we could see that a conclusion followed from its premises without knowing the general principle on account of which it followed, as we can move our arms effectively in definite purposive ways without knowing the laws of physiology which govern our motions or the laws of physics which make the selected motions

> [18] What Ewing is describing here is a priori intuition, sometimes referred to as a priori insight. (This is not intuition in the sense of a hunch or premonition.) Empiricists typically deny that there is any such thing.

the most effective ones for our practical purpose. The same applies whether the connection is such as to make the conclusion follow with certainty given the premises, or whether it is, as in most inductive arguments, such that the premises make the conclusion only probable. But, while logicians have easily agreed on the general principles governing deduction and we can see these to be completely self-evident, neither is the case as regards the general principles governing induction. Yet though neither the plain man nor even the logician is clear as to the fundamental laws behind the process, we can see in particular cases of induction that the truth of the premises makes the truth of the conclusion probable, as we can see that the truth of the premises makes the truth of the conclusion certain in particular cases of deduction. [19] "Intuition" as a source of knowledge or justified belief is often brushed aside with contempt, but the argument I have given at any rate shows that, if there are to be any valid inferences, there must be some intuitions.

> [19] Ewing is saying that particular inductive arguments can be seen to be rationally cogent, even if we cannot state a general principle in relation to which they are so. (See Discussion Question 3.)

Many philosophers have preferred to limit the term "intuition" to cases of certain knowledge, but there are many cases where something presents itself to one intuitively as deserving a certain degree of credence but falling short of certainty or where an intuition has some value but is confused and inextricably blended with erroneous assumptions or inferences. These cases are particularly plentiful in philosophy. It seems to me therefore preferable to use the term intuition to cover cases also where certainty is lacking. Anyone who dislikes this usage may substitute the term "ostensible intuition." For, whether all "intuitions" are said to be certain or not, we must at least admit that what is taken to be a certain intuition is not always really one. It is largely a matter of terminology whether we then say that it is not an intuition or say that it is an intuition but not certain. But it is clear that there are all sorts of degrees of subjective certainty and uncertainty in apparent intuitions. Similarly, the a priori in general must not be equated with the certain. Empirical propositions may be certain, as are many established by immediate experience; and there are many cases of apparent a priori insight where we cannot be quite certain whether what we seem to see to be a priori true is really so. But any uncertainty there is in the a priori lies in the defects of the mind that reasons. We can only be uncertain in such matters because we are or may be confused. In some cases as in mathematics the confusion can be removed quite easily, in others as in philosophy it can persist for generations.

The main argument of those who attack the notion of intuition is that apparent intuitions are liable to conflict with each other and there is then no means of deciding which is right. [20] But this is a mistake; we can in fact test them in various ways. We can consider whether they are capable of any clear and internally consistent statement. We can ask whether they fit into a coherent system with the rest of our well-established beliefs. We can also ask whether intuitions of the same kind have been confirmed in the past. We can ask whether an intuition stands or falls by itself or is a presupposition of a whole number of other beliefs which we cannot help holding, as some (though confused) intuition of the occurrence of causation or the uniformity of nature seems a necessary presupposition of all inductive beliefs. We can consider the plausibility of giving an alternative explanation of the intuitive belief. The result may then be negative or positive. It may be that our apparent intuition will evaporate when we think of the explanation, and then the latter is probably a correct one at least as to why *we* held the belief. Or it may be that the intuition will persist unshaken, in which case the explanation is probably at least inadequate. We can again consider whether the intuition repeats itself when considered in different contexts and different moods or with different examples.

So when two people have conflicting intuitions we need not suppose that there is just an irreducible

[20] This is perhaps the most standard objection to a priori intuition.

difference of intuitive faculty between them and that there is nothing more to be done about it. Arguments may well be available which without strictly proving either side to be wrong put a disputant into a position in which he can see better for himself whether he is right or wrong or at least partially confirm or cast doubt on the truth of his view. In general, the clearer we have made ourselves about a subject by inferential thought, by analysing the different factors involved and by clearing up our terminology, the more likely are we to have correct intuitions on the matter if such are available at all. Again, intellectual confusions may be revealed which were responsible for the truth of the belief in question. Thus a person who really sees that A is B may confuse B with C and will then think he sees intuitively that A is C. Some such conflicts may be caused simply or mainly by ambiguities of terminology or the attaching of different meanings to some word. And of course we need not deny that differences of intuition may sometimes be due on one side or even on both to "wishful thinking" or to the kind of cause which it is the business of the psycho-analyst (or of a patient and tactful friend) to remove. . . . We cannot of course settle all disputes in these ways, but neither can we in practice settle all disputes in science. The most we can say is that they are soluble in principle, though we may not have the ability to hit on the right way of solving a particular dispute. Similarly, there is no reason to believe that conflicts between rival intuitions would not all be capable of a solution if these methods were applied aright and with good will on both sides, though in fact we cannot so apply them. [21]

[21] Ewing's response is that there are many ways to attempt to resolve the dispute between opposed intuitions, even though none of these is guaranteed to succeed. Try to think how these would work in particular cases.

. . .

Discussion Questions

1. How might the claim that there are no synthetic a priori truths—that is, that no synthetic proposition is capable of being justified a priori—be restated in the form "all A's are B's"? One attempt, albeit a bit clumsy, would be "all synthetic propositions are incapable of

being justified a priori." Is the predicate of this claim included in its subject in any clear or obvious way? Is there any way that its truth can be seen to follow from the definitions of the terms involved? Assume that "synthetic" is defined as "nonanalytic," not in Ayer's mistaken and **question-begging** way (see Annotation 9 to the Ayer selection).

2. How do we acquire concepts like causality, substance, and others that do not seem to be derived from experience in any obvious way? Are they derived from experience in some unobvious way? Are they innate (and what exactly would that mean)? Is there a third alternative along the lines suggested by Ewing: that they are derived from a non-experiential awareness of features of oneself (note that this

is not introspection in any simple way, which would be a kind of experience) or from awareness of logical connections? Is Ewing just appealing to a broader notion of experience, and is there any problem with that?

3. Think of an actual instance of inductive reasoning: a case in which there have been many observations of A's that are B's under varied conditions and circumstances and no observations of A's that are not B's, and in which it is inferred that all A's are B's. How plausible is it that we have an a priori intuition (or at least "ostensible intuition") that the conclusion of the argument is probably true—that the premises of the argument support the conclusion in a way analogous to that which occurs in a deductive argument?

IS INDUCTION JUSTIFIED?

David Hume

David Hume (1711–1776), a Scottish philosopher and historian, is usually regarded as one of the most important and influential philosophers of all time. He did very important work in epistemology, metaphysics, ethics, and the philosophy of religion, producing a comprehensive philosophical position that is most distinctive for its skeptical tendencies—tendencies that are reflected in the present selection.

In this selection, Hume presents what is perhaps the first reasonably clear formulation of the problem of induction. His initial concern is with knowledge of causal relations, which he claims to be the only basis for knowledge of matters of fact that go beyond direct experience and memory. His view is that causal relations can themselves be known only through repeated experience of the causal sequence. But this raises in turn the problem of how repeated experience of thing or property A always being followed by thing or property B can justify the conclusion that A will probably always be followed by B (which is at least part of the meaning of the claim that A causes B, in the sense of being a causally **sufficient condition** for B). Hume's skeptical thesis is that there is no cogent reasoning that leads from such an experiential premise to this conclusion, so that inductive reasoning of this sort is in fact *not* justified. (It is important to realize that he is not claiming merely that inductive conclusions cannot be known with certainty: his stronger and much more startling claim is that there is no good reason at all to accept them even as probable.)

Skeptical Doubts Concerning the Operations of the Understanding, from *An Enquiry Concerning Human Understanding*

PART I

All the objects of human reason or inquiry may naturally be divided into two kinds, to wit, *relations of ideas,* and *matters of fact.* Of the first kind are the sciences of geometry, algebra, and arithmetic; and in short, every affirmation which is either intuitively or demonstratively certain. *That the square of the hypotenuse is equal to the squares of the two sides,* is a proposition which expresses a relation between these figures. *That three times five is equal to the half of thirty,* expresses a relation between these numbers. Propositions of this kind are discoverable by the mere operation of thought, without dependence on what is anywhere existent in the universe. Though there never was a circle or triangle in nature, the truths demonstrated by Euclid would for ever retain their certainty and evidence.①

> **①** This distinction is the main basis for the subsequent argument and needs to be considered carefully. "Relations of ideas" suggests the idea of analyticity, but Hume is also claiming that anything knowable a priori has this status—and also, in the next paragraph, that all such claims are necessary, since nothing contingent has this status. Thus Hume is assuming in effect that the three main distinctions (see the chapter introduction) coincide (in which case, among other things, there would be no synthetic a priori truths).

Matters of fact, which are the second objects of human reason, are not ascertained in the same manner; nor is our evidence of their truth, however great, of a like nature with the foregoing. The contrary of every matter of fact is still possible; because it can never imply a contradiction, and is conceived by the mind with the same facility and distinctness, as if ever so comfortable to reality. *That the sun will not rise tomorrow* is no less intelligible a proposition, and implies no more contradiction than the affirmation, *that it will rise.* We should in vain, therefore, attempt to demonstrate its falsehood. Were it demonstratively false, it would imply a contradiction, and could never be distinctly conceived by the mind.②

It may, therefore, be a subject worthy of curiosity, to inquire what is the nature of that evidence which assures us of any real existence and matter of fact, beyond the present testimony of our senses, or the records of our memory. . . .

All reasonings concerning matter of fact seem to be founded on the relation of *cause and effect.* By means of that relation alone we can go beyond the evidence of our memory and senses.③ If you were to ask a man, why he believes any matter of fact, which is absent; for instance, that his friend is in the country, or in France; he would give you a reason; and this reason would be some other fact; as a letter received from him, or the knowledge of his former resolutions and promises. A man finding a watch or any other machine in a desert island, would conclude that there had once been men in that island. All our reasonings concerning fact are of the same nature. And here it is constantly supposed that there is a connection between the present fact and that which is inferred from it. Were there

> **②** The primary meaning of "matters of fact" seems to be claims that can be denied without contradiction and so are contingent rather than necessary. But Hume is also saying that these are not knowable a priori, and also not relations of ideas and so not analytic, but rather synthetic. The overall implication is again that all three distinctions (a priori/a *posteriori,* necessary/contingent, analytic/synthetic) coincide, though Hume gives no real argument for this claim (a version of moderate empiricism).

> **③** Thus the claim is that any contingent fact that goes beyond direct sense perception or the memory of such perception can be known only through causal reasoning.

From An Enquiry Concerning Human Understanding, *1748.*

nothing to bind them together, the inference would be entirely precarious. The hearing of an articualte voice and rational discourse in the dark assures us of the presence of some person: Why? because these are the effects of the human make and fabric, and closely connected with it. If we anatomize all the other reasonings of this nature, we shall find that they are founded on the relation of cause and effect, and that this relation is either near or remote, direct or collateral. Heat and light are collateral effects of fire, and the one effect may justly be inferred from the other.

If we would satisfy ourselves, therefore, concerning the nature of that evidence, which assures us of matters of fact, we must inquire how we arrive at the knowledge of cause and effect.

I shall venture to affirm, as a general proposition, which admits of no exception, that the knowledge of this relation is not, in any instance, attained by reasonings a priori; but arises entirely from experience, when we find that any particular objects are constantly conjoined with each other. ④ Let an object be presented to a man of ever so strong natural reason and abilities; if that object be entirely new to him, he will not be able, by the most accurate examination of its sensible qualities, to discover any of its causes or effects. Adam, though his rational faculties be supposed, at the very first, entirely perfect, could not have inferred from the fluidity and transparency of water that it would suffocate him, or from the light and warmth of fire that it would consume him. No object ever discovers, by the qualities which appear to the senses, either the causes which produced it, or the effects which will arise from it; nor can our reason, unassisted by experience, ever draw any inference concerning real existence and matter of fact.

This proposition, *that causes and effects are discoverable, not by reason but by experience,* will readily be admitted with regard to such objects, as we remember to have once been altogether unknown to us; since we must be conscious of the utter inability, which we then lay under, of foretelling what would arise from them. Present two smooth pieces of marble to a man who has no tincture of natural philosophy; he will never discover that they will adhere together in

④ Thus A can be known to be the cause of B only by finding in experience that the two are constantly conjoined (in the right order), that is that A is always followed by B.

such a manner as to require great force to separate them in a direct line, while they make so small a resistance to a lateral pressure. Such events, as bear little analogy to the common course of nature, are also readily confessed to be known only by experience; nor does any man imagine that the explosion of gunpowder, or the attraction of a loadstone, could ever be discovered by arguments a priori. In like manner, when an effect is supposed to depend upon an intricate machinery or secret structure of parts, we make no difficulty in attributing all our knowledge of it to experience. Who will assert that he can give the ultimate reason, why milk or bread is proper nourishment for a man, not for a lion or a tiger?

But the same truth may not appear, at first sight, to have the same evidence with regard to events, which have become familiar to us from our first appearance in the world, which bear a close analogy to the whole course of nature, and which are supposed to depend on the simple qualities of objects, without any secret structure of parts. We are apt to imagine that we could discover these effects by the mere operation of our reason, without experience. We fancy, that were we brought on a sudden into this world, we could at first have inferred that one billiard ball would communicate motion to another upon impulse; and that we needed not to have waited for the event, in order to pronounce with certainty concerning it. Such is the influence of custom, that, where it is strongest, it not only covers our natural ignorance, but even conceals itself, and seems not to take place, merely because it is found in the highest degree.⑤

⑤ In the case of events that are similar enough to those with which we are familiar, we may seem to ourselves to have direct insights into what will cause what that do not depend on experience. Hume is saying that this is an illusion.

But to convince us that all the laws of nature, and all the operations of bodies without exception, are known only by experience, the following reflections may, perhaps, suffice. Were any object presented to us, and were we required to pronounce concerning the effect, which will result from it, without consulting past observation; after what manner, I beseech you, must the mind proceed in this operation? It must invent or imagine some event, which it ascribes to the object as its effect; and it is plain that this invention must be entirely arbitrary. The mind can never possibly find the effect in the supposed cause, by the most accurate scrutiny and examination. For the effect is totally different from the cause, and consequently can never be discovered in it. Motion in the second billiard ball is a quite distinct event from motion in the first: nor is there anything in the one to suggest the smallest hint of the other. A stone or piece of metal raised into the air, and left without any support, immediately falls: but to consider the matter a priori, is there anything we discover in this situation which can beget the idea of a downward, rather than an upward, or any other motion, in the stone or metal?

And as the first imagination or invention of a particular effect, in all natural operations, is arbitrary, where we consult not experience; so must we also esteem the supposed tie or connection between the cause and effect, which binds them together, and renders it impossible that any other effect could result from the operation of that cause. When I see, for instance, a billiard ball moving in a straight line towards another; even suppose motion in the second ball should by accident be suggested to me, as the result of their contact or impulse; may I not conceive, that a hundred different events might as well follow from that cause? May not both these balls remain at absolute rest? May not the first ball return in a straight line, or leap off from the second in any line or direction? All these suppositions are consistent and conceivable. Why then should we give the preference to one, which is no more consistent or conceivable than the rest? All our reasonings a priori will never be able to show us any foundation for this preference.

In a word, then, every effect is a distinct event from its cause. It could not, therefore, be discovered in the cause, and the first invention or conception of it, a priori, must be entirely arbitrary. And even after it is suggested, the conjunction of it with the cause must appear equally arbitrary; since there are always many other effects, which, to reason, must seem fully as consistent and natural. In vain, therefore, should we pretend to determine any single event, or infer any cause or effect, without the assitance of observation and experience.[6]

. . .

6 One important sort of causal relation that this does not seem to account for is that which involves unobservable entities, as in theoretical science. See the BonJour selection for a discussion of how such causal relations might be known.

PART II

But we have not yet attained any tolerable satisfaction with regard to the question first proposed. Each solution still gives rise to a new question as difficult as the foregoing, and leads us on to farther inquiries. When it is asked, *What is the nature of all our reasonings concerning matter of fact?* the proper answer seems to be, that they are founded on the relation of cause and effect. When again it is asked, *What is the foundation of all our reasonings and conclusions concerning that relation?* it may be replied in one word, *experience*. But if we still carry on our sifting humor, and ask, *What is the foundation of all conclusions from experience?* this implies a new question, which may be of more difficult solution and explication. . . .

I shall content myself, in this section, with an easy task, and shall pretend only to give a negative answer to the question here proposed. I say then, that, even after we have experience of the operations of cause and effect, our conclusions from that experience are *not* founded on reasoning, or any process of the understanding. This answer we must endeavor both to explain and to defend.

It must certainly be allowed, that nature has kept us at a great distance from all her secrets, and has afforded us only the knowledge of a few superficial qualities of objects; while she conceals from us those powers and principles on which the influence of those objects entirely depends. Our senses inform us of the color, weight, and consistence of bread; but neither sense nor reason can ever inform us of those qualities which fit it for the nourishment and support of a human body. Sight or feeling conveys an idea of the actual motion of bodies; but as to that wonderful force or power, which would carry on a moving body for ever in a continued change of place, and which bodies never lose but by communicating it to others; of this we cannot form the most distant conception. But notwithstanding this ignorance of natural powers and principles, we always presume, when we see like sensible qualities, that they have like secret powers, and expect that effects, similar to those which we have experienced, will follow from them. If a body of like color and consistence with that bread, which we have formerly eat, be presented to us, we make no scruple of repeating the experiment, and foresee, with certainty, like nourishment and support. Now this is a process of the mind or thought, of which I would willingly know the foundation. It is allowed on all hands that there is no known connection between the sensible qualities and the secret powers; and consequently, that the mind is not led to form such a conclusion concerning their constant and regular conjunction, by anything which it knows of their nature. ⑦

⑦ Hume might seem here to be suggesting that causal knowledge would be easier to obtain if it were somehow possible to directly observe these "secret powers." But this is misleading. Even if we could somehow observe the inner nature of things and not merely their "superficial qualities," the causal relations between those qualities and any further effects would still have to be established through experience in essentially the same way.

As to past *experience,* it can be allowed to give *direct* and *certain* information of those precise objects only, and that precise period of time, which fell under its cognizance: but why this experience should be extended to future times, and to other objects, which, for aught we know, may be only in appearance similar; this is the main question on which I would insist. The bread, which I formerly eat, nourished me; that is, a body of such sensible qualities was, at that time, endued with such secret powers: but does it follow, that other bread must also nourish me at another time, and that like sensible qualities must always be attended with like secret powers? The consequence seems no wise necessary. At least, it must be acknowledged that there is here a consequence drawn by the mind; that there is a certain step taken; a process of thought, and an inference, which wants to be explained. These two propositions are far from being the same, *I have found that such an object has always been attended with such an effect,* and *I foresee, that other objects, which are, in appearance, similar, will be attended with similar effects.* I shall allow, if you please, that the one proposition may justly be inferred from the other; I know, in fact, that it always is inferred. But if you insist that the inference is made by a chain of reasoning, I desire you to produce that reasoning. The connection between these propositions is not intuitive. There is required a medium, which may enable the mind to draw such an inference, if indeed it be drawn by reasoning and argument. What that medium is, I must confess, passes my comprehension; and it is incumbent on those to produce it, who assert that it really exists, and is the origin of all our conclusions concerning matter of fact. ⑧

This negative argument must certainly, in process of time, become altogether convincing, if many penetrating and able philosophers shall turn their inquiries this way and no one be ever able to discover any connecting proposition or intermediate step, which supports the understanding in this conclusion. But as the question is yet new, every reader may not trust so far to his own penetration, as to conclude, because an argument escapes his inquiry, that therefore it does not really exist. For this reason it may be requisite to venture upon a more difficult task: and enumerating all the branches of human knowledge, endeavor to show that none of them can afford such an argument.

All reasonings may be divided into two kinds, namely demonstrative reasoning, or that concerning relations of ideas, and moral reasoning, or that concerning matter of fact and existence. ⑨ That there are no demonstrative arguments in the case seems evident; since it implies no contradiction that the course of nature may change, and that an object, seemingly like those which we have experienced, may be attended with different or contrary effects. May I not clearly and distinctly conceive that a body, falling from the clouds, and which, in all other respects, resembles snow, has yet the taste of salt or feeling of fire? Is there any more intelligible proposition than to affirm, that all the trees will flourish in December and January, and decay in May and June? Now whatever is intelligible, and can be distinctly conceived, implies no contradiction, and can never be proved false by

⑧ Hume is claiming that there is no cogent reasoning of any sort from the observational premise that constant conjunction has been observed to the conclusion that the same sequence will occur in other cases. His first reason for this is a challenge to his opponent to produce such reasoning, to spell out in detail how an argument from that sort of premise to that sort of conclusion would go—something Hume is confident cannot be done.

⑨ His second and more important argument takes the form of a dilemma, relying on the distinction explained at the beginning of the selection. According to this distinction, there are only two possible sorts of reasoning: a priori reasoning and reasoning that appeals to experience. (Hume's use of the term "moral" to refer to the latter is an archaic usage that has nothing to do with the modern use of the term to refer to matters having to do with ethics.)

any demonstrative argument or abstract reasoning a priori. [10]

[10] A priori reasoning will not work because such reasoning depends in Hume's view on the avoidance of contradiction, and there is no contradiction in supposing that "the course of nature may change" in such a way that a sequence that has been experienced so far may cease to hold.

If we be, therefore, engaged by arguments to put trust in past experience, and make it the standard of our future judgment, these arguments must be probable only, or such as regard matter of fact and real existence, according to the division above mentioned. But that there is no argument of this kind, must appear, if our explication of that species of reasoning be admitted as solid and satisfactory. We have said that all arguments concerning existence are founded on the relation of cause and effect; that our knowledge of that relation is derived entirely from experience; and that all our experimental conclusions proceed upon the supposition that the future will be conformable to the past. To endeavor, therefore, the proof of this last supposition by probable arguments, or arguments regarding existence, must be evidently going in a circle, and taking that for granted, which is the very point in question. [11]

[11] And reasoning that appeals to experience will not work, since the only way that experience can support a general conclusion of the sort in question is by generalizing from repeated sequences in exactly the way that is at issue. Thus to appeal to any such reasoning (such as by arguing that inductive reasoning has been observed in the past to yield true conclusions and so is likely to do so in the future as well) would beg the question.

In reality, all arguments from experience are founded on the similarity which we discover among natural objects, and by which we are induced to expect effects similar to those which we have found to follow from such objects. And though none but a fool or madman will ever pretend to dispute the authority of experience, or to reject that great guide of human life, it may surely be allowed a philosopher to have so much curiosity at least as to examine the principle of human nature, which gives this mighty authority to experience, and makes us draw advantage from that similarity which nature has placed among different objects. From causes which appear *similar* we expect similar effects. This is the sum of all our experimental conclu-

sions. Now it seems evident that, if this conclusion were formed by reason, it would be as perfect at first, and upon one instance, as after ever so long a course of experience. But the case is far otherwise. . . . It is only after a long course of uniform experiments in any kind, that we attain a firm reliance and security with regard to a particular event. Now where is that process of reasoning which, from one instance, draws a conclusion, so different from that which it infers from a hundred instances that are nowise different from that single one? This question I propose as much for the sake of information, as with an intention of raising difficulties. I cannot find, I cannot imagine any such reasoning. But I keep my mind still open to instruction, if anyone will vouchsafe to bestow it on me.

Should it be said that, from a number of uniform experiments, we *infer* a connection between the sensible qualities and the secret powers; this, I must confess, seems the same difficulty, couched in different terms. The question still recurs, on what process of argument this *inference* is founded? Where is the medium, the interposing ideas, which join propositions so very wide of each other? It is confessed that the color, consistence, and other sensible qualities of bread appear not, of themselves, to have any connection with the secret powers of nourishment and support. For otherwise we could infer these secret powers from the first appearance of these sensible qualities, without the aid of experience; contrary to the sentiment of all philosophers, and contrary to plain matter of fact. Here, then, is our natural state of ignorance with regard to the powers and influence of all objects. How is this remedied by experience? It only shows us a number of uniform effects, resulting from certain objects, and teaches us that those particular objects, at that particular time, were endowed with such powers and forces. When a new object, endowed with similar sensible qualities, is produced, we expect similar powers and forces, and look for a like effect. From a body of like color and consistence with bread we expect like nourishment and support. But this surely is a step or progress of the mind, which wants to be explained. When a man says, *I have found, in all past instances, such sensible qualities conjoined with such secret powers:* And when he says, *Similar sensible qualities will always be conjoined with similar secret powers,* he is not guilty of a tautology, nor are these propositions in any respect the same. You say that the one proposition is an inference from the other. But you must confess that the inference is not intuitive; neither is it demonstrative: [12] Of what nature is it, then? To say it is experimental, is begging the question. For all inferences from experience suppose, as their foundation, that the future will resemble the past, and that similar powers will be conjoined with similar sensible qualities. If there be any suspicion that the course of nature may change, and that the past may be no rule for the future, all experience becomes useless, and can give rise to no inference or conclusion. It is impossible, therefore, that any arguments from experience can prove this resemblance of the past to the future; since all these arguments are founded on the supposition of that resemblance. Let the course of things be allowed hitherto ever so regular; that alone, without some new argument or inference, proves not that, for the future, it will continue so. In vain do you pretend to have learned the nature of bodies from your past experience. Their secret nature, and consequently all their effects and influence, may change, without any change in their sensible qualities. This happens sometimes, and with regard to some objects: Why may it not happen always, and with regard to all objects? What logic, what process of argument secures you against this supposition? My practice, you say, refutes my doubts. But you mistake the purport of my question. As an agent, I am quite satisfied in the point; but as a philosopher, who has some share of curiosity, I will not say scepticism, I want to learn the foundation of this inference. No reading, no inquiry has yet been able to remove my difficulty, or give me satisfaction in a matter of such importance. Can I do better than propose the difficulty to the public, even though, perhaps, I have small hopes of obtaining a solution? We shall, at least, by this means, be sensible of our ignorance, if we do not augment our knowledge.

I must confess that a man is guilty of unpardonable arrogance who concludes, because an argument has escaped his own investigation, that therefore it does not really exist. I must also confess that, though all the learned, for several ages, should have employed themselves in fruitless search upon any subject, it may still, perhaps, be rash to conclude positively that the subject must, therefore, pass all human comprehension. Even though we examine all the sources of our knowledge, and conclude them unfit for such a subject, there may still remain a suspicion, that the enumeration is not complete, or the examination not accurate. But with regard to the present subject, there are some considerations which seem to remove all this accusation of arrogance or suspicion of mistake.

It is certain that the most ignorant and stupid peasants—nay infants, nay even brute beasts—improve by experience, and learn the qualities of natural objects, by observing the effects which result from them. When a child has felt the sensation of pain from touching the flame of a candle, he will be careful not to put his hand near any candle; but will expect a similar effect from a cause which is similar in its sensible qualities and appearance. If you assert, therefore, that the understanding of the child is led into this conclusion by any process of argument or ratiocination, I may justly require you to produce that argument; nor have you any pretense to refuse so equitable a demand. You cannot say that the argument is abstruse, and may possibly escape your inquiry; since you confess that it is obvious to the capacity of a mere infant. If you hesitate, therefore, a moment, or if, after reflection, you produce any intricate or profound argument, you, in a manner, give up the question, and confess that it is not reasoning which engages us to suppose the past resembling the future, and to expect similar effects from causes which are, to appearance, similar. This is the proposition which I intended to enforce in the present section. If I be right, I pretend not to have made any mighty discovery. And if I be wrong, I must acknowledge myself to be indeed a very backward scholar; since I cannot now discover an argument which, it seems, was perfectly familiar to me long before I was out of my cradle. [13]

---

[12] To say that the inference is "intuitive" would be to say we have a direct a priori insight that the conclusion follows; to say it is "demonstrative" would be to say there is a more extended a priori argument involving intermediate steps. But both of these ways of justifying the inference depend, Hume thinks, on it being contradictory to accept the experiential premise and reject the conclusion—which, he has argued, is not the case here.

---

[13] Hume reinforces the challenge to his opponent by claiming that the reasoning in question, if it existed, could not be very difficult to specify, since it would have to be familiar even to young children (who obviously draw such conclusions).

Discussion Questions

1. Attempts are sometimes made to justify inductive reasoning by adding a further premise or principle to the argument: the premise that the future will probably resemble the past, or perhaps that unobserved cases will probably resemble observed cases. What would Hume's response be to such an attempt?

2. Hume seems to assume that any case in which one sort of event A was always followed (in the future as well) by another sort of event B would be a case of causation, but this is too simple a picture. Can you think of one or more common-sense examples in which it is plausible (apart from worries about induction) to suppose that A is always followed by B, but in which A is not the cause or even part of the cause of B? (Hint: think of cases where both A and B are caused by some third sort of event C.)

3. Look back at the discussion of abductive reasoning (theoretical or explanatory reasoning) in the BonJour selection. Could the acceptance of an inductive conclusion be justified by this sort of reasoning on the grounds that the existence of an objective regularity in nature is the best explanation of the observed regular sequence? What other explanations are possible for such an observed sequence? Does such an argument show that the inductive conclusion is probably true, given the truth of the premise? What do you think Hume would say about this sort of defense of induction? (This question is much harder and more complicated than most of the discussion questions.)

Wesley Salmon

Wesley Salmon (1925–2001) was an American philosopher who taught mainly at Indiana University, the University of Arizona, and the University of Pittsburgh. Salmon wrote widely in the philosophy of science, with his work on explanation and the related topic of causality being especially influential. In the following selection, Salmon restates the problem of induction as it grows out of Hume's discussion and then considers and evaluates a variety of possible solutions (some of which have been omitted here). In the process of doing this, he also offers a version of the moderate empiricist view of a priori knowledge that is somewhat different from that presented in the Ayer selection.

The Problem of Induction, from
The Foundations of Scientific Inference

We all believe that we have knowledge of facts extending far beyond those we directly perceive. The scope of our senses is severely limited in space and time; our immediate perceptual knowledge does not reach to events that happened before we were born, to events that are happening now in certain other places, or to any future events. We believe, nevertheless, that we have some kind of indirect knowledge of such facts. We know that a glacier once covered a large part of North America, that the sun continues to exist at night, and that the tides will rise and fall tomorrow. Science and common sense have at least this

From The Foundations of Scientific Inference *(Pittsburgh: University of Pittsburgh Press, 1967)*.

one thing in common: Each embodies knowledge of matters of fact that are not open to our direct inspection. Indeed, science purports to establish general laws or theories that apply to all parts of space and time without restriction. A "science" that consisted of no more than a mere summary of the results of direct observation would not deserve the name.

Hume's profound critique of induction begins with a simple and apparently innocent question: How do we acquire knowledge of the unobserved?* This question, as posed, may seem to call for an empirical answer. We observe that human beings utilize what may be roughly characterized as inductive or scientific methods of extending knowledge from the observed to the unobserved. The sciences, in fact, embody the most powerful and highly developed methods known, and we may make an empirical investigation of scientific methods much as we might for any other sort of human behavior. We may consider the historical development of science. We may study the psychological, sociological, and political factors relevant to the pursuit of science. We may try to give an exact characterization of the behavior of scientists. In doing all these things, however, important and interesting as they are, we will have ignored the *philosophical* aspect of the problem Hume raised. Putting the matter very simply, these empirical investigations may enable us to describe the ways in which people arrive at *beliefs* about unobserved facts, but they leave open the question of whether beliefs arrived at in this way actually constitute *knowledge*. It is one thing to describe how people go about seeking to extend their knowledge; it is quite another to claim that the methods employed actually do yield knowledge.

One of the basic differences between knowledge and belief is that knowledge must be founded upon evidence—i.e., it must be belief founded upon some rational justification. To say that certain methods yield knowledge of the unobserved is to make a cognitive claim for them. Hume called into question the justification of such cognitive claims. The answer cannot be found entirely within an empirical study of human behavior, for a *logical* problem has been raised. It is the problem of understanding the logical relationship between evidence and conclusion in logically correct inferences. It is the problem of determining whether the inferences by which we attempt to make the transition from knowledge of the observed to knowledge of the unobserved are logically correct. The fact that people do or do not use a certain type of inference is irrelevant to its justifiability. Whether people have confidence in the correctness of a certain type of inference has nothing to do with whether such confidence is justified. If we should adopt a logically incorrect method for inferring one fact from others, these facts would not actually constitute evidence for the conclusion we have drawn. The problem of induction is the problem of explicating the very concept of *inductive evidence*.

. . .

Consider a simple and highly artificial situation. Suppose a number of balls have been drawn from an urn, and that all of the black ones that have been drawn are licorice-flavored. . . . The problem—Hume's basic *philosophical* problem—is this: Given that all of the observed black balls have been licorice-flavored, and given that somehow the conclusion has been entertained that the unobserved black balls in the urn are also licorice-flavored, do the observed facts constitute sound *evidence* for that conclusion? Would we be *justified* in accepting that conclusion on the basis of the facts alleged to be evidence for it? [1]

> [1] This is perhaps not the best example. There is no reason to think that drawing from an urn reflects any real regularity in nature, which is what the problem of induction is mainly concerned with.

As a first answer to this question we may point out that the inference does conform to an accepted inductive principle, a principle saying roughly that observed instances conforming to a generalization constitute evidence for it. [2] It is, however, a very small step to the next question: What grounds have we for accepting this or any other inductive principle? Is there any reason or justification for placing confidence in the conclusions of inferences of this type? Given that the premises of this inference are true, and

> [2] That is, that observations of cases of A's that are also B's constitute evidence for the generalization that all A's are B's.

*David Hume, *Enquiry Concerning Human Understanding*.

given that the inference conforms to a certain rule, can we provide any rational justification for accepting its conclusion rather than, for instance, the conclusion that black balls yet to be drawn will taste like quinine?

It is well known that Hume's answer to this problem was essentially skeptical. It was his great merit to have shown that a justification of induction, if possible at all, is by no means easy to provide. In order to appreciate the force of his argument it is first necessary to clarify some terminological points. This is particularly important because the word *induction* has been used in a wide variety of ways.

For purposes of systematic discussion one distinction is fundamental, namely, the distinction between demonstrative and nondemonstrative inference. A *demonstrative* inference is one whose premises necessitate its conclusion; the conclusion cannot be false if the premises are true. All valid deductions are demonstrative inferences. A *nondemonstrative* inference is simply one that fails to be demonstrative. Its conclusion is not necessitated by its premises; the conclusion could be false even if the premises are true. A demonstrative inference is *necessarily truth-preserving;* a nondemonstrative inference is not.[3]

> [3] Notice that this so far says nothing about *why* particular arguments have the feature of being necessarily truth-preserving. It is also important to be clear that a demonstrative argument guarantees only that the conclusion will be true *if* the premises are true.

The category of nondemonstrative inferences, as I have characterized it, contains, among other things perhaps, all kinds of fallacious inferences. If, however, there is any kind of inference whose premises, although not necessitating the conclusion, do lend it weight, support it, or make it probable, then such inferences possess a certain kind of logical rectitude. It is not deductive validity, but it is important anyway. Inferences possessing it are *correct inductive inferences.*

Since demonstrative inferences have been characterized in terms of their basic property of necessary truth preservation, it is natural to ask how they achieve this very desirable trait. For a large group of demonstrative inferences, including those discussed under "valid deduction" in most logic texts, the answer is rather easy. Inferences of this type purchase necessary truth preservation by sacrificing any extension of content. The conclusion of such an inference says no more

than do the premises—often less. The conclusion cannot be false if the premises are true *because* the conclusion says nothing that was not already stated in the premises. The conclusion is a mere reformulation of all or part of the content of the premises. In some cases the reformulation is unanticipated and therefore psychologically surprising, but the conclusion cannot augment the content of the premises. Such inferences are *nonampliative;* an ampliative inference, then, has a conclusion with content not present either explicitly or implicitly in the premises.[4]

> [4] Salmon's view is that all logically valid arguments are "nonampliative" because the content of the conclusion is present, at least "implicitly," in the content of the premises—where this is supposed to explain why the conclusion must be true if the premises are true. (See the selections by Ayer and Ewing for more discussion of this issue.)

While it is easy to understand why nonampliative inferences are necessarily truth-preserving, the further question arises whether there are any necessarily truth-preserving inferences that are also ampliative. Is there any type of inference whose conclusion must, of necessity, be true if the premises are true, but whose conclusion says something not stated by the premises? Hume believed that the answer is negative and so do I, but it is not easy to produce an adequate defense of this answer. Let us see, however, what an affirmative answer would amount to.

Suppose there were an ampliative inference that is also necessarily truth-preserving. Consider the implication from its premises, $P_1, \ldots, P_k$, to its conclusion C. If the inference were an ordinary nonampliative deduction, this implication would be analytic and empty; but since the argument is supposed to be ampliative, the implication must be synthetic. At the same time, because the argument is supposed to be necessarily truth-preserving, this implication must be not only true but necessarily true. Thus, to maintain that there are inferences that are both ampliative and necessarily truth-preserving is tantamount to asserting that there are synthetic a priori truths. [5] This may be

> [5] The statement that all cases where the premises are true are cases where the conclusion is true would be a necessary truth (and, Salmon is assuming, thereby knowable a priori), but would be synthetic (in Kant's sense) because the predicate is not included in the subject.

seen in another way. Any ampliative inference can be made into a nonampliative one by adding a premise. In particular, if we add to the foregoing ampliative inference the synthetic a priori premise, "If P_1 and P_2 and . . . and P_k, then C," the resulting inference will be an ordinary valid nonampliative deduction. Consider our example once more; this time let us set it out more formally:

1. Some black balls from this urn have been observed.
   All observed black balls from this urn are licorice-flavored.
   All black balls in this urn are licorice-flavored.

This argument is clearly ampliative, for the premise makes a statement about observed balls only, while the conclusion makes a statement about the unobserved as well as the observed balls. It appears to be nondemonstrative as well, for it seems perfectly possible for the conclusion to be false even if the premises are true. We see no reason why someone might not have dropped a black marble in the urn which, when it is drawn, will be found to be tasteless. We could, however, rule out this sort of possibility by adding another premise:

2. Some black balls from this urn have been observed.
   All observed black balls in this urn are licorice-flavored.
   Any two balls in this urn that have the same color also have the same flavor.
   All black balls in this urn are licorice-flavored.

The additional premise has transformed the former nondemonstrative inference into a demonstrative inference, but we must also admit that we have transformed it into a nonampliative inference. If, however, the third premise of 2 were a synthetic a priori truth, the original inference, although ampliative, would have been necessarily truth-preserving and, hence, demonstrative. If the premise that transformed inference 1 into inference 2 were necessarily true, then it would be impossible for the conclusion of inference 1 to be false if the premises were true, for that would contradict the third premise of inference 2.

Hardly anyone would be tempted to say that the statement, "Any two balls in this urn that have the same color also have the same flavor," expresses a synthetic a priori truth. Other propositions have, however, been taken to be synthetic a priori. Hume and many of his successors noticed that typical inductive inferences, such as our example concerning licorice-flavored black balls, would seem perfectly sound if we could have recourse to some sort of principle of uniformity of nature. If we could only prove that the course of nature is uniform, that the future will be like the past, or that uniformities that have existed thus far will continue to hold in the future, then we would seem to be justified in generalizing from past cases to future cases—from the observed to the unobserved.[6] Indeed, Hume suggests that we presuppose in our inductive reasoning a principle from which the third premise of 2 would follow as a special case: "We always presume, when we see like sensible qualities, that they have like secret powers, and expect that effects, similar to those which we have experienced, will follow from them."* Again, "From causes which appear *similar* we expect similar effects. This is the sum of all our experimental conclusions."†

[6] No one has ever claimed that the conclusion of an inductive argument is guaranteed to be true, since it is beyond question that such conclusions are occasionally false. The most that seems reasonable is the claim that such a conclusion is *probably* true, but then all that would be required to justify such a result is the claim that nature is largely uniform or that uniformities observed in the past will *probably* continue in the future.

Hume's searching examination of the principle of uniformity of nature revealed no ground on which it could be taken as a synthetic a priori principle. For all we can know a priori, Hume argued, the course of nature might change, the future might be radically unlike the past, and regularities that have obtained in respect to observed events might prove completely inapplicable to unobserved cases. We have found by experience, of course, that nature has exhibited a high degree of uniformity and regularity so far, and we infer inductively that this will continue, but to use an inductively inferred generalization as a justification

*Hume, *Human Understanding* [p. 287].
†Ibid [p. 289].

for induction, as Hume emphasized, would be flagrantly circular. He concluded, in fact, that there are no synthetic a priori principles in virtue of which we could have demonstrative inferences that are ampliative. Hume recognized two kinds of reasoning: reasoning concerning relations of ideas and reasoning concerning matters of fact and existence. The former is demonstrative but nonampliative while the latter is ampliative but not necessarily truth-preserving.

If we agree that there are no synthetic a priori truths, then we must identify necessarily truth-preserving inference with nonampliative inference. All ampliative inference is nondemonstrative. This leads to an exhaustive trichotomy of inferences: valid deductive inference, correct inductive inference, and assorted fallacies. The first question is, however, whether the second category is empty or whether there are such things as correct inductive inferences. This is Hume's problem of induction. Can we show that any particular type of ampliative inference can be justified in any way? If so, it will qualify as correct induction.

Consider, then, any ampliative inference whatever. The example of the licorice-flavored black balls illustrates the point. We cannot show *deductively* that this inference will have a true conclusion given true premises. If we could, we would have proved that the conclusion must be true if the premises are. That would make it necessarily truth-preserving, hence, demonstrative. This, in turn, would mean that it was nonampliative, contrary to our hypothesis. Thus, if an ampliative inference could be justified deductively it would not be ampliative. It follows that ampliative inference cannot be justified deductively.

At the same time, we cannot justify any sort of ampliative inference *inductively*. To do so would require the use of some sort of nondemonstrative inference. But the question at issue is the justification of nondemonstrative inference, so the procedure would be question begging. Before we can properly employ a nondemonstrative inference in a justifying argument, we must already have justified that nondemonstrative inference.[7]

[7] These two paragraphs are Salmon's version of Hume's dilemma argument.

Hume's position can be summarized succinctly: We cannot justify any kind of ampliative inference. If it could be justified deductively it would not be ampliative. It cannot be justified nondemonstratively because that would be viciously circular. It seems, then, that there is no way in which we can extend our knowledge to the unobserved. We have, to be sure, many beliefs about the unobserved, and in some of them we place great confidence. Nevertheless, they are without rational justification of any kind!

This is a harsh conclusion, yet it seems to be supported by impeccable arguments. It might be called "Hume's paradox," for the conclusion, although ingeniously argued, is utterly repugnant to common sense and our deepest convictions. We *know* ("in our hearts") that we have knowledge of unobserved fact. The challenge is to show how this is possible.[8]

[8] To see just how "harsh" or "repugnant" this conclusion is, ask yourself how much of our knowledge would be undermined if induction were rejected, and how much would be left. (See Discussion Question 1.)

II. ATTEMPTED SOLUTIONS

It hardly needs remarking that philosophers have attempted to meet Hume's intriguing challenge in a wide variety of ways. . . . In this section I shall survey what seem to me to be the most important efforts to deal with the problem.

1. Inductive Justification. If Hume's arguments had never been propounded and we were asked why we accept the methods of science, the most natural answer would be, I think, that these methods have proved themselves by their results. We can point to astonishing technological advances, to vastly increased comprehension, and to impressive predictions. Science has provided us with foresight, control, and understanding. No other method can claim a comparable record of successful accomplishment. If methods are to be judged by their fruits, there is no doubt that the scientific method will come out on top.

Unfortunately, Hume examined this argument and showed that it is viciously circular. It is an example of an attempt to justify inductive methods inductively. From the premise that science has had considerable predictive success in the past, we conclude that it will continue to have substantial predictive success in the future. Observed cases of the application of scientific method have yielded successful prediction; therefore, as yet unobserved cases of the application of scientific method will yield successful predictions. This argument has the same structure as our black-balls-in-the-urn example; it is precisely the sort of ampliative inference from the observed to the unobserved whose justifiability is in question.

Consider the parallel case for a radically different sort of method. A crystal gazer claims that his method is the appropriate method for making predictions. When we question his claim he says, "Wait a moment; I will find out whether the method of crystal gazing is the best method for making predictions." He looks into his crystal ball and announces that future cases of crystal gazing will yield predictive success. If we should protest that his method has not been especially successful in the past, he might well make certain remarks about parity of reasoning. "Since you have used your method to justify your method, why shouldn't I use my method to justify my method? If you insist upon judging my method by using your method, why shouldn't I use my method to evaluate your method? By the way, I note by gazing into my crystal ball that the scientific method is now in for a very bad run of luck." [9]

9 Not all "methods" will automatically be self-justifying in this way: if crystal balls do sometimes give clear and definite answers to questions, then some of them might say that crystal balls are *not* reliable or might give no definite answer either way to this particular question. A method that undermined itself in this way would be even less defensible, but this does nothing to show that self-justification is enough for genuine justification.

The trouble with circular arguments is obvious: with an appropriate circular argument you can prove anything. . . .

4. Synthetic **a priori** *Principles.* A long philosophical tradition, dating back to antiquity, denies the empiricist claim that knowledge of the world rests solely upon observational evidence—that factual knowledge is limited to what we can observe and what we can infer therefrom. In the modern period, this rationalistic tradition is represented by men like Descartes and Leibniz who took their inspiration from the abstract aspect of modern physics. After Hume's devastating criticism of induction, Kant provided a more precise formulation, a fuller elaboration, and a more subtle defense of rationalism than any that had been given earlier (or, quite possibly, subsequently). As Kant himself testified, it was Hume who awakened him from his "dogmatic slumbers" and thereupon stimulated the *Critique of Pure Reason.*

The doctrine that there are synthetic a priori truths is, as I explained above, tantamount to the view that there are necessarily truth-preserving ampliative inferences. If we could find a *bona fide* demonstrative ampliative inference we would have a solution to Hume's problem of the ground of inference from the observed to the unobserved. This solution could be presented in either of two ways. First, one could assert that there are factual propositions that can be established by pure reason—without the aid of empirical evidence—and that these synthetic a priori propositions, in conjunction with premises established by observation, make it possible to deduce (nonampliatively) conclusions pertaining to unobserved matters of fact. Second, one could claim that these synthetic a priori propositions, although not added as premises to ampliative inferences to render them nonampliative, do instead provide a warrant for genuinely ampliative inferences from the observed to the unobserved. [10] . . .

In order to appreciate the philosophical issues involved in the attempt to justify induction by means of a synthetic a priori principle, we must introduce some reasonably precise definitions of key terms. Two pairs of concepts are involved: first, the distinction between *analytic* and *synthetic* statements, and second, the distinction between a priori and *a posteriori* statements. . . .

Although it is reasonable to maintain, I think, that all logical truths are analytic, there seem to be analytic statements that are not logical truths. [11]

For instance,

All bachelors are unmarried

is not [a logical truth]. However, given the definition,

10 The first of these alternatives has no plausibility at all, because it would mean that the inductive conclusion is guaranteed to be true whenever the observational premises are true—which we know is not the case (see Annotation 6). The second alternative might amount to the same thing, but it might also involve only a principle saying that the conclusion is probably true when the observational premises are true.

11 A *logical truth* is roughly one that is guaranteed to be true by virtue of its *form*. (We have omitted Salmon's more technical account, which amounts to the same thing.)

Bachelor = ₍df₎ unmarried adult male,

the foregoing statement can be transformed into a logical truth, for the definition gives license to substitute the *definiens*, "unmarried adult male," for the *definiendum* "bachelor." This substitution yields,

All unmarried adult males are unmarried,

which is a logical truth. To incorporate cases of this sort, we may define an *analytic statement* as one that is a logical truth or can be transformed into a logical truth by definitional substitution of *definiens* for *definiendum*. [12] The negation of an analytic truth is a *self-contradiction*. Any statement that is neither analytic nor self-contradictory is *synthetic*. . . .

Analytic statements, like logical truths, have been characterized as statements that are true in all possible worlds. I have already explained how I think this characterization applies to logical truths. When the class of analytic statements is constructed by augmenting logical truths with statements that can be reduced to logical truths by definitional substitution, it is evident that these additional statements are true in all possible worlds in just the same manner as are logical truths. A definitional substitution cannot, after all, alter the truth value of any statement. [13]

. . .

Analytic statements are often said, moreover, to be devoid of any factual content. Although there are difficulties in giving an adequate account of the concept of factual content, enough can be said to illuminate its relation to analytic statements. The basic feature seems to be that factual content of a statement is a measure of the capacity of that statement to *rule out* possibilities. In this respect,

it is a negative concept. In a state of total ignorance all possible states of affairs are live possibilities; any possible state of affairs might, for all we know, be the actual state of things. As knowledge accumulates, we realize that some of the possibilities are not actualized. The statements expressing our knowledge are incompatible with descriptions of various possible worlds, so we know that these possibilities are ruled out—our actual world does not coincide with any of these possibilities that are incompatible with what we know. Generally speaking, moreover, the greater our knowledge—the greater the factual content of the statements we know—the more possibilities are disqualified from being actual. Imagine, for instance, the inhabitants of Plato's famous cave, who are totally ignorant of the nature of the external world. They can imagine birds of all sorts, including ravens of various colors. When the emissary to the outer world returns and reports that all ravens are black, those who remained in the cave can rule out all possibilities that had room for ravens of other colors. The statement, "All ravens are black," has factual content because of the descriptions of possible worlds with which it is incompatible. If, however, the emissary should return and remark that every raven is either black or non-black, his statement would be totally lacking in content, and the permanent inhabitants of the cave—anxious for knowledge of the external world—would be justly furious with him for his empty report. His statement would lack content because it is compatible with every possibility. It is . . . a logical truth. . . . Since it is true under any possible circumstances and is not incompatible with any description of a possible world, its content is zero. Any analytic statement will, as we have seen above, share this characteristic. We are, therefore, entitled to assert that analytic statements have no factual content. [14] . . .

Let us now turn to the other distinction required for our discussion. A statement is a priori if its truth or falsity can be established without recourse to observational evidence; it is a posteriori if observational

[12] This is Salmon's main definition of "analytic." You should compare it to Kant's and Ayer's. ("All unmarried adult males are unmarried" is a logical truth because it is of the form "All FGH are F," and any claim of that form is necessarily true.) (See Discussion Question 2.)

[13] Salmon is here claiming both (a) that analytic truths are true in every possible world, that is, are necessary, and (b) that any claim that is true in every possible world is analytic. Of these, (a) is very obvious, but (b) is much less so if "analytic" is understood in the way just explained.

[14] This is similar to Ayer's notion of factual content, but perhaps a bit clearer. Does the fact that a claim has no factual content in this sense help to explain how it can be justified or known a priori (as Salmon seems to be suggesting)? How would such an explanation go?

evidence is needed to establish its truth or falsity. The distinction between a priori and a posteriori statements refers exclusively to the justification of statements and has nothing to do with discovery. The statements of arithmetic, for example, are regarded by most philosophers as a priori; the fact that children may learn arithmetic by counting physical objects (e.g., fingers) has nothing to do with the issue. Arithmetic statements can be established . . . without the aid of empirical observation or experiment, and this qualifies them as a priori. It is evident, moreover, that analytic statements, as they have been described above, are a priori. Since their truth follows from logical truths and definitions alone—that is, from syntactical and semantical considerations alone—observation and experiment are not required for their proof.

Most philosophers would acknowledge that many synthetic statements are a posteriori. It would seem that no amount of pure ratiocination would reveal whether I had eggs for breakfast this morning or whether there is a typewriter on the desk in the next office. Some sort of observation would seem to be indispensable. However, it is not nearly as evident that *all* synthetic statements are a posteriori. The doctrine that there are synthetic a priori statements is, I take it, the thesis of rationalism. It was maintained by Kant, as well as by many other philosophers both before and after him. The doctrine that all a priori statements are either analytic or self-contradictory is the thesis of empiricism as I understand it.[15]

[15] That is, moderate empiricism.

I know of no easy way to argue the question of whether there are any synthetic a priori statements. The history of human thought has provided many attempts to establish synthetic a priori truths, with a notable lack of success in my opinion. . . .

Descartes provides an especially clear example of the use of synthetic a priori principles to justify ampliative inference. Starting from his famous *cogito*, he set out to deduce a complete account of the real world. He never supposed that nonampliative deduction would be equal to the task; instead, he appealed to principles he considered evident to the natural light of reason: "Now it is manifest by the natural light that there must at least be as much reality in the efficient and total cause as in its effect. For, pray, whence can the effect derive its reality, if not from its cause?"*

The man who thought he could not be certain that 2 + 2 = 4 or that he had hands unless he could prove that God is not a deceiver found the foregoing principle so clear and distinct that it is impossible to conceive its falsity![16]

[16] Salmon is right that this is what Descartes's claim amounts to. Think back to Descartes and try to see clearly why this is so. (Would there be any plausibility to the claim that Descartes's principle is analytic?)

Contemporary philosophy has not been lacking in claims for the synthetic a priori status of a variety of statements, although frequently they seem to be far less fancy than those for which the traditional claim was made. A recent important text in the philosophy of science argues that the statement,

No event [temporally] precedes itself

qualifies for the position.† However, the author fails to consider the empirical hypothesis that the history of the universe is a closed cycle. If this were true, events would precede themselves. Since the statement in question is incompatible with an empirical hypothesis, it could be falsified empirically, and this means that it cannot be an a priori truth.[17] Another currently famous example is the statement,

[17] Is Salmon right about this example? (See Discussion Question 3.)

Anything colored is extended.

Again, it seems to me, the statement turns out on close examination to be a posteriori. It is a physical fact, established empirically, that the stimulus that normally gives rise to color sensations is a very short wave. We find, by experience, that short waves provide rather reliable indications of the surface characteristics of objects from which they are emitted or reflected. If our visual sensations were elicited by long waves, like radio waves, they would be found not to provide much useful information about surfaces from which they emanate; in particular, they would be rather uninformative about size. Under these circumstances, I seriously doubt that we would closely associate the

---

*Rene Descartes, "Of God: That He Exists," *Meditations,* III [p. 160]; the translation in this book varies slightly.

†Arthur Pap, *Introduction to the Philosophy of Science* (New York: The Free Press of Glencoe, 1962), p. 97.

qualities of color and extensiveness, for we do not as a matter of fact make a close association between auditory qualities and extension. These considerations provide grounds, I believe, for denying that the foregoing statement is actually synthetic a priori.[18]

Although Kant's attempt to supply a synthetic a priori grounding for ampliative inference was by no means the first nor the last, it is, in many respects, the most notable. According to his view, the statements of geometry and arithmetic are synthetic a priori. . . .

Kant's approach to the question of synthetic a priori principles is profoundly instructive. So convinced was he that geometry provided examples of synthetic a priori propositions that he did not need to tarry long over the question of whether there are any such things. Instead, he moved on the question of how they are possible. Synthetic a priori knowledge (if there is such) does exhibit a genuine epistemological mystery. After some exposure to formal logic one can see without much difficulty how linguistic stipulations can yield analytic statements that hold in any possible world. It is easy to see that "Snow is white or snow is not white" is true simply because of the meanings we attach to "or" and "not." Analytic a priori statements are no great mystery. Likewise, it is not too difficult to see how our senses can provide clues to the nature of physical reality, helping us to establish propositions that are true in some but not all possible worlds. Although there are epistemological problems of perception, like illusion, that must not be ignored, we can still understand in very general terms how there can be a posteriori knowledge of synthetic propositions. But how could we conceivably establish by pure thought that some logically consistent picture of the real world is false? How could we, without any aid of experience whatever, find out anything about our world in contradistinction to other possible worlds? Given a logically contingent formula—one that admits of true as well as false interpretations—how could we hope to decide on a completely a priori basis which of its interpretations are true and which

false?[19] The empiricist says it is impossible to do so, and in this I think he is correct. Nevertheless, it is tempting to endow various principles with the status of synthetic a priori truths. It was to Kant's great credit that he saw the urgency of the question: *How is this possible?*

Various causal principles, as we have seen, have been accorded the status of synthetic a priori truths—for example, the traditional *ex nihilo* principle, the principle of sufficient reason, and Descartes' principle that the cause must be as great as the effect.[20] Kant also, in addition to claiming that the propositions of arithmetic and geometry are synthetic a priori, maintained that the principle of universal causation—everything that happens presupposes something from which it follows according to a rule—is synthetic a priori. It is by means of this principle that he hoped to dispose of the problem of induction. However, Kant's attempt to explain the possibility of synthetic a priori propositions is unsatisfactory. The propositions of Euclidean geometry do not enjoy epistemological primacy; the propositions of arithmetic lack synthetic content,[21] and the physical world can be made intelligible in nondeterministic terms. Human powers of conception and visualization far exceed the limits Kant saw as necessary constraints upon the human intellect and as the source of synthetic a priori truths.

[18] Think carefully about why "everything colored is extended" seems to be knowable a priori—because color has to occupy some space, that is, some extension. Do the scientific considerations Salmon mentions have any tendency to show that the claim is really empirical (which is what he is suggesting)?

[19] Here Salmon does not get the issue quite right: The rationalist proponent of the synthetic a priori does think that some *logically* contingent or consistent claims—that is claims that are not necessary solely by virtue of their form—can be known to be true a priori. But he does not think that such claims are really contingent or consistent, but instead that they are necessary, even if not *formally* necessary. (See the Ewing selection, especially Annotation 1 and the corresponding text.) Thus a synthetic a priori claim is supposed to be true in every possible world and so would not tell us something "about our world in contradistinction to other possible worlds."

[20] The "*ex nihilo* principle" is the principle that something cannot come from nothing, and the principle of sufficient reason is the claim that everything that exists must have a cause or explanation. Both of these "principles" are often appealed to in discussions of the cosmological argument (see Chapter 2).

[21] See Kant, Ayer, and Ewing for discussions of the issue of whether arithmetical propositions such as $7 + 5 = 12$ are analytic or synthetic.

It is unfortunate that subsequent philosophers have paid little attention to Kant's central question: How are synthetic a priori propositions possible? Instead, the category of synthetic a priori propositions has too often become a convenient wastebasket for statements not readily classifiable as analytic or a posteriori. The contents of this wastebasket may, of course, turn out to be very handy in dealing with tough philosophical problems, but the crucial point is whether the wastebasket is really empty. It seems to me that all such statements can be shown, on careful examination, to be analytic or a posteriori, and that no convincing example of a synthetic a priori proposition has yet been produced. Even if this is so, of course, it does not prove that there are no synthetic a priori statements. It should, however, give us pause, and it does relieve us of any obligation to accept the positive rationalistic thesis that there are synthetic a priori propositions. It does place the burden of proof upon those who hope to escape Hume's problem of induction by way of a synthetic a priori principle. Moreover, even if a recalcitrant example were given— one that seemed to defy all analysis as either analytic or a posteriori—it might still be reasonable to suppose that we had not exercised sufficient penetration in dealing with it. If we are left with a total epistemological mystery on the question of how synthetic a priori propositions are possible, it might be wise to suppose it more likely that our analytic acumen is deficient than that an epistemological miracle has occurred. [22]

[22] This is perhaps Salmon's strongest argument against the existence of synthetic a priori claims. But it depends on the claim that the idea of analyticity can explain all clear cases of a priori justification and knowledge with no such mystery. (See Discussion Questions 2 and 3.)

5. The Principle of Uniformity of Nature. A substantial part of Hume's critique of induction rested upon his attack on the principle of the uniformity of nature. He argued definitively that the customary forms of inductive inference cannot be expected to yield correct predictions if nature fails to be uniform—if the future is not like the past—if like sensible qualities are not accompanied by like results.

> All inferences from experience suppose, as their foundation, that the future will resemble the past, and that similar powers will be conjoined with similar sensible qualities. If there be any suspicion that the course of nature may change, and that the past may be no rule for the future, all experience becomes useless, and can give rise to no inference or conclusion.*

He argued, moreover, that there is no logical contradiction in the supposition that nature is not uniform— that the regularities we have observed up to the present will fail in wholesale fashion in the future.

> It implies no contradiction that the course of nature may change, and that an object, seemingly like those which we have experienced, may be attended with different or contrary effects. May I not clearly and distinctly conceive that a body, falling from the clouds, and which, in all other respects, resembles snow, has yet the taste of salt or feeling of fire? Is there any more intelligible proposition than to affirm, that all the trees will flourish in December and January, and decay in May and June? Now whatever is intelligible, and can be distinctly conceived, implies no contradiction, and can never be proved false by any demonstrative argument . . . †

He argues, in addition, that the principle of uniformity of nature cannot be established by an inference from experience: "It is impossible, therefore, that any arguments from experience can prove this resemblance of the past to the future; since all these arguments are founded on the supposition of that resemblance."‡ [23] Throughout Hume's discussion there is, however, a strong suggestion that we might have full confidence in the customary inductive methods if nature were known to be uniform.

[23] To be plausible, as we have already seen, the claim would have to be that the future resembles the past to a substantial degree, not that it does so perfectly in the sense that all observed regularities also obtain in the future—since we know that this isn't true.

*David Hume, *Human Understanding,* [p. 290].
†Ibid. [pp. 288–89].
‡Ibid. [p. 290].

Kant attempted to deal with the problem of induction in just this way, by establishing a principle of uniformity of nature, in the form of the principle of universal causation, as a synthetic a priori truth. Kant claimed, in other words, that every occurrence is governed by causal regularities, and this general characteristic of the universe can be established by pure reason, without the aid of any empirical evidence. He did not try to show that the principle of universal causation is a principle of logic, for to do so would have been to show that it was analytic—not synthetic—and thus lacking in factual content. He did not reject Hume's claim that there is no logical contradiction in the statement that nature is not uniform; he did not try to prove his principle of universal causation by deducing a contradiction from its denial. He did believe, however, that this principle, while not a proposition of pure logic, is necessarily true nevertheless. [24] Hume, of course, argued against this alternative as well. He maintained not only that the uniformity of nature is not a logical or analytic truth, but also that it cannot be any other kind of a priori truth either. Even before Kant had enunciated the doctrine of synthetic a priori principles, Hume had offered strong arguments against them:

[24] Kant's claim is roughly that the mind orders experience so as to make the causal principle true within the realm of experience, though not necessarily of things as they exist in themselves outside of experience.

> I shall venture to affirm, as a general proposition, which admits of no exception, that the knowledge of this relation [of cause and effect] is not, in any instance, attained by reasonings a priori.*
>
> Adam, though his rational faculties be supposed, at the very first, entirely perfect, could not have inferred from the fluidity and transparency of water that it would suffocate him, or from the light and warmth of fire that it would consume him.†
>
> When we reason a priori, and consider merely any object or cause, as it appears to the mind, independent of all observation, it never could suggest to us the notion of any distinct object, such as its effect; much less, show us the inseparable and inviolable connexion between them. A man must be very sagacious who could discover by reasoning that crystal is the effect of heat, and ice of cold, without being previously acquainted with the operation of these qualities.‡
>
> Now whatever is intelligible, and can be distinctly conceived . . . can never be proved false by any . . . abstract reasoning a priori.§

Hume argues, by persuasive example and general principle, that nothing about the causal structure of reality can be established by pure reason. [25] He poses an incisive challenge to those who would claim the ability to establish a priori knowledge of a particular causal relation or of the principle of universal causation. In the foregoing discussion of synthetic a priori statements, I have given reasons for believing that Kant failed to overcome Hume's previous objections.

[25] These Humean arguments are not really answers to Kant's specific arguments (which, of course, Hume had never seen).

There is, however, another interesting issue that arises in connection with the principle of uniformity of nature. Suppose it could be established—never mind how—prior to a justification of induction. Would it then provide an adequate basis for a justification of induction? The answer is, I think, negative.

Even if nature is uniform to some extent, it is not absolutely uniform. The future is something like the past, but it is somewhat different as well. Total and complete uniformity would mean that the state of the universe at any given moment is the same as its state at any other moment. Such a universe would be a changeless, Parmenidean world. Change obviously does occur, so the future is not exactly like the past. There are some uniformities, it appears, but not a complete absence of change. The problem is how to ferret out the genuine uniformities. As a matter of actual fact, there are many uniformities *within experience* that we take to be mere coincidences, and there are others that seem to represent genuine causal

---

*Ibid. [p. 286].

†Ibid. [p. 286].

‡Ibid. [not included in the slection in this book].

§Ibid. [pp. 288–89].

regularities. For instance, in every election someone finds a precinct, say in Maryland, which has always voted in favor of the winning presidential candidate. Given enough precincts, one expects this sort of thing by sheer chance, and we classify such regularities as mere coincidences. By contrast, the fact that glass windowpanes break when bricks are hurled at them is more than mere coincidence. Causal regularities provide a foundation for inference from the observed to the unobserved; coincidences do not. We can predict with some confidence that the next glass window pane at which a brick is hurled will break; we take with a grain of salt the prediction of the outcome of a presidential election early on election night when returns from the above-mentioned precinct are in. The most that a principle of uniformity of nature could say is that there are some uniformities that persist into the future; if it stated that every regularity observed to hold within the scope of our experience also holds universally, it would be patently false. We are left with the problem of finding a sound basis for distinguishing between mere coincidence and genuine causal regularity.

Kant's principle of universal causation makes a rather weak and guarded statement. It asserts only that there exist causal regularities: "Everything that happens presupposes something from which it follows according to some rule." For each occurrence it claims only the existence of *some* prior cause and *some* causal regularity. It gives no hint as to how we are to find the prior cause or how we are to identify the causal regularity. It therefore provides no basis upon which to determine whether the inductive inferences we make are correct or incorrect. It would be entirely consistent with Kant's principle for us always to generalize on the basis of observed coincidences and always to fail to generalize on the basis of actual causal relations. It would be entirely consistent with Kant's principle, moreover, for us always to cite a co-incidentally preceding event as the cause instead of the event that is the genuine cause. Kant's principle, even if it could be established, would not help us to justify the assertion that our inductive inferences would always or usually be correct. It would provide no criterion to distinguish sound from unsound inductions. Even if Kant's program had succeeded in establishing a synthetic a priori principle of universal

causation, it would have failed to produce a justification of induction.[26]

[26] A major problem with Kant's view is that he really gives no account of how specific causal truths are known.

. . .

7. A Probabilistic Approach. It may seem strange in the extreme that this discussion of the problem of induction has proceeded at such great length without seriously bringing in the concept of probability. It is very tempting to react immediately to Hume's argument with the admission that we do not have *knowledge* of the unobserved. Scientific results are not established with absolute certainty. At best we can make probabilistic statements about unobserved matters of fact, and at best we can claim that scientific generalizations and theories are highly confirmed. We who live in an age of scientific empiricism can accept with perfect equanimity the fact that the quest for certainty is futile; indeed, our thanks go to Hume for helping to destroy false hopes for certainty in science.

Hume's search for a justification of induction, it might be continued, was fundamentally misconceived. He tried to find a way of proving that inductive inferences with true premises would have *true* conclusions. He properly failed to find any such justification precisely because it is the function of *deduction* to prove the truth of conclusions, given true premises. Induction has a different function. An inductive inference with true premises establishes its conclusions as *probable*. No wonder Hume failed to find a justification of induction. He was trying to make induction into deduction, and he succeeded only in proving the platitude that induction is not deduction. If we want to justify induction, we must show that inductive inferences establish their conclusions as probable, not as true.

The foregoing sort of criticism of Hume's arguments is extremely appealing, and it has given rise to the most popular sort of attempt, currently, to deal with the problem. In order to examine this approach, we must consider, at least superficially, the meaning of the concept of probability. Two basic meanings must be taken into account at present.

One leading probability concept identifies probability with frequency—roughly, the probable is that which happens often, and the improbable is that which happens seldom. Let us see what becomes of Hume's argument under this interpretation of probability. If we were to claim that inductive conclusions are probable in this sense, we would be claiming that inductive inferences with true premises often have true conclusions, although not always. Hume's argument shows, unhappily, that this claim cannot be substantiated. It was recognized long before Hume that inductive inferences cannot be expected always to lead to the truth. Hume's argument shows, not only that we cannot justify the claim that *every* inductive inference with true premises will have a true conclusion, but also, that we cannot justify the claim that *any* inductive inference with true premises will have a true conclusion. Hume's argument shows that, for all we can know, every inductive inference made from now on might have a false conclusion despite true premises. Thus, Hume has proved, we can show neither that inductive inferences establish their conclusions as true nor that they establish their conclusions as probable in the frequency sense. [27] The introduction of the frequency concept of probability gives no help whatever in circumventing the problem of induction, but this is no surprise, for we should not have expected it to be suitable for this purpose.

A more promising probability concept identifies probability with degree of rational belief. To say that a statement is probable in this sense means that one would be rationally justified in believing it; the degree of probability is the degree of assent a person would be rationally justified in giving. We are not, of course, referring to the degree to which anyone *actually* believes in the statement, but rather to the degree to which one could *rationally* believe it. Degree of actual belief is a purely psychological concept, but degree of rational belief is determined objectively by the evidence. To say that a statement is probable in this sense means that it is supported by evidence. But, so the argument goes, if a statement is the conclusion of an inductive inference with true premises, it is supported by evidence—by inductive evidence—this is part of what it *means* to be supported by evidence. The very

concept of evidence depends upon the nature of induction, and it becomes incoherent if we try to divorce the two. Trivially, then, the conclusion of an inductive inference is probable under this concept of probability. To ask, with Hume, if we should accept inductive conclusions is tantamount to asking if we should fashion our beliefs in terms of the evidence, and this, in turn, is tantamount to asking whether we should be rational. In this way we arrive at an "ordinary language dissolution" of the problem of induction. Once we understand clearly the meanings of such key terms as "rational," "probable," and "evidence," we see that the problem arose out of linguistic confusion and evaporates into the question of whether it is rational to be rational. Such tautological questions, if meaningful at all, demand affirmative answers. [28]

[28] The claim is that reasoning inductively is just what we mean by "rational" in this sort of case, so that inductive reasoning is guaranteed to be rational.

Unfortunately, the dissolution is not satisfactory. Its inadequacy can be exhibited by focusing upon the concept of inductive evidence and seeing how it figures in the foregoing argument. The fundamental difficulty arises from the fact that the very notion of inductive evidence is determined by the rules of inductive inference. If a conclusion is to be supported by inductive evidence, it must be the conclusion of a correct inductive inference with true premises. Whether the inductive inference is correct depends upon whether the rule governing that inference is correct. The relation of inductive evidential support is, therefore, inseparably bound to the correctness of rules of inductive inference. In order to be able to say whether a given statement is supported by inductive evidence we must be able to say which inductive rules are correct.

For example, suppose that a die has been thrown a large number of times, and we have observed that the side two came up in one sixth of the tosses. This is our "evidence" *e*. Let *h* be the conclusion that, "in the long run," side two will come up one sixth of the times. Consider the following three rules:

1. (Induction by enumeration) Given m/n of observed A are B, to infer that the "long run" relative frequency of B among A is m/n.

2. (A priori rule) Regardless of observed frequencies, to infer that the "long run" relative frequency of B among A is 1/k, where k is the number of possible outcomes—six in the case of the die.

[29] Here the first rule is just the standard conception of inductive reasoning, generalized slightly to cover also cases where some fraction of observed A's are B's (in the case where all observed A's are B's, m and n are the same number). The second rule is the so-called "principle of indifference"—which might be badly wrong if the dice are "loaded." The third rule is the intuitively bizarre rule which says that the truth is just the opposite of what the evidence so far seems to show.

3. (Counterinductive rule) Given m/n of observed A are B, to infer that the "long run" relative frequency of B among A is (n − m)/n . **[29]**

Under Rule 1, e is positive evidence for h; under Rule 2, e is irrelevant to h; and under Rule 3, e is negative evidence for h. In order to say which conclusions are supported by what evidence, it is necessary to arrive at a decision as to what inductive rules are acceptable. If Rule 1 is correct, the evidence e supports the conclusion h. If Rule 2 is correct, we are justified in drawing the conclusion h, but this is entirely independent of the observational evidence e; the same conclusions would have been sanctioned by Rule 2 regardless of observational evidence. If Rule 3 is correct, we are not only prohibited from drawing the conclusion h, but also we are permitted to draw a conclusion h' which is logically incompatible with h. Whether a given conclusion is *supported* by *evidence*—whether it would be *rational to believe* it on the basis of given evidence—whether it is *made probable* by virtue of its relation to given evidence—depends upon selection of the correct rule or rules from among the infinitely many rules we might conceivably adopt.

The problem of induction can now be reformulated as a problem about evidence. What rules ought we to adopt to determine the nature of inductive evidence? What rules provide suitable concepts of inductive evidence? If we take the customary inductive rules to define the concept of inductive evidence, have we adopted a proper concept of evidence? Would the

adoption of some alternative inductive rules provide a more suitable concept of evidence? These are genuine questions which need to be answered.

We find, moreover, that what appeared earlier as a pointless question now becomes significant and difficult. If we take the customary rules of inductive inference to provide a suitable definition of the relation of inductive evidential support, it makes considerable sense to ask whether it is rational to believe on the basis of evidence as thus defined rather than to believe on the basis of evidence as defined according to other rules. . . .

There is danger of being taken in by an easy equivocation. One meaning we may assign to the concept of inductive evidence is, roughly, the basis on which we ought to fashion our beliefs. Another meaning results from the relation of evidential support determined by whatever rule of inductive inference we adopt. It is only by supposing that these two concepts are the same that we suppose the problem of induction to have vanished. The problem of induction is still there; it is the problem of providing adequate grounds for the selection of inductive rules. We want the relation of evidential support determined by these rules to yield a concept of inductive evidence which is, in fact, the basis on which we ought to fashion our beliefs.**[30]**

[30] Thus if reasoning inductively just means whatever way of reasoning is rational in this sort of case, it will not be automatically true that this is following the first rule rather than one of the others or some further rule—so some further defense will be needed, which is just the problem of induction all over again. Whereas if reasoning inductively means following the first rule, then it cannot just be assumed that this is the rational way to proceed (where "rational" means roughly that a method will probably lead to true or reliable results).

. . .

8. Pragmatic Justification. Of all the solutions and dissolutions proposed to deal with Hume's problem of induction, Hans Reichenbach's attempt to provide a pragmatic justification seems to me the most fruitful and promising.* This approach accepts

*Hans Reichenbach, *Experience and Prediction* (Chicago: U. of Chicago Press, 1938), Chap. 5, and *The Theory of Probability* (Berkeley: U. of California Press, 1949), Chap. 11.

Hume's arguments up to the point of agreeing that it is impossible to establish, either deductively or inductively, that any inductive inferences will ever again have true conclusions. Nevertheless, Reichenbach claims, the standard method of inductive generalization can be justified. Although its *success* as a method of prediction cannot be established in advance, it can be shown to be superior to any alternative method of prediction.

The argument can be put rather simply. Nature may be sufficiently uniform in suitable respects for us to make successful inductive inferences from the observed to the unobserved. On the other hand, for all we know, she may not. Hume has shown that we cannot prove in advance which case holds. All we can say is that nature may or may not be uniform—if she is, induction works; if she is not, induction fails. Even in the face of our ignorance about the uniformity of nature, we can ask what would happen if we adopted some radically different method of inference. Consider, for instance, the method of the crystal gazer. Since we do not know whether nature is uniform or not, we must consider both possibilities. If nature is uniform, the method of crystal gazing might work successfully, or it might fail. We cannot prove a priori that it will not work. At the same time, we cannot prove a priori that it will work, even if nature exhibits a high degree of uniformity. Thus, in case nature is reasonably uniform, the standard inductive method *must* work while the alternative method of crystal gazing *may or may not* work. In this case, the superiority of the standard inductive method is evident. Now, suppose nature lacks uniformity to such a degree that the standard inductive method is a complete failure. In this case, Reichenbach argues, the alternative method must likewise fail. Suppose it did not fail—suppose, for instance, that the method of crystal gazing worked consistently. This would constitute an important relevant uniformity that could be exploited inductively. If a crystal gazer had consistently predicted future occurrences, we could infer inductively that he has a method of prediction that will enjoy continued success. The inductive method would, in this way, share the success of the method of crystal gazing, and would therefore be, contrary to hypothesis, successful. Hence, Reichenbach concludes, the standard inductive method will be successful *if any other method could succeed.* As a result, we have everything to gain

and nothing to lose by adopting the inductive method. If any method works, induction works. If we adopt the inductive method and it fails, we have lost nothing, for any other method we might have adopted would likewise have failed. Reichenbach does not claim to prove that nature is uniform, or that the standard inductive method will be successful. He does not postulate the uniformity of nature. He tries to show that the inductive method is the best method for ampliative inference, whether it turns out to be successful or not.[31]

[31] Reichenbach's claim is not that reasoning inductively will even *probably* lead to true conclusions, but only that it will do so if any method can succeed in this way. This is some justification, but is it enough to really solve the problem? (See Discussion Question 1.)

This ingenious argument, although extremely suggestive, is ultimately unsatisfactory. As I have just presented it, it is impossibly vague. I have not specified the nature of the standard inductive method. I have not stated with any exactness what constitutes success for the inductive method or any other. Moreover, the uniformity of nature is not an all-or-none affair. Nature appears to be uniform to some extent and also to be lacking in uniformity to some degree. As we have already seen, it is not easy to state a principle of uniformity that is strong enough to assure the success of inductive inference and weak enough to be plausible. The vagueness of the foregoing argument is not, however, its fundamental drawback. It can be made precise. . . . When it is made precise, as we shall see, it suffers the serious defect of equally justifying too wide a variety of rules for ampliative inference.[32]

[32] Reichenbach's basic claim is that the method of generalizing from experience ("positing" that the proportion of all A's that are B's is the same as the currently observed proportion and then correcting that posit as new observations come in) is guaranteed to succeed in the long run if success is possible, that is, if there is an objective regularity to be found. The problem is that there are many other methods that can be justified in the same way. (See Discussion Question 4.)

I have presented Reichenbach's argument rather loosely in order to make intuitively clear its basic strategy. The sense in which it is a pragmatic justification should be clear. Unlike many authors who have sought a justification of induction, Reichenbach does not try to prove the truth of any synthetic proposition. He recognizes that the problem concerns the justification of a rule, and rules are neither true nor false. Hence, he tries to show that the adoption of a standard inductive rule is practically useful in the attempt to learn about and deal with the unobserved. He maintains that this can be shown even though we cannot prove the truth of the assertion that inductive methods will lead to predictive success. This pragmatic aspect is, it seems to me, the source of the fertility of Reichenbach's approach. Even though his argument does not constitute an adequate justification of induction, it seems to me to provide a valid core from which we may attempt to develop a more satisfactory justification.

. . .

Discussion Questions

1. If Hume's skepticism about induction is correct, then we have no reason at all to think that any conclusion that depends on inductive reasoning is true. How implausible a result is this from the standpoint of common sense? Notice in thinking about this that at least most of the results of theoretical science are arrived at as the best explanations of inductively established observational regularities. Notice also that evidence for historical claims also depends on inductively established regularities pertaining to various sorts of evidence. (How much would it help to be told that although we have no good reason for thinking that inductive conclusions are true, the inductive method is still guaranteed to succeed in finding the truth if success is possible, which is what Reichenbach's pragmatic justification—see Discussion Question 4—amounts to?)

2. Are all plausible a priori justifiable claims analytic in Salmon's sense? Consider, for example, the claim that nothing can be red all over and green all over at the same time. Is this something that can be justified a priori? It is not a logical truth as it stands (since many claims of the form "nothing can be F all over and G all over at the same time" are false—think about this). Can it be made into a logical truth by giving definitions of one or more of its terms, presumably "red" and/or "green"? (Remember that to be acceptable, a definition must actually capture the meaning of the term.)

3. Salmon claims (see Annotation 17 and the corresponding text) that "No event temporally precedes itself" is not a synthetic a priori truth because it is incompatible with the "empirical hypothesis that the history of the universe is a closed cycle." Is he right about this? What would it mean for the history of the universe to be a "closed cycle" in a way that would show that the original claim is false? It could be that there is a sequence of kinds of events that repeats itself over and over, but this wouldn't mean that any individual event temporally precedes itself. Thus the claim has to be that when the cycle repeats itself the very same event occurs again, but at a later time (so that the earlier occurrence of that same event precedes the later occurrence). Is this really an empirical possibility? What sort of empirical evidence would tend to show that it was true? Is it even an intelligible possibility?

4. Think about the rationale for Reichenbach's pragmatic justification of induction. Can you see why the method described in Annotation 32 is guaranteed to eventually find an objective regularity in nature if one actually exists? Why is such success only guaranteed in the long run? Can you think of another method that is equally guaranteed to succeed in the long run, but that gives a significantly different answer in the short run (think here of cases where the observed proportion of A's that are B's is some fraction rather than all—see Annotation 29 and the associated text). Hint: what you want is a rule that deviates from the observed proportion but where the deviation gets smaller and smaller as the number of cases gets larger, so that in the long run—but not in the short run, which is where the method is always actually applied—the result arrived at will be the same as that of the inductive method. A further issue: how long a run is necessary for the inductive method to be guaranteed to succeed if success is possible?

CHAPTER 4

Minds and Bodies

The reading selections in this chapter fall into the general area of philosophy known as the philosophy of mind, focusing on the central problem in that area: the mind-body problem—an issue that the German philosopher Arthur Schopenhauer described, because of its combination of centrality and difficulty, as "the world knot." Philosophers attempt to untie this knot by making clear the nature of mind and the relation between *minds* and mental (or spiritual) states and events, on the one hand, and physical *bodies* and their physical or material states, on the other. The last section of the chapter examines the distinct but related issue of personal identity.

ARE MINDS AND MENTAL STATES DISTINCT FROM BODIES AND MATERIAL STATES?

It is abundantly obvious that people have conscious mental states, including such things as sensations and feelings of various kinds, but also conscious beliefs, desires, emotions, and so on; and if the mind is what these various states are states *of,* then it is also obvious that people have minds. At the same time, it is equally obvious that people have physical bodies, including in particular physical brains, involving various sorts of physical states and processes. The fundamental issue that the reading selections in this chapter are concerned with is the relation between these two aspects of persons: are minds and mental states distinct from bodies and physical or bodily states (as **dualism** claims), so that human beings are made up of two fundamentally different kinds of ingredients? Or are minds and mental states somehow nothing more than, **reducible** to, bodies and material states (as **materialism** claims)? In spite of a tendency in recent times to assume that the brain is central to mental activity and even perhaps in some way to be identified with the mind, in fact the connection between these two basic aspects of human persons is far from obvious. The starting point here is the realization, which only one group of philosophers (the logical behaviorists—discussed later) have ever denied, that conscious mental states do not *seem,* as we are aware of them, to be states of the brain or indeed physical states of any kind. Think here of a sensation of red or of the conscious thought that, say, philosophy is challenging: if these are just states of the brain (as J. J. C. Smart and Jerry Fodor, among others, both claim—though in different ways), this is surely not obvious just by reflecting on them. (One way to see this is to realize that they certainly do not present themselves as any *specific* states of the brain.) Moreover, as we will see, philosophers have often thought that there are arguments seemingly showing that mental states could not be identical to physical states of any kind, thus supporting a dualist account of minds and mental states.

Here it will help to focus on a simple example involving both mental and material states. Suppose that I walk out my front door and stop halfway to my car, noticing that it is cold and damp, that there are dark clouds, and that the wind seems to be increasing; I decide that it is probably going to be rainy and cold, so I walk back to the house to get my coat and an umbrella; and having done this, I start out again for the car. Here we have various mental states: *sensations* of cold, dampness, darkness, and windiness; perceptual *beliefs* about these matters and the further belief that it is going to be rainy and cold; and presumably a *desire* not to be wet and cold. And there are also various physical or material states: in addition to the physical condition of my environment, there is the physical *behavior* of my body in walking, stopping, turning my head, and walking again, together with the physical condition of my body and my various sensory organs: the coldness and dampness of my skin, the light waves striking my eyes, and so on.

Dualism

According to a dualist view, the mental states involved in this example are quite distinct from the physical or material states. On the most straightforward and historically prominent version of dualism, the mental states are states of one thing or entity or **substance,** the mind; and the physical or material states are states of a separate thing or entity or substance, the body. And a human being is thus in effect a kind of team composed of these two separate elements, operating (or at least seeming to operate) in tandem. This was the view of René Descartes (see the selection from his *Meditations* in Chapter 3), and it also seems to be the version of dualism that Keith Campbell and John Foster have mainly in mind in the following selections. But many of the more recent proponents of dualism, such as Frank Jackson and David Chalmers, have opted instead for an **attribute** or property dualism (the main reason being doubts as to whether there is any clear conception of what a mental or spiritual substance, as distinct from its states and properties, would amount to). Attribute dualism is the view that there are two fundamentally different kinds of attributes or properties or features, mental or spiritual attributes and material or physical attributes, but that all of these are attributes of the same underlying thing or substance. This substance is what we refer to as the body (or more likely a part of the body, namely the brain), but on this view, this substance is neither purely material nor purely mental in nature, since it has both kinds of properties. (The most obvious importance of the difference between substance and attribute dualism is that the survival of a person after the death of his body seems at least possible under substance dualism, but not under attribute dualism.)

A second issue that divides different versions of dualism and is the main focus of Campbell's discussion concerns the causal relations (if any) that exist between the mind and the body. Here the common-sense view is **interactionism:** the view that mental states causally influence physical states and that physical states causally influence mental states. Think about our example again, and in particular about the natural explanation of my behavior. Here we *seem* to have both causation of mental states by material states and causation of material states by mental states: The material states of cold, cloudiness, and windiness causally affected my bodily sense organs which in turn produced sensations reflecting these conditions and then the beliefs that they obtained. These beliefs, together with my standing desire not to be cold and wet, produced the further mental state of deciding to go back for my coat and umbrella. And this decision (or perhaps an intention—a further mental state—that resulted from it) in turn caused my material body to make the specific movements that it made while walking back into the house and then out again to the car. And there are innumerable such examples that illustrate our common assumption that our minds affect our bodies and that our bodies affect our minds.

Some dualists accept at face value the view that mind and body causally interact in these ways. Foster defends such a view, and thus must explain how immaterial and material things can causally interact. But other dualists, along with most materialists (see the discussion in the Fodor selection), question whether causal relations between such fundamentally different kinds of things are possible or even intelligible. Some dualists think that the view that mental states causally influence the material world—thus making it impossible in principle to adequately explain all material events in terms of other material events alone—is especially implausible, leading them to adopt the view that the causal relations between body and mind are one-way only: while bodily states can causally affect or even completely produce mental states, mental states cannot causally affect physical states. This view, called **epiphenomenalism,** is the view that Campbell eventually adopts, though this is not reflected very clearly in the selection here. (The epiphenomenalist cannot accept the common-sense explanation of my behavior in the example, since that explanation depends on causal relations in both directions.)

A third kind of dualism, once popular but now rarely if ever held, is **parallelism:** the view that there are no causal relations either way—that the mental realm is causally isolated from the physical realm. A parallelist obviously has to find some explanation for the *appearance* of causal interaction (as in the foregoing example), and historically the defenders of this view have appealed to God for this purpose: either God creates the mental and material realms in such a way that they run in parallel like two clocks, always in agreement with each other *(preestablished harmony)* or God constantly intervenes to keep the two in synch *(occasionalism).* You are not alone if you find parallelism difficult to take seriously. Epiphenomenalism, on the other hand, despite its disagreement with a fundamental aspect of the common-sense picture, is probably the most popular version of dualism in recent times; Foster, however, argues against it.[1]

The distinction between interactionism, epiphenomenalism, and parallelism is independent of and cuts across that between substance and attribute dualism, so that there are really six possible views: substance and attribute versions of each of the three alternatives with respect to causal relations. But the two versions of parallelism can safely be dismissed

---

[1]There is a fourth view that is at least logically possible: that the mind causally influences the body, but the body does not causally influence the mind. But this last possibility has never been advocated by anyone. See if you can figure out why.

as extremely implausible, leaving only the two versions each of the other two views pertaining to causation. And since the issue between substance and attribute versions receives substantially less discussion and is perhaps not even very well understood, the main issue dividing versions of dualism is that between interactionism and epiphenomenalism.

Materialism

While some philosophers, such as Campbell and Foster, still defend dualism, by far the most widely accepted general position in recent times has been materialism (or **physicalism**): the view that there is no separate dualist mind or separate dualist attributes, so that the mind and its mental states are in some way reducible to bodies and material states.[2] Here again, there are several different views.

One materialist position that was once widely held (roughly in the middle of the twentieth century) but is now held by virtually no one is **logical behaviorism:** the extremely implausible view that mental states are nothing more than bodily behavior and dispositions to such behavior (so that to be in pain is just to wince and moan and ask for help, or to be disposed to do these things; and to believe that it will rain is just to do or be disposed to do things like carrying an umbrella, deliberately not watering the lawn, and so on). According to the logical behaviorist, this identity between mental states, on the one hand, and behavior and dispositions to behave, on the other, is simply a matter of *definition:* what various mental state concepts *mean* is just behavior and dispositions to behave. Philosophical arguments against logical behaviorism have pointed out the logical possibility of people who mimic behavior perfectly but still are not really in the corresponding mental state or who experience states like pain but have so much control over their reactions that they are not even disposed to exhibit characteristic pain behavior. But the main problem is that the logical behaviorist is in effect denying that there are really conscious mental states at all—and also, perhaps even more implausibly, that such states ever cause or explain behavior in the way that seems to be reflected in our example. Both of these claims are extremely implausible (though remember that the epiphenomenalist version of dualism also accepts the second one). Fodor briefly discusses logical behaviorism, along with another version of behaviorism that simply denies the need to appeal to mental states in giving explanations of behavior, without necessarily denying the existence of such states in themselves.

A second, more recent version of materialism, though one that is also no longer widely held, is the **identity theory** (of mind and body), also known as *central state materialism.* According to this view, mental states and processes are nothing more than neurophysiological states and processes of the brain. But, in contrast to logical behaviorism, this is not supposed to be true by definition or simply by virtue of the common-sense meaning or content of mental-state concepts, nor is it reflected in our introspective experience of such states. It is obvious that the common-sense concepts of the various sorts of mental states can be understood perfectly well without having any idea that the states involved are in the brain or indeed have anything to do with the brain; and also, as mentioned, mental states do not present themselves introspectively as specific brain states. Instead, according to the identity theory, the identity between these two sorts of states is an *empirical* discov-

---

[2]If, that is, minds and mental states exist at all. There is one radical version of materialism, not represented in the selections in this volume, that denies the very existence of minds and mental states, holding that they are merely things advocated by a bad common-sense theory of human behavior (in roughly the same way that phlogiston was once advocated by a mistaken physical theory of how combustion works). This view is called *eliminative materialism.*

ery, analogous to the discovery that lightning (the visible flash in the sky) is identical to a certain sort of electrical discharge (again, not a matter of meaning or definition and also not something obvious just from the experience of lightning, but a discovery that required rather complicated empirical investigation).

But if the meanings of mental state concepts do not explicitly involve brain processes, then there must be some other account of the content of such concepts, or rather of the mental states and properties that they describe: one that is neutral between materialism and dualism in that it does not *require* but still *allows* the identity that is claimed by the identity theory to hold. (Compare the lightning case: if there were not an *independent* concept of what lightning is, there would be no idea of a kind of thing or process that could be *subsequently* discovered to be in fact a kind of electrical discharge.) Smart defends the identity theory, focusing mainly on conscious sensations, and tries to offer such a neutral account of mental properties (his "topic-neutral" account). Fodor also discusses the identity theory and suggests some problems with it, problems that in his view point toward yet a further materialist view.

This third materialist view, currently by far the most popular, is called **functionalism.** Like the identity theory, functionalism does not hold that mental states are material states simply as a matter of the definition or meaning or content of mental concepts, nor in a way that is obvious in our mental experience. Instead, like the identity theorist, the functionalist offers an account of mental concepts or equivalently of the essential nature of mental states that is in itself neutral between materialism and dualism, but then adds that it is material states, states of the brain, that in fact satisfy or realize this essential nature (at least in human beings).

The functionalist account of mental states grows out of Smart's "topic-neutral" account of the meaning of mentalistic concepts and also reflects certain aspects of the logical behaviorist view. According to this account, mental states are *functional* states, defined in terms of their functional or causal *role*. What characterizes a particular mental state is (a) the particular ways in which it is caused by external (mainly perceptual) *inputs,* (b) the particular ways in which it relates causally to other specific mental states (through inference, psychological association, and the like), and (c) the specific ways in which it causally produces behavioral *outputs*—with the scope and importance of these three aspects varying from state to state. Thus, for example, the belief that it is going to rain (a) is caused by various perceptual experiences (such as the experience of dark clouds and wind) and ultimately by the physical stimuli that lead to such experiences, (b) causally interacts with other mental states (such as the desire to stay dry or the belief that the lawn needs water), and (c) tends to lead (indirectly, via its relations to other mental states) to actions such as carrying an umbrella. According to the functionalist, to have the belief that it is going to rain just *is* to be in a state that realizes this causal, functional role (of which nothing like a complete characterization has been given here)—and any state that realizes this role, whether a brain state, a state of a dualist immaterial mind, or a state of some still further kind, *is* a belief that it is going to rain. And the same is true, with appropriate modifications of the causal role, for all other mental states—though some of these three main aspects of causal role will be more important for some specific kinds of mental states than for others.[3] The selection by Fodor offers an explanation and defense of functionalism.

---

[3]Smart's "topic-neutral account" can be seen as in effect the functionalist account of the sorts of states—mainly sensations—where component (a) of the causal role is so important that the other two components matter very little. To expand Smart's view in such a way as to account for states where components (b) and (c) are more important—states such as beliefs and desires—would be to turn his view into functionalism. In this way, the identity theory can be seen as a kind of early and incomplete version of functionalism, which is why it is no longer regarded as an independent alternative.

Summing up this rather complicated discussion, while there are many more positions that are theoretically possible, some of which were seriously held in earlier times, recent discussion in the philosophy of mind has tended to focus on a very small set of alternatives: interactionist and epiphenomenalist version of dualism, on the one hand (with the substance-attribute distinction lurking in the background), and the functionalist version of materialism, on the other.

Since it is clear that materialism in general and functionalism in particular are to be preferred on grounds of economy or simplicity if everything else is equal, the main issue is whether the functionalist view can adequately account for the features that mental states seem to have. As Fodor emphasizes, there are two main features of mental states that are relevant here: *intentional* content and *qualitative* content (though he lists them in the opposite order). A mental state is **intentional** insofar as it represents something else: my belief that my dog is in the backyard is a mental state that represents something about my dog and the backyard. The problem is to understand how such representation works: how my mind is able to reach out and grasp the world in this way. In contrast, my mental state of being in pain as a result of, for example, a sprained ankle does not represent anything, even though it is caused by the sprained ankle, but it does have a distinctive qualitative character or feel, an aspect of mental states that philosophers call a *quale* (plural **qualia**)—where part of this character is the very feature of being *conscious* at all. It is at least unclear how a merely material state can have this sort of distinctive experiential character. Thus the main issue, discussed in the remaining two sections of the chapter, is whether functionalism (or any materialist view) can account for intentional content and for conscious qualia.

ARE MENTAL STATES ANALOGOUS TO THE STATES OF A COMPUTER?

Since, as Fodor discusses, the program states of a computer are also functional states, another way to put the functionalist view is to say that mental states are analogous to computer states—thereby raising the possibility that a computer of the right sort might also be capable of intentional thought. The selection by Alan Turing explores and defends the idea that this will eventually be possible. While Turing is very optimistic about the possibility of machines thinking, John Searle, writing 30 years later, is quite convinced that machines like computers whose essential nature is to manipulate symbols not only cannot now think, but in principle never will—and hence that a functionalist view, which characterizes mental states in terms of computer-like states, cannot successfully account for the intentionality of mental states. Searle rests his case on his famous Chinese Room thought experiment, an experiment designed to emphasize the difference between the intrinsically meaningful elements of human thought and the intrinsically meaningless symbols that computers manipulate. Searle insists that genuine thought and intentionality require *intrinsic* meaning, something that neither a computer program nor, more generally, any state characterized merely in terms of functional role can ever yield. In a further selection, Fodor, still confident that functionalism can solve the intentionality problem, objects to Searle's Chinese Room thought experiment, arguing that a particular kind of program with particular kinds of inputs and outputs will indeed have contentful thoughts. The second selection by Searle responds to Fodor's objections.

Can Materialism Account for Qualitative Consciousness?

The selections in the final section of the chapter are concerned with the other main problem faced by functionalism (and indeed, like the problem of intentionality, by any materialist view): can such a view account for the particular qualitative character of mental states—or indeed for consciousness itself (which is really just a central aspect of any sort of qualitative character). The selection by Thomas Nagel, which has become widely recognized as presenting one fundamental challenge to materialism, raises the issue, among many others, of whether the qualitative character of experience—specifically the experience of a nonhuman creature, a bat—could be known on the basis of a knowledge of its material makeup (including a functional description of its states). This is something that seemingly should be possible if the material story is, as the materialist claims, the entire story. Both Frank Jackson and Laurence BonJour elaborate this point, developing it into what has become known as "the knowledge argument" against materialism or physicalism.

One response to the seeming cogency of the knowledge argument, advocated in the selection by David Lewis, is to retain the claim that all of reality is material or physical in character, that the physical account leaves nothing out, by denying the very existence of qualitative content or qualia (which Lewis refers to as phenomenal qualities). Another, quite different response would be to reevaluate dualism and try to solve some of its problems. David Chalmers suggests and tentatively defends just such a strategy, arguing that philosophers should be trying to find the **psychophysical laws** that will explain the relationship between minds and bodies.

WHAT IS REQUIRED FOR PERSONAL IDENTITY?

The selections in the final section of the chapter are concerned with the problem of personal identity: of what it is for a person existing at one time to be identical to—the very same person as—one who exists at another time. (This is a **metaphysical** issue and not an **epistemological** one: the question is what it is for such a relation of identity to exist, not how we can know or justifiably believe that it does.)

Two aspects of this issue require some clarification. First, the main issue is the identity of *persons* and not the identity of *humans*. A human is a certain kind of biological organism, a member of a certain animal species. Because life involves taking in and expelling material parts of various kinds, there is a question about what it is for a biological organism existing at one time to be identical to one existing at another time. But to resolve this question would not automatically settle the question of personal identity, since it is far from clear that a person, roughly the sort of being that has responsibilities and rights and cares about its own survival, is to be identified with a biological organism. On a dualist view with regard to the mind-body problem, as we have seen, there is more to a person than just a material body. And even to many of those who reject dualism, it seems possible that the same material body might house different persons at different times and that the same person might inhabit different material bodies at different times. (These possibilities are elaborated in the selections that follow.)

Second, what is at issue is *numerical identity* (being the very same individual entity), as opposed to what is sometimes called *qualitative identity* (being exactly similar in qualities and features). Another car that is the same make, model, and color as my car, with the same kinds of accessories, the very same kinds of scratches in the paint, and so forth, might perhaps be qualitatively identical to my car, but would still obviously be numerically distinct. And, on the other hand, my car is normally taken to be the numerically same individual entity at different times even though its qualities change as it ages, becomes dirty or is washed, acquires scratches and dents, and so forth.[4]

In addition to its theoretical interest, the issue of personal identity is practically important in two quite distinct ways. First, there is the issue of individual *survival*. Most people hope to survive into the future, and many are concerned with the possibility of survival after death. But for a person to survive seems, at first glance at least, to require that some later person be identical to the earlier one who survives, making it important for those concerned with survival to discover what such identity requires. (For example, could a resurrected person be genuinely the same person as one who died earlier, and if so, what specifically would this require?) On the other hand, there is the issue of the justifiability of such things as blame, praise, punishment, reward, etc. For a person to be justifiably blamed, praised, punished, or rewarded for some earlier action seems to require that he or she be the very same person as the one who actually performed that action, again making it important to figure out what such identity requires. (For example, is a victim of amnesia the same person who existed before the amnesia and perhaps performed some action worthy of one or more of these responses?)

What makes the problem of personal identity so difficult is that it seemingly cannot be solved by appealing to some identifiable entity that is literally the same throughout the history of the same person. The human body consists of material components that are constantly being exchanged for others, so that after a period of about seven years none of the specific material ingredients is identical to those existing earlier. Some have appealed to an immaterial mind or soul as the entity responsible for identity, but apart from doubts about the very existence of such an entity, it is far from clear that it remains literally identical through the history of a person—or that it matters whether or not this is so. (See John Locke's discussions of these issues.)

What then does personal identity require? The predominant tendency in recent discussions, growing out of Locke, is to appeal to *psychological* criteria of some sort: things like memories or apparent memories of earlier actions or experiences. Locke's own view, as defended in the first of the following selections, is that personal identity requires that the later person have the "same consciousness" as the earlier person with which he or she is identical: where this means at least roughly that the later person has an apparent memory of the earlier person's actions and experiences. The selection by Thomas Reid offers a number of objections to Locke's view. The selection by Bernard Williams then considers the issue of whether, as Locke suggests, a person inhabiting one human body could be

---

[4]The car example raises an issue that is related to though still distinct from the problem of personal identity: what is it for a material object to be the numerically identical or the same from one time to another, as its qualities change in various ways and as material parts get added or subtracted? No one would say that my car today is not the same car as my car yesterday just because it has received a new scratch or dent in the meantime—even though this presumably means that it is not the very same collection of atoms and molecules in the same arrangement (since some molecules have been scratched off and others rearranged). But suppose that many parts of the original car have been replaced: the tires, the muffler, one or more of the windows, parts of the engine or even the whole engine, some or all of the seats, and so on. At what point is the resulting car no longer numerically identical to the original car? And does the shift from identity to nonidentity happen gradually or all at once? There is also a closely analogous though still somewhat different problem for living things. What makes the issue of personal identity importantly different from either of these is that on most views a person is not just a material object or even a living body. It has also often been assumed (though Parfit will challenge this) that personal identity, unlike the identity of material objects or living things, could not in principle be a matter of degree.

identical to a later person inhabiting a different body—whether two people could "exchange bodies," arguing that the answer to this question is seriously uncertain. Finally, the selection by Derek Parfit argues that there are describable cases in which the issue of whether one person is identical with an earlier one has no clear and determinate answer, but also that the issue of identity is less important than it has usually been taken to be— and in particular that, contrary to what has usually been assumed, the survival of a person does *not* require that there be a later person to whom the surviving person is identical.

ARE MINDS AND MENTAL STATES DISTINCT FROM BODIES AND MATERIAL STATES?

Keith Campbell

Keith Campbell (1938–) is an Australian philosopher who has published widely in metaphysics as well as in the philosophy of mind. This reading is from Chapter 2 of *Body and Mind,* a book in which Campbell, unlike many contemporary philosophers of mind, treats dualism as a serious option and indeed ends up tentatively defending a particular version of dualism (more specifically, a version of epiphenomenalism).

In this reading, Campbell clarifies, motivates, and defends four claims, each of which, he claims, is initially plausible. Yet it is clear that all four cannot be true: that if any three of the claims are true, then the remaining one must be false. Campbell thus articulates one especially clear formulation of the mind-body problem. The second of these four claims is that the human mind is a spiritual thing. Therefore, if Campbell is right about the nature of the mind-body problem, a materialist view, a view according to which the mind just is some part or aspect of the body (usually the brain), would constitute a clear solution, because such a view rejects this second claim. For a materialist (such as J. J. C. Smart or Jerry Fodor), the mind-body problem becomes mainly the more specific problem of explaining *how* a purely material thing like a brain could have mental states or events like thoughts and sensations.

How the Mind-Body Problem Arises

(i) FOUR INCOMPATIBLE PROPOSITIONS

We can grasp what is baffling about the problem of mind and body, and discern a pattern in the rival solutions to it, by setting out four propositions which express in a nutshell the dilemma which confronts us.

1. The human body is a material thing.
2. The human mind is a spiritual thing.
3. Mind and body interact.
4. Spirit and matter do not interact.

. . . the Mind-Body problem carries with it the problems of what a mind and a body are: propositions (1) and (2) are a most succinct way of giving answers to these questions. Leaving out all detail which for our purposes is irrelevant, they assert an overarching difference of nature between mind and

From Body and Mind, *2nd ed. (Notre Dame: University of Notre Dame Press, 1984).*

body. This difference sets up the question of how mind and body relate to one another. . . .

There comes to be a Mind-Body problem when there comes to be reason for thinking that each of the four propositions is true. For the propositions are incompatible; there is a contradiction involved in asserting all four.

The four propositions form what is known as an *inconsistent tetrad.* That is to say, any three of them are mutually consistent and can all be true. But any three together entail that the fourth is false. It takes at least three of them to disprove the fourth, but any three are enough to dispose of the remaining one.

The incompatibility is strictly logical. From the joint assertion of all four we can derive a contradiction, and not just some proposition known to be false. For example, (1), (2), and (4) entail (5) Mind and body do not interact, and (3) and (5) together are a flat contradiction.

Now the Mind-Body problem is not the problem of finding some profound way to reconcile our four propositions. There is no profound way to reconcile the two sides of a contradiction. Showing how a contradiction can really be true is something that cannot be done. . . .

Rather, the Mind-Body problem consists in determining which of the four propositions is false. A satisfactory solution of the problem consists in identifying the false propositions (for there may be more than one), explaining how, despite their plausibility, they are nevertheless false, and filling out as far as possible the details of the true propositions which remain.

. . .

We explain the four propositions by discussing the technical terms involved.

"Material"

In calling the body "material" I mean that it shares the properties common to the most familiar objects of our environment, such as shoes, ships, and lumps of sealing wax, e.g., mass, position, volume, velocity; that it is composed entirely of the recognized material stuffs, e.g., carbon, nitrogen, oxygen, phosphorus; and that its responses to physical influences satisfy only the laws governing all matter, whether found in living organisms or in inanimate systems. Proposition (1), asserting the material nature of the body, thus asserts

that physiology is just a specially complicated branch of chemistry and physics—and chemistry in its turn reduces to physics.

Now physics changes from one year to the next, with the result that the sorts of events which conform to physical laws can change from one year to the next. What the claim to materiality amounts to changes as physics changes. In the eighteenth century, (1) would assert that all events involving the body can be explained by reference solely to impact and gravitation among particles. And this is false, for the body is electromagnetic as well as mechanical. In the twentieth century, (1) embraces electromagnetism, for that is part of contemporary physics. The content of the claim that an object is material is relative to the physics of the time it is made. This *relativity of materialism* is of great importance when we come to consider materialist doctrines of the mind.[1] The claim that, for example, the mind is the same thing as the (purely material) central nervous system, inherits the relativity of all materialism.

> **1** From the standpoint of eighteenth-century physics, the electromagnetic events in the body would not count as material events. Yet from the standpoint of twentieth-century physics, those very same events are material events. So the very meaning of the claim that the body is material varies with changes in our knowledge of physics. Is this a problem for the claim that the body is material?

There is another complication about materiality. A material thing need not always behave in accord with physical law. A stone which flies through the air under a miraculous divine propulsion would violate the dynamical laws governing the motion of stones. But it would remain a material thing for all that. A material thing can, without ceasing to be a material thing, respond to forces other than physical ones. The brain, without ceasing to be material, can act under the influence of an immaterial mind. What is necessary is that all *physical* forces acting on the object should always have their normal effect even if this is supplemented, from time to time, by supervening influences.[2]

> **2** Campbell claims here that a brain would still be a material thing even if it were affected by an immaterial force. Is there any problem with saying that a baseball is still a material thing even if some sort of spiritual force or entity (perhaps a poltergeist) is able to throw it across the yard?

. . .

If in a brain there are events which are not of a physical kind, then whether they are law-conforming or random, the brain in which they occur is not a purely material object.③ In saying that a body is purely material, we are committed to holding that only events of a physical kind occur within it, and that either there are no deviations from physical expectations beyond the limits allowed in quantum theory, or that influences other than physical ones are effective in it.

. . .

③ Campbell is referring to events that actually occur *in* the brain. In contrast to this view, dualism claims that an immaterial mental state is not an event in the brain, but only an event that can affect the brain from the outside (as the poltergeist might affect the baseball). So, on Campbell's view, the existence of immaterial mental states, even if they do affect brain states, does not mean that the brain itself is not material.

"Spiritual"

Saying what is meant by proposition (2), that the human mind is a spiritual thing, is no easy task. The spiritual is so elusive that it seems to evade definition no less than investigation. The mind seems to have, *as mind,* no special nature at all. It resists direct description. So we begin to specify the spiritual by contrasting it with matter. A spiritual object is one which does not have all the qualities of matter; it lacks at least some of: mass, volume, velocity, solidity. Many thinkers have defined the spiritual, in contrast to matter, as being completely non-spatial and hence as having *none* of matter's characteristic qualities. But if ghosts are any guide, it seems that mass and solidity are the ones that count, for ghosts would have position and shape.④

④ It is not clear how seriously Campbell intends the example of the ghost to be taken. Certainly he is not assuming that there actually are ghosts, but at most that a ghost is a good example of a spiritual thing.

Further, a spiritual thing is *not* composed of the ordinary material elements, and *not* subject to ordinary material laws. We need to proceed a little carefully here. A shaft of light is not composed of ordinary material elements. Nor is it solid. In both these ways it resembles a ghost. But its behavior does conform to physical laws and the particles which make it up play a part in the economy of the non-thinking, nonliving, spatiotemporal world. A shaft of light is therefore not spiritual. Likewise a magnetic field, even if it is a thing, is not spiritual. Though a magnetic field lacks most qualities of material things, it belongs to the inanimate space-time world. And any part of the inanimate space-time world is excluded from the realm of spirit.⑤

All this is negative. Just what features a spirit *does* have are still to be specified. We must give the spirit some positive qualities, else it will not be anything at all. For what does not exist is without material qualities, is not composed of material elements, is not subject to physical laws, and is no part of inanimate nature.

⑤ Spiritual things fail to conform to physical laws (but remember the point about the relativity of materialism—which laws are the physical laws?). Light and magnetic fields are still material, since they do conform to physical laws.

The choice of a positive defining characteristic for spirit must be made with some care. To preserve the contrast with matter, we will do best to pick a characteristic which material things do not have. And to give the term "spirit" a useful role in our thought, we will do best to pick a characteristic which men's minds do have, or at least seem to. And so as not to exclude partially developed or handicapped spirits by our definition, we must choose a characteristic broad enough in scope to embrace all the sorts of spirit we might wish to talk about. There are two characteristics which have appealed to philosophers as meeting these specifications: consciousness and intentionality.

Consciousness

Descartes defined the spiritual thing which is a man's mind as *res cogitans,* the thinking thing. By this he meant the thing which enters any conscious state, whether of thinking, feeling, or acting.

The problem for this definition was deep and dreamless sleep. If in sleep there is no consciousness then equally, by definition, there is no spirit. A man would have to be given a new spirit, and so be a different man, every time he woke up.⑥ Descartes, a

⑥ Think about this possibility: does your spirit (or mind) cease to exist whenever you are completely lacking in consciousness (as in dreamless sleep)? If this did happen, would you be a different person when you woke up?

bold and brave philosopher, confronted this problem squarely and affirmed that the mind is conscious at all times, even in sleep. We don't realize this, he believed, because we forget the greater part of our dreams.

It is true that we forget much of our dreaming. But there is no reason to think that at every moment of sleep, trance, or anesthesia, there is some conscious mental activity. The mind is active, perhaps, but not conscious.⑦ So the nearest we should go to Descartes' definition of spiritual substance is: a spiritual substance must be *capable* of consciousness. The spirit is something which can think, feel, and act. The intrinsic character of this thing capable of conscious thought, feeling, and action—what it's like when it's resting, so to speak—remains unspecified.

> ⑦ Descartes's solution is that, contrary to the way it may seem, a person's spirit or mind is in fact always conscious. Campbell rejects this view as unsupported, and holds instead merely that spirits or minds are always *capable* of consciousness (though perhaps still active in some other way—but what way?). The underlying issue is then the essential nature of mind or spirit (since it can't be actually being conscious).

So the whole account of spirit remains rather shadowy. A spirit is defined indirectly as something capable of consciousness, and consciousness is no more fully described than as "what it takes to think, feel, and act," that is, as what it takes to have a mind.

Intentionality

"Intentionality" is a technical notion. It is used to describe a peculiar and significant characteristic of mental states. A hope is not just a hope, it is a hope for something, more or less definite. I can hope to obtain the moon, or win the girl, or get to work on time. I cannot just hope. Despair is despair over something. I can despair over my son's addiction to drugs or my being shipwrecked and not rescued. I cannot just despair. Perception is perception of something; I don't just see, I see an object or event or circumstance. I see the car, or I see the car crashing, or I see that the car has crashed. When I think, I think about the problem in hand. Anger is anger at someone or something. Determination is determination to achieve something.⑧

Other terms, which have no connection with the mind, are like this too. A substance can't just be poisonous, it must be a poison for some sorts of creatures. I can't just collide, I must collide with something. But the peculiarity of the mental states is that they are directed on objects which need have no material existence. I cannot collide with a boat unless there is a boat to collide with. But I can be determined to rescue the drowning passengers even if there are no passengers. Being directed on objects which need have no material existence is what is significant when mental states are described as intentional.

> ⑧ An intentional state is one directed toward or *about* something else. It is thus a state that has an *object*: one whose very nature involves a reference to something else.

A mental state is determined by its intentional object; my hope is the hope it is, and not some other, because it has one intentional object and not some other. And these intentional objects need not, in any material sense, exist at all.⑨

Intentionality is thus a likely candidate for defining the spiritual. It seems to maintain the contrast of the spiritual with the material, for material descriptions are not intentional. And it seems also to give "spiritual" a real place in our thought, for it is the familiar capacities to think, decide, and hope, etc., which are described in intentional ways. . . . We might therefore try to define a spiritual thing as something which has intentional states.

> ⑨ So, for example, my thought about my dog is a different mental state than my thought about my daughter just because of the difference between what the two states are about (the two states have different intentional objects). And notice that a child's hope that Santa will bring lots of presents is a mental state directed toward something with no real existence at all.

There are nonetheless difficulties with this definition. Maybe not all mental states have intentionality. States of bodily feeling are one doubtful class. To itch is to be in a mental state. An itch in the small of my back has a location, but it does not seem to have an object in the way that a hope does. Moods are another doubtful class. Dread, depression, and light-heartedness seem to need no objects, although we might try to overcome this objection either by saying they have extremely general objects, such as the state of the world, or my condition and prospects. . . .

Another difficulty is that some material things may be describable in intentional terms. An intentional description differs from a material one and yet a material thing may have states which are intentionally described. Thus a computer may be calculating the square root of 493; "calculating the square root of 493" is an intentional description. The calculation is directed upon its solution and is identified by reference to it. And if the computer is calculating the integral square root of 493, it is directed upon a non-existent object. Yet the computer is a material thing. So even if our definition of spirit does refer to intentionality, it will have to include the negative reference to immateriality as well. [10]

[10] Is it literally true that the computer's activity has the integral square root of 493 as an object? Or is that just an interpretation we place on electronic activity that really isn't in itself about anything?

Attempts to supply the positive element in the definition of "spirit" using consciousness and intentionality tend to coincide. For the one leads to "something which is capable of thinking, feeling, and acting," while the other leads to "something with intentionally describable states," where thinking, feeling, and acting are exactly the activities to which intentional descriptions apply.

Both give us indirect descriptions in terms of capacities, and both require the negative supplement to keep matter and spirit distinct. [11] We can sum them up thus:

[11] Note that Campbell hasn't given any clear reason for thinking that being capable of consciousness isn't by itself, without the "negative supplement," an accurate characterization of the spiritual. (Unless he is suggesting that the computer is also capable of consciousness, which is surely far from obvious.)

"Spiritual" = "immaterial, and capable of mental life."

The idea of spirituality proves to add only immateriality to the idea of mentality. Proposition (2), which asserts the spirituality of the mind amounts to:

The mind is an immaterial thing capable of mental life.

The search for a direct positive definition of "spirit" which would enlarge our knowledge of non-material reality is thus a failure. So even if we decide, in the end, that the mind is a spiritual thing, we will remain in considerable ignorance.

The spirit eludes positive description except in terms of its capabilities. But does this really make it any different from matter? In pursuing the Mind-Body problem, we stumble here upon one of the most profound problems in metaphysics and the philosophy of science, i.e., the problem of the extent to which physical descriptions are descriptions of capacities possessed by objects whose inner reality remains unspecified. [12]

[12] Think for example of the physical property of solidity. A table is solid, but what exactly does that mean? It does not mean that the matter of the table is continuous, that there are no gaps between the particles of the table. But if saying that the table is solid just means that it resists penetration by other objects (including, for example, our hands), then we are apparently just describing a *capability* of the table, without saying anything about its "inner reality."

"Interaction"

In our four propositions, the only other technical term is "interact". It is quickly explained: two items interact if and only if each has an effect upon the other. In action, changes in one item cause changes in another. In interaction, the process is mutual. The interaction which particularly concerns us involves bodily causes of mental effects and mental causes of bodily effects.

(ii) THE INITIAL PLAUSIBILITY OF ALL FOUR PROPOSITIONS

We said earlier that there is a Mind-Body problem only because there is some reason to think that each one of the four members of our inconsistent tetrad is true. It is time to substantiate this claim by reviewing the case which can be made for each of the propositions considered independently.

1. The Body Is a Material Thing   This proposition asserts that the body is composed of ordinary matter. It is made up of atoms of familiar elements—carbon, oxygen, nitrogen, and so on. And those atoms are in turn composed of the same particles which make up such atoms wherever they are found. The proposition asserts further that the material making up the body, provided only physical forces are acting on it, obeys all and only the very physical laws of motion, combination, and dissolution which hold for inanimate matter.

13 Does it seem odd that Campbell would think that he even needs to argue for claim (1)? He wants to give explicit reasons for each one of the four claims, thereby defending their plausibility, even if the reasons are in some cases very obvious.

The grounds for 1. are scientific.13 The findings of chemistry and biochemistry all point in this direction. Now that chemistry has developed to the point where we can determine the elementary constitution of material things, we can affirm with confidence that the vital functions—for example, respiration, digestion, and temperature-conservation—involve no transmutation of elements into some new kind of living stuff. Now that biochemistry has made the stunning advances of recent years, we know that these processes proceed in accord with the very laws governing the behavior of matter in an inanimate environment. The unraveling of the DNA maze has enabled us to discover that even growth, replication, and the transmission of hereditary characteristics are processes of an ordinary chemical kind. The molecules involved are more complex, but the atoms gain no new nature in the living organism.

. . .

Wherever we have been able to isolate an organic process and judge with confidence just which physical forces are at work, we have found that the living matter's behavior has conformed with ordinary physics and ordinary chemistry. The human body, including its brain, is not different in constitution or atomic nature from its material environment. That is proposition 1., and its warrant is the success of the biochemistry and biophysics which affirm it.

Yet although a body is a material system, a man may not be. To settle the Mind-Body problem we must determine whether this material bodily system is sometimes or always subject to further, non-physical forces and influences, and if so, which ones.

2. The Mind Is a Spiritual Thing   That the mind thinks and feels, and that it is engaged in action, are not contentious propositions. They help to pick out what we are talking about when we talk about minds. There can be little more argument over them than over claims that dentists drill teeth and politicians are engaged in the affairs of state. . . .

So the crucial element of proposition 2. is the immateriality of the mind. There are four families of reasons upon which men have based their conviction that the mind is not material.

Traditional and Intuitive Grounds

The differences between men on the one hand and our inanimate environment on the other are so many and so striking that the materiality of the mind has seemed to most people an obvious impossibility. Men can see and hear, ponder and resolve, suffer and enjoy. They have a language and a culture. They can make plans, solve problems, and hunger and thirst after righteousness. They can anticipate and regret, hope and fear. They can love, they can be amused, they can make music, they can worship. They can be heroic or cruel or ambitious. In all of this they are utterly different from the rocks and puddles, furniture and utensils, and even plants and animals which make up our natural and artificial environment. Further, these differences are all ones in which mind plays a crucial part. It is clear that men have got something that floorboards lack; "mind" is the name of this extra possession. But floorboards are not deficient in materiality. They are fully and properly material things. What is more natural, then, but to conclude that the mind is not material? So has arisen the long Western tradition of contrasting man with the natural material realm. For Plato man comes into it as a prisoner, for Christians he journeys through it as a wayfarer, for contemporary Existentialists he finds himself thrown amid alien *things*.

. . .

Now this tradition of immaterialism, based as it is on a common sense which incorporates massive ignorance of the ways of the world, cannot by itself establish anything. Its importance is rather that of placing the responsibility of proof on him who denies the spiritual character of the mind. The structure of the argument is this:

> There are great differences between men and other material things.
> These differences require an explanation.
> The initially most plausible explanation is that men differ from material things in having a spirit responsible for what is distinctively human.

So he who denies the spirituality of the mind must show how something merely material can after all have all the human characteristics. [14]

[14] This is a rather weak argument. Even if the first two premises are easily defensible (and true), the third premise doesn't give much support to the conclusion, because the "initially most plausible explanation" could still easily be wrong. (See Discussion Question 2 for more on this argument.)

This first body of reasons, then, are more accurately described as reasons for believing the mind is spiritual in the absence of convincing proof to the contrary. We are here discussing initial plausibility; the initially plausible view of the mind is that it is spiritual, because the mind is responsible for such an astonishing range of phenomena. Attempts at passing beyond initial plausibility to positive demonstration that the mind is not material have taken three main forms:

Epistemic Grounds

We can come to know for ourselves, and not just by teaching or report, only if the thing known affects our minds. Now we can learn of the world in ways other than by the physical operation of the senses. The mind is affected by non-physical reality.

[15] Think about the claim that numbers are immaterial, that seven (not the word or the numeral, but the number seven itself) is an immaterial thing. Does that seem right? Can you think of any plausible account of what sort of material thing the number seven might be? (In the following paragraph, God is an even more obvious example of an immaterial thing, but unfortunately one whose existence is controversial at best—see Chapter 2.)

For example, mathematical knowledge is not sense knowledge. The eternal, immaterial numbers are not perceptible, yet we can know them. Numbers cannot have any effect upon matter, yet they can affect our minds. So minds cannot be material. [15]

Likewise men can, in this life by mystic union and in the life to come by beatific vision, come to a knowledge of God. But God is not perceptible. We do not come to know him by any transaction involving the senses.

Again, we can know non-physical aspects of material things. Men have the knowledge of good and evil. But the good and evil in things cannot be seen or felt. We come to the knowledge of values through the operation of a "higher" spiritual faculty. [16]

So, the argument runs, in at least these three cases the mind is open to influences which cannot affect matter. In consequence, the mind cannot be a purely material thing. Again, if the changes which consist in gaining knowledge of these kinds are not bodily changes, then the mind is a spiritual thing.

Logical Grounds

Many arguments have been developed attempting to show that the idea that the mind is material is logically impossible or incoherent. [17] These arguments fall into two distinct classes: Category Arguments and Mental-Object Arguments. Here is an example of each.

Category Arguments

Consider pains. The favorite materialist idea about pains is that they are states of the brain. Now a pain can be intense or weak, long-lived or short, continuous or intermittent, stinging or throbbing. But there is no sense at all in saying a pain is two inches long, or of high voltage, or has electric currents in it that are fast or slow. So the idea that a man can have a small, cubical, low voltage, circular current pain makes no more sense than the idea that a dog can have an odd, prime, factor-of-25 doghouse. Just as a doghouse is not the sort of thing that can be odd or prime or have any arithmetical property, so a pain is not the sort of thing which can have any physical property of the kind a brain-state has. [18] Doghouses and numbers, pains

[16] This argument assumes that the properties of being good and being evil are nonphysical or immaterial aspects of things that affect the mind (thereby allowing us to have knowledge of good and evil). Do we have knowledge of good and evil? If so, is there any way that the objects of that knowledge could be merely material features or aspects of material things? (Which features or aspects would they be?)

[17] Something is logically impossible if we can understand it, but it cannot possibly be true: that cubes are spherical or that some bachelor is married, for example. Something is incoherent if it does not make clear sense (and so cannot be assessed as either true or false). A plausible example is the claim that my stove is in pain. No claim of either kind can be true, but for quite different reasons.

[18] Is this too fast? Think about why it seems to be nonsense to say that a doghouse is odd or prime. Is it clearly nonsense in the same way to say that a pain has a specific electrical property?

and brain-states, come from different *categories*. To confuse categories is to talk nonsense; and nonsense cannot be true. We reach the same result whatever material item we choose to equate with a pain. And what holds for pains holds for anything mental. So the mind cannot be material.

Mental-Object Arguments

Take an afterimage. An afterimage is not nothing. There is a difference between someone who is having an afterimage and someone who is not. Suppose the afterimage is pale turquoise. Now it may be that nothing nearby, either inside or outside the head of the person having the afterimage, is pale turquoise. If there does happen to be something pale turquoise nearby, it is almost certainly not the afterimage. The afterimage is "in the mind," but it is not a material thing. So the mind in which it is, is not a material thing either. [19]

[19] When Campbell says that the afterimage is "not nothing," he is suggesting that it is something—an object or entity that would then seemingly have to be pale turquoise. But is the afterimage really an object or entity? (See Discussion Question 3.)

. . .

Empirical Grounds

Scientific investigation points to the materiality of the body. We must now ask whether any comparable body of research establishes the nature of the mind. The situation is a curious one. We might expect that just as biochemistry and biophysics yield a result for the body, so psychology would settle the question for the mind. But this is not so.

Psychological research has established, with hitherto unknown precision, many of the relationships between mental events and processes, for example, between expectation and perception. And it has explored relations between mental and physical events and processes, for example, in experiments concerning the threshold levels for perception. Psychologists develop theories of personality structure and motivation. They increase our knowledge of how people learn and how they cope with distress.

But psychological investigation does not yield a doctrine of the nature of the mind. Psychological technique does not determine whether or not the mind is material. The chief reason for this is that psychologists must operate principally with the data of stimulus and response, and these data do not specify the nature of the mind falling between them. . . . [20]

The empirical evidence urged for the spirituality of the mind is rather that of parapsychology, the unorthodox investigation of extraordinary capacities of mind. This evidence is of two types: that concerning paranormal psychological powers, such as telepathy and clairvoyance, and that concerning survival of death. Telepathy and clairvoyance involve gaining knowledge of the thoughts of another, or of matter of physical fact, without the use of normal sensory means. The evidence of survival is that involved in "communications" to a trance-medium of knowledge hitherto possessed only by a now deceased person.

If any of these phenomena are genuine, they establish that the mind is not merely material. They show that a mind can do what no material system can do. [21] Remembering the relativity of materialism, we may hope that a new physics and chemistry will be able to accommodate them. But until that happens, or computers start to display inexplicable paranormal powers, paranormal phenomena would provide the best of reasons for holding to the spiritual character of the mind.

Although the prima facie case for the mind's spirituality does not rest on a copious base of relevant scientific results, it is nevertheless many-sided and considerable. Of our four incompatible propositions, the first two together set up a duality in man's nature. This duality of matter and

[20] Think carefully about this point, which will be important in later selections. Campbell is saying that psychology studies stimulus and response but says nothing about the nature of the inner events that result from the stimuli and cause the responses. (Indeed, some interpretations of psychology—the various forms of *behaviorism*—deny the very existence of such inner events. This is discussed in the Fodor selection, later in the chapter.)

[21] Think carefully about this claim, which Campbell does not elaborate. Is there any clear reason why telepathy (nonsensory awareness of another person's thoughts) and clairvoyance (nonsensory awareness of physical states of affairs) are things that a material system could not do, assuming for the sake of the argument that it is capable of conscious awareness? What about communication with the dead? (Their existence may be immaterial, but does that of the person communicating with them have to be?)

spirit generates the problems of interaction between them which give to the Mind-Body conundrum its modern severity.

3. Mind and Body Interact   This proposition is one of those, supported by an enormous and ever growing mass of common experience, which form a starting point for investigation and speculation. We confirm the interaction of mind and body a hundred times a day. A hot stove burns my finger (bodily event), and in consequence I suffer pain (mental event). I take LSD (bodily event), and am afflicted with hallucinations (mental event). The stray light entering my eyes changes in composition, and I realize that the traffic light has changed to green. So bodily changes have mental effects.

Causal connections in the other direction, linking mind to body, are equally easy to find. I am suffering the pain of my burned finger (mental event), and this causes me to apply a burn cream (bodily event). My psychedelic hallucinations are terrifying, so I scream or go to the hospital. I realize the traffic lights have changed, so I accelerate.

We can bolster the case for mind-body interaction by more general considerations. If the pain in the example of the burn is not caused by the physical contact of flesh with hot stove, then either it has no cause at all, or it has some utterly mysterious and totally unconscious prior mental cause. Neither alternative has any great theoretical appeal. We might come to one of these positions as a last resort when all alternatives have been ruled out, but they have low rational priority.

Again, in considering the action of mind on body, we might eventually come to the conclusion that mental events of thinking and planning formed no part of the causal chain resulting in the appearance of Newton's *Principia* or the Concorde airliner. But we should arrive at this complicated and implausible position reluctantly, and only after fruitless exploration of every other avenue. 22

The claim that mind and body interact, well-confirmed though it be, may not be true. We may even come in the end to reject it. But if we deny mind-body interaction we must furnish a convincing account of how the illusion arises. We will need a powerful reinterpretation of all the evidence apparently supporting interaction. In the meantime, the initial plausibility of the view that both body acts on mind and mind acts on body is immense.

4. Spirit and Matter Do Not Interact   The Mind-Body problem, what Schopenhauer called the "world-knot", is complete when we see that there are good reasons for *denying* that matter and spirit can interact. The case for this is a dual one; it rests on theoretical considerations and on a concrete program of scientific research.

Theoretical Considerations

The theoretical consideration is simply stated: interaction of matter and spirit is a causal impossibility. To see the force of this idea, we must make some study of the philosophy of cause. In a causal sequence, there is at least an event c followed by another event e. If what is involved is a single causal link and not a whole chain, the events c and e must not be too remote from one another in space (some say they must be next to each other), nor too far separated in time (again, some say c and e must be simultaneous or immediately successive). To distinguish cause from mere coincidence the whole class C of events relevantly similar to c must be followed by events of class E, relevantly similar to e. . . .

The Pure Regularity Theory of Causes, which springs from the thought of David Hume, holds the causal relation between c and e to consist in no more than the existence of the class C-E of sequences of which c-e is an example. The Pure Regularity Theory identifies causal connection with regularity of sequence. 23 Since no limits can be placed on what sort of event can be in regular connection with what

---

22   Campbell gives examples of both bodily events causing mental events and of mental events causing bodily events, but he gives "more general considerations" only for bodily events causing mental events. Can a more general argument of a parallel sort be made for mental events causing bodily events as well, and would it be equally strong? (See Discussion Question 4.)

---

23   Suppose, for example, that my throwing a rock at a window is event c, and the event of the window breaking is event e. According to the "Pure Regularity Theory of Causes," the existence of a causal relation between c and e *consists in* the existence of a class of other similar rock throwings that are immediately followed by other similar window breakings. Nothing more than this regular sequence of events is required for causality.

other sort of event, there can, on this theory, be causal connections between any two events, no matter how diverse. No sort of connection can be a causal impossibility. Anything can be the cause of anything. In particular, provided that problems about their spatial relations can be ironed out, material events can be the cause of spiritual events and vice versa. [24]

[24] Causes and effects that are both material usually have to be spatially close or contiguous, basically because a material event cannot affect one that is distant from it. But it is not clear why there should be such a requirement for mental-physical or physical-mental causation—presumably there is some other kind of relation there (see Foster's discussion of this issue in the following selection).

Proposition 4. asserts that matter and spirit do not interact. Its theoretical support collapses entirely if the Pure Regularity Theory of cause is correct. To maintain the theoretical objection to interaction, the Pure Regularity Theory must be convicted of error. Here, as so often, the Mind-Body problem raises one of the crucial general questions of philosophy. This time it is the problem: What is a cause?

Let us consider, in brief compass, the objections to the Pure Regularity Theory on which the theoretical case against the interaction of matter with spirit relies.

In developed sciences, we do not rest content with the mere establishment of a regular succession among events, but seek to uncover the mechanisms, the mode of operation, whereby the cause-event issues in the effect-event. It is not enough to know that assembling a critical mass of radioactive uranium will give you an explosion; we want to know why this happens. The story of why this happens is an explanation connecting the nature of uranium with a series of processes which culminate in an explosion. This intervening series of processes is what, with a slight stretching of the word, we are calling the *"mechanism"* of the causal connection.

Connections which are not fundamental thus do not fit the Pure Regularity Theory, for they involve reference to a mechanism as well as to regular sequence. When our analysis comes to an end in "fundamental" connections, for example, an atomic nucleus absorbing a flying particle and then dividing, there are no intervening processes between cause and effect (or none we know about, anyway). That is what we mean when we call the connection fundamental. [25] We cannot say how or why a fundamental process occurs. In these cases we must rest content with equations giving accurate quantitative expression to what happens, where, and when. In the atomic absorption and division example, we specify what energies are released, in what direction, over what time. In this case too the Pure Regularity Theory does not cover the whole of what is required; it leaves out the requirement that the regularity must be given mathematical form. [26]

[25] Fundamental connections are those that involve no intervening processes. Do you see why any account that appeals to mechanisms (intervening processes) must *also* involve connections that are treated as fundamental in this sense?

[26] Campbell suggests that all fundamental connections must be expressible in mathematical form, but gives no clear reason for this claim. (Can you think of a reason?) This leads to an objection to the Pure Regularity Theory of Causes.

Now all causal ties either have a mechanism, or are fundamental and admit of mathematical expression. But the links between matter and spirit neither have a mechanism nor admit of mathematical expression. The reason lies in the impalpable character of spirit. We have no idea how a mechanism could "get a grip" on a spirit. The mechanism by which changes in the brain can "get a grip" on the heart and change its rate of beating is intelligible; but how could the brain get a grip on a spiritual mind, to give it fear? And further, because fear resists description in terms of place or direction, we have no "fear" equations linking brain and spirit, nor seem likely ever to have any. From which the conclusion drawn is: matter-spirit interaction is impossible. [27]

[27] Campbell argues that "the impalpable character of spirit" rules out both mechanisms and mathematical expression for causal ties between matter and spirit (in either direction). But it can be questioned whether the idea of a mechanism even makes sense here. (See Discussion Question 5.) Thus the main basis for the objection to dualism is the idea that fundamental causal connections must be mathematically expressible, a requirement for which no clear support has been offered.

These theoretical considerations are not absolutely compelling. They establish at most the *anomaly* of matter-spirit interaction. They show that any such interactions would be very different from the interactions characteristic of physical sciences, and very difficult to express properly. These strange connections would exist only in the fragment of the universe consisting of beings with minds. . . .

The importance of the theoretical considerations is in showing matter-spirit interactions to be mysterious oddities quite at variance with what we know of nature's workings. "Don't dabble in mysterious oddities any more than you must" is a sound principle of intellectual method. On this principle matter-spirit interaction must be accorded low rational priority. We must seek ways of avoiding the admission of such an idea to our theories. ⟨28⟩

⟨28⟩ How strong is this argument? One response might be that relations between spirits and bodies are a unique enough case to make it reasonable to tolerate or even expect anomalous causal relations.

Empirical Considerations

Even if we are prepared to countenance the possibility of matter-spirit interaction, there are investigations which point to the conclusion that there are in fact no such connections. We shall call this scientific evidence The Shadow of Physiology.

Brain activity is the crucial bodily factor in both learning of our environment (perception), and in living out our lives in that environment (action). The links of senses to brain, and brain to muscles show every sign of being physicochemical relations. So if spirit acts on matter in men, it acts through the brain. Yet the evidence suggests that nothing happens in a man save what conforms to physical and chemical law.

. . . Our ignorance of brains is still profound, but research based on the assumption that the brain obeys only physicochemical laws has not yet suffered a damaging reverse. There seems to be no room for spirit to get into the act, and no sign of its effects. The Shadow of Physiology is a shadow cast by a successful program of scientific research. ⟨29⟩

⟨29⟩ If there were events in the brain that were known to be inexplicable in material terms, then we might have to take seriously the possibility that spirit was sometimes the cause of them. Equally, if all events in the brain were known to be adequately explicable in material terms, then influence by immaterial spirits would be seemingly ruled out. The actual situation is between these two: some brain events have been adequately explained, but many more have not so far. The question is whether the degree of success so far is great enough to suggest as strongly, as Campbell claims, that all brain events will eventually be explained in material terms.

. . .

The Mind-Body problem is a problem because, as we have now seen, there are reasons for holding to each of the four propositions which make up our inconsistent tetrad. Competing solutions of the problem consist in competing ideas concerning which members of the tetrad should be rejected, and what should be put in their place. . . .

Discussion Questions

1. Philosophers often need to clarify the key terms of a discussion before proceeding to argue for a claim (you'll often need to do that when writing philosophy essays), and Campbell is engaged in just such clarification in the first few pages of this reading: clarifying "material," "spiritual," and "interaction." One obvious way to clarify a term is to give a definition.

   a. Think of some terms that are easy to define (for example, "bachelor" and "triangle"), and state the definition for each term. Next, contrast those terms with other terms that seem almost impossible to define (for example, "red" and "love"), and try to come up with a way to explain what the terms mean to someone who has never experienced the referent of the terms (for example, how would you explain "red" to a blind person).

   b. It would be very tempting, when explaining "love," to explain the actions of someone who loves. For example, one might say that when a mother loves her child, she acts in ways that benefit the child and feels happy when things go well for the child and sad when they don't. But these are all *consequences* of the love the mother has for the child instead of a definition of love. Is such an explanation of love adequate or not?

c. Campbell admits that "spirit eludes positive description except in terms of its capabilities. But does this make it any different from matter?" The clear suggestion is that matter too is ultimately described in terms of capacities instead of its "inner reality." Has Campbell then failed to provide an adequate clarification of the key terms "spirit" and "matter"?

2. Consider again Campbell's argument (pp. 320–21) for the conclusion that someone who denies that minds are spiritual must show how some merely material thing can have all the human characteristics. One odd feature is that the conclusion seems to be true for reasons independent of the premises: surely a materialist must explain how a merely material thing can have the features that people in fact have. But another odd feature is the relatively weak claim made by the third premise. Consider a somewhat different argument: one with the same first two premises, but change the third premise to: the *best possible explanation* is that men differ from material things in having a spirit responsible for what is distinctively human. How plausible is this new premise 3? What about premise 2 of the argument? What conclusion would follow from those three premises?

3. Think about the afterimage you would have after looking directly into a flash bulb. You are certainly having an experience (a conscious state), but is it one that involves the afterimage (whatever color it is) as an *object?* Must there be any object somewhere (not necessarily a material object) that really is pale turquoise in order for you to experience a pale turquoise afterimage? If so, what sort of object is it? If not, how is the character of the experience to be explained? (Suppose instead that you hallucinate a pink elephant. Does this require that there is an object or entity that is genuinely pink? Does it require that it genuinely be an elephant?)

4. One version of dualism, the one that Campbell eventually defends in the book from which this reading is drawn, is epiphenomenalism, which accepts body-to-mind causation but rejects mind-to-body causation. Though both directions of causation seem obvious from the standpoint of common sense, are they in fact equally obvious? Think again of Campbell's "general considerations" (p. 323) in support of body-to-mind causation. And now consider the following example: (a) someone throws a snowball at you, (b) you have the mental experience of the snowball approaching, (c) you desire not to be hit by it, and (d) you jump out of the way. Here the transition from (a) to (b) seems like a case of body-to-mind causation, and the transition from (c) to (d) seems like a case of mind-to-body causation (with the transition from (b) to (c) being an example of mind-to-mind causation). Campbell's argument is in effect that there is no view of how (b) is caused that is even minimally plausible other than that it is caused by the physical event (a). Is it equally true that there is no view of how (d) is caused that is even minimally plausible other than that it is caused by your mental state (c), or can you think of an alternative here? How plausible is it?

5. Think again about the issue of whether a *mechanism* can account for mind-body causation. Take the body-to-mind part of the case in the previous question: the approaching snowball (a) seems to cause a mental awareness of a snowball approaching (b). Clearly it would be possible to find further events or processes that intervene between (a) and (b), thus constituting at least part of a mechanism. On the physical side there would be reflected light striking the eye, the focusing of it on the retina, events in the optical nerve, and events in the visual cortex. On the mental side, there are presumably initial awareness of colors and shapes prior to recognition of the object as a snowball, and perhaps other processes as well. Suppose that we specify a lot of intervening events of these sorts. Could this ever yield an account of how body-to-mind causation is possible, or would the same problem still remain? And if the latter is the case, what exactly does this show?

John Foster

John Foster (1941–) teaches at Oxford University. He has written widely in metaphysics and epistemology, as well as in the philosophy of religion and philosophy of mind. Foster is a very independent thinker. In the preface to one of his books (*The Case for Idealism*, 1982), he responds to the idea that the book may not be very well received since it defends views so contrary to current philosophical fashion by saying that he takes "some comfort from the thought that whatever its failings, it is unlikely to be considered either platitudinous or unduly derivative."

In this selection, Foster defends dualism by responding to objections, all of which criticize the possibility that there could be causal relations between a physical body and a nonphysical mind. (He seems to have in mind substance dualism, the view that the mind is a nonphysical thing or substance—see the chapter introduction.) Foster uses the phrase *psychophysical causation* to refer to causal relations between mental (psychological) states and physical states.

A Defense of Dualism

[1] To say that mental states are "the logical product" of something physical (presumably brain states), is to say that talk about mental states is in some way just a redescription of those physical states. (Functionalism, discussed in the chapter introduction and many of the later selections, would be an example of such a view.) If that were so, then mental states would *not* have an existence independent of the relevant physical brain states. Foster's dualism insists that mental states can cause physical states (and vice versa), and so mental states can be related in ways expressible by laws of nature to physical states ("nomological" just means having to do with laws of nature).

By "dualism" I mean the thesis that the mind and its contents are radically nonphysical, that is, that they are neither themselves physical, nor the logical product of anything physical, nor, except causally or nomologically, dependent on anything physical.[1]

It is nowadays generally assumed that dualism has been discredited. Even those who see problems for the alternatives usually are unwilling to countenance dualism as a possible solution. I believe that dualism is correct. . . . I shall consider some of the main objections to dualism and try to show why they are ineffective.

. . .

Of course, I do not have space to consider all the objections. Some are nothing more than rhetoric (I would put into this category such objections as "non-physical entities are queer" and "postulating nonphysical entities is ontologically extravagant") . . .

. . . the . . . objections I consider all concern, in one way or another, the dualist's account of psychophysical causation—his account of the causal relations between body and mind.[2] Dualism itself, of course, does not entail that there are such relations. There is no contradiction in maintaining that the mind, as well as being nonphysical, is causally isolated from the physical world; and with the help of a suitable theism, it may even be possible to explain why things are empirically

[2] Psychophysical causation, according to dualism, is a causal relation between a physical state and a nonphysical psychological (mental) state. As Campbell suggests (and Fodor will agree), making sense of this relation is one main problem for dualism and for the interactionist version of dualism in particular.

From The Case for Dualism, *edited by John R. Smythies and John Beloff (Charlottsville, Va.: University Press of Virginia, 1989).*

organized as if there were psychophysical causation, when there is not. But since I do not want my defense of dualism to force me into such an eccentric position, I shall work on the assumption that parallelism, in this extreme form, is untenable and that mind and body are indeed causally related.③ This still leaves the dualist with a choice between interactionism, which takes the causal relations to run in both directions, and epiphenomenalism, which takes them to run only from body to mind. Here my sympathies, again in line with common sense, are with the interactionist. And consequently, I would feel at least very uncomfortable if there were something which obliged me to choose between abandoning dualism altogether and adopting its epiphenomenalist version. That I do face such a choice is the substance of the [final] objection.

③ If one sphere of existence is causally isolated from another sphere, then no thing in either sphere can causally affect any other thing in the other sphere. Parallelism (see the chapter introduction) is the view that the mental sphere of existence is in this way causally isolated from the physical sphere. (By "a suitable theism," Foster means theories about how God makes it look as though there are psychophysical causal relations even though there really aren't—again, see the chapter introduction.)

The Traditional Objection. Perhaps the oldest objection to dualism is that if the mind is nonphysical, the very idea of psychophysical causation—of the body causally affecting the mind or the mind causally affecting the body—is deeply puzzling, if not incoherent. How can such different kinds of thing—the physical and the nonphysical—come into causal contact? How can the material body gain purchase on the immaterial mind, or vice versa?④ However, put like this, I cannot see what the problem is supposed to be. Obviously, dualistic causation does not operate through physical contact, as when one billiard ball displaces another. But why should it not just be in the nature of things that in certain psychophysical conditions, certain types of neural event cause certain types of mental event, or vice versa? According to Thomas Nagel, we cannot understand how such causation would work. Nagel assumes, I think correctly, though contrary to Hume's account, that

④ Campbell (p. 324) characterized this problem with the question: how can the immaterial mind "get a grip" in the material body?

causation involves some kind of objective necessitation.⑤ He then argues, in effect, that so long as we think of mental and physical events as radically different in their intrinsic nature, such necessitation is incomprehensible: "what we cannot understand is *how* . . . the brain process necessitates the sensation." But what I cannot understand is how this "how"-question arises. . . . since the causation is direct (the brain event directly causing the mental event, or vice versa), there is no question of an intervening mechanism. Perhaps it is this very directness which Nagel finds puzzling. For in the physical world causal processes are, in general, spatiotemporally continuous, thus providing an intervening mechanism between a cause and any subsequent effect.⑥ But there is surely nothing incoherent or problematic about the notion of direct causation. And where causation is direct, I do not see in what sense there could be a question of how it operates, except as a request to specify the causally relevant properties and covering laws.

⑤ "Objective necessitation" suggests that there is some stronger kind of connection or relation between a cause and its effect than merely regular sequence or constant conjunction—that there is something about the causal event that *makes* the effect happen in some stronger way (surely the common-sense view). But if that were right, then there might be some specific limitations as to what kind of cause could do this in relation to any particular effect. Whereas if Hume's regularity theory is right, then there are no restrictions on what kind of thing can be a cause for any particular effect. (See Discussion Question 1.)

⑥ Foster is suggesting that purely physical causal relations are never direct because any such process is spatio-temporally continuous. Think of a continuous line: between any two points there is another point. Foster is saying that between any physical cause and any physical effect (no matter how close the two are spatio-temporally), there will always be intermediate causal steps. But this is not so for the supposedly direct causal relation between a mental event and a physical event, or vice versa.

The Problem of Causal Pairings. While the traditional objection to dualistic psychophysical causation is totally misconceived, there is a related objection which is more troublesome and for which, ironically, I have to take the credit. It is normally assumed that where two events are causally related, they are so wholly by virtue of the way in which, via their noncausal properties and relations, they fall under some natural law.⑦ Thus if, on a particular occasion, my heating of a lump of metal caused it to melt, it is assumed that what makes this true is that the metal was of a certain type and reached a certain temperature and that it is a law of nature (or a consequence of a law of nature) that whenever a lump of metal of that type reaches that temperature, it melts. However, when we apply this model to the case of psychophysical causation, dualistically conceived, we encounter a problem. Suppose that B is the event of Smith's brain being in state ϕ at time t and that E is a mental event of type ψ which occurs in Smith's mind a tenth of a second after t and as the direct causal result of B.⑧ What psychophysical law could we postulate to account for this causal episode? We might begin by postulating the law (L_1) that whenever a brain is in a state ϕ a mental event of type ψ occurs a tenth of a second later. But this would be inadequate. For suppose that Jones's brain is also in state ϕ at t, giving us the event B' which is a simultaneous duplicate of B, and that this causes in Jones's mind, a tenth of a second later, an event E' of type ψ which is a simultaneous duplicate of E. Ex hypothesi, B is the cause of E and B' is the cause of E' But the law L_1 does not account for these causal pairings. Because it only specifies the temporal relation between cause and effect, it is neutral between these pairings and the alternative, but false, hypothesis that B is the cause of E' and B' is the cause of E.⑨ The obvious remedy is to replace L_1 by the stronger law (L_2) that whenever a brain x is in state ϕ a mental event of type ψ occurs a tenth of a second later in that mind which x, or the x-containing organism, embodies—in other words, in the mind of that subject whose brain x is. L_2 would then yield the unique causal pairings of B with E and of B' with E'. But the problem with this is that, for a dualist, the relation of embodiment itself must be analyzed, wholly or partly, in causal terms: at least part of what makes a particular brain x the brain of a particular subject y is that things are psychophysically arranged in a way which gives x (and x alone) the capacity to have a direct causal influence on y (and y alone) and, for the interactionist, vice versa. It would be circular to account for this arrangement by laws like L_2 and, because of the original problem, impossible to account for it by laws like L_1.⑩ In view of this, it might seem that the right solution is to abandon dualism. For if we identified mental events with neural events, we could envisage laws that guaranteed unique causal pairings by specifying the precise spatiotemporal relation between cause and effect. Indeed, we could hope to account for psychophysical causation wholly in terms of the ordinary laws of physics and chemistry.

When I first wrote about this problem . . . I argued that the right response, for the dualist, was to postulate psychophysical laws restricted to particular pairs of brains and minds (or brains and subjects). Thus in the case of Smith and Jones, we can secure the correct causal pairings by postulating a separate law for each person—the law (relevant to Smith) that whenever brain x_1 is in state ϕ, a ψ event occurs a tenth of a second later in mind M_1 (or to subject S) and the law (relevant to Jones) that whenever brain x_2 is in state ϕ, a ψ event occurs a tenth of a second later in mind M_2 (or to subject J), where x_1 and M_1 are the brain and mind of Smith and x_2 and M_2 are the brain and mind of Jones.⑪ More recently, I have tried to meet the problem in a quite different way. I have argued that even in the physical realm we can envisage cases in which the fundamental laws do not account for the causal pairings. Thus suppose that, for a certain kind K of metal, it is a law that when any spherical K lump reaches a specified temperature, a flash occurs a tenth of a second later somewhere (unspecified) in the region of points no farther from the center of the sphere than twice its diameter. Suppose further that there is no stronger law which fixes the position of the flash more precisely. Now imagine the case in which two adjacent K spheres simultaneously reach the critical temperature and, a tenth of a second later, two flashes occur, both within the specified region for each sphere.[12]

---

[12] The idea is that the spheres are close enough to each other that the specified regions for each sphere overlap, making it possible for both flashes to occur in the area of overlap. In this case, the law will not determine which flash is caused by which spherical lump.

It is coherent and indeed plausible to suppose that each flash is the effect of just one of the sphere-temperatures and that each sphere-temperature is the cause of just one of the flashes. But the causal pairings are not determined by the law and the non-causal conditions, since each flash falls within the specified region for each sphere. From this I concluded that we should abandon the assumption that causal relations can be wholly accounted for in terms of non-causal properties and laws. And once this assumption is abandoned, the

---

[13] Thus, according to Foster, we should abandon the view that correct causal laws must always be able to determine which effect goes with which cause—in which case, the failure of the causal laws in the mind-body case to do this would no longer constitute an objection to dualistic psychophysical causation.

---

[14] "Law-transcendent" just means that the relevant laws do not determine which pairings are correct.

---

problem of psychophysical causal pairings no longer arises; it no longer matters if the pairing of B with E and B' and E' is not determined by the noncausal conditions and the covering law.[13]

Reviewing these alternative responses, I now think that in a sense, both were correct. On the one hand, the hypothetical case of the K spheres does indeed show that causal pairings can be law-transcendent;[14] and, in that respect, the original

objection to the dualist's position fails. On the other hand, it does seem quite plausible to envisage laws of the restricted kind as underlying the relation of embodiment. As we have said, at least part of what makes a particular brain x the brain of a particular mental subject y is that things are psychophysically arranged in a way which gives x (and x alone) the capacity to have a direct causal influence on y (and y alone)—and, for the interactionist, vice versa. It is hard to see in what this arrangement could consist except in certain psychophysical laws which specifically link x and y, and such laws would guarantee unique causal pairings.[15] At all events, it is clear that the dualist has sufficient resources to meet the objection.

---

[15] Since such a restricted law applies only to states of a single individual, the causes and effects are always events within the same individual, and thus no pairings of a cause in one person and an effect in another person would fall under the law. That the mind and body of a particular person are linked in this way is *described* by such a law, but not really *explained* by it.

. . .

An Objection to Dualistic Interactionism. Some dualists, while accepting that there are psychophysical causal relations, hold that they only run in one direction—from body to mind. They accept, for example, that if I am stung by a wasp, the subsequent pain is caused by the neural response which the sting induces, but they deny that if I decide to smoke my pipe, the subsequent bodily movements involving pipe and matches are caused by my decision. And, quite generally, they accept that a person's mental states are causally affected by the states of his body but deny that his mental states have any causal influence on the states of his body or on anything else in the physical world. This version of dualism is known as "epiphenomenalism," and the version it contrasts with, which accepts psychophysical causation in both directions, is known as "interactionism." I should add that most epiphenomenalists, as well as denying that the mind has any causal influence on the body, also deny that it has a causal influence on anything at all. In particular, they deny that mental states can cause, or contribute to the causation of, other mental states.

Like most other current philosophers, I regard epiphenomenalism as unnatural and implausible. In the first place, it is in radical conflict with our conception of ourselves as agents. If mental states have no causal influence on behavior, then behavior cannot be thought of as intentional in any decent sense, even if the subject happens to have certain intentions which it fulfills. And if behavior is not intentional, it does not qualify as action in a sense which distinguishes it from mere bodily movement. The epiphenomenalist might reply that the general conformity of our behavior to our intentions is not merely accidental; it is ensured by the very structure of our brains and their muscular extensions in the framework of physical and psychophysical law. But even so, the behavior would not be intentional in the requisite sense, since the intentions and the psychophysical laws that control their occurrence would be irrelevant to its production. [16] Second, human behavior exhibits certain complex regularities that call for explanation and that, at present, we explain (at least partly) in psychological terms. These psychological explanations . . . attribute a causal efficacy to the mental; they represent behavior as falling under the control of the subject's beliefs and desires, or under the control of the subject's decisions, which are responsive to (if not determined by) his beliefs and desires. And these explanations gain credence from the fact that, as well as being, in their own terms, successful, they cannot, at present, be replaced by non-psychological explanations that cover the same ground. [17] Third, it is difficult to see how, if epiphenomenalism were true, the mind could form a subject matter for overt discussion. Certainly, if mental states have no causal access to our speech centers, the notion of an introspective report collapses: even if the subject retains an introspective

knowledge of his mental states, his utterances would not count as expressing that knowledge if it contributes nothing to their production. But it is not even clear how, on the epiphenomenalistic view, our language, as a medium for our utterances, makes semantic contact with the mind at all. In what sense, for example, could the word "pain," as overtly used, be said to signify a certain type of sensation, if neither the occurrence of the sensations nor our introspective conception of their type affects the overt use. . . ? [18]

None of these points shows that epiphenomenalism is logically untenable, in the sense of being incoherent or self-contradictory . . . Nonetheless, we have, I think, very strong, and perhaps even conclusive, reasons for rejecting it. And, because of this, I should not want my defense of dualism to involve my acceptance of anything but an interactionist position.

It is at this point that the [final] objection arises. For there is an argument which purports to show that dualism of any but an epiphenomenalistic kind is scientifically unacceptable. The argument runs like this:

1. The body is a physical system.
2. As such, the body must be subject to ordinary physical laws.
3. Our theories as to what physical laws obtain are subject to revision. But our current scientific evidence strongly supports the view that at any level of description relevant to a theory of human behavior, these laws are, for all practical purposes, deterministic.
4. So we can reasonably conclude that any bodily event, of a sort which might be cited in a description or explanation of behavior, is causally determined by prior physical events and conditions.

[16] Foster offers three reasons to reject epiphenomenalism before going on to answer the scientific argument against interactionist dualism in the previous paragraph. The first objection is that on an epiphenomenalist view, bodily actions (like Foster picking up his pipe to smoke it) are never caused by mental states (like Foster deciding or intending to smoke). But this means that human behavior is *never* genuinely intentional—which surely conflicts with our "common-sense conception of ourselves as agents." (See Discussion Question 2.)

[17] A corollary of the previous objection is that if epiphenomenalism is true, then our current psychological explanations of human behavior by appeal to beliefs and desires, which seem to be highly successful, must in fact be mistaken.

[18] Remember that oral speech and writing are *physical* events (involving air pushed through the vocal cords or ink marks on paper). According to epiphenomenalism, a person's mental states of introspective knowledge cannot cause that person to say or write certain things, and so speech or writing could not in any way reflect or express such knowledge. And, even worse, it seems impossible for language to even refer to or describe mental events if it is entirely causally isolated from them—so that the word "pain" could not in fact refer to the kind of sensation that it seems to refer to.

5. But such a conclusion leaves no room for a nonphysical mind to have any causal influence on behavior.

6. Hence, on our present scientific evidence, we face a choice between epiphenomenalism and some kind of identity thesis (if only of the token-token variety). [19]

[19] What Foster means by "some kind of identity thesis" is any view according to which mental states are identical to brain states. This includes both the view (defended by Smart in the next selection) that all mental states of a given type are identical with brain states of a specific type (thus type-type identity) and the view that each individual mental state is identical with some individual brain state but not necessarily the same kind of brain state for each instance of the same kind of mental state (the "token-token" view, where a "token" is an individual instance of a type). Functionalism is a view of the latter sort (see the selection by Fodor) and so would also hold what Foster refers to as an "identity thesis."

[20] Philosophers are often in the position of having to decide which theory is more defensible (or less indefensible), since it is often difficult to make conclusive arguments. Foster's claim here is that any identity thesis is so implausible that epiphenomenalism looks good in comparison—in spite of the recently argued points against epiphenomenalism. (Foster's own objections to identity views have been omitted here, but similar objections are discussed in later selections.)

If it is correct, this argument constitutes an objection to dualistic interactionism. It also, on the face of it, constitutes an objection to dualism as such, if epiphenomenalism is, as I would concede, unacceptable. And, nowadays, it is normally as an objection to dualism, and in support of the identity thesis, that the argument is offered. But here we must be careful. It is true that epiphenomenalism is very implausible and, overtly expressed, may even be self-refuting. And this means that, other things being equal, we should reject it. But it does not mean that we should reject it at all costs. If the only alternative were the identity thesis, then, in my view, epiphenomenalism, despite its implausibility, would be the preferable option. . . . The choice between epiphenomenalism and the identity thesis only counts against dualism on the assumption, which I hold to be false, that epiphenomenalism is not only very implausible but less plausible than its rival. [20] There is also a

further point to bear in mind. If the identity thesis is only of a token-token kind, it is not clear how, even if it were coherent, it would avoid the implausibilities of epiphenomenalism. For if mental events have physical effects only by virtue of their physical properties, and if mental properties are not identical with physical properties, or with functional properties of a purely physicalistic kind, then mental properties are causally irrelevant. And if mental properties are causally irrelevant, the identity thesis does not accord the mind the kind of causal efficacy which common sense demands. It does not allow the mental an influence on behavior in any interesting sense. So to provide a genuine alternative to epiphenomenalism, the identity thesis would have to be of a full-blooded materialist form, involving, in addition to token-identity, some physicalistic construal of mental properties. This is something which defenders of token-identity do not always recognize. . . . [21]

[21] This is an objection to functionalism—one that you are not yet in a position to evaluate. (See Discussion Question 6 to the Fodor selection for further consideration of this objection.)

However, whether it is an objection to dualism as such or only to interactionism, I have to find some answer to the argument; for I am not willing to concede that epiphenomenalism and the identity thesis are the only empirically acceptable options. In fact, the error in the argument is not hard to identify. We must begin by distinguishing two ways in which science might provide evidence that the functioning of the body is wholly explicable in terms of deterministic physical law. The first way would be by direct research on the body itself—in particular, on the brain, since it is on brain activity, if on anything, that we might expect the mind to exert a direct causal influence. Thus, by monitoring neural activity in various parts of the brain (without disturbing normal functioning), scientists might build up a strong inductive case for the conclusion that the electrochemical state of any neuron at any time is determined by its immediately prior electrochemical state and the states of other neurons directly connected to it. [22] The second way would be by discovering, without reference to the functioning of the human body, that the rest of the

[22] "Determined by" here means something much stronger than "influenced by": it means that the cause in question completely accounts for the result, leaving no room for any other influence.

physical world seems to be subject to certain physical laws of a sort which, if they applied universally, would make the body a deterministic system. This is the evidence provided by the investigations of physics and chemistry into the properties of matter and energy in general. Now it is predominantly evidence of the second kind to which the argument appeals. The claim is not that a thorough sampling of brain activity reveals a wholly deterministic system, for no such sampling has been conducted. Rather, the claim is that the human body, including the brain, must be physically deterministic if it is to conform to those theories which apply to physical systems in general. But this evidence, just because it bears on the question of the human system only indirectly, is not decisive. It has to be weighed against what we know or have reason to believe, independently, about the relation between body and mind. . . . 23 When everything is taken into account, the most reasonable conclusion to draw is, surely, that through its attachment to a nonphysical mind, the brain is subject to certain influences which do not affect the other physical systems that science investigates and on whose behavior its nomological theories are based. It is conceivable that this conclusion will be called into question by future brain research (if it were, I should have to reconsider my rejection of epiphenomenalism). But as things stand, we are entitled to assume that it will not.

23 Evidence of the second kind (that the rest of the *physical* world is deterministic), therefore, doesn't help establish the crucial claim without evidence of the first kind (that any particular brain state is completely determined by some prior physical state). And it is clear that we don't yet have evidence of the first kind.

. . .

Discussion Questions

1. Is causality merely regular sequence or constant conjunction of events, as Hume's regularity theory (also discussed by Campbell) claims, or does genuine causation require some stronger relation between cause and effect (what Nagel—cited by Foster on page 328—refers to as "objective necessitation")? What might this stronger connection amount to, and how would we tell whether it was present? Can you think of a plausible example of regular succession where there seems to be no causal relation between the two events in question themselves? Is it possible to have a causal relation between two specific events *without* there being any relation of regular succession between the corresponding kinds of events?

2. Foster's first objection to epiphenomenalism (p. 331) is that if epiphenomenalism is true, then we aren't genuine agents (since being a genuine agent requires that our intentions are genuinely effective in causing our behavior)—which conflicts strongly with common sense. He considers the following response from an epiphenomenalist: our intentions *seem* from the standpoint of common sense to cause our behavior because the real cause of some particular bit of behavior (a brain state) is *also* the cause of the mental intention to behave in that way. Because we are not consciously aware of the brain state, we think that the intention is the cause of the behavior, but it is really just another effect of one cause (with the other effect being the behavior). Consider Foster's example of deciding to smoke his pipe. According to the interactionist dualist, his conscious decision to smoke caused his bodily movements to get his pipe. According to this epiphenomenalist response, a single brain state is responsible for *both* his bodily movements to get his pipe and his conscious decision to smoke, and thus his conscious decision to smoke is *not* the cause of his bodily movements to get his pipe. How plausible or implausible is this epiphenomenalist response, and why? Might the appearance that intentions cause actions be in this way only an illusion?

3. Do we have good reason to think that the material or physical world is *causally closed:* not causally influenced by anything that is not physical? See Foster's discussion of this point and also Campbell's discussion of what he calls "the shadow of physiology." Campbell in fact adopts epiphenomenalism on this basis (though this is not made clear in the selection here), while Foster rejects this reason as inadequate. Who is right?

J.J.C. Smart

J. J. C. Smart (1920–) is an Australian philosopher whose work has been very influential in the philosophy of mind, the philosophy of science, and ethics. He collaborated with Bernard Williams to write a well-respected book about **utilitarianism** (see Chapter 6).

This selection explains and defends what many philosophers have come to call the central state identity theory (or just the identity theory), the materialist or physicalist view that mental states are *strictly identical* to brain states or processes. This is *not* merely the view that mental states are caused by or correlated with brain states, since most dualist views accept and even insist on that. A proponent of the identity theory, on the other hand, insists that the mental states *just are* brain states, that there is only one state and not two, a single state that can be referred to with either a mental state description or a brain state description. Smart is obviously very motivated by a scientific point of view, one that takes the results of science very seriously and is very suspicious of anything outside the boundaries of scientific enquiry.

Sensations and Brain Processes

... Suppose that I report that I have at this moment a roundish, blurry-edged after-image which is yellowish towards its edge and is orange towards its center. What is it that I am reporting? One answer to this question might be that I am not reporting anything, that when I say that it looks to me as though there is a roundish yellowy-orange patch of light on the wall I am expressing some sort of *temptation,* the temptation to say that there *is* a roundish yellowy-orange patch on the wall (though I may know that there is not such a patch on the wall). ... Similarly, when I "report" a pain, I am not really reporting anything (or, if you like, I am reporting in a queer sense of "reporting"), but am doing a sophisticated sort of wince.[1] ... The suggestion I wish if possible to avoid is ... that "I am in pain" is a genuine report, and that what it reports is an irreducibly psychical something. And similarly the suggestion I wish to resist is also that to say "I have a yellowish-orange after-image" is to report something irreducibly psychical.[2]

Why do I wish to resist this suggestion? Mainly because of Occam's razor.[3] It seems to me that science is increasingly giving us a viewpoint whereby organisms are able to be seen as physicochemical mechanisms: it seems that even the behavior of man himself will one day be explicable in mechanistic terms. There does seem to be, so far as science is concerned, nothing in the world but increasingly complex arrangements of physical constituents. All except for one place: in consciousness. That is, for a full description of what is going on in a man you would

[1] The views described would be versions of logical behaviorism: the once widely accepted (but still extremely implausible) thesis that mental states are nothing more than overt behavior or dispositions to such behavior (see the chapter introduction). Smart eventually rejects this view.

[2] To say that the experience, whether of pain or the afterimage, is something irreducibly psychical is just to say that it is something more than physical, something that cannot be reduced to the physical.

[3] By citing **"Occam's razor,"** Smart appeals to a principle of parsimony, a principle that recommends simplicity in theory construction: don't multiply entities beyond necessity.

From The Philosophy of Mind, *edited by V. C. Chappell (Englewood Cliffs, N.J.: Prentice-Hall, 1962).*

have to mention not only the physical processes in his tissues, glands, nervous system, and so forth, but also his states of consciousness: his visual, auditory, and tactual sensations, his aches and pains. That these should be *correlated* with brain processes does not help, for to say that they are *correlated* is to say that they are something "over and above."④ You cannot correlate something with itself. You correlate footprints with burglars, but not Bill Sikes the burglar with Bill Sikes the burglar. So sensations, states of consciousness, do seem to be the one sort of thing left outside the physicalist picture, and for various reasons I just cannot believe that this can be so. That everything should be explicable in terms of physics (together of course with descriptions of the ways in which the parts are put together—roughly, biology is to physics as radio-engineering is to electromagnetism) except the occurrence of sensations seems to me to be frankly unbelievable. Such sensations would be "nomological danglers," to use Feigl's expression.⑤ It is not often realized how odd would be the laws whereby these nomological danglers would dangle. It is sometimes asked, "Why can't there by psychophysical laws which are of a novel sort, just as the laws of electricity and magnetism were novelties from the standpoint of Newtonian mechanics?" Certainly we are pretty sure in the future to come across new ultimate laws of a novel type, but I expect them to relate simple constituents: for example, whatever ultimate particles are then in vogue. I cannot believe that ultimate laws of nature could relate simple constituents to configurations consisting of perhaps billions of neurons (and goodness knows how many

> ④ A physicalist isn't satisfied with the claim that mental states are merely *correlated* with brain states. For a dualist could agree that mental states are correlated with brain states, since such a claim is consistent with the view that mental states are still something separate from brain states.

> ⑤ "Nomological" just means having to do with or in accordance with laws of nature. If sensations are nomological danglers, then they are caused by physical states according to laws but cannot cause physical states (and are thus "danglers" in relation to the physical world). Smart is assuming that the only dualist view that is even worth taking seriously is epiphenomenalism (see the introduction to this chapter).

billion billions of ultimate particles) all put together for all the world as though their main purpose in life was to be a negative feedback mechanism of a complicated sort. Such ultimate laws would be like nothing so far known in science. They have a queer "smell" to them. I am just unable to believe in the nomological danglers themselves, or in the laws whereby they would dangle. If any philosophical arguments seemed to compel us to believe in such things, I would suspect a catch in the argument.⑥ In any case it is the object of this paper to show that there are no philosophical arguments which compel us to be dualists.

> ⑥ As Smart admits later, he has given no real argument against dualism here, merely reported that he just can't believe it is true.

The above is largely a confession of faith, but it explains why I find [the logical behaviorist view] so congenial. For on this view there are, in a sense, no sensations. A man is a vast arrangement of physical particles, but there are not, over and above this, sensations or states of consciousness. There are just behavioral facts about this vast mechanism, such as that it expresses a temptation (behavior disposition) to say "there is a yellowish-red patch on the wall" or that it goes through a sophisticated sort of wince, that is, says "I am in pain."

Though for the reasons given above, I am very receptive to the above "expressive" account of sensation statements, I do not feel that it will quite do the trick. Maybe this is because I have not thought it out sufficiently, but it does seem to me as though, when a person says "I have an after-image," he *is* making a genuine report, and that when he says "I have a pain," he *is* doing more that "replace pain-behavior," and that "this more" is not just to say that he is in distress. I am not so sure, however, that to admit this is to admit that there are nonphysical correlates of brain processes. Why should not sensations just be brain processes of a certain sort? There are, of course, well-known (as well as lesser-known) philosophical objections to the view that reports of sensations are reports of brain-processes, but I shall try to argue that these arguments are by no means as cogent as is commonly thought to be the case.

Let me first try to state more accurately the thesis that sensations are brain-processes. It is not the thesis that, for example, "after-image" or "ache" means the same as "brain process of sort X" (where "X" is replaced by a description of a certain sort of brain process).⑦ It is that, in so far as "afterimage" or "ache" is a report of a process, it is a report of a process that *happens to be* a brain process. It follows that the thesis does not claim that sensation statements can be *translated* into statements about brain processes. Nor does it claim that the logic of a sensation statement is the same as that of a brain-process statement. All it claims is that in so far as a sensation statement is a report of something, that something is in fact a brain process. Sensations are

⑦ When someone says "A is B," the claim is sometimes based on an identity of meaning and sometimes not. For example, the claim that bachelors are unmarried adult males depends on and can be taken as a way of saying that "bachelor" *means the same as* "unmarried adult male." In contrast, the claim that the President of the United States in 2003 was George W. Bush is not based on an identity of meaning: a person could understand both expressions and not thereby know that they refer to the same entity.

nothing over and above brain processes. Nations are nothing "over and above" citizens, but this does not prevent the logic of nation statements being very different from the logic of citizen statements, nor does it insure the translatability of nation statements into citizen statements. (I do not, however, wish to assert that the relation of sensation statements to brain-process statements is very like that of nation statements to citizen statements. Nations do not just *happen to be* nothing over and above citizens, for example. I bring in the "nations" example merely to make a negative point: that the fact that the logic of A-statements is different from that of B-statements does not insure that A's are anything over and above B's.)

REMARKS ON IDENTITY

When I say that a sensation is a brain process or that lightning is an electric discharge, I am using "is" in the sense of *strict identity*. (Just as in the—in this case necessary—proposition "7 is identical with the smallest prime number greater than 5.")⑧ When I say that a sensation is a brain process or that lightning is an electric discharge I do not mean just that the sensation is somehow spatially or temporally continuous with the brain process or that the lightning is just spatially

or temporally continuous with the discharge. . . .

I shall now discuss various possible objections to the view that the processes reported in sensation statements are in fact processes in the brain. Most of us have met some of these objections in our first year as philosophy students. All the more reason to take a good look at them. Others of the objections will be more recondite and subtle.

Objection 1. Any illiterate peasant can talk perfectly well about his after-images, or how things look or feel to him, or about his aches and pains, and yet he may know nothing whatever about neurophysiology. A man may, like Aristotle, believe that the brain is an organ for cooling the body without any impairment of his ability to make true statements about his sensations. Hence the things we are talking about when we describe our sensations cannot be processes in the brain.⑨

Reply. . . . Consider lightning. Modern physical science tells us that lightning is a certain kind of electrical discharge due to ionization of clouds of water vapor in the atmosphere. This, it is now believed, is what the true nature of lightning is. Note that there are not two things: a flash of lightning and an electrical discharge. There is one thing, a flash of lightning, which is described scientifically as an electrical discharge to the earth from a cloud of ionized water molecules.⑩ The case is not at all like that of explaining a footprint by reference to a burglar. We say that what lightning really is, what its true nature as revealed by science is, is an electrical

⑧ Think carefully about this mathematical example. There is one (and only one) smallest prime number greater than 5, and that number is 7. You can refer to *that thing* with the label "7" or you can refer to it with the label "the smallest prime number greater than 5." Smart's claim that a sensation is a brain process is the claim that there are not two things, a sensation and a brain process, but that there is just one thing: one thing that you can refer to with the label "sensation" or with the label "brain process."

⑨ The assumption motivating this objection is that if there are two different labels for the same thing, then someone, even an illiterate peasant, who understands one of them would also understand the other and also know that they refer to the same thing. How plausible is this? (See Discussion Question 1.)

discharge. (It is not the true nature of a footprint to be a burglar.)

. . .

In short, the reply to Objection I is that there can be contingent statements of the form "A is identical with B," and a person may well know that something is an A without knowing that it is a B.⟦11⟧ An illiterate peasant might well be able to talk about his sensations without knowing about his brain processes, just as he can talk about lightning though he knows nothing of electricity.

. . . Again, "I see the Evening Star' does not *mean* the same as "I see the Morning Star," and yet "The Evening Star and the Morning Star are one and the same thing" is a contingent proposition. Possibly Objection 2 derives some of its apparent strength from a "Fido"— Fido theory of meaning. If the meaning of an expression were what the expression named, then of course it *would* follow from the fact that "sensation" and "brain-process" have different meanings that they cannot name one and the same thing.

Objection 3.   Even if Objection 1 [does] . . . not prove that sensations are something over and above brain-processes, [it does] prove that the qualities of sensations are something over and above the qualities of brain-processes. That is, it may be possible to get out of asserting the existence of irreducibly psychic processes, but not out of asserting the existence of irreducibly psychic *properties*. . . .

Indeed, it might be thought that the objection succeeds at one jump. For consider the property of "being a yellow flash." It might seem that this property lies inevitably outside the physicalist framework within

⟦10⟧ Notice again the claim of strict identity: there are not two things here but just one thing, described or referred to in two different ways. (The relation between the common-sense idea of lightning and the scientific account is an excellent analogy for understanding what Smart is saying about the relation between the common-sense idea of a sensation and the account in terms of brain processes.)

⟦11⟧ A **contingent** statement is one that could be true or could be false— and thus, unlike "all bachelors are unmarried," one that is not made true by the meaning of the terms in the statement. (The claim that lightning is a certain sort of electrical discharge is also viewed by Smart as contingent.)

which I am trying to work . . . I must therefore digress for a moment and indicate how I deal with secondary qualities. I shall concentrate on color.⟦12⟧

First of all, let me introduce the concept of a normal percipient. One person is more a normal percipient than another if he can make color discriminations that the other cannot. For example, if A can pick a lettuce leaf out of a heap of cabbage leaves, whereas B cannot though he can pick a lettuce leaf out of a heap of beetroot leaves, then A is more normal than B. (I am assuming that A and B are not given time to distinguish the leaves by their slight difference in shape, and so forth.) From the concept of "more normal than" it is easy to see how we can introduce the concept of "normal." Of course, Eskimos may make the finest discriminations at the blue end of the spectrum, Hottentots at the red end. In this case the concept of a normal percipient is a slightly idealized one, rather like that of "the mean sun" in astronomical chronology. There is no need to go into such subtleties now. I say that "This is red" means something roughly like "A normal percipient would not easily pick this out of a clump of geranium petals though he would pick it out of a clump of lettuce leaves."⟦13⟧ Of course it does not exactly mean this: a person might know the meaning of "red" without knowing anything about geraniums, or even about normal percipients. But the point is that a person can be *trained* to say "This is red" of objects which would not easily be picked out of geranium petals by a normal percipient, and so on. (Note that even a color-blind person can reasonably assert that something is red, though of course he needs to use another human being, not just himself, as his "color meter.") This account of secondary qualities explains their unimportance in physics. For obviously the discriminations and lack of discriminations made by a very complex neurophysiological mechanism are hardly likely to correspond to simple and nonarbitrary distinctions in nature.

⟦12⟧ The most famous proponent of the philosophical distinction between **primary** and **secondary** qualities is John Locke (see Chapter 3), who said that secondary qualities (color, taste, odor, sound as heard, temperature as felt) are mere powers in objects to cause us to have certain sensations.

⟦13⟧ This is a good example only if all geraniums are red. This isn't in fact true, but pretend that it is for the sake of the discussion.

I therefore elucidate colors as powers, in Locke's sense, to evoke certain sorts of discriminatory responses in human beings. They are also, of course, powers to cause sensations in human beings (an account still nearer Locke's). But these sensations, I am arguing, are identifiable with brain processes. [14]

Now how do I get over the objection that a sensation can be identified with a brain process only if it has some phenomenal property, not possessed by brain processes, whereby one-half of the identification may be, so to speak, pinned down? [15]

Reply. My suggestion is as follows. When a person says, "I see a yellowish-orange after-image," he is saying something like this: "*There is something going on which is like what is going on when* I have my eyes open, am awake, and there is an orange illuminated in good light in front of me, that is, when I really see an orange." . . . Notice that the italicized words, namely "there is something going on which is like what is going on when," are all quasilogical or topic-neutral words. [16] This explains why the ancient Greek peasant's reports about his sensations can be neutral between dualistic metaphysics or my materialistic metaphysics. It explains how sensations can be brain-processes and yet how a man who reports them need know nothing about brain-processes. For he reports them only very abstractly as "something going on which is like what is going on when. . . ." Similarly, a person may say "someone is in the room," thus reporting truly that the doctor is in the room, even though he has never heard of doctors. (There are not two people in the room: "someone" *and* the doctor.) This account of sensation statements also explains the singular elusiveness of "raw feels" [17]— why no one seems to be able to pin any properties on them. Raw feels, in my view, are colorless for the very same reason that *something* is colorless. This does not mean that sensations do not have plenty of properties, for if they are brain-processes they certainly have lots of neurological properties. It only means that in speaking of them as being like or unlike one another we need not know or mention these properties.

This, then, is how I would reply to Objection 3. The strength of my reply depends on the possibility of our being able to report that one thing is like another without being able to state the respect in which it is like. I do not see why this should not be so. If we think cybernetically about the nervous system we can envisage it as able to respond to certain likenesses of its internal processes without being able to do more. [18] It would be easier to build a machine which would tell us, say on a punched tape, whether or not two objects were similar, than it would be to build a machine which would report wherein the similarities consisted.

Objection 4. The after-image is not in physical space. The brain-process is. So the after-image is not a brain-process.

Reply. This is an *ignoratio elenchi*. [19] I am not arguing that the after-image is a brain-process, but that the experience of

---

[14] A discriminatory response is a kind of behavior and thus publicly observable; a sensation, on the other hand, is a mental event, not something that is publicly observable (except by observing the brain, if Smart's main claim turns out to be true).

[15] **Phenomenal properties** (also referred to as qualia) are the distinctive properties allegedly found in subjective experience, such as color or taste as directly experienced. The objection is that sensations have phenomenal properties; but brain processes do not have such properties; so sensations cannot be the same things as brain processes.

[16] By "quasilogical or topic-neutral," Smart means almost logical or devoid of specific content. He is thinking of these reports as very, very abstract in their content, saying only that two situations are similar in some unspecified way.

[17] "Raw feel" is just a way of referring to immediately experienced sensations as they are in themselves, prior to any conceptual description. The raw feel of sucking on a lemon is very different from the raw feel of sucking on a sugar cube, whether the difference can be described or not.

[18] It is one thing to say that we don't have words for phenomenal properties, but a very different thing to say that there are no phenomenal properties at all. Smart must make the latter claim to have an answer to the objection (think carefully about this). Is his claim plausible? (See Discussion Question 2.)

[19] An *ignoratio elenchi* is the mistake one makes when one argues for or objects to an irrelevant claim, as opposed to the one that is at issue.

having an after-image is a brain-process. It is the *experience* which is reported in the introspective report. Similarly, if it is objected that the after-image is yellowy-orange, my reply is that it is the experience of seeing yellowy-orange that is being described, and this experience is not a yellowy-orange something. So to say that a brain-process cannot be yellowy-orange is not to say that a brain-process cannot in fact be the experience of having a yellowy-orange after-image. There is, in a sense, no such thing as an after-image . . . , though there is such a thing as the experience of having an image, and this experience is described indirectly in material object language, not in phenomenal language, for there is no such thing. [20] We describe the experience by saying, in effect, that it is like the experience we have when, for example, we really see a yellow-orange patch on the wall. Trees and wallpaper can be green, but not the experience of seeing or imagining a tree or wallpaper. (Or if they are described as green or yellow this can only be in a derived sense.)

[20] Phenomenal language would directly describe phenomenal properties. Since Smart denies the existence of phenomenal properties, he also holds that there is no such thing as phenomenal language.

Objection 5. It would make sense to say of a molecular movement in the brain that it is swift or slow, straight or circular, but it makes no sense to say this of the experience of seeing something yellow.

Reply. So far we have not given sense to talk of experiences as swift or slow, straight or circular. But I am not claiming that "experience" and "brain-process" mean the same or even that they have the same logic. "Somebody" and "the doctor" do not have the same logic, but this does not lead us to suppose that talking about somebody telephoning is talking about someone over and above, say, the doctor. The ordinary man when he reports an experience is reporting that something is going on, but he leaves it open as to what sort of thing is going on, whether in a material solid medium or perhaps in some sort of gaseous medium, or even perhaps in some sort of nonspatial medium (if this makes sense). All that I am saying is that "experience" and "brain-process" may in fact refer to the same thing, and if so we may easily adopt a convention (which is not a change in our present

rules for the use of experience words but an addition to them) whereby it would make sense to talk of an experience in terms appropriate to physical processes. [21]

Objection 6. Sensations are private, brain processes are *public*. If I sincerely say, "I see a yellowish-orange after-image," and I am not making a verbal mistake, then I cannot be wrong. But I can be wrong about a brain-process. The scientist looking into my brain might be having an illusion. Moreover, it makes sense to say that two or more people are observing the same brain-process but not that two or more people are reporting the same inner experience.

Reply. This shows that the language of introspective reports has a different logic from the language of material processes. It is obvious that until the brain-process theory is much improved and widely accepted there will be no *criteria* for saying "Smith has an experience of such-and-such a sort" *except* Smith's introspective reports. [22] So we have adopted a rule of language that (normally) what Smith says goes.

. . .

If it is asked what is the difference between those brain processes which, in my view, are experiences and those brain processes which are not, I can only reply that it is at present unknown. . . . [23] But at the very least, we can classify the brain processes which are experiences as those brain processes which are, or might have been, causal

[21] Smart's claim is that after it is discovered that sensations are brain processes, the claim that they have properties like speed or direction could come to be meaningful even if they aren't at present. The underlying suggestion is that before this change occurs, such claims may be empty or unintelligible, but not absurd or nonsensical.

[22] The suggestion here is that after we come to realize that the identity theory is true, we could in principle tell when Smith is having a particular experience just by looking at his brain. (This idea will be important later on in the chapter.)

[23] This amounts to an expression of faith on Smart's part: there must be something about the physical differences between a brain process that is an experience (or is conscious) and one that is not. And whatever that difference turns out to be, it will be a purely physical difference, if Smart is right that an experience is just a brain process and nothing more.

conditions of those pieces of verbal behavior which we call reports of immediate experience.

I have now considered a number of objections to the brain-process thesis. I wish now to conclude with some remarks on the logical status of the thesis itself. U. T. Place seems to hold that it is a straight-out scientific hypothesis. If so, he is partly right and partly wrong. If the issue is between (say) a brain-process thesis and a heart thesis, or a liver thesis, or a kidney thesis, then the issue is a purely empirical one, and the verdict is overwhelmingly in favor of the brain. The right sorts of things don't go on in the heart, liver, or kidney, nor do these organs possess the right sort of complexity of structure. On the other hand, if the issue is between a brain-or-liver-or-kidney thesis (that is, some form of materialism) on the one hand and epiphenomenalism on the other hand, then the issue is not an empirical one. For there is no conceivable experiment which could decide between materialism and epiphenomenalism. [24] This latter issue is not like the average straight-out empirical issue in science, but like the issue between the nineteenth-century English naturalist Philip Gosse and the orthodox geologists and paleontologists of his day. According to Gosse, the earth was created about 4000 B.C. exactly as described in *Genesis,* with twisted rock strata, "evidence" of erosion, and so forth, and all sorts of fossils, all in their appropriate strata, just as if the usual evolutionist story had been true. Clearly this theory is in a sense irrefutable: no evidence can possibly tell against it. Let us ignore the theological setting in which Philip Gosse's hypothesis had been placed, thus ruling out objections of a theo-

[24] Think carefully about this claim and about the difference between the identity theory and epiphenomenalism. Is Smart right that there is no empirical way to decide between the two views? (See Discussion Question 3.)

logical kind, such as "what a queer God who would go to such elaborate lengths to deceive us." Let us suppose that it is held that the universe just *began* in 4004 B.C. with the initial conditions just everywhere as they were in 4004 B.C., and in particular that our own planet began with sediment in the rivers, eroded cliffs, fossils in the rocks, and so on. No scientist would ever entertain this as a serious hypothesis, consistent though it is with all possible evidence. The hypothesis offends against the principles of parsimony and simplicity. There would be far too many brute and inexplicable facts. Why are pterodactyl bones just as they are? No explanation in terms of the evolution of pterodactyls from earlier forms of life would any longer be possible. We would have millions of facts about the world as it was in 4004 B.C. that just have to be *accepted.*

The issue between the brain-process theory and epiphenomenalism seems to be of the above sort. (Assuming that a behavioristic reduction of introspective reports is not possible.) If it be agreed that there are no cogent philosophical arguments which force us into accepting dualism, and if the brain process theory and dualism are equally consistent with the facts, then the principles of parsimony and simplicity seem to me to decide overwhelmingly in favor of the brain-process theory. [25] As I pointed out earlier, dualism involves a large number of irreducible psychophysical laws (whereby the "nomological danglers" dangle) of a queer sort, that just have to be taken on trust, and are just as difficult to swallow as the irreducible facts about the paleontology of the earth with which we are faced on Philip Gosse's theory.

[25] The appeal to simplicity is relevant only if everything else is equal, if there are no other considerations either way. Contrary to Smart's claim here, some philosophers think that there are serious objections to physicalism (the knowledge argument discussed later in the chapter, for example). If so, these would override the appeal to simplicity.

Discussion Questions

1. It is common to have more than one way of referring to or describing the same thing: "George Washington" and "the first president of the United States" refer to the same thing (a person), but not in the same way. Make a list of examples of this sort of situation, trying to think of cases that are as different from each other as possible. If your list is comprehensive enough, there will be cases where someone could not understand either of two ways of re-

ferring to or describing the same thing without both understanding the other one and realizing that they are references to or descriptions of the same thing. But how often is this the case? How common are cases where one way of referring or describing could be understood without understanding the other? How common are cases where both could be understood without realizing that they refer to or describe the same thing?

2. Suppose that you are much better than one of your friends at identifying musical instruments simply by hearing the sound they produce: you can distinguish the sound of a viola from the sound of a cello or the sound of a guitar from the sound of a lute, but your friend cannot. It seems plausible to say that you are able to do this because either (a) your sensations are more differentiated than your friend's (a cello and a viola playing a given note produce qualitatively different sensations in you but the same ones in your friend) or (b) you are more sensitive to the differences between different sensations than your friend (though the cello and viola produce different sensations in each of you, you can recognize the difference but your friend cannot). Someone who accepts the existence of phenomenal properties will say that in case (a) your sensations have different phenomenal properties, while your friend's do not; and that in case (b), you are able to recognize a difference between two different phenomenal properties, but your friend is not. What will Smart have to say about these cases, since he denies the very existence of phenomenal properties? How plausible is his view? Are you in fact aware of phenomenal properties when you make such discriminations?

3. Suppose that for each kind of sensation, there is a kind of brain process that is at least correlated with it in the sense that they always occur at approximately the same times in the same persons. According to the identity theory, the sensation and the brain process are the very same entity; while according to epiphenomenalism, the brain process causes the sensation according to a law of nature (but the sensation itself has no further effect on anything physical). These seem to be very different views. Is Smart right that there is no way to decide empirically which is true: no observation or experiment of any sort that would provide evidence one way or the other?

ARE MENTAL STATES ANALOGOUS TO THE STATES OF A COMPUTER?

Jerry Fodor

Jerry Fodor (1935–) is an American philosopher who teaches at Rutgers University and has been one of the main contributors to the debates in the philosophy of mind (and allied fields, such as philosophy of language and cognitive science) in the last several decades. He argues that functionalism, the view that mental states are functional states defined in terms of causal role, is preferable to either dualism or various earlier versions of materialism. His argument for that claim proceeds by considering the other views in roughly their order of historical development and arguing that each is fatally flawed. Fodor's suggestion is that functionalism in effect combines the best features of previous theories into one view. The guiding constraint in his discussion is to find a theory that will justify and make sense of the practice and theorizing of working psychologists, people who explain our behavior by appealing to our mental states (think of the umbrella example in the chapter introduction).

This is a quite difficult article, and our annotations are therefore themselves longer and more complicated than for most other articles in this book. Be patient and try to work yourself gradually into an understanding of functionalism and of the issues that it raises.

The Mind-Body Problem

It is only rather recently that philosophers have become seriously interested in the methodological tenets of psychology. Psychological explanations of behavior refer liberally to the mind and to states, operations and processes of the mind. The philosophical difficulty comes in stating in unambiguous language what such references imply.

Traditional philosophies of mind can be divided into two broad categories: dualist theories and materialist theories. In the dualist approach the mind is a nonphysical substance. In materialist theories the mental is not distinct from the physical; indeed, all mental states, properties, processes and operations are in principle identical with physical states, properties, processes and operations. Some materialists, known as behaviorists, maintain that all talk of mental causes can be eliminated from the language of psychology in favor of talk of environmental stimuli and behavioral responses. Other materialists, the identity theorists, contend that there are mental causes and that they are identical with neurophysiological events in the brain.

In the past 15 years ① a philosophy of mind called functionalism that is neither dualist nor materialist has emerged from philosophical reflection on developments in artificial intelligence, computational theory, lin-

① As will emerge, it is at least somewhat misleading to describe functionalism as "neither dualist nor materialist." While the functionalist account of what it is to be a mental state is neutral between the two views, virtually all functionalists believe that it is material states that satisfy that account and actually constitute mental states—and much of the point of functionalism is to find an alternative to dualism that is more viable than earlier materialist views.

guistics, cybernetics, and psychology. All these fields, which are collectively known as the cognitive sciences, have in common a certain level of abstraction and a concern with systems that process information. Functionalism, which seeks to provide a philosophical account of this level of abstraction, recognizes the possibility that systems as diverse as human beings, calculating machines and disembodied spirits could all have mental states.② In the functionalist view the psychology of a system depends not on the stuff it is made of (living cells, metal or spiritual energy) but on how the stuff is put together. Functionalism is a difficult concept, and one way of coming to grips with it is to review the deficiencies of the dualist and materialist philosophies of mind it aims to displace.

② "Recognizes" is at least somewhat misleading here, since there are still many philosophers who would not regard this alleged possibility as genuine. (Whether or not it is possible that these other systems could genuinely have mental states obviously depends on what exactly a mental state is.)

The chief drawback of dualism is its failure to account adequately for mental causation. If the mind is nonphysical, it has no position in physical space. How, then, can a mental cause give rise to a behavioral effect that has a position in space? To put it another way, how can the nonphysical give rise to the physical without violating the laws of the conservation of mass, of energy and of momentum?③

③ Fodor actually raises two objections here, one concerning spatial position and the other invoking the various conservation laws. Neither is developed very fully, making it hard to assess how serious they are. See Discussion Question 1.

From Scientific American, *Vol. 262 (January 1990).*

The dualist might respond that the problems of how an immaterial substance can cause physical events is not much obscurer than the problem of how one physical event can cause another. Yet there is an important difference: there are many clear cases of physical causation but not one clear case of nonphysical causation. Physical interaction is something philosophers, like all other people, have to live with. Nonphysical interaction, however, may be no more than an artifact of the immaterialist construal of the mental. Most philosophers now agree that no argument has successfully demonstrated why mind-body causation should not be regarded as a species of physical causation. ④

4 This is somewhat misleading, in that it suggests that the nature of mind-body causation is the primary issue. In fact, the main issue is the nature of mental states themselves. If some materialist account is true, then obviously there will be no reason to regard mind-body causation as something other than physical causation. The arguments to the contrary are just the objections to materialist accounts—which Fodor himself discusses later.

Dualism is also incompatible with the practices of working psychologists. The psychologist frequently applies the experimental methods of the physical sciences to the study of the mind. If mental processes were different in kind from physical processes, there would be no reason to expect these methods to work in the realm of the mental. In order to justify their experimental methods many psychologists urgently sought an alternative to dualism. ⑤

5 How serious is this objection? It assumes in effect that there is good reason to think that the experimental methods of science will work only in application to physical things and processes, rather than applying more generally. (One key issue about this is whether the reports of introspection can be regarded as a kind of observation that can play a role in experiments.)

In the 1920s John B. Watson of Johns Hopkins University made the radical suggestion that behavior does not have mental causes. He regarded the behavior of an organism as its observable responses to stimuli, which he took to be the causes of its behavior. Over the next 30 years psychologists such as B. F. Skinner of Harvard University developed Watson's ideas into an elaborate world view in which the role of psychology was to catalogue the laws that determine causal relations between stimuli and responses. In this "radical behaviorist" view the problem of explaining the nature of the mind-body interaction vanishes; there is no such interaction. ⑥

Radical behaviorism has always worn an air of paradox. For better or worse, the idea of mental causation is deeply ingrained in our everyday language and in our ways of understanding our fellow men and ourselves. For example, people commonly attribute behavior to beliefs, to knowledge, and to expectations. Brown puts gas in his tank because he believes the car will not run without it. Jones writes not "acheive" but "achieve" because he knows the rule about putting *i* before *e*. Even when a behavioral response is closely tied to an environmental stimulus, mental processes often intervene. Smith carries an umbrella because the sky is cloudy, but the weather is only part of the story. There are apparently also mental links in the causal chain: observation and expectation. The clouds affect Smith's behavior only because he observes them and because they induce in him an expectation of rain. ⑦

6 Radical behaviorism is different from logical behaviorism (discussed later): it simply denies that mental states are in any way relevant to behavior, making it at least tempting to deny their very existence.

7 Thus the radical behaviorist must reject an enormous number of common-sense explanations of behavior as mistaken. Is it plausible to any serious degree that we are all as mistaken as that? (Notice that a radical behaviorist who advocates that view cannot consistently say that he does so because he *believes* it to be true.)

The radical behaviorist is unmoved by appeals to such cases. He is prepared to dismiss references to mental causes, however plausible they may seem, as the residue of outworn creeds. The radical behaviorist predicts that as psychologists come to understand more about the relations between stimuli and responses they will find it increasingly possible to explain behavior without postulating mental causes.

The strongest argument against behaviorism is that psychology has not turned out this way; the opposite has happened. As psychology has matured, the framework of mental states and processes that is apparently needed to account for experimental observations has grown all the more elaborate. Particularly in the case of human behavior psychological theories satisfying the methodological tenets of radical behaviorism have proved largely sterile, as would be expected if the postulated mental processes are real and causally effective.

Nevertheless, many philosophers were initially drawn to radical behaviorism because, paradoxes and all, it seemed better than dualism. Since a psychology committed to immaterial substances was unacceptable, philosophers turned to radical behaviorism because it seemed to be the only alternative materialist philosophy of mind. The choice as they saw it, was between radical behaviorism and ghosts.⑧

[8] Fodor's talk of "ghosts" is a way of mocking dualism. Think about Fodor's claim here that radical behaviorism was at least better than dualism. Are the objections to mind-body causation really so strong as to make it better to deny that mental states causally affect behavior at all?

By the early 1960s philosophers began to have doubts that dualism and radical behaviorism exhausted the possible approaches to the philosophy of mind. Since the two theories seemed unattractive, the right strategy might be to develop a materialist philosophy of mind that nonetheless allowed for mental causes. Two such philosophies emerged, one called logical behaviorism and the other called the central-state identity theory.

[9] This is slightly misleading. It would be better to say that logical behaviorism is a theory about the nature of mental states that relies on and advocates such a semantic theory. Notice in the following discussion that thirst (as opposed to a *sensation* of thirst) is a somewhat odd example— perhaps not really a *mental* state at all (as opposed to a physiological state).

Logical behaviorism is a semantic theory about what mental terms mean.⑨ The basic idea is that attributing a mental state (say thirst) to an organism is the same as saying that the organism is disposed to behave in a particular way (for example to drink if there is water available). On this view every mental ascription is equivalent in meaning to an if-then statement (called a behavioral hypothetical) that expresses a behavioral disposition. For example, "Smith is thirsty" might be taken to be equivalent to the dispositional statement "If there were water available, then Smith would drink some." By definition a behavioral hypothetical includes no mental terms. The if-clause of the hypothetical speaks only of stimuli and the then-clause speaks only of behavioral responses. Since stimuli and responses are

physical events, logical behaviorism is a species of materialism.

The strength of logical behaviorism is that by translating mental language into the language of stimuli and responses it provides an interpretation of psychological explanations in which behavioral effects are attributed to mental causes. Mental causation is simply the manifestation of a behavioral disposition. More precisely, mental causation is what happens when an organism has a behavioral disposition and the if-clause of the behavioral hypothetical expressing the disposition happens to be true. For example, the causal statement "Smith drank some water because he was thirsty" might be taken to mean "If there were water available, then Smith would drink some, and there was water available."

I have somewhat oversimplified logical behaviorism by assuming that each mental ascription can be translated by a unique behavioral hypothetical. Actually the logical behaviorist often maintains that it takes an open-ended set (perhaps an infinite set) of behavioral hypotheticals to spell out the behavioral disposition expressed by a mental term. The mental ascription "Smith is thirsty" might also be satisfied by a hypothetical "If there were orange juice available, then Smith would drink some" and by a host of other hypotheticals. In any event, the logical behaviorist does not usually maintain he can actually enumerate all the hypotheticals that correspond to a behavioral disposition expressing a given mental term. He only insists that in principle the meaning of any mental term can be conveyed by behavioral hypotheticals.⑩

[10] Think very carefully about what the logical behaviorist is claiming: that *all* there is to any mental state is the truth of a large set of hypothetical statements of this sort. On this view, there is no conscious inner experience involved at all.

The way the logical behaviorist has interpreted a mental term such as thirsty is modeled after the way many philosophers have interpreted a physical disposition such as fragility. The physical disposition "The glass is fragile" is often taken to mean something like "If the glass were struck, then it would break." By the same token the logical behaviorist's analysis of mental causation is similar to the received analysis of one kind of physical causation. The causal statement "The glass broke because it was fragile" is taken to mean something like "If the glass were struck, then it would break, and the glass was struck." [11]

By equating mental terms with behavioral dispositions the logical behaviorist has put mental terms on a par with the non-behavioral dispositions of the physical sciences. That is a promising move, because the analysis of non-behavioral dispositions is on relatively solid philosophical ground. An explanation attributing the breaking of a glass to its fragility is surely something even the staunchest materialist can accept. By arguing that mental terms are synonymous with dispositional terms, the logical behaviorist has provided something the radical behaviorist could not: a materialist account of mental causation. [12]

Nevertheless, the analogy between mental causation as construed by the logical behaviorist and physical causation goes only so far. The logical behaviorist treats the manifestation of a disposition as the sole form of mental causation, whereas the physical sciences recognize additional kinds of causation. There is the kind of causation where one physical event causes another, as when the breaking of a glass is attributed to its having been struck. In fact, explanations that involve event-event causation are presumably more basic than dispositional explanations, because the manifestation of a disposition (the breaking of a fragile glass) always involves event-event causation and not vice versa. In the realm of the mental many examples of event-event causation involve one mental state's causing another, and for this kind of causation logical behaviorism provides no analysis. As a result the logical behaviorist is committed to the tacit and implausible assumption that psychology requires a less robust notion of causation than the physical sciences require. [13]

Event-event causation actually seems to be quite common in the realm of the mental. Mental causes typically give rise to behavioral effects by virtue of

their interaction with other mental causes. For example, having a headache causes a disposition to take aspirin only if one also has the desire to get rid of the headache, the belief that aspirin exists, the belief that taking aspirin reduces headaches and so on. Since mental states interact in generating behavior, it will be necessary to find a construal of psychological explanations that posits mental processes: causal sequences of mental events. It is this construal that logical behaviorism fails to provide.

Such considerations bring out a fundamental way in which logical behaviorism is quite similar to radical behaviorism. It is true that the logical behaviorist, unlike the radical behaviorist, acknowledges the existence of mental states. Yet since the underlying tenet of logical behaviorism is that references to mental states can be translated out of psychological explanations by employing behavioral hypotheticals, all talk of mental states and processes is in a sense heuristic. The only facts to which the behaviorist is actually committed are facts about relations between stimuli and responses. In this respect logical behaviorism is just radical behaviorism in a semantic form. Although the former theory offers a construal of mental causation, the construal is Pickwickian. What does not really exist cannot cause anything, and the logical behaviorist, like the radical behaviorist, believes deep down that mental causes do not exist. [14]

[11] This appeal to dispositions is not without problems. While there is an initial sense of intelligibility, it is hard to see clearly what exactly, metaphysically, is being claimed about the glass itself when we say, for example, that the glass is fragile. (See Discussion Question 2.)

[12] As you will see later, Fodor seriously qualifies this claim. There is an important sense in which logical behaviorism fails to account for mental causation in a satisfactory way.

[13] This talk of the "robustness" of the logical behaviorist's notion of causation is really just an indirect way of getting at the point made just below that there really is no genuine mental causation involved at all.

[14] Now it has become clear that logical behaviorism cannot account for genuine mental causation, since it really denies that mental causes even exist (and so doesn't really acknowledge the existence of mental states, as was claimed at the start of this rather confusing paragraph).

An alternative materialist theory of the mind to logical behaviorism is the central-state identity theory. According to this theory, mental events, states and processes are identical with neurophysiological events in the brain, and the property of being in a certain mental state (such as having a headache or believing it will rain) is identical with the property of being in a certain neurophysiological state. On this basis it is easy to make sense of the idea that a behavioral effect might sometimes have a chain of mental causes; that will be the case whenever a behavioral effect is contingent on the appropriate sequence of neurophysiological events.

The central-state identity theory acknowledges that it is possible for mental causes to interact causally without ever giving rise to any behavioral effect, as when a person thinks for a while about what he ought to do and then decides to do nothing. If mental processes are neurophysiological, they must have the causal properties of neurophysiological processes. Since neurophysiological processes are presumably physical processes, the central-state identity theory ensures that the concept of mental causation is as rich as the concept of physical causation. [15]

> [15] Again, how "rich" each concept of causation is really isn't the point—instead just that the identity theory allows mental states to genuinely cause behavior and logical behaviorism does not.

The central-state identity theory provides a satisfactory account of what the mental terms in psychological explanations refer to, and so it is favored by psychologists who are dissatisfied with behaviorism. The behaviorist maintains that mental terms refer to nothing or that they refer to the parameters of stimulus-response relations. Either way the existence of mental entities is only illusory. The identity theorist, on the other hand, argues that mental terms refer to neurophysiological states. Thus he can take seriously the project of explaining behavior by appealing to its mental causes.

> [16] Here again Fodor is alluding to his guiding constraint for evaluating different philosophies of mind. According to the central-state identity theory (as contrasted with logical behaviorism), the kinds of states involved in psychological explanations (things like beliefs and desires and reasoning of various sorts—these are the "explanatory constructs") have genuine existence and can therefore function as genuine causes.

The chief advantage of the identity theory is that it takes the explanatory constructs of psychology at face value, which is surely something a philosophy of mind ought to do if it can. [16] The identity theory shows how the mentalistic explanations of psychology could be not mere heuristics but literal accounts of the causal history of behavior. Moreover, since the identity theory is not a semantic thesis, it is immune to many arguments that cast in doubt logical behaviorism. A drawback of logical behaviorism is that the observation "John has a headache" does not seem to mean the same thing as a statement of the form "John is disposed to behave in such and such a way." The identity theorist, however, can live with the fact that "John has a headache" and "John is in such and such a brain state" are not synonymous. The assertion of the identity theorist is not that these sentences mean the same thing but only that they are rendered true (or false) by the same neurophysiological phenomena.

The identity theory can be held either as a doctrine about mental particulars (John's current pain or Bill's fear of animals) or as a doctrine about mental universals, or properties (having a pain or being afraid of animals). The two doctrines, called respectively token physicalism and type physicalism, differ in strength and plausibility. Token physicalism maintains only that all the mental particulars that happen to exist are neurophysiological, whereas type physicalism makes the more sweeping assertion that all the mental particulars there could possibly be are neurophysiological. Token physicalism does not rule out the logical possibility of machines and disembodied spirits having mental properties. Type physicalism dismisses this possibility because neither machines nor disembodied spirits have neurons. [17]

Type physicalism is not a plausible doctrine about mental properties even if

> [17] Both of these views agree that a specific mental state (for example, John's current headache) is identical to a certain specific neurophysiological state. The issue between them is whether all headaches of that very same specific kind are identical to neurophysiological states of that very same specific kind—in which case only a being with a brain exactly like John's could have such a headache. And the underlying issue, which this formulation fails to bring out very clearly, is *why* that specific neurophysiological state is a headache of a certain specific sort: is it because of its very specific physical properties (which is what early versions of the identity theory at least seemed to say), or because of more abstract properties, including its structure of relations to other such states, that might be realized by other sorts of "brains"—including both machines like computers and disembodied spirits (if they existed—which Fodor doesn't for a moment really believe).

token physicalism is right about mental particulars. The problem with type physicalism is that the psychological constitution of a system seems to depend not on its hardware, or physical composition, but on its software, or program. Why should the philosopher dismiss the possibility that silicon-based Martians have pains, assuming that the silicon is properly organized? And why should the philosopher rule out the possibility of machines having beliefs, assuming that machines are correctly programmed? If it is logically possible that Martians and machines could have mental properties, then mental properties and neurophysiological processes cannot be identical, however much they may prove to be coextensive. [18]

What it all comes down to is that there seems to be a level of abstraction at which the generalizations of psychology are most naturally pitched. This level of abstraction cuts across differences in the physical composition of the systems to which psychological generalizations apply. In the cognitive sciences, at least, the natural domain for psychological theorizing seems to be all systems that process information. [19]

The problem with type physicalism is that there are possible information-processing systems with the same psychological constitution as human beings but not the same physical organization. In principle all kinds of physically different things could have human software.

This situation calls for a relational account of mental properties that abstracts them from the physical structure of their bearers. In spite of the objections to logical behaviorism that I presented above, logical behaviorism was at least on the right track in offering a relational interpretation of mental properties: to have a headache is to be disposed to exhibit a certain pattern of relations between the stimuli one encounters and the responses one exhibits. If that is what having a headache is, however, there is no reason in principle why only heads that are physically similar to ours can ache. Indeed, according to logical behaviorism, it is a necessary truth that any system that has our stimulus-response contingencies also has our headaches. [20]

All of this emerged 10 to 15 years ago as a nasty dilemma for the materialist program in the philosophy of mind. On the one hand the identity theorist (and not the logical behaviorist) had got right the causal character of the interactions of mind and body. On the other the logical behaviorist (and not the identity theorist) had got right the relational character of mental properties. Functionalism has apparently been able to resolve the dilemma. By stressing the distinction computer science draws between hardware and software the functionalist can make sense of both the causal and the relational character of the mental.

The intuition underlying functionalism is that what determines the psychological type to which a mental particular belongs is the causal role of the particular in the mental life of the organism. Functional individuation is differentiation with respect to causal role. A headache, for example, is identified with the type of mental state that among other things causes a disposition for taking aspirin in people who believe aspirin relieves a headache, causes a desire to rid oneself of the pain one is feeling, often causes someone who speaks English to say such things as "I have a headache" and is brought on by overwork, eyestrain, and tension. This list is presumably not complete. More will be known about the nature of a headache as psychological and physiological research discovers more about its causal role.

---

[18] That it is logically possible that machines can have mental properties or states is surely not as obvious as Fodor makes it sound. The Martian example is better: if they are sentient creatures like ourselves, then it is plausible to suppose that they can have beliefs and desires and also experience pain, even if their brains are very different from ours. That this is a matter of "programming" is again not obvious without more argument than has been given so far—this is essentially the functionalist claim, which Fodor will eventually defend, but hasn't yet. (To say that two properties are "coextensive" is to say that they apply to exactly the same things; this does not necessarily mean that they are really the same property, since the coextensiveness could be a coincidence.)

[19] Again, this is far from obviously correct. (Is your computer a system that processes information? Does it have mental or psychological states?)

[20] Fodor seems (?) to be endorsing this suggestion. The problem with it is that it at least seems to leave out the most obvious and important aspect of a headache: the conscious experience, the way it *feels*. (One standard objection to logical behaviorism is that a being could exhibit the same pattern of "stimulus-response contingencies" while having no relevant *experience* at all.)

Functionalism construes the concept of causal role in such a way that a mental state can be defined by its causal relations to other mental states. In this respect functionalism is completely different from logical behaviorism. Another major difference is that functionalism is not a reductionist thesis. It does not foresee, even in principle, the elimination of mentalistic concepts from the explanatory apparatus of psychological theories.

The difference between functionalism and logical behaviorism is brought out by the fact that functionalism is fully compatible with token physicalism. The functionalist would not be disturbed if brain events turn out to be the only things with the functional properties that define mental states. Indeed, most functionalists fully expect it will turn out that way. [21]

Since functionalism recognizes that mental particulars may be physical, it is compatible with the idea that mental causation is a species of physical causation. In other words, functionalism tolerates the materialist solution to the mind-body problem provided by the central-state identity theory. It is possible for the functionalist to assert both that mental properties are typically defined in terms of their relations and that interactions of mind and body are typically causal in however robust a notion of causality is required by psychological explanations. The logical behaviorist can endorse only the first assertion and the type physicalist only the second. As a result functionalism seems to capture the best features of the materialist alternatives to dualism. [22] It is no wonder that functionalism has become increasingly popular.

Machines provide good examples of two concepts that are central to functionalism: the concept that mental states are interdefined and the concept that they can be realized by many systems. [This can be illustrated by contrasting] a behavioristic Coke machine

[21] The description of causal role says nothing about the intrinsic character of the state—about what it is made of, for example—thus leaving open the possibility that it is a brain state, though not requiring that this be so. (Notice that it also seems to say nothing at all about what it feels like to be in such a state, or indeed that it feels any way at all.)

[22] Mental particulars are both defined in terms of relations and capable of genuinely causing other states.

with a mentalistic one. Both machines dispense a Coke for 10 cents. (The price has not been affected by inflation.) The states of the machines are defined by reference to their causal roles, but only [one] machine would satisfy the behaviorist. Its single state (*S0*) is completely specified in terms of stimuli and responses. *S0* is the state a machine is in if, and only if, given a dime as the input, it dispenses a Coke as the output. [23]

[23] *S0* isn't really an internal state of the machine in any interesting sense at all, nor does it involve much in the way of programming or information processing. It could involve just a small lever that is tripped by the dime as it falls into a bin and that then releases a Coke.

The [second] machine has interdefined states (*S1* and *S2*), which are characteristic of functionalism. *S1* is the state a machine is in if, and only if, (1) given a nickel, it dispenses nothing and proceeds to *S2*, and (2) given a dime, it dispenses a Coke and stays in *S1*. *S2* is the state a machine is in if, and only if, (1) given a nickel, it dispenses a Coke and proceeds to *S1*, and (2) given a dime, it dispenses a Coke and a nickel and proceeds to *S1*. What *S1* and *S2* jointly amount to is the machine's dispensing a Coke if it is given a dime, dispensing a Coke and a nickel if it is given a dime and a nickel and waiting to be given a second nickel if it has been given a first one. [24]

Since *S1* and *S2* are each defined by hypothetical statements, they can be viewed as dispositions. Nevertheless, they are not behavioral dispositions because the consequences an input has for a machine in *S1* or *S2* are not specified solely in terms of the output of the machine. Rather, the consequences also involve the machine's internal states.

[24] *S1* and *S2*, on the other hand, do involve information (about whether a nickel has been received since the last Coke was dispensed) and do play different roles in something at least roughly like a program.

Nothing about the way I have described the behavioristic and mentalistic Coke machines puts constraints on what they could be made of. Any system whose states bore the proper relations to inputs, outputs and other states could be one of these machines. No doubt it is reasonable to expect such a system to be constructed out of such things as wheels, levers and diodes (token physicalism for Coke machines). Similarly, it is reasonable to expect that our minds may prove to be neurophysiological (token physicalism for human beings).

Nevertheless, the software description of a Coke machine does not logically require wheels, levers and diodes for its concrete realization. By the same token, the software description of the mind does not logically require neurons. As far as functionalism is concerned a Coke machine with states *S1* and *S2* could be made of ectoplasm, if there is such stuff and if its states have the right causal properties. Functionalism allows for the possibility of disembodied Coke machines in exactly the same way and to the same extent that it allows for the possibility of disembodied minds. [25]

To say that *S1* and *S2* are interdefined and realizable by different kinds of hardware is not, of course, to say that a Coke machine has a mind. Although interdefinitions and functional specification are typical features of mental states, they are clearly not sufficient for mentality. What more is required is a question to which I shall return below.

Some philosophers are suspicious of functionalism because it seems too easy. Since functionalism licenses the individuation of states by reference to their causal role, it appears to allow a trivial explanation of any observed event *E*, that is, it appears to postulate an *E*-causer. For example, what makes the valves in a machine open? Why, the operation of anything that has the functionally defined property causing valves to open.

In psychology this kind of question-begging often takes the form of theories that in effect postulate homunculi with the selfsame intellectual capacities the theorist sets out to explain. [26] Such is the case when visual perception is explained by simply postulating psychological mechanisms that process visual information. The behaviorist has often charged the mentalist, sometimes justifiably, of mongering this kind of question-begging pseudo explanation. The charge will have to be met if functionally defined mental states are to have a serious role in psychological theories.

The burden of the accusation is not untruth but triviality. There can be no doubt that it is a valve opener that opens valves, and it is likely that visual perception is mediated by the processing of visual information. The charge is that such putative functional explanations are mere platitudes. The functionalist can meet this objection by allowing functionally defined theoretical constructs only where mechanisms exist that can carry out the function and only where he has some notion of what such mechanisms might be like. [27] One way of imposing this requirement is to identify the mental processes that psychology postulates with the operations of the restricted class of possible computers called Turing machines.

A Turing machine can be informally characterized as a mechanism with a finite number of program states. The inputs and outputs of the machine are written on a tape that is divided into squares each of which included a symbol from a finite alphabet. The machine scans the tape one square at a time. It can erase the symbol on a scanned square and print a new one in its place. The machine can execute only the elementary mechanical operations of scanning, erasing, printing, moving the tape and changing state. [28]

The program states of the Turing machine are defined solely in terms of input symbols on the tape, the output symbols on the tape, the elementary operations and the other states of the program. Each program

[25] "Ectoplasm" is a term once used to refer to spiritual stuff. Any material complex enough to allow for different states standing in the indicated relations could serve as the "inner states of the Coke machine." Of course, whatever holds and dispenses the Cokes, together with the Cokes themselves, would still presumably have to be material.

[26] A "homunculus" ("homunculi" is the plural) is just a little man or man-like being inside the person or the mind or the brain, who is introduced to perform some mysterious process. The point is that postulating a homunculus that, for example, computes sums obviously does nothing really to explain psychologically how people compute sums, because the inner action of the homunculus is just as mysterious as the overt one for which the explanation was originally sought.

[27] To speak of a "mechanism" does not necessarily mean a physical mechanism. The idea is rather that it is a process that is fully understood, for which no further issue of explanation arises. If we can describe a mechanism that processes visual information, then there is no further explanatory issue about how this is done.

[28] Anything that operates in an analogous way is a Turing machine—it needn't take this explicit form. (Or to put the point in reverse, anything is a Turing machine whose inner operations could be carried out by a device of this sort.)

state is therefore functionally defined by the part it plays in the overall operation of the machine. Since the functional role of a state depends on the relation of the state to other states as well as to inputs and outputs, the relational character of the mental is captured by the Turing-machine version of functionalism. Since the definition of a program state never refers to the physical structure of the system running the program, the Turing-machine version of functionalism also captures the idea that the character of a mental state is independent of its physical realization. A human being, a roomful of people, a computer and a disembodied spirit would all be a Turing machine if they operated according to a Turing-machine program. 29

29 Is the second Coke machine described above a Turing machine? That is, can you see how the operations of the machine could be carried out by a device of the sort described earlier? (See Discussion Question 3.)

The proposal is to restrict the functional definition of psychological states to those that can be expressed in terms of the program states of Turing machines. If this restriction can be enforced, it provides a guarantee that psychological theories will be compatible with the demands of mechanisms. Since Turing machines are very simple devices, they are in principle quite easy to build. Consequently by formulating a psychological explanation as a Turing-machine program the psychologist ensures that the explanation is mechanistic, even though the hardware realizing the mechanism is left open.

There are many kinds of computational mechanisms other than Turing machines, and so the formulation of a functionalist psychological theory in Turing-machine notation provides only a sufficient condition for the theory's being mechanically realizable. What makes the condition interesting, however, is that the simple Turing machine can perform many complex tasks. Although the elementary operations of the Turing machine are restricted, iterations of the operations enable the machine to carry out any well-defined computation on discrete symbols.

An important tendency in the cognitive sciences is to treat the mind chiefly as a device that manipulates symbols. 30 If a

30 Think carefully about this suggestion, which is in fact fairly pervasive in recent philosophy of mind. Could manipulation of symbols really be the main thing that the mind does? (See Discussion Question 4.)

mental process can be functionally defined as an operation on symbols, there is a Turing machine capable of carrying out the computation and a variety of mechanisms for realizing the Turing machine. Where the manipulation of symbols is important, the Turing machine provides a connection between functional explanation and mechanistic explanation.

The reduction of psychological theory to a program for a Turing machine is a way of exorcising the homunculi. 31 The reduction ensures that no operations have been postulated except those that could be performed by a familiar mechanism. Of course, the working psychologist usually cannot specify the reduction for each functionally individuated process in every theory he is prepared to take seriously. In practice the argument usually goes in the opposite direction; if the postulation of a mental operation is essential to some cherished psychological explanation, the theorist tends to assume that there must be a program for a Turing machine that will carry out that operation.

31 If every process and operation is performed by a mechanism (see Annotation 26), then there is no mystery left and thus no need for homunculi.

. . .

Such is the origin, the provenance and the promise of contemporary functionalism. How much has it actually paid off? This question is not easy to answer because much of what is now happening in the philosophy of mind and the cognitive sciences is directed at exploring the scope and limits of the functionalist explanation of behavior. I shall, however, give a brief overview.

An obvious objection to functionalism as a theory of the mind is that the functionalist definition is not limited to mental states and processes. Catalysts, Coke machines, valve openers, pencil sharpeners, mousetraps and ministers of finance are all in one way or another concepts that are functionally defined, but none is a mental concept such as pain, belief and desire. What, then, characterizes the mental? And can it be captured in a functionalist framework?

The traditional view in the philosophy of mind has it that mental states are distinguished by their having what are called either qualitative content or intentional content. I shall discuss qualitative content first.

It is not easy to say what qualitative content is; indeed, according to some theories, it is not even possible to say what it is because it can be known not by description but only by direct experience. I shall nonetheless attempt to describe it. Try to imagine looking at a blank wall through a red filter. Now change the filter to a green one and leave everything else exactly the way it was. Something about the character of your experience changes when the filter does, and it is this kind of thing that philosophers call qualitative content. I am not entirely comfortable about introducing qualitative content in this way, but it is a subject with which many philosophers are not comfortable. 32

> 32 The idea of qualitative content or qualia was explained in Annotation 15 to the Smart selection.

The reason qualitative content is a problem for functionalism is straightforward. Functionalism is committed to defining mental states in terms of their causes and effects. It seems, however, as if two mental states could have all the same causal relations and yet could differ in their qualitative content. Let me illustrate this with the classic puzzle of the inverted spectrum.

> 33 Think carefully about this example. At first you might think that if the same object looked differently colored to different people, then the difference would quickly be discovered. But if color words are learned by pointing at objects, then whatever differences there are in color experience will correlate systematically with differences in the way each person understands those words: two such people will agree in calling ripe tomatoes "red" even if they have totally different color experiences when they look at a ripe tomato. And hence their verbal descriptions will not reveal the difference. (Is there any other way in which it might be revealed?)

It seems possible to imagine two observers who are alike in all relevant psychological respects except that experiences having the qualitative content of red for one observer would have the qualitative content of green for the other. Nothing about their behavior need reveal the difference because both of them see ripe tomatoes and flaming sunsets as being similar in color and both of them call that color "red." 33 Moreover, the causal connection between their (qualitatively distinct) experiences and their other mental states could also be identical. Perhaps they both think of Little Red Riding Hood when they see ripe tomatoes, feel depressed when they see the color green and so on. It seems as if anything that could be packed into the notion of the causal role of their experiences could be shared by them, and yet the qualitative content of the experiences could be as different as you like. If this is possible, then the functionalist account does not work for mental states that have qualitative content. If one person is having a green experience while another person is having a red one, then surely they must be in different mental states. 34

> 34 If Tom and Sally are in this situation with respect to their experiences of ripe tomatoes, then their experiential states will be totally different even though the causal role of each of those states is exactly the same: it is caused by ripe tomatoes (and other things such as fire engines, fresh raw beef, etc.) and causes each of them to say "red" when asked what color is being experienced (and to do various other things depending on what else is going on). But then the functionalist account of mental states in terms of causal role is mistaken.

The example of the inverted spectrum is more than a verbal puzzle. Having qualitative content is supposed to be a chief factor in what makes a mental state conscious. Many psychologists who are inclined to accept the functionalist framework are nonetheless worried about the failure of functionalism to reveal much about the nature of consciousness. Functionalists have made a few ingenious attempts to talk themselves and their colleagues out of this worry, but they have not, in my view, done so with much success. (For example, perhaps one is wrong in thinking one can imagine what an inverted spectrum would be like.) As matters stand, the problem of qualitative content poses a serious threat to the assertion that functionalism can provide a general theory of the mental. 35

> 35 Look back here at the final objection to the identity theory discussed by Smart (p. 340): can functionalism explain why certain states defined by causal role are conscious and others (such as those involved in controlling breathing and other bodily processes) are not?

Functionalism has fared much better with the intentional content of mental states. Indeed, it is here that the major achievements of recent cognitive sciences are found. To say that a mental state has intentional content is to say that it has certain semantic properties. For example, for Enrico to believe Galileo was Italian apparently involves a three-way relation between Enrico, a belief and a proposition that is the content of the belief (namely the proposition that Galileo was Italian). In particular it is an essential property of Enrico's belief that it is about Galileo (and not about, say, Newton) and that it is true if, and only if, Galileo was indeed Italian. Philosophers are divided on how these considerations fit together, but it is widely agreed that beliefs involve semantic properties such as expressing a proposition, being true or false and being about one thing rather than another.

. . .

The current idea is that the semantic properties of a mental representation are determined by aspects of its functional role. In other words, a sufficient condition for having semantic properties can be specified in causal terms. This is the connection between functionalism and the representational theory of the mind. Modern cognitive psychology rests largely on the hope that these two doctrines can be made to support each other.

No philosopher is now prepared to say exactly how the functional role of a mental representation determines its semantic properties. Nevertheless, the functionalist recognizes three types of causal relation among psychological states involving mental representations, and they might serve to fit the semantic properties of mental representations. The three types are causal relations among mental states and stimuli, mental states and responses and some mental states and other ones.

Consider the belief that John is tall. Presumably the following facts, which correspond respectively to the three types of causal relation, are relevant to determining the semantic properties of the mental representation involved in the belief. First, the belief is a normal effect of certain stimulations, such as seeing John in circumstances that reveal his height. Second, the belief is the normal cause of certain behavioral effects, such as uttering "John is tall." Third, the belief is a normal cause of certain other beliefs and a normal effect of certain other beliefs. For example, anyone who believes John is tall is very likely also to believe someone is tall. Having the first belief is normally causally sufficient for having the second belief. And anyone who believes everyone in the room is tall and also be- lieves John is in the room will very likely believe John is tall. The third belief is a normal effect of the first two. In short, the functionalist maintains that the proposition expressed by a given mental representation depends on the causal properties of the mental states in which that mental representation figures. ③⑥

The concept that the semantic properties of mental representations are determined by aspects of their functional role is at the center of current work in the cognitive sciences. Nevertheless, the concept may not be true. Many philosophers who are unsympathetic to the cognitive turn in modern psychology doubt its truth, and many psychologists would probably reject it in the bald and unelaborated way that I have sketched it. Yet even in its sketched form, there is this much to be said in its favor: It legitimizes the notion of mental representation, which has become increasingly important to theorizing in every branch of the cognitive sciences. Recent advances in formulating and testing hypotheses about the character of mental representation in fields ranging from phonetics to computer vision suggest that the concept of mental representation is fundamental to empirical theories of the mind. ③⑦

The behaviorist has rejected the appeal to mental representation because it runs counter to his view of the explanatory mechanisms that can figure in psychological theories. Nevertheless, the science of mental representation is now flourishing. The history of science reveals that when a successful theory comes into conflict with a methodological scruple, it is generally the scruple that gives way. Accordingly, the functionalist has released the behaviorist constraints on psychological explanations. There is probably no better way to decide what is methodologically permissible in science than by investigating what successful science requires.

③⑥ All these things seem to be true of the belief that John is tall. The question is whether they are sufficient to characterize that mental state: whether any state that has this causal role will automatically be such a belief. (Remember that the second belief involved must also be identified in the same way.) How plausible is this? (See Discussion Question 5.)

③⑦ A mental representation is a mental state that has a content that describes or says something about some thing or situation. To think that baseball is an exciting sport is to have a mental representation whose content makes a specific claim about that specific game.

Discussion Questions

1. On page 342, Fodor raises two objections to dualist accounts of mental causation.
   a. One of these has to do with spatial location: why does a mental state, which according to the dualist does not have a spatial position, produce an effect at one spatial location rather than another—that is, affect one body rather than another? The selection from Foster contains one possible response to this objection (in his discussion of "the problem of causal pairings"). How plausible is this response? Can you think of any other response on behalf of the dualist?
   b. Fodor's second objection appeals to various conservation laws: consider, for example, the law of conservation of energy. Fodor's idea here is that causal transactions involve energy, so that if there were causal relations between mental states and physical states, energy would be either entering (if the mental state causally affects the physical state) or leaving (if the physical state causally affects the mental state) the physical realm, in either case violating the principle of conservation of energy—assuming that this applies to the physical realm taken by itself. Can you think of a way of understanding the law that would not be violated by such cases? How sure and on what basis are we that the law, understood in the way that Fodor has in mind, is true? (You may have to do a little research about the law of conservation of energy to answer this question.)
2. Think carefully about what it means for a glass to be *fragile*. Suppose that your mother has a favorite vase, and you've always been told to be very careful of this vase because it is fragile. At one level, you know what that means: this vase will break more easily than most, given similar treatment. But think carefully about what must be true of the vase itself. Perhaps that the molecules of the vase are more loosely bound to each other? A dispositional property of an object describes how that object will behave under certain circumstances, but many philosophers think that such a description is only the first stage of an

explanation of the behavior. One might also ask *why* the object behaves in that way in those circumstances, where the answer would appeal to some more fundamental, nondispositional property. Think about the analogous question for the behaviorist's dispositions. One answer would be that the disposition exists because of an underlying mental state, in which case the behaviorist hasn't accounted for mental states after all. Is there some other plausible answer that the behaviorist can give?

3. Try to figure out how a Turing machine would have to be programmed in order to serve as the inner processor of the Coke machine. The machine starts by scanning a blank square of the tape. There is a device of some sort that causes a specific symbol to be printed on the tape when a nickel is inserted and a different symbol for a dime (perhaps just the numerals "5" and "10"); and some further symbols (perhaps a Coke logo and a "minus 5") that cause another device to dispense a Coke or a nickel when they appear on the tape. (These additional devices are not part of the Turing machine, but rather represent its "input" and "output.") Your task is to describe a set of Turing machine states (*S0, S1, S2*, etc.—contrary to what Fodor's discussion suggests, you will need more than two), where *S0* is the starting state as it scans the blank tape before any money has been inserted. For each state, you need to say what the machine does when it is in that state and is looking at each of the five possible states of the tape (including a blank): it can erase the symbol that is there, write a new symbol (but only if the tape is previously blank), or leave that symbol unchanged; and it can move left or right along the tape or stay in the same place (but only one printing or erasing action and one movement per combination of state and symbol). You need to arrange the states so that the machine "knows" how much money has been inserted, prints the Coke symbol when it has received 10 cents, prints the "minus 5" symbol when change is due, and finishes the process by erasing all of the symbols so that the tape is blank again for the next time. Assume that the "input" device prints the relevant symbol on

the square that the machine is scanning if that square is blank and otherwise on the first blank square to the right. Assume also that the people attempting to buy Cokes never put more than 15 cents into the machine and put in more than 10 only if it is a nickel followed by a dime.

4. Fodor suggests (along with many others) that the operations of the mind may be manipulations of symbols. Here a symbol is something analogous to a word in language: something that stands for something, but not in virtue of its intrinsic character. Thus the word "bird" stands for birds, but not because of its intrinsic shape; that shape could just was well have stood for something entirely different or might just have been a meaningless squiggle. (In contrast, a drawing of a bird would stand for a bird because of its specific shape, and so would not in this sense be a symbol.) Fodor's suggestion is essentially that people think about and reason about things by virtue of having symbols in their minds or brains: not symbols of a "natural language" like English, but rather symbols in a "language of thought" that is perhaps innate. To think about birds is to be in a state analogous to having the word "bird" written on a mental blackboard; and to infer from the fact that something is a bird to the conclusion that it is warm-blooded is something like having an occurrence of the mental word "bird" cause an occurrence of the mental word "warm-blooded." One problem with this sort of view is whether and how the person in question *understands* the meanings of the symbols. Think of your computer: it contains symbols of an analogous sort (digital strings of 0 and 1), but does it understand what any of them mean? Is merely processing symbols enough for meaningful mental activity (such as think-

ing, reasoning, wondering, fearing, etc.)? (The first selection by Searle has more to say about this issue.)

5. Suppose that there is a mental state having the causal role that Fodor describes in the passage corresponding to Annotation 36—or perhaps some more elaborate causal role, with further causal relations added. Will the fact that it satisfies any such set of causal relations be enough to guarantee that it is the *conscious* thought that John is tall? Is there any clear reason why a state could not satisfy any causal role of this sort, however elaborate, and involve no consciousness at all?

6. Foster (p. 332) raises the objection that on a functionalist ("token-token identity") view, only the *physical* features of the brain state that satisfies the functional role required to be a particular mental state will causally affect other physical states, with the mentalistic description of the state being causally irrelevant. If this is so, then functionalism is objectionable from the standpoint of common sense in the same way that epiphenomenalism was, since it also implies that people's mental states do not causally affect their behavior. Is this a serious problem for functionalism? Would it make sense for a functionalist to attribute causal significance to the fact that a brain state satisfies a certain functional or causal role? If not, does this mean that the mental state is causally irrelevant, even though the brain state is not? Or is it enough that the brain state (which is the mental state) is causally relevant, even though its character as a mental state is not? (This is a *very* hard question, one that functionalists themselves often have little to say about—but still very much worth considering.)

A. M. Turing

Alan Turing (1912–1954), British mathematician and father of computer science, introduced the important concept of a Turing Machine in this article. Turing worked for the British government during World War II decoding enemy communications. (The most prestigious prize in the computing world today is the A. M. Turing prize, awarded every year and accompanied by $100,000.)

In this article, Turing considers the philosophical question "Can computers think?", a question that is indirectly important for assessing the functionalist view of mental states. Turing argues that the best way to approach this question is to reformulate it in terms of a distinctive game that he describes, "the imitation game"—and one important question about the article is whether this reformulation really captures the original question in an adequate way. (Because the article was written in 1950, at the beginning of the computer revolution, Turing sometimes offers analogies and explanations that people who are now more familiar with computers probably don't need.)

Computing Machinery and Intelligence

1. THE IMITATION GAME

I propose to consider the question "Can machines think?" This should begin with definitions of the meaning of the terms "machine" and "think." The definitions might be framed so as to reflect so far as possible the normal use of the words, but this attitude is dangerous. If the meaning of the words "machine" and "think" are to be found by examining how they are commonly used it is difficult to escape the conclusion that the meaning and the answer to the question, "Can machines think?" is to be sought in a statistical survey such as a Gallup poll. But this is absurd. Instead of attempting such a definition I shall replace the question by another, which is closely related to it and is expressed in relatively unambiguous words.

The new form of the problem can be described in terms of a game which we call the "imitation game." It is played with three people, a man (A), a woman (B), and an interrogator (C) who may be of either sex. The interrogator stays in a room apart from the other two. The object of the game for the interrogator is to determine which of the other two is the man and which is the woman. He knows them by labels X and Y, and at the end of the game he says either "X is A and Y is B" or "X is B and Y is A." The interrogator is allowed to put questions to A and B thus:

C: Will X please tell me the length of his or her hair?

From Mind, *Vol. LIX, No. 236, (1950).*

Now suppose X is actually A, then A must answer. It is A's object in the game to try to cause C to make the wrong identification. His answer might therefore be

"My hair is shingled, and the longest strands are about nine inches long."

In order that tones of voice may not help the interrogator the answers should be written, or better still, typewritten. The ideal arrangement is to have a teleprinter communicating between the two rooms. Alternatively the question and answers can be repeated by an intermediary. The object of the game for the third player (B) is to help the interrogator. The best strategy for her is probably to give truthful answers. She can add such things as "I am the woman, don't listen to him!" to her answers, but it will avail nothing as the man can make similar remarks.

We now ask the question, "What will happen when a machine takes the part of A in this game?" Will the interrogator decide wrongly as often when the game is played like this as he does when the game is played between a man and a woman? These questions replace our original, "Can machines think?"[1]

[1] Turing's account here of the modification of the game for the computer case is not at all clear. As emerges from the following discussion, he has in mind a game in which the interrogator is trying to decide which of the other two players (one a human of either gender and the other a computer) is the computer and which is the human. The human is trying to help him and so will answer truthfully, while the computer is programmed so as to attempt to fool him.

2. CRITIQUE OF THE NEW PROBLEM

As well as asking, "What is the answer to this new form of the question," one may ask, "Is this new question a worthy one to investigate?" This latter question we investigate without further ado, thereby cutting short an infinite regress.

The new problem has the advantage of drawing a fairly sharp line between the physical and the intellectual capacities of a man. No engineer or chemist claims to be able to produce a material which is indistinguishable from the human skin. It is possible that at some time this might be done, but even supposing this invention available we should feel there was little point in trying to make a "thinking machine" more human by dressing it up in such artificial flesh. The form in which we have set the problem reflects this fact in the condition which prevents the interrogator from seeing or touching the other competitors, or hearing their voices. Some other advantages of the proposed criterion may be shown up by specimen questions and answers. Thus:

> Q: Please write me a sonnet on the subject of the Forth Bridge.
> A: Count me out on this one. I never could write poetry.
> Q: Add 34957 to 70764.
> A: (Pause about 30 seconds and then give as answer) 105621.
> Q: Do you play chess?
> A: Yes.
> Q: I have K at my K1, and no other pieces. You have only K at K6 and R at R1. It is your move. What do you play?
> A: (After a pause of 15 seconds) R-R8 mate.

The question and answer method seems to be suitable for introducing almost any one of the fields of human endeavor that we wish to include. We do not wish to penalize the machine for its inability to shine in beauty competitions, nor to penalize a man for losing in a race against an airplane. The conditions of our game make these disabilities irrelevant. The "witnesses" can brag, if they consider it advisable, as much as they please about their charms, strength or heroism, but the interrogator cannot demand practical demonstrations.②

The game may perhaps be criticized on the ground that the odds are weighted too heavily against

the machine. If the man were to try and pretend to be the machine he would clearly make a very poor showing. He would be given away at once by slowness and inaccuracy in arithmetic. May not machines carry out something which ought to be described as thinking but which is very different from what a man does? This objection is a very strong one, but at least we can say that if, nevertheless, a machine can be constructed to play the imitation game satisfactorily, we need not be troubled by this objection.③

. . .

② Since what is at issue is whether the computer can *think*, other features like what it looks like or how fast it can run are irrelevant. Communicating via a teleprinter (or the more modern alternative of something like e-mail) is a way of setting aside these irrelevant matters.

③ So Turing is saying that being able to fool the interrogator often enough is a **sufficient condition** for deciding (reasonably) that the computer can think, even though perhaps not a **necessary condition**: there might be computers that do not succeed in the game but are still thinking in some other way.

3. THE MACHINES CONCERNED IN THE GAME

. . . the present interest in "thinking machines" has been aroused by a particular kind of machine, usually called an "electronic computer" or "digital computer." Following this suggestion we only permit digital computers to take part in our game.

This restriction appears at first sight to be a very drastic one. I shall attempt to show that it is not so in reality. To do this necessitates a short account of the nature and properties of these computers.

It may also be said that this identification of machines with digital computers, like our criterion for "thinking," will only be unsatisfactory if (contrary to my belief), it turns out that digital computers are unable to give a good showing in the game.

There are already a number of digital computers in working order, and it may be asked, "Why not try the experiment straight away? It would be easy to satisfy the conditions of the game. A number of interrogators could be used, and statistics compiled to show how often the right identification was given." The short answer is that we are not asking whether all digital computers would do well in the game nor whether the computers at present available would do well, but whether there are imaginable computers which would do well.④ But this is only the short answer. We shall see this question in a different light later.

④ Obviously computers have progressed a long way since Turing's time. But the real issue is whether some computer that is theoretically *possible* could pass the test. ("Imaginable" is a little too vague, since writers of science fiction often imagine things that aren't really possible.) Whether anyone ever bothers to actually build one doesn't matter, and still less whether it has been done so far.

4. DIGITAL COMPUTERS

The idea behind digital computers may be explained by saying that these machines are intended to carry out any operations which could be done by a human computer. The human computer is supposed to be following fixed rules; he has no authority to deviate from them in any detail.⑤ We may suppose that these rules are supplied in a book, which is altered whenever he is put on to a new job. He has also an unlimited supply of paper on which he does his calculations. . . . A digital computer can usually be regarded as consisting of three parts:

⑤ The comparison with a human being is inessential and seems rather odd nowadays. The main point is that the computer is supposed to follow clear, definite rules that say exactly what to do in every relevant situation, with no deviation whatsoever being allowed.

    (i) Store.
    (ii) Executive unit.
    (iii) Control.

The store is a store of information, and corresponds to the human computer's paper, whether this is the paper on which he does his calculations or that on which his book of rules is printed. Insofar as the human computer does calculations in his head a part of the store will correspond to his memory.

The executive unit is the part which carries out the various individual operations involved in a calculation. What these individual operations are will vary from machine to machine. Usually fairly lengthy operations can be done such as "Multiply 3540675445 by 7076345687" but in some machines only very simple ones such as "Write down 0" are possible.

We have mentioned that the "book of rules" supplied to the computer is replaced in the machine by a part of the store. It is then called the "table of instructions." It is the duty of the control to see that these instructions are obeyed correctly and in the right order. The control is so constructed that this necessarily happens.

The information in the store is usually broken up into packets of moderately small size. In one machine, for instance, a packet might consist of ten decimal digits. Numbers are assigned to the parts of the store in which the various packets of information are stored, in some systematic manner. A typical instruction might say—

"Add the number stored in position 6809 to that in 4302 and put the result back into the latter storage position."

. . . The control will normally take the instructions to be obeyed in the order of the positions in which they are stored, but occasionally an instruction such as

"Now obey the instruction stored in position 5606, and continue from there"

may be encountered, or again

"If position 4505 contains 0 obey next the instruction stored in 6707, otherwise continue straight on."

Instructions of these latter types are very important because they make it possible for a sequence of operations to be repeated over and over again until some condition is fulfilled, but in doing so to obey, not fresh instructions on each repetition, but the same ones over and over again.

. . .

The book of rules which we have described our human computer as using is of course a convenient fiction. Actual human computers really remember what they have got to do. If one wants to make a machine mimic the behavior of the human computer in some complex operation one has to ask him how it is done, and then translate the answer into the form of an instruction table. Constructing instruction tables is usually described as "programming." To "program a machine to carry out the operation A" means to put the appropriate instruction table into the machine so that it will do A.

An interesting variant on the idea of a digital computer is a "digital computer with a random element."

These have instructions involving the throwing of a die or some equivalent electronic process; one such instruction might for instance be, "Throw the die and put the resulting number into store 1000." Sometimes such a machine is described as having free will (though I would not use this phrase myself). It is not normally possible to determine from observing a machine whether it has a random element, for a similar effect can be produced by such devices as making the choices depend on the digits of the decimal for π.⑥

> ⑥ Containing such a random element is the only way that the computer could do two different things in exactly the same situation, thus making its behavior unpredictable in the way that human behavior often seems to be.

. . .

5. UNIVERSALITY OF DIGITAL COMPUTERS

The digital computers considered in the last section may be classified among the "discrete state machines." These are the machines which move by sudden jumps or clicks from one quite definite state to another. These states are sufficiently different for the possibility of confusion between them to be ignored. . . . As an example of a discrete state machine we might consider a wheel which clicks round through 120° once a second, but may be stopped by a lever which can be operated from outside; in addition a lamp is to light in one of the positions of the wheel. This machine could be described abstractly as follows: The internal state of the machine (which is described by the position of the wheel) may be q_1, q_2 or q_3. There is an input signal i_0 or i_1 (position of lever). The internal state at any moment is determined by the last state and input signal according to the table

		Last State		
		q_1	q_2	q_3
Input	i_0	q_2	q_3	q_1
	i_1	q_1	q_2	q_3

The output signals, the only externally visible indication of the internal state (the light) are described by the table.

State	q_1	q_2	q_3
Output	o_0	o_0	o_1

This example is typical of discrete state machines. They can be described by such tables provided they have only a finite number of possible states.⑦

. . .

Given the table corresponding to a discrete state machine it is possible to predict what it will do. There is no reason why this calculation should not be carried out by means of a digital computer. Provided it could be carried out sufficiently quickly the digital computer could mimic the behavior of any discrete state machine. The imitation game could then be played with the machine in question (as B) and the mimicking digital computer (as A) and the interrogator would be unable to distinguish them. Of course the digital computer must have an adequate storage capacity as well as working sufficiently fast. Moreover, it must be programmed afresh for each new machine which it is desired to mimic.⑧

> ⑦ Think carefully about this extremely simple example: what would be a verbal statement of the rules corresponding to the two inputs? The machine described doesn't do anything very useful, but it does illustrate the sort of rules that any computer will follow, with differences just being a matter of complexity. (The Coke machines described in the previous selection from Fodor are also discrete state machines.)

> ⑧ Think of a version of the imitation game that is played by the simple machine just described and by a computer. Suppose that the interrogator has terminals displaying the states of the machines, two buttons for each machine that send the two inputs (for the simple machine these would just control the lever), and a light for each. It would be very easy to program the computer so that it emulates the behavior of the simple machine.

This special property of digital computers, that they can mimic any discrete state machine, is described by saying that they are *universal* machines. The existence of machines with this property has the important consequence that, considerations of speed apart, it is unnecessary to design various new machines to do various computing processes. They can all be done with one digital computer, suitably programmed for each case. It will be seen that as a consequence of this all digital computers are in a sense equivalent.

We may now consider again the point raised at the end of §3. It was suggested tentatively that the question, "Can machines think?" should be replaced by "Are there imaginable digital computers which would do well in the imitation game?" If we wish we can make this superficially more general and ask "Are there discrete state machines which would do well?" But in view of the universality property we see that either of these questions is equivalent to this, "Let us fix our attention on one particular digital computer C. Is it true that by modifying this computer to have an adequate storage, suitably increasing its speed of action,

[9] This has come to be referred to as "the Turing Test" (see, for example, the Searle selection later in this section).

and providing it with an appropriate program, C can be made to play satisfactorily the part of A in the imitation game, the part of B being taken by a man?"[9]

6. CONTRARY VIEWS ON THE MAIN QUESTION

We may now consider the ground to have been cleared and we are ready to proceed to the debate on our question, "Can machines think?" and the variant of it quoted at the end of the last section. We cannot altogether abandon the original form of the problem, for opinions will differ as to the appropriateness of the substitution and we must at least listen to what has to be said in this connection.

It will simplify matters for the reader if I explain first my own beliefs in the matter. Consider first the more accurate form of the question. I believe that in about fifty years' time [that is, in about 2000] it will be possible to program computers, with a storage capacity of about 10^9, to make them play the imitation game so well that an average interrogator will not have more than 70 per cent chance of making the right identification after five minutes of questioning. The original question, "Can machines think?" I believe to be too meaningless to deserve discussion. Nevertheless I believe that at the end of the century the use of words and general educated opinion will have altered so much that one will be able to speak of machines thinking without expecting to be contradicted.[10] I believe further that no useful purpose is served by concealing these beliefs. The popular view that scientists proceed inexorably from well-established fact to well-established fact, never being influenced by any unproved conjecture, is quite mistaken. Provided it is made clear which are

proved facts and which are conjectures, no harm can result. Conjectures are of great importance since they suggest useful lines of research.

I now proceed to consider opinions opposed to my own.

(1) The Theological Objection. Thinking is a function of man's immortal soul. God has given an immortal soul to every man and woman, but not to any other animal or to machines. Hence no animal or machine can think.

I am unable to accept any part of this, but will attempt to reply in theological terms. . . . It appears to me that the argument quoted above implies a serious restriction of the omnipotence of the Almighty. It is admitted that there are certain things that He cannot do such as making one equal to two, but should we not believe that He has freedom to confer a soul on an elephant if He sees fit? We might expect that He would only exercise this power in conjunction with a mutation which provided the elephant with an appropriately improved brain to minister to the needs of this soul. An argument of exactly similar form may be made for the case of machines. It may seem different because it is more difficult to "swallow." But this really only means that we think it would be less likely that He would consider the circumstances suitable for conferring a soul. The circumstances in question are discussed in the rest of this paper. In attempting to construct such machines we should not be irreverently usurping His power of creating souls, any more than we are in the procreation of children: rather we are, in either case, instruments of His will providing mansions for the souls that He creates.[11]

[10] Notice that five minutes of questioning and only 30 percent success on the part of the computer amounts to a rather low standard, especially with respect to the time limitation. (If Turing meant that by 2000 everyone would agree that computers think in the very same sense that human beings do, do you think he was correct? Would you say that about your computer? See Discussion Question 1.)

[11] The suggestion is that if God is omnipotent, then he could give a soul to a computer. But would a computer with a soul still be a computer? (A dualist would say, of course, that if the resulting entity could think, the thinking would be done by the soul, not by the original computer. This may be mistaken, but talk about what God could do isn't really very relevant to the main issue.)

However, this is mere speculation. I am not very impressed with theological arguments whatever they may be used to support. Such arguments have often been found unsatisfactory in the past. In the time of Galileo it was argued that the texts, "And the sun stood still ... and hasted not to go down about a whole day" (Joshua x. 13) and "He laid the foundations of the earth, that it should not move at any time" (Psalm cv. 5) were an adequate refutation of the Copernican theory. With our present knowledge such an argument appears futile. When that knowledge was not available it made a quite different impression.

(2) The "Heads in the Sand" Objection. "The consequences of machines thinking would be too dreadful. Let us hope and believe that they cannot do so."⑫

⑫ Obviously this "objection" is no more than wishful thinking.

This argument is seldom expressed quite so openly as in the form above. But it affects most of us who think about it at all. We like to believe that Man is in some subtle way superior to the rest of creation. It is best if he can be shown to be *necessarily* superior, for then there is no danger of him losing his commanding position. The popularity of the theological argument is clearly connected with this feeling. It is likely to be quite strong in intellectual people, since they value the power of thinking more highly than others, and are more inclined to base their belief in the superiority of Man on this power.

I do not think that this argument is sufficiently substantial to require refutation. Consolation would be more appropriate: perhaps this should be sought in the transmigration of souls.

(3) The Mathematical Objection. There are a number of results of mathematical logic which can be used to show that there are limitations to the powers of discrete state machines. The best known of these results is known as Gödel's theorem, and shows that in any sufficiently powerful logical system statements can be formulated which can neither be proved nor disproved within the system, unless possibly the system itself is inconsistent. There are other, in some respects similar, results due to *Church, Kleene, Rosser,* and *Turing.* The latter result is the most convenient to consider, since it refers directly to machines, whereas the others can only be used in a comparatively indirect argument. . . . The result in question refers to a type of machine which is essentially a digital computer with an infinite capacity. It states that there are certain things that such a machine cannot do. If it is rigged up to give answers to questions as in the imitation game, there will be some questions to which it will either give a wrong answer, or fail to give an answer at all however much time is allowed for a reply. There may, of course, be many such questions, and questions which cannot be answered by one machine may be satisfactorily answered by another. We are of course supposing for the present that the questions are of the kind to which an answer "Yes" or "No" is appropriate, rather than questions such as "What do you think of Picasso?" The questions that we know the machines must fail on are of this type, "Consider the machine specified as follows. . . . Will this machine ever answer 'Yes' to any question?" The dots are to be replaced by a description of some machine in a standard form, which could be something like that used in Sec. 5. When the machine described bears a certain comparatively simple relation to the machine which is under interrogation, it can be shown that the answer is either wrong or not forthcoming. This is the mathematical result: it is argued that it proves a disability of machines to which the human intellect is not subject.⑬

⑬ The mathematical results that Turning is referring to are too complicated to explain here (though you might want to look them up). The crucial point is that it is possible to formulate questions that relate to the structure of a specific computer in such a way that this very computer will be either unable to answer them or will answer them wrongly.

The short answer to this argument is that although it is established that there are limitations to the powers of any particular machine, it has only been stated, without any sort of proof, that no such limitations apply to the human intellect. But I do not think this view can be dismissed quite so lightly. Whenever one of these machines is asked the appropriate critical question, and gives a definite answer, we know that this answer must be wrong, and this gives us a certain feeling of superiority. Is this feeling illusory? It is no doubt quite genuine, but I do not think too much importance should be attached to it. We too often give wrong answers to questions ourselves to be justified in being very pleased at such evidence of fallibility on the part of the machines. Further, our superiority can only be felt on such an occasion in relation to the one machine over which we have scored our petty triumph. There would be no question of triumphing simultaneously over *all* machines. In short, then, there might be men cleverer than any given machine, but then again there might be other machines cleverer again, and so on. [14]

- - -

(4)   The   Argument from Consciousness. This argument is very well expressed in Professor Jefferson's Lister Oration for 1949, from which I quote. "Not until a machine can write a sonnet or compose a concerto because of thoughts and emotions felt, and not by the chance fall of symbols, could we agree that machine equals brain—that is, not only write it but know that it had written it. No mechanism could feel (and not merely artificially signal, an easy contrivance) pleasure at its successes, grief when its valves fuse, be warmed by flattery, be made miserable by its mistakes, be charmed by sex, be angry or depressed when it cannot get what it wants."

This argument appears to be a denial of the validity of our test. According to the most extreme form of this view the only way by which one could be sure that a machine thinks is to be the machine and to feel oneself thinking. One could then describe these feelings to the world, but of course no one would be justified in taking any notice. Likewise according to this view the only way to know that a *man* thinks is to be that particular man. It is in fact the solipsist point of view. [15] It may be the most logical view to hold but it makes communication of ideas difficult. A is liable to believe "A thinks but B does not" while B believes "B thinks but A does not." Instead of arguing continually over this point it is usual to have the polite convention that everyone thinks.

I am sure that Professor Jefferson does not wish to adopt the extreme and solipsist point of view. Probably he would be quite willing to accept the imitation game as a test. The game (with the player B omitted) is frequently used in practice under the name of *viva voce* [16] to discover whether someone really understands something or has "learned it parrot fashion." Let us listen in to a part of such a *viva voce:*

> Interrogator: In the first line of your sonnet which reads "Shall I compare thee to a summer's day," would not "a spring day" do as well or better?
> Witness: It   wouldn't scan.
> Interrogator: How about "a winter's day." That would scan all right.
> Witness: Yes, but nobody wants to be compared to a winter's day.
> Interrogator: Would you say Mr. Pickwick reminded you of Christmas?
> Witness: In a way.
> Interrogator: Yet Christmas is a winter's day, and I do not think Mr. Pickwick would mind the comparison.
> Witness: I don't think you're serious. By a winter's day one means a typical winter's day, rather than a special one like Christmas.

And so on. What would Professor Jefferson say if the sonnet-writing machine was able to answer like this in the *viva voce?* I do not know whether he would regard the machine as "merely artificially signaling" these answers, but if the answers were as satisfactory and sustained as in the above passage I do not think he would describe it as "an easy contrivance." This phrase is, I think, intended to cover such devices as the inclusion in the machine of a record of someone reading a sonnet, with appropriate switching to turn it on from time to time.

In short then, I think that most of those who support the argument from consciousness could be

---

[14]   Human fallibility in general is not very relevant. The point is that while human beings can answer correctly the specific question that a given computer cannot, so can other computers. And the underlying issue is whether there are questions that a human being cannot answer correctly *for this specific sort of reason.* If it could be shown that such questions do not exist for humans, then this would show that human beings are fundamentally different from computers; but until this is done (and it is very hard to see how it could be), this objection has no real force.

---

[15]   Solipsism is the metaphysical view that the only thing that exists is the very mind considering the view. Turing's point is that someone who says that the only way to know that a computer can think is to be that computer will also have to say that the only way to know that a person thinks is to be that person—in which case he will be forced to conclude that other people, whose thought he does not experience, do not think either.

---

[16]   This literally means in a live voice, and refers to an oral examination (though obviously the computer is not supposed to actually give oral answers).

---

persuaded to abandon it rather than be forced into the solipsist position. They will then probably be willing to accept our test.[17]

[17] Turing's point is that being able to give answers of this sort, whether orally or in writing, would normally be taken to indicate thought and understanding. (Someone who denies this in general would have no good reason for thinking that anyone other than himself thinks and understands, thereby being committed to solipsism—presumably an absurd result.) So *if* a computer could give such answers, it seems to follow that there is as good a reason for ascribing thought and understanding to it as there is for other people. (See Discussion Question 2.)

I do not wish to give the impression that I think there is no mystery about consciousness. There is, for instance, something of a paradox connected with any attempt to localize it. But I do not think these mysteries necessarily need to be solved before we can answer the question with which we are concerned in this paper.

(5) Arguments from Various Disabilities. These arguments take the form, "I grant you that you can make machines do all the things you have mentioned but you will never be able to make one to do X." Numerous features X are suggested in this connection. I offer a selection:

> Be kind, resourceful, beautiful, friendly, have initiative, have a sense of humor, tell right from wrong, make mistakes, fall in love, enjoy strawberries and cream, make someone fall in love with it, learn from experience, use words properly, be the subject of its own thought, have as much diversity of behavior as a man, do something really new. . . .

No support is usually offered for these statements. I believe they are mostly founded on the principle of scientific induction. A man has seen thousands of machines in his lifetime. From what he sees of them he draws a number of general conclusions. They are ugly, each is designed for a very limited purpose, when required for a minutely different purpose they are useless, the variety of behavior of any one of them is very small, etc., etc. Naturally he concludes that these are necessary properties of machines in general.[18] Many of these limitations are associated with the very small storage capacity of most machines. . . . A few years ago, when very little had been heard of digital computers, it was possible to elicit much incredulity

concerning them, if one mentioned their properties without describing their construction. That was presumably due to a similar application of the principle of scientific induction. . . . The works and customs of mankind do not seem to be very suitable material to which to apply scientific induction. A very large part of space-time must be investigated if reliable results are to be obtained. Otherwise we may (as most English children do) decide that everybody speaks English, and that it is silly to learn French.

[18] This inductive argument would be one sort of reason for denying that computers can do the sorts of things in question, but is it the only reason or the best one? (If someone claimed that his computer is in love with him, would your only reason for skepticism be that the computers you are familiar with don't seem to be capable of love?)

. . .

The claim that "machines cannot make mistakes" seems a curious one. One is tempted to retort, "Are they any the worse for that?" But let us adopt a more sympathetic attitude, and try to see what is really meant. I think this criticism can be explained in terms of the imitation game. It is claimed that the interrogator could distinguish the machine from the man simply by setting them a number of problems in arithmetic. The machine would be unmasked because of its deadly accuracy. The reply to this is simple. The machine (programmed for playing the game) would not attempt to give the *right* answers to the arithmetic problems. It would deliberately introduce mistakes in a manner calculated to confuse the interrogator. . . .

The claim that a machine cannot be the subject of its own thought can of course only be answered if it can be shown that the machine has *some* thought with *some* subject matter. Nevertheless, "the subject matter of a machine's operations" does seem to mean something, at least to the people who deal with it. If, for instance, the machine was trying to find a solution of the equation $x^2 - 40_x - 11 = 0$ one would be tempted to describe this equation as part of the machine's subject matter at that moment. In this sort of sense a machine undoubtedly can be its own subject matter. It may be used to help in making up its own programs, or to predict the effect of alterations in its own structure. By observing the results of its own behavior it can modify its own programs so as to achieve some purpose more effectively. These are possibilities of the near future rather than Utopian dreams.[19]

[19] There is no doubt that computers can calculate results that are relevant to formulating programs or predicting their own behavior. But is a computer that does these things actually thinking about itself in the way that human beings think about themselves?

[20] This points to an important issue: even if the computer can do (or at least simulate doing) one of these things, does it do it *in the same way* as a human being does? And if not, does the fact that thought is involved in the human's doing that task in the specific way that he does it give any reason for thinking that thought is involved in the computer doing it in a quite different way? (See Discussion Question 3.)

. . .

The criticisms that we are considering here are often disguised forms of the argument from consciousness. Usually if one maintains that a machine *can* do one of these things, and describes the kind of method that the machine could use, one will not make much of an impression. It is thought that the method (whatever it may be, for it must be mechanical) is really rather base. . . . [20]

(6) Lady Lovelace's Objection. . . .

A variant of Lady Lovelace's objection states that a machine can "never do anything really new." This may be parried for a moment with the saw, "There is nothing new under the sun." Who can be certain that "original work" that he has done was not simply the growth of the seed planted in him by teaching, or the effect of following well-known general principles. A better variant of the objection says that a machine can never "take us by surprise." This statement is a more direct challenge and can be met directly. Machines take me by surprise with great frequency. This is largely because I do not do sufficient calculation to decide what to expect them to do, or rather because, although I do a calculation, I do it in a hurried, slipshod fashion, taking risks. Perhaps I say to myself, "I suppose the voltage here ought to be the same as there: anyway let's assume it is." Naturally I am often wrong, and the result is a surprise for me, for by the time the experiment is done these assumptions have been forgotten. These admissions lay me open to lectures on the subject of my vicious ways, but do not throw any doubt on my credibility when I testify to the surprises I experience.[21]

. . .

(8) The Argument from Informality of Behavior. It is not possible to produce a set of rules purporting to describe what a man should do in every conceivable set of circumstances. One might for instance have a rule that one is to stop when one sees a red traffic light, and to go if one sees a green one, but what if by some fault both appear together? One may perhaps decide that it is safest to stop. But some further difficulty may well arise from this decision later. To attempt to provide rules of conduct to cover every eventuality, even those arising from traffic lights, appears to be impossible. With all this I agree.

From this it is argued that we cannot be machines. I shall try to reproduce the argument, but I fear I shall hardly do it justice. It seems to run something like this. "If each man had a definite set of rules of conduct by which he regulated his life he would be no better than a machine. But there are no such rules, so men cannot be machines." The undistributed middle is glaring.[22] I do not think the argument is ever put quite like this, but I believe this is the argument used nevertheless. There may however be a certain confusion between "rules of conduct" and "laws of behavior" to cloud the issue. By "rules of conduct" I mean precepts such as "Stop if you see red lights," on which one can act, and of which one can be conscious. By "laws of behavior" I mean laws of nature as applied to man's body such as "if you pinch him he will squeak." . . . However, we cannot so easily convince ourselves of the absence of complete laws of behavior as of complete rules of conduct. The only way we know of for

[21] Obviously computers often surprise us, especially when we operate them in careless or sloppy ways. The issue that Lady Lovelace seems to be getting at is whether everything they do is in principle predictable, and the answer seems to be "yes"—unless the computer involves a random element like that described in the passage corresponding to Annotation 6. But do we have any very strong reason for thinking that human behavior isn't in principle predictable in the same way?

[22] By speaking of an "undistributed middle" (a bit of logical jargon not worth explaining here), Turing is pointing out that the argument given is fallacious. Compare: if it is raining, then the streets are wet; it is not raining; therefore, the streets are not wet (and imagine that a fire hydrant has been turned on and is spraying the vicinity).

finding such laws is scientific observation, and we certainly know of no circumstances under which we could say, "We have searched enough. There are no such laws."[23]

[23] The point is that we need not be aware of "laws of behavior" in order to in fact be following them. Since they might be very complicated, we can never be sure we have looked long enough.

. . .

7. LEARNING MACHINES

The reader will have anticipated that I have no very convincing arguments of a positive nature to support my views. If I had I should not have taken such pains to point out the fallacies in contrary views. Such evidence as I have I shall now give.

. . .

The only really satisfactory support that can be given for the view expressed at the beginning of Sec. 6, will be that provided by waiting for the end of the century and then doing the experiment described. But what can we say in the meantime? What steps should be taken now if the experiment is to be successful?

As I have explained, the problem is mainly one of programming. Advances in engineering will have to be made too, but it seems unlikely that these will not be adequate for the requirements. Estimates of the storage capacity of the brain vary from 10^{10} to 10^{15} binary digits. I incline to the lower values and believe that only a very small fraction is used for the higher types of thinking. Most of it is probably used for the retention of visual impressions. I should be surprised if more than 10^9 was required for satisfactory playing of the imitation game, at any rate against a blind man. (Note: The capacity of the *Encyclopedia Britannica,* eleventh edition, is 2×10^9.) A storage capacity of 10^7 would be a very practicable possibility even by present techniques. It is probably not necessary to increase the speed of operations of the machines at all. Parts of modern machines which can be regarded as analogues of nerve cells work about a thousand times faster than the latter. This should provide a "margin of safety" which could cover losses of speed arising in many ways. Our problem then is to find out how to program these machines to play the game. . . .

In the process of trying to imitate an adult human mind we are bound to think a good deal about the process which has brought it to the state that it is in. We may notice three components,

a. The initial state of the mind, say at birth,

b. The education to which it has been subjected,

c. Other experience, not to be described as education, to which it has been subjected.

Instead of trying to produce a program to simulate the adult mind, why not rather try to produce one which simulates the child's? If this were then subjected to an appropriate course of education one would obtain the adult brain. Presumably the child-brain is something like a notebook as one buys it from the stationers. Rather little mechanism, and lots of blank sheets. (Mechanism and writing are from our point of view almost synonymous.) Our hope is that there is so little mechanism in the child-brain that something like it can be easily programmed. The amount of work in the education we can assume, as a first approximation, to be much the same as for the human child.

. . .

It will not be possible to apply exactly the same teaching process to the machine as to a normal child. It will not, for instance, be provided with legs, so that it could not be asked to go out and fill the coal scuttle. Possibly it might not have eyes. But however well these deficiencies might be overcome by clever engineering, one could not send the creature to school without the other children making excessive fun of it. It must be given some tuition. We need not be too concerned about the legs, eyes, etc. The example of Miss Helen Keller shows that education can take place provided that communication in both directions between teacher and pupil can take place by some means or other.

We normally associate punishments and rewards with the teaching process. Some simple child-machines can be constructed or programmed on this sort of principle. The machine has to be so constructed that events which shortly preceded the occurrence of a punishment-signal are unlikely to be repeated, whereas a reward-signal increases the probability of repetition of the events which led up to it. These definitions do not presuppose any feelings on the part of the machine. . . . [24]

[24] Of course, computers do not really experience "punishments" as punishments. But a machine could be constructed whose program was such that it tended to repeat actions that elicited a designated "reward" input and not to repeat actions that elicited a different "punishment" input—with some of the relevant actions perhaps being determined by a random component. This would simulate learning, but would any real learning or understanding or thought be involved?

The use of punishments and rewards can at best be a part of the teaching process. . . . It is necessary therefore to have some other "unemotional" channels of communication. If these are available it is possible to teach a machine by punishments and rewards to obey orders given in some language, e.g., a symbolic language. These orders are to be transmitted through the "unemotional" channels. The use of this language will greatly diminish the number of punishments and rewards required.

. . .

An important feature of a learning machine is that its teacher will often be very largely ignorant of quite what is going on inside, although he may still be able to some extent to predict his pupil's behavior. This should apply most strongly to the later education of a machine arising from a child-machine of well-tried design (or program). This is in clear contrast with normal procedure when using a machine to do computations: one's object is then to have a clear mental picture of the state of the machine at each moment in the computation. This object can only be achieved with a struggle. The view that "the machine can only do what we know how to order it to do," appears strange in face of this. Most of the programs which we can put into the machine will result in its doing something that we cannot make sense of at all, or which we regard as completely random behavior. Intelligent behavior presumably consists in a departure from the completely disciplined behavior involved in computation, but a rather slight one, which does not give rise to random behavior, or to pointless repetitive loops. Another important result of preparing our machine for its part in the imitation game by a process of teaching and learning is that "human fallibility" is likely to be omitted in

a rather natural way, i.e., without special "coaching." Processes that are learned do not produce a hundred per cent certainty of result; if they did they could not be unlearned.

It is probably wise to include a random element in a learning machine. A random element is rather useful when we are searching for a solution of some problem. Suppose for instance we wanted to find a number between 50 and 200 which was equal to the square of the sum of its digits, we might start at 51 then try 52 and go on until we got a number that worked. Alternatively we might choose numbers at random until we got a good one. This method has the advantage that it is unnecessary to keep track of the values that have been tried, but the disadvantage that one may try the same one twice, but this is not very important if there are several solutions. The systematic method has the disadvantage that there may be an enormous block without any solutions in the region which has to be investigated first. Now the learning process may be regarded as a search for a form of behavior which will satisfy the teacher (or some other criterion). Since there is probably a very large number of satisfactory solutions the random method seems to be better than the systematic. It should be noticed that it is used in the analogous process of evolution. But there the systematic method is not possible. How could one keep track of the different genetical combinations that had been tried, so as to avoid trying them again?

We may hope that machines will eventually compete with men in all purely intellectual fields. But which are the best ones to start with? Even this is a difficult decision. Many people think that a very abstract activity, like the playing of chess, would be best. [25] It can also be maintained that it is best to provide the machine with the best sense organs that money can buy, and then teach it to understand and speak English. This process could follow the normal teaching of a child.

[25] A lot of work has been done on chess-playing machines. See Discussion Question 3.

Things would be pointed out and named, etc. Again I do not know what the right answer is, but I think both approaches should be tried.

We can only see a short distance ahead, but we can see plenty there that needs to be done.

Discussion Questions

1. Do you think that your computer (or the one you use in the library or a computer lab) actually thinks in the same sense that you do? When, for example, you play a game on it (perhaps with the computer as your opponent), is it in any way aware of what is going on? Or is it just a calculating machine? Suppose that the program for a computer game includes instructions that generate statements from the computer about how much it hates losing or gloating when it defeats you—does that give you any more reason to suppose that it is genuinely thinking? Perhaps most importantly, is there any good reason to think that computers are *conscious?*

2. Does the ability to simulate an apparently intelligent pattern of answers in response to questions provide a good reason for believing that a computer understands the questions and answers and so is thinking? Suppose that an encyclopedia program is able to answer questions and even to answer follow-up questions. Would that show that it is thinking, or might it be just a matter of mechanical information retrieval with no thought or understanding on the part of the computer? Is there some level of performance on such tasks that would make it much more reasonable to suppose that the computer is thinking than that it is merely operating mechanically, and if so, how might that level be specified?

3. Chess-playing programs have achieved a very high level of sophistication: they can easily defeat the average human player and can do very well even against the best human chess players in the world. Is this a good reason for thinking that a computer running such a program is thinking? One thing that seems to be true is that the computer program determines its moves in a very different way from human players, namely by calculating the results of very long strings of alternative moves in a way that no human is capable of. Suppose that in a given chess position, a human and a computer come up with the same excellent move. The human clearly does so by thinking about the position, thinking ahead for several moves but also employing general strategic ideas. The computer merely calculates all the possibilities for many more moves ahead than the human is capable of. Does the fact that it achieves the same result that the human achieves by thinking, but in this very different way, yield any strong reason for believing that the computer is thinking too? Why or why not?

4. Think about contemporary movies in which the issue of whether computers can think is either addressed or assumed. For example, in a movie called *Blade Runner,* there is a robot who acts as if "she" is a human. The film portrays her as "believing" that she is a human; she has been programmed with "memories" of a childhood and has pictures that purport to show her playing when she was a child. But she was never a child, since she was built as a full grown "woman": she has "skin," and she "bleeds" when cut (though her "blood" is presumably not chemically the same as human blood). She can move and talk and would clearly pass the Turing Test. She fools everyone in the movie (the character played by Harrison Ford even falls in love with her!). Assuming that such a case is really possible, what has to be true of this being in order for it to be true that she thinks? Must there be real consciousness involved, or is the mere behavior enough? If the simulation is good enough, would there be any way to tell what was really going on? Or is the fact that she might be behaviorally indiscernible from an actual human being enough by itself to show that she thinks and is conscious—which is essentially Turing's claim?

John R. Searle

John Searle (1932–) is an American philosopher who teaches at the University of California at Berkeley. Most of his work has focused on questions in the philosophy of mind, but he has also made important contributions to the philosophy of language and the philosophy of the social sciences.

Searle is perhaps most famous for his provocative thought experiment called "the Chinese Room." In this article, he uses the Chinese Room thought experiment to argue against a view that he calls Strong AI (**artificial intelligence**). While he never mentions functionalism explicitly, functionalism is in fact the philosophy of mind that underlies and supports strong AI. While Searle is still convinced that this thought experiment provides a compelling objection to the view that mental states can be entirely understood in terms of functional role, not everyone agrees: there has continued to be a lively debate about this thought experiment ever since Searle first published it in 1980. In this article, Searle also presents a positive alternative to functionalism: a view, still a version of materialism, according to which mental states are biological or neurobiological in character.

Is the Brain's Mind a Computer Program?

Can a machine think? Can a machine have conscious thoughts in exactly the same sense that you and I have? If by "machine" one means a physical system capable of performing certain functions (and what else can one mean?), then humans are machines of a special biological kind, and humans can think, and so of course machines can think.[1] And, for all we know, it might be possible to produce a thinking machine out of different materials altogether—say, out of silicon chips or vacuum tubes. Maybe it will turn out to be impossible, but we certainly do not know that yet.

In recent decades, however, the question of whether a machine can think has been given a different interpretation entirely. The question that has been posed in its place is, Could a machine think just by virtue of implementing a computer program? Is the program by itself constitutive of thinking?[2] This is a completely different question because it is not about the physical, causal properties of actual or possible physical systems but rather about the abstract, computational properties of formal computer programs that can be implemented in any sort of substance at all provided only that the substance is able to carry the program.

A fair number of researchers in artificial intelligence (AI) believe the answer to the second question is yes; that is, they believe that by designing the right programs with the right inputs and outputs, they are literally creating minds. They believe furthermore that they have a scientific test for determining success or failure: the Turing test devised by Alan M. Turing, the founding father of artificial intelligence. The Turing test, as currently understood, is simply this: If a computer can perform in such a way that an expert cannot distinguish its performance from that of a human who has a certain cognitive ability—say, the ability to do addition or to understand Chinese—then the computer also has that ability.[3] So the goal is to design programs that will

[1] This is of course not the ordinary notion of a "machine" and not the one that Searle is mainly interested in. Note also that he rejects dualism from the outset, though he offers no real argument against it here.

[2] If the program were *constitutive* of thinking, then simply running that program would, by itself, be logically sufficient for thinking (in the same way that being an unmarried adult male is logically sufficient for being a bachelor).

[3] Think carefully about this application of the Turing Test: a computer has a certain ability just in case an expert cannot tell on the basis of its responses to inputs that it is *not* a human exercising that very ability. (Clearly this would not be a good test if the time period involved were very short— say the 5 minutes specified by Turing. To make such a claim plausible, the requirement has to be that the difference between a human and the computer cannot be discerned even in an unlimited amount of time.)

From Scientific American, *Vol. 262, January, 1990.*

simulate human cognition in such a way as to pass the Turing test. What is more, such a program would not merely be a model of the mind: it would literally be a mind, in the same sense that a human mind is a mind.

By no means does every worker in artificial intelligence accept so extreme a view. A more cautious approach is to think of computer models as being useful in studying the mind in the same way that they are useful in studying the weather, economics or molecular biology. To distinguish these two approaches, I call the first strong AI and the second weak AI. It is important to see just how bold an approach strong AI is.

⸤4⸥ As Searle will make clear later, he means by "formal symbols" symbols with no *meaning* that plays any role in the computer's manipulation of them. (The earlier selection from Fodor expresses a view very similar to the one ascribed here to strong AI.)

Strong AI claims that thinking is merely the manipulation of formal symbols and that is exactly what the computer does: manipulate formal symbols. This view is often summarized by saying, "The mind is to the brain as the program is to the hardware."⸤4⸥

Strong AI is unusual among theories of the mind in at least two respects: it can be stated clearly, and it admits of a simple and decisive refutation. The refutation is one that any person can try for himself or her self. Here is how it goes. Consider a language you don't understand. In my case, I do not understand Chinese. To me Chinese writing looks like so many meaningless squiggles. Now suppose I am placed in a room containing baskets full of Chinese symbols. Suppose also that I am given a rule book in English for matching Chinese symbols with other Chinese symbols. The rules identify the symbols entirely by their shapes and do not require that I understand any of them.⸤5⸥ The rules might say such things as, "Take a squiggle-squiggle sign from basket number one and put it next to a squoggle-squoggle sign from basket number two."

⸤5⸥ If the rules identify the symbols by their shape (and order), then obviously the person in the room need not understand the meanings of the symbols in order to follow the rules.

Imagine that people outside the room who understand Chinese hand in small bunches of symbols and that in response I manipulate the symbols according to the rule book and hand back more small bunches of symbols. Now, the rule book is the "computer program." The people who wrote it are "programmers," and I am the "computer." The baskets full of symbols are the "data base," the small bunches that are handed in to me are "questions" and the bunches I then hand out are "answers."

Now suppose that the rule book is written in such a way that my "answers" to the "questions" are indistinguishable from those of a native Chinese speaker. For example, the people outside might hand me some symbols that unknown to me mean, "What's your favorite color?" and I might after going through the rules give back symbols that, also unknown to me, mean, "My favorite is blue, but I also like green a lot." I satisfy the Turing test for understanding Chinese.⸤6⸥ All the same, I am totally ignorant of Chinese. And there is no way I could come to understand Chinese in the system as described, since there is no way that I can learn the meanings of any of the symbols. Like a computer, I manipulate symbols, but I attach no meaning to the symbols.

⸤6⸥ In order to satisfy the requirements of strong AI for understanding Chinese, the person following these rules would have to be able to produce answers indiscernible from those of a native speaker of Chinese for an essentially unlimited group of questions of this sort. Obviously if this is so, then he will satisfy the Turing Test. (But again a relatively short version of the Turing Test might be passed by a person running a program that isn't fully adequate in this way: one that satisfactorily answers the questions that are in fact asked, but would not do so for other questions that don't happen to be asked in the time in question.) See Discussion Question 1.

The point of the thought experiment is this: If I do not understand Chinese solely on the basis of running a computer program for understanding Chinese, then neither does any other digital computer solely on that basis. Digital computers merely manipulate formal symbols according to rules in the program.

What goes for Chinese goes for other forms of cognition as well.⸤7⸥ Just manipulating the symbols is not by itself enough to guarantee cognition, perception, understanding, think-

⸤7⸥ By "cognition," Searle means thinking of any sort.

ing and so forth. And since computers, qua computers, are symbol-manipulating devices, merely naming the computer program is not enough to guarantee cognition.

This simple argument is decisive against the claims of strong AI. The first premise of the argument simply states the formal character of a computer program. Programs are defined in terms of symbol manipulations, and the symbols are purely formal, or "syntactic." The formal character of the program by the way, is what makes computers so powerful. The same program can be run on an indefinite variety of hardwares, and one hardware system can run an indefinite range of computer programs. Let me abbreviate this "axiom" as:

Axiom 1. *Computer programs are formal (syntactic).*

This point is so crucial that it is worth explaining in more detail. A digital computer processes information by first encoding it in the symbolism that the computer uses and then manipulating the symbols through a set of precisely stated rules. These rules constitute the program. For example, in Turing's early theory of computers, the symbols were simply 0's and 1's, and the rules of the program said such things as. "Print a 0 on the tape, move one square to the left and erase a 1." The astonishing thing about computers is that any information that can be stated in a language can be encoded in such a system and any information-processing task that can be solved by explicit rules can be programmed.⑧

⑧ See Fodor's discussion of a Turing machine in the earlier selection. It can be proved rigorously that anything that any computer can do can be done by a Turing machine with a sufficiently complicated program.

Two further points are important. First, symbols and programs are purely abstract notions: they have no essential physical properties to define them and can be implemented in any physical medium whatsoever. The 0's and 1's, qua symbols, have no essential physical properties and a fortiori have no physical, causal properties. I emphasize this point because it is tempting to identify computers with some specific technology—say, silicon chips—and to think that the issues are about the physics of silicon chips or to think that syntax identifies some physical phenomenon that might have as yet unknown causal powers, in the way that actual physical phenomena such as electromagnetic radiation or hydrogen atoms have physical, causal properties. The second point is that symbols are manipulated without reference to any meanings. The symbols of the program can stand for anything the programmer or user wants. In this sense the program has syntax but no semantics.⑨

⑨ The sense in which a program has **syntax** but no **semantics** is just that (as we have seen) the rules of the program make no reference to the *meanings* of the symbols (whether or not they have any), but only to their syntactical features: shape, order, and the like.

The next axiom is just a reminder of the obvious fact that thoughts, perceptions, understandings and so forth have a mental content. By virtue of their content they can be about objects and states of affairs in the world. If the content involves language, there will be syntax in addition to semantics, but linguistic understanding requires at least a semantic framework. If, for example, I am thinking about the last presidential election, certain words will go through my mind but the words are about the election only because I attach specific meanings to these words, in accordance with my knowledge of English. In this respect they are unlike Chinese symbols for me.⑩ Let me abbreviate this axiom as:

⑩ When we think, the process of thinking seems at least to fundamentally depend on the *meanings* or *contents* of our thoughts. We seem to understand what we are thinking about and to reason accordingly, rather than just manipulating symbols with no reference to their meanings. (See Discussion Question 2.)

Axiom 2. *Human minds have mental contents (semantics).*

Now let me add the point that the Chinese room demonstrated. Having the symbols by themselves—just having the syntax—is not sufficient for having the semantics. Merely manipulating symbols is not enough to guarantee knowledge of what they mean. I shall abbreviate this as:

Axiom 3. *Syntax by itself is neither constitutive of nor sufficient for semantics.*

At one level this principle is true by definition. One might, of course, define the terms syntax and semantics differently. The point is that there is a distinction between formal elements, which have no intrinsic meaning or content, and those phenomena that have intrinsic content.⟦11⟧ From these premises it follows that:

⟦11⟧ Something has *intrinsic* content if it has that content strictly because of features of the thing itself and not because of any relations or external connections it has with other things. Searle is suggesting that thoughts have intrinsic content in this way (though Fodor would deny this). But the essential point for the moment is that the syntactical features that a computer program relies on are independent of any sort of content. (See Discussion Question 3.)

⟦12⟧ Contrary to what Searle says here, it isn't at all obvious that anything that can be simulated computationally can be correctly described as a computer. (He later suggests that a stomach digesting pizza can be thus simulated, but it would be extremely odd to say that such a stomach is a computer.) But the main point here is that merely manipulating symbols in the way that an ordinary computer does is not enough for thinking.

⟦13⟧ Searle hasn't mentioned consciousness explicitly so far. But in fact the reason that it seems so obvious that the person in the Chinese room doesn't understand Chinese is that there seems to be no consciousness of the meanings of the Chinese characters present.

Conclusion 1. *Programs are neither constitutive of nor sufficient for minds.*

And that is just another way of saying that strong AI is false.

It is important to see what is proved and not proved by this argument.

First, I have not tried to prove that "a computer cannot think," since anything that can be simulated computationally can be described as a computer, and since our brains can at some levels be simulated, it follows trivially that our brains are computers and they can certainly think.⟦12⟧ But from the fact that a system can be simulated by symbol manipulation and the fact that it is thinking, it does not follow that thinking is equivalent to formal symbol manipulation.

Second, I have not tried to show that only biologically based systems like our brains can think. Right now those are the only systems we know for a fact can think, but we might find other systems in the universe that can produce conscious thoughts, and we might even come to be able to create thinking systems artificially.⟦13⟧ I regard this issue as up for grabs.

Third, strong AI's thesis is not that, for all we know, computers with the right programs might be thinking, that they might have some as yet undetected psychological properties; rather it is that they must be thinking because that is all there is to thinking.

Fourth, I have tried to refute strong AI so defined. I have tried to demonstrate that the program by itself is not constitutive of thinking because the program is purely a matter of formal symbol manipulation—and we know independently that symbol manipulations by themselves are not sufficient to guarantee the presence of meanings.⟦14⟧ That is the principle on which the Chinese room argument works.

⟦14⟧ And, as we have already seen, meaning (or content) appears to be essential to thinking as we ordinarily understand it.

. . .

. . . the Chinese room argument also refutes any strong AI claims made for the new parallel technologies that are inspired by and modeled on neural networks. Unlike the traditional von Neumann computer, which proceeds in a step-by-step fashion, these systems have many computational elements that operate in parallel and interact with one another according to rules inspired by neurobiology. Although the results are still modest, these "parallel distributed processing," or "connectionist" models raise useful questions about how complex, parallel network systems like those in brains might actually function in the production of intelligent behavior.

The parallel "brainlike" character of the processing, however, is irrelevant to the purely computational aspects of the process.⟦15⟧ Any function that can be computed on a parallel machine can also be computed on a serial machine. Indeed, because parallel machines are still rare, connectionist programs are usually run on traditional serial machines.

⟦15⟧ Even parallel processing still relies on manipulating formal symbols according to syntactical rules, and therefore does not involve or rely on meaning. The syntactical rules are more complex, but they are still merely syntactical.

Parallel processing, then, does not afford a way around the Chinese room argument.

What is more, the connectionist system is subject even on its own terms to a variant of the objection presented by the original Chinese room argument. Imagine that instead of a Chinese room, I have a Chinese gym: a hall containing many monolingual English-speaking men. These men would carry out the same operations as the nodes and synapses in a connectionist architecture . . . , and the outcome would be the same as having one man manipulate symbols according to a rule book. No one in the gym speaks a word of Chinese, and there is no way for the system as a whole to learn the meanings of any Chinese words. Yet with appropriate adjustments, the system could give the correct answers to Chinese questions. [16]

There are, as I suggested earlier, interesting properties of connectionist nets that enable them to simulate brain processes more accurately than traditional serial architecture does. But the advantages of parallel architecture for weak AI are quite irrelevant to the issues between the Chinese room argument and strong AI.

. . .

Many people who are impressed by this argument are nonetheless puzzled about the differences between people and computers. If humans are, at least in a trivial sense, computers, and if humans have a semantics, then why couldn't we give semantics to other computers? Why couldn't we program a Vax or a Cray so that it too would have thoughts and feelings? Or why couldn't some new computer technology overcome the gulf between form and content, between syntax and semantics? What, in fact, are the differences between animal brains and computer systems that enable the Chinese room argument to work against computers but not against brains? [17]

The most obvious difference is that the processes that define something as a computer—computational processes—are completely independent of any reference to a specific type of hardware implementation.

[16] The idea is that each person in the gym receives input symbols, both from outside and from other people in the gym, and then proceeds to follow his own set of rules about what symbols to supply as output, again both to the outside and to others in the gym. (One could just as well have many Chinese rooms with appropriate connections between them along which symbols can pass.)

[17] Here Searle assumes that it is the brain that thinks (and hence once again that dualism is false). Given this assumption, the question is then how and why the brain is able to do this, while computers relying on formal manipulation of symbols are not: what the brain has that such computers lack.

One could in principle make a computer out of old beer cans strung together with wires and powered by windmills.

But when it comes to brains, although science is largely ignorant of how brains function to produce mental states, one is struck by the extreme specificity of the anatomy and the physiology. Where some understanding exists of how brain processes produce mental phenomena—for example, pain, thirst, vision, smell—it is clear that specific neurobiological processes are involved. Thirst, at least of certain kinds, is caused by certain types of neuron firings in the hypothalamus, which in turn are caused by the action of a specific peptide, angiotensin II. The causation is from the "bottom up" in the sense that lower-level neuronal processes cause higher-level mental phenomena. Indeed, as far as we know, every "mental" event, ranging from feelings of thirst to thoughts of mathematical theorems and memories of childhood, is caused by specific neurons firing in specific neural architectures. [18]

[18] Searle's view is that mental states are "higher-level" properties of the brain that are produced by "lower-level" properties like neuron firings. Elsewhere he offers as an analogy the liquidity of a substance (such as water): just as liquidity is a higher-order property that is caused by the properties of the molecules that make up the substance, so also mental properties are higher-level properties that are caused by the lower-level, "neurobiological" properties of the brain.

But why should this specificity matter? After all, neuron firings could be simulated on computers that had a completely different physics and chemistry from that of the brain. The answer is that the brain does not merely instantiate a formal pattern or program (it does that, too), but it also *causes* mental events by virtue of specific neurobiological processes. Brains are specific biological organs, and their specific biochemical properties enable them to cause consciousness and other sorts of mental phenomena. Computer simulations of brain processes provide models of the formal aspects of these processes. But the simulation should not be confused with duplication. The computational model of mental processes is no more real than the computational model of any other natural phenomenon.

One can imagine a computer simulation of the action of peptides in the hypothalamus that is accurate down to the last synapse. But equally one can imagine a computer simulation of the oxidation of hydrocarbons in a car engine or the action of digestive processes in a stomach when it is digesting pizza. And the simulation is no more the real thing in the case of the brain than it is in the case of the car or the stomach. Barring miracles, you could not run your car by doing a computer simulation of the oxidation of gasoline, and you could not digest pizza by running the program that simulates such digestion. It seems obvious that a simulation of cognition will similarly not produce the effects of the neurobiology of cognition.[19]

[19] As these examples make clear, the simulation of a certain sort of process is not to be identified with the process itself.

All mental phenomena, then, are caused by neurophysiological processes in the brain. Hence,

[20] The statement that brains cause minds is highly misleading, since it makes it sound as though the mind is a separate entity from the brain, and this is not Searle's view. Rather, as we have seen, the idea is that specific neurobiological processes in the brain cause particular mental events. But Searle has really offered no clear reason for this view. How plausible is it? (See Discussion Question 4.)

Axiom   4.   *Brains cause minds.* [20]

In conjunction with my earlier derivation, I immediately derive, trivially,

Conclusion 2. *Any other system capable of causing minds would have to have causal power (at least) equivalent to those of brains.*

This is like saying that if an electrical engine is to be able to run a car as fast as a gas engine, it must have (at least) an equivalent power output. This conclusion says nothing about the mechanisms. As a matter of fact cognition is a biological phenomenon: mental states and processes are caused by brain processes. This does not imply that only a biological system could think but it does imply that any alternative system, whether made of silicon, beer cans or whatever, would have to have the relevant causal capacities equivalent to those of brains. So now I can derive:

Conclusion 3. *Any artifact that produced mental phenomena, any artificial brain, would have to be able to duplicate the specific causal powers of brains, and it could not do that just by running a formal program.* [21]

Furthermore. I can derive an important conclusion about human brains:

Conclusion 4. *The way that human brains actually produce mental phenomena cannot be solely by virtue of running a computer program.*

I first presented the Chinese room parable in the pages of *Behavioral and Brain Sciences* in 1980, where it appeared, as is the practice of the journal along with peer commentary, in this case, 26 commentaries. Frankly, I think the point it makes is rather obvious, but to my surprise the publication was followed by a further flood of objections that—more surprisingly—continues to the present day. The Chinese room argument clearly touched some sensitive nerve.

The thesis of strong AI is that any system whatsoever—whether it is made of beer cans, silicon chips or toilet paper—not only might have thoughts and feelings but *must* have thoughts and feelings, provided only that it implements the right program, with the right inputs and outputs. Now, that is a profoundly antibiological view, and one would think that people in AI would be glad to abandon it. Many of them, especially the younger generation, agree with me, but I am amazed at the number and vehemence of the defenders. Here are some of the common objections.[22]

[21] *If* Searle is right that mental states are biological phenomena, produced by specific properties of the brain, then he is right that only something with those same causal powers could produce such states. And if this is right, then the functionalist view that being a mental state involves only running the right program (having the right software) and not any specific hardware is mistaken.

[22] Think carefully about these objections. Many of them may seem sufficiently implausible as to not require much of an answer, but still try to spell out what the answer would be for a, b, d, and e, since those are not discussed further in this selection or the ones that follow. (See Discussion Question 5.) Objection g, as Searle says later, has already been answered, but be sure you see clearly what his answer to it is.

a. In the Chinese room you really do understand Chinese, even though you don't know it. It is, after all, possible to understand something without knowing that one understands it.
b. You don't understand Chinese, but there is an (unconscious) subsystem in you that does. It

is, after all, possible to have unconscious mental states, and there is no reason why your understanding of Chinese should not be wholly unconscious.

c. You don't understand Chinese, but the whole room does. You are like a single neuron in the brain, and just as such a single neuron by itself cannot understand but only contributes to the understanding of the whole system you don't understand, but the whole system does.

d. Semantics doesn't exist anyway; there is only syntax. It is a kind of prescientific illusion to suppose that there exist in the brain some mysterious "mental contents," "thought processes" or "semantics." All that exists in the brain is the same sort of syntactic symbol manipulation that goes on in computers. Nothing more.

e. You are not really running the computer program—you only think you are. Once you have a conscious agent going through the steps of the program, it ceases to be a case of implementing a program at all.

f. Computers would have semantics and not just syntax if their inputs and outputs were put in appropriate causal relation to the rest of the world. Imagine that we put the computer into a robot, attached television cameras to the robot's head, installed transducers connecting the television messages to the computer and had the computer output operate the robot's arms and legs. Then the whole system would have a semantics. [23]

23 The suggestion here is that a mental symbol comes to be meaningful or have a specific content by standing in a causal relation of the right sort to something, normally something outside the person. Thus for example, a mental symbol would come to mean *dog* (or have the content *dog*) by standing in the right sort of causal relation to dogs. Fodor elaborates this objection in the next selection.

g. If the program simulated the operation of the brain of a Chinese speaker, then it would understand Chinese. Suppose that we simulated the brain of a Chinese person at the level of neurons. Then surely such a system would understand Chinese as well as any Chinese person's brain.

And so on.

All of these arguments share a common feature: they are all inadequate because they fail to come to grips with the actual Chinese room argument. That argument rests on the distinction between the formal symbol manipulation that is done by the computer and the mental contents biologically produced by the brain, a distinction I have abbreviated—I hope not misleadingly—as the distinction between syntax and semantics. I will not repeat my answers to all of these objections, but it will help to clarify the issues if I explain the weaknesses of the most widely held objection, argument c—what I call the systems reply. (The brain simulator reply, argument g, is another popular one, but I have already addressed that one in the previous section.)

The systems reply asserts that of course *you* don't understand Chinese but the whole system—you, the room, the rule book, the bushel baskets full of symbols—does. When I first heard this explanation, I asked one of its proponents, "Do you mean the room understands Chinese?" His answer was yes. It is a daring move, but aside from its implausibility, it will not work on purely logical grounds. The point of the original argument was that symbol shuffling by itself does not give any access to the meanings of the symbols. But this is as much true of the whole room as it is of the person inside. One can see this point by extending the thought experiment. Imagine that I memorize the contents of the baskets and the rule book, and I do all the calculations in my head. You can even imagine that I work out in the open. There is nothing in the "system" that is not in me, and since I don't understand Chinese, neither does the system. [24]

24 Another way to put the point is to say that understanding Chinese involves being conscious of the appropriate meanings, and there is no reason at all for thinking that such a consciousness somehow exists in the room, apart from the consciousness of the symbol manipulator.

. . .

Because the points I have been making are rather obvious—syntax is not the same as semantics, brain processes cause mental phenomena—the question arises, How did we get into this mess? How could anyone have supposed that a computer simulation of a mental process must be the real thing? After all, the whole point of models is that they contain only certain features of the modeled domain and leave out the rest. No one expects to get wet in a pool filled with ping-pong-ball models of water molecules. So why would anyone think a computer model of thought processes would actually think?

Part of the answer is that people have inherited a residue of behaviorist psychological theories of the past generation. The Turing test enshrines the temptation to think that if something behaves as if it had certain mental processes, then it must actually have those mental processes. And this is part of the behaviorists' mistaken assumption that in order to be scientific, psychology must confine its study to externally observable behavior. Paradoxically, this residual behaviorism is tied to a residual dualism. Nobody thinks that a computer simulation of digestion would actually digest anything, but where cognition is concerned, people are willing to believe in such a miracle because they fail to recognize that the mind is just as much a biological phenomenon as digestion. The mind, they suppose, is something formal and abstract, not part of the wet and slimy stuff in our heads. The polemical literature in AI usually contains attacks on something the authors call dualism, but what they fail to see is that they themselves display dualism in a strong form, for unless one accepts the idea that the mind is completely independent of the brain or of any other physically specific system, one could not possibly hope to create minds just by designing programs. [25]

Historically, scientific developments in the West that have treated humans as just a part of the ordinary physical, biological order have often been opposed by various rear-guard actions—Copernicus and Galileo were opposed because they denied that the earth was the center of the universe; Darwin was opposed because he claimed that humans had descended from the lower animals. It is best to see strong AI as one of the last gasps of this antiscientific tradition, for it denies that there is anything essentially physical and biological about the human mind. The mind according to strong AI is independent of the brain. It is a computer program and as such has no essential connection to any specific hardware.

Many people who have doubts about the psychological significance of AI think that computers might be able to understand Chinese and think about numbers but cannot do the crucially human things, namely—and then follows their favorite human specialty—falling in love, having a sense of humor, feeling the angst of postindustrial society under late capitalism, or whatever. But workers in AI complain—correctly—that this is a case of moving the goal posts. As soon as an AI simulation succeeds, it ceases to be of psychological importance. In this debate, both sides fail to see the distinction between simulation and duplication. As far as simulation is concerned, there is no difficulty in programming my computer so that it prints out. "I love you, Suzy"; "Ha ha"; or "I am suffering the angst of postindustrial society under late capitalism." The important point is that simulation is not the same as duplication, and that fact holds as much import for thinking about arithmetic as it does for feeling angst. The point is not that the computer gets only to the 40-yard line and not all the way to the goal line. The computer doesn't even get started. It is not playing that game.

[25] This is a different use of the term dualism from the one that applied to Foster's view, since functionalists and proponents of strong AI do not think that thinking occurs in a substance distinct from the brain. What is true is that the functionalist account of what it is to be a mental state is not one that could only be satisfied by a brain, even though all actual functionalists believe that it is brains that actually run the relevant program. Thus functionalism allows the bare possibility of immaterial minds in a way that Searle's view does not.

Discussion Questions

1. Think carefully about the Turing Test for thinking. What (if anything) seems right about it? What (if anything) seems wrong about it? On what do you base your judgment that any one of your friends or family is thinking, either in general or about some specific thing? What if you met an alien from another planet? How would you judge whether it could think? On what basis do you believe that your pet can or cannot think? (Should we perhaps be more tentative in our judgments about each other than we ordinarily are?) How important is *con-*

sciousness to thinking? Can something think if it is not conscious? On what basis do you judge that someone or something is conscious?

2. Is it true, as Searle claims, that normal thinking essentially involves and depends on meaning or content? Think again about the umbrella example in the chapter introduction: I understand what rain is and also what an umbrella is, and it is because of this understanding that I am led to conclude that I should go back and get the umbrella to guard against the rain. Is there any way to understand examples of this kind that appeals only to formal manipulation of symbols?

3. Many philosophers have claimed that thoughts have *intrinsic* meaning or content, that any particular thought means what it does because of properties of the thought itself and not because of any external connections or relations it has to anything else. While that claim is controversial for thought, it is clearly false for the symbols of any ordinary language (such as English or French or Chinese). The English word "dog" and the French word "chien" have the same meaning, but there is nothing about the letters themselves or the way the letters are put together that requires those combinations of letters to have the meaning that they have or indeed to have any meaning at all. Their meaning is purely conventional, and thus results in some way from external facts about how they are used. Thus the word "dog" could have had the meaning that the word "alligator" has, and vice versa. Is there a difference between the way your thoughts are meaningful and the way language is meaningful? Could your *thought* of dogs have been instead a *thought* about alligators (which would seem to be possible if it is, as Fodor believes, just a mental symbol)?

4. Searle's view that mental states like thinking are caused by and essentially depend on the specific neurobiological properties of the brain has sometimes been characterized as the "meatist" theory of the mind—because according to it, thought depends on the distinctive sort of "meat" that the brain is made up of, rather than on merely formal structure as the functionalist claims. How plausible is this view (which does not follow in any direct way from Searle's arguments against functionalism and strong AI)? Can you see any reason for thinking that it is the specific "neurobiological" character of the brain that accounts for conscious thought—or any glimmer of an idea of how this might work?

5. Consider again objections a, b, d, and e to the Chinese Room thought experiment. Can any of these objections be spelled out and defended in a way that makes it a cogent objection? If so, how? If not, why not?

Jerry Fodor

This selection is taken from Fodor's reply to Searle's original presentation of the Chinese Room argument (in 1980)—which did not differ in any significant way from the later version contained in the previous selection. Fodor is specifically criticizing Searle's reply to what was referred to in the earlier version as the "robot reply," objection f in the list in the previous selection. This objection insists that while the Chinese Room argument may successfully show that some systems running the supposedly right program fail to genuinely involve mental states and processes, it fails to show that this is so for any such system. Consider a system in which the program operates a robot having perceptual and motor systems: systems for taking in information (for example a video camera and microphone) and the capability for movement (so that it could, for example, walk around or make things). The program running in such a robot would be the "brain" that coordinates the inputs (analogous to our sensory inputs) and the outputs (analogous to our actions). In this sort of case, there will be what Fodor refers to as "causal linkages" between the symbols involved in the formal manipulations that constitute the running of the program and the things in the outside world with which the robot interacts—thereby, Fodor claims, giving those symbols the semantic content or meaning that Searle claims is lacking.

Searle's response to the "robot reply" in the original article was to imagine that the system running the program inside the robot is replaced with a person who manipulates symbols in the same formal way as in the original Chinese Room. His claim is that there is still no genuine meaning or content to be found in the system. Fodor insists that there wouldn't be the *right kind* of causal linkages if a person was inside the robot manipulating symbols in this way, but that there might be the right kind of causal linkages if an internal computer was running the program.

Searle on What Only Brains Can Do

1. Searle is certainly right that instantiating the same program that the brain does is not, in and of itself, a sufficient condition for having those propositional attitudes characteristic of the organism that has the brain.① If some people in AI think that it is, they're wrong. As for the Turing test, it has all the usual difficulties with predictions of "no difference"; you can't distinguish the truth of the prediction from the insensitivity of the test instrument.*

2. However, Searle's treatment of the "robot reply" is quite unconvincing. Given that there are the right kinds of causal linkages between the symbols that the device manipulates and things in the world—including the afferent and efferent transducers of the device—it is quite unclear that intuition rejects ascribing propositional attitudes to it. All that Searle's example shows is that the kind of causal linkage he imagines—one that is, in effect, mediated by a man sitting in the head of a robot—is, unsurprisingly, not the right kind.②

3. We don't know how to say what the right kinds of causal linkage are. This, also, is unsurprising since we don't know how to answer the closely related question as to what kinds of connection between a formula and the world determine the interpretation under which the formula is employed. We don't have an answer to this question for *any* symbolic system; a fortiori, not for mental representations. These questions are closely related because, given the mental representation view, it is natural to assume that what

① "Propositional attitudes" is a standard label for mental states like belief and desire that involve an "attitude" toward a **proposition** (such as the proposition that it will rain tomorrow): accepting it (in the case of belief) or wanting it to be true (in the case of desire). Fodor here is agreeing with Searle that merely running the program in some way is not enough to yield genuine beliefs and desires. (Fodor also agrees that satisfying the Turing Test is not enough to show that whatever satisfies it is thinking, basically because the standards for the test might not be demanding enough.)

② Fodor is claiming that a device running such a program inside a robot might genuinely have beliefs and desires *if* there are the *right kinds* of *causal* connections between the symbols manipulated by the device and things in the world. Saying that **"intuition"** does not clearly reject the ascription of propositional attitudes to such a device is just saying that it does not seem clearly mistaken in the case where the program is *not* being run by a man inside the robot's head. (Thus Fodor rejects Searle's reply as irrelevant to the most important case.)

From Behavioral and Brain Sciences, *Vol. 3, September 1980.*

*I assume, for simplicity, that there is only one program that the brain instantiates (which, of course, there isn't). Notice, by the way, that even passing the Turing test requires doing more than *just* manipulating symbols. A device that can't run a typewriter can't play the game.

makes mental states intentional is primarily that they involve relations to semantically interpreted mental objects; again, relations of the right kind.③

④ There is a subtle argument lurking here. It is obvious that some symbolic formulas have meanings ("interpretations"), namely those that are employed in ordinary languages like English. Fodor admits that we don't understand how this works, but is suggesting that however it works for those languages, it can work in the same way for the "language of thought"—and that mental states are meaningful because they involve meaningful symbols in the "language of thought." (But the question still remains whether causal relations of the sort that might be involved in the robot case are enough to account for meaning or content in *any* case—whether that of a language of thought or that of more ordinary sorts of languages. See Discussion Question 1.)

④ Fodor agrees with Searle that meaning or content is an essential feature of mental states. His claim is that the best version of functionalism (or strong AI) does not claim that meaning or content arises from the formal manipulations of the symbols alone, but rather from the semantic properties of the mental symbols that depend on the sorts of external causal relations that the robot case involves.

4. It seems to me that Searle has misunderstood the main point about the treatment of intentionality in representational theories of the mind; this is not surprising since proponents of the theory—especially in AI—have been notably unlucid in expounding it. For the record, then, the main point is this: intentional properties of propositional attitudes are viewed as inherited from semantic properties of mental representations (and not from the functional role of mental representations, unless "functional role" is construed broadly enough to include symbol-world relations).④ In effect, what is proposed is a reduction of the problem *what makes mental states intentional* to the problem *what bestows semantic properties on (fixes the interpretation of) a symbol.* This reduction looks promising because we're going to have to answer the latter question anyhow (for example, in constructing theories of natural languages); and we need the notion of mental representation anyhow (for example, to provide appropriate domains for mental processes).

It may be worth adding that there is nothing new about this strategy. Locke, for example, thought (a) that the intentional properties of mental states are inherited from the semantic (referential) properties of mental representations; (b) that mental processes are formal (associative); and (c) that the objects from which mental states inherit their intentionality are the same ones over which mental processes are defined: namely ideas.⑤ It's my view that no serious alternative to this treatment of propositional attitudes has ever been proposed.

5. To say that a computer (or a brain) performs formal operations on symbols is not the same thing as saying that it performs operations on formal (in the sense of "uninterpreted") symbols. This equivocation occurs repeatedly in Searle's paper, and causes considerable confusion. If there are mental representations they must, of course, be interpreted objects; it is because they are interpreted objects that mental states are intentional. But the brain might be a computer for all that.⑥

⑤ Locke's "ideas" seem, however, to be *intrinsically* meaningful states or entities, rather than mere symbols that acquire a meaning through external causal relations. (See the discussion of intrinsic meaning in Discussion Question 3 for the previous selection by Searle, and also the selection from Locke in Chapter 3.)

⑥ Fodor's point here is that while the operations of a computer (or a brain that functions like a computer) are formal in the sense that they do not rely on the meanings of the symbols that they manipulate, this does not mean that those symbols have no meanings. Fodor agrees that they must have meanings if contentful mental states are to result, but, to repeat, thinks those meanings derive from external causal relations rather than from the formal manipulations.

6. This situation—needing a notion of causal connection, but not knowing which notion of causal connection is the right one—is entirely familiar in philosophy. It is, for example, extremely plausible that "a perceives b" can be true only where there is the right kind of causal connection between a and b. And we don't know what the right kind of causal connection is here either.

Demonstrating that some kinds of causal connection are the *wrong* kinds would not, of course, prejudice the claim. For example, suppose we interpolated a little man between a and b, whose function it is to report to a on the presence of b. We would then have (inter alia) a sort of causal link from a to b, but we wouldn't have the sort of causal link that is required for a to perceive b.⑦ It would, of course, be a fallacy to argue from the fact that this causal linkage fails to re-construct perception to the conclusion that *no* causal linkage would succeed. Searle's argument against the "robot reply" is a fallacy of precisely that sort.

⑦ For example, imagine a blind woman who has a little man (with normal vision) who sits on her shoulder constantly telling her what is going on around her. This may lead to her having lots of correct beliefs about what is going on in her environment. In such a case, there would be a kind of causal connection between the blind person's beliefs and the things in the environment, but it wouldn't be the right kind of causal connection for it to be true that she visually perceives or sees those things. Analogously, Fodor is claiming, the causal connections in the case where there is a person in a head of the robot aren't the right kind to produce genuine meaning.

7. It is entirely reasonable (indeed it must be true) that the right kind of causal relation is the kind that holds between our brains and our transducer mechanisms (on the one hand) and between our brains and distal objects (on the other).⑧ It would not begin to follow that *only* our brains can bear such relations to transducers and distal objects; and it would also not follow that being the same sort of thing our brain is (in any biochemical sense of "same sort") is a necessary condition for being in that relation; and it would also not follow that formal manipulations of symbols are not among the links in such causal chains. And, even if our brains *are* the only sorts of things that can be in that relation, the fact that they are might quite possibly be of no particular interest; that would depend on *why* it's true.

Searle gives no clue as to why he thinks the biochemistry is important for intentionality and, prima facie, the idea that what counts is how the organism is connected to the world seems far more plausible. After all, it's easy enough to imagine, in a rough and ready sort of way, how the fact that my thought is causally connected to a tree might bear on its being a thought about a tree. But it's hard to imagine how the fact that (to put it crudely) my thought is made out of hydrocarbons could matter, except on the unlikely hypothesis that only hydrocarbons can be causally connected to trees in the way that brains are.⑨

⑧ This "must be true" only on the assumption, which is not at all clearly right, that our brains involve symbols of the sort in question rather than (as Searle thinks) intrinsically contentful states.

⑨ That is, Searle has really given no reason for the "meatist" theory other than the objections to functionalism. His view would follow only if there is no other viable alternative, which is far from obviously true.

. . .

10. *Talking* involves performing certain formal operations on symbols: stringing words together. Yet, not everything that can string words together can talk. It does not follow from these banal observations that what we utter are uninterpreted sounds, or that we don't understand what we say, or that whoever talks talks nonsense, or that only hydrocarbons can assert—similarly, mutatis mutandis, if you substitute "thinking" for "talking."

Discussion Questions

1. How plausible (or implausible) is Fodor's view that the semantic properties (meanings) of mental symbols in the "language of thought" result from external causal relations of the sort that exist in the case of the robot? Suppose that there is a symbol involved in your mental operations—we may suppose that it is something analogous to the English word "dog" written on something analogous to a mental blackboard. By virtue of external perceptual and motor relations (and also the internal, purely formal processing), this symbol comes to stand in some complicated network of causal relations to real dogs in the world: perhaps it tends to be produced (written in a specific place on the "blackboard") when your sense organs are stimulated in the right ways by passing dogs and tends to produce bodily movements that depend also on states that according to Fodor are desires or aversions to animals (though these will also depend essentially on symbols whose meaningfulness raises the same problem). Let us suppose that the resulting network of causal relations is the right

one, whatever that may be, to result in this symbol meaning or standing for dogs. If you have no independent knowledge of these external causal relations (which you ordinarily wouldn't) but are only, as it were, aware of the symbol on the "blackboard," is there any way that you would be able to become aware of the meaning of the symbol in a way that could enable you to thereby have conscious thoughts about dogs? (This is a difficult and subtle question, but one very much worth thinking about.)

2. Fodor claims that the causal relations that occur in the version of the robot case where there is a person in the head of the robot running the program are "not the right kind" to yield meaning for the symbols involved, but that those that result when there is a computer running the program might be. The reason for thinking that the causal relations are not the right kind in the former version of the case is that the person has no awareness of the resulting meaning or content, whereas this reason does not apply in the version where there is no such person. But is there any plausible reason for thinking that whatever causal relations are involved in the computer case might not be duplicated in the person case?

John R. Searle

Searle first published the Chinese Room argument in *Behavioral and Brain Sciences* along with 27 commentaries and his response to those commentaries. The following selection consists of Searle's response to Fodor, together with a bit of material that comes earlier in his reply, further elaborating his biological (or "meatist") view of mental states.

Author's Response

Strong AI. One of the virtues of the commentaries is that they make clear the extreme character of the strong AI thesis. The thesis implies that of all known types of specifically biological processes, from mitosis and meiosis to photosynthesis, digestion, lactation, and the secretion of auxin, one and only one type is completely independent of the biochemistry of its origins, and that one is cognition. The reason it is independent is that cognition consists entirely of computational processes, and since those processes are purely formal, any substance whatever that is capable of instantiating the formalism is capable of cognition.① Brains just happen to be one of the indefinite number of different types of computers capable of cognition, but computers made of water pipes, toilet paper and stones, electric wires—anything solid and enduring enough to carry the right program—will

necessarily have thoughts, feelings, and the rest of the forms of intentionality, because that is all that intentionality consists in: instantiating the right programs. The point of strong AI is . . . that there isn't anything to intentionality other than instantiating the right program.

Now I find the thesis of strong AI incredible in every sense of the word. But it is not enough to find a thesis incredible, one has to have an argument, and I offer an argument that is very simple: instantiating a program could not be constitutive of intentionality,

① Searle is right that functionalism and strong AI make mental states independent of any specific facts about biochemistry. States of any kind, no matter what their composition or makeup might be, could play the role of symbols in formal manipulations (and also, in Fodor's version, stand in external causal relations as a result of input and output connections. But this is an "extreme" or surprising view only if one assumes that "cognition" is a biological process at least roughly on a par with things like digestion and photosynthesis—something that is by no means obviously the case.

From Behavioral and Brain Sciences, *Vol. 3, September 1980.*

because it would be possible for an agent to instantiate the program and still not have the right kind of intentionality.② That is the point of the Chinese room example. Much of what follows will concern the force of that argument.

② Think here of Fodor's response to this way of putting the objection.

* * * * *

Fodor agrees with my central thesis that instantiating a program is not a sufficient condition of intentionality. He thinks, however, that if we got the right causal links between the formal symbols and things in the world that would be sufficient. Now there is an obvious objection to this variant of the robot reply that I have made several times: the same thought experiment as before applies to this case. That is, no matter what outside causal impacts there are on the formal tokens, these are not by themselves sufficient to give the tokens any intentional content. No matter what caused the tokens, the agent still doesn't understand Chinese. Let the egg foo yung symbol be causally connected to egg foo yung in any way you like, that connection by itself will never enable the agent to interpret the symbol as meaning egg foo yung.③ To do that he would have to have, for example, some a*wareness* of the causal relation between the symbol and the referent; but now we are no longer explaining intentionality in terms of symbols and causes but in terms of symbols, causes, and intentionality, and we have abandoned both strong AI and the robot reply. Fodor's only answer to this is to say that it shows we haven't yet got the right kind of causal linkage. But what is the right kind, since the above argument applies to any kind? He says he can't tell us, but it is there all the same. Well I can tell him what it is: it is any form of causation sufficient to produce intentional content in the agent, sufficient to produce, for example, a visual experience, or a memory, or a belief, or a semantic interpretation of some word.④

③ Searle is talking here about the Chinese room (including the robot version with the man in the robot's head) and saying that external causal connections, no matter what they may be like, will never allow the person in the room (or in the robot's head) to attach any meaning to the characters he is manipulating. Fodor's response will be that the causal relations will never be of the right kind as long as such an agent is involved, but does he have any good reason for this claim?

Fodor's variant of the robot reply is therefore confronted with a dilemma. If the causal linkages are just matters of fact about the relations between the symbols and the outside world, they will never by themselves give any interpretation to the symbols; they will carry by themselves no intentional content.⑤ If, on the other hand, the causal impact is sufficient to produce intentionality in the agent, it can only be because there is something more to the system than the *fact* of the causal impact and the *symbol,* namely the intentional content that the impact produces in the agent. Either the man in the room doesn't learn the meaning of the symbol from the causal impact, in which case the causal impact adds nothing to the interpretation, or the causal impact teaches him the meaning of the word, in which case the cause is relevant only because it produces a form of intentionality that is something in addition to itself and the symbol.⑥ In neither case is symbol, or cause and symbol, constitutive of intentionality.

. . .

④ Specifying the result in this way doesn't do much to say what the right kind of causal linkage actually is. The more important claim is the one made earlier: that causal relations cannot yield meaning unless the person is aware of them (in which case intentionality is being presupposed, and the causal relations alone are not doing the job).

⑤ This reiterates the point that the external causal relations can yield meaning in a way that is accessible to the agent on the inside only if the agent has an independent awareness of them—with the further suggestion being that causal relations will result in meaning or content for an ordinary person only if that person is aware of them, which is normally not the case.

⑥ The other alternative making up the alleged dilemma is the possibility that the causal relations help to cause (rather than constituting) an independently meaningful intentional state (Searle means one that is intrinsically meaningful, more than just a symbol—presumably one that is dependent on the biochemical or neurobiological nature of the brain). In this case, the meaningful intentional state must be something more than just the symbol and the external causal relations, and it is this something more that is responsible for genuine meaning.

In what is perhaps his crucial point, **Fodor** suggests that we should think of the brain or the computer as performing formal operations only on *interpreted* and not just on *formal* symbols. But who does the interpreting? And what is an interpretation? If he is saying that for intentionality there must be intentional content in addition to the formal symbols, then I of course agree. Indeed, two of the main points of my argument are that in our own case we have the "interpretation," that is, we have intrinsic intentionality, and that the computer program could never by itself be sufficient for that. . . . [7]

[7] Thus the crucial issue between Searle and Fodor is not whether mental states have meaning or content, but where that meaning or content comes from. (See Discussion Question 2.)

Discussion Questions

1. Dilemmas usually start by stating a *disjunction,* an either-or statement, each side of which leads to a result that the view being criticized cannot accept. What is the disjunction that Searle has in mind when he says that Fodor's reply is confronted with a dilemma? Why is each side of the dilemma supposed to create a problem for Fodor's position?

2. Searle and Fodor agree that mental states have meaning or content, with the main issue between them being where that meaning or content comes from. Searle's "meatist" view holds that the content resides in intrinsically meaningful or contentful states, which are in turn a result of lower-level neurobiological or ultimately biochemical causes. Fodor's view is that content depends on mental symbols that become meaningful by being connected with external things of various kinds through causal linkages of the right kind. Both of these views seem to face problems. Can Searle explain *how* the underlying causes produce meaningful or contentful states and in particular what determines the specific meaning or content of such a state? Can Fodor explain how the meaning that allegedly results from external causal relations becomes accessible to the person in a way that allows it to play a role in conscious, meaningful thoughts of the sort we seem to have? Which of these views seems to you more promising—or is there any real hope for either of them? What would be the right response to a dualist who suggests that these problems simply show that materialist views cannot adequately account for conscious, meaningful mental content—and hence that some version of dualism must be true after all?

CAN MATERIALISM ACCOUNT FOR QUALITATIVE CONSCIOUSNESS?

Thomas Nagel

Thomas Nagel (1937–) is an American philosopher who has taught philosophy at Princeton and currently at New York University. He is very well known for his work in philosophy of mind and ethics. The ideas in this influential article still inform the debate in contemporary philosophy of mind.

It is notoriously difficult to define, explain, or give an account of consciousness. Nagel, using the conscious experiences of bats as an example, argues that conscious experiences are essentially tied to a subjective, first-person point of view. Since physical brain states are essentially objective, and thus accessible from many points of view, these claims cause problems for any view that claims that mental states are identical to or realized by brain states.

What Is It Like To Be a Bat?

Consciousness is what makes the mind-body problem really intractable. Perhaps that is why current discussions of the problem give it little attention or get it obviously wrong. The recent wave of reductionist euphoria has produced several analyses of mental phenomena and mental concepts designed to explain the possibility of some variety of materialism, psychophysical identification, or reduction.① But the problems dealt with are those common to this type of reduction and other types, and what makes the mind-body problem unique, and unlike the water-H_2O problem or the Turing machine-IBM machine problem or the lightning-electrical discharge, problem . . . , is ignored.

Every reductionist has his favorite analogy from modern science. It is most unlikely that any of these unrelated examples of successful reduction will shed light on the relation of mind to brain. But philosophers share the general human weakness for explanations of what is incomprehensible in terms suited for what is familiar and well understood, though entirely different. This has led to the acceptance of implausible accounts of the mental largely because they would permit familiar kinds of reduction.② I shall try to explain why the usual examples do not help us to understand the relation between mind and body—why,

> ① As reflected in the earlier selections by Smart and Fodor, many philosophers are tempted by the view that psychological states can be identified with or somehow reduced to physical brain states, with functionalism currently being the most widely accepted version of such a view. (Think again about why reductionism is so tempting: physical science in general has been very successful, and there have been many recent developments in neuroscience in particular. If mental states were just brain states, then it would be clear how to proceed with a scientific investigation of them.)

indeed, we have at present no conception of what an explanation of the physical nature of a mental phenomenon would be. Without consciousness the mind-body problem would be much less interesting. With consciousness it seems hopeless. The most important and characteristic feature of conscious mental phenomena is very poorly understood. Most reductionist theories do not even try to explain it. And careful examination will show that no currently available concept of reduction is applicable to it. Perhaps a new theoretical form can be devised for the purpose, but such a solution, if it exists, lies in the distant intellectual future.

Conscious experience is a widespread phenomenon. It occurs at many levels of animal life, though we cannot be sure of its presence in the simpler organisms, and it is very difficult to say in general what provides evidence of it. (Some extremists have been prepared to deny it even of mammals other than man.) No doubt it occurs in countless forms totally unimaginable to us, on other planets in other solar systems throughout the universe. But no matter how the form may vary, the fact that an organism has conscious experience *at all* means, basically, that there is something it is like to *be* that organism. There may be further implications about the form of the experience; there may even (though I doubt it) be implications about the behavior of the organism. But fundamentally an organism has conscious mental states if and only if there is something that it is like to be that organism—something it is like *for* the organism.③

We may call this the subjective character of experience. It is not captured by any of the familiar, recently

> ② There is no real objection to attempting to explain what is presently incomprehensible in terms of what is familiar and well understood. Nagel's point is that such attempts are unlikely to succeed if the things we are trying to understand are radically different in nature from the familiar and well understood ones—which he will argue to be so for conscious mental states.

From Mortal Questions *(Cambridge: Cambridge University Press, 1979).*

devised reductive analyses of the mental, for all of them are logically compatible with its absence. It is not analyzable in terms of any explanatory system of functional states, or intentional states, since these could be ascribed to robots or automata that behaved like people though they experienced nothing. It is not analyzable in terms of the causal role of experiences in relation to typical human behavior—for similar reasons. I do not deny that conscious mental states and events cause behavior, nor that they may be given functional characterizations. I deny only that this kind of thing exhausts their analysis. Any reductionist program has to be based on an analysis of what is to be reduced. If the analysis leaves something out, the problem will be falsely posed.④ It is useless to base the defense of materialism on any analysis of mental phenomena that fails to deal explicitly with their subjective character. For there is no reason to suppose that a reduction which seems plausible when no attempt is made to account for consciousness can be extended to include consciousness. Without some idea, therefore, of what the subjective character of experience is, we cannot know what is required of physicalist theory.

While an account of the physical basis of mind must explain many things, this appears to be the most difficult. It is impossible to exclude the phenomenological features of experience from a reduction in the same way that one excludes the phenomenal features of an ordinary substance from a physical or chemical reduction of it—namely, by explaining them as effects on the minds of human observers.⑤ If physicalism is to be defended, the phenomenological features must themselves be given a physical account. But when we examine their subjective character it seems that such a result is impossible. The reason is that every subjective phenomenon is essentially connected with a single point of view, and it seems inevitable that an objective, physical theory will abandon that point of view.

Let me first try to state the issue somewhat more fully than by referring to the relation between the subjective and the objective. . . . This is far from easy. Facts about what it is like to be an X are very peculiar, so peculiar that some may be inclined to doubt their reality, or the significance of claims about them. To illustrate the connection between subjectivity and a point of view, and to make evident the importance of subjective features, it will help to explore the matter in relation to an example that brings out clearly the divergence between the two types of conception, subjective and objective.

I assume we all believe that bats have experience. After all, they are mammals, and there is no more doubt that they have experience than that mice or pigeons or whales have experience. I have chosen bats instead of wasps or flounders because if one travels too far down the phylogenetic tree, people gradually shed their faith that there is experience there at all.⑥ Bats, although more closely related to us than those other

---

③ Nagel is pointing here to what he takes to be the essential feature of consciousness. If, for example, frogs have conscious experience, then there must be something that it is like *for the frog* to be a frog. (Whether we could ever *know* facts like this about frogs is not the issue here.)

---

④ Nagel's claim is that reductive accounts such as functionalism do not capture this essential subjective character of conscious experience: describing the causal role of a state does not tell us what it is like to be in that state. (An *analysis* of something, as Nagel is using the term, is an allegedly complete and detailed account of what it involves; thus, he is claiming, the functionalist analysis is incomplete and therefore mistaken.)

---

⑤ This is a crucial point: a reductive physical or chemical analysis of an ordinary substance like coffee need not include its taste (a phenomenal feature) because *the taste* of coffee is just the subjective response of a person who drinks the coffee and not an intrinsic feature of the coffee itself. The taste of the coffee is caused by the intrinsic features of the coffee, given the features of the taste capacities of the person (coffee could very easily taste differently to aliens). Nagel's point is that while physical reductions of many items can ignore phenomenological (experiential) features by in this way treating them as features of the person experiencing the item being reduced rather than features of that item itself, the physical reduction of mental states cannot ignore such features, since mental states are essentially experiential (and there is no independent observer to whom the feature in question could be transferred).

---

⑥ The use of the bat example is not really essential to the argument—indeed, as Nagel suggests later, the same problem arises in relation to other people with different sensory capacities. But it is surely quite plausible that bats do have conscious experience, so that there is something that it is like to be a bat.

species, nevertheless present a range of activity and a sensory apparatus so different from ours that the problem I want to pose is exceptionally vivid (though it certainly could be raised with other species). Even without the benefit of philosophical reflection, anyone who has spent some time in an enclosed space with an excited bat knows what it is to encounter a fundamentally *alien* form of life.

I have said that the essence of the belief that bats have experience is that there is something that it is like to be a bat. Now we know that most bats (the microchiroptera, to be precise) perceive the external world primarily by sonar, or echolocation, detecting the reflections, from objects within range, of their own rapid, subtly modulated, high-frequency shrieks. Their brains are designed to correlate the outgoing impulses with the subsequent echoes, and the information thus acquired enables bats to make precise discriminations of distance, size, shape, motion, and texture comparable to those we make by vision. But bat sonar, though clearly a form of perception, is not similar in its operation to any sense that we possess, and there is no reason to suppose that it is subjectively like anything we can experience or imagine.[7] This appears to create difficulties for the notion of what it is like to be a bat. We must consider whether any method will permit us to extrapolate to the inner life of the bat from our own case,* and if not, what alternative methods there may be for understanding the notion.

> **[7]** It is fairly natural to imagine the bat experiencing something like a visual image, perhaps a very schematic one like the picture on a radar screen. But there is no reason at all to think that this is a correct view of bat experience—or that it isn't. The point is that we just can't tell.

Our own experience provides the basic material for our imagination, whose range is therefore limited. It will not help to try to imagine that one has webbing on one's arms, which enables one to fly around at dusk and dawn catching insects in one's mouth; that one has very poor vision, and perceives the surrounding world by a system of reflected high-frequency sound signals; and that one spends the day hanging upside down by one's feet in an attic. Insofar as I can imagine this (which is not very far), it tells me only what it would be like for *me* to behave as a bat behaves. But that is not the question. I want to know what it is like for a *bat* to be a bat. Yet if I try to imagine this, I am restricted to the resources of my own mind, and those resources are inadequate to the task. I cannot perform it either by imagining additions to my present experience, or by imagining segments gradually subtracted from it, or by imagining some combination of additions, subtractions, and modifications.[8]

> **[8]** Nagel's reflections here about whether we could *imagine* what it is like to be a bat are somewhat misleading. Some critics of his argument have focused on this point and have argued that we could imagine many things about being a bat (by, for example, relying on the experience of blind people—as Nagel himself suggests in his second footnote). But remember that Nagel is just trying to defend the claim that phenomenal facts are essentially connected to a point of view (the first-person subjective point of view).

To the extent that I could look and behave like a wasp or a bat without changing my fundamental structure, my experiences would not be anything like the experiences of those animals. On the other hand, it is doubtful that any meaning can be attached to the supposition that I should posses the internal neurophysiological constitution of a bat. Even if I could by gradual degrees be transformed into a bat, nothing in my present constitution enables me to imagine what the experiences of such a future stage of myself thus metamorphosed would be like. The best evidence would come from the experiences of bats, if we only knew what they were like.[9]

> **[9]** If I could somehow engage in a "mind-meld" with a bat, so that I could have its experiences, then I would know what it was like to be that bat. But notice that the idea of such a mind-meld assumes that I would take up that first-person perspective, that subjective point of view.

So if extrapolation from our own case is involved in the idea of what it is like to be a bat, the extrapolation must be incompletable. We cannot form more than a schematic conception of what it *is* like. For example, we may ascribe general *types* of experience on

---

*By 'our own case' I do not mean just 'my own case', but rather the mentalistic ideas that we apply unproblematically to ourselves and other human beings.

the basis of the animal's structure and behavior. Thus we describe bat sonar as a form of three-dimensional forward perception; we believe that bats feel some versions of pain, fear, hunger, and lust, and that they have other, more familiar types of perception besides sonar. But we believe that these experiences also have in each case a specific subjective character, which it is beyond our ability to conceive. And if there is conscious life elsewhere in the universe, it is likely that some of it will not be describable even in the most general experiential terms available to us. (The problem is not confined to exotic cases, however, for it exists between one person and another. The subjective character of the experience of a person deaf and blind from birth is not accessible to me, for example, nor presumably is mine to him. This does not prevent us each from believing that the other's experience has such a subjective character.)[10]

> [10] The exact nature of the subjective character of another person's experience is not fully describable. Try describing the pain involved in a toothache or a broken arm to someone who has never had the experience in question. It is notoriously difficult to accurately describe pain. Are any two *sharp* pains, for example, exactly alike?

If anyone is inclined to deny that we can believe in the existence of facts like this whose exact nature we cannot possibly conceive, he should reflect that in contemplating the bats we are in much the same position that intelligent bats or Martians would occupy if they tried to form a conception of what it was like to be us. The structure of their own minds might make it impossible for them to succeed, but we know they would be wrong to conclude that there is not anything precise that it is like to be us: that only certain general types of mental state could be ascribed to us (perhaps perception and appetite would be concepts common to us both; perhaps not). We know they would be wrong to draw such a skeptical conclusion because we know what it is like to be us. And we know that while it includes an enormous amount of variation and complexity, and while we do not possess the vocabulary to describe it adequately, its subjective character is highly specific, and in some respects describable in terms that can be understood only by creatures like us. The fact that we cannot expect ever to accommodate in our language a detailed description of Martian or bat phenomenology should not lead us to dismiss as meaningless the claim that bats and Martians have experiences fully comparable in richness of detail to our own.[11] It would be fine if someone were to develop concepts and a theory that enabled us to think about those things; but such an understanding may be permanently denied to us by the limits of our nature. And to deny the reality or logical significance of what we can never describe or understand is the crudest form of cognitive dissonance.

> [11] The claim here is that our total inability to conceive of the nature of a fact is not itself a reason to conclude that there is no such fact (and so our inability to conceive of what it is like to be a bat is not itself a reason to conclude that there is no way it is to be a bat). The appeals to bats, and now Martians, are merely illustrations of the point. (The selection from BonJour will make use of the Martian example.)

This brings us to the edge of a topic that requires much more discussion than I can give it here: namely, the relation between facts on the one hand and conceptual schemes or systems of representation on the other. My realism about the subjective domain in all its forms implies a belief in the existence of facts beyond the reach of human concepts.[12] Certainly it is possible for a human being to believe that there are facts which humans never *will* possess the requisite concepts to represent or comprehend. Indeed, it would be foolish to doubt this, given the finiteness of humanity's expectations. After all, there would have been transfinite numbers even if everyone had been wiped out by the Black Death before Cantor discovered them. But one might also believe that there are facts which *could* not ever be represented or comprehended by human beings, even if the species lasted forever—simply because our structure does not permit us to operate with concepts of the requisite type.[13] This impossibility

> [12] A **realist** about the subjective domain (or any other domain) claims that things in that domain, such as experiences and beliefs and hopes and dreams, are real and have specific features, whether human beings or indeed anyone can conceptually describe them or not.

> [13] Nagel is here envisaging the possibility that there are concepts that we not only do not in fact have, but could not in principle have, simply because "our structure" does not permit us to have them. He is not claiming that this possibility is in fact definitely realized in the bat case, only that it might well be.

might even be observed by other beings, but it is not clear that the existence of such beings, or the possibility of their existence, is a precondition of the significance of the hypothesis that there are humanly inaccessible facts. (After all, the nature of beings with access to humanly inaccessible facts is presumably itself a humanly inaccessible fact.) Reflection on what it is like to be a bat seems to lead us, therefore, to the conclusion that there are facts that do not consist in the truth of propositions expressible in a human language. We can be compelled to recognize the existence of such facts without being able to state or comprehend them.

I shall not pursue this subject, however. Its bearing on the topic before us (namely, the mind-body problem) is that it enables us to make a general observation about the subjective character of experience. Whatever may be the status of facts about what it is like to be a human being, or a bat, or a Martian, these appear to be facts that embody a particular point of view.

I am not adverting here to the alleged privacy of experience to its possessor. The point of view in question is not one accessible only to a single individual. Rather it is a *type*. It is often possible to take up a point of view other than one's own, so the comprehension of such facts is not limited to one's own case. There is a sense in which phenomenological facts are perfectly objective: one person can know or say of another what the quality of the other's experience is. They are subjective, however, in the sense that even this objective ascription of experience is possible only for someone sufficiently similar to the object of ascription to be able to adopt his point of view—to understand the ascription in the first person as well as in the third, so to speak.⑭ The more different from oneself the other experiencer is, the less success one can expect with this enterprise. In our own case we occupy the relevant point of view, but we will have as

much difficulty understanding our own experience properly if we approach it from another point of view as we would if we tried to understand the experience of another species without taking up *its* point of view.*⑮

This bears directly on the mind-body problem. For if the facts of experience—facts about what it is like for the experiencing organism—are accessible only from one point of view, then it is a mystery how the true character of experiences could be revealed in the physical operation of that organism. The latter is a domain of objective facts *par excellence*—the kind that can be observed and understood from many points of view and by individuals with differing perceptual systems. There are no comparable imaginative obstacles to the acquisition of knowledge about bat neurophysiology by human scientists, and intelligent bats or Martians might learn more about the human brain than we ever will.⑯

⑭ I can objectively say about you that you are in pain, but what I *mean* when I say that depends largely on what I think pain is, given my first-person perspective. My own point of view makes an essential contribution to the meaning of my claim about your pain, and that is the way in which the claim is, in a sense, subjective.

⑮ One might initially think that it would be very hard to take anything but a first-person perspective in our own case, but for some people, other people's opinions are so important that the first-person perspective can sometimes get temporarily lost. (See Discussion Question 1.)

⑯ Physical facts, by virtue of being accessible from many different points of view, are clearly objective, in Nagel's sense of objectivity. And if he is right that experiential facts are essentially subjective, in the sense of being accessible from only one point of view, then there is an obvious difficulty in identifying an experiential fact with a physical fact.

---

*It may be easier than I suppose to transcend inter-species barriers with the aid of the imagination. For example, blind people are able to detect objects near them by a form of sonar, using vocal clicks or taps of a cane. Perhaps if one knew what that was like, one could by extension imagine roughly what it was like to possess the much more refined sonar of a bat. The distance between oneself and other persons and other species can fall anywhere on a continuum. Even for other persons the understanding of what it is like to be them is only partial, and when one moves to species very different from oneself, a lesser degree of partial understanding may still be available. The imagination is remarkable flexible. My point, however, is not that we cannot *know* what it is like to be a bat. I am not raising that epistemological problem. My point is rather that even to form a *conception* of what it is like to be a bat (and *a fortiori* to know what it is like to be a bat) one must take up the bat's point of view. If one can take it up roughly, or partially, then one's conception will also be rough or partial. Or so it seems in our present state of understanding.

. . .

In the case of experience, on the other hand, the connexion with a particular point of view seems much closer. It is difficult to understand what could be meant by the *objective* character of an experience, apart from the particular point of view from which its subject apprehends it. After all, what would be left of what it was like to be a bat if one removed the viewpoint of the bat? But if experience does not have, in addition to its subjective character, an objective nature that can be apprehended from many different points of view, then how can it be supposed that a Martian investigating my brain might be observing physical processes which were my mental processes (as he might observe physical processes which were bolts of lightning), only from a different point of view? How, for that matter, could a human physiologist observe them from another point of view?*

We appear to be faced with a general difficulty about psychophysical reduction. In other areas the process of reduction is a move in the direction of greater objectivity, toward a more accurate view of the real nature of things. This is accomplished by reducing our dependence on individual or species-specific points of view toward the object of investigation. We describe it not in terms of the impressions it makes on our senses, but in terms of its more general effects and of properties detectable by means other than the human senses. The less it depends on a specifically human viewpoint, the more objective is our description. It is possible to follow this path because although the concepts and ideas we employ in thinking about the external world are initially applied from a point of view that involves our perceptual apparatus, they are used by us to refer to things beyond themselves—toward which we *have* the phenomenal point of view. Therefore we can abandon it in favor of another, and still be thinking about the same things. [17]

Experience itself, however, does not seem to fit the pattern. The idea of moving from appearance to reality seems to make no sense here. What is the analogue in this case to pursuing a more objective understanding of the same phenomena by abandoning the initial subjective viewpoint toward them in favor of another that is more objective but concerns the same thing? Certainly it *appears* unlikely that we will get closer to the real nature of human experience by leaving behind the particularly of our human point of view and striving for a description in terms accessible to beings that could not imagine what it was like to be us. If the subjective character of experience is fully comprehensible only from one point of view, then any shift to greater objectivity—that is, less attachment to a specific viewpoint—does not take us nearer to the real nature of the phenomenon: it takes us farther away from it. [18]

In a sense, the seeds of this objection to the reducibility of experience are already detectable in successful cases of reduction; for in discovering sound to be, in reality, a wave phenomenon in air or other media, we leave behind one viewpoint to take up another, and the auditory, human or animal viewpoint that we leave behind remains unreduced. Members of radically different

[17] For example, our initial investigations of heat were tied to our experiential access to the property because our very conception of heat was largely defined in terms of our experience of heat (only largely, because other effects of heat were obvious from the beginning). But the more we studied the phenomenon, the more we were able to focus on heat in objects as the cause of our sensation of heat, leading gradually to our current conception of heat as mean kinetic energy—a conception that is very far removed from our experience of heat. We have progressed from the *subjective appearance* of heat to the *objective reality* of heat (*if* we are right now about what heat is).

[18] It is just not clear that experiences have the kind of gap between appearance and reality that properties and objects in the world have. It is not unreasonable to think that the appearance of an experience just *is* its reality, so that to abstract away from the appearance is to lose the reality.

---

*The problem is not just that when I look at the *Mona Lisa,* my visual experience has a certain quality, no trace of which is to be found by someone looking into my brain. For even if he did observe there a tiny image of the *Mona Lisa,* he would have no reason to identify it with the experience.

species may both understand the same physical events in objective terms, and this does not require that they understand the phenomenal forms in which those events appear to the senses of members of the other species. Thus it is a condition of their referring to a common reality that their more particular viewpoints are not part of the common reality that they both apprehend. The reduction can succeed only if the species-specific viewpoint is omitted from what is to be reduced. [19]

[19] Imagine here two people investigating the same group of physical objects, one by sight only and one by touch only. It seems plausible that they could agree on an objective description of the objects and their relations to each other, and that each of the two people could understand that objective description without understanding the way that the objects were experienced by the other person.

But while we are right to leave this point of view aside in seeking a fuller understanding of the external world, we cannot ignore it permanently, since it is the essence of the internal world, and not merely a point of view on it. Most of the neobehaviorism of recent philosophical psychology results from the effort to substitute an objective concept of mind for the real thing, in order to have nothing left over which cannot be reduced. [20] If we acknowledge that a physical theory of mind must account for the subjective character of experience, we must admit that no presently available conception gives us a clue how this could be done. The problem is unique. If mental processes are indeed physical processes, then there is something it

[20] Functionalism is the clearest example of such a "neobehaviorist" view ("neo" because it is not the same as the original behaviorist views discussed in the first Fodor selection).

[21] A materialist might deny that there is any mystery here at all: some brain processes are such that when a person undergoes them, there is something that it is like; we don't yet know exactly how that happens, but surely it does happen, every day with every experience. To a dualist, on the other hand, the mystery is vivid: what possible physical property or process could begin to account for the distinctively experiential aspect of our mental life? Why do some brain processes have such an experiential dimension, while others do not?

is like, intrinsically, to undergo certain physical processes. What it is for such a thing to be the case remains a mystery. [21]

What moral should be drawn from these reflections, and what should be done next? It would be a mistake to conclude that physicalism must be false. Nothing is proved by the inadequacy of physicalist hypotheses that assume a faulty objective analysis of mind. It would be truer to say that physicalism is a position we cannot understand because we do not at present have any conception of how it might be true. [22] Perhaps it will be thought unreasonable to require such a conception as a condition of understanding. After all, it might be said, the meaning of physicalism is clear enough: mental states are states of the body; mental events are physical events. We do not know *which* physical states and events they are, but that should not prevent us from understanding the hypothesis. What could be clearer than the words 'is' and 'are'?

But I believe it is precisely this apparent clarity of the word 'is' that is deceptive. Usually, when we are told that X is Y we know *how* it is supposed to be true, but that depends on a conceptual or theoretical background and is not conveyed by the 'is' alone. We know how both 'X' and 'Y' refer, and the kinds of things to which they refer, and we have a rough idea how the two referential paths might converge on a single thing, be it an object, a person, a process, an event or whatever. But when the two terms of the identification are very disparate it may not be so clear how it could be true. We may not have even a rough idea of how the two referential paths could converge, or what kind of things they might converge on, and a theoretical framework may have to be supplied to enable us to understand this. Without the framework, an air of mysticism surrounds the identification. [23]

This explains the magical flavor of popular presentations of fundamental scientific discoveries, given

[22] As you will see in the next two selections, others have taken these basic ideas from Nagel and used them to argue that physicalism is false. Nagel insists, however, that the proper conclusion is that our concepts are so inadequate that we are unable to understand how the claim that mental states are identical to physical states could be true—even though it still might be true.

out as propositions to which one must subscribe without really understanding them. For example, people are now told at an early age that all matter is really energy. But despite the fact that they know what 'is' means, most of them never form a conception of what makes this claim true, because they lack the theoretical background. [24]

At the present time the status of physicalism is similar to that which the hypothesis that matter is energy would have had if uttered by a pre-Socratic philosopher. We do not have the beginnings of a conception of how it might be true. In order to understand the hypothesis that a mental event is a physical event, we require more than an understanding of the word 'is'. The idea of how a mental and a physical term might refer to the same thing is lacking, and the usual analogies with theoretical identification in other fields fail to supply it. They fail because if we construe the reference of mental terms to physical events on the usual model, we either get a reappearance of separate subjective events as the effects through which mental reference to physical events is secured, or else we get a false account of how mental terms refer (for example, a causal behaviorist one). [25]

Strangely enough, we may have evidence for the truth of something we cannot really understand. Suppose a caterpillar is locked in a sterile safe by someone unfamiliar with insect metamorphosis, and weeks later the safe is reopened, revealing a butterfly. If the person knows that the safe has been shut the whole time, he has reason to believe that the butterfly is or was once the caterpillar, without having any idea in what sense this might be so. (One possibility is that the caterpillar contained a tiny winged parasite that devoured it and grew into the butterfly.) [26]

. . .

Very little work has been done on the basic question (from which mention of the brain can be entirely omitted) whether any sense can be made of experiences' having an objective character at all. Does it make sense, in other words, to ask what my experiences are *really* like, as opposed to how they appear to me? [27] We cannot genuinely understand the hypothesis that their nature is captured in a physical description unless we understand the more fundamental idea that they *have* an objective nature (or that objective processes can have a subjective nature).

I should like to close with a speculative proposal. It may be possible to approach the gap between subjective and objective from another direction. Setting aside temporarily the relation between the mind and the brain, we can pursue a more objective understanding of the mental in its own right. At present we are completely unequipped to

---

[23] To understand the claim that two "referential paths" converge on the same object, the way that the two paths work must be such as to make clear what it would be for them to converge. Nagel's claim is that we do not (yet?) have a clear understanding of how this could happen in the experience-brain process case. (See Discussion Question 2.)

[24] Think carefully about this example, focusing on specific kinds of energy (heat, electricity, the kinetic energy of a moving object, the potential energy of an object suspended above the Earth, etc.) and various sorts of matter (wood, water, metal, etc.). Is it clear what it means for matter to just *be* energy (not just to be convertible into energy)?

[25] How is the brain event that is to be identified with a mental event to be picked out? Either as the one that is experienced in a certain way (in which case the experiential dimension has not been accounted for—see Annotation 21), or else by something like causal or functional role (in which case the experiential dimension that is essential to a mental state has simply been ignored).

[26] Do we have any analogous evidence that our mental states just are physical brain states even though we don't understand how that could be true? (See Discussion Question 3.)

[27] Does it make sense to ask what an experience is really like as opposed to how it appears to be? Think, for example, about one of your recent pain experiences. Does it make any sense to say that the pain wasn't *really* as bad as it appeared to be or that it was *really* much worse than it appeared to be or perhaps even that it wasn't *really* a pain at all? It is hard to imagine that one of our experiences might be somewhat different from what it appears to be, but it is even harder to imagine that it is really something completely different.

think about the subjective character of experience without relying on the imagination—without taking up the point of view of the experiential subject. This should be regarded as a challenge to form new concepts and devise a new method—an objective phenomenology not dependent on empathy or the imagination.[28] Though presumably it would not capture everything, its goal would be to describe, at least in part, the subjective character of experiences in a form comprehensible to beings incapable of having those experiences.

We would have to develop such a phenomenology to describe the sonar experiences of bats; but it would also be possible to begin with humans. One might try, for example, to develop concepts that could be used to explain to a person blind from birth what it was like to see. One would reach a blank wall eventually, but it should be possible to devise a method of expressing in objective terms much more than we can at present, and with much greater precision. The loose intermodal analogies—for example, 'Red is like the sound of a trumpet'—which crop up in discussions of this subject are of little use. That should be clear to anyone who has both heard a trumpet and seen red. But structural features of perception might be more accessible to objective description, even though something would be left out. And concepts alternative to those we learn in the first person may enable us to arrive at a kind of understanding even of our own experience which is denied us by the very ease of description and lack of distance that subjective concepts afford.

Apart from its own interest, a phenomenology that is in this sense objective may permit questions about the physical* basis of experience to assume a more intelligible form. Aspects of subjective experience that admitted this kind of objective description might be better candidates for objective explanations of a more familiar sort. But whether or not this guess is correct, it seems unlikely that any physical theory of mind can be contemplated until more thought has been given to the general problem of subjective and objective. Otherwise we cannot even pose the mind-body problem without sidestepping it.

[28] These remarks by Nagel are very puzzling. He seemed earlier to be arguing that the content of mental terms is always essentially tied to the first-person perspective of someone capable of having the very experiences the term refers to. But such a view seems to entail that the content of mental terms can never be objective (since objective content is not essentially tied to a single perspective).

Discussion Questions

1. Imagine a rich, domineering mother, Ethel, who continually tells her daughter, Cassie, how she—Cassie—feels, for example, that she loves fashion and hates books, that she wants lots of money and feels no compassion for the poor. Isn't it possible, if Ethel were sufficiently forceful and insistent, and Cassie were sufficiently weak and timid, that Cassie would begin to some extent to take a third-person perspective on herself—that she would begin to believe about herself what her mother says about her? Suppose that you ask Cassie to go with you to donate time to help the poor. Cassie hesitates and you ask why. She says: "Mother says that helping the poor is a waste of time." As you press her for her own opinion,

*I have not defined the term 'physical'. Obviously it does not apply just to what can be described by the concepts of contemporary physics, since we expect further developments. Some may think there is nothing to prevent mental phenomena from eventually being recognized as physical in their own right. But whatever else may be said of the physical, it has to be objective. So if our idea of the physical ever expands to include mental phenomena, it will have to assign them an objective character—whether or not this is done by analyzing them in terms of other phenomena already regarded as physical. It seems to me more likely, however, that mental-physical relations will eventually be expressed in a theory whose fundamental terms cannot be placed clearly in either category.

instead of her mother's opinion, all she can do is rehearse what her mother has drilled into her. This might suggest that Cassie has somehow lost access to her first-person perspective on this issue. Does this seem possible to you? Think of different ways to elaborate the example, illustrating either the view that it is possible or the view that it is not.

2. Suppose you are familiar with what you think of as two "stars": one that you call "the morning star" because you see it in the morning, and another that you call "the evening star" because you see it in the evening. You assume that these two names refer to different things (that there are two "referential paths" leading to two distinct objects). But as you investigate further, you discover that both the morning star and the evening star are the planet Venus, which sometimes appears in the morning and sometimes in the evening. You would have discovered that two referential paths converge onto one object. Think how you might do this. One way might be by plotting the position of one "star" in relation to other celestial objects, independently of the Earth's movement and rotation, and then discovering that the position of the second "star" is the same. Another might be to travel to the first "star" in a rocket ship and keep track of it long enough to see that it appears later as the second "star." These possibilities make sense because the

"referential path" for each object fundamentally involves spatial location. Now think of the case of an experience and a brain process. The "referential path" for the experience does not involve spatial location (think about this), so the same sort of approach will not work. How then can we understand what it would be for the two "referential paths" to converge? What might a functionalist like Fodor say about this issue?

3. Philosophers vary widely in their attitude toward the claim that mental states are really physical states of some sort. Some think that we have very strong reasons to think that this is true—even if, as Nagel suggests, we are not yet in a position to understand how it is true, and possibly never will. A philosopher of this sort will regard the various objections to materialism as problems to be solved, but not as serious reasons to think that some version of dualism might be true after all. Other philosophers view the issue as much more open, with dualism being a serious possibility, one that should perhaps be accepted if the objections to materialist views cannot be adequately met. Who is right here? Is there any strong reason for thinking that materialism is true that is prior to and independent of the success of particular materialist views? (Some of the earlier selections contain suggestions about this.)

Frank Jackson

Frank Jackson (1943–) is an Australian philosopher best known for his work in philosophy of mind and metaphysics. He teaches at the Australian National University.

In this reading, Jackson returns to a thought experiment he had developed in an earlier paper in order to respond to objections made in the intervening years. This paper develops one of the clearest versions of what philosophers have come to call the *knowledge argument* against materialism, which Jackson claims here to provide a very good reason to reject the claim that mental states are nothing more than physical states. (Jackson has since changed his mind about this.)

What Mary Didn't Know

Mary is confined to a black-and-white room, is educated through black-and-white books and through lectures relayed on black-and-white television. In this way she learns everything there is to know about the physical nature of the world.①️ She knows all the physical facts about us and our environment, in a wide sense of 'physical' which includes everything in *completed* physics, chemistry, and neurophysiology, and all there is to know about the causal and relational facts consequent upon all this, including of course functional roles.②️ If physicalism is true, she knows all there is to know. For to suppose otherwise is to suppose that there is more to know than every physical fact, and that is just what physicalism denies.

Physicalism is not the noncontroversial thesis that the actual world is largely physical, but the challenging thesis that it is entirely physical.③️ This is why physicalists must hold that complete physical knowledge is complete knowledge simpliciter. . . .

It seems, however, that Mary does not know all there is to know. For when she is let out of the black-and-white room or given a color television, she will learn what it is like to see something red, say.④️ This is rightly described as *learning*—she will not say "ho, hum." Hence, physicalism is false. This is the knowledge argument against physicalism in one of its manifestations. This note is a reply to three objections to it mounted by Paul M. Churchland.

1. . . . CLARIFICATIONS

The knowledge argument does not rest on the dubious claim that logically you cannot imagine what sensing red is like unless you have sensed red. Powers of imagination are not to the point. The contention about Mary is not that, despite her fantastic grasp of neurophysiology and everything else physical, she *could not imagine* what it is like to sense red; it is that, as a matter of fact, she *would not know*. But if physicalism is true, she would know; and no great powers of imagination would be called for. Imagination is a faculty that those who *lack* knowledge need to fall back on.⑤️

. . . the knowledge Mary lacked which is of particular point for the knowledge argument against physicalism is *knowledge about the experiences of others,* not about her own. When she is let out, she has new experiences, color experiences she has never had before. It is not, therefore, an objection to physicalism that she learns *something* on being let out. Before she was let out, she could not have known facts about her experience of red, for there were no such

①️ An essential assumption in Jackson's thought experiment is that Mary has no color experiences at all. She has only black and white visual experiences. We have to suppose that she never cuts herself (and sees red blood) or looks in the mirror or at her own body (and sees pinkish skin). (It might be more plausible to suppose that Mary starts out color-blind and then later has an operation that gives her normal color vision.)

②️ Another essential assumption is that she knows *all* the physical facts about human beings. Obviously no one now knows all the physical facts about human beings, but this is a philosophical thought experiment. We are trying to think about what follows from these assumptions.

③️ If physicalism is true, then there are no real things or states or events that are anything but entirely physical—no nonphysical parts or aspects of things or states or events. Thus if Mary knows all the physical facts about human beings, she knows all the facts there are. (As Nagel observed in his final footnote, just exactly what it is to be physical is not as clear as one might think.)

④️ She will have an experience of red, and thus she will know something that she didn't know before: the sort of experiences that result from perceptual processes that she knew about earlier under physical descriptions. But what she has now learned cannot be a physical fact, since, by hypothesis, she already knew all the physical facts.

⑤️ Thus from Jackson's perspective, what Mary (or the bat investigator) might or might not be able to *imagine* is strictly irrelevant. Even if Mary somehow managed to imagine color experience perfectly, she would still have no way before she is let out of the room to *know* that her imaginative conception was correct.

From The Journal of Philosophy, *Vol. LXXXIII, No. 5 (May 1986).*

facts to know.⑥ That physicalist and nonphysicalist alike can agree on. After she is let out, things change; and physicalism can happily admit that she learns this; after all, some physical things will change, for instance, her brain states and their functional roles. The trouble for physicalism is that, after Mary sees her first ripe tomato, she will realize how impoverished her conception of the mental life of *others* has been *all along*. She will realize that there was, all the time she was carrying out her laborious investigations into the neurophysiologies of others and into the functional roles of their internal states, something about these people she was quite unaware of. All along their experiences (or many of them, those got from tomatoes, the sky, . . .) had a feature conspicuous to them but until now hidden from her. . . . ⑦ But she knew all the physical facts about them all along; hence, what she did not know until her release is not a physical fact about their experiences. But it is a fact about them. That is the trouble for physicalism.

II. CHURCHLAND'S THREE OBJECTIONS

(i) Churchland's first objection is that the knowledge argument contains a defect that "is simplicity itself." The argument equivocates on the sense of 'knows about'. How so? Churchland suggests that the following is "a conveniently tightened version" of the knowledge argument:

(1) Mary knows everything there is to know about brain states and their properties.

(2) It is not the case that Mary knows everything there is to know about sensations and their properties.

Therefore, by Leibniz's law,

(3) Sensations and their properties ≠ brain states and their properties.⑧

Churchland observes, plausibly enough, that the type or kind of knowledge involved in premise 1 is distinct from the kind of knowledge involved in premise 2. We might follow his lead and tag the first 'knowledge by description', and the second 'knowledge by acquaintance';⑨ but, whatever the tags, he is right that the displayed argument involves a highly dubious use of Leibniz's law.

My reply is that the displayed argument may be convenient, but it is not accurate. It is not the knowledge argument. Take, for instance, premise 1. The whole thrust of the knowledge argument is that Mary (before her release) does *not* know everything there is to know about brain

⑥ According to the thought experiment, Mary has no experiences of red before she leaves the room. But before leaving, she knows that other people have experiences of what they call "red" and also knows everything about the physical and neurophysiological states that such people are in when they have such experiences.

⑦ Her knowledge of other people's mental states included knowing all the physical facts about someone's brain when, for example, he or she experiences a ripe tomato (including whatever brain states a materialist would claim to be identical with those experiences). She also knew, since she knew all physical facts, that a particular person's experience of a ripe tomato is caused by the light bouncing off the tomato and entering his or her eyes, and also the wavelength of the light, etc. What she did not know and learns when she is let out is what these experiences were like for those who had them.

⑧ According to Leibniz's law, Bill Clinton is the same person as Chelsea's father if and only if everything that is true of Bill Clinton is also true of Chelsea's father. In other words, if any two items have all and only the same things true of them, then they aren't two after all but only one. Since there is something true of sensations that is not true of brain states, according to this argument, sensations cannot be the same thing as brain states.

⑨ "Knowledge by acquaintance" requires direct experience of something, whereas "knowledge by description" does not. I am directly acquainted with the taste of chocolate ice cream (and thus know what it tastes like.) But I am not directly acquainted with the pain of a broken arm, though I've been told that it is very painful. So I know by description instead of by acquaintance, that a broken arm is very painful. Churchland claims that Mary knows about brain states by description, while she fails to know the relevant sensations by acquaintance. If this "conveniently tightened" version is an accurate interpretation of Jackson's original argument, then Churchland has a good objection, since the premises support the conclusion only if 'know' means the same thing in both premises.

states and their properties, because she does not know about certain qualia associated with them. What is complete, according to the argument, is her knowledge of matters physical. A convenient and accurate way of displaying the argument is:

(1) Mary (before her release) knows everything physical there is to know about other people. [10]
(2) Mary (before her release) does not know everything there is to know about other people (because she *learns* something about them on her release).

Therefore,

(3) There are truths about other people (and herself) which escape the physicalist story.

[10] Including, obviously, everything about their brain states and their properties.

What is immediately to the point is not the kind, manner, or type of knowledge Mary has, but *what* she knows. What she knows beforehand is ex hypothesi everything physical there is to know, but is it everything there is to know? That is the crucial question. [11]

[11] "Ex hypothesi" just means according to the hypothesis being considered.

There is, though, a relevant challenge involving questions about kinds of knowledge. It concerns the *support* for premise 2′. The case for premise 2′ is that Mary learns something on her release, she acquires knowledge, and that entails that her knowledge beforehand (*what* she knew, never mind whether by description, acquaintance, or whatever) was incomplete. The challenge, mounted by David Lewis and Laurence Nemirow, is that on her release Mary does *not* learn something or acquire knowledge in the relevant sense. What Mary acquires when she is released is a certain representational or imaginative ability; it is knowledge how rather than knowledge that. Hence, a physicalist can admit that Mary acquires something very significant of a knowledge kind—which can hardly be denied—without admitting that this shows that her earlier factual knowledge is defective. She knew all *that* there was to know about the experiences of others beforehand, but lacked an ability until after her release. [12]

Now it is certainly true that Mary will acquire abilities of various kinds after her release. She will, for instance, be able to imagine what seeing red is like,

be able to remember what it is like, and be able to understand why her friends regarded her as so deprived (something which, until her release, had always mystified her). But is it plausible that that is *all* she will acquire? Suppose she received a lecture on skepticism about other minds while she was incarcerated. On her release she sees a ripe tomato in normal conditions, and so has a sensation of red. Her first reaction is to say that she now knows more about the kind of experiences others have when looking at ripe tomatoes. She then remembers the lecture and starts to worry. Does she really know more about what their experiences are like, or is she indulging in a wild generalization from one case? [13] In the end she decides she does know, and that skepticism is mistaken (even if, like so many of us, she is not sure how to demonstrate its errors). What was she to-ing and fro-ing about—her abilities? Surely not; her representational abilities were a known constant throughout. What else then was she agonizing about than whether or not she had gained factual knowledge of others? There would be nothing to agonize about if ability was *all* she acquired on her release. [14]

I grant that I have no *proof* that Mary acquires on her release, as well as abilities, factual knowledge about the experiences

[12] Lewis and Nemirow are claiming that what Mary acquires is the ability to imagine red or perhaps to represent it in one particular way, but that she does not learn any new facts. (Does this seem like a plausible claim?)

[13] What Mary is supposed to be worrying about here is whether she is justified in ascribing the new fact she has seemingly learned through her own experiences to the experiences of other people as well. (Think here of the inverted spectrum case as described in the first Fodor selection: one way to see the point is to suppose that Mary is worried about whether other people might have color experiences that are inverted in relation to hers—in which case she really hasn't learned what it is like for *them* to experience red.)

[14] Mary decides that this skeptical worry is not to be taken seriously. But Jackson's point is that there was at least a factual claim about the experiences of others about whose correctness she was uncertain, in which case the Lewis-Nemirow suggestion that she had acquired *only* a new imaginative or representational ability is mistaken. (See Discussion Question 1.)

of others—and not just because I have no disproof of skepticism. My claim is that the knowledge argument is a valid argument from highly plausible, though admittedly not demonstrable, premises to the conclusion that physicalism is false. And that, after all, is about as good an objection as one could expect in this area of philosophy.

(ii) Churchland's second objection . . . is that there must be something wrong with the argument, for it proves too much. Suppose Mary received a special series of lectures over her black-and-white television from a full-blown dualist, explaining the "laws" governing the behavior of "ectoplasm" and telling her about qualia. This would not affect the plausibility of the claim that on her release she learns something. So if the argument works against physicalism, it works against dualism too. [15]

My reply is that lectures about qualia over black-and-white television do not tell Mary all there is to know about qualia. They may tell her some things about qualia, for instance, that they do not appear in the physicalist's story, and that the quale we use 'yellow' for is nearly as different from the one we use 'blue' for as is white from black. But why should it be supposed that they tell her everything about qualia? On the other hand, it is plausible that lectures over black-and-white television might in principle tell Mary everything in the physicalist's story. You do not need color television to learn physics or functionalist psychology. To obtain a good argument against dualism (attribute dualism; ectoplasm is a bit of fun), the premise in the knowledge argument that Mary has the full story according to physicalism before her release, has to be replaced by a premise that she has the full story according to dualism. The former is plausible; the latter is not. Hence, there is no "parity of reasons" trouble for dualists who use the knowledge argument. [16]

(iii) Churchland's third objection is that the knowledge argument claims "that Mary could not even *imagine* what the relevant experience would be like, despite her exhaustive neuroscientific knowledge, and hence must still be missing certain crucial information" . . . , a claim he goes on to argue against.

But, as we emphasized earlier, the knowledge argument claims that Mary would not know what the relevant experience is like. What she could imagine is another matter. If her knowledge is defective, despite being all there is to know according to physicalism, then physicalism is false, whatever her powers of imagination.

[15] The objection is that if Mary does learn something new, it would still be something new even if she had also learned (and accepted) everything about a dualist view of mental states in the same way that she learned everything about physical things, again through black-and-white books and television. Therefore, Churchland is suggesting, the Mary example counts just as much against dualism as against materialism.

[16] Jackson's response is that while we have every reason to think that Mary's black-and-white educational process is adequate for her to acquire a complete account of the physical world, there is no reason to think that the same thing is true for nonphysical facts of the sort advocated by dualism. Is he right about this? (See Discussion Question 2.) (*Attribute dualism* is the version of dualism that holds that there are both physical and nonphysical *properties,* but not necessarily two different sorts of things or substances.)

Discussion Questions

1. It is hard to deny that Mary learns or acquires *something* new when she leaves the black-and-white room and experiences colors. But is it new *facts* that she learns? Or is it, as Lewis and Nemirow suggest, new *abilities* to imagine or represent? Or is it something still different? One way to think about this issue is to try to say what the new facts are, if indeed there are any. Can these new facts be linguistically formulated, and if so, how? If not, what does that show?

2. Jackson claims that while it is very plausible to suppose that Mary can learn everything about the physical description of the world in a black-and-white way, this is much less obviously plausible for a dualist account of mental states. How plausible is this claim? Does Jackson offer any real argument for it? Can you think of an argument? (One approach might be to appeal to Nagel's distinction between objective and subjective facts.)

Laurence BonJour

Laurence BonJour (1943–) is an American philosopher who teaches at the University of Washington in Seattle and is best known for his work in epistemology. He is a coeditor of this book.

BonJour claims that there is a compelling argument against physicalism or materialism, one that grows out of the main insights of the Nagel and Jackson selections. This paper is not published anywhere else, but a more complete version can be found at http://faculty.washington .edu/bonjour.

What Is It Like To Be a Human (Instead of a Bat)?

My purpose in this paper is to discuss and defend an objection to physicalist or materialist accounts of the mind—one that I believe to be essentially conclusive.① The argument in question is not new. A version of it seems to be lurking, along with much else, in Thomas Nagel's famous paper "What Is It Like to Be a Bat?";* and a somewhat more explicit version is to be found in a well-known paper by Frank Jackson.† Despite the efforts of Nagel and Jackson (and some others), however, I believe that the most compelling version of the argument has not emerged clearly, with the result that materialist replies that in fact fail to speak to its central point are often taken to be adequate. Thus one purpose of the present paper is to offer what I regard as a more perspicuous restatement of the Nagel-Jackson argument, one which shows clearly why the replies in question do not work. A second purpose is to suggest that the application of the argument is in fact very much wider than the case of phenomenal properties or qualia upon which both Nagel and Jackson focus, that it in fact applies just as well to the content of intentional mental states like thoughts and indeed to the general phenomenon of consciousness itself.

I

I begin with a brief and selective recapitulation of Nagel's and Jackson's presentations of the argument and of some of the critical responses they evoked, focusing on those raised by Paul Churchland.

Though, as we will see, there are several other balls in the air, the strand of Nagel's argument upon which I wish to focus goes at least approximately as follows: It is reasonable to assume that bats have conscious experience of some kind, that as Nagel puts it "there is something it is like to be a bat." But such experience is surely enormously different from our own in many ways, due to the very different "range of activity and sensory apparatus" possessed by bats, in particular their well-known capacity of perceiving the world and navigating through it via a kind of sonar resulting from the reflection of their own high-pitched cries. Nagel's question is whether we could ever come to know "what it is like to be a bat," and in particular whether we could do this on the basis of a thoroughgoing knowledge of the physical or material facts pertaining to bat physiology. His claim is that we could

① When BonJour refers to physicalist or materialist accounts of the mind, he has in mind not just what Fodor calls central state materialism, but also functionalist theories. Since most functionalists are what Fodor calls token physicalists, their claim is that each mental state is some brain state or other, that, in other words, there is nothing more to a mental state than the particular brain state that it is (including its physically specified causal role).

*Reprinted in this book, pp. 382–390.
†Frank Jackson, "What Mary Didn't Know," reprinted in this book, pp. 392–395.

not, and the suggested conclusion, which he himself never quite draws, is that physicalism is false.

As will emerge, I believe that the foregoing argument is essentially sound. But Nagel's version of it seems to me less perspicuous than it might be, largely because so many other ideas and suggestions are present in the paper as well, ideas and suggestions that are not even clearly compatible with the foregoing argument and that in any case seem to point in rather different directions. There is, first, the idea of a "point of view," with the suggestion that certain kinds of facts may be knowable only from a certain point of view and the accompanying distinction between various "subjective" points of view and the "objective" point of view characteristic of physical science. Secondly, there is the concern with conceptual limitations, and the suggestion that the main problem with regard to bats is that we may not have and may not be able to acquire the right concepts to capture bat experiences. Third, there is the suggestion that the right conclusion is not so much that physicalism is false as that we do not understand how it could be true—which might still be compatible, Nagel suggests, with having good or even compelling reasons to think that it is true. And, fourth, even the formulation that I have echoed in my title in terms of "what it is like to be a bat" is at least potentially misleading, in that it (along with the employment of the objective/subjective dichotomy) might suggest that the knowledge that we are lacking with respect to bats is not so much knowledge of *facts* as knowledge of what it would "feel like from the in-

2 BonJour is mentioning these points only to set them aside as irrelevant to the specific argument he is interested in.

side" to be a bat—thereby inviting the reasonably plausible response that this is not a sort of knowledge that physicalism could be expected to provide even if it were true. 2

Jackson's version of the argument focuses more clearly on what I regard as the central point. In the most compelling version, it imagines a brilliant scientist, Mary, who lives her entire life, acquires her education, and does all of her scientific work in a black-and-white environment, using black-and-white books and black-and-white television for all of her learning and research. In this way, we may suppose, she comes to have a complete knowledge of all the physical facts in neurophysiology and related fields, together with their deductive consequences, insofar as these are relevant— thus arriving at as complete an understanding of

3 The relevant point again is not that it is true that there is someone like Mary. It just has to be *possible* that there is someone like Mary: someone who knows all the physical facts about our brains, central nervous system, sense organs, and anything else that is relevant to the way we take in and process information.

human functioning as those sciences can provide. 3 In particular, Mary knows the functional roles of all of the various brain states, including those pertaining to sense perception, insofar as these are reflected in their causal relations to sensory inputs, behavioral outputs, and other such states. But despite all of this knowledge, Jackson suggests, Mary does not know all that there is to know about human mental states: for when she is released from her black-and-white environment and allowed to view the world normally, she will, by viewing objects like ripe tomatoes, "learn what it is like to see something red," and analogous things about other colors. But then, argues Jackson, her previous knowledge must have been incomplete, in spite of the fact that she had all the relevant physical information. Therefore, there is more to know about mental states than is contained in the physical account, from which it follows that the physicalist claim to give a complete account of mental states must be mistaken.

While this version of the argument is certainly less burdened with other distractions than Nagel's and is also once again, I believe, essentially sound, there are still problems. These may be examined by considering two objections to the Jackson version offered by Churchland.*

Churchland's first objection is that while Mary undoubtedly learns *something* new when she is released from her black-and-white environment, what she acquires is not *knowledge* in the same sense of that term in which the physicalist claims that she already

---

*Paul M. Churchland, "Reduction, Qualia, and the Direct Inspection of Brain States," *Journal of Philosophy,* volume 82 (1985), pp. 8–28.

knows all there is to know.④ The sense of "knowledge" in which physicalism guarantees that Mary's knowledge is complete is that she knows all true *propositions,* while the sort of knowledge that Mary acquires is:

④ According to this objection to Jackson's knowledge argument, "know" means something different in (a) than it does in (b): (a) if physicalism is true, Mary *knows* everything there is to know while still in her black-and-white room; (b) Mary did *not* know everything about human mental states, since she learned something new when she left her black-and-white room. See the selection from Jackson for a response to this argument.

a matter of having a representation of redness in some prelinguistic or sublinguistic medium of representation for sensory variables, or . . . a matter of being able to make certain sensory discriminations, or something along these lines.

Churchland's point may perhaps be put somewhat more clearly by saying that it is not the case, according to him, that what Mary is initially lacking and then later comes to acquire is a knowledge of certain *facts* or *truths* about human mental states, but that knowledge of facts or truths is all that the physical account could be expected to supply, even if physicalism were correct. I believe that Churchland's claim that Mary does not come to know any new facts or truths is mistaken, but this point is difficult to establish clearly within the context of Jackson's formulation of the argument: if she learns new facts or truths, what exactly are they?

Churchland's second objection turns on the intriguing suggestion that Mary, once she has learned to employ the concepts of a completed neuroscience in introspection, might be able to imaginatively extrapolate from her introspective awareness of her black-and-white experiences to the experiences she would have if she were in the brain states corresponding to color experience and thus might come to have a tentative idea of "what it is like to see something red." Jackson's response is that if physicalism were true, Mary should *know* what the experience is like, rather than merely having to imagine it. But I do not see why Churchland, if his point were otherwise sound, could not claim that Mary might indeed come to know in this way what the experience is like, albeit via a kind of imaginative inference rather than direct experience.⑤ Again, I believe that Churchland

is mistaken here: both about what Mary would be able to do and, more importantly, about the relevance of this issue to the central point of the argument. But Jackson's formulation of the argument makes it hard to clearly establish either of these things.

II

What is needed, in my judgment, is a version of the argument that, first, makes it clear that there are *facts* or *truths* about human mental states that someone in Mary's position does not and cannot know on the basis of purely physical knowledge, however complete that may be; and, second, avoids relatively intractable issues about what Mary might be able to imagine or imaginatively infer on the basis of her own experience.⑥ And the way to do this, I suggest, is in effect to invert Nagel's original example, in a way that he himself suggests in passing but does not develop: instead of imagining ourselves trying to know or comprehend the experiences of an alien form of life, we need instead to imagine an alien form of life trying to know or comprehend our experiences.

Suppose then that a brilliant Martian scientist comes to Earth to investigate, with our full cooperation, the nature and makeup of human beings.⑦ Being a Martian, he has, we may suppose, a quite different sensory apparatus from ours, but one which is still quite adequate, given his complete mastery of scien-

⑤ Churchland's suggestion here seems to be that Mary, by comparing the brain states corresponding to her black-and-white experiences with those corresponding to other people's color experiences might somehow be able to infer from the nature of her black-and-white experiences to the nature of those other experiences via a sort of proportion: this brain state (A) is to this black-and-white experience (B) as that other brain state (C) is to the other person's experience (D), where Mary knows A, B, and C. This seems very difficult; but BonJour's main claim about it, made later, is that it is irrelevant to the main issue.

⑥ BonJour begins here to develop a version of the knowledge argument against physicalism that avoids the problems that in his view afflict Nagel's and Jackson's version.

⑦ This again is just a philosophical thought experiment, and thus it need not be true, just possible, that there is such a brilliant Martian scientist.

tific reasoning, to arrive at a complete knowledge of any purely physical phenomenon. Thus, in time, the Martian arrives at an ideally complete knowledge of the physical facts concerning human beings, including those pertaining to causally defined functional roles. Does he thereby come to know all of the facts about human mental states such as experiences of color?

Suppose that I am one of the subjects studied by the Martian. On a particular occasion, I look at a newly mowed, well-watered, and healthy lawn and thereby have an experience of a certain specific phenomenal or sensuous property, one which is somewhere toward the middle of the range of such properties that I am accustomed to call "green." Shortly thereafter, I look at a newly painted fire engine and thereby have an experience of a second specific phenomenal or sensuous property, one which is somewhere toward the middle of the range of properties that I am accustomed to call "red." That on the first occasion I experience the first property and on the second occasion the second property, rather than the other way around, are simply facts about me in the most straightforward possible sense. Suppose that the Martian is present on both occasions and is carefully monitoring my physical and brain states with an elaborate set of instruments that he has devised for this purpose. He thereby, we may suppose, comes to know *everything* about those physical states, including their causal relations to other states, to as fine a level of detail as could possibly be relevant. Is he thereby able to know that I am experiencing the first sensuous property on the first occasion and the second sensuous property on the second occasion? [8]

[8] If physicalism is true, then BonJour's experience of green is identical to, nothing more than, some particular brain state. The Martian will know that the particular brain state in question is caused by the light reflected from the lawn and causes BonJour to say things like "this is green" (and also to behave in various other ways).

I have stipulated that the Martian does not possess senses like ours. In particular, he does not possess eyes and a faculty of vision like ours. Thus one thing that he cannot do is determine what property I am experiencing by looking at the relevant objects himself. Nor should he need to do this, since facts about his own experiences are of course no part of his supposedly complete physical account of humans in general and of me in particular. [9] (The same thing is in fact true of Mary: Though she happens to be a member of the species that she is investigating, her introspective awareness of her own experiences is still not a part of the ideally complete physical account of humans at which she arrives by the methods of physical science. This is why Churchland's speculations about her imaginative extrapolations are simply irrelevant to the issue.)

[9] Even if he did have eyes and could look at the lawn, he wouldn't know that we experience that frequency of light waves in the same way he does. (The parenthetical remark that follows is BonJour's response to the suggestion that Mary might be able to extrapolate to the color experiences from her own black-and-white experiences and a comparison of the two sorts of brain states.)

The Martian does not experience colors in the way and in the contexts that we do. But it is still possible that he is familiar in some other way with the specific phenomenal or sensuous properties in question, and it will help to focus the essential point if we suppose that this is so. Thus suppose that he does experience those very properties, albeit in some quite different causal context. Perhaps he experiences colors when he hears or otherwise senses vibrations in the air corresponding to music. Or perhaps he does have something like eyes and vision, but in relation to a quite different range of electromagnetic radiation, and thereby experiences all of the colors that we experience (and perhaps others?), but in relation to different objects and situations than those that cause our specific experiences. Thus, we may suppose, he has a perfectly good grasp of the *concepts* of having an experience of each of the two properties in question, and the issue is only whether he can apply those concepts correctly to me. [10]

[10] The Martian then knows what the experience of (what we call) red is like and what the experience of (what we call) green is like. If the Martian asks which brain state *is* the experience of red (using the Martian word) and which one *is* the experience of green (again using the Martian word), he understands the question.

We may even concede to the Martian one more quite useful piece of information, albeit one that he almost certainly could not in fact arrive at on his own.

Let us stipulate not only that he is familiar with color properties and possesses the concepts of having such experiences, but even that he somehow knows—perhaps God whispers it in his ear or appropriate alternative sense organ—that two specific color properties out of the ones with which he is familiar are in fact the two that I am experiencing on the two occasions in question (but not of course which is which). In addition, we may suppose that the Martian has solved the difficult problem of isolating the specific features of my neurophysiology that are relevant to the issue we are concerned with, so that he is able to focus on two relatively restricted brain states (perhaps characterized in functional terms) that are, supposing that physicalism is true, identical to my experiencing of the two colors.[11] Thus he is able to formulate to himself two pairs of propositions, one pair identifying the first of these restricted states with an experiencing of the first of the two properties and the second restricted state with an experiencing of the second of the two properties, and the other pair reversing these ascriptions. He thus knows, we are supposing, that the propositions in one of these pairs are true and those in the other pair false, but not which is which. Can he tell, solely on the basis of his complete physical knowledge, which is the correct pair?[12]

> [11] BonJour has given the Martian the benefit of every doubt, for the sake of the argument, by stipulating that the Martian knows that one or the other of the two brain states is the experience of green (as specified in Martian) and the other is the experience of red (as specified in Martian).

> [12] If we name the first brain state A and the second brain state B, and we name the experience of red R and the experience of green G (or let these be the Martian names), then one pair of propositions is A is R and B is G; and the other pair of propositions is A is G and B is R. If physicalism is true, the Martian should be able to tell, given his complete knowledge of all things physical, which pair of propositions is true.

In thinking about this question, it is important to be quite clear about the exact shape of the issue. If physicalism is true, I submit, then the Martian should not have to extrapolate or surmise or guess, in however educated a fashion, in order to determine which pair of propositions is the correct one. If the ideal physical account is indeed a *complete* account of all the facts concerning humans and their mental states, and if one of the two pairs of propositions is true and

the other false in relation to that subject-matter, then it seems to follow that the propositions of the true pair must be already *included* in some way in that account, and that the propositions in the other pair must be in some way *incompatible* with that account. And this would apparently mean in turn that the ideas or concepts of the two phenomenal or sensuous properties in question would have to be either already present in the physical account or somehow strictly definable on the basis of the physical ideas or concepts pertaining to the relevant physical states.[13] The former of these alternatives seems clearly mistaken, which is just to say that neither the physical description of the brain nor that of the human organism as a whole explicitly invokes the idea of sensuous or phenomenal color. And the latter alternative is equally implausible. One way to argue this point is to appeal to the familiar view that color concepts are essentially indefinable, a view that I believe to be correct. But even apart from this sort of appeal, the idea that the concepts of the various sensuous or phenomenal colors are strictly definable on the basis of physical concepts pertaining to brain states and other strictly physical states has, if anything, even less plausibility than the old phenomenalist idea that concepts pertaining to physical object are definable in purely sensory terms. I do not know how to strictly prove that no such definition is possible, but I know of no one who has ever seriously defended such a view, nor of any way to make it even minimally plausible.

> [13] This claim is crucial to BonJour's argument that the Martian scientist is unable to know which of the two pairs of propositions is the right one: color concepts have to either be part of the physical theory or definable in terms of physical concepts. (It is important to emphasize here that BonJour's argument is concerned with the qualitative *experience* of color, not with such things as the corresponding wavelength of light, which the Martian can of course know.)

Thus it seems utterly plain that the answer to our original question is "no." All that the Martian's physical knowledge can give him is increasingly complicated accounts of the structure of the two restricted brain states and of their structural and causal relations to each other and to other states and processes of the same kind. But all of this knowledge, however detailed and elaborate we may suppose it to be, would still be entirely compatible with the truth of either of the two pairs of propositions concerning the relations of brain states to my color experiences. Thus although the Martian scientist knows all the *physical* facts there are, he does not know all the *facts* there are, and it follows that physicalism is false. ⑭

⑭ This concludes BonJour's initial version of the knowledge argument, as applied to phenomenal properties or qualia: if physicalism is true, then the brilliant Martian scientist can know, on the basis of his complete physical knowledge, which of the two pairs of propositions concerning the relation of BonJour's brain states with Bon-Jour's color experiences is true; but the Martian scientist cannot know on this basis which pair is true; so physicalism is not true.

⑮ This claim was crucial to BonJour's defense of the claim that the Martian scientist should be able to know which pair of propositions is true.

I want to conclude this section by considering briefly one possible rejoinder on behalf of the physicalist, a rejoinder that attempts to evade the argument by denying that it is a consequence of the truth of physicalism that all of the facts about a given sort of thing must be logically contained in a complete physical account of that thing. ⑮ On the contrary, it might be argued, there are at least two sorts of facts about a thing, one of them perhaps a subclass of the other, that need not, even if physicalism is true, be contained in a complete physical account that is confined to that thing. One sort of fact pertains to the *function* or *purpose* of the thing: thus I could know all of the purely physical facts about a certain sort of object and still not know that it is a chair, because being a chair has to do with its function for human beings and not with its purely physical description. The other sort of fact pertains to classifications that are relative to human needs or purposes and perhaps also to some degree conventional or even arbitrary: thus, for example, I could know all of the physical facts about a thing, including the precise mean kinetic energy of its molecules, and still not know that it was hot rather than lukewarm, as classified by common sense, because the difference here has to do with a fuzzy and relatively arbitrary line that humans draw, mainly for reasons having to do with their own body temperatures, within an essentially continuous range of physical temperatures. Thus, the correctness of physicalism does not mean that a phys-icalist account of something must include all of the facts about it.

But what makes facts of the kinds suggested un-knowable on the basis of a complete physical description of the thing is that they implicitly have to do with *relations* between the thing in question and other things, in this case humans and their purposes and classifications, and it is obviously no surprise that a relational fact cannot be known via a complete de-scription of one of the related things alone. ⑯ And the reason that this point is irrelevant to the argu-ment against physicalism, forcing at most a minor clarification, is that it seems abundantly clear that having an experience of one phenomenal prop-erty rather than another on a given occasion is an in-trinsic property of a per-son, not one that is in any way relational. ⑰

⑯ Consider, for example, the relational fact that Seattle is north of Portland. A complete de-scription of Seattle by it-self will never reveal that relational fact.

⑰ An intrinsic property is one an object has inde-pendently of any facts about anything else, whereas a relational property is one an object has in part because of facts about other things.

III

My conclusion so far is that the physicalist or materi-alist view of human mental states is false, on the grounds that certain entirely obvious facts about the qualitative character of phenomenal experience are not captured by any imaginable physical account. I claim no great originality for the argument to this point, for I think that it is very close to what Nagel and especially Jackson had in mind, even though their specific formulations opened the door to irrelevant responses. But unlike Jackson and probably Nagel, I do not think that the force of the argument is re-stricted to phenomenal ex-periences, and I will devote the final two sections of the paper to a consideration of how it can be more widely applied, focusing in the present section on inten-tional states such as beliefs and desires. ⑱

⑱ Fodor claimed (p. 351) that the objec-tion that functionalism can't account for inten-tional states was more easily answered than the objection that functional-ism can't account for phenomenal states.

Even among those who are doubtful about the case of sensory experiences, it has often been supposed that a physicalist account of states like beliefs and desires is on a much sounder footing. This discussion has tended to focus on states of belief, but in the present discussion, I will avoid certain irrelevant problems by focusing on a simpler sort of state, though one that is still clearly intentional: the state of simply thinking about or envisaging something, of having it in mind.

Suppose then that on a particular occasion I am thinking about a certain species of animal, say dogs—not some specific dog, just dogs in general (but I mean domestic dogs, specifically, not dogs in the generic sense that includes wolves and coyotes). The Martian scientist is present and has his usual complete knowledge of my brain states. Can he tell on that basis alone what I am thinking about? Can he tell that I am thinking about dogs rather than about cats or radishes or typewriters or free will or nothing at all? It is surely far from obvious how he might do this. My suggestion is that he cannot, that no knowledge of the complexities of my brain state will enable him to pick out that specific content in the logically tight way required, and hence that physicalism is once again clearly shown to be false.

Before examining this issue, however, it is important to be somewhat clearer than has been necessary so far about the scope of the knowledge that the Martian is allowed to draw on for this purpose. It is natural and, I believe, essentially correct, to regard my having a thought about dogs as a purely internal property of me, one that does not depend in a constitutive way on external objects and situations or on my relations to them (though it may of course be a causal result of such things). This is reflected in the fact that I am able in general to tell "from the inside," simply by reflection, what I am thinking about, without needing to know anything about these external matters.[19] Thus the Martian should apparently be able to tell on the basis of my internal physiology alone that I am thinking about dogs.

Before arguing specifically that he cannot, I want to consider briefly some possible objections to this construal of the issue, growing out of recent work in the philosophy of language, which challenge the very idea that having a thought with a certain content is an internal property of the person. A full consideration of the various ideas and doctrines involved in these objections is once again obviously impossible within the confines of this paper. But I believe that it will nonetheless be relatively easy to see that they have no serious effect on the main line of argument being advocated here.

Consider, first, the idea of "the division of linguistic labor." In various papers, Putnam has suggested that I need not have any very clear and determinate conception of, for example, dogs in order to be thinking about them. It is enough, he seems to suggest, if I merely employ in my thinking the word "dog," with the reference of the word being determined by "the relevant group of experts."*[20] Thus, it might be suggested, it would not be at all surprising if the Martian scientist is unable to determine on the basis of my internal neurophysiology alone that I am thinking about dogs, for this fact depends on facts about the experts and not merely on my internal properties.

I think that it is far from obvious that someone who has no conception at all of what sort of thing a

> [19] Think about an alligator. Now think about Mars. Could you tell from the inside what you were thinking about? If the content of BonJour's thought just is some brain state or other, then, he is suggesting, the Martian should be able to tell what he is thinking just by knowing everything there is to know about that brain state.

> [20] This is a view sometimes referred to as an externalist theory of thought content, according to which the content of a thought is *constituted* (not just caused) by external matters (like the knowledge of experts). A person employs the mental word "dog," but what that mental word refers to depends on these external matters.

---

*See, for example, Hilary Putnam, "The Meaning of 'Meaning'," in his *Mind, Language and Reality* (Cambridge: Cambridge University Press, 1975).

dog is, not even that it is an animal as opposed to a vegetable or an inanimate or even an abstract object, can nonetheless be genuinely thinking about dogs solely by virtue of employing the word. I also doubt that the Martian scientist would find it any easier to determine that I am indeed employing, in the relevant sense, a certain word. But it is enough for present purposes to focus on someone like myself who has a much more detailed conception of a dog. I am not one of the relevant experts (though that would be a possible case too), so it is possible that there are actual non-dogs that I could not distinguish from dogs. This is to say that my conception, and probably anyone's conception, of dogs fails to be completely determinate. But this does nothing to solve the main problem, for we can still ask whether the Martian can tell what this somewhat indeterminate thought content is, and the correct answer, I suggest, will still be negative.

Another idea in the same vicinity is the causal theory of reference or perhaps of thought content generally. Again it is suggested that what I am thinking about is not determined by my internal state alone, but depends also on external relations, in this case causal relations, including the causal history of the words I employ.[21] Here too we may concede that there is something right about the point in question. It is at least plausible to think that part of what makes my thought pertain to dogs, the earthly species, rather than to creatures on some other planet that might be indistinguishable from earthly dogs even by the experts at the time in question even though biologically unrelated to them, is that I am causally related, partly or perhaps even entirely via the causal history of the word "dog," to earthly dogs and not to these other creatures. The only thing that we must resist is a *completely* externalist account of content, according to which my internal state possesses by itself no content at all and thus nothing that the Martian could fail

to know. And here it is enough, I think, to point out that a completely externalist view of content would be incompatible with the obvious fact pointed out earlier: on a completely externalist view, I would have from the inside no grasp at all of what I was thinking about, since I have in general no access to the relevant causal relations—a result that I take to be obviously and indeed monumentally absurd.*[22]

Despite the enormous complexity and subtlety of the recent work in this area, the foregoing is, I think, enough to show that the specific instance of the argument against physicalism that is under discussion in this section cannot be plausibly met by denying that the content of my thoughts is, to a sufficient degree to pose the problem, an internal property of me.[23] Any account of content that makes it accessible enough from the inside to avoid clear absurdity will also make it to that same degree internal, thereby posing a clear challenge to the Martian and hence to physicalism.

Suppose then, as seems undeniable, that when I am thinking about dogs, my state of mind has a definite internal or intrinsic albeit perhaps somewhat indeterminate content, roughly the idea of a medium-sized hairy animal of a distinctive shape, behaving in characteristic ways, and so forth. Is there any plausible way in which, contrary to my earlier suggestion, the Martian scientist might come to know this content on the basis of his purely physical knowledge of me? As with the earlier instance of the argument, we may set aside issues that are here irrelevant (though they may well have an independent significance of their own) by supposing that the Martian scientist has an independent grasp of a conception of

[21] This is a slightly different version of an externalist theory of thought content. Fodor seems to have some view of this sort in mind in his reply to Searle.

[22] See Discussion Question 1 to Fodor's response to Searle for more on this issue.

[23] BonJour's claim is that even if some of the content of his thought, when he is thinking about dogs, is external to him, it is obvious there is at least some of the content that is internal to him, and thus the Martian scientist should at least be able to know what that internal part is.

---

*A philosopher who shall remain nameless once conceded to me in the course of a discussion of this sort of issue that on his view, he could not tell from the inside that we were not in fact discussing quantum mechanics rather than the philosophy of language. It should be easy to see why this made it seem futile to go on with the discussion.

dogs that is essentially the same as mine, so that he is able to formulate to himself, but only as one possibility among many, the thesis that I am thinking about dogs, thus conceived. 24

[24] Again BonJour is attempting to give the Martian as much help as possible.

We may also suppose that he has isolated the particular brain state, again perhaps functionally characterized, that is according to the physicalist identical to my thought about dogs. Is there any way that he can get further than this?

The problem is essentially the same as before. The Martian will know a lot of broadly structural facts about the state in question, together with causal and structural facts about its relations to other such states. But it is clear that the various ingredients of my conception of dogs (such as the ideas of hairiness, of barking, and so on) will not be explicitly present in the physical account, and extremely implausible to think that they will be definable on the basis of the relevant physical concepts. Thus, it would seem, there is no way that the physical account of me can logically compel the conclusion that I am thinking about dogs to the exclusion of other alternatives. 25 The indicated conclusion, once again, is that the physical account leaves out a fundamental aspect of our mental lives, and hence that physicalism is false.

[25] The assumption again is that the Martian would know that BonJour is thinking in a certain way about dogs only if BonJour's conception of a dog is either explicitly present or definable in terms of the physical concepts included in the complete physical account of BonJour's brain.

IV

I want to consider one more application of our general line of argument, in some ways the most fundamental of all, but one that is fortunately capable of being dealt with very briefly. It is obvious that on any plausible version of physicalism, only some of our brain states will be identified with conscious mental states. There is no consciousness associated with those states, for example, that control breathing and heartbeat. But this suggests the issue of whether our Martian scientist, on the basis of his complete physical knowledge, can tell which brain states are conscious and which are not. 26 My suggestion, once again, is that there is no way that he can do this in the logically tight way that is required.

[26] This is the same issue that was originally raised by Smart. This line of argument about consciousness could be more fully developed in ways very similar to the original argument about color. Think about how it would go.

We may suppose, reasonably enough, that there is some structural difference between states that are conscious and states that are not, and hence that the Martian can divide our states into two groups, corresponding to this difference. But even if he can get this far, how can he possibly determine, as opposed to merely surmise or conjecture, that the states in one group involve consciousness and that those in the other do not? It is, if anything, even more obvious that consciousness is not explicitly mentioned as such in his complete physical account, nor definable in terms of things that are mentioned. And again, as with the case of phenomenal properties, I know of no one who has ever seriously suggested otherwise.

My conclusion is that the Martian scientist, in spite of possessing complete physical knowledge of me, could not know many important facts about my conscious mental life, nor indeed even that I have a conscious mental life at all. This means that the physical account is radically incomplete as an account of my complete personal makeup and hence that physicalism or materialism, as an account of human beings, is surely and irredeemably false.

Discussion Questions

1. Would it really be possible for Mary to infer to the nature of color experiences in the way explained in Annotation 5? Why does BonJour think that this possibility, if it is a genuine possibility, is still irrelevant to the main issue posed by his argument? Is he right about this?

2. Suppose someone responded to the Martian scientist argument in the following way: of course the Martian would know which pair of propositions was the true pair, since the Martian knows everything there is to know about BonJour and his brain. BonJour would reply

that the Martian only knows every *physical* fact about himself and his brain. At this point, it may seem that the only possible response the objector has is the following: well, sure, he knows all the physical facts, and since all facts are physical facts, he knows all the facts. But the objector cannot say that all facts are physical facts, since that presupposes the very thing at issue—in other words such a claim would **beg the question** in favor of physicalism. Does the objector (the one who insists that the Martian scientist would know which pair of propositions is the true pair) have anything better to say about how he might do this?

3. Is the content of your thoughts something that you have direct, internal access to, at least to some extent? If it is, is there any way that Fodor's view that thought content is determined by the external causal relations between symbols in your mind and external objects can account for the accessibility of thought content?

David Lewis

David Lewis (1941–2001) was a major American philosopher who taught at Princeton University. He is most well-known for his work in metaphysics, but also made important contributions to many other areas.

When J. J. C. Smart considered the problem of phenomenal properties 20 years earlier, before the knowledge argument was proposed, he was very confident that science would discover the physical facts that constituted these phenomenal properties. He was confident that sensations could be reduced to brain processes. But Lewis, writing 20 years later, says that the physicalist ultimately must deny the very existence of phenomenal properties in order to respond to the knowledge argument.

Knowing What It's Like

The most formidable challenge to any sort of materialism and functionalism comes from the friend of phenomenal qualia. He says we leave out the phenomenal aspect of mental life [1]: we forget that pain is a feeling, that there is something it is like to hold one's hand in a flame, that we are aware of something when we suffer pain, that we can recognize that something when it comes again. . . . So far, our proper reply is the one sketched in [Lewis's article "Mad Pain and Martian Pain"]: we deny none of that! We say to the friend of qualia that, beneath his tendentious jargon, he is just talking about pain and various aspects of its functional role. We have already said what we take pain to be; and we do not doubt that part of its causal role is to give rise to judgments that one is in pain, and part is to enable one to recognize pain (the same realizer of the same role) when it comes again. [2]

[1] Lewis himself advocates a functionalist version of materialism about the mind, which is why he uses "we" to refer to the proponents of the view being challenged.

[2] These are some of the many things that a functionalist might say when trying to account for pain, or any other experiential state.

From Philosophical Papers, *Vol. 1 (New York: Oxford University Press, 1983).*

So far, so good. But if he persists, the friend of qualia can succeed in escaping our unwelcome agreement; and when he does, we must reverse our strategy. Suppose he makes his case as follows.*

> You have not tasted Vegemite (a celebrated yeast-based condiment). So you do not know what it is like to taste Vegemite. And you never will, unless you taste Vegemite. (Or unless the same experience, or counterfeit traces of it, are somehow produced in you by artificial means.) No amount of the information whereof materialists and functionalists speak will help you at all. But if you taste Vegemite, *then* you will know what it is like. So you will have gained a sort of information that the materialists and functionalists overlook entirely. Call this *phenomenal information.* By qualia I mean the special subject matter of this phenomenal information.

Now we must turn eliminative.③ We dare not grant that there is a sort of information we overlook; or, in other words, that there are possibilities exactly alike in the respects we know of, yet different in some other way. That would be defeat. Neither can we credibly claim that lessons in physics, physiology, . . . could teach the inexperienced what it is like to taste Vegemite. Our proper answer, I think, is that knowing what it's like is not the possession of information at all. It isn't the elimination of any hitherto open possibilities. Rather, knowing what it's like is the possession of abilities: abilities to recognize, abilities to imagine, abilities to predict one's behavior by means of imaginative experiments. (Someone who knows what it's like to taste Vegemite can easily and reliably predict whether he would eat a second helping of Vegemite ice cream.) Lessons cannot impart these abilities—who would have thought they could? There is a state of knowing what it's like, sure enough. And Vegemite has a special power to produce that state. But phenomenal information and its special subject matter do not exist.④

③ That is, the functionalist must, according to Lewis, deny the very existence of the sort of phenomenal information to which Jackson's argument appeals. Pay close attention to exactly what is going to be eliminated.

④ On this view, knowing what it's like does not involve having any special sort of information, knowing any *facts,* but rather being able to *do* something: recognize, discriminate, predict. It is still perhaps a kind of knowing, but not a kind that involves information. (A similar point was made by Churchland, as discussed by Jackson and BonJour.)

Imagine a smart data bank. It can be told things, it can store the information it is given, it can reason with it, it can answer questions on the basis of its stored information. Now imagine a pattern-recognizing device that works as follows. When exposed to a pattern it makes a sort of template, which it then applies to patterns presented to it in future. Now imagine one device with both faculties, rather like a clock radio. There is no reason to think that any such device must have a third faculty: a faculty of making templates for patterns it has never been exposed to, using its stored information about these patterns. If it has a full description about a pattern but no template for it, it lacks an ability but it doesn't lack information. (Rather, it lacks information in usable form.) When it is shown the pattern it makes a template and gains abilities, but it gains no information. We might be rather like that.⑤

⑤ Think carefully about this analogy. The correlate of the "template" in our case is the sort of awareness that allows one to recognize previously experienced things and discriminate among them. But on Lewis's view, such an awareness does not involve any new information.

Discussion Questions

1. Lewis denies that "knowing what it is like" to have a certain experience involves coming to have any sort of new information. But then it seems that he must also deny that such experience involves becoming aware of distinctive phenomenal properties, for if it did, there would seemingly be information involved: that the experience involved one such phenomenal

---

*This is the "knowledge argument" of Frank Jackson. It appears also, in less purified form, in Thomas Nagel, "What Is It Like To Be a Bat?" *Philosophical Review* 83 (1974): 435–50 [pp. 382–390].

property rather than another. (See BonJour's version of the knowledge argument.) How plausible is it to deny the very existence of such properties? One part of this issue is how someone could predict whether he would eat another serving of Vegemite ice cream except by being familiar with the resulting phenomenal property and liking or disliking it.

2. Think again about the analogy that Lewis offers at the end of the selection. The device has all the information about some pattern that it has never been exposed to, but no "template" for it (and so would be unable to recognize it). But if it has all the information together with a general capacity for templates, *why* wouldn't it be able to arrive on that basis at a new "template" corresponding to the not-yet experienced pattern? What does the "template" involve, over and above the complete information about the pattern? Is this a good analogy for the relation between our qualitative experience and our physical brain states?

David J. Chalmers

David Chalmers (1966–) was born in Australia but has taught mainly in the United States, most recently at the University of Arizona in Tucson. He is best known for his work in the philosophy of mind.

In this selection, Chalmers distinguishes between the *hard problem* and the *easy problems* of consciousness. The easy problems ultimately have to do with how the brain does the various things it does, while the hard problem concerns how the brain gives rise to conscious experience. He argues that the results of neuroscience are insufficient to solve the hard problem of consciousness because of what he calls "the explanatory gap." Chalmers does not develop a version of dualism in any detail, but he seems to have in mind a version of **epiphenomenalism,** according to which conscious states or properties do not have any effect on the physical world.

The Puzzle of Conscious Experience

Conscious experience is at once the most familiar thing in the world and the most mysterious. There is nothing we know about more directly than consciousness, but it is extraordinarily hard to reconcile it with everything else we know. Why does it exist? What does it do? How could it possibly arise from neural processes in the brain? These questions are among the most intriguing in all of science.

From an objective viewpoint, the brain is relatively comprehensible. When you look at this page, there is a whir of processing: photons stirring your retina, electrical signals are passed up your optic nerve and between different areas of your brain, and

From Scientific American *(December 1995).*

eventually you might respond with a smile, a perplexed frown or a remark. But there is also a subjective aspect. When you look at the page, you are conscious of it, directly experiencing the images and words as part of your private, mental life. You have vivid impressions of colored flowers and vibrant sky.① At the same time, you may be feeling some emotions and forming some thoughts. Together

① While you have no vivid impressions of flowers and sky when looking at this page, you would have such impressions if you were looking at flowers and sky outside or at a picture of flowers and sky. Chalmers is pointing here to the same thing that Nagel was talking about when he said that there is "something that it is like" to, for example, see flowers and sky.

such experiences make up consciousness: the subjective, inner life of the mind.

For many years, consciousness was shunned by researchers studying the brain and the mind. The prevailing view was that science, which depends on objectivity, could not accommodate something as subjective as consciousness. The behaviorist movement in psychology, dominant earlier in this century, concentrated on external behavior and disallowed any talk of internal mental processes. Later, the rise of cognitive science focused attention on processes inside the head. Still, consciousness remained off-limits, fit only for late-night discussion over drinks.

Over the past several years, however, an increasing number of neuroscientists, psychologists and philosophers have been rejecting the idea that consciousness cannot be studied and are attempting to delve into its secrets. As might be expected of a field so new, there is a tangle of diverse and conflicting theories, often using basic concepts in incompatible ways. To help unsnarl the tangle, philosophical reasoning is vital.

The myriad views within the field range from reductionist theories, according to which consciousness can be explained by the standard methods of neuroscience and psychology, to the position of the so-called mysterians, who say we will never understand consciousness at all.② I believe that on close analysis both of these views can be seen to be mistaken and that the truth lies somewhere in the middle.

② A reductionist theory of consciousness reduces consciousness to something more familiar: for example, the central state identity theory reduces mental states to brain states, since mental states *just are* brain states. Some philosophers (usually materialists) think that all dualists are "mysterians." (Does that seem a fair thing to say about Foster or Campbell?)

Against reductionism I will argue that the tools of neuroscience cannot provide a full account of conscious experience, although they have much to offer. Against mysterianism I will hold that consciousness might be explained by a new kind of theory. The full details of such a theory are still out of reach, but careful reasoning and some educated inferences can reveal something of its general nature. For example, it will probably involve new fundamental laws, and the concept of information

may play a central role. These faint glimmerings suggest that a theory of consciousness may have startling consequences for our view of the universe and of ourselves.

THE HARD PROBLEM

Researchers use the word "consciousness" in many different ways. To clarify the issues, we first have to separate the problems that are often clustered together under the name. For this purpose, I find it useful to distinguish between the "easy problems" and the "hard problem" of consciousness. The easy problems are by no means trivial—they are actually as challenging as most in psychology and biology—but it is with the hard problem that the central mystery lies.

The easy problems of consciousness include the following: How can a human subject discriminate sensory stimuli and react to them appropriately? How does the brain integrate information from many different sources and use this information to control behavior? How is it that subjects can verbalize their internal states? Although all these questions are associated with consciousness, they all concern the objective mechanisms of the cognitive system. Consequently, we have every reason to expect that continued work in cognitive psychology and neuroscience will answer them.③

③ These are the kinds of questions that the scientist in Nagel's example could answer about bats and that BonJour's Martian scientist could answer about humans.

The hard problem, in contrast, is the question of how physical processes in the brain give rise to subjective experience. This puzzle involves the inner aspect of thought and perception: the way things feel for the subject. When we see, for example, we experience visual sensations, such as that of vivid blue. Or think of the ineffable sound of a distant oboe, the agony of an intense pain, the sparkle of happiness or the meditative quality of a moment lost in thought. All are part of what I am calling consciousness. It is these phenomena that pose the real mystery of the mind.④

④ The real mystery, according to Chalmers, is how something physical like the brain can "give rise to" or cause experiences like these.

To illustrate the distinction, consider a thought experiment devised by the Australian philosopher Frank Jackson.⑤ Suppose that Mary, a neuroscientist in the 23rd century, is the world's leading expert on the brain processes responsible for color vision. But Mary has lived her whole life in a black-and-white room and has never seen any other colors. She knows everything there is to know about physical processes in the brain—its biology, structure and function. This understanding enables her to grasp everything there is to know about the easy problems: how the brain discriminates stimuli, integrates information and produces verbal reports. From her knowledge of color vision, she knows the way color names correspond with wavelengths on the light spectrum. But there is still something crucial about color vision that Mary does not know: what it is like to experience a color such as red. It follows that there are facts about conscious experience that cannot be deduced from physical facts about the functioning of the brain.⑥

⑤ See the earlier selection by Jackson (and also BonJour's account of this argument).

⑥ Chalmers is assuming, with Jackson, that Mary's experience of red is a real conscious experience that Mary would have known about before only if she could have *deduced* an adequate description of it from physical facts about the brain. (Notice the similarity between this argument and BonJour's Martian scientist argument.)

Indeed, nobody knows why these physical processes are accompanied by conscious experience at all. Why is it that when our brains process light of a certain wavelength, we have an experience of deep purple? Why do we have an experience at all? Could not an unconscious automaton have performed the same tasks just as well? These are questions that we would like a theory of consciousness to answer.

⑦ In saying that consciousness "arises from" the brain, Chalmers is not saying, as the materialist does, that conscious states just are brain states. Instead, he is saying that conscious states are entirely caused by brain states (something that some versions of dualism would accept, but others would deny).

I am not denying that consciousness arises from the brain.⑦ We know, for example, that the subjective experience of vision is closely linked to processes in the visual cortex. It is the link itself that perplexes, however. Remarkably, subjective experience seems to emerge from a physical process. But we have no idea how or why this is.

IS NEUROSCIENCE ENOUGH?

Given the flurry of recent work on consciousness in neuroscience and psychology, one might think this mystery is starting to be cleared up. On closer examination, however, it turns out that almost all the current work addresses only the easy problems of consciousness. The confidence of the reductionist view comes from the progress on the easy problems, but none of this makes any difference where the hard problem is concerned.

Consider the hypothesis put forward by neurobiologist Francis Crick of the Salk Institute for Biological Studies in San Diego and Christof Koch of the California Institute of Technology. They suggest that consciousness may arise from certain oscillations in the cerebral cortex, which become synchronized as neurons fire 40 times per second. Crick and Koch believe the phenomenon might explain how different attributes of a single perceived object (its color and shape, for example), which are processed in different parts of the brain, are merged into a coherent whole. In this theory, two pieces of information become bound together precisely when they are represented by synchronized neural firings.

The hypothesis could conceivably elucidate one of the easy problems about how information is integrated in the brain. But why should synchronized oscillations give rise to a visual experience, no matter how much integration is taking place?⑧ This question involves the hard problem, about which the theory has nothing to offer. Indeed, Crick and Koch are agnostic about whether the hard problem can be solved by science at all.

⑧ The emphasis here is on *experience*. How can these oscillations be responsible for the distinctively subjective experience, the way it is for someone to, for example, *see* the color and shape of a perceived object?

The same kind of critique could be applied to almost all the recent work on consciousness. In his 1991 book *Consciousness Explained,* philosopher

Daniel C. Dennett laid out a sophisticated theory of how numerous independent processes in the brain combine to produce a coherent response to a perceived event. The theory might do much to explain how we produce verbal reports on our internal states, but it tells us very little about why there should be a subjective experience behind these reports. Like other reductionist theories, Dennett's is a theory of the easy problems.

The critical common trait among these easy problems is that they all concern how a cognitive or behavioral function is performed. All are ultimately questions about how the brain carries out some task—how it discriminates stimuli, integrates information, produces reports and so on. Once neurobiology specifies appropriate neural mechanisms, showing how the functions are performed, the easy problems are solved. The hard problem of consciousness, in contrast, goes beyond problems about how functions are performed. Even if every behavioral and cognitive function related to consciousness were explained, there would still remain a further mystery: Why is the performance of these functions accompanied by conscious experience? [9] It is this additional conundrum that makes the hard problem hard.

> [9] What is it about the performance of these functions, or any functions, that results in conscious experience, instead of no experience at all? (A closely related problem is why, in a particular case, there is one distinctive sort of experience rather than another.)

THE EXPLANATORY GAP

Some have suggested that to solve the hard problem, we need to bring in new tools of physical explanation: nonlinear dynamics, say, or new discoveries in neuroscience, or quantum mechanics. But these ideas suffer from exactly the same difficulty. Consider a proposal from Stuart R. Hameroff of the University of Arizona and Roger Penrose of the University of Oxford. They hold that consciousness arises from quantum-physical processes taking place in microtubules, which are protein structures inside neurons. It is possible (if not likely) that such a hypothesis will lead to an explanation of how the brain makes decisions or even how it proves mathematical theorems, as Hameroff and Penrose suggest. [10] But even if it does, the theory is silent about how these processes might give rise to conscious experience. Indeed, the same problem arises with any theory of consciousness based only on physical processing.

> [10] Think about this suggestion that the brain "makes decisions" or "proves mathematical theorems." Do you think that your brain does either of these things without *conscious* thought?

The trouble is that physical theories are best suited to explaining why systems have a certain physical structure and how they perform various functions. Most problems in science have this form; to explain life, for example, we need to describe how a physical system can reproduce, adapt and metabolize. But consciousness is a different sort of problem entirely, as it goes beyond the explanation of structure and function. [11]

> [11] Physical theories are inadequate to explain consciousness, because consciousness "goes beyond" the specific results that are explained by physical theories.

Of course, neuroscience is not irrelevant to the study of consciousness. For one, it may be able to reveal the nature of the neural correlate of consciousness—the brain processes most directly associated with conscious experience. It may even give a detailed correspondence between specific processes in the brain and related components of experience. [12] But until we know why these processes give rise to conscious experience at all, we will not have crossed what philosopher Joseph Levine has called the explanatory gap between physical processes and consciousness. Making that leap will demand a new kind of theory.

> [12] This is the sort of thing that Mary and the Martian scientist are depicted as knowing. But even if we knew exactly which brain state was correlated with some particular experiential state, without understanding *why* that particular brain state gives rise to any experiential state and indeed to that particular experiential state, we have still not solved the hard problem of consciousness.

A TRUE THEORY OF EVERYTHING

In searching for an alternative, a key observation is that not all entities in science are explained in terms of more basic entities. In physics, for example, space-time, mass and charge (among other things) are regarded as fundamental features of the world, as they are not reducible to anything simpler. Despite this irreducibility, detailed and useful theories relate these entities to one another in terms of fundamental laws. Together these features and laws explain a great variety of complex and subtle phenomena.

It is widely believed that physics provides a complete catalogue of the universe's fundamental features and laws. As physicist Steven Weinberg puts it in his 1992 book *Dreams of a Final Theory,* the goal of physics is a "theory of everything" from which all there is to know about the universe can be derived. But Weinberg concedes that there is a problem with consciousness. Despite the power of physical theory, the existence of consciousness does not seem to be derivable from physical laws. He defends physics by arguing that it might eventually explain what he calls the objective correlates of consciousness (that is, the neural correlates), but of course to do this is not to explain consciousness itself. If the existence of consciousness cannot be derived from physical laws, a theory of physics is not a true theory of everything. So a final theory must contain an additional fundamental component. [13]

[13] If the complete physical theory neither includes any reference to consciousness nor allows for the derivation of consciousness, then assuming that consciousness is real (that there really is consciousness), the complete physical theory cannot be a theory of *everything.*

Toward this end, I propose that conscious experience can be considered a fundamental feature, irreducible to anything more basic. The idea may seem strange at first, but consistency seems to demand it. In the 19th century it turned out that electromagnetic phenomena could not be explained in terms of previously known principles. As a consequence, scientists introduced electromagnetic charge as a new fundamental entity and studied the associated fundamental laws. Similar reasoning should apply to consciousness. If existing fundamental theories cannot encompass it, then something new is required. [14]

[14] Thus if Chalmers is right that consciousness cannot be reduced to anything physical, then it follows that a true theory of everything cannot be restricted to what we now understand as purely physical entities and processes.

When there is a fundamental property, there are fundamental laws. In this case, the laws must relate experience to elements of physical theory. These laws will almost certainly not interfere with those of the physical world; it seems that the latter form a closed system in their own right. Rather the laws will serve as a bridge, specifying how experience depends on underlying physical processes. It is this bridge that will cross the explanatory gap.

Thus, a complete theory will have two components: physical laws, telling us about the behavior of physical systems from the infinitesimal to the cosmological, and what we might call psychophysical laws, telling us how some of those systems are associated with conscious experience. These two components will constitute a true theory of everything. [15]

[15] Psychophysical laws will provide the bridge over the explanatory gap, relating the psychological (experiential) states to the physical (brain) states. But if these laws do not "interfere" with those of the physical world, so that physical laws form a "closed system," then conscious states do not influence the physical world—which amounts to epiphenomenalism.

SEARCHING FOR A THEORY

Supposing for the moment that they exist, how might we uncover such psychophysical laws? The greatest hindrance in this pursuit will be a lack of data. As I have described it, consciousness is subjective, so there is no direct way to monitor it in others. But this difficulty is an obstacle, not a dead end. For a start, each one of us has access to our own experiences, a rich trove that can be used to formulate theories. We can also plausibly rely on indirect information, such as subjects' descriptions of their experiences. Philosophical arguments and thought experiments also have a role to play. Such methods have limitations, but they give us more than enough to get started.

These theories will not be conclusively testable, so they will inevitably be more speculative than those of more conventional scientific disciplines. Nevertheless, there is no reason they should not be strongly constrained to account accurately for our own first-person experiences, as well as the evidence from subjects' reports. If we find a theory that fits the data better than any other theory of equal simplicity, we will have good reason to accept it. Right now we do not have even a single theory that fits the data, so worries about testability are premature. [16]

We might start by looking for high-level bridging laws, connecting physical processes to experience at an everyday level. The basic contour of such a law might be gleaned from the observation that when we are conscious of something, we are generally able to act on it and speak about it—which are objective, physical functions. Conversely, when some information is directly available for action and speech, it is generally conscious. Thus, consciousness correlates well with what we might call "awareness": the process by which information in the brain is made globally available to motor processes such as speech and bodily action. [17]

The notion may seem trivial. But as defined here, awareness is objective and physical, whereas consciousness is not. Some refinements to the definition of awareness are needed, in order to extend the concept to animals and infants, which cannot speak. But at least in familiar cases, it is possible to see the rough outlines of a psychophysical law: where there is awareness, there is consciousness, and vice versa.

To take this line of reasoning a step further, consider the structure present in the conscious experience. The experience of a field of vision, for example, is a constantly changing mosaic of colors, shapes and patterns and as such has a detailed geometric structure. The fact that we can describe this structure, reach out in the direction of many of its components and perform other actions that depend on it suggests that the structure corresponds directly to that of the information made available in the brain through the neural processes of awareness. [18]

Similarly, our experiences of color have an intrinsic three-dimensional structure that is mirrored in the structure of information processes in the brain's visual cortex. This structure is illustrated in the color wheels and charts used by artists. Colors are arranged in a systematic pattern—red to green on one axis, blue to yellow on another, and black to white on a third. Colors that are close to one anther on a color wheel are experienced as similar. It is extremely likely that they also correspond to similar perceptual representations in the brain, as part of a system of complex three-dimensional coding among neurons that is not yet fully understood. We can recast the underlying concept as a principle of structural coherence: the structure of conscious experience is mirrored by the structure of information in awareness, and vice versa. [19]

Another candidate for psychophysical law is a principle of organizational invariance. It holds that physical systems with the same abstract organization will give rise to the same kind of conscious experience, no matter what they are made of. For example, if the precise interactions between our neurons could be duplicated with silicon chips, the same conscious experience would arise. The idea is somewhat controversial, but

---

[16] The reason that the sorts of theories that Chalmers has in mind will not be "conclusively testable" is that the experiences of other people are not directly accessible and any single person's first-person experiences do not provide enough evidence for "conclusive" testing. (This is more or less the same reason that motivated behavioral psychologists to attempt to explain behavior without appealing to consciousness—see the discussion of "radical behaviorism" in the first Fodor selection.)

[17] Think carefully about what Chalmers says in what follows about "awareness." There is a natural, intuitive sense of the word that is different from the sense he develops here. But according to Chalmers's usage of the term, "awareness" is a physical process that does not in itself involve consciousness.

[18] The hypothesis that there is a correlation between our experience of colored shapes and the information processed by the brain is supported by our ability to perform physical actions that relate directly to the details of such experience—including giving a verbal description of it. (On an epiphenomenalist view, paradoxically enough, such a description cannot be caused by the experience itself, because that would be a case of consciousness causally affecting the physical world. See Discussion Question 3.)

[19] Here is an initial candidate for a very rough and approximate psychophysical law: one connecting the structure of conscious experience with the physical states involved in the neural process of "awareness"—remember that "awareness" is not a conscious state for Chalmers.

I believe it is strongly supported by thought experiments describing the gradual replacement of neurons by silicon chips. The remarkable implication is that consciousness might someday be achieved in machines.[20]

[20] This result would be remarkable from Chalmers's perspective because he firmly rejects the claim that consciousness *just is* some physical state or other, even though he thinks that it results from physical states. Thus a conscious machine would have non-physical properties. (Someone who accepted Searle's "meatist" theory would not accept that mere "abstract organization" is enough for consciousness.)

INFORMATION: PHYSICAL AND EXPERIENTIAL

The ultimate goal of a theory of consciousness is a simple and elegant set of fundamental laws, analogous to the fundamental laws of physics. The principles described above are unlikely to be fundamental, however. Rather they seem to be high-level psychophysical laws, analogous to macroscopic principles in physics such as those of thermodynamics or kinematics. What might the underlying fundamental laws be? No one knows, but I don't mind speculating.[21]

[21] Many important scientific theories started as speculations.

I suggest that the primary psychophysical laws may centrally involve the concept of information. The abstract notion of information, as put forward in the 1940s by Claude E. Shannon of the Massachusetts Institute of Technology, is that of a set of separate states with a basic structure of similarities and differences between them. We can think of a 10-bit binary code as an information state, for example. Such information states can be embodied in the physical world. This happens whenever they correspond to physical states (voltages, say); the differences between them can be transmitted along some pathway, such as a telephone line.

We can also find information embodied in conscious experience. The pattern of color patches in a visual field, for example, can be seen as analogous to that of the pixels covering a display screen. Intriguingly, it turns out that we find the same information states embedded in conscious experience and in underlying physical processes in the brain. The three-dimensional encoding of color spaces, for example, suggests that the information state in a color experience corresponds directly to an information state in the brain. We might even regard the two states as distinct aspects of a single information state, which is simultaneously embodied in both physical processing and conscious experience.

A natural hypothesis ensues. Perhaps information, or at least some information, has two basic aspects: a physical one and an experiential one. This hypothesis has the status of a fundamental principle that might underlie the relation between physical processes and experience. Wherever we find conscious experience, it exists as one aspect of an information state, the other aspect of which is embedded in a physical process in the brain.[22] This proposal needs to be fleshed out to make a satisfying theory. But it fits nicely with the principles mentioned earlier—systems with the same organization will embody the same information, for example—and it could explain numerous features of our conscious experience.

[22] The claim that *any* informational state has a conscious aspect would mean that even the sorts of informational states that are involved in monitoring things like breathing and heartbeat in human beings have such aspects, even though we do not seem to be consciously aware of them. Chalmers doesn't commit himself to such a view, but he considers the possibility. Does it sound plausible?

The idea is at least compatible with several others, such as physicist John A. Wheeler's suggestion that information is fundamental to the physics of the universe.[23] The laws of physics might ultimately be cast in informational terms, in which case we would have a satisfying congruence between the constructs in both physical and psychophysical laws. It may even be that a theory of physics and a theory of consciousness could eventually be consolidated into a single grander theory of information.

[23] What if we discovered that all purely physical states were, in fact, informational states, and that every informational state had a conscious aspect? Would there still be an explanatory gap between the physical realm and consciousness?

A potential problem is posed by the ubiquity of information. Even a thermostat embodies some information, for example, but is it conscious? There are at least two possible responses. First, we could constrain the fundamental laws so that only some information has an experiential aspect, perhaps depending on how it is physically processed. Second, we might bite the bullet and allow that all information has an experiential aspect—where there is complex information processing, there is complex experience, and where there is simple information processing, there is simple experience.[24] If this is so, then even a thermostat might have experiences, although they would be much simpler than even a basic color experience, and there would certainly be no accompanying emotions or thoughts. This seems odd at first, but if experience is truly fundamental, we might expect it to be widespread. In any case, the choice between these alternatives should depend on which can be integrated into the most powerful theory.

Of course, such ideas may be all wrong. On the other hand, they might evolve into a more powerful proposal that predicts the precise structure of our conscious experience from physical processes in our brains. If this project succeeds, we will have good reason to accept the theory. If it fails, other avenues will be pursued, and alternative fundamental theories may be developed. In this way, we may one day resolve the greatest mystery of the mind.

[24] To "bite the bullet" is to affirm a seemingly counter-intuitive or seemingly implausible implication of a view—the more implausible, the bigger the "bullet." It does seem extremely odd to say that a thermostat has experiences, and so affirming this consequence of the view that all physical states are informational, and all informational states have an experiential aspect would be "biting the bullet."

Discussion Questions

1. Suppose that the claim that every informational state has a conscious aspect is true. Consider the informational states of a thermometer. That thermometer would have states with at least some minimal conscious aspect. Does it follow from this supposition that "there is something it is like" to be a thermometer? Thomas Nagel has flirted with a view called **"panpsychism"** (the view that mind or consciousness is a fundamental feature of all of reality). To some, the view seems just crazy, while to others, it seems at least somewhat plausible. How would you argue for or against this view?

2. Can you think of other times in the history of science when there was an explanatory gap between two domains that seemed to be related? Think about the relation between biological descriptions of an organism (you, for example) and a description in terms of physics (maybe even quantum mechanics). The descriptions will be very different, but presumably they can each be a true description of you. Consider another example, made famous by Sir Arthur Eddington, of the two descriptions of a table: on the one hand you can describe the table in common-sense terms that will include its color and solidity and shape, etc.; while on the other hand, someone could give a description of the table in terms of the most advanced physics as a cloud of particles with large gaps between them and no properties like color. But the two descriptions are presumably of the same table. Is the common-sense description simply false? What is the relation between the two descriptions?

3. Chalmers seems to accept an epiphenomenalist version of dualism, probably of attribute dualism (see Annotation 16 to the Jackson selection). Think carefully about the implications of this view, including the one mentioned in Annotation 18. How implausible is such a view? Does it seem obvious that your conscious states do influence the physical world through your physical reactions to them, including both deliberate actions and things like wincing from pain? How might an epiphenomenalist respond to this objection? Are there, as Chalmers thinks, strong reasons to think that consciousness has no effect on the physical world, and if so, what are they?

WHAT IS REQUIRED FOR PERSONAL IDENTITY?

John Locke

The English philosopher John Locke (1632–1704) was one of the most influential philosophers of all time, making major contributions to epistemology, metaphysics, and political philosophy. (For more about Locke's rather colorful life, see the introduction to the selection from his *Second Treatise of Government,* in Chapter 7.)

In this selection from his *Essay Concerning Human Understanding,* Locke offers a very influential account of the nature of personal identity. Since Locke was, like Descartes, a **substance dualist,** holding that a human being consists of a material body together with an immaterial mind or soul, it would have been natural for him to hold that personal identity is just identity of body or identity of mind or perhaps identity of both. He rejects all of these possibilities, however, and claims instead that what makes a later person B identical with an earlier person A is the continuity of consciousness whereby B is conscious of (that is, presumably, has an apparent memory of) the various conscious states of A—or at least some of them. This requirement could, Locke thinks, be satisfied even if neither the material body nor the immaterial mind of B is identical to those of A.

Personal Identity

...**8.** An animal is a living organized body; and consequently the same animal, as we have observed, is the same continued life communicated to different particles of matter as they happen successively to be united to that organized living body.① And whatever is talked of other definitions, ingenuous observation puts it past doubt that the *idea* in our minds of which the sound *man* in our mouths is the sign, is nothing else but of an animal of such a certain form: since I think I may be confident that whoever should see a creature of his own shape and make, though it had no more reason all its life than a *cat* or a *parrot,* would call him still a *man;* or whoever should hear a *cat* or a *parrot* discourse, reason, and philosophize would call or think it nothing but a *cat* or a *parrot* and say the one was a dull irrational *man,* and the other a very intelligent rational *parrot.* . . .

. . . it is not the *idea* of a thinking or rational being alone that makes the *idea* of a *man* in most people's sense, but of a body so and so shaped, joined to it; and if that be the *idea* of a *man,* the same successive body not shifted all at once must, as well as the same immaterial spirit, go to the making of the same *man.*②

> ① An animal is not an individual substance, but rather "a living organized body." For an animal at one time to be identical to an animal at an earlier time is not for all of their material parts to be identical, but only for the matter at each stage to be so organized as to be part of the same continued life.

> ② What makes something a *man* (that is, a human being) is its having a living animal body of a certain distinctive sort, not anything specific about its mental or intellectual capabilities (though it must also have a mind or soul). Thus for a particular man at one time to be the same man as one at an earlier time is, Locke claims, for both the body and the soul to be the same. Souls, unlike bodies, do not in his view have parts that could be replaced, so sameness of soul means that the soul at one stage is the very same particular entity as the soul at a later stage.

From An Essay Concerning Human Understanding, *1694.*

9. This being premised, to find wherein *personal identity* consists, we must consider what *person* stands for; which, I think, is a thinking intelligent being that has reason and reflection and can consider itself as itself, the same thinking thing in different times and places; which it does only by that consciousness which is inseparable from thinking and, as it seems to me, essential to it: it being impossible for anyone to perceive without perceiving that he does perceive. When we see, hear, smell, taste, feel, meditate, or will anything, we know that we do so. Thus it is always as to our present sensations and perceptions, and by this everyone is to himself that which he calls *self:* it not being considered in this case whether the same *self* be continued in the same or divers substances. For since consciousness always accompanies thinking, and it is that that makes everyone to be what he calls *self,* and thereby distinguishes himself from all other thinking things: in this alone consists *personal identity,* i.e. the sameness of a rational being. And as far as this consciousness can be extended backwards to any past action or thought, so far reaches the identity of that *person:* it is the same *self* now it was then, and it is by the same *self* with this present one that now reflects on it, that that action was done.③

③ A *person,* on the other hand, is a conscious rational being that is aware of its own continued existence. And it is this awareness of being at one time the same conscious being that existed at an earlier time that, according to Locke, makes the later person identical with the earlier one. Thus the identity of a person reaches only as far into the past as its consciousness of its earlier self, including only those previous conscious states and actions that the later person is conscious of—that is, presumably, remembers—in a way that also includes a consciousness of its current states and actions.

10. But it is further inquired whether it be the same identical substance? This, few would think they had reason to doubt of, if these perceptions, with their consciousness, always remained present in the mind whereby the same thinking thing would be always consciously present and, as would be thought, evidently the same to itself. But that which seems to make the difficulty is this: that this consciousness being interrupted always by forgetfulness, there being no moment of our lives wherein we have the whole train of all our past actions before our eyes in one view, but even the best memories losing the sight of one part whilst they are viewing another; and we sometimes, and that the greatest part of our lives, not reflecting on our past selves, being intent on our present thoughts, and in sound sleep having no thoughts at all, or at least none with that consciousness which remarks our waking thoughts; I say, in all these cases, our consciousness being interrupted, and we losing the sight of our past *selves,* doubts are raised whether we are the same thinking thing, i.e. the same substance, or no.④ Which,

④ Is the mental substance (the mind or soul) at one stage of a person's life identical to that at a later stage of the same person's life? Locke suggests that partial failures of memory, times when one is attending only to what is going on in the present, and the complete absence of consciousness in sleep raise doubts about this (though he does not explain why).

however reasonable or unreasonable, concerns not *personal identity* at all: the question being what makes the same *person,* and not whether it be the same identical substance, which always thinks in the same person; which, in this case, matters not at all: different substances, by the same consciousness (where they do partake in it) being united into one person, as well as different bodies by the same life are united into one animal, whose *identity* is preserved in that change of substances by the unity of one continued life. For, it being the same consciousness that makes a man be himself to himself, *personal identity* depends on that only, whether it be annexed only to one individual substance, or can be continued in a succession of several substances. For as far as any intelligent being can repeat the *idea* of any past action with the same consciousness it had of it at first, and with the same consciousness it has of any present action, so far it is the same *personal self.* For it is by the consciousness it has of its present thoughts and actions that it is *self* to *itself* now, and so will be the same *self* as far as the same consciousness can extend to actions past or to come, and would be by distance of time or change of substance no more two *persons* than a man be two men by wearing other clothes today than he did yesterday, with a long or short sleep between: the same consciousness uniting those distant actions into the same *person,* whatever substances contributed to their production.⑤

⑤ The important point, however, is that whether or not the mental substance is identical makes no difference, on Locke's view, to personal identity. As long as the later person has the "same consciousness" of the thoughts and actions of the earlier person, the two are identical, even if this later consciousness exists in a different mental substance or soul than the one at the earlier stage. (What does it mean for the consciousness to be "the same"? See Discussion Question 1.)

11. That this is so, we have some kind of evidence in our very bodies, all whose particles, whilst vitally united to this same thinking conscious self so that we feel when they are touched and are affected by and conscious of good or harm that happens to them, are a part of our *selves,* i.e. of our thinking conscious *self.* Thus, the limbs of his body are to everyone a part of *himself;* he sympathizes and is concerned for them. Cut off a hand, and thereby separate it from that consciousness he had of its heat, cold, and other affections, and it is then no longer a part of that which is *himself,* any more than the remotest part of matter. Thus, we see the *substance* whereof *personal self* consisted at one time may be varied at another, without the change of personal *identity:* there being no question about the same person, though the limbs, which but now were a part of it, be cut off.⑥

⑥ Locke suggests that something analogous is true of parts of the body: a part of the body that is connected in the right way to the consciousness of oneself is a part of the person, while a part that has been severed and is no longer connected ceases to be a part of the person.

12. But the question is whether, if the same substance, which thinks, be changed, it can be the same person, or, remaining the same, it can be different persons.

And to this I answer, first, this can be no question at all to those who place thought in a purely material animal constitution, void of an immaterial substance. For, whether their supposition be true or no, it is plain they conceive personal identity preserved in something else than identity of substance, as animal identity is preserved in identity of life and not of substance.⑦ And therefore those who place thinking in an immaterial substance only, before they can come

to deal with these men, must show why personal identity cannot be preserved in the change of immaterial substances, or variety of particular immaterial substances, as well as animal identity is preserved in the change of material substances, or variety of particular bodies: unless they will say, it is one immaterial spirit that makes the same life in brutes, as it is one immaterial spirit that makes the same person in men; which the *Cartesians* at least will not admit, for fear of making brutes thinking things too.

⑦ Pursuing the issue further, Locke asks (or imagines an objector asking) whether there can be (a) different thinking substances (here not assumed to be necessarily immaterial minds) in the same person or (b) the same thinking substance in different people. His first response is that the answer to (a) is obviously "yes" for nondualists for whom the thinking entity is just the animal body (which can remain the same entity even if its material constituents change).

13. But next, as to the first part of the question, whether, if the same thinking substance (supposing immaterial substances only to think) be changed, it can be the same person, I answer: That cannot be resolved but by those who know what kind of substances they are that do think, and whether the consciousness of past actions can be transferred from one thinking substance to another. I grant, were the same consciousness the same individual action, it could not; but, it being but a present representation of a past action, why it may not be possible that that may be represented to the mind to have been which really never was, will remain to be shown. . . . But that which we call the *same consciousness* not being the same individual act, why one intellectual substance may not have represented to it, as done by itself, what it never did, and was perhaps done by some other agent . . . will be difficult to conclude from the nature of things. And that it never is so will by us, till we have clearer views of the nature of thinking substances, be best resolved into the goodness of God, who, as far as the happiness or misery of any of his sensible creatures is concerned in it, will not, by a fatal error of theirs, transfer from one to another that consciousness which draws reward or punishment with it. . . . But yet, to return to the question before us, it must be allowed that, if the same consciousness . . . can be

transferred from one thinking substance to another, it will be possible that two thinking substances may make but one person. For the same consciousness being preserved, whether in the same or different substances, the personal identity is preserved. ⑧

14. As to the second part of the question, whether, the same immaterial substance remaining, there may be two distinct persons, which question seems to me to be built on this: whether the same immaterial being, being conscious of the actions of its past duration, may be wholly stripped of all the consciousness of its past existence and lose it beyond the power of ever retrieving again and so, as it were beginning a new account from a new period, have a consciousness that cannot reach beyond this new state. All those who hold pre-existence are evidently of this mind, since they allow the soul to have no remaining consciousness of what it did in that pre-existent state, either wholly separate from body, or informing any other body; and if they should not, it is plain experience would be against them. So that, personal identity reaching no further than consciousness reaches, a pre-existent spirit, not having continued so many ages in a state of silence, must needs make different persons. . . . ⑨ Let anyone reflect upon himself and conclude that he has in himself an immaterial spirit, which is that which thinks in him and in the constant change of his body keeps him the same and is that which he calls

⑧ For a dualist, the answer to (a) will depend on whether it is possible for the consciousness of past actions (and states of mind) to be transferred from the mind or soul that actually did or experienced them to one that did not. Locke argues that there is no clear reason for thinking that this is not possible (though God might for moral reasons prevent this from actually happening in cases where reward or punishment would then seem appropriate).

⑨ With regard to part (b) of the question, the issue is whether a mind or soul could have the consciousness of its actions and states of mind entirely removed and then begin a new and different conscious life. Locke points out that those who accept the view (held by Plato, among others) that the soul has an existence before birth in another realm of which it is not conscious after birth must say that this is possible. (Locke never quite says that it is actually possible, but would probably say, as with part (a), that there is no clear reason to the contrary.)

himself; let him also suppose it to be the same soul that was in *Nestor* or *Thersites* at the siege of *Troy* (for souls being, as far as we know anything of them, in their nature indifferent to any parcel of matter, the supposition has no apparent absurdity in it), which it may have been, as well as it is now the soul of any other man; but he now having no consciousness of any of the actions either of *Nestor* or *Thersites,* does or can he conceive himself the same person with either of them? Can he be concerned in either of their actions, attribute them to himself, or think them his own, more than the actions of any other men that ever existed? So that, this consciousness not reaching to any of the actions of either of those men, he is no more one *self* with either of them than if the soul or immaterial spirit that now informs him had been created and began to exist, when it began to inform his present body, though it were never so true that the same spirit that informed *Nestor's* or *Thersites's* body were numerically the same that now informs his. For this would no more make him the same person with *Nestor* than if some of the particles of matter that were once a part of *Nestor* were now a part of this man: the same immaterial substance, without the same consciousness, no more making the same person by being united to any body than the same particle of matter, without consciousness, united to any body, makes the same person. But let him once find himself conscious of any of the actions of *Nestor,* he then finds himself the same person with *Nestor.* ⑩

⑩ If such a total removal of consciousness followed by a new and different consciousness is possible, then there is, Locke argues, no reason to say that the person in whom that soul resided before the removal and the one in whom it resided after the new consciousness has emerged are the same person: having Nestor's soul does not make one the same person as Nestor unless a consciousness of Nestor's actions (or states of mind) comes with it.

15. And thus we may be able, without any difficulty, to conceive the same person at the resurrection, though in a body not exactly in make or parts the same which he had here, the same consciousness going along with the soul that inhabits it. But yet the soul alone, in the change of bodies, would scarce, to anyone but to him that makes the soul the *man,* be enough to make the same *man.* For should the soul of a prince, carrying with it the consciousness of the prince's past

life, enter and inform the body of a cobbler as soon as deserted by his own soul, everyone sees he would be the same person with the prince, accountable only for the prince's actions; but who would say it was the same man? The body too goes to the making the man and would, I guess, to everybody, determine the man in this case, wherein the soul, with all its princely thoughts about it, would not make another man: but he would be the same cobbler to everyone besides himself. I know that in the ordinary way of speaking, the same person and the same man stand for one and the same thing. And indeed, everyone will always have a liberty to speak as he pleases and to apply what articulate sounds to what *ideas* he thinks fit, and change them as often as he pleases. But yet when we will inquire what makes the same *spirit, man,* or *person,* we must fix the *ideas* of *spirit, man,* or *person* in our minds; and having resolved with ourselves what we mean by them, it will not be hard to determine in either of them or the like when it is the *same* and when not. ⑪

> ⑪ This makes it possible for a person to be resurrected with a different body, as long as the soul involved has a consciousness of the original person's actions and states of mind. But while having the same consciousness is enough to make an individual human the same *person,* it is not enough to make it the same *man* (since being the same man requires having the same animal body). Thus the cobbler with the prince's soul and consciousness is the same *person* as the prince, but the same *man* as the cobbler—the requirements for identity depend on what sort of thing is in question.

16. But though the same immaterial substance or soul does not alone, wherever it be, and in whatsoever state, make the same man: yet, it is plain, consciousness, as far as ever it can be extended, should it be to ages past, unites existences and actions very remote in time into the same person, as well as it does the existence and actions of the immediately preceding moment, so that whatever has the consciousness of present and past actions is the same person to whom they both belong. Had I the same consciousness that I saw the ark and *Noah's* flood as that I saw an overflowing of the *Thames* last winter, or as that I write now, I could no more doubt that I that write this now, that saw the *Thames* overflowed last winter, and that viewed the flood at the general deluge, was the same *self,* place that *self* in what substance you please, than I that write

this am the same *myself* now whilst I write (whether I consist of all the same substance, material or immaterial, or no) that I was yesterday. For as to this point of being the same *self,* it matters not whether this present *self* be made up of the same or other substances, I being as much concerned and as justly accountable for any action that was done a thousand years since, appropriated to me now by this self-consciousness, as I am for what I did the last moment.

17. *Self* is that conscious thinking thing (whatever substance made up of, whether spiritual or material, simple or compounded, it matters not) which is sensible or conscious of pleasure and pain, capable of happiness or misery, and so is concerned for *itself,* as far as that consciousness extends. Thus everyone finds that, whilst comprehended under that consciousness, the little finger is as much a part of *itself* as what is most so. Upon separation of this little finger, should this consciousness go along with the little finger and leave the rest of the body, it is evident the little finger would be the *person,* the *same person;* and self then would have nothing to do with the rest of the body. As in this case it is the consciousness that goes along with the substance, when one part is separate from another, which makes the same *person* and constitutes this inseparable *self:* so it is in reference to substance remote in time. That with which the *consciousness* of this present thinking thing can join itself makes the same *person* and is one *self* with it, and with nothing else, and so attributes to *itself* and owns all the actions of that thing as its own, as far as that consciousness reaches, and no further; as everyone who reflects will perceive. ⑫

> ⑫ Locke reiterates his view: a person at one time is the same person as any earlier person, no matter how remote, of whose actions (and states of mind) it is conscious (that is, remembers) along with its own. It does not matter whether the substance or substances involved are the same. If consciousness of the right sort can reside in a little finger, then that little finger is a person.

18. In this *personal identity* is founded all the right and justice of reward and punishment: happiness and misery being that for which everyone is concerned for *himself,* not mattering what becomes of any substance not joined to or affected with that consciousness. For, as it is evident in the instance I gave but now, if the consciousness went along with the little finger when it was cut off, that would be the

same *self* which was concerned for the whole body yesterday, as making part of *itself,* whose actions then it cannot but admit as its own now. Though, if the same body should still live and immediately from the separation of the little finger have its own peculiar consciousness, whereof the little finger knew nothing, it would not at all be concerned for it as a part of *itself,* or could own any of its actions, or have any of them imputed to him. [13]

> [13] The justifiability of reward and punishment depend on personal identity, thus understood, not on sameness of substance. (Thus if the consciousness of having committed some crime remains with the little finger and not the rest of the body, it is only the little finger that can justifiably be punished.)

19. This may show us wherein *personal identity* consists: not in the identity of substance but, as I have said, in the identity of *consciousness,* wherein, if *Socrates* and the present mayor of *Queenborough* agree, they are the same person; if the same *Socrates* waking and sleeping do not partake of the same *consciousness, Socrates* waking and sleeping is not the same person. And to punish *Socrates* waking for what sleeping *Socrates* thought, and waking *Socrates* was never conscious of, would be no more of right than to punish one twin for what his brother-twin did, whereof he knew nothing, because their outsides were so like that they could not be distinguished; for such twins have been seen. [14]

> [14] If Socrates waking and Socrates sleeping have two different consciousnesses, neither including the actions and events included in the other, then there are in effect two persons in the same body. (This resembles cases of multiple personality, with which Locke was presumably not familiar. See Discussion Question 2.)

20. But yet possibly it will still be objected, suppose I wholly lose the memory of some parts of my life beyond a possibility of retrieving them, so that perhaps I shall never be conscious of them again: yet am I not the same person that did those actions, had those thoughts that I once was conscious of, though I have now forgot them? To which I answer that we must here take notice what the word *I* is applied to, which, in this case, is the man only. And the same man being presumed to be the same person, *I* is easily here supposed to stand also for the same person. But if it be possible for the same man to have distinct incommunicable con-

sciousness at different times, it is past doubt the same man would at different times make different persons; which, we see, is the sense of mankind in the solemnest declaration of their opinions, human laws not punishing the *mad man* for the *sober man's* actions, nor the *sober man* for what the *mad man* did, thereby making them two persons: which is somewhat explained by our way of speaking in *English* when we say such an one *is not himself,* or is *beside himself;* in which phrases it is insinuated, as if those who now, or at least first used them, thought that *self* was changed, the *self*-same person was no longer in that man. [15]

> [15] Someone who totally and irretrievably forgets some of his earlier actions is no longer the same person who did them—though he may still be the same man (human being).

. . .

22. But is not a man drunk and sober the same person, why else is he punished for the fact he commits when drunk, though he be never afterwards conscious of it? Just as much the same person as a man that walks and does other things in his sleep is the same person and is answerable for any mischief he shall do in it. Human laws punish both, with a justice suitable to their way of knowledge; because, in these cases, they cannot distinguish certainly what is real, what counterfeit; and so the ignorance in drunkenness or sleep is not admitted as a plea. For, though punishment be annexed to personality, and personality to consciousness, and the drunkard perhaps be not conscious of what he did, yet human judicatures justly punish him, because the fact is proved against him, but want of consciousness cannot be proved for him. But in the Great Day, wherein the secrets of all hearts shall be laid open, it may be reasonable to think no one shall be made to answer for what he knows nothing of, but shall receive his doom, his conscience accusing or excusing him. [16]

> [16] Human laws punish people for things that they can no longer remember, but this is unjust and is done only because it is too hard to determine whether a person can actually remember or not.

23. Nothing but consciousness can unite remote existences into the same person: the identity of substance will not do it; for whatever substance there is however framed, without consciousness there is no person; and a carcass may be a person, as well as any sort of substance be so, without consciousness.

. . .

24. Indeed [the self] may conceive the substance whereof it is now made up to have existed formerly, united in the same conscious being; but consciousness removed, that substance is no more *itself* or makes no more a part of it than any other substance, as is evident in the instance we have already given of a limb cut off, of whose heat or cold or other affections having no longer any consciousness, it is no more of a man's self than any other matter of the universe. In like manner it will be in reference to any immaterial substance which is void of that consciousness whereby I am my *self* to *myself.* If there be any part of its existence which I cannot upon recollection join with that present consciousness whereby I am now my *self,* it is in that part of its existence no more my *self* than any other immaterial being. For whatsoever any substance has thought or done, which I cannot recollect and by my consciousness make my own thought and action, it will no more belong to me, whether a part of me thought or did it, than if it had been thought or done by any other immaterial being anywhere existing.

25. I agree the more probable opinion is that this consciousness is annexed to and the affection of one individual immaterial substance.

But let men, according to their divers hypotheses, resolve of that as they please. This every intelligent being, sensible of happiness or misery, must grant: that there is something that is *himself* that he is concerned for and would have happy; that this *self* has existed in a continued duration more than one instant, and therefore it is possible may exist, as it has done, months and years to come, without any certain bounds to be set to its duration; and may be the same *self* by the same consciousness, continued on for the future. And thus, by this consciousness, he finds himself to be the *same self* which did such or such an action some years since, by which he comes to be happy or miserable now. In all which account of *self,* the same numerical substance is not considered as making the same *self,* but the same continued consciousness, in which several substances may have been united and again separated from it, which, whilst they continued in a vital union with that wherein this consciousness then resided, made a part of that same *self.* Thus any part of our bodies, vitally united to that which is conscious in us, makes a part of our *selves;* but upon separation from the vital union, by which that consciousness is communicated, that

which a moment since was part of our *selves* is now no more so than a part of another man's *self* is a part of me; and it is not impossible but in a little time may become a real part of another person. And so we have the same numerical substance become a part of two different persons, and the same person preserved under the change of various substances. Could we suppose any spirit wholly stripped of all its memory or consciousness of past actions, as we find our minds always are of a great part of ours, and sometimes of them all, the union or separation of such a spiritual substance would make no variation of personal identity, any more than that of any particle of matter does. Any substance vitally united to the present thinking being is a part of that very *same self* which now is; anything united to it by a consciousness of former actions makes also a part of the *same self* which is the same both then and now.

26. *Person,* as I take it, is the name for this *self.* Wherever a man finds what he calls *himself,* there, I think, another may say is the *same person.* It is a forensic term, appropriating actions and their merit, and so belongs only to intelligent agents, capable of a law, and happiness and misery.[17] This personality extends *itself* beyond present existence to what is past, only by consciousness; whereby it becomes concerned and accountable, owns and imputes to *itself* past actions, just upon the

> [17] That is, personhood, in Locke's view, has more to do with justice, rights, and law than with the metaphysical nature of the entities in question.

same ground and for the same reason that it does the present. All which is founded in a concern for happiness, the unavoidable concomitant of consciousness: that which is conscious of pleasure and pain desiring that that self that is conscious should be happy. And therefore whatever past actions it cannot reconcile or appropriate to that present *self* by consciousness, it can be no more concerned in than if they had never been done; and to receive pleasure or pain, i.e. reward or punishment, on the account of any such action, is all one as to be made happy or miserable in its first being, without any demerit at all. For supposing a man punished now for what he had done in another life, whereof he could be made to have no consciousness at all, what difference is there between that punishment and being created miserable? And therefore conformable to this, the Apostle tells us, that at the Great Day, when everyone shall *receive according to his doings, the secrets of all hearts shall be laid open.* The sentence shall be justified by the consciousness all persons shall have that they *themselves,* in what bodies soever they appear, or what substances soever that consciousness adheres to, are the *same* that committed those actions and deserve that punishment for them.

. . .

Discussion Questions

1. Locke speaks of a later individual having the "same consciousness" as an earlier one and so being the same person, but he does not explain very clearly what is required for the consciousness in question to be the *same,* though he does make it clear that the mind or soul in which the consciousness resides (assuming, as he mainly does, a dualist view) need not be the one that actually performed a certain action or experienced a certain state of mind in order for it to have the "same consciousness" of those things. Suppose that, over a period of time, person A has various experiences and performs various actions. Discuss whether in the following cases person B has the "same consciousness" in the sense required for person A and person B to be (according to Locke) the same person:

   a. At a later period of time, person B, entirely by coincidence (perhaps as a result of a brain tumor) comes to have apparent memories of having done or experienced some or all of the things that A did (and is conscious of these along with its own actions and experiences).

   b. At a later period of time, person B is hypnotized by a third person who is intimately familiar with A's life and experiences, and who brings it about by post-hypnotic suggestion that B has apparent memories of some or all of A's actions and experiences (and is conscious of these along with its own actions and experiences).

   c. As a result of brain trauma, person A entirely forgets its actions and experiences. At a later time, person B (whose body is the same living human body that was involved in person A and whose immaterial mind or soul is also the same as that of person A, but whose memory at first goes back only to the time of the trauma) has a second episode of brain trauma that produces, entirely by coincidence, apparent memories of having done and experienced some or all of the same things that A did or experienced (and is conscious of these along with its own actions and experiences).

   d. Person A comes to have no conscious memory of its earlier history, though memory traces of its actions and experiences remain stored in its brain or immaterial mind. After a lengthy period, these memory traces are reactivated and the person at that time (person B), who has the same human body and the same immaterial mind, comes to have conscious apparent memories of some or all of A's actions and experiences (and is conscious of these along with its own actions and experiences).

   e. Person A dies and its consciousness of its actions and experiences thereby ceases. But via a brain scan, a record of those actions and experiences is kept in storage in a computer. At a later time, that record is used to create new apparent memories of some or all of A's actions and experiences in person B, and person B is conscious of these along with its own actions and experiences. (Person B does not have the same human body as person A. Does it matter whether or not person B's immaterial mind or soul—if there is one—is the same?)

   f. At the end of the initial period, person A enters a Star Trek-style "transporter." The transporter scans both his body and his mind, making a complete and accurate record of both, and then destroys that body (and also A's immaterial mind, if there is one). The information about A is sent to a second transporter, which then creates a new body (and immaterial soul, if A had one), each qualitatively similar in every respect to A's, and programs it (or them) with A's memories, character traits, etc. The result of this process, person B, then exits the second transporter. It has conscious apparent memories of some or all of A's actions and experiences (and is conscious of these along with its own actions and experiences).

On the basis of your responses to these cases, try to formulate an explicit account of what is required for the consciousness of two persons to be the same in the sense required by Locke for them to be the same person.

2. Suppose that one body is seemingly inhabited by two or more very different personalities, having different character traits, behavior patterns, knowledge, or even different degrees of intelligence. (There are many alleged cases of this sort, which you may want to look up.) Supposing that none of these personalities is conscious of the others' actions (except indirectly, by being informed by others), is this a case of one body inhabited by multiple persons? Suppose that one of the personalities commits a serious crime, of which the other personalities are ignorant (and about which they express shock and horror when informed). Can the body in question be justly imprisoned for the crime?

Thomas Reid

Thomas Reid (1710–1796), a Scottish philosopher, was one of the founders of what became known as the "common sense" school of philosophy. He is best known for his contributions to epistemology, which are mainly focused on defending the common-sense view of our knowledge of the material world against what he sees as the skeptical tendencies to be found in his British predecessors, Locke, Berkeley, and Hume, as well as Descartes and others. In this selection, Reid discusses and criticizes Locke's account of personal identity. Reid's own view, which does not emerge clearly here, is that personal identity is unanalyzable or indefinable, so that no account of the sort that Locke attempts to give is possible.

Of Mr. Locke's Account of Personal Identity

In a long chapter upon identity and diversity, Mr. Locke has made many ingenious and just observations, and some which, I think, cannot be defended. I shall only take notice of the account he gives of our own personal identity. . . .

Identity . . . supposes the continued existence of the being of which it is affirmed, and therefore can be applied only to things which have a continued existence. While any being continues to exist, it is the same being; but two beings which have a different beginning or a different ending of their existence, cannot possibly be the same. To this I think Mr. Locke agrees.

He observes very justly, that to know what is meant by the same person, we must consider what the word *person* stands for; and he defines a person to be an intelligent being, endowed with reason and with consciousness, which last he thinks inseparable from thought.

From this definition of a person, it must necessarily follow, that while the intelligent being continues to exist and to be intelligent, it must be the same person. To say that the intelligent being is the person, and yet that the person ceases to exist, while the intelligent being continues, or that the person continues while the intelligent being ceases to exist, is, to my apprehension, a manifest contradiction.

From Essays on the Intellectual Powers of Man *(Cambridge, Mass.: The MIT Press, 1969).*

One would think that the definition of a person should perfectly ascertain the nature of personal identity, or wherein it consists, though it might still be a question how we come to know and be assured of our personal identity.

Mr. Locke tells us, however, "that personal identity, that is, the sameness of a rational being, consists in consciousness alone; and, as far as this consciousness can be extended backward to any past action or thought, so far reaches the identity or that person. So that whatever has the consciousness of present and past actions, is the same person to whom they belong."

This doctrine has some strange consequences, which the author was aware of. Such as, that if the same consciousness can be transferred from one intelligent being to another, which he thinks we cannot show to be impossible, then two or twenty intelligent beings may be the same person. And if the intelligent being may lose the consciousness of the actions done by him, which surely is possible, then he is not the person that did those actions; so that one intelligent being may be two or twenty different persons, if he shall so often lose the consciousness of his former actions.①

① Reid points out some of the consequences of Locke's view that Locke himself endorses. How strange (and thus implausible) are these?

There is another consequence of this doctrine, which follows no less necessarily, though Mr. Locke probably did not see it. It is, that a man may be, and at the same time not be, the person that did a particular action.

Suppose a brave officer to have been flogged when a boy at school, for robbing an orchard, to have taken a standard from the enemy in his first campaign, and to have been made a general in advanced life. Suppose also, which must be admitted to be possible, that when he took the standard, he was conscious of his having been flogged at school; and that when made a general, he was conscious of his taking the standard, but had absolutely lost the consciousness of his flogging.

These things being supposed, it follows, from Mr. Locke's doctrine, that he who was flogged at school is the same person who took the standard; and that he who took the standard is the same person who was made a general. Whence it follows, if there be any truth in logic, that the general is the same person with him who was flogged at school. But the general's consciousness does not reach so far back as his flogging, therefore, according to Mr. Locke's doctrine, he is not the person who was flogged. Therefore the general is, and at the same time is not, the same person with him who was flogged at school.②

② Reid's strongest objection to Locke is this counter-example, one which most have found utterly decisive. The underlying principle of logic is that identity (of any sort) is *transitive*: if A is identical to B, and B is identical to C, then A is identical to C. So the general must be identical to the schoolboy who was flogged, even though Locke's account says otherwise. (Is there a way to amend Locke's view so as to avoid this problem? See Discussion Question 1.)

Leaving the consequences of this doctrine to those who have leisure to trace them, we may observe, with regard to the doctrine itself;

1st, That Mr. Locke attributes to consciousness the conviction we have of our past actions, as if a man may now be conscious of what he did twenty years ago. It is impossible to understand the meaning of this, unless by consciousness be meant memory, the only faculty by which we have an immediate knowledge of our past actions.

Sometimes, in popular discourse, a man says he is conscious that he did such a thing, meaning that he distinctly remembers that he did it. It is unnecessary, in common discourse, to fix accurately the limits between consciousness and memory. . . .

But this ought to be avoided in philosophy, otherwise we confound the different powers of the mind, and ascribe to one what really belongs to another. If a man can be conscious of what he did twenty years, or twenty minutes ago, there is no use for memory, nor ought we to allow that there is any such faculty. The faculties of consciousness and memory are chiefly distinguished by this, that the first is an immediate knowledge of the present, the second an immediate knowledge of the past.

When, therefore, Mr. Locke's notion of personal identity is properly expressed, it is, that personal identity consists in distinct remembrance: for, even in the popular sense, to say that I am conscious of a past action, means nothing else than that I distinctly remember that I did it.③

③ Remember correctly or incorrectly—that is, *seem* to remember. To appeal to genuine memory would seemingly presuppose identity rather than explain it, since I can't genuinely remember doing or experiencing something unless I am in fact the same person who did or experienced it.

2dly, It may be observed, that in this doctrine, not only is consciousness confounded with memory, but which is still more strange, personal identity is confounded with the evidence which we have of our personal identity.

It is very true, that my remembrance that I did such a thing is the evidence I have that I am the identical person who did it. And this, I am apt to think, Mr. Locke meant: but to say that my remembrance that I did such a thing, or my consciousness, makes me the person who did it, is, in my apprehension, an absurdity too gross to be entertained by any man who attends to the meaning of it: for it is to attribute to memory or consciousness, a strange magical power of producing its object, though that object must have existed before the memory or consciousness which produced it.

Consciousness is the testimony of one faculty; memory is the testimony of another faculty: and to say that the testimony is the cause of the thing testified, this surely is absurd, if any thing be, and could not have been said by Mr. Locke, if he had not confounded the testimony with the thing testified.

When a horse that was stolen is found and claimed by the owner, the only evidence he can have, or that a judge or witnesses can have, that this is the very identical horse which was his property, is similitude.

But would it not be ridiculous from this to infer that the identity of a horse consists in similitude only? The only evidence I have that I am the identical person who did such actions, is, that I remember distinctly I did them; or, as Mr. Locke expresses it, I am conscious I did them. To infer from this, that personal identity consists in consciousness, is an argument, which, if it had any force, would prove the identity of a stolen horse to consist solely in similitude. ^④

4 Reid's view is that seeming to remember that I did something (or had a certain experience) is *evidence* that I am identical to the earlier person (supposing that there is one) who did (or experienced) the thing in question. But if it is evidence for identity, then it can't also be what identity consists in (since then it would be evidence for itself, which makes no sense).

3dly, Is it not strange that the sameness or identity of a person should consist in a thing which is continually changing, and is not any two minutes the same?

Our consciousness, our memory, and every operation of the mind, are still flowing like the water of a river, or like time itself. The consciousness I have this moment can no more be the same consciousness I had last moment, than this moment can be the last moment. Identity can only be affirmed of things which have a continued existence. Consciousness, and every kind of thought, is transient and momentary, and has no continued existence; and therefore, if personal identity consisted in consciousness, it would certainly follow, that no man is the same person any two moments of his life; and as the right and justice of reward and punishment is founded on personal identity, no man could be responsible for his actions. ^⑤

5 This is a looser and less obviously compelling objection, though one that is made more serious by Locke's failure to explain what having the "same consciousness" amounts to. Does the fact that consciousness itself is "transient and momentary" prevent persons at different times from having the same consciousness in the sense that Locke intends? See Discussion Question 2.

But though I take this to be the unavoidable consequence of Mr. Locke's doctrine concerning personal identity, and though some persons may have liked the doctrine the better on this account, I am far from imputing any thing of this kind to Mr. Locke. He was too good a man not to have rejected with abhorrence a doctrine which he believed to draw this consequence after it. ^⑥

4thly, There are many expressions used by Mr. Locke in speaking of personal identity, which to me are altogether unintelligible, unless we suppose that he confounded that sameness, or identity, which we ascribe to an individual,

6 What Locke would have "rejected with abhorrence" is the alleged consequence that no one is ever responsible for his actions since he is not the same person as the one who performed them. But Locke would *not* have agreed that this consequence follows from his view.

with the identity which in common discourse is often ascribed to many individuals of the same species.

When we say that pain and pleasure, consciousness and memory, are the same in all men, this sameness can only mean similarity, or sameness of kind; but that the pain of one man can be the same individual pain with that of another man, is no less impossible, than that one man should be another man; the pain felt by me yesterday, can no more be the pain I feel today, than yesterday can be this day; and the same thing may be said of every passion and of every operation of the mind. The same kind or species of operation may be in different men, or in the same man at different times; but it is impossible that the same individual operation should be in different men, or in the same man at different times.⑦

⑦ Reid seems right about this: the consciousness in an earlier person and a later one cannot be numerically the same event of consciousness.

When Mr. Locke therefore speaks of "the same consciousness being continued through a succession of different substances;" when he speaks of "repeating the idea of a past action, with the same consciousness we had of it at the first," and of "the same consciousness extending to actions past and to come;" these expressions are to me unintelligible, unless he means, not the same individual consciousness, but a consciousness that is similar, or of the same kind.

If our personal identity consists in consciousness, as this consciousness cannot be the same individually any two moments, but only of the same kind, it would follow, that we are not for any two moments the same individual persons, but the same kind of persons.⑧

As our consciousness sometimes ceases to exist, as in sound sleep, our personal identity must cease with it. Mr. Locke allows, that the same thing cannot have two beginnings of existence, so that our identity would be irrecoverably gone every time we cease to think, if it was but for a moment.⑨

⑧ Is merely having consciousness of the same specific kind enough to satisfy what Locke has in mind, or is there some further requirement? See Discussion Question 1 to the Locke selection.

⑨ Locke admits that there are gaps in consciousness, for example in dreamless sleep, but never says clearly why these do not destroy identity. Again, the issue is really what is required for consciousness to be the same in the relevant sense.

Discussion Questions

1. Consider again the sort of situation involved in Reid's case of the general, and suppose that the same sort of situation is repeated through the general's whole life: though there are many earlier actions and states of mind that the person at a given stage cannot remember, each such person can remember actions and states of mind at some earlier stage, and the person at that stage can remember actions and states of mind at still earlier stages, and so on, so that starting from the general and appealing to intermediate stages, one can trace back to the very beginning of the general's life (or nearly so) via links of memory. This is roughly what is sometimes referred to as *psychological continuity*. Is psychological continuity a **sufficient condition** for personal identity, in which case the general at the end of his human life would still be the same person as the young child at the beginning of that life? Is it a **necessary condition?** Why or why not?

2. Reid's second and third observations amount to pointing out that the consciousness of a person at one time and that of a person at another time are never numerically the same, but at most qualitatively the same—that is, exactly similar—or, more likely, qualitatively the same in certain limited respects. Reid takes this to show that it follows from Locke's view that a person is never identical from one moment to the next, let alone over more extended stretches of time. How might Locke reply to this objection? Who do you think is right?

Bernard Williams

Bernard Williams (1929–2003) was a British philosopher who taught mainly at Cambridge University. He made major contributions to many areas of philosophy, most importantly to ethics.

In this selection, Williams approaches the issue of personal identity by asking whether or not it is possible for two persons to "exchange" their material bodies by having the memories, character traits, and so on of one erased from his brain and transferred into the brain of the other, and vice versa. Thus after the exchange, the person inhabiting one of the bodies will seemingly satisfy the correct psychological requirement for personal identity (*if* there is one): it will stand in the same psychological relations to the previous actions, experiences, and character traits of the person that previously inhabited the other body that persons normally stand in to their own previous actions, experiences, and character traits; and again, vice versa. But does this mean that the bodies have genuinely been "exchanged," so that each of the persons now inhabits a new body? Williams gives one account of such a case that seems to support such a conclusion. He then contrasts it with a second account that agrees on the basic facts of the case, but portrays them in a quite different way that seems to support the conclusion that the bodies have not been "exchanged," but instead that each of the persons, still inhabiting the same body, have suffered a combination of amnesia and artificially induced memories and character traits. Williams very tentatively opts for the latter account of the case, while admitting that it is very hard to be sure which one is correct.

The Self and the Future

THE SELF AND THE FUTURE

Suppose that there were some process to which two persons, A and B, could be subjected as a result of which they might be said—question-beggingly—to have *exchanged bodies.* That is to say—less question-beggingly—there is a certain human body which is such that when previously we were confronted with it, we were confronted with person A, certain utterances coming from it were expressive of memories of the past experiences of A, certain movements of it partly constituted the actions of A and were taken as expressive of the character of A, and so forth; but now, after the process is completed, utterances coming from this body are expressive of what seem to be just those memories which previously we identified as memories of the past experiences of B, its movements partly constitute actions expressive of the character of B, and so forth; and conversely with the other body.①

There are certain important philosophical limitations on how such imaginary cases are to be con-

structed, and how they are to be taken when constructed in various ways. I shall mention two principal limitations, not in order to pursue them further here, but precisely in order to get them out of the way.

There are certain limitations, particularly with regard to character and mannerisms, to our ability to imagine such cases even in the most restricted sense of our being disposed to take the later performances of that body which was previously A's as expressive of B's character; if the previous A and B were extremely unlike one another both physically and psychologically, and if, say, in addition, they were of different sex, there might be grave difficulties in reading B's dispositions in any

① Supposing that the utterances and behavior are taken at face value, the person now in the body that was previously inhabited by person A has the same sort of memory of the previous actions and experiences of person B that person B would have had of them if the "exchange" had not taken place—whether this is understood as a complete or relatively complete memory of them (as Locke seems to suggest) or only as a relation of psychological continuity with earlier stages of B (see Discussion Question 1 to the Reid selection). The person in the body previously inhabited by person A also apparently has all the character traits of person B.

From Problems of the Self *(Cambridge: Cambridge University Press, 1973).*

possible performances of *A*'s body. Let us forget this, and for the present purpose just take *A* and *B* as being sufficiently alike (however alike that has to be) for the difficulty not to arise; after the experiment, persons familiar with *A* and *B* are just *overwhelmingly struck* by the *B*-ish character of the doings associated with what was previously *A*'s body, and conversely. Thus the feat of imagining an exchange of bodies is supposed possible in the most restricted sense. But now there is a further limitation which has to be overcome if the feat is to be not merely possible in the most restricted sense but also is to have an outcome which, on serious reflection, we are prepared to describe as *A* and *B* having changed bodies—that is, an outcome where, confronted with what was previously *A*'s body, we are prepared seriously to say that we are now confronted with *B*.

It would seem a necessary condition of so doing that the utterances coming from that body be taken as genuinely expressive of memories of *B*'s past. But memory is a causal notion; and as we actually use it, it seems a necessary condition of *x*'s present knowledge of *x*'s earlier experiences constituting memory of those experiences that the causal chain linking the experiences and the knowledge should not run outside *x*'s body.② Hence if utterances coming from a given body are to be taken as expressive of memories of the experiences of *B*, there should be some suitable causal link between the appropriate state of that body and the original happening of those experiences to *B*. One radical way of securing that condition in the imagined exchange case is to suppose . . . that the brains of *A* and of *B* are transposed. We may not need so radical a condition. Thus suppose it were possible to extract information from a man's brain and store it in a device while his brain was repaired, or even renewed, the information then being replaced: it would seem exag-

gerated to insist that the resultant man could not possibly have the memories he had before the operation.③ With regard to our knowledge of our own past, we draw distinctions between merely recalling, being reminded, and learning again, and those distinctions correspond (roughly) to distinctions between no new input, partial new input, and total new input with regard to the information in question; and it seems clear that the information-parking case just imagined would not count as new input in the sense necessary and sufficient for 'learning again'. Hence we can imagine the case we are concerned with in terms of information extracted into such devices from *A*'s and *B*'s brains and replaced in the other brain; this is the sort of model which, I think not unfairly for the present argument, I shall have in mind.

We imagine the following. The process considered above exists; two persons can enter some machine, let us say, and emerge changed in the appropriate ways. If *A* and *B* are the persons who enter, let us call the persons who emerge the *A-body-person* and the *B-body-person:* the *A*-body-person is that person (whoever it is) with whom I am confronted when, after the experiment, I am confronted with that body which previously was *A*'s body—that is to say, that person who would naturally be taken for *A* by someone who just saw this person, was familiar with *A*'s appearance before the experiment, and did not know about the happening of the experiment. A non-question-begging description of the experiment will leave it open which (if either) of the persons *A* and *B* the *A*-body-person is; the description of the experiment as 'persons changing bodies' of course implies that the *A*-body-person is actually *B*.④

② There are at least two requirements here for memory: First, the present beliefs and perhaps images must be *caused* by the earlier experiences (rather than, say, occurring at random and just happening by coincidence to fit those earlier experiences). Second, the causal relation must be of the right sort: if, for example, the person's present knowledge of his or her earlier experiences depends on being told about them by a second person (who was previously told about them by the original person at some intervening time), then this is not a case of memory.

③ In the case described, the information is removed, stored externally, and then replaced. The later knowledge is not caused in exactly the same way as ordinary memory knowledge (since the causal process involves external storage of the information for a time), but it also does not involve another person who remembers and then relates the information. By saying that it would "seem exaggerated" to say that the result in this case is not genuine memory, Williams is saying rather indirectly that the result is genuine memory (so that, contrary to what he seemed to say earlier, it is not a requirement for memory that the causal process does not run outside the person's body). See Discussion Question 1.

We take two persons *A* and *B* who are going to have the process carried out on them. (We can suppose, rather hazily, that they are willing for this to happen; to investigate at all closely at this stage why they might be willing or unwilling, what they would fear, and so forth, would anticipate some later issues.) We further announce that one of the two resultant persons, the *A*-body-person and the *B*-body-person, is going after the experiment to be given $100,000, while the other is going to be tortured. We then ask each of *A* and *B* to choose which treatment should be dealt out to which of the persons who will emerge from the experiment, the choice to be made (if it can be) on selfish grounds.

Suppose that *A* chooses that the *B*-body-person should get the pleasant treatment and the *A*-body-person the unpleasant treatment; and *B* chooses conversely (this might indicate that they thought that 'changing bodies' was indeed a good description of the outcome). The experimenter cannot act in accordance with both these sets of preferences, those expressed by *A* and those expressed by *B*. Hence there is one clear sense in which *A* and *B* cannot both get what they want: namely, that if the experimenter, before the experiment, announces to *A* and *B* that he intends to carry out the alternative (for example), of treating the *B*-body-person unpleasantly and the *A*-body-person pleasantly—then *A* can say rightly, 'That's not the outcome I chose to happen', and *B* can say rightly, 'That's just the outcome I chose to happen'. So, evidently, *A* and *B* before the experiment can each come to know either that the outcome he chose will be that which will happen, or that the one he chose will not happen, and in that sense they can get or fail to get what they wanted.⑤ But is it also true that when the experimenter proceeds after the experiment to act in accordance with one of the preferences and not the other, *then* one of *A* and *B* will have got what he wanted, and the other not?

> ④ So the *A*-body-person now apparently has the memories and character traits of person *B*; and the *B*-body-person now apparently has the memories and character traits of person *A*.

> ⑤ Since the choice is to be made on selfish grounds, each person apparently believes (rightly or wrongly) that after the process occurs he will be the person in the other body (so that the bodies will indeed have been exchanged). Whether they are right about this is a further issue.

There seems very good ground for saying so. For suppose the experimenter, having elicited *A*'s and *B*'s preference, says nothing to *A* and *B* about what he will do; conducts the experiment; and then, for example, gives the unpleasant treatment to the *B*-body-person and the pleasant treatment to the *A*-body-person. Then the *B*-body-person will not only complain of the unpleasant treatment as such, but will complain (since he has *A*'s memories) that that was not the outcome he chose, since he chose that the *B*-body-person should be well treated; and since *A* made his choice in selfish spirit, he may add that he precisely chose in that way because he did not want the unpleasant things to happen to *him*. The *A*-body-person meanwhile will express satisfaction both at the receipt of the $100,000, and also at the fact that the experimenter has chosen to act in the way that he, *B*, so wisely chose. These facts make a strong case for saying that the experimenter has brought it about that *B* did in the outcome get what he wanted and *A* did not. It is therefore a strong case for saying that the *B*-body-person really is *A*, and the *A*-body-person really is *B*; and therefore for saying that the process of the experiment really is that of changing bodies.⑥ For the same reasons it would seem that *A* and *B* in our example really did choose wisely, and that it was *A*'s bad luck that the choice he correctly made was not carried out, *B*'s good luck that the choice he correctly made was carried out. This seems to show that to care about what happens to me in the future is not necessarily to care about what happens to *this* body (the one I now have); and this in turn might be taken to show that in some sense of Descartes's obscure phrase, I and my body are 'really distinct' (though, of course, nothing in these considerations could support the idea that I could exist without a body at all).

> ⑥ The *A*-body-person, having *B*'s memories and character traits, will seem to himself to be *B*, and in particular will remember having opted for the result where the *A*-body-person receives the money rather than being tortured. Thus it will *seem* to that person that he received the result that he asked for (and to the other person that he did not). But it is again not yet decided whether each of them is correct in their assessments.

These suggestions seem to be reinforced if we consider the cases where *A* and *B* make other choices with regard to the experiment. Suppose that *A* chooses that the *A*-body-person should get the money, and the

B-body-person get the pain, and B chooses conversely. Here again there can be no outcome which matches the expressed preferences of both of them: they cannot both get what they want. The experimenter announces, before the experiment, that the A-body-person will in fact get the money, and the B-body-person will get the pain. So A at this stage gets what he wants (the announced outcome matches his expressed preference). After the experiment, the distribution is carried out as announced. Both the A-body-person and the B-body-person will have to agree that what is happening is in accordance with the preference that A originally expressed. The B-body-person will naturally express this acknowledgement (since he has A's memories) by saying that this is the distribution he chose; he will recall, among other things, the experimenter announcing this outcome, his approving it as what he chose, and so forth. However, he (the B-body-person) certainly does not like what is now happening to him, and would much prefer to be receiving what the A-body-person is receiving—namely, $100,000. The A-body-person will on the other hand recall choosing an outcome other than this one, but will reckon it good luck that the experimenter did not do what he recalls choosing. It looks, then, as though the A-body-person has got what he wanted, but not what he chose, while the B-body-person has got what he chose, but not what he wanted. So once more it looks as though they are, respectively, B and A; and that in this case the original choices of both A and B were unwise.⑦

⑦ Now, in light of their selfish preferences, each person apparently believes that the bodies will not be "exchanged" and so opts to have the person in his previous body treated well and the other person treated badly. After the process is complete, it *seems* to each that he made the wrong choice, because it seems to him that he is now in the other body.

Suppose, lastly, that in the original choice A takes the line of the first case and B of the second: that is, A chooses that the B-body-person should get the money and the A-body-person the pain, and B chooses exactly the same thing. In this case, the experimenter would seem to be in the happy situation of giving both persons what they want—or at least, like God, what they have chosen. In this case, the B-body-person likes what he is receiving, recalls choosing it, and congratulates himself on the wisdom of (as he puts it) his choice; while the A-body-person does not like what he is receiving, recalls choosing it, and is forced to acknowledge that (as he puts it) his choice was unwise. So once more we seem to get results to support the suggestions drawn from the first case.⑧

. . .

Let us now consider something apparently different. Someone in whose power I am tells me that I am going to be tortured tomorrow. I am frightened, and look forward to tomorrow in great apprehension. He adds that when the time comes, I shall not remember being told that this was going to happen to me, since shortly before the torture something else will be done to me which will make me forget the announcement. This certainly will not cheer me up, since I know perfectly well that I can forget things, and that there is such a thing as indeed being tortured unexpectedly because I had forgotten or been made to forget a prediction of the torture: that will still be a torture which, so long as I do know about the prediction, I look forward to in fear. He then adds that my forgetting the announcement will be only part of a larger process: when the moment of torture comes, I shall not remember any of the things I am now in a position to remember. This does not cheer me up, either, since I can readily conceive of being involved in an accident, for instance, as a result of which I wake up in a completely amnesiac state and also in great pain; that could certainly happen to me, I should not like it to happen to me, nor to know that it was going to happen to me. He now further adds that at the moment of torture I shall not only not remember the things I am now in a position to remember, but will have a different set of impressions of my past, quite different from the memories I now have. I do not think that this would cheer me up, either. For I can at least conceive the possibility, if not the concrete reality, of going completely mad, and thinking perhaps that I am George IV or somebody; and being told that some-

⑧ Now A apparently thinks that the "exchange" will occur and B does not, so each opts that the B-body-person after the process be treated well and the other person treated badly. When this is done, the B-body-person likes the result (and *seems* to himself to be A and to have made a wise choice), while the A-body-person does not like the result (and *seems* to himself to be B and to have made an unwise choice).

thing like that was going to happen to me would have no tendency to reduce the terror of being told authoritatively that I was going to be tortured, but would merely compound the horror. Nor do I see why I should be put into any better frame of mind by the person in charge adding lastly that the impressions of my past with which I shall be equipped on the eve of torture will exactly fit the past of another person now living, and that indeed I shall acquire these impressions by (for instance) information now in his brain being copied into mine. Fear, surely, would still be the proper reaction: and not because one did not know what was going to happen, but because in one vital respect at least one did know what was going to happen—torture, which one can indeed expect to happen to oneself, and to be preceded by certain mental derangements as well.⑨

If this is right, the whole question seems now to be totally mysterious. For what we have just been through is of course merely one side, differently represented, of the transaction which we considered before; and it represents it as a perfectly hateful prospect, while the previous considerations represented it as something one should rationally, perhaps even cheerfully, choose out of the options there presented. It is differently presented, of course, and in two notable respects; but when we look at these two differences of presentation, can we really convince ourselves that the second presentation is wrong or misleading, thus leaving the road open to the first version which at the time seemed so convincing? Surely not.

The first difference is that in the second version the torture is throughout represented as going to happen to *me:* 'you', the man in charge persistently says. Thus he is not very neutral. But should he have been neutral? Or, to put it another way, does his use of the second person have a merely emotional and rhetorical effect on me, making me afraid when further reflection would have shown that I had no reason to be? It is certainly not obviously so. The problem just is that through every step of his predictions I seem to be able

to follow him successfully. And if I reflect on whether what he has said gives me grounds for fearing that I shall be tortured, I could consider that behind my fears lies some principle such as this: that my undergoing physical pain in the future is not excluded by any psychological state I may be in at the time, with the platitudinous exception of those psychological states which in themselves exclude experiencing pain, notably (if it is a psychological state) unconsciousness. In particular, what impressions I have about the past will not have any effect on whether I undergo the pain or not. This principle seems sound enough.⑩

It is an important fact that not everything I would, as things are, regard as an evil would be something that I should rationally fear as an evil if it were predicted that it would happen to me in the future and also predicted that I should undergo significant psychological changes in the meantime. For the fact that I regard that happening, things being as they are, as an evil can be dependent on factors of belief or character which might themselves be modified by the psychological changes in question. Thus if I am appallingly subject to acrophobia, and am told that I shall find myself on top of a steep mountain in the near future, I shall to that extent be afraid; but if I am told that I shall be psychologically changed in the meantime in such a way as to rid me of my acrophobia (and as with the other prediction, I believe it), then I have no reason to be afraid of the predicted happening, or at least not the same reason. Again, I might look forward to meeting a certain person again with either alarm or excitement because of my memories of our past relations. In some part, these memories operate in connexion with my emotion, not only on the present time, but projectively forward: for it is to a meeting itself affected by the presence of those memories that I look forward. If I am convinced that when the time comes I shall not have those memories, then I shall not have just the same reasons as before for looking forward to that meeting with the one emotion or the other . . . .

Physical pain, however, the example which for simplicity (and not for any obsessional reason) I have taken, is absolutely minimally dependent on character or belief. No amount of change in my character or my beliefs would seem to affect substantially the nastiness of tortures applied to me; correspondingly, no degree of predicted change in my character and beliefs can unseat the fear of torture which, together with those changes, is predicted for me. [11]

11 Thus no description of such changes, Williams is claiming, can make it unreasonable for someone to fear the future pain.

. . .

I said that there were two notable differences between the second presentation of our situation and the first. The first difference, which we have just said something about, was that the man predicted the torture for *me,* a psychologically very changed 'me'. We have yet to find a reason for saying that he should not have done this, or that I really should be unable to follow him if he does; I seem to be able to follow him only too well. The second difference is that in this presentation he does not mention the other man, except in the somewhat incidental rôle of being the provenance of the impressions of the past I end up with. He does not mention him at all as someone who will end up with impressions of the past derived from me (and, incidentally, with $100,000 as well—a consideration which, in the frame of mind appropriate to this version, will merely make me jealous).

But why *should* he mention this man and what is going to happen to him? My selfish concern is to be told what is going to happen to me, and now I know: torture, preceded by changes of character, brain operations, changes in impressions of the past. The knowledge that one other person, or none, or many will be similarly mistreated may affect me in other ways, of sympathy, greater horror at the power of this tyrant, and so forth; but surely it cannot affect my expectations of torture? But—someone will say—this is to leave out exactly the feature which, as the first presentation of the case showed, makes all the difference: for it is to leave out the person who, as the first presentation showed, will be you. It is to leave out not merely a feature which should fundamentally affect your fears, but it is to leave out the very person for whom you are fearful. So of course, the objector will say, this makes all the difference. [12]

But can it? Consider the following series of cases. In each case we are to suppose that after what is described, *A* is, as before, to be tortured; we are also to suppose the person *A* is informed beforehand that just these things followed by the torture will happen to him:

12 The objection claims that the inclusion of the other person existing after the "exchange"—the person who in the description of the original case started in *A*'s body and after the process *seems* to be *B*—should remove *B*'s fear of the future torture by making it clear that it is *A* and not *B* who will in fact be tortured.

(i) *A* is subjected to an operation which produces total amnesia;
(ii) amnesia is produced in *A*, and other interference leads to certain changes in his character;
(iii) changes in his character are produced, and at the same time certain illusory 'memory' beliefs are induced in him: these are of a quite fictitious kind and do not fit the life of any actual person;
(iv) the same as (iii), except that both the character traits and the 'memory' impressions are designed to be appropriate to another actual person, *B*;
(v) the same as (iv), except that the result is produced by putting the information into *A* from the brain of *B*, by a method which leaves *B* the same as he was before;
(vi) the same happens to *A* as in (v), but *B* is not left the same, since a similar operation is conducted in the reverse direction.

I take it that no-one is going to dispute that A has reasons, and fairly straightforward reasons, for fear of pain when the prospect is that of situation (i); there seems no conceivable reason why this should not extend to situation (ii), and the situation (iii) can surely introduce no difference of principle—it just seems a situation which for more than one reason we should have grounds for fearing, as suggested above. Situation (iv) at least introduces the person B, who was the focus of the objection we are now discussing. But it does not seem to introduce him in any way which makes a material difference; if I can expect pain through a transformation which involves new 'memory'-impressions, it would seem a purely external fact, relative to that, that the 'memory'-impressions had a model. Nor, in (iv), do we satisfy a causal condition which I mentioned at the beginning for the 'memories' actually being memories; though notice that if the job were done thoroughly, I might well be able to elicit from the A-body-person the kinds of remarks about his previous expectations of the experiment—remarks appropriate to the original B—which so impressed us in the first version of the story. I shall have a similar assurance of this being so in situation (v), where, moreover, a plausible application of the causal condition is available. [13]

[13] In the original case, it was the B-body-person who was tortured, but this change makes no real difference. Cases (i)–(iv) here correspond to the successive steps in the original account of the non-exchange case, while cases (v) and (vi) reflect a similar non-exchange version of the second person's situation.

But two things are to be noticed about this situation. First, if we concentrate on A and the A-body-person, we do not seem to have added anything which from the point of view of his fears makes any material difference; just as, in the move from (iii) to (iv), it made no relevant difference that the new 'memory'-impressions which precede the pain had, as it happened, a model, so in the move from (iv) to (v) all we have added is that they have a model which is also their cause: and it is still difficult to see why that, to him looking forward, could possibly make the difference between expecting pain and not expecting pain. To illustrate that point from the case of character: if A is capable of expecting pain, he is capable of expecting pain preceded by a change in his dispositions—and to that expectation it can make no difference, whether that change in his dispositions is modelled on, or indeed indirectly caused by; the dispositions of some other person. If his fears can, as it were, reach through the change, it seems a mere trimming how the change is in fact induced. The second point about situation (v) is that if the crucial question for A's fears with regard to what befalls the A-body-person is whether the A-body-person is or is not the person B, then that condition has not yet been satisfied in situation (v): for there we have an undisputed B in addition to the A-body-person, and certainly those two are not the same person. [14]

But in situation (vi), we seemed to think, that is finally what he is. But if A's original fears could reach through the expected changes in (v), as they did in (iv) and (iii), then certainly they can reach through in (vi). Indeed, from the point of view of A's expectations and fears, there is less difference between (vi) and (v) than there is between (v) and (iv) or between (iv) and (iii). In those transitions, there were at least differences—though we could not see that they were really relevant differences—in the content or cause of what happened to him; in the present case there is absolutely no difference at all in what happens to him, the only difference being in what happens to someone else. If he can fear pain when (v) is predicted, why should he cease to when (vi) is? [15]

[14] The issue is whether the addition of the elements of cases (v) and (vi) makes any difference to whether the person (A, as the case is described) whose body will be tortured is unreasonable or mistaken in some way in expecting and fearing that he will be tortured. The additions in case (v) by themselves make no difference: B still exists in the B-body, so that it cannot be that A is now in the B-body.

[15] But if A is reasonably fearful of being tortured in cases (i)–(v), how can the additional ingredients in case (vi) make any difference? If the person in the A-body is still A in case (v), how can doing something to the other person and nothing at all further to A somehow bring it about in case (vi) that A is now in the B-body (and so should not fear the torture that will happen to the A-body)? The underlying principle being assumed here is that the identity of the person in the A-body cannot be affected by the existence or situation of another person in a different body. (Is this correct?)

I can see only one way of relevantly laying great weight on the transition from (v) to (vi); and this involves a considerable difficulty. This is to deny that, as I put it, the transition from (v) to (vi) involves merely the addition of something happening to *somebody else;* what rather it does, it will be said, is to involve the reintroduction of A himself, as the B-body-person; since he has reappeared in this form, it is for this person, and not for the unfortunate A-body-person, that A will have his expectations. This is to reassert, in effect, the viewpoint emphasised in our first presentation of the experiment. But this surely has the consequence that A should not have fears for the A-body-person who appeared in situation (v). For by the present argument, the A-body-person in (vi) is not A; the B-body-person is. But the A-body-person in (v) is, in character, history, everything, exactly the same as the *A*-body-person in (vi); so if the latter is not *A*, then neither is the former. **16** (It is this point, no doubt, that encourages one to speak of the difference that goes with (vi) as being, on the present view, the *reintroduction of A*.) But no-one else in (v) has any better claim to be *A*. So in (v), it seems, *A* just does not exist. This would certainly explain why *A* should have no fears for the state of things in (v)—though he might well have fears for the path to it. But it rather looked earlier as though he could well have fears for the state of things in (v). Let us grant, however, that that was an illusion, and that *A* really does not exist in (v); then does he exist in (iv), (iii), (ii), or (i)? It seems very difficult to deny it for (i) and (ii); are we perhaps to draw the line between (iii) and (iv)? **17**

16 To insist that the *B*-body-person in case (vi) is the original person *A* requires one to also say, Williams is arguing, that the *A*-body-person in case (v) was also not *A*—presumably because that person then had *B*'s memories and character traits. (But of course the *A*-body-person was also not *B*, since *B* still exists in the *B*-body in cases (i)–(v). So who is the person in the *A*-body, according to this view—which Williams does not accept? See Discussion Question 3.)

17 If *A* does not exist in case (v)—since he is neither the person in the *B*-body nor the person in the *A*-body, according to the view being considered—when in the sequence of cases does he cease to exist?

Here someone will say: you must not insist on drawing a line—borderline cases are borderline cases, and you must not push our concepts beyond their limits. But this well-known piece of advice, sensible as it is in many cases, seems in the present case to involve an extraordinary difficulty. It may intellectually comfort observers of *A*'s situation; but what is *A* supposed to make of it? To be told that a future situation is a borderline one for its being myself that is hurt, that it is conceptually undecidable whether it will be me or not, is something which, it seems, I can do nothing with; because, in particular, it seems to have no comprehensible representation in my expectations and the emotions that go with them. **18**

If I expect that a certain situation, *S*, will come about in the future, there is of course a wide range of emotions and concerns, directed on *S*, which I may experience now in relation to my expectation. Unless I am exceptionally egoistic, it is not a condition on my being concerned in relation to this expectation, that I myself will be involved in *S*—where my being 'involved' in *S* means that I figure in *S* as someone doing something at that time or having something done to me, or, again, that *S* will have consequences affecting me at that or some subsequent time. There are some emotions, however, which I will feel only if I will be involved in *S*, and fear is an obvious example.

18 The suggestion is that while person *A* does not exist in case (v) and clearly exists (in the *A*-body) before any of the changes involved in the sequence of cases have taken place, there is no clear line at which he ceases to exist. Some at least of the intervening cases are borderline cases where it is simply unclear whether *A* exists or not. Is this view really intelligible?

Now the description of *S* under which it figures in my expectations will necessarily be, in various ways, indeterminate; and one way in which it may be indeterminate is that it leaves open whether I shall be involved in *S* or not. Thus I may have good reason to expect that one of us five is going to get hurt, but no reason to expect it to be me rather than one of the others. My present emotions will be correspondingly affected by this indeterminacy. Thus, sticking to the egoistic concern involved in fear, I shall presumably be somewhat more cheerful than if I knew it was going to be me, somewhat less cheerful than if I had been left out altogether. Fear will be mixed with, and qualified by, apprehension; and so forth. These emotions revolve around the thought of the eventual determination of the indeterminacy; moments of straight fear focus on its really turning out to be me, of hope on its turning out not to be me. All the emotions are related to the coming about of what I expect: and what I expect in such a case just cannot come about save by coming about in one of the ways or another.

There are other ways in which indeterminate expectations can be related to fear. Thus I may expect (perhaps neurotically) that something nasty is going to happen to me, indeed expect that when it happens it will take some determinate form, but have no range, or no closed range, of candidates for the determinate form to rehearse in my present thought. Different from this would be the fear of something radically indeterminate—the fear (one might say) of a nameless horror. If somebody had such a fear, one could even say that he had, in a sense, a perfectly determinate expectation: if what he expects indeed comes about, there will be nothing more determinate to be said about it after the event than was said in the expectation. Both these cases of course are cases of *fear* because one thing that is fixed amid the indeterminacy is the belief that it is me to whom the things will happen.[19]

> [19] I can be afraid in varying degrees because it is indeterminate what will happen to me in a future situation, as long as it is clear that it is indeed me to whom the indeterminate things will happen.

. . .

Suppose now that there is an *S* with regard to which it is for conceptual reasons undecidable whether it involves me or not, as is proposed for the experimental situation by the line we are discussing. It is important that the expectation of *S* is not *indeterminate* in any of the ways we have just been considering. It is not like the nameless horror, since the fixed point of that case was that it was going to happen to the subject, and that made his state unequivocally fear. Nor is it like the expectation of the man who expects one of the five to be hurt; his fear was indeed equivocal, but its focus, and that of the expectation, was that when *S* came about, it would certainly come about in one way or the other. In the present case, fear (of the torture, that is to say, not of the initial experiment) seems neither appropriate, nor inappropriate, nor appropriately equivocal. Relatedly, the subject has an incurable difficulty about how he may think about *S*. If he engages in projective imaginative thinking (about how it will be for him), he implicitly answers the necessarily unanswerable question; if he thinks that he cannot engage in such thinking, it looks very much as if he also answers it, though in the opposite direction. Perhaps he must just refrain from such thinking; but is he just refraining from it, if it is incurably undecidable whether he can or cannot engage in it?[20]

> [20] But in the case where it is indeterminate whether I will be involved at all, I simply do not know, according to Williams, what to think—whether to be fearful to any degree or not. Notice that this is not a case of ignorance, not one in which I am there or not, but just do not know which. (Does this show, as Williams may seem to suggest, that the view that it is indeterminate whether I exist must be wrong?)

It may be said that all that these considerations can show is that fear, at any rate, does not get its proper footing in this case; but that there could be some other, more ambivalent, form of concern which would indeed be appropriate to this particular expectation, the expectation of the conceptually undecidable situation. There are, perhaps, analogous feelings that actually occur in actual situations. Thus material objects do occasionally undergo puzzling transformations which leave a conceptual shadow over their identity. Suppose I were sentimentally attached to an object to which this sort of thing then happened; it might be that I could neither feel about it quite as I did originally, nor be totally indifferent to it, but would have some other and rather ambivalent feeling towards it. Similarly, it may be said, toward the prospective sufferer of pain, my identity relations with whom are conceptually shadowed, I can feel neither as I would if he were certainly me, nor as I would if he were certainly not, but rather some such ambivalent concern.

But this analogy does little to remove the most baffling aspect of the present case—an aspect which has already turned up in what was said about the subject's difficulty in thinking either projectively or nonprojectively about the situation. For to regard the prospective pain-sufferer *just* like the transmogrified object of sentiment, and to conceive of my ambivalent distress about his future pain as just like ambivalent distress about some future damage to such an object, is of course to leave him and me clearly distinct from one another, and thus to displace the conceptual shadow from its proper place. I have to get nearer to him than that. But is there any nearer that I can get to him without expecting his pain? If there is, the analogy has not shown us it. We can certainly not get nearer by expecting, as it were, *ambivalent* pain; there is no place at all for that. There seems to be an obstinate bafflement to mirroring in my expectations a situation in which it is conceptually undecidable whether I occur.[21]

> [21] We might, Williams suggests, know how to think about the situation in which identity is indeterminate from a third-person perspective, but not from a first-person perspective.

The bafflement seems, moreover, to turn to plain absurdity if we move from conceptual undecidability to its close friend and neighbour, conventionalist decision. This comes out if we consider another description, overtly conventionalist, of the series of cases which occasioned the present discussion. This description would reject a point I relied on in an earlier argument—namely, that if we deny that the *A*-body-person in (vi) is *A* (because the *B*-body-person is), then we must deny that the *A*-body-person in (v) is *A*, since they are exactly similar. 'No', it may be said, 'this is just to assume that we say the same in different sorts of situation. No doubt when we have the very good candidate for being *A*—namely, the *B*-body-person—we call him *A*; but this does not mean that we should not call the *A*-body-person *A* in that other situation when we have no better candidate around. Different situations call for different descriptions.' This line of talk is the sort of thing indeed appropriate to lawyers deciding the ownership of some property which has undergone some bewildering set of transformations; they just have to decide, and in each situation, let us suppose, it has got to go to somebody, on as reasonable grounds as the facts and the law admit. But as a line to deal with a person's fears or expectations about his own future, it seems to have no sense at all. If *A*'s fears can extend to what will happen to the *A*-body-person in (v), I do not see how they can be rationally diverted from the fate of the exactly similar person in (vi) by his being told that someone would have a reason in the latter situation which he would not have in the former for deciding to call another person *A*. [22]

[22] And the view that it is a matter of convention, something that we are free to decide either way, whether *A* still exists in case (v) is, Williams suggests, absurd. When *A* worries about whether to be fearful about this situation, what he is worrying about is not something that can be settled in this essentially arbitrary way.

Thus, to sum up, it looks as though there are two presentations of the imagined experiment and the choice associated with it, each of which carries conviction, and which lead to contrary conclusions. The idea, moreover, that the situation after the experiment is conceptually undecidable in the relevant respect seems not to assist, but rather to increase, the puzzlement; while the idea (so often appealed to in these matters) that it is conventionally decidable is even worse. Following from all that, I am not in the least clear which option it would be wise to take if one were presented with them before the experiment. I find that rather disturbing.

. . .

I will end by suggesting one rather shaky way in which one might approach a resolution of the problem, using only the limited materials already available.

The apparently decisive arguments of the first presentation, which suggested that *A* should identify himself with the *B*-body-person, turned on the extreme neatness of the situation in satisfying, if any could, the description of 'changing bodies'. But this neatness is basically artificial; it is the product of the will of the experimenter to produce a situation which would naturally elicit, with minimum hesitation, that description. By the sorts of methods he employed, he could easily have left off earlier or gone on further. He could have stopped at situation (v), leaving *B* as he was; or he could have gone on and produced two persons each with *A*-like character and memories, as well as one or two with *B*-like characteristics. [23] If he had done either of those, we should have been in yet greater difficulty about what to say; he just chose to make it as easy as possible for us to find something to say. Now if we had some model of ghostly persons in bodies, which were in some sense actually moved around by certain procedures, we could regard the neat experiment just as the *effective* experiment: the one method that really did result in the ghostly persons' changing places without being destroyed, dispersed, or whatever. But we cannot seriously use such a model. The experimenter has not in the sense of that model *induced* a change of bodies; he has rather produced the one situation out of a range of equally possible situations which we should be most disposed to call a change of bodies. As against this, the principle that one's fears can extend to future pain whatever psychological changes precede it seems positively straightforward. Perhaps, indeed, it is not; but we need to be shown what is wrong with it. Until we are shown what is wrong with it, we should perhaps decide that if we were the person *A* then, if we were to decide selfishly, we should pass the pain to the *B*-body-person. It would be risky: that there is room for the notion of a *risk* here is itself a major feature of the problem.

[23] Presumably if there were two or more persons having *A*'s memories and character after the process is complete, they could not both be identical with the original *A*. See Discussion Question 4.

Discussion Questions

1. When the person in the *A*-body seems after the process is complete to remember *B*'s experiences, is this genuine memory? Obviously the process that produces such apparent memories is different from the normal case, but is it still similar enough (as Williams suggests) to make the results still count as genuine memories—which is apparently required if the resulting person is to be *B*?

2. Obviously there are many sorts of psychological changes that are compatible with the continued existence of the same person, but is this true for any sort of psychological change (as the second way of describing the case claims)? Is a person who has suffered severe and irreversible amnesia still identical to the person who existed before this happens? Is a person who after amnesia has new experiences and forms totally new character traits still identical with the earlier person? Or is there some degree of change that rules out continuing identity?

3. In the second version of the case, the person in the *A*-body in case (v) is not yet *B* (because *B* still exists) but also arguably no longer *A* (since all the changes to him that will lead to his being *B* in case (vi) have already taken place). What should we say about the identity of this person? If *A* and *B* before the process in case (v) were each worried about whether they would survive it, should either of them be reassured by knowing that the person in the *A*-body will exist after the process is completed? If so, which one (and why)?

4. Suppose that *A*'s memories and character traits are transferred into two or more other bodies (and that the original *A*-body is either destroyed or has the memories and character of someone else transferred into it). On the view that accepts exchange of bodies in the original case presented by Williams, what should we say about the persons having *A*'s memories and character in this new case? Is one of them identical to person *A*, and if so, how could we determine which one? If neither of them is identical to *A*, does this mean that *A* does not survive in this new case? If *A* were able before the process occurs to take steps that might harm or hurt these later persons, what should his attitude toward them be (and why)?

5. Would you be willing to undergo the process described by Williams in the original case if both of the resulting people received sufficiently large amounts of money? (Assume that there are no concerns about whether the process will succeed as described.) If, as in the original case, only one person will receive money and the other will be tortured (and you cannot escape the process occurring), who would you want to receive the money: the person (whoever it is) that ends up in your original body or the person (having your memories and character traits) in the new (to you) body? Would the fact that your present body has terminal cancer and the other body is perfectly healthy change your attitude toward undergoing the process (assuming that you can be guaranteed that the healthy body that ends up with your memories and character traits will not be tortured)? Try to give reasons for each of your answers.

Derek Parfit

Derek Parfit (1942–) is a British philosopher who has made major contributions to metaphysics and ethics. He teaches at Oxford University. In this selection, Parfit argues for two main theses: First, there are describable cases, some of which may be scientifically possible, in which there is no clearly right yes-or-no answer to the question of whether a future person is numerically identical to some previously existing person. Second, the issue of personal identity is much less important than it has usually seemed to be: in particular, the issues of (a) whether a previously existing person has *survived* in some future situation and (b) whether a future person is *responsible* for the actions of such a previously existing person do not depend on the question of identity in the way that has standardly been thought. These are views that some philosophers have found extremely paradoxical, and you should carefully consider his reasons for them.

Toward the end of section IV of the selection, Parfit draws a distinction between psychological *continuity* and psychological *connectedness*. Of these, psychological continuity is the weaker and less demanding relation. It holds between a series of persons (or "person-stages") existing at different times as long as there are *direct* psychological relations (one remembering the experiences of another, one intending an action that another does, and so forth) between them that overlap in such a way that any two successive persons or stages are connected by some of them. (How many such direct relations hold between the various stages is a matter of degree, as thus is psychological continuity itself.) Thus in Reid's example (p. 424), the direct relation of remembering an earlier experience holds between the general and the young officer who captured the standard and also between the young officer and the schoolboy. Since there are direct relations between any two of these stages, the whole series satisfies the requirement of psychological continuity to at least this degree. But psychological connectedness (also a matter of degree) requires direct relations between all the members of the series, not just between successive members. Thus the series consisting of the schoolboy, the young officer, and the general does not, as Reid describes it, possess psychological connectedness to any degree, since there are no direct psychological relations between the general and the schoolboy. (This assumes that the general does not remember any of the experiences of the schoolboy, does not act so as to fulfill any of the schoolboy's intentions, and so on.)

Personal Identity

We can, I think, describe cases in which, though we know the answer to every other question, we have no idea how to answer a question about personal identity. These cases are not covered by the criteria of personal identity that we actually use.

Do they present a problem?

It might be thought that they do not, because they could never occur. I suspect that some of them could. (Some, for instance, might become scientifically possible.) But I shall claim that even if they did they would present no problem.

My targets are two beliefs: one about the nature of personal identity, the other about its importance.

The first is that in these cases the question about identity must have an answer.

No one thinks this about, say, nations or machines. Our criteria for the identity of these do not cover certain cases. No one thinks that in these cases the questions "Is it the same nation?" or "Is it the same machine?" must have answers.

Some people believe that in this respect they are different. They agree that our criteria of personal identity do not cover certain cases, but they believe that the nature of their own identity through time is, somehow, such as to guarantee that in these cases questions about their identity must have answers. This belief

From Philosophical Review, *Vol. 80, No.1 (January, 1971).*

might be expressed as follows: "Whatever happens between now and any future time, either I shall still exist, or I shall not. Any future experience will either be *my* experience, or it will not." ①

| ① | Think carefully about this claim, which many philosophers have taken to be obviously correct. The claim is that there must always be a correct yes-or-no answer to the question of whether a person existing at one time still exists at some later time (and if the answer is "yes," it is also assumed, a definite answer as to *which* person at the later time is identical with that earlier existing person). |

This first belief—in the special nature of personal identity—has, I think, certain effects. It makes people assume that the principle of self-interest is more rationally compelling than any moral principle. And it makes them more depressed by the thought of aging and of death.

I cannot see how to disprove this first belief. I shall describe a problem case. But this can only make it seem implausible.

Another approach might be this. We might suggest that one cause of the belief is the projection of our emotions. When we imagine ourselves in a problem case, we do feel that the question "Would it be me?" must have an answer. But what we take to be a bafflement about a further fact may be only the bafflement of our concern. ②

| ② | Parfit is suggesting that what might seem to be factual uncertainty about whether or not I would exist in some possible situation (and if I do exist, which person I would be) may instead be a more general uncertainty about whether and how my normal concern for my own well-being applies to the case in question, if at all. |

I shall not pursue this suggestion here. But one cause of our concern is the belief which is my second target. This is that unless the question about identity has an answer, we cannot answer certain important questions (questions about such matters as survival, memory, and responsibility).

Against this second belief my claim will be this. Certain important questions do presuppose a question about personal identity. But they can be freed of this presupposition. And when they are, the question about identity has no importance.

I

We can start by considering the much discussed case of the man who, like an amoeba, divides.

Wiggins has recently dramatized this case.* He first referred to the operation imagined by Shoemaker.† We suppose that my brain is transplanted into someone else's (brainless) body, and that the resulting person has my character and apparent memories of my life. Most of us would agree, after thought, that the resulting person is me. I shall here assume such agreement.

Wiggins then imagined his own operation. My brain is divided, and each half is housed in a new body. Both resulting people have my character and apparent memories of my life.

What happens to me? There seem only three possibilities: (1) I do not survive; (2) I survive as one of the two people; (3) I survive as both. ③

| ③ | Think about this case before reading further: If this happened to you, would one of the resulting people be you (and if so, which one)? Does it make sense to say that both of them are you? Or have you ceased to exist (and if so, did you die)? |

The trouble with (1) is this. We agreed that I could survive if my brain were successfully transplanted. And people have in fact survived with half their brains destroyed. It seems to follow that I could survive if half my brain were successfully transplanted and the other half were destroyed. But if this is so, how could I *not* survive if the other half were also successfully transplanted? How could a double success be a failure? ④

| ④ | Do you agree that you would continue to exist (survive) if half your brain were successfully transplanted and the other half destroyed? (Notice that this assumes that the rest of your body does not matter for your survival as a person.) |

We can move to the second description. Perhaps one success is the maximum score. Perhaps I shall be one of the resulting people.

---

*David Wiggins, *Identity and Spatio-Temporal Continuity* (Oxford, 1967), p. 50.
†Sydney S. Shoemaker, *Self-Knowledge and Self-Identity* (Ithaca, N. Y., 1963), p. 22.

The trouble here is that in Wiggins' case each half of my brain is exactly similar, and so, to start with, is each resulting person. So how can I survive as only one of the two people? What can make me one of them rather than the other?⑤

⑤ The question is not how someone else could tell which one is me (an epistemological question), but rather why it would be true that one is and one is not me. (Can you think of an answer that a mind-body dualist might give to this question? See Discussion Question 1.)

It seems clear that both of these descriptions—that I do not survive, and that I survive as one of the people—are highly implausible. Those who have accepted them must have assumed that they were the only possible descriptions.

What about our third description: that I survive as both people?

It might be said, "If 'survive' implies identity, this description makes no sense—you cannot be two people. If it does not, the description is irrelevant to a problem about identity."

⑥ The result of the operation is two functioning bodies, each with its own separate functioning brain (though each is only half of the original brain) and separate resulting stream of conscious experience. Can any sense be made of the claim there is still only one person and not two?

I shall later deny the second of these remarks. But there are ways of denying the first. We might say, "What we have called 'the two resulting people' are not two people. They are one person. I do survive Wiggins' operation. Its effect is to give me two bodies and a divided mind."⑥

It would shorten my argument if this were absurd. But I do not think it is. It is worth showing why.

We can, I suggest, imagine a divided mind. We can imagine a man having two simultaneous experiences, in having each of which he is unaware of having the other.

We may not even need to imagine this. Certain actual cases, to which Wiggins referred, seem to be best described in these terms. These involve the cutting of the bridge between the hemispheres of the brain. The aim was to cure epilepsy. But the result appears to be, in the surgeon's words, the creation of "two separate spheres of consciousness,"* each of which controls one half of the patient's body. What is experienced in each is, presumably, experienced by the patient.⑦

There are certain complications in these actual cases. So let us imagine a simpler case.

Suppose that the bridge between my hemispheres is brought under my voluntary control. This would enable me to disconnect my hemispheres as easily as if I were blinking. By doing this I would divide my mind. And we can suppose that when my mind is divided I can, in each half, bring about reunion.

This ability would have obvious uses. To give an example: I am near the end of a maths exam, and see two ways of tackling the last problem. I decide to divide my mind, to work, with each half, at one of two calculations, and then to reunite my mind and write a fair copy of the best result.

What shall I experience?

When I disconnect my hemispheres, my consciousness divides into two streams. But this division is not something that I experience. Each of my two streams of consciousness seems to have been straightforwardly continuous with my one stream of consciousness up to the moment of division. The only changes in each stream are the disappearance of half my visual field and the loss of sensation in, and control over, half my body.⑧

Consider my experiences in what we can call my "right-handed" stream. I remember that I assigned my right hand to the longer calculation. This I now begin. In working at this calculation I can see, from the movements of my left hand, that I am also working at

⑦ The evidence for two separate spheres of consciousness involves experiments in which each eye (each one being connected to only one hemisphere of the brain) is shown only part of a phrase like "key ring." When this is done, the parts of the body under the control of the separate hemispheres respond in a way appropriate to the part of the phrase that the corresponding eye saw, but not to both parts together (thus selecting from a set of options a key or a wedding ring, but not a key ring). This at least suggests separate awarenesses in those two parts.

---

*R. W. Sperry, in *Brain and Conscious Experience,* ed. J. C. Eccles (New York, 1966), p. 299.

the other. But I am not aware of working at the other. So I might, in my right-handed stream, wonder how, in my left-handed stream, I am getting on.

My work is now over. I am about to reunite my mind. What should I, in each stream, expect? Simply that I shall suddenly seem to remember just having thought out two calculations, in thinking out each of which I was not aware of thinking out the other. This, I submit, we can imagine. And if my mind was divided, these memories are correct.⑨

In describing this episode, I assumed that there were two series of thoughts, and that they were both mine. If my two hands visibly wrote out two calculations, and if I claimed to remember two corresponding series of thoughts, this is surely what we should want to say.

If it is, then a person's mental history need not be like a canal, with only one channel. It could be like a river, with islands, and with separate streams.

To apply this to Wiggins' operation: we mentioned the view that it gives me two bodies and a divided mind. We cannot now call this absurd. But it is, I think, unsatisfactory.

There were two features of the case of the exam that made us want to say that only one person was involved. The mind was soon reunited, and there was only one body. If a mind was permanently divided and its halves developed in different ways, the point of speaking of one person would start to disappear. Wiggins' case, where there are also two bodies, seems to be over the borderline. After I have had his operation, the two "products" each have all the attributes of a

⑧ In fact, the right hemisphere controls the left side of the body, and the left hemisphere controls the right side of the body. A complication that Parfit does not mention but which is still worth thinking about is that speech and language use are normally controlled only by the left hemisphere—so that the right hemisphere and the left hand might not be able to do math problems, though this could perhaps be overcome through training.

⑨ Try to imagine what this would be like. (See Discussion Question 2.)

person. They could live at opposite ends of the earth. (If they later met, they might even fail to recognize each other.) It would become intolerable to deny that they were different people.

Suppose we admit that they are different people. Could we still claim that I survived as both, using "survive" to imply identity?

We could. For we might suggest that two people could compose a third. We might say, "I do survive Wiggins' operation as two people. They can be different people, and yet be me. . . ."

This is a possible way of giving sense to the claim that I survive as two different people, using "survive" to imply identity. But it keeps the language of identity only by changing the concept of a person. And there are obvious objections to this change.*⑩

The alternative, for which I shall argue, is to give up the language of identity. We can suggest that I survive as two different people without implying that I am these people.

When I first mentioned this alternative, I mentioned this objection: "If your new way of talking does not imply identity, it cannot solve our problem. For that is about identity. The problem is that all the possible answers to the question about identity are highly implausible."

We can now answer this objection.

We can start by reminding ourselves that this is an objection only if we have one or both of the beliefs which I mentioned at the start of this paper.

The first was the belief that to any question about personal identity, in any describable case, there must be a true answer. For those with this belief, Wiggins' case is doubly perplexing. If all the possible answers are implausible, it is hard to decide which of them is true, and hard even to keep the belief that one of them

⑩ Everything about the lives of each of the two could be as different from the other as for any two ordinary people. This is why it is "intolerable" to deny that they are separate people—and also why it seems absurd to say that the original person is somehow identical to both of them.

---

*Suppose the resulting people fight a duel. Are there three people fighting, one on each side, and one on both? And suppose one of the bullets kills. Are there two acts, one murder and one suicide? How many people are left alive? One? Two? (We could hardly say, "One and a half.") We could talk in this way. But instead of saying that the resulting people are the original person—so that the pair is a trio—it would be far simpler to treat them as a pair, and describe their relation to the original person in some new way. (I owe this suggested way of talking, and the objections to it, to Michael Woods.)

must be true. If we give up this belief, as I think we should, these problems disappear. We shall then regard the case as like many others in which, for quite unpuzzling reasons, there *is* no answer to a question about identity. (Consider "Was England the same nation after 1066?")⑪

⑪ There are many sorts of things for which it is clear that the question of whether such a thing at one time is identical with one at a later time need have no correct yes-or-no answer: nations after changes of government or major territorial additions or subtractions or large-scale populations changes; physical objects (a car, a house, a ship) after major additions or subtractions or alterations of parts; and even living things (a divided plant, a cloned individual). The issue is whether personal identity can be uncertain in the same way.

Wiggins' case makes the first belief implausible. It also makes it trivial. For it undermines the second belief. This was the belief that important questions turn upon the question about identity. . . .

Against this second belief my claim is this. Certain questions do presuppose a question about personal identity. And because these questions *are* important, Wiggins' case does present a problem. But we cannot solve this problem by answering the question about identity. We can solve this problem only by taking these important questions and prizing them apart from the question about identity. After we have done this, the question about identity (though we might for the sake of neatness decide it) has no further interest.⑫

⑫ The suggestion is that answering the question of identity is not really essential to answering these other questions, thus making it possible to formulate them in a way that is clearly independent of it.

Because there are several questions which presuppose identity, this claim will take some time to fill out.

We can first return to the question of survival. This is a special case, for survival does not so much presuppose the retaining of identity as seem equivalent to it. It is thus the general relation which we need to prize apart from identity. We can then consider particular relations, such as those involved in memory and intention.

"Will I survive?" seems, I said, equivalent to "Will there be some person alive who is the same person as me?"

If we treat these questions as equivalent, then the least unsatisfactory description of Wiggins' case is, I think, that I survive with two bodies and a divided mind.

Several writers have chosen to say that I am neither of the resulting people. Given our equivalence, this implies that I do not survive, and hence, presumably, that even if Wiggins' operation is not literally death, I ought, since I will not survive it, to regard it *as* death. But this seemed absurd.

It is worth repeating why. An emotion or attitude can be criticized for resting on a false belief, or for being inconsistent. A man who regarded Wiggins' operation as death must, I suggest, be open to one of these criticisms.

He might believe that his relation to each of the resulting people fails to contain some element which is contained in survival. But how can this be true? We agreed that he *would* survive if he stood in this very same relation to only *one* of the resulting people. So it cannot be the nature of this relation which makes it fail, in Wiggins' case, to be survival.⑬ It can only be its duplication.

⑬ Whatever is true about the relations between the original person and one of the resulting people, considered only by themselves, is not affected by the presence or absence of the second person. (But think again about what a dualist might say about this case. See Discussion Question 1.)

Suppose that our man accepts this, but still regards division as death. His reaction would now seem wildly inconsistent. He would be like a man who, when told of a drug that could double his years of life, regarded the taking of this drug as death. The only difference in the case of division is that the extra years are to run concurrently. This is an interesting difference. But it cannot mean that there are *no* years to run.⑭

⑭ This analogy doesn't seem very close. But it does seem paradoxical to say that the presence of the second person means that the original person does not survive, when otherwise he would have. Should he try to ensure his survival by taking steps in advance to make sure that one of the hemisphere transplants fails? (See Discussion Question 3.)

I have argued this for those who think that there must, in Wiggins' case, be a true answer to the question about identity. For them, we might add, "Perhaps the original person does lose his identity. But there may be other ways to do this than to die. One other way might be to multiply. To regard these as the same is to confuse nought with two."

. . .

My first conclusion, then, is this. The relation of the original person to each of the resulting people contains all that interests us—all that matters—in any ordinary case of survival. This is why we need a sense in which one person can survive as two.

One of my aims in the rest of this paper will be to suggest such a sense. But we can first make some general remarks.

II

Identity is a one-one relation. Wiggins' case serves to show that what matters in survival need not be one-one.

Wiggins' case is of course unlikely to occur. The relations which matter are, in fact, one-one. It is because they are that we can imply the holding of these relations by using the language of identity.

This use of language is convenient. But it can lead us astray. We may assume that what matters *is* identity and, hence, has the properties of identity.

In the case of the property of being one-one, this mistake is not serious. For what matters is in fact one-one. But in the case of another property, the mistake *is* serious. Identity is all-or-nothing. Most of the relations which matter in survival are, in fact, relations of degree. If we ignore this, we shall be led into quite ill-grounded attitudes and beliefs. [15]

15 A *one-one* relation is a relation that a thing of the relevant kind can have only to exactly one second thing. (The relation between numbers of *x* being half as large as *y* is one-one; while the relation of *x* being smaller than *y* is *one-many*, since a given number *x* is smaller than very many other numbers.) Parfit's point is that although in normal cases (not including hemisphere transplants and the like) the relation of identity and "the relations that matter in survival" (not yet specified) are alike in being one-one, they differ in that the relation of identity is all or nothing, while the "relations that matter" are (according to him) matters of degree.

The claim that I have just made—that most of what matters are relations of degree—I have yet to support. Wiggins' case shows only that these relations need not be one-one. The merit of the case is not that it shows this in particular, but that it makes the first break between what matters and identity. The belief that identity *is* what matters is hard to overcome. This is shown in most discussions of the problem cases which actually occur: cases, say, of amnesia or of brain damage. Once Wiggins' case has made one breach in this belief, the rest should be easier to remove.*

To turn to a recent debate: most of the relations which matter can be provisionally referred to under the heading "psychological continuity" (which includes causal continuity). My claim is thus that we use the language of personal identity in order to imply such continuity. This is close to the view that psychological continuity provides a criterion of identity.

Williams has attacked this view with the following argument. Identity is a one-one relation. So any criterion of identity must appeal to a relation which is logically one-one. Psychological continuity is not logically one-one. So it cannot provide a criterion. [16]†

Some writers have replied that it is enough if the relation appealed to is always in fact one-one.

I suggest a slightly different reply. Psychological continuity is a ground for speaking of identity when it is one-one.

16 Psychological continuity is similar to but more general than the relation of memory suggested by Locke. It is a relation in which the psychological states (apparent memories and others) at one stage are caused by and grow out of those at earlier stages in a way that is mostly gradual and continuous, rather than involving jumps or gaps. (See the introduction to this slection.)

If psychological continuity took a one-many or branching form, we should need, I have argued, to abandon the language of identity. So this possibility would not count against this view.

We can make a stronger claim. This possibility would count in its favor.

*Bernard Williams' "The Self and the Future," *Philosophical Review,* 79 (1970), 161–180 [pp.427–36], is relevant here. He asks the question "Shall I survive?" in a range of problem cases, and he shows how natural it is to believe (1) that this question must have an answer, (2) that the answer must be all-or-nothing, and (3) that there is a "risk" of our reaching the wrong answer. . . .
†"Personal Identity and Individuation," *Proceedings of the Aristotelian Society,* 57 (1956–1957), 229–253; also *Analysis,* 21 (1960–1961), 43–48.

The view might be defended as follows. Judgments of personal identity have great importance. What gives them their importance is the fact that they imply psychological continuity. This is why, whenever there is such continuity, we ought, if we can, to imply it by making a judgment of identity.

If psychological continuity took a branching form, no coherent set of judgments of identity could correspond to, and thus be used to imply, the branching form of this relation. But what we ought to do, in such a case, is take the importance which would attach to a judgment of identity and attach this importance directly to each limb of the branching relation. So this case helps to show that judgments of personal identity do derive their importance from the fact that they imply psychological continuity. It helps to show that when we can, usefully, speak of identity, this relation is our ground. [17]

17 It is possible, Parfit is suggesting, for the psychological states of more than one person at a given time to be psychologically continuous with the states of one and the same person at an earlier time (as in the hemisphere transplant case). Thus while identity requires and so implies psychological continuity, psychological continuity can exist without identity. And it is psychological continuity—with or without identity—that is, Parfit will claim, what really matters for issues like survival and responsibility.

This argument appeals to a principle which Williams put forward.* The principle is that an important judgment should be asserted and denied only on importantly different grounds.

Williams applied this principle to a case in which one man is psychologically continuous with the dead Guy Fawkes, and a case in which two men are. His argument was this. If we treat psychological continuity as a sufficient ground for speaking of identity, we shall say that the one man is Guy Fawkes. But we could not say that the two men are, although we should have the same ground. This disobeys the principle. The remedy is to deny that the one man is Guy Fawkes, to insist that sameness of the body is necessary for identity. [18]

Williams' principle can yield a different answer. Suppose we regard psychological continuity as more important than sameness of the body. And suppose that the one man really is psychologically (and causally) continuous with Guy Fawkes. If he is, it would disobey the principle to deny that he is Guy Fawkes, for we have the same important ground as in a normal case of identity. In the case of the two men, we again have the same important ground. So we ought to take the importance from the judgment of identity and attach it directly to this ground. We ought to say, as in Wiggins' case, that each limb of the branching relation is as good as survival. This obeys the principle. [19]

To sum up these remarks: even if psychological continuity is neither logically, nor always in fact, one-one, it can provide a criterion of identity. For this can appeal to the relation of *non-branching* psychological continuity, which is logically one-one.

18 This is Williams's remedy (not discussed in the selection in this book), not Parfit's. It would settle (whether correctly or not) the case where one of the two later persons has the same body as the earlier one, but not a case in which both bodies are different.

19 Thus where there are two (or more) later persons that are each psychologically continuous with one earlier one, none of them is identical to him but what really matters for survival (according to Parfit and yet to be explained) is realized by each of them.

The criterion might be sketched as follows. "X and Y are the same person if they are psychologically continuous and there is no person who is contemporary with either and psychologically continuous with the other." We should need to explain what we mean by "psychologically continuous" and say how much continuity the criterion requires. We should then, I think, have described a sufficient condition for speaking of identity.†

We need to say something more. If we admit that psychological continuity might not be one-one, we need to say what we ought to do if it were not one-one. Otherwise our account would be open to the objections that it is incomplete and arbitrary.

I have suggested that if psychological continuity took a branching form, we ought to speak in a new way, regarding what we describe as having the

*Analysis, 21 (1960–1961), 44.
†But not a necessary condition, for in the absence of psychological continuity bodily identity might be sufficient.

same significance as identity. This answers these objections. [20]

[20] So the claim is that *nonbranching* psychological continuity, psychological continuity where only one later person is psychologically continuous with a specified earlier one, is both necessary and sufficient for personal identity.

We can now return to our discussion. We have three remaining aims. One is to suggest a sense of "survive" which does not imply identity. Another is to show that most of what matters in survival are relations of degree. A third is to show that none of these relations needs to be described in a way that presupposes identity.

We can take these aims in the reverse order.

III

The most important particular relation is that involved in memory. This is because it is so easy to believe that its description must refer to identity. . . .

It may be a logical truth that we can only remember our own experiences. But we can frame a new concept for which this is not a logical truth. Let us call this "q-memory."

To sketch a definition I am q-remembering an experience if (1) I have a belief about a past experience which seems in itself like a memory belief, (2) someone did have such an experience, and (3) my belief is dependent upon this experience in the same way (whatever that is) in which a memory of an experience is dependent upon it.

[21] Others have used the term "quasi-memory." Condition 3 is vague and would need to be spelled out more fully in a complete account. But each of the persons whose states are psychologically continuous with those of an earlier person would have q-memories of his experiences—though not memories if there is more than one of them and if memory requires identity.

According to (1) q-memories seem like memories. So I q-remember *having* experiences. [21]

This may seem to make q-memory presuppose identity. One might say, "My apparent memory of *having* an experience is an apparent memory of *my* having an experience. So how could I q-remember my having other people's experiences?"

This objection rests on a mistake. When I seem to remember an experience, I do indeed seem to remember *having* it. But it cannot be a part of what I seem to remember about this experience that I, the person who now seems to remember it, am the person who had this experience. [22] That I am is something that I automatically assume. (My apparent memories sometimes come to me simply as the belief that *I* had a certain experience.) But it is something that I am justified in assuming only because I do not in fact have q-memories of other people's experiences.

[22] Actual identity is not the sort of thing that could be part of the content of the memory.

Suppose that I did start to have such q-memories. If I did, I should cease to assume that my apparent memories must be about my own experiences. I should come to assess an apparent memory by asking two questions: (1) Does it tell me about a past experience? (2) If so, whose?

Moreover (and this is a crucial point) my apparent memories would now come to me *as q-memories*. Consider those of my apparent memories which do come to me simply as beliefs about my past: for example, "I did that." If I knew that I could q-remember other people's experiences, these beliefs would come to me in a more guarded form: for example, "Someone—probably I—did that." I might have to work out who it was.

I have suggested that the concept of q-memory is coherent. Wiggins' case provides an illustration. The resulting people, in his case, both have apparent memories of living the life of the original person. If they agree that they are not this person, they will have to regard these as only q-memories. And when they are asked a question like "Have you heard this music before?" they might have to answer "I am sure that I q-remember hearing it. But I am not sure whether I remember hearing it. I am not sure whether it was I who heard it, or the original person."

We can next point out that on our definition every memory is also a q-memory. Memories are, simply, q-memories of one's own experiences. Since this is so, we could afford now to drop the concept of memory and use in its place the wider concept q-memory . . . . [23]

[23] All actual memories are also q-memories, but not all q-memories are actual memories.

But we must move on. We can next take the relation between an intention and a later action. It may be a logical truth that we can intend to perform only our own actions. But intentions can be redescribed as *q*-intentions. And one person could *q*-intend to perform another person's actions.

Wiggins' case again provides the illustration. We are supposing that neither of the resulting people is the original person. If so, we shall have to agree that the original person can, before the operation, *q*-intend to perform their actions. He might, for example, *q*-intend, as one of them, to continue his present career, and, as the other, to try something new. (I say "*q*-intend *as one of them*" because the phrase "*q*-intend that one of them" would not convey the directness of the relation which is involved. If I intend that someone else should do something, I cannot get him to do it simply by forming this intention. But if I am the original person, and he is one of the resulting people, I can.)

The phrase "*q*-intend *as one of them*" reminds us that we need a sense in which one person can survive as two. But we can first point out that the concepts of *q*-memory and *q*-intention give us our model for the others that we need: thus, a man who can *q*-remember could *q*-recognize, and be a *q*-witness of, what he has never seen; and a man who can *q*-intend could have *q*-ambitions, make *q*-promises, and be *q*-responsible for.

24 In order to have future-oriented *q*-states (such as intending that one of the persons who results from the transplants of the hemispheres of my brain goes on with my career and the other tries something new), I seemingly must have some way now of specifying each of the relevant future persons that those later persons will be able to recognize and apply to themselves when the time comes, or else the intention will be ineffective. Each of the future persons must be able to tell which specific things he or she is supposed to do according to the original intention.

To put this claim in general terms: many different relations are included within, or are a consequence of, psychological continuity. We describe these relations in ways which presuppose the continued existence of one person. But we could describe them in new ways which do not. 24

. . . What I shall try to describe is a way of thinking of our own identity through time which is more flexible, and less misleading, than the way in which we now think.

This way of thinking will allow for a sense in which one person can survive as two. A more important feature is that it treats survival as a matter of degree.

IV

We must first show the need for this second feature. I shall use two imaginary examples.

The first is the converse of Wiggins' case: fusion. Just as division serves to show that what matters in survival need not be one-one, so fusion serves to show that it can be a question of degree.

Physically, fusion is easy to describe. Two people come together. While they are unconscious, their two bodies grow into one. One person then wakes up.

The psychology of fusion is more complex. One detail we have already dealt with in the case of the exam. When my mind was reunited, I remembered just having thought out two calculations. The one person who results from a fusion can, similarly, *q*-remember living the lives of the two original people. None of their *q*-memories need be lost. 25

25 This is a little tricky. The fused person can remember each of the previous people doing whatever they did. But can he remember doing those things *himself*—even though this would require him to have been in two places at the same time?

But some things must be lost. For any two people who fuse together will have different characteristics, different desires, and different intentions. How can these be combined?

We might suggest the following. Some of these will be compatible. These can coexist in the one resulting person. Some will be incompatible. These, if of equal strength, can cancel out, and if of different strengths, the stronger can be made weaker. And all these effects might be predictable.

To give examples—first, of compatibility: I like Palladio and intend to visit Venice. I am about to fuse with a person who likes Giotto and intends to visit Padua. I can know that the one person we shall become will have both tastes and both intentions. Second, of incompatibility: I hate red hair, and always vote Labour. The other person loves red hair, and always votes Conservative. I can know that the one person we shall become will be indifferent to red hair, and a floating voter. 26

If we were about to undergo a fusion of this kind, would we regard it as death?

26 Think carefully about these examples, inventing some more of your own. How clear is it what states the fused person would have?

Some of us might. This is less absurd than regarding division as death. For after my division the two resulting people will be in every way like me, while after my fusion the one resulting person will not be wholly similar. This makes it easier to say, when faced with fusion, "I shall not survive," thus continuing to regard survival as a matter of all-or-nothing.

This reaction is less absurd. But here are two analogies which tell against it.

First, fusion would involve the changing of some

27 Would anyone welcome a treatment that changed his characteristics by melding them with those of an arbitrarily chosen other person in the way indicated?

of our characteristics and some of our desires. But only the very self-satisfied would think of this as death. Many people welcome treatments with these effects. 27

Second, someone who is about to fuse can have, beforehand, just as much "intentional control" over the actions of the resulting individual as someone who is about to marry can have, beforehand, over the actions of the resulting couple. And the choice of a partner for fusion can be just as well considered

28 How good an analogy is this? You at least have to imagine a marriage in which every choice and decision is made jointly.

as the choice of a marriage partner. The two original people can make sure (perhaps by "trial fusion") that they do have compatible characters, desires, and intentions. 28

I have suggested that fusion, while not clearly survival, is not clearly failure to survive, and hence that what matters in survival can have degrees.

To reinforce this claim we can now turn to a second example. This is provided by certain imaginary beings. These beings are just like ourselves except that they reproduce by a process of natural division.

We can illustrate the histories of these imagined beings with the aid of a diagram. The lines on the diagram represent the spatiotemporal paths which would be traced out by the bodies of these beings. We can call each single line (like the double line) a "branch"; and we can call the whole structure a "tree." And let us suppose that each "branch" corresponds to what is thought of as the life of one individual. These individuals are referred to as "A," "B + 1," and so forth.

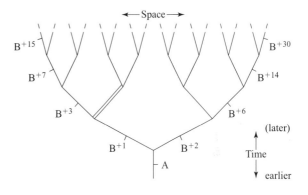

Now, each single division is an instance of Wiggins' case. So A's relation to both B + 1 and B + 2 is just as good as survival. But what of A's relation to B + 30?

I said earlier that what matters in survival could be provisionally referred to as "psychological continuity." I must now distinguish this relation from another, which I shall call "psychochological connectedness."

Let us say that the relation between a q-memory and the experience q-remembered is a "direct" relation. Another "direct" relation is that which holds between a q-intention and the q-intended action. A third is that which holds between different expressions of some lasting q-characteristic.

"Psychological connectedness," as I define it, requires the holding of these direct psychological relations. "Connectedness" is not transitive, since these relations are not transitive. Thus, if X q-remembers most of Y's life, and Y q-remembers most of Z's life, it does not follow that X q-remembers most of Z's life. And if X carries out the q-intentions of Y, and Y carries out the q-intentions of Z, it does not follow that X carries out the q-intentions of Z.

"Psychological continuity," in contrast, only requires overlapping chains of direct psychological relations. So "continuity" is transitive.㉙

To return to our diagram. A is psychologically continuous with B + 30. There are between the two continuous chains of overlapping relations. Thus, A has *q*-intentional control over B + 2, B + 2 has *q*-intentional control over B + 6, and so on up to B + 30. Or B + 30 can *q*-remember the life of B + 14, B + 14 can *q*-remember the life of B + 6, and so on back to A.*

㉙ A transitive relation is one such that if A has it to B and B has it to C, then A has it to C. Thus the relation of being a biological ancestor is transitive, while the relation of being someone's mother is not: if A is the mother of B and B is the mother of C, then A is *not* the mother of C. (See the introduction to this selection for more about the difference between psychological continuity and psychological connectedness.)

A, however, need *not* be psychologically connected to B + 30. Connectedness requires direct relations. And if these beings are like us, A cannot stand in such relations to every individual in his indefinitely long "tree." *Q*-memories will weaken with the passage of time, and then fade away. *Q*-ambitions, once fulfilled, will be replaced by others. *Q*-characteristics will gradually change. In general, A stands in fewer and fewer direct psychological relations to an individual in his "tree" the more remote that individual is. And if the individual is (like B + 30) sufficiently remote, there may be between the two *no* direct psychological relations.

Now that we have distinguished the general relations of psychological continuity and psychological connectedness, I suggest that connectedness is a more important element in survival. As a claim about our own survival, this would need more arguments than I have space to give. But it seems clearly true for my imagined beings. A is as close psychologically to B + 1 as I today am to myself tomorrow. A is as distant from B + 30 as I am from my great-great-grandson.㉚

Even if connectedness is not more important than continuity, the fact that one of these is a relation of degree is enough to show that what matters in survival can have degrees. And in any case the two relations are quite different. So our imagined beings would need a way of thinking in which this difference is recognized.

V

What I propose is this.

First, A can think of any individual, anywhere in his "tree," as "a descendant self." This phrase implies psychological continuity. Similarly, any later individual can think of any earlier individual on the single path which connects him to A as "an ancestral self."

Since psychological continuity is transitive, "being an ancestral self of" and "being a descendant self of" are also transitive.

To imply psychological connectedness I suggest the phrases "one of my future selves" and "one of my past selves."㉛

These are the phrases with which we can describe Wiggins' case. For having past and future selves is, what we needed, a way of continuing to exist which does not imply identity through time. The original person does, in this sense, survive Wiggins' operation: the two resulting people are his later selves. And they can each refer to him as "my past self." (They can share a past self without being the same self as each other.)

㉚ Not the best comparison, since there is no psychological continuity between a person and his children, grandchildren, etc. Is Parfit right that with regard to our own survival, psychological connectedness is more important than mere psychological continuity? (See Discussion Question 4.)

㉛ So being one of my future selves requires more than just being one of my descendant selves, as Parfit explains these concepts: all future selves are descendant selves, but not all descendant selves are future selves. The relation of being a descendant self is transitive: if B is a descendant self of A and C is a descendant self of B, then C is a descendant self of A. But the relation of being a future self is not transitive: B may be a future self of A and C a future self of B, without C being a future self of A (if both the relation between B and A and that between C and B are psychologically direct enough, but that between C and A is too indirect with few if any direct psychological relations).

---

*The chain of continuity must run in one direction of time. B + 2 is not, in the sense I intend, psychologically continuous with B + 1.

Since psychological connectedness is not transitive, and is a matter of degree, the relations "being a past self of" and "being a future self of" should themselves be treated as relations of degree. We allow for this series of descriptions: "my most recent self," "one of my earlier selves," "one of my distant selves," "hardly one of *my* past selves (I can only *q*-remember a few of his experiences)," and, finally, "not in any way one of *my* past selves—just an ancestral self."

This way of thinking would clearly suit our first imagined beings. But let us now turn to a second kind of being. These reproduce by fusion as well as by division. And let us suppose that they fuse every autumn and divide every spring. This yields the following diagram:

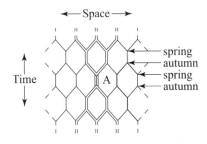

If A is the individual whose life is represented by the three-lined "branch," the two-lined "tree" represents those lives which are psychologically continuous with A's life. (It can be seen that each individual has his own "tree," which overlaps with many others.)

For the imagined beings in this second world, the phrases "an ancestral self" and "a descendant self" would cover too much to be of much use. (There may well be pairs of dates such that every individual who ever lived before the first date was an ancestral self of every individual who ever will live after the second date.) Conversely, since the lives of each individual last for only half a year, the word "I" would cover too little to do all of the work which it does for us. So part of this work would have to be done, for these second beings, by talk about past and future selves.[32]

. . .

32 This is a complicated example, and you will need to think about it carefully. If A is concerned about his own survival, what exactly is he concerned about (that is, what would it take to satisfy this concern)?

But let us look, finally, at a third kind of being.

In this world there is neither division nor union. There are a number of everlasting bodies, which gradually change in appearance. And direct psychological relations, as before, hold only over limited periods of time. This can be illustrated with a third diagram (which is found below). In this diagram the two shadings represent the degrees of psychological connectedness to their two central points.

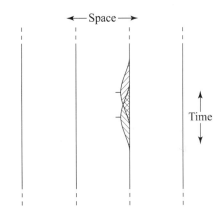

These beings could not use the way of thinking that we have proposed. Since there is no branching of psychological continuity, they would have to regard themselves as immortal. It might be said that this is what they are. But there is, I suggest, a better description.

Our beings would have one reason for thinking of themselves as immortal. The parts of each "line" are all psychologically continuous. But the parts of each "line" are not all psychologically connected. Direct psychological relations hold only between those parts which are close to each other in time. This gives our beings a reason for *not* thinking of each "line" as corresponding to one single life. For if they did, they would have no way of implying these direct relations. When a speaker says, for example, "I spent a period doing such and such," his hearers would not be entitled to assume that the speaker has any memories of this period, that his character then and now are in any way similar, that he is now carrying out any of the plans or intentions which he then had, and so forth. Because the word "I" would carry none of these implications, it would not have for these "immortal" beings the usefulness which it has for us.[33]

To gain a better way of thinking, we must revise the way of thinking that we proposed above. The revision is this. The distinction between successive selves can be made by reference, not to the branching of psychological continuity, but to the degrees of psychological connectedness. Since this connectedness is a matter of degree, the drawing of these distinctions can be left to the choice of the speaker and be allowed to vary from context to context.

On this way of thinking, the word "I" can be used to imply the greatest degree of psychological connectedness. When the connections are reduced, when there has been any marked change of character or style of life, or any marked loss of memory, our imagined beings would say, "It was not I who did that, but an earlier self." They could then describe in what ways, and to what degree, they are related to this earlier self.[34]

This revised way of thinking would suit not only our "immortal" beings. It is also the way in which we ourselves could think about our lives. And it is, I suggest, surprisingly natural.

One of its features, the distinction between successive selves, has already been used by several writers. To give an example, from Proust: "we are incapable, while we are in love, of acting as fit predecessors of the next persons who, when we are in love no longer, we shall presently have become. . . ."*

Although Proust distinguished between successive selves, he still thought of one person as being these different selves. This we would not do on the way of thinking that I propose. If I say, "It will not be me, but one of my future selves," I do not imply that I will be that future self. He is one of my later selves, and I am one of his earlier selves. There is no underlying person who we both are.

To point out another feature of this way of thinking. When I say, "There is no person who we both are," I am only giving my decision. Another person could say, "It will be you," thus deciding differently. There is no question of either of these decisions being a mistake. Whether to say "I," or "one of my future selves," or "a descendant self" is entirely a matter of choice. The matter of fact, which must be agreed, is only whether the disjunction applies. (The question "Are X and Y the same person?" thus becomes "Is X at least an ancestral [or descendant] self of Y?")[35]

VI

I have tried to show that what matters in the continued existence of a person are, for the most part, relations of degree. And I have proposed a way of thinking in which this would be recognized.

I shall end by suggesting two consequences and asking one question.

It is sometimes thought to be especially rational to act in our own best interests. But I suggest that the principle of self-interest has no force. There are only two genuine competitors in this particular field. One is the principle of biased rationality: do what will best achieve what you actually want. The other is the principle of impartiality: do what is in the best interests of everyone concerned.[36]

The apparent force of the principle of self-interest derives, I think, from these two other principles.

---

[33] That is, "I" (and "me" and "myself"), if used in the way indicated, would not capture for these beings the important part of what is captured by our use of these terms. I care about my past and my future (picked out as cases in which these terms, as used by me, would correctly apply). But, Parfit is suggesting, the beings in question would not care (or at least would have no reason to care) about their distant pasts and futures where all relations of psychological connectedness to their present selves are gone.

[34] Notice that this is a stronger requirement than we impose on the use of "I" (and related terms) even in our own situation: we often still use "I" to refer to a being with a seriously different character or life style or even the one who exists or will exist after a serious loss of memory.

[35] How plausible is this suggestion? Is it really just a matter of choice whether a future person with the same living body that you have but with a very different character or lifestyle is still you, is a future self, or is merely a descendant self—as opposed to saying that it is just a fact that the future person is still identical with you despite the various changes?

Within a Budding Grove (London, 1949), I, 226 (my own translation).

The principle of self-interest is normally supported by the principle of biased rationality. This is because most people care about their own future interests.

36 The difference between the first principle and the principle of self-interest is that "what you actually want" will normally include things that are in the interests of others and will not necessarily include things pertaining to your very remote future or descendant selves.

Suppose that this prop is lacking. Suppose that a man does not care what happens to him in, say, the more distant future. To such a man, the principle of self-interest can only be propped up by an appeal to the principle of impartiality. We must say, "Even if you don't care, you ought to take what happens to you then equally into account." But for this, as a special claim, there seem to me no good arguments. It can only be supported as part of the general claim, "You ought to take what happens to everyone equally into account."

The special claim tells a man to grant an *equal* weight to all the parts of his future. The argument for this can only be that all the parts of his future are *equally* parts of *his* future. This is true. But it is a truth too superficial to bear the weight of the argument. (To give an analogy: The unity of a nation is, in its nature, a matter of degree. It is therefore only a superficial truth that all of a man's compatriots are *equally* his compatriots. This truth cannot support a good argument for nationalism.)* **37**

I have suggested that the principle of self-interest has no strength of its own. If this is so, there is no special problem in the fact that what we ought to do can be against our interests. There is only the general problem that it may not be what we want to do.

The second consequence which I shall mention is implied in the first. Egoism, the fear not of near but of distant death, the regret that so much of one's *only* life should have gone by—these are not, I think, wholly natural or instinctive. They are all strengthened by the beliefs about personal identity which I have been attacking. If we give up these beliefs, they should be weakened. **38**

My final question is this. These emotions are bad, and if we weaken them we gain. But can we achieve this gain without, say, also weakening loyalty to, or love of, other particular selves? As Hume warned, the "refined reflections which philosophy suggests . . . cannot diminish . . . our vicious passions . . . without diminishing . . . such as are virtuous. They are . . . applicable to all our affections. In vain do we hope to direct their influence only to one side." **39**

That hope *is* vain. But Hume had another: that more of what is bad depends upon false belief. This is also my hope.

37 Parfit is saying that the fact that your distant future selves are still your selves gives you no good reasons to care about them as much as you do in fact care about your closer selves—or even, in the extreme case, to care about them at all. (See Discussion Question 4.)

38 The suggestion is that the concern about whether you will survive in the future should diminish as your future selves become psychologically more and more remote from your present self, perhaps eventually disappearing altogether. (See Discussion Question 4.)

39 At least part of what Parfit has in mind here has to do with caring about the future of other people.

Discussion Questions

1. Suppose that your brain is divided, and half of it is transplanted into another body, while the remaining half is left in your present body, so that there are two persons after the operation. Does the person whose body is your original body have a stronger claim to be identical to you than the other person, and if so, why? Suppose instead that both halves

*The unity of a nation we seldom take for more than what it is. This is partly because we often think of nations, not as units, but in a more complex way. If we thought of ourselves in the way that I proposed, we might be less likely to take our own identity for more than what it is. We are, for example, sometimes told, "It is irrational to act against your own interests. After all, it will be you who will regret it." To this we could reply, "No, not me. Not even one of my future selves. Just a descendant self."

are transplanted into new bodies. If consciousness involves a separate immaterial mind or soul, either (a) it somehow divides too, (b) it goes with one of the two halves and a new mind or soul somehow emerges for the other, or (c) it is destroyed, and both of the resulting persons have new minds or souls. Here the interesting case is (b): Does the (supposed) fact that one person has your original soul and the other does not give the one who does a stronger claim to be identical with you, and if so, why?

2. How would it seem from the standpoint of each of the separate streams of consciousness when the two streams that have been voluntarily divided in order to do two math problems are reunited (or are there such standpoints)? Would I still remember the two separate streams of consciousness *as separate?* Do you ever think about two things at the same time (perhaps a present conversation and a problem you are mulling in the background)? Might the combined memory of this be something like the memory in Parfit's case?

3. Do you survive if both parts of your brain are successfully transplanted into two new bodies? If you knew that the two parts of your brain were going to be transplanted, would it be reasonable for you to pay someone to destroy one of them or otherwise prevent the success of the operation, in order to bring it about that you survive? If you think that you survive when both are transplanted, would it be rational for you to pay to have this done in order to increase your overall chances of survival?

4. Suppose that you have good reason to believe that you will be alive 20 years into the future, and that you are in a position to take steps to make your future self happier, safer, and so forth. Should your degree of concern for that future self depend on how closely connected its psychological states will be to yours: how much of your experience it will remember, how similar its character traits and values will be, and so forth? Why or why not? Is there a point in the future (defined in terms of psychological connectedness and continuity, not time) when it is no longer reasonable for you to care *at all* about the well-being of your future self?

CHAPTER 5

Free Will and Moral Responsibility

The reading selections in this chapter focus on the perennial problem of free will. The main question here is whether human actions are normally—or even ever—the result of genuinely *free* choices in the way that seems to be required for those who do them to be *morally responsible*. The main reason, after all, that we are reluctant to punish someone who is thought to be insane, even for a crime that is very serious, is that we don't think that an insane person is really responsible in a moral sense for what he does. And the most obvious reason for this is that we think that an insane person is not really free. But are ordinary people really any freer than the insane person, however much they may differ from him in other ways? And even more fundamentally, what does it mean for an action to be genuinely free: what does free will really amount to?

ARE HUMAN ACTIONS GENUINELY FREE?
Hard Determinism

The initial reason for doubting that freedom genuinely exists is the thesis of **causal determinism:** the thesis that everything that happens, including all human actions, is rigidly determined by antecedent causes operating in accordance with laws of nature. If this is so, then any human action could in principle have been predicted thousands or millions of years before it occurred, given enough knowledge of the conditions at that time and of the relevant laws of nature. This seems to show that the person who performed the action could not in fact have done anything other than what he did, which in turn seems to many to show that the action was not free in the sense that moral responsibility requires. How, it is asked, can a person be morally blamed for doing something that was inevitable long before his birth? The view that accepts the thesis of causal determinism and argues in this way for the nonexistence of genuine freedom and moral responsibility is one version of **hard determinism.** Hard determinists often appeal more explicitly to *heredity* and *environment* as the deterministic causes of human actions. A view of this sort is suggested by Miles Corwin's account of Robert Harris and developed in detail by Robert Blatchford.

But is the thesis of causal determinism actually true? Arguments in favor of it that appeal to scientific success in explanation and prediction are less than conclusive, since there are still many, many things that cannot be explained and predicted in detail. Moreover, recent scientific developments in the field of quantum mechanics or quantum theory seem to offer strong reasons for thinking that causal determinism is in fact false. On the standard interpretation of quantum theory, there are certain physical events that are inherently random or chance in character, events for which there are no deterministic causes. An example here is radioactive decay: on the standard theory it is impossible in principle to predict when a particular radioactive atom will decay into another by emitting an alpha or beta particle because this is a random event that involves no underlying deterministic mechanism.

Contrary to what might initially be supposed, however, the rejection of causal determinism really does very little to strengthen the case for freedom. It raises at least the possibility that some human actions (or perhaps their immediate causes) might be *random* events, events that happen for no cause or reason at all, but unfortunately a random or randomly produced event is no more satisfactory as an instance of free action than one that is causally determined—indeed, perhaps even less so. If an action takes place at random, then something else could equally have happened at random, but it is still not the case that the person could have *done* otherwise in the sense that what he did was within his control. If, for example, your body suddenly starts doing things at random—perhaps attacking other people or doing other outrageous things—you seem to be no more responsible and as much a victim as anyone else. Thus a hard determinist whose main claim is that genuine freedom does not exist can in fact accept the existence of random events and the denial of causal determinism, while still insisting that this does nothing to establish the existence of freedom. (It is fairly standard, albeit a bit misleading, to refer to such a modified position as also a version of hard determinism, even though it no longer accepts causal determinism, and we will follow that usage here.)

Thus the most important argument for the denial of freedom does not in fact depend on whether causal determinism is true or not. Once it is realized that randomness is also incompatible with freedom, the defender of freedom is faced with a serious dilemma. It is at least plausible to assume that any event, including any human action, must be either causally determined or random. But according to the argument so far, neither of these alternatives is compatible with freedom, thus seemingly leading to the conclusion that freedom is not only nonexistent, but in fact entirely impossible. This, however, is a very difficult conclusion to swallow. Is it really believable that the very idea of freedom is somehow contradictory or unintelligible? Surely our overriding common-sense conviction that we at least sometimes act freely, especially as it arises in situations of difficult choice, could not be as totally mistaken as that?

Compatibilism (Soft Determinism)

This sort of reflection leads to the second main position on the free will problem: **compatibilism** (or **soft determinism**). Appealing to our common-sense judgments about which actions are free, the compatibilist rejects the claim that freedom and causal determinism are incompatible (while agreeing that freedom is incompatible with randomness). His view is that rather than being incompatible with causal determination, freedom is a special sort of causal determination: determination by the agent's own will or desires or psychological states. A person whose action is determined in this way could have done otherwise in the sense that if his desires had been different or if he had reasoned in a different way, he would have done otherwise. And this can be true even if both his action and the desires that led to it were causally determined. Thus freedom is compatible with determinism, and the free will problem essentially disappears. A compatibilist may also add that freedom requires the absence of external *constraints* (such as threats) and may even extend this to the absence of internal compulsions of various sorts. But there can be little doubt that on the compatibilist view, freedom genuinely exists in a wide range of cases. (Compatibilists standardly accept the possibility of random events on the scientific grounds already discussed, but insist that this possibility is irrelevant to the issue of freedom since random actions clearly aren't free.) David Hume and W. T. Stace present versions of compatibilism.

But is compatibilism really a satisfactory resolution of the problem? Paul Edwards raises doubts about the compatibilist account of "could have done otherwise" and about whether the sort of freedom advocated by compatibilists is really enough for moral responsibility. John Hospers argues in roughly the same vein, but with special attention to problems arising from the claims of psychoanalysis.

Libertarianism

Doubts of the sorts raised by Edwards and Hospers may lead back to hard determinism (this seems to be Edwards's conclusion, though Hospers is a little cagier), or they may lead instead to the third main position, namely **libertarianism:** the view that freedom is incompatible with causal determinism but nonetheless still genuinely exists. Since most libertarians also agree, for the reasons already discussed, that random actions are not free, a libertarian is apparently forced to find some third alternative to causal determination and randomness. Roderick Chisholm rather tentatively suggests such a view, and more detailed versions of it are offered by C. A. Campbell and Robert Nozick. Their basic suggestion is that a free action is one that is caused by the agent or self in a way that does not flow from his antecedent character or makeup and thus is not causally determined. The main problem is to explain why such "agent causation," since it is independent of the agent's formed character or anything else about him, isn't after all random, in which case the problem hasn't really been solved.

IS FREEDOM REQUIRED FOR MORAL RESPONSIBILITY?

The final two selections, by Galen Strawson and Susan Wolf, return to the issue of moral responsibility. Strawson questions whether people really are morally responsible in a deep or ultimate way, thus tending back toward hard determinism. Wolf, in contrast, argues that genuine moral responsibility requires something much less demanding than the sort of freedom that libertarians advocate: a kind of *sanity* that is seemingly compatible with determinism.

ARE HUMAN ACTIONS GENUINELY FREE?

Miles Corwin

Miles Corwin was until recently a reporter with the *Los Angeles Times*, focusing on crime. His account of Robert Harris and his crime is designed to bring out the difference in our reactions before and after we learn about Harris's childhood and about the ways in which he was mistreated. (Another way of presenting the story would have been to describe his childhood first and his crime second—think how that might have affected your reactions.) Corwin draws no very explicit conclusion, and certainly does not claim that the facts about Harris's childhood show that he should not be blamed or punished. But a determinist like Blatchford (see the following selection) would be very likely to make such a claim. (Robert Harris was executed in the gas chamber at San Quentin State Prison in California on April 21, 1992.)

Robert Harris

Consider the case of Robert Harris.

On the south tier of Death Row, in a section called 'Peckerwood Flats' where the white inmates are housed, there will be a small celebration the day Robert Alton Harris dies.

A group of inmates on the row have pledged several dollars for candy, cookies and soda. At the moment they estimate that Harris has been executed, they will eat, drink and toast to his passing.

"The guy's a misery, a total scumbag; we're going to party when he goes," said Richard (Chic) Mroczko, who lived in the cell next to Harris on San Quentin Prison's Death Row for more than a year. "He doesn't care about life, he doesn't care about others, he doesn't care about himself."

"We're not a bunch of Boy Scouts around here, and you might think we're pretty cold-blooded about the whole thing. But then, you just don't know the dude."

San Diego County Assistant Dist. Atty. Richard Huffman, who prosecuted Harris, said, "If a person like Harris can't be executed under California law and

federal procedure, then we should be honest and say we're incapable of handling capital punishment."

State Deputy Atty. Gen. Michael D. Wellington asked the court during an appeal hearing for Harris, "If this isn't the kind of defendant that justifies the death penalty, is there ever going to be one?"

What crime did Robert Harris commit to be considered the archetypal candidate for the death penalty? And what kind of man provokes such enmity that even those on Death Row . . . call for his execution?

On July 5, 1978, John Mayeski and Michael Baker had just driven through [a] fast-food restaurant and were sitting in the parking lot eating lunch. Mayeski and Baker . . . lived on the same street and were best friends. They were on their way to a nearby lake for a day of fishing.

At the other end of the parking lot, Robert Harris, 25, and his brother Daniel, 18, were trying to hotwire a [car] when they spotted the two boys. The Harris brothers were planning to rob a bank that afternoon and did not want to use their own car. When Robert Harris could not start the car, he pointed to the [car] where the 16-year-olds were eating and said to Daniel, "We'll take this one."

He pointed a . . . Luger at Mayeski, crawled into the back seat, and told him to drive east. . . .

From The Los Angeles Times *(May 6, 1982).*

Daniel Harris followed in the Harrises' car. When they reached a canyon area . . . , Robert Harris told the youths he was going to use their car in a bank robbery and assured them that they would not be hurt. Robert Harris yelled to Daniel to get the .22 caliber rifle out of the back seat of their car.

"When I caught up," Daniel said in a recent interview, "Robert was telling them about the bank robbery we were going to do. He was telling them that he would leave them some money in the car and all, for us using it. Both of them said they would wait on top of this little hill until we were gone, and then walk into town and report the car stolen." Robert Harris agreed.

"Michael turned and went through some bushes. John said, 'Good luck,' and turned to leave."

As the two boys walked away, Harris slowly raised the Luger and shot Mayeski in the back, Daniel said. Mayeski yelled: "Oh, God," and slumped to the ground. Harris chased Baker down a hill into a little valley and shot him four times.

Mayeski was still alive when Harris climbed back up the hill, Daniel said. Harris walked over to the boy, knelt down, put the Luger to his head and fired.

"God, everything started to spin," Daniel said. "It was like slow motion. I saw the gun, and then his head exploded like a balloon, . . . I just started running and running. . . . But I heard Robert and turned around.

"He was swinging the rifle and pistol in the air and laughing. God, that laugh made blood and bone freeze in me."

Harris drove [the] car to a friend's house where he and Daniel were staying. Harris walked into the house, carrying the weapons and the bag [containing] the remainder of the slain youth's lunch. Then, about 15 minutes after he had killed the two 16-year-old boys, Harris took the food out of the bag . . . and began eating a hamburger. He offered his brother an apple turnover, and Daniel became nauseated and ran to the bathroom.

"Robert laughed at me," Daniel said. "He said I was weak; he called me a sissy and said I didn't have the stomach for it."

Harris was in an almost lighthearted mood. He smiled and told Daniel that it would be amusing if the two of them were to pose as police officers and inform the parents that their sons were killed. Then, for the first time, he turned serious. He thought that somebody might have heard the shots and that police could

be searching for the bodies. He told Daniel that they should begin cruising the street near the bodies, and possibly kill some police in the area.

[Later, as they prepared to rob the bank,] Harris pulled out the Luger, noticed blood stains and remnants of flesh on the barrel as a result of the point-blank shot, and said, "I really blew that guy's brains out." And then, again, he started laughing.

. . . Harris was given the death penalty. He has refused all requests for interviews since the conviction.

"He just doesn't see the point of talking," said a sister . . . who has visited him three times since he has been on Death Row. "He told me he had his chance, he took the road to hell and there's nothing more to say."

. . . Few of Harris' friends or family were surprised that he ended up on Death Row. He had spent seven of the previous 10 years behind bars. Harris, who has an eighth-grade education, was convicted of car theft at 15 and was sentenced to a federal youth center. After being released, he was arrested twice for torturing animals and was convicted of manslaughter for beating a neighbor to death after a dispute.

Barbara Harris, another sister, talked to her brother at a family picnic on July 4, 1978. He had been out of prison less than six months, and his sister had not seen him in several years.

. . . Barbara Harris noticed his eyes, and she began to shudder. . . . "I thought, 'My God, what have they done to him?' He smiled, but his eyes were so cold, so totally flat. It was like looking at a rattlesnake or a cobra ready to strike. They were hooded eyes, with nothing but meanness in them.

"He had the eyes of a killer. I told a friend that I knew someone else would die by his hand."

The next day, Robert Harris killed the two youths. Those familiar with the case were as mystified as they were outraged by Harris' actions. Most found it incomprehensible that a man could be so devoid of compassion and conscience that he could kill two youths, laugh about their deaths and then casually eat their hamburgers. . . .

. . . Harris is a dangerous man on the streets and a dangerous man behind bars, said Mroczko, who spent more than a year in the cell next to Harris's. . . .

"You don't want to deal with him out there," said Mroczko, . . . "We don't want to deal with him in here."

During his first year on the row, Mroczko said, Harris was involved in several fights on the yard and was caught trying to supply a prisoner in an adjacent yard with a knife. During one fight, Harris was stabbed and the other prisoner shot by a guard. He grated on people's nerves and one night he kept the whole cell block awake by banging his shoe on a steel water basin and laughing hysterically.

An encounter with Harris always resulted in a confrontation. If an inmate had cigarettes, or something else Harris wanted, and he did not think "you could hold your mud," Mroczko said, he would try to take them.

Harris was a man who just did not know "when to be cool," he said. He was an obnoxious presence in the yard and in his cell, and his behavior precipitated unwanted attention from the guards. . . .

He acted like a man who did not care about anything. His cell was filthy, Mroczko said, and clothes, trash, tobacco and magazines were scattered on the floor. He wore the same clothes every day and had little interest in showers. Harris spent his days watching television in his cell, occasionally reading a Western novel.

---

[1] Think carefully at this point about your assessment of Harris: was he morally responsible for the crime described and did he deserve to be severely punished for it? (Reservations about the death penalty are not relevant to our present concerns.)

On the face of it, Harris is an "archetypal candidate" for blame. We respond to his heartlessness and viciousness with moral outrage and loathing. Does it matter to our reactions how he came to be so? [1]

We must now investigate the relevance of such historical considerations to the reactive attitudes. As it happens, the case of Robert Harris is again a vivid illustration.

"[During the interview] Barbara Harris put her palms over her eyes and said softly, 'I saw every grain of sweetness, pity and goodness in him destroyed. . . . It was a long and ugly journey before he reached that point.'"

Robert Harris' 29 years . . . have been dominated by incessant cruelty and profound suffering that he has both experienced and provoked. Violence presaged his birth, and a violent act is expected to end his life.

Harris was born Jan. 15, 1953, several hours after his mother was kicked in the stomach. She was 6½ months pregnant and her husband, an insanely jealous man, . . . came home drunk and accused her of infidelity. He claimed that the child was not his, threw her down and kicked her. She began hemorrhaging, and he took her to the hospital.

Robert was born that night. His heartbeat stopped at one point . . . but labor was induced and he was saved. Because of his premature birth, he was a tiny baby; he was kept alive in an incubator and spent months in the hospital.

His father was an alcoholic who was twice convicted of sexually molesting his daughters. He frequently beat his children . . . and often caused serious injury. Their mother also became an alcoholic and was arrested several times, once for bank robbery.

All of the children had monstrous childhoods. But even in the Harris family, . . . the abuse Robert was subjected to was unusual.

Before their mother died last year, Barbara Harris said, she talked incessantly about Robert's early years. She felt guilty that she was never able to love him; she felt partly responsible that he ended up on Death Row.

When Robert's father visited his wife in the hospital and saw his son for the first time, . . . the first thing he said was, "Who is the father of that bastard?" When his mother picked him up from the hospital . . . she said it was like taking a stranger's baby home.

The pain and permanent injury Robert's mother suffered as a result of the birth, . . . and the constant abuse she was subjected to by her husband, turned her against her son. Money was tight, she was overworked and he was her fifth child in just a few years. She began to blame all her problems on Robert, and she grew to hate the child.

"I remember one time we were in the car and Mother was in the back seat with Robbie in her arms. He was crying and my father threw a glass bottle at him, but it hit my mother in the face. The glass shattered and Robbie started screaming. I'll never forget it," she said. . . .

"Her face was all pink, from the mixture of blood and milk. She ended up blaming Robbie for all the hurt, all the things like that. She felt helpless and he was someone to vent her anger on."

. . . Harris had a learning disability and a speech problem, but there was no money for therapy. When he was at school he felt stupid and classmates teased him, his sister said, and when he was at home he was abused.

"He was the most beautiful of all my mother's children; he was an angel," she said. "He would just break your heart. He wanted love so bad he would beg for any kind of physical contact.

"He'd come up to my mother and just try to rub his little hands on her leg or her arm. He just never got touched at all. She'd just push him away or kick him. One time she bloodied his nose when he was trying to get close to her."

Barbara Harris put her head in her hands and cried softly. "One killer out of nine kids. . . . The sad thing is he was the most sensitive of all of us. When he was 10 and we all saw 'Bambi,' he cried and cried when Bambi's mother was shot. Everything was pretty to him as a child; he loved animals. But all that changed; it all changed so much."

. . . All nine children are psychologically crippled as a result of their father, she said, but most have been able to lead useful lives. But Robert was too young, and the abuse lasted too long, she said, for him ever to have had a chance to recover.

[At age 14] Harris was sentenced to a federal youth detention center [for car theft]. He was one of the youngest inmates there, Barbara Harris said, and he grew up "hard and fast."

. . . Harris was raped several times, his sister said, and he slashed his wrists twice in suicide attempts. He spent more than four years behind bars as a result of an escape, an attempted escape and a parole violation.

The centers were "gladiator schools," Barbara Harris said, and Harris learned to fight and be mean. By the time he was released from federal prison at 19, all his problems were accentuated. Everyone in the family knew that he needed psychiatric help.

The child who had cried at the movies when Bambi's mother dies had evolved into a man who was arrested several times for abusing animals. He killed cats and dogs, Daniel said, and laughed while torturing them with mop handles, darts and pellet guns. Once he stabbed a prize pig more than 1,000 times.

"The only way he could vent his feelings was to break or kill something," Barbara Harris said. "He took out all the frustrations of his life on animals. He had no feeling for life, no sense of remorse. He reached the point where there wasn't that much left of him."

. . . Harris' family is ambivalent about his death sentence. [Another sister said that] if she did not know her brother's past so intimately, she would support his execution without hesitation. Barbara has a 16-year-old son; she often imagines the horror of the slain boys' parents.

"If anyone killed my son, I'd try my damnedest, no matter what it took, to have my child revenged," Barbara Harris said. "I know how those parents must suffer every day.

"But Robbie in the gas chamber. . . ." She broke off in mid-sentence and stared out the window. "Well, I still remember the little boy who used to beg for love, for just one pat or word of kindness. . . . No I can't say I want my brother to die."

. . . Since Harris has been on Death Row, he has made no demands of time or money on his family. Harris has made only one request; he wants a dignified and serene ceremony after he dies—a ceremony in marked contrast to his life.

He has asked his oldest brother to take his ashes, to drive to the Sierras, hike to a secluded spot and scatter his remains in the trees.

No doubt this history gives pause to the reactive attitudes. Why does it do so? "No wonder Harris is as he is!" we think. What is the relevance of this thought?②

> ② Has your assessment of Harris changed at this point? How?

Discussion Questions

1. Was Robert Harris morally responsible for his crimes? Was he free in the sense that he could have done otherwise than he did when he shot the two boys? Was there some time earlier when he made a choice to become the kind of person who could do such a thing?

2. His sister reported that Robert had told her that "he had his chance, he took the road to hell, and there's nothing more to say." Does that suggest that he sees himself as having chosen this path? Is that relevant to whether he really had a choice?

Robert Blatchford

Robert Blatchford (1851–1943) was an English journalist and politician who helped found the British Labor Party and was a strong advocate of socialism. In this selection, he defends hard determinism, arguing that everything that a person does is determined by the combination of heredity and environment, and hence that no one is ever free to do other than he or she does or morally responsible or deserving of either blame or praise. Blatchford's motive for advocating this conclusion is intensely practical: he wants to convince us that even the "bottom dogs" in society, people (like Robert Harris) who seem utterly beyond redemption and entirely unworthy of sympathy or concern, are not responsible for the way they are and so do not deserve the punishments and other negative treatment they receive.

A Defense of Hard Determinism, from
Not Guilty: A Defense of the Bottom Dog

THE AUTHOR'S APOLOGY

. . . I claim that men should not be classified as good and bad, but as fortunate and unfortunate; that they should be pitied, and not blamed; helped instead of being punished.

I claim that since we do not hold a man worthy of praise for being born beautiful, nor of blame for being born ugly, neither should we hold him worthy of praise for being born virtuous, nor of blame for being born vicious.

I base this claim upon the self-evident and undeniable fact that man has no part in the creation of his own nature.

I shall be told this means that no man is answerable for his own acts.

That is exactly what it does mean.

But, it will be urged, every man has a free will to act as he chooses; and to deny that is to imperil all law and order, all morality and discipline.

I deny both these inferences, and I ask the reader to hear my case patiently, and to judge it on its merits.

. . .

From *Not Guilty: A Defense of the Bottom Dog* (New York: Boni and Liveright, 1918).

WHERE DO OUR NATURES COME FROM?

. . . I deal with heredity before environment, because it is needful to take them one at a time, and heredity comes first; as birth before schooling.

But we must not fall into the bad habit of thinking of heredity and environment apart from each other, for it is *both*, and not either of them that make man's character.

It is often said that neither heredity nor environment accounts for a man's conduct. And that is true. But it is true, also, that heredity *and* environment account for every quality in the human "make-up." A pianist, an artist, or a cricketer is "made as well as born," and so is every man. A good batsman is a good batsman for two reasons: (1) He was born with good sight, steady nerves, and sound sense, all of which he owes to his ancestors. (2) He has been well taught, or has practised well, and this practice, this endeavour to succeed, he owes to his inherited ambition, and to the precept and example of other men. So if a man plays a fiddle well, or steers a ship well, or devotes his life to charity, the excellence is always due to heredity *and* environment. For the cricketer would never have been a cricketer, nor the violinist a violinist, had he been born in a country where cricket and violin playing were unknown. And, on the other hand, a man bred amongst cricketers or musicians will never excel in music nor in cricket unless he has what is called "a gift"; and the gift is "heredity."

Now, what do we mean by "heredity"?

Heredity is "descent," or "breed." Heredity, as the word is here used, means those qualities which are handed down from one generation to the next. It means those qualities which a new generation inherits from the generation from whom it descends. It means all that "is bred in the bone." If a man inherits a Grecian nose, a violent temper, well-knit muscles, a love of excitement, or a good ear for music, from his father or mother, that quality or feature is part of his heredity. It is "bred in him."

Every quality a child possesses at the moment of birth, *every* quality of body or of mind, is inherited from his parents and their ancestors. And the whole of those qualities—which *are* the child—are what we call "heredity."

No child brings into the world one single quality of body or mind that has not been handed down to it by its ancestors.

And yet no two children are exactly alike, and no child is exactly like any one of its forbears.

This difference of children from each other and from the parent stock is called "variation."

. . .

Variation is due to the fact that every child has two parents. If these two parents were exactly alike, and if their ancestors had been all exactly alike, their children would be exactly like each other and like their parents.

But the father and mother are of different families, of different natures, and perhaps of different races. And the ancestors of the father and mother— millions in number—were all different from each other in nature and in descent.

Now, since a child inherits some qualities from its father and some from its mother, it follows that if the father and mother are different from each other, the child must differ from both, and yet resemble both. For he will inherit from the father qualities which the mother has not inherited from her ancestors, and he will inherit from the mother qualities which the father did not inherit from his ancestors. So the child will resemble both parents, without being an exact copy of either. It "varies" from both parents by inheriting from each.

. . .

ENVIRONMENT

What is environment?

When we speak of a man's environment we mean his surroundings, his experiences; all that he sees, hears, feels, and learns, from the instant that the lamp of life is kindled to the instant when the light goes out.

By environment we mean everything that develops or modifies the child or the man for good or for ill.

We mean his mother's milk; the home, and the state of life into which he was born. We mean the nurse who suckles him, the children he plays with, the school he learns in, the air he breathes, the water he drinks, the food he eats. We mean the games he plays, the work he does, the sights he sees, the sounds he hears. We mean the girls he loves, the woman he marries, the children he rears, the wages he earns. We mean the sickness that tries him, the griefs that sear him, the friends who aid and the enemies who wound him. We mean all his hopes and fears, his victories and defeats; his faiths and his disillusionments. We mean all the harm he does, and all the help he gives; all the ideals that beckon him, all the temptations that lure him; all his weepings and laughter, his kissings and cursings, his lucky hits and unlucky blunders: everything he does and suffers under the sun.

I go into all this detail because we must remember that everything that happens to a man, everything that influences him, is a part of his environment.

It is a common mistake to think of environment in a narrow sense, as though environment implied no more than poverty or riches. Everything outside our skin belongs to our environment.

Let us think of it again. Education is environment; religion is environment; business and politics are environment; all the ideals, conventions, and prejudices of race and class are environment; literature, science, and the Press are environment; music, history, and sport are environment; beauty and ugliness are environment; example and precept are environment;

war and travel and commerce are environment; sunshine and ozone, honour and dishonour, failure and success, are environment; love is environment.

I stress and multiply examples because the power of environment is so tremendous that we can hardly over-rate its importance.

A child is not born with a conscience; but with the rudiments of a conscience: the materials from which a conscience may or may not be developed—by environment.

A child is not born with capacities, but only with potentialities, or possibilities, for good or evil, which may or may not be developed—by environment.

A child is born absolutely without knowledge. Every atom of knowledge he gets must be got from his environment.

Every faculty of body or of mind grows stronger with use and weaker with disuse. This is as true of the reason and the will as of the muscles.

The sailor has better sight than the townsman, because his eyes get better exercise. The blind have sharper ears than ours, because they depend more on their hearing.

Exercise of the mind "alters the arrangement of the grey matter of the brain," and so alters the morals, the memory, and the reasoning powers.

Just as dumb-bells, rowing, or delving develop the muscles, thought, study, and conversation develop the brain.

And everything that changes, or develops, muscle or brain is a part of our environment.

There must be bounds to the powers of environment, but no man has yet discovered the limits, and few have dared to place them wide enough.

But the scope of environment is undoubtedly so great, as I shall try to prove, that, be the heredity what it may, environment has power to save or damn.

Let us think what it means to be born quite without knowledge. Let us think what it means to owe all that we learn to environment.

So it is. Were it not for the action of environment, for the help of other men and women, we should live and die as animals; without morality, without decency, without the use of tools, or arms, or arts, or letters. We should be savages, or superior kinds of apes. That we are civilised and cultured men and women we owe to the fellow-creatures who gave into our infant hands the key to the stored-up knowledge and experience of the race.

. . .

HOW HEREDITY AND ENVIRONMENT WORK

There are many who have some understanding of heredity and of environment when taken separately who fail to realise their effects upon each other.

The common cause of the stumbling is easy to remove.

It is often said that two men are differently affected by the same environment, or what seems to be the same environment, and that therefore there must be some power in men to "overcome" their environment.

. . . the contest between a man and his environment is really a contest between heredity and environment, and may be compared to the effort of a man to swim against a stream.

A given environment will affect two different men differently, because their heredity is different.

But remembering that we are born without any knowledge, and that we are born not with intellect nor conscience, but only with the rudiments of such, it must be insisted that the hereditary power to resist environment is very limited. So much so that we may amend our figure of the swimmer and the stream, and say that no man, howsoever strong and brave, could swim against a stream unless he had learnt to swim.

And the learning to swim is environment, and works against the contrary environment, typified by the stream.

Let us take the case of two children. One has bad and one good heredity. One is a healthy baby, born of moral stock. The other is a degenerate, born of immoral stock. We will call the healthy baby Dick, and the degenerate baby Harry.[1]

[1] That there are hereditary inclinations to immorality in the way suggested here is something many people would reject. But it is enough for Blatchford's purposes that some people are hereditarily more susceptible to environmental influences in the direction of immorality. And if even that isn't true, then the role of environment just becomes larger, which would not affect Blatchford's main conclusions.

They are taken at birth into an environment of theft, drunkenness, and vice. They are taught to lie, to steal, and to drink. They never hear any good, never see a good example.

Harry, the degenerate, will take to evil as a duck to water. Of that, I think, there is no question. But what of Dick, the healthy baby?

Dick is born without knowledge. He is also born with undeveloped propensities. He will learn evil. His propensities will be trained to evil. How is he to "overcome his environment and become good"? He *cannot*. What will happen in Dick's case is that he will become a different kind of criminal—a stronger and cleverer criminal than Harry.

But, I hear some one say, "we know that children, born of thieves and sots, and reared in bad surroundings, have turned out honest and sober men." And the inference is that they rose superior to their environment.

But that inference is erroneous. The *fact* is that these children were saved by some *good* environment, acting against the bad.

For there is hardly such a thing as an environment that is *all* bad. In the case of Dick and Harry we supposed an environment containing no good. But that was for the sake of illustration.

For the environment to be *all* bad, the child must be prevented from ever seeing a good deed, or reading a good book, or meeting a good man, woman, or child.

Now, we can imagine no town, nor slum, in which a child should never hear nor see anything good. He is almost certain at some time or other to encounter good influences.

And these good influences will affect a healthy child more strongly than they will affect a degenerate, just as the evil influences will affect him less fatally than they will affect a degenerate. Because the poor degenerate is born with a bias towards disease or crime.

Two children may be born of the same parents, reared in the same hovel, in the same slum, taught the same evil lesson. But they will meet different companions, and will have different experiences.

One may meet a good boy, or girl, or man, or woman, and may be influenced for good. The other may chance upon the very worst company.

. . . Would not the effects be very different? Yet at first sight the environment of the two boys would seem to be precisely alike.

And we shall always find that the man who rises above his environment has really been helped by good environment to overcome the bad environment. He has learnt some *good*. And that learning is part of his environment. He must have been *taught* some good if he knows any, for he was born destitute of knowledge.

. . .

It is a mistake to think of heredity as all good, or all bad. It is mixed. We inherit, *all* of us, good and bad qualities.

It is a mistake to think of environment as all good or all bad. It is mixed. There are always good and bad influences around every one of us.

It is a mistake to think that any two men ever did or can have exactly the same environment.

It is as impossible for the environment of any two men to be identical, as for their heredity to be identical. As there are no two men exactly alike, so there are no two men whose experiences are exactly alike. ②

Good and bad environment work against each other. All kinds of environment work with or against heredity. Different heredities make different natures; different natures are differently affected by similar environments. But the child, being born without knowledge and with rudimentary faculties, is, whatever his heredity, almost wholly at the mercy of his environment.

> ② This raises a problem about how Blatchford can be as sure as he is that two people with exactly the same heredity and environment will behave in exactly the same ways in the same circumstances. Even identical twins raised in the same house do not have exactly the same environment. How can this view be established if such cases never occur?

. . .

FREE WILL

The free will delusion has been a stumbling block in the way of human thought for thousands of years. Let us try whether common sense and common knowledge cannot remove it.

Free will is a subject of great importance to us in this case; and it is one we must come to with our eyes wide open and our wits wide awake; not because it is very difficult, but because it has been tied and twisted into a tangle of Gordian knots by twenty centuries full of wordy but unsuccessful philosophers.

The free will party claim that man is responsible for his acts, because his will is free to choose between right and wrong.

We reply that the will is not free, and that if it were a free man could not know right from wrong until he was taught.

As to the knowledge of good and evil the free will party will claim that conscience is an unerring guide. But . . . conscience does not and cannot tell us what is right and what is wrong: it only reminds us of the lessons we have learnt as to right and wrong.

The "still small voice" is not the voice of God: it is the voice of heredity and environment.

And now to the freedom of the will.

③ This is an overstatement. "Overruling" heredity and environment would suggest that they have no influence at all. But it would be enough for some degree of freedom if these things *influenced* but did not completely *determine* a person's actions—that is, if there were at least two significantly different alternatives open to him.

When a man says his will is free, he means that it is free of all control or interference: that it can over-rule heredity and environment.③

We reply that the will is ruled by heredity and environment.

The cause of all the confusion on this subject may be shown in a few words.

When the free will party say that man has a free will, they mean that he is free to act as he chooses to act.

There is no need to deny that. *But what causes him to choose?*

That is the pivot upon which the whole discussion turns.

The free will party seem to think of the will as something independent of the man, as something outside him. They seem to think that the will decides without the control of the man's reason.

If that were so, it would not prove the man responsible. "The will" would be responsible, and not the man. It would be as foolish to blame a man for the act of a "free" will, as to blame a horse for the action of its rider.④

④ This amounts to treating the will as an outside force. But essentially the same point could be made if a person's will made choices at random.

But I am going to prove to my readers, by appeals to their common sense and common knowledge, that the will is not free; and that it is ruled by heredity and environment.

To begin with, the average man will be against me. He knows that he chooses between two courses every hour, and often every minute, and he thinks his choice is free. But that is a delusion: his choice is not free. He can choose, and does choose. But he can only choose as his heredity and his environment cause him to choose. He never did choose and never will choose except as his heredity and his environment—his temperament and his training—cause him to choose. And his heredity and his environment have fixed his choice before he makes it.

The average man says "I know that I can act as I wish to act." But what causes him to wish?

The free will party say, "We know that a man can and does choose between two acts." But what settles the choice?

There is a cause for every wish, a cause for every choice; and every cause of every wish and choice arises from heredity, or from environment.

For a man acts always from temperament, which is heredity, or from training, which is environment.

And in cases where a man hesitates in his choice between two acts, the hesitation is due to a conflict between his temperament and his training, or, as some would express it, "between his desire and his conscience."

A man is practising at a target with a gun, when a rabbit crosses his line of fire. The man has his eye and his sights on the rabbit, and his finger on the trigger. The man's will is free. If he press the trigger the rabbit will be killed.

Now, how does the man decide whether or not he shall fire? He decides by feeling, and by reason.

He would like to fire, just to make sure that he could hit the mark. He would like to fire, because he would like to have the rabbit for supper. He would like to fire, because there is in him the old, old hunting instinct, to kill.

But the rabbit does not belong to him. He is not sure that he will not get into trouble if he kills it. Perhaps—if he is a very uncommon kind of man—he feels that it would be cruel and cowardly to shoot a helpless rabbit.

Well. The man's will is free. He can fire if he likes: he can let the rabbit go if he likes. How will he decide? On what does his decision depend?

His decision depends upon the relative strength of his desire to kill the rabbit, and of his scruples about cruelty, and the law.

Not only that, but, if we knew the man fairly well, we could guess how his free will would act before it acted. The average sporting Briton would kill the rabbit. But we know that there are men who would on no account shoot any harmless wild creature.

Broadly put, we may say that the sportsman would will to fire, and that the humanitarian would not will to fire.

Now, as both their wills are free, it must be something outside the wills that makes the difference.

Well. The sportsman will kill, because he is a sportsman: the humanitarian will not kill, because he is a humanitarian.

And what makes one man a sportsman and another a humanitarian? Heredity and environment: temperament and training.

One man is merciful, another cruel, by nature; or one is thoughtful and the other thoughtless, by nature. That is a difference of heredity.

One may have been taught all his life that to kill wild things is "sport"; the other may have been taught that it is inhuman and wrong: that is a difference of environment.

Now, the man by nature cruel or thoughtless, who has been trained to think of killing animals as sport, becomes what we call a sportsman, because heredity and environment have made him a sportsman.

The other man's heredity and environment have made him a humanitarian.

The sportsman kills the rabbit, because he is a sportsman, and he is a sportsman because heredity and environment have made him one.

That is to say the "free will" is really controlled by heredity and environment.⑤

Allow me to give a case in point. A man who had never done any fishing was taken out by a fisherman. He liked the sport, and for some months followed it eagerly. But one day an accident brought home to his mind the cruelty of catching fish with a hook, and he instantly laid down his rod, and never fished again.

⑤ Here again the issue is not whether the background (environment) of the sportsman and the humanitarian *influence* their choices (which seems obviously true), but instead whether they *determine* them completely (so that no meaningful alternatives are left). Do the foregoing discussion and the example that follows make as strong a case for the second of these claims as they do for the first of them?

Before the change he was always eager to go fishing if invited: after the change he could not be persuaded to touch a line. His will was free all the while. How was it that his will to fish changed to his will not to fish? It was the result of environment. He had learnt that fishing was cruel. This knowledge controlled his will.

But, it may be asked, how do you account for a man doing the thing he does not wish to do?

No man ever did a thing he did not wish to do. When there are two wishes the stronger rules.

Let us suppose a case. A young woman gets two letters by the same post; one is an invitation to go with her lover to a concert, the other is a request that she will visit a sick child in the slums. The girl is very fond of music, and is rather afraid of the slums. She wishes to go to the concert, and to be with her lover; she dreads the foul street and the dirty home, and shrinks from the risk of measles or fever. But she goes to the sick child, and she foregoes the concert. Why?

Because her sense of duty is stronger than her self-love.

Now, her sense of duty is partly due to her nature—that is, to her heredity—but it is chiefly due to environment. Like all of us, this girl was born without any kind of knowledge, and with only the rudiments of a conscience. But she has been well taught, and the teaching is part of her environment.

We may say that the girl is free to act as she chooses, but she *does* act as she has been *taught* that she *ought* to act. This teaching, which is part of her environment, controls her will.

We may say that a man is free to act as he chooses. He is free to act as *he* chooses, but *he* will choose as heredity and environment cause *him* to choose. For heredity and environment have made him that which he is.

A man is said to be free to decide between two courses. But really he is only free to decide in accordance with his temperament and training.

Brown is a Member of Parliament. He is given to understand that by suppressing his principles he may get a seat in the next Cabinet.

Brown is very anxious to get into the Cabinet. He is ambitious. His wife is ambitious. He wants to make a name; he wants to please his wife. But he has been taught that to sacrifice one's principles for a bribe is disgraceful.

Now, his ambition is part of his heredity; the things he has been taught are part of his environment.

The conflict in his mind is a conflict between the old Adam and the new; between the older egotism and the newer altruism. It is a conflict between good heredity and bad heredity; between heredity and environment; and the victory will be to the stronger.

If Brown is very ambitious, and not very conscientious, he will take the bribe. If his conscience is stronger than his ambition, he will refuse it. But to say that he is free to choose is a misuse of terms: he is only free to decide as the stronger of the two motives compels him to decide. And the motives arise from heredity and environment.

Macbeth was ambitious; but he had a conscience. He wanted Duncan's crown; but he shrank from treason and ingratitude. Ambition pulled him one way, honour pulled him the other way. The opposing forces were so evenly balanced that he seemed unable to decide. Was Macbeth free to choose? To what extent was he free? He was so free that he could arrive at no decision, and it was the influence of his wife that turned the scale to crime.

Was Lady Macbeth free to choose? She did not hesitate. Because her ambition was so much stronger than her conscience that she never was in doubt. She chose as her over-powering ambition compelled her to choose.

And most of us in our decisions resemble either Macbeth or his wife. Either our nature is so much stronger than our training, or our training is so much stronger than our nature, that we decide for good or evil as promptly as a stream decides to run down hill; or our nature and our training are so nearly balanced that we can hardly decide at all.

In Macbeth's case the contest is quite clear and easy to follow. He was ambitious, and his environment had taught him to regard the crown as a glorious and desirable possession. But environment had also taught him that murder, and treason, and ingratitude were wicked and disgraceful.

Had he never been taught these lessons, or had he been taught that gratitude was folly, that honour was weakness, and murder excusable when it led to power, he would not have hesitated at all. It was his environment that hampered his will.

. . .

We say that a drunkard and a lifelong abstainer are free to drink or to refuse a glass of whisky. But we know that in both cases the action of the free will is a foregone conclusion.

In all cases the action of the will depends upon the relative strength of two or more motives. The stronger motive decides the will; just as the heavier weight decides the balance of a pair of scales.

In Macbeth's case the balance seemed almost even: Lady Macbeth's persuasion brought down the scale on the wrong side.

If the will were free, it would be independent of the temperament and training, and so would act as freely in one case as in another. So that it would be as easy for the drunkard as for the lifelong abstainer to refuse to drink; as easy for the thief as for the Cardinal to be honest; as easy for Macbeth as for Lady Macbeth to seal the fate of Duncan.

But we all know that it is harder for one man than for another to be sober, or honest, or virtuous; and we all know that the sobriety, or honesty, or virtue of any man depends upon his temperament and training; that is to say, upon his heredity and his environment.⑥

> ⑥ That it is harder for one person to be sober than it is for another (which again seems obvious) doesn't yet show that what each person does is *entirely* determined by heredity and environment.

How, then, can we believe that free will is outside and superior to heredity and environment?

. . .

"What! Cannot a man be honest if he choose?" Yes, if he choose. But that is only another way of saying that he can be honest if his nature and his training lead him to choose honesty.

"What! Cannot I please myself whether I drink or refrain from drinking?" Yes. But that is only to say you will not drink because it pleases *you* to be sober. But it pleases another man to drink, because his desire for drink is strong, or because his self-respect is weak.

And you decide as you decide, and he decides as he decides, because you are *you*, and he is *he*; and heredity and environment made you both that which you are.

And the sober man may fall upon evil days, and may lose his self-respect, or find the burden of his trouble greater than he can bear, and may fly to drink for comfort, or oblivion, and may become a drunkard. Has it not been often so?

And the drunkard may, by some shock, or some disaster, or some passion, or some persuasion, regain his self-respect, and may renounce drink, and lead a sober and useful life. Has it not been often so?

And in both cases the freedom of the will is untouched: it is the change in the environment that lifts the fallen up, and beats the upright down.

We might say that a woman's will is free, and that she could, if she wished, jump off a bridge and drown herself. But she cannot *wish*. She is happy, and loves life, and dreads the cold and crawling river. And yet, by some cruel turn of fortune's wheel, she may become destitute and miserable; so miserable that she hates life and longs for death, and *then* she can jump into the dreadful river and die.

Her will was free at one time as at another. It is the environment that has wrought the change. Once she could not wish to die: now she cannot wish to live.

The apostles of free will believe that all men's wills are free. But a man can only will that which he is able to will. And one man is able to will that which another man is unable to will. To deny this is to deny the commonest and most obvious facts of life.⑦

> ⑦ Does the fact that one person can will things that a second person cannot will show that *everything* they will is determined—that there are *no* significant alternatives open to them?

The will is as free in one nation and in one class as in another. Who would more willingly return a blow, an Irish soldier, or an English Quaker? Who would be readier to stab a rival, an English curate, or a Spanish smuggler? The difference does not concern the freedom of the will: it is a difference of heredity and environment.

The wills of a priest and a sailor are free—free to make love in every port, and to swear in every breeze. The difference is one of environment.

The free will party look upon a criminal as a bad man, who could be good if he wished: *but he cannot wish*.

The free will party say that if Smith wills to drink he is bad. But we say that Smith drinks, and to drink is bad; but Smith drinks because he is Smith.

The free will party say, "then he was born bad." But we say "no: he was born Smith."

We all know that we can foretell the action of certain men in certain cases, because we know the men.

We know that under the same conditions Jack Sheppard would steal and Cardinal Manning would not steal. We know that under the same conditions the sailor would flirt with the waitress, and the priest would not; that the drunkard would get drunk, and the abstainer would remain sober. We know that Wellington would refuse a bribe, that Nelson would not run away, that Buonaparte would grasp at power, that Abraham Lincoln would be loyal to his country, that Torquemada would not spare a heretic. Why? If the will is free, how can we be sure, before a test arises, how the will must act?⑧

> ⑧ Does the fact that people's behavior is mostly predictable show that it is entirely determined? If it were completely predictable, so that we could be "sure" what each person will do in every situation, would this establish determinism? Is it clear that people's behavior is in fact *completely* predictable?

Simply because we know that heredity and environment have so formed and moulded men and women that under certain circumstances the action of their wills is certain.

Heredity and environment having made a man a thief, he will steal. Heredity and environment having made a man honest, he will not steal.

That is to say, heredity and environment have decided the action of the will, before the time has come for the will to act.

This being so—and we all know that it is so—what becomes of the sovereignty of the will?

Let any man that believes that he can "do as he likes" ask himself *why* he *likes,* and he will see the error of the theory of free will, and will understand why the will is the servant and not the master of the man: for the man is the product of heredity and environment, and these control the will.

As we want to get this subject as clear as we can, let us take one or two familiar examples of the action of the will.

Jones and Robinson meet and have a glass of whisky. Jones asks Robinson to have another. Robinson says, "no thank you, one is enough." Jones says, "all right: have another cigarette." Robinson takes the cigarette. Now, here we have a case where a man refuses a second drink, but takes a second smoke. Is it because he would like another cigarette, but would not like another glass of whisky? No. It is because he knows that it is *safer* not to take another glass of whisky.

How does he know that whisky is dangerous? He has learnt it—from his environment.

"But he *could* have taken another glass if he wished."

But he could not wish to take another, because there was something he wished more strongly—to be safe.

And why did he want to be safe? Because he had learnt—from his environment—that it was unhealthy, unprofitable, and shameful to get drunk. Because he had learnt—from his environment—that it is easier to avoid forming a bad habit than to break a bad habit when formed. Because he valued the good opinion of his neighbours, and also his position and prospects.

These feelings and this knowledge ruled his will, and caused him to refuse the second glass.

But there was no sense of danger, no well-learned lesson of risk to check his will to smoke another cigarette. Heredity and environment did not warn him against that. So, to please his friend, and himself, he accepted.

Now suppose Smith asks Williams to have another glass. Williams takes it, takes several, finally goes home—as he often goes home. Why?

Largely because drinking is a habit with him. And not only does the mind instinctively repeat an action, but, in the case of drink, a physical craving is set up, and the brain is weakened. It is easier to refuse the first glass than the second; easier to refuse the second than the third; and it is very much harder for a man to keep sober who has frequently got drunk.

So, when poor Williams has to make his choice, he has habit against him, he has a physical craving against him, and he has a weakened brain to think with.

"But Williams could have refused the first glass."

No. Because in his case the desire to drink, or to please a friend, was stronger than his fear of the danger. Or he may not have been so conscious of the danger as Robinson was. He may not have been so well taught, or he may not have been so sensible, or he may not have been so cautious. So that his heredity and environment, his temperament and training, led him to take the drink, as surely as Robinson's heredity and environment led him to refuse it.

And now, it is my turn to ask a question. If the will is "free," if conscience is a sure guide, how is it that the free will and the conscience of Robinson caused him to keep sober, while the free will and the conscience of Williams caused him to get drunk?

Robinson's will was curbed by certain feelings which failed to curb the will of Williams. Because in the case of Williams the feelings were stronger on the other side.

It was the nature and the training of Robinson which made him refuse the second glass, and it was the nature and the training of Williams which made him drink the second glass.

What had free will to do with it?

We are told that *every* man has a free will, and a conscience.

Now, if Williams had been Robinson, that is to say if his heredity and his environment had been exactly like Robinson's, he would have done exactly as Robinson did. ⑨

> **9** How does Blatchford know this is true?

It was because his heredity and environment were not the same that his act was not the same.

Both men had free wills. What made one do what the other refused to do?

Heredity and environment. To reverse their conduct we should have to reverse their heredity and environment.

. . .

Two boys work at a hard and disagreeable trade. One leaves it, finds other work, "gets on," is praised for getting on. The other stays at the trade all his life, works hard all his life, is poor all his life, and is respected as an honest and humble working man. . . .

What causes these two free wills to will so differently? One boy knew more than the other boy. He "knew better." All knowledge is environment. Both boys had free wills. It was in knowledge they differed: environment!

Those who exalt the power of the will, and belittle the power of environment, belie their words by their deeds.

For they would not send their children amongst had companions or allow them to read bad books. They would not say the children have free will and therefore have power to take the good and leave the bad.

They know very well that evil environment has power to pervert the will, and that good environment has power to direct it properly.

They know that children may be made good or bad by good or evil training, and that the will follows the training.

That being so, they must also admit that the children of other people may be made good or bad by training.

And if a child gets bad training, how can free will save it? Or how can it be blamed for being bad? It never had a chance to be good. That they know this is proved by their carefulness in providing their own children with better environment.

As I have said before, every church, every school, every moral lesson is a proof that preachers and teachers trust to good environment, and not to free will, to make children good. [10]

[10] Here again, freedom need not mean that the environment has no influence.

In this, as in so many other matters, actions speak louder than words.

That, I hope, disentangles the many knots into which thousands of learned men have tied the simple subject of free will; and disposes of the claim that man is responsible because his will is free. But there is one other cause of error, akin to the subject, on which I should like to say a few words.

We often hear it said that a man is to blame for his conduct because "he knows better."

It is true that men do wrong when they know better. Macbeth "knew better" when he murdered Duncan. But it is true, also, that we often think a man "knows better," when he does not know better.

For a man cannot be said to know a thing until he believes it. If I am told that the moon is made of green cheese, it cannot be said that I *know* it to be made of green cheese.

Many moralists seem to confuse the words "to know" with the words "to hear."

Jones reads novels and plays opera music on Sunday. The Puritan says Jones "knows better," when he means that Jones has been told that it is wrong to do those things.

But Jones does not know that it is wrong. He has heard someone say that it is wrong, but does not believe it. Therefore it is not correct to say that he knows it.

And, again, as to that matter of belief. Some moralists hold that it is wicked not to believe certain things, and that men who do not believe those things will be punished.

But a man cannot believe a thing he is told to believe: he can only believe a thing which he *can* believe; and he can only believe that which his own reason tells him is true.

It would be no use asking Sir Roger Ball to believe that the earth is flat. He *could not* believe it.

It is no use asking an agnostic to believe the story of Jonah and the whale. He *could not* believe it. He might pretend to believe it. He might try to believe it. But his reason would not allow him to believe it.

Therefore it is a mistake to say that a man "knows better," when the fact is that he has been told "better" and cannot believe what he has been told.

That is a simple matter, and looks quite trivial; but how much ill-will, how much intolerance, how much violence, persecution, and murder have been caused by the strange idea that a man is wicked because *his* reason *cannot* believe that which to another man's reason [is] quite true.

Free will has no power over a man's belief. A man cannot believe by will, but only by conviction. A man cannot be forced to believe. You may threaten him, wound him, beat him, burn him; and he may be frightened, or angered, or pained; but he cannot *believe*, nor can he be made to believe. Until he is convinced.⑪

[11] Opponents of hard determinism who believe there is free will do not usually think that it applies to beliefs. (This is an issue that arises in connection with Pascal's "wager"—see the selection by Kaufmann in Chapter 2.)

Now, truism as it may seem, I think it necessary to say here that a man cannot be convinced by abuse, nor by punishment. He can only be convinced by *reason*.

Yes. If we wish a man to believe a thing, we shall find a few words of reason more powerful than a million curses, or a million bayonets. To burn a man alive for failing to believe that the sun goes round the world is not to convince him. The fire is searching, but it does not seem to him to be relevant to the issue. He never doubted that fire would burn; but perchance his dying eyes may see the sun sinking down into the west, as the world rolls on its axis. He dies in his belief. And knows no "better."

SELF-CONTROL

The subject of self-control is another simple matter which has been made difficult by slovenly thinkers.

When we say that the will is not free, and that men are made by heredity and environment, we are met with the astonishing objection that if such were the case there could be no such things as progress or morality.

When we ask why, we are told that if a man is the creature of heredity and environment it is no use his making any effort: what is to be, will be.

But a man makes efforts because he wants something; and whether he be a "free agent," or a "creature of heredity and environment," he will continue to want things, and so he will continue to make efforts to get them.

"But," say the believers in free will, "the fact that he tries to get things shows that his will is free."

Not at all. The fact is that heredity and environment compel him to want things, and compel him to try for them.

The earth does not move of its own free will; but it moves. The earth is controlled by two forces: one is centrifugal force, the other is the force of gravity. Those two forces compel it to move, and to move in a certain path, or orbit.

"But a man does not move in a regular path or orbit." Neither does the earth. For every planet draws it more or less out of its true course. And so it is with man: each influence in his environment affects him in some way.

In every case the force of heredity compels us to move, and the force of environment controls or changes our movements.

And as this is a subject of great importance, and one upon which there is much confusion of thought, I shall ask my readers to give me their best attention, so that we may make it thoroughly clear and plain.

The control of man by heredity and environment is not the end of all effort; on the contrary, it is the beginning of all effort.

We do not say that the control of the earth by gravity and centrifugal force is the end of its motion: we know that it is the *cause* of its motion.

But, we shall be told, "the earth cannot resist. It is compelled to act. Man is free."

Man is not free. Man is compelled to act. Directly a child is born it begins to act. From that instant until the end of its life, it continues to act. It *must* act. It cannot cease from action. The force of heredity compels it to act.

And the nature of its actions is decided:

1. By the nature of the individual: which is his heredity.
2. By his experiences and training: which are his environment.

Therefore to cease from all action is impossible. Therefore it is nonsense to say that if we are creatures of heredity and environment we shall cease to act.

But, it may be said, a man can cease from action: he has power to kill himself.

Well: the earth has power to destroy itself if it is caused to destroy itself. And man cannot destroy himself unless he is caused to destroy himself.

For the nature of a man—through heredity—is to love life. No man destroys himself without a cause. He may go mad, he may be in great grief, he may be disappointed, jealous, angry. But there is always a cause when a man takes his own life. And, be the cause what it may, it belongs to environment. So that a man cannot even take his own life until heredity and environment cause him to do it.

But there is a second argument, to the effect that if we believe ourselves to be creatures of heredity and environment we shall cease to make any effort to be good, or to be better than we are.

Those who use such an argument do not understand the nature and power of environment. Environment is powerful for good as well as for evil.

Well. We have seen that it is impossible for us to cease to act. Now we are told that we shall cease to act well.

But our acting well or ill depends upon the nature of our heredity and environment.

If our heredity be good, and if our environment be good, we *must* act well: we cannot help it.

If our heredity be bad, and if our environment be bad, we must act ill: we cannot help it.

"What? Do you mean to say I cannot be good if I try?"

Is it not evident that you must have some good in you if you wish to try? That good is put there by heredity and environment.

"But even a bad man sometimes tries to be good."

That is slovenly thinking. A man who is *all* bad has no desire for good. Any man who has a desire for good is not all bad.

Therefore a man who is "bad" never tries to be good, and a man who tries to be good is not "bad." When it is said that a bad man tries to be good the idea is that a very imperfect man tries to be rather better.

And he tries to be rather better because heredity or environment causes him to wish to be rather better.

Before a man can wish to be good he must know what goodness is. All men are born destitute of knowledge. To know what goodness is he must learn. All learning is environment.

But when a man knows what is good, and wishes to be good, he will try to be good. He cannot help trying. And he will try just as hard, and just as long as his temperament and training cause him to try; and he will succeed in being just as good as his temperament

and training cause him to be. And his temperament is heredity, and his training is environment.[12]

[12] So how much a person tries is no more within his control than anything else.

It does not follow, then, that because a man is that which heredity and environment make him, he will be nothing, for they will *make* him something. It does not follow that he will be bad, for they will make him good or bad, as they are good or bad.

"Then," exclaims the confused opponent, "the man himself counts for nothing: he is a mere machine."

No. He is not a "mere machine": he is a mere man; and he counts for just as much as his heredity and environment amount to, for his heredity and environment are *he*.

"But to tell a youth that he is a creature of heredity and environment would discourage him." Not if he understood what was meant. As we want to get this subject perfectly clear let us put a speech in two ways.

A youth tells his father that he would like to be a painter. The father's reply may be varied as follows. First, let us suppose the father says:

"You will be just as good a painter as your heredity and environment allow, or compel you to be.

"If you have any hereditary talent for the art, so much the better. But painting requires something more than talent: it requires knowledge, and practice. The more knowledge and practice you get the better you will paint. The less hereditary talent you possess, the more knowledge and practice you will need. Therefore, if you want to be a good painter, you must work hard."

The second speech would leave out the word hereditary before the word talent, and would begin, "You will be just as a good a painter as your talent and industry will make you." Otherwise the speeches would not differ.

But are we to suppose that the first speech would discourage a boy who wanted to be a painter? Not at all: if the boy understood what heredity and environment mean. It tells him that he can only be as good a painter as *his* talent and *his* industry will make him. But it does not tell him what are the limits of his industry and talent, for nobody knows what the limits are. That can only be settled by trying.

To know that he cannot get more out of a gold reef than there is in it, does not discourage a miner. What he wants is to get all there is in it, and until he wants no more, or believes there is no more, he will keep on digging.

It is so with any human effort. We all know that we cannot do more than we can, whether we believe in free will or no. But we do not know how much we can do, and nobody can tell us. The only way is to try. And we try just as hard as our nature and our desire impel us to try, and just as long as any desire or any hope remains.

. . .

GUILTY OR NOT GUILTY?

We are to ask whether it is true that everything a man does is the only thing he could do, at the instant of his doing it.

This is a very important question, because if the answer is yes, all praise and all blame are undeserved.

All praise and *all* blame.

Let us take some revolting action as a test.

A tramp has murdered a child on the highway, has robbed her of a few coppers, and has thrown her body into a ditch.

"Do you mean to say that tramp could not help doing that? Do you mean to say he is not to blame? Do you mean to say he is not to be punished?"

Yes. I say all those things; and if all those things are not true this book is not worth the paper it is printed on.

Prove it? I have proved it. But I have only instanced venial acts, and now we are confronted with murder. And the horror of murder drives men almost to frenzy, so that they cease to think: they can only feel.

Murder. Yes, a brutal murder. It comes upon us with a sickening shock. . . . I have to plead for the *bottom* dog: the lowest, the most detested, the worst.

The tramp has committed a murder. Man would loathe him, revile him, hang him: God would cast him into outer darkness.

"Not," cries the pious Christian, "if he repent."

I make a note of the repentance and pass on.

The tramp has committed a murder. It was a cowardly and cruel murder, and the motive was robbery.

But I have proved that all motives and all powers; all knowledge and capacity, all acts and all words, are caused by heredity and environment.

I have proved that a man can only be good or bad as heredity and environment cause him to be good or bad; and I have proved these things because I have to claim that all punishments and rewards, all praise and blame, are undeserved.

. . .

Discussion Questions

1. What would Blatchford probably say about the case of Robert Harris, as described in the previous selection? How plausible is the resulting view of that case?

2. Blatchford gives reasons for thinking that heredity and especially environment influence people's choices, make it more difficult for them to do some things than others, and perhaps even rule out some choices entirely. Do any of these reasons, or any other reasons that he gives, make a strong case for the claim that what a person does is *entirely determined* by heredity and environment, so that no other alternative than what he did was genuinely possible for him?

3. If Blatchford's deterministic view is correct, does it follow that it is pointless to punish (or praise) people for what they do? Can you think of a justification for punishment that is compatible with hard determinism?

David Hume

David Hume (1711–1776), a Scottish philosopher and historian, is usually regarded as one of the most important and influential philosophers of all time. He did very important work in epistemology, metaphysics, ethics, and the philosophy of religion, producing a comprehensive philosophical position that is most distinctive for its skeptical tendencies.

In this selection, Hume defends compatibilism (or soft determinism), arguing that normal human actions are characterized by both necessity (causal determinism) and liberty (freedom). He claims that the view that necessity and liberty are incompatible results from misunderstandings of these concepts.

Of Liberty and Necessity, from *An Enquiry Concerning Human Understanding*

OF LIBERTY AND NECESSITY

Part I

It might reasonably be expected in questions which have been canvassed and disputed with great eagerness, since the first origin of science and philosophy, that the meaning of all the terms, at least, should have been agreed upon among the disputants; and our inquiries, in the course of two thousand years, been able to pass from words to the true and real subject of the controversy. For how easy may it seem to give exact definitions of the terms employed in reasoning, and make these definitions, not the mere sound of words, the object of future scrutiny and examination? But if we consider the matter more narrowly, we shall be apt to draw a quite opposite conclusion. From this circumstance alone, that a controversy has been long kept on foot, and remains still undecided, we may presume that there is some ambiguity in the expression, and that the disputants affix different ideas to the terms employed in the controversy. For as the faculties of the mind are supposed to be naturally alike in every individual; otherwise nothing could be more fruitless than to reason or dispute together; it were impossible, if men affix the same ideas to their terms, that they could so long form different opinions of the same subject; especially when they communicate their views, and each party turn themselves on all sides, in search

of arguments which may give them the victory over their antagonists. . . . ①

This has been the case in the long disputed question concerning liberty and necessity; and to so remarkable a degree that, if I be not much mistaken, we shall find, that all mankind, both learned and ignorant, have always been of the same opinion with regard to this subject, and that a few intelligible definitions would immediately have put an end to the whole controversy. . . .

> ① The idea that philosophical disputes result from confusions about the meanings of terms and can be resolved if these are clarified is one of the central doctrines of what has come to be known as the *analytic* school of philosophy. In this respect (and some others), Hume is plausibly viewed as one of the main influences on the analytic school.

I hope, therefore, to make it appear that all men have ever agreed in the doctrine both of necessity and of liberty, according to any reasonable sense, which can be put on these terms; and that the whole controversy has hitherto turned merely upon words. We shall begin with examining the doctrine of necessity.

It is universally allowed that matter, in all its operations, is actuated by a necessary force, and that every natural effect is so precisely determined by the energy of its cause that no other effect, in such particular circumstances, could possibly have resulted from it. The degree and direction of every motion is, by the laws of nature, prescribed with such exactness that a living creature may as soon arise from the shock of two bodies as motion in any other degree or direction than what is actually produced by it. Would we, therefore, form a just and precise idea of *necessity*, we

From An Enquiry Concerning Human Understanding, *1748*.

must consider whence that idea arises when we apply it to the operation of bodies.②

---

② Hume takes it to be beyond question that necessity (causal determinism) applies to the realm of material bodies. Thus he proposes to determine what necessity is by investigating what it amounts to in that realm.

It seems evident that, if all the scenes of nature were continually shifted in such a manner that no two events bore any resemblance to each other, but every object was entirely new, without any similitude to whatever had been seen before, we should never, in that case, have attained the least idea of necessity, or of a connection among these objects. We might say, upon such a supposition, that one object or event has followed another; not that one was produced by the other. The relation of cause and effect must be utterly unknown to mankind. . . . Our idea, therefore, of necessity and causation arises entirely from the uniformity observable in the operations of nature, where similar objects are constantly conjoined together, and the mind is determined by custom to infer the one from the appearance of the other. These two circumstances form the whole of that necessity, which we ascribe to matter. Beyond the constant *conjunction* of similar objects, and the consequent *inference* from one to the other, we have no notion of any necessity or connection.③

---

③ Hume's suggestion is that necessity as it applies to the realm of material bodies amounts to nothing more than (a) *constant conjunction* (events or objects of a specific kind being regularly followed by events or objects of another specific kind) together with (b) the consequent tendency of the mind to *infer* from the occurrence of one of these kinds of events or objects to the other.

If it appear, therefore, that all mankind have ever allowed, without any doubt or hesitation, that these two circumstances take place in the voluntary actions of men, and in the operations of mind; it must follow, that all mankind have ever agreed in the doctrine of necessity, and that they have hitherto disputed, merely for not understanding each other.

As to the first circumstance, the constant and regular conjunction of similar events, we may possibly satisfy ourselves by the following considerations. It is universally acknowledged that there is a great uniformity among the actions of men, in all nations and ages, and that human nature remains still the same, in

its principles and operations. The same motives always produce the same actions; the same events follow from the same causes. Ambition, avarice, self-love, vanity, friendship, generosity, public spirit: these passions, mixed in various degrees, and distributed through society, have been, from the beginning of the world, and still are, the source of all the actions and enterprises, which have ever been observed among mankind. Would you know the sentiments, inclinations, and course of life of the Greeks and Romans? Study well the temper and actions of the French and English: you cannot be much mistaken in transferring to the former *most* of the observations which you have made with regard to the latter. Mankind are so much the same, in all times and places, that history informs us of nothing new or strange in this particular. Its chief use is only to discover the constant and universal principles of human nature, by showing men in all varieties of circumstances and situations, and furnishing us with materials from which we may form our observations and become acquainted with the regular springs of human action and behavior. These records of wars, intrigues, factions, and revolutions, are so many collections of experiments, by which the politician or moral philosopher fixes the principles of his science, in the same manner as the physician or natural philosopher becomes acquainted with the nature of plants, minerals, and other external objects, by the experiments which he forms concerning them. Nor are the earth, water, and other elements, examined by Aristotle, and Hippocrates, more like to those which at present lie under our observation than the men described by Polybius and Tacitus are to those who now govern the world.

Should a traveler, returning from a far country, bring us an account of men, wholly different from any with whom we were ever acquainted; men, who were entirely divested of avarice, ambition, or revenge; who knew no pleasure but friendship, generosity, and public spirit; we should immediately, from these circumstances, detect the falsehood, and prove him a liar, with the same certainty as if he had stuffed his narration with stories of centaurs and dragons, miracles and prodigies. And if we would explode any forgery in history, we cannot make use of a more convincing argument, than to prove, that the actions ascribed to any person are directly contrary to the course of nature, and that no human motives, in such circumstances, could ever induce him to such a conduct.④ . . . So readily and universally do we acknowledge a uniformity in human motives and actions as well as in the operations of body.

④ The issue is then whether the two ingredients of necessity are also to be found in the realm of human actions. Hume's claim is that the first one is—and moreover, that no one really disputes this. Human actions occur in regular ways, and we would be suspicious of reports to the contrary.

. . .

We must not, however, expect that this uniformity of human actions should be carried to such a length as that all men, in the same circumstances, will always act precisely in the same manner, without making any allowance for the diversity of characters, prejudices, and opinions. Such a uniformity in every particular, is found in no part of nature. On the contrary, from observing the variety of conduct in different men, we are enabled to form a greater variety of maxims, which still suppose a degree of uniformity and regularity.

Are the manners of men different in different ages and countries? We learn thence the great force of custom and education, which mold the human mind from its infancy and form it into a fixed and established character. Is the behavior and conduct of the one sex very unlike that of the other? Is it thence we become acquainted with the different characters which nature has impressed upon the sexes, and which she preserves with constancy and regularity? Are the actions of the same person much diversified in the different periods of his life, from infancy to old age? This affords room for many general observations concerning the gradual change of our sentiments and inclinations, and the different maxims which prevail in the different ages of human creatures. Even the characters, which are peculiar to each individual, have a uniformity in their influence; otherwise our acquaintance with the persons and our observation of their conduct could never teach us their dispositions, or serve to direct our behavior with regard to them.⑤

⑤ People do not always act the same way in the same external circumstances. But this just shows that custom, education, and character are also causally relevant.

I grant it possible to find some actions, which seem to have no regular connection with any known motives, and are exceptions to all the measures of conduct which have ever been established for the government of men. But if we would willingly know what judgment should be formed of such irregular and extraordinary actions, we may consider the sentiments commonly entertained with regard to those irregular events which appear in the course of nature, and the operations of external objects. All causes are not conjoined to their usual effects with like uniformity. An artificer, who handles only dead matter, may be disappointed of his aim, as well as the politician, who directs the conduct of sensible and intelligent agents.

The vulgar, who take things according to their first appearance, attribute the uncertainty of events to such an uncertainty in the causes as makes the latter often fail of their usual influence; though they meet with no impediment in their operation. But philosophers, observing that, almost in every part of nature, there is contained a vast variety of springs and principles, which are hid, by reason of their minuteness or remoteness, find, that it is at least possible the contrariety of events may not proceed from any contingency in the cause, but from the secret operation of contrary causes. This possibility is converted into certainty by further observation, when they remark that, upon an exact scrutiny, a contrariety of effects always betrays a contrariety of causes, and proceeds from their mutual opposition. A peasant can give no better reason for the stopping of any clock or watch than to say that it does not commonly go right: but an artist easily perceives that the same force in the spring or pendulum has always the same influence on the wheels; but fails of its usual effect, perhaps by reason of a grain of dust, which puts a stop to the whole movement. From the observation of several parallel instances, philosophers form a maxim that the connection between all causes and effects is equally necessary, and that its seeming uncertainty in some instances proceeds from the secret opposition of contrary causes.

. . .

The philosopher, if he be consistent, must apply the same reasoning to the actions and volitions of intelligent agents. The most irregular and unexpected resolutions of men may frequently be accounted for by those who know every particular circumstance of their character and situation. A person of an obliging disposition gives a peevish answer; but he has the toothache, or has not dined. A stupid fellow discovers an uncommon alacrity in his carriage; but he has met with a sudden piece of good fortune. Or even when an action, as something happens, cannot be particularly accounted for, either by the person himself or by others; we know, in general, that the characters of men are, to a certain degree, inconstant and irregular. This is, in a manner, the constant character of human nature; though it be applicable, in a more particular manner, to some persons who have no fixed rule for their conduct, but proceed in a continued course of caprice and inconstancy. The internal principles and motives may operate in a uniform manner, notwithstanding these seeming irregularities; in the same manner as the winds, rain, clouds, and other variations of the weather are supposed to be governed by steady principles; though not easily discoverable by human sagacity and inquiry.⑥

⎡6⎤ In both realms (material bodies and human actions), there are exceptions to the general regularities of succession. Hume takes this to show, in both cases, only that there are further causes at work that have not yet been discovered.

Thus it appear, not only that the conjunction between motives and voluntary actions is as regular and uniform as that between the cause and effect in any part of nature; but also that this regular conjunction has been universally acknowledged among mankind, and has never been the subject of dispute, either in philosophy or common life. Now, as it is from past experience that we draw all inferences concerning the future, and as we conclude that objects will always be conjoined together which we find to have always been conjoined; it may seem superfluous to prove that this experienced uniformity in human actions is a source whence we draw *inferences* concerning them. But in order to throw the argument into a greater variety of lights we shall also insist, though briefly, on this latter topic.

The mutual dependence of men is so great in all societies that scarce any human action is entirely complete in itself, or is performed without some reference to the actions of others, which are requisite to make it answer fully the intention of the agent. The poorest artificer, who labors alone, expects at least the protection of the magistrate, to ensure him the enjoyment of the fruits of his labor. He also expects that, when he carries his goods to market, and offers them at a reasonable price, he shall find purchasers, and shall be able, by the money he acquires, to engage others to supply him with those commodities which are requisite for his subsistence. In proportion as men extend their dealings, and render their intercourse with others more complicated, they always comprehend, in their schemes of life, a greater variety of voluntary actions, which they expect, from the proper motives, to cooperate with their own. In all these conclusions they take their measures from past experience, in the same manner as in their reasonings concerning external objects; and firmly believe that men, as well as all the elements, are to continue, in their operations, the same that they have ever found them. A manufacturer reckons upon the labor of his servants for the execution of any work as much as upon the tools which he employs, and would be equally surprised were his expectations disappointed. In short, this experimental inference and reasoning concerning the actions of others enters so much into human life, that no man, while awake, is ever a moment without employing it. Have we not reason, therefore, to affirm that all mankind have always agreed in the doctrine of necessity according to the foregoing definition and explication of it?

Nor have philosophers ever entertained a different opinion from the people in this particular. For, not to mention that almost every action of their life supposes that opinion, there are even few of the speculative parts of learning to which it is not essential. What would become of *history,* had we not a dependence on the veracity of the historian according to the experience which we have had of mankind? How could *politics* be a science, if laws and forms of government had not a uniform influence upon society? Where would be the foundation of *morals,* if particular characters had no certain or determinate power to produce particular sentiments, and if these sentiments had no constant operation on actions? And with what pretense could we employ our *criticism* upon any poet or polite author, if we could not pronounce the conduct and sentiments of his actors either natural or unnatural to such characters, and in such circumstances? It seems almost impossible, therefore, to engage either in science or action of any kind without acknowledging the doctrine of necessity, and this *inference* from motive to voluntary actions, from characters to conduct.⑦

And indeed, when we consider how aptly *natural* and *moral* evidence link together, and form only one chain of argument, we shall make no scruple to allow that they are of the same nature, and derived from the same principles. A prisoner who has neither money nor interest, discovers the impossibility of his escape, as well when he considers the obstinacy of the goaler, as the walls and bars with which he is surrounded; and, in all attempts for his freedom, chooses rather to work upon the stone and iron of the one, than upon the inflexible nature of the other. The same prisoner, when conducted to the scaffold, foresees his death as certainly from the constancy and fidelity of his guards, as from the operation of the axe or wheel. His mind runs along a certain train of ideas: the refusal of the soldiers to consent to his escape; the action of the executioner; the separation of the head and body; bleeding, convulsive motions, and death. Here is a connected chain of natural causes and voluntary actions; but the mind feels no difference between them in passing from one link to another. Nor is less certain of the future event than if it were connected with the objects present to the memory or senses, by a train of causes, cemented together by what we are pleased to call a *physical* necessity. The same experienced union has the same effect on the mind, whether the united objects be motives, volition, and actions; or figure and motion. We may change the name of things; but their nature and their operation on the understanding never change.

Were a man, whom I know to be honest and opulent, and with whom I live in intimate friendship, to come into my house, where I am surrounded with my servants, I rest assured that he is not to stab me before he leaves it in order to rob me of my silver standish; and I no more suspect this event than the falling of the house itself, which is new, and solidly built and founded.—*But he may have been seized with a sudden and unknown frenzy.*—So may a sudden earthquake arise, and shake and tumble my house about my ears. I shall therefore change the suppositions. I shall say that I know with certainty that he is not to put his hand into the fire and hold it there till it be consumed: and this event, I think I can foretell with the same assurance, as that, if he throw himself out at the window, and meet with no obstruction, he will not remain a moment sus-

[7] Moreover, there is no doubt that in the realm of human actions, just as in the realm of material bodies, we rely on the patterns of uniformity to infer what people will do in various circumstances, given specified motives. Both ordinary actions in the world and the scholarly study of human actions depend essentially on these inferences.

pended in the air. No suspicion of an unknown frenzy can give the least possibility to the former event, which is so contrary to all the known principles of human nature. A man who at noon leaves his purse full of gold on the pavement at Charing Cross, may as well expect that it will fly away like a feather, as that he will find it untouched an hour after. Above one half of human reasonings contain inferences of a similar nature, attended with more or less degrees of certainty proportioned to our experience of the usual conduct of mankind in such particular situations.[8]

[8] Indeed, we often reason in a way that integrates regularities pertaining to material bodies with those pertaining to human actions, with no more uncertainty about the latter than about the former.

I have frequently considered, what could possibly be the reason why all mankind, though they have ever, without hesitation, acknowledged the doctrine of necessity in their whole practice and reasoning, have yet discovered such a reluctance to acknowledge it in words, and have rather shown a propensity, in all ages, to profess the contrary opinion. The matter, I think, may be accounted for after the following manner. If we examine the operations of body, and the production of effects from their causes, we shall find that all our faculties can never carry us farther in our knowledge of this relation than barely to observe that particular objects are *constantly conjoined* together, and that the mind is carried, by a *customary transition,* from the appearance of one to the belief of the other. But though this conclusion concerning human ignorance be the result of the strictest scrutiny of this subject, men still entertain a strong propensity to believe that they penetrate farther into the powers of nature, and perceive something like a necessary connection between the cause and the effect. When again they turn their reflections towards the operations of their own minds, and *feel* no such connection of the motive and the action; they are thence apt to suppose, that there is a difference between the effects which result from material force, and those which arise from thought and intelligence. But being once convinced that we know nothing farther of causation of any kind than merely the *constant conjunction* of objects, and the consequent *inference* of the mind from one to another, and finding that these two circumstances are universally allowed to have place in voluntary actions; we may be more easily led to own the same necessity common to all causes. And though this reasoning may contradict the systems of many philosophers, in ascribing necessity to the determinations of the will, we shall find, upon reflection, that they dissent from it in words only, not in their real sentiment. Necessity, according to the sense in which it is here taken, has never yet been rejected, nor can ever, I think, be rejected by any philosopher. . . .

It would seem, indeed, that men begin at the wrong end of this question concerning liberty and necessity, when they enter upon it by examining the faculties of the soul, the influence of the understanding, and the operations of the will. Let them first discuss a more simple question, namely, the operations of body and of brute unintelligent matter; and try whether they can there form any idea of causation and necessity, except that of a constant conjunction of objects, and subsequent inference of the mind from one to another. If these circumstances form, in reality, the whole of that necessity, which we conceive in matter, and if these circumstances be also universally acknowledged to take place in the operations of the mind, the dispute is at an end; at least, must be owned to be thenceforth merely verbal. But as long as we will rashly suppose, that we have some farther idea of necessity and causation in the operations of external objects; at the same time,

that we can find nothing farther in the voluntary actions of the mind; there is no possibility of bringing the question to any determinate issue, while we proceed upon so erroneous a supposition. The only method of undeceiving us is to mount up higher; to examine the narrow extent of science when applied to material causes; and to convince ourselves that all we know of them is the constant conjunction and inference above mentioned. We may, perhaps, find that it is with difficulty we are induced to fix such narrow limits to human understanding: but we can afterwards find no difficulty when we come to apply this doctrine to the actions of the will. For as it is evident that these have a regular conjunction with motives and circumstances and characters, and as we always draw inferences from one to the other, we must be obliged to acknowledge in words that necessity, which we have already avowed, in every deliberation of our lives, and in every step of our conduct and behavior. ⑨ *

⑨ One way in which people are led astray in these matters, Hume suggests, is by thinking that necessary connection of a sort that goes beyond the two elements he has indicated is perceivable in nature, but not in the actions of their own minds—that we can somehow perceive the causal connection itself, and not just the regularity that results from it. Hume denies that this is the case.

⑩ By the "doctrine of liberty," Hume means here the mistaken (according to him) idea that there is a kind of liberty pertaining to human actions that is distinct from and incompatible with causal necessity. His suggestion is that the plausibility of this idea results from its seeming, in a situation where a person is actually performing an action, that more than one alternative is possible, that even though he does one thing, he could just as well have done something else. Hume regards this as a kind of illusion, as shown by the fact that an external observer (or even the same person reflecting later) will find the action as regular and predictable as anything else.

*The prevalence of the doctrine of liberty may be accounted for, from another cause, viz., a false sensation or seeming experience which we have, or may have, of liberty or indifference, in many of our actions. The necessity of any action, whether of matter or of mind, is not, properly speaking, a quality in the agent, but in any thinking or intelligent being, who may consider the action; and it consists chiefly in the determination of his thoughts to infer the existence of that action from some preceeding objects; as liberty, when opposed to necessity, is nothing but the want of that determination, and a certain looseness or indifference, which we feel, in passing, or not passing, from the idea of one object to that of any succeeding one. Now we may observe, that, though, in *reflecting* on human actions, we seldom feel such a looseness, or indifference, but are commonly able to infer them with considerable certainty from their motives, and from the dispositions of the agent; yet it frequently happens, that, in *performing* the actions themselves, we are sensible of something like it. And as all resembling objects are readily taken for each other, this has been employed as a demonstrative and even intuitive proof of human liberty. We feel, that our actions are subject to our will, on most occasions; and imagine we feel, that the will itself is subject to nothing, because, when by a denial of it we are provoked to try, we feel, that it moves easily every way, and produces an image of itself . . . even on that side, on which it did not settle. This image, or faint motion, we persuade ourselves, could, at that time, have been completed into the thing itself; because, should that be denied, we find, upon a second trial, that, at present, it can. We consider not, that the fantastical desire of shewing liberty, is here the motive of our actions. And it seems certain, that, however we may imagine we feel a liberty within ourselves, a spectator can commonly infer our action from our motives and character; and even where he cannot, he concludes in general, that he might, were he perfectly acquainted with every circumstance of our situation and temper, and the most secret springs of our complexion and disposition. Now this is the very essence of necessity, according to the foregoing doctrine. ⑩

But to proceed in this reconciling project with regard to the question of liberty and necessity; the most contentious question of metaphysics, the most contentious science; it will not require many words to prove, that all mankind have ever agreed in the doctrine of liberty as well as in that of necessity, and that the whole dispute, in this respect also, has been hitherto merely verbal. For what is meant by liberty, when applied to voluntary actions? We cannot surely mean that actions have so little connection with motives, inclinations, and circumstances, that one does not follow with a certain degree of uniformity from the other, and that one affords no inference by which we can conclude the existence of the other. For these are plain and acknowledged matters of fact. By liberty, then, we can only mean *a power of acting or not acting, according to the determinations of the will;* that is, if we choose to remain at rest, we may; if we choose to move, we also may. Now this hypothetical liberty is universally allowed to belong to everyone who is not a prisoner and in chains. Here, then, is no subject of dispute. [11]

> [11] What then does liberty amount to, if not a denial of the regularity and inferability that everyone admits? Hume suggests that liberty means only acting (or not acting) according to the determinations of the will, that is, as one chooses. Since this is entirely compatible with the action and choice being causally determined, Hume thus *reconciles* liberty (freedom) with necessity (causal determinism).

Whatever definition we may give of liberty, we should be careful to observe two requisite circumstances; *first,* that it be consistent with plain matter of fact; *secondly,* that it be consistent with itself. If we observe these circumstances, and render our definition intelligible, I am persuaded that all mankind will be found of one opinion with regard to it.

. . .

Had not objects a regular conjunction with each other, we should never have entertained any notion of cause and effect; and this regular conjunction produces that inference of the understanding, which is the only connection, that we can have any comprehension of. Whoever attempts a definition of cause, exclusive of these circumstances, will be obliged either to employ unintelligible terms or such as are synonymous to the term which he endeavors to define. And if the definition above mentioned be admitted; liberty, when opposed to necessity, not to constraint, is the same thing with chance; which is universally allowed to have no existence. [12]

> [12] A liberty that was incompatible with necessity would amount to chance or randomness. Hume's claim, much more plausible then than now, is that genuine chance does not exist.

Part II

There is no method of reasoning more common, and yet none more blamable, than, in philosophical disputes, to endeavor the refutation of any hypothesis, by a pretense of its dangerous consequences to religion and morality. When any opinion leads to absurdities, it is certainly false; but it is not certain that an opinion is false, because it is of dangerous consequence. Such topics, therefore, ought entirely to be forborne; as serving nothing to the discovery of truth, but only to make the person of an antagonist odious. This I observe in general, without pretending to draw any advantage from it. I frankly submit to an examination of this kind, and shall venture to affirm that the doctrines, both of necessity and of liberty, as above explained, are not only consistent with morality, but are absolutely essential to its support.

Necessity may be defined two ways, conformably to the two definitions of *cause,* of which it makes an essential part. It consists either in the constant conjunction of like objects, or in the inference of the understanding from one object to another. Now necessity, in both these senses (which, indeed, are at bottom the same), has universally, though tacitly, in the schools, in the pulpit, and in common life, been allowed to belong to the will of man; and no one has ever pretended to deny that we can draw inferences concerning human actions, and that those inferences are founded on the experienced union of like actions, with like motives, inclinations, and circumstances. The only particular in which anyone can differ, is, that either, perhaps, he will refuse to give the name of necessity to this property of human actions: but as long as the meaning is understood, I hope the word can do no harm; or that he will maintain it possible to discover something farther in the operations of matter. But this, it must be acknowledged, can be of no consequence to morality or religion, whatever it may be to natural philosophy or metaphysics. We may here be mistaken in asserting that there is no idea of any other necessity or connection in the actions of body; but surely we ascribe nothing to the actions of the mind, but what everyone does, and must readily allow of. We change no circumstance in the received orthodox system with regard to the will, but only in that with regard to material objects and causes. Nothing, therefore, can be more innocent, at least, than this doctrine.

All laws being founded on rewards and punishments, it is supposed as a fundamental principle, that these motives have a regular and uniform influence on the mind, and both produce the good and prevent the evil actions. We may give to this influence what name we please; but, as it is usually conjoined with the action, it must be esteemed a *cause,* and be looked upon as an instance of that necessity, which we would here establish. 13

> 13 Necessity is also required to make sense of the practice of rewarding or punishing people, which assumes that such things will influence their behavior (and that of others) in a regular way.

The only proper object of hatred or vengeance is a person or creature, endowed with thought and consciousness; and when any criminal or injurious actions excite that passion, it is only by their relation to the person, or connection with him. Actions are, by their very nature, temporary and perishing; and where they proceed not from some *cause* in the character and disposition of the person who performed them, they can neither redound to his honor, if good; nor infamy, if evil. The actions themselves may be blamable; they may be contrary to all the rules of morality and religion. But the person is not answerable for them; and as they proceeded from nothing in him that is durable and constant, and leave nothing of that nature behind them, it is impossible he can, upon their account, become the object of punishment or vengeance. According to the principle, therefore, which denies necessity, and consequently causes, a man is as pure and untainted, after having committed the most horrid crime, as at the first moment of his birth, nor is his character anywise concerned in his actions, since they are not derived from it, and the wickedness of the one can never be used as a proof of the depravity of the other.

Men are not blamed for such actions as they perform ignorantly and casually, whatever may be the consequences. Why? but because the principles of these actions are only momentary, and terminate in them alone. Men are less blamed for such actions as they perform hastily and unpremeditatedly than for such as proceed from deliberation. For what reason? but because a hasty temper, though a constant cause or principle in the mind, operates only by intervals, and infects not the whole character. Again, repentance wipes off every crime, if attended with a reformation of life and manners. How is this to be accounted for? but by asserting that actions render a person criminal merely as they are proofs of criminal principles in the mind; and when, by an alteration of these principles, they cease to be just proofs, they likewise cease to be criminal. But, except upon the doctrine of necessity, they never were just proofs, and consequently never were criminal. 14

> 14 And blaming or punishing someone for an action only makes sense if the action flows in a regular way from the person's character, thus again presupposing causal necessity.

It will be equally easy to prove, and from the same arguments, that *liberty,* according to that definition above mentioned, in which all men agree, is also essential to morality, and that no human actions, where it is wanting, are susceptible of any moral qualities, or can be the objects either of approbation or dislike. For as actions are objects of our moral sentiment, so far only as they are indications of the internal character, passions, and affections; it is impossible that they can give rise either to praise or blame, where they proceed not from these principles, but are derived altogether from external violence. 15

> 15 Thus liberty in the compatibilist sense is essential to any sort of moral assessment of human actions.

. . .

Discussion Questions

1. Hume's view is that causal necessity, to the extent that we have any knowledge of it, amounts only to regular succession together with the tendency of the mind to infer from one of the regularly conjoined things to the other. He denies that any stronger sort of con-

nection between cause and effect is knowable. Does this seem right? Or does causality seem essentially to involve the idea that one event *makes* the other happen? Assess Hume's view on this point by thinking about a range of examples.

2. In the long footnote on page 478, Hume recognizes that in an actual situation of action, one's choice does not *seem* to be determined, but instead two or more options *seem* to be genuinely open. This sort of experience provides the basic argument for the existence of freedom in the libertarian sense that is incompatible with determinism. Is Hume right to reject it as an illusion? How should one decide this difficult issue?

3. Hume denies that chance or randomness genuinely exists. Suppose that he is mistaken about this (as the results of quantum mechanics seem to show). Would it then be plausible to identify a free action with one that results from chance? Does Hume's discussion suggest any further objections to such a view?

W. T. Stace

Walter Terence Stace (1886–1967) was an English philosopher who served in the British Civil Service in Ceylon and later taught at Princeton. Stace was an **empiricist** (see Chapter 3) and a **utilitarian** (see Chapter 6), but he also tried to make room in his philosophy for religious experience. In this selection, he defends a compatibilist (soft determinist) position, according to which freedom is not incompatible with causal determinism, but instead requires that an action be determined in the right way: by the person's own psychological states, rather than by something outside the person. His view is in many respects quite close to Hume's, though with many more examples and further arguments.

A Compatibilist Account of Free Will, from *Religion and the Modern Mind*

... I shall first discuss the problem of free will, for it is certain that if there is no free will there can be no morality. Morality is concerned with what men ought and ought not to do. But if a man has no freedom to choose what he will do, if whatever he does is done under compulsion, then it does not make sense to tell him that he ought not to have done what he did and that he ought to do something different. All moral precepts would in such case be meaningless. Also if he acts always under compulsion, how can he be held morally responsible for his actions? How can he, for example, be punished for what he could not help doing?

It is to be observed that those learned professors of philosophy or psychology who deny the existence of free will do so only in their professional moments and in their studies and lecture rooms. For when it comes to doing anything practical, even of the most trivial kind, they invariably behave as if they and others were free. They inquire from you at dinner whether you will choose this dish or that dish. They will ask a child why he told a lie, and will punish him for not having chosen the way of truthfulness. All of which is inconsistent with a disbelief in free will. This should cause us to suspect that the problem is not a real one; and this, I believe, is the case. The dispute is merely verbal, and is

From Religion and the Modern Mind *(Philadephia: Lippincott, 1952).*

due to nothing but a confusion about the meanings of words. It is what is now fashionably called a semantic problem.①

① Like Hume, Stace regards the free will problem as fundamentally arising from semantic confusion.

How does a verbal dispute arise? Let us consider a case which, although it is absurd in the sense that no one would ever make the mistake which is involved in it, yet illustrates the principle which we shall have to use in the solution of the problem. Suppose that someone believed that the word "man" means a certain sort of five-legged animal; in short that "five-legged animal" is the correct *definition* of man. He might then look around the world, and rightly observing that there are no five-legged animals in it, he might proceed to deny the existence of men. This preposterous conclusion would have been reached because he was using an incorrect definition of "man." All you would have to do to show him his mistake would be to give him the correct definition; or at least to show him that his definition was wrong. Both the problem and its solution would, of course, be entirely verbal. The problem of free will, and its solution, I shall maintain, is verbal in exactly the same way. The problem has been created by the fact that learned men, especially philosophers, have assumed an incorrect definition of free will, and then finding that there is nothing in the world which answers to their definition, have denied its existence. As far as logic is concerned, their conclusion is just as absurd as that of the man who denies the existence of men. The only difference is that the mistake in the latter case is obvious and crude, while the mistake which the deniers of free will have made is rather subtle and difficult to detect.

Throughout the modern period, until quite recently, it was assumed, both by the philosophers who denied free will and by those who defended it, that *determinism is inconsistent with free will.* If a man's actions were wholly determined by chains of causes stretching back into the remote past, so that they could be predicted beforehand by a mind which knew all the causes, it was assumed that they could not in that case be free.② This implies that a certain definition of actions done from free will was assumed, namely that they are actions *not* wholly determined by causes or predictable beforehand. Let us shorten this by saying that free will was defined as meaning inde-

terminism.③ This is the incorrect definition which has led to the denial of free will. As soon as we see what the true definition is we shall find that the question whether the world is deterministic, as Newtonian science implied, or in a measure indeterministic, as current physics teaches, is wholly irrelevant to the problem.④

Of course there is a sense in which one can define a word arbitrarily in any way one pleases. But a definition may nevertheless be called correct or incorrect. It is correct if it accords with a *common usage* of the word defined. It is incorrect if it does not. And if you give an incorrect definition, absurd and untrue results are likely to follow. For instance, there is nothing to prevent you from arbitrarily defining a man as a five-legged animal, but this is incorrect in the sense that it does not accord with the ordinary meaning of the word. Also it has the absurd result of leading to a denial of the existence of men. This shows that *common usage is the criterion for deciding whether a definition is correct or not.* And this is the principle which I shall apply to free will. I shall show that indeterminism is not what is meant by the phrase "free will" *as it is commonly used.* And I shall attempt to discover the correct definition by inquiring how the phrase is used in ordinary conversation.

Here are a few samples of how the phrase might be used in ordinary conversation. It will be noticed that they include cases in which the question whether a man acted with free will is asked in order to deter-

② Here is the basic reason why causal determinism seems to rule out free will: because it means that a person's actions are determined (and thus compelled) by causal antecedents (heredity and environment and ultimately whatever caused those) in a way that leaves him no real choice. Stace will reject this view.

③ This is too fast: to say that freedom is incompatible with determinism does not require saying that freedom just means indeterminism. Just as the compatibilist will say that freedom is *one sort* of determinism (an action being determined in one way rather than others), so a *libertarian* (who claims that freedom and determinism are incompatible and that freedom exists) can say that freedom is *one* sort of indeterminism.

④ A compatibilist need not insist that everything is determined and so need not deny that there are purely random events. (He will, however, deny that free actions are random events.)

mine whether he was morally and legally responsible for his acts.

Jones: I once went without food for a week.
Smith: Did you do that of your own free will?
Jones: No. I did it because I was lost in a desert and could find no food.

But suppose that the man who had fasted was Mahatma Gandhi. The conversation might then have gone:

Gandhi: I once fasted for a week.
Smith: Did you do that of your own free will?
Gandhi: Yes. I did it because I wanted to compel the British Government to give India its independence.

Take another case. Suppose that I had stolen some bread, but that I was as truthful as George Washington. Then, if I were charged with the crime in court, some exchange of the following sort might take place:

Judge: Did you steal the bread of your own free will?
Stace: Yes. I stole it because I was hungry.

Or in different circumstances the conversation might run:

Judge: Did you steal of your own free will?
Stace: No. I stole because my employer threatened to beat me if I did not.

At a recent murder trial in Trenton some of the accused had signed confessions, but afterwards asserted that they had done so under police duress. The following exchange might have occurred:

Judge: Did you sign this confession of your own free will?
Prisoner: No. I signed it because the police beat me up.

Now suppose that a philosopher had been a member of the jury. We could imagine this conversation taking place in the jury room.

Foreman of the Jury: The prisoner says he signed the confession because he was beaten, and not of his own free will.
Philosopher: This is quite irrelevant to the case. There is no such thing as free will.
Foreman: Do you mean to say that it makes no difference whether he signed because his conscience made him want to tell the truth or because he was beaten?

Philosopher: None at all. Whether he was caused to sign by a beating or by some desire of his own—the desire to tell the truth, for example—in either case his signing was causally determined, and therefore in neither case did he act of his own free will. Since there is no such thing as free will, the question whether he signed of his own free will ought not to be discussed by us.⑤

> **⑤** Someone like the "philosopher," who denies the existence of freedom, could still admit that the absence of freedom is clearer and more obvious in a case of external compulsion, like the one where the prisoner is forced to sign the confession.

The foreman and the rest of the jury would rightly conclude that the philosopher must be making some mistake. What sort of a mistake could it be? There is only one possible answer. The philosopher must be using the phrase "free will" in some peculiar way of his own which is not the way in which men usually use it when they wish to determine a question of moral responsibility. That is, he must be using an incorrect definition of it as implying action not determined by causes.⑥

> **⑥** The "philosopher" would of course deny that he was using an incorrect definition and would claim instead that people who say the uncoerced signing is free simply do not realize that it too was determined by antecedent causes.

Suppose a man left his office at noon, and were questioned about it. Then we might hear this:

Jones: Did you go out of your own free will?
Smith: Yes. I went out to get my lunch.

But we might hear:

Jones: Did you leave your office of your own free will?
Smith: No. I was forcibly removed by the police.

We have now collected a number of cases of actions which, in the ordinary usage of the English language, would be called cases in which people have acted of their own free will. We should also say in all these cases that they *chose* to act as they did. We should also say that they could have acted otherwise, if they had chosen. For instance, Mahatma Gandhi was not compelled to fast; he chose to do so. He could have eaten if he had wanted to. When Smith went out to get his lunch, he chose to do so. He could have stayed and done some more work, if he had wanted to.⑦ We have also collected a number of cases of the opposite kind. They are cases in which men were not able to exercise their free will. They had no choice. They were compelled to do as they did. The man in the desert did not fast of his own free will. He had no choice in the matter. He was compelled to fast because there was nothing for him to eat. And so with the other cases. It ought to be quite easy, by an inspection of these cases, to tell what we ordinarily mean when we say that a man did or did not exercise free will. We ought therefore to be able to extract from them the proper definition of the term. Let us put the cases in a table:

Free Acts	*Unfree Acts*
Gandhi fasting because he wanted to free India.	The man fasting in the desert because there was no food.
Stealing bread because one is hungry.	Stealing because one's employer threatened to beat one.
Signing a confession because one wanted to tell the truth.	Signing because the police beat one.
Leaving the office because one wanted one's lunch.	Leaving because forcibly removed.

It is obvious that to find the correct definition of free acts we must discover what characteristic is common to all the acts in the left-hand column, and is, at the same time, absent from all the acts in the right-hand column. This characteristic which all free acts have, and which no unfree acts have, will be the defining characteristic of free will.

Is being uncaused, or not being determined by causes, the characteristic of which we are in search? It

cannot be, because although it is true that all the acts in the right-hand column have causes, such as the beating by the police or the absence of food in the desert, so also do the acts in the left-hand column. Mr. Gandhi's fasting was caused by his desire to free India, the man leaving his office by his hunger, and so on. Moreover there is no reason to doubt that these causes of the free acts were in turn caused by prior conditions, and that these were again the results of causes, and so on back indefinitely into the past.⑧ Any physiologist can tell us the causes of hunger. What caused Mr. Gandhi's tremendously powerful desire to free India is no doubt more difficult to discover. But it must have had causes. Some of them may have lain in peculiarities of his glands or brain, others in his past experiences, others in his heredity, others in his education.⑨ Defenders of free will have usually tended to deny such facts. But to do so is plainly a case of special pleading, which is unsupported by any scrap of evidence. The only reasonable view is that all human actions, both those which are freely done and those which are not, are either wholly determined by causes, or at least as much determined as other events in nature. It may be true, as the physicists tell us, that nature is not as deterministic as was once thought. But whatever degree of determinism prevails in the world, human actions appear to be as much determined as anything else. And if this is so, it cannot be the case that what distinguishes actions freely chosen from those which are not free is that the latter are determined by causes while the former are not. Therefore, being uncaused or being undetermined by causes, must be an incorrect definition of free will.

What, then, is the difference between acts which are freely done and those which are not? What is the characteristic which is present to all the acts in the left-hand column and absent from all those in the right-hand column? Is it not obvious that, although

---

⑦ The compatibilist will say that a person whose action is caused by his own psychological states (which are in turn determined by antecedent causes stretching back into the past) still *could have done otherwise* in the sense that *if* the person had wanted to do something else (that is, if his psychological states had been different—which they could not have been, given the antecedent causes), he would have done that something else.

⑧ Stace is asserting that it is obvious that the actions we regard as free are just as causally determined as the ones we regard as unfree, so that determinism or lack of determinism does not mark the difference between them. Is the truth of determinism in the cases regarded as free as obvious as he thinks?

⑨ That Gandhi's actions were at least *influenced* by prior causes seems extremely plausible. Is it as obvious that they were *entirely* determined by such causes?

both sets of actions have causes, the causes of those in the left-hand column are *of a different kind* from the causes of those in the right-hand column? The free acts are all caused by desires, or motives, or by some sort of internal psychological states of the agent's mind. The unfree acts, on the other hand, are all caused by physical forces or physical conditions, outside the agent. Police arrest means physical force exerted from the outside; the absence of food in the desert is a physical condition of the outside world. We may therefore frame the following rough definitions. *Acts freely done are those whose immediate causes are psychological states in the agent. Acts not freely done are those whose immediate causes are states of affairs external to the agent.* [10]

> [10] Here is an explicit formulation of Stace's version of compatibilism. Some compatibilists would add a second requirement for freedom: that the acts not be externally *constrained* by something like a threat (which would be compatible with Stace's first requirement, since a threat operates by affecting the psychological states of the agent).

It is plain that if we define free will in this way, then free will certainly exists, and the philosopher's denial of its existence is seen to be what it is—nonsense. For it is obvious that all those actions of men which we should ordinarily attribute to the exercise of their free will, or of which we should say that they freely chose to do them, are in fact actions which have been caused by their own desires, wishes, thoughts, emotions, impulses, or other psychological states.

In applying our definition we shall find that it usually works well, but that there are some puzzling cases which it does not seem exactly to fit. These puzzles can always be solved by paying careful attention to the ways in which words are used, and remembering that they are not always used consistently. I have space for only one example. Suppose that a thug threatens to shoot you unless you give him your wallet, and suppose that you do so. Do you, in giving him your wallet, do so of your own free will or not? If we apply our definition, we find that you acted freely, since the immediate cause of the action was not an actual outside force but the fear of death, which is a psychological cause. Most people, however, would say that you did not act of your own free will but under compulsion. Does this show that our definition is wrong? I do not think so. Aristotle, who gave a solution of the problem of free will substantially the same as ours (though he did not use the term "free will") admitted that there are what he called "mixed" or borderline cases in which it is difficult to know whether we ought to call the acts free or compelled. In the case under discussion, though no actual force was used, the gun at your forehead so nearly approximated to actual force that we tend to say the case was one of compulsion. It is a borderline case. [11]

> [11] Some compatibilists would say that such an action is clearly not free to any meaningful extent because it is externally constrained. (But the person does still have some small latitude within which his choice determines the result: he can hand over the wallet or he can refuse—and be shot if the robber is serious.)

Here is what may seem like another kind of puzzle. According to our view an action may be free though it could have been predicted beforehand with certainty. But suppose you told a lie, and it was certain beforehand that you would tell it. How could one then say, "You could have told the truth"? The answer is that it is perfectly true that you could have told the truth *if you had wanted to*. In fact you would have done so, for in that case the causes producing your action, namely your desires, would have been different, and would therefore have produced different effects. It is a delusion that predictability and free will are incompatible. This agrees with common sense. For if, knowing your character, I predict that you will act honorably, no one would say when you do act honorably, that this shows you did not do so of your own free will. [12]

> [12] Stace reiterates the sense in which the person could have done otherwise, and makes the point that this sort of predictability is not ordinarily taken to rule out freedom. (Does it matter how *surely* and *exactly* predictable the action is?)

Since free will is a condition of moral responsibility, we must be sure that our theory of free will gives a sufficient basis for it. To be held morally responsible for one's actions means that one may be justly punished or rewarded, blamed or praised, for them. But it is not just to punish a man for what he cannot help doing. How can it be just to punish him for an action which it was certain beforehand that he would do? We have not attempted to decide whether, as a matter of fact, all events, including human actions, are completely determined. For that question is irrelevant to the problem of free will. But if we assume for the purposes of argument that complete determinism is true, but that we are nevertheless free, it may then be asked whether such a deterministic free will is compatible with moral responsibility. For it may seem unjust to punish a man for an action which it could have been predicted with certainty beforehand that he would do.

But that determinism is incompatible with moral responsibility is as much a delusion as that it is incompatible with free will. You do not excuse a man for doing a wrong act because, knowing his character, you felt certain beforehand that he would do it. Nor do you deprive a man of a reward or prize because, knowing his goodness or his capabilities, you felt certain beforehand that he would win it.

Volumes have been written on the justification of punishment. But so far as it affects the question of free will, the essential principles involved are quite simple. The punishment of a man for doing a wrong act is justified, either on the ground that it will correct his own character, or that it will deter other people from doing similar acts. [13] The instrument of punishment has been in the past, and no doubt still is, often unwisely used; so that it may often have done more harm than good. But that is not relevant to our present problem. Punishment, if and when it is justified, is justified only on one or both of the grounds just mentioned. The question then is how, if we assume determinism, punishment can correct character or deter people from evil actions.

> [13] This is a **utilitarian** justification for punishment: punishment is justified because it leads to better overall consequences than any of the alternatives.

Suppose that your child develops a habit of telling lies. You give him a mild beating. Why? Because you believe that his personality is such that the usual motives for telling the truth do not cause him to do so. You therefore supply the missing cause, or motive, in the shape of pain and the fear of future pain if he repeats his untruthful behavior. And you hope that a few treatments of this kind will condition him to the habit of truthtelling, so that he will come to tell the truth without the infliction of pain. You assume that his actions are determined by causes, but that the usual causes of truth-telling do not in him produce their usual effects. You therefore supply him with an artificially injected motive, pain and fear, which you think will in the future cause him to speak truthfully.

The principle is exactly the same where you hope, by punishing one man, to deter others from wrong actions. You believe that the fear of punishment will cause those who might otherwise do evil to do well.

We act on the same principle with non-human, and even with inanimate, things, if they do not behave in the way we think they ought to behave. The rose bushes in the garden produce only small and poor blooms, whereas we want large and rich ones. We supply a cause which will produce large blooms, namely fertilizer. Our automobile does not go properly. We supply a cause which will make it go better, namely oil in the works. The punishment for the man, the fertilizer for the plant, and the oil for the car, are all justified by the same principle and in the same way. The only difference is that different kinds of things require different kinds of causes to make them do what they should. Pain may be the appropriate remedy to apply, in certain cases, to human beings, and oil to the machine. It is, of course, of no use to inject motor oil into the boy or to beat the machine. [14]

> [14] Think carefully about this comparison: does treating people in a certain way require only the same sort of justification that is required for doing various things to plants or machines?

Thus we see that moral responsibility is not only consistent with determinism, but requires it. The assumption on which punishment is based is that human behavior is causally determined. If pain could not be a cause of truth-telling there would be no justification at all for punishing lies. If human actions and volitions were uncaused, it would be useless either to punish or reward, or indeed to do anything else to correct people's bad behavior. For nothing that you could do would in any way influence them. Thus moral responsibility would entirely disappear. If there were no determinism of human beings at all, their actions would be completely unpredictable and capricious, and therefore irresponsible. And this is in itself a strong argument against the common view of philosophers that free will means being undetermined by causes. [15]

> [15] Stace is assuming that the only alternative to a determinist account of free human actions is one according to which such actions are random in character.

. . .

Discussion Questions

1. Think carefully about the compatibilist account of the sense in which a person "could have done otherwise," applying it to some examples, and getting clear about how it is compatible with causal determinism. Is being able to do otherwise in this sense enough for freedom in the sense required for moral responsibility?

2. Is the person who hands over his wallet because another person has a gun to his head free in a meaningful sense? Could he have done otherwise? Should a compatibilist add the requirement that an action not be externally constrained? What should be said about different degrees of constraint?

3. Think about Blatchford's examples and the case of Robert Harris. What would Stace say about such cases? Do you think he is right?

4. Compare Stace's overall position with Blatchford's. They actually agree on quite a lot. What do they agree about? Where exactly are their points of disagreement, and who is right?

5. How successful is Stace's argument that his conception of free will makes sense of the assumption that free will is a condition of moral responsibility? His argument depends on showing that his view of free will can justify punishment. Is Stace's utilitarian justification for punishment enough to show that punishment is *morally* (as opposed to practically) justified?

Paul Edwards

Paul Edwards (1923–) is an American philosopher who taught previously at Columbia University and teaches currently at the New School for Social Research. Though perhaps best known as the editor-in-chief of the Macmillan *Encyclopedia of Philosophy* (1967), Edwards wrote widely on topics in the philosophy of religion, metaphysics, and ethics. In the following selection, he criticizes soft determinist or compatibilist views on the grounds that their account of freedom evades the deepest problems about free will and does not provide an acceptable basis for moral responsibility. His conclusion is that hard determinism is the correct position.

Hard and Soft Determinism

In his essay "The Dilemma of Determinism," William James makes a distinction that will serve as a point of departure for my remarks. He there distinguishes between the philosophers he calls "hard" determinists and those he labels "soft" determinists. The former, the hard determinists, James tells us, "did not shrink from such words as fatality, bondage of the will, necessitation and the like." He quotes a famous stanza from Omar Khayyám as representing this kind of determinism:

With earth's first clay they did the last man knead,
And there of the last harvest sowed the seed.
And the first morning of creation wrote
What the last dawn of reckoning shall read.

Another of Omar's verses expresses perhaps even better the kind of theory that James has here in mind:

Tis all a checker-board of nights and days,
Where destiny with men for pieces plays;
Thither and thither moves, and metes, and slays,
And one by one back to the closet lays.

James mentioned no names other than Omar Khayyám. But there is little doubt that among the

---

From Determinism and Freedom, *edited by Sidney Hook (New York: Collier Books, 1961).*

hard determinists he would have included Jonathan Edwards, Anthony Collins, Holbach, Priestley, Robert Owen, Schopenhauer, Freud, and also, if he had come a little earlier, Clarence Darrow.①

① And Robert Blatchford.

James of course rejected both hard and soft determinism, but for hard determinism he had a certain respect: the kind of respect one sometimes has for an honest, straightforward adversary. For soft determinism, on the other hand, he had nothing but contempt, calling it a "quagmire of evasion." "Nowadays," he writes, "we have a *soft* determinism which abhors harsh words, and repudiating fatality, necessity, and even predetermination, says that its real name is 'freedom.' " . . .

The theory James calls soft determinism, especially the Hume-Mill-Schlick variety of it, has been extremely fashionable during the last twenty-five years, while hardly anybody can be found today who has anything good to say for hard determinism.② In opposition to this contemporary trend, I should like to strike a blow on behalf of hard determinism in my talk today. I shall also try to bring out exactly what is really at issue between hard and soft determinism. I think the nature of this dispute has frequently been misconceived chiefly because many writers, including James, have a very inaccurate notion of what is maintained by actual hard determinists, as distinct from the bogey men they set up in order to score an easy victory.

② Soft determinism is also the view advocated by Stace.

To begin with, it is necessary to spell more fully the main contentions of the soft determinists. Since it is the dominant form of soft determinism at the present time, I shall confine myself to the Hume-Mill-Schlick theory. According to this theory there is in the first place no contradiction whatsoever between determinism and the proposition that human beings are sometimes free agents. When we call an action "free" we never in any ordinary situation mean that it was uncaused; and this emphatically includes the kind of action about which we pass moral judgments. By calling an action "free" we mean that the agent was not compelled or constained to perform it. Sometimes people act in a certain way because of threats or because they have been drugged or because of a posthypnotic suggestion or because of an irrational overpowering urge such as the one that makes a kleptomaniac steal something he does not really need. On such occasions human beings are not free agents.③ But on other occasions they act in certain ways because of their own rational desires, because of their own unimpeded efforts, because they have chosen to act in these ways. On these occasions they are free agents although their actions are just as much caused as actions that are not deemed free. In distinguishing between free and unfree actions we do not try to mark the presence and absence of causes but attempt to indicate the *kind* of causes that are present.

③ Edwards is here reporting the soft determinist view. But it is fairly clear that according to both Hume and Stace, the kleptomaniac acts freely (because his action is determined by his own psychological states or by his will). What would these two soft determinists say about these other cases?

Secondly there is no antithesis between determinism and moral responsibility. When we judge a person morally responsible for a certain action, we do indeed presuppose that he was a free agent at the time of the action. But the freedom presupposed is not the contracausal freedom about which indeterminists go into such ecstatic raptures.④ It is nothing more than the freedom already mentioned—the ability to act according to one's choices or desires. Since determinism is compatible with freedom in this sense, it is also compatible with moral responsibility. In other words, the world is after all wonderful: we can be determinists and yet go on punishing our enemies and our children, and we can go on blaming ourselves, all without a bad intellectual conscience.

④ That is, it is neither randomness nor some third alternative to determinism and randomness of the sort advocated by libertarians.

Mill, who was probably the greatest moralizer among the soft determinists, recognized with particular satisfaction the influence or alleged influence of one class of human desires. Not only, for example, does such lowly desire as my desire to get a new car influence my conduct. It is equally true, or so at least Mill believed, that my desire to become a more virtuous person does on occasion influence my actions. By suitable training and efforts my desire to change my character may in fact bring about the desired changes. If Mill were alive today he might point to contemporary psychiatry as an illustration of his point. Let us suppose that I have an intense desire to become famous, but that I also have an intense desire to become a happier and more lovable person who, among other things, does not greatly care about fame. Let us suppose, furthermore, that I know of a therapy that can transform fame-seeking and unlovable into lovable and fame-indifferent character structures. If, now, I have enough money, energy, and courage, and if a few other conditions are fulfilled, my desire may actually lead to a major change in my character. Since we can, therefore, at least to some extent, form our own character, determinism according to Mill is compatible not only with judgments of moral responsibility about this or that particular *action* flowing from an unimpeded desire, but also, within limits, with moral judgments about the *character* of human beings. ⑤

⑤ But of course whether or not I satisfy the conditions for being able to do this is itself determined.

I think that several of Mill's observations were well worth making and that James's verdict on his theory as a "quagmire of evasion" is far too derogatory. I think hard determinists have occasionally written in such a way as to suggest that they deny the causal efficacy of human desires and efforts. Thus Holbach wrote:

You will say that I feel free. This is an illusion, which may be compared to that of the fly in the fable, who, lighting upon the pole of a heavy carriage, applauded himself for directing its course. Man, who thinks himself free, is a fly who imagines he has power to move the universe, while he is himself unknowingly carried along by it.

There is also the following passage in Schopenhauer:

Every man, being what he is and placed in the circumstances which for the moment obtain, but which on their part also arise by strict necessity, can absolutely never do anything else than just what at that moment he does do. Accordingly, the whole course of a man's life, in all its incidents great and small, is as necessarily predetermined as the course of a clock. ⑥

⑥ Read these passages carefully. Is either Holbach or Schopenhauer denying in any clear way the "causal efficacy of human desires and efforts"—as opposed to just saying that these too are determined?

. . .

Furthermore there can be little doubt that Hume and Mill and Schlick were a great deal clearer about the relation between motives and actions than the hard determinists. . . .

But when all is said and done, there remains a good deal of truth in James's charge that soft determinism is an evasion. For a careful reading of their works shows that none of the hard determinists really denied that human desires, efforts, and choices make a difference in the course of events. Any remarks to the contrary are at most temporary lapses. This, then, is hardly the point at issue. If it is not the point at issue, what is? Let me at this stage imagine a hard determinist replying to a champion of the Hume-Mill theory: "You are right," he would say, "in maintaining that some of our actions are caused by our desires and choices. But you do not pursue the subject far enough. You arbitrarily stop at the desires and volitions. We must not stop there. We must go on to ask where *they* come from; and if determinism is true there can be no doubt about the answer to this question. Ultimately our desires and our whole character are derived from our inherited equipment and the environmental influences to which we were subjected at the beginning of our lives. It is clear that we had no hand in shaping either of these." ⑦ A hard determinist could quote a number of eminent supporters. "Our volitions and our desires," wrote Holbach in his little book *Good Sense*, "are never in our power. You think yourself free, because you do what you will; but are you free to will or not to will; to desire or not to desire?" And Schopenhauer expressed the same thought in the following epigram: "A man can surely do what he wills to do, but he cannot determine what he wills."

⑦ This is what Blatchford would say.

Let me turn once more to the topic of character transformation by means of psychiatry to bring out this point with full force. Let us suppose that both *A* and *B* are compulsive and suffer intensely from their neuroses. Let us assume that there is a therapy that could help them, which could materially change their character structure, but that it takes a great deal of energy and courage to undertake the treatment. Let us suppose that *A* has the necessary energy and courage while *B* lacks it. *A* undergoes the therapy and changes in the desired way. *B* just gets more and more compulsive and more and more miserable. Now, it is true that *A* helped form his own later character. But his starting point, his desire to change, his energy and courage, were already there. They may or may not have been the result of previous efforts on his own part. But there must have been a first effort, and the effort at that time was the result of factors that were not of his making.

The fact that a person's character is ultimately the product of factors over which he had no control is not denied by the soft determinists, though many of them don't like to be reminded of it when they are in a moralizing mood. Since the hard determinists admit that our desires and choices do on occasion influence the course of our lives, there is thus no disagreement between the soft and the hard determinists about the empirical facts. ⑧ However, some hard determinists infer from some of these facts that human beings are never morally responsible for their actions. The soft determinists, as already stated, do not draw any such inference. In the remainder of my paper I shall try to show just what it is that hard determinists are inferring and why, in my opinion, they are justified in their conclusion.

> ⑧ Think again of Blatchford and Stace. Is there any *empirical* issue, one capable of being settled by observation or experiment, about which they differ?

I shall begin by adopting for my purposes a distinction introduced by C. A. Campbell in his extremely valuable article "Is Free Will a Pseudo-Problem?"* in which he distinguishes between two conceptions of moral responsibility. Different persons, he says, require different conditions to be fulfilled before holding human beings morally responsible for what they do. First, there is what Campbell calls the ordinary unreflective person, who is rather ignorant and who is not greatly concerned with the theories of science, philosophy, and religion. If the unreflective person is sure that the agent to be judged was acting under coercion or constraint, he will not hold him responsible. If, however, he is sure that the action was performed in accordance with the agent's unimpeded rational desire, if he is sure that the action would not have taken place but for the agent's decision, then the unreflective person will consider ascription of moral responsibility justified. The fact that the agent did not ultimately make his own character will either not occur to him, or else it will not be considered a sufficient ground for withholding a judgment of moral responsibility.

In addition to such unreflective persons, continues Campbell, there are others who have reached "a tolerably advanced level or reflection."

> Such a person will doubtless be acquainted with the claims advanced in some quarters that causal law operates universally; or/and with the theories of some philosophies that the universe is throughout the expression of a single supreme principle; or/and with the doctrines of some theologians that the world is created, sustained and governed by an Omniscient and Omnipotent Being.

Such a person will tend to require the fulfillment of a further condition before holding anybody morally responsible. He will require not only that the agent was not coerced or constrained but also—and this is taken to be an additional condition—that he "could have chosen otherwise than he actually did." ⑨ I should prefer to put this somewhat differently, but it will not affect the main conclusion drawn by Campbell, with which I agree. The reflective person, I should prefer to express it, requires not only that the agent was not coerced; he also requires that the agent *originally chose his own character*—the character that now displays itself in his choices and desires and efforts. ⑩ Campbell concludes that determinism is indeed compatible with judgments of moral responsibility in the unreflective sense, but that it is incompatible with judgments of moral responsibility in the reflective sense.

> ⑨ Soft determinists, of course, accept this requirement—see Stace, pp. 483–4. The issue between them and Campbell (see the selection later in this chapter) is what the quoted phrase means.

> ⑩ Think carefully about this condition. What would it mean to choose your own character? On what basis would you make such a choice?

Although I do not follow Campbell in rejecting determinism, I agree basically with his analysis, with one other qualification. I do not think it is a question of the different senses in which the term is used by ignorant and unreflective people, on the one hand, and by those who are interested in science, religion, and philosophy, on the other. The very same persons, whether educated or uneducated, use it in certain contexts in the one sense and in other contexts in the other. Practically all human beings, no matter how much interested they are in science, religion, and philosophy, employ what Campbell calls the unreflective conception when they are dominated by violent emotions like anger, indignation, or hate, and especially when the conduct they are judging has been personally injurious to them. On the other hand, a great many people, whether they are educated or not, will employ what Campbell calls the reflective conception when they are not consumed with hate or anger—when they are judging a situation calmly and reflectively and when the fact that the agent did not ultimately shape his own character has been vividly brought to their attention. Clarence Darrow in his celebrated pleas repeatedly appealed to the jury on precisely this ground. If any of you, he would say, had been reared in an environment like that of the accused or had to suffer from his defective heredity, *you* would now be standing in the dock. I cannot refrain at this stage from reading a poem written by the hard determinist, A. E. Housman, which Darrow recited on such occasions. Its title is "The Culprit," and it is the soliloquy of a boy about to be hanged.

> The night my father got me
>   His mind was not on me;
> He did not plague his fancy
>   To muse if I should be
>   The son you see.
>
> The day my mother bore me
>   She was a fool and glad,
> For all the pain I cost her,
>   That she had borne the lad
>   That borne she had.
>
> My mother and my father
>   Out of the light they lie;
> The warrant could not find them,
>   And here 'tis only I
>   Shall hang so high.
>
> Oh let not man remember
>   The soul that God forgot,
> But fetch the county kerchief
>   And noose me in the knot,
>   And I will rot.

> For so the game is ended
>   That should not have begun,
> My father and my mother
>   They had a likely son,
>   And I have none.*

Darrow nearly always convinced the jury that the accused could not be held morally responsible for his acts; and certainly the majority of the jurors were relatively uneducated.

I have so far merely distinguished between two concepts of moral responsibility. I now wish to go a step farther and claim that only one of them can be considered, properly speaking, a moral concept. This is not an easy point to make clear, but I can at least indicate what I mean. We do not normally consider just any positive or negative feeling a "moral" emotion. Nor do we consider just any sentence containing the words "good" or "bad" expressions of "moral" judgment. . . . A feeling or judgment must in a certain sense be "impersonal" before we consider it moral. To this I would add that it must also be independent of violent emotions. Confining myself to judgments, I would say that a judgment was "moral" only if it was formulated in a calm and reflective mood, or at least if it is supported in a calm and reflective state of mind. If this is so, it follows that what Campbell calls the reflective sense of "moral responsibility" is the only one that qualifies as a properly moral use of the term. [11]

Before I conclude I wish to avoid a certain misunderstanding of my remarks. From the fact that human beings do not ultimately shape their own character, I said, it *follows* that they are never morally responsible. I do not mean that by reminding people of the ultimate causes of their character one makes them more charitable and less vengeful. Maybe one does, but that is not what I mean. I mean "follow" or "imply" in the same sense as, or in a sense closely akin to, that in which the conclusion of a valid syllogism follows from the premises. The effectiveness of Darrow's pleas does not merely

> [11] Edwards seems to be saying that anyone who approaches the issue in a "calm and reflective state of mind" will agree that the soft determinist's account of moral responsibility is inadequate. Do you think he is right about this?

show, I am arguing, how powerfully he could sway the emotions of the jurors. His pleas also brought into the open one of the conditions the jurors, like others, con-sider necessary on reflection before they hold an agent morally responsible. . . .

Discussion Questions

1. Assuming that freedom and moral responsibility do require that a person "could have done otherwise," is the compatibilist or soft determinist account of what this means the right one? Think of examples like those listed by Edwards on page 488 (before Annotation 3). Could the people in question have done otherwise in the compatibilist sense? If so, does this show that they are free and morally responsible, or does it show that the compatibilist account of "could have done otherwise" is not the right one for genuine freedom?

2. Consider now Edwards's alternative account of "could have done otherwise" (p. 490). If this is the right account, is anyone ever free and responsible? Can you even imagine how this requirement (which others have suggested too) could be satisfied? What would it be like to choose your own character—and on what basis would you make the choice? Can you think of any case where it seems plausible that you choose at least some significant part of your own character? Did the choice in question derive from other parts or aspects of your character?

John Hospers

John Hospers (1918–) is an American philosopher who taught at Brooklyn College and the University of Southern California. He has written on a wide variety of philosophical topics, especially in aesthetics, ethics, and political philosophy. In 1972, Hospers was the newly formed Libertarian Party's first candidate for president of the United States.

In the following selection, Hospers raises doubts about the compatibilist or soft determinist position, doubts that grow out of the claims of psychoanalysis concerning unconscious motivation. According to the compatibilist view, a person is free when he performs a particular action just in those cases where the action results from his own conscious will or desires—those cases where he does what he consciously wants to do. Such a view seems initially plausible because the occasions times when a person's action results from his own conscious will or desires are exactly the occasions when it seems to him from the inside that he is genuinely controlling his own behavior. But if, as psychoanalysis claims, there are actions that *seem* from the inside to be under conscious control but are in fact caused by events that happened long ago, operating through desires that are unconscious and not known to the person in question, then the conviction that a person is controlling his own behavior at those times appears to be merely an illusion.

Though Hospers gives many examples that presuppose the truth of psychoanalysis, he offers no reasons in this article for accepting these psychoanalytic claims, claims that are in fact highly controversial at best. Nonetheless, even the *possibility* that such claims might be true seems to raise doubts as to whether the compatibilist account of freedom (which in no way rules out actions caused by unconscious desires as being free) can be correct.

What Means This Freedom?

I am in agreement to a very large extent with the conclusions of Professor Edwards' paper, and am happy in these days of "soft determinism" to hear the other view so forcefully and fearlessly stated. As a preparation for developing my own views on the subject, I want to mention a factor that I think is of enormous importance and relevance: namely, unconscious motivation. There are many actions—not those of an insane person (however the term "insane" be defined), nor of a person ignorant of the effects of his action, nor ignorant of some relevant fact about the situation, nor in any obvious way mentally deranged—for which human beings in general and the courts in particular are inclined to hold the doer responsible, and for which, I would say, he should not be held responsible. The deed may be planned, it may be carried out in cold calculation, it may spring from the agent's character and be continuous with the rest of his behavior, and it may be perfectly true that he could have done differently *if* he had wanted to; nonetheless his behavior was brought about by unconscious conflicts developed in infancy, over which he had no control and of which (without training in psychiatry) he does not even have knowledge. He may even *think* he knows why he acted as he did, he may *think* he has conscious control over his actions, he may even *think* he is fully responsible for them; but he is not.① Psychiatric casebooks provide hundreds of examples. The law and common sense, though puzzled sometimes by such cases, are gradually becoming aware that they exist; but at this early stage countless tragic blunders still occur because neither the law nor the public in general is aware of the genesis of criminal actions. The mother blames her daughter for choosing the wrong men as candidates for husbands; but though the daughter thinks she is choosing freely and spends a considerable amount of time "deciding" among them, the identification with her sick father, resulting from Oedipal fantasies in early childhood, prevents her from caring for any but sick men, twenty or thirty years older than herself. Blaming her is beside the point; she cannot help it, and she cannot change it. Countless criminal acts are thought out in great detail; yet the participants are (without their own knowledge) acting out fantasies, fears, and defenses from early childhood, over whose coming and going they have no conscious control.

Now, I am not saying that none of these persons should be in jails or asylums. Often society must be protected against them. Nor am I saying that people should cease the practices of blaming and praising, punishing and rewarding; in general these devices are justified by the results ②— although very often they have practically no effect; the deeds are done from inner compulsion, which is not lessened when the threat of punishment is great. I am only saying that frequently persons we think responsible are not properly to be called so; we mistakenly think them responsible because we assume they are like those in whom no unconscious drive (toward this type of behavior) is present, and that their behavior can be changed by reasoning, exhorting, or threatening.

---

① Hospers is saying that an action that results in this way from unconscious motivation is one that satisfies the compatibilist requirement for freedom but is nonetheless neither free nor an action for which the person is morally responsible. He gives no explicit argument. Can you formulate one on his behalf?

② This is an appeal to the utilitarian justification of punishment. See Stace.

From Determinism and Freedom, *edited by Sidney Hook (New York: Collier Books, 1961).*

I

I have said that these persons are not responsible. But what is the criterion for responsibility? Under precisely what conditions is a person to be held morally responsible for an action? . . . There are several criteria that might be suggested:

1. The first idea that comes to mind is that responsibility is determined by the presence or absence of *premeditation*—the opposite of "premeditated" being, presumably, "unthinking" or "impulsive." But this will not do—both because some acts are not premeditated but responsible, and because some are premeditated and not responsible.

Many acts we call responsible can be as unthinking or impulsive as you please. If you rush across the street to help the victim of an automobile collision, you are (at least so we would ordinarily say) acting responsibly, but you did not do so out of premeditation; you saw the accident, you didn't think, you rushed to the scene without hesitation. It was like a reflex action. ③ But you acted responsibly: unlike the knee jerk, the act was the result of past training and past thought about situations of this kind; that is why you ran to help instead of ignoring the incident or running away. When something done originally from conviction or training becomes habitual, it becomes *like* a reflex action. As Aristotle said, Virtue should become second nature through habit: a virtuous act should be performed *as if* by instinct; this, far from detracting from its moral worth, testifies to one's mastery of the desired type of behavior; one does not have to make a moral effort each time it is repeated.

> ③ Is Hospers right that in such a case there is no premeditation at all, so that the action amounts to a sheer reflex?

There are also premeditated acts for which, I would say, the person is not responsible. Premeditation, especially when it is so exaggerated as to issue in no action at all, can be the result of neurotic disturbance or what we sometimes call an emotional "block," which the person inherits from long-past situations. In Hamlet's revenge on his uncle (I use this example because it is familiar to all of us), there was no lack, but rather a surfeit, of premeditation; his actions were so exquisitely premeditated as to make Freud and Dr. Ernest Jones look more closely to find out what lay behind them. The very premeditation camouflaged unconscious motives of which Hamlet himself was not aware. I think this is an important point, since it seems that the courts often assume that premeditation is a criterion of responsibility. If failure to kill his uncle had been considered a crime, every court in the land would have convicted Hamlet. ④ Again: a woman's decision to stay with her husband in spite of endless "mental cruelty" is, if she is the victim of an unconscious masochistic "will to punishment," one for which she is not responsible; she is the victim and not the agent, no matter how profound her con-

> ④ Does this psychoanalytic interpretation of the Hamlet story seem plausible? Is there an alternative account of what is going on under which Hamlet is free and responsible? How could we decide in a nonfictional case which is correct?

viction that she is the agent; she is caught in a masochistic web (of complicated genesis) dating back to babyhood, perhaps a repetition of a comparable situation involving her own parents. . . . Again: a criminal whose crime was carefully planned step by step is usually considered responsible, but as we shall see in later examples, the overwhelming impulse toward it, stemming from an unusually humiliating ego defeat in early childhood, was as compulsive as any can be.

2. Shall we say, then, that a person is not responsible for his act unless he can *defend it with reasons?* I am afraid that this criterion is no better than the previous one. First, intellectuals are usually better at giving reasons than nonintellectuals, and according to this criterion would be more responsible than persons acting from moral conviction not implemented by reasoning; yet it is very doubtful whether we should want to say that the latter are the more responsible. Second, the giving of reasons itself may be suspect. The reasons may be rationalizations camouflaging unconscious motives of which the agent knows nothing. Hamlet gave many reasons for not doing what he felt it was his duty to do: the time was not right, his uncle's soul might go to heaven, etc. His various "reasons" contradicted one another, and if an overpowering compulsion had not been present, the highly intellectual Hamlet would not have been taken in for a moment by these rationalizations. . . . One's intelligence and reasoning power do not enable one to escape from unconsciously motivated behavior; it only gives one greater facility in rationalizing that behavior; one's intelligence is simply used in the interests of the neurosis— it is pressed into service to justify with reasons what one does quite independently of the reasons.⑤

> ⑤ How could one tell the difference between a mere rationalization and a true reason?

If these two criteria are inadequate, let us seek others.

3. Shall we say that a person is responsible for his action unless it is the *result of unconscious forces* of which he knows nothing? Many psychoanalysts would probably accept this criterion. If it is not largely reflected in the language of responsibility as ordinarily used, this may be due to ignorance of fact: most people do not know that there are such things as unconscious motives and unconscious conflicts causing human beings to act. But it may be that if they did,

⑥ How could it be decided whether unconscious forces of this sort are involved and to what extent? What do you think a compatibilist would say about such cases? Does the fact that the motivation is unconscious make any difference from a compatibilist standpoint?

perhaps they would refrain from holding persons responsible for certain actions. ⑥

I do not wish here to quarrel with this criterion of responsibility. I only want to point out the fact that if this criterion is employed a far greater number of actions will be excluded from the domain of responsibility than we might at first suppose. Whether we are neat or untidy, whether we are selfish or unselfish, whether we provoke scenes or avoid them, even whether we can exert our powers of will to change our behavior—all these may, and often do, have their source in our unconscious life.

4. Shall we say that a person is responsible for his act unless it is *compelled*? Here we are reminded of Aristotle's assertion (*Nicomachean Ethics,* Book III) that a person is responsible for his act except for reasons of either ignorance or compulsion. Ignorance is not part of our problem here (unless it is unconsciously induced ignorance of facts previously remembered and selectively forgotten—in which case the forgetting is again compulsive), but compulsion is. How will compulsion do as a criterion? The difficulty is to state just what it means. When we say an act is compelled in a psychological sense, our language is metaphorical—which is not to say that there is no point in it or that, properly interpreted, it is not true. Our actions are compelled in a literal sense if someone has us in chains or is controlling our bodily movements. When we say that the storm compelled us to jettison the cargo of the ship (Aristotle's example), we have a less literal sense of compulsion, for at least it is open to us to go down with the ship. When psychoanalysts say that a man was compelled by unconscious conflicts to wash his hands constantly, this is also not a literal use of "compel"; for nobody forced his hands under the tap. Still, it is a typical example of what psychologists call *compulsive* behavior: it has unconscious causes inaccessible to introspection, and moreover nothing can change it—it is as inevitable for him to do it as it would be if someone were forcing his hands under the tap. In this it is exactly like the action of a powerful external force; it is just as little within one's conscious control. ⑦

In its area of application this interpretation of responsibility comes to much the same as the previous one. And this area is very great indeed. For if we cannot be held responsible for the infantile situations (in which we were after all passive victims), then neither, it would seem, can we be held responsible for compulsive actions occurring in adulthood that are inevitable consequences of those infantile situations.

⑦ Many compatibilists would accept the requirement for freedom that an action not be *externally* compelled (as in the example of a person who hands over his wallet because a robber threatens him with a gun), though Hume and Stace do not do so explicitly. Is Hospers right that the compulsive hand-washer's compulsion makes his action just as unavoidable (or even more so?) and hence prevents him from being free and responsible?

And, psychiatrists and psychoanalysts tell us, actions fulfilling this description are characteristic of all people some of the time and some people most of the time. Their occurrence, once the infantile events have taken place, is inevitable, just as the explosion is inevitable once the fuse has been lighted; there is simply more "delayed action" in the psychological explosions than there is in the physical ones.

(I have not used the word "inevitable" here to mean "causally determined," for according to such a definition every event would be inevitable if one accepted the causal principle in some form or other; and probably nobody except certain philosophers uses "inevitable" in this sense. Rather, I use "inevitable" in its ordinary sense of "cannot be avoided." To the extent, therefore, that adult neurotic manifestations *can* be avoided, once the infantile patterns have become set, the assertion that they are inevitable is not true.)

5. There is still another criterion, which I prefer to the previous ones, by which a man's responsibility for an act can be measured: the degree to which that act can (or could have been) *changed by the use of reasons.* Suppose that the man who washes his hands constantly does so, he says, for hygienic reasons, believing that if he doesn't do so he will be poisoned by germs. We now convince him, on the best medical authority, that his belief is groundless. Now, the test of his responsibility is whether the changed belief will result in changed behavior. If it does not, as with the compulsive hand washer, he is not acting responsibly,

but if it does, he is. It is not the *use* of reasons, but their *efficacy in changing behavior,* that is being made the criterion of responsibility. And clearly in

> **8** Here is a way of deciding whether (and to what extent?) unconscious motives are involved. Think how this would apply in the Hamlet case.

neurotic cases no such change occurs; in fact, this is often made the defining characteristic of neurotic behavior: it is unchangeable by any rational considerations. **8**

II

I have suggested these criteria to distinguish actions for which we can call the agent responsible from those for which we cannot. Even persons with extensive knowledge of psychiatry do not, I think, use any one of these criteria to the exclusion of the others; a conjunction of two or more may be used at once. But however they may be combined or selected in actual application, I believe we can make the distinction along some such lines as we have suggested.

But is there not still another possible meaning of "responsibility" that we have not yet mentioned? Even after we have made all the above distinctions, there remains a question in our minds whether we are, in the final analysis, *responsible for any of our actions at all.* The issue may be put this way: How can anyone be responsible for his actions, since they grow out of his character, which is shaped and molded and made what it is by influences—some hereditary, but most of them stemming from early parental environment—that were not of his own making or choosing? This question, I believe, still troubles many people who would agree to all the distinctions we have just made but still have the feeling that "this isn't all." They have the uneasy suspicion that there is a more ultimate sense, a "deeper" sense, in which we are *not* responsible for our actions, since we are not responsible for the character out of which those actions spring. This, of course, is the sense Professor Edwards was describing.

Let us take as an example a criminal who, let us say, strangled several persons and is himself now condemned to die in the electric chair. Jury and public alike hold him fully responsible (at least they utter the

words "he is responsible"), for the murders were planned down to the minutest detail, and the defendant tells the jury exactly how he planned them. But now we find out how it all came about; we learn of parents who rejected him from babyhood, of the childhood spent in one foster home after another, where it was always plain to him that he was not wanted; of the constantly frustrated early desire for affection, the hard shell of nonchalance and bitterness that he assumed to cover the painful and humiliating fact of being unwanted, and his subsequent attempts to heal these wounds to his shattered ego through defensive aggression.

> The criminal is the most passive person in this world, helpless as a baby in his motorically inexpressible fury. Not only does he try to wreak revenge on the mother of the earliest period of his babyhood; his criminality is based on the inner feeling of being incapable of making the mother even feel that the child seeks revenge on her. The situation is that of a dwarf trying to annoy a giant who superciliously refuses to see these attempts. . . . Because of his inner feeling of being a dwarf, the criminotic uses, so to speak, dynamite. Of that the giant must take cognizance. True, the "revenge" harms the avenger. He may be legally executed. However, the primary inner aim of forcing the giant to acknowledge the dwarf's fury is fulfilled.*

The poor victim is not conscious of the inner forces that exact from him this ghastly toll; he battles, he schemes, he revels in pseudo-aggression, he is miserable, but he does not know what works within him to produce these catastrophic acts of crime. His aggressive actions are the wriggling of a worm on a fisherman's hook. And if this is so, it seems difficult to say any longer, "He is responsible." Rather, we shall put him behind bars for the protection of society, but we shall no longer flatter our feeling of moral superiority by calling him personally responsible for what he did. **9**

> **9** Think here of Robert Harris, whose story is pretty close to the one Hospers imagines.

Let us suppose it were established that a man commits murder only if, sometime during the previ-

---

*Edmund Bergler, *The Basic Neurosis* (New York: Grune and Stratton, 1949), p. 305.

ous week, he has eaten a certain combination of foods—say, tuna fish salad at a meal also including peas, mushroom soup, and blueberry pie. What if we were to track down the factors common to all murders committed in this country during the last twenty years and found this factor present in all of them, and only in them? The example is of course empirically absurd; but may it not be that there is *some* combination of factors that regularly leads to homicide, factors such as are described in general terms in the above quotation? (Indeed the situation in the quotation is less fortunate than in our hypothetical example, for it is easy to avoid certain foods once we have been warned about them, but the situation of the infant is thrust on him; something has already happened to him once and for all, before he knows it has happened.) When such specific factors are discovered, won't they make it clear that it is foolish and pointless, as well as immoral, to hold human beings responsible for crimes? ⑩ . . .

(10) What should we say or think if such a discovery were made? Would it show clearly that none of the apparent murderers was really responsible?

When we know such things as these, we no longer feel so much tempted to say that the criminal is responsible for his crime; and we tend also (do we not?) to excuse him—not legally (we still confine him to prison) but morally; we no longer call him a monster or hold him personally responsible for what he did. Moreover, we do this in general, not merely in the case of crime: "You must excuse Grandmother for being irritable; she's really quite ill and is suffering some pain all the time." Or: "The dog always bites children after she's had a litter of pups; you can't blame her for it: she's not feeling well, and besides she naturally wants to defend them." Or: "She's nervous and jumpy, but do excuse her: she has a severe glandular disturbance."

Let us note that the more *thoroughly* and *in detail* we know the causal factors leading a person to behave as he does, the more we tend to exempt him from responsibility. When we know nothing of the man except what we see him do, we say he is an ungrateful cad who expects much of other people and does nothing in return, and we are usually indignant. When we learn that his parents were the same way and, having no guilt feelings about this mode of be-

havior themselves, brought him up to be greedy and avaricious, we see that we could hardly expect him to have developed moral feelings in this direction. When we learn, in addition, that he is not aware of being ungrateful or selfish, but unconsciously represses the memory of events unfavorable to himself, we feel that the situation is unfortunate but "not really his fault." When we know that this behavior of his, which makes others angry, occurs more constantly when he feels tense or insecure, and that he now feels tense and insecure, and that relief from pressure will diminish it, then we tend to "feel sorry for the poor guy" and say he's more to be pitied than censured. We no longer want to say that he is personally responsible; we might rather blame nature or his parents for having given him an unfortunate constitution or temperament. ⑪

(11) Hospers's suggestion is that a compatibilist view of freedom and responsibility is plausible only when the relevant causes are not known "thoroughly and in detail." Is he right about this? Is it true even if the causes are not unconscious motivations?

. . .

"But," a critic complains, "it's immoral to exonerate people indiscriminately in this way. I might have thought it fit to excuse somebody because he was born on the other side of the tracks, if I didn't know so many bank presidents who were also born on the other side of the tracks." Now, I submit that the most immoral thing in this situation is the critic's caricature of the conditions of the excuse. Nobody is excused merely because he was born on the other side of the tracks. But if he was born on the other side of the tracks *and* was a highly narcissistic infant to begin with *and* was repudiated or neglected by his parents *and* . . . (here we list a finite number of conditions), and if this complex of factors is *regularly* followed by certain behavior traits in adulthood, and moreover *unavoidably* so—that is, they occur no matter what he or anyone else tries to do—then we excuse him morally and say he is not responsible for his deed. If he is not responsible for *A*, a series of events occurring in his babyhood, then neither is he responsible for *B*, a series of things he does in adulthood, provided that *B* inevitably—that is, unavoidably—follows upon the occurrence of *A.* And according to psychiatrists and psychoanalysts, this often happens. [12]

But one may still object that so far we have talked only about neurotic behavior. Isn't nonneurotic or normal or not unconsciously motivated (or whatever you want to call it) behavior still within the area of responsibility? There are reasons for answering "No" even here, for the normal person no more than the neurotic one has caused his own character, which makes him what he is. Granted that neurotics are not responsible for their behavior (that part of it which we call neurotic) because it stems from undigested infantile conflicts that they had no part in bringing about, and that are external to them just as surely as if their behavior had been forced on them by a malevolent deity; . . . but the so-called normal person is equally the product of causes in which his volition took no part. And if, unlike the neurotic's, his behavior is changeable by rational considerations, and if he has the will power to overcome the effects of an unfortunate early environment, this again is no credit to him; he is just lucky. If energy is available to him in a form in which it can be mobilized for constructive purposes, this is no credit to him, for this too is part of his psychic legacy. Those of us who can discipline ourselves and develop habits of concentration of purpose tend to blame those who cannot, and call them lazy and weak-willed; but what we fail to see is that they literally *cannot* do what we expect; if their psyches were structured like ours, they could, but as they are burdened with a tyrannical super-ego (to use psychoanalytic jargon for the moment), and a weak defenseless ego whose energies are constantly consumed in fighting endless charges of the super-ego, they simply cannot do it, and it is irrational to expect it of them. We cannot with justification blame them for their inability, any more than we can congratulate ourselves for our ability. This lesson is hard to learn, for we constantly and naïvely assume that other people are constructed as we ourselves are.

[12] The crucial claim here is that the behavior is unavoidable "no matter what he . . . tries to do." Does this mean that he wills or desires to do something else, but still can't help doing the thing in question—in which case, the action doesn't seem to satisfy the compatibilist requirements for freedom and responsibility, and so isn't a problem for the compatibilist? Is there some other way of understanding what Hospers is saying here?

For example: A child raised under slum conditions, whose parents are socially ambitious and envy families with money, but who nevertheless squander the little they have on drink, may simply be unable in later life to mobilize a drive sufficient to overcome these early conditions. Common sense would expect that he would develop the virtue of thrift; he would make quite sure that he would never again endure the grinding poverty he had experienced as a child. But in fact it is not so: the exact conditions are too complex to be specified in detail here, but when certain conditions are fulfilled (concerning the subject's early life), he will always thereafter be a spendthrift, and no rational considerations will be able to change this. He will listen to the rational considerations and see the force of these, but they will not be able to change him, even if he tries; he cannot change his wasteful habits any more than he can lift the Empire State Building with his bare hands. We moralize and plead with him to be thrifty, but we do not see how strong, how utterly overpowering, and how constantly with him, is the opposite drive, which is so easily manageable with us. But he is possessed by the all-consuming, all-encompassing urge to make the world see that he belongs, that he has arrived, that he is just as well off as anyone else, that the awful humiliations were not real, that they never actually occurred, for isn't he now able to spend and spend? The humiliation must be blotted out; and conspicuous, fleshy, expensive, and wasteful buying will do this; it shows the world what the world must know! True, it is only for the moment; true, it is in the end self-defeating, for wasteful consumption is the best way to bring poverty back again; but the person with an overpowering drive to mend a lesion to his narcissism cannot resist the avalanche of that drive with his puny rational consideration. A man with his back against the wall and a gun at his throat doesn't think of what may happen ten years hence. (Consciously, of course, he knows nothing of this drive; all that appears to consciousness is its shattering effects; he knows only that he must keep on spending—not why—and that he is unable to resist.) He hasn't in him the psychic capacity, the energy to stem the tide of a drive that at that moment is all-powerful. We, seated comfortably away from this flood, sit in judgment on him and blame him and exhort him and criticize him; but he, carried along by the flood, cannot do otherwise than he does. He may fight with all the strength of which he is capable, but it is not enough. And we, who are rational enough at least to exonerate a man in a situation of "overpowering impulse" when we recognize it to be one, do not even recognize this as an example of it; and so, in addition to being swept away in the flood that childhood conditions rendered inevitable, he must also endure our lectures, our criticisms, and our moral excoriation. [13]

> [13] Here Hospers's view is very close to Blatchford's (and does not depend on the idea of unconscious motivation): whether or not a person is susceptible to rational persuasion or can overcome the effects of his environment is itself determined by environment and heredity. A person who cannot do this should thus not be blamed.

But, one will say, he could have overcome his spendthrift tendencies; some people do. Quite true: some people do. They are lucky. They have it in them to overcome early deficiencies by exerting great effort, and they are capable of exerting the effort. Some of us, luckier still, can overcome them with but little effort; and a few, the luckiest, haven't the deficiencies to overcome. It's all a matter of luck. The least lucky are those who can't overcome them, even with great effort, and those who haven't the ability to exert the effort.

But, one persists, it isn't a matter simply of luck; it *is* a matter of effort. Very well then, it's a matter of effort; without exerting the effort you may not overcome the deficiency. But whether or not you are the kind of person who has it in him to exert the effort is a matter of luck.

All this is well known to psychoanalysts. They can predict, from minimal cues that most of us don't notice, whether a person is going to turn out to be lucky or not. "The analyst," they say, "must be able to use the residue of the patient's unconscious guilt so as to remove the symptom or character trait that creates the guilt. The guilt must not only be present, but *available* for use, *mobilizable.* If it is used up (absorbed) in criminal activity, or in an excessive amount of self-damaging tendencies, then it cannot be used for therapeutic purposes, and the prognosis is negative." Not all philosophers will relish the analyst's way of putting the matter, but at least as a physician he can soon detect whether the patient is lucky or unlucky—and he knows that whichever it is, it *isn't the patient's fault.* The patient's conscious volition cannot remedy the deficiency. Even whether he will co-operate with the analyst is really out of the patient's hands: if he continually projects the denying-mother fantasy on the analyst and unconsciously identifies him always with the cruel, harsh forbidder of the nursery, thus frustrating any attempt at impersonal observation, the sessions are useless; yet if it happens that way, he can't help that either. That fatal projection is not under his control; whether it occurs or not depends on how his unconscious identifications have developed since his infancy. He can try, yes—but the ability to try enough for the therapy to have effect is also beyond his control; the capacity to try more than just so much is either there or it isn't—and either way "it's in the lap of the gods."

The position, then, is this: if we *can* overcome the effects of early environment, the ability to do so is itself a product of the early environment. We did not give ourselves this ability; and if we lack it we cannot be blamed for not having it. Sometimes, to be sure, moral exhortation brings out an ability that is there but not being used, and in this lies its *occasional* utility; but very often its use is pointless, because the ability is not there. The only thing that can overcome a desire, as Spinoza said, is a stronger contrary desire; and many times there simply is no wherewithal for producing a stronger contrary desire. Those of us who do have the wherewithal are lucky. [14]

> [14] Those who are able to exert enough effort to overcome the effects of environment (and heredity) are also that way as a result of heredity and environment. They deserve no credit for this capacity, but are simply lucky to have it.

There is one possible practical advantage in remembering this. It may prevent us (unless we are compulsive blamers) from indulging in righteous indignation and committing the sin of spiritual pride, thanking God that we are not as this publican here. And it will protect from our useless moralizings those who are least equipped by nature for enduring them. As with responsibility, so with deserts. Someone commits a crime and is punished by the state; "he deserved it," we say self-righteously—as if we were moral and he immoral, when in fact we are lucky and he is unlucky—forgetting that there, but for the grace of God and a fortunate early environment, go we. Or, as Clarence Darrow said in his speech for the defense in the Loeb-Leopold case:

> I do not believe that people are in jail because they deserve to be. . . . I know what causes the emotional life. . . . I know it is practically left out

of some. Without it they cannot act with the rest. They cannot feel the moral shocks which safeguard others. Is [this man] to blame that his machine is imperfect? Who is to blame? I do not know. I have never in my life been interested so much in fixing blame as I have in relieving people from blame. I am not wise enough to fix it.*

III

I want to make it quite clear that I have not been arguing for determinism. Though I find it difficult to give any sense to the term "indeterminism," because I do not know what it would be like to come across an uncaused event, let us grant indeterminists everything they want, at least in words—influences that suggest but do not constrain, a measure of acausality in an otherwise rigidly causal order, and so on—whatever these phrases may mean. With all this granted, exactly the same situation faces the indeterminist and the determinist; all we have been saying would still hold true. "Are our powers innate or acquired?"

> Suppose the powers are declared innate; then the villain may sensibly ask whether he is responsible for what he was born with. A negative reply is inevitable. Are they then acquired? Then the ability to acquire them—was *that* innate? or acquired? It is innate? Very well then. . . . †

The same fact remains—that we did not cause our characters, that the influences that made us what we are are influences over which we had no control and of whose

[15] Though Hospers sounds like a determinist, he is willing to allow for the possibility that there might be some degree of indeterminism. His response is that this makes no real difference to the point that a person does not and cannot shape his own character.

very existence we had no knowledge at the time. This fact remains for "determinism" and "indeterminism" alike. And it is this fact to which I would appeal, not the specific tenets of traditional forms of "determinism," which seem to me, when analyzed, empirically empty. [15]

"But," it may be asked, "isn't it your view that nothing ultimately *could* be other than it is? And isn't this deterministic? And isn't it deterministic if you say that human beings could never act otherwise than they do, and that their desires and temperaments could not, when you consider their antecedent conditions, be other than they are?"

I reply that all these charges rest on confusions.

. . .

What of the charge that we could never have acted otherwise than we did? This, I submit, is simply not true. Here the exponents of Hume-Mill-Schlick-Ayer "soft determinism" are quite right. I could have gone to the opera today instead of coming here; that is, if certain conditions had been different, I should have gone. I could have done many other things instead of what I did, if some condition or other had been different, specifically if my desire had been different. . . . [16]

[16] Hospers is saying that the compatibilist account of "could have done otherwise" is the right one—not because it is enough for freedom and responsibility, but simply because it is the only account available.

Well, then, could we ever have, not acted, but *desired* otherwise than we did desire? This gets us once again to the heart of the matter we were discussing in the previous section. [Bertrand] Russell said, "We can do as we please but we can't please as we please." But I am persuaded that even this statement conceals a fatal mistake. Let us follow the same analysis through. "I could have done *X*" means "I should have done *X* if I had wanted to." "I could have wanted *X*" by the same analysis would mean "I should have wanted *X* if I had wanted to"—which seems to make no sense at all. (What does Russell want? To please as he doesn't please?)

What does this show? It shows, I think, that the only meaningful context of "can" and "could have" is that of *action*. "Could have acted differently" makes sense; "could have desired differently," as we have just seen, does not. Because a word or phrase makes good sense in one context, let us not assume that it does so in another. [17]

I conclude, then, with the following suggestion: that we operate on two levels of moral discourse, which

---

*Levin, *op. cit.,* pp. 439–40, 469.
†W. I. Matson, "The Irrelevance of Free-will to Moral Responsibility," *Mind,* LXV (October 1956), p. 495.

we shouldn't confuse; one (let's call it the upper level) is that of actions; the other (the lower, or deeper, level)

[17] Russell's remark expresses a standard response to the compatibilist account of "could have done otherwise": it isn't enough that a person could have done something else if he had wanted or desired to, as long as the desire or want was itself determined and so not within the person's control. This suggests that freedom requires control over one's own wants or desires—being able to have the desires or wants that one desires or wants to have. Hospers dismisses this as senseless, but is he right? (See Discussion Question 3.)

is that of the springs of action. Most moral talk occurs on the upper level. It is on this level that the Hume-Mill-Schlick-Ayer analysis of freedom fully applies. As we have just seen, "can" and "could" acquire their meaning on this level; so, I suspect, does "freedom." So does the distinction between compulsive and non-compulsive behavior, and among the senses of "responsibility," discussed in the first section of this paper, according to which we are responsible for some things and not for others. All these distinctions are perfectly valid on this level (or in this dimension) of moral discourse; and it is, after all, the usual one—we are practical beings interested in changing the course of human behavior, so it is natural enough that 99 per cent of our moral talk occurs here.

But when we descend to what I have called the lower level of moral discourse, as we occasionally do in thoughtful moments when there is no immediate need for action, then we must admit that we are ultimately the kind of persons we are because of conditions occurring outside us, over which we had no control. But while this is true, we should beware of extending the moral terminology we used on the other level to this

one also. "Could" and "can," as we have seen, no longer have meaning here. "Right" and "wrong," which apply only to actions, have no meaning here either. I suspect that the same is true of "responsibility," for now that we have recalled often forgotten facts about our being the product of outside forces, we must ask in all seriousness what would be added by saying that we are not *responsible* for our own characters and temperaments. What would it mean even? Has it a significant opposite? What would it be like to be responsible for one's own character? What possible situation is describable by this phrase? Instead of saying that it is *false* that we are responsible for our own characters, I should prefer to say that the utterance is meaningless—meaningless in the sense that it describes no possible situation, though it *seems* to because the word "responsible" is the same one we used on the upper level, where it marks a real distinction. If this is so, the result is that *moral* terms—at least the terms "could have" and "responsible"—simply drop out on the lower level. What remains, shorn now of moral terminology, is the point we tried to bring out in Part II: whether or not we have personality disturbances, whether or not we have the ability to overcome deficiences of early environment, is like the answer to the question whether or not we shall be struck down by a dread disease: "it's all a matter of luck." It is important to keep this in mind, for people almost always forget it, with consequences in human intolerance and unnecessary suffering that are incalculable. [18]

[18] What is the relation between these two "levels of moral discourse" supposed to be? Does what he says about the lower or deeper level mean that the higher level is ultimately mistaken and not to be taken seriously? Why or why not?

Discussion Questions

1. A good deal of Hospers's argument rests on claims made by psychoanalysis, especially the claim that unconscious motivations and other sorts of unconscious states exist. How could the truth of such claims be established? (See Annotation 8 and the corresponding part of the selection for a possible suggestion.) How plausible do you think such claims are?

2. Were unconscious motivations involved in the case of Robert Harris, and if so, were they so

strong as to make his action inevitable and entirely beyond his control? Why or why not?

3. There is a version of compatibilism called "hierarchical compatibilism" that attempts to meet the sort of objection to compatibilism that arises from cases like the compulsive hand-washer. According to hierarchical compatibilists, it is not enough for freedom and moral responsibility that an action be caused by the agent's wants or desires, or even that there also

be no external constraint. They add the additional requirement that the person also have a *second-order desire* to have the first-order desire that leads to the action. Thus a compulsive hand-washer is free only if he not only wants to repeatedly wash his hands but wants to want this—even though this second-order desire is also determined. But does this really solve the problem? Why couldn't the second-order desire also be compulsive? Do we have to consider third-order desires, and so on?

4. Hospers says that he is not defending hard determinism, but he clearly states that "we did not cause our characters, that the influences that made us what we are are influences over which we had no control and of whose very existence we had no knowledge at the time." Does this view seem right to you? Can you think of ways that you seem to influence your own character? Can you think of aspects of your character that are traceable to your history in such a way that while you *might* be able to change them, it would take a lot of work? Compare and contrast, for example, the background that produced Robert Harris with the background that produced Mother Teresa (or choose other examples of your own). Are all characters equally controlled by background?

Roderick M. Chisholm

Roderick M. Chisholm (1916–1999) was an American philosopher who taught at Brown University. Chisholm was one of the most important figures in Anglo-American philosophy in the second half of the twentieth century, with his main work falling in epistemology and metaphysics.

In the following short commentary on the essays by Edwards and Hospers, Chisholm focuses on the crucial issue of whether actions are *avoidable*, that is whether an agent "could have done otherwise." He formulates an argument for the hard determinist conclusion that people are never morally responsible for any of their actions (because they are never free in the sense of having been able to have done otherwise) and considers whether it is possible to avoid this conclusion by rejecting one of the premises of the argument. A hard determinist will accept the conclusion of this argument (Step (5) in the article), while a compatibilist will reject premise (2)—see Annotation 2. The rejection of premise (4) of the argument (which Chisholm discusses but does not adopt here) points toward the libertarian idea of "agent causation," which Chisholm defends in his later work and which is defended by Campbell and Nozick in the selections that follow.

Responsibility and Avoidability

Edwards and Hospers hold that there is an important sense in which we may be said *not* to be morally responsible for any of our acts of choices. I propose the following as an explicit formulation of their reasoning:

From Determinism and Freedom, *edited by Sidney Hook (New York: Collier Books, 1961).*

1. If a choice is one we could not have avoided making, then it is one for which we are not morally responsible.

2. If we make a choice under conditions such that, given those conditions, it is (causally but not logically) impossible for the choice not to be made, then the choice is one we could not have avoided making.

3. Every event occurs under conditions such that, given those conditions, it is (causally but not logically) impossible for that event not to occur.
4. The making of a choice is the occurrence of an event.
5. We are not morally responsible for any of our choices.

If we wish to reject the conclusion (5)—and for most of us (5) is difficult to accept—we must reject at least one of the premises.

Premise (1), I think, may be interpreted as a logical truth. If a man is responsible for what he did, then we may say, "He *could* have done otherwise." And if we may say, "He couldn't help it," then he is not responsible for what he did. ①

Many philosophers would deny (2), substituting a weaker account of avoidability. A choice is avoidable, they might say, provided only it is such that, *if* the agent had reflected further, or had reflected on certain things on which in fact he did not reflect, he would *not* have made the choice. To say of a choice that it "could *not* have been avoided," in accordance with this account, would be to say that, even if the agent *had* reflected further, on anything you like, he would all the same have made the choice.② But such conditional accounts of *avoidability* ("An act or choice is avoidable provided only it is such that, *if* the agent were to do so-and-so, the act or choice would not occur") usually have this serious defect: the antecedent clause ("if the agent were to do so-and-so") refers to some act or choice, or to the fail-

① By "a logical truth," Chisholm means a necessary truth, one that is true in every possible world. Perhaps the single thing about which all views on the free will problem agree is that moral responsibility (and freedom) require avoidability in this sense.

② Chisholm is talking here about the compatibilist or soft determinist account of avoidability, though he formulates it a bit differently from the formulations we have seen before. To say that free actions are those that result from the agent's will (Hume) or are caused by the agent's psychological states (Stace) doesn't quite make clear that the action would have been different had the agent's process of reflection and deliberation been different, though this is surely what Hume and Stace intend.

ure to perform some act or to make some choice; hence we may ask, concerning the occurrence or nonoccurrence of this act or choice, whether or not *it* is avoidable. Thus one who accepted (5) could say that, if the agent's failure to reflect further was itself unavoidable, his choice was also unavoidable. And no such conditional account of *avoidability* seems adequate to the use of "avoidable" and "unavoidable" in questions and statements such as these.③

③ The problem with compatibilism is that even if the choice would have been different if the process of deliberation had been different, that process was *itself* causally determined, according to the compatibilist, and so could not have been different—in which case neither it nor what resulted from it was avoidable in a meaningful sense.

If we accept a conditional account of avoidability, we may be tempted to say, of course, that it would be a *misuse* of "avoidable" to ask whether the nonoccurrence of the antecedent event ("the agent does so-and-so") is avoidable. But the philosopher who accepts (5) may well insist that, since the antecedent clause refers to an act or a choice, the use of "avoidable" in question is *not* a misuse.

What, then, if we were to deny (3)? Suppose that some of our choices do not satisfy (3)—that when they are made they are *not* made under any conditions such that it is (causally) impossible (though logically possible) for them not to be made. If there are choices of this sort, then they are merely fortuitous or capricious. And if they are merely fortuitous or capricious, if they "just happen," then, I think, we may say with Blanshard that we are *not* morally responsible for them. Hence denying (3) is not the way to avoid (5).④

④ Chisholm is saying here that an event for which there are not causally sufficient conditions (conditions such that it is impossible for that event not to occur given the laws of nature), can only be a random or chance event. But if human choices are random events, then the person is also not responsible for them (or free in making them). They are in a sense avoidable, but not in a way that gives the person any *control* over them.

We seem confronted, then, with a dilemma: either our choices have sufficient causal conditions or they do not; if they do have sufficient causal conditions they are not avoidable; if they do not, they are fortuitous or capricious; and therefore, since our choices are either unavoidable or fortuitous, we are not morally responsible for them. ⑤

⑤ This sums up the central core of the free will problem. As discussed in the introduction to this chapter, a libertarian view of freedom and moral responsibility must apparently reject both sides of this dilemma and thus must find a third alternative to causal determinism and randomness.

There are philosophers who believe that by denying the rather strange-sounding premise (4) we can escape the dilemma. Insisting on something like "the primacy of practical reason," they would say that since we are certain that (5) is false we must construct a metaphysical theory about the self, a theory denying (4) and enabling us to reconcile (3) and the denial of (5). I say "metaphysical" because it seems to be necessary for the theory to replace (4) by sentences using such terms as "active power," "the autonomy of the will," "prime mover," or "higher levels of causality"—terms designating something to which we apparently need not refer when expressing the conclusions of physics and the natural sciences. But I believe we cannot know whether such theories enable us to escape our dilemma. For it seems impossible to conceive what the relation is that, according to these theories, holds between the "will," "self," "mover," or "active power," on the one hand, and the bodily events this power is supposed to control, on the other—the relation between the "activities" of the self and the events described by physics. ⑥

⑥ Think carefully about just how premise (4) is required to make the argument valid. To say that the making of a choice is not an event is an attempt to avoid having to say either that it is causally determined or random. The suggestion, not spelled out very fully here, is that free choices result from the will or self—from the *agent*—in a way that does not involve any further event about which the previous dilemma arises.

I am dissatisfied, then, with what philosophers have proposed as alternatives to premises (1) through (4) above, but since I feel certain that (5) is false I also feel certain that at least one of the premises is false.

Discussion Questions

1. Suppose that causal determinism is true (since random events, if there are any, really don't matter to the main issue), and think carefully about the compatibilist account of avoidability (see Annotations 2 and 3). As spelled out by Chisholm, the compatibilist says that a choice could have been different if the person's process of deliberation had been different, but also says that the process of deliberation was itself determined. Think now about some event other than a human choice: it also could have been different, in a sense, if its causes had been different; and they could have been different if their causes had been different; and so on, back into time. Is there any difference between the sense in which human actions or choices could have been different, according to the compatibilist, and the sense in which other kinds of events could have been different?

2. Chisholm says that the conclusion of the argument that he formulates is "for most of us . . . difficult to accept." How difficult to accept does it seem to you? Might it be that people are never really free or responsible? Try to imagine going through the world and making choices, some of them difficult ones, while bearing in mind all the time that everything you do is determined and not free. Does this lead to a coherent outlook, or would there be a fundamental conflict in your thinking? Is this a reason to think that freedom exists after all?

C. A. Campbell

Charles Arthur Campbell (1897–1974) was a Scottish philosopher who taught at the University of Glasgow and the University of North Wales. He is best known for his work on the free will problem, but he also made important contributions to ethics and the philosophy of religion. In the following selection, he attempts to elaborate and defend a libertarian view of free will. Campbell's view is a version of the doctrine of agent causation. The central idea is that a free choice (in his case the choice of whether or not to exert the effort required to overcome the balance of one's desires and do what one perceives to be the morally right thing) is caused by the agent or self, but not by some specific event (or set of events) occurring within the agent—because otherwise one could ask for the cause of that event, and so on, leading either to causal determinism or to one or more random events.

In Defence of Free Will

... Let us begin by noting that the problem of free will gets its urgency for the ordinary educated man by reason of its close connection with the conception of moral responsibility. When we regard a man as morally responsible for an act, we regard him as a legitimate object of moral praise or blame in respect of it. But it seems plain that a man cannot be a legitimate object of moral praise or blame for an act unless in willing the act he is in some important sense a 'free' agent. Evidently free will in some sense, therefore, is a pre-condition of moral responsibility. . . .

We raise the question at once, therefore, what are the conditions, in respect of freedom, which must attach to an act in order to make it a morally responsible act? It seems to me that the fundamental conditions are two. I shall state them with all possible brevity, for we have a long road to travel.

The first condition is the universally recognised one that the act must be *self*-caused, *self*-determined. But it is important to accept this condition in its full rigour. The agent must be not merely *a* cause but the *sole* cause of that for which he is deemed morally responsible. If entities other than the self have also a causal influence upon an act, then that act is not one for which we can say without qualification that the *self* is morally responsible. If in respect of it we hold the self responsible at all, it can only be for some feature of the act—assuming the possibility of disengaging such a feature—of which the self *is* the sole cause. I do not see how this conclusion can be evaded. But it has awkward implications which have led not a

few people to abandon the notion of individual moral responsibility altogether.[1]

This first condition, however, is quite clearly not sufficient. It is possible to conceive an act of which the agent is the sole cause, but which is at the same time an act *necessitated* by the agent's nature. . . . In the case of such an act, where the agent could not do otherwise than he did, we must all agree, I think, that it would be inept to say that he *ought* to have done otherwise and is thus morally blameworthy, or *ought not* to have done otherwise and is thus morally praiseworthy. It is perfectly true that we do sometimes hold a person morally responsible for an act, even when we believe that he, being what he now is, virtually could not do otherwise. But underlying that judgment is always the assumption that the person has *come* to be what he now is in virtue of past acts of will in which he *was* confronted by real alternatives, by genuinely open possibilities: and, strictly speaking, it is in respect of these *past* acts of his that we praise or blame the agent *now*.[2] For ultimate analysis, the agent's power of alternative action would seem to be an inexpugnable condition of

[1] Think about this very strong requirement: can you think of an action that is caused solely by your self, with no causal influence by anything else? (A further question is whether it even makes sense to think of a self—as opposed to one or more of its states, such as desires or motives—as a cause.)

[2] Campbell adds the requirement that the person could have done otherwise, which means on his view that the nature of the self or agent did not necessitate the action in question—or else that the nature that does necessitate the action was itself a result of one or more earlier choices, in which the self or agent could have done otherwise.

From In Defence of Free Will *(London: George Allen & Unwin LTD, 1967).*

his liability to moral praise or blame, i.e. of his moral responsibility.

We may lay down, therefore, that an act is a 'free' act in the sense required for moral responsibility only if the agent (*a*) is the sole cause of the act; and (*b*) could exert his causality in alternative ways. . . .

And now, the conditions of free will being defined in these general terms, we have to ask whether human beings are in fact capable of performing free acts; and if so, where precisely such acts are to be found. In order to prepare the way for an answer, it is desirable, I think, that we should get clear at once about the significance of a certain very familiar, but none the less formidable, criticism of free will which . . . the Libertarian has to meet. This is the criticism which bases itself upon the facts of heredity on the one hand and of environment on the other. I may briefly summarize the criticism as follows.

Every historic self has an hereditary nature consisting of a group of inborn propensities, in range more or less common to the race, but specific to the individual in their respective strengths. With this equipment the self just *happens* to be born. Strictly speaking, it antedates the existence of the self proper, i.e. the existence of the self-conscious subject, and it is itself the effect of a series of causes leading back to indefinitely remote antiquity. It follows, therefore, that any of the self's choices that manifests the influence of his hereditary nature is not a choice of which *he*, the actual historic self, is the sole cause. The choice is determined, at least in part, by factors external to the self. The same thing holds good of 'environment'. Every self is born and bred in a particular physical and social environment, not of his own choosing, which plays upon him in innumerable ways, encouraging this propensity, discouraging that, and so on. Clearly any of the self's choices that manifests the influence of environmental factors is likewise a choice which is determined, at least in part, by factors external to the self. But if we thus grant, as seems inevitable, that heredity and environment are external influences, where shall we find a choice in the whole history of a self that is not subject to external influence? Surely we must admit that every particular act of choice bears the marks of the agent's hereditary nature and environmental nurture; in which case a free act, in the sense of an act determined solely by the self, must be dismissed as a mere chimaera.③

. . .

The externality of these influences is taken for granted in our reflective practical judgments upon persons. On those occasions when we are in real earnest about giving a critical and considered estimate of a man's moral calibre—as, e.g., in any serious biographical study—we impose upon ourselves as a matter of course the duty of enquiring with scrupulous care into his hereditary propensities and environmental circumstances, with a view to discovering how far his conduct is influenced by these factors. And having traced these influences, we certainly do not regard the result as having no bearing on the question of the man's moral responsibility for his conduct. On the contrary, the very purpose of the enquiry is to enable us, by due appreciation of the *external* influences that affect his conduct, to gain as accurate a view as possible of that which can justly be attributed to the man's own *self*-determination. The allowances that we all of us do in practice make for hereditary and environmental influences in passing judgment on our fellows would be meaningless if we did not suppose these influences to be in a real sense 'external' to the self.

Now the recognition of this externality is, of course, a [serious] matter for the Libertarian. For the Libertarian, as we saw, accepts condition (*a*) . . . i.e. that an act is free only if it is determined by the self and nothing but the self. . . . We know now that condition (*a*) is not fulfilled by any act in respect of which inheritance or environment exerts a causal influence. For that type of influence has been shown to be in a real sense external to the self. The free act of which we are in search has therefore got to be one into which influences of this kind do not enter at all.④

Moreover, one encouraging portent has emerged in the course of our brief discussion. For we noticed that our reflective practical judgments on persons, while fully recognizing the externality of the influence of heredity and environment, do nevertheless presuppose throughout that there *is something* in conduct which is genuinely self-determined; something which

③ This sounds most like Blatchford. But all the other authors so far in this chapter, with the sole exception of Chisholm, would agree pretty closely.

④ Again, this is a *very* strong requirement—one that may seem quite impossible to satisfy.

the agent contributes solely on his own initiative, unaffected by external influences; something for which, accordingly, he may justly be held morally responsible. That conviction may, of course, be a false one. But the fact of its widespread existence can hardly be without significance for our problem.

Let us proceed, then, by following up this clue. Let us ask, why do human beings so obstinately persist in believing that there is an indissoluble core of purely *self*-originated activity which even heredity and environment are powerless to affect? There can be little doubt, I think, of the answer in general terms. They do so, at bottom, because they feel certain of the existence of such activity from their immediate practical experience of themselves.⑤ Nor can there be in the end much doubt, I think, in what function of the self that activity is to be located. There seems to me to be one, and only one, function of the self with respect to which the agent can even pretend to have an assurance of that absolute self-origination which is here at issue. But to render precise the nature of that function is obviously of quite paramount importance: and we can do so, I think, only by way of a somewhat thorough analysis—which I now propose to attempt—of the experiential situation in which it occurs, viz., the situation of 'moral temptation'.

⑤ Campbell is referring to the actual experience of choice, especially in a situation in which one is pulled in more than one way.

It is characteristic of that situation that in it I am aware of an end A which I believe to be morally right, and also of an end B, incompatible with A, towards which, in virtue of that system of conative dispositions which constitutes my 'character' as so far formed, I entertain a strong desire. There may be, and perhaps must be, desiring elements in my nature which are directed to A also. But what gives to the situation its specific character as one of moral temptation is that the urge of our desiring nature towards the right end, A, is felt to be *relatively* weak. We are sure that if our desiring nature is permitted to issue directly in action, it is end B that we shall choose. That is what is meant by saying, as William James does, that end B is 'in the line of least resistance' relatively to our conative dispositions. The expression is, of course, a metaphorical one, but it serves to describe, graphically enough, a situation of which we all have frequent experience, viz., where we recognize a specific end as that towards which the 'set' of our desiring nature most strongly inclines us, and which we shall indubitably choose if no inhibiting factor intervenes.⑥

But inhibiting factors, we should most of us say, *may* intervene: and that in two totally different ways which it is vital to distinguish clearly. The inhibiting factor may be of the nature of another desire (or aversion), which operates by changing the balance of the desiring situation. Though at one stage I desire B, which I believe to be wrong, more strongly than I desire A, which I believe to be right, it may happen that before action is taken I become aware of certain hitherto undiscerned consequences of A which I strongly desire, and the result may be that now not B but A presents itself to me as the end in the line of least resistance. Moral temptation is here overcome by the simple process of ceasing to be a moral temptation.⑦

⑥ The morally wrong action, B, is supposed to be the one that your "desiring nature" would choose and thus the one that you want most, all things considered—the one that accords with the overall balance of your desires. You may have some desire to do the morally right thing, A, but not enough, by itself, to overcome the stronger desire for B. Everyone has experienced situations that at least *seem* to fit this specification, and you should think of an example of your own.

⑦ New information or just a change of mind may alter the balance of desire in favor of A. Acting in accord with the new balance of desire would be simply doing what follows most naturally from one's "desiring nature" and would not, in Campbell's view, be a genuine example of free choice.

That is one way, and probably by far the commoner way, in which an inhibiting factor intervenes. But it is certainly not regarded by the self who is confronted by moral temptation as the *only* way. In such situations we all believe, rightly or wrongly, that even although B *continues* to be in the line of least resistance, even although, in other words, the situation remains one with the characteristic marks of moral temptation, we *can* nevertheless align ourselves with A. We can do so, we believe, because we have the power to introduce a new energy, to make what we call an 'effort of will', whereby we are able to act contrary to the felt balance of mere desire, and to achieve the higher end despite the fact that it continues to be in the line of greater resistance relatively to our desiring nature. The self in practice believes that it has this power; and believes, moreover, that the decision rests solely with its self, here and now, whether this power be exerted or not. ⑧

⑧ Note carefully that Campbell is here describing only what we all believe in a situation of this sort: that it is within one's power to exert the effort to overcome the overall balance of desire in favor of B and do A instead. Is he right that this is what everyone believes in such a situation?

Now the objective validity or otherwise of this belief is not at the moment in question. I am here merely pointing to its existence as a psychological fact. No amount of introspective analysis, so far as I can see, even tends to disprove that we do as a matter of fact believe, in situations of moral temptation, that it rests with our self absolutely to decide whether we exert the effort of will which will enable us to rise to duty, or whether we shall allow our desiring nature to take its course.

I have now to point out, further, how this act of moral decision, at least in the significance which it has for the agent himself, fulfils in full the two conditions which we found it necessary to lay down at the beginning for the kind of 'free' act which moral responsibility presupposes.

For obviously it is, in the first place, an act which the agent believes he could perform in alternative ways. He believes that it is genuinely open to him to put forth effort—in varying degrees, if the situation admits of that—or withhold it altogether. And when he *has* decided—in whatever way—he remains convinced that these alternative courses were really open to him. ⑨

⑨ *If* a person really does have the ability to put forth this special sort of effort (and also, of course, not to do it), then whether or not he does so is controlled by him alone and not to any degree determined by other causes.

It is perhaps a little less obvious, but, I think, equally certain, that the agent believes the second condition to be fulfilled likewise, i.e. that the act of decision is determined *solely* by his self. It appears less obvious, because we all realize that formed character has a great deal to do with the choices that we make; and formed character is, without a doubt, partly dependent on the external factors of heredity and environment. But it is crucial here that we should not

misunderstand the precise nature of the influence which formed character brings to bear upon the choices that constitute conduct. No one denies that it determines, at least largely, what things we desire, and again how greatly we desire them. It may thus fairly be said to determine the felt balance of desires in the situation of moral temptation. But all that that amounts to is that formed character prescribes the nature of the situation *within* which the act of moral decision takes place. It does not in the least follow that it has any influence whatsoever in determining the act of decision itself—the decision as to whether we shall exert effort or take the easy course of following the bent of our desiring nature: take, that is to say, the course which, in virtue of the determining influence of our character as so far formed, we feel to be in the line of least resistance.

When one appreciates this, one is perhaps better prepared to recognize the fact that the agent himself in the situation of moral temptation does not, and indeed could not, regard his formed character as having any influence whatever upon his act of decision as such. For the very nature of that decision, as it presents itself to him, is as to whether he will or will not permit his formed character to dictate his action. In other words, the agent distinguishes sharply between the self which makes the decision, and the self which, as formed character, determines not the decision but the situation within which the decision takes place. Rightly or wrongly, the agent believes that through his act of decision he can oppose and transcend his own formed character in the interest of duty. We are therefore obliged to say, I think, that the agent *cannot* regard his formed character as in any sense a determinant of the act of decision as such. The act is felt to be a genuinely creative act, originated by the self *ad hoc,* and by the self alone. ⑩

⑩ While formed character determines the balance of one's desires, the choice as to whether to exert the effort to overcome that balance of desires or not cannot be due to formed character—*if* such a thing really occurs.

Here then, if my analysis is correct, in the function of moral decision in situations of moral temptation, we have an act of the self which at least *appears to the agent* to satisfy both of the conditions of freedom which we laid down at the beginning. The vital question now is, is this 'appearance' true or false? Is the act of decision really what it appears to the agent to be, determined solely by the self, and capable of alternative forms of expression? If it is, then we have here a free act which serves as an adequate basis for moral responsibility. We shall be entitled to regard the agent as morally praiseworthy or morally blameworthy according as he decides to put forth effort or to let his desiring nature have its way. We shall be entitled, in short, to judge the agent as he most certainly judges himself in the situation of moral temptation. If, on the other hand, there is good reason to believe that the agent is the victim of illusion in supposing his act of decision to bear this character, then in my opinion the whole conception of moral responsibility must be jettisoned altogether. For it seems to me certain that there is no other function of the self that even looks as though it satisfied the required conditions of the free act.

Now in considering the claim to truth of this belief of our practical consciousness, we should begin by noting that the onus of proof rests upon the critic who rejects this belief. Until cogent evidence to the contrary is adduced, we are entitled to put our trust in a belief which is so deeply embedded in our experience as practical beings as to be, I venture to say, ineradicable from it. Anyone who doubts whether it is ineradicable may be invited to think himself imaginatively into a situation of moral temptation as we have above described it, and then to ask himself whether in that situation he finds it possible to *disbelieve* that his act of decision has the characteristics in question. I have no misgivings about the answer. It is possible to disbelieve only when we are thinking abstractly about the situation; not when we are living through it, either actually or in imagination. This fact certainly establishes a strong prima facie presumption in favour of the Libertarian position. [11] Nevertheless I agree that we shall have to weigh carefully several criticisms of high authority before we can feel justified in asserting free will as an ultimate and unqualified truth.

> [11] Campbell claims that a person cannot help believing in such a situation that he does have the ability in question, that whether he chooses to exert the effort or not is not determined by his formed character. His claim is that this is enough to create "a strong prima facie presumption" in favor of libertarianism, thereby putting the burden of proof strongly on the opposing position. Is he right about this?

Fortunately for our purpose, however, there are some lines of criticism which, although extremely influential in the recent past, may at the present time be legitimately ignored. . . .

. . . Libertarianism is certainly inconsistent with a rigidly determinist theory of the physical world. It is idle to pretend that there can be open possibilities for psychical decision, while at the same time holding that the physical events in which such decisions manifest themselves are determined in accordance with irrevocable law. But whereas until a few years ago the weight of scientific authority was thrown overwhelmingly on the side of a universal determinism of physical phenomena, the situation has, as everybody knows, profoundly altered during the present century more especially since the advent of Planck's Quantum Theory and Heisenberg's Principle of Uncertainty. Very few scientists to-day would seek to impugn free will on the ground of any supposed implications of the aims or achievements of physical science. . . .

I may turn at once, therefore, to lines of argument which do still enjoy a wide currency among anti-Libertarians. And I shall begin with one which, though it is a simple matter to show its irrelevance to the Libertarian doctrine as I have stated it, is so extremely popular that it cannot safely be ignored.

The charge made is that the Libertarian view is incompatible with the *predictability* of human conduct. For we do make rough predictions of people's conduct, on the basis of what we know of their character, every day of our lives, and there can be no doubt that the practice, within certain limits, is amply justified by results. Indeed if it were not so, social life would be reduced to sheer chaos. The close relationship between character and conduct which prediction postulates really seems to be about as certain as anything can be. But the Libertarian view, it is urged, by ascribing to the self a mysterious power of decision uncontrolled by character, and capable of issuing in acts inconsistent with character, denies that continuity between character and conduct upon which prediction depends. If Libertarianism is true, prediction is impossible. But prediction *is* possible, therefore Libertarianism is untrue. [12]

> [12] Here is an obvious objection to libertarianism, one that is raised by Blatchford.

My answer is that the Libertarian view is perfectly compatible with prediction within certain limits, and that there is no empirical evidence at all that prediction is in fact possible beyond these limits. The following considerations will, I think, make the point abundantly clear.

(1)   There is no question, on our view, of a free will that can will just anything at all. The range of possible choices is limited by the agent's character in every case; for nothing can be an object of possible choice which is not suggested by either the agent's desires or his moral ideals, and these depend on 'character' for us just as much as for our opponents. We have, indeed explicitly recognized at an earlier stage that character determines the situation within which the act of moral decision takes place, although not the act of moral decision itself. This consideration obviously furnishes a broad basis for at least approximate predictions. [13]

[13]   Freedom, according to Campbell, involves a choice between one's overall balance of desires and the demands of morality. Since both one's desires and one's conception of morality are a part of the formed character that is a result of heredity and environment, there will still be a basis for many approximate predictions: predictions that a person will not do a wide range of things that are favored by neither desire nor morality and that his action will fall within a certain range (one that includes both the desired option and the one favored by morality).

(2)   There is *one* experiential situation, and *one only,* on our view, in which there is any possibility of the act of will not being in accordance with character; viz. the situation in which the course which formed character prescribes is a course in conflict with the agent's moral ideal: in other words, the situation of moral temptation. Now this is a situation of comparative rarity. Yet with respect to all other situations in life we are in full agreement with those who hold that conduct is the response of the agent's formed character to the given situation. Why should it not be so? There could be no reason, on our view any more than on another, for the agent even to consider deviating from the course which his formed character prescribes and he most strongly desires, *unless* that course is believed by him to be incompatible with what is right. [14]

(3)   Even within that one situation which is relevant to free will, our view can still recognize a certain basis for prediction. In that situation our character as so far formed prescribes a course opposed to duty, and an effort of will is required if we are to deviate from that course. But of course we are all aware that a greater effort of will is required in proportion to the degree in which we have to transcend our formed character in order to will the right. Such action is, as we say, 'harder'. But if action is 'harder' in proportion as it involves deviation from formed character, it seems reasonable to suppose that, on the whole, action will be of rarer occurrence in that same proportion: though perhaps we may not say that at any level of deviation it becomes flatly impossible. It follows that even with respect to situations of moral temptation we may usefully employ our knowledge of the agent's character as a clue to prediction. It will be a clue of limited, but of by no means negligible, value. It will warrant us in predicting, e.g., of a person who has become enslaved to alcohol, that he is unlikely, even if fully aware of the moral evil of such slavery, to be successful immediately and completely in throwing off its shackles. Predictions of this kind we all make often enough in practice. And there seems no reason at all why a Libertarian doctrine should wish to question their validity. [15]

[14]   Thus, if situations of choice between desire and morality are fairly rare, most actions will be predictable on the basis for formed character. (Does this mean that we are free and morally responsible on only these fairly rare occasions?)

[15]   Think very hard about this point: if it is very hard to overcome the balance of desire that results from formed character, is a person who fails to do so still free and morally responsible? Isn't his action very largely determined by formed character, which is in turn determined by environment and heredity, leaving very little room for freedom?

Now when these three considerations are borne in mind, it becomes quite clear that the doctrine we are defending is compatible with a very substantial measure of predictability indeed. And I submit that there is not a jot of empirical evidence that any larger measure than this obtains in fact.

Let us pass on then to consider a much more interesting and, I think, more plausible criticism. It is constantly objected against the Libertarian doctrine that it is fundamentally *unintelligible.* Libertarianism holds that the act of moral decision is the *self's* act, and yet insists at the same time that it is not influenced by any of those determinate features in the self's nature which go to constitute its 'character'. But, it is asked, do not these two propositions contradict one another? Surely a *self*-determination which is determination by something other than the self's *character* is a contradiction in terms? What meaning is there in the conception of a 'self' in abstraction from its 'character'? If you really wish to maintain, it is urged, that the act of decision is not determined by the self's character, you ought to admit frankly that it is not determined by the *self* at all. But in that case, of course, you will not be advocating a freedom which lends any kind of support to moral responsibility; indeed very much the reverse. [16]

> [16] There is one obvious way in which a choice that does not accord with the agent's character seems to be possible: if the choice is simply random. But a random choice would not be the act of the self in any sense relevant to moral responsibility. Thus another way to put the problem is to say that it is hard to understand how a choice can be neither the result of formed character nor random. If it is neither of these, where does it come from?

Now this criticism, and all of its kind, seem to me to be the product of a simple, but extraordinarily pervasive, error: the error of confining one's self to the categories of the external observer in dealing with the actions of human agents. Let me explain.

It is perfectly true that the standpoint of the external observer, which we are obliged to adopt in dealing with physical processes, does not furnish us with even a glimmering of a notion of what can be meant by an entity which acts causally and yet not through any of the determinate features of its character. So far as we confine ourselves to external observation, I agree that this notion must seem to us pure nonsense. But then we are *not* obliged to confine ourselves to external observation in dealing with the human agent. Here, though here alone, we have the inestimable advantage of being able to apprehend operations from the *inside,* from the standpoint of *living experience.* But if we do adopt this internal standpoint—surely a proper standpoint, and one which we should be only too glad to adopt if we could in the case of other entities—the situation is entirely changed. We find that we not merely can, but constantly do, attach meaning to a causation which is the self's causation but is yet not exercised by the self's

character. We have seen as much already in our analysis of the situation of moral temptation. When confronted by such a situation, we saw, we are certain that it lies with our *self* to decide whether we shall let our character as so far formed dictate our action or whether we shall by effort oppose its dictates and rise to duty. We are certain, in other words, that the act is *not* determined by our *character*, while we remain equally certain that the act *is* determined by our *self.*

Or look, for a further illustration (since the point we have to make here is of the very first importance for the whole free will controversy), to the experience of effortful willing itself, where the act of decision has found expression in the will to rise to duty. In such an experience we are certain that it is our self which makes the effort. But we are equally certain that the effort does not flow from that system of conative dispositions which we call our formed character; for the very function that the effort has for us is to enable us to act against the 'line of least resistance', i.e. to act in a way *contrary* to that to which our formed character inclines us. [17]

> [17] Campbell appeals to our experience of actually making choices in this way. But even if he is right (is he?) that our experience seems to support the view that such choices actually occur, this isn't enough to *explain* what is going on: what determination by the self but not by the formed character or nature of the self really amounts to.

I conclude, therefore, that those who find the Libertarian doctrine of the self's causality in moral decision inherently unintelligible find it so simply because they restrict themselves, quite arbitrarily, to an inadequate standpoint: a standpoint from which, indeed, a genuinely creative activity, if it existed, never *could* be apprehended.

It will be understood, of course, that it is no part of my purpose to deny that the act of moral decision is in *one* sense 'unintelligible'. If by the 'intelligibility' of an act we mean that it is capable, at least in principle, of being inferred as a consequence of a given ground, then naturally my view is that the act in question is '*un*intelligible'. But that, presumably, is not the meaning of 'intelligibility' in the critic's mind when he says that the Libertarian holds an 'unintelligible' doctrine. If it were all he meant, he would merely be pointing out that Libertarianism is not compatible with Determinism! And that tautologous pronouncement would hardly deserve the title of 'criticism'.

. . .

What is required of the critic, of course, if he is to make good his case, is a reasoned justification of his cavalier attitude towards the testimony of practical self-consciousness. That is the primary desideratum. And the lack of it in the bulk of Determinist literature is in my opinion something of a scandal. Without it, the criticism we have just been examining is sheer dogmatism. It is, indeed, dogmatism of a peculiarly perverse kind. For the situation is, in effect, as follows. From our practical self-consciousness we gain a notion of a genuinely creative act—which might be defined as an act which nothing determines save the agent's doing of it. Of such a character is the act of moral decision as we experience it. But the critic says 'No! This sort of thing cannot be. A person cannot without affront to reason be conceived to be the author of an act which bears, *ex hypothesi,* no intelligible relation to his character. A mere intuition of practical self-consciousness is the solitary prop of this fantastic notion, and surely that is quite incapable of bearing the weight that you would thrust upon it.' Now observe the perversity! The critic says, excluding the evidence of practical self-consciousness, the notion makes nonsense. In other words, excluding the only evidence there ever *could* be for such a notion, the notion makes nonsense! For, of course, if there should be such a thing as creative activity, there is absolutely no other way save an intuition of practical self-consciousness in which we could become aware of it. Only from the inside, from the standpoint of the agent's living experience, can 'activity' possibly be apprehended. So that what the critic is really doing is to condemn a notion as nonsensical on the ground that the only evidence for it is the only evidence there ever could be for it. [18]

[18] Again the real problem is not so much whether there is evidence for the existence of such choices as how to explain what such a choice would amount to and how it would be arrived at.

. . .

Discussion Questions

1. Clearly, on Campbell's view, a person who exerts the effort needed to overcome the balance of his desires has acted freely. Is the action of a person who chooses *not* to exert this effort and so does what he most desires to do also a free action (so that people would not be morally responsible only when they do the right thing)? Why or why not? What if the desires opposed to morality are very strong (see Annotation 15 and the associated text)?
2. Does the idea of agent causation, in general and in Campbell's specific version, really make sense? How is the choice fixed or arrived at if it is not a result of formed character (and also not random)?
3. On Campbell's view, a person is free and morally responsible only in situations where there is a conflict between desire and morality (and perhaps only when he follows morality and not desire). Is this a plausible view of freedom? Is there any way to expand Campbell's view so as to allow a wider range of free choices?

Robert Nozick

Robert Nozick (1938–2002) taught philosophy for many years at Harvard and was a major figure in twentieth century philosophy. He made important contributions to many areas, but was perhaps best known for his book *Anarchy, State, and Utopia* (from which two of the selections in Chapter 7 on political philosophy are exerpted). Nozick was also famous for his lively style and his knack for devising striking and intuitively engaging examples.

In the following selection, Nozick defends a libertarian position that, like Campbell's, is a version of agent causation. On Nozick's account, free actions arise from situations in which an agent *assigns* weights to reasons favoring various alternatives (rather than simply acting in accord with the antecedently most weighty reasons).

Choice and Indeterminism, from *Philosophical Explanations*

WEIGH(T)ING REASONS

Making some choices feels like this. There are various reasons for and against doing each of the alternative actions or courses of action one is considering, and it seems and feels as if one could do any one of them. In considering the reasons, mulling them over, one arrives at a view of which reasons are more important, which ones have more weight. One decides which reasons to act on; or one may decide to act on none of them but to seek instead a new alternative since none previously considered was satisfactory.

After the choice, however, others will say we were caused to act by the considerations which were (or turned out to be) more weighty. And it is not just others. We too, in looking back at our past actions, will see which reasons swayed us and will view (accepting) those considerations as having caused us to act as we did. Had we done the other act, though, acting on the opposing considerations, we (along with the others) would have described those considerations as causing us to do that other act. Whichever act we do, the (different) background considerations exist which can be raised to causal status. Which considerations will be so raised depends upon which act we do. Does the act merely show which of the considerations was the weightier cause, or does the decision make one of them weightier?

The reasons do not come with previously given precisely specified weights; the decision process is not one of discovering such precise weights but of assigning them. The process not only weighs reasons,

From Philosophical Explanations *(Cambridge, Mass.: Harvard University Press, 1981).*

it (also) weights them. At least, so it sometimes feels. This process of weighting may focus narrowly, or involve considering or deciding what sort of person one wishes to be, what sort of life one wishes to lead. ①

What picture of choice emerges if we take seriously the feeling that the (precise) weights to be assigned to reasons is "up to us"? It is causally undetermined (by prior factors) which of the acts we will decide to do. It may be causally determined that certain reasons are reasons (in the one direction or the other), but there is no prior causal determination of the precise weight each reason will have in competition with others.② Thus, we need not hold that every possible reason is available to every person at every time or historical period. Historians and anthropologists delineate how certain ideas and considerations can be outside the purview of some societies, some of whose reasons would not count as reasons for us. (Yet, there does remain the question of whether an innovator couldn't have recognized as a reason something outside the purview of others in his society.) Psychology,

> ① Think of a situation involving a choice between two or more alternatives, where there are reasons for each of the alternatives, but where it is uncertain how much weight the various reasons should have. One might think that the agent in such a situation is trying to figure out what weights the various reasons already possess, but Nozick's suggestion is that there are no antecedent weights to be discovered, so that they have to be assigned.

> ② As was also acknowledged by Campbell, the reasons that an agent finds relevant may be determined by antecedent causes. It is only the weights of the reasons that are claimed not to be determined when there is a genuinely free choice.

sociobiology, and the various social sciences, on this view, will offer causal explanations of why something is or is not a reason for a person (in a situation). They will not always be able to explain why the reasons get the precise weights they do. Compare the way art historians treat style; not every style is equally available to every artist in every period, yet within a style creative choices are made, and some artistic revolutions introduce new stylistic possibilities.

It is neither necessary nor appropriate, on this view, to say the person's action is uncaused. As the person is deciding, mulling over reasons R_A which are reasons for doing act A and over R_B which are reasons for doing act B, it is undetermined which act he will do. In that very situation, he could do A and he could do B. He decides, let us suppose, to do act A. It then will be true that he was caused to do act A by (accepting) R_A. However, had he decided to do act B, it then would have been R_B that caused him to do B. Whichever he decides upon, A or B, there will be a cause of his doing it, namely R_A or R_B. His action is not (causally) determined, for in that very situation he could have decided differently; if the history of the world had been replayed up until that point, it could have continued with a different action. With regard to his action the person has what has been termed contra-causal freedom—we might better term it contra-deterministic.③

Thus, we draw a distinction between an action's being caused, and its being causally determined. Some philosophers would deny this distinction, maintaining that whenever one event causes another, there holds a general law in accordance with which it does so: some specification of the first event (along with other conditions which hold) always is and would be followed by an event of the same type as the second. It is a metaphysical thesis that the root notion of causality, producing or making something happen, can operate only through such lawlike universality.④ If this were correct, . . . then causality necessarily would involve causal determination: under exactly the same conditions repeated, exactly the same thing would have (again) to happen. According to the view that distinguishes causality

---

③ Nozick is saying that the action is still caused by the reason to which the agent assigns the greater weight, even though not causally *determined* (since it was not determined that this reason would be assigned greater weight).

---

from causal determination, an act can be done because of something and have a cause even though in exactly the same conditions another act could have been done. It is common, in retrospect, to see what caused us to act as we did. Although we can retrospectively identify a cause, this does not mean our action was causally determined; had we acted differently in that situation (as we could have) we retrospectively would have identified a different cause— R_B instead of R_A.⑤

The weights of reasons are inchoate until the decision. The decision need not bestow exact quantities, though, only make some reasons come to outweigh others. A decision establishes inequalities in weight, even if not precise weights.

These bestowed weights (or comparative weightings of reasons) are not so evanescent as to disappear immediately after the very decision that bestows them. They set up a framework within which we make future decisions, not eternal but one we tentatively are committed to. The process of decision fixes the weights reasons are to have. The situation resembles that of precedents within a legal system; an earlier decision is not simply ignored though it may be overturned for reason, the decision represents a tentative commitment to make future decisions in accordance with the weights it establishes, and so on.

The claim that we always do what we most prefer or always act from the strongest motive is sometimes said to be empty of content, since the preference or the strength of motive is identified by what the person does. If the claim is to have empirical content, it must sometimes be possible to discover what a person's preference or strongest motive is via some other situation, to independently identify it in order then to check in this situation whether the person is doing

---

④ Nozick is saying that his view cannot accept this metaphysical thesis. This is akin to Chisholm's suggestion that a free choice might not be an event, where events are things that either occur according to general laws or else are random.

---

⑤ But this is somewhat misleading. The cause of the action isn't really R_A by itself, but rather R_A with an assigned weight that exceeds that of R_B. And there is a general law that a more weighty reason will triumph over a less weighty one. It is the assigning of weights that is the ultimate cause of the action, and that assigning is *neither* determined nor caused on Nozick's view.

what he most prefers or has the strongest motive to do.⑥ Defenders of the claim do point out other situations (of choice or answering questions) where the relevant preference or motive can be identified; so the truth of the claim in this decision situation is testable, given the assumption that the preference or motive is stable from the one situation to the other. However, if our conception of the bestowal of weights (with a commitment that lingers) holds true, then these independent "tests" are to be interpreted differently. We do not always act on what was a preexistingly strongest preference or motive; it can become strongest in the process of making the decision, thereafter having greater weight (in other future decisions) than the reasons it vanquished. The prior independent test of a preference therefore need not discover one that existed; it may establish a preference which then consistently carries over into a new decision situation. The testing procedure cannot show that we always act on a preexistingly strongest preference or motive.⑦

Only when there are opposed reasons for different actions is it necessary to arrive at a weighting; otherwise, one can just do what all the reasons favor. However, neither group of these opposed reasons need be moral; decisions that involve a conflict of duty or other moral motives with (nonmoral) desires are only a subclass of the free decisions.⑧ Shall we say, though, that every free decision involves a conflict of some sort, with reasons pulling in different directions? The reasons in conflict need not then have indeterminate weight, for a free decision may "act out" an earlier weighting decision as precedent. (But is there always present a reason of indeterminate weight to reexamine and overturn an earlier precedent, which reason itself must be given a determinate lesser weight in the decision to follow the precedent?) Even though it will include no interesting cases we especially want to judge, still, we may formulate the theory to avoid the uncomfortable consequence that actions in the face of no contrary reasons are not free ones.⑨

. . .

NONRANDOM WEIGHTING

Granting the coherence of the conception wherein the process of decision bestows weights, still, is that free will? An action's being non-determined . . . is not sufficient for it to be free—it might just be a random act. If we acted in the way uranium 238 emits alpha particles, determinism would be false but (unless we are greatly mistaken about uranium 238) we would not thereby have free will. What makes the bestowal of weights on reasons any different? If that too is a random act, then is acting on those weights in that very decision other than random? Acting on those same weights later will not be random, but is it better than any other determined act if it traces its history back not to causes before birth but to a recent random weighting of reasons?⑩

⑥ Blatchford, among others, claims that a person always acts from his antecedently strongest motive. Nozick questions how this motive is to be identified (since to say that it is just whatever motive he ends up acting on would reduce the claim to the trivial thesis that he acts on whatever motive he acts on—hardly something anyone would deny). Thus some other way of identifying the antecedently strongest motive is needed.

⑦ One solution to this problem is to identify the antecedently strongest motive by what the person says or does on some other occasion. Nozick responds that this procedure cannot distinguish between an antecedently strongest motive and one that is created by an assignment on the occasion of the question or previous action—and thus cannot support Blatchford's claim. (Is there any other way to identify an *antecedently* strongest motive, one that distinguishes it from a motive that *becomes* strongest only by being assigned greater weight?)

⑧ Thus Nozick's conception of free choice is broader than Campbell's, in that morality need not be the reason for one of the alternatives. (In a footnote that we have deleted, Nozick explicitly refers to the Campbell article from which the previous selection was taken.)

⑨ Campbell's view also seemed to have the consequence that we are free only where there are competing choices. Nozick is suggesting that this is implausible and that it can be avoided by adopting the suggestion in the preceding parenthetical remark.

⑩ Thus the idea of assigning weights to reasons has not yet avoided the central problem for libertarianism: that of finding a third alternative to determinism and randomness.

How can the giving of weights be other than random? Since (by hypothesis) there is no cause for giving or bestowing these particular weights on reasons rather than other weights, must it be merely a random act when these are bestowed? . . . If the absence of causation entailed randomness, then the denial of (contra-causal) free will would follow immediately. However, 'uncaused' does not entail 'random'. To be sure, the theorist of free will still has to explain wherein the act not causally determined is nonrandom, but at least there is room for this task.

In what way is the bestowal of weights not simply random? There may be causes limiting the reasons on which (nonzero) weight can be bestowed, and the interval within which these weights fall may similarly be limited. However, although it is not a random matter that the weights bestowed fall within this range, neither is that decided by the person. [11] The question remains: how is her decision among the alternatives causally open to her (the alternatives it is not causally determined she won't choose) not simply a random matter?

First, the decision may be self-subsuming; the weights it bestows may fix general principles that mandate not only the relevant act but also the bestowing of those (or similar) weights. The bestowal of weights yields both the action and (as a subsumption, not a repetition) that very bestowal. For example, consider the policy of choosing so as to track bestness: if the act weren't best you wouldn't do it, while if it were best you would. The decision to follow this policy may itself be an instance of it, subsumed under it. [12]

[11] The limitations on the reasons and the interval would themselves be causally determined.

[12] A random occurrence is sometimes thought of as one that happens for no reason. Nozick is suggesting that there might, in a way, be a reason for the assigning of weights: it might operate via a general principle that is *self-subsuming,* that is, whose adoption is an instance of itself. Nozick's example is the general policy or principle of choosing in such a way as to "track bestness," that is, do whatever is morally best. Adopting that principle is itself arguably an instance of doing what is morally best, so that the principle is self-subsuming. (Another way to put this is to say that the principle adopted may provide a reason for the adoption of that very principle.)

Consider a self-subsuming decision that bestows weights to reasons on the basis of a then chosen conception of oneself and one's appropriate life, a conception that includes bestowing those weights and choosing that conception (where the weights also yield choosing that self-conception). Such a self-subsuming decision will not be a random brute fact; it will be explained as an instance of the very conception and weights chosen. (I do not say that all of one's choices or all that bestow weights are self-subsuming in this way; however, the other ones that are based on weights previously given in such decisions, revokable weights, will inherit autonomy.) It will no more be a random brute fact than is the holding of a fundamental deep explanatory law that subsumes and thereby explains itself. . . . A self-subsuming decision does not happen inexplicably, it is not random in the sense of being connected to no weighted reasons (including the self-subsuming ones then chosen). But although it doesn't happen just randomly, still, there are different and conflicting self-subsuming decisions that could be made; just as there are different fundamental, self-subsuming laws that could hold true, could have held true. Is it not arbitrary then that one self-subsuming decision is made rather than another? Won't it be left inexplicable why this one was made (rather than another one)? [13]

[13] Such a self-subsuming decision may be as general as a choice of an overall kind of life: live the morally best life, where adopting that principle is part of living the morally best life. But while there is in this odd way a reason for the adoption of such a principle or conception of one's life, in the interesting cases there will be alternative choices that would have similarly been self-subsuming. So why isn't the choice between these arbitrary—that is, random?

UNDERSTANDING AND EXPLAINING FREE CHOICES

. . .

The moral I wish to draw is this: we can have an explanation and understanding of why something occurred even when we do not know of any reason why it, rather than something else, occurred that time, in that instance. Even when the event is random, its occurrence need not be inexplicable; it can be seen as an event, one of a type to be expected, arising from a mechanism or system that, in a way we may have better or worse understanding of, yields such events among others.

I am not suggesting that free decisions are random happenings from a chance mechanism with a well-defined probability distribution . . . over the various alternative actions. The process of choice among alternative actions is different; there are not fixed factual probabilities for each action, there is no such dispositional propensity or limit of long-run frequencies or whatever. Rather, there is a process operating wherein each alternative action could be yielded, and one of them was. This time, the process gave rise to that particular alternative. (Compare: this time the random system yielded that particular event.)

To be sure, we do not want to say simply that there is a process which could give rise to any of the alternative actions—we want to know more about the process, we want to delineate and understand it, we want to know how it works.

. . .

In what . . . way . . . can we understand the process of making free choices? By making them, perhaps.[14] We might interpret those theorists who pointed to our choices not as trying to prove that we made free choices but as ostensively explaining the notion, showing its intelligibility. Were they saying that we understand free choice and agency by virtue of making free choices as agents? . . . Our problem is that we are puzzled about the nature of free choices, so any inside knowledge we may have of such choices due to and in making them obviously hasn't served to clear up our puzzles about their nature. It is tempting to say our puzzlement stems from supposing we must be able discursively to say or describe what a free choice is like, yet the fact that we cannot, when we are directly acquainted with them, doesn't interfere with understanding them. But too many ineffabilities spoil the philosophical broth. Since I do not myself have even the feeling of understanding, I will continue the (discursive) attempts at explanation.[15]

[14] This is Campbell's suggestion.

. . . We have said already that the decision process (sometimes) bestows weights on the reasons for and against the various alternatives, and that this bestowal of weights is self-subsuming and so to that extent not random. Still, there can be different self-subsuming bestowals of weight. Although after one occurs we will be able retrospectively to give a reason as the cause (though without causal determination), can anything be said about why that one self-subsuming decision is made rather than another? No, the weights are bestowed in virtue of weights that come into effect in the very act of bestowal. This is the translation into this context of the notion of reflexivity: the phenomenon, such as reference or a law's holding, has an "inside" character when it holds or occurs in virtue of a feature bestowed by its holding or occurring.

The free decision is reflexive; it holds in virtue of weights bestowed by its holding. An explanation of why the act was chosen will have to refer to its being chosen. However, not every act you do is a minor miracle of reflexive self-subsumption, only the ones involving choice of fundamental principles and self-conception. (Yet since such a choice is revokable, do later choices reaffirm it, and so also involve reflexive self-subsumption?)[16]

[15] But experiencing such a choice doesn't really explain how it works and in particular how it can be neither determined nor random. Nozick concedes that he doesn't really even seem to himself to understand this.

[16] To say that the assignment of weights is *reflexive* is to say that it is adopted by virtue of itself.

Suppose a process of decision can have these features, bestowing weights in a self-subsuming fashion which is reflexive. The decision then does not simply dangle there at random—we can see the many ties and connections it has (including internal ones); the particular decision is not inexplicable—we see it as something that could arise from a process of this sort.

More might be demanded, however; it might be demanded that the theorist of free will show how the decision is causally determined. Otherwise, it will be said, the character and nature of the decision will remain mysterious. But clearing up any mystery in that way would come at the cost of the act's contra-causal freedom. No adequate condition on explanation or understanding necessitates . . . causal explanation. . . . Free will is to be explained differently, by delineating a decision process that can give rise to various acts in a nonrandom nonarbitrary way; whichever it gives rise to—and it could give rise to any one of several—will happen nonarbitrarily. These remarks are independent of the particular process we have delineated here, involving the bestowal of weights, reflexive self-subsumption, and so on. What is inappropriate is to demand that a free choice be explained in a way that shows it is unfree.

The theme of the bestowal of weights to reasons, in a situation of no preexistingly determinate weights, seems to me phenomenologically accurate and proper to emphasize. [17] I have more worries about terming this bestowal nonarbitrary and nonrandom because it is self-subsuming and reflexive. This position has too much the flavor of applying shiny new tools and ideas everywhere, as a magic key—except that some of the applications depend, perhaps, upon these ideas being not so well understood, not so shiny. So we should be somewhat wary of this use of the themes of self-subsumption and reflexiveness to delineate the nonarbitrary nature of a free choice. They do have the right flavor, though. . . .

---

[17] To say that this picture seems "phenomenologically accurate" is to say that it seems to accurately reflect what goes on in an actual *experience* of free choice.

COULD ONE HAVE BESTOWED OTHERWISE?

. . . Another way in which bestowal of weight upon reasons can be nonarbitrary is that the self can synthesize itself around this bestowing: "I value things in this way." If in that reflexive self-reference, the I synthesizes itself (in part) around the act of bestowing weight on reasons, then it will not be arbitrary or random that *that* self bestowed those weights. [18]

The process of decision can yield the intentional doing of different actions, and it would have if different weights had been assigned, which could have happened. But does it follow that the person could have done otherwise, that it was within the person's power to bestow different weights, as opposed to that merely happening? In what way could the person have *done* otherwise, not merely been the arena in which otherwise happened?

It would be fruitless to embark upon the theoretical regress wherein a different intentional action of bestowing weights occurs with its own separate weights which have to be bestowed by a still separate act. And why is it asked only if another bestowal could have been done; why is it not similarly asked whether the bestowal that did occur was a doing or merely a happening? Maybe it is possible for weights somehow to just happen to get bestowed on reasons; however, when the bestowal is anchored and tied in the way we have described, to a formed self-conception (even if formed just then), if it is self-subsuming and reflexive, leading to later (revokable) commitment, then it is a doing, not a happening merely. If all that context and stage setting . . . does not make it an action, what alternative conception of action is being presupposed? The actual bestowal of weights on reasons is a doing and not merely a happening; another and alternative bestowal of weights on reasons could have occurred instead—this one wasn't causally determined, and others aren't causally excluded—with all of the accompanying context and stage setting appropriate to it, so that alternative bestowal too would have been a doing and not merely a happening. The person could have bestowed differently. . . . [19]

---

[18] If the assignment of weights is a part of creating or constituting the sort of self that one chooses to be, then there will be another (related) way that it is nonrandom: it reflects the very nature of the resulting self. (But there would still be alternative choices that would reflect the nature of alternative selves, still making it unclear why the choice of self isn't itself random.)

---

[19] Nozick is saying that the choice of self was something the person *did*, not something that merely happened to him (either as a result of causal determination or randomness). Thus the person could have done otherwise in the sense that he could have chosen a different self with corresponding assignment of weights. (But this still doesn't explain just how the choice is made if it is neither causally determined nor random.)

Discussion Questions

1. Is Nozick right that his view seems "phenomenologically accurate"? Think of a realistic example or two and try to spell out just how Nozick's view of such a case differs from that of either the hard or soft determinist.
2. Does the idea of self-subsumption solve the problem of why the assigning of weights isn't random? Does it even contribute to a solution of this problem? Why or why not?
3. Nozick concedes that he does not "have even the feeling of understanding" with regard to the question of how a free choice really works, how it is different from either determinism or randomness. Assuming that no one is in any better position in this respect, how serious a problem is this for libertarianism? Is it possible that we have good reasons for thinking that there are such choices and perhaps even that we can tell which ones they are, even if we don't really understand their nature?

IS FREEDOM REQUIRED FOR MORAL RESPONSIBILITY?

Galen Strawson

Galen Strawson (1952–) teaches philosophy at the University of Reading in England. Strawson has written on a variety of philosophical topics, especially the philosophy of mind, issues concerning causation, and the free will problem. He is the son of the perhaps even better known British philosopher P. F. Strawson.

In the following selection, Strawson, in addition to offering a useful summary of the main positions on the free will problem, argues that moral responsibility (and freedom) in the most ultimate sense would require a kind of control over one's own nature or character that it is impossible to have. His view is thus a version of what we have called *hard determinism*—though a hard determinism that is not committed to the thesis of causal determinism itself, but simply argues that whether or not causal determinism is true there is no logical room for freedom.

Free Will

'Free will' is the conventional name of a topic that is best discussed without reference to the will. Its central questions are 'What is it to act (or choose) freely?', and 'What is it to be morally responsible for one's actions (or choices)?' These two questions are closely connected, for freedom of action is necessary for moral responsibility, even if it is not sufficient.

Philosophers give very different answers to these questions, hence also to two more specific questions about ourselves: (1) Are we free agents? and (2) Can we be morally responsible for what we do? Answers to (1) and (2) range from 'Yes, Yes' to 'No, No'—via

From Routledge Encyclopedia of Philosophy, *edited by Edward Craig (New York: Routledge, Ltd., 1998).*

'Yes, No' and various degrees of 'Perhaps', 'Possibly', and 'In a sense'. (The fourth pair of outright answers, 'No, Yes', is rare, but appears to be accepted by some Protestants.)① Prominent among the 'Yes, Yes' sayers are the *compatibilists,* who hold that free will is compatible with *determinism.* Briefly, determinism is the view that everything that happens is necessitated by what has already gone before, in such a way that nothing can happen otherwise than it does. According to compatibilists, freedom is compatible with determinism because freedom is essentially just a matter of not being constrained or hindered in certain ways when one acts or chooses. Thus normal adult human beings in normal circumstances are able to act and choose freely. No one is holding a gun to their heads. They are not drugged, or in chains, or subject to a psychological compulsion. They are therefore wholly free to choose and act even if their whole physical and psychological make-up is entirely determined by things for which they are in no way ultimately responsible—starting with their genetic inheritance and early upbringing.

> ① You should be able to figure out roughly what views these answers reflect. The "Yes, No" answer might be given by someone who accepts the compatibilist account of freedom as the only intelligible one, but thinks that it is still inadequate for genuine moral responsibility. The Protestant view in question is the idea that everything a person does is predestined by God, but that people are still responsible at least in the sense that they can be appropriately rewarded or punished.

Incompatibilists hold that freedom is not compatible with determinism. They point out that if determinism is true, then every one of one's actions was determined to happen as it did before one was born. They hold that one cannot be held to be truly free and finally morally responsible for one's actions in this case. They think compatibilism is a 'wretched subterfuge. . . . a petty word-jugglery', as Kant put it. It entirely fails to satisfy our natural convictions about the nature of moral responsibility.

The incompatibilists have a good point, and may be divided into two groups. *Libertarians* answer 'Yes, Yes' to questions (1) and (2). They hold that we are indeed free and fully morally responsible agents, and that determinism must therefore be false. Their great difficulty is to explain why the falsity of determinism is any better than the truth of determinism when it comes to establishing our free agency and moral responsibility. For suppose that not every event is determined, and that some events occur randomly, or as a matter of chance. How can our claim to moral responsibility be improved by the supposition that it is partly a matter of chance or random outcome that we and our actions are as they are?②

> ② Thus the libertarian, as we have seen, must seemingly find a third alternative to determinism and randomness.

The second group of incompatibilists is less sanguine. They answer 'No, No' to questions (1) and (2). They agree with the libertarians that the truth of determinism rules out genuine moral responsibility, but argue that the falsity of determinism cannot help. Accordingly, they conclude that we are not genuinely free agents or genuinely morally responsible, whether determinism is true or false. One of their arguments can be summarized as follows. When one acts, one acts in the way one does because of the way one is. So to be truly morally responsible for one's actions, one would have to be truly responsible for the way one is: one would have to be *causa sui,* or the cause of oneself, at least in certain crucial mental respects. But nothing can be *causa sui*—nothing can be the ultimate cause of itself in any respect. So nothing can be truly morally responsible.③

> ③ This is essentially the view of Blatchford and Edwards—and also in the end of Strawson himself.

Suitably developed, this argument against moral responsibility seems very strong. But in many human beings, the experience of choice gives rise to a conviction of absolute responsibility that is untouched by philosophical arguments. This conviction is the deep and inexhaustible source of the free will problem; powerful arguments that seem to show that we cannot be morally responsible in the ultimate way that we suppose keep coming up against equally powerful psychological reasons why we continue to believe that we are ultimately morally responsible.④

1. COMPATIBILISM

Do we have free will? It depends what you mean by the word 'free'. More than two hundred senses of the word have been distinguished: the history of the discussion of free will is rich and remarkable. David Hume called the problem of free will 'the most contentious question of metaphysics, the most contentious science'.

> ④ As we have seen, this psychological conviction, especially as it arises in situations of actual choice, is the most basic reason for believing in free will.

According to *compatibilists,* we do have free will. They propound a sense of the word 'free' according to which free will is compatible with *determinism,* even though determinism is the view that the history of the universe is fixed in such a way that nothing can happen otherwise than it does because everything that happens is necessitated by what has already gone before.

Suppose tomorrow is a national holiday. You are considering what to do. You can climb a mountain or read Lao Tse. You can mend your bicycle or go to the zoo. At this moment you are reading . . . philosophy. You are free to go on reading or stop now. You have started on this sentence, but you don't have to . . . finish it.

In this situation, as so often in life, you have a number of options. Nothing forces your hand. It seems natural to say that you are *entirely* free to choose what to do. And, given that nothing hinders you, it seems natural to say that you act entirely freely when you actually do (or try to do) what you have decided to do.

Compatibilists claim that this is the right thing to say. They believe that to have free will, to be a free agent, to be free in choice and action, is simply to be free from *constraints* of certain sorts. Freedom is a matter of not being physically or psychologically forced or compelled to do what one does. Your character, personality, preferences, and general motivational set may be entirely determined by events for which you are in no way responsible (by your genetic inheritance, upbringing, subsequent experience, and so on). But you do not have to be in control of any of these things in order to have compatibilist freedom. They do not constrain or compel you, because compatibilist freedom is just a matter of being able to choose and act in the way one prefers or thinks best *given how one is.* As its name declares, it is compatible with determinism. It is compatible with determinism even though it follows from determinism that every aspect of your character, and everything you will ever do, was already inevitable before you were born.

If determinism does not count as a constraint or compulsion, what does? Compatibilists standardly take it that freedom can be limited by such things as imprisonment, by a gun at one's head, or a threat to the life of one's children, or a psychological obsession and so on.

It is arguable, however, that compatibilist freedom is something one continues to possess undiminished so long as one can choose or act in any way at all. One continues to possess it in any situation in which one is not actually panicked, or literally compelled to do what one does, in such a way that it is not clear that one can still be said to choose or act at all (as when one presses a button, because one's finger is actually forced down on the button).

Consider pilots of hijacked aeroplanes. They usually stay calm. They *choose* to comply with the hijackers' demands. They act responsibly, as we naturally say. They are able to do other than they do, but they choose not to. They do what they most want to do, all things considered, in the circumstances in which they find themselves.

All circumstances limit one's options in some way. It is true that some circumstances limit one's options much more drastically than others; but it does not follow that one is not free to choose in those circumstances. Only literal compulsion, panic, or uncontrollable impulse really removes one's freedom to choose, and to (try to) do what one most wants to do given one's character or personality. Even when one's finger is being forced down on the button, one can still act freely in resisting the pressure, and in many other ways.⑤

> ⑤ Strawson is saying that the central compatibilist view that we found in Hume and Stace (that a free action is one that results from one's own will or psychological processes) does not really justify excluding cases of constraint or compulsion from the class of free actions. His point is essentially the same that was made by Stace when he described such cases as "borderline cases": they involve some degree of freedom in that one still has options, even though very limited ones.

Most of us are free to choose throughout our waking lives, according to the compatibilist conception of freedom. We are free to choose between the options that we perceive to be open to us. (Sometimes we would rather not face options, but are unable to avoid awareness of the fact that we do face them.) One has options even when one is in chains, or falling through space. Even if one is completely paralysed, one is still free in so far as one is free to choose to think about one thing rather than another. Sartre observed that there is a sense in which we are 'condemned' to freedom, not free not to be free.

Of course one may well not be able to do everything one wants—one may want to fly unassisted, vapourize every gun in the United States by an act of thought, or house all those who sleep on the streets of Calcutta by the end of the month. But few have supposed that free will, or free agency, is a matter of being able to do everything one wants. That is one possible view of what it is to be free; but according to the compatibilists, free will is simply a matter of having genuine options and opportunities for action, and being able to choose between them according to what one wants or thinks best.

It may be said that dogs and other animals can be free agents, according to this basic account of compatibilism. Compatibilists may reply that dogs can indeed be free agents. And yet we do not think that dogs can be free or morally responsible in the way we can be. So compatibilists need to say what the relevant difference is between dogs and ourselves.

Many suppose that it is our capacity for self-conscious thought that makes the crucial difference, because it makes it possible for us to be explicitly aware of ourselves as facing choices and engaging in processes of reasoning about what to do. This is *not* because being self-conscious can somehow liberate one from the facts of determinism; if determinism is true, one is determined to have whatever self-conscious thoughts one has, whatever their complexity. Nevertheless, many are inclined to think that a creature's explicit self-conscious awareness of itself as chooser and agent can constitute it as a free agent in a fundamental way that is unavailable to any unself-conscious agent. [6]

[6] Is there any good reason for thinking that self-consciousness is relevant to freedom in this way?

Compatibilists can agree with this. They can acknowledge and incorporate the view that self-conscious awareness of oneself as facing choices can give rise to a kind of freedom that is unavailable to unself-conscious agents. They may add that human beings are sharply marked off from dogs by their capacity to act for reasons that they explicitly take to be moral reasons. In general, compatibilism has many variants. According to Harry Frankfurt's version, for example, one has free will if one wants to be moved to action by the motives that do in fact move one to action. [7] On this view, freedom is a matter of having a personality that is harmonious in a certain way. Freedom in this sense is clearly compatible with determinism.

[7] This is the hierarchical compatibilist view that was mentioned earlier in Discussion Question 3 for the Hospers selection.

Compatibilism has been refined in many ways, but this gives an idea of its basis. 'What more could free agency possibly be?', compatibilists like to ask. And this is a very powerful question.

2.   INCOMPATIBILISM

Those who want to secure the conclusion that we are free agents do well to adopt a compatibilist theory of freedom, for determinism is unfalsifiable, and may be true. [8] . . . Many, however, think that the compatibilist account of things does not even touch the real problem of free will. They believe that all compatibilist theories of freedom are patently inadequate.

[8] Strawson means here that the failure to find causes doesn't establish that there aren't any. Even in the case of quantum theory, some still think that underlying deterministic causes (so-called "hidden variables") will eventually be found.

What is it, they say, to define freedom in such a way that it is compatible with determinism? It is to define it in such a way that a creature can be a free agent even if all its actions throughout its life are determined to happen as they do by events that have taken place before it is born; so that there is a clear sense in which it could not at any point in its life have done otherwise than it did. This, they say, is certainly not free will. More importantly, it is not a sufficient basis for true moral responsibility. One cannot possibly be truly or ultimately morally responsible for what one does if everything one does is ultimately a deterministic outcome of events that took place before one was born; or (more generally) a deterministic outcome of events for whose occurrence one is in no way ultimately responsible.

These anti-compatibilists or *incompatibilists* divide into two groups: the *libertarians* and the *no-*

freedom theorists or *pessimists* about free will and moral responsibility.⑨ The libertarians think that the compatibilist account of freedom can be improved on.

⑨ "No-freedom theorists" are hard determinists, as that term has been used here.

They hold (1) that we do have free will, (2) that free will is not compatible with determinism, and (3) that determinism is therefore false. But they face an extremely difficult task: they have to show how *indeterminism* (the falsity of determinism) can help with free will and, in particular, with moral responsibility.

The pessimists or no-freedom theorists do not think that this can be shown. They agree with the libertarians that the compatibilist account of free will is inadequate, but they do not think it can be improved on. They agree that free will is not compatible with determinism, but deny that indeterminism can help to make us (or anyone else) free. They believe that free will, of the sort that is necessary for genuine moral responsibility, is probably impossible.

The pessimists about free will grant what everyone must: that there is a clear and important compatibilist sense in which we can be free agents (we can be free, when unconstrained, to choose and to do what we want or think best, given how we are). But they insist that this compatibilist sense of freedom is not enough: it does not give us what we want, in the way of free will; nor does it give us what we believe we have. And it is not as if the compatibilists have missed something. The truth is that nothing can give us what

⑩ This "absolute, buckstopping" idea of freedom is essentially the one being advocated by Campbell and Nozick: one in which the agent or self is ultimately responsible for free choices, but without those choices depending on its formed character or nature (which would make them instead dependent on heredity and environment). Strawson denies that this sort of freedom is possible, though without yet giving a reason.

we (think we) want, or what we ordinarily think we have. All attempts to furnish a stronger notion of free will fail. We cannot be morally responsible, in the absolute, buck-stopping way in which we often unreflectively think we are. We cannot have 'strong' free will of the kind that we would need to have, in order to be morally responsible in this way.⑩

The fundamental motor of the free will debate is the worry about moral responsibility. If no one had this worry, it is doubtful whether the problem of free will would be a famous philosophical problem. The rest of this discussion will therefore be organized around the question of moral responsibility.

First, though, it is worth remarking that the worry about free will does not have to be expressed as a worry about the grounds of moral responsibility. A commitment to belief in free will may be integral to feelings that are extremely important to us independently of the issue of moral responsibility: feelings of gratitude, for example, and perhaps of love. One's belief in strong free will may also be driven simply by the conviction that one is or can be *radically self-determining* in one's actions (in a way that is incompatible with determinism) and this conviction need not involve giving much—or any—thought to the issue of moral responsibility. It seems that a creature could conceive of itself as radically self-determining without having any conception of moral right or wrong at all—and so without being any sort of moral agent.

3.   PESSIMISM

One way of setting out the no-freedom theorists' argument is as follows.

(1)   When you act, you do what you do, in the situation in which you find yourself, because of the way you are.

It seems to follow that

(2)   To be truly or ultimately morally responsible for what you *do*, you must be truly or ultimately responsible for the way you *are*, at least in certain crucial mental respects. (Obviously you don't have to be responsible for the way you are in all respects. You don't have to be responsible for your height, age, sex, and so on. But it does seem that you have to be responsible for the way you are at least in certain mental respects. After all, it is your overall mental make-up that leads you to do what you do when you act.)

But

(3)   You cannot be ultimately responsible for the way you are in any respect at all, so you

cannot be ultimately morally responsible for what you do.

Why is that you cannot be ultimately responsible for the way you are? Because

(4) To be ultimately responsible for the way you are you would have to have intentionally brought it about that you are the way you are, in a way that is impossible.

The impossibility is shown as follows. Suppose that

(5) You have somehow intentionally brought it about that you are the way you now are, in certain mental respects: suppose that you have intentionally brought it about that you have a certain mental nature N, and that you have brought this about in such a way that you can now be said to be ultimately responsible for having nature N. (The limiting case of this would be the case in which you had simply endorsed your existing mental nature N from a position of power to change it.)

For this to be true

11 Step (6) is the crucial step in the argument. It claims that a choice of one's own nature (perhaps via the adoption of a principle for assigning weights to reasons, as discussed by Nozick) *must* be based on intentions or preferences that derive from one's previous nature. The implicit idea is that otherwise it would be random and so not anything for which the person would be responsible.

(6) You must already have had a certain mental nature N_{-1}, in the light of which you intentionally brought it about that you now have nature N. (If you did not already have a certain mental nature, then you cannot have had any intentions or preferences, and even if you did change in some way, you cannot be held to be responsible for the way you now are.)11

But then

(7) For it to be true that you and you alone are truly responsible for how you now are, you must be truly responsible for having had the nature N_{-1} in the light of which you intentionally brought it about that you now have nature N.

So

(8) You must have intentionally brought it about that you had that nature N_{-1}. But in that case, you must have existed already with a prior nature. N_{-2}, in the light of which you intentionally brought it about that you had the nature N_{-1}.

And so on. Here one is setting off on a potentially infinite regress. In order for one to be truly or ultimately responsible for *how one is,* in such a way that one can be truly morally responsible for *what one does,* something impossible has to be true: there has to be, and cannot be, a starting point in the series of acts of bringing it about that one has a certain nature—a starting point that constitutes an act of ultimate self-origination. 12

There is a more concise way of putting the point: in order to be truly morally responsible for what one does, it seems that one would have to be the ultimate cause or origin of oneself, or at least of some crucial part of one's mental nature. One would have to be *causa sui,* in the old terminology. But nothing can be truly or ultimately *causa sui* in any respect at all. Even if the property of being *causa sui* is allowed to belong (unintelligibly) to God, it cannot plausibly be supposed to be possessed by ordinary finite human beings. . . .

In fact, nearly all of those who believe in strong free will do so without any conscious thought that it requires ultimate self-origination. Nevertheless, this is the only thing that could actually ground the kind of strong free will that is regularly believed in, and it does seem that one way in which the belief in strong free will manifests itself is in the very vague and (necessarily) unexamined belief that many have that they

12 Since an infinite regress of natures is impossible, there must be a starting point in which one constitutes one's own nature for the first time, on the basis of no previous nature. Strawson claims that this is impossible. In the following paragraph, this claim is elaborated by appeal to the allegedly impossible idea of causing oneself. (Notice that, contrary to what Strawson may seem to suggest, Nozick does not need to claim that one can be the cause of one's self in *every* respect. It is enough for Nozick's purposes if there are certain aspects of one's self that one brings into being without these being either shaped by one's previous self or random.)

are somehow or other radically responsible for their general mental nature, or at least for certain crucial aspects of it.

The pessimists' argument may seem contrived, but essentially the same argument can be given in a more natural form as follows. (i) It is undeniable that one is the way one is, initially, as a result of heredity and early experience. (ii) It is undeniable that these are things for which one cannot be held to be in any way responsible (this might not be true if there were reincarnation, but reincarnation would just shift the problem backwards). (iii) One cannot at any later stage of one's life hope to accede to true or ultimate responsibility for the way one is by trying to change the way one already is as a result of one's heredity and previous experience. For one may well try to change oneself, but (iv) both the particular way in which one is moved to try to change oneself, and the degree of success in one's attempt at change, will be determined by how one already is as a result of heredity and previous experience. And (v) any further changes that one can bring about only after one has brought about certain initial changes will in turn be determined, via the initial changes, by heredity and previous experience. (vi) This may not be the whole story, for it may be that some changes in the way one is are traceable to the influence of indeterministic or random factors. But (vii) it is foolish to suppose that indeterministic or random factors, for which one is *ex hypothesi* in no way responsible, can in themselves contribute to one's being truly or ultimately responsible for how one is. ⒔

⒔ Here is a simpler version of the argument, one that Blatchford and Edwards would endorse. Nozick (and Campbell) would reject step (iv), claiming that one can sometimes change one's self in ways not determined by one's previously formed character.

The claim, then, is not that people cannot change the way they are. They can, in certain respects (which tend to be exaggerated by North Americans and underestimated, perhaps, by members of many other cultures). The claim is only that people cannot be supposed to change themselves in such a way as to be or become truly or ultimately responsible for the way they are, and hence for their actions. One can put the point by saying that the way you are is, ultimately, in every last detail, a matter of luck—good or bad.

4. MORAL RESPONSIBILITY

Two main questions are raised by the pessimists' arguments. First, is it really true that one needs to be self-creating or *causa sui* in some way, in order to be truly or ultimately responsible for what one does, as step (2) of the pessimists' argument asserts? Addressing this question will be delayed until §6, because a more basic question arises: What notion of responsibility is being appealed to in this argument? What exactly is this 'ultimate' responsibility that we are held to believe in . . . ? And if we do believe in it, what makes us believe in it?

One dramatic way to characterize the notion of ultimate responsibility is by reference to the story of heaven and hell: 'ultimate' moral responsibility is responsibility of such a kind that, if we have it, it *makes sense* to propose that it could be just to punish some of us with torment in hell and reward others with bliss in heaven. It makes sense because what we do is absolutely up to us. The words 'makes sense' are stressed because one certainly does not have to believe in the story of heaven and hell in order to understand the notion of ultimate responsibility that it is used to illustrate. Nor does one have to believe in the story of heaven and hell in order to believe in ultimate responsibility (many atheists have believed in it). One does not have to have heard of it. ⒕

⒕ The last point here is worth underlining: Strawson is using the idea of heaven and hell to illustrate what "ultimate moral responsibility" is supposed to be like. But he is *not* saying that the existence of heaven and hell—or God—is required for ultimate moral responsibility to exist or for the idea of it to be intelligible.

The story is useful because it illustrates the *kind* of absolute or ultimate responsibility that many have supposed—and do suppose—themselves to have. It becomes particularly vivid when one is specifically concerned with moral responsibility, and with questions of desert: but it serves equally well to illustrate the sense of radical freedom and responsibility that may be had by a self-conscious agent that has no concept of morality. And one does not have to refer to the story of heaven and hell in order to describe the sorts of everyday situation that seem to be primarily influential in giving rise to our belief in ultimate responsibility. Suppose you set off for a shop on the eve of a national holiday, intending to buy a cake with your last ten pound note. Everything is closing down. There is one cake left: it costs ten pounds. On the steps of the shop someone is shaking an Oxfam tin.[15] You stop, and it seems completely clear to you that it is entirely up to you what you do next. That is, it seems clear to you that you are truly, radically free to choose, in such a way that you will be ultimately responsible for whatever you do choose. You can put the money in the tin, or go in and buy the cake, or just walk away. (You are not only completely free to choose. You are not free not to choose.)

> [15] Oxfam is an international charitable and emergency relief organization.

Standing there, you may believe that determinism is true. You may believe that in five minutes' time you will be able to look back on the situation and say, of what you will by then have done, 'It was determined that I should do that'. But even if you do believe this, it does not seem to undermine your current sense of the absoluteness of your freedom, and of your moral responsibility for your choice.

One diagnosis of this phenomenon is that one cannot really believe that determinism is true, in such situations of choice, and cannot help thinking that the falsity of determinism might make freedom possible. But the feeling of ultimate responsibility seems to remain inescapable even if one does not think this, and even if one has been convinced by the entirely general argument against ultimate responsibility given in §3. Suppose one accepts that no one can be in any way *causa sui,* and yet that one would have to be *causa sui* (in certain crucial mental respects) in order to be ultimately responsible for one's actions. This does not seem to have any impact on one's sense of one's radical freedom and responsibility, as one stands there, wondering what to do. One's radical responsibility seems to stem simply from the fact that one is fully conscious of one's situation, and knows that one can choose, and believes that one action is morally better than the other. This seems to be immediately enough to confer full and ultimate responsibility. And yet it cannot really do so, according to the pessimists. For whatever one actually does, one will do what one does because of the way one is, and the way one is is something for

which one neither is nor can be responsible, however self-consciously aware of one's situation one is.

The example of the cake may be artificial, but similar situations of choice occur regularly in human life. They are the experiential rock on which the belief in ultimate responsibility is founded. The belief often takes the form of belief in specifically moral, desert-implying responsibility. But, as noted, an agent could have a sense of ultimate responsibility without possessing any conception of morality, and there is an interesting intermediate case: an agent could have an irrepressible experience of ultimate responsibility, and believe in objective moral right and wrong, while still denying the coherence of the notion of desert.[16]

> [16] Strawson seems (?) to be saying that the experience, though "irrepressible," would be mistaken (since if the notion of desert is incoherent, then the idea of ultimate responsibility—which implies desert—really makes no sense).

5. METAPHYSICS AND MORAL PSYCHOLOGY

We now have the main elements of the problem of free will. It is natural to start with the compatibilist position; but this has only to be stated to trigger the objection that compatibilism cannot possibly satisfy our intuitions about moral responsibility. According to this objection, an incompatibilist notion of free will is essential in order to make sense of the idea that we are genuinely morally responsible. But this view, too, has only to be stated to trigger the pessimists' objection that indeterministic occurrences cannot possibly contribute to moral responsibility: one can hardly be supposed to be more truly morally responsible for one's choices and actions or character if indeterministic occurrences have played a part in their causation than if they have not played such a part. Indeterminism gives rise to unpredictability, not responsibility. It cannot help in any way at all.

The pessimists therefore conclude that strong free will is not possible, and that ultimate responsibility is not possible either. So no punishment or reward is ever truly just or fair, when it comes to moral matters.

. . .

Now the argument may cycle back to compatibilism. Pointing out that 'ultimate' moral responsibility is obviously impossible, compatibilists may claim that we should rest content with the compatibilist account of things—since it is the best we can do. But this claim reactivates the incompatibilist objection, and the cycle continues.

There is an alternative strategy at this point; quit the traditional metaphysical circle for the domain of *moral psychology*. The principal positions in the traditional metaphysical debate are clear. No radically new option is likely to emerge after millennia of debate. The interesting questions that remain are primarily psychological: Why do we believe we have strong free will and ultimate responsibility? . . . What is it like to live with this belief? What are its varieties? How might we be changed by dwelling intensely on the view that ultimate responsibility is impossible?

A full answer to these questions is beyond the scope of this [article] but one fundamental cause of our belief in ultimate responsibility has been mentioned. It lies in the experience of choice that we have as self-conscious agents who are able to be fully conscious of what they are doing when they deliberate about what to do and make choices. (We choose between the Oxfam box and the cake; or we make a difficult, morally neutral choice about which of two paintings to buy.) This raises an interesting question: Is it true that any possible self-conscious creature that faces choices and is fully aware of the fact that it does so must experience itself as having strong free will, or as being radically self-determining, simply in virtue of the fact that it is a self-conscious agent (and whether or not it has a conception of moral responsibility)? It seems that we cannot live or experience our choices as determined, even if determinism is true. But perhaps this is a human peculiarity, not an inescapable feature of any possible self-conscious agent. And perhaps it is not even universal among human beings. ⑰

⑰ What would it be like to have the opposite experience: to experience one's choices as determined? Do people ever have such an experience?

. . .

6. CHALLENGES TO PESSIMISM

The preceding discussion attempts to illustrate the internal dynamic of the free will debate, and to explain why the debate is likely to continue for as long as

human beings can think. The basic point is this: powerful logical or metaphysical reasons for supposing that we cannot have strong free will keep coming up against equally powerful psychological reasons why we cannot help believing that we do have it. The pessimists' or no-freedom theorists' conclusions may seem irresistible during philosophical discussion, but they are likely to lose their force, and seem obviously irrelevant to life, when one stops philosophizing.

Various challenges to the pessimists' argument have been proposed, some of which appear to be supported by the experience or 'phenomenology' of choice. One challenge grants that one cannot be ultimately responsible for one's mental nature—one's character, personality, or motivational structure—but denies that it follows that one cannot be truly morally responsible for what one does (it therefore challenges step (2) of the argument set out in §3).

This challenge has at least two versions. One has already been noted: we are attracted by the idea that our capacity for fully explicit self-conscious deliberation, in a situation of choice, suffices by itself to constitute us as truly morally responsible agents in the strongest possible sense. The idea is that such full self-conscious awareness somehow renders irrelevant the fact that one neither is nor can be ultimately responsible for any aspect of one's mental nature. On this view, the mere fact of one's self-conscious presence in the situation of choice can confer true moral responsibility; it may be undeniable that one is, in the final analysis, wholly constituted as the sort of person one is by factors for which one cannot be in any way ultimately responsible; but the threat that this fact appears to pose to one's claim to true moral responsibility is simply obliterated by one's self-conscious awareness of one's situation. ⑱

⑱ Why would a self-conscious awareness of deliberation be enough for responsibility if the results of that determination are still determined by a nature over which one has no ultimate control?

The pessimists reply: This may correctly describe a strong source of *belief* in ultimate (moral) responsibility, but it is not an account of something that could *constitute* ultimate (moral) responsibility. When one acts after explicit self-conscious deliberation, one acts for certain reasons. But which reasons finally weigh with one is a matter of one's mental nature, which is something for which one cannot be in any way ultimately responsible.[19] One can certainly be a morally responsible agent in the sense of being aware of distinctively moral considerations when one acts. But one cannot be morally responsible in such a way that one is ultimately deserving of punishment or reward for what one does.

[19] This is essentially the reply that Blatchford and Edwards would give.

The conviction that fully explicit self-conscious awareness of one's situation can be a sufficient foundation of strong free will is extremely powerful. The no-freedom theorists' argument seems to show that it is wrong, but it is a conviction that runs deeper than rational argument, and it survives untouched, in the everyday conduct of life, even after the validity of the no-freedom theorists' argument has been admitted.[20]

[20] Is this conviction as strong as Strawson claims? Does it even exist?

Another version of the challenge runs as follows. The reason why one can be truly or ultimately (morally) responsible for what one does is that one's *self*—what one might call the 'agent self'—is, in some crucial sense, independent of one's general *mental nature* (one's character, personality, motivational structure, and so on). One's mental nature *inclines* one to do one thing rather than another, but it does not thereby *necessitate* one to do one thing rather than the other. . . . As an agent-self, one incorporates a power of free decision that is independent of all the particularities of one's mental nature in such a way that one can, after all, count as truly and ultimately morally responsible in one's decisions and actions even though one is not ultimately responsible for any aspect of one's mental nature.[21]

[21] This is the Campbell-Nozick view. How compelling is Strawson's reply (in the following paragraph)?

The pessimists reply: Even if one grants the validity of this conception of the agent-self for the sake of argument, it cannot help to establish ultimate moral responsibility. According to the conception, the agent-self decides in the light of the agent's mental nature but is not determined by the agent's mental nature. The following question immediately arises: *Why* does the agent-self decide as it does? The general answer is clear. Whatever the agent-self decides, it decides as it does because of the overall way it is; and this neces-

sary truth returns us to where we started. For once again, it seems that the agent-self must be responsible for being the way it is, in order to be a source of true or ultimate responsibility. But this is impossible, for the reasons given in §3; nothing can be *causa sui* in the required way. Whatever the nature of the agent-self, it is ultimately a matter of luck (or, for those who believe in God, a matter of grace). It may be proposed that the agent-self decides as it does partly or wholly because of the presence of indeterministic occurrences in the decision process. But it is clear that indeterministic occurrences can never be a source of true (moral) responsibility.

Some believe that free will and moral responsibility are above all a matter of being governed in one's choices and actions by reason—or by Reason with a capital 'R'. But possession of the property of being governed by Reason cannot be a ground of radical moral responsibility as ordinarily understood. It cannot be a property that makes punishment (for example) ultimately just or fair for those who possess it, and unfair for those who do not possess it. Why not? Because to be morally responsible, on this view, is simply to possess one sort of motivational set among others. It is to value or respond naturally to rational considerations—which are often thought to include moral considerations by those who propound this view. It is to have a general motivational set that may be attractive, and that may be more socially beneficial than many others. But there is no escape from the fact that someone who does possess such a motivational set is simply lucky to possess it—if it is indeed a good thing— while someone who lacks it is unlucky.[22]

[22] This would be a version of compatibilism, but importantly different from the ones discussed so far, in the emphasis on reason.

This may be denied. It may be said that some people struggle to become more morally responsible, and make an enormous effort. Their moral responsibility is then not a matter of luck; it is their own hard-won achievement.

The pessimists' reply is immediate. Suppose you are someone who struggles to be morally responsible, and make an enormous effort. Well, that, too, is a matter of luck. You are lucky to be someone who has a character of a sort that disposes you to make that sort of effort. . . .

In the end, luck swallows everything. This is one way of putting the point that there can be no ultimate responsibility, given the natural, strong conception of responsibility that was characterized at the beginning of §4. Relative to that conception, no punishment or reward is ever ultimately just or fair, however natural or useful or otherwise humanly appropriate it may be or seem.

The facts are clear, and they have been known for a long time. When it comes to the metaphysics of free will. André Gide's remark is apt: 'Everything has been said before, but since nobody listens we have to keep going back and beginning all over again.' It seems that the only freedom that we can have is compatibilist freedom. If—since—that is not enough for ultimate responsibility, we cannot have ultimate responsibility. The only alternative to this conclusion is to appeal to God and mystery—this in order to back up the claim that something that appears to be provably impossible is not only possible but actual.

The debate continues; some have thought that philosophy ought to move on. There is little reason to expect that it will do so, as each new generation arises bearing philosophers gripped by the conviction that they can have ultimate responsibility. Would it be a good thing if philosophy did move on, or if we became more clear-headed about the topic of free will than we are? It is hard to say.

Discussion Questions

1. Think carefully through the arguments for hard determinism that Strawson gives on pages 523–525. How would a compatibilist reply? How would Nozick and Campbell reply? Which view do you find most plausible, and why?

2. Strawson says in several places that the Campbell-Nozick view is impossible. Does he have any clear argument for this claim—over and above the challenge (already seen earlier) to explain how free choices of the sort they attempt to describe can fail to be determined by the antecedent nature of the self without being random?

Susan Wolf

Susan Wolf (1952–) teaches philosophy at the University of North Carolina-Chapel Hill (and previously at the University of Maryland and Johns Hopkins University). Her work focuses on ethics, with special attention to issues concerning free will and moral responsibility. In the following selection, she challenges the idea that genuine moral responsibility requires the sort of freedom that Campbell and Nozick advocate, and that Strawson regards as impossible. Instead, she suggests, moral responsibility requires something weaker: a *deep self* that is *sane* in the sense of being able to accurately understand right and wrong and revise itself accordingly.

Sanity and the Metaphysics of Responsibility

Philosophers who study the problems of free will and responsibility have an easier time than most in meeting challenges about the relevance of their work to ordinary, practical concerns. Indeed, philosophers

From Responsibility, Character, and the Emotions: New Essays in Moral Psychology, *edited by Ferdinand David Schoeman (Cambridge: Cambridge University Press, 1988).*

who study these problems are rarely faced with such challenges at all, since questions concerning the conditions of responsibility come up so obviously and so frequently in everyday life. Under scrutiny, however, one might question whether the connections between philosophical and nonphilosophical concerns in this area are real.

In everyday contexts, when lawyers, judges, parents, and others are concerned with issues of responsibility, they know, or think they know, what in general the conditions of responsibility are. Their questions are questions of application: Does this or that particular person meet this or that particular condition? Is this person mature enough, or informed enough, or sane enough to be responsible? Was he or she acting under posthypnotic suggestion or under the influence of a mind-impairing drug? It is assumed, in these contexts, that normal, fully developed adult human beings are responsible beings. The questions have to do with whether a given individual falls within the normal range.[1]

[1] Some of these questions (the ones about posthypnotic suggestion or mind-altering drugs) might be asked by a version of compatibilism that requires that free actions not be influenced in these ways (perhaps under the general heading of "compulsion"). This might also extend to some issues involving sanity. Considerations having to do with maturity or information, on the other hand, have no obvious bearing on the issue of freedom.

By contrast, philosophers tend to be uncertain about the general conditions of responsibility, and they care less about dividing the responsible from the nonresponsible agents than about determining whether, and if so why, any of us are ever responsible for anything at all.

In the classroom, we might argue that the philosophical concerns grow out of the nonphilosophical ones, that they take off where the nonphilosophical questions stop. In this way, we might convince our students that even if they are not plagued by the philosophical worries, they ought to be. If they worry about whether a person is mature enough, informed enough, and sane enough to be responsible, then they should worry about whether that person is metaphysically free enough, too.

The argument I make here, however, goes in the opposite direction. My aim is not to convince people who are interested in the apparently nonphilosophical conditions of responsibility that they should go on to worry about the philosophical conditions as well, but rather to urge those who already worry about the philosophical problems not to leave the more mundane, prephilosophical problems behind. In particular, I suggest that the mundane recognition that *sanity* is a condition of responsibility has more to do with the murky and apparently metaphysical problems which surround the issue of responsibility than at first meets the eye. Once the significance of the condition of sanity is fully appreciated, at least some of the apparently insuperable metaphysical aspects of the problem of responsibility will dissolve.

My strategy is to examine a recent trend in philosophical discussions of responsibility, a trend that tries, but I think ultimately fails, to give an acceptable analysis of the conditions of responsibility. It fails due to what at first appear to be deep and irresolvable metaphysical problems. It is here that I suggest that the condition of sanity comes to the rescue. What at first appears to be an impossible requirement for responsibility—the requirement that the responsible agent have created her- or himself—turns out to be the vastly more mundane and noncontroversial requirement that the responsible agent must, in a fairly standard sense, be sane.

FRANKFURT . . . AND TAYLOR

The trend I have in mind is exemplified by the writings of Harry Frankfurt . . . and Charles Taylor. I will briefly discuss each of their separate proposals, and then offer a composite view that, while lacking the subtlety of any of the separate accounts, will highlight some important insights and some important blind spots they share.

In his seminal article "Freedom of the Will and the Concept of a Person,"* Harry Frankfurt notes a distinction between freedom of action and freedom of the will. A person has freedom of action, he points out, if she (or he) has the freedom to do whatever she wills to do—the freedom to walk or sit, to vote liberal or conservative,

---

*Harry Frankfurt, "Freedom of the Will and the Concept of a Person," *Journal of Philosophy* LXVIII (1971), 5–20.

to publish a book or open a store, in accordance with her strongest desires. Even a person who has freedom of action may fail to be responsible for her actions, however, if the wants or desires she has the freedom to convert into action are themselves not subject to her control. Thus, the person who acts under posthypnotic suggestion, the victim of brainwashing, and the kleptomaniac might all possess freedom of action. In the standard contexts in which these examples are raised, it is assumed that none of the individuals is locked up or bound. Rather, these individuals are understood to act on what, at one level at least, must be called *their own desires*. Their exemption from responsibility stems from the fact that their own desires (or at least the ones governing their actions) are not up to them. These cases may be described in Frankfurt's terms as cases of people who possess freedom of action, but who fail to be responsible agents because they lack freedom of the will.②

② Frankfurt's view is a version of hierarchical compatibilism. See Discussion Question 3 for the Hospers selection.

Philosophical problems about the conditions of responsibility naturally focus on an analysis of this latter kind of freedom: What *is* freedom of the will, and under what conditions can we reasonably be thought to possess it? Frankfurt's proposal is to understand freedom of the will by analogy to freedom of action. As freedom of action is the freedom to do whatever one wills to do, freedom of the will is the freedom to will whatever one wants to will. To make this point clearer, Frankfurt introduces a distinction between first-order and second-order desires. First-order desires are desires to do or to have various things; second-order desires are desires about what desires to have or what desires to make effective in action. In order for an agent to have both freedom of action and freedom of the will, that agent must be capable of governing his or her actions by first-order desires *and* capable of governing his or her first-order desires by second-order desires.③

. . .

Frankfurt's . . . account may be understood as [a] development of the intuition that in order to be re-sponsible for one's actions, one must be responsible for the self that performs these actions. Charles Taylor, in an article entitled "Responsibility for Self,"* is concerned with the same intuition. Although Taylor does not describe his view in terms of different levels or types of desire, his view is related, for he claims that our freedom and re-sponsibility depend on our ability to reflect on, criticize, and revise our selves. Like Frankfurt . . . Taylor seems to believe that if the characters from which our actions flowed were simply and permanently *given* to us, implanted by heredity, environment, or God, then we would be mere vehicles through which the causal forces of the world traveled, no more responsible than dumb animals or young children or machines. But like the others, he points out that, for most of us, our characters and desires are not so brutely implanted—or, at any rate, if they are, they are subject to revision by our own reflecting, valuing, or second-order desiring selves. We human beings—and as far as we know, only we human beings—have the ability to step back from ourselves and decide whether we are the selves we want to be. Because of this, these philosophers think, we are responsible for our selves and for the actions that we produce.④

③ Thus a person who has a compulsive first-order desire (for example, the desire to take drugs as a result of an addiction), and who also has a second-order desire not to have that first-order desire, but is unable to overcome the first-order desire (and so unable to satisfy the second-order desire) would not be free on Frankfurt's view.

④ This at least suggests the sort of control over the nature of one's self that Nozick is advocating and that Strawson claims to be impossible.

Although there are subtle and interesting differences [between] the accounts of Frankfurt . . . and Taylor, my concern is with features of their views that are common to them. . . . [Both] share the idea that responsible agency involves something more than intentional agency. [Both] agree that if we are responsible agents, it is not just because our actions are within the control of our wills, but because, in addition, our wills are not just psychological states *in* us, but expressions of characters that come *from* us, or that at any rate are

*Charles Taylor, "Responsibility for Self," in A. E. Rorty, ed., *The Identities of Persons* (Berkeley: University of California Press, 1976), pp. 281–99.

acknowledged and affirmed *by* us. For Frankfurt, this means that our wills must be ruled by our second-order desires; . . . for Taylor, that our wills must issue from selves that are subject to self-assessment and redefinition in terms of a vocabulary of worth. In one way or another, [both of] these philosophers seem to be saying that the key to responsibility lies in the fact that responsible agents are those for whom it is not just the case that their actions are within the control of their wills, but also the case that their wills are within the control of their *selves* in some deeper sense. Because, at one level, the differences [between] Frankfurt . . . and Taylor may be understood as differences in the analysis or interpretation of what it is for an action to be under the control of this deeper self, we may speak of their separate positions as variations of one basic view about responsibility: the *deep-self view.*

THE DEEP-SELF VIEW

Much more must be said about the notion of a deep self before a fully satisfactory account of this view can be given. Providing a careful, detailed analysis of that notion poses an interesting, important, and difficult task in its own right. The degree of understanding achieved by abstraction from the views of Frankfurt . . . and Taylor, however, should be sufficient to allow us, to recognize some important virtues as well as some important drawbacks of the deep-self view.

One virtue is that this view explains a good portion of our pretheoretical intuitions about responsibility. It explains why kleptomaniacs, victims of brainwashing, and people acting under posthypnotic suggestion may not be responsible for their actions, although most of us typically are. In the cases of people in these special categories, the connection between the agents' deep selves and their wills is dramatically severed—their wills are governed not by their deep selves, but by forces external to and independent from them.⑤ A different intuition is that we adult human beings can be responsible for our actions in a way that dumb animals, infants, and machines can-

⑤ Not fully "external to and independent from" the *persons,* since the compulsive desires are still internal to them. Think carefully about why the desires in question are supposed to be "external to and independent of" "their deep selves."

not. Here the explanation is not in terms of a split between these beings' deep selves and their wills; rather, the point is that these beings *lack* deep selves altogether. Kleptomaniacs and victims of hypnosis exemplify individuals whose selves are *alienated* from their actions; lower animals and machines, on the other hand, do not have the sorts of selves from which actions *can* be alienated, and so they do not have the sort of selves from which, in the happier cases, actions can responsibly flow.⑥

⑥ Think about the difference, as you understand it, between an animal and a normal adult human being. Both seem to have desires and to act on them. So exactly what is it that the animal does not have? Try to spell this out, following the suggestions of Frankfurt and Taylor.

At a more theoretical level, the deep-self view has another virtue: It responds to at least one way in which the fear of determinism presents itself.

A naive reaction to the idea that everything we do is completely determined by a causal chain that extends backward beyond the times of our births involves thinking that in that case we would have no control over our behavior whatsoever. If everything is determined, it is thought, then what happens happens, whether we want it to or not. A common, and proper, response to this concern points out that determinism does not deny the causal efficacy an agent's desires might have on his or her behavior. On the contrary, determinism in its more plausible forms tends to affirm this connection, merely adding that as one's behavior is determined by one's desires, so one's desires are determined by something else.⑦

⑦ This is the compatibilist view. (By *fatalism,* in the next sentence, Wolf means roughly the view that everything that happens is inevitable, that nothing could have been other than it was.)

Those who were initially worried that determinism implied fatalism, however, are apt to find their fears merely transformed rather than erased. If our desires are governed by something else, they might say, they are not *really* ours after all—or, at any rate, they are ours in only a superficial sense.

The deep-self view offers an answer to this transformed fear of determinism, for it allows us to distinguish cases in which desires are determined by forces foreign to oneself from desires which are determined *by* one's self—by one's "real," or second-order desiring, . . . or deep self, that is. Admittedly, there are cases, like that of the kleptomaniac or the victim of hypnosis, in which the agent acts on desires that "belong to" him or her in only a superficial sense. But the proponent of the deep-self view will point out that even if determinism is true, ordinary adult human action can be distinguished from this. Determinism implies that the desires which govern our actions are in turn governed by something else, but that something else will, in the fortunate cases, be our own deeper selves.

This account of responsibility thus offers a response to our fear of determinism; but it is a response with which many will remain unsatisfied. Even if my actions are governed by my desires and my desires are governed by my own deeper self, there remains the question: Who, or what, is responsible for this deeper self? The response above seems only to have pushed the problem further back.

Admittedly, some versions of the deep-self view, including Frankfurt's and Taylor's, seem to anticipate this question by providing a place for the ideal that an agent's deep self may be governed by a still deeper self. Thus, for Frankfurt, second-order desires may themselves be governed by third-order desires, third-order desires by fourth-order desires, and so on. Also, Taylor points out that, as we can reflect on and evaluate our prereflective selves, so we can reflect on and evaluate the selves who are doing the first reflecting and evaluating, and so on. However, this capacity to recursively create endless levels of depth ultimately misses the criticism's point.

First of all, even if there is no *logical* limit to the number of levels of reflection or depth a person may have, there is certainly a psychological limit—it is virtually impossible imaginatively to conceive a fourth-, much less an eighth-order, desire. More important, no matter how many levels of self we posit, there will still, in any individual case, be a last level—a deepest self about whom the question "What governs it?" will arise, as problematic as ever. If determinism is true, it implies that even if my actions are governed by my desires, and my desires are governed by my deepest self, my deepest self will still be governed by something that must, logically, be external to myself altogether. Though I can step back from the values my parents and teachers have given me and ask whether these are the values I really

want, the "I" that steps back will itself be a product of the parents and teachers I am questioning.[8]

The problem seems even worse when one sees that one fares no better if determinism is false. For if my deepest self is not determined by something external to myself, it will still not be determined by *me*. Whether I am a product of carefully controlled forces or a result of random mutations, whether there is a complete explanation of my origin or no explanation at all, *I* am not, in any case, responsible for my existence; I am not in control of my deepest self.

Thus, though the claim that an agent is responsible for only those actions that are within the control of his or her deep self correctly identifies a necessary condition for responsibility—a condition that separates the hypnotized and the brainwashed, the immature and the lower animals from ourselves, for example—it fails to provide a sufficient condition of responsibility that puts all fears of determinism to rest. For one of the fears invoked by the thought of determinism seems to be connected to its implication that we are but intermediate links in a causal chain, rather than ultimate, self-initiating sources of movement and change. From the point of view of one who has this fear, the deep-self view seems merely to add loops to the chain, complicating the picture but not really improving it. From the point of view of one who has this fear, responsibility seems to require being a prime mover unmoved, whose deepest self is itself neither random *nor* externally determined, but is rather determined *by* itself—who is, in other words, self-created. [9]

At this point, however, proponents of the deep-self view may wonder whether this fear is legitimate. For although people evidently can be brought to the point where they feel that responsible agency requires them to be ultimate sources of power, to the point where it seems that nothing short of self-creation will do, a return to the internal standpoint of

[8] Thus the deepest self is still determined by something external to it. (Like Strawson, Wolf rejects the idea—found in Nozick—that one could choose some aspects of one's self in a way that is not determined by those that antecedently exist.)

[9] This is what Strawson refers to as a "*causa sui.*" (Nozick's view is in effect that a person can be "self-created" in some respects, though not in all.)

the agent whose responsibility is in question makes it hard to see what good this metaphysical status is supposed to provide or what evil its absence is supposed to impose.

From the external standpoint, which discussions of determinism and indeterminism encourage us to take up, it may appear that a special metaphysical status is required to distinguish us significantly from other members of the natural world. But proponents of the deep-self view will suggest this is an illusion that a return to the internal standpoint should dispel. The possession of a deep self that is effective in governing one's actions is a sufficient distinction, they will say. For while other members of the natural world are not in control of the selves that they are, we, possessors of effective deep selves, are in control. We can reflect on what sorts of beings we are, and on what sorts of marks we make on the world. We can change what we don't like about ourselves, and keep what we do. Admittedly, we do not create ourselves from nothing. But as long as we can revise ourselves, they will suggest, it is hard to find reason to complain. Harry Frankfurt writes that a person who is free to do what he wants to do and also free to want what he wants to want has "all the freedom it is possible to desire or to conceive." This suggests a rhetorical question: If you are free to control your actions by your desires, and free to control your desires by your deeper desires,

> [10] What answer would a libertarian give to this question?

and free to control those desires by still deeper desires, what further kind of freedom can you want? [10]

THE CONDITION OF SANITY

Unfortunately, there is a further kind of freedom we can want, which it is reasonable to think necessary for responsible agency. The deep-self view fails to be convincing when it is offered as a complete account of the conditions of responsibility. To see why, it will be helpful to consider another example of an agent whose responsibility is in question.

JoJo is the favorite son of Jo the First, an evil and sadistic dictator of a small, undeveloped country. Because of his father's special feelings for the boy, JoJo is given a special education and is allowed to accompany his father and observe his daily routine. In light of this treatment, it is not surprising that little JoJo

takes his father as a role model and develops values very much like Dad's. As an adult, he does many of the same sorts of things his father did, including sending people to prison or to death or to torture chambers on the basis of whim. He is not *coerced* to do these things, he acts according to his own desires. Moreover, these are desires he wholly *wants* to have. When he steps back and asks, "Do I really want to be this sort of person?" his answer is resoundingly "Yes," for this way of life expresses a crazy sort of power that forms part of his deepest ideal.

In light of JoJo's heritage and upbringing—both of which he was powerless to control—it is dubious at best that he should be regarded as responsible for what he does. It is unclear whether anyone with a childhood such as his could have developed into anything but the twisted and perverse sort of person that he has become. However, note that JoJo is someone whose actions are controlled by his desires and whose desires are the desires he wants to have: That is, his actions are governed by desires that are governed by and expressive of his deepest self. [11]

> [11] How plausible is it that JoJo is less responsible or has less control over the sort of person he becomes than those who are raised in a more normal way? What would the various views we have considered say about JoJo?

The Frankfurt- . . . Taylor strategy that allowed us to differentiate our normal selves from the victims of hypnosis and brainwashing will not allow us to differentiate ourselves from the son of Jo the First. In the case of these earlier victims, we were able to say that although the actions of these individuals, were, at one level, in control of the individuals themselves, these individuals themselves, qua agents, were not the selves they more deeply wanted to be. In this respect, these people were unlike our happily more integrated selves. However, we cannot say of JoJo that his self, qua agent, is not the self he wants it to be. It *is* the self he wants it to be. From the inside, he feels as integrated, free, and responsible as we do.

Our judgment that JoJo is not a responsible agent is one that we can make only from the outside—from reflecting on the fact, it seems, that his deepest self is not up to him. Looked at from the outside, however, our situation seems no different from his—for in the last analysis, it is not up to any of us to have the deepest selves we do. Once more, the problem seems metaphysical—and not just metaphysical, but insuperable. For, as I mentioned before, the problem is independent of the truth of determinism. Whether we are determined or undetermined, we cannot have created our deepest selves. Literal self-creation is not just empirically, but logically impossible.

If JoJo is not responsible because his deepest self is not up to him, then we are not responsible either. Indeed, in that case responsibility would be impossible for anyone to achieve. But I believe the appearance that literal self-creation is required for freedom and responsibility is itself mistaken.

The deep-self view was right in pointing out that freedom and responsibility require us to have certain distinctive types of control over our behavior and our selves. Specifically, our actions need to be under the control of our selves, and our (superficial) selves need to be under the control of our deep selves. Having seen that these types of control are not enough to guarantee us the status of responsible agents, we are tempted to go on to suppose that we must have yet another kind of control to assure us that even our deepest selves are somehow up to us. But not all the things necessary for freedom and responsibility must be types of power and control. We may need simply to *be* a certain way, even though it is not within our power to determine whether we are that way or not.

Indeed, it becomes obvious that at least one condition of responsibility is of this form as soon as we remember what, in everyday contexts, we have known all along—namely, that in order to be responsible, an agent must be *sane*. It is not ordinarily in our power to determine whether we are or are not sane. Most of us, it would seem, are lucky, but some of us are not. Moreover, being sane does not necessarily mean that one has any type of power or control an insane person lacks. Some insane people, like JoJo and some actual political leaders who resemble him, may have complete control of their actions, and even complete control of their acting selves. The desire to be sane is thus not a desire for another form of control; it is rather a desire that one's self be connected to the world in a certain way—we could even say it is a desire that one's self be *controlled by* the world in certain ways and not in others.

12 Is it as clear as Wolf thinks that JoJo is *insane* in a sense that is relevant to moral responsibility?

This becomes clear if we attend to the criteria for sanity, that have historically been dominant in legal questions about responsibility. According to the M'Naughten Rule, a person is sane if (1) he knows what he is doing and (2) he knows that what he is doing is, as the case may be, right or wrong. Insofar as one's desire to be sane involves a desire to know what one is doing—or more generally, a desire to live in the real world—it is a desire to be controlled (to have, in this case, one's *beliefs* controlled) by perceptions and sound reasoning that produce an accurate conception of the world, rather than by blind or distorted forms of response. The same goes for the second constituent of sanity—only, in this case, one's hope is that one's *values* be controlled by processes that afford an accurate conception of the world.* 13 Putting these two conditions together, we may understand sanity, then, as the minimally sufficient ability cognitively and normatively to recognize and appreciate the world for what it is.

13 If JoJo is insane, it is because he fails to meet the second of these conditions, not the first. What if he does know the difference between right and wrong, but prefers to do things that are morally wrong? Is he still insane? (Note that Wolf is apparently assuming (a) that there are objectively correct moral values, and (b) that normal people have some way of knowing what they are, of having their judgments about value shaped by the objective truth. There is more discussion of these issues in Chapter 6.)

There are problems with this definition of sanity, at least some of which will become obvious in what follows, that make it ultimately unacceptable either as a gloss on or an improvement of the meaning of the term in many of the contexts in which it is used. The definition offered does seem to bring out the interest sanity has for us in connection with issues of responsibility,

---

*Strictly speaking, perception and sound reasoning may not be enough to ensure the ability to achieve an accurate conception of what one is doing and especially to achieve a reasonable normative assessment of one's situation. Sensitivity and exposure to certain realms of experience may also be necessary for these goals. For the purpose of this essay, I understand "sanity" to include whatever it takes to enable one to develop an adequate conception of one's world. In other contexts, however, this would be an implausibly broad construction of the term.

however, and some pedagogical as well as stylistic purposes will be served if we use sanity hereafter in this admittedly specialized sense.

THE SANE DEEP-SELF VIEW

So far I have argued that the conditions of responsible agency offered by the deep-self view are necessary but not sufficient. Moreover, the gap left open by the deep-self view seems to be one that can be filled only by a metaphysical, and, as it happens, metaphysically impossible addition. I now wish to argue, however, that the condition of sanity, as characterized above, is sufficient to fill the gap. In other words, the deep-self view, supplemented by the condition of sanity, provides a satisfying conception of responsibility. The conception of responsibility I am proposing, then, agrees with the deep-self view in requiring that a responsible agent be able to govern her (or his) actions by her desires and to govern her desires by her deep self. In addition, my conception insists that the agent's deep self be sane, and claims that this is *all* that is needed for responsible agency. By contrast to the plain deep-self view, let us call this new proposal the *sane deep-self view*.

It is worth noting, to begin with, that this new proposal deals with the case of JoJo and related cases of deprived childhood victims in ways that better match our pretheoretical intuitions. Unlike the plain deep-self view, the sane deep-self view offers a way of explaining why JoJo is not responsible for his actions without throwing our own responsibility into doubt. For, although like us, JoJo's actions flow from desires that flow from his deep self, unlike us, JoJo's deep self is itself insane. Sanity, remember, involves the ability to know the difference between right and wrong, and a person who, even on reflection, cannot see that having someone tortured because he failed to salute you is wrong plainly lacks the requisite ability. ⑭

Less obviously, but quite analogously, this new proposal explains why we give less than full responsibility to persons who, though acting badly, act in ways that are strongly encouraged by their societies—the slaveowners of the 1850s, the Nazis of the 1930s, and many male chauvinists of our fathers' generation, for example. These are people, we imagine, who falsely believe that the ways in which they are acting are morally acceptable, and so, we may assume, their behavior is expressive of or at least in accordance with these agents' deep selves. But their false beliefs in the moral permissibility of their actions and the false values from which these beliefs derived may have been inevitable, given the social circumstances in which they developed. If we think that the agents could not help but be mistaken about their values, we do not blame them for the actions those values inspired.*

It would unduly distort ordinary linguistic practice to call the slaveowner, the Nazi, or the male chauvinist even partially or locally insane. Nonetheless, the reason for withholding blame from them is at bottom the same as the reason for withholding it from JoJo. Like JoJo, they are, at the deepest level, unable cognitively and normatively to recognize and appreciate the world for what it is. In our sense of the term, their deepest selves are not fully sane. ⑮

The sane deep-self view thus offers an account of why victims of deprived childhoods as well as victims of misguided societies may not be responsible for their actions, without implying that we are not responsible for ours. The actions of these others are governed by mistaken conceptions of value that the agents in question cannot help but have.

> ⑭ JoJo is (by our lights) mistaken in a deep and important way. Is this enough to show that he (or his deep self) is insane (and so not responsible)? Does it matter that he arrived at his mistaken beliefs in the way that he did, or would anyone who held such beliefs automatically qualify as insane?

> ⑮ Again, it is clear (again, by our lights) that such people are seriously mistaken. But is this enough to show that they are less than fully *sane?* Does any serious mistake about morality qualify as a form of insanity? If not, why not?

---

*Admittedly, it is open to question whether these individuals were in fact unable to help having mistaken values, and indeed, whether recognizing the errors of their society would even have required exceptional independence or strength of mind. This is presumably an empirical question, the answer to which is extraordinarily hard to determine. My point here is simply that *if* we believe they are unable to recognize that their values are mistaken, we do not hold them responsible for the actions that flow from these values, and *if* we believe their ability to recognize their normative errors is impaired, we hold them less than fully responsible for the relevant actions.

Since, as far as we know, our values are not, like theirs, unavoidably mistaken, the fact that these others are not responsible for their actions need not force us to conclude that we are not responsible for ours.

But it may not yet be clear why sanity, in this special sense, should make such a difference—why, in particular, the question of whether someone's values are unavoidably *mistaken* should have any bearing on their status as responsible agents. The fact that the sane deep-self view implies judgments that match our intuitions about the difference in status between characters like JoJo and ourselves provides little support for it if it cannot also defend these intuitions. So we must consider an objection that comes from the point of view we considered earlier which rejects the intuition that a relevant difference can be found.

Earlier, it seemed that the reason JoJo was not responsible for his actions was that although his actions were governed by his deep self, his deep self was not up to him. But this had nothing to do with his deep self's being mistaken or not mistaken, evil or good, insane or sane. If JoJo's values are unavoidably mistaken, our values, even if not mistaken, appear to be just as unavoidable. When it comes to freedom and responsibility, isn't it the unavoidability, rather than the mistakenness, that matters?

Before answering this question, it is useful to point out a way in which it is ambiguous: The concepts of avoidability and mistakenness are not unequivocally distinct. One may, to be sure, construe the notion of avoidability in a purely metaphysical way. Whether an event or state of affairs is unavoidable under this construal depends, as it were, on the tightness of the causal connections that bear on the event's or state of affairs' coming about. In this sense, our deep selves do seem as unavoidable for us as JoJo's and the others' are for them. For presumably we are just as influenced by our parents, our cultures, and our schooling as they are influenced by theirs. In another sense, however, our characters are not similarly unavoidable.

In particular, in the cases of JoJo and the others, there are certain features of their characters that they cannot avoid *even though these features are seriously mistaken, misguided, or bad*. This is so because, in

our special sense of the term, these characters are less than fully sane. Since these characters lack the ability to know right from wrong, they are unable to revise their characters on the basis of right and wrong, and so their deep selves lack the resources and the reasons that might have served as a basis for self-correction. Since the deep selves *we* unavoidably have, however, are sane deep selves—deep selves, that is, that unavoidably *contain* the ability to know right from wrong—we unavoidably do have the resources and reasons on which to base self-correction. What this means is that though in one sense we are no more in control of our deepest selves than JoJo et al., it does not follow in our case, as it does in theirs, that we would be the way we are, even if it is a bad or wrong way to be. However, if this does not follow, it seems to me, our absence of control at the deepest level should not upset us.(16)

Consider what the absence of control at the deepest level amounts to for us: Whereas JoJo is unable to control the fact that, at the deepest level, he is not fully sane, we are not responsible for the fact that, at the deepest level,

> **16** Think carefully here about what the difference between JoJo and us really amounts to, on Wolf's view. Can he *alter* his own self (perhaps by deciding that he has been too lenient with his citizens and changing accordingly)? (See Discussion Question 3.)

we are. It is not up to us to *have* minimally sufficient abilities cognitively and normatively to recognize and appreciate the world for what it is. Also, presumably, it is not up to us to have lots of other properties, at least to begin with—a fondness for purple, perhaps, or an antipathy for beets. As the proponents of the plain deep-self view have been at pains to point out, however, we do, if we are lucky, have the ability to revise our selves in terms of the values that are held by or constitutive of our deep selves. If we are lucky enough both to have this ability and to have our deep selves be sane, it follows that although there is much in our characters that we did not choose to have, there is nothing irrational or objectionable in our characters that we are compelled to keep.

Being sane, we are able to understand and evaluate our characters in a reasonable way, to notice what there is reason to hold on to, what there is reason to eliminate, and what, from a rational and reasonable standpoint, we may retain or get rid of as we please. Being able as well to govern our superficial selves by our deep selves, then, we are able to change the things we find there is reason to change. This being so, it seems that although we may not be *metaphysically* responsible for ourselves—for, after all, we did not create ourselves from nothing—we are *morally* responsible for ourselves, for we are able to understand and appreciate right and wrong, and to change our characters and our actions accordingly.

SELF-CREATION, SELF-REVISION, AND SELF-CORRECTION

At the beginning of this chapter, I claimed that recalling that sanity was a condition of responsibility would dissolve at least some of the appearance that responsibility was metaphysically impossible. To see how this is so, and to get a fuller sense of the sane deep-self view, it may be helpful to put that view into perspective by comparing it to the other views we have discussed along the way.

As Frankfurt . . . and Taylor showed us, in order to be free and responsible we need not only to be able to control our actions in accordance with our desires, we need to be able to control our desires in accordance with our deepest selves. We need, in other words, to be able to *revise* ourselves—to get rid of some desires and traits, and perhaps replace them with others on the basis of our deeper desires or values or reflections. However, consideration of the fact that the selves who are doing the revising might themselves be either brute products of external forces or arbitrary outputs of random generation made us wonder whether the capacity for self-revision was enough to assure us of responsibility—and the example of JoJo added force to the suspicion that it was not. Still, if the ability to revise ourselves is not enough, the ability to create ourselves does not seem necessary either. Indeed, when you think of it, it is unclear why anyone should want self-creation. Why should anyone be disappointed at having to accept the idea that one has to get one's start somewhere? It is an idea that most of us have lived with quite contentedly all along. What we do have reason to want, then, is something more than the ability to revise ourselves, but less than the ability to create ourselves. Implicit in the sane deep-self view

is the idea that what is needed is the ability to *correct* (or improve) ourselves.

Recognizing that in order to be responsible for our actions, we have to be responsible for our selves, the sane deep-self view analyzes what is necessary in order to be responsible for our selves as (1) the ability to evaluate ourselves sensibly and accurately, and (2) the ability to transform ourselves insofar as our evaluation tells us to do so. We may understand the exercise of these abilities as a process whereby we *take* responsibility for the selves that we are but did not ultimately create. The condition of sanity is intrinsically connected to the first ability; the condition that we be able to control our superficial selves by our deep selves is intrinsically connected to the second. [17]

> [17] So JoJo fails to be morally responsible because he lacks ability (1). There is no reason to think that he lacks ability (2).

The difference between the plain deep-self view and the sane deep-self view, then, is the difference between the requirement of the capacity for self-revision and the requirement of the capacity for self-correction. Anyone with the first capacity can *try* to take responsibility for himself or herself. However, only someone with a sane deep self—a deep self that can see and appreciate the world for what it is—can self-evaluate sensibly and accurately. Therefore, although insane selves can try to take responsibility for themselves, only sane selves will properly be accorded responsibility.

TWO OBJECTIONS CONSIDERED

At least two problems with the sane deep-self view are so glaring as to have certainly struck many readers. In closing, I shall briefly address them. First, some will be wondering how, in light of my specialized use of the term "sanity," I can be so sure that "we" are any saner than the nonresponsible individuals I have discussed. What justifies my confidence that, unlike the slaveowners, Nazis, and male chauvinists, not to mention JoJo himself, we are able to understand and appreciate the world for what it is? The answer to this is that nothing justifies this except widespread intersubjective agreement and the considerable success we have in getting around in the world and satisfying our needs. These are not sufficient grounds for the smug assumption that we are in a position to see the truth about *all* aspects of ethical and social life. Indeed, it seems more reasonable to expect that time will reveal blind spots in our cognitive and normative outlook, just as it has revealed errors in the outlooks of those who have lived before. But our judgments of responsibility can only be made from here, on the basis of the understandings and values that we can develop by exercising the abilities we do possess as well and as fully as possible. [18]

[18] Will any such "blind spots" mean that we are also less than fully sane? Are we responsible only to the extent that we are sane? (And how can we ever know what extent that is?)

If some have been worried that my view implicitly expresses an overconfidence in the assumption that we are sane and therefore right about the world, others will be worried that my view too closely connects sanity with being right about the world, and fear that my view implies that anyone who acts wrongly or has false beliefs about the world is therefore insane and so not responsible for his or her actions. This seems to me to be a more serious worry, which I am sure I cannot answer to everyone's satisfaction.

First, it must be admitted that the sane deep-self view embraces a conception of sanity that is explicitly normative. But this seems to me a strength of that view, rather than a defect. Sanity *is* a normative concept, in its ordinary as well as in its specialized sense, and severely deviant behavior, such as that of a serial murderer or a sadistic dictator, does constitute evidence of a psychological defect in the agent. The suggestion that the most horrendous, stomach-turning crimes could be committed only by an insane person— an inverse of Catch–22, as it were—must be regarded as a serious possibility, despite the practical problems that would accompany general acceptance of that conclusion.

But, it will be objected, there is no justification, in the sane deep-self view, for regarding only horrendous and stomach-turning crimes as evidence of insanity in its specialized sense. If sanity is the ability cognitively and normatively to understand and appreciate the world for what it is, then *any* wrong action or false belief will count as evidence of the absence of that ability. This point may also be granted, but we must be careful about what conclusion to draw. To be sure,

when someone acts in a way that is not in accordance with acceptable standards of rationality and reasonableness, it is always appropriate to look for an explanation of why he or she acted that way. The hypothesis that the person was unable to understand and appreciate that an action fell outside acceptable bounds will always be a possible explanation. Bad performance on a math test always suggests the possibility that the testee is stupid. Typically, however, other explanations will be possible, too—for example, that the agent was too lazy to consider whether his or her action was acceptable, or too greedy to care, or, in the case of the math testee, that he or she was too occupied with other interests to attend class or study. Other facts about the agent's history will help us decide among these hypotheses.

This brings out the need to emphasize that sanity, in the specialized sense, is defined as the *ability* cognitively and normatively to understand and appreciate the world for what it is. According to our commonsense understandings, having this ability is one thing and exercising it is another—at least some wrongacting, responsible agents presumably fall within the gap. The notion of "ability" is notoriously problematic, however, and there is a long history of controversy about whether the truth of determinism would show our ordinary ways of thinking to be simply confused on this matter. [19] At this point, then, metaphysical concerns may voice themselves again—but at least they will have been pushed into a narrower, and perhaps a more manageable, corner.

The sane deep-self view does not, then, solve all the philosophical problems connected to the topics of free will and responsibility. If anything, it highlights some of the practical and empirical problems, rather than solves them. It may, however, resolve some of the

[19] The idea here is that one can be mistaken about values and still be responsible as long as one has the *ability* to arrive at the correct view. But if everything about us, including the nature of our deep selves, is determined, what does it mean to say that a person could have arrived at the correct view even though he didn't? Are we back to something like a compatibilist view: he would have arrived at the correct view if he had thought about things differently (even though he was determined from long before his birth to think in just the way that he did)?

philosophical, and particularly, some of the metaphysical problems, and reveal how intimate are the connections between the remaining philosophical problems and the practical ones.

Discussion Questions

1. What is a deep self? How does it differ from a shallower self (or shallower aspects of the self)? Is it clear that animals do not have deep selves, and if so, why? Why is having a deep self an essential requirement for moral responsibility? Why is it better from the standpoint of moral responsibility to have a shallow self that is determined by a deep self that is in turn determined by external factors than to have only a shallow self that is determined by those same external factors?

2. Do you think JoJo is insane and so not morally responsible? What are the requirements for what might be called moral sanity that he fails to meet? Will anyone who commits really horrendous crimes be morally insane and so not responsible, in Wolf's view? Is this a plausible result?

3. There is no reason to deny that JoJo has as much capacity for *self-alteration* as we do: he can judge some feature of his character to be morally mistaken and perhaps alter it accordingly (if the rest of his deep self is such as to make this possible). We can do the same, with the only difference being that we (by our own lights) have more accurate perceptions of moral values to guide our attempts at self-alteration (so we are capable of self-*correction*, alteration in the direction of moral improvement, and JoJo isn't). This is an important difference between us and JoJo, but does it make us morally responsible in a way that he isn't? Why or why not?

CHAPTER 6

Morality and Moral Problems

The selections in this chapter are concerned with issues pertaining to ethics, or moral philosophy: the philosophical study of what makes actions morally right or morally wrong (and also of other kinds of moral value pertaining to such things as ends or character). The most fundamental question is whether there are general moral standards that are objectively correct, and if so, what they are. The first main section of the chapter is concerned with views that challenge the existence of objectively or universally correct interpersonal moral standards; the second with three general accounts of the content of such standards; and the third with the way in which such standards apply to concrete moral problems (and with other ideas that may shed light on such problems).

IS MORALITY RELATIVE?
ARE WE MOTIVATED ONLY BY SELF-INTEREST?

Many people, especially but not only students, are highly suspicious of **moral objectivism:** the idea that there are objective or universal moral truths. For many of them the preferred alternative is some form of **moral relativism.** This is the view (a) that there are moral truths of a sort, but also (b) that moral truth is relative to something, such as to the individual, to the society or culture, to the historical era, etc., rather than being objective or universal. Here part (a) is crucial, for there is a third alternative to moral objectivism and moral relativism that very few people find palatable: **moral nihilism,** the view that there are no moral truths of any sort, that morality is just a mistake or illusion. The moral nihilist does not, of course, deny the obvious fact that people have moral *opinions;* his claim is just that none of these opinions are ever true or correct in any way, so that there is no good reason why anyone's choices should be guided or restricted by them.

Thus one requirement for a significant version of moral relativism is that it not turn out to really amount to moral nihilism. This would be so if, for example, someone were to advocate a version of individual relativism according to which the moral truth for a given individual is determined by whatever moral opinions he has at the moment, however ill-considered and fleeting they may be: since anything he thinks is morally acceptable will be morally acceptable for him, it is hard to see how such a view could guide or restrict his behavior in any way—in which case it is really not distinct from moral nihilism. Thus a version of individual relativism that is clearly distinct from moral nihilism will have to impose constraints on allowable moral opinions (for example, that they be carefully considered and reasonably consistent over time).[1]

It is a striking fact about the current state of moral discussion that despite the popularity of relativist views among nonphilosophers, very few philosophers find them plausible. Whether or not you ultimately agree, you should try to understand the reasons for this widespread philosophical rejection of relativism. Many of the most important of these are presented in the two selections by James Rachels, one concerned with cultural relativism and the other with versions of individual relativism.

A slightly more specific interpretation of cultural relativism is suggested by the arguments presented by Glaucon in Plato's *Republic* for the claim that there are no reasons to act according to the moral rules of your society (to act justly), but that there are reasons to act in such a way as to be *perceived* as acting according to those rules, while in fact breaking those rules. The view of morality presumed by these arguments is a kind of conventionalism, according to which moral rules derive from the tacit consent of people living together. This particular version of cultural relativism is not argued for, but is only in the background of the discussion of whether we are better off, whether it is in our self-interest, to behave morally or immorally. Another common assumption reflected in Plato's discussion is that the requirements of self-interest and morality often conflict. This is the very assumption that Plato's positive view challenges: according to Plato, it is always in our self-interest to behave morally.

A different sort of challenge to the idea of objective or universal moral truths is posed by egoism. Here there are two distinct, but related views. First, there is **psychological egoism,** the view that as a matter of psychological fact, no one is *capable* of pursuing anything but his own selfish interests. Second, there is **ethical egoism,** the view that no one is ever morally obligated to act in any way that is contrary to his own interests (since a person cannot be *morally obligated* to do anything that is psychologically impossible)—and perhaps, even less plausibly, that people are morally obligated to pursue their own best interests. Ethical egoism, in either of these versions, would, if correct, amount in a way to an objective moral truth, but it would mean that there are no objective moral truths of the more familiar sort that restrain people's selfish behavior by appeal to the interests and rights of others. The selection by Joel Feinberg offers a detailed critique of psychological egoism, which Feinberg claims to appear plausible only as a result of confusions of various sorts. (If psychological egoism is rejected, then there is no clear rationale of any sort for ethical egoism.)

---

[1]Moral opinions satisfying such constraints could perhaps guide or restrict the individual's behavior, but a further question is *why* he should be guided or restricted by them. Does this depend on his having an opinion to *that* effect (which he might not have) or does it not depend on *his* moral opinions at all (in which case it seems to be offered as an *objective* moral truth, if it is claimed to be true at all—thus undermining the claim of relativism).

WHAT IS THE BEST THEORY OF MORALITY: UTILITARIANISM, DEONTOLOGICAL VIEWS, OR VIRTUE ETHICS?

The reading selections in the second and most important section of the chapter are concerned with three competing accounts of what the objectively or universally true moral principles, assuming that there are any, actually say.

Utilitarianism: Morality Depends on Consequences

The first and in many ways most obvious of these views is utilitarianism, with the most straightforward version of utilitarianism being **act utilitarianism:** the view that the morally correct action in any situation of choice is the one out of the available alternatives that produces the best overall consequences, the most utility (for all who are affected by it, in the indefinitely long run). (Act utilitarianism is thus one version of **consequentialism:** the view that the moral correctness or acceptability of an action is determined by its consequences.) The selection by Jeremy Bentham presents a straightforward version of **hedonistic** act utilitarianism, the historically most prominent version of utilitarianism, according to which the relevant sort of utility that makes actions good (or bad) is the pleasure or happiness (as contrasted with pain or unhappiness) they lead to. The selection by John Stuart Mill then presents a revised and more subtle version of act utilitarianism, one that, among other things, recognizes different *qualities* (as opposed to quantities) of pleasure or happiness.

Mill's discussion has also been taken by some to suggest an importantly different sort of utilitarian view, **rule utilitarianism,** according to which (a) the morally correct action in a given situation is determined by a set of general rules, and (b) the correct set of rules is the one whose general observance leads to the greatest utility. The rough idea here is that everyone following a rule like "never tell lies" might produce more utility overall even if conformity to this rule produced less utility in some specific cases. The selection by J. J. C. Smart discusses the issue between these two versions of utilitarianism, arguing that there is no good rationale for rule utilitarianism. Finally, the selection from Bernard Williams offers some further criticisms of utilitarianism.

It is also worth adding here that while hedonistic versions of utilitarianism are the most prominent, both in these readings and in general, there are two other accounts of utility that different versions of utilitarianism accept: According to **ideal utilitarianism,** there are many different sorts of **intrinsic good,** things that are good in themselves or for their own sake as opposed to being merely good as a means to something else (**instrumental good**), with pleasure or happiness being only one—or perhaps two—of these (knowledge, on some views, is another). The fundamental moral principle of ideal utilitarianism is then that the sum of all these goods should be maximized, either by each action (the act version) or by the set of rules (the rule version). And a third, much more recently developed account of utility defines it in terms of the satisfaction of *preferences,* with the morally correct action or set of rules being the one that maximizes the satisfaction of preferences.

Deontological Views: Morality Depends on Duties and Rights

The second main sort of view is a **deontological** moral theory, according to which the rightness or wrongness of an action is determined, not by its consequences, but just by the kind of action it is—with the crucial claim being that some sorts of actions are morally unacceptable no matter what results they may lead to in terms of utility. Here the most influential view by far is that of Immanuel Kant, so much so indeed that the main alternative to utilitarianism is often referred to as a Kantian moral theory. The selection from Kant offers an account of this sort of position, centering around several supposedly equivalent versions of what Kant regards as the fundamental principle of morality: the **categorical imperative.** The following selection by Onora O'Neill then discusses the contrast between utilitarian and Kantian views in relation to a specific moral issue: the issue of moral obligations with respect to famine relief.

One deontological idea that plays a relatively minor explicit role in Kant's view but that has come to be very prominent in recent moral discussion is the idea of moral **rights.** (What makes this a deontological moral concept is that rights are normally taken to override considerations of utility in that it is morally wrong to violate a person's right to something even if doing so produces better overall results.) The selection from David T. Ozar explains and develops the idea of moral rights.

Virtue Ethics: Morality Depends on Character Traits

A third sort of moral view has very ancient roots but has been revived as a main view only fairly recently (and is, far more than the other two views, still in the process of development). This view centers around the idea of **moral virtues:** morally valuable traits of individual character, such as courage, temperance, charity, and so on. There are two importantly different versions of virtue ethics, making weaker and stronger claims. The weaker view presents itself less as a rival than as a supplement to utilitarian and Kantian views: it insists that there are important moral questions that go beyond that of the morally right or acceptable choice of action. One of these questions is what sort of person one should be, with the idea of moral virtue playing a major role in the answer. In contrast, a second, more ambitious version of virtue ethics attempts to provide an alternative account of morally correct or acceptable actions as those that would be adopted by an ideally virtuous person. The selection from Aristotle offers the historically most influential account of the nature of moral virtue, while the selection from Rosalind Hursthouse defends a version of the second, more ambitious version of virtue ethics, contrasting it with utilitarian and Kantian views.

How Do General Moral Concepts
Apply to Concrete Issues?

Much of the most important recent work in moral philosophy has been of a less abstract and more down-to-earth character, focusing on specific moral problems that are the subject of political and moral controversy. Discussions of this sort often appeal to general moral views like utilitarianism, but they also invoke more specific moral ideas that arise out of reflection on the specific issue in question. The final section of this chapter presents a modest sampling of this work: the selection from Judith Jarvis Thomson presents a very influential account of the problem of abortion; the selection from Philippa Foot investigates the moral permissibility of various forms of euthanasia; the selection from Thomas Nagel investigates issues pertaining to the morality of specific kinds of actions in the context of war; and the selection from Tom Regan argues for the existence of animal rights of a demanding sort that would make many of our ways of dealing with animals morally impermissible.

MORAL INVESTIGATION: THE METHOD OF REFLECTIVE EQUILIBRIUM

There is one other matter that needs to be discussed before proceeding: a general method of thinking about moral questions that has come to be very widely accepted among philosophers, at least in its general outlines. This method is motivated by two general facts that are also widely acknowledged: first, that moral claims are rarely if ever so obviously and straightforwardly true that they can simply be accepted on that basis; and, second, that while nonmoral facts can be relevant in various ways to moral issues, the truth of moral claims is always logically independent of such nonmoral facts and incapable of being settled by appeal to them.

How then can the truth or correctness of moral claims be assessed on a rational basis? The starting point here is the realization that while, as already noted, such claims are rarely just obviously true, they are very frequently matters about which we have opinions of varying degrees of strength that are not inferred from other moral opinions but are instead direct or immediate. Thus, for example, upon observing a simple case of theft (or, importantly, having such a case described in some detail), most people will judge immediately and noninferentially that the thief's action was wrong. (They may *also* infer this result from more general principles, but this will not normally be the sole basis or even the main basis for the resulting belief.) Such immediate, noninferential moral opinions have come to be referred to as *moral intuitions.*

The essential input for the method of reflective equilibrium is moral intuitions pertaining to many different matters: intuitions about specific cases, whether actual or invented, together with intuitions about more general principles at various levels of generality. There is no doubt that we do have such intuitions and that many of them are matters of substantial agreement among different persons. But there is also no doubt that the intuitions of different people about the same issue can conflict with each other—and also, even more interestingly, that the intuitions of a single person about different issues and at different levels can conflict among themselves. Thus even if it is assumed that people have some capacity for moral insight and thus that their carefully considered moral intuitions have some claim to be correct, it is obvious that not all such intuitions are correct. The hope, however, is that by reflectively weighing such intuitions against each other, discarding those that seem to be in conflict with many others, and perhaps refining or adjusting others to avoid such conflicts, an overall coherent package of specific claims and principles of varying degrees of generality can be arrived at. And then the overall view of this sort that best preserves the clearest and strongest moral intuitions (and also, perhaps, explains away many of the intuitions that it has to reject as mistaken) will have, according to this view, the strongest claim to be correct. This perhaps somewhat idealized result is referred to as *reflective equilibrium:* "equilibrium" because the sorts of conflicts that make one's moral views unstable and subject to change have, for the moment anyway, been eliminated. And thus the philosopher's main goal in thinking about moral issues is to seek and (it is hoped) achieve such reflective equilibrium.

Perhaps no one can seriously claim to have achieved this result in a fully satisfactory way. But implicit appeals to this method pervade the readings that follow, with intuitions about various sorts of cases and examples being cited as reasons for or against a particular moral view.

IS MORALITY RELATIVE? ARE WE MOTIVATED ONLY BY SELF-INTEREST?

James Rachels

James Rachels (1941–2003) was an American philosopher best known for his work in both theoretical and applied ethics. He taught at several different universities, spending the longest time at the University of Alabama-Birmingham. In this selection, he explains and criticizes cultural relativism, arguing that the typical reasons advanced for the view fail to support it and that the view has implausible consequences. Moreover, he argues, there is not nearly as much moral disagreement as most defenders of cultural relativism claim there is.

The Challenge of Cultural Relativism

Morality differs in every society, and is a convenient term for socially approved habits.

RUTH BENEDICT, *PATTERNS OF CULTURE* (1934)

1. HOW DIFFERENT CULTURES HAVE DIFFERENT MORAL CODES

Darius, a king of ancient Persia, was intrigued by the variety of cultures he encountered in his travels. He had found, for example, that the Callatians (a tribe of Indians) customarily ate the bodies of their dead fathers. The Greeks, of course, did not do that—the Greeks practiced cremation and regarded the funeral pyre as the natural and fitting way to dispose of the dead. Darius thought that a sophisticated understanding of the world must include an appreciation of such differences between cultures. One day, to teach this lesson, he summoned some Greeks who happened to be present at his court and asked them what they would take to eat the bodies of their dead fathers. They were shocked, as Darius knew they would be, and replied that no amount of money could persuade them to do such a thing. Then Darius called in some Callatians, and while the Greeks listened asked them what they

From The Elements of Moral Philosophy, *Chapter 2 (Philadelphia: Temple University Press, 1986).*

would take to burn their dead fathers' bodies. The Callatians were horrified and told Darius not even to mention such a dreadful thing.

This story, recounted by Herodotus in his *History,* illustrates a recurring theme in the literature of social science: different cultures have different moral codes. What is thought right within one group may be utterly abhorrent to the members of another group, and vice versa. Should we eat the bodies of the dead or burn them? If you were a Greek, one answer would seem obviously correct; but if you were a Callatian, the opposite would seem equally certain.

It is easy to give additional examples of the same kind. Consider the Eskimos. They are a remote and inaccessible people. Numbering only about 25,000, they live in small, isolated settlements scattered mostly along the northern fringes of North America and Greenland. Until the beginning of this century, the outside world knew little about them. Then explorers began to bring back strange tales.

Eskimo customs turned out to be very different from our own. The men often had more than one wife, and they would share their wives with guests, lending them for the night as a sign of hospitality. Moreover, within a community, a dominant male might demand—and get—regular sexual access to other men's wives. The women, however, were free to break these arrangements simply by leaving their husbands and taking up with new partners—free, that is, so long as their former husbands chose not to make trouble. All in all, the Eskimo practice was a volatile scheme that bore little resemblance to what we call marriage.

But it was not only their marriage and sexual practices that were different. The Eskimos also seemed to have less regard for human life. Infanticide, for example, was common. Knud Rasmussen, one of the most famous early explorers, reported that he met one woman who had borne twenty children but had killed ten of them at birth. Female babies, he found, were especially liable to be destroyed, and this was permitted simply at the parents' discretion, with no social stigma attached to it. Old people also, when they became too feeble to contribute to the family, were left out in the snow to die. So there seemed to be, in this society, remarkably little respect for life.

To the general public, these were disturbing revelations. Our own way of living seems so natural and right that for many of us it is hard to conceive of others living so differently. And when we do hear of such things, we tend immediately to categorize those other peoples as "backward" or "primitive." But to anthropologists and sociologists, there was nothing particularly surprising about the Eskimos. Since the time of Herodotus, enlightened observers have been accustomed to the idea that conceptions of right and wrong differ from culture to culture. If we assume that *our* ideas of right and wrong will be shared by all peoples at all times, we are merely naive.

2. CULTURAL RELATIVISM

To many thinkers, this observation—"Different cultures have different moral codes"—has seemed to be the key to understanding morality. The idea of universal truth in ethics, they say, is a myth.① The customs of different societies are all that exist. These customs cannot be said to be "correct" or "incorrect," for that implies we have an independent standard of right and wrong by which they may be judged. But there is no such independent standard; every standard is culture-bound. The great pioneering sociologist William Graham Sumner, writing in 1906, put the point like this:

> The "right" way is the way which the ancestors used and which has been handed down. The tradition is its own warrant. It is not held subject to verification by experience. The notion of right is in the folkways. It is not outside of them, of independent origin, and brought to test them. In the folkways, whatever is, is right. This is because they are traditional, and therefore contain in themselves the authority of the ancestral ghosts. When we come to the folkways we are at the end of our analysis.

This line of thought has probably persuaded more people to be skeptical about ethics than any other single thing. *Cultural Relativism,* as it has been called, challenges our ordinary belief in the objectivity and universality of moral truth. It says, in effect, that there is no such thing as universal truth in ethics; there are only the various cultural codes, and nothing more. Moreover, our own code has no special status; it is merely one among many.

As we shall see, this basic idea is really a compound of several different thoughts. It is important to separate the various elements of the theory because, on analysis, some parts of the theory turn out to be correct, whereas others seem to be mistaken. As a beginning, we may distinguish the following claims, all of which have been made by cultural relativists:

1. Different societies have different moral codes.
2. There is no objective standard that can be used to judge one societal code better than another.
3. The moral code of our own society has no special status; it is merely one among many.
4. There is no "universal truth" in ethics—that is, there are no moral truths that hold for all peoples at all times.
5. The moral code of a society determines what is right within that society; that is, if the moral code of a society says that a certain action is right, then that action *is* right, at least within that society.
6. It is mere arrogance for us to try to judge the conduct of other peoples. We should adopt

---

① By "universal truth in ethics," Rachels means objective (or "absolute") ethical truth: ethical truths that are true in the same nonrelative way that scientific truths or at least simple, purely factual historical truths are true.

an attitude of tolerance toward the practices of other cultures.②

② Think carefully about the relations among these claims. Claim 1 is in itself a nonmoral, factual claim, while all the others are moral claims of one sort or another. The central claim of cultural relativism is Claim 5.

Although it may seem that these six propositions go naturally together, they are independent of one another, in the sense that some of them might be true even if others are false. In what follows, we will try to identify what is correct in Cultural Relativism, but we will also be concerned to expose what is mistaken about it.

3. THE CULTURAL DIFFERENCES ARGUMENT

Cultural Relativism is a theory about the nature of morality. At first blush it seems quite plausible. However, like all such theories, it may be evaluated by subjecting it to rational analysis; and when we analyze Cultural Relativism we find that it is not so plausible as it first appears to be.

The first thing we need to notice is that at the heart of Cultural Relativism there is a certain *form of argument.* The strategy used by cultural relativists is to argue from facts about the differences between cultural outlooks to a conclusion about the status of morality. Thus we are invited to accept this reasoning:

1. The Greeks believed it was wrong to eat the dead, whereas the Callatians believed it was right to eat the dead.
2. Therefore, eating the dead is neither objectively right nor objectively wrong. It is merely a matter of opinion, which varies from culture to culture.

Or, alternatively:

1. The Eskimos see nothing wrong with infanticide, whereas Americans believe infanticide is immoral.
2. Therefore, infanticide is neither objectively right nor objectively wrong. It is merely a matter of opinion, which varies from culture to culture.

Clearly, these arguments are variations of one fundamental idea. They are both special cases of a more general argument, which says:

1. Different cultures have different moral codes.
2. Therefore, there is no objective "truth" in morality. Right and wrong are only matters of opinion, and opinions vary from culture to culture.

We may call this the *Cultural Differences Argument.* To many people, it is very persuasive. But from a logical point of view, is it a *sound* argument?③

It is not sound. The trouble is that the conclusion does not really follow from the premise—that is, even if the premise is true, the conclusion still might be false. The premise concerns what people *believe:* in some societies, people believe one thing; in other societies, people believe differently. The conclusion, however, concerns *what really is the case.* The trouble is that this sort of conclusion does not follow logically from this sort of premise.

③ To say that an argument is *sound* is to say both that the premise or premises are true and that the argument is *valid* in the sense that the conclusion genuinely follows from the premises (in other words, that it is impossible for the premises to be true and the conclusion false).

Consider again the example of the Greeks and Callatians. The Greeks believed it was wrong to eat the dead; the Callatians believed it was right. Does it follow, *from the mere fact that they disagreed,* that there is no objective truth in the matter? No, it does not follow; for it *could* be that the practice was objectively right (or wrong) and that one or the other of them was simply mistaken.

To make the point clearer, consider a very different matter. In some societies, people believe the earth is flat. In other societies, such as our own, people believe the earth is (roughly) spherical. Does it follow, *from the mere fact that they disagree,* that there is no "objective truth" in geography? Of course not; we would never draw such a conclusion because we realize that, in their beliefs about the world, the members of some societies might simply be wrong. There is no reason to think that if the world is round everyone must know it. Similarly, there is no reason to think that if there is moral truth everyone must know it. The fundamental mistake in the Cultural Differences Argument is that it attempts to derive a substantive conclusion about a subject (morality) from the mere fact that people disagree about it.

It is important to understand the nature of the point that is being made here. We are *not* saying (not yet, anyway) that the conclusion of the argument is false. Insofar as anything being said here is concerned, it is still an open question whether the conclusion is true. We *are* making a purely logical point and saying that the conclusion does not *follow from* the premise. This is important, because in order to determine whether the conclusion is true, we need arguments in its support. Cultural Relativism proposes this argument, but unfortunately the argument turns out to be fallacious. So it proves nothing.④

> ④ As with other arguments, the conclusion might still in fact be true even if the argument is unsound.

4. THE CONSEQUENCES OF TAKING CULTURAL RELATIVISM SERIOUSLY

Even if the Cultural Differences Argument is invalid, Cultural Relativism might still be true. What would it be like if it were true?

In the passage quoted above, William Graham Sumner summarizes the essence of Cultural Relativism. He says that there is no measure of right and wrong other than the standards of one's society: "The notion of right is in the folkways. It is not outside of them, of independent origin, and brought to test them. In the folkways, whatever is, is right."

Suppose we took this seriously. What would be some of the consequences?

1. We could no longer say that the customs of other societies are morally inferior to our own. This, of course, is one of the main points stressed by Cultural Relativism. We would have to stop condemning other societies merely because they are "different." So long as we concentrate on certain examples, such as the funerary practices of the Greeks and Callatians, this may seem to be a sophisticated, enlightened attitude.

However, we would also be stopped from criticizing other, less benign practices. Suppose a society waged war on its neighbors for the purpose of taking slaves.⑤ Or suppose a society was violently anti-Semitic and its leaders set out to destroy the Jews. Cultural Relativism would preclude us from saying that either of these practices was wrong. We would not even be able to say that a society tolerant of Jews is *better* than the anti-Semitic society, for that would imply some sort of transcultural standard of comparison. The failure to condemn *these* practices does not seem "enlightened"; on the contrary, slavery and anti-Semitism seem wrong *wherever* they occur. Nevertheless, if we took Cultural Relativism seriously, we would have to admit that these social practices also are immune from criticism.

> ⑤ An even more obvious example might be the practice of slavery in the pre-Civil War American South. Is it really impossible (as the cultural relativist must claim) for us to say intelligibly that the practices of that society were in an important way morally inferior to those of our present society?

2. We could decide whether actions are right or wrong just by consulting the standards of our society. Cultural Relativism suggests a simple test for determining what is right and what is wrong: all one has to do is ask whether the action is in accordance with the code of one's society. Suppose a resident of South Africa is wondering whether his country's policy of *apartheid*—rigid racial segregation—is morally correct. All he has to do is ask whether this policy conforms to his society's moral code. If it does, there is nothing to worry about, at least from a moral point of view.⑥

> ⑥ Apartheid is no longer practiced in South Africa, but we can still ask whether a person living under apartheid could have correctly decided that racial segregation was morally acceptable simply by appealing to the standard actually accepted there.

This implication of Cultural Relativism is disturbing because few of us think that our society's code is perfect—we can think of ways it might be improved. Yet Cultural Relativism would not only forbid us from criticizing the codes of *other* societies; it would stop us from criticizing our *own*. After all, if right and wrong are relative to culture, this must be true for our own culture just as much as for others.

3. The idea of moral progress is called into doubt.

Usually, we think that at least some changes in our society have been for the better. (Some, of course, may have been changes for the worse.) Consider this example: Throughout most of Western history the place of women in society was very narrowly circumscribed. They could not own property; they could not vote or hold political office; with a few exceptions, they were not permitted to have paying jobs; and generally they were under the almost absolute control of their husbands. Recently much of this has changed, and most people think of it as progress.

If Cultural Relativism is correct, can we legitimately think of this as progress? Progress means replacing a way of doing things with a *better* way. But by what standard do we judge the new ways as better? If the old ways were in accordance with the social standards of their time, then Cultural Relativism would say it is a mistake to judge them by the standards of a different time. Eighteenth-century society was, in effect, a different society from the one we have now. To say that we have made progress implies a judgment that present-day society is better, and that is just the sort of transcultural judgment that, according to Cultural Relativism, is impermissible.

Our idea of social *reform* will also have to be reconsidered. A reformer such as Martin Luther King, Jr., seeks to change his society for the better. Within the constraints imposed by Cultural Relativism, there is one way this might be done. If a society is not living up to its own ideals, the reformer may be regarded as acting for the best: the ideals of the society are the standard by which we judge his or her proposals as worthwhile. But the "reformer" may not challenge the ideals themselves, for those ideals are by definition correct. According to Cultural Relativism, then, the idea of social reform makes sense only in this very limited way.

These three consequences of Cultural Relativism have led many thinkers to reject it as implausible on its face. It does make sense, they say, to condemn some practices, such as slavery and anti-Semitism, wherever they occur. It makes sense to think that our own society has made some moral progress, while admitting that it is still imperfect and in need of reform. Because Cultural Relativism says that these judg-ments make no sense, the argument goes, it cannot be right.

5. WHY THERE IS LESS DISAGREEMENT THAN IT SEEMS

The original impetus for Cultural Relativism comes from the observation that cultures differ dramatically in their views of right and wrong. But just how much do they differ? It is true that there are differences. However, it is easy to overestimate the extent of those differences. Often, when we examine what *seems* to be a dramatic difference, we find that the cultures do not differ nearly as much as it appears.

Consider a culture in which people believe it is wrong to eat cows. This may even be a poor culture, in which there is not enough food; still, the cows are not to be touched. Such a society would *appear* to have values very different from our own. But does it? We have not yet asked why these people will not eat cows. Suppose it is because they believe that after death the souls of humans inhabit the bodies of animals, especially cows, so that a cow may be someone's grandmother. Now do we want to say that their values are different from ours? No; the difference lies elsewhere. The difference is in our belief systems, not in our values. We agree that we shouldn't eat Grandma; we simply disagree about whether the cow *is* (or could be) Grandma.[7]

> [7] Thus if the members of our culture came to believe that cows were reincarnations of relatives or friends, they would also presumably think that it was wrong to eat them.

The general point is this. Many factors work together to produce the customs of a society. The society's values are only one of them. Other matters, such as the religious and factual beliefs held by its members and the physical circumstances in which they must live, are also important. We cannot conclude, then, merely because customs differ, that there is a disagreement about *values*. The difference in customs may be attributable to some other aspect of social life. Thus there may be less disagreement about values than there appears to be.

Consider the Eskimos again. They often kill perfectly normal infants, especially girls. We do not approve of this at all; a parent who did this in our society would be locked up. Thus there appears to be a great difference in the values of our two cultures. But suppose we ask *why* the Eskimos do this. The explanation is not that they have less affection for their children or less respect for human life. An Eskimo family will always protect its babies if conditions permit. But they live in a harsh environment, where food is often in short supply. A fundamental postulate of Eskimo thought is: "Life is hard, and the margin of safety small." A family may want to nourish its babies but be unable to do so.

As in many "primitive" societies, Eskimo mothers will nurse their infants over a much longer period of time than mothers in our culture. The child will take nourishment from its mother's breast for four years, perhaps even longer. So even in the best of times there are limits to the number of infants that one mother can sustain. Moreover, the Eskimos are a nomadic people—unable to farm, they must move about in search of food. Infants must be carried, and a mother can carry only one baby in her parka as she travels and goes about her outdoor work. Other family members can help, but this is not always possible.

Infant girls are more readily disposed of because, first, in this society the males are the primary food providers—they are the hunters, according to the traditional division of labor—and it is obviously important to maintain a sufficient number of food gatherers. But there is an important second reason as well. Because the hunters suffer a high casualty rate, the adult men who die prematurely far outnumber the women who die early. Thus if male and female infants survived in equal numbers, the female adult population would greatly outnumber the male adult population. Examining the available statistics, one writer concluded that "were it not for female infanticide . . . there would be approximately one-and-a-half times as many females in the average Eskimo local group as there are food-producing males."

So among the Eskimos, infanticide does not signal a fundamentally different attitude toward children. Instead, it is a recognition that drastic measures are sometimes needed to ensure the family's survival. Even then, however, killing the baby is not the first option considered. Adoption is common; childless couples are especially happy to take a more fertile couple's "surplus." Killing is only the last resort. I emphasize this in order to show that the raw data of the anthropologists can be misleading; it can make the differences in values between cultures appear greater than they are. The Eskimos' values are not all that different from our values. It is only that life forces upon them choices that we do not have to make. ⑧

> ⑧ How much of the difference in behavior between our society and traditional Eskimo society can be explained in this way? See Discussion Question 1.

6. HOW ALL CULTURES HAVE SOME VALUES IN COMMON

It should not be surprising that, despite appearances, the Eskimos are protective of their children. How could it be otherwise? How could a group survive that did *not* value its young? This suggests a certain argument, one which shows that all cultural groups must be protective of their infants:

1. Human infants are helpless and cannot survive if they are not given extensive care for a period of years.
2. Therefore, if a group did not care for its young, the young would not survive, and the older members of the group would not be replaced. After a while the group would die out.
3. Therefore, any cultural group that continues to exist must care for its young. Infants that are *not* cared for must be the exception rather than the rule.

Similar reasoning shows that other values must be more or less universal. Imagine what it would be like for a society to place no value at all on truth telling. When one person spoke to another, there would be no presumption at all that he was telling the truth—for he could just as easily be speaking falsely. Within that society, there would be no reason to pay attention to what anyone says. (I ask you what time it is, and you say "Four o'clock." But there is no presumption that you are speaking truly; you could just as easily have said the first thing that came into your head. So I have no reason to pay attention to your answer—in fact, there was no point in my asking you in the first place!) Communication would then be extremely difficult, if not impossible. And because complex societies cannot exist without regular communication among their members, society would become impossible. It follows that in any complex society there *must* be a presumption in favor of truthfulness. There may of course be exceptions to this rule: there may be situations in which it is thought to be permissible to lie. Nevertheless, these will be exceptions to a rule that *is* in force in the society.

Let me give one further example of the same type. Could a society exist in which there was no prohibition on murder? What would this be like? Suppose people were free to kill other people at will, and no one thought there was anything wrong with it. In such a "society," no one could feel secure. Everyone would have to be constantly on guard. People who wanted to survive would have to avoid other people as much as possible. This would inevitably result in individuals trying to become as self-sufficient as possible—after all, associating with others would be dangerous. Society on any large scale would collapse. Of course, people might band together in smaller groups with others that they *could* trust not to harm them. But notice what this means: they would be forming smaller societies that *did* acknowledge a rule against murder. The prohibition of murder, then, is a necessary feature of all societies.

There is a general theoretical point here, namely, that *there are some moral rules that all societies will have in common, because those rules are necessary for society to exist.* The rules against lying and murder are two examples. And in fact, we do find these rules in force in all viable cultures. Cultures may differ in what they regard as legitimate exceptions to the rules, but this disagreement exists against a background of agreement on the larger issues. Therefore, it is a mistake to overestimate the amount of difference between cultures. Not *every* moral rule can vary from society to society.⑨

9 Is the fact that certain moral principles seem to be essential to any imaginable society enough to show that they are objectively true: that any society is *morally* required to follow them?

7. WHAT CAN BE LEARNED FROM CULTURAL RELATIVISM

At the outset, I said that we were going to identify both what is right and what is wrong in Cultural Relativism. Thus far I have mentioned only its mistakes: I

have said that it rests on an invalid argument, that it has consequences that make it implausible on its face, and that the extent of cultural disagreement is far less than it implies. This all adds up to a pretty thorough repudiation of the theory. Nevertheless, it is still a very appealing idea, and the reader may have the feeling that all this is a little unfair. The theory *must* have something going for it, or else why has it been so influential? In fact, I think there *is* something right about Cultural Relativism, and now I want to say what that is. There are two lessons we should learn from the theory, even if we ultimately reject it.

1. Cultural Relativism warns us, quite rightly, about the danger of assuming that all our preferences are based on some absolute rational standard. They are not. Many (but not all) of our practices are merely peculiar to our society, and it is easy to lose sight of that fact. In reminding us of it, the theory does a service.

Funerary practices are one example. The Callatians, according to Herodotus, were "men who eat their fathers"—a shocking idea, to us at least. But eating the flesh of the dead could be understood as a sign of respect. It could be taken as a symbolic act that says: We wish this person's spirit to dwell within us. Perhaps this was the understanding of the Callatians. On such a way of thinking, burying the dead could be seen as an act of rejection, and burning the corpse as positively scornful. If this is hard to imagine, then we may need to have our imaginations stretched. Of course we may feel a visceral repugnance at the idea of eating human flesh in any circumstances. But what of it? This repugnance may be, as the relativists say, only a matter of what is customary in our particular society.

There are many other matters that we tend to think of in terms of objective right and wrong, but that are really nothing more than social conventions. Should women cover their breasts? A publicly exposed breast is scandalous in our society, whereas in other cultures it is unremarkable. Objectively speaking, it is neither right nor wrong—there is no objective reason why either custom is better. Cultural Relativism begins with the valuable insight that many of our practices are like this—they are only cultural products.⑩ Then it

10 It is entirely consistent with the existence of objective morality that there are many issues, including some that have been thought to be morally significant, about which there is no objective moral truth.

goes wrong by concluding that, because *some* practices are like this, *all* must be.

2. The second lesson has to do with keeping an open mind. In the course of growing up, each of us has acquired some strong feelings: we have learned to think of some types of conduct as acceptable, and others we have learned to regard as simply unacceptable. Occasionally, we may find those feelings challenged. We may encounter someone who claims that our feelings are mistaken. For example, we may have been taught that homosexuality is immoral, and we may feel quite uncomfortable around gay people and see them as alien and "different." Now someone suggests that this may be a mere prejudice; that there is nothing evil about homosexuality; that gay people are just people, like anyone else, who happen, through no choice of their own, to be attracted to others of the same sex. But because we feel so strongly about the matter, we may find it hard to take this seriously. Even after we listen to the arguments, we may still have the unshakable feeling that homosexuals *must,* somehow, be an unsavory lot.

Cultural Relativism, by stressing that our moral views can reflect the prejudices of our society, provides an antidote for this kind of dogmatism. When he tells the story of the Greeks and Callatians, Herodotus adds:

> For if anyone, no matter who, were given the opportunity of choosing from amongst all the nations of the world the set of beliefs which he thought best, he would inevitably, after careful consideration of their relative merits, choose that of his own country. Everyone without exception believes his own native customs, and the religion he was brought up in, to be the best.

Realizing this can result in our having more open minds. We can come to understand that our feelings are not necessarily perceptions of the truth—they may be nothing more than the result of cultural conditioning. Thus when we hear it suggested that some element of our social code is *not* really the best and we find ourselves instinctively resisting the suggestion, we might stop and remember this. Then we may be more open to discovering the truth, whatever that might be.

We can understand the appeal of Cultural Relativism, then, even though the theory has serious shortcomings. It is an attractive theory because it is based on a genuine insight—that many of the practices and attitudes we think so natural are really only cultural products. Moreover, keeping this insight firmly in view is important if we want to avoid arrogance and have open minds. These are important points, not to be taken lightly. But we can accept these points without going on to accept the whole theory. [11]

> [11] To accept these points does not force us to accept any part of the theory, let alone the whole theory.

Discussion Questions

1. Rachels argues that apparent moral disagreement can often be accounted for by appeal to differences in factual beliefs or in the physical circumstances within which different cultures exist, without supposing that the underlying moral beliefs or values are really different. How well does this work in relation to the contrast between our culture and traditional Eskimo culture, as Rachels describes it? If our physical circumstances came to be closely similar to those of the Eskimos, would we then decide—without any change in our underlying moral beliefs and principles—that treating infants and old people in the way the Eskimos did is morally acceptable? Or would there still be a conflict between the demands of morality and the requirements of survival?

2. The cultural relativist view is that an individual should follow the moral standards of his society or culture. But it is arguable that many individuals in the modern world are members of more than one society or at least more than one group, with different groups often accepting different moral standards. Think of illustrations of this problem. Is there any way in such a situation to decide which group's moral standards the individual should follow?

3. Does cultural relativism allow for genuine moral disagreement between two (or more) individuals: a situation in which such individuals hold different moral views that are genuinely opposed to each other in such a way that both (or all) of them cannot be correct? Consider here both (a) two individuals from

the same culture and (b) two individuals from different cultures. In (a), there can be a genuine disagreement of a sort, but is it really a moral disagreement, and is it plausible that this is the only way in which moral disagreement is possible? Can there be even this sort of moral disagreement (if it really is that) in (b)? If not, how implausible a result is this?

4. The central claim of cultural relativism is that the moral code of a particular society *determines* what is right (and wrong) for individuals in that society (claim 5 on p. 547). This seems to mean that individuals are morally bound by the standards of their culture, morally required to follow those standards. But can the cultural relativist account for the truth of *this* moral claim? What if there is a culture, call it the Objectivists, whose moral code includes the claim that their moral claims are objectively true. The Objectivists do *not* say that people should follow the standards of their own cultures, since some culture's moral codes are wrong. If cultural relativism is true, then the Objectivist's culture *determines* the moral truth for those people, and so, for them, objectivism is true. Is this result consistent with the truth of cultural relativism?

James Rachels

In this selection, Rachels discusses two views that make moral judgments depend, in different ways, on the approval or disapproval of particular individuals. According to Simple Subjectivism, moral judgments are simply statements that a given individual approves or disapproves of a particular action. According to Emotivism, moral judgments (which really aren't judgments at all) are *expressions* of individual approval or disapproval, but make no claim that could be either true or false. Both of these views are versions of individual (as opposed to cultural) relativism, though perhaps not the only possible versions of this general view (see Discussion Question 2).

Subjectivism in Ethics

Take any action allow'd to be vicious: Wilful murder, for instance. Examine it in all lights, and see if you can find that matter of fact, or real existence, which you call *vice*. . . . You can never find it, till you turn your reflexion into your own breast, and find a sentiment of disapprobation, which arises in you, toward this action. Here is a matter of fact; but 'tis the object of feeling, not reason.

DAVID HUME, *A TREATISE OF HUMAN NATURE*
(1740)

From The Elements of Moral Philosophy, *Chapter 3 (Philadelphia: Temple University Press, 1986).*

1. THE BASIC IDEA OF ETHICAL SUBJECTIVISM

The Reverend Jerry Falwell, founder of the Moral Majority, said in a television interview: "Homosexuality is immoral. The so-called 'gay rights' are not rights at all, because immorality is not right. God hates homosexuality, and so do we. But we do not hate the homosexual; we want to help him by helping him overcome his sin."

Falwell speaks for a large number of Americans who feel that there is something deeply objectionable about homosexuality. In other societies, of course, people have other views. The rulers of present-day Iran agree with Falwell and take his view to an extreme: there, homosexuals may be castrated or killed or both. . . . In England, on the other hand, a more tolerant attitude is taken, and all legal penalties were removed . . . decades ago. What attitude are we to take? One possibility is that we might agree with Falwell and say that homosexuality is in fact immoral. Or we might disagree and say that in fact homosexuality is *not* immoral. But there is a third alternative. We might say something like this:

> Falwell is expressing his own personal opinion, and many may agree with him. But others may have different opinions. Where morality is concerned, there are no "facts," and no one is "right." He has his opinion; others have their opinions; and that's the end of it.

This is the basic thought behind *Ethical Subjectivism.* Ethical Subjectivism is the idea that our moral opinions are based on our feelings, and nothing more. On this view, there is no such thing as "objective" right or wrong. It is a fact that some people are homosexual and some are heterosexual; but it is not a fact that one is good and the other bad. So when someone such as Falwell says that homosexuality is wrong, he is not stating a fact about homosexuality. Instead, he is merely saying something about his feelings toward it.

Of course, Ethical Subjectivism is not simply an idea about the evaluation of homosexuality. It applies to all moral matters. To take a different example, it is a fact that Hitler and his henchmen exterminated millions of innocent people; but according to Ethical Subjectivism, it is not a fact that what they did was evil. When we say their actions were evil, we are not stating a fact about those actions; rather, we are saying that we have negative feelings toward them.① Exactly the same applies to any moral judgment whatever.

① Whereas Hitler and his henchmen presumably had positive feelings about what they did, which they could have expressed by saying that their actions were morally good or morally admirable.

We should be clear about what *kind* of theory this is. Ethical Subjectivism is not a theory about what things are good and what things are bad. It does not try to tell us how we should live or what moral opinions we should accept. It is not that sort of theory. Instead, it is a theory about *the nature of moral judgments.* It says that no matter what moral judg-

ments we make, we are only expressing our personal feelings, and nothing more. People who accept this theory will still have moral opinions, of course—they might be in favor of gay rights or opposed to them. But whichever stance they choose, they will not believe their choice represents the "truth." They will recognize that their opinions merely represent their own personal feelings.

2. THE EVOLUTION OF THE THEORY

Often the development of a philosophical idea will proceed through several stages. At first the idea will be put forward in a crude, simple form, and many people will find it attractive for one reason or another. But then the idea will be subjected to critical analysis, and it will be discovered to have serious defects. Arguments against the idea will be found. At this point some people may be so impressed with the objections that they abandon the idea altogether, concluding that it cannot be right. Others, however, may continue to have confidence in the basic idea, and so they will try to refine it—giving it a new, improved formulation—so that it will not be vulnerable to the objections. For a time it may appear that the theory has been saved. But then new arguments may be found that cast doubt on the new version of the theory. Once again the new objections may cause some to abandon the idea, while others may keep the faith and try to salvage the theory by formulating still another "improved" version. The whole process of revision and criticism will then start over again.

The theory of Ethical Subjectivism has developed in just this way. It began as a simple idea—in the words of David Hume, that morality is a matter of sentiment rather than fact. But as objections were raised to the theory, and as its defenders tried to answer the objections, the theory evolved into something much more sophisticated.

3. THE FIRST STAGE: SIMPLE SUBJECTIVISM

As we have already observed, Ethical Subjectivism is a theory about the nature of moral judgments. The simplest version of the theory, which states the main idea but does not attempt to refine it very much, is this: when a person says that something is morally good or bad, this means that he or she approves of that thing, or disapproves of it, and nothing more. In other words:

"X is morally acceptable"
"X is right" } all mean:
"X is good" "I (the speaker)
"X ought to be done" approve of X"

And similarly:

"X is morally unacceptable"
"X is wrong" } all mean:
"X is bad" "I (the speaker)
"X ought not to be done" disapprove of X"

We might call this version of the theory *Simple Subjectivism*. It expresses the basic idea of Ethical Subjectivism in a plain, uncomplicated form, and many people have found it attractive.② However, Simple Subjectivism is open to several rather obvious objections, because it has implications that are contrary to what we know to be the case (or at least, contrary to what we *think* we know to be the case) about the nature of moral evaluation. Let me mention [two] of the most prominent objections.

2 Probably it should be added that the approval or disapproval is of a *moral* sort rather than some other kind (such as aesthetic approval or disapproval).

1. We are sometimes wrong in our evaluations. None of us is infallible, we can make mistakes; and when we discover that we are mistaken, we may want to change our judgments. But if Simple Subjectivism were correct, this would be impossible—because Simple Subjectivism implies that each of us is infallible.

Consider Falwell again, who says homosexuality is immoral. According to Simple Subjectivism, what he is saying is that he, Falwell, disapproves of homosexuality. Now of course it is possible that he is not speaking sincerely—it is possible that he really does not disapprove of homosexuality, that he is merely playing to his conservative audience. But *if we assume he is speaking sincerely*—if we assume he really does disapprove of it—then it follows that what he says is true. So long as he is honestly representing his own feelings, he cannot be mistaken.

Thus the following argument may be offered against Simple Subjectivism:

(1) If Simple Subjectivism is correct, then each of us is infallible in our moral judgments, at least so long as we are speaking sincerely.

(2) However, we are not infallible. We may be mistaken, even when we are speaking sincerely.

(3) Therefore, Simple Subjectivism cannot be correct.③

2. The second argument against Simple Subjectivism is based on the idea that this theory cannot account for the fact of *disagreement* in ethics. Dan Bradley was formerly the director of the United States Legal Services Administration; he resigned in 1982 in order to "come out of the closet" and publicly acknowledge his homosexuality. (He was the highest government official to have done this, and so his declaration was widely publicized.) Bradley insists that homosexuality is not immoral. On the face of it, it appears that Bradley and Falwell disagree. But consider what Simple Subjectivism implies about this situation.

3 Notice that this treats the moral judgment as merely the factual claim that one does approve (or disapprove). Does anything follow about what the individual person who makes the judgment is *morally* required to do? If not, in what sense is it really a moral judgment?

According to Simple Subjectivism, when Bradley says that homosexuality is not immoral, he is merely making a statement about his attitude—he is saying that he, Bradley, does not disapprove of homosexuality. Would Falwell disagree with that? No, Falwell would *agree* that Bradley does not disapprove of homosexuality. At the same time, when Falwell says that homosexuality is immoral, he is only saying that he, Falwell, disapproves of it. And why should Bradley disagree with *that*? In fact, Bradley would certainly acknowledge that Falwell disapproves of homosexuality. Thus according to Simple Subjectivism, there is no disagreement between them—each would acknowledge the truth of what the other is saying! Surely, the argument goes, there is something wrong here, for surely Falwell and Bradley *do* disagree about whether homosexuality is immoral.

There is a kind of eternal frustration implied by Simple Subjectivism: Falwell and Bradley are deeply opposed to one another; yet they cannot even state their positions in a way that joins the issue.

Bradley may *try* to deny what Falwell says, by denying that homosexuality is immoral, but according to Simple Subjectivism he succeeds only in changing the subject.

The argument may be summarized like this:

(1) When one person says "X is morally acceptable" and someone else says "X is morally unacceptable," they are disagreeing.

(2) However, if Simple Subjectivism were correct, there would be no disagreement between them.

(3) Therefore, Simple Subjectivism cannot be correct.④

④ This is perhaps the most serious objection to Simple Subjectivism and indeed to most versions of individual relativism. The underlying idea is that it is just obvious that people really do have moral disagreements, so that a view that cannot account for this must be wrong.

. . .

These arguments, and others like them, show that Simple Subjectivism is a flawed theory: it cannot be maintained, at least not in such a crude form. In the face of such arguments, some thinkers have chosen to reject the whole idea of Ethical Subjectivism. Others, however, have worked to produce a better version of the theory, one that would not be vulnerable to these objections.

4. THE SECOND STAGE: EMOTIVISM

The improved version was a theory that came to be known as *Emotivism*. Developed chiefly by the American philosopher Charles L. Stevenson (1908–1979), Emotivism has been one of the most influential theories of ethics in the twentieth century. It is a far more subtle and sophisticated theory than Simple Subjectivism.

Emotivism begins with the observation that language is used in a variety of ways. One of its principal uses is in stating facts, or at least in stating what we believe to be facts. Thus we may say:

"Abraham Lincoln was President of the United States."
"I have an appointment at four o'clock."
"Gasoline costs $1.19 per gallon."
"Shakespeare is the author of *Hamlet*."

And so on. In each case, we are saying something that is either true or false, and the purpose of our utterance is, typically, to convey information to the listener.

However, there are other purposes for which language may be used. For example, suppose I say to you "Close the door!" This utterance is neither true nor false. It is not a *statement* of any kind; it is a *command,* which is something altogether different. Its purpose is not to convey information; rather, its purpose is *to get you to do something.* In giving you a command, I am not trying to alter your beliefs; instead I am trying to influence your conduct.

Or consider utterances such as these, which are neither statements of fact nor commands:

"Hurrah for Abraham Lincoln!"
"Would that gasoline did not cost so much!"
"Alas!"
"Damn Hamlet!"

These are perfectly familiar, common types of sentences that we understand easily enough. But none of them is "true" or "false." (It would make no sense to say "It is true that hurrah for Abraham Lincoln" or "It is false that alas.") Again, these sentences are not used to state facts; instead, they are used to express the speaker's attitudes.

We need to note clearly the difference between *reporting* an attitude and *expressing* the same attitude. If I say "I like Abraham Lincoln," I am reporting the fact that I have a positive attitude toward him. The statement is a statement of fact, which is either true or false. On the other hand, if I shout "Hurrah for Lincoln!" I am not stating any sort of fact. I am expressing an attitude, but I am not reporting that I have it.

Now, with these points in mind, let us turn our attention to moral language. According to Emotivism, moral language is not fact-stating language; it is not typically used to convey information. Its purpose is entirely different. It is used, first, as a means of influencing people's behavior: if someone says "You ought not to do that," he is *trying to stop you from doing it.* Thus the utterance is more like a command than a statement of fact; it is as though he had said "Don't do that!" Second, moral language is used to express (*not* report) one's attitude. Saying "Lincoln was a good man" is not like saying

"I approve of Lincoln," but it *is* like saying "Hurrah for Lincoln!" ⑤

⑤ Here are two characterizations of what moral statements say or express, characterizations that are by no means obviously equivalent to each other. In most cases, a command is one thing, and an expression of attitude is quite something else, making it at least a little unclear how moral judgments can do both of these things.

The difference between Emotivism and Simple Subjectivism should now be obvious. Simple Subjectivism interpreted ethical sentences as statements of fact, of a special kind—namely, as reports of the speaker's attitude. According to Simple Subjectivism, when Falwell says "Homosexuality is immoral," this means the same as "I (Falwell) disapprove of homosexuality"—a statement of fact about his attitude. Emotivism, on the other hand, would deny that his utterance states any fact at all, even a fact about himself. Instead, Emotivism interprets his utterance as equivalent to something such as "Homosexuality—yecch!" or "Do not engage in homosexual acts!" or "Would that there were no homosexuals."

Now this may seem to be a trivial, nitpicking difference that isn't worth bothering with. But from a theoretical point of view, it is actually a very big and important difference. One way to see this is to consider again the [two] arguments against Simple Subjectivism. While those arguments were severely embarrassing to Simple Subjectivism, they do not affect Emotivism at all.

1. The first argument was that if Simple Subjectivism is correct, then we are all infallible in our moral judgments; but we certainly are not infallible; therefore, Simple Subjectivism cannot be correct.

This argument is effective only because Simple Subjectivism interprets moral judgments as statements that can be true or false. "Infallible" means that one's judgments are always true; and Simple Subjectivism assigns moral judgments a meaning that *will* always be true, so long as the speaker is speaking sincerely. That is why, on that theory, people turn out to be infallible. Emotivism, on the other hand, does not interpret moral judgments as statements that are true-or-false; and so the same argument will not work against it. Because commands and expressions of attitude are not true-or-false, people cannot be "infallible" with respect to them. ⑥

2. The second argument had to do with moral disagreement. If Simple Subjectivism is correct, then when one person says "X is morally acceptable" and someone else says "X is morally unacceptable," they are not really disagreeing. They are, in fact, talking about entirely different things—each is making a statement about his or her own attitude with which the other can readily agree. But, the argument goes, people who say such things *are* disagreeing with one another, and so Simple Subjectivism cannot be correct.

Emotivism emphasizes that there is more than one way in which people may disagree. If I believe that Lee Harvey Oswald acted alone in the assassination of John Kennedy and you believe there was a conspiracy, it is a disagreement over the facts—I believe something to be true that you believe to be false. But consider a different type of disagreement. Suppose I favor strict gun-control legislation and you are opposed to it. Here we disagree, but in a different sense. It is not our beliefs that are in conflict but our desires. (You and I may agree about all the facts surrounding the gun-control controversy and still take different sides concerning what we want to see happen.) In the first kind of disagreement, we believe different things, both of which cannot be true. In the second, we want different things, both of which cannot happen. Stevenson calls this second one a *disagreement in attitude,* and he contrasts it with disagreement *about* attitudes. You and I may agree in all our judgments about our attitudes—we agree that you are opposed to gun control, and we agree that I am for it. But we still disagree *in* our attitudes. Moral disagreements, says Stevenson, are like this: they are disagreements in attitude. ⑦ Simple Subjectivism could not explain moral disagreement

⑥ Note that according to Emotivism, people are still morally infallible in the sense that they cannot be mistaken in their moral judgments (even though they also cannot be correct). Is this first argument still an objection to the view, in relation to, for example, cases like Hitler?

⑦ This is a disagreement of a sort, but still one where the two views do not conflict in a way that would mean that one of them must be mistaken. Does this yield a plausible account of actual cases of apparent moral disagreement? (See Discussion Question 1.)

because, once it interpreted moral judgments as statements *about* attitudes, the disagreement vanished.

. . .

Simple Subjectivism was an attempt to capture the basic idea of Ethical Subjectivism and express it in an acceptable form. It ran into trouble because it assumed that moral judgments *report* attitudes; that is why it was vulnerable to the counterarguments. Emotivism was a superior theory because it jettisoned the troublesome assumption and replaced it with a more sophisticated view of how moral language works. But as we shall see, Emotivism also had its problems. One of the main problems was that Emotivism could not account for the place of reason in ethics.

5. EMOTIVISM, REASON, AND "MORAL FACTS"

. . . a moral judgment—or for that matter *any* kind of value judgment—must be supported by good reasons. If someone tells you that a certain action would be wrong, for example, you may ask *why* it would be wrong, and if there is no satisfactory answer, you may reject that advice as unfounded. In this way, moral judgments are different from mere expressions of personal preference. If someone says "I like coffee," she does not need to have a reason—she may be making a statement about her personal taste, and nothing more. But moral judgments require backing by reasons, and in the absence of such reasons, they are merely arbitrary. This is a point about the *logic* of moral judgment. It is not merely that it would be a good thing to have reasons for one's moral judgments. The point is stronger than that. One *must* have reasons, or else one is not making a moral judgment at all. This is part of what the moral concepts mean. To say "It would be morally wrong to do X, but there is no reason why it would be wrong" is a self-contradiction.⑧

> ⑧ Think carefully about this claim. Perhaps Rachels is right that something cannot be morally wrong for no reason at all, but is there anything objectionable about saying that something is wrong just because of the sort of thing it is, without there being any further, independent reason?

If the connection between moral judgments and reasons is a necessary and important one, then any adequate theory of the nature of moral judgment should be able to give some account of the connection. It is at just this point that Emotivism fails.

What can an emotivist say about reasons? Remember that for the emotivist, a moral judgment is like a command—it is primarily a verbal means of trying to influence people's attitudes and conduct. The view of reasons that naturally goes with this basic idea is that reasons are any considerations that will have the desired effect, that will influence attitudes and conduct in the desired way. Suppose I am trying to convince you that Goldbloom is a bad man (I am trying to influence your attitude toward him) and you are resisting the idea. Knowing you are anti-Semitic, I say: "Goldbloom is a Jew!" That does the trick; your attitude toward him changes, and you agree that he is a scoundrel. It would seem that for the emotivist, then, the fact that Goldbloom is Jewish is, at least in some contexts, a reason in support of the judgment that he is a bad man. In fact, Stevenson takes exactly this view. In his classic work *Ethics and Language* (1944), he says: "*Any* statement about *any* fact which *any* speaker considers likely to alter attitudes may be adduced as a reason for or against an ethical judgment."⑨

> ⑨ Must anyone who accepts Emotivism say what Stevenson did about this issue? Couldn't it be said that even in relation to attitudes, some kinds of considerations just don't count as genuine reasons? (But what would make this so?)

Obviously, something had gone wrong. Not just any fact can count as a reason in support of just any judgment. For one thing, the fact must be relevant to the judgment, and psychological influence does not necessarily bring relevance with it. (Jewishness is irrelevant to viciousness, regardless of the psychological connections in anyone's mind.) There is a small lesson and a larger lesson to be learned from this. The small lesson is that a particular moral theory, Emotivism, seems to be deeply flawed, and with it, the whole idea of Ethical Subjectivism is brought into doubt. The larger lesson has to do with the importance of reason in ethics.

Hume emphasized that if we examine wicked actions—"wilful murder, for instance"—we will find no "matter of fact" corresponding to the wickedness. The universe, apart from our attitudes, contains no such facts. This realization has often been taken as cause for despair, because people assume this must mean that values have no "objective" status. But why should Hume's observation come as a surprise? Values are not the kinds of things that *could* exist in the way that stars and planets exist. (What would a "value," thus conceived, be like?) A fundamental mistake, which many people fall into when they think about this subject, is to assume just two possibilities:

1. There are moral facts, in the same way that there are facts about stars and planets; or
2. Our "values" are nothing more than the expression of our subjective feelings.

This is a mistake because it overlooks a crucial third possibility. People have not only feelings but reason, and that makes a big difference. It may be that:

3. Moral truths are truths of reason; that is, a moral judgment is true if it is backed by better reasons than the alternatives.

This seems to be indisputable—even the emotivists recognized the need to give *some* account of the place of reason in ethics. Thus if we want to understand the nature of ethics, it is reason that we must focus on.

A truth of ethics is a conclusion that is backed by reasons: the "correct" answer to a moral question is simply the answer that has the weight of reason on its side.⑩ Such truths are objective in the sense that they are true independently of what we might want or think. We cannot make something good or bad just by wishing it to be so, because we cannot merely will that the weight of reason on its side or against it. And we can be wrong about what is good or bad, because we can be wrong about what reason commends. Reason says what it says, regardless of our opinions or desires.

⑩ What makes such reasons relevant to a moral claim or judgment if they are not reasons for thinking that it is true in some further way? (See Discussion Question 3.)

6. THE EXAMPLE OF HOMOSEXUALITY

Solving moral problems, then, is largely a matter of weighing up the reasons, or arguments, that can be given for or against the various alternatives. Consider again the dispute about homosexuality. Is Falwell right? The key idea is that *we may determine whether homosexuality (or anything else, for that matter) is morally acceptable or unacceptable by formulating and assessing the arguments that can be given regarding it.* If we can produce good reasons for thinking this practice is wrong and show that the arguments in its support are unsound, then we have proven it wrong, regardless of what attitude one might have. On the other hand, if a stronger case can be made on the other side, then it is *not* wrong, regardless of what one's attitude might be.

If we consider the relevant reasons, what do we find? In opposition to Falwell, it may be said that homosexuals are pursuing the only way of life that affords them a chance of happiness. Sex is a particularly strong urge—it isn't hard to understand why—and few people are able to fashion a happy life without satisfying their sexual needs. Moreover, individuals do not choose their sexual orientations; both homosexuals and heterosexuals find themselves to be what they are without having exercised any option in the matter. Thus to say that people should not express their homosexuality is, more often than not, to condemn them to unhappy lives.

If it could be shown that in pursuing their way of life homosexuals pose some sort of threat to the rest of society, that would be a powerful argument for the other side. And in fact, people who share Falwell's view have often claimed as much. But when examined dispassionately, those claims have always turned out to have no factual basis. Apart from the nature of their sexual relationships, there is no known difference between homosexuals and heterosexuals in their moral characters or in their contributions to society. The idea that homosexuals are somehow sinister characters proves to be a myth similar to the myth that black people are lazy, or that Jews are avaricious.

The case against homosexuality thus reduces to the familiar claim that it is "unnatural," or to the claim—often made by followers of Falwell—that it is a threat to "family values." As for the first argument, it is hard to know what to make of it because the notion of "unnaturalness" is so vague. What exactly does it mean? It might be taken as a statistical notion—in this sense, a human quality is unnatural if it is not shared by most people. Homosexuality would be unnatural in this sense, but so would left-handedness. Clearly, this is no reason to judge it bad; rare qualities might even be good.

If "unnatural" is not a statistical notion, what other sense might it have? The word has a sinister sound to it, so perhaps it should be understood as a term of evaluation. Perhaps in this context "unnatural" means something like "contrary to what a person ought to be." But in this sense, to say that something is wrong because it is unnatural is utterly vacuous; it is to say that one ought not to be thus-and-so because one ought not to be thus-and-so! If no better understanding of "unnatural" can be found, this argument will have to be rejected. [11]

[11] Can you think of any other way of understanding what "unnatural" might mean here? If so, does it yield any clear basis for thinking that homosexuality is morally wrong?

But what of the claim, often heard from religious fundamentalists, that homosexuality is contrary to "family values"? Falwell and others like him often say that their condemnation of homosexuality is part of their general support of "the family," as is their condemnation of divorce, abortion, pornography, adultery, and so forth. But how, exactly, is homosexuality opposed to family values? It might be said that if everyone were homosexual, there would be no families because there would be no children. (After all, children are the products of heterosexual unions.) This ignores the evident fact that many homosexuals want children and are even willing to undertake a period of heterosexual activity in order to have them. But even leaving this aside, the existence of a minority of homosexuals in society hardly poses a danger to families, because homosexuals, as a group, are no greater a threat to the lives and institutions of other people than are the members of any other group. (There have always been homosexuals; but has there ever been a society in which the institution of the family was brought down or even seriously damaged by them? No.)

Perhaps there are other arguments in support of Falwell's point of view, but I do not know what they could be. The evidence at hand, however, suggests that his view, no matter how firmly held, is not supported by reason. But my main point is not about homosexuality; that is only an example, although an important one. The main point is this: in considering a question of morality, one must ask *why* a moral judgment should, or should not, be accepted. One might have strong feelings, of course, and one might choose to ignore reason and go with those feelings. But in doing so, one would be opting out of moral thinking. Moral thinking and moral conduct are a matter of weighing reasons and being guided by them. That is why, in focusing on attitudes and feelings, Ethical Subjectivism seems to be going in the wrong direction.

Discussion Questions

1. Consider an example of what appears to be genuine moral disagreement: Becky thinks abortion is morally wrong in a serious way, while Tom thinks it is morally permissible (and therefore not wrong). Consider the account that would be given of this apparent disagreement by (a) Simple Subjectivism and (b) Emotivism. Does either view offer a plausible account of a disagreement of this sort: one that plausibly reflects what actually seems to be going on? Does either view allow one of the two to say that the other is mistaken (as they each presumably want to say)?

2. According to cultural relativism, the moral view held by a society is binding on the members of that society in the sense that they are morally required to conform to it. Does either of the versions of individual relativism that Rachels discusses make the moral judgments of an individual binding on that individual in an analogous way, so that the individual is morally required to conform to his own moral judgments? If not, can you devise a different version of individual relativism that has such a result? (Think here of the analogy with cultural relativism.) If you can, then consider further how well it can answer the objections that Rachels raises.

3. Rachels suggests that true or correct moral statements are those that are supported by the strongest reasons. One way in which a reason may support a claim is by making it more likely that the claim is true in some further, independent way (such as by corresponding to reality). But Rachels denies that moral claims are true in such a way. How then can we understand what makes a reason offered for such a moral claim a good one? (This is a *very* hard question—one to which there may be no very straightforward answer.)

Plato

Plato (469–399 B.C.) was (along with Aristotle) one of the two major Ancient Greek philosophers (see Chapter 1 for more information about Plato). In this selection, taken from the *Republic,* Glaucon presents arguments for the conclusion that it is better to be unjust than to be just, where by acting justly he can be taken to mean acting morally or rightly. The arguments presented by Glaucon purport to show that the rewards for any person are greatest if he or she acts unjustly (immorally) while being *perceived* as acting justly (morally). One underlying assumption of these arguments is that the only justification for the moral rules of a society is the tacit consent given by the citizens to live according to these rules because that is better than living at the mercy of some few strong citizens who would dominate many others: most people are likely to suffer less with these rules than they would without them. While that underlying assumption is not argued for in this selection, it is important to keep the issues distinct: it may be true that we are better off, in some narrow sense, if we behave immorally, but there may still be an objective reason to act morally, whether it is in our interest or not; or we may be better off if we behave according to the moral rules, whether there is any objective justification for them or not. Glaucon claims that he is presenting these arguments because he hopes that Socrates will be able to show what is wrong with them, and the selection ends with a very short summary of Plato's account (from later in the dialogue) of why the view that it is better to be unjust (immoral) than to be just (moral) is mistaken.

Are We Better Off Behaving Morally or Immorally?

Socrates, [Glaucon] broke out, you have made a show of proving that justice is better than injustice in every way. Is that enough, or do you want us to be really convinced?

Certainly I do, if it rests with me.

Then you are not going the right way about it. I want to know how you classify the things we call good. Are there not some which we should wish to have, not for their consequences, but just for their own sake, such as harmless pleasures and enjoyments that have no further result beyond the satisfaction of the moment?

Yes, I think there are good things of that description.

And also some that we value both for their own sake and for their consequences—things like knowledge and health and the use of our eyes?

Yes.

And a third class which would include physical training, medical treatment, earning one's bread as a doctor or otherwise—useful, but burdensome things, which we want only for the sake of the profit or other benefit they bring.[1]

Yes, there is that third class. What then?

In which class do you place justice?

[1] In more contemporary terminology, philosophers distinguish between things that are merely instrumentally good (good only for their results—Glaucon's third class), things that are intrinsically good (good just because of what they are themselves, regardless of their results—the first class), and things that are both intrinsically good and instrumentally good (the second class).

From The Republic of Plato, *translated by Francis MacDonald Cornford (New York: Oxford University Press, 1973).*

I should say, in the highest, as a thing which anyone who is to gain happiness must value both for itself and for its results.

According to this last view, justice is similar in one way to money: it is good for its results (what you can get for it), but not good in itself, while justice is dissimilar to money in that being just is itself difficult and unpleasant, whereas having money is not itself unpleasant.

Well, that is not the common opinion. Most people would say it was one of those things, tiresome and disagreeable in themselves, which we cannot avoid practising for the sake of reward or a good reputation.②

I know, said I; that is why Thrasymachus has been finding fault with it all this time and praising injustice. But I seem to be slow in seeing his point.

Listen to me, then, and see if you agree with mine. . . . nothing so far said about justice and injustice has been established to my satisfaction. I want to be told what each of them really is, and what effect each has, in itself, on the soul that harbours it, when all rewards and consequences are left out of account. So here is my plan, if you approve. I shall revive Thrasymachus' theory. First, I will state what is commonly held about the nature of justice and its origin; secondly, I shall maintain that it is always practised with reluctance, not as good in itself, but as a thing one cannot do without; and thirdly, that this reluctance is reasonable, because the life of injustice is much the better life of the two—so people say. That is not what I think myself, Socrates; only I am bewildered by all that Thrasymachus and ever so many others have dinned into my ears; and I have never yet heard the case for justice stated as I wish to hear it. You, I believe, if anyone, can tell me what is to be said in praise of justice in and for itself; that is what I want. Accordingly, I

③ Glaucon wants an argument for the claim that justice itself, not merely the consequences of being just, is an intrinsic good for the person who is acting justly.

shall set you an example by glorifying the life of injustice with all the energy that I hope you will show later in denouncing it and exalting justice in its stead.③ Will that plan suit you?

Nothing could be better, I replied. Of all subjects this is one on which a sensible man must always be glad to exchange ideas.

Good, said Glaucon. Listen then, and I will begin with my first point: the nature and origin of justice.

What people say is that to do wrong is, in itself, a desirable thing; on the other hand, it is not at all desirable to suffer wrong, and the harm to the sufferer outweighs the advantage to the doer.④ Consequently, when men have had a taste of both, those who have not the power to seize the advantage and escape the harm decide that they would be better off if they made a compact neither to do wrong nor to suffer it.

④ Think carefully about the claim that "to do wrong is, in itself, a desirable thing." What exactly do "they" mean when they say that? Why would someone *want* to do wrong?

Hence they began to make laws and covenants with one another; and whatever the law prescribed they called lawful and right. That is what right or justice is and how it came into existence; it stands half-way between the best thing of all—to do wrong with impunity—and the worst, which is to suffer wrong without the power to retaliate. So justice is accepted as a compromise, and valued, not as good in itself, but for lack of power to do wrong; no man worthy of the name, who had that power, would ever enter into such a compact with anyone; he would be mad if he did.⑤

⑤ The suggestion here is that acting justly is nothing but acting according to the law, and the law is binding not because it is good or just itself, but only because citizens have tacitly consented to laws as a way to control people (the motivation for the consent is the idea that living in a society with laws is better than suffering the resulting chaos of a society with no laws). But if this is the right way to think about justice, could laws themselves be unjust? (See Discussion Question 1.)

That, Socrates, is the nature of justice according to this account, and such the circumstances in which it arose.

The next point is that men practise it against the grain, for lack of power to do wrong. How true that is, we shall best see if we imagine two men, one just, the other unjust, given full licence to do whatever they like, and then follow them to observe where each will be led by his desires. We shall catch the just man taking the same road as the unjust; he will be moved by self-interest, the end which it is natural to every creature to pursue as good, until forcibly turned aside by law and custom to respect the principle of equality.⑥

⑥ The following thought experiment is designed to defend the claim that *the only* reason that people ever act justly is that they are afraid of suffering the negative consequences that result from acting unjustly. Before you consider the thought experiment, think about the claim itself. Does it seem true?

Now, the easiest way to give them that complete liberty of action would be to imagine them possessed of the talisman found by Gyges, the ancestor of the famous Lydian. The story tells how he was a shepherd in the King's service. One day there was a great storm, and the ground where his flock was feeding was rent by an earthquake. Astonished at the sight, he went down into the chasm and saw, among other wonders of which the story tells, a brazen horse, hollow, with windows in its sides. Peering in, he saw a dead body, which seemed to be of more than human size. It was naked save for a gold ring, which he took from the finger and made his way out. When the shepherds met, as they did every month, to send an account to the King of the state of his flocks, Gyges came wearing the ring. As he was sitting with the others, he happened to turn the bezel of the ring inside his hand. At once he became invisible, and his companions, to his surprise, began to speak of him as if he had left them. Then, as he was fingering the ring, he turned the bezel outwards and became visible again. With that, he set about testing the ring to see if it really had this power, and always with the same result: according as he turned the bezel inside or out he vanished and reappeared. After this discovery he contrived to be one of the messengers sent to the court. There he seduced the Queen, and with her help murdered the King and seized the throne.

Now suppose there were two such magic rings, and one were given to the just man, the other to the unjust. No one, it is commonly believed, would have such iron strength of mind as to stand fast in doing right or keep his hands off other men's goods, when he could go to the market-place and fearlessly help himself to anything he wanted, enter houses and sleep with any woman he chose, set prisoners free and kill men at his pleasure, and in a word go about among men with the powers of a god.⑦ He would behave no better than the other; both would take the same course. Surely this would be strong proof that men do

right only under compulsion; no individual thinks of it as good for him personally, since he does wrong whenever he finds he has the power. Every man believes that wrong-doing pays him personally

⑦ Does it seem right that anyone with such a ring would act in such a way? Would you always take what is not yours if you could get away with it? Would everyone you know act in such a way?

much better, and, according to this theory, that is the truth. Granted full licence to do as he liked, people would think him a miserable fool if they found him refusing to wrong his neighbours or to touch their belongings, though in public they would keep up a pretence of praising his conduct, for fear of being wronged themselves.⑧ So much for that.

Finally, if we are really to judge between the two lives, the only way is to

⑧ Notice that the claim is not only that people would behave unjustly if they could get away with it, but that they would be fools to do anything but that. How plausible is this thought experiment? (See Discussion Question 2.)

contrast the extremes of justice and injustice. We can best do that by imagining our two men to be perfect types, and crediting both to the full with the qualities they need for their respective ways of life. To begin with the unjust man: he must be like any consummate master of a craft, a physician or a captain, who, knowing just what his art can do, never tries to do more, and can always retrieve a false step. The unjust man, if he is to reach perfection, must be equally discreet in his criminal attempts, and he must not be found out, or we shall think him a bungler; for the highest pitch of injustice is to seem just when you are not. So we must endow our man with the full complement of injustice; we must allow him to have secured a spotless reputation for virtue while committing the blackest crimes; he must be able to retrieve any mistake, to defend himself with convincing eloquence if his misdeeds are denounced, and, when force is required, to bear down all opposition by his courage and strength and by his command of friends and money.

Now set beside this paragon the just man in his simplicity and nobleness, one who, in Aeschylus' words, 'would be, not seem, the best.' There must, indeed, be no such seeming; for if his character were apparent, his reputation would bring him honours and rewards, and then we should not know whether it was for their sake that he was just or for justice's sake alone. He must be stripped of everything but justice, and denied every advantage the other enjoyed. Doing no wrong, he must have the worst reputation for wrong-doing, to test whether his virtue is proof against all that comes of having a bad name; and under this lifelong imputation of wickedness, let him hold on his course of justice unwavering to the point of death.⑨ And so, when the two men have carried their justice and injustice to the last extreme, we may judge which is the happier.

> ⑨ The claim here is that the best comparison of the just and the unjust life is one which characterizes the unjust life as one that *appears* to be just and the just life as one that *appears* to be unjust. What reason does Glaucon give for that requirement? Does it seem right?

My dear Glaucon, I exclaimed, how vigorously you scour these two characters clean for inspection, as if you were burnishing a couple of statues!

I am doing my best, he answered. Well, given two such characters, it is not hard, I fancy, to describe the sort of life that each of them may expect; and if the description sounds rather coarse, take it as coming from those who cry up the merits of injustice rather than from me. They will tell you that our just man will be thrown into prison, scourged and racked, will have his eyes burnt out, and, after every kind of torment, be impaled. That will teach him how much better it is to seem virtuous than to be so. In fact those lines of Aeschylus I quoted are more fitly applied to the unjust man, who, they say, is a realist and does not live for appearances: 'he would be, not seem' unjust,

> reaping the harvest sown
> In those deep furrows of the thoughtful heart
> Whence wisdom springs.

With his reputation for virtue, he will hold offices of state, ally himself by marriage to any family he may choose, become a partner in any business, and, having no scruples about being dishonest, turn all these advantages to profit. If he is involved in a lawsuit, public or private, he will get the better of his opponents, grow rich on the proceeds, and be able to help his friends and harm his enemies. Finally, he can make sacrifices to the gods and dedicate offerings with due magnificence, and, being in a much better position than the just man to serve the gods as well as his chosen friends, he may reasonably hope to stand higher in the favour of heaven. So much better, they say, Socrates, is the life prepared for the unjust by gods and men.⑩

> ⑩ Qualify the claim just a bit to say that *most* unjust people who appear to be just will be happier than *most* just people who appear to be unjust. This claim is supposed to show why it is reasonable for people to use the ring of Gyges to act immorally. (See Discussion Question 3.)

Here Glaucon ended, and I was meditating a reply, when his brother Adeimantus exclaimed:

Surely, Socrates, you cannot suppose that that is all there is to be said.

Why, isn't it? said I.

The most essential part of the case has not been mentioned, he replied.

Well, I answered, there is a proverb about a brother's aid. If Glaucon has failed, it is for you to make good his shortcomings; though, so far as I am concerned, he has said quite enough to put me out of the running and leave me powerless to rescue the cause of justice.

Nonsense, said Adeimantus; there is more to be said, and you must listen to me. If we want a clear view of what I take to be Glaucon's meaning, we must study the opposite side of the case, the arguments used when justice is praised and injustice condemned. When children are told by their fathers and all their pastors and masters that it is a good thing to be just, what is commended is not justice in itself but the respectability it brings. They are to let men see how just they are, in order to gain high positions and marry well and win all the other advantages which Glaucon mentioned, since the just man owes all these to his good reputation.⑪

> ⑪ Suppose that it is true that we train our children to be just by citing the rewards of justice. Is that a good reason to think that justice is merely instrumentally good? (See Feinberg's moral education argument in the following selection.)

In this matter of having a good name, they go farther still: they throw in the favourable opinion of heaven, and can tell us of no end of good things with which they say the gods reward piety. . . .

Besides all this, think of the way in which justice and injustice are spoken of, not only in ordinary life, but by the poets. All with one voice reiterate that self-control and justice, admirable as they may be, are difficult and irksome, whereas vice and injustice are pleasant and very easily to be had; it is mere convention to regard them as discreditable. They tell us that dishonesty generally pays better than honesty. They will cheerfully speak of a bad man as happy and load him with honours and social esteem, provided he be rich and otherwise powerful; while they despise and disregard one who has neither power nor wealth, though all the while they acknowledge that he is the better man of the two. 12

> 12 This is another, slightly different aspect to this view of our human nature. Is it accurate? Do we despise weak and poor people even though we recognize that they are better than the strong and prosperous people?

Most surprising of all is what they say about the gods and virtue: that heaven itself often allots misfortunes and a hard life to the good man, and gives prosperity to the wicked. Mendicant priests and soothsayers come to the rich man's door with a story of a power they possess by the gift of heaven to atone for any offence that he or his ancestors have committed with incantations and sacrifice, agreeably accompanied by feasting. If he wishes to injure an enemy, he can, at a trifling expense, do him a hurt with equal ease, whether he be an honest man or not, by means of certain invocations and spells which, as they profess, prevail upon the gods to do their bidding. In support of all these claims they call the poets to witness. Some, by way of advertising the easiness of vice, quote the words: 'Unto wickedness men attain easily and in multitudes; smooth is the way and her dwelling is very near at hand. But the gods have ordained much sweat upon the path to virtue'* and a long road that is rough and steep.

Others, to show that men can turn the gods from their purpose, cite Homer: 'Even the gods themselves listen to entreaty. Their hearts are turned by the entreaties of men with sacrifice and humble prayers and libation and burnt offering, whensoever anyone transgresses and does amiss.'† They produce a whole farrago of books in which Musaeus and Orpheus, described as descendants of the Muses and the Moon, prescribe their ritual; and they persuade entire communities, as well as individuals, that, both in this life and after death, wrongdoing may be absolved and purged away by means of sacrifices and agreeable performances which they are pleased to call rites of initiation. These deliver us from punishment in the other world, where awful things are in store for all who neglect to sacrifice.

Now, my dear Socrates, when all this stuff is talked about the estimation in which virtue and vice are held by heaven and by mankind, what effect can we suppose it has upon the mind of a young man quick-witted enough to gather honey from all these flowers of popular wisdom and to draw his own conclusions as to the sort of person he should be and the way he should go in order to lead the best possible life? In all likelihood he would ask himself, in Pindar's words: 'Will the way of right or the by-paths of deceit lead me to the higher fortress,' where I may entrench myself for the rest of my life? For, according to what they tell me, I have nothing to gain but trouble and manifest loss from being honest, unless I also get a name for being so; whereas, if I am dishonest and provide myself with a reputation for honesty, they promise me a marvellous career. Very well, then; since 'outward seeming,' as wise men inform me, 'overpowers the truth' and decides the question of happiness, I had better go in for appearances wholeheartedly. . . . You may say it is not so easy to be wicked without ever being found out. Perhaps not; but great things are never easy. Anyhow, if we are to reach happiness, everything we have been told points to this as the road to be followed. 13 We will form secret societies to save us from exposure; besides, there are men who teach the art of winning over popular assemblies and courts of law; so that, one way or another, by persuasion or violence, we shall get the better of our neighbours without being punished. You might object that the gods are not to be deceived and are beyond the reach of violence. 14

> 13 If it is true that the best results (whether from gods or other people) come from appearing to be just while really being unjust, then that is what we have reason to do.

> 14 The objection is that the gods are not fooled by appearances. The truly unjust person who appears to be just might fool other humans, but he or she will not be able to fool the gods. How compelling is this objection?

---

*Hesiod, *Works and Days,* 287.
†*Iliad* ix. 497.

But suppose that there are no gods, or that they do not concern themselves with the doings of men; why should we concern ourselves to deceive them? Or, if the gods do exist and care for mankind, all we know or have ever heard about them comes from current tradition and from the poets who recount their family history, and these same authorities also assure us that they can be won over and turned from their purpose 'by sacrifice and humble prayers' and votive offerings. We must either accept both these statements or neither. If we are to accept both, we had better do wrong and use part of the proceeds to offer sacrifice. By being just we may escape the punishment of heaven, but we shall be renouncing the profits of injustice; whereas by doing wrong we shall make our profit and escape punishment into the bargain, by means of those entreaties which win over the gods when we transgress and do amiss. But then, you will say, in the other world the penalty for our misdeeds on earth will fall either upon us or upon our children's children. We can counter that objection by reckoning on the great efficacy of mystic rites and the divinities of absolution, vouched for by the most advanced societies and by the descendants of the gods who have appeared as poets and spokesmen of heavenly inspiration.

What reason, then, remains for preferring justice to the extreme of injustice, when common belief and the best authorities promise us the fulfilment of our desires in this life and the next, if only we conceal our ill-doing under a veneer of decent behaviour? ⑮ The

⑮ Think about whether there could be a reason for choosing to be just under these conditions.

upshot is, Socrates, that no man possessed of superior powers of mind or person or rank or wealth will set any value on justice; he is more likely to laugh when he hears it praised. So, even one who could prove my case false and were quite sure that justice is best, far from being indignant with the unjust, will be very ready to excuse them. He will know that, here and there, a man may refrain from wrong because it revolts some instinct he is graced with or because he has come to know the truth; no one else is virtuous of his own will; it is only lack of spirit or the infirmity of age or some other weakness that makes men condemn the iniquities they have not the strength to practise. This is easily seen: give such a man the power, and he will be the first to use it to the utmost.

What lies at the bottom of all this is nothing but the fact from which Glaucon, as well as I, started upon this long discourse. We put it to you, Socrates, with all respect, in this way. All you who profess to sing the praises of right conduct, from the ancient heroes whose legends have survived down to the men of the present day, have never denounced injustice or praised justice apart from the reputation, honours, and rewards they bring; but what effect either of them in itself has upon its possessor when it dwells in his soul unseen of gods or men, no poet or ordinary man has ever yet explained. No one has proved that a soul can harbour no worse evil than injustice, no greater good than justice. Had all of you said that from the first and tried to convince us from our youth up, we should not be keeping watch upon our neighbours to prevent them from doing wrong to us, but everyone would keep a far more effectual watch over himself, for fear lest by wronging others he should open his doors to the worst of all evils. ⑯

⑯ If we trained our children to be just by teaching them that acting unjustly will cause them harm, will soil their soul, then each person would take responsibility for keeping him or herself clean, for genuinely acting justly, regardless of appearances.

That, Socrates, is the view of justice and injustice which Thrasymachus and, no doubt, others would state, perhaps in even stronger words. For myself, I believe it to be a gross perversion of their true worth and effect; but, as I must frankly confess, I have put the case with all the force I could muster because I want to hear the other side from you. You must not be content with proving that justice is superior to injustice; you must make clear what good or what harm each of them does to its possessor, taking it simply in itself and, as Glaucon required, leaving out of account the reputation it bears. For unless you deprive each of its true reputation and attach to it the false one, we shall say that you are praising or denouncing nothing more than the appearances in either case, and recommending us to do wrong without being found out; and that you hold with Thrasymachus that right means what is good for someone else, being the interest of the stronger, and wrong is what really pays, serving one's own interest at the expense of the weaker. You have agreed that justice belongs to that highest class of good things which are worth having not only for their consequences, but much more for their own sakes—things like sight and hearing, knowledge, and health, whose value is genuine and intrinsic, not dependent on opinion. So I want you, in commending justice, to consider only how justice, in itself, benefits a man who has it in him, and how injustice harms him, leaving rewards and reputation out of account.[17] I might put up with others dwelling on those outward effects as a reason for praising the one and condemning the other; but from you, who have spent your life in the study of this question, I must beg leave to demand something better. You must not be content merely to prove that justice is superior to injustice, but explain how one is good, the other evil, in virtue of the intrinsic effect each has on its possessor, whether gods or men see it or not.

[17] Socrates is challenged, remember, to argue that justice itself, not the mere appearance of justice, is a good thing, that being just is good for the person whether he or she appears just or not.

. . .

THE VIRTUES IN THE INDIVIDUAL

. . . [Socrates:] we shall conclude that a man is just in the same way that a state was just. And we have surely not forgotten that justice in the state meant that each of the three orders in it was doing its own proper work. So we may henceforth bear in mind that each one of us likewise will be a just person, fulfilling his proper function, only if the several parts of our nature fulfil theirs.[18]

[18] Plato has argued in other parts of the dialogue that a state is just only if the three different kinds of citizens (rulers, soldiers, and ordinary people) fulfill their proper functions. The just person, analogously, has three different parts of his or her nature which also fulfill their proper function. (See Discussion Question 5.)

Certainly.

And it will be the business of reason to rule with wisdom and forethought on behalf of the entire soul; while the spirited element ought to act as its subordinate and ally. The two will be brought into accord, as we said earlier, by that combination of mental and bodily training which will tune up one string of the instrument and relax the other, nourishing the reasoning part on the study of noble literature and allaying the other's wildness by harmony and rhythm.[19] When both have been thus nurtured and trained to know their own true functions, they must be set in command over the appetites, which form the greater part of each man's soul and are by nature insatiably covetous. They must keep watch lest this part, by battening on the pleasures that are called bodily, should grow so great and powerful that it will no longer keep to its own work, but will try to enslave the others and usurp a dominion to which it has no right, thus turning the whole of life upside down.[20] At the same time, those two together will be the best of guardians for the entire soul and for the body against all enemies from without: the one will take counsel, while the other will do battle, following its ruler's commands and by its own bravery giving effect to the ruler's designs.

[19] Reason, our thinking, cognitive faculty, is the part of our nature that is analogous to the philosopher-kings who are the rulers of the state; and spirit, our willing conative faculty is analogous to the guardians who are the soldiers of the state. Just as our spirit is supposed to act in support of what reason dictates, the soldiers are supposed to act in support of what the rulers command.

[20] The third part of our nature is our appetite, our desires for bodily pleasures, and this part of our nature is analogous to the farmer and merchant, the ordinary folk who carry on the business of the state. These three parts of our nature each have a proper function, according to Plato's theory of our nature. Just as the three different kinds of people each have a proper function.

Yes, that is all true.

And so we call an individual brave in virtue of this spirited part of his nature, when, in spite of pain or pleasure, it holds fast to the injunctions of reason about what he ought or ought not to be afraid of.

True.

And wise in virtue of that small part which rules and issues these injunctions, possessing as it does the knowledge of what is good for each of the three elements and for all of them in common.

Certainly.

And, again, temperate by reason of the unanimity and concord of all three, when there is no internal conflict between the ruling element and its two subjects, but all are agreed that reason should be ruler.

Yes, that is an exact account of temperance, whether in the state or in the individual.

Finally, a man will be just by observing the principle we have so often stated.[21]

Necessarily.

[21] In a just person, reason rules by invoking the spirit to control the appetites according to what is good for each part and what is good for the whole person.

Now is there any indistinctness in our vision of justice, that might make it seem somehow different from what we found it to be in the state?

I don't think so.

Because, if we have any lingering doubt, we might make sure by comparing it with some commonplace notions. Suppose, for instance, that a sum of money were entrusted to our state or to an individual of corresponding character and training, would anyone imagine that such a person would be specially likely to embezzle it?

No.

And would he not be incapable of sacrilege and theft, or of treachery to friend or country; never false to an oath or any other compact; the last to be guilty of adultery or of neglecting parents or the due service of the gods?

Yes.

And the reason for all this is that each part of his nature is exercising its proper function, of ruling or of being ruled.

Yes, exactly.

Are you satisfied, then, that justice is the power which produces states or individuals of whom that is true, or must we look further?

There is no need; I am quite satisfied.

And so our dream has come true—I mean the inkling we had that, by some happy chance, we had lighted upon a rudimentary form of justice from the very moment when we set about founding our commonwealth. . . . But in reality justice, . . . is not a matter of external behaviour, but of the inward self and of attending to all that is, in the fullest sense, a man's proper concern. The just man does not allow the several elements in his soul to usurp one another's functions; he is indeed one who sets his house in order, by self-mastery and discipline coming to be at peace with himself, and bringing into tune those three parts, like the terms in the proportion of a musical scale, the highest and lowest notes and the mean between them, with all the intermediate intervals. Only when he has linked these parts together in well-tempered harmony and has made himself one man instead of many, will he be ready to go about whatever he may have to do, whether it be making money and satisfying bodily wants, or business transactions, or the affairs of state. In all these fields when he speaks of just and honourable conduct, he will mean the behaviour that helps to produce and to preserve this habit of mind; and by wisdom he will mean the knowledge which presides over such conduct. Any action which tends to break down this habit will be for him unjust; and the notions governing it he will call ignorance and folly.[22]

[22] Justice then involves the proper ordering of the three parts of a person's nature and is only derivatively related to the external behavior of a person. A just person will behave justly (morally) as a consequence of being a just person.

That is perfectly true, Socrates.

Good, said I. I believe we should not be thought altogether mistaken, if we claimed to have discovered the just man and the just state, and wherein their justice consists.

Indeed we should not.

Shall we make that claim, then?

Yes, we will.

So be it, said I. Next, I suppose, we have to consider injustice.

Evidently.

This must surely be a sort of civil strife among the three elements, whereby they usurp and encroach upon one another's functions and some one part of the soul rises up in rebellion against the whole, claiming a supremacy to which it has no right because its nature fits it only to be the servant of the ruling principle. Such turmoil and aberration we shall, I think, identify with injustice, intemperance, cowardice, ignorance, and in a word with all wickedness.

Exactly.

And now that we know the nature of justice and injustice, we can be equally clear about what is meant by acting justly and again by unjust action and wrong-doing.

How do you mean?

Plainly, they are exactly analogous to those wholesome and unwholesome activities which respectively produce a healthy or unhealthy condition in the body; in the same way just and unjust conduct produce a just or unjust character. Justice is produced in the soul, like health in the body, by establishing the elements concerned in their natural relations of control and subordination, whereas injustice is like disease and means that this natural order is inverted. 23

23 Injustice then primarily involves the lack of proper ordering of the three parts of a person's nature. Injustice, on this view, is a kind of sickness. As a result of such sickness, an unjust person will behave immorally.

Quite so.

It appears, then, that virtue is as it were the health and comeliness and well-being of the soul, as wickedness is disease, deformity, and weakness.

True.

And also that virtue and wickedness are brought about by one's way of life, honourable or disgraceful.

That follows.

So now it only remains to consider which is the more profitable course: to do right and live honourably and be just, whether or not anyone knows what manner of man you are, or to do wrong and be unjust, provided that you can escape the chastisement which might make you a better man.

But really, Socrates, it seems to me ridiculous to ask that question now that the nature of justice and injustice has been brought to light. People think that all the luxury and wealth and power in the world cannot make life worth living when the bodily constitution is going to rack and ruin; and are we to believe that, when the very principle whereby we live is deranged and corrupted, life will be worth living so long as a man can do as he will, and wills to do anything rather than to free himself from vice and wrongdoing and to win justice and virtue?

Yes, I replied, it is a ridiculous question.

Discussion Questions

1. While there are many different theories about the source and nature of justice (see Chapter 7 for more discussion of the issue), the idea that justice is created by people banding together and agreeing to follow laws or rules is an initially persuasive one. (The idea that the source of morality as a whole is similarly conventional is less initially persuasive, but not completely unreasonable.) Think carefully about this view of justice: is justice actually created by such agreement or is merely the enforcement of justice effected by such agreement? Do people agree to the particular laws *because* they think that the laws reflect justice? If that is right, then justice is prior to the creation of laws, not subsequent to the creation of laws. Which comes first, justice or laws? (This is a version of the Euthyphro question: see Chapter 1.)

2. The intuitive thought experiment involving the ring of Gyges supports the claim that people behave justly only because they want to avoid the negative consequences of being caught behaving unjustly. How plausible are the claims made in that thought experiment? Is it so obvious that someone who could become invisible would consistently behave unjustly? Think carefully about the details of different situations to see what makes most sense, given your experience and understanding of yourself and others.

3. Suppose that the best evaluation of the relative merits of the just and unjust life requires thinking of each life as appearing to be what it's not: the just life appears to be unjust and the unjust life appears to be just. Consider the claim that most such unjust lives will be happier than most such just lives. Does that seem true? Consider the claim that most such unjust lives will be better for the person living the life than most such just lives. Does that seem true? What is the relation between the two claims? Surely happier lives are better lives, but might there be other ways for a life to be better than for it to be happier? Think about the case described on page 565 of the just person who appears to be unjust. Even if such a life is less happy than it would be had it appeared to be just, might the life be better in some other way? What exactly needs to be said about the rela-

tive merits of these two kinds of lives in order to make it reasonable for someone who had the ring of Gyges to engage in unjust activity?

4. According to Plato, it is always in our self-interest to behave morally. If Plato is right, then everyone has a reason to behave morally, but suppose that Plato is wrong. Suppose that it is *not* always in our self-interest to behave morally. Suppose that the requirements of morality demand that we act in ways that further the interests of others and sometimes that requirement is in direct conflict with our own self-interest. Do we thereby lose any reason to behave morally in such cases?

5. Plato's argument that it is better to be just than to be unjust depends on an analogy be-tween the parts of a person and the parts of the state: a person is just to the extent that the three different parts of his or her nature fulfill their proper function, *because* a state is just to the extent that its three different kinds of citizens fulfill their proper functions. Think carefully about arguments by analogy: they are strongest when the things being compared are very similar, especially with respect to those features relevant to the point at issue; and they are weaker when the things being compared are more dissimilar, again, especially with respect to features relevant to the point at issue. What about this particular analogy between parts of a state and parts of a person: is it strong or weak?

Joel Feinberg

Joel Feinberg (1926–2004) was an American legal, moral, and political philosopher who taught at UCLA, Princeton, Rockefeller University, and the University of Arizona. In the following selection, Feinberg explains and criticizes *psychological egoism:* the view that people always act from selfish or egoistic motives, giving special attention to the *hedonistic* version of egoism, according to which people always aim at their own pleasure or happiness. Feinberg argues that there are no good arguments in favor of psychological egoism, and that the superficial plausibility of the view rests on confusion.

Psychological Egoism

A. THE THEORY

1. "Psychological egoism" is the name given to a theory widely held by ordinary people, and at one time almost universally accepted by political economists, philosophers, and psychologists, according to which all human actions when properly understood can be seen to be motivated by selfish desires. More precisely, psychological egoism is the doctrine that the only thing anyone is capable of desiring or pursuing ultimately (as an end in itself) is his *own*

From Reason and Responsibility, *edited by Joel Feinberg (Belmont, CA.: Wadsworth, 1996).*

self-interest. No psychological egoist denies that people sometimes do desire things other than their own welfare—the happiness of other people, for example; but all psychological egoists insist that people are capable of desiring the happiness of others only when they take it to be a *means* to their own happiness. In short, purely altruistic and benevolent actions and desires do not exist; but people sometimes appear to be acting unselfishly and disinterestedly when they take the interests of others to be means to the promotion of their own self-interest.

2. This theory is called *psychological* egoism to indicate that it is not a theory about what *ought* to be the case, but rather about what, as a matter of fact, *is* the case. That is, the theory claims to be a description of

psychological facts, not a prescription of ethical ideals. It asserts, however, not merely that all men do as a contingent matter of fact "put their own interests first," but also that they are capable of nothing else, human nature being what it is. Universal selfishness is not just an accident or a coincidence on this view, rather, it is an unavoidable consequence of psychological laws.

The theory is to be distinguished from another doctrine, so-called "ethical egoism," according to which all people *ought* to pursue their own well-being.

---

① These are two distinct views. But psychological egoism might be used as an argument for ethical egoism, by appealing to the principle that "ought implies can" (that is, that one cannot be obligated to do something that one is not able to do). From this it would follow that one cannot have a moral obligation to act in an unselfish way if psychological egoism is true—in which case, any moral obligations there are could only be egoistic ones.

This doctrine, being a prescription of what *ought* to be the case, makes no claim to be a psychological theory of human motives; hence the word "ethical" appears in its name to distinguish it from *psychological* egoism. ①

3. There are a number of types of motives and desires which might reasonably be called "egoistic" or "selfish," and corresponding to each of them is a possible version of psychological egoism. Perhaps the most common version of the theory is that apparently held by Jeremy Bentham.* According to this version, all persons have only one ultimate motive in all their voluntary behavior and that motive is a selfish one; more specifically, it is one particular kind of selfish motive—namely, a desire for one's own *pleasure*. According to this version of the theory, "the only kind of ultimate desire, is the desire to get or to prolong pleasant experiences, and to avoid or to cut short unpleasant experiences for oneself."† This form of psychological egoism is often given the cumbersome name—*psychological egoistic hedonism*.

B. PRIMA FACIE REASONS IN SUPPORT OF THE THEORY

4. Psychological egoism has seemed plausible to many people for a variety of reasons, of which the following are typical:②

a. "Every action of mine is prompted by motives or desires or impulses which are *my* motives and not somebody else's. This fact might be expressed by saying

---

② As Feinberg will explain, none of these arguments is very compelling. See if you can figure out now what is wrong with them.

---

that whenever I act I am always pursuing my own ends or trying to satisfy my own desires. And from this we might pass on to—'I am always pursuing something for myself or seeking my own satisfaction.' Here is what seems like a proper description of a man acting selfishly, and if the description applies to all actions of all men, then it follows that all men in all their actions are selfish."‡

b. It is a truism that when a person gets what he wants he characteristically feels pleasure. This has suggested to many people that what we really want in every case is our own pleasure, and that we pursue other things only as a means.

c. *Self-Deception.* Often we deceive ourselves into thinking that we desire something fine or noble when what we really want is to be thought well by others or to be able to congratulate ourselves, or to be able to enjoy the pleasures of good conscience. It is a well-known fact that people tend to conceal their true motives from themselves by camouflaging them with words like "virtue," "duty," etc. Since we are so often misled concerning both our own real motives and the real motives of

---

*See his *Introduction to the Principles of Morals and Legislation* (1789), Chap. I, first paragraph: "Nature has placed mankind under the governance of two sovereign masters, *pain* and *pleasure.* It is for them alone to point out what we ought to do, as well as to determine what we shall do. . . . They govern us in all we do, in all we say, in all we think: every effort we can make to throw off our subjection will serve but to demonstrate and confirm it."

†C. D. Broad, *Ethics and the History of Philosophy* (New York: The Humanities Press, 1952), p. 218.

‡Austin Duncan-Jones, *Butler's Moral Philosophy* (London; Penguin Books, 1952), p. 96. Duncan-Jones goes on to reject this argument. See p. 512f.

others, is it not reasonable to suspect that we might *always* be deceived when we think motives disinterested and altruistic? . . .

d. *Moral Education.* Morality, good manners, decency, and other virtues must be teachable. Psychological egoists often notice that moral education and the inculcation of manners usually utilize what Bentham calls the "sanctions of pleasure and pain." Children are made to acquire the civilizing virtues only by the method of enticing rewards and painful punishments. Much the same is true of the history of the race. People in general have been inclined to behave well only when it is made plain to them that there is "something in it for them." Is it not then highly probable that just such a mechanism of human motivation as Bentham describes must be presupposed by our methods of moral education?

C. CRITIQUE OF PSYCHOLOGICAL EGOISM: CONFUSIONS IN THE ARGUMENTS

5. Non-Empirical Character of the Arguments. If the arguments of the psychological egoist consisted for the most part of carefully acquired empirical evidence (well-documented reports of controlled experiments, surveys, interviews, laboratory data, and so on), then the critical philosopher would have no business carping at them. After all, since psychological egoism purports to be a scientific theory of human motives, it is the concern of the experimental psychologist, not the philosopher, to accept or reject it. But as a matter of fact, empirical evidence of the required sort is seldom presented in support of psychological egoism. Psychologists, on the whole, shy away from generalizations about human motives which are so sweeping and so vaguely formulated that they are virtually incapable of scientific testing. It is usually the "armchair scientist" who holds the theory of universal selfishness, and his usual arguments are either based simply on his "impressions" or else are largely of a non-empirical sort. The latter are often shot full of a very subtle kind of logical confusion, and this makes their criticism a matter of special interest to the analytic philosopher.

6. The psychological egoist's first argument (4a, above) is a good example of logical confusion. It be-

gins with a truism—namely, that all of my motives and desires are *my* motives and desires and not someone else's. (Who would deny this?) But from this simple tautology nothing whatever concerning the nature of my motives or the objective of my desires can possibly follow. . . . What the eogoist must prove is not merely:

(i) Every voluntary action is prompted by a motive of the agent's own.

but rather:

(ii) Every voluntary action is prompted by a motive of a quite particular kind, viz. a selfish one.

Statement (i) is obviously true, but it cannot all by itself give any logical support to statement (ii).③

③ Statement (i) is compatible with the agent's motive being an entirely unselfish one: for example, the desire to help someone else entirely for their own sake.

The source of the confusion in this argument is readily apparent. It is not the genesis of an action or the *origin* or its motives which makes it a "selfish" one, but rather the "purpose" of the act or the *objective* of its motives; *not where the motive comes from* (in voluntary actions it always comes from the agent) but *what it aims at* determines whether or not it is selfish. There is surely a valid distinction between voluntary behavior, in which the agent's action is motivated by purposes of his own, and *selfish* behavior in which the agent's motives are of one exclusive sort. . . .

7. But if argument 4a fails to prove its point, argument 4b does no better. From the fact that all our successful actions (those in which we get what we were after) are accompanied or followed by pleasure it does not follow, as the egoist claims, that the *objective* of every action is to get pleasure for oneself. To begin with, the premise of the argument is not, strictly speaking, even true. Fulfillment of desire (simply getting what one was after) is no guarantee of satisfaction (pleasant feelings of gratification in the mind of the agent). Sometimes when we get what we want we *also* get, as a kind of extra dividend, a warm, glowing feeling of contentment; but often, far too often, we get no dividend at all, or, even worse, the bitter taste of ashes. Indeed, it has been said that the characteristic psychological problem of our time is

the *dissatisfaction* that attends the fulfillment of our very most powerful desires.

Even if we grant, however, for the sake of argument, that getting what one wants *usually* yields satisfaction, the egoist's conclusion does not follow. We can concede that we normally get pleasure (in the sense of satisfaction) when our desires are satisfied, no matter what our desires are for; but it does not follow from this roughly accurate generalization that the only thing we ever desire is our own satisfaction. . . . ④

④ Thus, to use the same example, I might have a desire to help someone else for their own sake and feel pleasure because I am able to bring about that result. The pleasure I feel would thus derive from the satisfaction of my *independent* desire to help that person, so that it would make no sense to say that my only desire is for that pleasure.

8. Disinterested Benevolence. . . . Not only is argument [4b] fallacious; it also provides us with a suggestion of a counterargument to show that its conclusion (psychological egoistic hedonism) is false. Not only is the presence of pleasure (satisfaction) as a by-product of an action no proof that the action was selfish; in some special cases it provides rather conclusive proof that the action was *unselfish*. For in those special cases the fact that we get pleasure from particular action *presupposes that we desired something else*—something other than our own pleasure—as an end in itself and not merely as a means to our own pleasant state of mind.

This way of turning the egoistic hedonist's argument back on him can be illustrated by taking a typical egoist argument, one attributed (perhaps apocryphally) to Abraham Lincoln, and then examining it closely.

> Mr. Lincoln once remarked to a fellow-passenger on an old-time mud-coach that all men were prompted by selfishness in doing good. His fellow-passenger was antagonizing this position when they were passing over a corduroy bridge that spanned a slough. As they crossed this bridge they espied an old razor-backed sow on the bank making a terrible noise because her pigs had got into the slough and were in danger of drowning. As the old coach began to climb the hill, Mr. Lincoln called out, "Driver, can't you stop just a moment?" Then Mr. Lincoln jumped out, ran back and lifted the little pigs out of the mud and water and placed them on the bank. When he returned, his companion remarked: "Now Abe, where does selfishness come in on this little episode?" "Why, bless your soul Ed, that was the very essence of selfishness. I should have had no peace of mind all day had I gone on and left that suffering old sow worrying over those pigs. I did it to get peace of mind, don't you see?"*

If Lincoln had cared not a whit for the welfare of the little pigs and their "suffering" mother, but only for his own "peace of mind," it would be difficult to explain how he could have derived pleasure from helping them. The very fact that he did feel satisfaction as a result of helping the pigs presupposes that he had a preexisting desire for something other than his own happiness. Then when *that* desire was satisfied, Lincoln of course derived pleasure. The *object* of Lincoln's desire was not pleasure; rather pleasure was the *consequence* of his preexisting desire for something else. If Lincoln had been wholly indifferent to the plight of the little pigs as he claimed, how could he possibly have derived any pleasure from helping them? . . . He could not have achieved peace of mind from rescuing the pigs, had he not a prior concern—on which his peace of mind depended— for the welfare of the pigs for its own sake.⑤

⑤ If Lincoln had no *independent* concern for the welfare of the pigs (or their mother), it would be inexplicable why his own peace of mind would be disturbed if they were not helped. Thus it makes no sense to say that he is only concerned about his own peace of mind.

In general, the psychological hedonist analyzes apparent benevolence into a desire for "benevolent pleasure." No doubt the benevolent person does get pleasure from his benevolence, but in most cases, this is only because he has previously desired the good of some person, or animal, or mankind at large. Where there is no such desire, benevolent conduct is not generally found to give pleasure to the agent.

9. Malevolence. Difficult cases for the psychological egoist include not only instances of disinterested benevolence, but also cases of "disinterested malevolence." Indeed, malice and hatred are generally no more "selfish" than benevolence. Both are motives

---

*Quoted from the *Springfield* (Illinois) *Monitor,* by F. C. Sharp in his *Ethics* (New York: Appleton-Century, 1928), p. 75.

likely to cause an agent to sacrifice his own interests—in the case of benevolence, in order to help someone else, in the case of malevolence in order to harm someone else. The selfish person is concerned ultimately only with his own pleasure, happiness, or power, the benevolent person is often equally concerned with the happiness of others; to the malevolent person, the *injury* of another is often an end in itself—an end to be pursued sometimes with no thought for his own interests. There is reason to think that people have as often sacrificed themselves to injure or kill others as to help or to save others, and with as much "heroism" in the one case as in the other.⑥ . . .

> ⑥ Thus the actions of the malevolent person make sense only because he has a desire to harm someone else that is independent of any desire for his own happiness: it is because of this independent desire that he may be unable to be happy unless that person suffers.

10. Lack of Evidence for Universal Self-Deception.   The more cynical sort of psychological egoist who is impressed by the widespread phenomenon of self-deception (see 4c above) cannot be so quickly disposed of, for he has committed no *logical* mistakes. We can only argue that the acknowledged frequency of self-deception is insufficient evidence for his universal generalization. His argument is not fallacious, but inconclusive.

No one but the agent himself can ever be certain what conscious motives really prompted his action, and where motives are disreputable, even the agent may not admit to himself the true nature of his desires. Thus, for every apparent case of altruistic behavior, the psychological egoist can argue, with some plausibility, that the true motivation *might* be selfish, appearance to the contrary. Philanthropic acts are really motivated by the desire to receive gratitude; acts of self-sacrifice, when truly understood, are seen to be motivated by the desire to feel self-esteem; and so on. We must concede to the egoist that all apparent altruism might be deceptive in this way; but such a sweeping generalization requires considerable empirical evidence, and such evidence is not presently available.⑦

> ⑦ Is it even possible that there is always a selfish motive in any case of apparent altruism? See Discussion Question 1.

11. The "Paradox of Hedonism" and Its Consequences for Education.   The psychological egoistic Hedonist (e.g., Jeremy Bentham) has the simplest possible theory of human motivation. According to this variety of egoistic theory, all human motives without exception can be reduced to one—namely, the desire for one's own pleasure. But this theory, despite its attractive simplicity, or perhaps because of it, involves one immediately in a paradox. Astute observers of human affairs from the time of the ancient Greeks have often noticed that pleasure, happiness, and satisfaction are states of mind which stand in a very peculiar relation to desire. An exclusive desire for happiness is the surest way to prevent happiness from coming into being. Happiness has a way of "sneaking up" on persons when they are preoccupied with other things; but when persons deliberately and single-mindedly set off in pursuit of happiness, it vanishes utterly from sight and cannot be captured. This is the famous "paradox of hedonism": the single-minded pursuit of happiness is necessarily self-defeating, for *the way to get happiness is to forget it;* then perhaps it will come to you. If you aim exclusively at pleasure itself, with no concern for the things that bring pleasure, then pleasure will never come. To derive satisfaction, one must ordinarily first desire something other than satisfaction, and then find the means to get what one desires.

To feel the full force of the paradox of hedonism the reader should conduct an experiment in his imagination. Imagine a person (let's call him "Jones") who is, first of all, devoid of intellectual curiosity. He has no desire to acquire any kind of knowledge for its own sake, and thus is utterly indifferent to questions of science, mathematics, and philosophy. Imagine further that the beauties of nature leave Jones cold: he is unimpressed by the autumn foliage, the snowcapped mountains, and the rolling oceans. Long walks in the country on spring mornings and skiing forays in the winter are to him equally a bore. Moreover, let us suppose that Jones can find no appeal in art. Novels are dull, poetry a pain, paintings nonsense and music just noise. Suppose further that Jones has neither the participant's nor the spectator's passion for baseball, football, tennis, or any other sport. Swimming to him is a cruel aquatic form of calisthenics, the sun only a cause of sunburn. Dancing is coeducational idiocy, conversation a waste of time, the other sex an unappealing mystery. Politics is a fraud, religion mere superstition; and the misery of millions of underprivileged human beings is nothing to be concerned with or excited about. Suppose finally that Jones has no talent for any kind of handicraft, industry, or commerce, and that he does not regret that fact.

What then is Jones interested in? He must desire something. To be sure, he does. Jones has an overwhelming passion for, a complete preoccupation with, his own happiness. The one exclusive desire of his life is *to be happy.* It takes little imagination at this point to see that Jones's one desire is bound to be frustrated. People who—like Jones—most hotly pursue their own happiness are the least likely to find it. Happy people are those who successfully pursue such things as aesthetic or religious experience, self-expression, service to others, victory in competitions, knowledge, power, and so on. If none of these things in themselves and for their own sakes mean anything to a person, if they are valued at all then only as a means to one's own pleasant states of mind—then that pleasure can never come. The way to achieve happiness is to pursue something else. ⑧

> ⑧ Does Jones's state of mind even make sense? See Discussion Question 2.

Almost all people at one time or another in their lives feel pleasure. Some people (though perhaps not many) really do live lives which are on the whole happy. But if pleasure and happiness presuppose desires for something other than pleasure and happiness, then the existence of pleasure and happiness in the experience of some people proves that those people have strong desires for something other than their own happiness—egoistic hedonism to the contrary.

The implications of the "paradox of hedonism" for educational theory should be obvious. The parents least likely to raise a happy child are those who, even with the best intentions, train their child to seek happiness directly. How often have we heard parents say:

> I don't care if my child does not become an intellectual, or a sports star, or a great artist. I just want her to be a plain average sort of person. Happiness does not require great ambitions and great frustrations; it's not worth it to suffer and become neurotic for the sake of science, art, or do-goodism. I just want my child to be happy.

This can be a dangerous mistake, for it is the child (and the adult for that matter) without "outer-directed" interests who is the most likely to be unhappy. The pure egoist would be the most wretched of persons.

. . .

As for moral education, it is probably true that punishment and reward are indispensable means of inculcation. But if the child comes to believe that the *sole* reasons for being moral are that he will escape the pain of punishment thereby and/or that he will gain the pleasure of a good reputation, then what is to prevent him from doing the immoral thing whenever he is sure that he will not be found out? While punishment and reward then are important tools for the moral educator, they obviously have their limitations. Beware of the man who does the moral thing only out of fear of pain or love of pleasure. He is not likely to be wholly trustworthy. Moral education is truly successful when it produces persons who are willing to do the right thing *simply because it is right,* and not merely because it is popular or safe. ⑨

> ⑨ Notice that this is a quite different point from the preceding one. There is nothing impossible or necessarily self-defeating about being motivated to be moral only by the promise of rewards and the threat of punishment. The point is just that a person who acts only for such reasons isn't really concerned with morality as such at all.

12. Pleasure as Sensation. One final argument against psychological hedonism should suffice to put that form of the egoistic psychology to rest once and for all. The egoistic hedonist claims that all desires can be reduced to the single desire for one's own *pleasure.* Now the word "pleasure" is ambiguous. On the one hand, it can stand for a certain indefinable, but very familiar and specific kind of sensation, or more accurately, a property of sensations; and it is generally, if not exclusively, associated with the senses. For example, certain taste sensations such as sweetness, thermal sensations of the sort derived from a hot bath or the feel of the August sun while one lies on a sandy beach, erotic sensations, olfactory sensations (say) of the fragrance of flowers or perfume, and tactual and kinesthetic sensations from a good massage, are all pleasant in this sense. Let us call this sense of "pleasure," which is the converse of "physical pain," pleasure$_1$.

On the other hand, the word "pleasure" is often used simply as a synonym for "satisfaction" (in the sense of gratification, not mere desire fulfillment). In this sense, the existence of pleasure presupposes the prior existence of desire. Knowledge, religious experience, aesthetic expression, and other so-called "spiritual activities" often give pleasure in this sense. In fact, as we have seen, we tend to get pleasure in this sense whenever we get what we desire, no matter what we desire. The masochist even derives pleasure (in the sense of "satisfaction") from his own physically painful sensations. Let us call the sense of "pleasure" which means "satisfaction"—pleasure$_2$.

Now we can evaluate the psychological hedonist's claim that the sole human motive is a desire for one's own pleasure, bearing in mind (as he often does not) the ambiguity of the word "pleasure." First, let us take the hedonist to be saying that it is the desire for pleasure$_1$ (pleasant sensation) which is the sole ultimate desire of all people and the sole desire capable of providing a motive for action. Now I have little doubt that all (or most) people desire their own pleasure, *sometimes*. But even this familiar kind of desire occurs, I think, rather rarely. When I am very hungry, I often desire to eat, or, more specifically, to eat this piece of steak and these potatoes. Much less often do I desire to eat certain morsels simply for the sake of the pleasant gustatory sensations they might cause. I have, on the other hand, been motivated in the latter way when I have gone to especially exotic (and expensive) French or Chinese restaurants; but normally, pleasant gastronomic sensations are simply a happy consequence or by-product of my eating, not the antecedently desired objective of my eating. There are, of course, others who take gustatory sensations far more seriously: the *gourmet* who eats only to savor the textures and flavors of fine foods, and the wine fancier who "collects" the exquisitely subtle and very pleasant tastes of rare old wines. Such people are truly absorbed in their taste sensations when they eat and drink, and there may even be some (rich) persons whose desire for such sensations is the sole motive for eating and drinking.

It should take little argument, however, to convince the reader that such persons are extremely rare.[10]

Similarly, I usually derive pleasure from taking a hot bath, and on occasion (though not very often) I even decide to bathe simply for the sake of such sensations. Even if this is equally true of everyone, however, it hardly provides grounds for inferring that *no one*

[10] It is in fact pretty hard to imagine a person of this sort who really cares only about the pleasurable sensations (and not at all about the fact that the wine is rare and costly).

ever bathes from *any* other motive. It should be empirically obvious that we sometimes bathe simply in order to get clean, or to please others, or simply from habit.

The view then that we are never after anything in our actions but our own pleasure[11]—that all people are complete "gourmets" of one sort or another—is not only morally cynical; it is also contrary to common sense and everyday experience. In fact, the view that pleasant sensations play such an enormous role in human affairs is so patently false on the available evidence, that we must conclude that the psychological hedonist has the other sense of "pleasure"—satisfaction—in mind when he states his thesis. If, on the other hand, he really does try to reduce the apparent multitude of human motives to the one desire for pleasant sensations, then the abundance of historical counter-examples justifies our rejection out of hand of his thesis. It surely seems incredible that the Christian martyrs were ardently pursuing their own pleasure when they marched off to face the lions, or that what the Russian soldiers at Stalingrad "really" wanted when they doused themselves with gasoline, ignited themselves, and then threw the flaming torches of their own bodies on German tanks, was simply the experience of pleasant physical sensations.

[11] Pleasure$_1$, that is.

13. Pleasure as Satisfaction. Let us consider now the other interpretation of the hedonist's thesis, that according to which it is one's own pleasure$_2$ (satisfaction) and not merely pleasure$_1$ (pleasant sensation) which is the sole ultimate objective of all voluntary behavior. In one respect, the "satisfaction thesis" is even less plausible than the "physical sensation thesis"; for the latter at least is a genuine empirical hypothesis, testable in experience, though contrary to the facts which experience discloses. The former, however, is so confused that it cannot even be completely stated without paradox. It is, so to speak, defeated in its own formulation. Any attempted explication of the theory that all men at all times desire only their own satisfaction leads to an *infinite regress* in the following way:

"All men desire only satisfaction."
"Satisfaction of what?"
"Satisfaction of their desires."
"Their desires for what?"
"Their desires for satisfaction."

"Satisfaction of what?"

"Their desires."

"For what?"

"For satisfaction"—etc., *ad infinitum.*

In short, psychological hedonism interpreted in this way attributes to all people as their sole motive a wholly vacuous and infinitely self-defeating desire. The source of this absurdity is in the notion that satisfaction can, so to speak, feed on itself, and perform the miracle of perpetual self-regeneration in the absence of desires for anything other than itself. [12]

To summarize the argument of sections 12 and 13: The word "pleasure" is

[12] Thus pleasure₂ essentially presupposes the existence of desires for something other than pleasure, with satisfaction resulting when these desires are satisfied.

ambiguous. Pleasure₁ means a certain indefinable characteristic of physical sensation. Pleasure₂ refers to the feeling of satisfaction that often comes when one gets what one desires whatever be the nature of that which one desires. Now, if the hedonist means pleasure₁ when he says that one's own pleasure is the ultimate objective of all of one's behavior, then his view is not supported by the facts. On the other hand, if he means pleasure₂, then his theory cannot even be clearly formulated, since it leads to the following infinite regress: "I desire only satisfaction of my desire for satisfaction of my desire for satisfaction . . . etc., *ad infinitum.*" I conclude then that psychological hedonism (the most common form of psychological egoism), however interpreted, is untenable.

. . .

Discussion Questions

1. Feinberg argues that there is no adequate evidence for the claim that apparent cases of altruism always actually involve selfish motives, but seems to concede that this might still possibly be the case (see the passage at Annotation 7)—even if the desire for the pleasure that results from the satisfaction of an independent altruistic desire is set aside for the reasons already discussed (see Annotations 4 and 5). Is this really a serious (as opposed to a merely logical) possibility? Think of various cases of apparent altruism and try to imagine what the supposed selfish motive might be. ("The desire to receive gratitude"

doesn't seem to always apply in a realistic way, since there is often no one from whom gratitude could be realistically expected. And it is hard to see why one should feel self-esteem as a result of an altruistic action unless one independently values altruism.)

2. Does it really even make sense to desire only one's own happiness (as Jones is said to do in the passage at Annotation 8)? What does happiness amount to if it does not involve having or being able to do various things that one likes or values—that is, various things for which one has independent desires?

What Is the Best Theory of Morality?

Utilitarianism: Morality Depends on Consequences

Jeremy Bentham

Jeremy Bentham (1748–1832) was an English moral, political, and legal philosopher, and the founder of the utilitarian approach to ethics. Bentham's main concern was with practical legal and social reform along utilitarian lines, and he became the leader of an important group of reformers (the "Philosophical Radicals"), whose influence led to significant changes in British law, particularly in the area of criminal law. In the following selection from his most important work, Bentham presents, explains, and defends a hedonistic version of act utilitarianism based on the *principle of utility,* which he regards as the only reasonable basis for moral judgments.

From *An Introduction to the Principles of Morals and Legislation*

CHAPTER I.

Of the Principle of Utility.

I. Nature has placed mankind under the governance of two sovereign masters, *pain* and *pleasure.* It is for them alone to point out what we ought to do, as well as to determine what we shall do. On the one hand the standard of right and wrong, on the other the chain of causes and effects, are fastened to their throne. They govern us in all we do, in all we say, in all we think: every effort we can make to throw off our subjection, will serve but to demonstrate and confirm it. In words a man may pretend to abjure their empire: but in reality he will remain subject to it all the while. The *principle of utility** recognises this subjection, and assumes it for the foundation of that system, the object of which is to rear the fabric of felicity by the hands of reason and of law. Systems which attempt to question it, deal in sounds instead of sense, in caprice instead of reason, in darkness instead of light.

But enough of metaphor and declamation: it is not by such means that moral science is to be improved.

II. The principle of utility is the foundation of the present work: it will be proper therefore at the outset to give an explicit and determinate account of what is meant by it. By the principle of utility is meant that principle which approves or disapproves of every action whatsoever, according to the tendency which it appears to have to augment or diminish the happiness of the party whose interest is in question: or, what is the same thing in other words, to promote or to oppose that happiness.① I say of every action whatsoever; and therefore not only of every action of a private individual, but of every measure of government.

> ① As will become clear later, the party in question is the entire community.

III. By utility is meant that property in any object, whereby it tends to produce benefit, advantage, pleasure, good, or happiness, (all this in the present case comes to the same thing) or (what comes again to the same thing) to prevent the happening of mischief, pain, evil, or unhappiness to the party whose interest is considered: if that party be the community in general, then the happiness of the community: if a particular individual, then the happiness of that individual.②

> ② Bentham clearly assumes that all varieties of pleasure and happiness amount to the same thing; and similarly for pain and unhappiness. See the previous selection from Feinberg for some doubts about this.

IV. The interest of the community is one of the most general expressions that can occur in the phraseology of morals: no wonder that the meaning of it is often lost. When it has a meaning, it is this. The community is a fictitious *body,* composed of the individual persons who are considered as constituting as it were its *members.* The interest of the community then is,

---

From An Introduction to the Principles of Morals and Legislation, *1823.*

---

*Note by the Author, July 1822.

To this denomination has of late been added, or substituted, the *greatest happiness* or *greatest felicity* principle: this for shortness, instead of saying at length *that principle* which states the greatest happiness of all those whose interest is in question, as being the right and proper, and only right and proper and universally desirable, end of human action: of human action in every situation, and in particular in that of a functionary or set of functionaries exercising the powers of Government. . . .

what?—the sum of the interests of the several members who compose it.

V. It is in vain to talk of the interest of the community, without understanding what is the interest of the individual. A thing is said to promote the interest, or to be *for* the interest, of an individual, when it tends to add to the sum total of his pleasures: or, what comes to the same thing, to diminish the sum total of his pains.

③ What Bentham presumably means here (as suggested by the previous footnote) is that the morally right action is the one whose tendency in favor of happiness as opposed to unhappiness is the *greatest* of the available alternatives: the action that *maximizes* the net balance of pleasure or happiness over pain or unhappiness. (Notice that in a sufficiently unfortunate situation, this net balance might still be negative—that is, all the alternatives might produce more unhappiness than happiness.)

VI. An action then may be said to be conformable to the principle of utility, or, for shortness sake, to utility, (meaning with respect to the community at large) when the tendency it has to augment the happiness of the community is greater than any it has to diminish it.③

VII. A measure of government (which is but a particular kind of action, performed by a particular person or persons) may be said to be conformable to or dictated by the principle of utility, when in like manner the tendency which it has to augment the happiness of the community is greater than any which it has to diminish it.

. . .

X. Of an action that is conformable to the principle of utility one may always say either that it is one that ought to be done, or at least that it is not one that ought not to be done. One may say also, that it is right it should be done; at least that it is not wrong it should be done: that it is a right action; at least that it is not a wrong action.④ When thus interpreted, the words *ought,* and *right* and *wrong,* and others of that stamp, have a meaning: when otherwise, they have none.

XI. Has the rectitude of this principle been ever formally contested? It should seem that it had, by those who have not known what they have been meaning. Is it susceptible of any direct proof? it should seem not: for that which is used to prove every thing else, cannot itself be proved: a chain of proofs must have their commencement somewhere. To give such proof is as impossible as it is needless.⑤

XII. Not that there is or ever has been that human creature breathing, however stupid or perverse, who has not on many, perhaps on most occasions of his life, deferred to it. By the natural constitution of the human frame, on most occasions of their lives men in general embrace this principle, without thinking of it: if not for the ordering of their own actions, yet for the trying of their own actions, as well as of those of other men. There have been, at the same time, not many, perhaps, even of the most intelligent, who have been disposed to embrace it purely and without reserve. There are even few who have not taken some occasion or other to quarrel with it, either on account of their not understanding always how to apply it, or on account of some prejudice or other which they were afraid to examine into, or could not bear to part with. For such is the stuff that man is made of: in principle and in practice, in a right track and in a wrong one, the rarest of all human qualities is consistency.

XIII. When a man attempts to combat the principle of utility, it is with reasons drawn, without his being aware of it, from that very principle itself*. His arguments, if they prove any thing, prove not that the principle is *wrong,* but that, according to the applications he supposes to be made of it, it is *misapplied.* Is it possible for a man to move the earth? Yes; but he must first find out another earth to stand upon.

④ Why does Bentham say that an action that conforms to his principle might *merely* be "not one that ought not to be done"? He seems to be allowing here for the possibility that there might be two or more actions that are *equally* good from the standpoint of utility, in which case each of them would be permitted (it would be "not one that ought not to be done"), but no particular one of them would be required ("one that ought to be done").

⑤ What Bentham seems to be saying here is that the principle of utility is **self-evident,** that one can see that it is true just by understanding the content of the principle.

---

*'The principle of utility, (I have heard it said) is a dangerous principle: it is dangerous on certain occasions to consult it.' This is as much as to say, what? that it is not consonant to utility, to consult utility: in short, that it is *not* consulting it, to consult it.

XIV. To disprove the propriety of it by arguments is impossible; but, from the causes that have been mentioned, or from some confused or partial view of it, a man may happen to be disposed not to relish it. Where this is the case, if he thinks the settling of his opinions on such a subject worth the trouble, let him take the following steps, and at length, perhaps, he may come to reconcile himself to it.

1. Let him settle with himself, whether he would wish to discard this principle altogether; if so, let him consider what it is that all his reasonings (in matters of politics especially) can amount to?⑥

2. If he would, let him settle with himself, whether he would judge and act without any principle, or whether there is any other he would judge and act by?

3. If there be, let him examine and satisfy himself whether the principle he thinks he has found is really any separate intelligible principle; or whether it be not a mere principle in words, a kind of phrase, which at bottom expresses neither more nor less than the mere averment of his own unfounded sentiments; that is, what in another person he might be apt to call caprice?

4. If he is inclined to think that his own approbation or disapprobation, annexed to the idea of an act, without any regard to its consequences, is a sufficient foundation for him to judge and act upon, let him ask himself whether his sentiment is to be a standard of right and wrong, with respect to every other man, or whether every man's sentiment has the same privilege of being a standard to itself?

5. In the first case, let him ask himself whether his principle is not despotical, and hostile to all the rest of human race?

6. In the second case, whether it is not anarchial, and whether at this rate there are not as many different standards of right and wrong as there are men? and whether even to the same man, the same thing, which is right to-day, may not (without the least change in its nature) be wrong to-morrow? and whether the same

> ⑥ In what follows, Bentham claims in effect that there is no rational alternative to the principle of utility: appeal to arbitrary individual preference is unacceptable (whether one person's preference is despotically applied to everyone or each person's preferences are given the same status, leading to moral chaos); and there is no basis other than utility on which the reflective acceptance of a principle could be grounded.

thing is not right and wrong in the same place at the same time? and in either case, whether all argument is not at an end? and whether, when two men have said, 'I like this,' and 'I don't like it,' they can (upon such a principle) have any thing more to say?

7. If he should have said to himself, No: for that the sentiment which he proposes as a standard must be grounded on reflection, let him say on what particulars the reflection is to turn? if on particulars having relation to the utility of the act, then let him say whether this is not deserting his own principle, and borrowing assistance from that very one in opposition to which he sets it up: or if not on those particulars, on what other particulars?

8. If he should be for compounding the matter, and adopting his own principle in part, and the principle of utility in part, let him say how far he will adopt it?

9. When he has settled with himself where he will stop, then let him ask himself how he justifies to himself the adopting it so far? and why he will not adopt it any farther?

10. Admitting any other principle than the principle of utility to be a right principle, a principle that it is right for a man to pursue; admitting (what is not true) that the word *right* can have a meaning without reference to utility, let him say whether there is any such thing as a *motive* that a man can have to pursue the dictates of it: if there is, let him say what that motive is, and how it is to be distinguished from those which enforce the dictates of utility: if not, then lastly let him say what it is this other principle can be good for?⑦

> ⑦ Here is a further consideration: since people can be motivated only by pleasure and pain, there would be no motive to follow any other sort of principle. (This is a version of the doctrine of psychological hedonism—see Feinberg—though Bentham does not insist on the egoistic version, which would undermine his own view.)

CHAPTER II.

Of Principles Adverse to That of Utility.

I. If the principle of utility be a right principle to be governed by, and that in all cases, it follows from what has been just observed, that whatever principle differs from it in any case must necessarily be a wrong one. To prove any other principle, therefore, to be a wrong one, there needs no more than just to show it to be what it is, a principle of which the dictates are in some point or other different from those of the principle of utility: to state it is to confute it.⑧

II. A principle may be different from that of utility in two ways: 1. By being constantly opposed to it: this is the case with a principle which may be termed the principle of *asceticism*. 2. By being sometimes opposed to it, and sometimes not, as it may happen: this is the case with another, which may be termed the principle of *sympathy* and *antipathy*.

III. By the principle of asceticism I mean that principle which, like the principle of utility, approves or disapproves of any action, according to the tendency which it appears to have to augment or diminish the happiness of the party whose interest is in question; but in an inverse manner: approving of actions in as far as they tend to diminish his happiness; disapproving of them in as far as they tend to augment it.

. . .

IX. The principle of asceticism seems originally to have been the reverie of certain hasty speculators, who having perceived, or fancied, that certain pleasures, when reaped in certain circumstances, have, at the long run, been attended with pains more than equivalent to them, took occasion to quarrel with every thing that offered itself under the name of pleasure. Having then got thus far, and having forgot the point which they set out from, they pushed on, and went so much further as to think it meritorious to fall in love with pain. Even this, we see, is at bottom but the principle of utility misapplied.⑨

X. The principle of utility is capable of being consistently pursued; and it is but tautology to say, that the more consistently it is pursued, the better it must ever be for humankind. The principle of asceti-cism never was, nor ever can be, consistently pursued by any living creature. Let but one tenth part of the inhabitants of this earth pursue it consistently, and in a day's time they will have turned it into a hell.

XI. Among principles adverse to that of utility, that which at this day seems to have most influence in matters of government, is what may be called the principle of sympathy and antipathy. By the principle of sympathy and antipathy, I mean that principle which approves or disapproves of certain actions, not on account of their tending to augment the happiness, nor yet on account of their tending to diminish the happiness of the party whose interest is in question, but merely because a man finds himself disposed to approve or disapprove of them: holding up that approbation or disapprobation as a sufficient reason for itself, and disclaiming the necessity of looking out for any extrinsic ground. . . . ⑩

XII. It is manifest, that this is rather a principle in name than in reality: it is not a positive principle of itself, so much as a term employed to signify the negation of all principle. What one expects to find in a principle is something that points out some external consideration, as a means of warranting and guiding the internal sentiments of approbation and disapprobation: this expectation is but ill fulfilled by a proposition, which does neither more nor less than hold up each of those sentiments as a ground and standard for itself.

XIII. In looking over the catalogue of human actions (says a partizan of this principle) in order to determine which of them are to be marked with the seal of disapprobation, you need but to take counsel of your own feelings: whatever you find in yourself a propensity to condemn, is wrong for that very reason. For the same reason it is also meet for punishment: in what proportion it is adverse to utility, or whether it be adverse to utility at all, is a matter that makes no difference. In that same *proportion* also is it meet for punishment: if you hate much, punish much: if you hate little, punish little: punish as you hate. If you hate

---

⑧ Again the assumption seems to be that the principle of utility is self-evidently true, so that Bentham can appeal to it in refuting opposing views.

⑨ The "principle of asceticism," which says that one should choose the action that produces the *least* utility, seems simply perverse. Bentham suggests that those who purport to adopt it (does anyone really do so?) are misapplying the principle of utility, by generalizing from cases where short-term pleasure leads to a greater long-term pain.

⑩ The principle of sympathy and antipathy is Bentham's label for the moral view that assesses the rightness or wrongness of actions simply by appeal to one's immediate inclination to approve or disapprove of them—what is sometimes referred to as moral intuition. As we have already seen, his view is that there is no rational basis apart from utility for such inclinations.

not at all, punish not at all: the fine feelings of the soul are not to be overborne and tyrannized by the harsh and rugged dictates of political utility.

XIV. The various systems that have been formed concerning the standard of right and wrong, may all be reduced to the principle of sympathy and antipathy. One account may serve for all of them. They consist all of them in so many contrivances for avoiding the obligation of appealing to any external standard, and for prevailing upon the reader to accept of the author's sentiment or opinion as a reason for itself. The phrases different, but the principle the same.* ⑪

XV. It is manifest, that the dictates of this principle will frequently coincide with those of utility, though perhaps without intending any such thing.

Probably more frequently than not: and hence it is that the business of penal justice is carried on upon that tolerable sort of footing upon which we see it carried on in common at this day. For what more natural or more general ground of hatred to a practice can there be, than the mischievousness of such practice? What all men are exposed to suffer by, all men will be disposed to hate. It is far yet, however, from being a constant ground: for when a man suffers, it is not always that he knows what it is he suffers by.

⑪ This footnote lists a variety of ways of formulating what Bentham regards as essentially the same appeal to unargued and fundamentally irrational moral inclinations or intuitions. (Is he right that these all amount to the same thing?)

---

*It is curious enough to observe the variety of inventions men have hit upon, and the variety of phrases they have brought forward, in order to conceal from the world, and, if possible, from themselves, this very general and therefore very pardonable self-sufficiency.

1. One man says, he has a thing made on purpose to tell him what is right and what is wrong; and that it is called a *moral sense:* and then he goes to work at his ease, and says, such a thing is right, and such a thing is wrong—why? 'because my moral sense tells me it is.'

2. Another man comes and alters the phrase: leaving out *moral,* and putting in *common,* in the room of it. He then tells you, that his common sense teaches him what is right and wrong, as surely as the other's moral sense did: meaning by common sense, a sense of some kind or other, which, he says, is possessed by all mankind: the sense of those, whose sense is not the same as the author's, being struck out of the account as not worth taking. This contrivance does better than the other; for a moral sense, being a new thing, a man may feel about him a good while without being able to find it out: but common sense is as old as the creation; and there is no man but would be ashamed to be thought not to have as much of it as his neighbours. . . .

3. Another man comes, and says, that as to a moral sense indeed, he cannot find that he has any such thing: that however he has an *understanding,* which will do quite as well. This understanding, he says, is the standard of right and wrong: it tells him so and so. All good and wise men understand as he does: if other men's understandings differ in any point from his, so much the worse for them: it is a sure sign they are either defective or corrupt.

4. Another man says, that there is an eternal and immutable Rule of Right: that that rule of right dictates so and so: and then he begins giving you his sentiments upon any thing that comes uppermost: and these sentiments (you are to take for granted) are so many branches of the eternal rule of right.

5. Another man, or perhaps the same man (it's no matter) says, that there are certain practices conformable, and others repugnant, to the Fitness of Things; and then he tells you, at his leisure, what practices are conformable and what repugnant: just as he happens to like a practice or dislike it.

6. A great multitude of people are continually talking of the Law of Nature; and then they go on giving you their sentiments about what is right and what is wrong: and these sentiments, you are to understand, are so many chapters and sections of the Law of Nature.

7. Instead of the phrase, Law of Nature, you have sometimes, Law of Reason, Right Reason, Natural Justice, Natural Equity, Good Order. Any of them will do equally well. This latter is most used in politics. The three last are much more tolerable than the others, because they do not very explicitly claim to be any thing more than phrases: they insist but feebly upon the being looked upon as so many positive standards of themselves, and seem content to be taken, upon occasion, for phrases expressive of the conformity of the thing in question to the proper standard, whatever that may be. . . .

It is upon the principle of antipathy that such and such acts are often reprobated on the score of their being *unnatural:* the practice of exposing children, established among the Greeks and Romans, was an unnatural practice. Unnatural, when it means any thing, means unfrequent: and there it means something; although nothing to the present purpose. But here it means no such thing: for the frequency of such acts is perhaps the great complaint. It therefore means nothing; nothing, I mean, which there is in the act itself. All it can serve to express is, the disposition of the person who is talking of it: the disposition he is in to be angry at the thoughts of it. Does it merit his anger? Very likely it may: but whether it does or no is a question, which, to be answered rightly, can only be answered upon the principle of utility.

. . .

A man may suffer grievously, for instance, by a new tax, without being able to trace up the cause of his sufferings to the injustice of some neighbour, who has eluded the payment of an old one.

XVI. The principle of sympathy and antipathy is most apt to err on the side of severity. It is for applying punishment in many cases which deserve none: in many cases which deserve some, it is for applying more than they deserve. There is no incident imaginable, be it ever so trivial, and so remote from mischief, from which this principle may not extract a ground of punishment. Any difference in taste: any difference in opinion: upon one subject as well as upon another. No disagreement so trifling which perseverance and altercation will not render serious. Each becomes in the other's eyes an enemy, and, if laws permit, a criminal. This is one of the circumstances by which the human race is distinguished (not much indeed to its advantage) from the brute creation.

XVII. It is not, however, by any means unexampled for this principle to err on the side of lenity. A near and perceptible mischief moves antipathy. A remote and imperceptible mischief, though not less real, has no effect. . . .

XIX. There are two things which are very apt to be confounded, but which it imports us carefully to distinguish:—the motive or cause, which, by operating on the mind of an individual, is productive of any act: and the ground or reason which warrants a legislator, or other by-stander, in regarding that act with an eye of approbation.⑫ When the act happens, in the particular instance in question, to be productive of effects which we approve of, much more if we happen to observe that the same motive may frequently be productive, in other instances, of the like effects, we are apt to transfer our approbation to the motive itself, and to assume, as the just ground for the approbation we bestow on the act, the circumstance of its originating from that motive. It is in this way that the sentiment of antipathy has often been considered as a just ground of action. Antipathy, for instance, in such or such a case, is the cause of an action which is attended with good effects: but this does not make it a right ground of action in that case, any more than in any other. Still farther. Not only the effects are good, but the agent sees beforehand that they will be so. This may make the action indeed a perfectly right action: but it does not make antipathy a right ground of action. For the same sentiment of antipathy, if implicitly deferred to, may be, and very frequently is, productive of the very worst effects. Antipathy, therefore, can never be a right ground of action. . . . ⑬ The only right ground of action, that can possibly subsist, is, after all, the consideration of utility, which, if it is a right principle of action, and of approbation, in any one case, is so in every other. Other principles in abundance, that is, other motives, may be the reasons why such and such an act *has* been done: that is, the reasons or causes of its being done: but it is this alone that can be the reason why it might or ought to have been done. Antipathy or resentment requires always to be regulated, to prevent its doing mischief:

⑫ Suppose I save a child from drowning because I want a reward that has been offered for such actions, not because I have any real concern for the child's welfare. The result of my action is morally good, and a legislator or bystander should therefore approve of it on that basis. But the motive operating on my mind is the desire for money, which has nothing to do with the reason why the action is good and does not in itself deserve moral approval.

⑬ Because even where antipathy may lead to the right results, it does so for a bad reason—one that will lead to incorrect results in other cases.

Continued

The mischief common to all these ways of thinking and arguing (which, in truth, as we have seen, are but one and the same method, couched in different forms of words) is their serving as a cloke, and pretence, and aliment, to despotism: if not a despotism in practice, a despotism however in disposition: which is but too apt, when pretence and power offer, to show itself in practice. The consequence is, that with intentions very commonly of the purest kind, a man becomes a torment either to himself or his fellow-creatures. If he be of the melancholy cast, he sits in silent grief, bewailing their blindness and depravity: if of the irascible, he declaims with fury and virulence against all who differ from him; blowing up the coals of fanaticism, and branding with the charge of corruption and insincerity, every man who does not think, or profess to think, as he does.

If such a man happens to possess the advantages of style, his book may do a considerable deal of mischief before the nothingness of it is understood. . . .

to be regulated by what? always by the principle of utility. The principle of utility neither requires nor admits of any other regulator than itself.

. . .

CHAPTER IV.

Value of a Lot of Pleasure or Pain, How to be Measured.

I. Pleasures then, and the avoidance of pains, are the *ends* which the legislator has in view: it behoves him therefore to understand their *value*. Pleasures and pains are the *instruments* he has to work with: it behoves him therefore to understand their force, which is again, in other words, their value.

II. To a person considered *by himself*, the value of a pleasure or pain considered *by itself*, will be greater or less, according to the four following circumstances:

1. Its *intensity*.
2. Its *duration*.
3. Its *certainty* or *uncertainty*.
4. Its *propinquity* or *remoteness*. [14]

[14] The first two of these are the most obvious features bearing on the utility or disutility of pleasures and pains: how intense they are and how long they last. "Certainty or uncertainty" really pertains to our knowledge that the pleasure or pain will result from the action in question, not to the pain or pleasure itself; Bentham is just pointing out the obvious fact that we can base a decision only on what we *believe* will result. "Propinquity or remoteness" has to do with how close the result in question is in time; Bentham seems to be suggesting that a temporally distant pleasure or pain should count for less than one that will occur sooner.

III. These are the circumstances which are to be considered in estimating a pleasure or a pain considered each of them by itself. But when the value of any pleasure or pain is considered for the purpose of estimating the tendency of any *act* by which it is produced, there are two other circumstances to be taken into the account; these are,

5. Its *fecundity*, or the chance it has of being followed by sensations of the *same* kind: that is, pleasures, if it be a pleasure: pains, if it be a pain.

6. Its *purity*, or the chance it has of *not* being followed by sensations of

the *opposite* kind: that is, pains, if it be a pleasure: pleasures, if it be a pain. [15]

These two last, however, are in strictness scarcely to be deemed properties of the pleasure or the pain itself; they are not, therefore, in strictness to be taken into the account of the value of that pleasure or that pain. They are in strictness to be deemed properties only of the act, or other event, by which such pleasure or pain has been produced; and accordingly are only to be taken into the account of the tendency of such act or such event.

IV. To a *number* of persons, with reference to each of whom the value of a pleasure or a pain is considered, it will be greater or less, according to seven circumstances: to wit, the six preceding ones; *viz.*

1. Its *intensity*.
2. Its *duration*.
3. Its *certainty* or *uncertainty*.
4. Its *propinquity* or *remoteness*.
5. Its *fecundity*.
6. Its *purity*.

And one other; to wit:

7. Its *extent;* that is, the number of persons to whom it *extends;* or (in other words) who are affected by it.

V. To take an exact account then of the general tendency of any act, by which the interests of a community are affected, proceed as follows. Begin with any one person of those whose interests seem most immediately to be affected by it: and take an account,

1. Of the value of each distinguishable *pleasure* which appears to be produced by it in the *first* instance.
2. Of the value of each *pain* which appears to be produced by it in the *first* instance.
3. Of the value of each pleasure which appears to be produced by it *after* the first. This

[15] As Bentham proceeds to say, "fecundity" and "purity" are not really qualities of the pleasures or pains themselves. It would be clearer to put his point here by saying that all of the consequences of an action in terms of pleasure and pain must be counted in assessing it, including of course pleasures and pains that are caused by earlier pleasures and pains.

constitutes the *fecundity* of the first *pleasure* and the *impurity* of the first *pain.*

4. Of the value of each *pain* which appears to be produced by it after the first. This constitutes the *fecundity* of the first *pain,* and the *impurity* of the first pleasure.

5. Sum up all the values of all the *pleasures* on the one side, and those of all the pains on the other. The balance, if it be on the side of pleasure, will give the *good* tendency of the act upon the whole, with respect to the interests of that *individual* person; if on the side of pain, the *bad* tendency of it upon the whole.⟨16⟩

6. Take an account of the *number* of persons whose interests appear to be concerned; and repeat the above process with respect to each. *Sum up* the numbers expressive of the degrees of *good* tendency, which the act has, with respect to each individual, in regard to whom the tendency of it is *good* upon the whole: do this again with respect to each individual, in regard to whom the tendency of it is *bad* upon the whole. Take the *balance;* which, if on the side of *pleasure,* will give the general *good tendency* of the act, with respect to the total number or community of individuals concerned; if on the side of pain, the general *evil tendency,* with respect to the same community.⟨17⟩

VI. It is not to be expected that this process should be strictly pursued previously to every moral judgment, or to every legislative or judicial operation. It may, however, be always kept in view: and as near as the process actually pursued on these occasions approaches to it, so near will such process ap-proach to the character of an exact one.⟨18⟩

VII. The same process is alike applicable to pleasure and pain, in whatever shape they appear: and by whatever denomination they are distinguished: to pleasure, whether it be called *good* (which is properly the cause or instrument of pleasure) or *profit* (which is distant pleasure, or the cause or instrument of distant pleasure,) or *convenience,* or *advantage, benefit, emolument, happiness,* and so forth: to pain, whether it be called *evil,* (which corresponds to *good*) or *mischief,* or *inconvenience,* or *disadvantage,* or *loss,* or *unhappiness,* and so forth.

VIII. Nor is this a novel and unwarranted, any more than it is a useless theory. In all this there is nothing but what the practice of mankind, wheresoever they have a clear view of their own interest, is perfectly conformable to. An article of property, an estate in land, for instance, is valuable, on what account? On account of the pleasures of all kinds which it enables a man to produce, and what comes to the same thing the pains of all kinds which it enables him to avert. But the value of such an article of property is universally understood to rise or fall according to the length or shortness of the time which a man has in it: the certainty or uncertainty of its coming into possession; and the nearness or remoteness of the time at which, if at all, it is to come into possession. As to the *intensity* of the pleasures which a man may derive from it, this is never thought of, because it depends upon the use which each particular person may come to make of it; which cannot be estimated till the particular pleasures he may come to derive from it, or the particular pains he may come to exclude by means of it, are brought to view. For the same reason, neither does he think of the *fecundity* or *purity* of those pleasures.

. . .

⟨16⟩ Thus Bentham assumes that all pleasures and pains for a given individual are *commensurable:* that the positive and negative values they represent can be combined in one total. It is suggested here and made clear in the following paragraph that these values are to be thought of in numerical terms.

⟨17⟩ He also assumes, even more controversially, that positive and negative values pertaining to different people can be combined in one numerically expressed total.

⟨18⟩ Strictly carrying out this process in a real-life case would require enormous expenditures of time and effort (if it could be done at all—see Discussion Question 2). This would be wasteful and inefficient, and so mistaken according to the principle of utility itself, since the resources involved would produce more pleasure or avoidance of pain if used in other ways than is gained by figuring out the best action with complete precision.

Discussion Questions

1. Bentham seems to regard the principle of utility as self-evidently correct. Does this amount to any more than saying that he (and many others) have a strong inclination or intuition in favor of this principle? If so, Bentham seems to be appealing to the very principle of sympathy or antipathy that he wants to reject. Is there any way of assessing moral claims that does not appeal, directly or indirectly, to such moral inclinations or intuitions? (See the discussion of the method of reflective equilibrium in the introduction to this chapter.)

2. Consider a choice between two actions, A and B, assuming that only your own utility is in question. Action A involves going out with friends, having pizza and beer, and going to a concert; but it also involves considerable expense, driving in heavy traffic, etc. Action B involves staying home with your significant other, eating food you prepare yourself, drinking lemonade, watching a movie on cable, and relaxing, with little effort or expense. (You may need to adjust the examples to make them better fit your particular desires and tastes.) How plausible is it that the various pleasures and pains (including various sorts of discomfort) involved in each of these cases can be combined into two total net values that are reasonably precise and can be numerically compared with each other?

3. How feasible is the larger utilitarian calculation Bentham describes? Suppose you are considering a choice between two different actions, each of which will cause a variety of pleasures and pains (or states of happiness and unhappiness) for many different individuals. (Try to think of a specific, fairly detailed example of your own here.) Is there any way to arrive at a total net value of each action for all the different individuals involved by combining all of their different sorts of pleasure and pain (or happiness and unhappiness) into one total?

4. One slightly more specific problem for such calculations: suppose that one alternative action leads to the *death* of one or more people, while the other does not. How should death be figured into the calculation? How much pleasure or happiness does it take to offset someone's death (or how much pain of other sorts is it equivalent to)? Is there any clear answer to this question?

5. One moral value that is often regarded as very important is justice (or fairness). What role, if any, does justice play in a utilitarian evaluation of alternative actions? Suppose one action produces a certain amount of positive utility (pleasure or happiness) that is divided fairly evenly among the members of the relevant community, while a second action produces an amount of utility that is slightly greater, but most of which is enjoyed by a small group of people, with most of the members of the community receiving very little. Which action will apparently be preferred according to the principle of utility? Does this seem like the right result (an appeal to moral intuition)? Can you think of any response to this objection on behalf of utilitarianism?

John Stuart Mill

John Stuart Mill (1806–1873) was a British philosopher who made important contributions to many areas of philosophy, including epistemology, logic, ethics, and political philosophy. His father, James Mill, was a close follower of Bentham. In the following selection, Mill defends a version of hedonistic utilitarianism, but one that departs from Bentham in assessing pleasures by their quality as well as quantity and that also contains some passages that seem to move in the direction of rule utilitarianism. Mill also offers a controversial "proof" of the principle of utility.

From *Utilitarianism*

CHAPTER I

General Remarks

There are few circumstances among those which make up the present condition of human knowledge more unlike what might have been expected, or more significant of the backward state in which speculation on the most important subjects still lingers, than the little progress which has been made in the decision of the controversy respecting the criterion of right and wrong. From the dawn of philosophy, the question concerning the *summum bonum,* or, what is the same thing, concerning the foundation of morality, has been accounted the main problem in speculative thought, has occupied the most gifted intellects and divided them into sects and schools carrying on a vigorous warfare against one another. And after more than two thousand years the same discussions continue, philosophers are still ranged under the same contending banners, and neither thinkers nor mankind at large seem nearer to being unanimous on the subject than when the youth Socrates listened to the old Protagoras and asserted (if Plato's dialogue be grounded on a real conversation) the theory of utilitarianism against the popular morality of the so-called sophist.①

> ① The reference is to Plato's dialogue *Protagoras.*

. . .

To inquire how far the bad effects of this deficiency have been mitigated in practice, or to what extent the moral beliefs of mankind have been vitiated or made uncertain by the absence of any distinct recognition of an ultimate standard, would imply a complete survey and criticism of past and present ethical doctrine. It would, however, be easy to show that whatever steadiness or consistency these moral beliefs have attained has been mainly due to the tacit influence of a standard not recognized. Although the nonexistence of an acknowledged first principle has made ethics not so much a guide as a consecration of men's actual sentiments, still, as men's sentiments, both of favor and of aversion, are greatly influenced

From Utilitarianism, published 1861.

by what they suppose to be the effects of things upon their happiness, the principle of utility, or, as Bentham latterly called it, the greatest happiness principle, has had a large share in forming the moral doctrines even of those who most scornfully reject its authority. . . .

On the present occasion, I shall, without further discussion of the other theories, attempt to contribute something toward the understanding and appreciation of the "utilitarian" or "happiness" theory, and toward such proof as it is susceptible of. It is evident that this cannot be proof in the ordinary and popular meaning of the term. Questions of ultimate ends are not amenable to direct proof. Whatever can be proved to be good must be so by being shown to be a means to something admitted to be good without proof. . . .

. . . Before . . . I attempt to enter into the philosophical grounds which can be given for assenting to the utilitarian standard, I shall offer some illustrations of the doctrine itself, with the view of showing more clearly what it is, distinguishing it from what it is not, and disposing of such of the practical objections to it as either originate in, or are closely connected with, mistaken interpretations of its meaning. . . .

CHAPTER II

What Utilitarianism Is

. . .

The creed which accepts as the foundation of morals "utility" or the "greatest happiness principle" holds that actions are right in proportion as they tend to promote happiness; wrong as they tend to produce the reverse of happiness. By happiness is intended pleasure and the absence of pain; by unhappiness, pain and the privation of pleasure. To give a clear view of the moral standard set up by the theory, much more requires to be said; in particular, what things it includes in the ideas of pain and pleasure, and to what extent this is left an open question. But these supplementary explanations do not affect the theory of life on which this theory of morality is grounded—namely, that pleasure and freedom from pain are the only things desirable as ends; and that all desirable things (which are as numerous in the utilitarian as in any other scheme) are desirable either for pleasure inherent in themselves or as means to the promotion of pleasure and the prevention of pain.②

> **②** Pleasure (and the avoidance of pain) is thus, for Mill, the only **intrinsic good,** with other things being valuable either for the pleasure they involve or for their **instrumental** value in leading to pleasure (or the avoidance of pain).

Now such a theory of life excites in many minds, and among them in some of the most estimable in feeling and purpose, inveterate dislike. To suppose that life has (as they express it) no higher end than pleasure—no better and nobler object of desire and pursuit—they designate as utterly mean and groveling, as a doctrine worthy only of swine, to whom the followers of Epicurus were, at a very early period, contemptuously likened; and modern holders of the doctrine are occasionally made the subject of equally polite comparisons by its German, French, and English assailants.

When thus attacked, the Epicureans have always answered that it is not they, but their accusers, who represent human nature in a degrading light, since the accusation supposes human beings to be capable of no pleasures except those of which swine are capable. If this supposition were true, the charge could not be gainsaid, but would then be no longer an imputation; for if the sources of pleasure were precisely the same to human beings and to swine, the rule of life which is good enough for the one would be good enough for the other. The comparison of the Epicurean life to that of beasts is felt as degrading, precisely because a beast's pleasures do not satisfy a human being's conceptions of happiness. Human beings have faculties more elevated than the animal appetites and, when once made conscious of them, do not regard anything as happiness which does not include their gratification.③ . . . It must

> **③** Mill suggests not only that human beings are capable of experiencing kinds of pleasure that animals are incapable of experiencing (which is obvious), but also that nothing will count as human happiness that does not include these "higher" pleasures. The rationale for this last point is not yet clear.

be admitted, however, that utilitarian writers in general have placed the superiority of mental over bodily pleasures chiefly in the greater permanency, safety, uncostliness, etc., of the former—that is, in their circumstantial advantages rather than in their intrinsic nature.④ And on all these points utilitarians have fully proved their case; but they might have taken the other and, as it may be called, higher ground with entire consistency. It is quite compatible with the principle of utility to recognize the fact that some kinds of pleasure are more desirable and more valuable than others. It would be absurd that, while in estimating all other things quality is considered as well as quantity, the estimation of pleasure should be supposed to depend on quantity alone.⑤

If I am asked what I mean by difference of quality in pleasures, or what makes one pleasure more valuable than another, merely as a pleasure, except its being greater in amount, there is but one possible answer. Of two pleasures, if there be one to which all or almost all who have experience of both give a decided preference, irrespective of any feeling of moral obligation to prefer it, that is the more desirable pleasure. If one of the two is, by those who are competently acquainted with both, placed so far above the other that they prefer it, even though knowing it to be attended with a greater amount of discontent, and would not resign it for any quantity of the other pleasure which their nature is capable of, we are justified in ascribing to the preferred enjoyment a superiority in quality so far outweighing quantity as to render it, in comparison, of small account.⑥

> **④** Here is one rationale for the claim that "higher" pleasures are more valuable for human beings: they are instrumentally superior to bodily pleasures, in that they last longer, involve fewer risks (of pains and unpleasant experiences), and are less costly (again in terms of pains and unpleasant experiences, not just money).

> **⑤** While not rejecting the previous point, Mill suggests a different and more controversial reason for preferring "higher" to "lower" pleasures: "higher" pleasures are superior in *quality* to "lower" pleasures, where this means that a given quantity of a higher pleasure is preferable *in terms of its intrinsic pleasureableness alone* to the same or even a somewhat greater quantity of a "lower" pleasure.

> **⑥** Mill seems to present the appeal to what has been described as "a jury of pleasure testers" as giving the very meaning of the claim that one pleasure is of a better quality than another, but it seems better to regard this as simply a practical test or criterion. One problem here is whether the "competence" of such jurors can be decided in a way that does not beg the question at issue. (See Discussion Question 1.)

Now it is an unquestionable fact that those who are equally acquainted with and equally capable of appreciating and enjoying both do give a most marked preference to the manner of existence which employs their higher faculties. Few human creatures would consent to be changed into any of the lower animals for a promise of the fullest allowance of a beast's pleasures; no intelligent human being would consent to be a fool, no instructed person would be an ignoramus, no person of feeling and conscience would be selfish and base, even though they should be persuaded that the fool, the dunce, or the rascal is better satisfied with his lot than they are with theirs. They would not resign what they possess more than he for the most complete satisfaction of all the desires which they have in common with him. . . . Whoever supposes that this preference takes place at a sacrifice of happiness—that the superior being, in anything like equal circumstances, is not happier than the inferior—confounds the two very different ideas of happiness and content. It is indisputable that the being whose capacities of enjoyment are low has the greatest chance of having them fully satisfied; and a highly endowed being will always feel that any happiness which he can look for, as the world is constituted, is imperfect. But he can learn to bear its imperfections, if they are at all bearable; and they will not make him envy the being who is indeed unconscious of the imperfections, but only be-

> **⑦** Note that the issue is not just whether it is "better to be a human being dissatisfied than a pig satisfied" (where this means that anyone familiar with both sorts of lives would choose the former), but whether this is so because the human life is superior in terms of pleasure or happiness. Mill cannot simply assume that pleasure or happiness is the only basis for this choice.

cause he feels not at all the good which those imperfections qualify. It is better to be a human being dissatisfied than a pig satisfied; better to be Socrates dissatisfied than a fool satisfied. And if the fool, or the pig, are of a different opinion, it is because they only know their own side of the question. The other party to the comparison knows both sides.⑦

. . .

According to the greatest happiness principle, as above explained, the ultimate end, with reference

to and for the sake of which all other things are desirable—whether we are considering our own good or that of other people—is an existence exempt as far as possible from pain, and as rich as possible in enjoyments, both in point of quantity and quality; the test of quality and the rule for measuring it against quantity being the preference felt by those who, in their opportunities of experience, to which must be added their habits of self-consciousness and self-observation, are best furnished with the means of comparison. This, being according to the utilitarian opinion the end of human action, is necessarily also the standard of morality, which may accordingly be defined "the rules and precepts for human conduct," by the observance of which an existence such as has been described might be, to the greatest extent possible, secured to all mankind; and not to them only, but, so far as the nature of things admits, to the whole sentient creation.⑧

> **⑧** There are at least three different issues raised by this passage: (1) Is it true that happiness and enjoyment are the ultimate ends of human life in the sense that they capture everything that people actually aim at? (See the selection from Nozick in Chapter 8 for more on this issue.) (2) Even if this were true, does it follow that happiness is thereby the standard of morality—that people *ought* to be guided only by the pursuit of happiness (their own and that of others)? (3) If circumstances do not allow all of mankind and even "the whole sentient creation" to be maximally happy, does utilitarianism have anything to say about how the choice of who is to be happy (and to what degree), and who is not, is to be made?

. . .

I must again repeat what the assailants of utilitarianism seldom have the justice to acknowledge, that the happiness which forms the utilitarian standard of what is right in conduct is not the agent's own happiness but that of all concerned. As between his own happiness and that of others, utilitarianism requires him to be as strictly impartial as a disinterested and benevolent spectator. In the golden rule of Jesus of Nazareth, we read the complete spirit of the ethics of utility. "To do as you would be done by," and "to love your neighbor as yourself," constitute the ideal perfection of utilitarian morality. . . . ⑨

It may not be superfluous to notice a few more of the common misapprehensions of utilitarian ethics, even those which are so obvious and gross that it might appear impossible for any person of candor and intelligence to fall into them; since persons, even of considerable mental endowment, often give themselves so little trouble to understand the bearings of any opinion against which they entertain a prejudice, and men are in general so little conscious of this voluntary ignorance as a defect that the vulgarest misunderstandings of ethical doctrines are continually met with in the deliberate writings of persons of the greatest pretensions both to high principle and to philosophy. . . .

9 Since all that matters is achieving the greatest total, utilitarianism does not allow a person to give *any* preference to his own happiness or well-being (or that of his family and friends)—nor to be any more concerned about his own projects and commitments than about those of anyone else. How reasonable a requirement is this? (See the selection from Williams later in this chapter.)

. . . utility is often summarily stigmatized as an immoral doctrine by giving it the name of "expediency," and taking advantage of the popular use of that term to contrast it with principle. But the expedient, in the sense in which it is opposed to the right, generally means that which is expedient for the particular interest of the agent himself. . . . When it means anything better than this, it means that which is expedient for some immediate object, some temporary purpose, but which violates a rule whose observance is expedient in a much higher degree. The expedient, in this sense, instead of being the same thing with the useful, is a branch of the hurtful. Thus it would often be expedient, for the purpose of getting over some momentary embarrassment, or attaining some object immediately useful to ourselves or others, to tell a lie. But inasmuch as the cultivation in ourselves of a sensitive feeling on the subject of veracity is one of the most useful, and the enfeeblement of that feeling one of the most hurtful, things to which our conduct can be instrumental; and inasmuch as any, even unintentional, deviation from truth does that much toward weakening the trustworthiness of human assertion, which is not only the principal support of all present social well-being, but the insufficiency of which does more than any one thing that can be named to keep back civilization, virtue, everything on which human happiness on the largest scale depends—we feel that the violation, for a present advantage, of a rule of such transcendent expediency is not expedient, and that he who, for the sake of convenience to himself or to some other individual, does what depends on him to deprive mankind of the good, and inflict upon them the evil, involved in the greater or less reliance which they can place in each other's word, acts the part of one of their worst enemies. Yet that even this rule, sacred as it is, admits of possible exceptions is acknowledged by all moralists; the chief of which is when the withholding of some fact (as of information from a malefactor, or of bad news from a person dangerously ill) would save an individual (especially an individual other than oneself) from great and unmerited evil, and when the withholding can only be effected by denial. But in order that the exception may not extend itself beyond the need, and may have the least possible effect in weakening reliance on veracity, it ought to be recognized and, if possible, its limits defined; and, if the principle of utility is good for anything, it must be good for weighing these conflicting utilities against one another and marking out the region within which one or the other preponderates. **10**

10 Perhaps the central objection to act utilitarianism is that it would sanction violating various common-sense moral rules (rules that seem to be supported by our intuitive moral convictions, such as the rule not to lie, not to break promises, etc.) whenever even a small gain in utility would result. A response to this objection is that when the damaging effects of such actions on valuable practices and social institutions are added in, such violations will be justified only in very unusual cases, where it is no longer clear that they are objectionable. Does this work? (See Discussion Question 3.)

Again, defenders of utility often find themselves called upon to reply to such objections as this—that there is not time, previous to action, for calculating and weighing the effects of any line of conduct on the general happiness. . . . The answer to the objection is that there has been ample time, namely, the whole past duration of the human species. During all that time mankind have been learning by experience the tendencies of actions; on which experience all the prudence as well as all the morality of life are dependent. People talk as if the commencement of this course of experience had hitherto been put off, and as if, at the moment when some man feels tempted to meddle with the property or life of another, he had to begin considering for the first time whether murder and theft are injurious to human happiness. . . . There is no difficulty in proving any ethical standard whatever to work ill if we suppose universal idiocy to be conjoined with it; but on any hypothesis short of that, mankind must by this time have acquired positive beliefs as to the effects of some actions on their happiness; and the beliefs which have thus come down are the rules of morality for the multitude, and for the philosopher until he has succeeded in finding better. That philosophers might easily do this, even now, on many subjects; that the received code of ethics is by no means of divine right; and that mankind have still much to learn as to the effects of actions on the general happiness, I admit or rather earnestly maintain. The corollaries from the principle of utility, like the precepts of every practical art, admit of indefinite improvement, and, in a progressive state of the human mind, their improvement is perpetually going on. But to consider the rules of morality as improvable is one thing; to pass over the intermediate generalization entirely and endeavor to test each individual action directly by the first principle is another. It is a strange notion that the acknowledgment of a first principle is inconsistent with the admission of secondary ones. To inform a traveler respecting the place of his ultimate destination is not to forbid the use of landmarks and direction-posts on the way. The proposition that happiness is the end and aim of morality does not mean that no road ought to be laid down to that goal, or that persons going thither should not be advised to take one direction rather than another. Men really ought to leave off talking a kind of nonsense on this subject, which they would neither talk nor listen to on other matters of practical concernment. Nobody argues that the art of navigation is not founded on astronomy because sailors cannot wait to calculate the Nautical Almanac. Being rational creatures, they go to sea with it ready calculated; and all rational creatures go out upon the sea of life with their minds made up on the common questions of right and

wrong, as well as on many of the far more difficult questions of wise and foolish. And this, as long as foresight is a human quality, it is to be presumed they will continue to do. Whatever we adopt as the fundamental principle of morality, we require subordinate principles to apply it by; the impossibility of doing without them, being common to all systems, can afford no argument against any one in particular; but gravely to argue as if no such secondary principles could be had, and as if mankind had remained till now, and always must remain, without drawing any general conclusions from the experience of human life is as high a pitch, I think, as absurdity has ever reached in philosophical controversy. [11]

. . . It is not the fault of any creed, but of the complicated nature of human affairs, that rules of conduct cannot be so framed as to require no exceptions, and that hardly any kind of action can safely be laid down as either always obligatory or always condemnable. . . . There exists no moral system under which there do not arise unequivocal cases of conflicting obligation. These are the real difficulties, the knotty points both in the theory of ethics and in the conscientious guidance of personal conduct. . . . If utility is the ultimate source of moral obligations, utility may be invoked to decide between them when their demands are incompatible. Though the application of the standard may be difficult, it is better than none at all; while in other systems, the moral laws all claiming independent authority, there is no common umpire entitled to interfere between them; their claims to precedence one over another rest on little better than sophistry, and, unless determined, as they generally are, by the unacknowledged influence of consideration of utility, afford a free scope for the action of personal desires and partialities. We must remember that only in these cases of conflict between sec-

[11] Even act utilitarianism can sanction the use of general rules of morality in cases where it is too difficult or costly or time-consuming to do a full utilitarian calculation (a point also made by Bentham). The issue between act and rule utilitarianism is whether one should ever follow such a rule even when it is clear that it will not produce the greatest utility in the situation in question. (See the following selection from Smart for more on this.)

12 Here Mill seems to be saying that a utilitarian calculation should be made only where the "secondary rules" conflict. This would mean that in the absence of conflict, the relevant secondary rule should always be followed—even in cases where it does not lead to the greatest utility, which suggests the rule utilitarian view (see the chapter introduction and the following selection by Smart). But he may only be saying that an appeal to a utilitarian calculation is not required ("requisite") where there is no conflict but is still permitted and perhaps even desirable where feasible—which would still be an act utilitarian view.

ondary principles is it requisite that first principles should be appealed to. There is no case of moral obligation in which some secondary principle is not involved; and if only one, there can seldom be any real doubt which one it is, in the mind of any person by whom the principle itself is recognized. 12

CHAPTER IV

Of What Sort of Proof the Principle of Utility Is Susceptible

It has already been remarked that questions of ultimate ends do not admit of proof, in the ordinary acceptation of the term. To be incapable of proof by reasoning is common to all first principles, to the first premises of our knowledge, as well as to those of our conduct. But the former, being matters of fact, may be the subject of a direct appeal to the faculties which judge of fact—namely, our senses and our internal consciousness. Can an appeal be made to the same faculties on questions of practical ends? Or by what other faculty is cognizance taken of them?

Questions about ends are, in other words, questions what things are desirable. The utilitarian doctrine is that happiness is desirable, and the only thing desirable, as an end; all other things beings only desirable as means to that end. What ought to be required of this doctrine, what conditions is it requisite that the doctrine should fulfill—to make good its claim to be believed?

The only proof capable of being given that an object is visible is that people actually see it. The only proof that a sound is audible is that people hear it; and so of the other sources of our experience. In like manner, I apprehend, the sole evidence it is possible to produce that anything is desirable is that

people do actually desire it. 13 If the end which the utilitarian doctrine proposes to itself were not, in theory and in practice, acknowledged to be an end, nothing could ever convince any person that it was so. No reason can be given why the general happiness is desirable, except that each person, so far as he believes it to be attainable, desires his own happiness. This, however, being a fact, we have not only all the proof which the case admits of, but all which it is possible to require, that happiness is a good, that each person's happiness is a good to that person, and the general happiness, therefore, a good to the aggregate of all persons. Happiness has made out its title as *one* of the ends of conduct and, consequently, one of the criteria of morality. 14

But it has not, by this alone, proved itself to be the sole criterion. To do that, it would seem, by the same rule, necessary to show, not only that people desire happiness, but that they never desire anything else. Now it is palpable that they do desire things which, in common language, are decidedly distinguished from happiness. They desire, for example, virtue and the absence of vice no less really than pleasure and the absence of pain. The desire of virtue is not as universal, but it is as authentic a fact as the desire of happiness. And hence the opponents of the utilitarian standard deem that they have a right to infer that there are other ends of human action besides happiness, and that happiness is not the standard of approbation and disapprobation.

13 This is the first stage of Mill's "proof," purporting to establish that happiness is desirable in the sense of being an intrinsic good for all people (given the further premise that all people in fact desire their own happiness). Think about the cogency of this argument, and in particular about the analogy between visibility or audibility and the relevant sense of "desirability." (See Discussion Question 4.)

14 Here is the second stage of the argument: if the happiness of each person is an intrinsic good for that person (supposedly established in the first stage), then "the general happiness" of all people is an intrinsic good for "the aggregate of all people." Does this, as Mill seems to be claiming, establish that individual people should aim at "the general happiness" (as utilitarianism claims)? (See Discussion Question 4.)

But does the utilitarian doctrine deny that people desire virtue, or maintain that virtue is not a thing to be desired? The very reverse. It maintains not only that virtue is to be desired, but that it is to be desired disinterestedly, for itself. Whatever may be the opinion of utilitarian moralists as to the original conditions by which virtue is made virtue, however they may believe (as they do) that actions and dispositions are only virtuous because they promote another end than virtue, yet this being granted, and it having been decided, from considerations of this description, what *is* virtuous, they not only place virtue at the very head of the things which are good as means to the ultimate end, but they also recognize as a psychological fact the possibility of its being, to the individual, a good in itself, without looking to any end beyond it; and hold that the mind is not in a right state, not in a state conformable to utility, not in the state most conducive to the general happiness, unless it does love virtue in this manner—as a thing desirable in itself, even although, in the individual instance, it should not produce those other desirable consequences which it tends to produce, and on account of which it is held to be virtue. ⑮ This opinion is not, in the smallest degree, a departure from the happiness principle. The ingredients of happiness are very various, and each of them is desirable in itself, and not merely when considered as swelling an aggregate. The principle of utility does not mean that any given pleasure, as music, for instance, or any given exemption from pain, as for example health, is to be looked upon as means to a collective something termed happiness, and to be desired on that account. They are desired and desirable in and for themselves; besides being means, they are a part of the end. Virtue, according to the utilitarian doctrine, is not naturally and originally part of the end, but it is capable of becoming so; and in those who live it disinterestedly it has become so, and is desired and cherished, not as a means to happiness, but as a part of their happiness.

. . . Life would be a poor thing, very ill provided with sources of happiness, if there were not this provision of nature by which things originally indifferent, but conducive to, or otherwise associated with, the satisfaction of our primitive desires, become in themselves sources of pleasure more valuable than the primitive pleasures, both in permanency, in the space of human existence that they are capable of covering, and even in intensity.

Virtue, according to the utilitarian conception, is a good of this description. There was no original desire of it, or motive to it, save its conduciveness to pleasure, and especially to protection from pain. But through the association thus formed it may be felt a good in itself, and desired as such with as great intensity as any other good. . . .

It results from the preceding considerations that there is in reality nothing desired except happiness. Whatever is desired otherwise than as a means to some end beyond itself, and ultimately to happiness, is desired as itself a part of happiness, and is not desired for itself until it has become so. . . .

We have now, then, an answer to the question, of what sort of proof the principle of utility is susceptible. If the opinion which I have now stated is psychologically true—if human nature is so constituted as to desire nothing which is not either a part of happiness or a means of happiness—we can have no other proof, and we require no other, that these are the only things desirable. If so, happiness is the sole end of human action, and the promotion of it the test by which to judge of all human conduct; from whence it necessarily follows that it must be the criterion of morality, since a part is included in the whole.

And now to decide whether this is really so, whether mankind do desire nothing for itself but that which is a pleasure to them, or of which the absence is a pain, we have evidently arrived at a question of fact and experience, dependent, like all similar questions, upon evidence. It can only be determined by practiced self-consciousness and self-observation, assisted by observation of others. I believe that these sources

⑮ It is clearly compatible with utilitarianism that something other than happiness (such a virtue) be desired as an instrumental means to the end of happiness. Somewhat more surprisingly, it is also compatible with utilitarianism to hold that more utility will be produced if virtue is desired as an end in itself, as intrinsically valuable, rather than being explicitly sought only as a means to happiness. (But this might just mean that it is valuable for people to believe *falsely* that virtue is an intrinsic good.)

of evidence, impartially consulted, will declare that desiring a thing and finding it pleasant, aversion to it and thinking of it as painful, are phenomena entirely inseparable or, rather, two parts of the same phenomenon—in strictness of language, two different modes of naming the same psychological fact; that to think of an object as desirable (unless for the sake of its consequences) and to think of it as pleasant are one and the same thing; and that to desire anything except in proportion as the idea of it is pleasant is a physical and metaphysical impossibility. [16]

. . .

[16] Mill argues, that if virtue is desired as an end in itself, then realizing that end becomes in itself a source of pleasure or happiness, so that it becomes "part of happiness," in which case it is still only pleasure or happiness that is desired. (Here he seems to be making the mistake discussed at the end of the earlier selection from Feinberg: the pleasure or happiness (Feinberg's pleasure$_2$) that results when a desire for something is satisfied cannot be the main end of that desire, for it is only because there is an *independent* desire for that thing that pleasure results when the desire is satisfied.)

Discussion Questions

1. Suppose you are attempting to assess the relative quality of two pleasures: the pleasure of attending an opera and the pleasure of eating pizza. Mill says this question should be decided by appealing to a jury composed of people who have experienced both pleasures or, he says a bit later, are "competently acquainted with both." How is it to be decided which people qualify to be members of this jury? Clearly merely having some brief exposure to both pizza and opera is not enough, especially for opera, which seems to be an "acquired taste." But then how much exposure is required to produce "competent acquaintance" with something like opera (or other "higher" pleasures)? Clearly we cannot say that a person is not "competently acquainted" with a "higher" pleasure unless he or she prefers it (in general) to "lower" pleasures, since that would load the dice in favor of the "higher" pleasures.

2. Even if the utilitarian calculation were possible under Bentham's view (see Discussion Questions 2 and 3 to the Bentham selection), is it still possible given Mill's recognition of qualities as well as quantities of pleasure? How are qualities to be figured into the calculation? Can pleasures of different quality be combined into one total, and if so, how? (Remember how differences of quality are supposed to be determined: does this plausibly yield a numerical ranking that could perhaps be multiplied with the quantitative value?)

3. One objection to act utilitarianism is that it would allow or indeed require actions such as telling lies or breaking promises whenever even a slight gain in utility results from doing so. Suppose, for example, that you have promised a friend that you will go to a movie with him, but that you are invited at the last minute to go to a concert with a different friend instead. Suppose also that it is clear to you that you will enjoy the concert enough more than the movie that the total utility (allowing for both the disappointment and unhappiness

experienced by the first friend and the increased happiness experienced by the second friend) will be greater if you break the promise and go to the concert. (Assume there is no way to reschedule the movie in a satisfactory way with the first friend.) Act utilitarianism seems to say that you should go to the concert, but this seems to be the wrong choice according to most people's moral convictions. Mill suggests (see the passage at Annotation 10) that your calculation should also include the negative value resulting from the effect of your action on the valuable practice of relying on other people's promises: this practice allows people to coordinate their actions in ways that lead to a great deal of pleasure and happiness, and the breaking of promises tends to undermine the practice by making people less willing to rely on it. There is no doubt that this additional consideration *might* be enough to alter the result of the utilitarian calculation if

the original difference in utility was small enough. But how plausible is it that it will make enough difference in most or all cases to avoid a serious conflict between act utilitarianism and our considered moral convictions?

4. How compelling are the two stages of Mill's "proof" of the principle of utility (see Annotations 13 and 14)? A further hint for the first stage: "visible" means "able to be seen," but does "desirable" (in the sense relevant to intrinsic value) mean "able to be desired"? And for the second stage, does it follow from the fact that something is a good for "the aggregate of persons" that it is a good for each individual member of that aggregate (something that such an individual should aim at, rather than aiming at his or her own individual good)? Indeed, what is it for something to be a good for "the aggregate of persons" when only individual people and not aggregates ever make choices or act?

J.J.C.Smart

John Jamieson Carswell Smart (1920–) is a British-born philosopher who has done virtually all his professional work and teaching in Australia. Smart has made major contributions to the philosophy of mind, the philosophy of science, and ethics, and is perhaps the most important recent proponent of act utilitarianism. In the following selection, Smart discusses the issues that divide act utilitarianism (which he refers to as "extreme utilitarianism") and rule utilitarianism (which he refers to as "restricted utilitarianism"). He argues that an act utilitarian can still appeal to moral "rules of thumb," and that once this is realized, there is no remaining justification for giving rules the more fundamental status that is advocated by rule utilitarianism.

Extreme and Restricted Utilitarianism

I

Utilitarianism is the doctrine that the rightness of actions is to be judged by their consequences. What do we mean by 'actions' here? Do we mean par-

ticular actions or do we mean classes of actions? According to which way we interpret the word 'actions' we get two different theories, both of which merit the appellation 'utilitarian.'

1. If by 'actions' we mean particular individual actions we get the sort of doctrine held by Bentham, Sidgwick, and Moore. According to this doctrine we test individual actions by their consequences, and gen-

eral rules, like 'keep promises,' are mere rules of thumb which we use only to avoid the necessity of estimating the probable consequences of our actions at every step. The rightness or wrongness of keeping a promise on a particular occasion depends only on the goodness or badness of the consequences of keeping or of breaking the promise on that particular occasion. Of course part of the consequences of breaking the promise, and a part to which we will normally ascribe decisive importance, will be the weakening of faith in the institution of promising. However, if the goodness of the consequences of breaking the rule is *in toto* greater than the goodness of the consequences of keeping it, then we must break the rule, irrespective of whether the goodness of the consequences of *everybody's* obeying the rule is or is not greater than the consequences of *everybody's* breaking it. To put it shortly, rules do not matter, save *per accidens* as rules of thumb and as *de facto* social institutions with which the utilitarian has to reckon when estimating consequences. I shall call this doctrine 'extreme utilitarianism.'[1]

> [1] As already noted, this is Smart's term for what is more standardly referred to as "act utilitarianism."

2. A more modest form of utilitarianism has recently become fashionable. The doctrine is to be found in Toulmin's book *The Place of Reason in Ethics,* in Nowell-Smith's *Ethics* (though I think Nowell-Smith has qualms), in John Austin's *Lectures on Jurisprudence* (Lecture II), and even in J. S. Mill, if Urmson's interpretation of him is correct. . . . Part of its charm is that it appears to resolve the dispute in moral philosophy between intuitionists and utilitarians in a way which is very neat. The above philosophers hold, or seem to hold, that moral rules are more than rules of thumb. In general the rightness of an action is *not* to be tested by evaluating its consequences but only by considering whether or not it falls under a certain rule. Whether the rule is to be considered an acceptable moral rule, is, however, to be decided by considering the consequences of adopting the rule. Broadly, then, actions are to be tested by rules and rules by consequences. The only cases in which we must test an individual action directly by its consequences are (*a*) when the action comes under two different rules, one of which enjoins it and one of which forbids it, and (*b*) when there is no rule whatever that governs the given case. I shall call this doctrine 'restricted utilitarianism.'[2]

It should be noticed that the distinction I am making cuts across, and is quite different from, the distinction commonly made between hedonistic and ideal utilitarianism. Bentham was an extreme hedonistic utilitarian and Moore an extreme ideal utilitarian, and Toulmin (perhaps) could be classified as a restricted ideal utilitarian. A hedonistic utilitarian holds that the goodness of the consequences of an action is a function only of their pleasurableness and an ideal utilitarian, like Moore, holds that pleasurableness is not even a necessary condition of goodness.[3] Mill seems, if we are to take his remarks about higher and lower pleasures seriously, to be neither a pure hedonistic nor a pure ideal utilitarian. He seems to hold that pleasurableness is a necessary condition for goodness, but that goodness is a function of other qualities of mind as well. Perhaps we can call him a quasi-ideal utilitarian. When we say that a state of mind is good I take it that we are expressing some sort of *rational preference.* When we say that it is pleasurable I take it that we are saying that it is enjoyable, and when we say that something is a higher pleasure I take it that we are saying that it is more truly, or more deeply, enjoyable. I am doubtful whether 'more deeply enjoyable' does not just mean 'more enjoyable, even though not more enjoyable on a first look,' and so I am doubtful whether quasi-ideal utilitarianism, and possibly ideal utilitarianism too, would not collapse into hedonistic utilitarianism on a closer scrutiny of the logic of words like 'preference,' 'pleasure,' 'enjoy,' 'deeply enjoy,' and so on. However, it is beside the point of the present paper to go into these questions. I am here concerned only with the issue between extreme and restricted utilitarianism and am ready to concede that both forms of utilitarianism can be either hedonistic or nonhedonistic.

> [2] And this is his term for what is more standardly referred to as "rule utilitarianism."

> [3] Moore's view was (a) that "good" is an indefinable term standing for an immediately recognizable quality that is possessed by many things besides pleasure or happiness (such as knowledge); and (b) that the right action is the one that produces the maximal amount of total goodness.

The issue between extreme and restricted utilitarianism can be illustrated by considering the remark 'But suppose everyone did the same.' . . . To say that you ought not to do an action A because it would have bad results if everyone (or many people) did action A

---

④ For an act utilitarian, the utility that would result if other people acted in the same way as the action being evaluated is relevant only to the extent that the action in question will lead or tend to lead to others acting in the same way, where the results of those other, similar actions will then be part of the results of the original action. (Rarely if ever would one action result in everyone acting in that way or anything very close to that, making it at least misleading to speak of "the causal form" of "the universalization principle.")

⑤ For a rule utilitarian, in contrast to an act utilitarian, the assessment of the action depends essentially on the assessment of the results of *everyone* acting that way, that is, of everyone following a rule requiring such an action—independently of any question of whether one action of that sort would tend to causally produce others. (Since the results of everyone acting in the way in question would depend on what other rules people also follow, it is better, as discussed in the Introduction to this chapter, to think in terms of the consequences of everyone following a comprehensive set of rules. An action is then morally correct if it is sanctioned by a rule in the set that leads to the maximum of utility.)

may be merely to point out that while the action A would otherwise be the optimific one, nevertheless when you take into account that doing A will probably cause other people to do A too, you can see that A is not, on a broad view, really optimific. If this causal influence could be avoided (as may happen in the case of a secret desert island promise) then we would disregard the universalisation principle. This is the causal form of the principle.④ A person who accepted the universalisation principle in its hypothetical form would be one who was concerned only with what would happen *if* everyone did the action A: he would be totally unconcerned with the question of whether in fact everyone would do the action A. That is, he might say that it would be wrong not to vote because it would have bad results if everyone took this attitude, and he would be totally unmoved by arguments purporting to show that my refusing to vote has no effect whatever on other people's propensity to vote. Making use of [this] distinction, we can say that an extreme utilitarian would apply the universalisation principle in the causal form, while a restricted utilitarian would apply it in the hypothetical form.⑤

How are we to decide the issue between extreme and restricted utilitarianism? I wish to repudiate at the outset that milk and water approach which describes itself sometimes as 'investigating what is implicit in the common moral consciousness' and sometimes as 'investigating how people ordinarily talk about morality.' We have only to read the newspaper correspondence about capital punishment or about what should be done with Formosa [Taiwan] to realise that the common moral consciousness is in part made up of superstitious elements, of morally bad elements, and of logically confused elements. I address myself to good hearted and benevolent people and so I hope that if we rid ourselves of the logical confusion the superstitious and morally bad elements will largely fall away. For even among good hearted and benevolent people it is possible to find superstitious and morally bad reasons for moral beliefs. These superstitious and morally bad reasons hide behind the protective screen of logical confusion. With people who are not logically confused but who are openly superstitious or morally bad I can of course do nothing. That is, our ultimate pro-attitudes may be different. Nevertheless I propose to rely on *my own* moral consciousness and to appeal to *your* moral consciousness and to forget about what people ordinarily say. . . .

II

For an extreme utilitarian moral rules are rules of thumb. In practice the extreme utilitarian will mostly guide his conduct by appealing to the rules ('do not lie,' 'do not break promises,' etc.) of common sense morality. This is not because there is anything sacrosanct in the rules themselves but because he can argue that probably he will most often act in an extreme utilitarian way if he does not think as a utilitarian. For one thing, actions have frequently to be done in a hurry. Imagine a man seeing a person drowning. He jumps in and rescues him. There is no time to reason the matter out, but usually this will be the course of action which an extreme utilitarian would recommend if he did reason the matter out. If, however, the man drowning had been drowning in a river near Berchtesgaden in 1938, and if he had had the well known black forelock and moustache of Adolf Hitler, an extreme utilitarian would, if he had time, work out the probability of the man's being the villainous dictator, and if the probability were high enough he would, on extreme utilitarian grounds, leave him to drown. The rescuer, however, has not time. He trusts to his instincts and dives in and rescues the man. And this trusting to instincts and to moral rules can be justified on extreme utilitarian grounds.[6] Furthermore, an extreme utilitarian who knew that the drowning man was Hitler would nevertheless praise the rescuer, not condemn him. For by praising the man he is strengthening a courageous and benevolent disposition of mind, and in general this disposition has great positive utility. (Next time, perhaps, it will be Winston Churchill that the man saves!) We must never forget that an extreme utilitarian may praise actions which he knows to be wrong. Saving Hitler was wrong, but it was a member of a class of actions which are generally right, and the motive to do actions of this class is in general an optimific one. In considering questions of praise and blame it is not the expediency of the praised or blamed action that is at issue, but the expediency of the praise. It can be expedient to praise an inexpedient action and inexpedient to praise an expedient one.[7]

Lack of time is not the only reason why an extreme utilitarian may, on extreme utilitarian principles, trust to rules of common sense morality. He knows that in particular cases where his own interests are involved his calculations are likely to be biased in his own favour. Suppose that he is unhappily married

and is deciding whether to get divorced. He will in all probability greatly exaggerate his own unhappiness (and possibly his wife's) and greatly underestimate the harm done to his children by the break up of the family. He will probably also underestimate the likely harm done by the weakening of the general faith in marriage vows. So probably he will come to the correct extreme utilitarian conclusion if he does not in this instance think as an extreme utilitarian but trusts to common sense morality.[8]

There are many more and subtle points that could be made in connection with the relation between extreme utilitarianism and the morality of common sense. . . . One further point raised by Sidgwick in this connection is whether an (extreme) utilitarian ought on (extreme) utilitarian principles to propagate (extreme) utilitarianism among the public. As most people are not very philosophical and not good at empirical calculations, it is probable that they will most often act in an extreme utilitarian way if they do not try to think as extreme utilitarians.[9] We have seen how easy it would be to misapply the extreme utilitarian criterion in the case of divorce. Sidgwick seems to think it quite probable that an extreme utilitarian should not propagate his doctrine too widely. However, the great danger to humanity comes nowadays on the plane of public morality—not private morality. There is a greater danger to humanity from the hydrogen bomb than from an increase of the divorce rate, regrettable though that might be, and there seems no doubt

---

[6] As noted by both Bentham and Mill, maximal utility is very unlikely to be achieved by doing a full utilitarian calculation for every action. One reason is that there is often not enough time (or enough information). Thus adopting and generally following "rules of thumb" (those such that following them will produce more utility than other rules or sets of rules of the same kind) is itself a choice that will be sanctioned by the act utilitarian principle—even though it is bound to lead to less than optimal results and perhaps even very bad results in some cases.

[7] This is a subtle point. Praising an action is itself an action and therefore should be assessed on utilitarian grounds. This leads to the result that we should praise (or blame), not the actions that are in themselves right (or wrong) in terms of utility, but rather those actions the praising (or blaming) of which will produce the most utility—which will normally be those that follow from the rules of thumb that are most conducive to utility.

[8] Another reason for relying on rules of thumb is that personal bias (or perhaps other, similar sorts of problems) is likely to lead to an incorrect utilitarian calculation. (Notice that Smart is assuming that the rules of "common sense morality" are in fact those that will tend to produce the greatest utility if used in this way—something that is not clearly or obviously correct.)

[9] Here is another tricky question: should the act utilitarian try to convince people in general that act utilitarianism is correct: that is, try to convince them to believe what he thinks is true? Since this is just another action to be assessed, according to act utilitarianism, in the same way, it follows that the act utilitarian should do this only if it produces the best results in terms of utility—which might very well not be the case if people are not very good at the relevant sorts of calculations.

that extreme utilitarianism makes for good sense in international relations. . . . I myself have no hesitation in saying that on extreme utilitarian principles we ought to propagate extreme utilitarianism as widely as possible. But Sidgwick had respectable reasons for suspecting the opposite.

The extreme utilitarian, then, regards moral rules as rules of thumb and as sociological facts that have to be taken into account when deciding what to do, just as facts of any other sort have to be taken into account. But in themselves they do not justify any action.

III

The restricted utilitarian regards moral rules as more than rules of thumb for short-circuiting calculations of consequences. Generally, he argues, consequences are not relevant at all when we are deciding what to do in a particular case. In general, they are relevant only to deciding what rules are good reasons for acting in a certain way in particular cases. This doctrine is possibly a good account of how the modern unreflective twentieth century Englishman often thinks about morality, but surely it is monstrous as an account of how it is most rational to think about morality. Suppose that there is a rule R and that in 99% of cases the best possible results are obtained by acting in accordance with R. Then clearly R is a useful rule of thumb; if we have not time or are not impartial enough to assess the consequences of an action it is an extremely good bet that the thing to do is to act in accordance with R. But is it not monstrous to suppose that if we *have* worked out the consequences and if we have perfect faith in the impartiality of our calculations, and if we *know* that in this instance to break R will have better results than to keep it, we should nevertheless obey the rule? Is it not to erect R into a sort of idol if we keep it when breaking it will prevent, say, some avoidable misery? Is not this a form of superstitious rule-worship (easily explicable psychologically) and not the rational thought of a philosopher? ⑩

The point may be made more clearly if we consider Mill's comparison of moral rules to the tables in the nautical almanac. . . . This comparison of Mill's is adduced by Urmson as evidence that Mill was a restricted utilitarian, but I do not think that it will bear this interpretation at all. (Though I quite agree with Urmson that many other things said by Mill are in har-

mony with restricted rather than extreme utilitarianism. Probably Mill had never thought very much about the distinction and was arguing for utilitarianism, restricted or extreme, against other and quite non-utilitarian forms of moral argument.) Mill says: 'Nobody argues that the art of navigation is not founded on astronomy, because sailors cannot wait to calculate the Nautical Almanack. Being rational creatures, they go out upon the sea of life with their minds made up on the common questions of right and wrong, as well as on many of the far more difficult questions of wise and foolish. . . . Whatever we adopt as the fundamental principle of morality, we require subordinate principles to apply it by.' Notice that this is, as it stands, only an argument for subordinate principles as rules of thumb. The example of the nautical almanack is misleading because the information given in the almanack is in all cases the same as the information one would get if one made a long and laborious calculation from the original astronomical data on which the almanack is founded. Suppose, however, that astronomy were different. Suppose that the behaviour of the sun, moon and planets was very nearly as it is now, but that on rare occasions there were peculiar irregularities and discontinuities, so that the almanack gave us rules of the form 'in 99% of cases where the observations are such and such you can deduce that your position is so and so.' Furthermore, let us suppose that there were methods which enabled us, by direct and laborious calculation from the original astronomical data, not using the rough and ready tables of the almanack, to get our correct position in 100% of cases. Seafarers might use the almanack because they never had time for the long calculations and they were content with a 99% chance of success in calculating their positions. Would it not be absurd, however, if they *did* make the direct calculation, and

⑩ Here is the fundamental problem for rule utilitarianism: why should a given rule be followed even when the person is completely sure that doing something else will lead to greater utility? That rule is, we are assuming, one that produces maximal results in terms of utility when generally followed (or a member of a comprehensive set of rules that has this feature), but why does that matter if following it will not produce the best results in the case actually in question? (As Smart proceeds to argue, Mill's navigational example does not support such a result.)

finding that it disagreed with the almanack calculation, nevertheless they ignored it and stuck to the almanack conclusion? Of course the case would be altered if there were a high enough probability of making slips in the direct calculation: then we might stick to the almanack result, liable to error though we knew it to be, simply because the direct calculation would be open to error for a different reason, the fallibility of the computer. This would be analogous to the case of the extreme utilitarian who abides by the conventional rule against the dictates of his utilitarian calculations simply because he thinks that his calculations are probably affected by personal bias. But if the navigator were sure of his direct calculations would he not be foolish to abide by his almanack? I conclude, then, that if we change our suppositions about astronomy and the almanack (to which there are no exceptions) to bring the case into line with that of morality (to whose rules there are exceptions), Mill's example loses its appearance of supporting the restricted form of utilitarianism. Let me say once more that I am not here concerned with how ordinary men think about morality but with how they ought to think. We could quite well imagine a race of sailors who acquired a superstitious reverence for their almanack, even though it was only right in 99% of cases, and who indignantly threw overboard any man who mentioned the possibility of a direct calculation. But would this behaviour of the sailors be rational?

Let us consider a much discussed sort of case in which the extreme utilitarian might go against the conventional moral rule. I have promised to a friend, dying on a desert island from which I am subsequently rescued, that I will see that his fortune (over which I have control) is given to a jockey club. However, when I am rescued I decide that it would be better to give the money to a hospital, which can do more good with it. It may be argued that I am wrong to give the money to the hospital. But why? (*a*) The hospital can do more good with the money than the jockey club can. (*b*) The present case is unlike most cases of promising in that no one except me knows about the promise. In breaking the promise I am doing so with complete secrecy and am doing nothing to weaken the general faith in promises. That is, a factor, which would normally keep the extreme utilitarian from promise breaking even in otherwise unoptimific cases, does not at present operate. (*c*) There is no doubt a slight weakening in my own character as an habitual promise keeper, and moreover psychological tensions will be set up in me every time I am asked what the man made me promise him to do. For clearly I shall have to say that he made me promise to give the money to the hospital, and, since I am an habitual truth teller, this will go very much against the grain with me.⑪ Indeed I am pretty sure that in practice I myself would keep the promise. But we are not discussing what my moral habits would probably make me do; we are discussing what I ought to do. Moreover, we must not forget that even if it would be most rational of me to give the money to the hospital it would also be most rational of you to punish or condemn me if you did, most improbably, find out the truth (e.g. by finding a note washed ashore in a bottle). Furthermore, I would agree that though it was most rational of me to give the money to the hospital it would be most rational of you to condemn me for it. We revert again to Sidgwick's distinction between the utility of the action and the utility of the praise of it.⑫

... It will be useful ... to consider one other example. ... Suppose that during hot weather there is an edict that no water must be used for watering gardens. I have a garden and I reason that most people are sure to obey the edict, and that as the amount of water that I use will be by itself negligible no harm will be done if I use the water secretly. So I do use the water,

⑪ Here are two further, closely related things that the act utilitarian can appeal to in trying to show that his view does not conflict with our considered moral convictions in cases like this one: first, the effects of breaking the promise on the agent's moral character (because it will, as a matter of psychological fact, make it easier for him to break promises in other cases, even where such an action does not produce greater utility); and, second, the disutility resulting from the psychological conflict and discomfort experienced by the agent.

⑫ Smart seems to suggest that the right action in the case as described is to break the promise. But it does not follow (see Annotation 7 and the corresponding passage) that the person should not be condemned (or even punished) if he is caught doing this—once again the choice of whether to praise or condemn or neither (as well as the choice whether or reward or punish or neither) are separate choices, themselves to be assessed in the same utilitarian way.

thus producing some lovely flowers which give happiness to various people. Still, you may say, though the action was perhaps optimific, it was unfair and wrong.⑬

13 A rule utilitarian might say that because the rule of obeying such edicts produces maximal results when followed (or is a member of a set that produces maximal results when followed), the edict ought to be obeyed even in a case where doing so does not maximize utility. This is one way to try to allow for fairness or justice within a broadly utilitarian view.

There are several matters to consider. Certainly my action should be condemned. We revert once more to Sidgwick's distinction. A right action may be rationally condemned. Furthermore, this sort of offence is normally found out. If I have a wonderful garden when everybody else's is dry and brown there is only one explanation. So if I water my garden I am weakening my respect for law and order, and as this leads to bad results an extreme utilitarian would agree that I was wrong to water the garden. Suppose now that the case is altered and that I can keep the thing secret: there is a secluded part of the garden where I grow flowers which I give away anonymously to a home for old ladies. Are you still so sure that I did the wrong thing by watering my garden? However, this is still a weaker case than that of the hospital and the jockey club. There will be tensions set up within myself: my secret knowledge that I have broken the rule will make it hard for me to exhort others to keep the rule. These psychological ill effects in myself may be not inconsiderable: directly and indirectly they may lead to harm which is at least of the same order as the happiness that the old ladies get from the flowers. You can see that on an extreme utilitarian view there are two sides to the question.⑭

14 That is, for an act utilitarian, the case could go either way, depending on the details with regard to these various matters. Whereas for a rule utilitarian, it might be that there is no uncertainty at all (if the optimal rule or set of rules says to always follow such edicts). Smart is suggesting that the right result does in fact depend on these uncertain details, so that the rule utilitarian view on which the issue is clear is itself mistaken.

. . .

I now pass on to a type of case which may be thought to be the trump card of restricted utilitarianism. Consider the rule of the road. It may be said that since all that matters is that everyone should do the same it is indifferent which rule we have, 'go on the left hand side' or 'go on the right hand side.' Hence the only *reason* for going on the left hand side in British countries is that this is the rule. Here the rule does seem to be a reason, in itself, for acting in a certain way. I wish to argue against this. The rule in itself is not a reason for our actions. We would be perfectly justified in going on the right hand side if (*a*) we knew that the rule was to go on the left hand side, and (*b*) we were in a country peopled by super-anarchists who always on principle did the opposite of what they were told. This shows that the rule does not give us a reason for acting so much as an indication of the probable actions of others, which helps us to find out what would be our own most rational course of action. If we are in a country not peopled by anarchists, but by non-anarchist extreme Utilitarians, we expect, other things being equal, that they will keep rules laid down for them. Knowledge of the rule enables us to predict their behaviour and to harmonise our own actions with theirs. The rule 'keep to the left hand side,' then, is not a logical *reason* for action but an anthropological *datum* for planning actions.⑮

15 Obviously "keep to the left hand side" is not itself a moral rule.

I conclude that in every case if there is a rule R the keeping of which is in general optimific, but such that in a special sort of circumstances the optimific behaviour is to break R, then in these circumstances we should break R. Of course we must consider all the less obvious effects of breaking R, such as reducing people's faith in the moral order, before coming to the conclusion that to break R is right: in fact we shall rarely come to such a conclusion. Moral rules, on the extreme utilitarian view, are rules of thumb only, but they are not bad rules of thumb. But if we *do* come to the conclusion that we should break the rule and if we have weighed in the balance our own fallibility and liability to personal bias, what good reason remains for keeping the rule? I can understand 'it is optimific' as a reason for action, but why should 'it is a member of a class of actions which are usually optimific' or 'it is a member of a class of actions which as a class are more optimific than any alternative general class' be a good reason? . . .

Discussion Questions

1. Consider again the case of the broken promise formulated by Smart at Annotation 11. (a) According to your considered moral convictions, what is the right choice to make in this case? (b) What does the act utilitarian view say is the right result? This will require assessing all the relevant results in terms of utility, including those mentioned in Annotation 11. Does this case constitute a serious objection to act utilitarianism? Does it constitute a good argument for rule utilitarianism?

2. Here is another fairly standard sort of problem case for act utilitarianism: Suppose that a series of horrible, apparently racially motivated murders of members of a minority group have been committed in some city, and the police are unable to catch the person or persons responsible. Tensions are rising, and there is a serious threat of riots and open conflict between the minority group and the larger majority group. You are the detective in charge of the case, and are in a position to successfully frame an innocent member of the majority group for some of the murders. Moreover, this person has no family, no regular job, and contributes little to the community. Should you frame this person, bringing about their conviction and eventual execution for the crimes in question, thereby relieving much of the tension and also perhaps deterring people on both sides who might otherwise be motivated to commit further murders or engage in other sorts of violence?

   a. What would an act utilitarian like Smart say about such a case, considering all of the relevant factors, and remembering that framing the innocent person is an action to be assessed entirely in terms of its consequences, according to act utilitarianism? (Fill in further details of the case or consider different alternatives if you need to.)

   b. What might a rule utilitarian say about this case?

3. One problem with rule utilitarianism, not mentioned by Smart, is the possibility of more complicated rules, specifying exceptions to the main rule where they lead to increased utility. Thus one might have a rule that says to keep promises unless breaking them can be done in secret and with increased utility; or a rule that says that innocent people should not be punished unless they can be successfully framed (so that everyone thinks they are guilty), and increased utility again results. If such rules are allowable, then rule utilitarianism does not really succeed in avoiding these standard problems for utilitarianism. Is there any reason a rule utilitarian can give for excluding rules of this sort? Indeed, is there any reason for excluding the principle of utility itself as the relevant rule (understanding that this will lead to frequent reliance on rules of thumb in the way that Smart discusses)? (If this is an acceptable rule, then there may well turn out to be no real difference at all between act and rule utilitarianism.)

Bernard Williams

Bernard Williams (1929–2003) was a British philosopher who taught mainly at Cambridge University. Williams made important contributions to many areas of philosophy, most importantly to ethics, where his subtle criticisms of both utilitarianism and Kantianism reflect a distinctively skeptical temperament. In the following selection from his most influential discussion of utilitarianism, Williams poses two widely discussed problem cases and argues, among other things, that utilitarianism fails to give adequate weight to a person's own individual projects and commitments.

A Critique of Utilitarianism

NEGATIVE RESPONSIBILITY: AND TWO EXAMPLES

Although I have defined a state of affairs being *accessible* to an agent in terms of the actions which are *available* to him, nevertheless it is the former notion which is really more important for consequentialism.① Consequentialism is basically indifferent to whether a state of affairs consists in what I do, or is produced by what I do, where that notion is itself wide enough to include, for instance, situations in which other people do things which I have made them do, or allowed them to do, or encouraged them to do, or given them a chance to do. All that consequentialism is interested in is the idea of these doings being *consequences* of what I do, and that is a relation broad enough to include the relations just mentioned, and many others.

. . . There are certain situations in which the causation of the situation, the relation it has to what I do, is in no way remote or problematic in itself, and entirely justifies the claim that the situation is a consequence of what I do: for instance, it is quite clear, or reasonably clear, that if I do a certain thing, this situation will come about, and if I do not, it will not. So from a consequentialist point of view it goes into the calculation of consequences along with any other state of affairs accessible to me. Yet from some, at least, non-consequentialist points of view, there is a vital difference between some such situations and others: namely, that in some a vital link in the production of the eventual outcome is provided by *someone else's* doing something. But for consequentialism, all causal connexions are on the same level, and it makes no difference, so far as that goes, whether the causation of a

> ① Consequentialism is the more general view of which utilitarianism is the most important species: the view that the morally best action is the one that produces the best total consequences.

From Utilitarianism: For and Against, *by J. J. C. Smart and Bernard Williams (Cambridge: Cambridge University Press, 1973).*

given state of affairs lies through another agent, or not.②

. . . It is because consequentialism attaches value ultimately to states of affairs, and its concern is with what states of affairs the world contains, that it essentially involves the notion of *negative responsibility:* that if I am ever responsible for anything, then I must be just as much responsible for things that I allow or fail to prevent, as I am for things that I myself, in the more everyday restricted sense, bring about. Those things also must enter my deliberations, as a responsible moral agent, on the same footing. What matters is what states of affairs the world contains, and so what matters with respect to a given action is what comes about if it is done, and what comes about if it is not done, and those are questions not intrinsically affected by the nature of the causal linkage, in particular by whether the outcome is partly produced by other agents.

The strong doctrine of negative responsibility flows directly from consequentialism's assignment of ultimate value to states of affairs. Looked at from another point of view, it can be seen also as a special application of something that is favoured in many moral outlooks not themselves consequentialist—something which, indeed, some thinkers have been disposed to regard as the essence of morality itself: a principle of impartiality. Such a principle will claim that there can be no relevant difference from a moral point of view which consists just in the fact, not further explicable in general terms, that benefits or harms accrue to one person rather than to another—'it's me' can never in itself be a morally comprehensible reason. This principle, familiar with regard to the reception of harms and benefits, we can see consequentialism as extending to their production: from the moral point of view, there is no comprehensible difference which consists just in my bringing about a certain outcome rather than someone else's producing it. . . .

> ② Thus, for example, if someone else deliberately harms another person in a way that I could have prevented, then the resulting harm is just as much a consequence of my action (or inaction) as harm that I deliberately produce myself.

... Now, ... let us look more concretely at two examples, to see what utilitarianism might say about them, what we might say about utilitarianism and, most importantly of all, what would be implied by certain ways of thinking about the situations. ...

(1)   George, who has just taken his Ph.D. in chemistry, finds it extremely difficult to get a job. He is not very robust in health, which cuts down the number of jobs he might be able to do satisfactorily. His wife has to go out to work to keep them, which itself causes a great deal of strain, since they have small children and there are severe problems about looking after them. The results of all this, especially on the children, are damaging. An older chemist, who knows about this situation, says that he can get George a decently paid job in a certain laboratory, which pursues research into chemical and biological warfare. George says that he cannot accept this, since he is opposed to chemical and biological warfare. The older man replies that he is not too keen on it himself, come to that, but after all George's refusal is not going to make the job or the laboratory go away; what is more, he happens to know that if George refuses the job, it will certainly go to a contemporary of George's who is not inhibited by any such scruples and is likely if appointed to push along the research with greater zeal than George would. Indeed, it is not merely concern for George and his family, but (to speak frankly and in confidence) some alarm about this other man's excess of zeal, which has led the older man to offer to use his influence to get George the job ... George's wife, to whom he is deeply attached, has views (the details of which need not concern us) from which it follows that at least there is nothing particularly wrong with research into CBW. What should he do?

(2)   Jim finds himself in the central square of a small South American town. Tied up against the wall are a row of twenty Indians, most terrified, a few defiant, in front of them several armed men in uniform. A heavy man in a sweat-stained khaki shirt turns out to be the captain in charge and, after a good deal of questioning of Jim which establishes that he got there by accident while on a botanical expedition, explains that the Indians are a random group of the inhabitants who, after recent acts of protest against the government, are just about to be killed to remind other possible protes-

tors of the advantages of not protesting. However, since Jim is an honoured visitor from another land, the captain is happy to offer him a guest's privilege of killing one of the Indians himself. If Jim accepts, then as a special mark of the occasion, the other Indians will be let off. Of course, if Jim refuses, then there is no special occasion, and Pedro here will do what he was about to do when Jim arrived, and kill them all. Jim, with some desperate recollection of schoolboy fiction, wonders whether if he got hold of a gun, he could hold the captain, Pedro and the rest of the soldiers to threat, but it is quite clear from the set-up that nothing of that kind is going to work: any attempt at that sort of thing will mean that all the Indians will be killed, and himself. The men against the wall, and the other villagers, understand the situation, and are obviously begging him to accept. What should he do?③

③ Williams's whole discussion focuses on these two examples. You should try to decide, before reading further, (a) what the right action is in each case, and (b) what you think a utilitarian would say about them. (Williams has mainly act utilitarianism in mind, but you can think about whether some version of rule utilitarianism might yield a different result.)

To these dilemmas, it seems to me that utilitarianism replies, in the first case, that George should accept the job, and in the second, that Jim should kill the Indian. Not only does utilitarianism give these answers but, if the situations are essentially as described and there are no further special factors, it regards them, it seems to me, as *obviously* the right answers.④ But many of us would certainly wonder whether, in (1), that could possibly be the right answer at all; and in the case of (2), even one who came to think that perhaps that was the answer, might well wonder whether it was obviously the answer. Nor is it just a question of the rightness or obviousness of these answers. It is also a question of what sort of considerations come into finding the answer. A feature of utilitarianism is that it cuts out a kind of consideration which for some others makes a difference to what they feel about such cases: a consideration involving the idea, as we might first and very simply put it, that each of us is specially responsible for what *he* does, rather

④ Be sure you understand clearly why this is so.

than for what other people do.⑤ This is an idea closely connected with the value of integrity. It is

⑤ Here is a basic anti-consequentialist and anti-utilitarian idea: that the morality of a person's action depends primarily on what he or she actually does—the specific kind of action performed (and the consequences that result directly from that without any intervention from other persons)—and much less on other consequences that the action leads to as a result of the actions of others. (See the following selection from Kant for a version of such a view.)

often suspected that utilitarianism, at least in its direct forms, makes integrity as a value more or less unintelligible. I shall try to show that this suspicion is correct. Of course, even if that is correct, it would not necessarily follow that we should reject utilitarianism; perhaps, as utilitarians sometimes suggest, we should just forget about integrity, in favour of such things as a concern for the general good. However, if I am right, we cannot

merely do that, since the reason why utilitarianism cannot understand integrity is that it cannot coherently describe the relations between a man's projects and his actions.

TWO KINDS OF REMOTER EFFECT

A lot of what we have to say about this question will be about the relations between my projects and

⑥ By "projects," Williams means a person's ends or goals or purposes, especially those to which more importance is attached, that are broader in scope, and that persist over a long period of time.

other people's projects.⑥ But before we get on to that, we should first ask whether we are assuming too hastily what the utilitarian answers to the dilemmas will be. In terms of more direct effects of the possible decisions, there

does not indeed seem much doubt about the answer in either case; but it might be said that in terms of more remote or less evident effects counterweights might be found to enter the utilitarian scales. Thus the effect on George of a decision to take the job might be invoked, or its effect on others who might know of his decision. The possibility of there being more beneficent labours in the future from which he might be barred or disqualified, might be mentioned; and so forth. Such effects—in particular, possible effects on the agent's character, and effects on the public at large—are often

invoked by utilitarian writers dealing with problems about lying or promise-breaking, and some similar considerations might be invoked here.

There is one very general remark that is worth making about arguments of this sort. The certainty that attaches to these hypotheses about possible effects is usually pretty low; in some cases, indeed, the hypothesis invoked is so implausible that it would scarcely pass if it were not being used to deliver the respectable moral answer, as in the standard fantasy that one of the effects of one's telling a particular lie is to weaken the disposition of the world at large to tell the truth. The demands on the certainty or probability of these beliefs as beliefs about particular actions are much milder than they would be on beliefs favouring the unconventional course.⑦ . . .

⑦ The point is that the likelihood of these further sorts of remote consequences is rarely great enough to make it plausible that taking note of them will alter the overall utilitarian assessment.

Leaving aside that very general point, I want to consider now two types of effect that are often invoked by utilitarians, and which might be invoked in connexion with these imaginary cases. The attitude or tone involved in invoking these effects may sometimes seem peculiar; but that sort of peculiarity soon becomes familiar in utilitarian discussions, and indeed it can be something of an achievement to retain a sense of it.

First, there is the psychological effect on the agent. Our descriptions of these situations have not so far taken account of how George or Jim will be after they have taken the one course or the other; and it might be said that if they take the course which seemed at first the utilitarian one, the effects on them will be in fact bad enough and extensive enough to cancel out the initial utilitarian advantages of that course. Now there is one version of this effect in which, for a utilitarian, some confusion must be involved, namely that in which the agent feels bad, his subsequent conduct and relations are crippled and so on, *because he thinks that he has done the wrong thing*—for if the balance of outcomes was as it appeared to be *before* invoking this effect, then he has not (from the utilitarian point of view) done the wrong thing. So that version of the effect, for a rational and utilitarian agent, could not possibly make any difference to the assessment of right and wrong.⑧ However, perhaps he is not a thoroughly rational agent, and is disposed to have bad feelings, whichever he decided to do. Now such feelings, which are from a strictly utilitarian point of view irrational—nothing, a utilitarian can point out, is advanced by having them—cannot, consistently, have any great weight in a utilitarian calculation. I shall consider in a moment an argument to suggest that they should have no weight

⟦8⟧ There is no good reason for the person to be distressed if he has indeed, as utilitarianism claims, done the right thing. (And also, it might be added, no reason for his moral character to be affected in undesirable ways.)

at all in it. But short of that, the utilitarian could reasonably say that such feelings should not be encouraged, even if we accept their existence, and that to give them a lot of weight is to encourage them. Or, at the very best, even if they are straightforwardly and without any discount to be put into the calculation, their weight must be small: they are after all (and at best) one man's feelings.

That consideration might seem to have particular force in Jim's case. In George's case, his feelings represent a larger proportion of what is to be weighed, and are more commensurate in character with other items in the calculation. In Jim's case, however, his feelings might seem to be of very little weight compared with other things that are at stake. . . .

If, then, one is really going to regard one's feelings from a strictly utilitarian point of view, Jim should give very little weight at all to his; it seems almost indecent, in fact, once one has taken that point of view, to suppose that he should give any at all. . . .

The psychological effect on the agent was the first of two general effects considered by utilitarians, which had to be discussed. The second is in general a more substantial item, but it need not take so long, since it is both clearer and has little application to the present cases. This is the *precedent effect*. As Burke rightly emphasized, this effect can be important: that one morally *can* do what someone has actually done, is a psychologically effective principle, if not a deontically valid one. For the effect to operate, obviously some conditions must hold on the publicity of the act and on such things as the status of the agent . . . ; what these may be will vary evidently with circumstances.⟦9⟧

In order for the precedent effect to make a difference to a utilitarian calculation, it must be based upon a confusion. For suppose that there is an act which would be the best in the circumstances, except that doing it will encourage by precedent other people to do things which will not be the best things to do. Then the situation of those other people must be relevantly different from that of the original agent; if it were not, then in doing the same as what would be the best course for the original agent, they would necessarily do the best thing themselves. But if the situations are in this way relevantly different, it must be a confused perception which takes the first situation, and the agent's course in it, as an adequate precedent for the second.

⟦9⟧ By "the status of the agent," Williams means things such as whether the person in question is especially prominent or respected, since an action by a person who is especially conspicuous in these ways will be more likely to influence others. (To say that the principle "that one *can* do what someone has actually done" is not "deontically" valid is just to say that it does not reflect good moral reasoning: what another person has done can still be morally unacceptable, for him and for you.)

However, the fact that the precedent effect, if it really makes a difference, is in this sense based on a confusion, does not mean that it is not perfectly real, nor that it is to be discounted: social effects are by their nature confused in this sort of way. What it does emphasize is that calculations of the precedent effect have got to be realistic, involving considerations of how people are actually likely to be influenced. In the present examples, however, it is very implausible to think that the precedent effect could be invoked to make any difference to the calculation. Jim's case is extraordinary enough, and it is hard to imagine who the recipients of the effect might be supposed to be; while George is not in a sufficiently public situation or role for the question to arise in that form, and in any case one might suppose that the motivations of others on such an issue were quite likely to be fixed one way or another already.

No appeal, then, to these other effects is going to make a difference to what the utilitarian will decide about our examples. Let us now look more closely at the structure of those decisions.

INTEGRITY

The situations have in common that if the agent does not do a certain disagreeable thing, someone else will, and in Jim's situation at least the result, the state of affairs after the other man has acted, if he does, will be worse than after Jim has acted, if Jim does. The same, on a smaller scale, is true of George's case. I have already suggested that it is inherent in consequentialism that it offers a strong doctrine of negative responsibility: if I know that if I do X, O_1 will eventuate, and if I refrain from doing X, O_2 will, and that O_2 is worse than O_1, then I am responsible for O_2 if I refrain voluntarily from doing X. 'You could have prevented it', as will be said, and truly, to Jim, if he refuses, by the relatives of the other Indians. . . .

That may be enough for us to speak, in some sense, of Jim's responsibility for that outcome, if it occurs; but it is certainly not enough, it is worth noticing, for us to speak of Jim's *making* those things happen. For granted this way of their coming about, he could have made them happen only by making Pedro shoot, and there is no acceptable sense in which his refusal makes Pedro shoot. If the captain had said on Jim's refusal, 'you leave me with no alternative', he would have been lying, like most who use that phrase. While the deaths, and the killing, may be the outcome of Jim's refusal, it is misleading to think, in such a case, of Jim having an *effect* on the world through the medium (as it happens) of Pedro's acts; for this is to leave Pedro out of the picture in his essential role of one who has intentions and projects, projects for realizing which Jim's refusal would leave an opportunity.

⑩ It is Pedro, not Jim, who will have an effect on the world if he kills the prisoners.

Instead of thinking in terms of supposed effects of Jim's projects on Pedro, it is more revealing to think in terms of the effects of Pedro's projects on Jim's decision. This is the direction from which I want to criticize the notion of negative responsibility.

. . .

What projects does a utilitarian agent have? As a utilitarian, he has the general project of bringing about maximally desirable outcomes; how he is to do this at any given moment is a question of what causal levers, so to speak, are at that moment within reach. The desirable outcomes, however, do not just consist of agents carrying out *that* project; there must be other more basic or lower-order projects which he and other

agents have, and the desirable outcomes are going to consist, in part, of the maximally harmonious realization of those projects ('in part', because one component of a utilitarianly desirable outcome may be the occurrence of agreeable experiences which are not the satisfaction of anybody's projects). Unless there were first-order projects, the general utilitarian project would have nothing to work on, and would be vacuous. ⑪ What do the more basic or lower-order projects comprise? Many will be the obvious kinds of desires for things for oneself, one's family, one's friends, including basic necessities of life, and in more relaxed circumstances, objects of taste. Or there may be pursuits and interests of an intellectual, cultural or creative character. . . .

⑪ This point is closely related to Feinberg's distinction between two senses of pleasure (see pp. 576–7). Happiness in any meaningful sense corresponds to Feinberg's pleasure₂ and presupposes the existence of other sorts of desires and commitments besides just seeking happiness—what Williams refers to as projects. A particular agent might aim only at the maximal satisfaction of other people's projects, but that could not be everyone's only aim, for then there would be no more specific projects to be realized.

Beyond these, someone may have projects connected with his support of some cause: Zionism, for instance, or the abolition of chemical and biological warfare. Or there may be projects which flow from some more general disposition towards human conduct and character, such as a hatred of injustice, or of cruelty, or of killing.

. . . Utilitarianism would do well then to acknowledge the evident fact that among the things that make people happy is not only making other people happy, but being taken up or involved in any of a vast range of projects, or—if we waive the evangelical and moralizing associations of the word—commitments. One can be committed to such things as a person, a cause, an institution, a career, one's own genius, or the pursuit of danger.

Now none of these is itself the *pursuit of happiness:* by an exceedingly ancient platitude, it is not at all clear that there could be anything which was just that, or at least anything that had the slightest chance of being successful. Happiness, rather, requires being involved in, or at least content with, something else.*⑫ It is not impossible for utilitarianism to accept that point: it does not have to be saddled with a naïve and absurd philosophy of mind about the relation between desire and happiness. What it does have to say is that if such commitments are worth while, then pursuing the projects that flow from them, and realizing some of those projects, will make the person for whom they are worth while, happy. It may be that to claim that is still wrong: it may well be that a commitment can make sense to a man (can make sense of his life) without his supposing that it will make him *happy.* But that is not the present point; let us grant to utilitarianism that all worthwhile human projects must conduce, one way or another, to happiness. The point is that even if that is true, it does not follow, nor could it possibly be true, that those projects are themselves projects of pursuing happiness. One has to believe in, or at least want, or quite minimally, be content with, other things, for there to be anywhere that happiness can come from.

⑫ See Feinberg's discussion of Jones, the man who aims only at happiness (p. 575).

Utilitarianism, then, should be willing to agree that its general aim of maximizing happiness does not imply that what everyone is doing is just pursuing happiness. On the contrary, people have to be pursuing other things. What those other things may be, utilitarianism, sticking to its professed empirical stance, should be prepared just to find out. No doubt some possible projects it will want to discourage, on the grounds that their being pursued involves a negative balance of happiness to others: though even there, the unblinking accountant's eye of the strict utilitarian will have something to put in the positive column, the satisfactions of the destructive agent. Beyond that, there will be a vast variety of generally beneficent or at least harmless projects; and some no doubt, will take the form not just of tastes or fancies, but of what I have called 'commitments'. It may even be that the utilitarian researcher will find that many of those with commitments, who have really identified themselves with objects outside themselves, who are thoroughly involved with other persons, or institutions, or activities or causes, are actually happier than those whose projects and wants are not like that. If so, that is an important piece of utilitarian empirical lore.

. . .

Let us now go back to the agent as utilitarian, and his higher-order project of maximizing desirable outcomes. At this level, he is committed only to that: what the outcome will actually consist of will depend entirely on the facts, on what persons with what projects and what potential satisfactions there are within calculable reach of the causal levers near which he finds himself. His own substantial projects and commitments come into it, but only as one lot among others—they potentially provide one set of satisfactions among those which he may be able to assist from where he happens to be. He is the agent of the satisfaction system who happens to be at a particular point at a particular time: in Jim's case, our man in South America. His own decisions as a utilitarian agent are a function of all the satisfactions which he can affect from where he is: and this means that the projects of others, to an indeterminately great extent, determine his decision.

This may be so either positively or negatively. It will be so positively if agents within the causal field of his decision have projects which are at any rate harmless, and so should be assisted. It will equally be so, but negatively, if there is an agent within the causal field whose projects are harmful, and have to be frustrated to maximize desirable outcomes. So it is with Jim and the soldier Pedro. On the utilitarian view, the undesirable projects of other people as much determine, in this negative way, one's decisions as the desirable ones do positively: if those people were not there, or had different projects, the causal nexus would be different, and it is the actual state of the causal nexus which determines the decision. The determination to an indefinite degree of my decisions by other people's projects is just another aspect of my

---

*This does not imply that there is no such thing as the project of pursuing pleasure. Some writers who have correctly resisted the view that all desires are desires for pleasure, have given an account of pleasure so thoroughly adverbial as to leave it quite unclear how there could be a distinctively hedonist way of life at all. Some room has to be left for that, though there are important difficulties both in defining it and living it. Thus (particularly in the case of the very rich) it often has highly ritual aspects, apparently part of a strategy to counter boredom.

unlimited responsibility to act for the best in a causal framework formed to a considerable extent by their projects. ⑬

The decision so determined is, for utilitarianism, the right decision. But what if it conflicts with some project of mine? This, the utilitarian will say, has already been dealt with: the satisfaction to you of fulfilling your project, and any satisfactions to others of your so doing, have already been through the calculating device and have been found inadequate. Now in the case of many sorts of projects, that is a perfectly reasonable sort of answer. But in the case of projects of the sort I have called 'commitments', those with which one is more deeply and extensively involved and identified, this cannot just by itself be an adequate answer, and there may be no adequate answer at all. For, to take the extreme sort of case, how can a man, as a utilitarian agent, come to regard as one satisfaction among others, and a dispensable one, a project or attitude round which he has built his life, just because someone else's projects have so structured the causal scene that that is how the utilitarian sum comes out?

The point here is not, as utilitarians may hasten to say, that if the project or attitude is that central to his life, then to abandon it will be very disagreeable to him and great loss of utility will be involved. . . . The point is that he is identified with his actions as flowing from projects and attitudes which in some cases he takes seriously at the deepest level, as what his life is about (or, in some cases, this section of his life—seriousness is not necessarily the same as persistence). It is absurd to demand of such a man, when the sums come in from the utility network which the projects of others have in part determined, that he should just step aside from his own project and decision and acknowledge the decision which utilitarian calculation requires. It is to alienate him in a real sense from his actions and the source of his action in his own convictions. It is to make him into a channel between the input of everyone's projects, including

⑬ Though the utilitarian agent will in the normal case have projects and commitments of his own, these play no more role in the overall utilitarian calculation than any of the projects and commitments of others that he is in a position to affect either positively or negatively. How much weight his own projects will have depends on what those other projects and his relationship to them turn out to be.

his own, and an output of optimific decision; but this is to neglect the extent to which *his* actions and *his* decisions have to be seen as the actions and decisions which flow from the projects and attitudes with which he is most closely identified. It is thus, in the most literal sense, an attack on his integrity. ⑭

⑭ Thus even a person's deepest and most serious projects and commitments must, from a utilitarian point of view, be sacrificed if that is the way that the overall calculation comes out. Is this, as Williams claims, an *absurd* result that violates the person's *integrity?*

These sorts of considerations do not in themselves give solutions to practical dilemmas such as those provided by our examples; but I hope they help to provide other ways of thinking about them. In fact, it is not hard to see that in George's case, viewed from this perspective, the utilitarian solution would be wrong. Jim's case is different, and harder. But if (as I suppose) the utilitarian is probably right in this case, that is not to be found out just by asking the utilitarian's questions. Discussions of it—and I am not going to try to carry it further here—will have to take seriously the distinction between my killing someone, and its coming about because of what I do that someone else kills them: a distinction based, not so much on the distinction between action and inaction, as on the distinction between my projects and someone else's projects. At least it will have to start by taking that seriously, as utilitarianism does not; but then it will have to build out from there by asking why that distinction seems to have less, or a different, force in this case than it has in George's. One question here would be how far one's powerful objection to killing people just is, in fact, an application of a powerful objection to their being killed. Another dimension of that is the issue of how much it matters that the people at risk are actual, and there, as opposed to hypothetical, or future, or merely elsewhere. ⑮

There are many other considerations that could come into such a question, but the immediate point of all this is to draw one particular contrast with utili-

⑮ Think carefully about how looking at things from this other perspective is supposed to clearly lead to an opposite result in the case involving George. Is Williams right that it probably doesn't change the result in the case of Jim, and if so, why? (Think about the suggestions that he tentatively offers here.)

tarianism: that to reach a grounded decision in such a case should not be regarded as a matter of just discounting one's reactions, impulses and deeply held projects in the face of the pattern of utilities, nor yet merely adding them in—but in the first instance of trying to understand them.

Of course, time and circumstances are unlikely to make a grounded decision, in Jim's case at least, possible. It might not even be decent. Instead of thinking in a rational and systematic way either about utilities or about the value of human life, the relevance of the people at risk being present, and so forth, the presence of the people at risk may just have its effect. The significance of the immediate should not be underesti-

mated. Philosophers, not only utilitarian ones, repeatedly urge one to view the world *sub specie aeternitatis,* [16] but for most human purposes that is not a good *species* to view it under. If we are not agents of the universal satisfaction system, we are not primarily janitors of any system of values, even our own: very often, we just act, as a possibly confused result of the situation in which we are engaged. That, I suspect, is very often an exceedingly good thing. . . .

[16] Under the aspect of (or from the point of view of) eternity—essentially from a God's eye point of view. To adopt such a point of view is to abandon one's own distinctive point of view, as defined by one's own projects and commitments.

Discussion Questions

1. After considering the George and Jim cases and seeing what Williams says, what is the right action in each of the two main cases that he describes, and why? Does either case constitute a clear **counter-example** to utilitarianism?

2. Is utilitarianism an unreasonably demanding moral position? Is it reasonable to expect people to give no more weight to their own projects and commitments than to those of others—in Mill's words, to be strictly impartial between one's own happiness and that of anyone else? Think carefully about the implications that such a view would have in various situations.

DEONTOLOGICAL VIEWS: MORALITY DEPENDS ON DUTIES AND RIGHTS

Immanuel Kant

German philosopher Immanuel Kant (1724–1804) was one of the most important and influential philosophers of all time. Kant made major contributions to epistemology, metaphysics, ethics, the philosophy of religion, aesthetics, and many other areas. His central concern was to explain and vindicate the authority and autonomy of reason, both theoretical (pertaining to factual and especially scientific knowledge of the world) and practical (pertaining to action and morality).

In the following selection from the first of his major ethical works, Kant attempts to derive and defend what he regards as the fundamental principle of morality: the *categorical imperative.* The starting point is the idea that morality must not depend on any motive or goal that might not be shared by others, but must instead be valid for any rational being. Kant attempts to show in effect that this very requirement can by itself lead to the moral principle he is seeking. He offers several different formulations of this principle; these are supposed to amount to the same thing, but this is by no means obviously the case.

From *Foundations of The Metaphysics of Morals*

FIRST SECTION / TRANSITION FROM THE COMMON RATIONAL KNOWLEDGE OF MORALS TO THE PHILOSOPHICAL

Nothing in the world—indeed nothing even beyond the world—can possibly be conceived which could be called good without qualification except a *good will.*① Intelligence, wit, judgment, and the other talents of the mind, however they may be named, or courage, resoluteness,

> ① By a "good will," Kant means one that is motivated only by the demands of moral duty (not a will that is benevolent or generous, as the phrase is more standardly used).

and perseverance as qualities of temperament, are doubtless in many respects good and desirable. But they can become extremely bad and harmful if the will, which is to make use of these gifts of nature and which in its special constitution is called character, is not good. It is the same with the gifts of fortune. Power, riches, honor, even health, general well-being, and the contentment with one's condition which is called happiness, make for pride and even arrogance if there is not a good will to correct their influence on the mind and on its principles of action so as to make it universally conformable to its end.② It need hardly be mentioned that the sight of a being adorned with no feature of a pure and good will, yet enjoying uninterrupted prosperity, can never give pleasure to a rational impartial observer. Thus the good will seems to constitute the indispensable condition even of worthiness to be happy.

> ② All of these things can, in the absence of a good will, lead to actions and results that are morally bad.

Some qualities seem to be conducive to this good will and can facilitate its action, but, in spite of that, they have no intrinsic unconditional worth. They rather presuppose a good will, which limits the high esteem which one otherwise rightly has for them and prevents their being held to be absolutely good. Moderation in emotions and passions, self-control, and calm deliberation not only are good in many respects but even seem to constitute a part of the inner worth of the person. But however unconditionally they were esteemed by the ancients, they are far from being good without qualification. For without the principle of a good will they can become extremely bad, and the coolness of a villain makes him not only far more dangerous but also more directly abominable in our eyes than he would have seemed without it.③

> ③ Again, the point is that the various character traits in question can lead to moral badness or evil if not accompanied by a good will.

The good will is not good because of what it effects or accomplishes or because of its adequacy to achieve some proposed end; it is good only because of its willing, i.e., it is good of itself. And, regarded for itself, it is to be esteemed incomparably higher than anything which could be brought about by it in favor of any inclination or even of the sum total of all inclinations. Even if it should happen that, by a particularly unfortunate fate or by the niggardly provision of a step-motherly nature, this will should be wholly lacking in power to accomplish its purpose, and if even the greatest effort should not avail it to achieve anything of its end, and if there remained only the good will (not as a mere wish but as the summoning of all the means in our power), it would sparkle like a jewel in its own right, as something that had its full worth in itself. Usefulness or fruitlessness can neither diminish nor augment this worth. . . .

We have, then, to develop the concept of a will which is to be esteemed as good of itself without regard to anything else. It dwells already in the natural sound understanding and does not need so much to be taught as only to be brought to light. In the estimation of the total worth of our actions it always takes first place and is the condition of everything else. In order to show

---

From Kant: Foundations of the Metaphysics of Morals, *edited by Robert Paul Wolff (New York: The Bobbs-Merrill Company, Inc., 1969).*

this, we shall take the concept of duty. It contains that of a good will, though with certain subjective restrictions and hindrances; but these are far from concealing it and making it unrecognizable, for they rather bring it out by contrast and make it shine forth all the brighter.

I here omit all actions which are recognized as opposed to duty, even though they may be useful in one respect or another, for with these the question does not arise at all as to whether they may be carried out *from* duty, since they conflict with it. I also pass over the actions which are really in accordance with duty and to which one has no direct inclination, rather executing them because impelled to do so by another inclination. For it is easily decided whether an action in accord with duty is performed from duty or for some selfish purpose. It is far more difficult to note this difference when the action is in accordance with duty and, in addition, the subject has a direct inclination to do it. For example, it is in fact in accordance with duty that a dealer should not overcharge an inexperienced customer, and wherever there is much business the prudent merchant does not do so, having a fixed price for everyone, so that a child may buy of him as cheaply as any other. Thus the customer is honestly served. But this is far from sufficient to justify the belief that the merchant

has behaved in this way from duty and principles of honesty. His own advantage required this behavior; but it cannot be assumed that over and above that he had a direct inclination to the purchaser and that, out of love, as it were, he gave none an advantage in price over another. Therefore the action was done neither from duty nor from direct inclination but only for a selfish purpose.④

④ The shopkeeper's action conforms to the demands of moral duty (that is, the shopkeeper does what duty would require), but the action still has no moral worth if done only from the motive of self-interest. The shopkeeper has done the right thing for the wrong reason. (Contrary to what the wording of the last sentence might suggest, Kant is not saying that this must always be the case.)

. . .

To be kind where one can is duty, and there are, moreover, many persons so sympathetically constituted that without any motive of vanity or selfishness they find an inner satisfaction in spreading joy, and rejoice in the contentment of others which they have made possible. But I say that, however dutiful and ami-

able it may be, that kind of action has no true moral worth. It is on a level with [actions arising from] other inclinations, such as the inclination to honor, which, if fortunately directed to what in fact accords with duty and is generally useful and thus honorable, deserve praise and encouragement but no esteem. For the maxim⑤ lacks the moral import of an action done not from inclination but from duty. But assume that the mind of that friend to mankind was clouded by a sorrow of his own which extinguished all sympathy with the lot of others and that he still had the power to benefit others in dis-

⑤ The *maxim* is the practical principle that the agent is subjectively following: to do a certain sort of thing in a certain sort of situation for a certain sort of reason. In effect, it is a generalized version of the person's conscious intention in doing the action.

tress, but that their need left him untouched because he was preoccupied with his own need. And now suppose him to tear himself, unsolicited by inclination, out of this dead insensibility and to perform this action only from duty and without any inclination—then for the first time his action has genuine moral worth. Furthermore, if nature has put little sympathy in the heart of a man, and if he, though an honest man, is by temperament cold and indifferent to the sufferings of others, perhaps because he is provided with special gifts of patience and fortitude and expects or even requires that others should have the same—and such a man would certainly not be the meanest product of nature—would not he find in himself a source from which to give himself a far higher worth than he could have got by having a good-natured temperament? This is unquestionably true even though nature did not make him philanthropic, for it is just here that the worth of the character is brought out, which is morally and incomparably the highest of all: he is beneficent not from inclination but from duty.⑥

⑥ Persons who help or benefit others because they have a spontaneous inclination toward sympathy (or benevolence or generosity) are, like the shopkeeper, doing what they want to do and not acting out of duty; thus their actions, while worthy of praise and encouragement, have no real *moral* worth. The person worthy of moral esteem is the one who has no desire or inclination at all to help anyone, who "is by temperament cold and indifferent," but who helps others out of moral duty alone. (See Discussion Question 1.)

. . .

[Thus the first proposition of morality is that to have moral worth an action must be done from duty.] The second proposition is: An action performed from duty does not have its moral worth in the purpose which is to be achieved through it but in the maxim by which it is determined. Its moral value, therefore, does not depend on the realization of the object of the action but merely on the principle of volition by which the action is done without any regard to the objects of the faculty of desire. From the preceding discussion it is clear that the purposes we may have for our actions and their effects as ends and incentives of the will cannot give the actions any unconditional and moral worth. Wherein, then, can this worth lie, if it is not in the will in relation to its hoped-for effect? It can lie nowhere else than in the principle of the will, irrespective of the ends which can be realized by such action.⑦ . . .

| ⑦ Kant concludes that moral value must derive from a principle of action that does not depend on any purpose or goal toward which we may have an inclination. (This should be *very* puzzling at this point: how can such a principle have any definite content if not in relation to some purpose or goal?) |

The third principle, as a consequence of the two preceding, I would express as follows: Duty is the necessity of an action executed from respect for law. I can certainly have an inclination to the object as an effect of the proposed action, but I can never have respect for it precisely because it is a mere effect and not an activity of a will. Similarly, I can have no respect for any inclination whatsoever, whether my own or that of another; in the former case I can at most approve of it and in the latter I can even love it, i.e., see it as favorable to my own advantage. But that which . . . does not serve my inclination but overpowers it or at least excludes it from being considered in making a choice—in a word, law itself—can be an object of respect and thus a command. Now as an act from duty wholly excludes the influence of inclination and therewith every object of the will, nothing remains which can determine the will objectively except the law, and nothing subjectively except pure respect for this practical law. This subjective element is the maxim that I ought to follow such a law even if it thwarts all my inclinations.⑧

. . .

But what kind of a law can that be, the conception of which must determine the will without reference to the expected result? Under this condition alone the will can be called absolutely good without qualification. Since I have robbed the will of all impulses which could come to it from obedience to any law, nothing remains to serve as a principle of the will except universal conformity of its action to law as such. That is, I should never act in such a way that I could not also will that my maxim should be a universal law.⑨ Mere conformity to law as such (without assuming any particular law applicable to certain actions) serves as the principle of the will, and it must serve as such a principle if duty is not to be a vain delusion and chimerical concept. . . .

| ⑧ Thus a dutiful action must derive from respect for (moral) law, not from any specific inclinations that the person might happen to have. (Again, how does this moral or practical law come to have any specific content?) |

| ⑨ Lacking any specific purpose, the content of the moral law can only derive from the fact that it is supposed to be a *universal* law, a law that governs all rational beings. Thus the fundamental moral requirement (elaborated much further later on) is that the maxim of my action must be capable of being a universal law that a rational being can will to hold. (While this is a bit more specific, it is still unclear at this point how it will result in any definite content.) |

SECOND SECTION / TRANSITION FROM THE POPULAR MORAL PHILOSOPHY TO THE METAPHYSICS OF MORALS

. . .

Everything in nature works according to laws. Only a rational being has the capacity of acting according to the conception of laws, i.e., according to principles. This capacity is will. Since reason is required for the derivation of actions from laws, will is nothing else than practical reason.⑩ If reason infallibly determines the will, the actions which such a being recognizes as objectively necessary are also

| ⑩ That is, will is the faculty in us that derives practical results (actions) from the requirements of reason. |

subjectively necessary. That is, the will is a faculty of choosing only that which reason, independently of inclination, recognizes as practically necessary, i.e., as good. . . .

The conception of an objective principle so far as it constrains a will, is a command (of reason), and the formula of this command is called an *imperative.*

All imperatives are expressed by an "ought" and thereby indicate the relation of an objective law of reason to a will which is not in its subjective constitution necessarily determined by this law. This relation is that of constraint. Imperatives say that it would be good to do or to refrain from doing something, but they say it to a will which does not always do something simply because it is presented as a good thing to do. Practical good is what determines the will by means of the conception of reason and hence not by subjective causes but, rather, objectively, i.e., on grounds which are valid for every rational being as such. It is distinguished from the pleasant as that which has an influence on the will only by means of a sensation from merely subjective causes, which hold only for the senses of this or that person and not as a principle of reason which holds for everyone.[11]

⟦11⟧ An imperative, as a command of reason, holds for any rational being. When pleasure influences the will, this does not normally involve any command of reason and will vary from person to person, because different people find different things pleasant.

. . .

All imperatives command either hypothetically or categorically. The former present the practical necessity of a possible action as a means to achieving something else which one desires (or which one may possibly desire). The categorical imperative would be one which presented an action as of itself objectively necessary, without regard to any other end.[12]

Since every practical law presents a possible action as good and thus as necessary for a subject practically determinable by reason, all imperatives

⟦12⟧ Hypothetical imperatives depend on actual or possible desires (inclinations), while categorical imperatives do not. (Given the previous discussion, it follows that an imperative of morality must be categorical rather than hypothetical, because it cannot depend on any specific desire or inclination.)

are formulas of the determination of action which is necessary by the principle of a will which is in any way good. If the action is good only as a means to something else, the imperative is hypothetical; but if it is thought of as good in itself, and hence as necessary in a will which of itself conforms to reason as the principle of this will, the imperative is categorical.

The imperative thus says what action possible to me would be good, and it presents the practical rule in relation to a will which does not forthwith perform an action simply because it is good, in part because the subject does not always know that the action is good and in part (when he does know it) because his maxims can still be opposed to the objective principles of practical reason.

The hypothetical imperative, therefore, says only that the action is good to some purpose, possible or actual. In the former case it is a problematical, in the latter an assertorical, practical principle. The categorical imperative, which declares the action to be of itself objectively necessary without making any reference to a purpose, i.e., without having any other end, holds as an apodictical (practical) principle.[13]

We can think of that which is possible through the mere powers of some rational being as a possible purpose of any will. As a consequence, the principles of action, in so far as they are thought of as necessary to attain a possible purpose which can be achieved by them, are in reality infinitely numerous. . . .

There is one end, however, which we may presuppose as actual in all rational beings so far as imperatives apply to them, i.e., so far as they are dependent beings; there is one purpose not only which they *can* have but which we can presuppose that they all *do* have by a

⟦13⟧ A "problematical" practical principle says that a person should do some particular action *if* that person has the purpose or end to which that action is in fact a means. An "assertorical" practical principle says of a person who in fact does have a particular purpose or end that he definitely should do the action that is a means to that purpose or end. (This assumes that there is only one relevant means or one that is clearly better than any other.) An "apodictical" practical purpose says that some action (which may be the "action" of *not* doing some particular thing) should *necessarily* be done by any rational being, no matter what specific purposes or ends he may have.

necessity of nature. This purpose is happiness. The hypothetical imperative which represents the practical necessity of action as means to the promotion of happiness is an assertorical imperative. We may not expound it as merely necessary to an uncertain and a merely possible purpose, but as necessary to a purpose which we can a priori and with assurance assume for everyone because it belongs to his essence. Skill in the choice of means to one's own highest welfare can be called prudence in the narrowest sense. Thus the imperative which refers to the choice of means to one's own happiness, i.e., the precept of prudence, is still only hypothetical; the action is not absolutely commanded but commanded only as a means to another end.

Finally, there is one imperative which directly commands a certain conduct without making its condition some purpose to be reached by it. This imperative

14 Since there are no specific purposes or ends in question, a categorical imperative cannot concern the relation of the action to such an end. Kant concludes that it can only concern the *form* of the action: the general kind of action that it is. (But it is still not clear at this point what this means.)

is categorical. It concerns not the material of the action and its intended result but the form and the principle from which it results.**14** What is essentially good in it consists in the intention, the result being what it may. This imperative may be called the imperative of morality.

Volition according to these three principles is plainly distinguished by dissimilarity in the constraint to which they subject the will. In order to clarify this dissimilarity, I believe that they are most suitably named if one says that they are either rules of skill, counsels of prudence, or commands (laws) of morality, respectively. . . .

The question now arises: how are all these imperatives possible? This question does not require an answer as to how the action which the imperative commands can be performed but merely as to how the constraint of the will, which the imperative expresses in the problem, can be conceived. How an imperative of skill is possible requires no particular discussion. Whoever wills the end, so far as reason has decisive influence on his action, wills also the indispensably necessary means to it that lie in his power.**15** . . .

If it were only easy to give a definite concept of happiness, the imperatives of prudence would com-

pletely correspond to those of skill. . . . For it could be said in this case as well as in the former that whoever wills the end wills also (necessarily according to reason) the only means to it which are in his power. But it is a misfortune that the concept of happiness is so indefinite that, although each person wishes to attain it, he can never definitely and self-consistently state what it is he really wishes and wills.**16** . . .

To see how the imperative of morality is possible is, then, without doubt the only question needing an answer. It is not hypothetical, and thus the objectively conceived necessity cannot be supported by any presupposition, as was the case with the hypothetical imperatives. But it must not be overlooked that it cannot be shown by any example (i.e., it cannot be empirically shown) whether or not there is such an imperative. . . . we cannot show with certainty by any example that the will is here determined by the law alone without any other incentives, even though this appears to be the case. For it is always possible that secret fear of disgrace, and perhaps also obscure apprehension of other dangers, may have had an influence on the will. Who can prove by experience the nonexistence of a cause when experience shows us only that we do not perceive the cause? But in such a case the so-called moral imperative, which as such appears to be categorical and unconditional, would be actually only a pragmatic precept which makes us attentive to our own advantage and teaches us to consider it.**17**

Thus we shall have to investigate purely a priori the possibility of a categorical imperative, for we do not have the advantage

15 It would make no sense to will an end without willing an "indispensably necessary means," so any rational being that wills the end also wills the means—which is what a "rule of skill" (a problematical principle) says.

16 The analogous point holds for most "counsels of prudence" (assertorical principles). But for the key case where the goal is happiness, the uncertainty pertaining to both the nature of happiness and the means required to attain it make it quite possible for a rational being to will the end and fail to will the means—as we often discover later, to our regret.

17 The possibility of categorical imperatives cannot be established empirically by citing actual cases of actions where there is no specific end or purpose, since it is always possible that there is some underlying end (such as fear of disgrace) that even the agent in question is unaware of.

that experience would give us the reality of this imperative, so that the [demonstration of its] possibility would be necessary only for its explanation and not for its establishment. In the meantime, this much may at least be seen: the categorical imperative alone can be taken as a practical *law,* while all the others may be called principles of the will but not laws. This is because what is necessary merely for the attainment of an arbitrary purpose can be regarded as itself contingent, and we get rid of the precept once we give up the purpose, whereas the unconditional command leaves the will no freedom to choose the opposite. Thus it alone implies the necessity which we require of a law.

. . .

In attacking this problem, we will first inquire whether the mere concept of a categorical imperative does not also furnish the formula containing the proposition which alone can be a categorical imperative. . . . [18]

[18] Here is the key idea, already hinted at earlier (see Annotation 9 and the corresponding passage): the very idea of a *categorical* imperative, one not deriving from any specific end or purpose, will also determine the content of such an imperative.

If I think of a hypothetical imperative as such, I do not know what it will contain until the condition is stated [under which it is an imperative]. But if I think of a categorical imperative, I know immediately what it contains. For since the imperative contains besides the law only the necessity that the maxim* should accord with this law, while the law contains no condition to which it is restricted, there is nothing remaining in it except the universality of law as such to which the maxim of the action should conform; and in effect this conformity alone is represented as necessary by the imperative.

There is, therefore, only one categorical imperative. It is: Act only according to that maxim by which you can at the same time will that it should become a universal law. [19]

. . .

The universality of law according to which effects are produced constitutes what is properly called nature in the most general sense (as to form), i.e., the existence of things so far as it is determined by universal laws. [By analogy], then, the universal imperative of duty can be expressed as follows: Act as though the maxim of your action were by your will to become a universal law of nature.

We shall now enumerate some duties, adopting the usual division of them into duties to ourselves and to others and into perfect and imperfect duties. [20]

1. A man who is reduced to despair by a series of evils feels a weariness with life but is still in possession of his reason sufficiently to ask whether it would not be contrary to his duty to himself to take his own life. Now he asks whether the maxim of his action could become a universal law of nature. His maxim, however, is: For love of myself, I make it my principle to shorten my life when by a longer duration it threatens more evil than satisfaction. But it is questionable whether this principle of self-love could become a universal law of nature. One immediately sees a contradiction in a system of nature whose law would be to destroy life by the feeling whose special office is to impel the improvement of life. In this case it would not exist as nature; hence that maxim cannot obtain as a law of nature,

[19] According to the idea of the categorical imperative, the maxim of the action must conform to a universal law, one valid for all rational beings. Since there is no basis for any more specific content, the categorical imperative can say only that the maxim of one's action must be such as to make this possible: something that could be a universal law and could be willed by the agent to have this status. This is Kant's first formulation of the categorical imperative.

[20] A perfect duty is one that *strictly* requires certain specific actions, with no choice or leeway; an imperfect duty is one that can be fulfilled in several different ways, among which the agent may choose, and thus no one of which is strictly required.

*A maxim is the subjective principle of acting and must be distinguished form the objective principle, i.e., the practical law. The former contains the practical rule which reason determines according to the conditions of the subject (often its ignorance or inclinations) and is thus the principle according to which the subject acts. The law, on the other hand, is the objective principle valid for every rational being, and the principle by which it ought to act, i.e., an imperative.

and thus it wholly contradicts the supreme principle of all duty. [21]

[21] Kant's claim is that the maxim of this proposed action could not be a universal law because it is **contradictory** when made universal. But it is hard to see just what the contradiction is supposed to be. (See Discussion Question 2.)

2. Another man finds himself forced by need to borrow money. He well knows that he will not be able to repay it, but he also sees that nothing will be loaned him if he does not firmly promise to repay it at a certain time. He desires to make such a promise, but he has enough conscience to ask himself whether it is not improper and opposed to duty to relieve his distress in such a way. Now, assuming he does decide to do so, the maxim of his action would be as follows: When I believe myself to be in need of money, I will borrow money and promise to repay it, although I know I shall never do so. Now this principle of self-love or of his own benefit may very well be compatible with his whole future welfare, but the question is whether it is right. He changes the pretension of self-love into a universal law and then puts the question: How would it be if my maxim became a universal law? He immediately sees that it could never hold as a universal law of nature and be consistent with itself; rather it must necessarily contradict itself. For the universality of a law which says that anyone who believes himself to be in need could promise what he pleased with the intention of not fulfilling it would make the promise itself and the end to be accomplished by it impossible; no one would believe what was promised to him but would only laugh at any such assertion as vain pretense. [22]

[22] Here again the claim is that the maxim of the action becomes contradictory when made universal. This is a more plausible case in that there is a way in which the universalized maxim would (probably?) be self-defeating. But is it really *contradictory*? (See Discussion Question 2.)

3. A third finds in himself a talent which could, by means of some cultivation, make him in many respects a useful man. But he finds himself in comfortable circumstances and prefers indulgence in pleasure to troubling himself with broadening and improving his fortunate natural gifts. Now, however, let him ask whether his maxim of neglecting his gifts, besides agreeing with his propensity to idle amusement, agrees

also with what is called duty. He sees that a system of nature could indeed exist in accordance with such a law, even though man (like the inhabitants of the South Sea Islands) should let his talents rust and resolve to devote his life merely to idleness, indulgence, and propagation—in a word, to pleasure. But he cannot possibly will that this should become a universal law of nature or that it should be implanted in us by a natural instinct. For, as a rational being, he necessarily wills that all his faculties should be developed, inasmuch as they are given to him for all sorts of possible purposes. [23]

[23] The (alleged) problem is different in this case: the maxim can be made universal without contradiction, but (it is claimed) the person cannot *will* this universalized maxim to be a law because any rational being necessarily wills something that contradicts it (so that the problem is still contradiction, but this time within the will itself, rather than within the universalized maxim). (But why must a rational being will that all his faculties be developed—indeed, is this even possible? See Discussion Question 3.)

4. A fourth man, for whom things are going well, sees that others (whom he could help) have to struggle with great hardships, and he asks, "What concern of mine is it? Let each one be as happy as heaven wills, or as he can make himself; I will not take anything from him or even envy him; but to his welfare or to his assistance in time of need I have no desire to contribute." If such a way of thinking were a universal law of nature, certainly the human race could exist, and without doubt even better than in a state where everyone talks of sympathy and good will, or even exerts himself occasionally to practice them while, on the other hand, he cheats when he can and betrays or otherwise violates the rights of man. Now although it is possible that a universal law of nature according to that maxim could exist, it is nevertheless impossible to will that such a principle should hold everywhere as a law of nature. For a will which resolved this would conflict with itself, since instances can often arise in which he would need the love and sympathy of others, and in which he would have robbed himself, by such a law of nature springing from his own will, of all hope of the aid he desires. [24]

[24] The second case of an alleged conflict within the will itself is again more plausible. But is it really true that no one could fail to will that he be helped when in need? (See Discussion Question 3.)

The foregoing are a few of the many actual duties, or at least of duties we hold to be actual, whose derivation from the one stated principle is clear. We must be able to will that a maxim of our action become a universal law; this is the canon of the moral estimation of our action generally. Some actions are of such a nature that their maxim cannot even be *thought* as a universal law of nature without contradiction, far from it being possible that one could will that it should be such. In others this internal impossi-

25 Kant summarizes the two sorts of ways that the categorical imperative can fail to be satisfied by the maxim of an action. The first is said to correspond to perfect duties, the second to imperfect duties: on Kant's view, one may never commit suicide in the face of misfortune or make a promise while knowing that one will not be able to keep it; but one has a choice of which talents to develop (not all can be fully developed) and of which people to help (no one person can help everyone).

bility is not found, though it is still impossible to *will* that their maxim should be raised to the universality of a law of nature, because such a will would contradict itself. We easily see that the former maxim conflicts with the stricter or narrower (imprescriptible) duty, the latter with broader (meritorious) duty. 25 Thus all duties, so far as the kind of obligation (not the object of their action) is concerned, have been completely exhibited by these examples in their dependence on the one principle.

When we observe ourselves in any transgression of a duty, we find that we do not actually will that our maxim should become a universal law. That is impossible for us; rather, the contrary of this maxim should remain as a law generally, and we only take the liberty of making an exception to it for ourselves or for the sake of our inclination, and for this one occasion. Consequently, if we weighed everything from one and the same standpoint, namely, reason, we would come upon a contradiction in our own will, viz., that a certain principle is objectively necessary as a universal law and yet subjectively does not hold universally but rather admits exceptions. . . .

We have thus at least established that if duty is a concept which is to have significance and actual legislation for our actions, it can be expressed only in categorical imperatives and not at all in hypothetical ones. For every application of it we have also clearly exhibited the content of the categorical imperative which must contain the principle of all duty (if there is such). This is itself very much. But we are not yet advanced far enough to prove a priori that that kind of imperative really exists, that there is a practical law which of itself commands absolutely and without any incentives, and that obedience to this law is duty. 26

26 The reason for the uncertainty expressed here is not entirely clear. Perhaps the idea is that the ultimate point of the moral law is not yet clear. Specific purposes or ends have been ruled out, but Kant will suggest that there is a certain unconditional end that any rational being must have.

. . .

The will is thought of as a faculty of determining itself to action in accordance with the conception of certain laws. Such a faculty can be found only in rational beings. That which serves the will as the objective ground of its self-determination is an end, and, if it is given by reason alone, it must hold alike for all rational beings. On the other hand, that which contains the ground of the possibility of the action, whose result is an end, is called the means. The subjective ground of desire is the incentive, while the objective ground of volition is the motive. Thus arises the distinction between subjective ends, which rest on incentives, and objective ends, which depend on motives valid for every rational being. Practical principles are formal when they disregard all subjective ends; they are material when they have subjective ends, and thus certain incentives, as their basis. The ends which a rational being arbitrarily proposes to himself as consequences of his action are material ends and are without exception only relative, for only their relation to a particularly constituted faculty of desire in the subject gives them their worth. And this worth cannot, therefore, afford any universal principles for all rational beings or valid and necessary principles for every volition. That is, they cannot give rise to any practical laws. All these relative ends, therefore, are grounds for hypothetical imperatives only.

But suppose that there were something the existence of which in itself had absolute worth, something which, as an end in itself, could be a ground of definite laws. In it and only in it could lie the ground of a possible categorical imperative, i.e., of a practical law. 27

27 Think again about the idea of a truly categorical imperative: one that is binding on any rational being, no matter what specific purposes it may or may not have. An end that had *absolute* worth could be the basis for such an imperative; and, Kant is saying, *only* an end with such worth could supply such a basis. In what follows, Kant proclaims (is there any real argument?) that rational beings are themselves ends with absolute as opposed to merely conditional worth.

Now, I say, man and, in general, every rational being exists as an end in himself and not merely as a means to be arbitrarily used by this or that will. In all his actions, whether they are directed to himself or to other rational beings, he must always be regarded at the same time as an end. All objects of inclinations have only a conditional worth, for if the inclinations and the needs founded on them did not exist, their object would be without worth. The inclinations themselves as the sources of needs, however, are so lacking in absolute worth that the universal wish of every rational being must be indeed to free himself completely from them. 28 Therefore, the worth of any objects to be obtained by our actions is at all times conditional. Beings whose existence does not depend on our will but on nature, if they are not rational beings, have only a relative worth as means and are therefore called "things";

28 This claim reveals some of the austere character of Kant's thought: according to him, a rational being would want to have no contingent inclinations at all—no desires for anything that does not have absolute worth. (What would life be like for such a being?)

on the other hand, rational beings are designated "persons" because their nature indicates that they are ends in themselves, i.e., things which may not be used merely as means. Such a being is thus an object of respect and, so far, restricts all [arbitrary] choice. Such beings are not merely subjective ends whose existence as a result of our action has a worth for us, but are objective ends, i.e., beings whose existence in itself is an end. Such an end is one for which no other end can be substituted, to which these beings should serve merely as means. 29 For, without them, nothing of absolute worth could be found, and if all worth is conditional and thus contingent, no supreme practical principle for reason could be found anywhere.

Thus if there is to be a supreme practical principle and a categorical imperative for the human will, it must be one that forms an objective principle of the will from the conception of that which is necessarily an end for everyone because it is an end in itself. Hence this objective principle can serve as a universal practical law. The ground of this principle is: rational nature exists as an end in itself. Man necessarily thinks of his own existence in this way; thus far it is a subjective principle of human actions. Also every other rational being thinks of his existence by means of the same rational ground which holds also for myself; thus it is at the same time an objective principle from which, as a supreme practical ground, it must be possible to derive all laws of the will. The practical imperative, therefore, is the following: Act so that you treat humanity, whether in your own person or in that of another, always as an end and never as a means only. 30 Let us now see whether this can be achieved.

29 The existence of a rational being is an end in itself. It is thus a fundamental mistake to regard or treat such a being as merely a means to something else (which could only be something with merely contingent, conditional worth).

30 Here is the second formulation of the categorical imperative, supposedly just another formulation of the same underlying moral law. It is important to stress that persons are never to be treated "as a means *only,*" that is, never *merely* as a means—not that they may never be treated in any respect as a means (which would make most forms of human interaction impossible).

To return to our previous examples:

First, according to the concept of necessary duty to one's self, he who contemplates suicide will ask himself whether his action can be consistent with the idea of humanity as an end in itself. If, in order to escape from burdensome circumstances, he destroys himself, he uses a person merely as a means to maintain a tolerable condition up to the end of life. Man, however, is not a thing, and thus not something to be used merely as a means; he must always be regarded in all his actions as an end in himself. Therefore, I cannot dispose of man in my own person so as to mutilate, corrupt, or kill him. 31 (It belongs to ethics proper to define more accurately this basic principle so as to avoid all misunderstanding, e.g., as to the amputation of limbs in order to preserve myself, or to exposing my life to danger in order to save it; I must, therefore, omit them here.)

31 On the surface, this is a different reason for the moral unacceptability of suicide in the face of misfortune: it treats a person (the person who commits suicide) as a means to the end of escaping the misfortune in question. (But is this really so? See Discussion Question 4.)

Second, as concerns necessary or obligatory duties to others, he who intends a deceitful promise to others sees immediately that he intends to use another man merely as a means, without the latter containing the end in himself at the same time. For he whom I want to use for my own purposes by means of such a promise cannot possibly assent to my mode of acting against him and cannot contain the end of this action in himself. This conflict against the principle of other men is even clearer if we cite examples of attacks on their freedom and property. For then it is clear that he who transgresses the rights of men intends to make use of the persons of others

32 This is the clearest example of the application of the second version of the categorical imperative—and probably the best and clearest of all of Kant's discussions of specific examples.

merely as a means, without considering that, as rational beings, they must always be esteemed at the same time as ends, i.e., only as beings who must be able to contain in themselves the end of the very same action. **32**

Third, with regard to contingent (meritorious) duty to one's self, it is not sufficient that the action not conflict with humanity in our person as an end in itself; it must also harmonize with it. Now in humanity there are capacities for greater perfection which belong to the end of nature with respect to humanity

33 How clear is Kant's reasoning in this case? Why does treating one's own humanity as an end in itself require developing one's talents? (See Discussion Question 5.)

in our own person; to neglect these might perhaps be consistent with the preservation of humanity as an end in itself but not with the furtherance of that end. **33**

Fourth, with regard to meritorious duty to others, the natural end which all men have is their own happiness. Humanity might indeed exist if no one contributed to the happiness of others, provided he did not

intentionally detract from it; but this harmony with humanity as an end in itself is only negative rather than positive if everyone does not also endeavor, so far as he can, to further the ends of others. For the ends of any person, who is an end in himself, must as far as possible also be my end, if that conception of an end in itself is to have its full effect on me. **34**

34 Why does the fact (assuming that it is a fact) that another person is an end in himself mean that his ends must also be my ends? Also, how strong is this requirement? (See Discussion Question 6.)

This principle of humanity and of every rational creature as an end in itself is the supreme limiting condition on freedom of the actions of each man. It is not borrowed from experience, first, because of its universality, since it applies to all rational beings generally and experience does not suffice to determine anything about them; and, secondly, because in experience humanity is not thought of (subjectively) as the end of men, i.e., as an object which we of ourselves really make our end. Rather it is thought of as the objective end which should constitute the supreme limiting condition of all subjective ends, whatever they may be. Thus this principle must arise from pure reason. . . .

If we now look back upon all previous attempts which have ever been undertaken to discover the principle of morality, it is not to be wondered at that they all had to fail. Man was seen to be bound to laws by his duty, but it was not seen that he is subject only to his own, yet universal, legislation, and that he is only bound to act in accordance with his own will, which is, however, designed by nature to be a will giving universal laws. For if one thought of him as subject only to a law (whatever it may be), this necessarily implied some interest as a stimulus or compulsion to obedience because the law did not arise from his will. Rather, his will was constrained by something else according to a law to act in a certain way. By this strictly necessary consequence, however, all the labor of finding a supreme ground for duty was irrevocably lost, and one never arrived at duty but only at the necessity of action from a certain interest. This might be his own interest or that of another, but in either case the imperative always had to be conditional and could not at all serve as a moral command. This principle I will call the principle of *autonomy* of the will in contrast to all other principles which I accordingly count under *heteronomy.* ㉟

㉟ This is a different way of putting the point that only a moral law that arises from the will of a rational being as such (and so is a principle of *autonomy*) can be unconditionally binding. Basing moral principles on anything else (principles of *heteronomy*—literally, being under the dominion of another) will fail to show why rational beings are obliged to follow them.

The concept of each rational being as a being that must regard itself as giving universal law through all the maxims of its will, so that it may judge itself and its actions from this standpoint, leads to a very fruitful concept, namely, that of a *realm of ends.*

By "realm" I understand the systematic union of different rational beings through common laws. Because laws determine ends with regard to their universal validity, if we abstract from the personal difference of rational beings and thus from all content of their private ends, we can think of a whole of all ends in systematic connection, a whole of rational beings as ends in themselves as well as of the particular ends which each may set for himself. This is a realm of ends, which is possible on the aforesaid principles. For all rational beings stand under the law that each of them should treat himself and all others never merely as means but in every case also as an end in himself. Thus there arises a

㊱ Here is one more, supposedly equivalent formulation of Kant's central moral idea, which leads to one more formulation of the categorical imperative. But exactly what this version adds to the previous two is not particularly clear.

systematic union of rational beings through common objective laws. This is a realm which may be called a realm of ends (certainly only an ideal), because what these laws have in view is just the relation of these beings to each other as ends and means. ㊱

. . .

Morality, therefore, consists in the relation of every action to that legislation through which alone a realm of ends is possible. This legislation, however, must be found in every rational being. It must be able to arise from his will, whose principle then is to take no action according to any maxim which would be inconsistent with its being a universal law and thus to act only so that the will through its maxims could regard itself at the same time as universally lawgiving.

If now the maxims do not by their nature already necessarily conform to this objective principle of rational beings as universally lawgiving, the necessity of acting according to that principle is called practical constraint, i.e., duty. Duty pertains not to the sovereign in the realm of ends, but rather to each member, and to each in the same degree.

The practical necessity of acting according to this principle, i.e., duty, does not rest at all on feelings, impulses, and inclinations; it rests merely on the relation of rational beings to one another, in which the will of a rational being must always be regarded as legislative, for otherwise it could not be thought of as an end in itself. Reason, therefore, relates every maxim of the will as giving universal laws to every other will and also to every action toward itself; it does so not for the sake of any other practical motive or future advantage but rather from the idea of the dignity of a rational being who obeys no law except that which he himself also gives.

. . .

The three aforementioned ways of presenting the principle of morality are fundamentally only so many formulas of the very same law, and each of them unites the others in itself. There is, nevertheless, a difference in them, but the difference is more subjectively than objectively practical, for it is intended to bring an idea of reason closer to intuition (by means of a certain analogy) and thus nearer to feeling. All maxims have:

1. A form, which consists in universality; and in this respect the formula of the moral imperative requires that the maxims be chosen as though they should hold as universal laws of nature.
2. A material, i.e., an end; in this respect the formula says that the rational being, as by its nature an end and thus as an end in itself, must serve in every maxim as the condition restricting all merely relative and arbitrary ends.
3. A complete determination of all maxims by the formula that all maxims which stem from autonomous legislation ought to harmonize with a possible realm of ends as with a realm of nature.

There is a progression here like that through the categories of the unity of the form of the will (its universality), the plurality of material (the objects, i.e., the ends), and the all-comprehensiveness or totality of the system of ends. But it is better in moral evaluation to follow the rigorous method and to make the universal formula of the categorical imperative the basis: Act according to the maxim which can at the same time make itself a universal law. But if one wishes to gain a hearing for the moral law, it is very useful to bring one and the same action under the three stated principles and thus, so far as possible, to bring it nearer to intuition.

We can now end where we started, with the concept of an unconditionally good will. That will is absolutely good which cannot be bad, and thus it is a will whose maxim, when made a universal law, can never conflict with itself. Thus this principle is also its supreme law: Always act according to that maxim whose universality as a law you can at the same time will. This is the only condition under which a will can never come into conflict with itself, and such an imperative is categorical. Because the validity of the will, as a universal law for possible actions, has an analogy with the universal connection of the existence of things under universal laws, which is the formal element of nature in general, the categorical imperative can also be expressed as follows: Act according to maxims which can at the same time have themselves as universal laws of nature as their object. Such, then, is the formula of an absolutely good will.

. . .

Discussion Questions

1. Is Kant right that a person who helps other people out of duty alone is morally superior to someone who acts out of an inclination toward sympathy, generosity, benevolence, etc.? Can you think of any way in which he might defend this claim?

2. In applying the first version of the categorical imperative (see Annotation 19) to the suicide and promising examples, Kant claims that the maxims of the actions in question are *contradictory* when universalized. Is he right about this in either of these cases? The promising case is the more plausible of the two, but is there really a contradiction in supposing that everyone borrows money and promises to repay, but never does so? It is very *unlikely* that people would be gullible enough to continue to lend money under such circumstances, but is it really impossible that they could be that gullible?

3. In the second two cases (talent and charity), Kant claims that though universalizing the maxim can be done without contradiction, *willing* the universalized maxim leads to a conflict or contradiction within the will itself. Clearly this depends on his claim that there are other, conflicting things that a rational being necessarily wills. How plausible is his claim, in each of the two cases, that *any* rational being necessarily wills the other things in question? Can you imagine a rational being that does not do so?

4. Is a person who commits suicide in order to escape misfortune of some serious sort (ill health, financial catastrophe, loss of a loved one, etc.) using himself as merely a means to an end? What is the end and in what way is the person being used as a means to it? Can you see how someone might argue in some of these cases that suicide is consistent with or even required by the idea that the person is an end in himself?

5. Why does the idea that people are ends in themselves require developing one's talents? Does Kant have any clear argument for this claim? What does he mean in this discussion by the "end of nature with respect to humanity"? Does this suggest using humanity as a means to some further end that is not the end of the person in question but of *nature* (and what does "nature" mean here)?

6. One objection to utilitarianism (see the selection from Williams) was that it required giving the projects and desires of other people the same consideration as one's own. Someone sympathetic to Kant's view might put this point by saying that utilitarianism views people merely as means to the achievement of the greatest overall total of happiness. But does Kant himself fall into the same problem

by saying that "the ends of any person, who is an end in himself, must as far as possible also be my end"? How much of a limitation is expressed by "as far as possible"?

Onora O'Neill

Onora O'Neill (1941–) is a British philosopher (born in Northern Ireland), who has made important contributions to moral and political philosophy, bioethics, issues pertaining to international justice, and the philosophy of Kant. O'Neill taught for many years in the United States at Barnard College, before returning to Britain to teach at the University of Essex and Cambridge University. In 1999, she was made a life peer in the British House of Lords.

In the following selection, O'Neill explores the contrast between utilitarian and Kantian approaches to moral questions by exploring what each view would say about an issue that has only fairly recently become a focus of philosophical discussion: the issue of moral obligations pertaining to famine and famine relief. In the part of her discussion devoted to Kant, she focuses on what is often regarded as the most useful and suggestive formulation of the categorical imperative, namely the version that requires treating people always as ends in themselves and never merely as means.

The Moral Perplexities of Famine Relief

§1 Is Famine a New Moral Problem?

. . . when we wonder what we or others should do about global famine there don't seem to be familiar literary or religious traditions or philosophical discussions to which to turn. This is not because famine is new, but because there is today far more that we (or others) can do—or refrain from doing—that will affect the course of any famine there may be. Through history, millions have died of sheer starvation and of malnutrition or from illnesses that they might have survived with better nourishment. And whenever there were such deaths, nearby survivors may have realized that they might have helped prevent deaths and may either have done so or wondered whether they should. But nobody considered whether to prevent faraway deaths. Distance made an important difference, and with few exceptions there was nothing to be done for the victims of faraway famines.

In a global economy things are different. Corn from the North American prairies could be (and has been) distributed to the starving in Bangladesh or Somalia. Longer-term policies that affect economic development, fertility levels, and agricultural productivity may hasten or postpone far-off famines or make them more or less severe. Consequently, we now face moral questions about whether we ought to do some of these newly possible actions. Ought we (or others) to try to distribute food or aid or to introduce technical improvements? Who should foot the bill and suffer the other costs? To whom (if anyone) should aid be given and to whom should it be denied? How much hardship or sacrifice is demanded of those who have the means to help, if any?①

. . .

§6 Limiting The Discussion

I shall consider only two potentially morally acceptable theories. I have chosen these two because they are leading contenders for being morally acceptable theories.

From Matters of Life and Death, *edited by T. Regan (New York: McGraw Hill, 1980).*

One of these theories is utilitarianism; the other is a (simplified) version of Kantian ethics. Probably most serious writers on ethics in the English-speaking world today view some form of one of these two theories as likely to be a morally acceptable theory. I am going to present each of these theories and then see whether each has the scope and precision to answer some of the moral problems that famines raise. . . .

> 1 You will be better prepared to assess what the moral views to be explored say about this issue if you think about it at least some on your own before proceeding. Does the situation of famine and the possibility of famine relief create any clear and definite moral obligations—and if so, what are they?

UTILITARIAN APPROACHES TO SOME FAMINE PROBLEMS

§12 Bentham And Utilitarianism

The first person to call himself a "utilitarian" was an eighteenth-century polemicist and philosopher named Jeremy Bentham (1748–1832). Bentham is now best known for having written a work with the forbidding title *Introduction to the Principles of Morals and Legislation.* But his aim was anything but forbidding. What he wanted was to increase human happiness; and he hoped that legal and moral reform undertaken in a systematic and organized way would do so. His object, he wrote, was "to rear the fabric of felicity by the hands of reason and law." The first principle of this task he called the Principle of Utility, and he stated that he meant by this

> that principle which approves or disapproves of every action whatsoever, according to the tendency which it appears to have to augment or diminish the happiness of the party whose interest is in question.*

If faced with a decision, we should, according to Bentham's moral theory, ask ourselves which act is most likely to most increase the happiness of the person or persons affected. Legislators should ask which law would make most of those who have to live under it most happy. If we can discover the act or law that will do most for the happiness of the affected parties, then we have found the act that is right and required.

If we accept the Principle of Utility, we will solve problems by working out which of the many courses of action we might take will produce most happiness. That course of action is obligatory, and if more than one action is likely to yield maximal happiness, then it would be obligatory to do one or other of them, though perhaps it would not be morally important which was picked.

Bentham realized that his theory required decision makers to go through long calculations in order to work out which available action (or legislation) would produce the greatest happiness. He was undaunted. He thought we could list the available courses of action, and then work out how much happiness each would produce. He pointed out seven different aspects of happiness or pleasure that calculations should reckon with. If an act would affect only oneself, then one should consider the *intensity* of the pleasure or happiness; its *duration;* its *certainty* or *uncertainty* (counting unlikely pleasures like winning lotteries at a lower rate than sure things); its *propinquity* or *remoteness* (counting the pleasures we expect to enjoy soon at a higher rate); its *fecundity,* by which he meant its likelihood of being followed by more, similar pleasures; and its *purity,* which is the degree to which the pleasure is unmixed with pains. If an act would affect others as well as oneself, it becomes necessary to work out the pleasure's *extent* also, which is the number of persons who will be affected pleasurably or painfully by the proposed act. . . .

. . . Bentham's calculus requires that we make calculations for which we *nearly always* lack the necessary information. We often are unsure how much happiness an act will produce, and how much unhappiness. In fact, we don't know how we are supposed to measure happiness. We often don't know who will be affected, to what extent, or for how long. Bentham apparently didn't find this sort of problem baffling. He was lifelong in the thick of political controversy taking determined stands in favor of one or another proposal for reform on the basis of utility calculations he felt able to make. He agitated tirelessly for reform of harsh or pointless laws, for the extension of the franchise, and for the abolition of slavery. When he died in 1832, some of the reforms he had advocated had

---

*J. Bentham, *Introduction to the Principles of Morals and Legislation,* Oxford, 1789, Ch. I. [579]

already been enacted by the British Parliament; others were fought for and achieved in the following decades.

If we assess Bentham's system soberly and discount some of his enthusiasm, we might conclude that its scope is large but its precision spurious. For if we can't do the calculations, we won't get answers at all.

§13 Mill and Utilitarianism

Bentham's successors, including some of his warmest admirers, were more skeptical about the felicific calculus.② Even though they thought utilitarian moral theory right in principle, they doubted that moral decisions could be made a matter of calculation. The most famous of these successors was John Stuart Mill (1806–1873), whose main work in ethics has as its very title the word 'utilitarianism'. Like Bentham, John Stuart Mill took as the main principle of his moral theory the Greatest Happiness Principle. He formulated it as "actions are right in proportion as they tend to promote happiness, wrong as they tend to produce the reverse of happiness."

② "The felicific calculus" is O'Neill's label for the calculation of the overall total of pleasure and happiness (including negative values for pain and unhappiness) that results from various alternative actions. ("Felicity" just means happiness.)

John Stuart Mill, even though he had grown up in Bentham's shadow and had been groomed as the heir to Bentham's reforming crusade, was not merely a disciple. He doubted that it was possible to make calculations of any precision about the amount of pleasure to be expected from each possible course of action. Pleasures, he thought, may vary in quality as well as in amount. And if some pleasures are of higher quality than others, then it is impossible to add them together, just as it is impossible to add together Bentham's height and John Stuart Mill's weight. To add things together they must be measured in the same units, or in units that (like inches and centimeters) can be reduced to one another. But on Mill's view, some pleasures are *irreducibly* superior to others. "It is better," he wrote, "to be a human being dissatisfied than a

pig satisfied; better to be Socrates dissatisfied than a fool satisfied." However intense, fecund, long, or pure, the swinish or foolish pleasures are, they do not in Mill's view outweigh the pleasures of a nobler and more reflective life. This is shown, he claims, by the fact that all who have experience both of higher and of brutish pleasures prefer the former.

This division between Bentham and Mill did not end the influence of utilitarianism in moral thought. Utilitarianism of one form or another is advocated by many different thinkers. There are still some (mostly economists and decision theorists) who hope for Benthamite precision in handling problems. But there are more who regard utilitarianism in a humane rather than a scientific way. This majority does not claim that precise calculations of pleasure can be made to guide every decision, but only that we can bring informed judgment to bear on the question of which action is most likely to enhance human happiness, and that if we can identify such an action with reasonable certainty, we ought to embark on it, while if we can identify actions that seem likely to produce misery, we should avoid them. I shall now consider what such a humane version of utilitarianism would tell us about our moral duties towards those who do or may suffer famine.

§14 Some Utilitarian Arguments About Famine

I shall now take the simplified utilitarian moral theory outlined in the last section and show how it can be and has been used to draw diametrically opposed conclusions about what affluent persons (ourselves, for example) ought to do about famines that they could help to relieve. I will try to use this embarrassing result as the basis for an assessment of utilitarianism. . . .

To reach the opposing conclusions, I shall draw on the arguments of two well known recent articles about moral problems raised by the prospect of famine. The first of these articles is Garrett Hardin's "Lifeboat Ethics: The Case Against Helping the Poor," which argues that the affluent ought not to relieve famine. The second is Peter Singer's "Famine, Affluence and Morality," which argues that the affluent ought to relieve famine.*

---

*G. Hardin, "Lifeboat Ethics: The Case Against Helping the Poor; P. Singer, "Famine, Affluence and Morality," both are reprinted in W. Aiken and H. La Follette, *World Hunger and Moral Obligation,* Englewood Cliffs, N.J., Prentice-Hall, 1977.

Neither of these articles relies on an argument acceptable *only* to utilitarians. Both authors assume only a more general *consequentialist* position. Consequentialist moral theories regard acts as obligatory if they have better results than all other available acts. Some consequentialists are not utilitarians, since they think that there are other things besides human happiness and human suffering that are good and bad. For example, some consequentialists think that the existence of beauty, even when nobody is there to enjoy it, is a good thing, and that therefore we ought to try to make sure that there are beautiful things even if we believe that no human will survive to enjoy them. However, since all serious consequentialists have shared the utilitarian view that human happiness and misery are respectively good and bad, many of their conclusions can also be reached from utilitarian assumptions. The bad results to which both Hardin and Singer allude in their arguments about famine relief are results that *any* utilitarian thinks bad—namely the misery that famines cause. So Hardin's and Singer's conclusions can be reached by that special form of consequentialist argument that is utilitarian. Their conclusions do not depend on there being anything other than human happiness that is good, or anything other than human misery that is bad. Each argument can be framed as a straightforwardly utilitarian argument.

§15 A Utilitarian Argues Against Relieving Famine

Hardin's argument can be summarized as follows. The citizens of affluent countries are like passengers in a lifeboat around which other, desperate, shipwrecked persons are swimming. The people in the lifeboat can help some of those in the water. But if the citizens of affluent countries help some of the starving, this will, unlike many lifeboat rescues, have bad effects. To begin with, according to Hardin, the affluent countries will then have less of a safety margin, like an over-laden lifeboat. This alone might be outweighed by the added happiness of those who have been rescued. But the longer-run effects are bad for everyone. The rescued will assume that they are secure, will multiply their numbers and so make future rescues impossible. It is better, from a utilitarian point of view, to lose some lives now than to lose more lives later. So no rescue attempt should be made.

Hardin's (and others') use of the lifeboat metaphor has been widely criticized. Persons in lifeboats have (often) some title to their seats. Rescue operations in lifeboats endanger the rescuers. There are few interests that those inside a boat share with the drowning. By contrast, it is not clear that affluent persons and nations are entitled to all they have. Some of it may have been acquired by exploiting poorer nations or persons; even if it has been acquired by standard market procedures, the terms of trade are often (and perhaps unfairly) weighted in favor of the powerful. Further, it is not clear that attempts at famine relief present any serious danger to the affluent. Some forms of famine relief may even benefit the donors—for example, if by sending more food relief, the prosperous give up diets that leave them fat and prone to heart attacks, then they too will be healthier. Finally, the interests of the rich and poor are often congruent, while those of the rescued and the drowning are diametrically opposed. Everybody has an interest in the preservation of peace and in the prevention of ecocatastrophes.③ But though the analogy between affluent nations and lifeboats has these limitations, Hardin's main point can be stated without depending on the metaphor.

> ③ Think carefully about each of these alleged disanalogies between the lifeboat example and the famine case. How much do they undermine Hardin's argument?

His main claim is that famine relief *encourages* population growth to a level that cannot be indefinitely sustained. If we pool our resources with the poor of this world, soon nobody will have a safety margin and even local and temporary crop failures will have a drastic effect. If we pooled resources, we should all, aptly enough, be in the same boat; and the boat would not be stormworthy.

Hardin's view is that once population has been increased by the added children of those who would otherwise not have survived to have children at all, the total amount of suffering will be larger than the suffering from unrelieved famine of a smaller number of people. He writes:

> If poor countries received no food from outside, the rate of their population growth would be periodically checked by crop failures and famines. But if they can always draw on a world food bank in time of need, their population can continue to

grow unchecked, and so will their "need" for aid. In the short run a world food bank may diminish that need, but in the long run it actually increases the need without limit.*

Hardin's view of famine is harsh, but reasoned. He thinks that feeding the hungry is merely likely to lead to population growth and greater suffering in the future. Feeding the hungry preserves lives and happiness now, but costs great loss of life and misery in the future. The prosperous not merely may but ought, if they are utilitarians, to leave the starving to themselves, to die or to survive as best they may.④

---

④ How plausible is it that the results in terms of pleasure and happiness minus pain and suffering will be greater if people are allowed to starve than for any available alternative? Are there more complicated alternatives that Hardin should consider? (See Discussion Question 1.)

Singer, however, thinks that the prosperous have an obligation to try to feed the hungry. He starts from the assumption that

> if it is in our power to prevent something bad from happening, without thereby sacrificing anything of comparable moral importance, we ought, morally, to do it.† ⑤

---

⑤ Though Singer is in fact a utilitarian, here he invokes a principle that captures only the negative side of utilitarianism, as it were: the obligation to avoid pain and suffering wherever the cost is less than the gain. Nothing is said about the obligation to maximize pleasure and happiness, not just avoid pain and suffering.

He then points out that contributing to famine relief, even contributing a large proportion of a prosperous income, say 50 percent, does not sacrifice anything of comparable importance. But it does help prevent the misery and loss of life that famines produce. So, he concludes, the prosperous ought to help feed the hungry and ought to do so up to that point at which they have indeed reduced their own standard of living so far that something of comparable moral importance would be sacrificed by further giving.

This conclusion too can be reached by a quite explicitly utilitarian route. For what makes famine bad, as Singer and all utilitarians agree, is that it causes acute human suffering; and what makes the sacrifices of the prosperous less bad is that they cause much less acute human suffering. (Compare what it would be like to have no car with what it would be like to go without half the food you now eat.) So if we think that we ought to do acts that will prevent or reduce suffering, or still better, produce happiness, then it seems that there is little doubt that we ought to relieve famine, even if it costs us a fair amount of minor unhappiness to do so.⑥

---

⑥ This seems to understate rather seriously what follows from Singer's principle: if we must help until the cost of helping reaches the point at which it would be as bad as the suffering prevented, much more than "minor unhappiness" will be required.

---

§17 Why Do Hardin and Singer Reach Incompatible Conclusions?

Reading Hardin and Singer presents any utilitarian and any consequentialist with a dilemma. For it seems that their starting points are not very different, but that they have come to incompatible conclusions. I believe this is due to their divergent views about the effects of attempts at famine relief and not to a difference over moral theory.

Hardin pays attention to the long-term effects of uncontrolled population growth. He is a pessimistic neo-Malthusian who thinks that there is no method to curtail population growth except by letting famines run their "natural" course. With luck, this experience may educate the survivors of "irresponsible" populations so that they then do curb the size of their families; but only the reality of famine can teach this lesson. If Hardin thought there was another less painful way in which population growth could be curbed, he would presumably have to modify his conclusion. For the suffering of those who would die of famine need not then be outweighed by the future suffering of those born as the result of unchecked population growth.

---

*G. Hardin, in W. Aiken and H. La Follette, *op. cit.,* p. 17.
†*P. Singer, in W. Aiken and H. La Follette, *op. cit.,* p. 24.

Singer is an optimistic neo-Malthusian who tends to underestimate the long-range effects of saving persons from famine without being able to prevent population growth that might later outstrip available resources. In a later appendix to his article, he modifies his view and claims that the obligation of the prosperous to the starving is an obligation to give aid that checks rather than promotes population growth. He is even prepared to think that countries that take no steps to reduce their population growth should not be given aid.* Here his conclusion is much closer to Hardin's. Unless we can resolve disputes about the facts and future of population growth, we cannot resolve the dispute between Singer and Hardin.

§18 The Uncertainty of Consequences

One of the many similarities between Hardin's and Singer's work is that both shift easily between talking about the obligations of nations and those of individuals. This ambidexterity has been a part of the utilitarian tradition of moral thought ever since Bentham wrote *Principles of Morals and Legislation.* It is one of the strengths of the utilitarian moral thought that it can be so generally applied; its scope is large. The actions of individuals, the policies of nations, and the activities of groups (ranging from multinational corporations to famine-relief charities to government departments) all affect human happiness. So the acts of all these agents and agencies can be morally assessed by the same arguments. But this enormous scope of utilitarian moral theory is no help unless we can know fairly precisely what effects proposed acts would have. A conscientious utilitarian, even one who does not credit Benthamite calculations, must try to work out the effects of his or her actions; and as we have seen in the case of Hardin and Singer, it is hard to work these out at all, let alone with precision, when we deliberate about famine relief.

This imprecision is reflected in the great diversity of (often incompatible) policies for which utilitarian arguments are offered. At the most general level, passionate utilitarian arguments have been made *both* for centralized economic planning *and* for reliance on free markets. At a less global level, utilitarians repeatedly disagree about policies and actions.

Consider, for example, the following policy for the distribution of famine relief that some utilitarians advocate. William and Paul Paddock in *Famine—1975!* suggest that famine relief should be allocated on a *triage* principle.† When resources are limited they should be given to those who can benefit most. The term 'triage' is taken from military medicine. In medical contexts it means that the worst injured should be left to die and the walking wounded left to hobble. All care should go to the third, in-between group. In the case of famine, this means that aid should be concentrated on those countries that have the best chance of survival if aided but won't survive otherwise. Triage is a policy that seeks to maximize the number of survivors. Lives are to be sacrificed, but only for the sake of preserving more lives by concentrating resources where they will do the most good.

Utilitarians would probably endorse the triage principle *if* they thought all lives tended on average to be equally happy. The preservation of life is necessary for the existence of happy lives, so that if other things were equal (which they seldom are) preserving as many lives as possible would produce the greatest total amount of happiness. Only if some of the lives to be preserved were likely to be on balance painful would utilitarians advocate that they not be preserved. By the same token, utilitarians would oppose 'heroic' medical measures to prolong painful lives; they do not value life itself but the happiness of lives. It does not bother utilitarians that triaging sacrifices some lives for the sake of others. For utilitarians, biological life is no end in itself, but a means to the enjoyment of living. And where a greater total of happiness or enjoyment would be achieved by triaging populations or countries, it is not merely permissible but a duty to adopt this policy. Happiness should be maximized even if doing so costs some lives.

However, it is far from clear that triaging would in fact maximize happiness. First, lives are *not* all equally

---

*Ibid., p. 34.
†*W. and P. Paddock, *Famine—1975!,* Boston, Little, Brown, 1967

happy, and if not all lives can be preserved, utilitarians would prefer policies that ensure that those whose prospects are happiest, rather than those whose survival is easiest to secure, are helped. Second, it is difficult to see how triaging can legitimately be applied beyond the medical context. For there are no clear standards to determine who is the "best risk." Any nation or region might be made more likely to survive if given the right sort of help. Some nations or regions seem to need more help, but since we lack a scientific account of the methods for achieving economic development (though theories are legion), we don't really know whom it will be hardest to save in the long run. In this century some seemingly desperate countries have achieved steady economic growth, and others that seemed as well placed have not. So it is not obvious whom the triagers should reject as hopeless cases, whom they should dismiss as walking wounded, and whom they should help. Thus it is unclear whether utilitarians would on reflection endorse a triaging policy.[7]

> [7] Think carefully about this question. Is there any real hope, in the face of the problems that O'Neill points out, that a utilitarian can reach a reasonably clear and justified decision about whether some specific version of the moral policy of triaging is the right solution to the famine problem?

Alternatively, consider some of the following dilemmas that individual utilitarians might meet while thinking about famine. In all of these examples, suppose that A is a moderately prosperous utilitarian who sincerely wants to use his extra money to help relieve famine and save lives, which he reasonably judges would greatly reduce human misery. A might wonder whether to try to send money to a poor family in a poor country. But how is he to be sure that they get the money, and that it doesn't fall into the hands of some nonneedy local official, who uses it to worsen the situation of others, perhaps by buying imported goods, leaving those who formerly sold to him without a customer? Might not the result of A's generosity also worsen the position of those needy families whom he cannot benefit, who find that the going price of goods has risen beyond their means because benefited families can afford to pay more and have driven up the price? Or suppose A thinks that the way to benefit the poor is to purchase the products of needy nations and areas. Might not this encourage production for fickle export markets, retard the development of local self-sufficiency, and make people more vulnerable in hard years? If A buys Brazilian coffee despite its high price, can he be sure whom he is benefiting? Might not he be encouraging the development of a one-crop economy with all its potential for disaster? Or suppose that in order to encourage development in the Arab world, A advocates (and, as a consumer, follows) policies that are heavily dependent on importing OPEC oil. May not this policy fuel nothing more productive of human happiness and life than the Middle East arms race? Or suppose A hopes to assist, through work in a multinational corporation, the introduction of more modern industrial processes in some under-developed economy. How can he be sure that this will not lead to a developed enclave within a traditional economy that, on the whole, causes friction for many, unemployment for some, and gain for a few who were not in the first place the most needy? Or suppose A is an economic planner in a socialist country. Hoping to improve welfare by raising per capita meat consumption, he institutes heavy grain purchases (for animal fodder) on the world market, which prevent increased cereal production from benefiting the hungrier peoples and drive up world cereal prices. Once more, the net effect of an act intended to increase happiness may be to increase rather than reduce human misery. The conundrums can be multiplied again and again. The point is that if we are to try to work out the consequences of our actions as utilitarian theory demands we should, we shall repeatedly find ourselves confronted with impossible calculations. Utilitarianism offers us spurious precision in moral argument.[8]

> [8] This is one fundamental objection to utilitarianism in this area and many others: that it is simply impossible to determine what the right action is from a utilitarian standpoint or even to come to a reasonable estimate or approximation.

The reasons for these difficulties lie deep in the structure of utilitarian theory and are not likely to be remedied by further research. For utilitarians do not say that one should look *just* at the fairly local effects of one's own act. After all, if the aim is to maximize human happiness and to minimize human misery, then there is no point in basing one's calculations on the false assumption that the consequences of one's own act can be isolated. There is no point, for example, in aiding poor countries if the good effects of the aid are outweighed by bad effects, such as propping up a regime that opposes change and economic growth. There is no point, on utilitarian calculations, in spending all one's efforts in lobbying for reduced "defense" spending so that swords can be beaten into plowshares if the result is likely to be either that no reduction takes place but that one has no time to make more modest contributions to human happiness, or, on the other hand, that a reduction takes place but produces increased unemployment and no plowshares, while leading arms purchasers to turn to different sellers. For utilitarians, it is *results,* not *intentions,* that count, and the calculation of results must therefore be taken seriously. I can know my intentions fairly clearly, but I can never be sure about all the effects of my own acts or of an institution's policies.

The very comprehensive and systematic structure that makes utilitarian moral theory attractive to many people becomes on reflection one of its nightmares. We may often be fairly clear about the short-term effect on nearby people of what we propose to do. But we are seldom clear about the total effect or tendency of acts or policies in an economically interdependent world where we might affect the lives of persons thousands of miles or many generations away. We face in our own time decisions about energy policy that will deeply affect future lives. If we leave a world of nuclear radiation or terrorism, or of fossil-fuel famine, or of health- and crop-destroying pollution, we shall make future persons more miserable—or less happy—than they might have been had we made different decisions. Yet, which of us can be sure (including the disputing experts) which decision is likely to have the happiest results? Difficulties of calculations affect persons and agencies (from corner stores to nation states to the United Nations). They produce an uncomfortable feeling that we cannot make the most needed calculations, so can never say: "This is the way to minimize misery, so this ought to be done." Where there is no limit to the number of consequences, nearby or remote, that we ought to consider, conclusions seem to evaporate, not to crystallize. Utilitarians may start out wanting to be realists who soberly calculate the outcomes and the odds; but there seems to be no natural stopping point before they find themselves trying to be futurologists who seek to uncover the impact of their actions, or that of their insti-

tutions, in a vast and complex causal web that extends indefinitely into the future. ⑨

A serious utilitarian faces a morally strenuous life. Every decision is a moral decision, since any act affects human happiness or prevents another act that might affect human happiness. A utilitarian can never say: "I've done my duty." However great one's contribution has been, it is likely that there are further miseries one could in part reduce without causing oneself or others comparable misery. As each misery is vanquished there will be another waiting for one's ministrations. ⑩ And so utilitarianism comes to seem not the most precise but at once the vaguest and the most demanding of moral theories. Utilitarian arguments founder, not just occasionally but systematically, on our uncertainty about calculating the effects of our own acts when combined with others'. Research might help a bit, but it would not resolve the indeterminacy in all cases. This is a standard difficulty of utilitarian moral theory, but it appears much graver in thinking about a problem like famine, where particularly long and intricate causal chains must *nearly always* be considered. Utilitarians can get nowhere unless they are reasonably sure about the effects acts they consider are likely to have. If utilitarians do not know this, then they have no way of telling whether a proposed act or policy is obligatory, forbidden, or neither. ⑪ . . .

⑨ Part of the problem is the need to consider consequences indefinitely into the future. This problem cannot be adequately dealt with by saying—as Bentham seems to suggest— that consequences in the distant future should be "discounted": weighted less heavily than temporally closer ones. Even if they count for less, distant future consequences may well be more important to the correct overall result simply because there are so many of them.

⑩ From a utilitarian standpoint, there are moral obligations pertaining to *everything* we do, with actions that are acceptable but not obligatory occurring only in the rare case where several actions are tied in their utilitarian value. And the point is not just that this is demanding, but that it is intuitively implausible that things are really like that.

⑪ O'Neill is right that this problem is especially conspicuous with regard to an issue like famine. But are there any very serious choices to which it does not apply? (See Discussion Question 2.)

KANTIAN APPROACHES TO SOME FAMINE PROBLEMS

§22 A Simplified Account of Kant's Ethics

Kant's moral theory has acquired the reputation of being forbiddingly difficult to understand and, once understood, excessively demanding in its requirements. I don't believe that this reputation has been wholly earned, and I am going to try to undermine it. In §§23–26 I shall try to reduce some of the difficulties, and in §§27–30 I shall try to show the implications of a Kantian moral theory for action toward those who do or may suffer famine. Finally, I shall compare Kantian and utilitarian approaches and assess their strengths and weaknesses.

The main method by which I propose to avoid some of the difficulties of Kant's moral theory is by explaining only one part of the theory. This does not seem to me to be an irresponsible approach in this case. One of the things that makes Kant's moral theory hard to understand is that he gives a number of different versions of the principle that he calls the Supreme Principle of Morality, and these different versions don't look at all like one another. They also don't look at all like the utilitarians' Greatest Happiness Principle. But the Kantian principle is supposed to play a similar role in arguments about what to do.

Kant calls his Supreme Principle the *Categorical Imperative;* its various versions also have sonorous names. One is called the Formula of Universal Law; another is the Formula of the Kingdom of Ends. The one on which I shall concentrate is known as the *Formula of the End in Itself.* To understand why Kant thinks that these picturesquely named principles are equivalent to one another takes quite a lot of close and detailed analysis of Kant's philosophy. I shall avoid this and concentrate on showing the implications of this version of the Categorical Imperative.

§23 The Formula of the End in Itself

Kant states the Formula of the End in Itself as follows:

> Act in such a way that you always treat humanity, whether in your own person or in the person of

any other, never simply as a means but always at the same time as an end.*

To understand this we need to know what it is to treat a person as a means or as an end. According to Kant, each of our acts reflects one or more *maxims.* The maxim of the act is the principle on which one sees oneself as acting. A maxim expresses a person's policy, or if he or she has no settled policy, the principle underlying the particular intention or decision on which he or she acts. Thus, a person who decides "This year I'll give 10 percent of my income to famine relief" has as a maxim the principle of tithing his or her income for famine relief. In practice, the difference between intentions and maxims is of little importance, for given any intention, we can formulate the corresponding maxim by deleting references to particular times, places, and persons. In what follows I shall take the terms 'maxim' and 'intention' as equivalent.

Whenever we act intentionally, we have at least one maxim and can, if we reflect, state what it is. (There is of course room for self-deception here—"I'm only keeping the wolf from the door" we may claim as we wolf down enough to keep ourselves overweight, or, more to the point, enough to feed someone else who hasn't enough food.)

When we want to work out whether an act we propose to do is right or wrong, according to Kant, we should look at our maxims and not at how much misery or happiness the act is likely to produce, and whether it does better at increasing happiness than other available acts. We just have to check that the act we have in mind will not use anyone as a mere means, and, if possible, that it will treat other persons as ends in themselves.

§24 Using Persons as Mere Means

To use someone as a *mere means* is to involve them in a scheme of action *to which they could not in principle consent.*[12] Kant does not say that there is anything wrong about using someone as a means. Evidently we have to do so in any cooperative scheme of action. If I cash a check I use the teller as a means, without whom I could not lay my hands on the cash;

---

*I. Kant, *Groundwork of the Metaphysic of Morals,* tr. H. H. Paton, New York, Harper Torchbooks, 1964, p. 96.

the teller in turn uses me as a means to earn his or her living. But in this case, each party consents to her or his part in the transac-

[12] This is a helpful suggestion as to what it is to treat a person as a "mere means," one that is supported to some extent by Kant's own discussion. Does it capture all of the relevant cases? Think here of Kant's own examples, though some of those are, as we have seen, debatable in themselves. (And see Discussion Question 3.)

tion. Kant would say that though they use one another as means, they do not use one another as *mere* means. Each person assumes that the other has maxims of his or her own and is not just a thing or a prop to be manipulated.

But there are other situations where one person uses another in a way to which the other could not in principle consent. For example, one person may make a promise to another with every intention of breaking it. If the promise is accepted, then the person to whom it was given must be ignorant of what the promisor's intention (maxim) really is. If one knew that the promisor did not intend to do what he or she was promising, one would, after all, not accept or rely on the promise. It would be as though there had been no promise made. Successful false promising depends on deceiving the person to whom the promise is made about what one's real maxim is. And since the person who is deceived doesn't know that real maxim, he or she can't in principle consent to his or her part in the proposed scheme of ac-

[13] So any action that depends essentially on deceiving another person will be one to which the person in question "could not in principle consent." Is it plausible that all actions that have this feature are morally objectionable? (See Discussion Question 4.)

tion. The person who is deceived is, as it were, a prop or a tool—a mere means—in the false promisor's scheme. A person who promises falsely treats the acceptor of the promise as a prop or a thing and not as a person. In Kant's view, it is this that makes false promising wrong. [13]

One standard way of using others as mere means is by deceiving them. By getting someone involved in a business scheme or a criminal activity on false pretenses, or by giving a misleading account of what one is about, or by making a false promise or a fraudulent contract, one involves another in something to which he or she in principle cannot consent, since the

scheme requires that he or she doesn't know what is going on. Another standard way of using others as mere means is by coercing them. If a rich or powerful person threatens a debtor with bankruptcy unless he or she joins in some scheme, then the creditor's intention is to coerce; and the debtor, if coerced, cannot consent to his or her part in the creditor's scheme. To make the example more specific: If a moneylender in an Indian village threatens not to renew a vital loan unless he is given the debtor's land, then he uses the debtor as a mere means. He co-erces the debtor, who cannot truly consent to this "offer he can't refuse." (Of course the outward form of such transactions may look like ordinary commercial dealings, but we know very well that some offers and demands couched in that form are coercive.) [14]

[14] Think carefully about this further suggestion. Does *any* sort of pressure on another person's choice count as *coercion*—and if not, how much is required? Is there a reasonably clear line here? (See Discussion Question 5.)

In Kant's view, acts that are done on maxims that require deception or coercion of others, and so cannot have the consent of those others (for consent precludes both deception and coercion), are wrong. When we act on such maxims, we treat others as mere means, as things rather than as ends in themselves. If we act on such maxims, our acts are not only wrong but unjust: such acts wrong the particular others who are deceived or coerced.

§25 Treating Persons as Ends in Themselves

Duties of justice are, in Kant's view (as in many others'), the most important of our duties. When we fail in these duties, we have used some other or others as mere means. But there are also cases where, though we do not use others as mere means, still we fail to use them as ends in themselves in the fullest possible way. To treat someone as an end in him or herself requires in the first place that one not use him or her as mere means, that one respect each as a rational person with his or her own maxims. But beyond that, one may also seek to foster others' plans and maxims by sharing some of their ends. To act beneficently is to seek others' happiness, therefore to intend to achieve some of the things that those others aim at with their maxims. If I want to make others happy, I will adopt maxims that not merely do not manipulate them but that foster some of their plans and activities. Beneficent acts try to achieve what others want. However, we cannot seek everything that others want; their wants are too numerous and diverse, and, of course, sometimes incompatible. It follows that beneficence has to be selective. [15]

---

[15] To what extent do we have to seek things that others seek or foster their plans and activities in order to satisfy this part of Kant's requirement? How much is required to be "reasonably benefi-cent," as O'Neill says fur-ther on? Does Kant's view yield an answer to this question that is at least reasonably clear?

There is then quite a sharp distinction between the requirements of justice and of beneficence in Kantian ethics. Justice requires that we act on *no* maxims that use others as mere means. Beneficence requires that we act on *some* maxims that foster others' ends, though it is a matter for judgment and discretion which of their ends we foster. Some [ends] no doubt ought not to be fostered because it would be unjust to do so. Kantians are not committed to working interminably through a list of happiness-producing and misery-reducing acts; but there are some acts whose obligatoriness utilitarians may need to debate as they try to compare total outcomes of different choices, to which Kantians are stringently bound. Kantians will claim that they have done nothing wrong if none of their acts is unjust, and that their duty is complete if in addition their life plans have in the circumstances been reasonably beneficent.

In making sure that they meet all the demands of justice, Kantians do not try to compare all available acts and see which has the best effects. They consider only the proposals for action that occur to them and check that these proposals use no other as mere means. If they do not, the act is permissible; if omitting the act would use another as mere means, the act is obligatory. [16] Kant's

---

[16] An act that uses another person as a mere means is morally forbidden. One that would if *not* performed use another person as a mere means is morally required. (Can you think of an example of this?) If an action has neither of these features, then both performing it and not performing it are morally permissible—assuming that the agent has somewhere, though not necessarily with this specific action or inaction, satisfied the requirements of "reasonable beneficence."

---

theory has less scope than utilitarianism. Kantians do not claim to discover whether acts whose maxims they don't know fully are just. They may be reluctant to judge others' acts or policies that cannot be regarded as the maxim of any person or institution. They cannot rank acts in order of merit. Yet, the theory offers more precision than utilitarianism when data are scarce. One can usually tell whether one's act would use others as mere means, even when its impact on human happiness is thoroughly obscure.

§26 Kantian Deliberations on Famine Problems

The theory I have just sketched may seem to have little to say about famine problems. For it is a theory that forbids us to use others as mere means but does not require us to direct our benevolence first to those who suffer most. A conscientious Kantian, it seems, has only to avoid being unjust to those who suffer famine and can then be beneficent to those nearer home. He or she would not be obliged to help the starving, even if no others were equally distressed. [17]

---

[17] The issue here is whether all sorts of beneficence are morally on a par, as long as the overall total is great enough—or whether not treating others as mere means requires helping or at least trying to help those in greater need.

Kant's moral theory does make less massive demands on moral agents than utilitarian moral theory. On the other hand, it is somewhat clearer just what the more stringent demands are, and they are not negligible. We have here a contrast between a theory that makes massive but often indeterminate demands and a theory that makes fewer but less unambiguous demands and leaves other questions, in particular the allocation of beneficence, unresolved. We have also a contrast between a theory whose scope is comprehensive and one that is applicable only to persons acting intentionally and to those institutions that adopt policies, and so maxims. Kantian ethics is silent about the moral status of unintentional action; utilitarians seek to assess all consequences regardless of the intentions that led to them.

§27 Kantian Duties of Justice in Times of Famine

In famine situations, Kantian moral theory requires unambiguously that we do no injustice. We should not act on any maxim that uses another as mere means, so we should neither deceive nor coerce others. Such a requirement can become quite exacting when the means of life are scarce, when persons can more easily be coerced, and when the advantage of gaining more than what is justly due to one is great. I shall give a list of acts that on Kantian principles it would be unjust to do, but that one might be strongly tempted to do in famine conditions.

I will begin with a list of acts that one might be tempted to do as a member of a famine-stricken population. First, where there is a rationing scheme, one ought not to cheat and seek to get more than one's share—any scheme of cheating will use someone as mere means. Nor may one take advantage of others' desperation to profiteer or divert goods onto the black market or to accumulate a fortune out of others' misfortunes. Transactions that are outwardly sales and purchases can be coercive when one party is desperate. All the forms of corruption that deceive or put pressure on others are also wrong: hoarding unallocated food, diverting relief supplies for private use, corruptly using one's influence to others' disadvantage. Such requirements are far from trivial and frequently violated in hard times. In severe famines, refraining from coercing and deceiving may risk one's own life and require the greatest courage. [18]

Second, justice requires that in famine situations one still try to fulfill one's duties to particular others. For example, even in times of famine, a person has duties to try to provide for dependents. These duties may, tragically, be unfulfillable. [19] If they are, Kantian ethical theory would not judge wrong the acts of a person who had done her or his best. There have no doubt been times in human history where there was nothing to be done except abandon the weak and old or . . . leave children to fend for themselves as best they might. But providing the supporter of dependents acts on maxims of attempting to meet their claims, he or she uses no others as mere means to his or her own survival and is not unjust. A conscientious attempt to meet the particular obligations one has undertaken may also require of one many further maxims of self-restraint and of endeavor—for example, it may require a conscientious attempt to avoid having (further) children; it may require contributing one's time and effort to programs of economic development. Where there is no other means to fulfill particular obligations, Kantian principles may require a generation of sacrifice. They will not, however, require one to seek to maximize the happiness of later generations but only to establish the modest security and prosperity needed for meeting present obligations.

The obligations of those who live with or near famine are undoubtedly stringent and exacting; for those who live further off it is rather harder to see what a Kantian moral theory demands. Might it not, for example, be permissible to do nothing at all about those suffering famine? Might one not ensure that one does nothing unjust to the victims of famine by adopting no maxims whatsoever that mention them? To do so would, at the least, require one to refrain from certain deceptive and coercive practices frequently employed during the European exploration and economic penetration of the now under-developed world and still not unknown. For example, it would be unjust to "purchase" valuable lands and resources from persons who don't understand commercial transactions or exclusive property rights or mineral rights, so do not understand that their acceptance of trinkets destroys their traditional economic pattern and way of life. The old adage "trade follows the flag" reminds us to how great an extent the economic penetration of the less-developed countries involved elements of coercion and deception, so was on Kantian principles unjust (regardless of whether or not the net effect has benefited the citizens of those countries).

Few persons in the developed world today find themselves faced with the possibility of adopting on a grand scale maxims of deceiving or coercing persons living in poverty. But at least some people find that their jobs require them to make decisions about investment and aid policies that enormously affect the lives of those nearest to famine. What does a

[18] Think carefully about each of these examples. Again there is a difficult issue of just when coercion (or an unacceptable level of coercion) occurs. Is making people pay for the food that they need a form of coercion? Why or why not?

[19] Not to attempt to fulfill an obligation resulting from an explicit agreement of some sort would be a fairly clear case of using the other person as a mere means. Is it clear how this extends to other sorts of duties one may be thought to have to particular people, such as duties to one's children? If I am unwilling to endure sacrifice in order to feed my children in a time of famine, have I thereby used them as a mere means, and if so, how?

commitment to Kantian moral theory demand of such persons?

It has become common in writings in ethics and social policy to distinguish between one's *personal responsibilities* and one's *role responsibilities.* So a person may say, "As an individual I sympathize, but in my official capacity I can do nothing"; or we may excuse persons' acts of coercion because they are acting in some particular capacity—e.g., as a soldier or a jailer. On the other hand, this distinction isn't made or accepted by everyone. At the Nuremberg trials of war criminals, the defense "I was only doing my job" was disallowed, at least for those whose command position meant that they had some discretion in what they did. Kantians generally would play down any distinction between a person's own responsibilities and his or her role responsibilities. They would not deny that in any capacity one is accountable for certain things for which as a private person one is not accountable. For example, the treasurer of an organization is accountable to the board and has to present periodic reports and to keep specified records. But if she fails to do one of these things for which she is held accountable she will be held responsible for that failure—it will be imputable to her as an individual. When we take on positions, we *add* to our responsibilities those that the job requires; but we do not lose those that are already required of us. Our social role or job gives us, on Kant's view, no license to use others as mere means; even business executives and aid officials and social revolutionaries will act unjustly, so wrongly, if they deceive or coerce—however benevolent their motives.

If persons are responsible for all their acts, it follows that it would be unjust for aid officials to coerce persons into accepting sterilization, wrong for them to use coercive power to achieve political advantages (such as military bases) or commercial advantages (such as trade agreements that will harm the other country). It would be wrong for the executives of large corporations to extort too high a price for continued operation employment and normal trading. Where a less-developed country is pushed to exempt a multinational corporation from tax laws, or to construct out of its meager tax revenues the infrastructure of roads, harbors, or airports (not to mention executive mansions) that the corporation—but perhaps not the country—

needs, then one suspects that some coercion has been involved. [20]

The problem with such judgments—and it is an immense problem—is that it is hard to identify coercion and deception in complicated institutional settings. It is not hard to understand what is coercive about one person threatening another with serious injury if he won't comply with the first person's suggestion. But it is not at all easy to tell where the outward forms of political and commercial negotiation—which often involve an element of threat—have become coercive. I can't here explore this fascinating question. But I think it is at least fairly clear that the preservation of the outward forms of negotiation, bargaining, and voluntary consent do *not* demonstrate that there is no coercion, especially when one party is vastly more powerful or the other in dire need. Just as our judiciary has a long tradition of voiding contracts and agreements on grounds of duress or incompetence of one of the parties, so one can imagine a tribunal of an analogous sort rejecting at least some treaties and agreements as coercive, despite the fact that they were negotiated between "sovereign" powers or their representatives. In particular, where such agreements were negotiated with some of the cruder deceptions and coercion of the early days of European economic expansion or the subtler coercions and deceptions of contemporary superpowers, it seems doubtful that the justice of the agreement could be sustained.

Justice, of course, is not everything, even for Kantians. But its demands are ones that they can reasonably strive to fulfill. They may have some uncertain moments—for example, does advocating cheap raw materials mean advocating an international trade system in which the less developed will continue to suffer the pressures of the developed world—or is it a benevolent policy that will maximize world trade and benefit all parties, while doing no one an injustice? But for Kantians, the important moral choices are above all those in which one acts directly, not those in which one decides which patterns of actions to encourage in others or in those institutions that one can influence. And such moral decisions include deci-

[20] Once again there is the issue of how much pressure constitutes coercion. Is any case of asking for something in return for help a case of coercion—and if not, where does the line fall?

sions about the benevolent acts that one will or will not do.

§28 Kantian Duties of Beneficence in Times of Famine

The grounds of duties of beneficence are that such acts not merely don't use others as mere means but are acts that develop or promote others' ends and that, in particular, foster others' capacities to pursue ends, to be autonomous beings.

Clearly there are many opportunities for beneficence. But one area in which the *primary* task of developing others' capacity to pursue their own ends is particularly needed is in the parts of the world where extreme poverty and hunger leave people unable to pursue *any* of their other ends. Beneficence directed at putting people in a position to pursue whatever ends they may have has, for Kant, a stronger claim on us than beneficence directed at sharing ends with those who are already in a position to pursue varieties of ends. It would be nice if I bought a tennis racquet to play with my friend who is tennis mad and never has enough partners; but it is more important to make people able to plan their own lives to a minimal extent. It is nice to walk a second mile with someone who requests one's company; better to share a cloak with someone who may otherwise be too cold to make any journey. Though these suggestions are not a detailed set of instructions for the allocation of beneficence by Kantians, they show that relief of famine must stand very high among duties of beneficence. [21]

---
[21] Here is an argument that we are, from a Kantian standpoint, obligated to try to help those whose need is greater, that their claim on our beneficence is greater. How compelling is it?

---

§29 The Limits of Kantian Ethics: Intentions and Results

Kantian ethics differs from utilitarian ethics both in its scope and in the precision with which it guides action. Every action, whether of a person or of an agency, can be assessed by utilitarian methods, provided only that information is available about all the consequences of the act. The theory has unlimited scope, but, owing to lack of data, often lacks precision. Kantian ethics has a more restricted scope. Since it assesses actions by looking at the maxims of agents, it can only assess intentional acts. This means that it is most at home in assessing individuals' acts; but it can be extended to assess acts of agencies that (like corporations and governments and student unions) have decision-making procedures. It can do nothing to assess patterns of action that reflect no intention or policy, hence it cannot assess the acts of groups lacking decision-making procedures, such as the student movement, the women's movement, or the consumer movement.

It may seem a great limitation of Kantian ethics that it concentrates on intentions to the neglect of results. It might seem that all conscientious Kantians have to do is to make sure that they never intend to use others as mere means, and that they sometimes intend to foster others' ends. And, as we all know, good intentions sometimes lead to bad results, and correspondingly, bad intentions sometimes do no harm, or even produce good. If Hardin is right, the good intentions of those who feed the starving lead to dreadful results in the long run. If some traditional arguments in favor of capitalism are right, the greed and selfishness of the profit motive have produced unparalleled prosperity for many.

But such discrepancies between intentions and results are the exception and not the rule. For we cannot just *claim* that our intentions are good and do what we will. Our intentions reflect what we expect the immediate results of our action to be. Nobody credits the "intentions" of a couple who practice neither celibacy nor contraception but still insist "we never meant to have (more) children." Conception is likely (and known to be likely) in such cases. Where people's expressed intentions ignore the normal and predictable results of what they do, we infer that (if they are not amazingly ignorant) their words do not express their true intentions. The Formula of the End in Itself applies to the intentions on which one acts—not to some prettified version that one may avow. Provided this intention—the agent's real intention—uses no other as mere means, he or she does nothing unjust. If some of his or her intentions foster others' ends, then he or she is sometimes beneficent. It is therefore possible for people to test their proposals by Kantian arguments even when they lack the comprehensive causal knowledge that utilitarianism requires. Conscientious Kantians can work out whether they will be doing wrong by some act even though they know that their foresight is limited and that they may cause some harm or fail to cause some benefit. But they will not cause harms that they can foresee without this being reflected in their intentions.

RESPECT FOR LIFE: A COMPARISON OF KANTIAN AND UTILITARIAN VIEWS

§30 Utilitarianism and Respect for Life

From the differing implications that Kantian and utilitarian moral theories have for our actions towards those who do or may suffer famine, we can discover two sharply contrasting views of the value of human life. Utilitarians value happiness and the absence or reduction of misery. As a utilitarian one ought (if conscientious) to devote one's life to achieving the best possible balance of happiness over misery. If one's life plan remains in doubt, this will be because the means to this end are often unclear. But whenever the causal tendency of acts is clear, utilitarians will be able to discern the acts they should successively do in order to improve the world's balance of happiness over unhappiness.

This task is not one for the faint-hearted. First, it is dauntingly long, indeed interminable. Second, it may at times require the sacrifice of happiness, and even of lives, for the sake of a greater happiness. Such sacrifice may be morally required not only when the person whose happiness or even whose life is at stake volunteers to make the sacrifice. It may be necessary to sacrifice some lives for the sake of others. As our control over the means of ending and preserving human life has increased, analogous dilemmas have arisen in many areas for utilitarians. Should life be preserved at the cost of pain when modern medicine makes this possible? Should life be preserved without hope of consciousness? Should triage policies, because they may maximize the number of survivors, be used to determine who should be left to starve? Should population growth be fostered wherever it will increase the total of human happiness—or on some

views so long as average happiness is not reduced? All these questions can be fitted into utilitarian frameworks and answered *if* we have the relevant information. And sometimes the answer will be that human happiness demands the sacrifice of lives, including the sacrifice of unwilling lives. Further, for most utilitarians, it makes no difference if the unwilling sacrifices involve acts of injustice to those whose lives are to be lost. It might, for example, prove necessary for maximal happiness that some persons have their allotted rations, or their hard-earned income, diverted for others' benefit. Or it might turn out that some generations must sacrifice comforts or liberties and even lives to rear "the fabric of felicity" for their successors. Utilitarians do not deny these possibilities, though the imprecision of our knowledge of consequences often blurs the implications of the theory. If we peer through the blur, we see that the utilitarian view is that lives may indeed be sacrificed for the sake of a greater good even when the persons are not willing. There is nothing wrong with using another as a mere means provided that the end for which the person is so used is a happier result than could have been achieved any other way, taking into account the misery the means have caused. In utilitarian thought, persons are not ends in themselves. Their special moral status derives from their being means to the production of happiness. Human life has therefore a high though derivative value, and one life may be taken for the sake of greater happiness in other lives, or for ending of misery in that life. Nor is there any deep difference between ending a life for the sake of others' happiness by not helping (e.g., by triaging) and doing so by harming. Because the distinction between justice and beneficence is not sharply made within utilitarianism, it is not possible to say that triaging is a matter of not benefiting, while other interventions are a matter of injustice.

Utilitarian moral theory has then a rather paradoxical view of the value of human life. Living, conscious humans are (along with other sentient beings) necessary for the existence of everything utilitarians value. But it is not their being alive but the state of their consciousness that is of value. Hence, the best results may require certain lives to be lost—by whatever means—for the sake of the total happiness and absence of misery that can be produced.

§31 Kant and Respect for Persons

Kantians reach different conclusions about human life. Human life is valuable because humans (and conceivably other beings, e.g., angels or apes) are the bearers of rational life. Humans are able to choose and to plan. This capacity and its exercise are of such value that they ought not to be sacrificed for anything of lesser value. Therefore, no one rational or autonomous creature should be treated as mere means for the enjoyment or even the happiness of another. We may in Kant's view justifiably—even nobly—risk or sacrifice our lives for others. For in doing so we follow our own maxim and nobody uses us as mere means. But no others may use either our lives or our bodies for a scheme that they have either coerced or deceived us into joining. For in doing so they would

fail to treat us as rational beings; they would use us as mere means and not as ends in ourselves.

It is conceivable that a society of Kantians, all of whom took pains to use no other as mere means, would end up with less happiness or with fewer persons alive than would some societies of complying utilitarians. For since the Kantians would be strictly bound only to justice, they might without wrongdoing be quite selective in their beneficence and fail to maximize either survival rates or happiness, or even to achieve as much of either as a strenuous group of utilitarians, who somehow make the right calculations. On the other hand, nobody will have been made an instrument of others' survival or happiness in the society of complying Kantians.

. . .

Discussion Questions

1. Hardin seems to be arguing for the conclusion that affluent countries should not help those suffering from famine (and similar problems, such as widespread disease) at all—not just that this is not morally required, but that it would be morally wrong from a utilitarian standpoint to do so. How plausible is his argument? How much does it depend on a choice between no help at all and a very great level of help that might put the affluent countries themselves in jeopardy? Are there intermediate levels of help that do better from a utilitarian standpoint than either of these extreme alternatives? If so, is it fairly clear where the best alternative lies?

2. Think of several examples of reasonably serious moral choices, and think of the possible consequences that different actions might have in the fairly distant future. How often in such cases are we in a position to make a confident assessment of the utilitarian value of those distant consequences? How often can someone make such a choice from a utilitarian standpoint with any very great confidence that he is doing the right thing?

3. What does the "in principle" part of O'Neill's suggested Kantian requirement that one not involve a people in "a scheme of action to which they could not in principle consent" amount to? Could one, for example, consent

in principle to being treated as a slave? Why or why not?

4. Is any action that essentially involves deceiving another person thereby immoral? Is it immoral to lure someone to a surprise party in their honor (something that essentially involves deceiving them—and to which they could not in principle consent, since that would destroy the surprise)? Can you think of other actions with this feature that do not seem morally objectionable? Is there any way for a Kantian to draw a clear line between deception that is morally permissible and deception that is not?

5. There are many sorts of actions where coercion—or at least something that looks a lot like coercion—seems to be essentially involved, but that nonetheless seem morally permissible. A store, by having prices for its merchandise (and antishoplifting devices) might be said to coerce its customers into paying for what they want. Law enforcement authorities might be said to use the threat of various sorts of punishment to coerce citizens into complying with the law. Teachers might be said to coerce students into working hard with the threat of low grades. Is there any reasonably clear way to draw a line between cases of coercion (or pressure) that are morally acceptable and those that use others merely as means?

David T. Ozar

David T. Ozar (1942–) is an American philosopher who teaches at Loyola University, where he is also the Director of Loyola's Center for Ethics. He has written widely on rights and on the ethics of health care. In this selection, Ozar explains the general concept of rights, distinguishes moral rights from conventional rights (such as legal rights), and discusses the issue of whether there are universal moral rights that all human beings have (and if so, what the basis for such rights might be).

Rights: What They Are and Where They Come From

1. RIGHTS TALK

Rights talk is one way of trying to talk, think, and reason about what individuals and communities ought and ought not to do. That is, rights talk is one area of moral discourse. There are many other ways of trying to analyze the various kinds of situations that arise in our lives when an action or policy is good or bad, right or wrong, moral or immoral. But in the Western world at the present time, rights talk is one of the most common ways of formulating moral issues, whether the issues involve only individuals or are between individuals and communities or even when they involve the relationships of whole communities with one another. For this reason it is very important to understand rights talk and to see how it can be used to explain the moral components of the situations we face in our lives.

It is possible, of course, that rights talk only gets at part of the whole moral picture and misses something crucial. If this is so, it will need to be patched up or amended or possibly even replaced. Talk about rights, then, is only one way to deal with critical ethical issues. But even people who think that rights talk probably does not tell the whole moral story would have to begin their arguments by looking carefully at social issues from the perspective of rights. . . .

From Philosophical Issues in Human Rights: Theories and Applications, *edited by Patricia H. Werhane, A.R. Gini, and David T. Ozar (New York: Random House, 1986).*

2. WHAT ARE RIGHTS?

No simple definition of the form "a right is a . . ." can adequately explain this complex concept. Instead we need to ask ourselves two closely related questions: (1) What do we imply when we make the statement "A has a right, R, of some sort"? and (2) What conditions must be fulfilled for such a statement to be true?

First of all, when we say that someone has a right of some sort, we are, as already noted, talking about what ought or ought not to be done. Rights talk is one kind of moral discourse. It is used to inform people of their obligations and to give explanations of our own and others' choices and actions.

Second, to speak about a right, any right, is to say that there is *someone* who *has* such a right. A right always has reference to an actor—or, in philosophical jargon, an "agent"—a being that acts and is acted upon. Rights do not exist independently, unattached, as it were. In most cases the agent will be an individual human being; that is, ordinarily it is human beings that *have* rights. Whether nonhuman animals can have rights and whether a *group* of human beings, functioning as a single entity, can have rights are questions for debate. We also ask whether beings from another solar system or galaxy could have rights. We will return to this question again shortly.

Third, to say that someone, A, has a right, R, of some sort is to imply that someone else, B, has an *obligation* of some sort, to do or to refrain from some act relative to A. That is, rights are *relational*. This is not necessarily to say that all rights have their basis in relationships; we will discuss various proposed bases of rights in a moment. The point being made here is rather that a right *is* a relationship; it is a relationship between a person who has the right and others who have corresponding obligations to act or to refrain. ①

① As this suggests, the idea of someone having a *right* seems to make no real sense unless there are others who have correlative *duties*. (But the reverse does not seem to be the case: not every duty entails a corresponding right. Kant's duty of beneficence is one example of an alleged duty to which there is no corresponding right: no one in particular has a right to any given person's beneficence.)

Fourth, rights have a special *overriding* character. As Gregory Vlastos has put it, rights take precedence over many other sorts of moral considerations.* When we say that someone has a right, our words imply that the moral considerations that are the basis of this statement are more important than any other kinds of moral considerations that might be relevant to the situation.

What other kinds of moral considerations might be relevant? In general they fall into two categories: rules and consequences. For many people obligations to act or to refrain from acting frequently derive from a set of fundamental rules of conduct. These rules may be simple rather straightforward rules like those we often use to instruct our children: Do not lie; do not steal; do not harm other persons; keep your promises; help those in need; develop your talents; and so on. Or they may be much more *abstract* rules like the two tests of moral action proposed by the German philosopher Immanuel Kant (1724–1804): (1) "I ought never to act except in such a way that I can also will that my maxim should become a universal law"; (2) "Act in such a way that you always treat humanity, whether in your own person or in the person of any other, never simply as a means, but always at the same time as an end."†

On the other hand, for many other people the point of our obligation is to bring about by our actions the greatest amount of good, the greatest improvement in well-being for people, that we can. In this view, the key to correct judgments about what ought and ought not to be done is a careful analysis of the consequences that can be expected from the various actions that might be performed. This approach claims that, of the actions available to us in a particular situation, that action ought to be performed that brings about the highest level of well-being for the people affected. There are many complications with this approach, regarding how the good and evil consequences of the same act are to be taken into account together, especially if they are experienced and evaluated differently by different people. But for many people such reflections on the consequences of our actions are the basis of people's obligations to do or refrain. ②

② Utilitarianism is, of course, one example of such a consequentialist view.

When we say that someone has a right, we imply that the moral considerations that are the basis of this statement about rights are more important than rules of conduct that might be relevant, and that these moral considerations also outweigh in importance the consequences of the particular actions under consideration. As a matter of fact, when we talk about a right, we are talking about something that takes precedence over other moral considerations in two ways. Rights have a *double* overriding character. First, if A has a right of some sort, then B's obligation to do or to refrain takes precedence over other moral considerations relevant to B's own choice of his or her best or most required action. That is, B may not simply disregard an obligation based on A's right without moral fault; and, with few exceptions, the only considerations that can possibly have comparable moral weight for B are considerations based on the rights of other, third, parties or, to a more limited extent, on B's own rights. ③

③ This overriding character of rights makes it tempting to formulate any allegedly serious moral claim as a right. But the fact that rights in this way override other moral considerations suggests that it will be harder to establish the existence of rights than to establish the existence of other sorts of moral considerations—and hence that we should be suspicious of claims of rights that are put forth without any clear basis.

*Gregory Vlastos, "Justice and Equality," in *Social Justice,* ed. Richard Brandt (Englewood Cliffs, N.J.: Prentice-Hall, 1962), pp. 31–72.
†Immanuel Kant, *Groundwork of the Metaphysic of Morals,* trans. H. J. Paton (New York: Harper & Row, 1964), p. 70; p. 96.

The second overriding feature of a right concerns the rest of us. To say that A has a right of some sort implies not only that B has an obligation of some sort to do or refrain. It implies, too, that the rest of us also have some measure of obligation to see to it, within certain limits, that B acts or refrains accordingly. The limits of this obligation are determined in turn by our own rights, by B's rights, and possibly by other moral considerations, depending on the circumstances. But the point is that the rest of us are affected by the fact, if it *is* a fact, that A has certain rights vis-á-vis B. Henry Shue expresses this point forcefully when he says that a right provides the rational basis for A to demand that the enjoyment of the substance of that right be "socially guaranteed against standard threats."* This overriding character of rights will be studied further in Section 6 below.

Fifth, to say that A has a right that B act or refrain in some way is to say not only that B has an obligation in this regard, but that B owes this to A. If B fails to act or refrain accordingly, B is not only failing to act as morality requires; B is failing A.

Suppose, by contrast, that B had an obligation of some other sort to be generous toward A but that A did not have a right to this. If B fails to be generous, B acts immorally, but B does not fail A, for B did not *owe* A anything. But if A has *a right,* then if B fails to act or refrain as obligated, B fails A because B owed something to A and did not carry it out. This is why rights are sometimes partially defined as justified claims upon other persons to act or to refrain, and why the legal theorist Hohfeld called them claim-rights.†

By the same token, if A has a right and if the rest of us fail to carry out our corresponding obligations to see to it that B acts or refrains accordingly, then we have not only failed to act as morality requires but we have failed A as well. For A's right is also a *claim* on the rest of us; it is something we *owe* A. It justifies a *demand* on the rest of us—a demand that we see to it, within proper limits, that B acts or refrains accordingly.④

Sixth, since there is never a moral obligation to do what is simply impossible, it follows that it is never the case that A has a right that B do what is impossible or that B refrain from what B cannot possibly avoid. This is a feature of the very notion of a right, and it is such a feature because it is a feature of the very notion of moral obligation. It makes no sense—and more specifically it is an example of what has been called a "category mistake"—to try to say that B has an obligation to do something or avoid something that it is simply impossible for B to do or avoid.

In a similar way, the concept of a right makes no sense when the acting or refraining to which it refers is impossible. Suppose that an argument is made that everyone in the world has a right to sufficient food to maintain a minimal level of functioning. But suppose that it is known that the earth simply cannot produce enough food for everyone in the world to maintain that level of functioning. Then it follows (assuming that no other source of food is available) that we cannot meaningfully say that there is an obligation to provide such food. But if we cannot meaningfully say there is an obligation to do X, how can we meaningfully say that someone has a *right* that X be done? In such cases talk of rights is not exactly false; it is, like talk of obligations in such cases, just empty.‡⑤

> ④ Do rights always support this sort of demand? One related issue here is the scope of this "we": does it extend to all humankind, or is it restricted to some smaller community (and if so, which one)?

> ⑤ This point is somewhat more controversial: do genuine rights just disappear when it becomes impossible to satisfy them? (See Discussion Question 1.) Another issue about the specific right mentioned here is who would have the corresponding duty.

---

*Henry Shue, *Basic Rights* (Princeton: Princeton University Press, 1981), p. 13. For another highly respected treatment of this aspect of rights, see the title essay of Ronald Dworkin's book, *Taking Rights Seriously* (Cambridge, Mass.: Harvard University Press, 1977), pp. 184–205.

†One of the most famous analyses of rights and related concepts within Anglo-American law is Wesley Hohfeld, *Fundamental Legal Conceptions* (New Haven: Yale University Press, 1919; 1964). . . .

‡In some cases we are in the position of being unable to determine whether what a proposed right refers to is impossible or not. Consequently we don't know if the proposed right is empty or not; and we cannot either accept it as true or reject it as false. . . . Since such cases involve matters of overriding moral significance, morality requires that we try to get answers to our unanswered questions so we can learn what we ought and ought not to do.

Seventh, if A has a right, A has the option *not to exercise* that right and also the option to waive that right in particular cases and, possibly, altogether. How are we to understand these features of rights? Suppose that A lends B $100 with the clear understanding that B will repay the money within two months. After the two months have passed, A has a right to be repaid. A may justifiably demand that B repay the sum, and B's obligation to repay it would override a number of other moral considerations regarding B's use of the money. Except in very unusual circumstances, for example, B would be acting immorally to spend $100 to buy a gift for a friend when A had a right to be repaid the $100. In addition A could reasonably appeal to the rest of us to assist him or her in getting the money repaid.

But it is no contradiction of the notion of having a right that A might choose not to exercise that right. That is, A might choose not to demand that B pay back the money at the end of two months. A might permit B to pay the money back whenever it was convenient for B, or whenever A actually had need of the money. In such circumstances A retains the right but chooses not to exercise it at a certain time or for a certain period of time.

While the difference between A's not exercising a right and A's waiving a right [is] fairly clear in the case of A's right to repayment, there are many puzzles in the notions of waiving and not exercising rights. For example, how could an accused citizen not exercise his or her constitutional right to counsel or to a jury trial without also waiving that right in that case? And what are we to say about children, for example, who presumably have various rights but who are not competent to choose to waive or not exercise them? Can another person choose for them to exercise or not exercise, to waive or not waive, *their* rights? May every failure by a right holder to exercise a particular right be treated by the rest of us as a *choice* not to exercise the right; that is, does the responsibility for exercise always fall first on the right holder? May a pattern of failure to exercise a right eventually be interpreted as a waiving of the right? Finally, are there rights that cannot be waived, which are—as the more traditional language expresses it—"inalienable"?[6]

6 For example, can a person waive his right not to be enslaved (thereby perhaps making slavery morally acceptable)? What about the right not to be killed?

3. CONVENTIONAL RIGHTS AND MORAL RIGHTS

We have been examining what we imply when we say of someone that he or she has a right of some sort. Now let us look at the kinds of conditions that must be fulfilled for a statement of this sort to be true.

To determine if a statement of the form "A has a right, R, of some sort" is true; we must look at two quite different sets of conditions. Some rights are verified by reference to a social rule or rule system or an institutional framework of some sort. Such rights are called *conventional* rights because the existence of such rights depends upon the existence of particular social rules, rule systems, and institutions, whose existence depends in turn on the *acceptance* of these rules, rule systems, and institutions by the parties involved. The important point for present purposes is that many rights depend for their existence on such social rules, rule systems, and institutions. To determine whether a statement of the form "A has a conventional right, R" is true, we must determine whether the social rule, rule system, or institution referred to in the statement actually exists—i.e., is accepted by the relevant parties as described—and also whether the right identified in the statement actually derives from this rule, rule system, or institution.

On the other hand, many people, philosophers and nonphilosophers alike, hold that there are rights of another kind that exist as part of the moral nature of things, independently of anyone's choosing. These rights are sometimes called natural rights, sometimes human rights, sometimes moral rights. When they are called natural rights the emphasis may be on their being part of the nature of things, but this expression is also used to indicate that the basis of such rights lies in "human nature"—a stable and fundamental set of characteristics thought to be built into every human being. This, in turn, has prompted some thinkers to wonder if the notion of such rights depends on there being a "builder" (i.e., a God) who "makes" human beings. This position raises a number of philosophical questions. Therefore other thinkers have called these sorts of rights human rights, rights we have just because we are human beings. However, even if the idea of such rights is that everyone who is human has them, in fact they are not recognized, or recognized equally, everywhere. Thus they are also called moral rights, rights that everyone *should* recognize everywhere and in all circumstances, but rights that in fact are not always exercised. We shall employ the expression "moral rights" here. Thus if we say that A has a particular moral right, we are saying that A has this right as part of the moral nature of things. The existence of this right is not dependent on anyone's choice or acceptance of it. It is not even dependent on A's choice or acceptance of it, so A cannot choose not to have this right and cannot choose to waive it, a notion that we have traditionally expressed by saying that moral rights are inalienable.⑦

> ⑦ Contrary to what Ozar suggests here, it is not generally held that all moral rights are in this way inalienable.

4. ARE THERE UNIVERSAL MORAL RIGHTS?

A moral (human, natural) right, we have said, is a right that exists as part of the moral nature of things and independently of anyone's choosing or agreeing that there be such a right. Many people believe that human beings have some such rights, and they believe that *all* human beings have them. They believe, in other words, that there are some moral rights that are *universal* among human beings. In this and the following sections we shall explore this widespread conviction that there are universal moral rights. We will examine a number of those features of human beings and of human life that have been proposed as the basis of such rights, and we will explain as well some of the problems with these defenses of universal moral rights.

a. The Great Machine and Its Slave It will be helpful to begin our discussion of universal moral rights with a case. The following somewhat fanciful story can illuminate how deep are our convictions about the existence of universal moral rights.

> Suppose that in some future age it became possible to harness all of the world's technology to a single master computer that could then direct all the world's productive processes to produce and distribute the resources necessary for every human being on earth to live a secure and comfortable life. Let us also assume that the master computer has been programmed to carry out its task in an ecologically sound manner, so there is

no risk to future members of the human community. Let us also assume that the Great Machine is completely dependable, that there is no risk of malfunction in our submitting the well-being of the whole human race to its direction.

But there is one problem. With so many complex processes to control and integrate at once, the Great Machine must have the permanent and total use of a living human brain in order to carry out the reasoning processes that are necessary for its work. Some human being must be hooked up to the Great Machine for it to do its job. This person will continue to live in comfort, but his or her brain will be totally taken over by the Great Machine. There is no way that this function could be shared among a group of persons with lesser effects on each; and there is no point to someone's doing it only for a while and then handing it over to someone else because, once programmed by the Great Machine, a human brain could never be used again for living an ordinary human life. Slavery to the Great Machine is total and permanent.

Let us assume that there are no volunteers to be the Great Machine's slave. Would it be morally justifiable to enslave an unwilling human being to the Great Machine in order to achieve so high a level of well-being and so much opportunity for growth and fullness of life for everyone else on earth? (Let us postulate that a fair and equitable procedure for selecting this person would be available, so there would be no moral problem with the selection process itself.) Would it be moral to enslave someone to the Great Machine?⑧

> ⑧ An act utilitarian would seemingly have to answer "yes" to this question. As we saw earlier, cases like this provide one of the standard objections to act utilitarianism—which can now be put by saying that act utilitarians apparently cannot recognize moral rights (since for them, any alleged right could always be overridden by considerations of utility.)

Many people would respond to this case by saying that we would be acting immorally, indeed profoundly immorally, if we were to make someone a slave to the Great Machine against the person's will, regardless of the benefits for everyone else. Many of those who would respond in this way would explain their response by saying that every human being has certain moral rights that would be violated if he was enslaved to the Great Machine against his will. But what reasons are there for saying there are universal moral rights?

b. "Endowed by Their Creator" One possible account of the basis of universal moral rights is that these rights have been given to mankind by God. This is the basis Thomas Jefferson identified in the Declaration of Independence. "We hold these Truths to be self-evident, that all Men are created equal, that they are endowed by their Creator with certain unalienable Rights. . . ." Critics of this approach could begin, of course, by asking for reasons supporting the claim that there is a God who has created mankind. But let us pass over that point in order to focus more directly on a different aspect of Jefferson's reasoning.

Jefferson does not appeal to the Scriptures or any other source of authoritative religious teaching to support his claim that God has endowed every human being with rights. He says instead that it is "self-evident." By this he surely means "obvious to everyone." In other words, Jefferson thought that there is evidence that is plain for everyone to see which points to the existence of universal moral rights. But what evidence? Clearly Jefferson believed that there are features of human beings or of human life that lead unerringly to this conclusion.

Jefferson does not give us much help in identifying these features, and it may seem that we have made little progress by examining the words of the Declaration. But there is something important to be learned from it. Even those who locate the basis of universal moral rights in God's choice to create the human race in a certain way have features of human beings in mind—the clues that tell us that, created thus, human beings do possess universal moral rights. That is, belief in the divine origin of universal human rights is not an answer to our question about the basis of the belief that humans have such rights.

It is, at most, an urgent reason for trying to answer this question.*

c. Features Shared by All Human Beings Of the specific features of human beings that have been proposed as the basis of moral rights, the two most often mentioned are human freedom and human rationality. Human beings are free. That is, they make choices, and these choices derive in significant measure from the person himself or herself. Consequently human beings are special, different from every other species on this planet, and different specifically by addition: They perform a kind of activity that no other species performs. Our treatment of human beings, it is argued, must therefore be special as well. Human beings may not simply be used, as the other beings on the planet are used, in the fulfillment of one's own purposes. Our actions toward human beings must recognize that they are choosers, that they have their own purposes. To treat human beings without concern for their choices and purposes is to treat them as they are not, as if they were not choosers. Rights, then, according to this pattern of reasoning, are ways of respecting the choices and purposes of other human beings.

On the other hand, some thinkers emphasize human rationality. Human beings are not merely sensors of the world around them. They are knowers, judgers, creators, communicators. They do not just react to stimuli; they put information together to form generalized truths about the world. They use these truths to understand each new situation that arises. Consequently they are also able to reshape the world and to share their experiences of the world with one another in language, symbol, and culture. Human beings are thus again special among the beings of this planet, and special by addition by performing activities that other beings do not. Therefore they must be treated specially, as originators of understanding, as shapers of the world around them, as builders of

---

*If there were explicit mention of universal human rights in the Judeo-Christian Scriptures or in the sacred writings of other religious traditions, then of course those for whom these are authoritative accounts of the true nature of things would have conclusive evidence of the existence of universal human rights. But the Judeo-Christian Scriptures and the sacred writings of most other religious traditions antedate the development of rights talk by hundreds of years or more. Consequently the support given to the notion of universal human rights within the various religious traditions must derive from theological reflection upon older teachings regarding human beings and human life. It is hard to see how such theological reflection could support the claim that there are universal human rights without, again, trying to identify the features of human beings and human life in which the truth of this claim is most evidenced. So even in the context of theological reflection of this sort, our questions in this section must still be addressed.

human community. According to this pattern of reasoning, rights protect these special activities of the human species.⑨

⑨ It is plausible to suppose that these features distinguish human beings from at least most other earthly species. But is it clear *why* these features are supposed to yield the moral rights in question? (See Discussion Question 2.) It has sometimes been suggested that intelligent mammals like dolphins might have such features; another possibility is nonhuman extraterrestrials.

Nevertheless, critics of these two approaches argue, neither choice nor the activities of reason are universal within the human species. Infants do not make choices or perform acts of rationality of the sort just described. Even young children do not make choices or judgments with such independence that we think it improper to override their choices or set aside their judgments. Also, those with severe mental illnesses can lose the capacity to reason correctly and to make genuine choices. The comatose and even those who are sleeping do not perform acts of choice or reasoning.

Does this mean that a human being's moral rights start and stop as the relevant forms of activity begin and end? That is certainly not the way in which moral rights are ordinarily understood. Does it mean that some members of the human species do not have rights—infants, most young children, the mentally ill, the comatose, those who are asleep? Clearly, if this is the case, we should not go on speaking of *universal* moral rights.⑩

⑩ Here is one fundamental issue about alleged human rights: do they extend even to those humans who do not have the special features that are allegedly the basis for them (and if so, why)? (See the Regan selection in the final section of the chapter for more discussion of this issue.)

Another approach would be to look at features that we are certain are universal characteristics of the human species. All of us have the same number of chromosomes, or at least are the same within a small range. But this is true for every species; all members of each species have the same genetic makeup, within a certain range. It must be the specifics of our make-up as humans, not just the fact that all of us have approximately the same make-up, that are important. Human beings are all bipeds and have opposite thumbs and many other genetic traits in common. But

neither these two features nor any of a host of other common biological characteristics of human beings seem significant enough from a moral point of view to serve as the basis of moral rights.

All human beings who are living are, of course, alive and are subject to pain and to death. Life, pain, and death are surely matters of moral importance. Could the importance to human beings of maintaining life, avoiding death, and averting or at least minimizing pain serve as the basis of universal moral rights? The problem with this approach is that the net seems to be too wide. If vulnerability to pain and death is the basis of moral rights, all human beings are indeed included, but so are most animals of other species. The suggestion that nonhuman animals have moral rights is an important topic for moral discourse, but most defenders of universal moral rights for human beings hold, at a minimum, that the moral rights of human beings are stronger, broader, different in some way from whatever rights nonhuman animals might have.⑪

⑪ At least most nonhuman animals; as we have seen, there may be exceptions.

Some defenders of universal moral rights have held that the basis of these rights is "human dignity" or "human worth," which is surely something that human beings do not share with nonhuman animals. But a problem with this approach is the difficulty of determining just what features of human beings are referred to by the expressions "human dignity" and "human worth." If human beings are said to have dignity or worth because they are free and/or rational, then moral rights based on dignity or worth will not be universal, for the reasons explained above. If human beings have dignity or worth for some other reason, it needs to be explained; and the expressions "dignity" and "worth" alone do not provide any clear clues to this explanation.

We seem to be at an impasse. Either there are moral rights that some humans have, and possibly only some of the time, or there are moral rights that all humans have, but most nonhuman animals have the same rights as well. If we stopped at this point, we would have to give up our original idea—that there are moral rights that all human beings have precisely "because they are human."

But several other approaches to this issue have been developed. In the next section we will examine the bilevel approach and the potentiality approach. In the following section, recent work growing out of re-lational interpretations of "human dignity" and "human worth" will be explored.

d. Bilevel and Potentiality Approaches Some moral theorists have responded to the problems posed in the previous section by frankly conceding that the fullest notion of moral rights applies properly only to those human beings who are capable of free choice and rationality. Fetuses, infants, and small children up to a certain point of development do not have moral rights; neither do the permanently comatose and those members of the human species who, for what-ever reason and regardless of their chronological age, have never become capable of choice and rational activity.

But this is not to say that humans in these cate-gories are altogether without rights. That will depend on two other factors. First, in some bilevel theories, all members of the human species have moral rights of a diminished sort because of their vulnerability to pain and death. Those humans who lack moral rights in the fullest sense will therefore still have moral rights in this diminished sense. For example, it might be a vio-lation of someone's moral rights to torture him or her, even though the person being tortured does not have full moral rights.

But these rights are not in principle different from the rights of nonhuman animals. The obligation not to torture is simply an application of a more general ob-ligation not to treat cruelly any being that can experi-ence intense pain. The only difference is that, with our more complex psyches, human vulnerability to certain forms of pain is broader than that of nonhuman ani-mals. Consequently, the obligations implied by rights of this sort will be likely to have a broader scope when their referents are human beings than when their ref-erents are nonhuman animals.

Secondly, in all theories that attribute full moral rights only to those human beings capable of acts of choice and rationality, other human beings may still have extensive conventional rights. Among these rights may be legal rights and rights based on other social rule systems. Even more important, however, are rights that derive from the free commitments of free, rational humans. For example, a young child may have a conventional right to care by his or her parents by reason of acts of commitment on their part

in keeping the child rather than offering him or her for adoption. In a similar way, the permanently com-atose patient may have conventional rights vis-á-vis various health care personnel who have freely under-taken his or her care and are therefore committed to provide it.

Such conventional rights are dependent for their existence on the choices and commitments of free, ra-tional human beings. They are nevertheless important moral features of the lives of those members of the human species who are not free and rational them-selves, and who therefore lack, according to bilev-el approaches, full moral rights.[12]

> [12] One issue here is what should be said about the moral status of nonfree and nonrational humans who are not in this way the objects of actual choices and com-mitments by free and ra-tional humans.

Bilevel approaches frequently mark the distinc-tion between those members of the human species who have full moral rights and those who do not by saying that the former are human *persons* while the latter, though certainly human, are not persons. This way of marking the distinction would be informative if we had a clear sense, independently of this discus-sion, of how persons differ from other beings. In re-cent debates about moral rights, however, the term *person* has often been used with little explanation of what features of human beings it refers to. So we must still ask what distinguishes human *persons,* who have full moral rights, from other members of the species who do not. But that is just our original question again in a new language.

In sum, the bilevel theories respond to the prob-lems raised in the preceding section by setting aside universality. Only human beings fulfilling certain con-ditions have full moral rights. The rights of other members of the human species and the obligations that are owed them will depend upon other matters.

A second response to the problems discussed above focuses on the notion of potentiality. There are universal moral rights, this view holds, because the basis of moral rights is the *potential* for free and ra-tional acts. Human beings have this potential from the moment of their conception. For, from that moment on, they are continually developing in the direction of performing such acts. They retain this potential, inso-far as we can be certain of our judgments about it, until the moment when they die. For even those who are comatose may still have this potential, at least up to the point at which we can certify that all their higher brain functions, which are necessary for free and rational acts, have ceased. At that point, they not only no longer have moral rights but they are also no longer living human beings.

There are a number of arguments that can be given in support of this view. First, it is difficult to identify any point in the development of a human being at which so radical a change takes place that it makes sense for us to say that he or she is a person afterward, but was not before that moment, or that he or she now has full moral rights, but did not have full moral rights before then. What exists and unfolds continually throughout this developmental process is precisely the potential to perform acts of freedom and rationality. Therefore, it is argued, the potentiality approach represents our actual experience of human life much more accurately than the bilevel approach. Obviously, the potentiality approach also accords much better than the bilevel approach with the centuries-old conviction that if there are any moral rights, they are universal moral rights.

Another point that favors the potentiality approach is the fact that if there are any moral rights, none of us believes that they exist only when a person is awake or cease to exist when a person goes to sleep. But what is it about a person that endures through waking and sleeping alike? It is, the holders of this position argue, precisely the person's *potentiality* for these actions that, when awake, he or she performs. ⑬

⑬ Is the sense of potentiality that pertains to people who are asleep the same as that which pertains to a newly born infant (or a fetus)?

One objection to the potentiality theory focuses on those members of the human species who are born or become severely retarded, and whose level of mental functioning is therefore such that they cannot perform acts of freedom and rationality—that is, they do not have the potentiality for such acts. These members of the human species would seem not to have moral rights according to the potentiality theory as we have explained it; yet surely they are still human beings. How then can the potentiality theorist claim that there are *universal* human rights?

Some supporters of the potentiality approach have responded to this objection by arguing that beside freedom and rationality there are other distinctive and characteristic activities of human beings that are morally significant. The ability to appreciate and to respond to affection, for example, characterizes even those who are extremely retarded. This potentiality combines with the potentiality for free and rational acts as the basis of universal moral rights. This addition of a new feature as the basis of moral rights must be carefully weighed, however. The fact that there is such potential and that it is universal among human beings, or even nearly so, does not automatically demonstrate that there are moral rights connected with it.

A more radical objection concerns the notion of potentiality itself. What *is* a potentiality? A potentiality, says the objection, is not a "something" that can be possessed by a human being. When we talk of people's potentialities, it is simply a more convenient way of saying that we have expectations and consider it probable that these people will act in a certain way in the future. We base such predictions either on the individuals' own past acts or on their membership in a class of beings who have acted in the predicted way. But none of this involves attributing to an individual a special *feature* of his or her make-up that should be called a potentiality. Much less, then, should we be drawn into considering this "feature" of the individual's make-up to be the basis of anything else, including moral rights.

A related objection points out that the potentiality theorists claim to have demonstrated *actual* rights. That is, they imply that other persons *actually have* obligations to act or refrain in certain ways. But how can human activities, however morally significant, that are merely *potential* give rise to rights and, thus, obligations that are fully *actual*?

To answer these two objections, the potentiality theorists must demonstrate that our language about human potentialities in fact refers to real and actual features of human beings. Much work still needs to be done to develop such demonstrations. But potentiality theorists believe that they are forthcoming.

e. Relational Approaches to the Existence of Moral Rights Instead of focusing on features of individual human beings, a number of rights theorists have focused on features of human life together. Could the widespread conviction that there are universal moral rights have its foundation in key relationships in which all human beings participate? Many philosophic traditions have stressed the idea that we cannot describe the essential elements of the human make-up by looking at human individuals in isolation from one another. To be connected with other human beings is a fundamental part of what it is to be human. But before this idea can become useful to us it must be made much more specific and concrete. What kinds of relations between human beings are being referred to; and why should we think they are the basis of moral rights? A number of theorists have proposed answers to these questions. We will focus briefly on the work of three contemporary English-speaking philosophers: A. I. Melden, Gregory Vlastos, and Bernard Williams.

In his book, *Rights and Persons,* A. I. Melden argues that we will not find some single feature of human beings that can serve as the basis of moral rights. Rather, the basis of moral rights lies in the whole context of our efforts to support one another and to be supported by one another in the pursuit of our interests. It is a fundamental truth of the human make-up that we pursue our interests, and an equally fundamental truth that we pursue them together with other human beings. Each of us assists and supports the others, and each is assisted and supported by the others. There is no pursuit of interests by human beings other than this. Relatedness to other human beings is not only something we absolutely need in order to achieve our interests. It is also, Melden's work suggests, an essential element of the very significance of human pursuits and achievements, so that these are inconceivable without it.*

In "Justice and Equality" Gregory Vlastos adds to our understanding of the relational approach. Vlastos points out that there are certain instances and features of human persons' valuations of one another that do not involve comparison of persons or the grading of persons one above or below the other. That is, among the ways in which human beings relate to one another,

there is at least one relationship in which people are not graded or compared, as contrasted with the myriad human relationships where grading, ranking, and comparison of people in terms of their abilities, performances, and other attributes are appropriate. Vlastos does not try to name that distinctive relationship. But he does identify it by saying that in this relationship what is valued in one human being by another is "human worth."

While Vlastos does not claim that the following description exhausts what we mean by human worth, he does claim that these two elements will be part of any complete description of it: (*a*) "the enjoyment of value in all the forms in which it can be experienced by human beings," which he calls well-being for short and (*b*) "conscious choices and deliberate decisions [and also] subtler modulations and more spontaneous expressions of individual preference," which Vlastos gathers together under the simple label "freedom."†

Now let us pause and ask what these two accounts of human relationships can tell us about moral rights. The relationship that Vlastos describes clearly implies rights and obligations between the participants. The relationship consists in an unconditional affirmation of the worth of the other in his or her well-being and freedom. No one could consistently affirm such a relationship with another human being while failing to take into account the other's well-being and freedom in concrete actions, or even while simply weighing his or her own actions in terms of the other's abilities, performances, or other attributes. In other words, in this relationship the other party has rights. 14

14 Such an unconditional affirmation of the worth of other humans is very close to what Kant seems to mean by regarding other humans as ends in themselves. Thus the ascription of moral rights to others can be argued to be a clear implication of Kant's view.

Vlastos holds that this relationship is pervasive within the human community, and that every member of the human community therefore has moral rights. To this claim it might be objected that the rights Vlastos

---

*A. I. Melden, *Rights and Persons* (Berkeley: University of California Press, 1977).

†Gregory Vlastos, "Justice and Equality," in *Social Justice,* ed. Richard Brandt (Englewood Cliffs, N.J.: Prentice-Hall, 1962), pp. 48–53.

has demonstrated exist only among those who have this unconditional relationship, and that this relation-

<hr>

[15] Kant would, of course, deny that regarding other humans in this way is *morally* optional; in his view, such a stance toward other humans is the most fundamental moral requirement. (What might Kant—or Vlastos—say about the problem of humans who are incapable of experiencing value or making deliberate decisions?)

<hr>

ship is optional—a matter of choice. Consequently, it could be argued, these are really conventional rather than moral rights, and we have no reason as yet for thinking that they are universal rights. [15]

On the other hand, the relatedness between human beings that Melden has described is clearly universal, involving all

members of the human species who have or are capable of having interests. It is also clearly not a matter of convention but an essential element of the human make-up. An objector to Melden's position would claim, however, that if this relatedness is merely the factual truth that we need one another in pursuing our interests, then we have not yet learned anything about rights or obligations. The fact that we need one another does not by itself demonstrate that we have *obligations* to respond to one another's needs.

Is there any relationship that has the universality and necessity of Melden's interdependency and, at the same time, an explicit moral dimension like Vlastos's unconditional affirmation of human worth? Bernard Williams has made a valuable suggestion along these lines in his well-known paper, "The Idea of Equality." Williams begins his argument about the basis of human equality in a manner very similar to Vlastos, with an opening distinction between "the technical or professional attitude" and "the human approach." In professional relations and in the world of work, a person's actions are judged by others according to various professional or technical titles, such as "laborer" or "waiter" or "assistant manager." He writes:

> The technical or professional attitude is that which regards the man solely under that title, the human approach that which regards him as *a man who has* that title (among others), willingly, unwillingly, through lack of alternatives, with pride, etc.

This human approach involves looking at the person not simply as "the surface to which a certain label can be applied," but trying to "see the world (including the label) from his point of view.*

Every one of us who makes this imaginative identification with the perspective of another human being recognizes in making it that the other's perspective has value, worth, and moral significance. The only way to exclude this valuing of the other's perspective as a center of experience is to refuse to view things from his or her perspective. But this refusal does not eliminate the possibility of such identification; the relationship of valuing the other's perspective is always available. The only other option would be to deny this possibility, but that denial would fly in the face of undoubted and rational[ly] justified convictions about the nature of human beings.

Moreover, while not all human beings are able, at all times, to identify with another's perspective in this way, all human beings are centers of experience and are thus capable of being identified with and having their perspectives valued. Those who are sleeping, retarded, or in severe pain are centers of experience and have a point of view that others can identify with and experience as valuable. So, too, are infants and, more than likely, fetuses during much of their development. Even the comatose may be active centers of experience, especially experience of pain and helplessness. Thus, while the initiator of the relationship may not include all human beings, its term is universal. That is, all human beings count; they all have shoes into which we can put ourselves. From this vantage point we experience each of them—all other persons—as valuable. [16]

<hr>

[16] Is this enough to distinguish all human beings from "higher" animals of various sorts?

<hr>

More reflection and argument would be needed to demonstrate fully that in this universal relationship of unconditional valuing lies the basis of universal moral rights. The suggestions of Melden and Vlastos, for example, might now be linked with what Williams has proposed. There will also be many objections to answer. But in the fuller development of Williams's proposal we may have a rational basis for universal moral rights.

<hr>

*Bernard A. O. Williams, "The Idea of Equality," in *Philosophy, Politics, and Society,* second series ed. Peter Laslett and W. G. Runciman (London: Basil Blackwell, 1962), p. 117. . . .

5. RIGHTS AND CONSEQUENCES

Rights talk, as we said earlier, is one way of talking, thinking, and reasoning about what individuals and communities ought and ought not to do. Rights talk is one kind of moral discourse. Another important kind of moral discourse looks at the morality of individuals' and communities' actions in terms of their consequences. This approach to moral reasoning and reflection is often called consequentialism.

According to consequentialism, sound moral reasoning is a comparative process. First, we must identify the alternative courses of action that are available and determine what the likely consequences of each will be. Second, we must evaluate each of these sets of consequences both positively and negatively, on the basis of some appropriate evaluative criterion. Then, finally, we must compare the sets of consequences to determine which of them produces the highest level of the appropriate criterion when both positive and negative consequences have been taken into account. The action that produces this best set of consequences of all those available is the action that, according to the consequentialist approach, ought to be undertaken.

. . .

For rights theorists who hold that the basis of all sound moral reasoning lies in people's fundamental moral rights, analyses of morality in terms of the consequences of individuals' and groups' actions cannot correctly inform us about what ought and ought not to be done unless these analyses are derived in turn from a more fundamental understanding of moral rights. For there are certain actions that clearly ought or ought not to be done *regardless of the consequences.* This means, necessarily, that consequences cannot be the most fundamental basis of what ought and ought not to be done. Such theorists frequently cite cases analogous to that of the Great Machine, discussed above, in arguing for this position. The consequentialists, according to such rights theorists, would surely be committed to not only permitting but even requiring that someone be forced to be the slave of the machine. For, they argue, the great benefits of doing so for millions of people would surely outweigh the costs, in the form of a life without use of one's own brain, for the person enslaved. However, since such enslavement of even one person is clearly immoral, they argue, the consequentialist approach is surely inadequate by itself. Morality requires that no one be enslaved to the Great Machine, even if the consequences of doing so would be better for everyone except the person so enslaved.

On the other side, consequentialists often hold that a rights theory is either based on consequentialism or mistaken. They defend this claim by arguing that whenever a moral decision involves competing rights, we resolve the matter by examining the consequences of the actions available and identifying the action that has the best, most desirable consequences.

Why, then, we might ask a consequentialist, do we speak of rights? Why has rights talk become so important a part of moral discourse? Because, says the consequentialist, some kinds of valued things are the preconditions of our being able to achieve all our other values. Life, health, the absence of coercion and of certain other kinds of interference, self-respect, a sense of ourselves as thinking and choosing beings— these particular values are values we *must* have in significant measure before we can achieve the other things and have the other experiences that we value in life, no matter what these other values and valued experiences are. Therefore, within our evaluation of our possible actions, these values are assigned a special place. It is not necessarily the case that we value them more. It is rather that they are preconditions of the others, and therefore they must be secured first before the others can even be possible. This very real priority of the preconditions of all else we value is the reason for assigning a special name to these things, namely rights, and for according them special weight in our moral reflections. Thus, says the consequentialist, rights talk has a useful role to play within moral discourse; but it is consequences, not rights, which are the true basis of our judgments of what ought and ought not to be done.[17]

We leave it to the reader to reflect further on these two views of the place of rights talk within moral

[17] This consequentialist approach is similar to rule utilitarianism, and it faces the same important problem: that there is no clear consequentialist justification for recognizing a right when it is clear (as it sometimes will be) that better consequences can be achieved by violating it. But, the proponent of rights will argue, a right that can be overridden in this way by an appeal to consequences is not really a right at all.

discourse. Are rights or consequences the deepest basis of our judgments about what ought and ought not to be done? Or is there some other?

6. POSITIVE RIGHTS, NEGATIVE RIGHTS, AND LIBERTARIANISM

To say that A has a right is to imply, as we indicated above, that someone else, B, has an obligation of some sort to do or to refrain from some act relative to A. Some contemporary rights theorists have drawn a sharp distinction between rights that imply an obligation of B to act, which are frequently called positive rights, and rights that imply only an obligation of B to refrain, which are called negative rights.

The expressions *positive rights* and *negative rights* are surely awkward; for it is not really the rights that are "positive" or "negative" (whatever that would mean) but rather the obligations implied by the rights. In addition to this awkwardness of terminology, there is also a serious dispute among rights theorists about the validity and importance of the distinction itself.

One group of moral theorists who claim that the distinction between positive and negative rights is of the highest importance are known as libertarians. The libertarian position has been explained in several ways. One way to explain it is to say that the basis of all sound moral judgments is a single fundamental moral rule: Respect people's liberty. This means that we are not to interfere with others' acting on the basis of their own goals, values, and purposes; we are to leave them free to do as they please so long as in exercising their liberty they do not interfere with the rights of others similarly to be left alone. [18]

[18] Respecting people's liberty in this sense involves also respecting their life—and, at least arguably, respecting the property they acquire through exercising their liberty (without illegitimately infringing on the liberty or lives of others). The selections from Locke and Nozick in Chapter 7 present versions of such a view.

It is easy to see why this theory of morality is also often expressed as a rights theory—every person has a fundamental right not to be interfered with in acting on the basis of his or her own goals, values, and purposes. This fundamental libertarian right is obviously a "negative right," a right implying obligations on the part of others only to refrain from interfering. Libertarians claim that the only moral rights are negative rights, namely this fundamental right and any more specific negative rights that might be derived from it. There are no moral rights that are positive rights; all positive rights that anyone might have are conventional rights, based on people's voluntary agreements to undertake the obligations involved.

Libertarian theorists expand on this fundamental rule or right in a variety of ways. But most of them would accept the following statement as a starting point for developing more narrowly focused obligations:

1. It is never moral to interfere with actions of a competent adult (who is not interfering with someone else) simply to bring about better consequences.
2. It is moral to interfere with the actions of someone who is interfering with someone else, for the purpose of ending that interference and/or securing appropriate restitution and/or punishment.
3. All other obligations between persons shall be by voluntary agreement of the parties involved so that the arrangements so agreed upon are conventional rights and obligations.
4. The obligation not to interfere applies not only to the body but also the mind, and to the property of every person.
5. When the exercise of liberty conflicts with another exercise of liberty (that is, when a fundamental right conflicts with another fundamental right), then that action or policy is to be preferred that preserves the greatest total liberty for everyone involved.

Not all rights theorists agree with the libertarians, however, that the only moral rights are negative rights. Some theorists have defended the view that all moral rights involve both "positive" and "negative" obligations—that is, obligations both to act and to refrain.

One such argument challenges the claim that there is a significant distinction between actions and omissions of actions. If the line marking the distinction between an action and an omission cannot be maintained, or if it should prove to have no moral significance, then the claim that the only moral rights are negative rights will lose its significance. [19]

A second argument supporting this view builds on the implication that in the case of any *moral* right, each of us has some measure of obligation to see to it that the relevant actions and omissions are carried out. This means that even rights that at first seem to imply only obligations not to interfere in fact also imply obligations to act positively to prevent or deter interference in circumstances where it is likely. Consequently, it is argued, so-called negative rights involve both obligations to refrain and obligations to take action.[20]

[19] If you are about to run someone over with your car, is avoiding that result an omission (not hitting him) or an action (stepping on the brake or swerving away)? This suggests that many cases of not interfering with others can be described either way. But does this really undermine the distinction between positive and negative rights in a serious way? (See Discussion Question 3.)

[20] Not everyone agrees that negative rights always involve such positive obligations. But even if they do, there is still a difference between a view according to which the only positive obligations are to help others secure or defend their negative rights and one according to which there are other positive obligations and corresponding rights as well: rights to receive something from others that goes beyond this sort of help.

Finally, some theorists who accept the distinction between positive and negative rights argue forcefully for the importance of positive moral rights. These thinkers, who are strong critics of libertarianism, claim that positive rights and the obligations they entail are essential for human development. Negative rights create, at best, "benign neglect" for those unable to exercise their rights, because negative rights allow only those who are aggressive in pursuing their liberty and who happen to have the needed resources to succeed, and then often at the expense of others. One way to formulate this argument, for example, is to show that those whose basic needs are not filled, when sufficient resources are available so that their needs *could* be filled, are deprived of the very equality of opportunity that many libertarians stress, or they are deprived of the psychological possibility of fulfilling goals other than survival. Another way is to challenge the claim implicit in libertarianism that we have no positive moral relationships to one another to start with. Social interaction, it is argued, is an inseparable part of the make-up of each of us, so

that the libertarian's "fundamental" negative rights are themselves already grounded in and dependent upon the fulfillment of positive moral relations between persons.[21]

[21] The selection by Rawls in Chapter 7 defends a version of this view. One issue about positive rights of this sort is who has the corresponding obligation (which we have seen to be essential to a meaningful right). (See Discussion Question 4.)

7. CONFLICTING RIGHTS AND OTHER OBLIGATIONS

In some moral theories, moral rights are the basis of all moral obligations. In such theories it is worth asking whether all moral rights have the same weight or whether some rights can take precedence over others when both cannot be fulfilled simultaneously. By the same token, it is important to determine whether the obligations implied by a given right all have the same moral weight or not.

To take a simple example, suppose Mr. Jones tells Dr. Smith, "If it's cancer, Doctor, don't tell me." Jones, let us assume, has a right to know the truth about his condition, and also a right, let us assume, to define the terms of his relationship with Dr. Smith. What is the morally best thing for Dr. Smith to do when these rights conflict? Or suppose it is the rights of two bearers of rights that are in conflict. If a fetus has a right not to be killed and a woman the right to control what happens to her body, for example, then the morality of an elective abortion is a matter of conflicting rights of distinct rights bearers. Is there any basis in rights theory for ranking rights in order to resolve such conflicts?

Some rights theorists have held that no priorities can be assigned among the most general or fundamental moral rights. But as more narrowly focused rights are derived from them, these latter will have to be weighed and ranked against one another, since they will sometimes be in conflict in concrete situations. The basis for their ranking will be the extent to which each of them fulfills and/or hinders the value expressed in the fundamental rights—e.g., human freedom, rationality, fundamental relationships between human beings, or whatever.

A number of recent arguments of this sort claim a special moral significance for human needs and tie them closely to the most important moral rights. But the notion of human needs is not a simple one. The many things that people call needs are not of equal moral significance. So a moral theory that ranks rights in terms of needs must rank needs as well and must explain why they are so ranked. Such theories are not necessarily circular; but when carefully developed, they are necessarily more complicated than one might first expect.

Another way of assigning priorities among rights is based on the claim that there are some moral rights that must be fulfilled before any others can be fulfilled. Henry Shue calls such rights basic rights and argues that they include the rights to subsistence and security and certain forms of freedom. These "basic rights" must rank first, Shue argues, because they are preconditions of all other rights; without them, the fulfillment of other rights is impossible.* (Shue also proposes a ranking of obligations derived from his thesis about the "basicness" of the basic rights. Shue divides human concerns into four categories, in ascending order of moral significance: preference satisfaction, cultural enrichment, nonbasic rights, basic rights. He offers a priority principle that says, firstly and obviously, that a person must rank obligations deriving from basic rights ahead of obligations deriving from nonbasic rights, and secondly that a person is morally obligated to sacrifice his or her own preferences and cultural enrichment, for example, if this is necessary to secure another's nonbasic rights and is morally obligated to sacrifice all three, if necessary, to secure another person's basic rights.)† ㉒

In mixed theories in which moral rights are not the only basis of moral obligations, or in consequentialist theories in which, as we have indicated, the concept of moral rights may well have a place, but always a derivative one, the ranking of particular rights in relation to one another (and of obligations based on rights in relation to other obligations) will depend upon the precise nature of the theory under study. Little general guidance can be offered beyond stessing the importance of determining the precise basis of rights and other moral considerations in each particular theory as it is applied to concrete issues and situations, for the ranking of these factors will depend on this.

· · ·

㉒ Since Shue's basic rights include some that are positive (such as the rights to subsistence and security), this yields the result that people are morally required not to devote resources to pursuing their own projects and interests so long as anyone's "basic rights" are unsatisfied. One issue about this is the scope of the community within which this obligation holds. (See Discussion Question 5.)

Discussion Questions

1. Suppose that person A has an obligation (perhaps resulting from a contract or agreement of some sort) to give person B a certain amount of money at a designated time, and that person B has a corresponding right against person A that this be done. If it is impossible at the time in question for person A to pay person B the required amount, does this mean that there is no obligation and so no right? Suppose that A will never be able to pay (perhaps because he will no longer be alive). Does it matter *why* person A was unable to fulfill the obligation? (Think of different possibilities here.) If payment is genuinely impossible, then obviously A will not in fact fulfill the obligation, but is there any reason to think that B's right has not still been violated?—in which case it and the corresponding obligation must still exist.

2. Ozar (along with many others) suggests that it is the specific features of freedom and rationality that result in at least normally developed humans having moral rights (such as, at least, the rights to life and to liberty). But he says very little about why this is supposed to be so, beyond just remarking that these features make humans "special among the beings of this planet." Even assuming that this last claim is correct, it isn't very clear how the claim of rights is supposed to follow. Can you

*Henry Shue, *Basic Rights* (Princeton University Press, 1980).
†Shue, pp. 114–119.

see any further reason or argument here? (This is an extremely hard question, but one very much worth thinking about.)

3. Ozar suggests that the distinction between negative and positive rights depends on that between omissions of actions and actions, and so may be undermined if the latter distinction turns out to be questionable (as in the case described in Annotation 19). But another way to put the distinction is in terms of negative rights not to be interfered with (except to prevent interference with others) and positive rights to be given some positive benefit or assistance. Investigate the clarity and sharpness of this distinction by thinking of various rights that people are claimed to have and trying to see if they fall clearly into one or the other of these two categories.

4. It is often claimed that all human beings have moral rights to minimally adequate nutrition, housing, and clothing, among others. One question about such alleged rights is who has the corresponding duties. One possible answer is "society" or "the community." But apart from concerns about the size or scope of the relevant society or community (does it include all humans or even all rational beings of any sort, or is it more limited in size?), some will object that society has no resources of its own, but only those derived from individuals in some way (as by taxation). Could society have an obligation to provide everyone with the things in question (assuming that they are unable to provide them for themselves) without some or all of the members of society having such an obligation? If not, what is the basis for the latter obligation—especially as it extends, for example, to people in distant countries? Is this a serious objection to the idea of (nonconventional) positive rights? (Is there any analogous problem about negative rights?)

5. Does each person have a moral obligation not to devote resources to his own projects and interests until and unless the basic rights of all human beings (or perhaps even all rational creatures) have been fulfilled (which seems to mean, for Shue, that their basic needs have been met). What would the implications of such a view be in the area of famine relief? What if we discovered, in the process of space exploration, a large planet full of exceptionally needy rational beings (does it matter whether they are biologically human?)? (Think here about Williams's objection to utilitarianism: that it fails to give adequate weight to a person's own projects and commitments. To what extent does a similar objection apply to Shue's view of rights?)

VIRTUE ETHICS: MORALITY DEPENDS ON CHARACTER TRAITS

Aristotle

Aristotle (384–322 B.C.) was a Greek philosopher and one of the most important and influential philosophers of all time—quite possibly the most important and influential of all. He was a student of Plato, tutored Alexander the Great, and later founded his own philosophical school, the Lyceum. In the writings that have survived, almost none of which were intended for publication in their current state, Aristotle makes important contributions to virtually every area of philosophy including logic, metaphysics, epistemology, the philosophy of mind, ethics, political philosophy, and aesthetics.

In the selection that follows, taken from his most important ethical work, Aristotle argues that human happiness (or flourishing) consists in action according to virtue, and proceeds to give an account of the moral virtues. His famous view is that a virtue consists in a mean between two opposed vices, one of these involving an excess and the other a deficiency of the relevant quality. Though Aristotle's thought has provided much of the inspiration for contemporary virtue ethics, it is a matter of scholarly controversy (which cannot be pursued here) whether he held a view of this sort himself.

The italicized headings in the selection were added by the translator and do not come from Aristotle.

From *The Nichomachean Ethics*

BOOK I: THE GOOD FOR MAN

Subject of Our Inquiry

All human activities aim at some good: some goods subordinate to others

1. Every art and every inquiry, and similarly every action and pursuit, is thought to aim at some good; and for this reason the good has rightly been declared to be that at which all things aim. But a certain difference is found among ends; some are activities, others are products apart from the activities that produce them. Where there are ends apart from the actions, it is the nature of the products to be better than the activities. . . .

The science of the good for man is politics

2. If, then, there is some end of the things we do, which we desire for its own sake (everything else being desired for the sake of this), and if we do not choose everything for the sake of something else (for at that rate the process would go on to infinity, so that our desire would be empty and vain), clearly this must be the good and the chief good.① Will not the knowledge of it, then, have a great influence on life? Shall we not, like archers who have a mark to aim at,

> ① Not everything can be desired only for the sake of something else. Thus some things must be **intrinsic goods**, desirable for their own sakes. Aristotle assumes further that there is one and only one intrinsic good for the sake of which everything else is desired. (How plausible is this assumption?)

be more likely to hit upon what is right? If so, we must try, in outline at least, to determine what it is, and of which of the sciences or capacities it is the object. It would seem to belong to the most authoritative art and that which is most truly the master art. And politics appears to be of this nature; for it is this that ordains which of the sciences should be studied in a state, and which each class of citizens should learn and up to what point they should learn them.② . . .

> ② Here "politics" is roughly the study of what is good or best for an organized community. Underlying this is Aristotle's assumption that the good for human beings essentially involves participation in such a community.

What Is the Good for Man?

It is generally agreed to be happiness, but there are various views as to what happiness is. . . .

4. Let us resume our inquiry and state, in view of the fact that all knowledge and every pursuit aims at some good, what it is that we say political science aims at and what is the highest of all goods achievable by action. Verbally there is very general agreement; for both the general run of men and people of superior refinement say that it is happiness, and identify living well and faring well with being happy③; but with regard to what happiness is they differ, and the many do not give the same account as the wise. For the former think it is some plain and obvious thing, like pleasure, wealth, or hon-

> ③ The Greek word here translated as "happiness" is "*eudaimonia,*" also sometimes translated as "human flourishing." It refers to whatever sort of life is most desirable or satisfactory, with no implication that this will be one of pleasure or enjoyment.

From The Nichomachean Ethics, *translated by David Ross, revised by Ackrill and Urmson (Oxford: Oxford University Press, 1980).*

our; they differ, however, from one another—and often even the same man identifies it with different things, with health when he is ill, with wealth when he is poor; but, conscious of their ignorance, they admire those who proclaim some great thing that is above their comprehension. Now some thought that apart from these many goods there is another which is good in itself and causes and goodness of all these as well. . . .

Discussion of the popular views that the good is pleasure, honour, wealth . . .

5. . . . To judge from the lives that men lead, most men, and men of the most vulgar type, seem (not without some ground) to identify the good, or happiness, with pleasure; which is the reason why they love the life of enjoyment. For there are, we may say, three prominent types of life—that just mentioned, the political, and thirdly the contemplative life. Now the mass of mankind are evidently quite slavish in their tastes, preferring a life suitable to beasts. . . . A consideration of the prominent types of life shows that people of superior refinement and of active disposition identify happiness with honour; for this is, roughly speaking, the end of the political life. But it seems too superficial to be what we are looking for, since it is thought to depend on those who bestow honour rather than on him who receives it, but the good we divine to be something of one's own and not easily taken from one. Further, men seem to pursue honour in order that they may be assured of their merit; at least it is by men of practical wisdom that they seek to be honoured, and among those who know them, and on the ground of their virtue; clearly, then, according to them, at any rate, virtue is better. . . . ④

④ The Greek word here translated as "virtue" is "*aretē*," also sometimes translated as "excellence." (The "*aretē*" of a thing of a certain kind is whatever makes it a *good* thing of that kind.) Virtue is then excellence of human character. People are honored for their excellences, but not only for moral excellence.

The good must be something final and self-sufficient. Definition of happiness reached by considering the characteristic function of man

7. Let us again return to the good we are seeking, and ask what it can be . . . we call that which is in itself worthy of pursuit more final than that which is worthy of pursuit for the sake of something else, and that which is never desirable for the sake of something else more final than the things that are desirable both in themselves and for the sake of that other thing, and therefore we call final without qualification that which is always desirable in itself and never for the sake of something else.

Now such a thing happiness, above all else, is held to be; for this we choose always for itself and never for the sake of something else, but honour, pleasure, reason, and every virtue we choose indeed for themselves (for if nothing resulted from them we should still choose each of them), but we choose them also for the sake of happiness, judging that through them we shall be happy. Happiness, on the other hand, no one chooses for the sake of these, nor, in general, for anything other than itself.⑤

⑤ This is essentially a matter of definition: happiness is whatever has this status. (What this is, we do not yet know.)

From the point of view of self-sufficiency the same result seems to follow; for the final good is thought to be self-sufficient. Now by self-sufficient we do not mean that which is sufficient for a man by himself, for one who lives a solitary life, but also for parents, children, wife, and in general for his friends and fellow citizens, since man is born for citizenship. . . . the self-sufficient we now define as that which when isolated makes life desirable and lacking in nothing; and such we think happiness to be; and further we think it most desirable of all things, not a thing counted as one good thing among others—if it were so counted it would clearly be made more desirable by the addition of even the least of goods; for that which is added becomes an excess of goods, and of goods the greater is always more desirable. Happiness, then, is something final and self-sufficient, and is the end of action.

Presumably, however, to say that happiness is the chief good seems a platitude, and a clearer account of what it is is still desired. This might perhaps be given, if we could first ascertain the function of man. For just as for a flute-player, a sculptor, or any artist, and, in general, for all things that have a function or activity, the good and the 'well' is thought to reside in the function, so would it seem to be for man, if he has a function. Have the carpenter, then, and the tanner certain functions or activities, and has man none? Is he born without a function? Or as eye, hand, foot, and in general each of the parts evidently has a function, may one lay it down that man similarly has a function apart from all these? ⑥ What then can this be? Life seems to belong even to plants, but we are seeking what is peculiar to man. Let us exclude, therefore, the life of nutrition and growth. Next there would be a life of perception, but *it* also seems to be shared even by the horse, the ox, and every animal. There remains, then, an active life of the element that has a rational principle. . . . ⑦ Now if the function of man is an activity of soul which follows or implies a rational principle, . . . and if any action is well performed when it is performed in accordance with the appropriate excellence: if this is the case, human good turns out to be activity of soul exhibiting excellence, and if there are more than one excellence, in accordance with the best and most complete. ⑧

> ⑥ The function (*ergon*) of something is its characteristic activity in virtue of the kind of thing that it is.

> ⑦ Aristotle argues that the function of a human being must be something that is not shared with lower forms of life: an active life involving reason or rationality, rather than just nutrition or perception.

> ⑧ Thus human happiness or flourishing is rational activity in accordance with the best and most complete excellence or virtue.

But we must add 'in a complete life'. For one swallow does not make a summer, nor does one day; and so too one day, or a short time, does not make a man blessed and happy.

. . .

Our definition is confirmed by current beliefs about happiness

8. . . . The characteristics that are looked for in happiness seem also, all of them, to belong to what we have defined happiness as being. For some identify happiness with virtue, some with practical wisdom, others with a kind of philosophic wisdom, others with these, or one of these, accompanied by pleasure or not without pleasure; while others include also external prosperity. . . .

With those who identify happiness with virtue or some one virtue our account is in harmony; for to virtue belongs virtuous activity. But it makes, perhaps, no small difference whether we place the chief good in possession or in use, in state of mind or in activity. For the state of mind may exist without producing any good result, as in a man who is asleep or in some other way quite inactive, but the activity cannot; for one who has the activity will of necessity be acting, and acting well. . . . ⑨

> ⑨ Aristotle insists that happiness essentially involves *activity*; it is not enough to simply possess traits of mind that would lead to virtuous activity, but which are never in fact used.

Their life is also in itself pleasant. For pleasure is a state of *soul,* and to each man that which he is said to be a lover of is pleasant; e.g. not only is a horse pleasant to the lover of horses, and a spectacle to the lover of sights, but also in the same way just acts are pleasant to the lover of justice and in general virtuous acts to the lover of virtue. Now for most men their pleasures are in conflict with one another because these are not by nature pleasant, but the lovers of what is noble find pleasant the things that are by nature pleasant; and virtuous actions are such, so that these are pleasant for such men as well as in their own nature. Their life, therefore, has no further need of pleasure as a sort of adventitious charm, but has its pleasure in itself. For, besides what we have said, the man who does not rejoice in noble actions is not even good; since no one would call a man just who did not enjoy acting justly, nor any man liberal who did not enjoy liberal actions; and similarly in all other cases. If this is so, virtuous actions must be in themselves pleasant. ⑩ But they are also *good* and *noble,* and have each of these attributes in the highest degree, since the good man judges well about these attributes. . . . Happiness then is the best, noblest, and most pleasant thing in the world. . . . For all these properties belong to the best activities; and these, or one—the best—of these, we identify with happiness.

> ⑩ A virtuous person will take pleasure in virtuous actions as such, without the need for external pleasure as a motivation.

Yet evidently . . . it needs the external goods as well; for it is impossible, or not easy, to do noble acts without the proper equipment. In many actions we use friends and riches and political power as instruments; and there are some things the lack of which takes the lustre from happiness—good birth, goodly children, beauty; for the man who is very ugly in appearance or ill-born or solitary and childless is not very likely to be happy, and perhaps a man would be still less likely if he had thoroughly bad children or friends or had lost good children or friends by death. . . . happiness seems to need this sort of prosperity in addition; for which reason some identify happiness with good fortune, though others identify it with virtue.⑪

> ⑪ For the Greeks, happiness involved more than the right inner states of mind or even the right motivations for actions; a substantial degree of success was also required, so that even a person with the best sort of character could have their happiness destroyed by external bad fortune of various sorts.

. . .

Kinds of Virtue

Division of the faculties, and resultant division of virtue into intellectual and moral

13. Since happiness is an activity of soul in accordance with perfect virtue, we must consider the nature of virtue; for perhaps we shall thus see better the nature of happiness. . . .

BOOK II: MORAL VIRTUE

Moral Virtue, How Produced, in What Medium and in What Manner Exhibited

Moral virtue, like the arts, is acquired by repetition of the corresponding acts

1. Virtue, then, being of two kinds, intellectual and moral, intellectual virtue in the main owes both its birth and its growth to teaching (for which reason it requires experience and time), while moral virtue comes about as a result of habit. . . . From this it is also plain that none of the moral virtues arises in us by nature; for nothing that exists by nature can form a habit contrary to its nature. . . . Neither by nature, then, nor contrary to nature do the virtues arise in us; rather we are adapted by nature to receive them, and are made perfect by habit.⑫

> ⑫ Human nature is in itself receptive to either virtue or vice; which one of these it acquires depends on how it is exercised and what habits it eventually forms.

Again, of all the things that come to us by nature we first acquire the potentiality and later exhibit the activity . . . ; but the virtues we get by first exercising them, as also hap-

pens in the case of the arts as well. For the things we have to learn before we can do them, we learn by doing them, e.g. men become builders by building and lyre-players by playing the lyre; so too we become just by doing just acts, temperate by doing temperate acts, brave by doing brave acts.⑬

> ⑬ This might seem paradoxical: how can you do something in order to learn how to do it? Aristotle will explain on page 661.

. . .

Again, it is from the same causes and by the same means that every virtue is both produced and destroyed, and similarly every art. . . . by doing the acts that we do in our transactions with other men we become just or unjust, and by doing the acts that we do in the presence of danger, and by being habituated to feel fear or confidence, we become brave or cowardly. The same is true of appetites and feelings of anger; some men become temperate and good-tempered, others self-indulgent and irascible, by behaving in one way or the other in the appropriate circumstances. Thus, in one word, states of character arise out of like activities. This is why the activities we exhibit must be of a certain kind; it is because the states of character correspond to the differences between these. It makes no small difference, then, whether we form habits of one kind or of another from our very youth; it makes a very great difference, or rather *all* the difference.⑭

> ⑭ Thus people become virtuous by practicing virtuous behavior *before* the corresponding character traits have been formed (and vicious in the same way).

These acts cannot be prescribed exactly, but must avoid excess and defect

2. Since, then, the present inquiry does not aim at theoretical knowledge like the others (for we are inquiring not in order to know what virtue is, but in order to become good, since otherwise our inquiry would have been of no use), we must examine the nature of actions, namely how we ought to do them; for these determine also the nature of the states of character that are produced. . . . But this must be agreed upon beforehand, that the whole account of matters of conduct must be given in outline and not precisely, as we said at the very beginning that the accounts we demand must be in accordance with the subject-matter; matters concerned with conduct and questions of what is good for us have no fixity, any more than matters of health.

15 As Aristotle said in an earlier passage omitted from this selection, an adequate discussion should have "as much clearness as the subject-matter admits of"—he claims that ethics does not admit of the same degree of clarity as, for example, logic or science.

The general account being of this nature, the account of particular cases is yet more lacking in exactness; for they do not fall under any art or precept, but the agents themselves must in each case consider what is appropriate to the occasion, as happens also in the art of medicine or of navigation. 15

But though our present account is of this nature we must give what help we can. First, then, let us consider this, that it is the nature of such things to be destroyed by defect and excess, as we see in the case of strength and of health (for to gain light on things imperceptible we must use the evidence of sensible things); exercise either excessive or defective destroys the strength and similarly drink or food which is above or below a certain amount destroys the health, while that which is proportionate both produces and increases and preserves it. So too is it, then, in the case of temperance and courage and the other virtues. For the man who flies from and fears everything and does not stand his ground against anything becomes a coward, and the man who fears nothing at all but goes to meet every danger becomes rash; and similarly the man who indulges in every pleasure and abstains from none becomes self-indulgent, while the

16 Here is the first appearance of a view to be extensively developed in what follows: virtuous character traits are intermediate between excess and deficiency.

man who shuns every pleasure, as boors do, becomes in a way insensible; temperance and courage, then, are destroyed by excess and defect, and preserved by the mean. 16

. . .

Pleasure in doing virtuous acts is a sign that the virtuous disposition has been acquired: a variety of considerations show the essential connexion of moral virtue with pleasure and pain

3. We must take as a sign of states of character the pleasure or pain that supervenes upon acts; for the man who abstains from bodily pleasures and delights in this very fact is temperate, while the man who is annoyed at it is self-indulgent, and he who stands his ground against things that are terrible and delights in this or at least is not pained is brave, while the man who is pained is a coward. For moral excellence is concerned with pleasures and pains; it is on account of the pleasure that we do bad things, and on account of the pain that we abstain from noble ones. Hence we ought to have been brought up in a particular way from our very youth . . . so as both to delight in and to be pained by the things that we ought; this is the right education. 17

17 As noted earlier, a virtuous person will find virtuous actions pleasurable in themselves, whereas one who does the right thing but finds it onerous does not yet possess the corresponding virtue.

Again, if the virtues are concerned with actions and passions, and every passion and every action is accompanied by pleasure and pain, for this reason also virtue will be concerned with pleasures and pains. This is indicated also by the fact that punishment is inflicted by these means; for it is a kind of cure, and it is the nature of cures to be effected by contraries.

. . .

That virtue, then, is concerned with pleasures and pains, and that by the acts from which it arises it is both increased and, if they are done differently, destroyed . . . let this be taken as said.

The actions that produce moral virtue are not good in the same sense as those that flow from it: the latter must fulfil certain conditions not necessary in the case of the arts

4. The question might be asked, what we mean by saying that we must become just by doing just acts, and temperate by doing temperate acts; for if men do just and temperate acts, they are already just and temperate, exactly as, if they do what is in accordance with the laws of grammar and of music, they are grammarians and musicians. 18

18 Aristotle raises an objection to the view that virtues are acquired by doing actions of the corresponding sort: one who acts in the corresponding ways (for example, courageously or temperately) must already have the corresponding virtue, and so cannot acquire it in that way.

Or is this not true even of the arts? It is possible to do something that is in accordance with the laws of grammar, either by chance or under the guidance of another. A man will be a grammarian, then, only when he has both said something grammatical and said it grammatically; and this means doing it in accordance with the grammatical knowledge in himself.

Again, the case of the arts and that of the virtues are not similar; for the products of the arts have their goodness in themselves, so that it is enough that they should have a certain character, but if the acts that are in accordance with the virtues have themselves a certain character it does not follow that they are done justly or temperately. The agent also must be in a certain condition when he does them; in the first place he must have knowledge, secondly he must choose the acts, and choose them for their own sakes, and thirdly his action must proceed from a firm and unchangeable character. These are not reckoned in as conditions of the possession of the arts, except the bare knowledge; but as a condition of the possession of the virtues knowledge has little or no weight, while the other conditions count not for a little but for everything, i.e. the very conditions which result from often doing just and temperate acts.

Actions, then, are called just and temperate when they are such as the just or the temperate man would do; but it is not the man who does these that is just and temperate, but the man who also does them *as* just and temperate men do them. It is well said, then, that it is by doing just acts that the just man is produced, and by doing temperate acts the temperate man; without doing these no one would have even a prospect of becoming good. [19]

[19] But the previous objection is mistaken. Just as in the arts, a person can do the sorts of actions in question, can act in a given case as the virtuous person would act, without yet having the formed character trait. (Such a person does not do the virtuous action *as* the virtuous person would because the act is not produced in the same way in that it does not arise out of the same trait of character.)

But most people do not do these, but take refuge in theory and think they are being philosophers and will become good in this way, behaving somewhat like patients who listen attentively to their doctors, but do none of the things they are ordered to do. As the latter will not be made well in body by such a course of treatment, the former will not be made well in soul by such a course of philosophy.

Definition of Moral Virtue

The genus of moral virtue: it is a state of character, not a passion, nor a faculty

5. Next we must consider what virtue is. Since things that are found in the soul are of three kinds—passions, faculties, states of character—virtue must be one of these. By passions I mean appetite, anger, fear, confidence, envy, joy, friendly feeling, hatred, longing, emulation, pity, and in general the feelings that are accompanied by pleasure or pain; by faculties the things in virtue of which we are said to be capable of feeling these, e.g. of becoming angry or being pained or feeling pity; by states of character the things in virtue of which we stand well or badly with reference to the passions, e.g. with reference to anger we stand badly if we feel it violently or too weakly, and well if we feel it moderately; and similarly with reference to the other passions. [20]

[20] Aristotle distinguishes states of the soul into three general and supposedly exhaustive categories. (How plausible is this?)

Now neither the virtues nor the vices are *passions,* because we are not called good or bad on the ground of our passions, but are so called on the ground of our virtues and our vices, and because we are neither praised nor blamed for our passions (for the man who feels fear or anger is not praised, nor is the man who simply feels anger blamed, but the man who feels it in a certain way), but for our virtues and our vices we *are* praised or blamed.

Again, we feel anger and fear without choice, but the virtues are modes of choice or involve choice. Further, in respect of the passions we are said to be moved, but in respect of the virtues and the vices we are said not to be moved but to be disposed in a particular way.

For these reasons also they are not *faculties;* for we are neither called good or bad, nor praised or blamed, for the simple capacity of feeling the passions; again, we have the faculties by nature, but we are not made good or bad by nature; we have spoken of this before.

If, then, the virtues are neither passions nor faculties, all that remains is that they should be *states of character.*

Thus we have stated what virtue is in respect of its genus. [21]

[21] Aristotle argues by elimination that virtues are states of character. (This may seem too obvious to need saying, but not if virtues are just human excellences.) This is the *genus* (general category) within which virtue falls, but does not yet say what specific sorts of states of character the virtues are.

The differentia of moral virtue: it is a disposition to choose the mean

6. We must, however, not only describe virtue as a state of character, but also say what sort of state it is. We may remark, then, that every virtue or excellence both brings into good condition the thing of which it is the excellence and makes the work of that thing be done well; e.g. the excellence of the eye makes both the eye and its work good; for it is by the excellence of the eye that we see well. . . . Therefore, if this is true in every case, the virtue of man also will be the state of character which makes a man good and which makes him do his own work well. [22]

[22] By comparison with other cases, human virtues will be states of character that allow people to do their essential work or functions well.

How this is to happen we have stated already, but it will be made plain also by the following consideration of the specific nature of virtue. In everything that is continuous and divisible it is possible to take more, less, or an equal amount, and that either in terms of the thing itself or relatively to us; and the equal is an intermediate between excess and defect. By the intermediate in the object I mean that which is equidistant from each of the extremes, which is one and the same for all men; by the intermediate relatively to us that which is neither too much nor too little—and this is not one, nor the same for all. For instance, if ten is many and two is few, six is the intermediate, taken in terms of the object; for it exceeds and is exceeded by an equal amount; this is intermediate according to arithmetical proportion. But the intermediate relatively to us is not to be taken so; if ten pounds are too much for a particular person to eat and two too little, it does not follow that the trainer will order six pounds; for this also is perhaps too much for the person who is to take it, or too little. . . . Thus a master of any art avoids excess and defect, but seeks the intermediate and chooses this—the intermediate not in the object but relatively to us. [23]

If it is thus, then, that every art does its work well—by looking to the intermediate and judging its works by this standard (so that we often say of good works of art that it is not possible either to take away or to add anything, implying that excess and defect destroy the goodness of works of art, while the mean preserves it; and good artists, as we say, look to this in their work), and if, further, virtue is more exact and better than any art, as nature also is, then virtue must have the quality of aiming at the intermediate. I mean moral virtue; for it is this that is concerned with passions and actions, and in these there is excess, defect, and the intermediate. For instance, both fear and confidence and appetite and anger and pity and in general pleasure and pain may be felt both too much and too little, and in both cases not well; but to feel them at the right times, with reference to the right objects, towards the right people, with the right motive, and in the right way, is what is both intermediate and best, and this is characteristic of virtue. [24] Similarly with regard to actions also there is excess, defect, and the intermediate. Now virtue is concerned with passions and actions, in which excess is a form of failure, and so is defect, while the intermediate is praised and is a form of success; and being praised and being successful are both characteristics of virtue. Therefore virtue is a kind of mean, since, as we have seen, it aims at what is intermediate.

Again, it is possible to fail in many ways . . . , while to succeed is possible only in one way (for which reason also one is easy and the other difficult—to miss the mark easy, to hit it difficult); for these reasons also, then, excess and defect are characteristic of vice, and the mean of virtue;

For men are good in but one way, but bad in many.

Virtue, then, is a state of character concerned with choice, lying in a mean, i.e. the mean relative to

[23] And this in turn involves avoiding both excess and defect (deficiency) and finding the appropriate intermediate action or *mean*—but with the important qualification that the relevant mean is to be determined in relation to the person and the situation, not just mathematically.

[24] Here is the general formula for virtuous action, with what is right being determined in each case by avoiding both excess and deficiency in the dimension in question and thereby finding the appropriate mean.

us, this being determined by a rational principle, and by that principle by which the man of practical wisdom would determine it. ⟨25⟩ Now it is a mean between two vices, that which depends on excess and that which depends on defect; and again it is a mean because the vices respectively fall short of or exceed what is right in both passions and actions, while virtue both finds and chooses that which is intermediate. Hence in respect of what it is, i.e. the definition which states its essence, virtue is a mean, with regard to what is best and right an extreme.

⟨25⟩ And here finally is the definition of virtue. The translation is misleading in that the word translated as "rational principle" (*logos*) does not necessarily suggest that there is a principle in the sense of a clear rule, but only that the determination is done in a rational way, through reason.

But not every action nor every passion admits of a mean; for some have names that already imply badness, e.g., spite, shamelessness, envy, and in the case of actions adultery, theft, murder; for all of these and suchlike things imply by their names that they are themselves bad, and not the excesses or deficiencies of them. It is not possible, then, ever to be right with regard to them: one must always be wrong. . . . It would be . . . absurd, then, to expect that in unjust, cowardly, and voluptuous action there should be a mean, an excess, and a deficiency. . . . of the actions we have mentioned there is no mean nor any excess and deficiency, but however they are done they are wrong; for in general there is neither a mean of excess and deficiency, nor excess and deficiency of a mean.

The above proposition illustrated by reference to particular virtues

7. . . . With regard to feelings of fear and confidence courage is the mean; of the people who exceed, he who exceeds in fearlessness has no name (many of the states have no name), while the man who exceeds in confidence is rash, and he who exceeds in fear and falls short in confidence is a coward. With regard to pleasures and pains—not all of them, and not so much with regard to the pains—the mean is temperance, the excess self-indulgence. Persons deficient with regard to the pleasures are not often found; hence such persons also have received no name. But let us call them 'insensible'.

With regard to giving and taking of money the mean is liberality, the excess and the defect prodigality and meanness. In these actions people exceed and fall short in contrary ways; the prodigal exceeds in spending and falls short in taking, while the mean man exceeds in taking and falls short in spending. (At present we are giving a mere outline or summary, and are satisfied with this; later these states will be more exactly determined.) ⟨26⟩ With regard to money there are also other dispositions—a mean, magnificence (for the magnificent man differs from the liberal man; the former deals with large sums, the latter with small ones), an excess, tastelessness and vulgarity, and a deficiency, niggardliness; these differ from the states opposed to liberality, and the mode of their difference will be stated later.

⟨26⟩ Some, but not all, of these more detailed accounts are included later in this selection.

With regard to honour and dishonour the mean is proper pride, the excess is known as a sort of 'empty vanity', and the deficiency is undue humility; and as we said liberality was related to magnificence, differing from it by dealing with small sums, so there is a state similarly related to proper pride, being concerned with small honours while that is concerned with great. For it is possible to desire honour as one ought, and more than one ought, and less, and the man who exceeds in his desires is called ambitious, the man who falls short unambitious, while the intermediate person has no name. . . .

With regard to anger also there is an excess, a deficiency, and a mean. Although they can scarcely be said to have names, yet since we call the intermediate person good-tempered let us call the mean good temper; of the persons at the extremes let the one who exceeds be called irascible, and his vice irascibility, and the man who falls short an unirascible sort of person, and the deficiency unirascibility.

There are also three other means, which have a certain likeness to one another, but differ from one another: for they are all concerned with intercourse in words and actions, but differ in that one is concerned with truth in this sphere, the other two with pleasantness; and of this one kind is exhibited in giving amusement, the other in all the circumstances of life. We must therefore speak of these too, that we may the better see that in all things the mean is praiseworthy, and the extremes neither praiseworthy nor right, but worthy of blame. Now most of these states also have no names, but we must try, as in the other cases, to invent names ourselves so that we may be clear and easy to follow. With regard to truth, then, the intermediate is a truthful sort of person and the mean may be called truthfulness, while the pretence which exaggerates is boastfulness and the person characterized by it a boaster, and that which understates is mock modesty and the person characterized by it mock-modest.[27]

[27] As this suggests, Aristotle has at least primarily in mind a person's descriptions of himself and his own qualities.

With regard to pleasantness in the giving of amusement the intermediate person is ready-witted and the disposition ready wit, the excess is buffoonery and the person characterized by it a buffoon, while the man who falls short is a sort of boor and his state is boorishness. With regard to the remaining kind of pleasantness, that which is exhibited in life in general, the man who is pleasant in the right way is friendly and the mean is friendliness, while the man who exceeds is an obsequious person if he has no end in view, a flatterer if he is aiming at his own advantage, and the man who falls short and is unpleasant in all circumstances is a quarrelsome and surly sort of person.

There are also means in the passions and concerned with the passions; since shame is not a virtue, and yet praise is extended to the modest man. For even in these matters one man is said to be intermediate, and another to exceed, as for instance the bashful man who is ashamed of everything; while he who falls short or is not ashamed of anything at all is shameless, and the intermediate person is modest. Righteous indignation is a mean between envy and spite, and these states are concerned with the pain and pleasure that are felt at the fortunes of our neighbours; the man who is characterized by righteous indignation is pained at undeserved good fortune, the envious man, going beyond him, is pained at all good fortune, and the spiteful man falls so far short of being pained that he even rejoices. . . . *

BOOK III: MORAL VIRTUE

Inner Side of Moral Virtue: Conditions of Responsibility for Action

Praise and blame attach to voluntary actions, i.e. actions done (1) not under compulsion, and (2) with knowledge of the circumstances

1. Since virtue is concerned with passions and actions, and on voluntary passions and actions praise and blame are bestowed, on those that are involuntary pardon, and sometimes also pity, to distinguish the voluntary and the involuntary is presumably necessary for those who are studying the nature of virtue, and useful also for legislators with a view to the assigning both of honours and of punishments.

Those things, then, are thought involuntary, which take place by force or owing to ignorance; and that is compulsory of which the moving principle is outside, being a principle in which nothing is contributed by the person who acts—or, rather, is acted upon, e.g. if he were to be carried somewhere by a wind, or by men who had him in their power.[28]

[28] So something could be *involuntary* without being *compulsory*. One example would be an action due to ignorance (for example, shooting people who were, unbeknownst to you, standing behind the targets at your shooting range), where the "moving principle" (immediate cause) is still within the person rather than outside.

But with regard to the things that are done from fear of greater evils or for some noble object (e.g. if a tyrant were to order one to do something base, having one's parents and children in his power, and if one did the action they were to be saved, but otherwise would be put to death), it may be debated whether such actions are involuntary or voluntary. Something of the sort happens also with regard to the throwing of goods overboard in a storm; for in the abstract no one throws goods away voluntarily, but on condition of its securing the safety of himself and his crew any sensible man does so. Such actions, then, are mixed, but are more like voluntary actions; for they are worthy of

*Aristotle must mean that while the envious man is pained at the good fortune of others, whether deserved or not, the spiteful man is pleased at the *bad* fortune of others, whether deserved or not. But if he had stated this in full, he would have seen that there is no real opposition.

choice at the time when they are done, and the end of an action is relative to the occasion. Both the terms, then, 'voluntary' and 'involuntary', must be used with reference to the moment of action.... ㉙

___

㉙ In these cases, the person is not ignorant of the situation and does have a choice about what to do, which makes the action more like an ordinary case of a voluntary action. What makes such actions seem less than fully voluntary is that the range of available choices is restricted by circumstances in an unfortunate way: in the ship case, no choice is available that will save both the goods and the people.

___

㉚ It would be odd to call something done out of ignorance but which the person does not later regret involuntary, but also not quite right to call it voluntary either. Aristotle suggests that it should have a label of its own, but does not suggest one here.

___

Everything that is done by reason of ignorance is *not* voluntary; it is only what produces pain and regret that is *in*voluntary. For the man who has done something owing to ignorance, and feels not the least vexation at his action, has not acted voluntarily, since he did not know what he was doing, nor yet involuntarily, since he is not pained. Of people, then, who act by reason of ignorance he who regrets is thought an involuntary agent, and the man who does not regret may, since he is different, be called a not voluntary agent; for, since he differs from the other, it is better that he should have a name of his own. ㉚

...

Since that which is done by force or by reason of ignorance is involuntary, the voluntary would seem to be that of which the moving principle is in the agent him-

___

㉛ This is a definition of what it is for an action to be voluntary.

___

self, he being aware of the particular circumstances of the action.... ㉛

Moral virtue implies that the action is done (3) by choice: the object of choice is the result of previous deliberation

2. Both the voluntary and the involuntary having been delimited, we must next discuss choice; for it is thought to be most closely bound up with virtue, and to discriminate characters better than actions do.

Choice, then, seems to be voluntary, but not the same thing as the voluntary; the latter extends more widely. For both children and the lower animals share in voluntary action, but not in choice, and acts done on the spur of the moment we describe as voluntary, but not as chosen.

...

But neither is it wish, though it seems near to it; for choice cannot relate to impossibles, and if any one said he chose them he would be thought silly; but there may be a wish even for impossibles, e.g. for immortality. And wish may relate to things that could in no way be brought about by one's own efforts, e.g. that a particular actor or athlete should win in a competition; but no one chooses such things, but only the things that he thinks could be brought about by his own efforts. Again, wish relates rather to the end, choice to the means; for instance, we wish to be healthy, but we choose the acts which will make us healthy, and we wish to be happy and say we do, but we cannot well say we choose to be so; for, in general, choice seems to relate to the things that are in our own power.

...

What, then, or what kind of thing is it, since it is none of the things we have mentioned? It seems to be voluntary, but not all that is voluntary to be an object of choice. Is it, then, what has been deliberated about before? At any rate choice involves a rational principle and thought. Even the name seems to suggest that it is what is chosen before other things. ㉜

___

㉜ Aristotle says that the category of choice is narrower than the category of the voluntary and suggests that choice involves rational deliberation. ("Rational principle" is again misleading in the way indicated in Annotation 25.)

___

The nature of deliberation and its objects: choice is deliberate desire of things in our own power

3. Do we deliberate about everything, and is everything a possible subject of deliberation, or is deliberation impossible about some things? We ought presumably to call not what a fool or a madman would deliberate about, but what a sensible man would deliberate about, a subject of deliberation....

We deliberate about things that are in our power and can be done ... the things that are brought about by our own efforts, but not always in the same way, are the things about which we deliberate, e.g. questions of medical treatment or of money-making. . . . Deliberation is concerned with things that happen in a certain way for the most part, but in which the event is obscure, and with things in which it is indeterminate. . . .

We deliberate not about ends but about means. For a doctor does not deliberate whether he shall heal, nor an orator whether he shall convince, nor a statesman whether he shall produce law and order, nor does any one else deliberate about his end. Having set the end, they consider how and by what means it is to be attained; and if it seems to be produced by several means they consider by which it is most easily and best produced, while if it is achieved by one only they consider how it will be achieved by this and by what means *this* will be achieved, till they come to the first cause, which is the order of discovery is last. ㉝

㉝ Deliberation has to do with means to an end rather than ends themselves and involves working back from the end until some action that is within one's direct power is reached (the "first cause"). (While this may be the most typical case, is it as clear as he thinks that we cannot also deliberate about ends?)

. . . And if we come on an impossibility, we give up the search, e.g. if we need money and this cannot be got; but if a thing appears possible we try to do it. By 'possible' things I mean things that might be brought about by our own efforts. . . . It seems, then, . . . that man is a moving principle of actions; now deliberation is about the things to be done by the agent himself, and actions are for the sake of things other than themselves. . . .

The same thing is deliberated upon and is chosen, except that the object of choice is already determinate, since it is that which has been decided upon as a result of deliberation that is the object of choice. For everyone ceases to inquire how he is to act when he has brought the moving principle back to himself and to the ruling part of himself; for this is what chooses.

. . .

We are responsible for bad as well as for good actions
5. The end, then, being what we wish for, the means what we deliberate about and choose, actions concerning means must be according to choice and voluntary. Now the exercise of the virtues is concerned with means. Therefore virtue also is in our own power, and so too vice. ㉞ For where it is in our power to act

it is also in our power not to act, and *vice versa;* so that, if to act, where this is noble, is in our power, not to act, which will be base, will also be in our power, and if not to act, where this is noble, is in our power, to act, which will be base, will also be in our power. Now if it is in our power to do noble or base acts, and likewise in our power not to do them, and this was what being good or bad meant, then it is in our power to be virtuous or vicious.

The saying that 'no one is voluntarily wicked nor involuntarily happy' seems to be partly false and partly true; for no one is involuntarily happy, but wickedness is voluntary. ㉟ Or else we shall have to dispute what has just been said, at any rate, and deny that man is a moving principle or begetter of his actions, as of children. But if these facts are evident and we cannot refer actions to moving principles other than those in ourselves, the acts whose moving principles are in us must themselves also be in our power and voluntary.

Witness seems to be borne to this both by individuals in their private capacity and by legislators themselves; for these punish and take vengeance on those who do wicked acts (unless they have acted under compulsion or as a result of ignorance for which they are not themselves responsible), while they honour those who do noble acts, as though they meant to encourage the latter and deter the former. But no one is encouraged to do the things that are neither in our power nor voluntary; it is assumed that there is no gain in being persuaded not to be hot or in pain or hungry or the, like since we shall experience these feelings none the less. ㊱ Indeed, we punish a man for his very ignorance, if he is thought responsible for the

㉞ There is some possibility of verbal confusion here. In saying that virtues are concerned with means, Aristotle is saying that they are concerned with ways of producing ends (not "means" in the sense of intermediates between excess and deficiency, as discussed earlier). Since means are deliberately and so voluntarily chosen, it follows that whether a person acts virtuously is something that is within his power. (How clear is it that virtue has only to do with means in this sense?)

㉟ No one is involuntarily happy because no one regrets happiness even if it is produced accidentally, out of ignorance (see Annotation 30). The more important point is that wickedness is voluntary, which follows from what has just been said.

ignorance, as when penalties are doubled in the case of drunkenness; for the moving principle is in the man

36 Aristotle cites the ways in which noble (virtuous) acts are honored and wicked actions punished as corroborating evidence for the claim that virtuous (and vicious) actions are within a person's voluntary control.

himself, since he had the power of not getting drunk and his getting drunk was the cause of his ignorance. And we punish those who are ignorant of anything in the laws that they ought to know and that is not difficult, and so too in the case of anything else that they are thought to be ignorant of through carelessness; we assume that it is in their power not to be ignorant, since they have the power of taking care.

But perhaps a man is the kind of man not to take care. Still they are themselves by their slack lives responsible for becoming men of that kind, and men are themselves responsible for being unjust or self-indulgent, in that they cheat or spend their time in drinking-bouts and the like; for it is activities exercised on particular objects that make the corresponding character. This is plain from the case of people training for any contest or action; they practise the activity the whole time. Now not to know that it is from the exercise of activities on particular objects that states of character are produced is the mark of a thoroughly senseless person. Again, it is irrational to suppose that a man who acts unjustly does not wish to be unjust or a man who acts self-indulgently to be self-indulgent. But if *without* being ignorant a man does the things which will make him unjust, he will be unjust voluntarily. Yet it does not follow that if he wishes he will cease to be unjust and will be just. For neither does the man who is ill become well on those terms. We may suppose a case in which he is ill voluntarily, through living incontinently and disobeying his doctors. In that case it was *then* open to him not to be ill, but not now, when he has thrown away his chance, just as when you have let a stone go it is too late to recover it; but that it was in your power to throw it, since the moving principle was in you. So, too, to the unjust and to the self-indulgent man it was open at the beginning not to become men of this kind, and so they are unjust and self-indulgent voluntarily; but now that they have become so it is not possible for them not to be so. **37**

. . .

With regard to the virtues *in general* we have stated their genus in outline, viz. that they are means and that they are states of character, and that they tend, and by their own nature, to the doing of the acts by which they are produced, and that they are in our power and voluntary, and act as the right rule prescribes. But actions and states of character are not voluntary in the same way; for we are masters of our actions from the beginning right to the end, if we know the particular facts, but though we control the beginning of our states of character the gradual progress is not obvious, any more than it is in illnesses; because it was in our power, however, to act in this way or not in this way, therefore the states are voluntary.

Let us take up the several virtues, however, and say which they are and what sort of things they are concerned with and how they are concerned with them; at the same time it will become plain how many they are. And first let us speak of courage.

37 But to say that virtuous actions and so virtue itself is within voluntary control is *not* to say that people are at every moment of their lives capable of acting virtuously. If someone has failed to form the right sorts of habits by acting in accord with virtue, the time may come when he is unable to act virtuously. But this is still a result within his voluntary control in the sense that it results from *earlier* voluntary actions.

Courage

Courage concerned with the feelings of fear and confidence—strictly speaking, with the fear of death in battle

6. That it is a mean with regard to feelings of fear and confidence has already been made evident; and plainly the things we fear are fearful things, and these are, to speak without qualification, evils; for which reason people even define fear as expectation of evil. Now we fear all evils, e.g. disgrace, poverty, disease, friendlessness, death, but the brave man is not thought to be concerned with all; for to fear some things is even right and noble, and it is base not to fear them— e.g. disgrace; he who fears this is good and modest, and he who does not is shameless. . . . Poverty and disease we perhaps ought not to fear, nor in general the things that do not proceed from vice and are not due to a man himself. But not even the man who is fearless of these is brave. . . . With what sort of fearful things, then, is the brave man concerned? Surely with the greatest; for no one is more likely than he to stand his ground against what is awe-inspiring. Now death is the most fearful of all things; for it is the end, and nothing is thought to be any longer either good or bad for the dead. But the brave man would not seem to be concerned even with death in *all* circumstances, e.g. at sea or in disease. In what circumstances, then? Surely in the noblest. Now such deaths are those in

___

38 The aspect of Greek thought that finds war to be the greatest and most noble human activity is unlikely to be very plausible to modern readers. But most of what Aristotle says about courage can be applied to other situations of danger as well.

___

battle; for these take place in the greatest and noblest danger. . . . Properly, then, he will be called brave who is fearless in face of a noble death, and of all emergencies that involve death; and the emergencies of war are in the highest degree of this kind. . . . 38

The motive of courage is the sense of honour: characteristics of the opposite vices, cowardice and rashness

7. . . . Of the faults that are committed, one consists in fearing what we should not, another in fearing as we should not, another in fearing when we should not, and so on; and so too with respect to the things that inspire confidence. The man, then, who faces and who fears the right things and from the right motive, in the right way and at the right time, and who feels confidence under the corresponding conditions, is brave; for the brave man feels and acts according to the merits of the case and in whatever way the rule directs. Now the end of every activity is conformity to the corresponding state of character. This is true, therefore, of the brave man as well as of others. But courage is noble. Therefore the end also is noble; for each thing is defined by its end. Therefore it is for a noble end that the brave man endures and acts as courage directs.

Of those who go to excess he who exceeds in fearlessness has no name (we have said previously that many states of character have no names), but he would be a sort of madman or insensitive to pain if he feared nothing, neither earthquakes nor the waves . . . while the man who exceeds in confidence about what really is fearful is rash. 39 The rash man, however, is also thought to be boastful and only a pretender to courage; at all events, as the brave man *is* with regard

to what is fearful, so the rash man wishes to *appear;* and so he imitates him in situations where he can. Hence also most of them are a mixture of rashness and cowardice; for, while

___

39 So there are supposedly two sorts of excess in the direction of absence of fear. How clear is the distinction between them?

___

in these situations they display confidence, they do not hold their ground against what is really fearful. The man who exceeds in fear is a coward; for he fears both what he ought not and as he ought not, and all the similar characterizations attach to him. He is lacking also in confidence; but he is more conspicuous for his excess of fear in painful situations. The coward, then, is a despairing sort of person; for he fears everything. The brave man, on the other hand, has the opposite disposition; for confidence is the mark of a hopeful disposition. The coward, the rash man, and the brave man, then, are concerned with the same objects but are differently disposed towards them; for the first two exceed and fall short, while the third holds the middle, which is the right, position; and rash men are precipitate, and wish for dangers beforehand but draw back when they are in them, while brave men are excited in the moment of action, but collected beforehand.

As we have said, then, courage is a mean with respect to things that inspire confidence or fear, in the circumstances that have been stated; and it chooses or endures things because it is noble to do so, or because it is base not to do so. But to die to escape from poverty or love or anything painful is not the mark of a brave man, but rather of a coward; for it is softness to fly from what is troublesome, and such a man endures death not because it is noble but to fly from evil.

. . .

Temperance

Temperance is limited to certain pleasures of touch

10. After courage let us speak of temperance; for these seem to be the virtues of the irrational parts. We have said that temperance is a mean with regard to pleasures (for it is less, and not in the same way, concerned with pains); self-indulgence also is manifested in the same sphere. Now, therefore, let us determine with what sort of pleasures they are concerned. We may assume the distinction between bodily pleasures and those of the soul, such as love of honour and love of learning; for the lover of each of these delights in that of which he is a lover, the body being in no way affected, but rather the mind; but men who are concerned with such pleasures are called neither temperate nor self-indulgent. . . .

Temperance must be concerned with bodily pleasures, but not all even of these; for those who delight in objects of vision, such as colours and shapes and painting, are called neither temperate nor self-indulgent; yet it would seem possible to delight even in these either as one should or to excess or to a deficient degree.

. . .

. . . Temperance and self-indulgence are concerned with the kind of pleasures that the other animals share in, which therefore appear slavish and brutish; these are touch and taste. But even of taste they appear to make little or no use; for the business of taste is the discriminating of flavours, which is done by wine-tasters and people who season dishes; but they hardly take pleasure in making these discriminations, or at least self-indulgent people do not, but in the actual enjoyment, which in all cases comes through touch, both in the case of food and in that of drink and in that of sexual intercourse. . . . Thus the sense with which self-indulgence is connected is the most widely shared of the senses; and self-indulgence would seem to be justly a matter of reproach, because it attaches to us not as men but as animals. To delight in such things, then, and to love them above all others, is brutish. . . .

Characteristics of temperance and its opposites, self-indulgence and 'insensibility'

11. . . . Plainly, then, excess with regard to pleasures is self-indulgence and is culpable; with regard to pains one is not, as in the case of courage, called temperate for facing them or self-indulgent for not doing so, but the self-indulgent man is so called because he is pained more than he ought at not getting pleasant things (even his pain being caused by pleasure), and the temperate man is so called because he is not pained at the absence of what is pleasant and at his abstinence from it.

The self-indulgent man, then, craves for all pleasant things or those that are most pleasant, and is led by his appetite to choose these at the cost of everything else; hence he is pained both when he fails to get them and when he is merely craving for them (for appetite involves pain). . . . People who fall short with regard to pleasures and delight in them less than they should are hardly found; for such insensibility is not human. . . . The temperate man occupies a middle position with regard to these objects. For he neither enjoys the things that the self-indulgent man enjoys most—but rather dislikes them—nor in general the things that he should not, nor anything of this sort to excess, nor does he feel pain or craving when they are absent, or does so only to a moderate degree, and not more than he should, nor when he should not, and so on; but the things that, being pleasant, make for health or for good condition, he will desire moderately and as he should, and also other pleasant things if they are not hindrances to these ends, or contrary to what is noble, or beyond his means. For he who neglects these conditions loves such pleasures more than they are worth, but the temperate man is not that sort of person, but the sort of person that the right rule prescribes. **40**

> **40** Here again the Greek word (*logos*) does not mean that there is a definite rule, only that the choice is made on rational grounds.

. . .

BOOK IV: MORAL VIRTUE

. . .

The Virtue Concerned with Anger

Good temper

5. Good temper is a mean with respect to anger; the middle state being unnamed, **41** and the extremes almost without a name as well, we place good temper in the middle position, though it inclines towards the deficiency, which is without a name. The excess might be called a sort of 'irascibility'. For the passion is anger, while its causes are many and diverse.

> **41** Unnamed until Aristotle named it "good temper."

The man who is angry at the right things and with the right people, and, further, as he ought, when he ought, and as long as he ought, is praised. This will be the good-tempered man, then, since good temper is praised. For the good-tempered man tends to be unperturbed and not to be led by passion, but to be angry in the manner, at the things, and for the length of time, that the rule dictates;㊷ but he is thought to err rather in the direction of deficiency; for the good-tempered man is not revengeful, but rather tends to make allowances.

㊷ Here again, "the rule" just means rationality, with no implication that there is a definite rule that could be formulated as such.

The deficiency, whether it is a sort of 'unirascibility' or whatever it is, is blamed. For those who are not angry at the things they should be angry at are thought to be fools, and so are those who are not angry in the right way, at the right time, or with the right persons; for such a man is thought not to feel things nor to be pained by them, and, since he does not get angry, he is thought unlikely to defend himself; and to endure being insulted and put up with insult to one's friends is slavish.

The excess can be manifested in all the points that have been named (for one can be angry with the wrong persons, at the wrong things, more than is right, too quickly, or too long); yet *all* are not found in the same person. Indeed they could not; for evil destroys even itself, and if it is complete becomes unbearable. Now *hot-tempered* people get angry quickly and with the wrong persons and at the wrong things and more than is right, but their anger ceases quickly—which is the best point about them. This happens to them because they do not restrain their anger but retaliate openly owing to their quickness of temper, and then their anger ceases. By reason of excess *choleric* people are quick-tempered and ready to be angry with everything and on every occasion; whence their name. *Sulky* people are hard to appease, and retain their anger long; for they repress their passion. But it ceases when they retaliate; for revenge relieves them of their anger, producing in them pleasure instead of pain. If this does not happen they retain their burden; for owing to its not being obvious no one even reasons with them, and to digest one's anger in oneself takes time. Such people are most troublesome to themselves and to their dearest friends. We call *bad-tempered* those who are angry at the wrong things, more than is right, and longer, and cannot be appeased until they inflict vengeance or punishment.㊸

㊸ So there is more than one way to be "bad-tempered."

To good temper we oppose the excess rather than the defect; for not only is it commoner (since revenge is the more human), but bad-tempered people are worse to live with.

What we have said in our earlier treatment of the subject is plain also from what we are now saying; viz. that it is not easy to define how, with whom, at what, and how long one should be angry, and at what point right action ceases and wrong begins. For the man who strays a little from the path, either towards the more or towards the less, is not blamed; since sometimes we praise those who exhibit the deficiency, and call them good-tempered, and sometimes we call angry people manly, as being capable of ruling. How far, therefore, and how a man must stray before he becomes blameworthy, it is not easy to state in words; for the decision depends on the particular facts and on perception.㊹ But so much at least is plain, that the middle state is praiseworthy—that in virtue of which we are angry with the right people, at the right things, in the right way, and so on, while the excesses and defects are

㊹ So there is no clearly defined rule, nothing that could avoid the need for rational judgment.

blameworthy—slightly so if they are present in a low degree, more if in a higher degree, and very much if in a high degree. Evidently, then, we must cling to the middle state.—Enough of the states relative to anger.

. . .

BOOK VI: INTELLECTUAL VIRTUE

Introduction

Reasons for studying intellectual virtue: intellect divided into the contemplative and the calculative

1. Since we have previously said that one ought to choose that which is intermediate, not the excess nor the defect, and that the intermediate is determined by the dictates of the right rule, let us discuss the nature of these dictates. In all the states of character we have mentioned, as in all other matters, there is a mark to which the man who has the rule looks, and heightens or relaxes his activity accordingly, and there is a standard which determines the mean states which we say are intermediate between excess and defect, being in accordance with the right rule.㊺ But such a statement, though true, is by no means clear; for not only

㊺ Here we have several more places where the translation suggests some sort of explicit rule, but what is in fact said by Aristotle is only that reason or rationality or good judgment is involved.

here but in all other pursuits which are objects of knowledge it is indeed true to say that we must not exert ourselves nor relax our efforts too much or too little, but to an intermediate extent and as the right rule dictates; but if a man had only this knowledge he would be none the wiser—e.g. we should not know what sort of medicines to apply to our body if someone were to say 'all those which the medical art prescribes, and which agree with the practice of one who possesses the art'. Hence it is necessary with regard to the states of the soul also, not only that this true statement should be made, but also that it should be determined what is the right rule and what is the standard that fixes it.

. . .

The proper object of contemplation is truth; that of calculation is truth corresponding with right desire

2. The virtue of a thing is relative to its proper work. Now there are three things in the soul which control action and truth—sensation, reason, desire.

46 Aristotle's view is that while lower animals may react to sensation, they do not act in the sense that involves deliberate choice.

Of these sensation originates no action; this is plain from the fact that the lower animals have sensation but no share in action.[46]

What affirmation and negation are in thinking, pursuit and avoidance are in desire; so that since moral virtue is a state of character concerned with choice, and choice is deliberate desire, therefore both the reasoning must be true and the desire right, if the choice is to be good, and the latter must pursue just what the former asserts. Now this kind of intellect and of truth is practical; of the intellect which is contemplative, not practical nor productive, the good and the bad state are truth and falsity respectively (for this is the work of everything intellectual); while of the part which is practical and intellectual the good state is truth in agreement with right desire.

The origin of action—its efficient, not its final cause—is choice, and that of choice is desire and reasoning with a view to an end. This is why choice cannot exist either without reason and intellect or without a moral state; for good action and its opposite cannot exist without a combination of intellect and character. Intellect itself, however, moves nothing, but only the

intellect which aims at an end and is practical; . . . for good action is an end, and desire aims at this. . . .

Practical wisdom—knowledge of how to secure the ends of human life

5. Regarding *practical wisdom*[47] we shall get at the truth by considering who are the persons we credit with it. Now it is thought to be a mark of a man of practical wisdom to be able to deliberate well

47 "Practical wisdom" (*phronesis*) is the rational capacity that is aimed at attaining ends in a correct and virtuous way.

about what is good and expedient for himself, not in some particular respect, e.g. about what sorts of thing conduce to health or to strength, but about what sorts of thing conduce to the good life in general. This is shown by the fact that we credit men with practical wisdom in some particular respect when they have calculated well with a view to some good end which is one of those that are not the object of any art. It follows that in the general sense also the man who is capable of deliberating has practical wisdom. Now no one deliberates about things that are invariable, or about things that it is impossible for him to do. Therefore, since scientific knowledge involves demonstration, but there is no demonstration of things whose first principles are variable (for all such things might actually be otherwise), and since it is impossible to deliberate about things that are of necessity, practical wisdom cannot be scientific knowledge or art; not science because that which can be done is capable of being otherwise, not art because action and making are different kinds of thing. The remaining alternative, then, is that it is a true and reasoned state of capacity to act with regard to the things that are good or bad for man. For while making has an end other than itself, action cannot; for good action itself is its end. . . .

Practical wisdom, then, must be a reasoned and true state of capacity to act with regard to human goods. . . .

Happiness

Happiness is good activity, not amusement

6. Now that we have spoken of the virtues, the forms of friendship, and the varieties of pleasure, what remains is to discuss in outline the nature of happiness, since this is what we state the end of human affairs to be. Our discussion will be the more concise if we first sum up what we have said already. We said, then, that it is not a state; for if it were it might belong to someone who was asleep throughout his life, living the life of a plant, or, again, to someone who was suffering the greatest misfortunes. If these implications are unacceptable, and we must rather class happiness as an activity, as we have said before, and if some activities are necessary, and desirable for the sake of something else, while others are so in themselves, evidently happiness must be placed among those desirable in themselves, not among those desirable for the sake of something else; for happiness does not lack anything, but is self-sufficient. Now those activities are desirable in themselves from which nothing is sought beyond the activity. And of this nature virtuous actions are thought to be; for to do noble and good deeds is a thing desirable for its own sake.

Pleasant amusements also are thought to be of this nature: we choose them not for the sake of other things; for we are injured rather than benefited by them, since we are led to neglect our bodies and our property. But most of the people who are deemed happy take refuge in such pastimes, which is the reason why those who are ready-witted at them are highly esteemed at the courts of tyrants; they make themselves pleasant companions in the tyrants' favourite pursuits, and that is the sort of man they want. Now these things are thought to be of the nature of happiness because people in despotic positions spend their leisure in them, but perhaps such people prove nothing; for virtue and reason, from which good activities flow, do not depend on despotic position; nor, if these people, who have never tasted pure and generous pleasure, take refuge in the bodily pleasure, should these for that reason be thought more desirable; for boys, too, think the things that are valued among themselves are the best. It is to be expected, then, that, as different things seem valuable to boys and to men, so they should to bad men and to good. Now, as we have often maintained, those things are both valuable and pleasant which are such to the good man; and to each man the activity in accordance with his own state is most desirable, and therefore to the good man that which is in accordance with virtue. Happiness, therefore, does not lie in amusement; it would, indeed, be strange if the end were amusement, and one were to take trouble and suffer hardship all one's life in order to amuse oneself. For, in a word, everything that we choose we choose for the sake of something else—except happiness, which is an end. Now to exert oneself and work for the sake of amusement seems silly and utterly childish. But to amuse oneself in order that one may exert oneself . . . seems right; for amusement is a sort of relaxation, and we need relaxation because we cannot work continuously. Relaxation, then, is not an end; for it is taken for the sake of activity. [48]

[48] How good are Aristotle's reasons for rejecting the view that the life of enjoyment or amusement is the happy life?

The happy life is thought to be virtuous; now a virtuous life requires exertion, and does not consist in amusement. And we say that serious things are better than laughable things and those connected with amusement, and that the activity of the better of any two things—whether it be two elements of our being or two men—is the more serious; but the activity of the better is *ipso facto* superior and more of the nature of happiness. And any chance person—even a slave—can enjoy the bodily pleasures no less than the best man; but no one assigns to a slave a share in happiness—unless he assigns to him also a share in human life. For happiness does not lie in such occupations, but, as we have said before, in virtuous activities.

Happiness in the highest sense is the contemplative life

7. If happiness is activity in accordance with virtue, it is reasonable that it should be in accordance with the highest virtue; and this will be that of the best thing in us. Whether it be reason or something else that is this element which is thought to be our natural ruler and guide and to take thought of things noble and divine, whether it be itself also divine or only the most divine element in us, the activity of this in accordance with its proper virtue will be perfect happiness. . . . this activity is contemplative. . . .

Now this would seem to be in agreement both with what we said before and with the truth. For, firstly, this activity is the best (since not only is reason the best thing in us, but the objects of reason are the best of knowable objects); and, secondly, it is the most continuous, since we can contemplate truth more continuously than we can *do* anything. And we think happiness ought to have pleasure mingled with it, but the activity of philosophic wisdom is admittedly the pleasantest of virtuous activities; at all events the pursuit of it is thought to offer pleasures marvellous for their purity and their enduringness, and it is to be expected that those who know will pass their time more pleasantly than those who inquire. And the self-sufficiency that is spoken of must belong most to the contemplative activity. For while a philosopher, as well as a just man or one possessing any other virtue, needs the necessaries of life, when they are sufficiently equipped with things of that sort the just man needs people towards whom and with whom he shall act justly, and the temperate man, the brave man, and each of the others is in the same case, but the philosopher, even when by himself, can contemplate truth, and the better the wiser he is; he can perhaps do so better if he has fellow workers, but still he is the most self-sufficient. And this activity alone would seem to be loved for its own sake; for nothing arises from it apart from the contemplating, while from practical activities we gain more or less apart from the action. And happiness is thought to depend on leisure; for we are busy that we may have leisure, and make war that we may live in peace. Now the activity of the practical virtues is exhibited in political or military affairs, but the actions concerned with these seem to be unleisurely. Warlike actions are completely so (for no one chooses to be at war, or provokes war, for the sake of being at war; anyone would seem absolutely murderous if he were to make enemies of his friends in order to bring about battle and slaughter); but the action of the statesman also is unleisurely, and aims—beyond the political action itself—at despotic power and honours, or at all events happiness, for him and his fellow citizens—a happiness different from political action, and evidently sought as being different. So if among virtuous actions political and military actions are distinguished by nobility and greatness, and these are unleisurely and aim at an end and are not desirable for their own sake, but the activity of reason, which is contemplative, seems both to be superior in serious worth and to aim at no end beyond itself, and to have its pleasure proper to itself (and this augments the activity), and the self-sufficiency, leisureliness, unweariedness (so far as this is possible for man), and all the other attributes ascribed to the supremely happy man are evidently those connected with this activity, it follows that this will be the complete happiness of man, if it be allowed a complete term of life (for none of the attributes of happiness is *in*complete). (49)

> (49) Aristotle's view is that the best sort of life for a human being, the one that most perfectly achieves happiness (*eudaimonia*) is the contemplative life. How good are the reasons he offers?

Discussion Questions

1. How plausible do you find Aristotle's idea that by acting as a virtuous person would act, you will acquire the relevant virtues? Consider the virtue of charity: the charitable person makes charitable contributions *because of* the character trait of charity. Suppose that Carol makes charitable contributions only to gain her father's approval. Doesn't it seem as though Carol could act that way for years without acquiring the virtue of charity? But consider another example: we typically teach our children to share, trying to create in them the character trait of generosity (the stable disposition to give accompanied by the relevantly appropriate emotional responses). Might that kind of training be successful? How do people acquire the kind of character traits that Aristotle is talking about?

2. Aristotle is surely right that we deliberate about means: we think about what we should do to reach our goals, to realize our ends. Suppose you have a goal of finishing college with a double major in biology and philosophy in fewer than five years. You have a better chance of reaching that goal if you think carefully about what steps to take in those five years to reach that goal. But what about the goal itself? Do you deliberate about ends? Think about some of your ends, your goals. How did you choose them? Did you deliberate about them? Did you just find yourself wanting to achieve them without questioning whether you should want to achieve them? Some philosophers think that it makes no sense to deliberate about ends—that it makes sense to deliberate only about means to ends. What do you think?

3. Aristotle assumes that you should be punished or praised only for things within your voluntary control. Does that seem right? Think of the conditions for excusing behavior: if a bank teller gives the money to a robber who points a gun at her, we do not punish the bank teller. Why not? If someone breaks the law, but it is established that he was insane, we do not punish him. Why not? But suppose that determinism is true, and your skills, abilities, and all of your actions are completely determined by your heredity and your environment. In what sense is your behavior voluntary? Should you be praised for doing well in college if your actions are completely determined by your heredity and your environment? (See Chapter 5 for further discussion of these issues.)

4. Aristotle thinks the best thing about us is our reason: the person who most closely approximates the excellence that is distinctively human is the one who spends most of his life in contemplation. What do you think about that view? What do you think about the view that a life of enjoyment or amusement is a less than excellent life? Do you think that there is something else about us, other than reason, that is "the best thing about us"? Do some lives more clearly involve human flourishing than other lives?

Rosalind Hursthouse

Rosalind Hursthouse (1943–) teaches at the University of Auckland in New Zealand, having previously taught in both England and the United States. She is a major figure in the recently developed area of virtue ethics, defending a view that she characterizes as "neo-Aristotelian."

In the following selection, Hursthouse defends the thesis that virtue ethics, in addition to giving an account of good and bad character and of what it means for a human being to live well or flourish, can also give an account of which actions are right or wrong in particular situations, thereby providing a genuine alternative to the accounts provided by utilitarian and deontological (Kantian) ethics.

Normative Virtue Ethics

A common belief concerning virtue ethics is that it does not tell us what we should do. This belief is sometimes manifested merely in the expressed assumption that virtue ethics, in being 'agent-centred' rather than 'act-centred', is concerned with Being rather than Doing, with good (and bad) character rather than right (and wrong) action, with the question 'What sort of person should I be?' rather than the question 'What should I do?' On this assumption, 'virtue ethics' so-called does not figure as a normative rival to utilitarian and deontological ethics; rather, its (fairly) recent revival is seen as having served the useful purpose of reminding moral philosophers that the elaboration of a normative theory may fall short of giving a full account of our moral life. Thus prompted, deontologists have turned to Kant's long neglected 'Doctrine of Virtue', and utilitarians, largely abandoning the old debate about rule- and act-utilitarianism, are showing interest in the general-happiness-maximizing consequences of inculcating such virtues as friendship, honesty, and loyalty.

On this assumption, it seems that philosophers who 'do virtue ethics', having served this purpose, must realize that they have been doing no more than

From *How Should One Live?*, edited by Roger Crisp (New York: Oxford University Press, 1996).

supplementing normative theory, and should now decide which of the two standard views they espouse. . . . But anyone who wants to espouse virtue ethics as a rival to deontological or utilitarian ethics (finding it distinctly bizarre to suppose that Aristotle espoused either of the latter) will find this common belief voiced against her as an objection: 'Virtue ethics does not, because it cannot, tell us what we should do.

> **1** This is one standard objection to virtue ethics.

Hence it cannot be a normative rival to deontology and utilitarianism.'①

This paper is devoted to defending virtue ethics against this objection.

1. RIGHT ACTION

What grounds might someone have for believing that virtue ethics cannot tell us what we should do? It seems that sometimes the ground is no more than the claim that virtue ethics is concerned with good (and bad) character rather than right (and wrong) action. But that claim does no more than highlight an interesting contrast between virtue ethics on the one hand, and deontology and utilitarianism on the other; the former is agent-centred, the latter (it is said) are act-centred. It does not entail that virtue ethics has nothing to say about the concept of right action, nor about which actions are right and which wrong. Wishing to highlight a different contrast, the one between utilitarianism and deontology, we might equally well say, 'Utilitarianism is concerned with good (and bad) states of affairs rather than right (and wrong) action', and no one would take that to mean that utilitarianism, unlike deontology, had nothing to say about right action, for what utilitarianism does say is so familiar.

Suppose an act-utilitarian laid out her account of right action as follows:

> **2** Here and elsewhere, "iff" is a standard philosophical abbreviation meaning "if and only if."

U1. An action is right iff it promotes the best consequences.②

This premiss provides a specification of right action, forging the familiar utilitarian link between the concepts of *right action* and *best consequences,* but gives one no guidance about how to act until one knows

what to count as the best consequences. So these must be specified in a second premiss, for example:

U2. The best consequences are those in which happiness is maximized, which forges the familiar utilitarian link between the concepts of *best consequences* and *happiness.**

Many different versions of deontology can be laid out in a way that displays the same basic structure. They begin with a premiss providing a specification of right action:

D1. An action is right iff it is in accordance with a correct moral rule or principle.

Like the first premiss of act-utilitarianism, this gives one no guidance about how to act until, in this case, one knows what to count as a correct moral rule (or principle). So this must be specified in a second premiss which begins

D2. A correct moral rule (principle) is one that . . . , and this may be completed in a variety of ways, for example:

(i) is on the following list (and then a list does follow)

or

(ii) is laid on us by God

or

(iii) is universalizable

or

(iv) would be the object of choice of all rational beings

and so on.③

> **3** Here (iii) and (iv) reflect aspects of Kant's position. For a consideration of a view like (ii), see the selection from Plato's dialogue *Euthyphro* in Chapter 1. A view that merely gives a list is unlikely to be very compelling without some further account of how the list is arrived at (which is then likely to replace the list as the main account).

Although this way of laying out fairly familiar versions of utilitarianism and deontology is hardly controversial, it is worth noting that it suggests some infelicity in the slogan 'Utilitarianism begins

---

*Variations on utilitarianism are not my concern here. I am ignoring rule-utilitarianism, and assuming my reader to be well aware of the fact that different utilitarians may specify *best consequences* in different ways. . . .

with (or takes as its fundamental concept etc.) the Good, whereas deontology begins with the Right.' If the concept a normative ethics 'begins with' is the one it uses to specify right action, then utilitarianism might be said to begin with the Good (if we take this to be the 'same' concept as that of the *best*), but we should surely hasten to add 'but only in relation to consequences; not, for instance, in relation to *good* agents, or to living *well*'.④

④ Utilitarianism certainly does not begin with the idea of a good agent (or one who lives well)—and has little to say about it except that a good agent will follow the principle of utility (or, for rule utilitarianism, conform to rules that maximize utility). Proponents of virtue ethics will suggest that this is a clearly inadequate account of human flourishing.

And even then, we shall not be able to go on to say that most versions of deontology 'begin with' the Right, for they use the concept of moral rule or principle to specify right action. . . .

And if the dictum is supposed to single out, rather vaguely, the concept which is 'most important', then the concepts of *consequences* or *happiness* seem as deserving of mention as the concept of the Good for utilitarianism, and what counts as most important (if any one concept does) for deontologists would surely vary from case to case. For some it would be God, for others universalizability, for others the Categorical Imperative, for others rational acceptance, and so on.

It is possible that too slavish an acceptance of this slogan, and the inevitable difficulty of finding a completion of 'and virtue ethics begins with . . .' which does not reveal its inadequacy, has contributed to the belief that virtue ethics cannot provide a specification of right action. . . . But if the question is 'How can virtue ethics specify right action?', the answer is easy:

> V1. An action is right iff it is what a virtuous agent would characteristically (i.e. acting in character) do in the circumstances.

This specification rarely, if ever, silences those who maintain that virtue ethics cannot tell us what we should do. On the contrary, it tends to provoke irritable laughter and scorn. '*That*'s no use', the objectors say. 'It gives us no guidance whatsoever. Who are the virtuous agents?' But if the failure of the first premise of a normative ethics which forges a link between the concept of right action and a concept distinctive of that ethics may provoke scorn because it provides no practical guidance, why not direct a similar scorn at the first premises of act-utilitarianism and deontology in the form in which I have given them? Of each of them I remarked . . . that they gave us no guidance. Utilitarianism must specify what are to count as the best consequences, and deontology what is to count as a correct moral rule, producing a second premise, before any guidance is given. And similarly, virtue ethics must specify who is to count as a virtuous agent. So far, the three are all in the same position.

Of course, if the virtuous agent can only be specified as an agent disposed to act in accordance with moral rules, as some have assumed, then virtue ethics collapses back into deontology and is no rival to it.⑤ So let us add a subsidiary premise to this skeletal outline, with the intention of making it clear that virtue ethics aims to provide a non-deontological specification of the virtuous agent via a specification of the virtues, which will be given in its second premise:

⑤ The main issue is not whether thesis V1 is true, but rather what makes it true. A Kantian (or a utilitarian or a holder of any other sort of moral view) can accept it as true as long as he defines "a virtuous agent" as someone who conforms to the Kantian moral rules (or those of utilitarianism or whatever other view). But the virtue ethicist wants to start with an *independently* defined conception of a virtuous agent (as roughly the ideal exemplification of the moral virtues) and then define the morally right action as whatever that agent does in the circumstances in question.

> V1a. A virtuous agent is one who acts virtuously, that is, one who has and exercises the virtues.
> V2. A virtue is a character trait that . . .

This second premise of virtue ethics might, like the second premise of some versions of deontology, be completed simply by enumeration ('a virtue is one of the following', and then the list is given). Or we might, not implausibly, interpret the Hume of the second *Enquiry* as espousing virtue ethics. According to him, a virtue is a character trait (of human beings) that is useful or agreeable to its possessor or to others (inclusive 'or' both times). The standard neo-Aristotelian completion claims that a virtue is a character trait a human being needs for *eudaimonia,* to flourish or live well.⑥

⏹ **6** Think carefully about these different ways of filling out V2 and their relation to V1a and V1. Are any of them definite enough for V1 to yield fairly precise results as to which actions are right?

Here, then, we have a specification of right action, whose structure closely resembles those of act-utilitarianism and many forms of deontology. Given that virtue ethics can come up with such a specification, can it still be maintained that it, unlike utilitarianism and deontology, cannot tell us what we should do? Does the specification somehow fail to provide guidance in a way that the other two do not?

At this point, the difficulty of identifying the virtuous agent in a way that makes VI action-guiding tends to be brought forward again. Suppose it is granted that deontology has just as much difficulty in identifying the correct moral rules as virtue ethics has in identifying the virtues and hence the virtuous agent. Then the following objection may be made.

'All the same,' it may be said, if we imagine that that has been achieved—perhaps simply by enumeration—deontology yields a set of clear prescriptions which are readily applicable ("Do not lie", "do not steal", "do not inflict evil or harm on others", "Do help others", "Do keep promises", etc.). But virtue ethics yields only the prescription "Do what the virtuous agent (the one who is honest, charitable, just, etc.) would do in these circumstances." And this gives me no guidance unless I am (and know I am) a virtuous agent myself (in which case I am hardly in need of it). If I am less than fully virtuous, I shall have no idea what a virtuous agent would do, and hence cannot apply the only prescription that virtue ethics has given me. (Of course, act-utilitarianism also yields a single prescription. "Do what maximises happiness", but there are no *parallel* difficulties in applying that.) So there is the way in which V1 fails to be action-guiding where deontology and utilitarianism succeed.'⑦

⏹ **7** How plausible is the claim that only a virtuous agent can know what a virtuous agent would do in a particular situation?

It is worth pointing out that, if I acknowledge that I am far from perfect, and am quite unclear what a virtuous agent would do in the circumstances in which I find myself, the obvious thing to do is to go and ask one, should this be possible. This is far from being a trivial point, for it gives a straightforward explanation of an aspect of our moral life which should not be ignored, namely the fact that we do seek moral guidance from people who we think are morally better than ourselves. When I am looking for an excuse to do something I have a horrid suspicion is wrong, I ask my moral inferiors (or peers if I am bad enough), 'Wouldn't you do such and such if you were in my shoes?' But when I am anxious to do what is right, and do not see my way clear, I go to people I respect and admire—people who I think are kinder, more honest, more just, wiser, than I am myself—and ask them what they would do in my circumstances. How utilitarianism and deontology would explain this fact, I do not know; but, as I said, the explanation within the terms of virtue ethics is straightforward. If you want to do what is right, and doing what is right is doing what a virtuous agent would do in the circumstances, then you should find out what she would do if you do not already know.⑧

⏹ **8** One problem here is whether it is possible to identify fully or optimally virtuous people with enough confidence to make it possible to use their advice as a criterion for the right action. (Another problem is raised in Discussion Question 1.)

Moreover, seeking advice from virtuous people is not the only thing an imperfect agent trying to apply the single prescription of virtue ethics can do. For it is simply false that, in general, 'if I am less than fully virtuous, then I shall have no idea what a virtuous agent would do', as the objection claims. Recall that we are assuming that the virtues have been enumerated, as the deontologist's rules have been. The latter have been enumerated as, say, 'Do not lie', 'Do not inflict evil or harm', etc.; the former as, say, honesty, charity, justice, etc. So, *ex hypothesi,* a virtuous agent is one who is honest, charitable, just, etc. So what she characteristically does is act honestly, charitably, justly, etc., and not dishonestly, uncharitably, unjustly. So given an enumeration of the virtues, I may well have a perfectly good idea of what the virtuous person would do in my circumstances despite my own imperfection. Would she lie in her teeth to acquire an unmerited advantage? No, for that would be to act both dishonestly and unjustly. Would she help the naked man by the roadside or pass by on the other side? The former, for she acts charitably. Might she keep a deathbed promise even though living people would benefit from its being broken? Yes, for she acts justly. And so on. ⑨

> ⑨ There are two problems lurking here that you should think about: first, whether it is always or at least usually pretty clear what a particular virtue would require in a given situation; and second, how to deal with situations where different virtues point in different directions (which Hursthouse discusses later on).

2. MORAL RULES

The above response to the objection that V1 fails to be action-guiding clearly amounts to a denial of the oft-repeated claim that virtue ethics does not come up with any rules (another version of the thought that it is concerned with Being rather than Doing and needs to be supplemented with rules). We can now see that it comes up with a large number; not only does each virtue generate a prescription—act honestly, charitably, justly—but each vice a prohibition—do not act dishonestly, uncharitably, unjustly. Once this point about virtue ethics is grasped (and it is remarkable how often it is overlooked), can there remain any reason for thinking that virtue ethics cannot tell us what we should do? Yes. The reason given is, roughly, that rules such as 'Act honestly', 'Do not act uncharitably', etc. are, like the rule 'Do what the virtuous agent would do', still the wrong sort of rule, still somehow doomed to fail to provide the action guidance supplied by the rules (or rule) of deontology and utilitarianism.

But how so? It is true that these rules of virtue ethics (henceforth 'v-rules') are couched in terms, or concepts, which are certainly 'evaluative' in *some* sense, or senses, of that difficult word. Is it this which dooms them to failure? Surely not, unless many forms of deontology fail too.* If we concentrate on the single example of lying, defining lying to be 'asserting what you believe to be untrue, with the intention of deceiving your hearer(s)', then we might, for a mo-

ment, preserve the illusion that a deontologist's rules do not contain 'evaluative' terms. But as soon as we remember that few deontologists will want to forego principles of non-maleficence or beneficence, the illusion vanishes. For those principles, and their corresponding rules ('Do no evil or harm to others', 'Help others', 'Promote their well-being'), rely on terms or concepts which are at least as 'evaluative' as those employed in the v-rules. Few deontologists rest content with the simple quasi-biological 'Do not kill', but more refined versions of that rule such as 'Do not murder', or 'Do not kill the innocent', once again employ 'evaluative' terms, and 'Do not kill unjustly' is itself a particular instantiation of a v-rule. ⑩

> ⑩ The point of the objection is that a rule that requires further evaluation does not yield a clear guide to action by itself, since what it says to do will depend on the result of that further evaluation. This poses a serious problem only if the further evaluation is difficult to make.

Supposing this point were granted, a deontologist might still claim that the v-rules are markedly inferior to deontological rules as far as providing guidance for children is concerned. Granted, adult deontologists must think hard about what really constitutes harming someone, or promoting their well-being, or respecting their autonomy, or murder, but surely the simple rules we learnt at our mother's knee are indispensable? How could virtue ethics plausibly seek to dispense with these and expect toddlers to grasp 'Act charitably, honestly, and kindly', 'Don't act unjustly', and so on? Rightly are these concepts described as 'thick'! Far too thick for a child to grasp. ⑪

> ⑪ A "thick" moral concept is one that involves description as well as evaluation: "good" or "right" are thin moral concepts, while "generous" or "honest" are thick ones.

Strictly speaking, this claim about learning does not really support the *general* claim that v-rules fail to provide action-guidance, but the claim about learning,

---

*Forms of utilitarianism which aim to be entirely value-free or empirical, such as those which define happiness in terms of the satisfaction of actual desires or preferences, regardless of their content, or as a mental state whose presence is definitively established by introspection, seem to me the least plausible, but I accept that anyone who embraces them may consistently complain that v-rules give inferior action-guidance in virtue of containing 'evaluative' terms. But any utilitarian who wishes to employ any distinction between the higher and lower pleasures, or rely on some list of goods (such as autonomy, friendship, knowledge of important matters) in defining happiness, must grant that even her single rule is implicitly 'evaluative'.

arising naturally as it does in the context of the general claim, is one I am more than happy to address. For it pinpoints a condition of adequacy that any normative ethics must meet, namely that such an ethics must not only come up with action-guidance for a clever rational adult but also generate some account of moral education, of how one generation teaches the next what they should do. But an ethics inspired by Aristotle is unlikely to have forgotten the question of moral education, and the objection fails to hit home. First, the implicit empirical claim that toddlers are taught *only* the deontologist's rules, not the 'thick' concepts, is false. Sentences such as 'Don't do that, it hurts, you mustn't be *cruel*', 'Be *kind* to your brother, he's only little', 'Don't be so *mean, so greedy*' are commonly addressed to toddlers. Secondly, why should a proponent of virtue ethics deny the significance of such mother's-knee rules as 'Don't lie', 'Keep promises', 'Don't take more than your fair share', 'Help others'? Although it is a mistake, I have claimed, to define a virtuous agent simply as one disposed to act in accordance with moral rules, it is a very understandable mistake, given the obvious connection between, for example, the exercise of the virtue of honesty and refraining from lying. Virtue ethicists want to emphasize the fact that, if children are to be taught to be honest, they must be taught to prize the truth, and that *merely* teaching them not to lie will not achieve this end. But they need not deny that to achieve this end teaching them not to lie is useful, even indispensable. [12]

> [12] This echoes Aristotle's idea that a person first becomes virtuous by acting in the way prescribed by the virtue even if not yet for the reason that the virtuous person acts.

So we can see that virtue ethics not only comes up with rules (the v-rules, couched in terms derived from the virtues and vices), but further, does not exclude the more familiar deontologists' rules. The theoretical distinction between the two is that the familiar rules, and their applications in particular cases, are given entirely different backings. According to virtue ethics, I must not tell this lie, since it would be dishonest, and dishonesty is a vice; must not break this promise, since it would be unjust, or a betrayal of friendship, or, perhaps (for the available virtue and vice terms do not neatly cover every contingency), simply because no virtuous person would. [13]

However, the distinction is not merely theoretical. It is, indeed, the case that, with respect to a number of familiar examples, virtue ethicists and deontologists tend to stand shoulder to shoulder against utilitarians, denying that, for example, this lie can be told, this promise broken, this human being killed because the consequences of so doing will be generally happiness-maximizing. But, despite a fair amount of coincidence in action-guidance between deontology and virtue ethics, the latter has its own distinctive approach to the practical problems involved in dilemmas.

> [13] Contrast this with Kant's account (on the basis of the version of the categorical imperative that says not to treat others as mere means) of why a person should not tell lies and should keep promises. (See Discussion Question 2.)

3. THE CONFLICT PROBLEM

It is a noteworthy fact that, in support of the general claim that virtue ethics cannot tell us what we should do, what is often cited is the 'conflict problem'. The requirements of different virtues, it is said, can point us in opposed directions. Charity prompts me to kill the person who would (truly) be better off dead, but justice forbids it. Honesty points to telling the hurtful truth, kindness and compassion to remaining silent or even lying. And so on. So virtue ethics lets us down just at the point where we need it, where we are faced with the really difficult dilemmas and do not know what to do. [14]

In the mouth of a utilitarian, this may be a comprehensible criticism, for, as is well known, the only conflict that classical utilitarianism's one rule can generate is the tiresome logical one between the two occurrences of 'greatest' in its classical statement. [15] But it is strange to find the very same criticism

> [14] This is the most important objection to the sort of view that Hursthouse is advocating.

> [15] Hursthouse is referring to the formula that one should produce "the greatest good for the greatest number," the second part of which raises the issue of how the good consequences are to be distributed among people. But this is not a serious conflict for the standard utilitarian view, since it is clear that what is required is maximizing the good consequences (happiness or whatever else they may be), no matter how they are distributed.

coming from deontologists, who are notoriously faced with the same problem. 'Don't kill', 'Respect autonomy', 'Tell the truth', 'Keep promises' may all conflict with 'Prevent suffering' or 'Do no harm', which is precisely why deontologists so often reject utilitarianism's deliverances on various dilemmas. Presumably, they must think that deontology can solve the 'conflict problem' and, further, that virtue ethics cannot. Are they right?

With respect to a number of cases, the deontologist's strategy is to argue that the 'conflict' is merely apparent, or *prima facie.* The proponent of virtue ethics employs the same strategy: according to her, many of the putative conflicts are merely apparent, resulting from a misapplication of the virtue or vice terms. Does kindness require not telling hurtful truths? Sometimes, but in *this* case, what has to be understood is that one does people no kindness by concealing this sort of truth from them, hurtful as it may be. Or, in a different case, the importance of the truth in question puts the consideration of hurt feelings out of court, and the agent does not show herself to be unkind, or callous, by speaking out. Does charity require that I kill the person who would be better off dead but who wants to stay alive, thereby conflicting with justice? Not if, in Foot's words, '[a] man does not lack charity because he refrains from an act of injustice which would have been for someone's good'.*

One does not have to agree with the three judgements expressed here to recognize this as a *strategy* available to virtue ethics, any more than one has to agree with the particular judgements of deontologists who, for example, may claim that one rule outranks another, or that a certain rule has a certain exception clause built in, when they argue that a putative case of conflict is resolvable. Whether an individual has resolved a putative moral conflict or dilemma rightly is one question; whether a normative ethics has the wherewithal to resolve it is an entirely different question, and it is the latter with which we are concerned here.

The form the strategy takes within virtue ethics provides what may plausibly be claimed to be the deep explanation of why, in some cases, agents do not know the answer to 'What should I do in these circumstances?' despite the fact that there *is* an answer. Trivially, the explanation is that they lack moral knowledge of what to do in this situation; but why? In what way? The lack, according to virtue ethics' strategy, arises from lack of moral wisdom, from an inadequate grasp of what is involved in acting *kindly* (unkindly) or *charitably* (uncharitably), in being *honest,* or *just,* or *lacking in charity,* or, in general, of how the virtue (and vice) terms are to be correctly applied.[16]

> [16] Hursthouse's suggestion here seems to be that when properly understood, the different virtues do not conflict, so that any appearance of conflict results from less than complete understanding. How plausible is this claim (which she seems to retreat from later)? (See Discussion Question 3.)

Here we come to an interesting defence of the v-rules, often criticized as being too difficult to apply for the agent who lacks moral wisdom.† The defence relies on an (insufficiently acknowledged) insight of Aristotle's—namely that moral knowledge, unlike mathematical knowledge, cannot be acquired merely by attending lectures and is not characteristically to be found in people too young to have much experience of life. Now *if* right action were determined by rules that any clever adolescent could apply correctly, how could this be so? Why are there not moral whiz-kids, the way there are mathematical (or quasi-mathematical) whiz-kids? But if the rules that determine right action are, like the v-rules, very difficult to apply correctly, involving, for instance, a grasp of the *sort* of truth that one does people no kindness by concealing, the explanation is readily to hand. Clever adolescents do not, in general, have a good grasp of that sort of thing. And *of course* I have to say 'the sort of truth that . . .' and 'that sort of thing', relying on my readers' knowledgeable uptake. For if I could define either sort, then,

---

*P. Foot, *Virtues and Vices* (Oxford, 1978), p. 60, n. 12.

†This could well be regarded as another version of the criticism discussed earlier, that the v-rules somehow fail to provide action-guidance.

once again, clever adolescents could acquire moral wisdom from textbooks.

So far, I have described one strategy available to virtue ethics for coping with the 'conflict problem', a strategy that consists in arguing that the conflict is merely apparent, and can be resolved. . . . I have been talking so far as though examples of putative dilemmas and examples of putative conflict between the requirements of different virtues (or deontologists' rules) coincided. But it may seem to many, as it does to me, that there are certain (putative) dilemmas which can only be described in terms of (putative) conflict with much artifice and loss of relevant detail.

Let us, therefore, consider the problem of moral dilemmas without bothering about whether they can be described in the simple terms of a conflict between the requirements of two virtues (or two deontologists' rules). Most of us, it may be supposed, have our own favoured example(s), either real or imaginary, of the case (or cases) where we see the decision about whether to do A or B as a very grave matter, have thought a great deal about what can be said for and against doing A, and doing B, and have still not managed to reach a conclusion which we think is the right one. How, if at all, does virtue ethics direct us to think about such cases?

4. DILEMMAS AND NORMATIVE THEORY

As a preliminary to answering that question, we should consider a much more general one, namely 'How should any normative ethics direct us to think about such cases?' This brings us to the topic of normative theory.

It is possible to detect a new movement in moral philosophy, a movement which has already attracted the name 'anti-theory in ethics'. Its various representatives have as a common theme the rejection of normative ethical theory. . . . What is meant by a 'normative theory' in this context is not easy to pin down, but, roughly, a normative theory is taken to be a set (possibly one-membered in the case of utilitarianism) of general principles which provide a *decision procedure* for all questions about how to act morally. [17]

Part of the point of distinguishing a normative ethics by calling it a normative 'theory' is that a decent theory, as we know from science, enables us to answer questions that we could not answer before we had it. It is supposed to resolve those difficult dilemmas in which, it is said, our moral intuitions clash, and, prior to our grasp of the theory, we do not know what we should do. And a large part of the motivation for subscribing to 'anti-theory in ethics' is the belief that we should not be looking to science to provide us with our model of moral knowledge. Our 'intuitions' in ethics do not play the same role *vis-à-vis* the systematic articulation of moral knowledge as our 'observations' play *vis-à-vis* the systematic articulation of scientific knowledge; many of the goals appropriate to scientific knowledge—universality, consistency, completeness, simplicity—are not appropriate to moral knowledge; the acquisition of moral knowledge involves the training of the emotions in a way that the acquisition of scientific knowledge does not; and so on. [18]

Clearly, many different issues are involved in the question of the extent to which moral knowledge should be modelled on scientific knowledge. The one I want to focus on here is the issue of whether a normative ethics should provide a decision procedure which enables us to resolve all moral dilemmas. Should it, to rephrase the question I asked above, (1) direct us to think about moral dilemmas in the belief that they

[17] It might be better to describe such a decision procedure as a goal for normative theory or as what would be accomplished by an ideal normative theory. If this is supposed to be a procedure that can clearly and unequivocally resolve all questions of this sort, few if any philosophers (though Bentham may be an exception) would seriously claim to have given one.

[18] It is doubtful that this analogy with science really provides very much of the motivation for seeking a normative theory. The idea is rather, first, that it seems plausible to suppose that there is a right answer to all such questions; and, second, that if we cannot say how to determine what that right answer is, then our understanding is to that extent incomplete (and the practical guidance offered by the view is to that extent incomplete). (But the first claim especially can be questioned.)

must have a resolution, and that it is the business of the normative ethics in question to provide one? Or should it (2) have built into it the possibility of there being, as David Wiggins puts it, some 'absolutely undecidable questions—e.g. cases where . . . nothing could count as *the* reasonable practical answer',* counting questions about dilemmas of the sort described as amongst them? Or should it (3) be sufficiently flexible to allow for a comprehensible disagreement on this issue between two proponents of the normative ethics in question?

If we are to avoid modelling normative ethics mindlessly on scientific theory, we should not simply assume that the first position is the correct one. But rejection of such a model is not enough to justify the second position either. Someone might believe that for *any* dilemma there must be something that counts as the right way out of it, without believing that normative ethics remotely resembles scientific theory. . . . More particularly, someone might believe on religious grounds that if I find myself, through no fault of my own, confronted with a dilemma (of the sort described), there must be something that counts as the right way out of it. . . .† ⑲ It seems to me that a normative ethics should be able to accommodate such differences, and so I subscribe to the third position outlined above.

> ⑲ Can you think of a way in which actions for which you *are* clearly at fault might lead to a moral dilemma to which there is no right solution—where whatever you do will be wrong?

Which position utilitarians and deontologists might espouse is not my concern here; I want to make clear how it is that virtue ethics is able to accommodate the third.

Let us return to V1—'An action is right iff it is what a virtuous agent would characteristically do in the circumstances.' This makes it clear that if two people disagree about the possibility of irresolvable moral dilemmas, their disagreement will manifest itself in what they say about the virtue of agents. So let us suppose that two candidates for being virtuous agents are each faced with their own case of the same dilemma. . . . And, after much thought, one does A and the other does B.

Now, those who believe that there cannot be irresolvable dilemmas (of the sort described) can say that, in the particular case, at least one agent, say the one who did A, thereby showed themselves to be lacking in virtue, perhaps in that practical wisdom which is an essential aspect of each of the 'non-intellectual' virtues. . . . Or they can say that at least one agent must have been lacking in virtue, without claiming to know which. ⑳

But those who believe that there are, or may be, irresolvable dilemmas can suppose that both agents are not merely candidates for being, but actually are, virtuous agents. For to believe in such dilemmas is to believe in cases in which even the perfect practical wisdom that the most idealized virtuous agent has does not direct her to do, say, A rather than B. And then the fact that these virtuous agents acted differently, despite being in the same circumstances, *determines* the fact that there is no answer to the question 'What is *the* right thing to do in these circumstances?' For if it is true both that *a* virtuous agent would do A, and that *a* virtuous agent would do B (as it is, since, *ex hypothesi,* one did do A and the other B), then both A and B are, in the circumstances, right, according to V1. ㉑

> ⑳ One way to deal with the conflict of virtues problem, which Hursthouse may be suggesting here, is to appeal to a supposed higher-order virtue of practical wisdom (Aristotle's *phronesis*) that is essentially the capacity to adjudicate between the competing claims of lower-order virtues (like kindness, fairness, loyalty, honesty, etc.). The question is whether it is clear enough what practical wisdom would amount to and how it would work for this to be a real solution to the problem.

> ㉑ To say that both actions are right is to say that there is no moral objection to doing either one of them. See Discussion Question 4.

The acceptance of this should not be taken as a counsel of despair, nor as an excuse for moral irresponsibility. It does not license coin-tossing when one

---

*D. Wiggins, 'Truth, Invention and the Meaning of Life', *Proceedings of the British Academy* 62 (1976), 371, my italics. . . .
†I am assuming that the qualification 'through no fault of my own' is all-important, since I cannot imagine why anyone should think (except through oversight) that there must always be a right action I can do to get myself out of any mess that I have got myself into through previous wrongdoing.

is faced with a putative dilemma, for the moral choices we find most difficult do not come to us conveniently labelled as 'resolvable' or 'irresolvable'. I was careful to specify that the two candidates for being virtuous agents acted only 'after much thought'. It will always be necessary to think very hard before accepting the idea that a particular moral decision does not have one right issue, and, even on the rare occasions on which she eventually reached the conclusion that this is such a case, would the virtuous agent toss a coin? Of course not.

. . .

The acceptance of the possibility of irresolvable dilemmas within virtue ethics (by those of us who do accept it) should not be seen in itself as conceding much to 'pluralism'. If I say that I can imagine a case in which two virtuous agents are faced with a dilemma, and one does A while the other does B, I am not saying that I am imagining a case in which the two virtuous agents each think that what the other does is wrong (vicious, contrary to virtue) because they have radically different views about what is required by a certain virtue, or about whether a certain character trait is a vice, or about whether something is to be greatly valued or of little importance. I am imagining a case in which my two virtuous agents have the same 'moral views' about everything, up to and including the view that, in this particular case, neither decision is *the* right one, and hence neither is wrong. Each recognizes the propriety of the other's reason for doing what she did—say, 'To avoid *that* evil', 'To secure *this* good'—for her recognition of the fact that this is as good a moral reason as her own (say, 'To avoid *this* evil', 'To secure *that* good') is what forced each to ac-

cept the idea that the dilemma was irresolvable in the first place. Though each can give such a reason for what they did (A in one case, B in the other), neither attempts to give 'the moral reason' why they did one *rather than* the other. The 'reason' for or explanation of *that* would be, if available at all, in terms of psychological autobiography ('I decided to sleep on it, and when I woke up I just found myself thinking in terms of doing A', or 'I just felt terrified at the thought of doing A: I'm sure this was totally irrational, but I did, so I did B').*

The topic of this chapter has been the view that virtue ethics cannot be a normative rival to utilitarianism and deontology because 'it cannot tell us what we should do'. In defending the existence of normative virtue ethics I have not attempted to argue that it can 'tell us what we should do' in such a way that the difficult business of acting well is made easy for us. I have not only admitted but welcomed the fact that, in some cases, moral wisdom is required if the v-rules are to be applied correctly and apparent dilemmas thereby resolved (or indeed identified, since a choice that may seem quite straightforward to the foolish or wicked may rightly appear difficult, calling for much thought, to the wise). Nor have I attempted to show that virtue ethics is guaranteed to be able to resolve every dilemma. It seems bizarre to insist that a normative ethics must be able to do this prior to forming a reasonable belief that there cannot be irresolvable dilemmas, but those who have formed such a belief may share a normative ethics with those who have different views. . . . A normative ethics, I suggested, should be able to accommodate both views on this question, as virtue ethics does, not model itself mindlessly on scientific theory.

Discussion Questions

1. Clearly Hursthouse is right that we often seek moral advice from other people, and particularly from people we especially respect or admire from a moral standpoint. But what do we want from such people? Is it simply direct advice as to what to do (based on what they would do), as Hursthouse's account would seem to suggest? Or don't we instead want them to give us *reasons* in favor of some action (often for more than one alternative), reasons that we then attempt to evaluate for ourselves? (The latter alternative would suggest

---

*It must be remembered that, *ex hypothesi*, these are things said by virtuous agents about what they did when confronted with an irresolvable dilemma. Of course they would be very irresponsible accounts of why one had done A rather than B in a resolvable case.

that there are moral considerations that are more fundamental than what a virtuous person does: the rules or principles or standards that he himself is following. How might Hursthouse reply to this objection?)

2. Consider the example of making a deliberately insincere promise to someone (as in borrowing money while not really intending to repay). Kant says that this is morally wrong because it treats the other person as a mere means. Hursthouse's view says that it is wrong because an ideally virtuous person would not do such a thing. Each might agree in part with the other view: Kant can say that an ideally virtuous person would not act in this way *because* it would involve treating another as a mere means; while Hursthouse can say that it is wrong to treat another as a mere means *because* an ideally virtuous person would not do this. Thus they might agree on the moral result, while differing as to the most fundamental reason for it. Who is right about this latter issue?

3. How plausible is Hursthouse's suggestion that the different virtues do not conflict with each other when properly understood? Make a list of virtues for yourself, and try to think of situations where they seem to conflict. How plausible is it that such conflicts can always be resolved by understanding each virtue in the right way—as opposed to understanding, perhaps via practical wisdom, that one virtue overrides another in a given case? (This last result would *not* mean that the overridden virtue does not conflict with the one that overrides it, for otherwise there would be no point of speaking of one overriding the other.)

4. Could it happen that through no fault of the agent, there are serious moral objections to *any* action available—in which case even what the ideally virtuous person does will not be right without serious qualification? (Think here especially of Williams's case of Jim, on page 605.) If this were so, then a morally right action could not be defined as whatever an ideally virtuous person would do (since even an ideally virtuous person would do something). How serious an objection is this to Hursthouse's version of virtue ethics?

How Do General Moral Concepts Apply to Concrete Issues?

Judith Jarvis Thomson

Judith Jarvis Thomson (1929–) is an American philosopher who teaches at the Massachusetts Institute of Technology. She has made important contributions to both ethics and metaphysics.

In the following selection (which is perhaps the single piece of work for which Thomson is best known) she defends the thesis that abortion is often (but not always) morally permissible, even on the assumption (which she does not accept) that the fetus (the prenatal organism) is a person from the moment of conception, and even in cases where the mother's life is not threatened. (Here it is important to distinguish the moral concept of a person from the biological concept of a member of the human species. There is no doubt that the fetus is biologically human, but what Thomson is assuming for the sake of the argument is that it is also a being with the kind of moral status, including rights, that we ascribe to at least most humans, but might also ascribe to beings of other species, such as perhaps dolphins or extraterrestrials.)

A Defense of Abortion

Most opposition to abortion relies on the premiss that the foetus is a human being, a person, from the moment of conception. The premiss is argued for, but, as I think, not well. Take, for example, the most common argument. We are asked to notice that the development of a human being from conception through birth into childhood is continuous; then it is said that to draw a line, to choose a point in this development and say 'before this point the thing is not a person, after this point it is a person' is to make an arbitrary choice, a choice for which in the nature of things no good reason can be given. It is concluded that the foetus is, or anyway that we had better say it is, a person from the moment of conception. But this conclusion does not follow. Similar things might be said about the development of an acorn into an oak tree, and it does not follow that acorns are oak trees, or that we had better say they are. Arguments of this form are sometimes called 'slippery slope arguments'— the phrase is perhaps self-explanatory—and it is dismaying that opponents of abortion rely on them so heavily and uncritically.①

> **① ** Think carefully about this analogy. What we would say about the stages between an acorn and an oak tree is reasonably clear: they are intermediate stages, more than acorns but not yet oak trees. But what should be said about the stages intermediate between something that has no moral status or moral rights and a full-blown person who has both? Can something be more than a nonperson but not yet a full-fledged person (and if so, what sort of moral status and rights would it have)?

I am inclined to agree, however, that the prospects for 'drawing a line' in the development of the foetus look dim. I am inclined to think also that we shall probably have to agree that the foetus has already become a human person well before birth. Indeed, it comes as a surprise when one first learns how early in its life it begins to acquire human characteristics. By the tenth week, for example, it already has a face, arms and legs, fingers and toes; it has internal organs, and brain activity is detectable.② On the other hand, I think that the premiss is false, that the foetus is not a person from the moment of conception. A newly fertilized ovum, a newly implanted clump of cells, is no more a person than an acorn is an oak tree. But I shall not discuss any of this. For it seems to me to be of great interest to ask what happens if, for the sake of argument, we allow the premiss.③ How, precisely, are we supposed to get from there to the conclusion that abortion is morally impermissible? Opponents of abortion commonly spend most of their time establishing that the foetus is a person, and hardly any time explaining the step from there to the impermissibility of abortion. Perhaps they think the step too simple and obvious to require much comment. Or perhaps instead they are simply being economical in argument. Many of those who defend abortion rely on the premiss that the foetus is not a person, but only a bit of tissue that will become a person at birth; and why pay out more arguments than you have to? Whatever the explanation, I suggest that the step they take is neither easy nor obvious, that it calls for closer examination than it is commonly given, and that when we do give it this closer examination we shall feel inclined to reject it.

> **② ** These characteristics are much more clearly relevant to biological humanity than to personhood.

> **③ ** The premise, that is, that the fetus is a person from the moment of conception. Thomson proposes to assume, for the sake of the argument, that this is so, even though she doesn't really accept it.

I propose, then, that we grant that the foetus is a person from the moment of conception. How does the argument go from here? Something like this, I take it. Every person has a right to life. So the foetus has a right to life. No doubt the mother has a right to decide what shall happen in and to her body; everyone would grant that. But surely a person's right to life is stronger and more stringent than the mother's right to decide what happens in and to her body, and so outweighs it. So the foetus may not be killed; an abortion may not be performed.

It sounds plausible. But now let me ask you to imagine this. You wake up in the morning and find

From Philosophy and Public Affairs *Vol. I, No. 1 (Fall 1971).*

yourself back to back in bed with an unconscious violinist. A famous unconscious violinist. He has been found to have a fatal kidney ailment, and the Society of Music Lovers has canvassed all the available medical records and found that you alone have the right blood type to help. They have therefore kidnapped you, and last night the violinist's circulatory system was plugged into yours, so that your kidneys can be used to extract poisons from his blood as well as your own. The director of the hospital now tells you, 'Look, we're sorry the Society of Music Lovers did this to you—we would never have permitted it if we had known. But still, they did it, and the violinist now is plugged into you. To unplug you would be to kill him. But never mind, it's only for nine months. By then he will have recovered from his ailment, and can safely be unplugged from you.' Is it morally incumbent on you to accede to this situation? No doubt it would be very nice of you if you did, a great kindness. But do you *have* to accede to it? What if it were not nine months, but nine years? Or longer still? What if the director of the hospital says, 'Tough luck, I agree, but you've now got to stay in bed, with the violinist plugged into you, for the rest of your life. Because remember this. All persons have a right to life,

> ④ This famous analogy is central to Thomson's argument, and you should think about it very carefully. One thing to notice is that there are also disanalogies between the case of pregnancy and the violinist case, as Thomson presents it. You should ask yourself how important these are and also whether the violinist case could be modified so as to eliminate some or all of them. (See Discussion Question 1.)

and violinists are persons. Granted you have a right to decide what happens in and to your body, but a person's right to life outweighs your right to decide what happens in and to your body. So you cannot ever be unplugged from him.' I imagine you would regard this as outrageous, which suggests that something really is wrong with that plausible-sounding argument I mentioned a moment ago. ④

In this case, of course, you were kidnapped; you didn't volunteer for the operation that plugged the violinist into your kidneys. Can those who oppose abortion on the ground I mentioned make an exception for a pregnancy due to rape? Certainly. They can say that persons have a right to life only if they didn't come into existence because of rape; or they can say that all per-

sons have a right to life, but that some have less of a right to life than others, in particular, that those who came into existence because of rape have less. But these statements have a rather unpleasant sound. Surely the question of whether you have a right to life at all, or how much of it you have, shouldn't turn on the question of whether or not you are the product of a rape. And in fact the people who oppose abortion on the ground I mentioned do not make this distinction, and hence do not make an exception in case of rape. ⑤

> ⑤ Many people do think that the fact that a pregnancy resulted from rape is morally significant, but *why* is this so (if it is)? Does it have any bearing on whether or not the fetus is a person? Is it perhaps relevant in some other way?

Nor do they make an exception for a case in which the mother has to spend the nine months of her pregnancy in bed. They would agree that would be a great pity, and hard on the mother; but all the same, all persons have a right to life, the foetus is a person, and so on. I suspect, in fact, that they would not make an exception for a case in which, miraculously enough, the pregnancy went on for nine years, or even the rest of the mother's life.

Some won't even make an exception for a case in which continuation of the pregnancy is likely to shorten the mother's life; they regard abortion as impermissible even to save the mother's life. Such cases are nowadays very rare, and many opponents of abortion do not accept this extreme view. All the same, it is a good place to begin: a number of points of interest come out in respect to it.

1. Let us call the view that abortion is impermissible even to save the mother's life 'the extreme view'. I want to suggest first that it does not issue from the argument I mentioned earlier without the addition of some fairly powerful premises. Suppose a woman has become pregnant, and now learns that she has a cardiac condition such that she will die if she carries the baby to term. What may be done for her? The foetus, being a person, has a right to life, but as the mother is a person too, so has she a right to life. Presumably they have an equal right to life. How is it supposed to come out that an abortion may not be performed? If mother and child have an equal right to life, shouldn't we perhaps flip a coin? Or should we add to the mother's right to life her right to decide what happens in and to her body, which everybody seems to be ready to grant—

the sum of her rights now outweighing the foetus's right to life?

The most familiar argument here is the following. We are told that performing the abortion would be directly killing* the child, whereas doing nothing would not be killing the mother, but only letting her die. Moreover, in killing the child, one would be killing an innocent person, for the child has committed no crime, and is not aiming at his mother's death. And then there are a variety of ways in which this might be continued. (1) But as directly killing an innocent person is always and absolutely impermissible, an abortion may not be performed. Or, (2) as directly killing an innocent person is murder, and murder is always and absolutely impermissible, an abortion may not be performed. Or, (3) as one's duty to refrain from directly killing an innocent person is more stringent than one's duty to keep a person from dying, an abortion may not be performed. Or, (4) if one's only options are directly killing an innocent person or letting a person die, one must prefer letting the person die, and thus an abortion may not be performed.†

Some people seem to have thought that these are not further premises which must be added if the conclusion is to be reached, but that they follow from the very fact that an innocent person has a right to life. But this seems to me to be a mistake, and perhaps the simplest way to show this is to bring out that while we must certainly grant that innocent persons have a right to life, the theses in (1) to (4) are all false. Take (2), for example. If directly killing an innocent person is murder, and thus is impermissible, then the mother's directly killing the innocent person inside her is murder, and thus is impermissible. But it cannot seriously be thought to be murder if the mother performs an abortion on herself to save her life. It cannot seriously be said that she *must* refrain, that she *must* sit passively by and wait for her death. Let us look again at the case of you and the violinist. There you are, in bed with the violinist, and the director of the hospital says to you, 'It's all most distressing, and I deeply sympathize, but you see this is putting an additional strain on

your kidneys, and you'll be dead within the month. But you *have* to stay where you are all the same. Because unplugging you would be directly killing an innocent violinist, and that's murder, and that's impermissible.' If anything in the world is true, it is that you do not commit murder, you do not do what is impermissible, if you reach around to your back and unplug yourself from that violinist to save your life.⑥

> ⑥ Is it, as Thomson seems to think, more obvious that the mother can save her own life than that someone else can act so as to do it for her—and analogously in the violinist case? Why?

The main focus of attention in writings on abortion has been on what a third party may or may not do in answer to a request from a woman for an abortion. This is in a way understandable. Things being as they are, there isn't much a woman can safely do to abort herself. So the question asked is what a third party may do, and what the mother may do, if it is mentioned at all, is deduced, almost as an afterthought, from what it is concluded that third parties may do. But it seems to me that to treat the matter in this way is to refuse to grant to the mother that very status of person which is so firmly insisted on for the foetus. For we cannot simply read off what a person may do from what a third party may do. Suppose you find yourself trapped in a tiny house with a growing child. I mean a very tiny house, and a rapidly growing child—you are already up against the wall of the house and in a few minutes you'll be crushed to death. The child on the other hand won't be crushed to death; if nothing is done to stop him from growing he'll be hurt, but in the end he'll simply burst open the house and walk out a free man. Now I could well understand it if a bystander were to say, 'There's nothing we can do for you. We cannot choose between your life and his, we cannot be the ones to decide who is to live, we cannot intervene.' But it cannot be concluded that you too can do nothing, that you cannot attack it to save your life. However innocent the child may be, you do not have to wait passively while it crushes you to

---

*The term 'direct' in the arguments I refer to is a technical one. Roughly, what is meant by 'direct killing' is either killing as an end in itself, or killing as a means to some end, for example, the end of saving someone else's life. . . .

†The thesis in (4) is in an interesting way weaker than those in (1), (2), and (3): they rule out abortion even in cases in which both mother *and* child will die if the abortion is not performed. By contrast, one who held the view expressed in (4) could consistently say that one needn't prefer letting two persons die to killing one.

death. Perhaps a pregnant woman is vaguely felt to have the status of house, to which we don't allow the right of self-defence. But if the woman houses the child, it should be remembered that she is a person who houses it.

I should perhaps stop to say explicitly that I am not claiming that people have a right to do anything whatever to save their lives. I think, rather, that there are drastic limits to the right of self-defence. If someone threatens you with death unless you torture someone else to death, I think you have not the right, even to save your life, to do so. But the case under consideration here is very different. In our case there are only two people involved, one whose life is threatened, and one who threatens it. Both are innocent: the one who is threatened is not threatened because of any fault, the one who threatens does not threaten because of any fault. For this reason we may feel that we bystanders cannot intervene. But the person threatened can.⑦

> ⑦ The (rather fanciful) example in the previous paragraph is a case of an *innocent threat:* someone who is a threat to someone else's life (or well-being) through no fault of their own. Thomson's claim is that a person can defend themselves from an innocent threat even if it requires harming or even killing the innocent person who poses the threat. Is this right? (See Discussion Question 2.)

In sum, a woman surely can defend her life against the threat to it posed by the unborn child, even if doing so involves its death. And this shows not merely that the theses in (1) to (4) are false; it shows also that the extreme view of abortion is false, and so we need not canvass any other possible ways of arriving at it from the argument I mentioned at the outset.

2. The extreme view could of course be weakened to say that while abortion is permissible to save the mother's life, it may not be performed by a third party, but only by the mother herself. But this cannot be right either. For what we have to keep in mind is that the mother and the unborn child are not like two tenants in a small house which has, by an unfortunate mistake, been rented to both: the mother *owns* the house. The fact that she does adds to the offensiveness of deducing that the mother can do nothing from the supposition that third parties can do nothing. But it does more than this: it casts a bright light on the supposition that

third parties can do nothing. Certainly it lets us see that a third party who says 'I cannot choose between you' is fooling himself if he thinks this is impartiality. If Jones has found and fastened on a certain coat, which he needs to keep him from freezing, but which Smith also needs to keep him from freezing, then it is not impartiality that says 'I cannot choose between you' when Smith owns the coat. Women have said again and again 'This body is *my* body!' and they have reason to feel angry, reason to feel that it has been like shouting into the wind. Smith, after all, is hardly likely to bless us if we say to him, 'Of course it's your coat, anybody would grant that it is. But no one may choose between you and Jones who is to have it.'⑧

> ⑧ One key premise of Thomson's argument is that the mother *owns* her body (as the person hooked up to the violinist also does). Does this seem right? (In examples like the coat example, it is important to insist that the ownership in question is itself morally legitimate, not in any way morally questionable, as some cases of ownership might be—for example ownership resulting from exploitation or fraud.)

We should really ask what it is that says 'no one may choose' in the face of the fact that the body that houses the child is the mother's body. It may be simply a failure to appreciate this fact. But it may be something more interesting, namely the sense that one has a right to refuse to lay hands on people, even where it would be just and fair to do so, even where justice seems to require that somebody do so. Thus justice might call for somebody to get Smith's coat back from Jones, and yet you have a right to refuse to be the one to lay hands on Jones, a right to refuse to do physical violence to him. This, I think, must be granted. But then what should be said is not 'no one may choose', but only '*I* cannot choose', and indeed not even this, but '*I* will not *act*', leaving it open that somebody else can or should, and in particular that anyone in a position of authority, with the job of securing people's rights, both can and should. So this is no difficulty. I have not been arguing that any given third party must accede to the mother's request that he perform an abortion to save her life, but only that he may.

I suppose that in some views of human life the mother's body is only on loan to her, the loan not being one which gives her any prior claim to it. One who held this view might well think it impartiality to say 'I cannot choose'. But I shall simply ignore this possibility. My own view is that if a human being has any just, prior claim to anything at all, he has a just, prior claim to his own body. And perhaps this needn't be argued for here anyway, since, as I mentioned, the arguments against abortion we are looking at do grant that the woman has a right to decide what happens in and to her body.

But although they do grant it, I have tried to show that they do not take seriously what is done in granting it. I suggest the same thing will reappear even more clearly when we turn away from cases in which the mother's life is at stake, and attend, as I propose we now do, to the vastly more common cases in which a woman wants an abortion for some less weighty reason than preserving her own life.

3. Where the mother's life is not at stake, the argument I mentioned at the outset seems to have a much stronger pull. 'Everyone has a right to life, so the unborn person has a right to life.' And isn't the child's right to life weightier than anything other than the mother's own right to life, which she might put forward as ground for an abortion?

This argument treats the right to life as if it were unproblematic. It is not, and this seems to me to be precisely the source of the mistake.

For we should now, at long last, ask what it comes to, to have a right to life. In some views having a right to life includes having a right to be given at least the bare minimum one needs for continued life. But suppose that what in fact *is* the bare minimum a man needs for continued life is something he has no right at all to be given? If I am sick unto death, and the only thing that will save my life is the touch of Henry Fonda's cool hand on my fevered brow, then all the same, I have no right to be given the touch of Henry Fonda's cool hand on my fevered brow. It would be frightfully nice of him to fly in from the West Coast to provide it. It would be less nice, though no doubt well meant, if my friends flew out to the West Coast and carried Henry Fonda back with them. But I have no right at all against anybody that he should do this for me. Or again, to return to the story I told earlier, the fact that for continued life that violinist needs the continued use of your kidneys does not establish that he

has a right to be given the continued use of your kidneys. He certainly has no right against you that *you* should give him continued use of your kidneys. For nobody has any right to use your kidneys unless you give him such a right; and nobody has the right against you that you shall give him this right—if you do allow him to go on using your kidneys, this is a kindness on your part, and not something he can claim from you as his due. Nor has he any right against anybody else that *they* should give him continued use of your kidneys. Certainly he had no right against the Society of Music Lovers that they should plug him into you in the first place. And if you now start to unplug yourself, having learned that you will otherwise have to spend nine years in bed with him, there is nobody in the world who must try to prevent you, in order to see to it that he is given something he has a right to be given.⑨

> ⑨ In Thomson's view, the right to life (the one we ascribe to persons) is not a *positive* right to receive whatever minimum aid is needed to preserve life (the use of someone's kidneys or Henry Fonda's hand). (For the distinction between positive and negative rights, see the Ozar selection.)

Some people are rather stricter about the right to life. In their view, it does not include the right to be given anything, but amounts to, and only to, the right not to be killed by anybody. But here a related difficulty arises. If everybody is to refrain from killing that violinist, then everybody must refrain from doing a great many different sorts of things. Everybody must refrain from slitting his throat, everybody must refrain from shooting him—and everybody must refrain from unplugging you from him. But does he have a right against everybody that they shall refrain from unplugging you from him? To refrain from doing this is to allow him to continue to use your kidneys. It could be argued that he has a right against us that *we* should allow him to continue to use your kidneys. That is, while he had no right against us that we should give him the use of your kidneys, it might be argued that he anyway has a right against us that we shall not now intervene and deprive him of the use of your kidneys. I shall come back to third-party interventions later. But certainly the violinist has no right against you that *you* shall allow him to continue to use your kidneys. As I said, if you do allow him to use them, it is a kindness on your part, and not something you owe him. ⑩

---

⑩ If the violinist has no right to the use of your kidneys, then it seems to follow that you can prevent him from using them and perhaps—to be discussed later—that others can help you in this. Thus the violinist's right to life is not a right to noninterference of any sort. (As shown also by the earlier example of the coat that each of two people need, one owns, and the other currently is wearing.)

---

⑪ Thomson is saying that the intuition that all *persons* (not necessarily all humans) have a right to life is strong enough that any acceptable account of this right must yield this result (this may in fact follow immediately from the concept of a person).

The difficulty I point to here is not peculiar to the right to life. It reappears in connection with all the other natural rights; and it is something which an adequate account of rights must deal with. For present purposes it is enough just to draw attention to it. But I would stress that I am not arguing that people do not have a right to life—quite to the contrary, it seems to me that the primary control we must place on the acceptability of an account of rights is that it should turn out in that account to be a truth that all persons have a right to life. ⑪ I am arguing only that having a right to life does not guarantee having either a right to be given the use of or a right to be allowed continued use of another person's body—even if one needs it for life itself. So the right to life will not serve the opponents of abortion in the very simple and clear way in which they seem to have thought it would.

4. There is another way to bring out the difficulty. In the most ordinary sort of case, to deprive someone of what he has a right to is to treat him unjustly. Suppose a boy and his small brother are jointly given a box of chocolates for Christmas. If the older boy takes the box and refuses to give his brother any of the chocolates, he is unjust to him, for the brother has been given a right to half of them. But suppose that, having learned that otherwise it means nine years in bed with that violinist, you unplug yourself from him. You surely are not being unjust to him, for you gave him no right to use your kidneys, and no one else can have given him any such right. But we have to notice that in unplugging yourself, you are killing him; and violinists, like everybody else, have a right to life, and

thus in the view we were considering just now, the right not to be killed. So here you do what he supposedly has a right you shall not do, but you do not act unjustly to him in doing it.

The emendation which may be made at this point is this: the right to life consists not in the right not to be killed, but rather in the right not to be killed unjustly. ⑫ This runs a risk of circularity, but never mind: it would enable us to square the fact that the violinist has a right to life with the fact that you do not act unjustly toward him in unplugging yourself, thereby killing him. For if you do

---

⑫ So, in Thomson's view, the right to life is a right to noninterference of a certain sort: the right not to be killed *unjustly.* (This does not, of course, settle the question of what counts as unjust killing.)

---

not kill him unjustly, you do not violate his right to life, and so it is no wonder you do him no injustice.

But if this emendation is accepted, the gap in the argument against abortion stares us plainly in the face: it is by no means enough to show that the foetus is a person, and to remind us that all persons have a right to life—we need to be shown also that killing the foetus violates its right to life, i.e. that abortion is unjust killing. And is it?

I suppose we may take it as a datum that in a case of pregnancy due to rape the mother has not given the unborn person a right to the use of her body for food and shelter. Indeed, in what pregnancy could it be supposed that the mother has given the unborn person such a right? It is not as if there were unborn persons drifting about the world, to whom a woman who wants a child says 'I invite you in'.

But it might be argued that there are other ways one can have acquired a right to the use of another person's body than by having been invited to use it by that person. Suppose a woman voluntarily indulges in intercourse, knowing of the chance it will issue in pregnancy, and then she does become pregnant; is she not in part responsible for the presence, in fact the very existence, of the unborn person inside her? No doubt she did not invite it in. But doesn't her partial responsibility for its being there itself give it a right to the use of her body? If so, then her aborting it would be more like the boy's taking away the chocolates, and less like your unplugging yourself from the violinist—doing so would be depriving it of what what it does have a right to, and thus would be doing it an injustice. ⑬

And then, too, it might be asked whether or not she can kill it even to save her own life: If she voluntarily called it into existence, how can she now kill it, even in self-defence?

13 Thomson is suggesting this view, not fully endorsing it. One way to assess it is to imagine a version of the violinist case that involves you doing something that you know in advance might lead to you being hooked up to the violinist. (See Discussion Question 3.)

The first thing to be said about this is that it is something new. Opponents of abortion have been so concerned to make out the independence of the foetus, in order to establish that it has a right to life, just as its mother does, that they have tended to overlook the possible support they might gain from making out that the foetus is *dependent* on the mother, in order to establish that she has a special kind of responsibility for it, a responsibility that gives it rights against her which are not possessed by any independent person—such as an ailing violinist who is a stranger to her.

On the other hand, this argument would give the unborn person a right to its mother's body only if her pregnancy resulted from a voluntary act, undertaken in full knowledge of the chance a pregnancy might result from it. It would leave out entirely the unborn person whose existence is due to rape. Pending the availability of some further argument, then we would be left with the conclusion that unborn persons whose

14 According to Thomson, this is the clearest case in which abortion is not unjust killing and so does not violate the fetus's right to life. She is not saying that it is the only case.

existence is due to rape have no right to the use of their mothers' bodies, and thus that aborting them is not depriving them of anything they have a right to and hence is not unjust killing. 14

And we should also notice that it is not at all plain that this argument really does go even as far as it purports to. For there are cases and cases, and the details make a difference. If the room is stuffy, and I therefore open a window to air it, and a burglar climbs in, it would be absurd to say, 'Ah, now he can stay, she's given him a right to the use of her house—for she is partially responsible for his presence there, having voluntarily done what enabled him to get in, in full knowledge that there are such things as burglars, and that burglars burgle.' It would be still more absurd to

say this if I had had bars installed outside my windows, precisely to prevent burglars from getting in, and a burglar got in only because of a defect in the bars. It remains equally absurd if we imagine it is not a burglar who climbs in, but an innocent person who blunders or falls in. . . .

It seems to me that the argument we are looking at can establish at most that there are *some* cases in which the unborn person has a right to the use of its mother's body, and therefore *some* cases in which abortion is unjust killing. There is room for much discussion and argument as to precisely which, if any. But I think we should side-step this issue and leave it open, for at any rate the argument certainly does not establish that all abortion is unjust killing.

5. There is room for yet another argument here, however. We surely must all grant that there may be cases in which it would be morally indecent to detach a person from your body at the cost of his life. Suppose you learn that what the violinist needs is not nine years of your life, but only one hour: all you need do to save his life is to spend one hour in that bed with him. Suppose also that letting him use your kidneys for that one hour would not affect your health in the slightest. Admittedly you were kidnapped. Admittedly you did not give anyone permission to plug him into you. Nevertheless it seems to me plain you *ought* to allow him to use your kidneys for that hour—it would be indecent to refuse.

Again, suppose pregnancy lasted only an hour, and constituted no threat to life or health. And suppose that a woman becomes pregnant as a result of rape. Admittedly she did not voluntarily do anything to bring about the existence of a child. Admittedly she did nothing at all which would give the unborn person a right to the use of her body. All the same it might well be said, as in the newly emended violinist story, that she *ought* to allow it to remain for that hour—that it would be indecent in her to refuse. 15

15 "Morally indecent" because what is needed to keep the unborn person (under Thomson's original assumption) alive costs the mother so little. One way to defend this point would be to appeal to Kant's duty of beneficence, deriving from the requirement to treat other persons as ends-in-themselves: could you be regarding another person as an end-in-himself and still be unwilling to make even this minimal effort to save him?

Now some people are inclined to use the term 'right' in such a way that it follows from the fact that you ought to allow a person to use your body for the hour he needs, that he has a right to use your body for the hour he needs, even though he has not been given that right by any person or act. They may say that it follows also that if you refuse, you act unjustly toward him. This use of the term is perhaps so common that it cannot be called wrong; nevertheless it seems to me to be an unfortunate loosening of what we would do better to keep a tight rein on. Suppose that box of chocolates I mentioned earlier had not been given to both boys jointly, but was given only to the older boy. There he sits, stolidly eating his way through the box, his small brother watching enviously. Here we are likely to say 'You ought not to be so mean. You ought to give your brother some of those chocolates.' My own view is that it just does not follow from the truth of this that the brother has any right to any of the chocolates. If the boy refuses to give his brother any, he is greedy, stingy, callous—but not unjust. I suppose that the people I have in mind will say it does follow that the brother has a right to some of the chocolates, and thus that the boy does act unjustly if he refuses to give his brother any. But the effect of saying this is to obscure what we should keep distinct, namely the difference between the boy's refusal in this case and the boy's refusal in the earlier case, in which the box was given to both boys jointly, and in which the small brother thus had what was from any point of view clear title to half.

A further objection to so using the term 'right' that from the fact that A ought to do a thing for B, it follows that B has a right against A that A do it for him, is that it is going to make the question of whether or not a man has a right to a thing turn on how easy it is to provide him with it; and this seems not merely unfortunate, but morally unacceptable. Take the case of Henry Fonda again. I said earlier that I had no right to the touch of his cool hand on my fevered brow, even though I needed it to save my life. I said it would be frightfully nice of him to fly in from the West Coast to provide me with it, but that I had no right against him that he should do so. But suppose he isn't on the West Coast. Suppose he has only to walk across the room, place a hand briefly on my brow—and lo, my life is saved. Then surely he ought to do it, it would be indecent to refuse. Is it to be said 'Ah, well, it follows that in this case she has a right to the touch of his hand on her brow, and so it would be an injustice in him to refuse?' So that I have a right to it when it is easy for him to provide it, though no right when it's hard? It's rather a shocking idea that anyone's rights should fade away and disappear as it gets harder and harder to accord them to him.[16]

[16] Thomson is appealing here to the moral intuition that *rights* override other sorts of considerations—and so could not depend on how easy they are to satisfy. (See the selection from Ozar for a discussion of how rights override other moral considerations.)

So my own view is that even though you ought to let the violinist use your kidneys for the one hour he needs, we should not conclude that he has a right to do so—we should say that if you refuse, you are, like the boy who owns all the chocolates and will give none away, self-centred and callous, indecent in fact, but not unjust. And similarly, that even supposing a case in which a woman pregnant due to rape ought to allow the unborn person to use her body for the hour he needs, we should not conclude that he has a right to do so; we should conclude that she is self-centred, callous, indecent, but not unjust, if she refuses. The complaints are no less grave; they are just different. However, there is no need to insist on this point. If anyone does wish to deduce 'he has a right' from 'you ought', then all the same he must surely grant that there are cases in which it is not morally required of you that you allow that violinist to use your kidneys, and in which he does not have a right to use them, and so also for mother and unborn child. Except in such cases as the unborn person has a right to demand it—and we were leaving open the possibility that there may be such cases—nobody is morally *required* to make large sacrifices, of health, of all other interests and concerns, of all other duties and commitments, for nine years, or even for nine months, in order to keep another person alive.

6. We have in fact to distinguish between two kinds of Samaritan: the Good Samaritan and what we might call the Minimally Decent Samaritan. The story of the Good Samaritan, you will remember, goes like this:

> A certain man went down from Jerusalem to Jericho, and fell among thieves, which stripped him of his raiment, and wounded him, and departed, leaving him half dead.

And by chance there came down a certain priest that way; and when he saw him, he passed by on the other side.

And likewise a Levite, when he was at the place, came and looked on him, and passed by on the other side.

But a certain Samaritan, as he journeyed, came where he was; and when he saw him he had compassion on him.

And went to him, and bound up his wounds, pouring in oil and wine, and set him on his own beast, and brought him to an inn, and took care of him.

And on the morrow, when he departed, he took out two pence, and gave them to the host, and said unto him, 'Take care of him; and whatsoever thou spendest more, when I come again, I will repay thee.'

(Luke 10: 30–5)

The Good Samaritan went out of his way, at some cost to himself, to help one in need of it. We are not told what the options were, that is, whether or not the priest and the Levite could have helped by doing less than the Good Samaritan did, but assuming they could have, then the fact they did nothing at all shows they were not even Minimally Decent Samaritans, not because they were not Samaritans, but because they were not even minimally decent.

These things are a matter of degree, of course, but there is a difference, and it comes out perhaps most clearly in the story of Kitty Genovese, who, as you will remember, was murdered while thirty-eight people watched or listened, and did nothing at all to help her. A Good Samaritan would have rushed out to give direct assistance against the murderer. Or perhaps we had better allow that it would have been a Splendid Samaritan who did this, on the ground that it would have involved a risk of death for himself. But the thirty-eight not only did not do this, they did not even trouble to pick up a phone to call the police. Minimally Decent Samaritanism would call for doing at least that, and their not having done it was monstrous.[17]

[17] Again a Kantian argument seems relevant: could anyone who refused even to make a phone call seriously claim to be treating Kitty Genovese as an end-in-herself?

After telling the story of the Good Samaritan, Jesus said 'Go, and do thou likewise.' Perhaps he meant that we are morally required to act as the Good Samaritan did. Perhaps he was urging people to do more than is morally required of them. At all events it seems plain that it was not morally required of any of the thirty-eight that he rush out to give direct assistance at the risk of his own life, and that it is not morally required of anyone that he give long stretches of his life—nine years or nine months—to sustaining the life of a person who has no special right (we were leaving open the possibility of this) to demand it.

Indeed, with one rather striking class of exceptions, no one in any country in the world is *legally* required to do anywhere near as much as this for anyone else. The class of exceptions is obvious. My main concern here is not the state of the law in respect to abortion, but it is worth drawing attention to the fact that in no state in this country is any man compelled by law to be even a Minimally Decent Samaritan to any person; there is no law under which charges could be brought against the thirty-eight who stood by while Kitty Genovese died. By contrast, in most states in this country women are compelled by law to be not merely Minimally Decent Samaritans, but Good Samaritans to unborn persons inside them. This doesn't by itself settle anything one way or the other, because it may well be argued that there should be laws in this country—as there are in many European countries—compelling at least Minimally Decent Samaritanism. But it does show that there is a gross injustice in the existing state of the law. And it shows also that the groups currently working against liberalization of abortion laws, in fact working toward having it declared unconstitutional for a state to permit abortion, had better start working for the adoption of Good Samaritan laws generally, or earn the charge that they are acting in bad faith.

I should think, myself, that Minimally Decent Samaritan laws would be one thing, Good Samaritan laws quite another, and in fact highly improper. But we are not here concerned with the law. What we should ask is not whether anybody should be compelled by law to be a Good Samaritan, but whether we must accede to a situation in which somebody is being compelled—by nature, perhaps—to be a Good Samaritan. We have, in other words, to look now at third-party interventions. I have been arguing that no person is morally required to make large sacrifices to sustain the life of another who has no right to demand them, and this even where the sacrifices do not include life itself; we are not morally required to be Good Samaritans or anyway Very Good Samaritans to one another. But what if a man cannot extricate himself from such a situation? What if he appeals to us to extricate him? It seems to me plain that there are cases in which we can, cases in which a Good Samaritan would extricate him. There you are, you were kidnapped, and nine years in bed with that violinist lie ahead of you. You have your own life to lead. You are sorry, but you simply cannot see giving up so much of your life to the sustaining of his. You cannot extricate yourself, and ask us to do so. I should have thought that—in light of his having no right to the use of your body—it was obvious that we do not have to accede to your being forced to give up so much. We can do what you ask. There is no injustice to the violinist in our doing so.⑱

⑱ There is no injustice because you have done nothing to give the violinist any right to use your kidneys. (Think of ways in which the situation might be different in this respect.) And minimal decency (like Kant's duty of beneficence) does not require a sacrifice this great.

7. Following the lead of the opponents of abortion, I have throughout been speaking of the foetus merely as a person, and what I have been asking is whether or not the argument we began with, which proceeds only from the foetus's being a person, really does establish its conclusion. I have argued that it does not.

But of course there are arguments and arguments, and it may be said that I have simply fastened on the wrong one. It may be said that what is important is not merely the fact that the foetus is a person, but that it is a person for whom the woman has a special kind of responsibility issuing from the fact that she is its mother. And it might be argued that all my analogies are therefore irrelevant—for you do not have that special kind of responsibility for that violinist, Henry Fonda does not have that special kind of responsibility for me. And our attention might be drawn to the fact that men and women both *are* compelled by law to provide support for their children.

I have in effect dealt (briefly) with this argument in section 4 above; but a (still briefer) recapitulation now may be in order. Surely we do not have any such 'special responsibility' for a person unless we have as-

sumed it, explicitly or implicitly. If a set of parents do not try to prevent pregnancy, do not obtain an abortion, and then at the time of birth of the child do not put it out for adoption, but rather take it home with them, then they have assumed responsibility for it, they have given it rights, and they cannot *now* withdraw support from it at the cost of its life because they now find it difficult to go on providing for it. But if they have taken all reasonable precautions against having a child, they do not simply by virtue of their biological relationship to the child who comes into existence have a special responsibility for it. They may wish to assume responsibility for it, or they may not wish to. And I am suggesting that if assuming responsibility for it would require large sacrifices, then they may refuse. A Good Samaritan would not refuse—or anyway, a Splendid Samaritan, if the sacrifices that had to be made were enormous. But then so would a Good Samaritan assume responsibility for that violinist; so would Henry Fonda, if he is a Good Samaritan, fly in from the West Coast and assume responsibility for me.⑲

⑲ Thomson is saying, among other things, that a merely biological relationship is not enough to give the mother a special responsibility for the child. Here again, one way to think about this claim is to imagine a corresponding variation of the violinist example.

8. My argument will be found unsatisfactory on two counts by many of those who want to regard abortion as morally permissible. First, while I do argue that abortion is not impermissible, I do not argue that it is always permissible. There may well be cases in which carrying the child to term requires only Minimally Decent Samaritanism of the mother, and this is a standard we must not fall below. I am inclined to think it a merit of my account precisely that it does *not* give a general yes or a general no. It allows for and supports our sense that, for example, a sick and desperately frightened fourteen-year-old schoolgirl, pregnant due to rape, may *of course* choose abortion, and that any law which rules this out is an insane law. And it also allows for and supports our sense that in other cases resort to abortion is even positively indecent. It would be indecent in the woman to request an abortion, and indecent in a doctor to perform it, if she is in her seventh month, and wants the abortion just to avoid the nuisance of postponing a trip abroad. The very fact that the arguments I have been drawing at-

tention to treat all cases of abortion, or even all cases of abortion in which the mother's life is not at stake, as morally on a par ought to have made them suspect at the outset.[20]

[20] Thus Thomson's argument does not seem to support "a woman's right to choose" as this is currently understood, at least not as a moral right. (The issue of whether abortion should be *legally* permitted is not directly addressed directly by anything Thomson says. See the end of the following selection by Foot for brief discussion of the difference between moral issues and legal ones.)

Secondly, while I am arguing for the permissibility of abortion in some cases, I am not arguing for the right to secure the death of the unborn child. It is easy to confuse these two things in that up to a certain point in the life of the foetus it is not able to survive outside the mother's body; hence removing it from her body guarantees its death. But they are importantly different. I have argued that you are not morally required to spend nine months in bed, sustaining the life of that violinist; but to say this is by no means to say that if, when you unplug yourself, there is a miracle and he survives, you then have a right to turn round and slit his throat. You may detach yourself even if this costs him his life; you have no right to be guaranteed his death, by some other means, if unplugging yourself does not kill him. There are some people who will feel dissatisfied by this feature of my argument. A woman may be utterly devastated by the thought of a child, a bit of herself, put out for adoption and never seen or heard of again. She may therefore want not merely that the child be detached from her, but more, that it die. Some opponents of abortion are inclined to regard this as beneath contempt—thereby showing insensitivity to what is surely a powerful source of despair. All the same, I agree that the desire for the child's death is not one which anybody may gratify, should it turn out to be possible to detach the child alive.

At this place, however, it should be remembered that we have only been pretending throughout that the foetus is a human being from the moment of conception. A very early abortion is surely not the killing of a person, and so is not dealt with by anything I have said here.

Discussion Questions

1. Here are two obvious differences between the violinist case and a standard abortion case (these are not the only ones): (1) A pregnant woman is able to move fairly freely, continue to work, and engage in various other activities, whereas the person hooked up to the violinist must remain in bed. (2) The violinist is described as famous, and so is presumably especially talented and thereby valuable, whereas nothing of this sort is known to pertain to a normal fetus. Try to imagine a version of the violinist case that is closer to a normal pregnancy in these respects (not an abnormal pregnancy that is closer to the violinist case), and then see if any of the changes make a difference to your intuitive assessment of the case.

2. Here is another example of an innocent threat: An innocent 5-year old is about to push a button that will set off a bomb that will kill several people. You can't get there in time to physically restrain the child from pressing the button, but you can stop him from doing so by shooting him with a gun that you already have in your hand. Assume that it is certain beyond any reasonable doubt that the child is going to immediately press the button (perhaps it looks like a button in a game that the child likes to play), and also that none of the people involved, including the child, is in any way responsible for the situation being as it is. Is it morally acceptable to shoot the child to prevent the bomb from going off? Does it matter how many others will be killed if it does? Does it matter whether you are one of them? What if the bomb will also kill the child?

3. Here is a modified version of the violinist case: Suppose that, rather than being kidnapped at random, you were kidnapped from a concert of classical music, and that you knew in advance (a) that there was a group attempting to help musicians with damaged kidneys and (b) that there was a good chance that some of the people attending the concert would be kidnapped to be hooked up to such musicians. Is

this enough to make it the case that you have given the violinist a right to the use of your kidneys? Does it matter what the odds of being thus kidnapped are (assuming that you know them)? What if you could have greatly reduced the probability of being kidnapped for this purpose by purchasing a more expensive ticket to the concert, but you chose in fact to buy only a cheaper ticket? What if it were part of the agreement you made in purchasing the ticket that there would be a certain probability of being hooked up to a musician, and that you agreed to remain hooked up for nine months if this should happen (as a condition of getting the ticket)?

4. Suppose that a person who cannot swim has fallen into the water and is about to drown.

You are standing on shore, and there is a system available that will automatically locate the person, fasten a rope to him, and pull him to shore (without drowning or otherwise harming him in the process). But the system needs to be activated by pressing a button. Are you violating the person's right to life if you do not press the button? Are you being "morally indecent" by not doing so? Does it matter if there are other people who could press the button, and some of them are closer to it than you? Does it matter how far you have to walk to reach the button (still assuming that you can get there in time) and how much inconvenience will be involved for you? Should people in your situation be *legally* required to press the button (if no one else does it first)?

(Philippa Foot)

Philippa Foot (1920–) is a British philosopher who has made many important contributions to moral philosophy. In the following selection, she explores the question of whether euthanasia (which she defines as bringing about a person's death for the good of that person) is ever morally permissible. She concludes that it clearly is in some cases (but not in all cases), and then also considers briefly the separate but related issue of whether some forms of euthanasia should be legalized. In doing so, Foot seems to assume a moral view that strongly resembles Kant's: one that invokes duties of justice and charity (Kant's beneficence).

Euthanasia

The widely used *Shorter Oxford English Dictionary* gives three meanings for the word 'euthanasia': the first, 'a quiet and easy death'; the second, 'the means of procuring this'; and the third, 'the action of inducing a quiet and easy death'. It is a curious fact that no one of the three gives an adequate definition of the word as it is usually understood. For 'euthanasia' means much more than a quiet and easy death, or the means of procuring it, or the action of inducing it. The definition

specifies only the manner of death, and if this were all that was implied a murderer, careful to drug his victim, could claim that his act was an act of euthanasia. We find this ridiculous because we take it for granted that in euthanasia it is death itself, not just the manner of death, that must be kind to the one who dies.

. . .

Let us insist, then, that when we talk about euthanasia we are talking about a death understood as a good or happy event for the one who dies. This stipulation follows etymology, but is itself not exactly in line with current usage, which would be captured by the

From Virtues and Vices, *edited by Philippa Foot (Los Angeles: University of California Press, 1978).*

condition that the death should *not* be an evil rather than that it *should* be a good. That this is how people talk is shown by the fact that the case of Karen Ann Quinlan and others in a state of permanent coma is often discussed under the heading of 'euthanasia'.① Perhaps it is not too late to object to the use of the word 'euthanasia' in this sense. . . . For if we say that the death must be supposed to be a good to the subject we can also specify that it shall be for his sake that an act of euthanasia is performed. If we say merely that death shall not be an evil to him, we cannot stipulate that benefiting him shall be the motive where euthanasia is in question. Given the importance of the question, For whose sake are we acting? it is good to have a definition of euthanasia which brings under this heading only cases of opting for death for the sake of the one who dies. Perhaps what is most important is to say either that euthanasia is to be for the good of the subject or at least that death is to be no evil to him. . . . However, in this paper it is the first condition that will be understood, with the additional proviso that by an act of euthanasia we mean one of inducing or otherwise opting for death for the sake of the one who is to die.

A few lesser points need to be cleared up. In the first place it must be said that the word 'act' is not to be taken to exclude omission: we shall speak of an act of euthanasia when someone is deliberately allowed to die, for his own good, and not only when positive measures are taken to see that he does. The very general idea we want is that of a choice of action or inaction directed at another man's death and causally effective in the sense that, in conjunction with actual circumstances, it is a sufficient condition of death. . . . ②

A second, and definitely minor, point about the definition of an act of euthanasia concerns the question of fact versus belief. It has already been implied

> ① Karen Ann Quinlan was a young woman who suffered irreversible brain damage (apparently as a result of mixing alcohol and tranquilizers at a party), but who was kept alive by a respirator. Her parents eventually succeeded in having the respirator removed, but she surprisingly remained alive for several years before finally dying. Since she was incapable of any further experience, death was arguably neither a good nor an evil for her.

> ② Thus choosing *not* to use technology such as a respirator still counts as an act.

that one who performs an act of euthanasia thinks that death will be merciful for the subject since we have said that it is on account of this thought that the act is done. But is it enough that he acts with this thought, or must things actually be as he thinks them to be? If one man kills another, or allows him to die, thinking that he is in the last stages of a terrible disease, though in fact he could have been cured, is this an act of euthanasia or not? Nothing much seems to hang on our decision about this. The same condition has got to enter into the definition whether as an element in reality or only as an element in the agent's belief. And however we define an act of euthanasia culpability or justifiability will be the same: if a man acts through ignorance his ignorance may be culpable or it may not.③

> ③ If it is morally permissible to deliberately kill someone or allow him to die because it is for his own good, it will presumably also be morally permissible to do so because you justifiably and non-culpably believe that this is so, even if in fact it isn't. The only issue is whether the latter case should be called "euthanasia" or instead perhaps "attempted euthanasia" (since you mean to be doing something that is better for that person, even though it actually isn't).

These are relatively easy problems to solve, but one that is dauntingly difficult has been passed over in this discussion of the definition, and must now be faced. It is easy to say, as if this raised no problems, that an act of euthanasia is by definition one aiming at the *good* of the one whose death is in question, and that it is *for his sake* that his death is desired. But how is this to be explained? Presumably we are thinking of some evil already with him or to come on him if he continues to live, and death is thought of as a release from this evil. But this cannot be enough. Most people's lives contain evils such as grief or pain, but we do not therefore think that death would be a blessing to them. On the contrary, life is generally supposed to be a good even for someone who is unusually unhappy or frustrated. How is it that one can ever wish for death for the sake of the one who is to die? This difficult question is central to the discussion of euthanasia, and we shall literally not know what we are talking about if we ask whether acts of euthanasia defined as we have defined them are ever morally permissible without first understanding better the reason for saying that life is a good, and the possibility that it is not always so.

If a man should save my life he would be my benefactor. In normal circumstances this is plainly true; but does one always benefit another in saving his life? It seems certain that he does not. Suppose, for instance, that a man were being tortured to death and was given a drug that lengthened his sufferings; this would not be a benefit but the reverse. Or suppose that in a ghetto in Nazi Germany a doctor saved the life of someone threatened by disease, but that the man once cured was transported to an extermination camp; the doctor might wish for the sake of the patient that he had died of the disease. Nor would a longer stretch of life always be a benefit to the person who was given it. Comparing Hitler's camps with those of Stalin, Dmitri Panin observes that in the latter the method of extermination was made worse by agonies that could stretch out over months.

> Death from a bullet would have been bliss compared with what many millions had to endure while dying of hunger. The kind of death to which they were condemned has nothing to equal it in treachery and sadism.*

4 How bad do the prospects for a person's life have to be for it to be better for them to die sooner rather than later? Is there any way to draw a clear line or distinction that could be reasonably applied by someone other than the person in question?

These examples show that to save or prolong a man's life is not always to do him a service: it may be better for him if he dies earlier rather than later. It must therefore be agreed that while life is normally a benefit to the one who has it, this is not always so.**4**

The judgement is often fairly easy to make—that life is or is not a good to someone—but the basis for it is very hard to find. When life is said to be a benefit or a good, on what grounds is the assertion made?

The difficulty is underestimated if it is supposed that the problem arises from the fact that one who is dead has nothing, so that the good someone gets from being alive cannot be compared with the amount he would otherwise have had. For why should this particular comparison be necessary? Surely it would be enough if one could say whether or not someone whose life was prolonged had more good than evil in the extra stretch of time. Such estimates are not always possible, but frequently they are; we say, for example, 'He was very happy in those last years', or, 'He had little but unhappiness then'. If the balance of good and evil determined whether life was a good to someone we would expect to find a correlation in the judgements. In fact, of course, we find nothing of the kind. First, a man who has no doubt that existence is a good to him may have no idea about the balance of happiness and unhappiness in his life, or of any other positive and negative factors that may be suggested. So the supposed criteria are not always operating where the judgement is made. And secondly the application of the criteria gives an answer that is often wrong. Many people have more evil than good in their lives; we do not, however, conclude that we would do these people no service by rescuing them from death.

To get around this last difficulty Thomas Nagel has suggested that experience itself is a good which must be brought in to balance accounts.

> . . . life is worth living even when the bad elements of experience are plentiful, and the good ones too meager to outweigh the bad ones on their own. The additional positive weight is supplied by experience itself, rather than by any of its contents.†

This seems implausible because if experience itself is a good it must be so even when what we experience is wholly bad, as in being tortured to death. How should one decide how much to count for this experiencing; and why count anything at all?**5**

Others have tried to solve the problem by arguing that it is a man's desire for life that makes us call life a good: if he wants to live then anyone who prolongs his life does him a benefit. Yet someone may

5 Contrary to what Foot may be suggesting here, Nagel is not in fact claiming that the good constituted by experience itself (just having experiences of any sort) is great enough to outweigh wholly bad contents of experience. But she is right that it seems very hard to assign any definite value to the supposed goodness of experience itself.

*Dmitri Panin, *The Notebooks of Sologdin* (London, 1976), pp. 66–7.
†Thomas Nagel, 'Death', in James Rachels, ed., *Moral Problems* (New York, 1971), p. 362.

cling to life where we would say confidently that it would be better for him if he died, and he may admit it too. Speaking of those same conditions in which, as he said, a bullet would have been merciful, Panin writes,

> I should like to pass on my observations concerning the absence of suicides under the extremely severe conditions of our concentration camps. The more that life became desperate, the more a prisoner seemed determined to hold onto it.*

One might try to explain this by saying that hope was the ground of this wish to survive for further days and months in the camp. But there is nothing unintelligible in the idea that a man might cling to life though he knew those facts about his future which would make any charitable man wish that he might die.⑥

___

⑥ It might seem irrational to cling to life in such a situation, but is there any clear reason or argument that this is so?

___

The problem remains, and it is hard to know where to look for a solution. Is there a conceptual connexion between *life* and *good?* Because life is not always a good we are apt to reject this idea, and to think that it must be a contingent fact that life is usually a good, as it is a contingent matter that legacies are usually a benefit, if they are. Yet it seems not to be a contingent matter that to save someone's life is ordinarily to benefit him. The problem is to find where the conceptual connexion lies.⑦

___

⑦ Foot is suggesting that it is a necessary rather than contingent truth that life is a good thing except under very extreme circumstances. (She is assuming that necessary truths are always matters of "conceptual connection," which is a version of the moderate empiricist view discussed in the a priori knowledge section of Chapter 3.)

___

It may be good tactics to forget for a time that it is euthanasia we are discussing and to see how *life* and *good* are connected in the case of living beings other than men. Even plants have things done to them that are harmful or beneficial, and what does them good must be related in some way to their living and dying. Let us therefore consider plants and animals, and then come back to human beings. At least we shall get away from the temptation to think that the connexion between life and benefit must everywhere be a matter of happiness and unhappiness or of pleasure and pain; the idea being absurd in the case of animals and impossible even to formulate for plants.

In case anyone thinks that the concept of the beneficial applies only in a secondary or analogical way to plants, he should be reminded that we speak quite straightforwardly in saying, for instance, that a certain amount of sunlight is beneficial to most plants. What is in question here is the habitat in which plants of particular species flourish, but we can also talk, in a slightly different way, of what does them good, where there is some suggestion of improvement or remedy. What has the beneficial to do with sustaining life? It is tempting to answer, 'everything', thinking that a healthy condition just is the one apt to secure survival. In fact, however, what is beneficial to a plant may have to do with reproduction rather than survival of the individual member of the species. Nevertheless there is a plain connexion between the beneficial and the life-sustaining even for the individual plant; if something makes it better able to survive in conditions normal for that species it is ipso facto good for it. We need go no further, and could go no further, in explaining why a certain environment or treatment is good for a plant than to show how it helps this plant to survive.

This connexion between the life-sustaining and the beneficial is reasonably unproblematic, and there is nothing fanciful or zoomorphic in speaking of benefiting or doing good to plants. A connexion with its survival can make something beneficial to a plant. But this is not, of course, to say that we count life as a good to a plant. We may save its life by giving it what is beneficial; we do not benefit it by saving its life.

A more ramified concept of benefit is used in speaking of animal life. New things can be said, such as that an animal is better or worse off for something that happened, or that it was a good or bad thing for it that it did happen. And new things count as benefit. In the first place, there is comfort, which often is, but need not be, related to health. . . . And secondly an animal can be benefited by having its life saved. 'Could you do anything for it?' can be answered by, 'Yes, I managed to save its life.' Sometimes we may

___

understand this, just as we would for a plant, to mean that we had checked some disease. But we can also do something for an animal by scaring away its predator. If we do this, it is a good thing for the animal that we did, unless of course it immediately meets a more unpleasant end by some other means. Similarly, on the bad side, an animal may be worse off for our intervention, and this not because it pines or suffers but simply because it gets killed.

The problem that vexes us when we think about euthanasia comes on the scene at this point. For if we can do something for an animal—can benefit it—by relieving its suffering but also by saving its life, where does the greater benefit come when only death will end pain? It seemed that life was a good in its own right; yet pain seemed to be an evil with equal status and could therefore make life not a good after all. Is it only life without pain that is a good when animals are concerned? This does not seem a crazy suggestion when we are thinking of animals, since unlike human beings they do not have suffering as part of their normal life.⁸ But it is perhaps the idea of ordinary life that matters here. We would not say that we had done anything for an animal if we had merely kept it alive, either in an unconscious state or in a condition where, though conscious, it was unable to operate in an ordinary way; and the fact is that animals in severe and continuous pain simply do not operate normally. So we do not, on the whole, have the option of doing the animal good by saving its life though the life would be a life of pain.⁹ No doubt there are borderline cases, but that is no problem. We are not trying to make new judgements possible, but rather to find the principle of the ones we do make.

When we reach human life the problems seem even more troublesome. For now we must take quite new things into account, such as the subject's own view of his life. It is arguable that this places extra constraints on the solution: might it not be counted as a necessary condition of life's being a good to a man that he should see it as such? Is there not some difficulty about the idea that a benefit might be done to him by the saving or prolonging of his life even though he himself wished for death? Of course he might have a quite mistaken view of his own prospects, but let us ignore this and think only of cases where it is life as he knows it that is in question. Can we think that the prolonging of this life would be a benefit to him even though he would rather have it end than continue? It seems that this cannot be ruled out. That there is no simple incompatibility between life as a good and the wish for death is shown by the possibility that a man should wish himself dead, not for his own sake, but for the sake of someone else. And if we try to amend the thesis to say that life cannot be a good to one who wishes *for his own sake* that he should die, we find the crucial concept slipping through our fingers. As Bishop Butler pointed out long ago not all ends are either benevolent or self-interested. Does a man wish for death for his own sake in the relevant sense if, for instance, he wishes to revenge himself on another by his death? Or what if he is proud and refuses to stomach dependence or incapacity even though there are many good things left in life for him? The truth seems to be that the wish for death is sometimes compatible with life's being a good and sometimes not, which is possible because the description 'wishing for death' is one covering diverse states of mind from that of the determined suicide, pathologically depressed, to that of one who is surprised to find that the thought of a fatal accident is viewed with relief. On the one hand, a man may see his life as a burden but go about his business in a more or less ordinary way; on the other hand, the wish for death may take the form of a rejection of everything that is in life, as it does in severe depression. It seems reasonable to say that life is not a good to one permanently in the latter state, and we must return to this topic later on.

When are we to say that life is a good or a benefit to a man? The dilemma that faces us is this. If we say that life as such is a good we find ourselves refuted by the examples given at the beginning of this discussion. We therefore incline to think that it is as bringing good things that life is a good, where it is a good. But

---

⑧ Foot here means emotional rather than physical suffering. It is imaginable that a person (or an animal) might live his whole life without experiencing physical pain intense enough to be called suffering. But it is just about unimaginable that a normal person could fail to experience emotional suffering at the death of loved ones, the failure of cherished projects, etc.—which is why suffering is a part of a normal human life.

⑨ Pretty obviously this depends on the degree of pain involved.

if life is a good only because it is the condition of good things why is it not equally an evil when it brings bad things? And how can it be a good even when it brings more evil than good?

It should be noted that the problem has here been formulated in terms of the balance of good and evil, not that of happiness and unhappiness, and that it is not to be solved by the denial (which may be reasonable enough) that unhappiness is the only evil or happiness the only good. In this paper no view has been expressed about the nature of goods other than life itself. The point is that on any view of the goods and evils that life can contain, it seems that a life with more evil than good could still itself be a good. [10]

[10] Foot is not saying here merely that such a life could be (perhaps irrationally) preferred to death by someone; she is saying that such a preference might in fact be correct.

It may be useful to review the judgements with which our theory must square. Do we think that life can be a good to one who suffers a lot of pain? Clearly we do. What about severely handicapped people; can life be a good to them? Clearly it can be, for even if someone is almost completely paralysed, perhaps living in an iron lung, perhaps able to move things only by means of a tube held between his lips, we do not rule him out of order if he says that some benefactor saved his life. Nor is it different with mental handicap. There are many fairly severely handicapped people—such as those with Down's Syndrome (Mongolism)—for whom a simple affectionate life is possible. What about senility? Does this break the normal connexion between life and good? Here we must surely distinguish between forms of senility. Some forms leave a life which we count someone as better off having than not having, so that a doctor who prolonged it would benefit the person concerned. With some kinds of senility this is however no longer true. There are some in geriatric wards who are barely conscious, though they can move a little and swallow food put into their mouths. To prolong such a state, whether in the old or in the very severely mentally handicapped is not to do them a service or confer a benefit. But of course it need not be the reverse: only if there is suffering would one wish for the sake of the patient that he should die. [11]

It seems, therefore, that merely being alive even without suffering is not a good, and that we must

make a distinction similar to that which we made when animals were our topic. But how is the line to be drawn in the case of men? What is to count as ordinary human life in the relevant sense? If it were only the very senile or very ill who were said not to have this life it might seem right to describe it in terms of *operation*. But it will be hard to find the sense in which the men described by Panin were not operating, given that they dragged themselves out to the forest to work. What is it about the life that the prisoners were living that makes us put it on the other side of the dividing line from that of most of the physically or mentally handicapped and of some severely ill or suffering patients? It is not that they were in captivity, for life in captivity can certainly be a good. Nor is it merely the unusual nature of their life. In some ways the prisoners were living more as other men do than the patient in the iron lung.

The idea we need seems to be that of life which is ordinary human life in the following respect—that it contains a minimum of basic human goods. What is ordinary in human life—even in very hard lives—is that a man is not driven to work far beyond his capacity; that he has the support of a family or community; that he can more or less satisfy his hunger; that he has hopes for the future; that he can lie down to rest at night. [12] Such things were denied to the men in the Vyatlag camps described by Panin; not even rest at night was allowed them when they were tormented by bed-bugs, by noise and stench, and by routines such as body-searches and bath-parades—arranged for the night time so that work norms would not be reduced. Disease too can so take over a man's life that the normal human goods disappear. When a patient is so overwhelmed by pain or nausea that he cannot eat with pleasure, if he can eat at all, and is out of the reach of even the most loving voice, he no longer has

[11] Sometimes it is said that death in such a situation is better for the person because it preserves their "dignity." (This was said even about Karen Ann Quinlan.) How plausible is this sort of suggestion?

[12] Think carefully about this list of ingredients of an "ordinary human life." Are they all equally important? Since they all seem to be to some extent matters of degree, what degree of each is required? Could having more of one compensate to some extent for a deficiency in another?

ordinary human life in the sense in which the words are used here. And we may now pick up a thread from an earlier part of the discussion by remarking that crippling depression can destroy the enjoyment of ordinary goods as effectively as external circumstances can remove them.

The suggested solution to the problem is, then, that there is a certain conceptual connexion between *life* and *good* in the case of human beings as in that of animals and even plants. Here, as there, however, it is not the mere state of being alive that can determine, or itself count as, a good, but rather life coming up to some standard of normality. It was argued that it is as part of ordinary life that the elements of good that a man may have are relevant to the question of whether saving his life counts as benefiting him. Ordinary human lives, even very hard lives, contain a minimum of basic goods, but when these are absent the idea of life is no longer linked to that of good. And since it is in this way that the elements of good contained in a man's life are relevant to the question of whether he is benefited if his life is preserved, there is no reason why it should be the balance of good and evil that counts. ⑬

13 So the claim is that a life that contains enough of these basic ingredients to constitute an ordinary human life is good for the person who lives it, even if the overall balance in his life between good and evil is in favor of evil, perhaps even strongly so.

It should be added that evils are relevant in one way when, as in the examples discussed above, they destroy the possibility of ordinary goods, but in a different way when they invade a life from which the goods are already absent for a different reason. So, for instance, the connexion between *life* and *good* may be broken because consciousness has sunk to a very low level, as in extreme senility or severe brain damage. In itself this kind of life seems to be neither good nor evil, but if suffering sets in one would hope for a speedy end.

This, admittedly inadequate, discussion of the sense in which life is normally a good, and of the reasons why it may not be so in some particular case, completes the account of what euthanasia is here taken to be. An act of euthanasia, whether literally act or rather omission, is attributed to an agent who opts for the death of another because in his case life seems to be an evil rather than a good. ⑭ The question now to be asked is whether acts of euthanasia are ever justifiable. But there are two topics here rather than one. For it is one thing to say that some acts of euthanasia considered only in themselves and their results are morally unobjectionable, and another to say that it would be all right to legalise them. Perhaps the practice of euthanasia would allow too many abuses, and perhaps there would be too many mistakes. Moreover the practice might have very important and highly undesirable side effects, because it is unlikely that we could change our principles about the treatment of the old and the ill without changing fundamental emotional attitudes and social relations. ⑮ The topics must, therefore, be treated separately. In the next part of the discussion, nothing will be said about the social consequences and possible abuses of the practice of euthanasia, but only about acts of euthanasia considered in themselves.

14 Thus Foot's view is apparently that any person whose life contains enough of the basic ingredients to count as an ordinary human life is not better off dead in a way that would make killing him or letting him die an act of euthanasia—no matter what other sorts and degrees of evil his life may contain. (See Discussion Question 1.)

15 The point here is that law is a practical and relatively blunt instrument, one that may have repercussions (some of them unexpected) that go well beyond the specific issue in question. This is one reason why not every moral truth should automatically be enshrined in law.

What we want to know is whether acts of euthanasia, defined as we have defined them, are ever morally permissible. To be more accurate, we want to know whether it is ever sufficient justification of the choice of death for another that death can be counted a benefit rather than harm, and that this is why the choice is made.

It will be impossible to get a clear view of the area to which this topic belongs without first marking the distinct grounds on which objection may lie when one man opts for the death of another. There are two different virtues whose requirements are, in general, contrary to such actions. An unjustified act of killing, or allowing to die, is contrary to justice or to charity, or to both virtues, and the moral failings are distinct. Justice has to do with what men *owe* each other in the way of noninterference and positive service. When used in this wide sense, which has its history in the doctrine of the cardinal virtues, justice is not especially connected with, for instance, law courts but with the whole area of rights, and duties corresponding to rights. Thus murder is one form of injustice, dishonesty another, and wrongful failure to keep contracts a third; chicanery in a law court or defrauding someone of his inheritance are simply other cases of injustice. Justice as such is not directly linked to the good of another, and may require that something be rendered to him even where it will do him harm, as Hume pointed out when he remarked that a debt must be paid even to a profligate debauchee who 'would rather receive harm than benefit from large possessions'.* Charity, on the other hand, is the virtue which attaches us to the good of others. An act of charity is in question only where something is not demanded by justice, but a lack of charity and of justice can be shown where a man is denied something which he both needs and has a right to;

⌐16⌐ Charity here corresponds to Kant's duty of beneficence (and justice to his more stringent duty of justice).

both charity and justice demand that widows and orphans are not defrauded, and the man who cheats them is neither charitable nor just. ⌐16⌐

It is easy to see that the two grounds of objection to inducing death are distinct. A murder is an act of injustice. A culpable failure to come to the aid of someone whose life is threatened is normally contrary, not to justice, but to charity. But where one man is under contract, explicit or implicit, to come to the aid of another injustice too will be shown. Thus

⌐17⌐ Thus one may unjustly kill someone but also unjustly allow him to die. (Compare Thomson's discussion of murder as unjust killing in the preceding selection.)

injustice may be involved either in an act or an omission, and the same is true of a lack of charity; charity may demand that someone be aided, but also that an unkind word not be spoken. ⌐17⌐

The distinction between charity and justice will turn out to be of first importance when voluntary and

nonvoluntary euthanasia are distinguished later on. This is because of the connexion between justice and rights, and something should now be said about this. I believe it is true to say that wherever a man acts unjustly he has infringed a right, since justice has to do with whatever a man is owed, and whatever he is owed is his as a matter of right. Something should therefore be said about the different kinds of rights. The distinction commonly made is between having a right in the sense of having a liberty, and having a 'claim-right' or 'right of recipience'. The best way to understand such a distinction seems to be as follows. To say that a man has a right in the sense of liberty is to say that no one can demand that he not do the thing which he has the right to do. The fact that he has a right to do it consists in the fact that a certain kind of objection does not lie against his doing it. Thus a man has a right in this sense to walk down a public street or park his car in a public parking space. It does not follow that no one else may prevent him from doing so. If for some reason I want a certain man not to park in a certain place I may lawfully park there myself or get my friends to do so, thus preventing him from doing what he has a right (in the sense of a liberty) to do. ⌐18⌐

It is different, however, with a claim-right. This is the kind of right which I have in addition to a liberty when, for example, I

⌐18⌐ I can prevent him from parking there, but I cannot demand that he not park there, since he has a liberty to do so (as also do I).

have a private parking space; now others have duties in the way of noninterference, as in this case, or of service, as in the case where my claim-right is to goods or services promised to me. Sometimes one of these rights gives other people the duty of securing to me that to which I have a right, but at other times their duty is merely to refrain from interference. If a fall of snow blocks my private parking space there is normally no obligation for anyone else to clear it away. Claim rights generate duties; sometimes these duties are duties of noninterference; sometimes they are duties of service. If your right gives me the duty not to interfere with you I have 'no right' to do it; similarly, if your right gives me the duty to provide something

---

*David Hume, *Treatise,* book III, part II, section 1.

for you I have 'no right' to refuse to do it. What *I* lack is the right which is a liberty: I am not 'at liberty' to interfere with you or to refuse the service. ⑲

⑲ "Claim-rights" are the sort of rights discussed in the selection by Ozar.

Where in this picture does the right to life belong? No doubt people have the right to live in the sense of a liberty, but what is important is the cluster of claim-rights brought together under the title of the right to life. The chief of these is, of course, the right to be free from interferences that threaten life. If other people aim their guns at us or try to pour poison into our drink we can, to put it mildly, demand that they desist. And then there are the services we can claim from doctors, health officers, bodyguards, and firemen; the rights that depend on contract or public arrangement. Perhaps there is no particular point in saying that the duties these people owe us belong to the right to life; we might as well say that all the services owed to anyone by tailors, dressmakers, and couturiers belong to a right called the right to be elegant. But contracts such as those understood in the patient–doctor relationship come in in an important way when we are discussing the rights and wrongs of euthanasia, and are therefore mentioned here.

Do people have the right to what they need in order to survive, apart from the right conferred by special contracts into which other people have entered for the supplying of these necessities? Do people in the underdeveloped countries in which starvation is rife have the right to the food they so evidently lack? ⑳ Joel Feinberg, discussing this question, suggests that they should be said to have 'a claim', distinguishing this from a 'valid claim', which gives a claim-right.

⑳ Such rights would be positive rather than negative rights. (See the discussion of this distinction by Ozar.)

> The manifesto writers on the other side who seem to identify needs, or at least basic needs, with what they call 'human rights', are more properly described, I think, as urging upon the world community the moral principle that *all* human needs ought to be recognized as *claims* (in the customary *prima facie* sense) worthy of sympathy and serious consideration right now, even though, in many cases, they cannot yet plausibly be treated as *valid* claims, that is, as grounds of any other people's duties. This way of talking avoids the anomaly of ascribing to all human beings now, even those in pre-industrial societies, such 'economic and social rights' as 'periodic holidays with pay'.*

This seems reasonable, though we notice that there are some actual rights to service which are not based on anything like a contract, as for instance the right that children have to support from their parents and parents to support from their children in old age, though both sets of rights are to some extent dependent on existing social arrangements. ㉑

㉑ The rights mentioned in the last paragraph would be positive rights based on social conventions. (Does the latter of them in particular clearly exist in all cases, no matter what the specific relations and agreements between parents and children may be?) Feinberg, in the quoted passage, *may* only be suggesting (like Ozar) that a right cannot exist unless it is possible to fulfill it. But is it obvious that the rights he mentions do exist once it is possible to fulfill them, and if so, why?

Let us now ask how the right to life affects the morality of acts of euthanasia. Are such acts sometimes or always ruled out by the right to life? This is certainly a possibility; for although an act of euthanasia is, by our definition, a matter of opting for death for the good of the one who is to die, there is, as we noted earlier, no simple connexion between that to which a man has a right and that which is for his good. It is true that men have the right only to the kind of thing that is, in general, a good: we do not think that people have the right to garbage or polluted air. Nevertheless, a man may have the right to something which he himself would be better off without; where rights exist it is a man's will that counts not his or anyone else's estimate of benefit or harm. ㉒ So the duties complementary to the right to life—the general duty of noninter-

㉒ A right may be waived (as discussed in Ozar), and it may even be reasonable in some cases to assume that it would be waived (as in the case of garbage). But it is still up to the person who has the right whether or not to do this.

---

*Feinberg, 'Human rights', Gorovitz, *Moral Problems in Medicine*, p. 465.

ference and the duty of service incurred by certain persons—are not affected by the quality of a man's life or by his prospects. Even if it is true that he would be, as we say, 'better off dead', so long as he wants to live this does not justify us in killing him and may not justify us in deliberately allowing him to die. All of us have the duty of noninterference, and some of us may have the duty to sustain his life. Suppose, for example, that a retreating army has to leave behind wounded or exhausted soldiers in the wastes of an arid or snow-bound land where the only prospect is death by starvation or at the hands of an enemy notoriously cruel. It has often been the practice to accord a merciful bullet to men in such desperate straits. But suppose one of them demands that he should be left alive? It seems clear that his comrades have no right to kill him, though it is a quite different question as to whether they should give him a life-prolonging drug. The right to life can sometimes give a duty of positive service, but does not do so here. What it does give is the right to be left alone.

Interestingly enough we have arrived by way of a consideration of the right to life at the distinction normally labelled 'active' versus 'passive' euthanasia, and often thought to be irrelevant to the moral issue.* Once it is seen that the right to life is a distinct ground of objection to certain acts of euthanasia, and that this right creates a duty of noninterference more widespread than the duties of care there can be no doubt about the relevance of the distinction between passive and active euthanasia. Where everyone may have the duty to leave someone alone, it may be that no one has the duty to maintain his life, or that only some people do.

Where then do the boundaries of the 'active' and 'passive' lie? In some ways the words are themselves misleading, because they suggest the difference between act and omission which is not quite what we want. Certainly the act of shooting someone is the kind of thing we were talking about under the heading of 'interference', and omitting to give him a drug a case of refusing care. But the act of turning off a respirator should surely be thought of as no different from the decision not to start it; if doctors had decided

that a patient should be allowed to die, either course of action might follow, and both should be counted as passive rather than active euthanasia if euthanasia were in question.[23] The point seems to be that interference in a course of treatment is not the same as other interference in a man's life, and particularly if the same body of people are responsible for the treatment and for its discontinuance. In such a case we could speak of the disconnecting of the apparatus as killing the man, or of the hospital as allowing him to die. By and large, it is the act of killing that is ruled out under the heading of noninterference, but not in every case.

Doctors commonly recognise this distinction, and the grounds on which some philosophers have denied it seem untenable. James Rachels, for instance, believes that if the difference between active and passive is relevant anywhere, it should be relevant everywhere, and he has pointed to an example in which it seems to make no difference which is done. If someone saw a child drowning in a bath it would seem just as bad to let it drown as to push its head under water.† If 'it makes no difference' means that one act would be as iniquitous as the other this is true. It is not that killing is *worse* than allowing to die, but that the two are contrary to distinct virtues, which gives the possibility that in some circumstances one is impermissible and the other permissible. In the circumstances invented by Rachels, both are wicked: it is contrary to justice to push the child's head under the water— something one has no right to do. To leave it to drown is not contrary to justice, but is a particularly glaring example of lack of charity. Here it makes no practical difference because the requirements of justice and charity coincide; but in the case of the retreating army

[23] Active euthanasia is where one deliberately acts to end someone's life for his own good, while passive euthanasia is where one brings about his death for the same reason by not doing something (or not continuing to do something, as in the case of a respirator) to prevent it. The distinction is morally significant because the right to life involves a general duty of noninterference but not a general duty to render aid.

---

*See, for example, James Rachels, 'Active and Passive Euthanasia', *New England Journal of Medicine* 292, no. 2 (9 Jan. 1975): 78–80.
†Ibid.

they did not: charity would have required that the wounded soldier be killed had not justice required that he be left alive.*⟨24⟩ In such a case it makes all the difference whether a man opts for the death of another in a positive action, or whether he allows him to die. An analogy with the right to property will make the point clear. If a man owns something he has the right to it even when its possession does him harm,

⟨24⟩ So the point is that in Rachels's case, the two acts in question are equally wrong, but wrong for different reasons—leaving open the possibility that those reasons may not apply equally to other cases (such as the wounded soldier case). (See Discussion Question 2 for a fuller discussion of Rachels's example.)

and normally we have no right to take it from him. But if one day it should blow away, maybe nothing requires us to get it back for him; we could not deprive him of it, but we may allow it to go. This is not to deny that it will often be an unfriendly act or one based on an arrogant judgement when we refuse to do what he wants. Nevertheless, we would be within our rights, and it might be that no moral objection of any kind would lie against our refusal.

It is important to emphasise that a man's rights may stand between us and the action we would dearly like to take for his sake. They may, of course, also prevent action which we would like to take for the sake of others, as when it might be tempting to kill one man to save several. But it is interesting that the limits of allowable interference, however uncertain, seem stricter in the first case than the second. Perhaps there are no cases in which it would be all right to kill a man against his will *for his own sake* unless they could equally well be described as cases of allowing him to die, as in the example of turning off the respirator. However, there are circumstances, even if these are very rare, in which one man's life would justifiably be sacrificed to save others, and 'killing' would be the only description of what was being done. For instance, a vehicle which had gone out of control might be steered from a path on which it would kill more than one man to a path on which it would kill one.⟨25⟩ But it would not be permissible to steer a vehicle towards someone in order to kill him, against his will, for his own good. An analogy with property rights again

⟨25⟩ This is a famous and widely discussed case. See Discussion Question 3 for a fuller consideration of it.

illustrates the point. One may not destroy a man's property against his will on the grounds that he would be better off without it; there are however circumstances in which it could be destroyed for the sake of others. If his house is liable to fall and kill him that is his affair; it might, however, without injustice be destroyed to stop the spread of a fire.

We see then that the distinction between active and passive, important as it is elsewhere, has a special importance in the area of euthanasia. . . .

So far we have said very little about the right to service as opposed to the right to noninterference, though it was agreed that both might be brought under the heading of 'the right to life'. What about the duty to preserve life that may belong to special classes of persons such as bodyguards, firemen, or doctors? Unlike the general public they are not within their rights if they merely refrain from interfering and do not try to sustain life. The subject's claim-rights are two-fold as far as they are concerned and passive as well as active euthanasia may be ruled out here if it is against his will. This is not to say that he has the right to any and every service needed to save or prolong his life; the rights of other people set limits to what may be demanded, both because they have the right not to be interfered with and because they may have a competing right to services. Furthermore one must enquire just what the contract or implicit agreement amounts to in each case. Firemen and bodyguards presumably have a duty which is simply to preserve life, within the limits of justice to others and of reasonableness to themselves. With doctors it may however be different, since their duty relates not only to preserving life but also to the relief of suffering. It is not clear what a doctor's duties are to his patient if life can be prolonged only at the cost of suffering or suffering relieved only by measures that shorten life. George Fletcher has argued

*It is not, however, that justice and charity conflict. A man does not lack charity because he refrains from an act of injustice which would have been for someone's good.

that what the doctor is under contract to do depends on what is generally done, because this is what a patient will reasonably expect.* This seems right. If procedures are part of normal medical practice then it seems that the patient can demand them however much it may be against his interest to do so. Once again it is not a matter of what is 'most humane'.

That the patient's right to life may set limits to permissible acts of euthanasia seems undeniable. If he does not want to die no one has the right to practise active euthanasia on him, and passive euthanasia may also be ruled out where he has a right to the services of doctors or others. 26

> 26 Here is the first definite conclusion in the article: active euthanasia that is *involuntary* (which the person in question definitely wants not to happen) is morally unacceptable, as is passive euthanasia in the specific case where the person has on some basis a right to the assistance needed to preserve life (but perhaps not in other cases—an issue still to be considered).

Perhaps few will deny what has so far been said about the impermissibility of acts of euthanasia, simply because we have so far spoken about the case of one who positively wants to live, and about his rights; whereas those who advocate euthanasia are usually thinking either about those who wish to die or about those whose wishes cannot be ascertained either because they cannot properly be said to have wishes or because, for one reason or another, we are unable to form a reliable estimate of what they are. The question that must now be asked is whether the latter type of case, where euthanasia though not *in*voluntary would again be *non*voluntary, is different from the one discussed so far. 27 Would we have the right to kill someone for his own good so

> 27 As Foot uses the term, euthanasia is *nonvoluntary* both in the case where it is *involuntary* (because the person has expressed a positive preference not to die) and in the case where there is no known preference either way. The clearest example of this last situation would be the case of a person in a coma (not necessarily an irreversible one).

long as we had no idea that he positively wished to live? And what about the life-prolonging duties of doctors in the same circumstances? This is a very difficult problem. On the one hand, it seems ridiculous to suppose that a man's right to life is something which generates duties only where he has signalled that he wants to live; as a borrower does indeed have a duty to return something lent on indefinite loan only if the lender indicates that he wants it back. On the other hand, it might be argued that there is something illogical about the idea that a right has been infringed if someone incapable of saying whether he wants it or not is deprived of something that is doing him harm rather than good. Yet on the analogy of property we would say that a right has been infringed. Only if someone had earlier told us that in such circumstances he would not want to keep the thing could we think that his right had been waived. Perhaps if we could make confident judgements about what anyone in such circumstances would wish, or what he would have wished beforehand had he considered the matter, we could agree to consider the right to life as 'dormant', needing to be asserted if the normal duties were to remain. But as things are we cannot make any such assumption; we simply do not know what most people would want, or would have wanted, us to do unless they tell us. 28 This is certainly the case so far as active measures to end life are concerned. Possibly it is different, or will become different, in the matter of being kept

> 28 Could it ever be reasonable to simply assume that a person, if he could express a preference, would want to die? And even if this were somehow reasonable, would it be the same as his actually having expressed such a preference?

alive, so general is the feeling against using sophisticated procedures on moribund patients, and so much is this dreaded by people who are old or terminally ill. Once again the distinction between active and passive euthanasia has come on the scene, but this time because most people's attitudes to the two are so different. It is just possible that we might presume, in the absence of specific evidence, that someone would not

---

*George Fletcher, 'Legal Aspects of the Decision not to Prolong Life', *Journal of the American Medical Association* 203, no. 1 (1 Jan. 1968): 119–22.

wish, beyond a certain point to be kept alive; it is certainly not possible to assume that he would wish to be killed. [29]

[29] Foot suggests that people in general find not being kept alive less objectionable than being killed, making it perhaps easier to assume that they would wish for passive euthanasia. But is even this assumption ever clearly enough right to justify a person who would otherwise have a duty to prolong life acting on it? (See Discussion Question 4.)

In the last paragraph we have begun to broach the topic of voluntary euthanasia, and this we must now discuss. What is to be said about the case in which there is no doubt about someone's wish to die? Either he has told us beforehand that he would wish it in circumstances such as he is now in, and has shown no sign of a change of mind, or else he tells us now, being in possession of his faculties and of a steady mind. We should surely say that the objections previously urged against acts of euthanasia, which it must be remembered were all on the ground of rights, had disappeared. It does not seem that one would infringe someone's right to life in killing him with his permission and in fact at his request. Why should someone not be able to waive his right to life, or rather, as would be more likely to happen, to cancel some of the duties of noninterference that this right entails? (He is more likely to say that he should be killed by this man at this time in this manner, than to say that anyone may kill him at any time and in any way.) Similarly someone may give permission for the destruction of his property, and request it. The important thing is that he gives a critical permission, and it seems that this is enough to cancel the duty normally associated with the right. If someone gives you permission to destroy his property it can no longer be said that you have no right to do so, and I do not see why it should not be the same with taking a man's life. An objection might be made on the ground that only God has the right to take life, but in this paper religious as opposed to moral arguments are being left aside. Religion apart, there seems to be no case to be made out for an infringement of rights if a man who wishes to die is allowed to die or even killed. But of course it does not follow that there is no moral objection to it. Even with property, which is after all a relatively small matter, one might be wrong to destroy what one had the right to destroy. For, apart from its value to other people, it

might be valuable to the man who wanted it destroyed, and charity might require us to hold our hand where justice did not. [30]

Let us review the conclusion of this part of the argument, which has been about nonvoluntary euthanasia and the right to life. It has been argued that from this side come stringent restrictions on the acts of euthanasia that could be morally permissible. Active nonvoluntary euthanasia is ruled out by that part of the right to life which creates the duty of noninterference though passive nonvoluntary euthanasia is not necessarily ruled out, except where the right to life-preserving action has been created by some special condition such as a contract between a man and his doctor. Voluntary euthanasia is another matter: as the preceding paragraph suggested, no right is infringed if a man is allowed to die or even killed at his own request.

Turning now to the other objection that normally holds against inducing the death of another, that it is against charity, or benevolence, we must tell a very different story. Charity is the virtue that gives attachment to the good of others, and because life is normally a good, charity normally demands that it should be saved or prolonged. But as we so defined an act of euthanasia that it seeks a man's death for his own sake—for his good—charity will normally speak in favour of it. This is not, of course, to say that charity can require an act of euthanasia which justice forbids, but if an act of euthanasia is not contrary to justice—that is, it does not infringe rights—charity will rather be in its favour than against. [31]

[30] Suppose that a person whose life is not so bad as to no longer be a good for him nonetheless waives his right to life or even asks someone to kill him (perhaps in a moment of depression). According to Foot, it is still *uncharitable,* and so morally wrong, to kill him. (Is this enough to make it *murder*—as it seems intuitively to be?)

[31] In a case of euthanasia, by definition, the person's life is not a good for him, making charity no longer an objection. Thus if the person genuinely wants to die, there seems to be no objection to euthanasia—active or passive—from the standpoint of charity. Indeed, charity may require it.

Once more the distinction between nonvoluntary and voluntary euthanasia must be considered. Could it ever be compatible with charity to seek a man's death although he wanted to live, or at least had not let us know that he wanted to die? I have argued that in such circumstances active euthanasia would infringe his right to life, but passive euthanasia would not do so, unless he had some special right to life-preserving service from the one who allowed him to die. What would charity dictate? Obviously when a man wants to live there is a presumption that he will be benefited if his life is prolonged, and if it is so the question of euthanasia does not arise. But it is, on the other hand, possible that he wants to live where it would be better for him to die: perhaps he does not realise the desperate situation he is in, or perhaps he is afraid of dying. So, in spite of a very proper resistance to refusing to go along with the man's own wishes in the matter of life and death, someone might justifiably refuse to prolong the life even of someone who asked him to prolong it, as in the case of refusing to give the wounded soldier a drug that would keep him alive to meet a terrible end. And it is even more obvious that charity does not always dictate that life should be prolonged where a man's own wishes, hypothetical or actual, are not known. ⟨32⟩

⟨32⟩ So passive involuntary euthanasia may be morally permissible where the person has no special right to the aid needed to keep him alive—and even more clearly in the case where no preference either way has been expressed.

So much for the relation of charity to nonvoluntary passive euthanasia, which was not, like nonvoluntary active euthanasia, ruled out by the right to life. Let us now ask what charity has to say about voluntary euthanasia both active and passive. It was suggested in the discussion of justice that if of sound mind and steady desire a man might give others the *right* to allow him to die or even to kill him, where otherwise this would be ruled out. But it was pointed out that this would not settle the question of whether the act was morally permissible, and it is this that we must now consider. Could not charity speak against what justice allowed? Indeed it might do so. For while the fact that a man wants to die suggests that his life is wretched, and while his rejection of life may itself tend to take the good out of things he might have enjoyed, nevertheless his wish to die might here be opposed for his own sake just as it might be if suicide were in question. Perhaps there is hope that his mental condition will improve. Perhaps he is mistaken in thinking his disease is incurable. Perhaps he wants to die for the

sake of someone else on whom he feels he is a burden, and we are not ready to accept this sacrifice whether for ourselves or others. In such cases, and there will surely be many of them, it could not be for his own sake that we kill him or allow him to die, and therefore euthanasia as defined in this paper would not be in question. But this is not to deny that there could be acts of voluntary euthanasia both passive and active against which neither justice nor charity would speak.

We have now considered the morality of euthanasia both voluntary and nonvoluntary, and active and passive. The conclusion has been that nonvoluntary active euthanasia (roughly, killing a man against his will or without his consent) is never justified; that is to say, that a man's being killed for his own good never justifies the act unless he himself has consented to it. A man's rights are infringed by such an action, and it is therefore contrary to justice. However, all the other combinations, nonvoluntary passive euthanasia, voluntary active euthanasia, and voluntary passive euthanasia are sometimes compatible with both justice and charity. But the strong condition carried in the definition of euthanasia adopted in this paper must not be forgotten; an act of euthanasia as here understood is one whose purpose is to benefit the one who dies. ⟨33⟩

⟨33⟩ Think carefully about all of these results, remembering that the nonvoluntary category includes both the case where the person prefers not to die and the case where no preference either way has been expressed.

In the light of this discussion let us look at our present practices. Are they good or are they bad? And what changes might be made, thinking now not only of the morality of particular acts of euthanasia but also of the indirect effects of instituting different practices, of the abuses to which they might be subject and of the changes that might come about if euthanasia became a recognised part of the social scene?

The first thing to notice is that it is wrong to ask whether we should introduce the practice of euthanasia as if it were not something we already had. In fact we do have it. For instance it is common, where the medical prognosis is very bad, for doctors to recommend against measures to prolong life, and particularly where a process of degeneration producing one medical emergency after another has already set in. If these doctors are not certainly within their legal rights this is something that is apt to come as a surprise to them as to the general public. It is also obvious that euthanasia is often practised where old people are concerned. If someone very old and soon to die is attacked by a disease that makes his life wretched, doctors do not always come in with life-prolonging drugs. Perhaps poor patients are more fortunate in this respect than rich patients, being more often left to die in peace; but it is in any case a well recognised piece of medical practice, and a form of euthanasia.[34]

> [34] All these cases are cases of passive, not active, euthanasia. They are also cases where it is not clearly involuntary, though it may be nonvoluntary. It is also important to note that they are usually not very clearly identified as cases of euthanasia (and might face more legal obstacles if they were).

. . .

What we must consider, even if only briefly, is the possibility that euthanasia, genuine euthanasia, and not contrary to the requirements of justice or charity, should be legalised over a wider area. Here we are up against the really serious problem of abuse. Many people want, and want very badly, to be rid of their elderly relatives and even of their ailing husbands or wives. Would any safeguards ever be able to stop them describing as euthanasia what was really for their own benefit? And would it be possible to prevent the occurrence of acts which were genuinely acts of euthanasia but morally impermissible because infringing the rights of a patient who wished to live or whose wishes were unknown?

Perhaps the furthest we should go is to encourage patients to make their own contracts with a doctor by making it known whether they wish him to prolong their lives in case of painful terminal illness or of incapacity. A document such as the Living Will seems eminently sensible, and should surely be allowed to give a doctor following the previously expressed wishes of the patient immunity from legal proceedings by relatives.[35] Legalising active euthanasia is, however, another matter. Apart from the special repugnance doctors feel towards the idea of a lethal injection, it may be of the very greatest importance to keep a psychological barrier up against killing. Moreover it is active euthanasia which is the most liable to abuse. . . . In the first place it would be hard to devise procedures that would protect people from being persuaded into giving their consent. And secondly the possibility of active voluntary euthanasia might change the social scene in ways that would be very bad. As things are, people do, by and large, expect to be looked after if they are old or ill. This is one of the good things that we have, but we might lose it, and be much worse off without it. It might come to be expected that someone likely to need a lot of looking after should call for the doctor and demand his own death. Something comparable could be good in an extremely poverty-stricken community where the children genuinely suffered from lack of food; but in rich societies such as ours it would surely be a spiritual disaster. Such possibilities should make us very wary of supporting large measures of euthanasia, even where moral principle applied to the individual act does not rule it out.[36]

> [35] The possibility of abuse by people who desire the person's death for other reasons is the main concern here. Does the idea of a Living Will provide an adequate safeguard against this?

> [36] Think carefully about the sorts of concerns that Foot lists in the latter part of this paragraph. How compelling are they, given the very real possibility that a restriction to passive euthanasia may lead to a great deal of suffering in some cases that could be avoided through active euthanasia?

Discussion Questions

1. Is Foot right in her view that no life that meets the minimal standards for an "ordinary human life" could fail to be a good for the person who lives it, no matter what other evils his life may contain—where this means that killing such a person or letting him die could never count as euthanasia? Think of some examples here.

2. James Rachels imagines a person who intends to murder his young nephew in order to receive an inheritance that would otherwise go to the

victim. In one case, the murder is actually carried out by pushing the victim's head underwater during a bath. In a second case, the victim accidentally hits his head in the bath and drowns, with the would-be murderer merely looking on and refraining from saving him. Rachels claims that the two cases are morally on a par: that the action in the first case and the inaction in the second are equally wrong and equally blameworthy. Is he right about this? What if the victim were not a person (such as a young relative) to whom the would-be murderer might seem to have an obligation of care? Especially with the modification just suggested, is what the would-be murderer does in the two cases wrong for the same reason or for importantly different reasons (which might then yield different results in other cases, whether or not they do in this one)?

3. Here is a version of the sort of case discussed by Foot in the passage at Annotation 25: You are driving a subway train through a tunnel. Suddenly you see ahead of you several people who have inadvertently wandered onto the tracks and will surely be killed if you continue in the direction you are going. Given the speed of the train, there is not enough time to stop before this happens. But there is a side track onto which you can steer, avoiding killing the people on the main track but killing a single repairman who happens to be working there. What is the morally correct choice, and why? (How would you justify your action to a person who will be killed, if you somehow had time to do so?) Does it matter how many people are on the main track (as long as it is more than one)?

4. Is it ever clearly reasonable to assume that a person who is unable to actually express a preference would prefer to die if he were able to make a choice? Is the assumption that the person would prefer to die more likely to be reasonable, as Foot claims, where it is passive rather than active euthanasia that is in question?

Thomas Nagel

Thomas Nagel (1937–) is an American philosopher who has taught at Princeton and presently at New York University. He has made important contributions to a wide range of areas, including the philosophy of mind, ethics, metaphysics, epistemology, and social philosophy. In the following selection, written during the Vietnam War, Nagel's concern is with the moral justification for restrictions on the morality of war (of the sort contained in the Geneva Convention) and more generally with the issue of what means can be employed in pursuing a war that is otherwise just. In relation to these issues, Nagel defends an "absolutist" position (a deontological view somewhat similar to Kant's) against a utilitarian view, but suggests that where the utilitarian stakes are high enough, there may be moral "blind alleys" where a person, through no fault of his own, is faced with a situation where no available alternative is morally acceptable. (It is worth saying that discussions of this issue, perhaps more than most, tend to rely on historical examples that are impossible to fully explain in the article or the annotations; more information about these is readily available in encyclopedias, history texts, and on the Internet—though it is important not to believe everything that is claimed on various websites, which can be either seriously slanted or simply unreliable.)

War and Massacre

From the apathetic reaction to atrocities committed in Vietnam by the United States and its allies, one may conclude that moral restrictions on the conduct of war command almost as little sympathy among the general public as they do among those charged with the formation of U.S. military policy.* Even when restrictions on the conduct of warfare are defended, it is usually on legal grounds alone: their moral basis is often poorly understood. I wish to argue that certain restrictions are neither arbitrary nor merely conventional, and that their validity does not depend simply on their usefulness. There is, in other words, a moral basis for the rules of war, even though the conventions now officially in force are far from giving it perfect expression.

① The Mylai massacre was probably the most notorious and widely discussed atrocity on the American side in the Vietnam War. An American army company entered a Vietnamese hamlet, expecting to find an enemy Viet Cong battalion. Meeting no opposition, the soldiers proceeded to slaughter several hundred women, children, and old men.

② Under the traditional doctrine of the just war, military action of any sort is morally permissible only if the overall cause is just. But there are also specific sorts of actions that are morally impermissible even when undertaken in pursuit of a just cause.

I

No elaborate moral theory is required to account for what is wrong in cases like the Mylai massacre, since it did not serve, and was not intended to serve, any strategic purpose.① Moreover, if the participation of the United States in the Indo-Chinese war is entirely wrong to begin with, then that engagement is incapable of providing a justification for *any* measures taken in its pursuit—not only for the measures which are atrocities in every war, however just its aims.②

But this war has revealed attitudes of a more general kind, which influenced the conduct of earlier wars as well. After it has ended, we shall still be faced with the problem of how warfare may be conducted, and the attitudes that have resulted in the specific conduct of this war will not have disappeared. Moreover, similar problems can arise in wars or rebellions fought for very different reasons, and against very different opponents. It is not easy to keep a firm grip on the idea of what is not permissible in warfare, because while some military actions are obvious atrocities, other cases are more difficult to assess, and the general principles underlying these judgments remain obscure. Such obscurity can lead to the abandonment of sound intuitions in favor of criteria whose rationale may be more obvious.③ If such a tendency is to be resisted, it will require a better understanding of the restrictions than we now have.

③ Nagel probably means criteria of a more pragmatic sort, ones that would permit many actions that seem intuitively not to be morally acceptable.

I propose to discuss the most general moral problem raised by the conduct of warfare: the problem of means and ends. In one view, there are limits on what may be done even in the service of an end worth pursuing—and even when adherence to the restriction may be very costly. A person who acknowledges the force of such restrictions can find himself in acute moral dilemmas. He may believe, for example, that by torturing a prisoner he can obtain information necessary to prevent a disaster, or that by obliterating one village with bombs he can halt a campaign of terrorism. If he believes that the gains from a certain measure will clearly outweigh its costs, yet still suspects that he ought not to adopt it, then he is in a dilemma produced by the conflict between two disparate categories of moral reason: categories that may be called *utilitarian* and *absolutist*.

Utilitarianism gives primacy to a concern with what will *happen*. Absolutism gives primacy to a concern with what one is *doing*.④ The conflict between them arises because the alternatives we face are rarely just choices between *total outcomes:* they are also

From Mortal Questions *(Cambridge: Cambridge University Press, 1979).*

---

*This essay was completed in 1971. Direct U.S. military involvement in the Vietnam War lasted from 1961 to 1973. Hence the present tense.

choices between alternative pathways or measures to be taken. When one of the choices is to do terrible

[4] Utilitarianism is, as we have seen, concerned only with consequences, while what Nagel describes as "absolutism" (perhaps not the best label) is a deontological view according to which certain kinds of actions are morally unacceptable, whether or not they produce the best overall consequences.

things to another person, the problem is altered fundamentally; it is no longer merely a question of which outcome would be worse.

Few of us are completely immune to either of these types of moral intuition, though in some people, either naturally or for doctrinal reasons, one type will be dominant and the other suppressed or weak. But it is perfectly possible to feel the force of both types of reason very strongly; in that case the moral dilemma in certain situations of crisis will be acute, and it may appear that every possible course of action or inaction is unacceptable for one reason or another.

II

Although it is this dilemma that I propose to explore, most of the discussion will be devoted to its absolutist component. The utilitarian component is straightforward by comparison, and has a natural appeal to anyone who is not a complete skeptic about ethics. Utilitarianism says that one should try, either individually or through institutions, to maximize good and minimize evil (the definition of these categories need not enter into the schematic formulation of the view), and that if faced with the possibility of preventing a great evil by producing a lesser, one should choose the lesser evil. There are certainly problems about the formulation of utilitarianism, and much has been written about it, but its intent is morally transparent. Nevertheless, despite the additions and refinements, it continues to leave large portions of ethics unaccounted for. I do not suggest that some form of absolutism can account for them all, only that an examination of ab-

solutism will lead us to see the complexity, and perhaps the incoherence, of our moral ideas.

Utilitarianism certainly justifies *some* restrictions on the conduct of warfare. There are strong utilitarian reasons for adhering to any limitation which seems natural to most people—particularly if the limitation is widely accepted already. An exceptional measure which seems to be justified by its results in a particular conflict may create a precedent with disastrous long-term effects.* It may even be argued that war involves violence on such a scale that it is never justified on utilitarian grounds—the consequences of refusing to go to war will never be as bad as the war itself would be, even if atrocities were not committed. Or in a more sophisticated vein it might be claimed that a uniform policy of never resorting to military force would do less harm in the long run, if followed consistently, than a policy of deciding each case on utilitarian grounds (even though on occasion particular applications of the pacifist policy might have worse results than a specific utilitarian decision).[5] But I shall not consider these arguments, for my concern is with reasons of a different kind, which may remain when reasons of utility and interest fail.†

[5] This would be quite plausible if everyone adopted such a policy. But how plausible is it that such a policy will produce the best overall results in the long run even in a world where other nations do not follow it? (See Discussion Question 1.)

In the final analysis, I believe that the dilemma cannot always be resolved. While not every conflict between absolutism and utilitarianism creates an insoluble dilemma, and while it seems to me certainly right to adhere to absolutist restrictions unless the utilitarian considerations favoring violation are overpoweringly weighty and extremely certain—nevertheless, when that special condition is met, it may become impossible to adhere to an absolutist position. What I shall offer, therefore, is a somewhat qualified defense of absolutism. I believe it underlies a valid and fundamental type of moral

---

*Straightforward considerations of national interest often tend in the same direction: the inadvisability of using nuclear weapons seems to be overdetermined in this way.

†These reasons, moreover, have special importance in that they are available even to one who denies the appropriateness of utilitarian considerations in international matters. He may acknowledge limitations on what may be done to the soldiers and civilians of other countries in pursuit of his nation's military objectives, while denying that one country should in general consider the interests of nationals of other countries in determining its policies.

judgment—which cannot be reduced to or overridden by other principles. And while there may be other

> ⑥ As we have seen earlier, there is no action, however horrible its consequences, that might not be justified from a utilitarian standpoint if the consequences of all the other alternatives were worse.

principles just as fundamental, it is particularly important not to lose confidence in our absolutist intuitions, for they are often the only barrier before the abyss of utilitarian apologetics for large-scale murder. ⑥

III

One absolutist position that creates no problems of interpretation is pacifism: the view that one may not kill another person under any circumstances, no matter what good would be achieved or evil averted thereby. The type of absolutist position that I am going to discuss is different. Pacifism draws the conflict with utilitarian considerations very starkly. But there are other views according to which violence may be undertaken, even on a large scale, in a clearly just cause, so long as certain absolute restrictions on the character and direction of that violence are observed. The line is drawn somewhat closer to the bone, but it exists.

The philosopher who has done most to advance contemporary philosophical discussion of such a view, and to explain it to those unfamiliar with its extensive treatment in Roman Catholic moral theology, is G.E.M. Anscombe. In 1958 Miss Anscombe published a pamphlet entitled *Mr. Truman's Degree,* on the occasion of the award by Oxford University of an honorary doctorate to Harry Truman. The pamphlet explained why she had opposed the decision to award that degree, recounted the story of her unsuccessful opposition, and offered some reflections on the his-

> ⑦ Perhaps as a means to the destruction of enemy morale and will to resist; as an end, either to weaken the enemy nation or perhaps for revenge (which seems to have been an important motive for some actions in World War II, such as the fire-bombing of Dresden.)

tory of Truman's decision to drop atom bombs on Hiroshima and Nagasaki, and on the difference between murder and allowable killing in warfare. She pointed out that the policy of deliberately killing large numbers of civilians either as a means or as an end in itself⑦ did not originate

with Truman, and was common practice among all parties during World War II for some time before Hiroshima. The Allied area bombings of German cities by conventional explosives included raids which killed more civilians than did the atomic attacks; the same is true of certain fire-bomb raids on Japan.

The policy of attacking the civilian population in order to induce an enemy to surrender, or to damage his morale, seems to have been widely accepted in the civilized world, and seems to be accepted still, at least if the stakes are high enough. It gives evidence of a moral conviction that the deliberate killing of noncombatants—women, children, old people—is permissible if enough can be gained by it. This follows from the more general position that any means can in principle be justified if it leads to a sufficiently worthy end. Such an attitude is evident not only in the more spectacular current weapons systems but also in the day-to-day conduct of the nonglobal war in Indo-China: the indiscriminate destructiveness of antipersonnel weapons, napalm, and aerial bombardment; cruelty to prisoners; massive relocation of civilians; destruction of crops; and so forth. An absolutist position opposes to this the view that certain acts cannot be justified no matter what the consequences. Among those acts is murder—the deliberate killing of the harmless: civilians, prisoners of war, and medical personnel.⑧

> ⑧ Deliberately killing people for some reason other than self-defense is usually viewed as a clear case of not regarding them as ends-in-themselves. If the purpose is to produce some further result (such as lowering of enemy morale), then it seems to be a way of using them merely as means to an end.

In the present war such measures are sometimes said to be regrettable, but they are generally defended by reference to military necessity and the importance of the long-term consequences of success or failure in the war. I shall pass over the inadequacy of this consequentialist defense in its own terms. (That is the dominant form of moral criticism of the war, for it is part of what people mean when they ask, 'Is it worth it?') I am concerned rather to account for the inappropriateness of offering any defense of that kind for such actions.

Many people feel, without being able to say much more about it, that something has gone seriously wrong when certain measures are admitted into consideration in the first place. The fundamental mistake is made there, rather than at the point where the overall benefit of some monstrous measure is judged to outweigh its disadvantages, and it is adopted. An account of absolutism might help us to understand this. If it is not allowable to *do* certain things, such as killing unarmed prisoners or civilians, then no argument about what will happen if one does not do them can show that doing them would be all right.

Absolutism does not, of course, require one to ignore the consequences of one's acts. It operates as a limitation on utilitarian reasoning, not as a substitute for it. An absolutist can be expected to try to maximize good and minimize evil, so long as this does not require him to transgress an absolute prohibition like that against murder. But when such a conflict occurs, the prohibition takes complete precedence over any consideration of consequences.⑨ Some of the results of this view are clear enough. It requires us to forgo certain potentially useful military measures, such as the slaughter of hostages and prisoners or indiscriminate attempts to reduce the enemy civilian population by starvation, epidemic infectious diseases like anthrax and bubonic plague, or mass incineration. It means that we cannot deliberate on whether such measures are justified by the fact that they will avert still greater evils, for as intentional measures they cannot be justified in terms of any consequences whatever.

⑨ Robert Nozick and others have described deontological restrictions (such as rights) as "side constraints" on the pursuit of consequences: limitations that rule out certain sorts of actions even if they would lead to the best consequences.

Someone unfamiliar with the events of this century might imagine that utilitarian arguments, or arguments of national interest, would suffice to deter measures of this sort. But it has become evident that such considerations are insufficient to prevent the adoption and employment of enormous antipopulation weapons once their use is considered a serious moral possibility. The same is true of the piecemeal wiping out of rural civilian populations in airborne antiguerrilla warfare. Once the door is opened to calculations of utility and national interest, the usual speculations about the future of freedom, peace, and economic prosperity can be brought to bear to ease the consciences of those responsible for a certain number of charred babies.⑩

For this reason alone it is important to decide what is wrong with the frame of mind which allows such arguments to begin. But it is also important to understand absolutism in the cases where it genuinely conflicts with utility. Despite its appeal, it is a paradoxical position, for it can require that one refrain from choosing the lesser of two evils when that is the only choice one has. And it is additionally paradoxical because, unlike pacifism, it permits one to do horrible things to people in some circumstances but not in others.

⑩ There are two issues here. One is whether utilitarian calculations, correct performed, genuinely sanction such actions. A second is whether natural human bias in favor of one's own interests sometimes or even frequently leads to mistaken utilitarian calculations that *seem* to justify morally horrendous actions. (If this were so, there would—as we saw earlier in the discussion of utilitarianism, albeit in a different context—be a utilitarian argument against making decisions on an explicitly utilitarian basis, particular in certain kinds of cases.)

IV

Before going on to say what, if anything, lies behind the position, there remain a few relatively technical matters which are best discussed at this point.

First, it is important to specify as clearly as possible the kind of thing to which absolutist prohibitions can apply. We must take seriously the proviso that they concern what we deliberately do to people. There could not, for example, without incoherence, be an absolute prohibition against *bringing about* the death of an innocent person. For one may find oneself in a situation in which, no matter what one does, some innocent people will die as a result. I do not mean just that there are cases in which someone will die no matter what one does, because one is not in a position to affect the outcome one way or the other. That, it is to be hoped, is one's relation to the deaths of most innocent people. I have in mind, rather, a case in which someone is bound to die, but who it is will depend on what one does. Sometimes these situations have natural causes, as when too few resources (medicine, lifeboats) are available to rescue everyone threatened with a certain catastrophe. Sometimes the situations are manmade, as when the only way to control a campaign of terrorism is to employ terrorist tactics against the community from which it has arisen. Whatever one does in cases such as these, some innocent people will die as a result. If the absolutist prohibition forbade doing what would result in the deaths of innocent people, it would have the consequence that in such cases nothing one could do would be morally permissible. [11]

> [11] The subway case discussed in Discussion Question 3 to the Foot selection is an example of this sort. So also is the case of an innocent threat (see Discussion Question 2 to the Thomson selection) where it is people other than oneself who are threatened (since it is not in the same way clearly unacceptable to do nothing and allow oneself to be killed).

This problem is avoided, however, because what absolutism forbids is *doing* certain things to people, rather than bringing about certain *results.* Not everything that happens to others as a result of what one does is something that one has *done* to them. Catholic moral theology seeks to make this distinction precise in a doctrine known as the law of double effect, which asserts that there is a morally relevant distinction between bringing about or permitting the death of an innocent person deliberately, either as an end in itself or as a means, and bringing it about or permitting it as a side effect of something else one does deliberately. In the latter case, even if the outcome is foreseen, it is not murder, and does not fall under the absolute prohibition, though of course it may still be wrong for other reasons (reasons of utility, for example). Briefly, the principle states that one is sometimes permitted knowingly to bring about or permit as a side-effect of one's actions something which it would be absolutely impermissible to bring about or permit deliberately as an end or as a means. In application to war or revolution, the law of double effect permits a certain amount of civilian carnage as a side-effect of bombing munitions plants or attacking enemy soldiers. And even this is permissible only if the cost is not too great to be justified by one's objectives. [12]

However, despite its importance and its usefulness in accounting for certain plausible moral judgments, I do not believe that the law of double effect is a generally applicable test for the consequences of an absolutist position. Its own application is not always clear, so that it introduces uncertainty where there need not be uncertainty.

In Indo-China, for example, there is a great deal of aerial bombardment, strafing, spraying of napalm, and employment of pellet- or needle-spraying antipersonnel weapons against rural villages in which guerrillas are suspected to be hiding, or from which small-arms fire has been received. The majority of those killed and wounded in these aerial attacks are reported to be women and children, even when some combatants are caught as well. However, the government regards these civilian casualties as a regrettable side-effect of what is a legitimate attack against an armed enemy.

It might be thought easy to dismiss this as sophistry: if one bombs, burns, or strafes a village containing a hundred people, twenty of whom one believes to be guerrillas, so that by killing most of them one will be statistically likely to kill most of the guerrillas, then is not one's attack on the group of one hundred a *means* of destroying the guerrillas, pure and simple? If one makes no attempt to discriminate between guerrillas and civilians, as is impossible in an aerial attack on a small village, then one cannot regard as a mere side-effect the deaths of those in the group that one would not have bothered to kill if more selective means had been available.

The difficulty is that this argument depends on one particular description of the act, and the reply might be that the means used against the guerrillas is not: killing everybody in the village—but rather: obliteration bombing of the *area* in which the twenty guerrillas are known to be located. If there are civilians in the area as well, they will be killed as a side-effect of such action.* [13]

> [12] It is important to be clear that it may be known in advance that such a side effect will definitely occur. What makes it a side effect, rather than a means, is that it contributes nothing to accomplishing the end of the action. Thus if a munitions plant is bombed and a civilian walking by is killed, the death of the civilian contributes nothing to the aim of destroying the plant: it would be destroyed as effectively (or ineffectively, as the case may be) if the civilian were not there.

---

*This counter-argument was suggested by Rogers Albritton.

Because of casuistical problems like this, I prefer to stay with the original, unanalyzed distinction between what one does to people and what merely happens to them as a result of what one does. The law of double effect provides an approximation to that distinction in many cases, and perhaps it can be sharpened to the point where it does better than that. Certainly the original distinction itself needs clarification, particularly since some of the things we do to people involve things happening to them as a result of other things we do. In a case like the one discussed, however, it is clear that by bombing the village one slaughters and maims the civilians in it. Whereas by giving the only available medicine to one of two sufferers from a disease, one does not kill the other or deliberately allow him to die, even if he dies as a result.

The second technical point is this. The absolutist focus on actions rather than outcomes does not merely introduce a new, outstanding item into the catalogue of evils. That is, it does not say that the worst thing in the world is the deliberate murder of an innocent person. For if that were all, then one could presumably justify one such murder on the ground that it would prevent several others, or ten thousand on the ground that they would prevent a hundred thousand more. That is a familiar argument. But if this is allowable, then there is no absolute prohibition against murder after all. Absolutism requires that we *avoid* murder at all costs, not that we *prevent* it at all costs.[14]

It would also be possible to adopt a deontological position less stringent than absolutism, without falling into utilitarianism. There are two ways in which someone might acknowledge the moral relevance of the distinction between deliberate and nondeliberate killing, without being an absolutist. One would be to count murder as a specially bad item in the catalogue of evils, much worse than accidental death or nondeliberate killing. But the other would be to say that deliberately killing an innocent is impermissible unless it is the only way to prevent some very large evil (say the deaths of fifty innocent people). Call this the *threshold* at which the prohibition against murder is overridden. The position is not absolutist, obviously, but it is also not equivalent to an assignment of utilitarian disvalue to murder equal to the disvalue of the threshold. This is easily seen. If a murder had the disvalue of fifty accidental deaths, it would still be permissible on utilitarian grounds to commit a murder to prevent one other murder, plus some lesser evil like a broken arm. Worse still, we would be required on utilitarian grounds to prevent one murder even at the cost of forty-nine accidental deaths that we could otherwise have prevented. These are not in fact consequences of a deontological prohibition against murder with a threshold, because it does not say that the occurrence of a certain kind of act is a bad thing, and therefore to be prevented, but rather tells everyone to *refrain* from such acts, except under certain conditions.[15] In fact, it is perfectly compatible with a deontological prohibition against murder to hold that, considered as an outcome, a murder has *no* more disvalue than an accidental death. While the admission of thresholds would reduce the starkness of the conflicts discussed here, I do not think it would make them disappear, or change their basic character. They would persist in the clash between any deontological requirement and utilitarian values somewhat lower than its threshold.

Finally, let me remark on a frequent criticism of absolutism that depends on a misunderstanding. It is sometimes suggested that such prohibitions depend

---

13 Which is the right description of this case? (See Discussion Question 2.) (In the following sentence, the adjective "casuistical" refers to the science or art of resolving moral questions through the comparison and analysis of similar and dissimilar cases—a process that at least lends itself to rationalization and sophistry.)

14 Thus the absolutist view is that murder cannot be justified even to prevent a larger number of murders. Murder is *absolutely* forbidden (thus the term "absolutism"), not just an especially bad occurrence to be weighed against others.

15 Nagel is suggesting a qualified absolutist position: certain actions are forbidden unless they are necessary to prevent bad consequences that exceed some threshold of badness. Obviously the extent to which this departs from pure absolutism (and moves at least roughly in the direction of utilitarianism) depends in very large part on where the threshold falls. Most philosophers with absolutist sympathies would accept only very high or strong thresholds, assuming that they were willing to accept such a position at all. (See Discussion Question 3.)

on a kind of moral self-interest, a primary obligation to preserve one's own moral purity, to keep one's hands clean no matter what happens to the rest of the world. If this were the position, it might be exposed to the charge of self-indulgence. After all, what gives one man a right to put the purity of his soul or the cleanness of his hands above the lives or welfare of large numbers of other people? It might be argued that a public servant like Truman has no right to put himself first in that way; therefore if he is convinced that the alternatives would be worse, he must give the order to drop the bombs, and take the burden of those deaths on himself, as he must do other distasteful things for the general good.

But there are two confusions behind the view that moral self-interest underlies moral absolutism. First, it is a confusion to suggest that the need to preserve one's moral purity might be the *source* of an obligation. For if by committing murder one sacrifices one's moral purity or integrity, that can only be because there is *already* something wrong with murder. The general reason against committing murder cannot therefore be merely that it makes one an immoral person. Secondly, the notion that one might sacrifice one's moral integrity justifiably, in the service of a sufficiently worthy end, is an incoherent notion. For if one were justified in making such a sacrifice (or even morally required to make it), then one would not be sacrificing one's moral integrity by adopting that course: one would be preserving it.[16]

> [16] Compare Williams's discussion of the attempt by utilitarians to avoid intuitively unacceptable results by appealing to a person's moral discomfort at doing something that would otherwise lead to the best consequences (see Annotation 8 to the Williams selection and the corresponding passage).

Moral absolutism is not unique among moral theories in requiring each person to do what will preserve his own moral purity in all circumstances. This is equally true of utilitarianism, or of any other theory which distinguishes between right and wrong. Any theory which defines the right course of action in various circumstances and asserts that one should adopt that course, *ipso facto* asserts that one should do what will preserve one's moral purity, simply because the right course of action *is* what will preserve one's moral purity in those circumstances. Of course utilitarianism does not assert that this is *why* one should

adopt that course, but we have seen that the same is true of absolutism.

V

It is easier to dispose of false explanations of absolutism than to produce a true one. A positive account of the matter must begin with the observation that war, conflict, and aggression are relations between persons. The view that it can be wrong to consider merely the overall effect of one's action on the general welfare comes into prominence when those actions involve relations with others. A man's acts usually affect more people than he deals with directly, and those effects must naturally be considered in his decisions. But if there are special principles governing the manner in which he should *treat* people, that will require special attention to the particular persons toward whom the act is directed, rather than just to its total effect.

Absolutist restrictions in warfare appear to be of two types: restrictions on the class of persons at whom aggression or violence may be directed and restrictions on the manner of attack, given that the object falls within that class. These can be combined, however, under the principle that hostile treatment of any person must be justified in terms of something *about that person* which makes the treatment appropriate. Hostility is a personal relation, and it must be suited to its target. One consequence of this condition will be that certain persons may not be subjected to hostile treatment in war at all, since nothing about them justifies such treatment. Others will be proper objects of hostility only in certain circumstances, or when they are engaged in certain pursuits. And the appropriate manner and extent of hostile treatment will depend on what is justified by the particular case.[17]

> [17] This is an intuitively appealing standard, but one that may be difficult to apply with very clear results in actual cases.

A coherent view of this type will hold that extremely hostile behavior toward another is compatible with treating him as a person—even perhaps as an end in himself. This is possible only if one has not automatically stopped treating him as a person as soon as one starts to fight with him. If hostile, aggressive, or combative treatment of others always violated the condition that they be treated as human beings, it would be difficult to make further distinctions on that score *within* the class of hostile actions. That point of view, on the level of international relations, leads to the position that if complete pacifism is not accepted, no holds need be barred at all, and we may slaughter and massacre to our hearts' content, if it seems advisable. Such a position is often expressed in discussions of war crimes.

But the fact is that ordinary people do not believe this about conflicts, physical or otherwise, between individuals, and there is no more reason why it should be true of conflicts between nations. There seems to be a perfectly natural conception of the distinction between fighting clean and fighting dirty. To fight dirty is to direct one's hostility or aggression not at its proper object, but at a peripheral target which may be more vulnerable, and through which the proper object can be attacked indirectly. This applies in a fist fight, an election campaign, a duel, or a philosophical argument. If the concept is general enough to apply to all these matters, it should apply to war—both to the conduct of individual soldiers and to the conduct of nations.

Suppose that you are a candidate for public office, convinced that the election of your opponent would be a disaster, that he is an unscrupulous demagogue who will serve a narrow range of interests and seriously infringe the rights of those who disagree with him; and suppose you are convinced that you cannot defeat him by conventional means. Now imagine that various unconventional means present themselves as possibilities: you possess information about his sex life which would scandalize the electorate if made public; or you learn that his wife is an alcoholic or that in his youth he was associated for a brief period with a proscribed political party, and you believe that this information could be used to blackmail him into withdrawing his candidacy; or you can have a team of your supporters flatten the tires of a crucial subset of his supporters on election day; or you are in a position to stuff the ballot boxes; or, more simply, you can have him assassinated. What is wrong with these methods, given that they will achieve an overwhelmingly desirable result? [18]

[18] Think about this question before proceeding with the reading: are each of the suggested actions morally unacceptable in this case, and if so, why? Are they morally unacceptable to the same degree? If not, what accounts for the difference?

There are, of course, many things wrong with them: some are against the law; some infringe the pro-

cedures of an electoral process to which you are presumably committed by taking part in it; very importantly, some may backfire, and it is in the interest of all political candidates to adhere to an unspoken agreement not to allow certain personal matters to intrude into a campaign. But that is not all. We have in addition the feeling that these measures, these methods of attack, are *irrelevant* to the issue between you and your opponent, that in taking them up you would not be directing yourself to that which makes him an object of your opposition. You would be directing your attack not at the true target of your hostility, but at peripheral targets that happen to be vulnerable.

The same is true of a fight or argument outside the framework of any system of regulations or law. In an altercation with a taxi driver over an excessive fare, it is inappropriate to taunt him about his accent, flatten one of his tires, or smear chewing gum on his windshield; and it remains inappropriate even if he casts aspersions on your race, politics, or religion, or dumps the contents of your suitcase into the street.

The importance of such restrictions may vary with the seriousness of the case; and what is unjustifiable in one case may be justified in a more extreme one. But they all derive from a single principle: that hostility or aggression should be directed at its true object. This means both that it should be directed at the person or persons who provoke it and that it should aim more specifically at what is provocative about them. The second condition will determine what form the hostility may appropriately take.

It is evident that some idea of the relation in which one should stand to other people underlies this principle, but the idea is difficult to state. I believe it is roughly this: whatever one does to another person intentionally must be aimed at him as a subject, with the intention that he receive it as a subject. It should manifest an attitude to *him* rather than just to the situation, and he should be able to recognize it and identify himself as its object. The procedures by which such an attitude is manifested need not be addressed to the person directly. Surgery, for example, is not a form of personal confrontation but part of a medical treatment that can be offered to a patient face to face and received by him as a response to his needs and the natural outcome of an attitude toward *him*.

Hostile treatment, unlike surgery, is already addressed *to* a person, and does not take its interpersonal meaning from a wider context. But hostile acts can serve as the expression or implementation of only a limited range of attitudes to the person who is attacked. Those attitudes in turn have as objects certain real or presumed characteristics or activities of the person which are thought to justify them. When this background is absent, hostile or aggressive behavior can no longer be intended for the reception of the victim as a subject. Instead it takes on the character of a purely bureaucratic operation. This occurs when one attacks someone who is not the true object of one's hostility—the true object may be someone else, who can be attacked through the victim; or one may not be manifesting a hostile attitude toward anyone, but merely using the easiest available path to some desired goal. One finds oneself not facing or addressing the victim at all, but operating on him—without the larger context of personal interaction that surrounds a surgical operation.

If absolutism is to defend its claim to priority over considerations of utility, it must hold that the maintenance of a direct interpersonal response to the people one deals with is a requirement which no advantages can justify one in abandoning. The requirement is absolute only if it rules out any calculation of what would justify its violation. I have said earlier that there may be circumstances so extreme that they render an absolutist position untenable. One may find then that one has no choice but to do something terrible. Nevertheless, even in such cases absolutism retains its force in that one cannot claim *justification* for the violation. It does not become *all right*.

As a tentative effort to explain this, let me try to connect absolutist limitations with the possibility of justifying *to the victim* what is being done to him. If one abandons a person in the course of rescuing several others from a fire or a sinking ship, one *could* say to him, 'You understand, I have to leave you to save the others.' Similarly, if one subjects an unwilling child to a painful surgical procedure, one can say to him, 'If you could understand, you would realize that I am doing this to help you.' One could *even* say, as one bayonets an enemy soldier, 'It's either you or me.' But one cannot really say while torturing a prisoner, 'You understand, I have to pull out your fingernails because it is absolutely essential that we have the names of your confederates'; nor can one say to

the victims of Hiroshima, 'You understand, we have to incinerate you to provide the Japanese government with an incentive to surrender.' [19]

This does not take us very far, of course, since a utilitarian would presumably be willing to offer justifications of the latter sort to his victims, in cases where he thought they were sufficient. They are really justifications to the world at large, which the victim, as a reasonable man, would be expected to appreciate. However, there seems to me something wrong with this view, for it ignores the possibility that to treat someone else horribly puts you in a special relation to him, which may have to be defended in terms of other features of your relation to him. The suggestion needs much more development; but it may help us to understand how there may be requirements which are absolute in the sense that there can be no justification for violating them. If the justification for what one did to another person had to be such that it could be offered to him specifically, rather than just to the world at large, that would be a significant source of restraint.

If the account is to be deepened, I would hope for some results along the following lines. Absolutism is associated with a view of oneself as a small being interacting with others in a large world. The justifications it requires are primarily interpersonal. Utilitarianism is associated with a view of oneself as a benevolent bureaucrat distributing such benefits as one can control to countless other beings, with whom one may have various relations or none. The justifications it requires are primarily administrative. The argument between the two moral attitudes may depend on the relative priority of these two conceptions.

VI

Some of the restrictions on methods of warfare which have been adhered to from time to time are to be explained by the mutual interests of the involved parties: restrictions on weaponry, treatment of prisoners, etc. But that is not all there is to it. The conditions of directness and relevance which I have argued apply to

[19] This is again related to Kant's idea of treating the other person as an end in himself. But again it may be hard to apply in actual cases in a way that yields clear and sharp results.

relations of conflict and aggression apply to war as well. I have said that there are two types of absolutist restrictions on the conduct of war: those that limit the legitimate targets of hostility and those that limit its character, even when the target is acceptable. I shall say something about each of these. As will become clear, the principle I have sketched does not yield an unambiguous answer in every case.

First let us see how it implies that attacks on some people are allowed, but not attacks on others. It may seem paradoxical to assert that to fire a machine gun at someone who is throwing hand grenades at your emplacement is to treat him as a human being. Yet the relation with him is direct and straightforward. The attack is aimed specifically against the threat presented by a dangerous adversary, and not against a peripheral target through which he happens to be vulnerable but which has nothing to do with that threat. For example, you might stop him by machine-gunning his wife and children, who are standing nearby, thus distracting him from his aim of blowing you up and enabling you to capture him. But if his wife and children are not threatening your life, that would be to treat them as means with a vengeance.

This, however, is just Hiroshima on a smaller scale. One objection to weapons of mass annihilation— nuclear, thermonuclear, biological, or chemical—is that their indiscriminateness disqualifies them as direct instruments for the expression of hostile relations. In attacking the civilian population, one treats neither the military enemy nor the civilians with that minimal respect which is owed to them as human beings. This is clearly true of the direct attack on people who present no threat at all. But it is also true of the character of the attack on those who *are* threatening you, i.e., the government and military forces of the enemy. Your aggression is directed against an area of vulnerability quite distinct from any threat presented by them which you may be justified in meeting. You are taking aim at them through the mundane life and survival of their countrymen, instead of aiming at the destruction of their military capacity. And of course it does not require hydrogen bombs to commit such crimes.

This way of looking at the matter also helps us to understand the importance of the distinction between combatants and noncombatants, and the irrelevance of much of the criticism offered against its intelligibility and moral significance. According to an absolutist position, deliberate killing of the innocent is murder, and in warfare the role of the innocent is filled by noncombatants. This has been thought to raise two sorts of problems: first, the widely imagined difficulty of making a division, in modern warfare, between combatants and noncombatants; second, problems deriving from the connotation of the word 'innocence'.

Let me take up the latter question first.* In the absolutist position, the operative notion of innocence is not moral innocence, and it is not opposed to moral guilt. If it were, then we would be justified in killing a wicked but noncombatant hairdresser in an enemy city who supported the evil policies of his government, and unjustified in killing a morally pure conscript who was driving a tank toward us with the profoundest regrets and nothing but love in his heart. But moral innocence has very little to do with it, for in the definition of murder 'innocent' means 'currently harmless', and it is opposed not to 'guilty' but to 'doing harm'. It should be noted that such an analysis has the consequence that in war we may often be justified in killing people who do not deserve to die, and unjustified in killing people who do deserve to die, if anyone does.

So we must distinguish combatants from noncombatants on the basis of their immediate threat or harmfulness. I do not claim that the line is a sharp one, but it is not so difficult as is often supposed to place individuals on one side of it or the other. Children are not combatants even though they may join the armed forces if they are allowed to grow up. Women are not combatants just because they bear children or offer comfort to the soldiers. More problematic are the supporting personnel, whether in or out of uniform, from drivers of munitions trucks and army cooks to civilian munitions workers and farmers. I believe they can be plausibly classified by applying the condition that the prosecution of conflict must direct itself to the cause of danger, and not to what is peripheral. The

*What I say on this subject derives from Anscombe.

threat presented by an army and its members does not consist merely in the fact that they are men, but in the fact that they are armed and are using their arms in the pursuit of certain objectives. Contributions to their arms and logistics are contributions to this threat; contributions to their mere existence as men are not. It is therefore wrong to direct an attack against those who merely serve the combatants' needs as human beings, such as farmers and food suppliers, even though survival as a human being is a necessary condition of efficient functioning as a solider. [20]

This brings us to the second group of restrictions: those that limit what may be done even to combatants. These limits are harder to explain clearly. Some of them may be arbitrary or conventional, and some may have to be derived from other sources; but I believe that the condition of directness and relevance in hostile relations accounts for them to a considerable extent.

Consider first a case which involves both a protected class of noncombatants and a restriction on the measures that may be used against combatants. One provision of the rules of war which is universally recognized, though it seems to be turning into a dead letter in Vietnam, is the special status of medical personnel and the wounded in warfare. It might be more efficient to shoot medical officers on sight and to let the enemy wounded die rather than be patched up to fight another day. But someone with medical insignia is supposed to be left alone and permitted to tend and retrieve the wounded. I believe this is because medical attention is a species of attention to completely general human needs, not specifically the needs of a combat soldier, and our conflict with the soldier is not with his existence as a human being.

By extending the application of this idea, one can justify prohibitions against certain particularly cruel weapons: starvation, poisoning, infectious diseases (supposing they could be inflicted on combatants only), weapons designed to main or disfigure or torture the opponent rather than merely to stop him. It is not, I think, mere casuistry to claim that such weapons attack the men, not the soldiers. The effect of dumdum bullets, for example, is much more extended than necessary to cope with the combat situation in which they are used. They abandon any attempt to discriminate in their effects between the combatant and the human being. [21] For this reason the use of flamethrowers and napalm is an atrocity in all circumstances that I can imagine, whoever the target may be. Burns are both extremely painful and extremely disfiguring—far more than any other category of wound. That this well-known fact plays no (inhibiting) part in the determination of U.S. weapons policy suggests that moral sensitivity among public officials has not increased markedly since the Spanish Inquisition.*

Finally, the same condition of appropriateness to the true object of hostility should limit the scope of attacks on an enemy country: its economy, agriculture, transportation system, and so forth. Even if the parties to a military conflict are considered to be not armies

[20] How clear is this distinction between combatants and noncombatants? Does it matter how eagerly the people in question support the war—for example, whether the farmers have made special efforts to increase production so as to make their troops better fed and so more effective? Does it make any difference whether attacking the enemy army's food supply is the most effective or perhaps even the only very feasible way to prosecute the war? (Similar questions can be asked about the medical personnel discussed in the following paragraph.)

[21] A "dum-dum" bullet is one that is designed to expand on impact, thereby producing a larger and more likely fatal wound.

---

*Beyond this I feel uncertain. Ordinary bullets, after all, can cause death, and nothing is more permanent than that. I am not at all sure why we are justified in trying to kill those who are trying to kill us (rather than merely in trying to stop them with force which may also result in their deaths). It is often argued that incapacitating gases are a relatively humane weapon (when not used, as in Vietnam, merely to make people easier to shoot). Perhaps the legitimacy of restrictions against them must depend on the dangers of escalation, and the great utility of maintaining *any* conventional category of restriction so long as nations are willing to adhere to it.

Let me make clear that I do not regard my argument as a defense of the moral immutability of the Hague and Geneva Conventions. Rather, I believe that they rest partly on a moral foundation, and that modifications of them should also be assessed on moral grounds.

or governments but entire nations (which is usually a grave error), that does not justify one nation in warring against every aspect or element of another nation. That is not justified in a conflict between individuals, and nations are even more complex than individuals, so the same reasons apply. Like a human being, a nation is engaged in countless other pursuits while waging war, and it is not in those respects that it is an enemy.[22]

[22] Even if those other pursuits contribute in indirect ways to the war effort.

The burden of the argument has been that absolutism about murder has a foundation in principles governing all one's relations to other persons, whether aggressive or amiable, and that these principles and that absolutism, apply to warfare as well, with the result that certain measures are impermissible no matter what the consequences.* I do not mean to romanticize war. It is sufficiently utopian to suggest that when nations conflict they might rise to the level of limited barbarity that typically characterizes violent conflict between individuals, rather than wallowing in the moral pit where they appear to have settled, surrounded by enormous arsenals.

VI

Having described the elements of the absolutist position, we must now return to the conflict between it and utilitarianism. Even if certain types of dirty tactics become acceptable when the stakes are high enough, the most serious of the prohibited acts, like murder and torture, are not just supposed to require unusually strong justification. They are supposed *never* to be done, because no quantity of resulting benefit is thought capable of *justifying* such treatment of a person.

The fact remains that when an absolutist knows or believes that the utilitarian cost of refusing to adopt a prohibited course will be very high, he may hold to his refusal to adopt it, but he will find it difficult to feel that a moral dilemma has been satisfactorily resolved. The same may be true of someone who rejects an absolutist requirement and adopts instead the course yielding the most acceptable consequences. In either case, it is possible to feel that one has acted for reasons insufficient to justify violation of the opposing principle. In situations of deadly conflict, particularly where a weaker party is threatened with annihilation or enslavement by a stronger one, the argument for resorting to atrocities can be powerful, and the dilemma acute.

There may exist principles, not yet codified, which would enable us to resolve such dilemmas. But then again there may not. We must face the pessimistic alternative that these two forms of moral intuition are not capable of being brought together into a single, coherent moral system, and that the world can present us with situations in which there is no honorable or moral course for a man to take, no course free of guilt and responsibility for evil.

The idea of a moral blind alley is a perfectly intelligible one. It is possible to get into such a situation by one's own fault, and people do it all the time. If, for example, one makes two incompatible promises or commitments—becomes engaged to two people, for example—then there is no course one can take which is not wrong, for one must break one's promise to at least one of them. Making a clean breast of the whole thing will not be enough to remove one's reprehensibility. The existence of such cases is not morally disturbing, however, because we feel that the situation was not unavoidable: one had to do something wrong in the first place to get into it. But what if the world itself, or someone else's actions, could face a previously innocent person with a choice between morally abominable courses of action, and leave him no way to escape with his honor? Our intuitions rebel at the idea, for we feel that the constructibility of such a case must show a contradiction in our moral views. But it is not in itself a contradiction to say that someone can do X or not do X, and

---

*It is possible to draw a more radical conclusion, which I shall not pursue here. Perhaps the technology and organization of modern war are such as to make it impossible to wage as an acceptable form of interpersonal or even international hostility. Perhaps it is too impersonal and large-scale for that. If so, then absolutism would in practice imply pacifism, given the present state of things. On the other hand, I am skeptical about the unstated assumption that a technology dictates its own use.

that for him to take either course would be wrong. It merely contradicts the supposition that *ought* implies *can*—since presumably one ought to refrain from what is wrong, and in such a case it is impossible to do so. Given the limitations on human action, it is naïve to suppose that there is a solution to every moral problem with which the world can face us. We have always known that the world is a bad place. It appears that it may be an evil place as well.㉓

㉓ Try to think of examples of this sort. How plausible is it that every available alternative is morally unacceptable? (See Discussion Question 4.)

Discussion Questions

1. How plausible is the suggestion that a policy of never resorting to warfare, no matter what other countries may do, is justified from a utilitarian standpoint? Here it is important to consider the possibility that the threat of a military response may deter a wide range of aggressive actions that might otherwise be much more commonly employed.

2. Consider again the sort of case described in the passage corresponding to Annotation 13: You are attempting to destroy an enemy force that is known to be located in a certain general location, and the most effective means is to bomb the whole area, thereby killing the enemy soldiers, but also killing any enemy noncombatants that may happen to be there. Is such an action justified in any of the following range of cases, and if so, where (if at all) does it stop being justified (and why)?:

   a. the area is small, and you have no knowledge of any enemy noncombatants located there;

   b. the area is much larger, and you have no knowledge of enemy noncombatants located there;

   c. the area is known to contain a small number of noncombatants, who have been warned to leave by the time of the proposed bombing (and have a reasonable chance to do so);

   d. the area is known to contain a small number of noncombatants, who either have not been warned or do not have enough time to leave;

   e. the area is known to contain noncombatants equal in number to the enemy force and with no chance to leave in time;

   f. the area is known to contain noncombatants much larger in numbers than the enemy force and again with no chance to leave in time;

   g. the area is known to contain a number of noncombatants that is many, many times larger than the enemy force and once again with no chance to leave in time;

   h. the area is the entire enemy country containing millions and millions of people, again with no chance to leave.

3. Suppose that you know that a bomb has been planted somewhere in an urban area and will go off in 24 hours unless defused first. Suppose also that the only way to discover the location of the bomb in time is to severely torture an enemy soldier (or perhaps a terrorist) until he reveals its location. (He is stubborn and tough and will endure a lot of suffering before giving up the information, but it is virtually certain that he will eventually do so if tortured with the available methods.) Do you think it is morally permissible to torture him for this purpose? What answer would be given by a utilitarian view? What answer would be given by the law of double effect? Under an absolutist view with a threshold, the answer would depend on the number of people who will be killed by the bomb (and perhaps also on what other sorts of damage it would do): does such a view seem plausible in relation to this case, and if so, where should the threshold be set? (Would different sorts of envisaged actions require different thresholds? Suppose, for example, that the only way to get him to talk is to torture his children.)

4. The case described in the previous question, with the stipulation that the bomb will kill very large numbers of innocent people, is a fairly plausible example of one where many people would be tempted to say that there is no morally acceptable action available: torture is absolutely unacceptable according to many views, but so is letting large numbers of innocent people be killed when it is possible to

prevent it. Is this the right conclusion? Does it make sense to say that every available alternative is wrong, so that you will be acting in a seriously immoral way whatever you do? Or, as others think, must it be the case that the least bad of the alternatives (whether judged on utilitarian grounds or in some other way) *must* be morally acceptable?

Tom Regan

Tom Regan (1938–) is an American philosopher who teaches at North Carolina State University. He is one of the foremost proponents of animal rights, and has made other important contributions to moral philosophy as well. In the following selection, Regan argues for the view that animals of the sorts that are raised to be used for food, used for laboratory experiments, and hunted have the same inherent worth as human beings and therefore have rights, rights that are flagrantly violated by the ways in which humans treat them. His argument proceeds by examining a set of different moral theories and the views of the status of animals that they generate. His conclusion is that a rights-based moral theory is the most adequate, and that there no justification within such a theory for restricting rights to human beings.

The Case for Animal Rights

I regard myself as an advocate of animal rights—as a part of the animal rights movement. That movement, as I conceive it, is committed to a number of goals, including:

The total abolition of the use of animals in science;

The total dissolution of commercial animal agriculture;

The total elimination of commercial and sport hunting and trapping.

There are, I know, people who profess to believe in animal rights but do not avow these goals. Factory farming, they say, is wrong—it violates animals' rights—but traditional animal agriculture is all right. Toxicity tests of cosmetics on animals violates their rights, but important medical research—cancer research, for example—does not. The clubbing of baby seals is abhorrent, but not the harvesting of adult seals. I used to think I understood this reasoning. Not any more. You don't change unjust institutions by tidying them up.

What's wrong—fundamentally wrong—with the way animals are treated isn't the details that vary from case to case. It's the whole system. The forlornness of the veal calf is pathetic, heart wrenching[1]; the pulsing pain of the chimp with electrodes planted deep in her brain is repulsive; the slow, tortuous death of the raccoon caught in the leg-hold trap is agonizing. But what is wrong isn't the pain, isn't the suffering, isn't the deprivation. These compound what's wrong. Sometimes—often—they make it much, much worse. But they are not the fundamental wrong.

[1] The case of veal calves is one of the most widely discussed examples in the literature on moral issues pertaining to the treatment of animals. In order to produce tender, pale-colored meat, veal calves are fed a liquid diet that is deficient by design in iron and fiber and are confined in crates that severely limit their movement and interaction with other animals. These conditions result in what is described as "chronic stress," together with anemia and various physical disorders.

From In Defense of Animals, *edited by Peter Singer* (Oxford: Blackwell, 1985).

The fundamental wrong is the system that allows us to view animals as *our resources,* here for *us*—to be eaten, or surgically manipulated, or exploited for sport or money.② Once we ac-cept this view of animals—as our resources—the rest is as predictable as it is re-grettable. Why worry about their loneliness, their pain, their death? Since animals exist for us, to benefit us in one way or another, what harms them really doesn't matter—or matters only if it starts to bother us, makes us feel a trifle uneasy when we eat our veal escalope, for example. So, yes, let us get veal calves out of soli-tary confinement, give them more space, a little straw, a few companions. But let us keep our veal escalope.

> ② That is, in Kantian terms, animals are often treated merely as means and not at all as ends in themselves.

But a little straw, more space and a few compan-ions won't eliminate—won't even touch—the basic wrong that attaches to our viewing and treating these animals as our resources. A veal calf killed to be eaten after living in close confinement is viewed and treated in this way: but so, too, is another who is raised (as they say) 'more humanely'. To right the wrong of our treatment of farm animals requires more than making rearing methods 'more humane'; it requires the total dissolution of commercial animal agriculture.

How we do this, whether we do it or, as in the case of animals in science, whether and how we abol-ish their use—these are to a large extent political questions. People must change their beliefs before they change their habits. Enough people, especially those elected to public office, must believe in change—must want it—before we will have laws that protect the rights of animals. This process of change is very complicated, very demanding, very exhausting, calling for the efforts of many hands in education, publicity, political organization and activity, down to the licking of envelopes and stamps. As a trained and practising philosopher, the sort of contribution I can make is limited but, I like to think, important. The currency of philosophy is ideas—their meaning and rational foundation—not the nuts and bolts of the leg-islative process, say, or the mechanics of community organization. That's what I have been exploring over the past ten years or so in my essays and talks and, most recently, in my book, *The Case for Animal Rights.* I believe the major conclusions I reach in the book are true because they are supported by the weight of the best arguments. I believe the idea of ani-mal rights has reason, not just emotion, on its side.

In the space I have at my disposal here I can only sketch, in the barest outline, some of the main features of the book. Its main themes—and we should not be surprised by this—involve asking and answering deep, foundational moral questions about what moral-ity is, how it should be understood and what is the best moral theory, all considered. I hope I can convey something of the shape I think this theory takes. The attempt to do this will be (to use a word a friendly critic once used to describe my work) cerebral, per-haps too cerebral. But this is misleading. My feelings about how animals are sometimes treated run just as deep and just as strong as those of my more volatile compatriots. Philosophers do—to use the jargon of the day—have a right side to their brains. If it's the left side we contribute (or mainly should), that's because what talents we have reside there.

How to proceed? We begin by asking how the moral status of animals has been understood by thinkers who deny that animals have rights. Then we test the mettle of their ideas by seeing how well they stand up under the heat of fair criticism. If we start our thinking in this way, we soon find that some people believe that we have no duties directly to animals, that we owe nothing to them, that we can do nothing that wrongs them. Rather, we can do wrong acts that in-volve animals, and so we have duties regarding them, though none to them. Such views may be called indi-rect duty views. By way of illustration: suppose your neighbour kicks your dog. Then your neighbour has done something wrong. But not to your dog. The wrong that has been done is a wrong to you. After all, it is wrong to upset people, and your neighbour's kick-ing your dog upsets you. So you are the one who is wronged, not your dog. Or again: by kicking your dog your neighbour damages your property. And since it is wrong to damage another person's property, your neighbour has done something wrong—to you, of course, not to your dog. Your neighbour no more wrongs your dog than your car would be wronged if the windshield were smashed. Your neighbour's duties involving your dog are indirect duties to you. More generally, all of our duties regarding animals are indi-rect duties to one another—to humanity.③

How could someone try to justify such a view? Someone might say that your dog doesn't feel anything and so isn't hurt by your neighbour's kick, doesn't care about the pain since none is felt, is as unaware of anything as is your windshield. Someone might say this, but no rational person will, since, among other considerations, such a view will commit anyone who holds it to the position that no human being feels pain either—that human beings also don't care about what happens to them.④ A second possibility is that though both humans and your dog are hurt when kicked, it is only human pain that matters. But, again, no rational person can believe this. Pain is pain wherever it occurs. If your neighbour's causing you pain is wrong because of the pain that is caused, we cannot rationally ignore or dismiss the moral relevance of the pain that your dog feels.⑤

Philosophers who hold indirect duty views—and many still do—have come to understand that they must avoid the two defects just noted: that is, both the view that animals don't feel anything as well as the idea that only human pain can be morally relevant. Among such thinkers the sort of view now favoured is one or other form of what is called *contractarianism.*

Here, very crudely, is the root idea: morality consists of a set of rules that individuals voluntarily agree to abide by, as we do when we sign a contract (hence the name contractarianism). Those who understand and accept the terms of the contract are covered directly; they have rights created and recognized by, and protected in, the contract. And these contractors can also have protection spelled out for others who, though they lack the ability to understand morality and so cannot sign the contract themselves, are loved or cherished by those who can. Thus young children, for example, are unable to sign contracts and lack rights. But they are protected by the contract none the less because of the sentimental interests of others, most notably their parents. So we have, then, duties involving these children, duties regarding them, but no duties to them. Our duties in their case are indirect duties to other human beings, usually their parents.⑥

As for animals, since they cannot understand contracts, they obviously cannot sign; and since they cannot sign, they have no rights. Like children, however, some animals are the objects of the sentimental interest of others. You, for example, love your dog or cat. So those animals that enough people care about (companion animals, whales, baby seals, the American bald eagle), though they lack rights themselves, will be protected because of the sentimental interests of people. I have, then, according to contractarianism, no duty directly to your dog or any other animal, not even the duty not to cause them pain or suffering; my duty not to hurt them is a duty I have to those people who care about what happens to them. As for other animals, where no or little sentimental interest is present—in the case of farm animals, for example, or laboratory rats—what duties we have grow weaker and weaker, perhaps to vanishing point. The pain and death they endure, though real, are not wrong if no one cares about them.⑦

When it comes to the moral status of animals, contractarianism could be a hard view to refute if it were an adequate theoretical approach to the moral status of human beings. It is not adequate in this latter respect, however, which makes the question of its adequacy in the former case, regarding animals, utterly

③ It is unlikely that very many pet owners have this attitude toward their pets. But it is a very common attitude toward animals raised for food or used in laboratory research.

④ Regan's point is that the same general sort of behavioral evidence that shows that people other than oneself feel pain and want to avoid it is also available in relation to animals. While there are some differences (mainly the human capacity for verbal expression), it is hard to see how anyone could reasonably hold the view that other humans do indeed feel pain but animals do not.

⑤ Obviously there are many differences between humans and other sorts of animals. But do any of these plausibly support the view that although human pain is of great moral significance, animal pain is morally irrelevant? (See Discussion Question 1.)

⑥ As Regan says, this is a relatively crude version of a view that has been developed in much more complicated and subtle ways. Many of its proponents would not be satisfied with the view that children have no rights and are protected only in this indirect way.

⑦ Whether such behavior is justified by such a contractarian view, there can be little doubt that this picture accurately reflects the way in which animals are treated: some are serious objects of moral concern, while others are almost entirely ignored in this respect (with the latter group being much larger than the former).

moot. For consider: morality, according to the (crude) contractarian position before us, consists of rules that people agree to abide by. What people? Well, enough to make a difference—enough, that is, *collectively* to have the power to enforce the rules that are drawn up in the contract. That is very well and good for the signatories but not so good for anyone who is not asked to sign. And there is nothing in contractarianism of the sort we are discussing that guarantees or requires that everyone will have a chance to participate equally in framing the rules of morality. The result is that this approach to ethics could sanction the most blatant forms of social, economic, moral and political injustice, ranging from a repressive caste system to systematic racial or sexual discrimination. Might, according to this theory, does make right. Let those who are the victims of injustice suffer as they will. It matters not so long as no one else—no contractor, or too few of them—cares about it. Such a theory takes one's moral breath away . . . as if, for example, there would be nothing wrong with apartheid in South Africa if few white South Africans were upset by it. A theory with so little to recommend it at the level of the ethics of our treatment of our fellow humans cannot have anything more to recommend it when it comes to the ethics of how we treat our fellow animals.⑧

⑧ Remember again that this is only a crude version of the contract view. But any version of it will have to deal with the issue of who is a party to the supposed contract and who is not (and also of what happens when there are different, perhaps conflicting contracts).

The version of contractarianism just examined is, as I have noted, a crude variety, and in fairness to those of a contractarian persuasion it must be noted that much more refined, subtle and ingenious varieties are possible. For example, John Rawls, in his *A Theory of Justice,* sets forth a version of contractarianism that forces contractors to ignore the accidental features of being a human being—for example, whether one is white or black, male or female, a genius or of modest intellect. Only by ignoring such features, Rawls believes, can we ensure that the principles of justice that contractors would agree upon are not based on bias or prejudice. Despite the improvement a view such as Rawls's represents over the cruder forms of contractarianism, it remains deficient: it systematically denies that we have direct duties to those human beings who do not have a sense of justice—young children, for instance, and many mentally retarded humans. And yet it seems reasonably certain that, were we to torture a young child or a retarded elder, we would be doing something that wronged him or her, not something that would be wrong if (and only if) other humans with a sense of justice were upset. And since this is true in the case of these humans, we cannot rationally deny the same in the case of animals.⑨

⑨ In fact, Rawls does not present his view as a general account of morality, but only more narrowly of justice as it pertains to the basic structure of society; and even for that narrower issue, it is not clear that Regan's account is entirely accurate. But Rawls does seem to assume from the outset that animals are not part of the relevant community (the one whose members are parties to the agreement). (See Chapter 7 for more about Rawls's view.)

Indirect duty views, then, including the best among them, fail to command our rational assent. Whatever ethical theory we should accept rationally, therefore, it must at least recognize that we have some duties directly to animals, just as we have some duties directly to each other. The next two theories I'll sketch attempt to meet this requirement.

The first I call the cruelty-kindness view. Simply stated, this says that we have a direct duty to be kind to animals and a direct duty not to be cruel to them. Despite the familiar, reassuring ring of these ideas, I do not believe that this view offers an adequate theory. To make this clearer, consider kindness. A kind person acts from a certain kind of motive—compassion or concern, for example. And that is a virtue. But there is no guarantee that a kind act is a right act. If I am a generous racist, for example, I will be inclined to act kindly towards members of my own race, favouring their interests above those of others. My kindness would be real and, so far as it goes, good. But I trust it is too obvious to require argument that my kind acts may not be above moral reproach—may, in fact, be positively wrong because rooted in injustice. So kindness, notwithstanding its status as a virtue to be encouraged, simply will not carry the weight of a theory of right action.

Cruelty fares no better. People or their acts are cruel if they display either a lack of sympathy for or, worse, the presence of enjoyment in another's suffering. Cruelty in all its guises is a bad thing, a tragic human failing. But just as a person's being motivated by kindness does not guarantee that he or she does what is right, so the absence of cruelty does not ensure that he or she avoids doing what is wrong. Many people who perform abortions, for example, are not cruel, sadistic people. But that fact alone does not settle the terribly difficult question of the morality of abortion. The case is no different when we examine the ethics of our treatment of animals. So, yes, let us be for kindness and against cruelty. But let us not suppose that being for the one and against the other answers questions about moral right and wrong. [10]

> [10] Probably no one seriously advocates this view as a general moral theory. But many people do seem to assume something like it as a moral account of how animals should be treated.

Some people think that the theory we are looking for is utilitarianism. A utilitarian accepts two moral principles. The first is that of equality: everyone's interests count, and similar interests must be counted as having similar weight or importance. White or black, American or Iranian, human or animal—everyone's pain or frustration matter, and matter just as much as the equivalent pain or frustration of anyone else. The second principle a utilitarian accepts is that of utility: do the act that will bring about the best balance between satisfaction and frustration for everyone affected by the outcome. [11]

> [11] Regan seems to be assuming a preference-satisfaction version of utilitarianism (see the introduction to this chapter). But the main points he is making would apply just as well to a hedonistic version (or to a version that recognizes many sorts of good).

As a utilitarian, then, here is how I am to approach the task of deciding what I morally ought to do: I must ask who will be affected if I choose to do one thing rather than another, how much each individual will be affected, and where the best results are most likely to lie—which option, in other words, is most likely to bring about the best results, the best balance between satisfaction and frustration. That option, whatever it may be, is the one I ought to choose. That is where my moral duty lies.

The great appeal of utilitarianism rests with its uncompromising *egalitarianism:* everyone's interests count and count as much as the like interests of everyone else. The kind of odious discrimination that some forms of contractarianism can justify—discrimination based on race or sex, for example—seems disallowed in principle by utilitarianism, as is speciesism, systematic discrimination based on species membership.

The equality we find in utilitarianism, however, is not the sort an advocate of animal or human rights should have in mind. Utilitarianism has no room for the equal moral rights of different individuals because it has no room for their equal inherent value or worth. What has value for the utilitarian is the satisfaction of an individual's interests, not the individual whose interests they are. A universe in which you satisfy your desire for water, food and warmth is, other things being equal, better than a universe in which these desires are frustrated. And the same is true in the case of an animal with similar desires. But neither you nor the animal have any value in your own right. Only your feelings do. [12]

> [12] Thus, as it has sometimes been put, people (and animals) are for utilitarianism only locations where pleasure or good results or preference satisfaction occurs and are valuable only as means to these ends.

Here is an analogy to help make the philosophical point clearer: a cup contains different liquids, sometimes sweet, sometimes bitter, sometimes a mix of the two. What has value are the liquids: the sweeter the better, the bitterer the worse. The cup, the container, has no value. It is what goes into it, not what they go into, that has value. For the utilitarian you and I are like the cup; we have no value as individuals and thus no equal value. What has value is what goes into us, what we serve as receptacles for; our feelings of satisfaction have positive value, our feelings of frustration negative value.

Serious problems arise for utilitarianism when we remind ourselves that it enjoins us to bring about the best consequences. What does this mean? It doesn't mean the best consequences for me alone, or for my family or friends, or any other person taken individually. No, what we must do is, roughly, as follows: we must add up (somehow!) the separate satisfactions and frustrations of everyone likely to be affected by our choice, the satisfactions in one column, the frustrations in the other. We must total each column for each of the options before us. That is what it means to say the theory is aggregative. And then we must choose that option which is most likely to bring about the best balance of totalled satisfactions over totalled frustrations. Whatever act would lead to this outcome is the one we ought morally to perform—it is where our moral duty lies. And that act quite clearly might not be the same one that would bring about the best results for me personally, or for my family or friends, or for a lab animal. The best aggregated consequences for everyone concerned are not necessarily the best for each individual.

That utilitarianism is an aggregative theory—different individuals' satisfactions or frustrations are added, or summed, or totalled—is the key objection to this theory. My Aunt Bea is old, inactive, a cranky, sour person, though not physically ill. She prefers to go on living. She is also rather rich. I could make a fortune if I could get my hands on her money, money she intends to give me in any event, after she dies, but which she refuses to give me now. In order to avoid a huge tax bite, I plan to donate a handsome sum of my profits to a local children's hospital. Many, many children will benefit from my generosity, and much joy will be brought to their parents, relatives and friends. If I don't get the money rather soon, all these ambitions will come to naught. The once-in-a-lifetime opportunity to make a real killing will be gone. Why, then, not kill my Aunt Bea? Oh, of course I *might* get caught. But I'm no fool and, besides, her doctor can be counted on to co-operate (he has an eye for the same investment and I happen to know a good deal about his shady past). The deed can be done . . . professionally, shall we say. There is *very* little chance of getting caught. And as for my conscience being guilt-ridden, I am a resourceful sort of fellow and will take more than sufficient comfort—as I lie on the beach at Acapulco—in contemplating the joy and health I have brought to so many others. ⑬

⑬ This is another version of a standard sort of objection to utilitarianism.

Suppose Aunt Bea is killed and the rest of the story comes out as told. Would I have done anything wrong? Anything immoral? One would have thought that I had. Not according to utilitarianism. Since what I have done has brought about the best balance between totalled satisfaction and frustration for all those affected by the outcome, my action is not wrong. Indeed, in killing Aunt Bea the physician and I did what duty required.

This same kind of argument can be repeated in all sorts of cases, illustrating, time after time, how the utilitarian's position leads to results that impartial people find morally callous. It *is* wrong to kill my Aunt Bea in the name of bringing about the best results for others. A good end does not justify an evil means. Any adequate moral theory will have to explain why this is so. Utilitarianism fails in this respect and so cannot be the theory we seek.

What to do? Where to begin anew? The place to begin, I think, is with the utilitarian's view of the value of the individual—or, rather, lack of value. In its place, suppose we consider that you and I, for example, do have value as individuals—what we'll call *inherent value.* To say we have such value is to say that we are something more than, something different from, mere receptacles. Moreover, to ensure that we do not pave the way for such injustices as slavery or sexual discrimination, we must believe that all who have inherent value have it equally, regardless of their sex, race, religion, birthplace and so on. Similarly to be discarded as irrelevant are one's talents or skills, intelligence and wealth, personality or pathology, whether one is loved and admired or despised and loathed. The genius and the retarded child, the prince and the pauper, the brain surgeon and the fruit vendor, Mother Teresa and the most unscrupulous used-car salesman—all have inherent value, all possess it equally, and all have an equal right to be treated with respect, to be treated in ways that do not reduce them to the status of things, as if they existed as resources for others. My value as an individual is independent of my usefulness to you. Yours is not dependent on your usefulness to me. For either of us to treat the other in ways that fail to show respect for the other's independent value is to act immorally, to violate the individual's rights. ⑭

⑭ This is very close to Kant's view that human beings are ends in themselves, and Regan makes reasonably clear how this leads to the conclusion that they have rights. (See Ozar's discussion of these points in the deontology section.)

Some of the rational virtues of this view—what I call the rights view—should be evident. Unlike (crude) contractarianism, for example, the rights view *in principle* denies the moral tolerability of any and all forms of racial, sexual or social discrimination; and unlike utilitarianism, this view *in principle* denies that we can justify good results by using evil means that violate an individual's rights—denies, for example, that it could be moral to kill my Aunt Bea to harvest beneficial consequences for others. That would be to sanction the disrespectful treatment of the individual in the name of the social good, something the rights view will not—categorically will not—ever allow.

The rights view, I believe, is rationally the most satisfactory moral theory. It surpasses all other theories in the degree to which it illuminates and explains the foundation of our duties to one another—the domain of human morality. On this score it has the best reasons, the best arguments, on its side. Of course, if it were possible to show that only human beings are included within its scope, then a person like myself, who believes in animal rights, would be obliged to look elsewhere.

But attempts to limit its scope to humans only can be shown to be rationally defective. Animals, it is true, lack many of the abilities humans possess. They can't read, do higher mathematics, build a bookcase or make *baba ghanoush*. Neither can many human beings, however, and yet we don't (and shouldn't) say that they (these humans) therefore have less inherent value, less of a right to be treated with respect, than do others. It is the *similarities* between those human beings who most clearly, most non-controversially have such value (the people reading this, for example), not our differences, that matter most. And the really crucial, the basic similarity is simply this: we are each of us the experiencing subject of a life, a conscious creature having an individual welfare that has importance to us whatever our usefulness to others.

We want and prefer things, believe and feel things, recall and expect things. And all these dimensions of our life, including our pleasure and pain, our enjoyment and suffering, our satisfaction and frustration, our continued existence or our untimely death—all make a difference to the quality of our life as lived, as experienced, by us as individuals. As the same is true of those animals that concern us (the ones that are eaten and trapped, for example), they too must be viewed as the experiencing subjects of a life, with inherent value of their own. [15]

[15] Being "the experiencing subject of a life" is thus Regan's proposal for the basic characteristic that gives a being inherent worth and rights. He is not trying to decide just which animals have this characteristic (whether, for example, fish or even insects do), but is claiming only that the sorts of animals that are standardly used for food, used in laboratory experiments, and hunted do: animals like cows, sheep, chimpanzees, dogs, rabbits, etc. To what extent is this clearly so (given Regan's account here)? (See Discussion Question 2.)

Some there are who resist the idea that animals have inherent value. "Only humans have such value," they profess. How might this narrow view be defended? Shall we say that only humans have the requisite intelligence, or autonomy, or reason? But there are many, many humans who fail to meet these standards and yet are reasonably viewed as having value above and beyond their usefulness to others. Shall we claim that only humans belong to the right species, the species *Homo sapiens?* But this is blatant speciesism. [16] Will it be said, then, that all—and only—humans have immortal souls? Then our opponents have their work cut out for them. I am myself not ill-disposed to the proposition that there are immortal souls. Personally, I profoundly hope I have one. But I would not want to rest my position on a controversial ethical issue on the even more controversial question about who or what has an immortal soul. That is to dig one's hole deeper, not to climb out. Rationally, it is better to resolve moral issues without making more controversial assumptions than are needed. The question of who has inherent value is such a question, one that is resolved more rationally without the introduction of the idea of immortal souls than by its use. [17]

[16] "Speciesism" is the analogue of racism and sexism: holding that members of certain groups are worthy of moral concern or have rights just because they are members of those groups (while others do not just because they are members of different groups), without identifying any difference between these groups that is morally relevant to the issues in question. Humans may have a different moral status from animals, but any such claim must point to some other difference between them—not just to the fact that humans belong to one species and animals belong to other species. (See the discussion of the difference between the concept of a human and the concept of a person in the selection from Thomson.)

[17] If there are immortal souls, is there any clear philosophical (as opposed to religious) reason for thinking that at least some animals do not also have them?

Well, perhaps some will say that animals have some inherent value, only less than we have. Once again, however, attempts to defend this view can be shown to lack rational justification. What could be the basis of our having more inherent value than animals? Their lack of reason, or autonomy, or intellect?

Only if we are willing to make the same judgement in the case of humans who are similarly deficient.

18   Here is Regan's most compelling argument for his claim: we attribute inherent worth and rights to at least some humans whose characteristics are not significantly different from those possessed by animals. Regan takes this to show that the animals have inherent worth as well, but that is not the only possible alternative here. (See Discussion Question 3.)

But it is not true that such humans—the retarded child, for example, or the mentally deranged—have less inherent value than you or I. Neither, then, can we rationally sustain the view that animals like them in being the experiencing subjects of a life have less inherent value. *All* who have inherent value have it *equally,* whether they be human animals or not. 18

Inherent value, then, belongs equally to those who are the experiencing subjects of a life. Whether it belongs to others—to rocks and rivers, trees and glaciers, for example—we do not know and may never know. But neither do we need to know, if we are to make the case for animal rights. We do not need to know, for example, how many people are eligible to vote in the next presidential election before we can know whether I am. Similarly, we do not need to know how many individuals have inherent value before we can know that some do. When it comes to the case for animal rights, then, what we need to know is whether the animals that, in our culture, are routinely eaten, hunted and used in our laboratories, for example, are like us in being subjects of a life. And we do know this. We do know that many—literally, billions and billions—of these animals are the subjects of a life in the sense explained and so have inherent value if we do. And since, in order to arrive at the best theory of our duties to one another, we must recognize our equal inherent value as individuals, reason—not sentiment, not emotion—reason compels us to recognize the equal inherent value of these animals and, with this, their equal right to be treated with respect.

That, *very* roughly, is the shape and feel of the case for animal rights. Most of the details of the supporting argument are missing. They are to be found in the book to which I alluded earlier. Here, the details go begging, and I must, in closing, limit myself to [two] final points.

The first is how the theory that underlies the case for animal rights shows that the animal rights movement is a part of, not antagonistic to, the human rights movement. The theory that rationally grounds the rights of animals also grounds the rights of humans. Thus those involved in the animal rights movement are partners in the struggle to secure respect for human rights—the rights of women, for example, or minorities, or workers. The animal rights movement is cut from the same moral cloth as these.

Second, having set out the broad outlines of the rights view, I can now say why its implications for farming and science, among other fields, are both clear and uncompromising. In the case of the use of animals in science, the rights view is categorically abolitionist. Lab animals are not our tasters; we are not their kings. Because these animals are treated routinely, systematically as if their value were reducible to their usefulness to others, they are routinely, systematically treated with a lack of respect, and thus are their rights routinely, systematically violated. This is just as true when they are used in trivial, duplicative, unnecessary or unwise research as it is when they are used in studies that hold out real promise of human benefits. We can't justify harming or killing a human being (my Aunt Bea, for example) just for these sorts of reason. Neither can we do so even in the case of so lowly a creature as a laboratory rat. It is not just refinement or reduction that is called for, not just larger, cleaner cages, not just more generous use of anaesthetic or the elimination of multiple surgery, not just tidying up the system. It is complete replacement. The best we can do when it comes to using animals in science is—not to use them. That is where our duty lies, according to the rights view.

As for commercial animal agriculture, the rights view takes a similar abolitionist position. The fundamental moral wrong here is not that animals are kept in stressful close confinement or in isolation, or that their pain and suffering, their needs and preferences are ignored or discounted. All these *are* wrong, of course, but they are not the fundamental wrong. They are symptoms and effects of the deeper, systematic wrong that allows these animals to be viewed and treated as lacking independent value, as resources for us—as, indeed, a renewable resource. Giving farm animals more space, more natural environments, more companions does not right the fundamental wrong, any more than giving lab animals more anaesthesia or bigger, cleaner cages would right the fundamental wrong in their case. Nothing less than the total dissolution of commercial animal agriculture will do this, just as, for similar reasons I won't develop at length here, morality requires nothing less than the total elimination of hunting and trapping for commercial and sporting ends. The rights view's implications, then, as I have said, are clear and uncompromising. ⑲

. . .

⑲ Even if animals do have inherent worth (that is, are ends-in-themselves), does it follow that they can never be *used* in any way: as food, for laboratory experiments, as targets for hunting, as pets, for labor of various sorts (as saddle horses, guide dogs, etc.)? (See Discussion Question 4.)

Discussion Questions

1. Despite the many differences between humans and animals, it is highly plausible to think that animals experience pain and indeed that they experience pains of various kinds that are broadly similar to those that humans experience. Suppose you have a choice between an action that will result in a specific sort of moderately severe pain for a human being and an alternative action that will result in a very similar pain for an animal of one of the specific kinds that Regan is mainly concerned with: for example, a cow, pig, dog, or chimpanzee. Most people would choose the action that results in the pain for the animal rather than the one that results in the pain for the human, but is there a clear reason that supports this choice (assuming no special concern or relation to either one)? Why (if at all) is human pain morally more significant than animal pain? (And how much more significant is it?: Does even a small amount of human pain outweigh a very large amount of animal pain? What exactly is the correct tradeoff between the two?)

2. Look carefully at Regan's elaboration (in the passage at Annotation 15) of the elements involved in being "the experiencing subject of a life." To what extent do these all apply straightforwardly and without any serious uncertainty to animals of the sort that Regan is primarily concerned with? Do cows have preferences and expectations and memories? Do they enjoy things and experience frustration? Do they attach importance to their own wel-

fare? Do they have any conception of an "untimely death" (which seems required for the prospect of such a death to make any difference to "the quality of . . . life as lived")? The answer to each of these questions is probably: yes, to some degree (though with much greater doubts about the last two). But how plausible is it that the varying degrees make no difference at all to their "inherent value"? Is Regan right in thinking, as he apparently does, that inherent worth is an all-or-nothing matter, rather than a matter of degree?

3. Suppose you are dealing with an animal (say, a dog) and with a human who is severely retarded or brain damaged so as to be exactly at the same level of intelligence or autonomy (or the more specific characteristics that Regan lists in discussing inherent worth) as the animal. What should your moral attitude be to these two individuals? One alternative, the one favored by Regan, is to accord them each the same degree of inherent worth and the same rights that you accord to normal humans. A second alternative, which he rejects without much in the way of specific argument, would be to accord them each the same lesser degree of worth and rights (perhaps in proportion to their degree of rationality or autonomy or other characteristics as compared to normal humans). And the third alternative is to find some justification for according them very different degrees of worth and rights, the same for the human as normal humans, but much less for the animal. Is the second alternative

clearly wrong, and if so, why? Can you think of any way to defend the third alternative?

4. Kant's principle, which Regan seems to be influenced by, is that it is never permissible to treat humans beings *merely* as means, not that they can never be treated as means in any respect. It is at least initially plausible that what this requires is giving appropriate weight to the interests and needs of others, rather than just to your own interests and needs. Given that animals arguably have interests and needs that are different in important ways from those pertaining to humans, is it possible that some or all of the ways in which we use animals might be morally acceptable after all, according to the Kantian principle? Think about specific cases here (such as the ones listed in Annotation 19).

The Legitimacy of Government and the Nature of Justice

The selections in this chapter are concerned with two central issues in the general area of philosophy known as political philosophy: first, whether and how the very existence of government is morally justified or *legitimate;* and, second, what it is for a society and its governing institutions to be *just* with respect to the distribution of benefits and burdens among its citizens.

WHAT IS THE JUSTIFICATION FOR GOVERNMENT?

Perhaps the most conspicuous features of governments are that they (a) control and restrict the behavior of the citizens they govern and (b) extract economic resources from those citizens. Governments employ *coercive* means for both of these purposes: force and the threat of force. In doing this, the agents of the government behave in ways that would obviously be morally objectionable if practiced by private citizens or by groups such as gangs, organized criminals, or even corporations. And the question is what (if anything) makes the existence of governments and the coercive power that they exercise morally legitimate in a way that private exercises of otherwise similar power would not be. How are governments different from gangs or organized criminals, which might also exert control over a particular area and force the people living there to pay for "protection"?

A further, related question is whether and to what extent obedience to the mandates of government by citizens is itself, to some degree at least, morally required. The fact that behaving (or not behaving) in a certain way is required by law is often taken to be a reason to act accordingly, but is it (always or ever) a *moral* reason, and if so, why? The obvious alternative is that obedience to government is merely a matter of prudence—which would mean that there is no reason not to break the law if one can get away with doing so.

A once popular answer to these questions, though one for which there is little to be said from a philosophical standpoint, is the doctrine of the *divine right* of kings: the view that rulers are in some way anointed by God and rule on the basis of his authority, with obedience to government thereby morally required as an instance of the more general principle that obedience to God is morally required. There are many problems with such a view, but perhaps the most obvious is that of determining who in fact has the status of being thus divinely anointed—a problem obviously made more practically serious by the frequent occasions in which one ruler is overthrown by another in ways—such as coups or assassinations—that would seemingly be illegitimate if the ruler who is overthrown were divinely anointed. (If the ruler who is overthrown was anointed by God, then presumably the new ruler was not, and so is illegitimate.)

As the doctrine of divine right came to be seen as more and more dubious, philosophers looked for an alternative, and some of them found it in the idea that government originates in an agreement, a *social contract,* among the future citizens to leave the *state of nature* that existed previously and form a government. On this view, the fundamental justification for governmental authority is traced to the *consent* of those to whom it applies, with the moral requirement to obey the resulting government being thus a specific instance of the more general moral obligation to conform to agreements which one has deliberately and freely entered into.

There are many questions that can be raised about social contract theories: whether such an event of agreement ever actually took place, what its terms were if it did, and, most importantly, whether and why it should still apply to those later citizens who were not directly involved. Thomas Hobbes and John Locke offer two extremely influential and significantly different accounts of the social contract. David Hume, while agreeing that such an agreement could in principle be the basis of legitimate government, questions whether the authority of existing governments can be justified in this way. His contrary suggestion is that the justification for government derives simply from its *utility:* from the fact that having a government of a certain specific sort produces better overall consequences for all the people involved than any alternative (including both anarchy and other specific governments). Thus Hume, on this issue at least, is a **utilitarian.** (See Chapter 6 for more discussion of the general utilitarian view.)

WHAT IS THE NATURE OF SOCIAL JUSTICE?

One of the main results of social institutions in general and governments in particular is the *distribution* of goods of various kinds, most conspicuously economic ones, among the various people who live in the society in question. It seems clear that not all such distributions are equally acceptable from a moral standpoint and in particular that some of them treat various individuals or groups in ways that are *unjust.* It is thus at least a necessary condition for the acceptability of a set of social institutions that it satisfy the standards of *distributive justice.*

But just what are those standards? What sort of distribution does justice require? One answer that has seemed obviously right to some thinkers, but that few if any actual societies have ever realized, is **egalitarianism:** the view that justice requires that economic goods and other benefits be distributed *equally* among all citizens. Other views advocate unequal distribution on the basis of such criteria as moral merit, contribution to society, and the like. And it is obvious that societies have often in practice distributed benefits on the basis of such criteria as social class, racial or ethnic distinctions, and gender—though few if any philosophers have ever defended distributions of this sort.

Robert Nozick and John Rawls offer influential and very different answers to this question of what justice requires with respect to distribution. Nozick appeals simply to the absence of injustice in the *process* through which a given distribution was produced, with any distribution that is produced via individually just steps itself counting as just. On his view, distributive justice does not require any particular *pattern* of distribution, since free choices by individuals that are in no way individually unjust could lead to widely varying patterns of distribution, including ones that depart quite far from equality. Rawls, on the other hand, presents and argues for two abstract principles of justice, the more important one being that departures from an equal distribution are acceptable only if they benefit those members of society who are least well off. Such a view will not lead to an equal distribution, because giving additional incentives to those who are especially talented or productive may raise overall production to such a degree that even the least well off are still better off than they would have been under a more equal distribution. But the degree of inequality that is compatible with justice will still be much less for Rawls than for Nozick. A further selection from Nozick offers criticisms of Rawls, while the selection from Thomas Scanlon criticizes Nozick and partially defends Rawls.

WHAT IS THE JUSTIFICATION FOR GOVERNMENT?

Thomas Hobbes

One of the earliest and most influential versions of the general idea of a social contract as the basis for government is that presented by the English philosopher Thomas Hobbes (1588–1679) in his *Leviathan*. Hobbes lived through the English Civil War of 1642–1649, which ended with the beheading of King Charles I. He was also a spectator from a greater distance of much other war and turmoil, most strikingly that involved in the devastating Thirty Years War of 1618–1648 on the European continent. It is thus hardly surprising that he attaches great, indeed overriding value to stability, order, and peace.

Hobbes's presentation and defense of his version of a social contract begins with his conception of the situation in which human beings would exist in the absence of government: the *state of nature*. As we will see, Hobbes viewed the state of nature as a state of war of "all against all" in which human life would accordingly, in his famous phrase, be "solitary, poor, nasty, brutish, and short." It is to escape such a state that he envisions people agreeing among themselves to create a *commonwealth* by conferring all their power and authority on a *sovereign* (which might be either one person or a group of people, though Hobbes clearly favored the former alternative).

Most of Hobbes's conception of the status and power of the sovereign can be seen as following directly from the goal of escaping the state of nature and, just as important, guaranteeing (or coming as close to a guarantee as possible) that there will be no relapse into such a condition. It is for this reason that the powers of the sovereign must, according to him, be *absolute,* where this includes not only such things as control of all military power and its use, total lawmaking and judicial power, the power of censorship, and the like, but also the even more extreme idea that each subject shall view the sovereign's actions as though they were his own. But even absolute power turns out to have some surprising limitations. And there is always the concern that the sovereign's power will be eroded, leading to a collapse of the commonwealth and a return to the state of nature. It is this above all that Hobbes wants to guard against.

The Social Contract, from *Leviathan*

OF THE NATURAL CONDITION OF MANKIND AS CONCERNING THEIR FELICITY, AND MISERY ①

① This section contains Hobbes's description of the state of nature. What assumptions is he making about human beings, especially their psychology, and about the world they inhabit? (By *prudence,* Hobbes means something broader than is meant nowadays: wisdom in general with regard to practical matters.)

Nature hath made men so equal, in the faculties of body, and mind; as that though there be found one man sometimes manifestly stronger in body, or of quicker mind than another; yet when all is reckoned together, the difference between man, and man, is not so considerable, as that one man can thereupon claim to himself any benefit, to which another may not pretend, as well as he. For as to the strength of body, the weakest has strength enough to kill the strongest, either by secret machination, or by confederacy with others, that are in the same danger as himself.

And as to the faculties of the mind, (setting aside the arts grounded upon words, and especially that skill of proceeding upon general, and infallible rules, called science; which very few have, and but in few things; as being not a native faculty, born with us . . .) I find yet a greater equality amongst men, than that of strength. For prudence, is but experience; which equal time, equally bestows on all men, in those things they equally apply themselves unto. . . .

From this equality of ability, ariseth equality of hope in the attaining of our ends. And therefore if any two men desire the same thing, which nevertheless they cannot both enjoy, they become enemies; and in the way to their end, (which is principally their own conservation, and sometimes their delectation only) endeavour to destroy, or subdue one another. And from hence it comes to pass, that where an invader hath no more to fear, than another man's single power; if one plant, sow, build, or possess a convenient seat, others may probably be expected to come prepared with forces united, to dispossess, and deprive him, not only of the fruit of his labour, but also of his life, or liberty. And the invader again is in the like danger of another.

And from this diffidence ② of one another, there is no way for any man to secure himself, so reasonable, as anticipation;

② By *diffidence,* Hobbes means just fear and distrust of others—now an archaic meaning.

that is, by force, or wiles, to master the persons of all men he can, so long, till he see no other power great enough to endanger him: and this is no more than his own conservation requireth, and is generally allowed. Also because there be some, that taking pleasure in contemplating their own power in the acts of conquest, which they pursue farther than their security requires; if others, that otherwise would be glad to be at ease within modest bounds, should not by invasion increase their power, they would not be able, long time, by standing only on their defence, to subsist. And by consequence, such augmentation of domin-

From Leviathan *(1651).*

ion over men, being necessary to a man's conservation, it ought to be allowed him.

Again, men have no pleasure (but on the contrary a great deal of grief) in keeping company, where there is no power able to over-awe them all. For every man looketh that his companion should value him at the same rate he sets upon himself: and upon all signs of contempt, or undervaluing, naturally endeavours, as far as he dares (which amongst them that have no common power to keep them in quiet, is far enough to make them destroy each other) to extort a greater value from his contemners, by damage; and from others, by the example.

So that in the nature of man, we find three principal causes of quarrel. First, competition; secondly, diffidence; thirdly, glory.

The first, maketh man invade for gain; the second, for safety; and the third, for reputation. The first use violence, to make themselves masters of other men's persons, wives, children, and cattle; the second, to defend them; the third, for trifles, as a word, a smile, a different opinion, and any other sign of undervalue, either direct in their persons, or by reflection in their kindred, their friends, their nation, their profession, or their name.③

> ③ What does Hobbes mean by *glory,* and why does the desire for it (allegedly) lead people to attack each other? Are they being rational in doing so? (Would having glory make a person safer in the state of nature?)

Hereby it is manifest, that during the time men live without a common power to keep them all in awe, they are in that condition which is called war; and such a war, as is of every man, against every man. For War, consisteth not in battle only, or the act of fighting; but in a tract of time, wherein the will to contend by battle is sufficiently known. . . .

Whatsoever therefore is consequent to a time of war, where every man is enemy to every man; the same is consequent to the time, wherein men live without other security, than what their own strength, and their own invention shall furnish them withal. In such condition, there is no place for industry; because the fruit thereof is uncertain: and consequently no culture of the earth; no navigation, nor use of the commodities that may be imported by sea; no commodious building; no instruments of moving, and removing such things as require much force; no knowledge of the face of the earth; no account of time; no arts; no letters; no society; and which is worst of all, continual fear, and danger of violent death; and the life of man, solitary, poor, nasty, brutish, and short.

. . .

To this war of every man against every man, this also is consequent; that nothing can be unjust. The notions of right and wrong, justice and injustice have there no place. Where there is no common power, there is no law: where no law, no injustice. Force, and fraud, are in war the two cardinal virtues. Justice, and injustice are none of the faculties neither of the body, nor mind. If they were, they might be in a man that were alone in the world, as well as his senses, and passions. They are qualities, that relate to men in society, not in solitude. It is consequent also to the same condition, that there be no propriety, no dominion, no *mine* and *thine* distinct; but only that to be every man's, that he can get; and for so long, as he can keep it.④ And thus much for the ill condition, which many by mere nature is actually placed in; though with a

> ④ What is Hobbes saying here about the nature and source of right and wrong, justice and injustice, and property rights? Is he correct that each of these cannot exist apart from society?

possibility to come out of it, consisting partly in the passions, partly in his reason.

The passions that incline men to peace, are fear of death; desire of such things as are necessary to commodious living; and a hope by their industry to obtain them. And reason suggesteth convenient articles of peace, upon which men may be drawn to agreement.

OF THE FIRST AND SECOND NATURAL LAWS, AND OF CONTRACTS

The RIGHT OF NATURE, which writers commonly call *jus naturale,* is the liberty each man hath, to use his own power, as he will himself, for the preservation of his own nature; that is to say, of his own life; and consequently, of doing any thing, which in his own judgment, and reason, he shall conceive to be the aptest means thereunto.

. . .

A LAW OF NATURE (*lex naturalis*) is a precept, or general rule, found out by reason, by which a man is forbidden to do that, which is destructive of his life, or taketh away the means of preserving the same; and to omit that, by which he thinketh it may be best preserved. . . . ⑤

⑤ By a *law of nature* Hobbes seems to mean a requirement of rational prudence or rational self-interest (not a divine command or a principle of objective morality). A *right of nature* is a liberty established on the same basis.

And because the condition of man, (as hath been declared in the precedent chapter) is a condition of war of every one against every one; in which case every one is governed by his own reason; and there is nothing he can make use of, that may not be a help unto him, in preserving his life against his enemies; it followeth, that in such a condition, every man has a right to every thing: even to one another's body. And therefore, as long as this natural right of every man to every thing endureth, there can be no security to any man, (how strong or wise soever he be) of living out the time, which nature ordinarily alloweth men to live. And consequently it is a precept, or general rule of reason, *that every man, ought to endeavour peace, as far as he has hope of obtaining it; and when he cannot obtain it, that he may seek, and use, all helps, and advantages of war.* The first branch of which rule, containeth the first, and fundamental law of nature; which is, *to seek peace, and follow it.* The second, the sum of the right of nature; which is, *by all means we can, to defend ourselves.*

From this fundamental law of nature, by which men are commanded to endeavor peace, is derived this second law; *that a man be willing, when others are so too, as farforth, as for peace, and defence of himself he shall think it necessary, to lay down this right to all things; and be contented with so much liberty against other men, as he would allow other men against himself.* For as long as every man holdeth this right, of doing any thing he liketh; so long are all men in the condition of war. But if other men will not lay down their right, as well as he; then there

is no reason for any one, to divest himself of his: for that were to expose himself to prey, (which no man is bound to) rather than to dispose himself to peace. . . . ⑥

Whensoever a man transferreth his right, or renounceth it; it is either in consideration of some right reciprocally transferred to himself; or for some other good he hopeth for thereby. For it is a voluntary act: and of the voluntary acts of every man, the object is some *good to himself.* . . .

The mutual transferring of right, is that which men call CONTRACT.

. . . one of the contractors, may deliver the thing contracted for on his part, and leave the other to perform his part at some determinate time after, and in the mean time be trusted; and then the contract on his part, is called PACT, or COVENANT: or both parts may contract now, to perform hereafter. . . . ⑦

If a covenant be made, wherein neither of the parties perform presently, but trust one another; in the condition of mere nature, (which is a condition of war of every man against every man) upon any reasonable suspicion, it is void: but if there be a common power set over them both, with right and force sufficient to compel performance, it is not void. For he that performeth first, has no assurance the other will perform after; because the bonds of words are too weak to bridle men's ambition, avarice, anger, and other passions, without the fear of some coercive power; which in the condition of mere nature, where all men are

⑥ Hobbes thinks that no one could rationally prefer a state of war. Peace is obviously preferable *if* it can be obtained in a way that does not expose a person to even more risk than the state of war. Think about whether and how this might be done, given Hobbes's conception of the state of nature. (If someone lives close enough to attack you and has enough strength to succeed if you are caught off guard, can you afford not to attack him first?)

⑦ What is needed in order to escape the state of nature is an agreement—a *contract*—in which people mutually surrender their natural rights to attack each other in pursuit of their own survival. Such a contract is a *covenant* in Hobbesian terminology because it involves promises of future performance. (It wouldn't be good enough merely to promise not to attack right now.)

equal, and judges of the justness of their own fears, cannot possibly be supposed. And therefore he which performeth first, does but betray himself to his enemy; contrary to the right (he can never abandon) of defending his life, and means of living.⑧

⑧ Here is Hobbes's fundamental reason for thinking that peace is impossible on this basis so long as people continue to be in a state of nature. Refraining from attacking (when a person has a favorable opportunity, such as while the other person is asleep) in return for a promise that other persons will not attack in the future (when circumstances are favorable to them) cannot be a rational thing to do because there is not and cannot be any way to guarantee the other person's future performance. (See Discussion Question 1.)

But in a civil estate, where there is a power set up to constrain those that would otherwise violate their faith, that fear is no more reasonable; and for that cause, he which by the covenant is to perform first, is obliged so to do.

. . .

OF OTHER LAWS OF NATURE

From that law of nature, by which we are obliged to transfer to another, such rights, as being retained, hinder the peace of mankind, there followeth a third; which is this, *that men perform their covenants made:* without which, covenants are in vain, and but empty words; and the right of all men to all things remaining, we are still in the condition of war.

And in this law of nature, consisteth the fountain and original of JUSTICE. For where no covenant hath preceded, there hath no right been transferred, and every man has right to every thing; and consequently, no action can be unjust. But when a covenant is made, then to break it is *unjust;* and the definition of INJUSTICE, is no other than *the not performance of covenant.* And whatsoever is not unjust, is *just.*⑨

⑨ Notice that Hobbes seems to be saying here that justice and injustice are concerned *only* with the keeping and not keeping of covenants. This is a rather narrow conception of justice, too narrow for many philosophers.

But because covenants of mutual trust, where there is fear of not performance on either part, (as hath been said in the former chapter) are invalid; though the original of justice be the making of covenants; yet injustice actually there can be none, till the cause of such fear be taken away; which while men are in the natural condition of war, cannot be done. Therefore before the names of just, and unjust can have place, there must be some coercive power, to compel men equally to the performance of their covenants, by the terror of some punishment, greater than the benefit they expect by the breach of their covenant. . . .

OF THE CAUSES, GENERATION, AND DEFINITION OF A COMMONWEALTH

The final cause, end, or design of men, (who naturally love liberty and dominion over others) in the introduction of that restraint upon themselves (in which we see them live in commonwealths) is the foresight of their own preservation, and of a more contented life thereby; that is to say, of getting themselves out from that miserable condition of war, which is necessarily consequent (as hath been shown) to the natural passions of men, when there is no visible power to keep them in awe, and tie them by fear of punishment to the performance of their covenants, and observation of those laws of nature set down in the [previous two] chapters.

For the laws of nature (as *justice, equity, modesty, mercy,* and (in sum) *doing to others, as we would be done to,*) of themselves, without the terror of some power, to cause them to be observed, are contrary to our natural passions, that carry us to partiality, pride, revenge, and the like. And covenants, without the sword, are but words, and of no strength to secure a man at all. . . .⑩

⑩ Hobbes seems to be saying here that agreements are mere words and so have no moral force unless they can be socially enforced. Does that seem right?

Nor is it the joining together of a small number of men, that gives them this security; because in small numbers, small additions on the one side or the other, make the advantage of strength so great, as is sufficient to carry the victory; and therefore gives encouragement to an invasion. . . .

Nor is it enough for the security, which men desire should last all the time of their life, that they be governed, and directed by one judgment, for a limited time; as in one battle, or one war. For though they obtain a victory by their unanimous endeavour against a foreign enemy; yet afterwards, when either they have no common enemy, or he that by one part is held for an enemy, is by another part held for a friend, they must needs by the difference of their interests dissolve, and fall again into a war amongst themselves.⑪

⑪ Might something less extreme than Hobbes's eventual proposal—joining into a smaller group or choosing a temporary leader—be enough to yield security? Perhaps temporarily—but not, Hobbes argues, in the long run.

. . .

The only way to erect such a common power, as may be able to defend them from the invasion of foreigners, and the injuries of one another, and thereby to secure them in such sort, as that by their own industry, and by the fruits of the earth, they may nourish themselves and live contentedly; is, to confer all their power and strength upon one man, or upon one assembly of men, that may reduce all their wills, by plurality of voices, unto one will: which is as much as to say, to appoint one man, or assembly of men, to bear their person; and even one to own, and acknowledge himself to be author of whatsoever he that so beareth their person, shall act, or cause to be acted, in those things which concern the common peace and safety; and therein to submit their wills, every one to his will, and their judgments, to his judgment. This is more than consent, or concord; it is a real unity of them all, in one and the same person, made by covenant of every man with every man, in such manner, as if every man should say to every man, *I authorise and give up my right of governing myself, to this man, or to this assembly of men, on this condition, that thou give up thy right to him, and authorize all his actions in like manner.* This done, the multitude so united in one person, is called a COMMONWEALTH. . . . This is the generation of that great LEVIATHAN, or rather (to speak more reverently) of that *mortal god,* to which we owe under the *immortal God,* our peace and defence. For by this authority, given him by every particular man in the commonwealth, he hath the use of so much power and strength conferred on him, that by terror thereof, he is enabled to form the wills of them all, to peace at home, and mutual aid against their enemies abroad. And in him consisteth the essence of the commonwealth; which (to define it,) is *one person, of whose acts a great multitude, by mutual covenants one with another, have made themselves every one the author, to the end he may use the strength and means of them all, as he shall think expedient, for their peace and common defence.*

And he that carrieth this person, is called SOVEREIGN, and said to have sovereign power; and every one besides, his SUBJECT.⑫

The attaining to this sovereign power, is by two ways. One, by natural force; as when a man maketh his children, to submit themselves, and their children to his government, as being able to destroy them if they refuse; or by war subdueth his enemies to his will, giving them their lives on that condition. The other, is when men agree amongst themselves, to submit to some man, or assembly of men, voluntarily, on confidence to be protected by him against all others. This latter, may be called a political commonwealth, or commonwealth by *institution;* and the former, a commonwealth by *acquisition.* . . .⑬

⑫ Thus the only viable solution, in Hobbes's view, is for all or almost all those in a given area to surrender all their rights of self-defense and all their power and authority to one *sovereign* (either a single person or a group, but we will speak as though it is a single person), thereby creating a *commonwealth.*

⑬ A second and rather different way (listed first in this paragraph) in which the authority of a sovereign over a particular group of people can be established is by force, by conquest. In this way, a commonwealth established in one area or over one group might be extended to another area or group. (Consider, in light of this, the issue of what might happen if most of the people in a given area agree to institute a sovereign, but a few refuse to go along.)

OF THE RIGHTS OF SOVEREIGNS BY INSTITUTION

A *commonwealth* is said to be *instituted,* when a *multitude* of men do agree, and *covenant, every one, with every one,* that to whatsoever *man,* or *assembly of men,* shall be given by the major part, the *right to present* the person of them all, (that is to say, to be their *representative*) every one, as well he that *voted for it,* as he that *voted against it,* shall *authorize* all the actions and judgments, of that man, or assembly of men, in the same manner, as if they were his own, to the end, to live peaceably amongst themselves, and be protected against other men. ⑭

⑭ How should we think of the power of the sovereign (who may, Hobbes suggests, be chosen by a majority vote of those who agree to the creation of a commonwealth)? This passage gives the core of Hobbes's answer: each person agrees to authorize the judgments and actions of the sovereign "as if they were his own." Think about this idea very carefully. It has some surprising consequences, as we will see shortly.

From this institution of a commonwealth are derived all the *rights,* and *faculties* of him, or them, on whom the sovereign power is conferred by the consent of the people assembled.

First, because they covenant, it is to be understood, they are not obliged by former covenant to any thing repugnant hereunto. And consequently they that have already instituted a commonwealth, being thereby bound by covenant, to own the actions, and judgments of one, cannot lawfully make a new covenant, amongst themselves, to be obedient to any other, in any thing whatsoever, without his permission. . . .

Secondly, because the right of bearing the person of them all, is given to him they make sovereign, by covenant only of one to another, and not of him to any of them; there can happen no breach of covenant on the part of the sovereign; and consequently none of his subjects, by any pretence of forfeiture, can be freed from his subjection. That he which is made sovereign maketh no covenant with his subjects beforehand, is manifest; because either he must make it with the whole multitude, as one party to the covenant; or he must make a several covenant with every man. With the whole, as one party, it is impossible; because as yet they are not one person: and if he make so many several covenants as there be men, those covenants after he hath the sovereignty are void, because what act soever can be pretended by any one of them for breach thereof, is the act both of himself, and of all the rest, because done in the person, and by the right of every one of them in particular. ⑮ Besides, if any one, or more of them, pretend a breach of the covenant made by the sovereign at his institution; and

others, or one other of his subjects, or himself alone, pretend there was no such breach, there is in this case, no judge to decide the controversy; it returns therefore to the sword again; and every man recovereth the right of protecting himself by his own strength, contrary to the design they had in the institution. . . .

Thirdly, because the major part hath by consenting voices declared a sovereign; he that dissented must now consent with the rest; that is, be contented to avow all the actions he shall do, or else justly be destroyed by the rest. For if he voluntarily entered into the congregation of them that were assembled, he sufficiently declared thereby his will, (and therefore tacitly covenanted) to stand, to what the major part should ordain. . . . And whether he be of the congregation, or not; and whether his consent be asked, or not, he must either submit to their decrees, or be left in the condition of war he was in before; wherein he might without injustice be destroyed by any man whatsoever. ⑯

⑯ Here we have the explicit answer to the question of what happens to those who disagree about the formation of the commonwealth or the choice of the sovereign.

⑮ Can the sovereign violate the covenant that establishes the commonwealth? Hobbes's surprising answer is that he cannot because he is not a party to it at all. Think carefully about the reason he gives. (Presumably the idea is that the sovereign *qua sovereign* is not and cannot be a party to the covenant, not that the person or group that later becomes the sovereign might not have been such a party.)

Fourthly, because every subject is by this institution author of all the actions, and judgments of the sovereign instituted; it follows, that whatsoever he doth, it can be no injury to any of his subjects; nor ought he to be by any of them accused of injustice. For he that doth any thing by authority from another, doth therein no injury to him by whose authority he acteth; but by this institution of a commonwealth, every particular man is author of all the sovereign doth; and consequently he that complaineth of injury from his sovereign, complaineth of that whereof he himself is author; and therefore ought not to accuse any man but himself; no nor himself of injury; because to do injury to one's self, is impossible. It is true that they that have sovereign power, may commit iniquity; but not injustice, or injury in the proper signification.

Fifthly, and consequently to that which was said last, no man that hath sovereign power can justly be put to death, or otherwise in any manner by his subjects punished. For seeing every subject is author of the actions of his sovereign; he punisheth another, for the actions committed by himself.⒄

17 In this paragraph and the preceding one are two alleged, very surprising consequences of each subject agreeing to regard the actions of the sovereign as his own: the sovereign cannot injure (that is, wrongly harm) the subjects; and the sovereign may not be justly punished by the subjects for any of his actions.

And because the end of this institution, is the peace and defence of them all; and whosoever has right to the end, has right to the means; it belongeth of right, to whatsoever man, or assembly that hath the sovereignty, to be judge both of the means of peace and defence; and also of the hindrances, and disturbances of the same; and to do whatsoever he shall think necessary to be done, both beforehand, for the preserving of peace and security, by prevention of discord at home, and hostility from abroad; and, when peace and security are lost, for the recovery of the same. And therefore,

Sixthly, it is annexed to the sovereignty, to be judge of what opinions and doctrines are averse, and what conducing to peace; and consequently, on what occasions, how far, and what, men are to be trusted withal, in speaking to multitudes of people; and who shall examine the doctrines of all books before they be published. For the actions of men proceed from their opinions; and in the well-governing of opinions, consisteth the well-governing of men's actions, in order to their peace, and concord. And though in matter of doctrine, nothing ought to be regarded but the truth; yet this is not repugnant to regulating of the same by peace. For doctrine repugnant to peace, can no more be true, than peace and concord can be against the law of nature. . . .

Seventhly, is annexed to the sovereignty, the whole power of prescribing the rules, whereby every man may know, what goods he may enjoy, and what actions he may do, without being molested by any of his fellow-subjects; and this is it men call *propriety* [property]. . . .

Eighthly, is annexed to the sovereignty, the right of judicature; that is to say, of hearing and deciding all controversies, which may arise concerning law, either civil, or natural; or concerning fact. For without the decision of controversies, there is no protection of one subject, against the injuries of another; . . . and to every man remaineth, from the natural and necessary appetite of his own conservation, the right of protecting himself by his private strength, which is the condition of war; and contrary to the end for which every commonwealth is instituted.

Ninthly, is annexed to the sovereignty, the right of making war and peace with other nations, and commonwealths; that is to say, of judging when it is for the public good, and how great forces are to be assembled, armed, and paid for that end; and to levy money upon the subjects, to defray the expenses thereof. . . .

Tenthly, is annexed to the sovereignty, the choosing of all counsellors, ministers, magistrates, and officers, both in peace, and war. For seeing the sovereign is charged with the end, which is the common peace and defence, he is understood to have power to use such means, as he shall think most fit for his discharge.

Eleventhly, to the sovereign is committed the power of rewarding with riches, or honour; and of punishing with corporal, or pecuniary punishment, or with ignominy every subject according to the law he hath formerly made; or if there be no law made, according as he shall judge most to conduce to the encouraging of men to serve the commonwealth, or deterring of them from doing disservice to the same.

Lastly, considering what values men are naturally apt to set upon themselves; what respect they look for from others; and how little they value other men; from whence continually arise amongst them, emulation, quarrels, factions, and at last war, to the destroying of one another, and diminution of their strength against a common enemy; it is necessary that there be laws of honour. . . . To the sovereign therefore it belongeth also to give titles of honour; and to appoint what order of place, and dignity, each man shall hold; and what signs of respect, in public or private meetings, they shall give to one another.

These are the rights, which make the essence of sovereignty; and which are the marks, whereby a man may discern in what man, or assembly of men, the sovereign power is placed, and resideth. For these are incommunicable, and inseparable. . . .⒅

18 The rest of the powers of the sovereign are more obvious, given the basic rationale of enabling him to preserve peace and avoid a return to the state of nature.

But a man may here object, that the condition of subjects is very miserable; as being obnoxious to the lusts, and other irregular passions of him, or them that have so unlimited a power in their hands. And commonly that they live under a monarch, think it the fault of monarchy; and they that live under the government of democracy, or other sovereign assembly, attribute all the inconvenience to that form of commonwealth; whereas the power in all forms, if they be perfect enough to protect them, is the same; not considering that the estate of man can never be without some incommodity or other; and that the greatest, that in any form of government can possibly happen to the people in general, is scarce sensible, in respect to the miseries, and horrible calamities, that accompany a civil war, or that dissolute condition of masterless men, without subjection to laws, and a coercive power to tie their hands from rapine and revenge. . . . 19

> 19 Here is Hobbes's reply to the many that would object to the idea of an absolute sovereign, citing the various evils that often flow from such a system. He makes two points: first, that however bad those evils may be, the state of nature is much, much worse; and, second, that an absolute sovereign is the only way to *guarantee* (or come as close as possible to a guarantee) that such a horrible state will not recur.

OF THE LIBERTY OF SUBJECTS

. . .

To come now to the particulars of the true liberty of a subject; that is to say, what are the things, which though commanded by the sovereign, he may nevertheless, without injustice, refuse to do; we are to consider, what rights we pass away, when we make a commonwealth; or (which is all one,) what liberty we deny ourselves, by owning all the actions (without exception) of the man, or assembly we make our sovereign. . . .

. . . it is manifest, that every subject has liberty in all those things, the right whereof cannot by covenant be transferred. I have shewn before . . . that covenants, not to defend a man's own body, are void. Therefore,

If the sovereign command a man (though justly condemned,) to kill, wound, or maim himself; or not to resist those that assault him; or to abstain from the use of food, air, medicine, or any other thing, without which he cannot live; yet hath that man the liberty to disobey.

If a man be interrogated by the sovereign, or his authority, concerning a crime done by himself, he is not bound (without assurance of pardon) to confess it; because no man (as I have shown . . .) can be obliged by covenant to accuse himself.

Again, the consent of a subject to sovereign power, is contained in these words, *I authorize, or take upon me, all his actions;* in which there is no restriction at all, of his own former natural liberty: for by allowing him to *kill me,* I am not bound to kill myself when he commands me. It is one thing to say, *kill me, or my fellow, if you please;* another thing to say, *I will kill myself, or my fellow.* It followeth therefore, that

No man is bound by the words themselves, either to kill himself, or any other man; and consequently, that the obligation a man may sometimes have, upon the command of the sovereign to execute any dangerous, or dishonourable office, dependeth not on the words of our submission; but on the intention, which is to be understood by the end thereof. When therefore our refusal to obey, frustrates the end for which the sovereignty was ordained; then there is no liberty to refuse: otherwise there is.

Upon this ground, a man that is commanded as a soldier to fight against the enemy, though his sovereign have right enough to punish his refusal with death, may nevertheless in many cases refuse, without injustice; as when he substituteth a sufficient soldier in his place: for in this case he deserteth not the service of the commonwealth. And there is allowance to be made for natural timorousness; not only to women, (of whom no such dangerous duty is expected,) but also to men of feminine courage. . . .when the defence of the commonwealth, requireth at once the help of all that are able to bear atms, every one is obliged; because otherwise the institution of the commonwealth, which they have not the purpose, or courage to preserve, was in vain.

To resist the sword of the commonwealth, in defence of another man, guilty, or innocent, no man hath liberty; because such liberty, takes away from the sovereign, the means of protecting us; and is therefore destructive of the very essence of government. But in case a great many men together, have already resisted the sovereign power unjustly, or committed some capital crime, for which every one of them expecteth death, whether have they not the liberty then to join together, and assist, and defend one another? Certainly they have: for they but defend their lives, which the guilty man may as well do, as the innocent. There was indeed injustice in the first breach of their duty; their bearing of arms subsequent to it, though it be to maintain what they have done, is no new unjust act. And if it be only to defend their persons, it is not unjust at all. But the offer of pardon taketh from them, to whom it is offered, the plea of self-defence, and maketh their perserverance in assisting, or defending the rest, unlawful. [20]

[20] Do the subjects of the commonwealth have any liberties left (beyond those that the sovereign may choose to allow them)? Somewhat surprisingly, they do—indeed liberties that could obviously threaten the very stability of the commonwealth. To see why Hobbes says this, you need to think again about the rationale for the original agreement, as viewed from the standpoint of each individual person.

As for other liberties, they depend on the silence of the law. In cases where the sovereign has prescribed no rule, there the subject hath the liberty to do, or forbear, according to his own discretion. And therefore such liberty is in some places more, and in some less; and in some times more, in other times less, according as they that have the sovereignty shall think most convenient. . . .

The obligation of subjects to the sovereign, is understood to last as long, and no longer, than the power lasteth, by which he is able to protect them. For the right men have by nature to protect themselves, when none else can protect them, can by no covenant be relinquished. [21] The sovereignty is the soul of the commonwealth; which once departed from the body, the members do no more receive their motion from it. The end of obedience is protection; which, wheresoever a man seeth it, either in his own, or in another's sword, nature applieth his obedience to it, and his endeavour to maintain it. And though sovereignty, in the intention of them that make it, be immortal; yet is it in its own nature, not only subject to violent death, by foreign war; but also through the ignorance, and passions of men, it hath in it, from the very institution, many seeds of a natural mortality, by intestine discord.

[21] Here is another fundamental limitation to the sovereign's absolute power, one that again follows from the very rationale of the social contract.

. . .

OF THOSE THINGS THAT WEAKEN, OR TEND TO THE DISSOLUTION OF A COMMONWEALTH [22]

Though nothing can be immortal, which mortals make; yet, if men had the use of reason they pretend to, their commonwealths might be secured, at least, from perishing by internal diseases. For by the nature of their institution, they are designed to live, as long as mankind, or as the laws of nature, or as justice itself, which gives them life. . . .

[22] Hobbes was very conscious of the potential fragility of a commonwealth, and in this section warns of various things that could lead to its collapse. Some of these are obvious in light of the previous discussion, but others suggest what Hobbes's objections would have been to other forms of government.

Amongst the *infirmities* therefore of a commonwealth, I will reckon in the first place, those that arise from an imperfect institution, and resemble the diseases of a natural body, which proceed from a defectuous procreation.

Of which, this is one, *that a man to obtain a kingdom, is sometimes content with less power, than to the peace, and defence of the commonwealth is necessarily required.* From whence it cometh to pass, that when the exercise of the power laid by, is for the public safety to be resumed, it hath the resemblance of an unjust act; which disposeth great numbers of men (when occasion is presented) to rebel. . . .

In the second place, I observe the *diseases* of a commonwealth, that proceed from the poison of seditious doctrines, whereof one is, *That every private man is judge of good and evil actions.* This is true in the condition of mere nature, where there are no civil laws; and also under civil government, in such cases as are not determined by the law. But otherwise it is manifest, that the measure of good and evil actions, is the civil law; and the judge the legislator, who is always representative of the commonwealth. From this false doctrine, men are disposed to debate with themselves, and dispute the commands of the commonwealth; and afterwards to obey, or disobey them, as in their private judgments they shall think fit. Whereby the commonwealth is distracted and *weakened.*

Another doctrine repugnant to civil society, is, that *whatsoever a man does against his conscience, is sin;* and it dependeth on the presumption of making himself judge of good and evil. For a man's conscience, and his judgment is the same thing; and as the judgment, so also the conscience may be erroneous. Therefore, though he that is subject to no civil law, sinneth in all he does against his conscience, because he has no other rule to follow but his own reason; yet it is not so with him that lives in a commonwealth; because the law is the public conscience, by which he hath already undertaken to be guided. Otherwise in such diversity, as there is of private consciences, which are but private opinions, the commonwealth must needs be distracted, and no man dare to obey the sovereign power, farther than it shall seem good in his own eyes.

. . .

A fourth opinion, repugnant to the nature of a commonwealth, is this, *that he that hath the sovereign power, is subject to the civil laws.* It is true, that sovereigns are all subject to the laws of nature. . . . But to those laws which the sovereign himself, that is, which the commonwealth maketh, he is not subject. For to be subject to laws, is to be subject to the commonwealth, that is to the sovereign representative, that is to himself; which is not subjection, but freedom from the laws. Which error, because it setteth the laws above the sovereign, setteth also a judge above him, and a power to punish him; which is to make a new sovereign; and again for the same reason a third, to punish the second; and so continually without end, to the confusion, and dissolution of the commonwealth.

A fifth doctrine, that tendeth to the dissolution of a commonwealth, is, *that every private man has an absolute propriety in his goods; such, as excludeth the right of the sovereign.* Every man has indeed a propriety that excludes the right of every other subject: and he has it only from the sovereign power; without the protection whereof, every other man should have equal right to the same. But if the right of the sovereign also be excluded, he cannot perform the office they have put him into; which is, to defend them both from foreign enemies, and from the in-

juries of one another; and consequently there is no longer a commonwealth.

. . .

There is a sixth doctrine, plainly, and directly against the essence of a commonwealth; and it is this, *that the sovereign power may be divided.* For what is it to divide the power of a commonwealth, but to dissolve it; for powers divided mutually destroy each other. And for these doctrines, men are chiefly beholding to some of those, that making profession of the laws, endeavour to make them depend upon their own learning, and not upon the legislative power.[23]

. . .

Lastly, when in a war (foreign or intestine,) the enemies get a final victory; so as (the forces of the commonwealth keeping the field no longer), there is no farther protection of subjects in their loyalty; then is the commonwealth DISSOLVED, and every man at liberty to protect himself by such courses as his own discretion shall suggest unto him. For the sovereign, is the public soul, giving life and motion to the commonwealth; which expiring, the members are governed by it no more, than the carcase of a man, by his departed (though immortal) soul. For though the right of a sovereign monarch cannot be extinguished by the act of another; yet the obligation of the members may. For he that wants protection, may seek it any where; and when he hath it, is obliged (without fraudulent pretence of having submitted himself out of fear,) to protect his protection as long as he is able. But when the power of an assembly is once suppressed, the right of the same perisheth utterly; because the assembly itself is extinct; and consequently, there is no possibility for the sovereignty to re-enter.

[23] Here (and in the discussion of the fourth opinion) is Hobbes's objection to a doctrine that lies at the heart of the United States Constitution: the idea of division (and balance) of power. He is not saying that such a government will collapse at once, but that it essentially involves a possibility that can lead to its own destruction and hence a return to the state of nature. What response might a proponent of the American system of government give to Hobbes?

Discussion Questions

1. In thinking about the problem of trying to achieve peace in the state of nature, it is helpful to appeal to the following kind of reasoning, typical of that which is studied in *rational choice theory*. Suppose that person A has a neighbor, person B, the two being approximately equal in strength and other relevant capacities. Suppose that A and B attempt to achieve peace by entering into an agreement not to attack each other. Suppose also that there are easily identifiable times when an attack by one on the other is virtually certain to succeed (when the potential victim is asleep, for example). Focusing now on a situation in which B is in such a vulnerable condition, consider the choices available to A: he can keep the agreement or he can attack B anyway (presumably destroying him). When the situation is reversed, B has the same two choices. Each of their two choices has two possible results, depending on what the other person does, yielding the following *decision-theoretic matrix* of choices and outcomes:

	B keeps the agreement	B attacks
A keeps the agreement	At least temporary peace	A is killed; B is more secure
A attacks	B is killed; A is more secure	Return to a state of war

Think now of the values of these results for each of the two parties. Even temporary peace is better than war, but war is better than death. And the death of the other person is better than temporary peace because it removes all threat as far as that person is concerned. This yields the following "payoff" matrix, where the numbers represent the *ordinal* value of the results (1 is best), with the value for A being listed first:

	B keeps the agreement	B attacks
A keeps the agreement	2, 2	4, 1
A attacks	1, 4	3, 3

Look at this from A's perspective: whatever B chooses, A does better by attacking than by keeping the agreement. And the same thing is true for B. Thus the rational, self-interested choice for each of them is apparently to attack—even though by doing so each of them ends up with the next-to-worst possible outcome. (Notice that it is being assumed that the two choices are made independently of each other—but this seems to be true in the state of nature.) This is a version of what has become known as "the prisoner's dilemma" (named after a different example in which each of two accused criminals must decide whether or not to "rat" on the other). It seems to capture pretty well what Hobbes has in mind in his discussion of the state of nature.

Explain how this provides a rationale for instituting a sovereign, that is, how having a sovereign over A and B would solve the problem. Is there any other way out of this situation, one where the parties remain in the state of nature? This might involve some basis on which a person could choose to keep such an agreement without violating his own rational self-interest. One thing to consider here is how this argument might be affected by the presence of other people. Suppose that there are other persons, C, D, E, and so on, who are witnessing from afar the proceedings between A and B. How might they react to A's making one choice or the other, and how might such reactions alter the value of the overall outcome of each choice for A?

2. There is a problem lurking in Hobbes's view, about which he says very little—the problem of enforcement. Suppose that a commonwealth has been formed and you have been chosen by majority vote (or even unanimous consent) to be the sovereign. Perhaps we put a little hat on your head and say "Congratulations! You're the sovereign." You proceed to formulate and announce various rules requiring people not to attack each other, to pay taxes, to serve in the police or army, and so forth. These rules require your subjects to do various things that they might otherwise prefer not to do. How are you to enforce them? Suppose that you call a violation of a rule to

someone's attention and point at your hat, but they shrug their shoulders and continue doing whatever they were doing. What can you do? You aren't strong enough by yourself to enforce the rules with very much chance of success, especially if the rule breakers band together to resist. What you need is a group of enforcers—a posse. But how can you get one if people won't obey your commands? Is there any solution to this problem, or does Hobbes's account of how government is created fall apart right at the beginning? Here it might help to think about how the leaders of groups that aren't legally constituted get and maintain power—groups such as street gangs and the like.

3. Hobbes holds a view of human nature according to which human beings are self-interested individuals for whom society is of value only if and to the extent that it leads to greater security or other concrete advantages (such as economic exchange). Others have held views according to which human beings are essentially social creatures, incapable of having satisfactory lives outside of society. What do you think about this question? Is Hobbes right? If not, how seriously does this undermine his arguments?

John Locke

The English philosopher John Locke (1632–1704) offers in his *Second Treatise of Government* an account of the idea of a social contract that has been even more influential than the one given by Hobbes. (In case you are wondering, the *First Treatise* was a critique of the view that the political authority of kings derives from "divine right.") Locke lived a bit later than Hobbes and was more extensively involved in practical politics than almost any other philosopher. He was an adviser and assistant to the Earl of Shaftesbury, who was one of the leaders of the movement (following the restoration of the British monarchy after Cromwell) that attempted to prevent the eventual James II from ascending the British throne because of his Roman Catholic views. Shaftesbury eventually had to flee the country in 1683 to avoid execution for treason, and Locke soon followed. Shaftesbury died in exile, but Locke returned to England with William and Mary at the time of the "Glorious Revolution" of 1688–1689 (in which the Stuart monarchy was quickly and bloodlessly overthrown). Locke subsequently served in the resulting government in several important positions. The two *Treatises* were written at least in part as a justification of the political movement that culminated in the Glorious Revolution.

Like Hobbes, Locke begins his account of the origin and justification of government with an account of the state of nature, but a state of nature that is substantially less fearsome than the one Hobbes portrays. In Locke's view, people in the state of nature are capable of living in at least relative peace, in large part because they are capable of understanding through reason a moral *law of nature* (which Locke views as laid down by God), a law that each of them is morally entitled to enforce. Problems can still arise, however: some people may ignore the moral law and be powerful enough to get away with it, and even those who recognize it may be biased in their own favor in their interpretation of it. These problems are serious enough, in Locke's view, to motivate the formation of a community and the institution of a government empowered to take over the enforcement of the law of nature. But they do not justify conferring absolute power on the government, a situation that in Locke's view would be *worse* than the state of nature. Instead, the powers of the government are limited and are conferred on it only provisionally, with the people retaining the right to overthrow the government and replace it with another if it exceeds its proper authority or violates their rights.

Here we see Locke's rationale for the Glorious Revolution. His view was also one major influence on the American Founding Fathers at the time of the American Revolution and is reflected clearly in the Declaration of Independence.

The Social Contract, from *Second Treatise of Government*

OF THE STATE OF NATURE

4. To understand political power, right, and derive it from its original, we must consider what state all men are naturally in, and that is, *a state of perfect freedom* to order their actions, and dispose of their possessions and persons, as they think fit, within the bounds of the law of nature; without asking leave, or depending upon the will of any other man.

A *state also of equality,* wherein all the power and jurisdiction is reciprocal, no one having more than another; there being nothing more evident, than that creatures of the same species and rank, promiscuously born to all the same advantages of nature, and the use of the same faculties, should also be equal one amongst another without subordination or subjection; unless the lord and master of them all should, by any manifest declaration of his will, set one above another, and confer on him, by an evident and clear appointment, an undoubted right to dominion and sovereignty.

. . .

6. But though this be *a state of liberty,* yet *it is not a state of licence:* though man in that state have an uncontrollable liberty to dispose of his person or possessions, yet he has not liberty to destroy himself, or so much as any creature in his possession, but where some nobler use than its bare preservation calls for it. The *state of nature* has a law of nature to govern it, which

obliges every one: And reason, which is that law, teaches all mankind, who will but consult it, that being all *equal and independent,* no one ought to harm another in his life, health, liberty, or possessions. For men being all the workmanship of one omnipotent and infinitely wise Maker; all the servants of one sovereign master, sent into the world by his order, and about his business; they are his property, whose workmanship they are, made to last during his, not another's pleasure. And being furnished with like faculties, sharing all in one community of nature, there cannot be supposed any such subordination among us, that may authorize us to destroy another, as if we were made for one another's uses, as the inferior ranks of creatures are for ours. Every one, as he is *bound to preserve himself,* and not to quit his station willfully, so by the like reason, when his own preservation comes not in competition, ought he, as much as he can, *to preserve the rest of mankind,* and may not, unless it be to do justice to an offender, take away or impair the life, or what tends to the preservation of life, the liberty, health, limb, or goods of another.①

7. And that all men may be restrained from invading others rights, and from doing hurt to one another, and the law of nature be observed, which willeth the peace and *preservation of all mankind,* the *execution* of the law of nature is, in that state, put into every man's hands, whereby every one has a right to punish the transgressors of that law to such a degree as may hinder its violation. For the *law of nature* would, as all other laws that concern men in this world, be in vain,

From Second Treatise of Government *(1690).*

if there were no body that in the state of nature had a *power to execute* that law, and thereby preserve the innocent and restrain offenders. And if any one in the state of nature may punish another for any evil he has done, every one may do so. For in that *state of perfect equality,* where naturally there is no superiority or jurisdiction of one over another, what any may do in prosecution of that law, every one must needs have a right to do.②

8. And thus, in the state of nature, *one man comes by a power over another;* but yet no absolute or arbitrary power, to use a criminal, when he has got him in his hands, according to the passionate heats, or boundless extravagancy of his own will; but only to retribute to him, so far as calm reason and conscience dictate, what is proportionate to his *transgression;* which is so much as may serve for reparation and *restraint.* For these two are the only reasons, why one man may lawfully do harm to another, which is that we call *punishment.*③ In transgressing the law of nature, the offender declares himself to live by another rule than that of reason and common equity, which is that measure God has set to the actions of men, for their mutual security; and so he becomes dangerous to mankind, the tye, which is to secure them from injury and violence, being slighted and broken by him. Which being a trespass against the whole species, and the peace and safety of it, provided for by the law of nature; every man upon this score, by the right he hath to preserve mankind in general, may restrain, or, where it is necessary, destroy things noxious to them, and so may bring such evil on any one, who hath transgressed that law, as may make him repent the doing of it, and thereby deter him, and by his example others, from doing the like mischief. And in this case, and upon this ground, *every man hath a right to punish the offender, and be executioner of the law of nature.*

. . .

10. Besides the crime which consists in violating the law, and varying from the right rule of reason, whereby a man so far becomes degenerate, and declares himself to quit the principles of human nature, and to be a noxious creature, there is commonly injury done to some person or other, and some other man receives damage by his transgression, in which case he who hath received any damage, has besides the right of punishment common to him with other men, a particular right to seek *reparation* from him that has done it. And any other person who finds it just, may also join with him that is injured, and assist him in recovering from the offender so much as may make satisfaction for the harm he has suffered.

11. . . . And thus it is, that every man, in the state of nature, has a power to kill a murderer, both to deter others from doing the like injury, which no reparation can compensate, by the example of the punishment that attends it from every body, and also *to secure* men from the attempts of a criminal, who having renounced reason, the common rule and measure, God hath given to mankind, hath by the unjust violence and slaughter he hath committed upon one, declared war against all mankind; and therefore may be destroyed as a *lion* or a *tiger,* one of those wild savage beasts, with whom men can have no society nor security. . . .④

13. To this strange doctrine, viz. That *in the state of nature every one has the executive power* of the law of nature, I doubt not

---

**① ** This paragraph presents Locke's conception of the law of nature, which he later summarizes as the idea that "all, as much as may be, should be preserved" (§ 183, not included in this selection). Unlike Hobbes's "laws of nature," which are fundamentally prudential in character, the Lockean law of nature is a moral law, laid down by God, but in Locke's view still discernible by human reason, without the need to appeal to religious authority (which would be unavailable in the state of nature).

**② ** But who is to enforce such a law, in the absence of a government? Whereas Hobbes thinks that there can be no meaningful morality or justice outside of society, Locke's view is that the very existence of the law of nature brings with it a right to *execute* (that is, enforce) it, a right that is equally shared by all in the situation of equality and independence that defines the state of nature. As he makes clear in what follows, this right of execution is not limited to self-defense, but extends also to protecting others from violations of their rights and punishing the offender.

**③ ** Locke offers two justifications for punishment: *reparation* to the injured party and *restraint* of the criminal from committing similar offenses. These are said to be limited to what is "proportionate" to the crime. (How clear a limitation is this?)

**④ ** Restraint may involve also *deterring* others from committing similar crimes.

but it will be objected, that it is unreasonable for men to be judges in their own cases, that self-love will make men partial to themselves and their friends: And on the other side, that ill nature, passion and revenge will carry them too far in punishing others; and hence nothing but confusion and disorder will follow, and that therefore God hath certainly appointed government to restrain the partiality and violence of men. I easily grant, that civil government is the proper remedy for the inconveniencies of the state of nature, which must certainly be great, where men may be judges in their own case, since it is easy to be imagined, that he who was so unjust as to do his brother an injury, will scarce be so just as to condemn himself for it: 5 But I shall desire those who make this objection to remember, that *absolute monarchs* are but men, and if government is to be the remedy of those evils, which necessarily follow from men's being judges in their own cases, and the state of nature is therefore not to be endured,

5 Here is the first main rationale for leaving the state of nature and instituting government: even those who recognize the law of nature may be biased in their application of it, favoring themselves and their friends and exaggerating the degree of punishment that is justified to those who harm them. (But Locke proceeds to argue that a Hobbesian absolute sovereign not only fails to solve this problem but actually makes it worse.)

I desire to know what kind of government that is, and how much better it is than the state of nature, where one man commanding a multitude, has the liberty to be judge in his own case, and may do to all his subjects whatever he pleases, without the least liberty to any one to question or control those who execute his pleasure? and in whatsoever he doth, whether led by reason, mistake or passion, must be submitted to? Much better it is in the state of nature, wherein men are not bound to submit to the unjust will of another: And if he that judges, judges amiss in his own, or any other case, he is answerable for it to the rest of mankind.

. . .

OF THE STATE OF WAR

16. The *state of war* is a state of *enmity* and *destruction:* And therefore declaring by word or action, not a passionate and hasty, but a sedate settled design upon another man's life, *puts him in a state of war* with him against whom he has declared such an intention, and so has exposed his life to the other's power to be taken away by him, or any one that joins with him in his defence, and espouses his quarrel: it being reasonable and just I should have a right to destroy that which threatens me with destruction. For *by the fundamental law of nature, man being to be preserved* as much as possible, when all cannot be preserved, the safety of the innocent is to be preferred: And one may destroy a man who makes war upon him, or has discovered an enmity to his being, for the same reason that he may kill a *wolf* or a *lion;* because such men are not under the ties of the common law of reason, have no other rule, but that of force and violence, and so may be treated as beasts of prey, those dangerous and noxious creatures, that will be sure to destroy him whenever he falls into their power. 6

6 A state of war comes to exist when one person makes it clear that he does not accept the restrictions imposed by the law of nature. Locke first focuses on the case where such a person threatens an innocent person's life.

17. And hence it is, that he who attempts to get another man into his absolute power, does thereby *put himself into a state of war* with him; it being to be understood as a declaration of a design upon his life. For I have reason to conclude, that he who would get me into his power without my consent, would use me as he pleased when he got me there, and destroy me too when he had a fancy to it; for no body can desire to *have me in his absolute power* unless it be to compel me by force to that which is against the right of my freedom, i.e. make me a slave. To be free from such force is the only security of my preservation; and reason bids me look on him, as an enemy to my preservation, who would take away that freedom which is the fence to it; so that he who makes an *attempt to enslave* me, thereby puts himself into a state of war with me. He that, in the state of nature, *would take away the freedom* that belongs to any one in that state, must necessarily be supposed to have a design to take away every thing else, that *freedom* being the foundation of all the rest: As he that, in the state of society, would take away the freedom belonging to those of that society or commonwealth, must be supposed to design to take away from them every thing else, and so be looked on as *in a state of war.*

18. This makes it lawful for a man to *kill a thief,* who has not in the least hurt him, nor declared any design upon his life, any farther, than by the use of force, so to get him in his power, as to take away his money, or what he pleases, from him; because using force, where he has no right, to get me into his power, let his pretence be what it will, I have no reason to suppose, that he, who would *take away my liberty,* would not, when he had me in his power, take away every thing else. And therefore it is lawful for me to treat him as one who has put *himself into a state of war* with me, i.e. kill him if I can; for to that hazard does he justly expose himself, whoever introduces a state of war, and is aggressor in it.⑦

> ⑦ The law of nature also guarantees rights to freedom and property (which Locke views as acquired when a person "mixes his labor" with unowned parts of the world). Thus a person who fails to respect those specific rights also shows that he does not recognize the law of nature in general and so, Locke says, may be justifiably killed.

19. And here we have the plain *difference between the state of nature and the state of war;* which however some men have confounded, are as far distant, as a state of peace, good will, mutual assistance and preservation, and a state of enmity, malice, violence and mutual destruction, are one from another. Men living together according to reason, without a common superior on earth, with authority to judge between them, is *properly the state of nature.* But force, or a declared design of force, upon the person of another, where there is no common superior on earth to appeal to for relief, *is the state of war:* And it is the want of such an appeal gives a man the right of war even against an aggressor, though he be in society and a fellow subject. Thus a *thief,* whom I cannot harm, but by appeal to the law, for having stolen all that I am worth, I may kill, when he sets on me to rob me but of my horse or coat; because the law, which was made for my preservation, where it cannot interpose to secure my life from present force, which, if lost, is capable of no reparation, permits me my own defence, and the right of war, a liberty to kill the aggressor, because the aggressor allows not time to appeal to our common judge, nor the decision of the law, for remedy in a case where the mischief may be irreparable. *Want of a common judge with authority, puts all men in a state of* nature: *Force without right, upon a man's person, makes a state of war,* both where there is, and is not, a common judge.⑧

. . .

21. To avoid this *state of war* (wherein there is no appeal but to heaven, and wherein every the least difference is apt to end, where there is no authority to decide between the contenders) is *one great reason of men's putting themselves into society,* and quitting the state of nature. For where there is an authority, a power on earth, from which relief can be had by *appeal,* there the continuance of the *state of war* is excluded, and the controversy is decided by that power. . . .⑨

> ⑧ Thus for Locke, unlike Hobbes, there is a clear distinction between the state of nature and a state of war. The state of nature may degenerate into a state of war, but this is in no way necessary or inevitable.

> ⑨ But the risk of such a state of war is still a second main rationale for leaving the state of nature in favor of organized society.

OF POLITICAL OR CIVIL SOCIETY

87. Man being born, as has been proved, with a title to perfect freedom, and an uncontrolled enjoyment of all the rights and privileges of the law of nature, equally with any other man, or number of men in the world, hath by nature a power, not only to preserve his property, that is, his life, liberty, and estate, against the injuries and attempts of other men; but to judge of and punish the breaches of that law in others, as he is persuaded the offence deserves, even with death itself, in crimes where the heinousness of the fact, in his opinion, requires it. But because no *political* society can be, nor subsist, without having in itself the power to preserve the property, and, in order thereunto, punish the offences of all those of that society; there and there only is *political society,* where every one of the members hath quitted his natural power, resigned it up into the hands of the community in all cases that excludes him not from appealing for protection to the law established by it. And thus all private judgment of every particular member being excluded, the community comes to be umpire by settled standing rules, indifferent, and the same to all parties; and by men having authority from the community, for the execution of those rules, decides all the differences that may

happen between any members of that society concerning any matter of right; and punishes those offences which any member hath committed against the society, with such penalties as the law has established, whereby it is easy to discern, who are, and who are not, in *political society* together. Those who are united into one body, and have a common established law and judicature to appeal to, with authority to decide controversies between them, and punish offenders, *are in civil society* one with another: but those who have no such common appeal, I mean on earth, are still in the state of nature, each being, where there is no other, judge for himself, and executioner: which is, as I have before shewed, the perfect *state of nature.* [10]

[10] Political society exists, by definition, only where people have surrendered to a community (and ultimately to a particular government) their natural right to enforce the law of nature and punish transgressions.

88. And thus the commonwealth comes by a power to set down what punishment shall belong to the several transgressions which they think worthy of it, committed amongst the members of that society, (which is the *power of making laws*) as well as it has the power to punish any injury done unto any of its members, by any one that is not of it, (which is the power of war and peace) and all this for the preservation of the property of all the members of that society, as far as is possible. But though every man who has entered into civil society, and is become a member of any commonwealth, has thereby quitted his power to punish offences against the law of nature, in prosecution of his own private judgment; yet with the judgment of offences, which he has given up to the legislative in all cases where he can appeal to the magistrate, he has given a right to the commonwealth to employ his force, for the execution of the judgments of the commonwealth whenever he shall be called to it; which indeed are his own judgments, they being made by himself, or his representative. And herein we have the original of the legislative and executive power of civil society, which is to judge by standing laws, how far offences are to be punished, when committed within the commonwealth; and also to determine, by occasional judgments founded on the present circumstances of the fact, how far injuries from without are to be vindicated; and in both these to employ all the force of all the members, when there shall be need. [11]

89. Whenever therefore any number of men are so united into one society, as to quit every one his executive power of the law of nature, and to resign it to the public, there and there only is a political, or civil society. And this is done, wherever any number of men, in the state of nature, enter into society to make one people, one body politic, under one supreme government; or else when any one joins himself to, and incorporates with any government already made. For hereby he authorizes the society, or, which is all one, the legislative thereof, to make laws for him, as the public good of the society shall require; to the execution whereof, his own assistance . . . is due. And this puts men out of a state of nature into that of a commonwealth, by setting up a judge on earth, with authority to determine all the controversies, and redress the injuries that may happen to any member of the commonwealth: which judge is the legislative, or magistrate appointed by it. And wherever there are any number of men, however associated, that have no such decisive power to appeal to, there they are still in the state of nature.

[11] In this way, the community acquires from the individuals that compose it the power (a) to make laws defining crimes and determining the punishment for them, and (b) to enforce those laws, using the force of its members, as needed. Here (a) is the source of the legislative power and (b) the source of the executive power.

90. Hence it is evident, that absolute monarchy, which by some men is counted the only government in the world, is indeed inconsistent with civil society, and so can be no form of civil government at all; for the end of civil society being to avoid and remedy these inconveniencies of the state of nature, which necessarily follow from every man's being judge in his own case, by setting up a known authority, to which every one of that society may appeal upon any injury received, or controversy that may arise, and which every one of the society ought to obey; wherever any persons are, who have not such an authority to appeal to for the decision of any difference between them, there those persons are still *in the state of nature.* And so is every *absolute prince,* in respect of those who are under his dominion.

91. For he being supposed to have all, both legislative and executive power in himself alone, there is no judge to be found, no appeal lies open to any one, who may fairly, and indifferently, and with authority decide, and from whose decision relief and redress

may be expected of any injury or inconveniency that may be suffered from the prince, or by his order: so that such a man, however intitled, *czar,* or *grand seignior,* or how you please, is as much in *the state of nature,* with all under his dominion, as he is with the rest of mankind. For wherever any two men are, who have no standing rule, and common judge to appeal to on earth, for the determination of controversies of right betwixt them, there they are still *in the state of nature,* and under all the inconveniencies of it, with only this woful difference to the subject, or rather slave of an absolute prince; that whereas in the ordinary state of nature he has a liberty to judge of his right, and, according to the best of his power, to maintain it; now, whenever his property is invaded by the will and order of his monarch, he has not only no appeal, as those in society ought to have, but, as if he were degraded from the common state of rational creatures, is denied a liberty to judge of, or to defend his right; and so is exposed to all the misery and inconveniencies that a man can fear from one, who being in the unrestrained state of nature, is yet corrupted with flattery, and armed with power.⑫

⑫ Locke reiterates and further elaborates his objection to absolute monarchy as a form of government: far from escaping the state of nature, the subjects of an absolute monarch are still in a state of nature in relation to him, but even less able to defend themselves.

. . .

OF THE BEGINNING OF POLITICAL SOCIETIES

95. Men being, as has been said, by nature, all free, equal, and independent, no one can be put out of this estate, and subjected to the political power of another, without his own consent. The only way, whereby any one divests himself of his natural liberty, and puts on the *bonds of civil society,* is by agreeing with other men to join and unite into a community, for their comfortable, safe, and peaceable living one amongst another, in a secure enjoyment of their properties, and a greater security against any, that are not of it. This any number of men may do, because it injures not the freedom of the rest; they are left as they were in the liberty of the state of nature. When any number of men have so *consented to make one community or government,* they

are thereby presently incorporated, and make *one body politic,* wherein the *majority* have a right to act and conclude the rest.⑬

96. For when any number of men have, by the consent of every individual, made a *community,* they have thereby made that *community* one body, with a power to act as one body, which is only by the will and determination of the majority. For that which acts any community, being only the *consent* of the individuals of it, and it being necessary to that which is one body to move one way, it is necessary the body should move that way whither the greater force carries it, which is the *consent of the majority:* or else it is impossible it should act or continue one body, one community, which the consent of every individual that united into it, agreed that it should; and so every one is bound by that consent to be concluded by the majority. And therefore we see, that in assemblies, impowered to act by positive laws, where no number is set by that positive law which impowers them, the *act of the majority* passes for the act of the whole, and of course determines, as having, by the law of nature and reason, the power of the whole.

97. And thus every man, by consenting with others to make one body politic under one government, puts himself under an obligation, to every one of that society, to submit to the determination of the majority, and to be concluded by it; or else this *original compact,* whereby he with others incorporate into one society, would signify nothing, and be no compact, if he be left free, and under no other ties than he was in before in the state of nature. For what appearance would there be of any compact? What new engagement if he were no farther tied by any decrees of the society, than he himself thought fit, and did actually consent to? This would be still as great a liberty, as he himself had before his compact, or any one else in the state of nature hath, who may submit himself, and consent to any acts of it if he thinks fit.

98. For if *the consent of the majority* shall not, in reason, be received as *the act of the whole,* and conclude every individual; nothing but the consent of every individual can make any thing to be the act of

⑬ A political or civil society (two terms for the same thing) comes into being, according to Locke, only when a group of people all agree voluntarily to surrender the liberty and rights they have in the state of nature and unite into a community.

the whole; But such a consent is next to impossible ever to be had. . . . Such a constitution as this would make the mighty *leviathan* of a shorter duration than the feeblest creatures, and not let it outlast the day it was born in: which cannot be supposed, till we can think, that rational creatures should desire and constitute societies only to be dissolved. For where the majority cannot conclude the rest, there they cannot act as one body, and consequently will be immediately dissolved again. [14]

[14] The actions of such a community are to be determined by majority rule, since to require unanimity would make it futile to form a community in the first place. As is implicit here and more explicit later, Locke views the act of uniting into a community—unlike the formation of a specific sort of government—as irrevocable. If people could withdraw whenever they disapprove of the community action, then the formation of the community would have no real force.

99. Whosoever therefore out of a state of nature unite into a community, must be understood to give up all the power, necessary to the ends for which they unite into society, to the majority of the community, unless they expressly agreed in any number greater than the majority. And this is done by barely agreeing to *unite into one political society,* which is *all the compact* that is, or needs be, between the individuals, that enter into, or make up a commonwealth. And thus that, which begins and actually *constitutes any political society,* is nothing, but the consent of any number of freemen capable of a majority, to unite and incorporate into such a society. And this is that, and that only, which did, or could give beginning to any lawful government in the world.

. . .

OF THE ENDS OF POLITICAL SOCIETY AND GOVERNMENT

123. If man in the state of nature be so free, as has been said; if he be absolute lord of his own person and possessions, equal to the greatest, and subject to no body, why will he part with his freedom? why will he give up this empire, and subject himself to the dominion and control of any other power? To which it is obvious to answer, that though in the state of nature he hath such a right, yet the enjoyment of it is very uncertain, and constantly exposed to the invasion of others. For all being kings as much as he, every man his equal, and

the greater part no strict observers of equity and justice, the enjoyment of the property he has in this state is very unsafe, very unsecure. This makes him willing to quit this condition, which, however free, is full of fears and continual dangers: and it is not without reason, that he seeks out, and is willing to join in society with others, who are already united, or have a mind to unite, for the mutual preservation of their lives, liberties, and estates, which I call by the general name, property.

124. The great and *chief end,* therefore, of men's uniting into commonwealths, and putting themselves under government, is *the preservation of their property.* [15] To which in the state of nature there are many things wanting.

[15] As the previous sentence makes clear, "property" for Locke includes life and liberty, as well as property in the ordinary sense.

First, There wants an established, settled, known law, received and allowed by common consent to be the standard of right and wrong, and the common measure to decide all controversies between them. For though the law of nature be plain and intelligible to all rational creatures; yet men being biassed by their interest, as well as ignorant for want of studying it, are not apt to allow of it as a law binding to them in the application of it to their particular cases.

125. *Secondly,* In the state of nature there wants *a known and indifferent judge,* with authority to determine all differences according to the established law. For every one in that state being both judge and executioner of the law of nature, men being partial to themselves, passion and revenge is very apt to carry them too far, and with too much heat, in their own cases; as well as negligence, and unconcernedness, to make them too remiss in other men's.

126. *Thirdly,* In the state of nature, there often wants power to back and support the sentence when right, and to give it due execution. They who by any injustice offended, will seldom fail, where they are able, by force to make good their injustice; such resistance many times makes the punishment dangerous, and frequently destructive, to those who attempt it. [16]

[16] These three points spell out more fully the difficulties pertaining to enforcing the law of nature in the state of nature.

127. Thus mankind, notwithstanding all the privileges of the state of nature, being but in an ill condition, while they remain in it, are quickly driven

into society. Hence it comes to pass that we seldom find any number of men live any time together in this state. The inconveniencies that they are therein exposed to, by the irregular and uncertain exercise of the power every man has of punishing the transgressions of others, make them take sanctuary under the established laws of government, and therein seek *the preservation of their property*. It is this makes them so willingly give up every one his single power of punishing, to be exercised by such alone, as shall be appointed to it amongst them; and by such rules as the community, or those authorized by them to that purpose, shall agree on. And in this we have the original *right and rise of both the legislative and executive power,* as well as of the governments and societies themselves.

128. For in the state of nature, to omit the liberty he has of innocent delights, a man has two powers.

The first is to do whatsoever he thinks fit for the preservation of himself and others within the permission of the *law of nature:* by which law, common to them all, he and all the rest of *mankind are one community,* make up one society, distinct from all other creatures. And, were it not for the corruption and viciousness of degenerate men, there would be no need of any other; no necessity that men should separate from this great and natural community, and by positive agreements combine into smaller and divided associations.

The other power a man has in the state of nature, is the *power to punish the crimes* committed against that law. Both these he gives up, when he joins in a private, if I may so call it, or particular politic society, and incorporates into any commonwealth, separate from the rest of mankind.

129. The first *power,* viz. *of doing whatsoever he thought fit for the preservation of himself,* and the rest of mankind, *he gives up* to be regulated by laws made by the society, so far forth as the preservation of himself and the rest of that society shall require; which laws of the society in many things confine the liberty he had by the law of nature.

130. *Secondly,* The *power of punishing he wholly gives up,* and engages his natural force, (which he might before employ in the execution of the law of nature, by his own single authority, as he thought fit) to assist the executive power of the society, as the law thereof shall require. For being now in a new state, wherein he is to enjoy many conveniencies, from the

labour, assistance, and society of others in the same community, as well as protection from its whole strength; he is to part also, with as much of his natural liberty, in providing for himself, as the good, prosperity, and safety of the society shall require; which is not only necessary, but just, since the other members of the society do the like.⟨17⟩

⟨17⟩ Why do you think that one of these powers is, in Locke's view, wholly given up when entering into society, while the other is only partially given up? What is the rationale for this difference?

131. But though men, when they enter into society, give up the equality, liberty, and executive power they had in the state of nature, into the hands of the society, to be so far disposed of by the legislative, as the good of the society shall require; yet it being only with an intention in every one the better to preserve himself, his liberty and property; (for no rational creature can be supposed to change his condition with an intention to be worse) the power of the society, or legislative constituted by them, *can never be supposed to extend farther, than the common good;* but is obliged to secure every one's property, by providing against those three defects above mentioned, that made the state of nature so unsafe and uneasy. And so whoever has the legislative or supreme power of any commonwealth, is bound to govern by established standing laws, promulgated and known to the people, and not by extemporary decrees; by indifferent and upright judges, who are to decide controversies by those laws; and to employ the force of the community at home, *only in the execution of such laws;* or abroad to prevent or redress foreign injuries, and secure the community from inroads and invasion. And all this to be directed to no other *end,* but the *peace, safety,* and *public good* of the people.⟨18⟩

⟨18⟩ Can the supreme power use the power that men have given up to enhance the wealth of a few at the expense of the many?

. . .

OF THE EXTENT OF THE LEGISLATIVE POWER

134. The great end of men's entering into society being the enjoyment of their properties in peace and safety, and the great instrument and means of that being the laws established in that society; *the first and*

fundamental positive law of all commonwealths *is the establishing of the legislative* power; as the *first and fundamental natural law,* which is to govern even the legislative itself, *is the preservation of the society,* and (as far as will consist with the public good) of every person in it.[19] This *legislative* is not only *the supreme power* of the commonwealth, but sacred and unalterable in the hands where the community have once placed it; nor can any edict of any body else, in what form soever conceived, or by what power soever backed, have the force and obligation of a law, which has not its *sanction from* that *legislative* which the public has chosen and appointed; for without this the law could not have that, which is absolutely necessary to its being a *law, the consent of the society;* over whom no body can have a power to make laws, but by their own consent, and by authority received from them; and therefore all the obedience, which by the most solemn ties any one can be obliged to pay, ultimately terminates in this supreme power, and is directed by those laws which it enacts; nor can any oaths to any foreign power whatsoever, or any domestic subordinate power, discharge any member of the society from his *obedience to the legislative,* acting pursuant to their trust; nor oblige him to any obedience contrary to the laws so enacted, or farther than they do allow; it being ridiculous to imagine one can be tied ultimately to obey any power in the society, which is not the supreme.[20]

135. Though the legislative, whether placed in one or more, whether it be always in being, or only by intervals, though it be the supreme power in every commonwealth; yet,

First, It is *not,* nor can possibly be absolutely *arbitrary* over the lives and fortunes of the people. For it being but the joint power of every member of the so-

> [19] "Positive law" is man-made law, as opposed to natural law. And the most fundamental such law is the one that establishes and delineates the lawmaking authority or authorities of the society. (In many societies, this would be the most important part of a written constitution.)

> [20] "The legislative" (that is the persons or bodies in whom the legislative power is placed) constitutes the supreme authority within the society, from which any other legitimate authorities must ultimately derive their power.

ciety given up to that person, or assembly, which is legislator, it can be no more than those persons had in a state of nature before they entered into society, and gave up to the community. For no body can transfer to another more power than he has in himself; and no body has an absolute arbitrary power over himself, or over any other, to destroy his own life, or take away the life or property of another. A man, as has been proved, cannot subject himself to the arbitrary power of another; and having in the state of nature no arbitrary power over the life, liberty, or possession of another, but only so much as the law of nature gave him for the preservation of himself and the rest of mankind; this is all he doth, or can give up to the commonwealth, and by it to the legislative power, so that the legislative can have no more than this. Their power, in the utmost bounds of it, is *limited to the public good* of the society. It is a power, that hath no other end but preservation, and therefore can never have a right to destroy, enslave, or designedly to impoverish the subjects. The obligations of the law of nature cease not in society, but only in many cases are drawn closer, and have by human laws known penalties annexed to them, to enforce their observation. Thus the law of nature stands as an eternal rule to all men, legislators as well as others. The rules that they make for other men's actions, must, as well as their own and other men's actions, be conformable to the law of nature, i.e. to the will of God, of which that is a declaration; and the *fundamental law of nature being the preservation of mankind,* no human sanction can be good or valid against it.[21]

> [21] Even the powers of the legislative authority are severely limited, according to Locke. He proceeds to enumerate four main restrictions. First, even the legislative authority does not and cannot legitimately have arbitrary, unlimited power over the citizens. Think carefully about how this follows from the source of the legislative power.

136. *Secondly,* The legislative or supreme authority cannot assume to itself a power to rule, by extemporary, arbitrary decrees, but *is bound to dispense justice,* and decide the rights of the subject, *by promulgated, standing laws, and known authorised judges.* For the law of nature being unwritten, and so no-where to be found, but in the minds of men; they who through passion, or interest, shall miscite, or misapply it, cannot so easily be convinced of their mistake, where there is no established judge: and so

it serves not, as it ought, to determine the rights, and fence the properties of those that live under it; especially where every one is judge, interpreter, and executioner of it too, and that in his own case: and he that has right on his side having ordinarily but his own single strength, hath not force enough to defend himself from injuries, or to punish delinquents. To avoid these inconveniencies, which disorder men's properties in the state of nature, men unite into societies, that they may have the united strength of the whole society to secure and defend their properties, and may have standing rules to bound it, by which every one may know what is his. To this end it is that men give up all their natural power to the society which they enter into, and the community put the legislative power into such hands as they think fit: with this trust, that they shall be governed by *declared laws,* or else their peace, quiet, and property will still be at the same uncertainty, as it was in the state of nature.

137. Absolute arbitrary power, or governing without *settled standing laws,* can neither of them consist with the ends of society and government, which men would not quit the freedom of the state of nature for, and tie themselves up under, were it not to preserve their lives, liberties, and fortunes, and by *stated rules* of right and property to secure their peace and quiet. It cannot be supposed that they should intend, had they a power so to do, to give to any one, or more, an *absolute arbitrary power* over their persons and estates, and put a force into the magistrate's hand to execute his unlimited will arbitrarily upon them. This were to put themselves into a worse condition than the state of nature, wherein they had a liberty to defend their right against the injuries of others, and were upon equal terms of force to maintain it, whether invaded by a single man, or many in combination. Whereas by supposing they have given up themselves to the absolute arbitrary power and will of a legislator, they have disarmed themselves, and armed him, to make a prey of them when he pleases. . . . 22

22 Second, the legislative authority must govern by "settled standing laws," not arbitrary or ad hoc decrees. Part of the reason for this is by now obvious. But there is a further, underlying rationale: one of the purposes for leaving the state of nature is to avoid the situation where the natural law is subject to different interpretations, leading to conflict and insecurity.

138. *Thirdly,* The *supreme power cannot take* from any man part of his property without his own consent. For the preservation of property being the end of government, and that for which men enter into society, it necessarily supposes and requires, that the people should *have property,* without which they must be supposed to lose that, by entering into society, which was the end for which they entered into it; too gross an absurdity for any man to own. *Men* therefore *in society having property,* they have such right to the goods, which by the law of the community are theirs, that no body hath a right to take their substance or any part of it from them, without their own consent; without this they have no property at all. For I have truly no property in that, which another can by right take from me, when he pleases, against my consent. Hence it is a mistake to think, that the *supreme or legislative power* of any commonwealth can do what it will, and dispose of the estates of the subject arbitrarily, or take any part of them at pleasure. . . . 23

23 Third, Locke says that the legislative authority cannot take property from people without their consent. The rationale is that preserving property was the main end of instituting society and government in the first place. This seems to make it uncertain how a government can pay its own necessary expenses. In the following paragraph, however, Locke seems to say that majority consent of the people or their representatives is enough to satisfy this requirement. (In thinking about this, remember the broad conception of "property" pointed out in Annotation 15.)

140. It is true, governments cannot be supported without great charge, and it is fit every one who enjoys his share of the protection, should pay out of his estate his proportion for the maintenance of it. But still it must be with his own consent, i.e. the consent of the majority, giving it either by themselves, or their representatives chosen by them. For if any one shall claim a *power to lay* and levy *taxes* on the people, by his own authority, and without such consent of the people, he thereby invades the *fundamental law of property,* and subverts the end of government. For what property have I in that, which another may by right take when he pleases, to himself?

141. *Fourthly,* The *legislative cannot transfer the power of making laws* to any other hands. For it being but a delegated power from the people, they who have it cannot pass it over to others. The people alone can

appoint the form of the commonwealth, which is by constituting the legislative, and appointing in whose hands that shall be. And when the people have said, we will submit to rules, and be governed by laws made by such men, and in such forms, no body else can say other men shall make laws for them; nor can the people be bound by any laws, but such as are enacted by those whom they have chosen, and authorized to make laws for them. The power of the legislative being derived from the people by a positive voluntary grant and institution, can be no other than what that positive grant conveyed, which being only to make laws, and not to make legislators, the legislative can have no power to transfer their authority of making laws and place it in other hands. 24

> 24 Fourth, the legislative authority cannot transfer its fundamental lawmaking power to someone else (which does not rule out the delegation of subsidiary powers). Whoever exercises that power in effect has it on loan from the people, but does not own it in a way that would allow giving it to someone else.

. . .

OF THE LEGISLATIVE [AND] EXECUTIVE POWER OF THE COMMONWEALTH

143. The legislative power is that, which has a right *to direct how the force of the commonwealth* shall be employed for preserving the community and the members of it. But because those laws which are constantly to be executed, and whose force is always to continue, may be made in a little time; therefore there is no need, that the legislative should be always in being, not having always business to do. And because it may be too great a temptation to human frailty, apt to grasp at power, for the same persons, who have the power of making laws, to have also in their hands the power to execute them, whereby they may exempt themselves from obedience to the laws they make, and suit the law, both in its making and execution, to their own private advantage, and thereby come to have a distinct interest from the rest of the community, contrary to the end of society and government: therefore in well ordered commonwealths, where the good of the whole is so considered, as it ought, the legislative power is put into the hands of divers persons, who, duly assembled, have by themselves, or jointly with

others, a power to make laws; which when they have done, being separated again, they are themselves subject to the laws they have made; which is a new and near tie upon them, to take care that they make them for the public good.

144. But because the laws, that are at once, and in a short time made, have a constant and lasting force, and need a *perpetual execution,* or an attendance thereunto: therefore it is necessary there should be a *power always in being,* which should see to the execution of the laws that are made, and remain in force. And thus the legislative and executive power come often to be separated. 25

> 25 In Locke's view, the executive power is subsidiary to the legislative and exists only for essentially practical reasons. (Think of how this compares to the presidency in the American system of government.)

. . .

OF THE SUBORDINATION OF THE POWERS OF THE COMMONWEALTH

149. Though in a constituted commonwealth, standing upon its own basis, and acting according to its own nature, that is, acting for the preservation of the community, there can be but *one supreme power,* which is the *legislative,* to which all the rest are and must be subordinate; yet the legislative being only a fiduciary power to act for certain ends, there remains still *in the people a supreme power to remove or alter the legislative,* when they find the legislative act contrary to the trust reposed in them. For all *power given with trust* for the attaining an end, being limited by that end; whenever that end is manifestly neglected or opposed, the trust must necessarily be forfeited, and the power devolve into the hands of those that gave it, who may place it anew where they shall think best for their safety and security. 26 And thus the *community* perpetually *retains a supreme power* of saving themselves from

> 26 Here is the fundamental difference between Locke and Hobbes: whereas for Hobbes power is conferred on the sovereign irrevocably, for Locke the power is merely *entrusted* to the government to act for specific ends—a trust that can be revoked by the people if the government fails to perform satisfactorily, especially if it exceeds its proper authority by invading the rights of the subjects.

the attempts and designs of any body, even of their legislators, whenever they shall be so foolish, or so wicked, as to lay and carry on designs against the liberties and properties of the subject. For no man, or society of men, having a power to deliver up their preservation, or consequently the means of it, to the absolute will and arbitrary dominion of another; whenever any one shall go about to bring them into such a slavish condition, they will always have a right to preserve what they have not a power to part with; and to rid themselves of those who invade this fundamental, sacred, and unalterable law of self-preservation, for which they entered into society. And thus the community may be said in this respect to be *always the supreme power,* but not as considered under any form of government, because this power of the people can never take place till the government be dissolved.

. . .

OF THE DISSOLUTION OF GOVERNMENT

211. He that will with any clearness speak of the *dissolution of government,* ought in the first place to distinguish between the *dissolution of the society* and the *dissolution of the government.* That which makes the community, and brings men out of the loose state of nature into *one politic society,* is the agreement which every one has with the rest to incorporate, and act as one body, and so be one distinct commonwealth. The usual, and almost only way whereby *this union is dissolved,* is the inroad of foreign force making a conquest upon them. For in that case, (not being able to maintain and support themselves, as *one entire* and *independent body*) the union belonging to that body which consisted therein, must necessarily cease, and so every one return to the state he was in before, with a liberty to shift for himself, and provide for his own safety, as he thinks fit, in some other society. . . .[27]

[27] One way in which a government can be dissolved is by foreign conquest, in which case the community is dissolved also, and people are back in the state of nature.

212. Besides this overturning from without, *governments are dissolved from within.*

First, When the *legislative is altered.* Civil society being a state of peace, amongst those who are of it, from whom the state of war is excluded by the umpirage, which they have provided in their legislative, for the ending all differences that may arise amongst any of them; it is in their legislative, that the members of a commonwealth are united, and combined together into one coherent living body. This *is the soul that gives form, life, and unity* to the commonwealth: from hence the several members have their mutual influence, sympathy, and connexion; and therefore, when the legislative is broken, or dissolved, dissolution and death follows. For, *the essence and union of the society* consisting in having one will, the legislative, when once established by the majority, has the declaring, and as it were keeping of that will. The *constitution of the legislative* is the first and fundamental act of society, whereby provision is made for the *continuation of their union,* under the direction of persons, and bonds of laws, made by persons authorized thereunto, by the consent and appointment of the people; without which no one man, or number of men, amongst them, can have authority of making laws that shall be binding to the rest. When any one, or more, shall take upon them to make laws, whom the people have not appointed so to do, they make laws without authority, which the people are not therefore bound to obey; by which means they come again to be out of subjection, and may constitute to themselves a new legislative, as they think best, being in full liberty to resist the force of those, who without authority would impose any thing upon them. Every one is at the disposure of his own will, when those who had, by the delegation of the society, the declaring of the public will, are excluded from it, and others usurp the place, who have no such authority or delegation.[28]

[28] Since the constitution of the supreme legislative authority is the fundamental act that establishes a government, any alteration in the legislative authority destroys the legitimacy of the government. This might involve an attempted transfer of legislative power by the original legislative authority to a new one, or it might involve illegitimate usurpation of that power by some other person or body.

. . .

221. There is, therefore, secondly, another way whereby *governments are dissolved,* and that is, when

the legislative, or the prince either of them, act contrary to their trust.㉙

㉙ By "the prince," Locke means the executive power (which he assumes will usually be held by a constitutionally limited monarch).

First, The *legislative acts against the trust* reposed in them, when they endeavour to invade the property of the subject, and to make themselves, or any part of the community, masters, or arbitrary disposers of the lives, liberties, or fortunes of the people.

222. The reason why men enter into society, is the preservation of their property; and the end why they choose and authorize a legislative, is, that there may be laws made, and rules set, as guards and fences to the properties of all the members of the society: to limit the power, and moderate the dominion, of every part and member of the society. For since it can never be supposed to be the will of the society, that the legislative should have a power to destroy that, which every one designs to secure, by entering into society, and for which the people submitted themselves to legislators of their own making, whenever the *legislators endeavour to take away and destroy the property of the people,* or to reduce them to slavery under arbitrary power, they put themselves into a state of war with the people, who are thereupon absolved from any farther obedience, and are left to the common refuge, which God hath provided for all men, against force and violence. Whensoever therefore the *legislative* shall transgress this fundamental rule of society; and either by ambition, fear, folly or corruption, *endeavour to grasp* themselves, *or put into the hands of any other an absolute power* over the lives, liberties, and estates of the people; by this breach of trust they *forfeit the power,* the people had put into their hands, for quite contrary ends, and it devolves to the people, who have a right to resume their original liberty, and, by the establishment of a new legislative, (such as they shall think fit) provide for their own safety and security, which is the end for which they are in society. What I have said here, concerning the legislative in general, holds true also concerning the supreme executor, who having a double trust put in him, both to have a part in the legislative, and the supreme execution of the law, acts against both, when he goes about to set up his own arbitrary will, as the law of the society. . . .㉚

223. To this perhaps it will be said, that the people being ignorant, and always discontented, to lay the foundation of government in the unsteady opinion and uncertain humour of the people, is to expose it to certain ruin; and *no government will be able long to subsist,* if the people may set up a new legislative, whenever they take offence at the old one.㉛ To this I answer, quite the contrary. People are not so easily got out of their old forms as some are apt to suggest. They are hardly to be prevailed with to amend the acknowledged faults in the frame they have been accustomed to. And if there be any original defects, or adventitious ones introduced by time, or corruption: it is not an easy thing to get them changed, even when all the world sees there is an opportunity for it. This slowness and aversion in the people to quit their old constitutions, has in the many revolutions which have been seen in this kingdom, in this and former ages, still kept us to, or, after some interval of fruitless attempts, still brought us back again to, our old legislative of king, lords, and commons: and whatever provocations have made the crown be taken from some of our princes heads, they never carried the people so far as to place it in another line.

224. But it will be said, this *hypothesis* lays a *ferment for* frequent *rebellion.* To which I *answer,*

First, No more than any other *hypothesis:* for when the people are made miserable, and find themselves *exposed to the ill usage of arbitrary power,* cry up their governors as much as you will, for *sons of Jupiter;* let them be sacred or divine, descended, or authorized from heaven; give them out for whom or what you please, the same will happen. *The people generally ill treated,* and contrary to right, will be ready upon any occasion to ease themselves of a burden that sits heavy upon them. They will wish, and seek for the

㉚ Here Locke spells out the most important way in which either the legislative or the executive authority may violate the trust placed in them by the people, thereby justifying rebellion: by attempting to assume arbitrary, unlimited power over the people.

㉛ Here we have in effect the objection that Hobbes would have made to Locke's view: that sanctioning the overthrow of the government by the people whenever they are unhappy with it will make government too unstable to survive very long. Consider very carefully Locke's reply (in this and the immediately following paragraphs).

opportunity, which in the change, weakness, and accidents of human affairs, seldom delays long to offer itself. He must have lived but a little while in the world, who has not seen examples of this in his time; and he must have read very little, who cannot produce examples of it in all sorts of governments in the world.

225. *Secondly,* I answer, such *revolutions happen* not upon every little mismanagement in public affairs. *Great mistakes* in the ruling part, many wrong and inconvenient laws, and all the slips of human frailty, will be *borne by the people* without mutiny or murmur. But if a long train of abuses, prevarications and artifices, all tending the same way, make the design visible to the people, and they cannot but feel what they lie under, and see whither they are going; it is not to be wondered, that they should then rouse themselves, and endeavour to put the rule into such hands which may secure to them the ends for which government was at first erected; and without which, ancient names, and specious forms, are so far from being better, that they are much worse, than the state of nature, or pure anarchy; the inconveniencies being all as great and as near, but the remedy farther off and more difficult.

226. *Thirdly,* I answer, that *this doctrine* of a power in the people of providing for their safety anew, by a new legislative, when their legislators have acted contrary to their trust, by invading their property, is the *best fence against rebellion,* and the probablest means to hinder it. For *rebellion* being an opposition, not to persons, but authority, which is founded only in the constitutions and laws of the government; those, whoever they be, who by force break through, and by force justify their violation of them, are truly and properly *rebels.* [32] For when men, by entering into society and civil government, have excluded force, and introduced laws for the preservation of property, peace, and unity amongst themselves; those who set up force again in opposition to the laws, do *rebellare,* that is, bring back again the state of war, and are properly rebels: Which they who are in power, (by the pretence they have to authority, the temptation of force they have in their hands, and the flattery of those about them) being likeliest to do; the properest way to prevent the evil, is

[32] Locke makes the rhetorical point that those who attempt to violate the constitution and legitimate restrictions on the powers of the government are the real rebels, not the people who resist such attempts.

to shew them the danger and injustice of it, who are under the greatest temptation to run into it.

227. In both the forementioned cases, when either the legislative is changed, or the legislators act contrary to the end for which they were constituted, those who are guilty are *guilty of rebellion;* for if any one by force takes away the established legislative of any society, and the laws by them made pursuant to their trust, he thereby takes away the umpirage, which every one had consented to, for a peaceable decision of all their controversies, and a bar to the state of war amongst them. They who remove, or change the legislative, take away this decisive power, which no body can have but by the appointment and consent of the people; and so destroying the authority which the people did, and no body else can set up, and introducing a power which the people hath not authorized, they actually *introduce a state of war,* which is that of force without authority; and thus by removing the legislative established by the society, (in whose decisions the people acquiesced and united, as to that of their own will) they untie the knot, and *expose the people anew to the state of war.* And if those, who by force take away the legislative, are *rebels,* the *legislators* themselves, as has been shewn, can be no less esteemed so; when they, who were set up for the protection and preservation of the people, their liberties and properties, shall by force invade and endeavour to take them away; and so they putting themselves into a state of war with those who made them the protectors and guardians of their peace, are properly, and with the greatest aggravation, *rebellantes,* rebels.

. . .

240. Here, it is like, the common question will be made, *Who shall be judge,* whether the prince or legislative act contrary to their trust? This, perhaps, ill-affected and factious men may spread amongst the people, when the prince only makes use of his due prerogative. To this I reply, "The people shall be judge"; for who shall be *judge* whether his trustee or deputy acts well, and according to the trust reposed in him, but he who deputes him, and must by having deputed him, have still a power to discard him, when he fails in his trust? If this be reasonable in particular cases of private men, why should it be otherwise in that of the greatest moment, where the welfare of millions is concerned, and also where the evil, if not

prevented, is greater, and the redress very difficult, dear, and dangerous?

. . .

242. If a controversy arise betwixt a prince and some of the people, in a matter where the law is silent, or doubtful, and the thing be of great consequence, I should think the proper *umpire,* in such a case, should be the body of the *people:* for in cases where the prince hath a trust reposed in him, and is dispensed from the common ordinary rules of the law; there, if any men find themselves aggrieved, and think the prince acts contrary to, or beyond that trust, who so proper to *judge* as the body of the *people,* (who, at first, lodged that trust in him) how far they meant it should extend? ③③ But if the prince, or whoever they be in the administration, decline that way of determination, the appeal then lies no where but to heaven; force between either persons, who have no known superior on earth, or which permits no appeal to a judge on earth, being properly a state of war, wherein the appeal lies only to heaven; and in that state the *injured party must judge* for himself, when he will think fit to make use of that appeal, and put himself upon it.

③③ Here is a crucial issue: who decides whether the government has violated the trust placed in it in the ways indicated? Locke's answer is that the people are the final judge—where this presumably means a majority of the people.

243. To conclude, The *power that every individual gave the society,* when he entered into it, can never revert to the individuals gain, as long as the society lasts, but will always remain in the community; because without this there can be no community, no commonwealth, which is contrary to the original agreement: so also when the society hath placed the legislative in any assembly of men, to continue in them and their successors, with direction and authority for providing such successors, the *legislative can never revert to the people* whilst that government lasts: Because, having provided a legislative with power to continue for ever, they have given up their political power to the legislative, and cannot resume it. But if they have set limits to the duration of their legislative, and made this supreme power in any person, or assembly, only temporary; or else, when by the miscarriages of those in authority, it is forfeited; upon the forfeiture, or at the determination of the time set, *it reverts to the society,* and the people have a right to act as supreme, and continue the legislative in themselves; or erect a new form, or under the old form place it in new hands, as they think good. ③④

③④ Locke says explicitly that the dissolution of the government does not mean the dissolution of the community, but instead means that the people have the right to form a new government or to act as the government (that is, the legislative authority) themselves, if they so choose.

Discussion Questions

1. Hobbes argued that the sovereign was not and could not be a party to the social contract and hence could not violate it. Explain how Locke answers Hobbes's argument on this point by in effect having two stages involved in the social contract: the first where the community is formed and the second where the actual government (mainly the legislative authority) is constituted.

2. Locke's conception of the state of nature is very different from that presented by Hobbes. Explain the main differences and consider what these reveal about their contrasting views of essential human psychology. What reasons might each of them have offered in opposition to the other? Who do you think is right (or at least closer to the truth)?

3. Do you think that the sort of situation in which a social contract was explicitly agreed to, as described by either Hobbes or Locke, ever actually occurred in human history? If so, when? If not, does this mean that their accounts have no real relevance to the issue of whether the governments that actually exist in the world have legitimate authority?

4. If the law of nature (as described by Locke) does genuinely exist, then we are all obliged to preserve as much as we can, so that someone who recklessly destroys property and life would be in violation of the natural law. Do

you think that a law of nature of this general sort genuinely exists? Does the answer to this question depend essentially on whether there is a God, or might such a moral law exist even if it were not created by the commands of a deity?

5. Locke in effect offers two different criteria for when a government can be legitimately overthrown by the people: (a) an objective criterion (when it fails to carry out the purposes for which it was instituted or exceeds its legitimate powers, one case of which is transferring the legislative power illegitimately); and (b) a subjective criterion (when it loses the confidence of the people because they judge, rightly or wrongly, that it has done one or more of these things). Consider which of these two criteria is primary by considering what is the right result when they diverge: when (a) is satisfied but (b) is not, or when (b) is satisfied but (a) is not.

David Hume

One of the more trenchant criticisms of Locke's appeal to the idea of a social contract, and of social contract theories generally, was produced about 60 years later (1748) by his fellow "British empiricist" David Hume (1711–1176). (See earlier articles by Hume in this book for more about him.) Hume recognizes the appeal of the idea that the legitimacy of government must rest on the sort of consent that would be involved in a social contract, and he does not deny either (a) that something like consent (or at least acquiescence) must have been the original basis for government in the very distant past or (b) that the actual consent of the people, if it were genuinely obtained, would be a just foundation for government. But he denies that the legitimacy of the governments that in fact exist in the world, in his time or ours, can reasonably be viewed as resting to any significant degree on actual consent. Hume also considers and rejects the idea that *tacit consent,* consent manifested by such things as voluntarily remaining in the country in question, can provide an acceptable substitute for an actual, explicit agreement. (One possible response to these criticisms would be to insist that governments whose authority does not rest on consent have no legitimate authority at all; Hume does not explicitly mention such a view, but would surely have regarded it as too absurd to be taken seriously.)

Hume also offers a "more philosophical" refutation of the appeal to a social contract or to popular consent, by asking what the basis for the supposed obligations to keep contracts or adhere to promises might be. His claim is that the only basis for such obligations is their *utility* to society. But the duty of allegiance to reasonably satisfactory governments can also be based directly on social utility, making the detour through the ideas of a social contract or of popular consent unnecessary. (His view is thus a version of utilitarianism, similar to Bentham's and Mill's (see Chapter 6), and subject to many of the same objections.)

Of the Original Contract

As no party, in the present age, can well support itself, without a philosophical or speculative system of principles, annexed to its political or practical one; we accordingly find, that each of the factions, into which this nation is divided, has reared up a fabric of the former kind, in order to protect and cover that scheme of actions, which it pursues.

From Of the Original Contract *(1748).*

The people being commonly very rude builders, especially in this speculative way, and more especially still, when actuated by party-zeal; it is natural to imagine, that their workmanship must be a little unshapely, and discover evident marks of that violence and hurry, in which it was raised. The one party, by tracing up government to the Deity, endeavour to render it so sacred and inviolate, that it must be little less than sacrilege, however tyrannical it may become, to touch or invade it, in the smallest article. The other party, by founding government altogether on the consent of the People, suppose that there is a kind of *original contract,* by which the subjects have tacitly reserved the power of resisting their sovereign, whenever they find themselves aggrieved by that authority, with which they have, for certain purposes, voluntarily entrusted him. These are the speculative principles of the two parties; and these too are the practical consequences deduced from them.①

> ① Hume here summarizes the two views concerning the justification of government that were current in Great Britain in the mid-1700s: the Lockean appeal to a revocable social contract and the older idea of divine right (usually restricted to monarchical governments).

I shall venture to affirm, *That both these* systems *of speculative principles are just; though not in the sense, intended by the parties:* And, *That both the* schemes *of practical consequences are prudent; though not in the extremes, to which each party, in opposition to the other, has commonly endeavoured to carry them.*

That the Deity is the ultimate author of all government will never be denied by any, who admit a general providence, and allow, that all events in the universe are conducted by an uniform plan, and directed to wise purposes. As it is impossible for the human race to subsist, at least in any comfortable or secure state, without the protection of government; this institution must certainly have been intended by that beneficent Being, who means the good of all his creatures: And as it has universally, in fact, taken place, in all countries, and all ages; we may conclude, with still greater certainty, that it was intended by that omniscient Being, who can never be deceived by any event or operation. But since he gave rise to it, not by any particular or miraculous interposition, but by his concealed and universal efficacy; a sovereign cannot, properly speaking, be called his vice-regent, in any other sense than every power or force, being derived from him, may be said to act by his commission. Whatever actually happens is comprehended in the general plan or intention of providence; nor has the greatest and most lawful prince any more reason, upon that account, to plead a peculiar sacredness or inviolable authority, than an inferior magistrate, or even an usurper, or even a robber and a pyrate. The same divine superintendant, who, for wise purposes, invested a Titus or a Trajan with authority, did also, for purposes, no doubt, equally wise, though unknown, bestow power on a Borgia or an Angria. The same causes, which gave rise to the sovereign power in every state, established likewise every petty jurisdiction in it, and every limited authority. A constable, therefore, no less than a king, acts by a divine commission, and possesses an indefeasible right.②

> ② Though he is elsewhere skeptical about such claims, Hume here concedes the existence of God and thus the apparent divine sanction for human governments, though giving this claim the ironic twist that governments or leaders of any sort have an equal claim to divine sanction.

When we consider how nearly equal all men are in their bodily force, and even in their mental powers and faculties, till cultivated by education; we must necessarily allow, that nothing but their own consent could, at first, associate them together, and subject them to any authority. The people, if we trace government to its first origin in the woods and deserts, are the source of all power and jurisdiction, and voluntarily, for the sake of peace and order, abandoned their native liberty, and received laws from their equal and companion. The conditions, upon which they were willing to submit, were either expressed, or were so clear and obvious, that it might well be esteemed superfluous to express them. If this, then, be meant by the *original contract,* it cannot be denied, that all government is, at first, founded on a contract, and that the most ancient rude combinations of mankind were formed chiefly by that principle. In vain, are we asked in what records this charter of our liberties is registered. It was not written on parchment, nor yet on leaves or barks of trees. It preceded the use of writing and all the other civilized arts of life.③ But we trace it plainly in the nature of man, and in the equality, or something approaching equality, which we find in all the individuals of that species. The force, which now prevails, and which is founded on fleets and armies, is plainly political, and derived from authority, the effect of established government. A man's natural force consists only in the vigour of his limbs, and the firmness of his courage; which could never subject multitudes to the command of one. Nothing but their own consent, and their sense of the advantages resulting from peace and order, could have had that influence.

③ Hume concedes that some sort of consent or agreement must have been involved when government first originated, but points out at once that there is no record of any sort of the terms of such an agreement.

Yet even this consent was long very imperfect, and could not be the basis of a regular administration. The chieftain, who had probably acquired his influence during the continuance of war, ruled more by persuasion than command; and till he could employ force to reduce the refractory and disobedient, the society could scarcely be said to have attained a state of civil government. No compact or agreement, it is evident, was expressly formed for general submission; an idea far beyond the comprehension of savages: Each exertion of authority in the chieftain must have been particular, and called forth by the present exigencies of the case: The sensible utility, resulting from his interposition, made these exertions become daily more frequent; and their frequency gradually produced an habitual, and, if you please to call it so, a voluntary, and therefore precarious, acquiescence in the people.④

④ Nor, he argues, is there any reason to think that such an original act of consent involved anything like an explicit and detailed contract, as opposed to piecemeal and ad hoc accretions of authority.

But philosophers, who have embraced a party (if that be not a contradiction in terms) are not contented with these concessions. They assert, not only that government in its earliest infancy arose from consent or rather the voluntary acquiescence⑤ of the people; but also, that, even at present, when it has attained full maturity, it rests on no other foundation. They affirm, that all men are still born equal, and owe allegiance to no prince or government, unless bound by the obligation and sanction of a *promise*. And as no man, without some equivalent, would forego the advantages of his native liberty, and subject himself to the will of another; this promise is always understood to be conditional, and imposes on him no obligation, unless he meet with justice and protection from his sovereign. These advantages the sovereign promises him in return; and if he fail in the execution, he has broken, on his part, the articles of engagement, and has thereby freed his subject from all obligations to allegiance. Such, according to these philosophers, is the foundation of authority in every government; and such the right of resistance, possessed by every subject.⑥

⑤ Take careful note of the two very different terms Hume employs here: actual "consent" and mere "voluntary acquiescence" are very different things, with the latter being much less clearly a basis for legitimate authority than the former.

⑥ Hume here summarizes the main ideas of the Lockean view.

But would these reasoners look abroad into the world, they would meet with nothing that, in the least, corresponds to their ideas, or can warrant so refined and philosophical a system. On the contrary, we find, every where, princes, who claim their subjects as their property, and assert their independent right of sovereignty, from conquest or succession. We find also, every where, subjects, who acknowledge this right in their prince, and suppose themselves born under obligations of obedience to a certain sovereign, as much as under the ties of reverence and duty to certain parents. These connexions are always conceived to be equally independent of our consent, in Persia and China; in France and Spain; and even in Holland and England, wherever the doctrines above-mentioned have not been carefully inculcated. Obedience or subjection becomes so familiar, that most men never make any enquiry about its origin or cause, more than about the principle of gravity, resistance, or the most universal laws of nature. Or if curiosity ever move them; as soon as they learn, that they themselves and their ancestors have, for several ages, or from time immemorial, been subject to such a form of government or such a family; they immediately acquiesce, and acknowledge their obligation to allegiance. Were you to preach, in most parts of the world, that political connexions are founded altogether on voluntary consent or a mutual promise, the magistrate would soon imprison you, as seditious, for loosening the ties of obedience; if your friends did not before shut you up as delirious, for advancing such absurdities. It is strange, that an act of the mind, which every individual is supposed to have formed, and after he came to the use of reason too, otherwise it could have no authority; that this act, I say, should be so much unknown to all of them, that, over the face of the whole earth, there scarcely remain any traces or memory of it.⑦

> ⑦ One problem is that the idea of such a contract is recognized and accepted almost nowhere else in the world. How then, Hume asks, can it be the basis for the actual authority of governments?

But the contract, on which government is founded, is said to be the *original contract;* and consequently may be supposed too old to fall under the knowledge of the present generation. If the agreement, by which savage men first associated and conjoined their force, be here meant, this is acknowledged to be real; but being so ancient, and being obliterated by a thousand changes of government and princes, it cannot now be supposed to retain any authority. If we would say any thing to the purpose, we must assert, that every particular government, which is lawful, and which imposes any duty of allegiance on the subject, was, at first, founded on consent and a voluntary compact. But besides that this supposes the consent of the fathers to bind the children, even to the most remote generations, (which republican writers will never allow) besides this, I say, it is not justified by history or experience, in any age or country of the world.⑧

> ⑧ It will not work to say that the relevant contract is the supposed original one, now forgotten. For why would it retain its authority after so long a time and so many changes? And (a serious problem for any social contract view), why would such a contract continue to bind people after those who actually agreed to it are dead and gone?

Almost all the governments, which exist at present, or of which there remains any record in story, have been founded originally, either on usurpation or conquest, or both, without any presence of a fair consent, or voluntary subjection of the people. When an artful and bold man is placed at the head of an army or faction, it is often easy for him, by employing, sometimes violence, sometimes false pretences, to establish his dominion over a people a hundred times more numerous than his partizans. He allows no such open communication, that his enemies can know, with certainty, their number or force. He gives them no leisure to assemble together in a body to oppose him. Even all those, who are the instruments of his usurpation, may wish his fall; but their ignorance of each other's intention keeps them in awe, and is the sole cause of his security. By such arts as these, many governments have been established; and this is all the *original contract,* which they have to boast of.

The face of the earth is continually changing, by the encrease of small kingdoms into great empires, by the dissolution of great empires into smaller kingdoms, by the planting of colonies, by the migration of tribes. Is there any thing discoverable in all these events, but force and violence? Where is the mutual agreement or voluntary association so much talked of?⑨

> ⑨ Actual governments are almost all founded originally on "usurpation or conquest," making it unclear how a contract can be supposed to play any role.

. . .

Let not the establishment at the *Revolution* deceive us, or make us so much in love with a philosophical origin to government, as to imagine all others monstrous and irregular. Even that event was far from corresponding to these refined ideas. It was only the succession, and that only in the regal part of the government, which was then changed: And it was only the majority of seven hundred, who determined that change for near ten millions. I doubt not, indeed, but the bulk of those ten millions acquiesced willingly in the determination: But was the matter left, in the least, to their choice? Was it not justly supposed to be, from that moment, decided, and every man punished, who refused to submit to the new sovereign? How otherwise could the matter have ever been brought to any issue or conclusion? ⑩

> ⑩ Indeed, Hume argues, even the government established by the "Glorious Revolution" in Great Britain was founded on force or the threat of force—contrary to the view held by many (apparently including Locke) that it was a clear case of a social contract. The vast majority of the people may have *acquiesced* to the governmental change, but they had no reasonable choice as to whether to consent or not.

. . .

It is in vain to say, that all governments are or should be, at first, founded on popular consent, as much as the necessity of human affairs will admit. This favours entirely my pretension. I maintain, that human affairs will never admit of this consent; seldom of the appearance of it. But that conquest or usurpation, that is, in plain terms, force, by dissolving the ancient governments, is the origin of almost all the new ones, which were ever established in the world. And that in the few cases, where consent may seem to have taken place, it was commonly so irregular, so confined, or so much intermixed either with fraud or violence, that it cannot have any great authority.

My intention here is not to exclude the consent of the people from being one just foundation of government where it has place. It is surely the best and most sacred of any. I only pretend, that it has very seldom had place in any degree, and never almost in its full extent. And that therefore some other foundation of government must also be admitted. ⑪

> ⑪ Some other foundation must be admitted *if,* as Hume is assuming, it is not reasonable to say that virtually all governments are illegitimate.

. . .

When a new government is established, by whatever means, the people are commonly dissatisfied with it, and pay obedience more from fear and necessity, than from any idea of allegiance or of moral obligation. The prince is watchful and jealous, and must carefully guard against every beginning or appearance of insurrection. Time, by degrees, removes all these difficulties, and accustoms the nation to regard, as their lawful or native princes, that family, which, at first, they considered as usurpers or foreign conquerors. In order to found this opinion, they have no recourse to any notion of voluntary consent or promise, which, they know, never was, in this case, either expected or demanded. The original establishment was formed by violence, and submitted to from necessity. The subsequent administration is also supported by power, and acquiesced in by the people, not as a matter of choice, but of obligation. They imagine not, that their consent gives their prince a title: But they willingly consent, because they think, that, from long possession, he has acquired a title, independent of their choice or inclination.

Should it be said, that, by living under the dominion of a prince, which one might leave, every individual has given a *tacit* consent to his authority, and promised him obedience; it may be answered, that such an implied consent can only have place, where a man imagines, that the matter depends on his choice. But where he thinks (as all mankind do who are born under established governments) that by his birth he owes allegiance to a certain prince or certain form of government; it would be absurd to infer a consent or choice, which he expressly, in this case, renounces and disclaims. ⑫

> ⑫ Social contract theorists have sometimes appealed to the idea of *tacit consent:* the idea that people, by remaining in a particular country rather than going elsewhere, have thereby tacitly or implicitly consented to the authority of the existing government. One problem with this is that people who do not realize that they have any choice cannot reasonably be said to have consented. Another, in the following paragraph, is that emigrating to another country is not a reasonable option for most people.

Can we seriously say, that a poor peasant or artizan has a free choice to leave his country, when he knows no foreign language or manners, and lives from day to day, by the small wages which he acquires? We may as well assert, that a man, by remaining in a vessel, freely consents to the dominion of the master; though he was carried on board while asleep, and must leap into the ocean, and perish, the moment he leaves her.

. . .

The truest *tacit* consent of this kind, that is ever observed, is when a foreigner settles in any country, and is beforehand acquainted with the prince, and government, and laws, to which he must submit: Yet is his allegiance, though more voluntary, much less expected or depended on, than that of a natural born subject. On the contrary, his native prince still asserts a claim to him. And if he punish not the renegade, when he seizes him in war with his new prince's commission; this clemency is not founded on the municipal law, which in all countries condemns the prisoner; but on the consent of princes, who have agreed to this indulgence, in order to prevent reprisals. ⑬

> ⑬ Hume also points out that the clearest case of tacit consent would be that of a person who deliberately comes to a country and settles there. But in fact, no one thinks that such a person has a *stronger* duty of allegiance than a native citizen.

. . .

Suppose, that an usurper, after having banished his lawful prince and royal family, should establish his dominion for ten or a dozen years in any country, and should preserve so exact a discipline in his troops, and so regular a disposition in his garrisons, that no insurrection had ever been raised, or even murmur heard, against his administration: Can it be asserted, that the people, who in their hearts abhor his treason, have tacitly consented to his authority, and promised him allegiance, merely because, from necessity, they live under his dominion? Suppose again their native prince restored, by means of an army, which he levies in foreign countries: They receive him with joy and exultation, and shew plainly with what reluctance they had submitted to any other yoke. I may now ask, upon what foundation the prince's title stands? Not on popular consent surely: For though the people willingly acquiesce in his authority, they never imagine, that their consent made him sovereign. They consent; because they apprehend him to be already, by birth, their lawful sovereign. And as to that tacit consent, which may now be inferred from their living under his dominion, this is no more than what they formerly gave to the tyrant and usurper.[14]

> [14] The idea of tacit consent fails to discriminate among various governments that might be thought to differ in legitimacy: as long as they are all firmly in power, they will receive the same degree of tacit consent.

. . .

But would we have a more regular, at least a more philosophical, refutation of this principle of an original contract or popular consent; perhaps, the following observations may suffice.

All *moral* duties may be divided into two kinds. The *first* are those, to which men are impelled by a natural instinct or immediate propensity, which operates on them, independent of all ideas of obligation, and of all views, either to public or private utility. Of this nature are, love of children, gratitude to benefactors, pity to the unfortunate. When we reflect on the advantage, which results to society from such humane instincts, we pay them the just tribute of moral approbation and esteem: But the person, actuated by them, feels their power and influence, antecedent to any such reflection.

The *second* kind of moral duties are such as are not supported by any original instinct of nature, but

are performed entirely from a sense of obligation, when we consider the necessities of human society, and the impossibility of supporting it, if these duties were neglected. It is thus *justice* or a regard to the property of others, *fidelity* or the observance of promises, become obligatory, and acquire an authority over mankind. For as it is evident, that every man loves himself better than any other person, he is naturally impelled to extend his acquisitions as much as possible; and nothing can restrain him in this propensity, but reflection and experience, by which he learns the pernicious effects of that licence, and the total dissolution of society which must ensue from it. His original inclination, therefore, or instinct, is here checked and restrained by a subsequent judgment or observation.

The case is precisely the same with the political or civil duty of *allegiance* as with the natural duties of justice and fidelity. Our primary instincts lead us, either to indulge ourselves in unlimited freedom, or to seek dominion over others: And it is reflection only which engages us to sacrifice such strong passions to the interests of peace and public order. A small degree of experience and observation suffices to teach us, that society cannot possibly be maintained without the authority of magistrates, and that this authority must soon fall into contempt, where exact obedience is not payed to it. The observation of these general and obvious interests is the source of all allegiance, and of that moral obligation, which we attribute to it.

What necessity, therefore, is there to found the duty of *allegiance* or obedience to magistrates on that of *fidelity* or a regard to promises, and to suppose, that it is the consent of each individual, which subjects him to government; when it appears, that both allegiance and fidelity stand precisely on the same foundation, and are both submitted to by mankind, on account of the apparent interests and necessities of human society? We are bound to obey our sovereign, it is said; because we have given a tacit promise to that purpose. But why are we bound to observe our promise? . . . The obligation to allegiance being of like force and authority with the obligation to fidelity, we gain nothing by resolving the one into the other. The general interests or necessities of society are sufficient to establish both.[15]

If the reason be asked of that obedience, which we are bound to pay to government, I readily answer, *because society could not otherwise subsist:* And this answer is clear and intelligible to all mankind. Your answer is, *because we should keep our word.* But besides, that no body, till trained in a philosophical system, can either comprehend or relish this answer: Besides this, I say, you find yourself embarrassed, when it is asked, *why we are bound to keep our word?* Nor can you give any answer, but what would, immediately, without any circuit, have accounted for our obligation to allegiance.

But *to whom is allegiance due? And who is our lawful sovereign?* This question is often the most difficult of any, and liable to infinite discussions. When people are so happy, that they can answer, *Our present sovereign, who inherits, in a direct line, from ancestors, that have governed us for many ages;* this answer admits of no reply; even though historians, in tracing up to the remotest antiquity, the origin of that royal family, may find, as commonly happens, that its first authority was derived from usurpation and violence. . . .

The general obligation, which binds us to government, is the interest and necessities of society; and this obligation is very strong. The determination of it to this or that particular prince or form of government is frequently more uncertain and dubious. Present possession has considerable authority in these cases, and greater than in private property; because of the disorders which attend all revolutions and changes of government.

[15] Hume now raises the background issue of the basis for the duty to adhere to contracts or agreements or promises. His claim is that it is not grounded in natural human instincts, but rather in perceived utility to society. But a duty to obey a solidly established, reasonably satisfactory government could be arrived at on the same basis of social utility, making the appeal to a social contract needlessly indirect (in addition to all its other problems).

We shall only observe, before we conclude, that, though an appeal to general opinion may justly, in the speculative sciences of metaphysics, natural philosophy, or astronomy, be deemed unfair and inconclusive, yet in all questions with regard to morals, as well as criticism, there is really no other standard, by which any controversy can ever be decided. And nothing is a clearer proof, that a theory of this kind is erroneous, than to find, that it leads to paradoxes, repugnant to the common sentiments of mankind, and to the practice and opinion of all nations and all ages. The doctrine, which founds all lawful government on an *original contract,* or consent of the people, is plainly of this kind; nor has the most noted of its partizans, in prosecution of it, scrupled to affirm, *that absolute monarchy is inconsistent with civil society, and so can be no form of civil government at all; and that the supreme power in a state cannot take from any man, by taxes and impositions, any part of his property, without his own consent or that of his representatives.* What authority any moral reasoning can have, which leads into opinions so wide of the general practice of mankind, in every place but this single kingdom, it is easy to determine.[16]

[16] Hume argues that the implications of the social contract view are too out of keeping with "the common sentiments of mankind" and with prevailing practice to have any real plausibility.

. . .

New discoveries are not to be expected in these matters. If scarce any man, till very lately, ever imagined that government was founded on compact, it is certain, that it cannot, in general, have any such foundation.

. . .

Discussion Questions

1. Is Hume right (in his implicit suggestion) that the view that almost all actual governments fail to possess legitimate authority is too absurd to be taken seriously? Might it be that actual consent is the only legitimate basis for governmental authority, even if it has seldom (or ever?) been completely realized?

2. In Plato's dialogue *Crito,* Socrates argues that by remaining in Athens and accepting the numerous benefits of Athenian citizenship, he has incurred an obligation to obey the laws of Athens and accept the verdict of the Athenian authorities—even when they sentence him to death. This amounts to an appeal to the idea

of tacit consent. How compelling are Hume's objections to this idea? Consider in particular how much it matters whether or not Socrates was explicitly aware of the choice as to whether to stay in Athens or leave.

3. Hume is surely right that few if any of the governments that were actually in power in his time had been created by a social contract, as opposed to arising in various ways by force and coercion. Is the same thing true today? For example, did the ratification of the United States Constitution (in 1787–1790) constitute something approaching a social contract? Might the establishment of a new government in Iraq, if all goes well, constitute such a contract?

4. Is Hume right that social utility provides the only basis for a duty to adhere to contracts or agreements or to keep promises? Does the fact that some institution or pattern of behavior can be justified on the basis of social utility create as strong an obligation to support it as would an explicit contract or promise? Why or why not? (Think of examples here.)

WHAT IS SOCIAL JUSTICE?

Robert Nozick

Robert Nozick (1938–2002), for many years a professor at Harvard, was a major figure in twentieth-century philosophy, making contributions to many areas but most importantly to political philosophy and epistemology. Nozick is perhaps most famous for his engaging style and his knack for devising striking and intuitively engaging examples, one of them being the Wilt Chamberlain example that appears in this selection.

In *Anarchy, State, and Utopia,* Nozick develops a broadly *libertarian* political philosophy: one that emphasizes the value of human liberty and voluntary choice, is suspicious of governmental power, and demands a clear justification for governmental actions that restrict such liberty. Nozick's position includes an account of the justification of government in relation to the state of nature in the tradition of Hobbes and Locke. The present selection offers an abstract outline of an account of distributive justice, together with forceful criticisms of opposing accounts. Nozick calls his account of justice "the entitlement theory." Its central idea is that the justice or injustice of a distribution of property or other goods among the members of a society depends entirely on the justice of the specific transactions through which that distribution was produced, including both acquisitions of previously unowned things and transfers of owned things from one person to another. This means, he argues, that there is no structurally specified *pattern* of distribution, whether simple equality or something more complicated, that is required by justice. From Nozick's standpoint, views that insist on such a pattern are objectionable both (a) because they must interfere massively and continuously in people's lives in order to maintain the pattern and (b) because much of this interference amounts to a denial that even those who have received an allotment of money or goods according to the chosen pattern are free to do with them what they choose (since doing so is very likely to upset the pattern).

The Entitlement Theory of Justice, from *Anarchy, State, and Utopia*

. . . The term "distributive justice" is not a neutral one. Hearing the term "distribution," most people presume that some thing or mechanism uses some principle or criterion to give out a supply of things. Into this process of distributing shares some error may have crept. So it is an open question, at least, whether *re*distribution should take place; whether we should do again what has already been done once, though poorly. However, we are not in the position of children who have been given portions of pie by someone who now makes last minute adjustments to rectify careless cutting. There is no *central* distribution, no person or group entitled to control all the resources, jointly deciding how they are to be doled out. What each person gets, he gets from others who give to him in exchange for something, or as a gift. In a free society, diverse persons control different resources, and new holdings arise out of the voluntary exchanges and actions of persons. There is no more a distributing or distribution of shares than there is a distributing of mates in a society in which persons choose whom they shall marry. The total result is the product of many individual decisions which the different individuals involved are entitled to make. . . . ① We shall speak of people's holdings; a principle of justice in holdings describes (part of) what justice tells us (requires) about holdings. . . .

> ① Nozick objects that the usual understanding of the issue of distributive justice and the term itself involves a highly questionable assumption: that people's holdings of various sorts are the result of a central process of distribution by a central authority, which is thus assumed to have legitimate control over what is distributed. (Can you think of a situation, perhaps a more limited one, in which such an assumption would be legitimate?)

THE ENTITLEMENT THEORY

The subject of justice in holdings consists of three major topics. The first is the *original acquisition of holdings,* the appropriation of unheld things. This includes the issues of how unheld things may come to be held, the process, or processes, by which unheld things may come to be held, the things that may come to be held by these processes, the extent of what comes to be held by a particular process, and so on. We shall refer to the complicated truth about this topic, which we shall not formulate here, as the principle of justice in acquisition.② The second topic concerns the *transfer of holdings* from one person to another. By what processes may a person transfer holdings to another? How may a person acquire a holding from another who holds it? Under this topic come general descriptions of voluntary exchange, and gift and (on the other hand) fraud, as well as reference to particular conventional details fixed upon in a given society. The complicated truth about this subject . . . we shall call the principle of justice in transfer. (And we shall suppose it also includes principles governing how a person may divest himself of a holding, passing it into an unheld state.)

> ② Justice in acquisition has to do with how previously unheld (that is, unowned) things can come to be legitimately held. Genuinely unheld things are relatively rare in the modern world. Try to think of some examples of things to which Nozick's principle might apply.

If the world were wholly just, the following . . . definition would exaustively cover the subject of justice in holdings.

1. A person who aquires a holding in accordance with the principle of justice in acqustion is entitled to that holding.
2. A person who aquires a holding in accordance with the principle of justice in transfer, from someone else entitled to the holding, is entitled to the holding.
3. No one is entitled to the holding except by (repeated) applications of 1 and 2.

The complete principle of distributive justice would say simply that a distribution is just if everyone is

From Anarchy, State, and Utopia *(New York: Basic Books, 1974).*

entitled to the holdings they possess under the distribution.③

③ Obviously Nozick has not even begun to say what the details of such principles might look like. He is describing only the general structure of such a theory of justice.

A distribution is just if it arises from another just distribution by legitimate means. The legitimate means of moving from one distribution to another are specified by the principle of justice in transfer. The legitimate first "moves" are specified by the principle of justice in acquisition. Whatever arises from a just situation by just steps is itself just. The means of change specified by the principle of justice in transfer preserve justice. As correct rules of inference are truth-preserving, and any conclusion deduced via repeated application of such rules from only true premises is itself true, so the means of transition from one situation to another specified by the principle of justice in transfer are justice-preserving, and any situation actually arising from repeated transitions in accordance with the principle from a just situation is itself just.④ The parallel between justice-preserving transformations and truth-preserving transformations illuminates where it fails as well as where it holds. That a conclusion could have been deduced by truth-preserving means from premisses that are true suffices to show its truth. That from a just situation a situation *could* have arisen via justice-preserving means does *not* suffice to show its justice. The fact that a thief's victims voluntarily *could* have presented him with gifts does not entitle the thief to his ill-gotten gains. Justice in holdings is historical; it depends upon what actually has happened. We shall return to this point later.

④ Thus the justice of a distribution of holdings depends only on the justice of the transitions via which it was arrived at, according to the two (unstated) principles of justice in acquisition and transfer. A distribution of holdings (property) could thereby be just even if the shares of different people or different groups of people were very unequal.

Not all actual situations are generated in accordance with the two principles of justice in holdings: the principle of justice in acquisition and the principle of justice in transfer. Some people steal from others, or defraud them, or enslave them, seizing their product and preventing them from living as they choose, or forcibly exclude others from competing in exchanges.

None of these are permissible modes of transition from one situation to another. And some persons acquire holdings by means not sanctioned by the principle of justice in acquisition. The existence of past injustice (previous violations of the first two principles of justice in holdings) raises the third major topic under justice in holdings: the rectification of injustice in holdings. If past injustice has shaped present holdings in various ways, some identifiable and some not, what now, if anything, ought to be done to rectify these injustices? What obligations do the performers of injustice have toward those whose position is worse than it would have been had the injustice not been done? Or, than it would have been had compensation been paid promptly? How, if at all, do things change if the beneficiaries and those made worse off are not the direct parties in the act of injustice, but, for example, their descendants? Is an injustice done to someone whose holding was itself based upon an unrectified injustice? How far back must one go in wiping clean the historical slate of injustices? What may victims of injustice permissibly do in order to rectify the injustices being done to them, including the many injustices done by persons acting through their government?⑤ I do not know of a thorough or theoretically sophisticated treatment of such issues. Idealizing greatly, let us suppose theoretical investigation will produce a principle of rectification. This principle uses historical information about previous situations and injustices done in them (as defined by the first two principles of justice and rights against interference), and information about the actual course of events that flowed from these injustices, until the present, and it yields a description (or descriptions) of holdings in the society. The principle of rectification presumably will make use of its best estimate of subjunctive information about what would have occurred (or a probability distribution over what might have occurred, using the expected value) if the injustice had not taken place. If the actual description of holdings turns our not to be one of the descriptions yielded by the principle, then one of the descriptions yielded must be realized.

⑤ As Nozick suggests, how and to what extent past injustices should be rectified is a very complicated and difficult issue. You should think about it further by considering actual cases of past injustice and asking what, if anything, can and should be done to rectify them.

The general outlines of the theory of justice in holdings are that the holdings of a person are just if he is entitled to them by the principles of justice in acquisition and transfer, or by the principle of rectification of injustice (as specified by the first two principles).

---
6 Thus the justice of a set of holdings does not depend at all, according to Nozick's view, on any considerations beyond these principles (such as the structure or pattern of the resulting distribution).

If each person's holdings are just, then the total set (distribution) of holdings is just.**6** To turn these general outlines into a specific theory we would have to specify the details of each of the three principles of justice in holdings: the principle of acquisition of holdings, the principle of transfer of holdings, and the principle of rectification of violations of the first two principles. I shall not attempt that task here. . . .

HISTORICAL PRINCIPLES AND END-RESULT PRINCIPLES

The general outlines of the entitlement theory illuminate the nature and defects of other conceptions of distributive justice. The entitlement theory of justice in distribution is *historical;* whether a distribution is just depends upon how it came about. In contrast, *current time-slice principles* of justice hold that the justice of a distribution is determined by how things are distributed (who has what) as judged by some *structural* principle(s) of just distribution. A utilitarian who judges between any two distributions by seeing which has the greater sum of utility and, if the sums tie, applies some fixed equality criterion to choose the more equal distribution, would hold a current time-slice principle of justice. As would someone who had a fixed schedule of trade-offs between the sum of happiness and equality. According to a current time-slice principle, all that needs to be looked at, in judging the justice of a distribution, is who ends up with what. . .

Most persons do not accept current time-slice principles as constituting the whole story about distributive shares. They think it relevant in assessing the justice of a situation to consider not only the distribution it embodies, but also how that distribution came about. If some persons are in prison for murder or war crimes, we do not say that to assess the justice of the distribution in the society we must look only at what this person has, and that person has, and that person

has, . . . at the current time. We think it relevant to ask whether someone did something so that he *deserved* to be punished, deserved to have a lower share. Most will agree to the relevance of further information with regard to punishments and penalties. . . .

We construe the position we discuss too narrowly by speaking of *current* time-slice principles. Nothing is changed if structural principles operate upon a time sequence of current time-slice profiles and, for example, give someone more now to counterbalance the less he has had earlier. . . . Henceforth, we shall refer to such unhistorical principles of distributive justice, including the current time-slice principles, as *end-result principles* or *end-state principles.***7**

In contrast to end-result principles of justice, *historical principles* of justice hold that past circumstances or actions of people can create differential entitlements or differential deserts to things. . . .

---
7 Strict egalitarianism (the view that each person should have an equal share of holdings) is the most obvious example of such an "end-state principle" of justice. Can you think of others?

PATTERNING

The entitlement principles of justice in holdings that we have sketched are historical principles of justice. To better understand their precise character, we shall distinguish them from another subclass of the historical principles. Consider, as an example, the principle of distribution according to moral merit. This principle requires that total distributive shares vary directly with moral merit; no person should have a greater share than anyone whose moral merit is greater. . . . Or consider the principle that results by substituting "usefulness to society" for "moral merit" in the previous principle. . . . Let us call a principle of distribution *patterned* if it specifies that a distribution is to vary along with some natural dimension, weighted sum of natural dimensions, or . . . ordering of natural dimensions.**8** And let us say a distribution is patterned if it accords with some patterned principle. . . .

---
8 Think of other examples of patterned principles of justice. (Don't limit yourself to ones that you find plausible.) It is fairly natural to expand the category of patterned principles to include end-state principles as well, since these also involve a pattern, though not a historical one. Nozick sometimes seems to do this.

Almost every suggested principle of distributive justice is patterned: to each according to his moral merit, or needs, or marginal product, or how hard he tries, or the weighted sum of the foregoing, and so on. The principle of entitlement we have sketched is *not* patterned. There is no one natural dimension or weighted sum or combination of a small number of natural dimensions that yields the distributions generated in accordance with the principle of entitlement. The set of holdings that results when some persons receive their marginal products, others win at gambling, others receive a share of their mate's income, others receive gifts from foundations, others receive interest on loans, others receive gifts from admirers, others receive returns on investment, others make for themselves much of what they have, others find things, and so on, will not be patterned. . . .

To think that the task of a theory of distributive justice is to fill in the blank in "to each according to his _____" is to be predisposed to search for a pattern; and the separate treatment of "from each according to his _____" treats production and distribution as two separate and independent issues. On an entitlement view these are *not* two separate questions. Whoever makes something, having bought or contracted for all other held resources used in the process (transferring some of his holdings for these cooperating factors), is entitled to it. The situation is *not* one of something's getting made, and there being an open question of who is to get it. Things come into the world already attached to people having entitlements over them.⑨ From the point of view of the historical entitlement conception of justice in holdings, those who start afresh to complete "to each according to his _____" treat objects as if they appeared from nowhere, out of nothing. . . .

HOW LIBERTY UPSETS PATTERNS

It is not clear how those holding alternative conceptions of distributive justice can reject the entitlement conception of justice in holdings. For suppose a distribution favored by one of these non-entitlement conceptions is realized. Let us suppose it is your favorite one and let us call this distribution D_1.⑩; perhaps everyone has an equal share, perhaps shares vary in accordance with some dimension you treasure. Now suppose that Wilt Chamberlain⑪ is greatly in demand by basketball teams, being a great gate attraction. (Also suppose contracts run only for a year, with players being free agents.) He signs the following sort of contract with a team: In each home game, twenty-five cents from the price of each ticket of admission goes to him. . . . The season starts, and people cheerfully attend his team's games; they buy their tickets, each time dropping a separate twenty-five cents of their admission price into a special box with Chamberlain's name on it. They are excited about seeing him play; it is worth the total admission price to them. Let us suppose that in one season one million persons attend his home games, and Wilt Chamberlain winds up with $250,000, a much larger sum than the average income and larger even than anyone else has. Is he entitled to this income? Is this new distribution D_2, unjust? If so, why? There is *no* question about whether each of the people was entitled to the control over the resources they held in D_1; because that was the distribution . . . that (for the purposes of argument) we assumed was acceptable. Each of these persons *chose* to give twenty-five cents of their money to Chamberlain. They could have spent it on going to the movies, or on candy bars, or on copies of *Dissent* magazine, or of *Monthly Review*. But they all, at least one million of them, converged on giving it to Wilt Chamberlain in exchange for watching him play basketball. If D_1 was a just distribution, and people voluntarily moved from it to D_2, transferring parts of their shares they were given under D_1 (what was it for if not to do something with?), isn't D_2 also just? ⑫ If the people were entitled to dispose of the resources to which they were entitled (under D_1), didn't this include their being entitled to give it to,

⑩ Here by "your favorite one," Nozick really just means whatever one the proponent of a patterned view thinks is correct.

⑪ Wilt Chamberlain was a famous basketball player of the 1960s and 1970s, one of the most dominant offensive players ever. The details of his career are worth looking up, for those who care about such things. But for current students, Michael Jordan or Shaquille O'Neill might be better examples.

or exchange it with, Wilt Chamberlain? Can anyone else complain on grounds of justice? Each other person already has his legitimate share under D_1. Under D_1, there is nothing that anyone has that anyone else has a claim of justice against. After someone transfers something to Wilt Chamberlain, third parties *still* have their legitimate shares; *their* shares are not changed. . . .

12 Here is one of Nozick's basic objections to patterned views: if D_1 is a just distribution and if people are justly free to do as they like with their just allotments, then how can the resulting distribution D_2 be unjust (as the theory that advocates D_1 must seemingly say that it is, since D_2 differs from D_1)?

Why might someone work overtime in a society in which it is assumed their needs are satisfied? Perhaps because they care about things other than needs. . . . Thus, persons either must do without some extra things that they want, or be allowed to do something extra to get some of these things. On what basis could the inequalities that would eventuate be forbidden? Notice also that small factories would spring up in a socialist society, unless forbidden. I melt down some of my personal possessions (under D_1) and build a machine out of the material. I offer you, and others, a philosophy lecture once a week in exchange for your cranking the handle on my machine, whose products I exchange for yet other things, and so on. (The raw materials used by the machine are given to me by others who possess them under D_1, in exchange for hearing lectures.) Each person might participate to gain things over and above their allotment under D_1. Some persons even might want to leave their job in socialist industry and work full time in this private sector. . . . [Thus] private property even in means of production would occur in a socialist society that did not forbid people to use as they wished some of the resources they are given under the socialist distribution D_1. The socialist society would have to forbid capitalist acts between consenting adults.

The general point illustrated by the Wilt Chamberlain example and the example of the entrepreneur in a socialist society is that no end-state principle or distributional patterned principle of justice can be continuously realized without continuous interference with people's lives. Any favored pattern would be transformed into one unfavored by the principle, by people choosing to act in various ways; for example, by people exchanging goods and services with other people, or giving things to other people, things the transferrers are entitled to under the favored distributional pattern. To maintain a pattern one must either continually interfere to stop people from transferring resources as they wish to, or continually (or periodically) interfere to take from some persons resources that others for some reason chose to transfer to them. . . . **13**

13 Nozick regards such continued interference as unacceptable in itself. But it also seems to conflict with the idea that people genuinely own and so can freely control what they receive according to the favored pattern.

REDISTRIBUTION AND PROPERTY RIGHTS

Apparently, patterned principles allow people to choose to expend upon themselves, but not upon others, those resources they are entitled to (or rather, receive) under some favored distributional pattern D_1. For if each of several persons chooses to expend some of his D_1 resources upon one other person, then that other person will receive more than his D_1 share, disturbing the favored distributional pattern. Maintaining a distributional pattern is individualism with a vengeance! Patterned distributional principles do not give people what entitlement principles do, only better distributed. For they do not give the right to choose what to do with what one has; they do not give the right to choose to pursue an end involving (intrinsically, or as a means) the enhancement of another's position. To such views, families are disturbing; for within a family occur transfers that upset the favored distributional pattern. Either families themselves become units to which distribution takes place . . . (on what rationale?) or loving behavior is forbidden. . . .

Proponents of patterned principles of distributive justice focus upon criteria for determining who is to receive holdings; they consider the reasons for which someone should have something, and also the total picture of holdings. Whether or not it is better to give than to receive, proponents of patterned principles ignore giving altogether. In considering the distribution of goods, income, and so forth, their theories are theories of recipient justice; they completely ignore any right a person might have to give something to someone. Even in exchanges where each party is simultaneously giver and recipient, patterned principles of justice focus only upon the recipient role and its supposed rights.

Thus discussions tend to focus on whether people (should) have a right to inherit, rather than on whether people (should) have a right to bequeath [14] or on whether persons who have a right to hold also have a right to choose that others hold in their place. I lack a good explanation of why the usual theories of

14 Inheritance (via bequeathing) is the most important example here. Are restrictions on inheritance (perhaps via taxation) compatible with the idea that the person who bequeaths something to another legitimately owns it (whether via a patterned distribution or in some other way)?

distributive justice are so recipient oriented; ignoring givers and transferrers and their rights is of a piece with ignoring producers and their entitlements. But why is it *all* ignored?

Patterned principles of distributive justice necessitate *re*distributive activities. The likelihood is small that any actual freely-arrived-at set of holdings fits a given pattern; and the likelihood is nil that it will continue to fit the pattern as people exchange and give. From the point of view of an entitlement theory, redistribution is a serious matter indeed, involving, as it does, the violation of people's rights. (An exception is those takings that fall under the principle of the rectification of injustices.) From other points of view, also, it is serious.

Taxation of earnings from labor is on a par with forced labor. Some persons find this claim obviously true: taking the earnings of *n* hours labor is like taking *n* hours from the person; it is like forcing the person to work *n* hours for another's purpose. Others find the claim absurd. But even these, *if* they object to forced labor, would oppose forcing unemployed hippies to work for the benefit of the needy. And they would also object to forcing each person to work five extra hours each week for the benefit of the needy. . . .

The man who chooses to work longer to gain an income more than sufficient for his basic needs prefers some extra goods or services to the leisure and activities he could perform during the possible non-working hours; whereas the man who chooses not to work the extra time prefers the leisure activities to the extra goods or services he could acquire by working more. Given this, if it would be illegitimate for a tax system to seize some of a man's leisure (forced labor)

for the purpose of serving the needy, how can it be legitimate for a tax system to seize some of a man's goods for that purpose? Why should we treat the man whose happiness requires certain material goods or services differently from the man whose preferences and desires make such goods unnecessary for his happiness? Why should the man who prefers seeing a movie (and who has to earn money for a ticket) be open to the required call to aid the needy, while the person who prefers looking at a sunset (and hence need earn no extra money) is not? . . .

When end-result principles of distributive justice are built into the legal structure of a society, they (as do most patterned principles) give each citizen an enforceable claim to some portion of the total social product; that is, to some portion of the sum total of the individually and jointly made products. This total product is produced by individuals laboring, using means of production others have saved to bring into existence, by people organizing production or creating means to produce new things or things in a new way. It is on this batch of individual activities that patterned distributional principles give each individual an enforceable claim. Each person has a claim to the activities and the products of other persons, independently of whether the other persons enter into particular relationships that give rise to these claims, and independently of whether they voluntarily take these claims upon themselves, in charity or in exchange for something.

Whether it is done through taxation on wages or on wages over a certain amount, or through seizure of profits, or through there being a big *social pot* so that it's not clear what's coming from where and what's going where, patterned principles of distributive justice involve appropriating the actions of other persons. Seizing the results of someone's labor is equivalent to seizing hours from him and directing him to carry on various activities. [15] If people force you to do certain work, or unrewarded work, for a certain period of time, they decide what you are to do and what purposes your work is to serve apart from your decisions. This process whereby they take this decision from you makes them a *part-owner*

15 Is there a morally important difference between (a) taking the results of someone's work away from them and using it to achieve some end and (b) requiring the person to work for the same number of hours directly to achieve that end? If so, what is it?

of you; it gives them a property right in you. Just as having such partial control and power of decision, by right, over an animal or inanimate object would be to have a property right in it.

End-state and most patterned principles of distributive justice institute (partial) ownership by others of people and their actions and labor. These principles involve a shift from the classical liberals' notion of self-ownership to a notion of (partial) property rights in *other* people.

. . .

LOCKE'S THEORY OF ACQUISITION

Before we turn to consider other theories of justice in detail, we must introduce an additional bit of complexity into the structure of the entitlement theory. This is best approached by considering Locke's attempt to specify a principle of justice in acquisition. [16] Locke views property rights in an unowned object as originating through someone's mixing his labor with it. This gives rise to many questions. What are the boundaries of what labor is mixed with? If a private astronaut clears a place on Mars, has he mixed his labor with (so that he comes to own) the whole planet, the whole uninhabited universe, or just a particular plot? . . .

Why does mixing one's labor with something make one the owner of it? Perhaps because one owns one's labor, and so one comes to own a previously unowned thing that becomes permeated with what one owns. Ownership seeps over into the rest. But why isn't mixing what I own with what I don't own a way of losing what I own rather than a way of gaining what I don't? If I own a can of tomato juice and spill it in the sea so that its molecules (made radioactive, so I can check this) mingle evenly throughout the sea, do I thereby come to own the sea, or have I foolishly dissipated my tomato juice? Perhaps the idea, instead, is that laboring on something improves it and makes it more valuable; and anyone is entitled to own a thing whose value he has created. . . . Ignore the fact that laboring on something may make it less valuable (spraying pink enamel paint on a piece of driftwood

[16] Nozick's view is similar to Locke's (in a part of the *Second Treatise of Government* omitted from the selection included earlier). But he rejects the idea that "mixing one's labor" with something is the key to acquisition.

that you have found). Why should one's entitlement extend to the whole object rather than just to the *added value* one's labor has produced? . . .

It will be implausible to view improving an object as giving full ownership to it, if the stock of unowned objects that might be improved is limited. For an object's coming under one person's ownership changes the situation of all others. [17] Whereas previously they were at liberty . . . to use the object, they now no longer are. This change in the situation of others (by removing their liberty to act on a previously unowned object) need not worsen their situation. If I appropriate a grain of sand from Coney Island, no one else may now do as they will with *that* grain of sand. But there are plenty of other grains of sand left for them to do the same with. Or if not grains of sand, then other things. Alternatively, the things I do with the grain of sand I appropriate might improve the position of others, counterbalancing their loss of the liberty to use that grain. The crucial point is whether appropriation of an unowned object worsens the situation of others.

[17] Nozick is saying not just that an act of acquiring a previously unowned object where the supply of such objects is limited "changes the situation of all others" (which is obvious), but that it changes it in a way that may be morally objectionable. Think very carefully about this point. It seems to amount to saying that people stand in a morally significant relation even to unowned objects. Why might this be so?

Locke's proviso that there be "enough and as good left in common for others" . . . is meant to ensure that the situation of others is not worsened. . . . It is often said that this proviso once held but now no longer does. But there appears to be an argument for the conclusion that if the proviso no longer holds, then it cannot ever have held so as to yield permanent and inheritable property rights. Consider the first person Z for whom there is not enough and as good left to appropriate. The last person Y to appropriate left Z without his previous liberty to act on an object, and so worsened Z's situation. So Y's appropriation is not allowed under Locke's proviso. Therefore the next to last person X to appropriate left Y in a worse position, for X's act ended permissible appropriation. Therefore X's appropriation wasn't permissible. But then the appropriator two from last, W, ended permissible appropriation and so, since it worsened X's position, W's appropriation wasn't permissible. And so on back to the first person *A* to appropriate a permanent property right.[18]

[18] Think very carefully about this rather tricky argument: does it show that if it is even *possible* for the supply of an unowned thing to run out, then there was never, even at the beginning, "enough and as good" left for others?

This argument, however, proceeds too quickly. Someone may be made worse off by another's appropriation in two ways: first, by losing the opportunity to improve his situation by a particular appropriation or any one; and second, by no longer being able to use freely (without appropriation) what he previously could. A *stringent* requirement that another not be made worse off by an appropriation would exclude the first way if nothing else counterbalances the diminution in opportunity, as well as the second. A *weaker* requirement would exclude the second way, though not the first. With the weaker requirement, we cannot zip back so quickly from *Z* to *A,* as in the above argument; for though person *Z* can no longer *appropriate,* there may remain some for him to use as before. In this case *Y*'s appropriation would not violate the weaker Lockean condition.[19] . . . It is arguable that no one legitimately can complain if the weaker provision is satisfied. . . .

[19] Nozick's suggestion is that the weaker condition is the right one, that the more stringent one is too stringent. Do you think he is right about this, and if so, why?

Is the situation of persons who are unable to appropriate (there being no more accessible and useful unowned objects) worsened by a system allowing appropriation and permanent property? Here enter the various familiar social considerations favoring private property: it increases the social product by putting means of production in the hands of those who can use them most efficiently (profitably); experimentation is encouraged, because with separate persons controlling resources, there is no one person or small group whom someone with a new idea must convince to try it out; private property enables people to decide on the pattern and types of risks they wish to bear, leading to specialized types of risk bearing; private property protects future persons by leading some to hold back resources from current consumption for future markets; it provides alternate sources of employment for unpopular persons who don't have to convince any one person or small group to hire them, and so on. These considerations enter a Lockean theory to support the claim that appropriation of private property satisfies the intent behind the "enough and as good left over" proviso, *not* as a utilitarian justification of property. They enter to rebut the claim that because the proviso is violated no natural right to private property can arise by a Lockean process. The difficulty in working such an argument to show that the proviso is satisfied is in fixing the appropriate base line for comparison. Lockean appropriation makes people no worse off than they would be *how?* . . .[20]

[20] Nozick's suggestion is that the system of private property does not leave people worse off than they would have been if acquisition of unowned objects did not occur, even though they no longer have much opportunity for acquisition of unowned objects themselves. But he recognizes the problem of what the appropriate "baseline" for this comparison is: must people be no worse off than they would have been in a state of nature (easy to satisfy) or no worse off than they would have been in another social system without private property (perhaps substantially more difficult to satisfy)?

THE PROVISO

Whether or not Locke's particular theory of appropriation can be spelled out so as to handle various difficulties, I assume that any adequate theory of justice in acquisition will contain a proviso similar to the weaker of the ones we have attributed to Locke. A process normally giving rise to a permanent bequeathable property right in a previously unowned thing will not do so if the position of others no longer at liberty to use the thing is thereby worsened. It is important to specify *this* particular mode of worsening the situation of others, for the proviso does not encompass other modes. It does not include the worsening due to more limited opportunities to appropriate (the first way above, corresponding to the more stringent condition), and it does not include how I "worsen" a seller's position if I appropriate materials to make some of what he is selling, and then enter into competition with him. Someone whose appropriation otherwise would violate the proviso still may appropriate provided he compensates the others so that their situation is not thereby worsened; unless he does compensate these others, his appropriation will violate the proviso of the principle of justice in acquisition and will be an illegitimate one. 21 A theory of appropriation incorporating this Lockean proviso will handle correctly the cases (objections to the theory lacking the proviso) where someone appropriates the total supply of something necessary for life.

A theory which includes this proviso in its principle of justice in acquisition must also contain a more complex principle of justice in transfer. Some reflection of the proviso about appropriation constrains later actions. If my appropriating all of a certain substance violates the Lockean proviso, then so does my appropriating some and purchasing all the rest from others who obtained it without otherwise violating the Lockean proviso. If the proviso excludes someone's appropriating all the drinkable water in the world, it also excludes his purchasing it all. (More weakly, and messily, it may exclude his charging certain prices for some of his supply.) This proviso (almost?) never will come into effect; the more someone acquires of a scarce substance which others want, the higher the price of the rest will go, and the more difficult it will become for him to acquire it all. . . .

Each owner's title to his holding includes the historical shadow of the Lockean proviso on appropriation. This excludes his transferring it into an agglomeration that does violate the Lockean proviso and excludes his using it in a way, in coordination with others or independently of them, so as to violate the proviso by making the situation of others worse than their baseline situation. Once it is known that someone's ownership runs afoul of the Lockean proviso, there are stringent limits on what he may do with (what it is difficult any longer unreservedly to call) "his property." Thus a person may not appropriate the only water hole in a desert and charge what he will. Nor may he charge what he will if he possesses one, and unfortunately it happens that all the water holes in the desert dry up, except for his. This unfortunate circumstance, admittedly no fault of his, brings into operation the Lockean proviso and limits his property rights. Similarly, an owner's property right in the only island in an area does not allow him to order a castaway from a shipwreck off his island as a trespasser, for this would violate the Lockean proviso.

. . .

21 Nozick concludes that the correct account of justice will include a restriction on acquisition of unowned objects of the sort indicated in the previous annotation, but without resolving the issue raised there. Is he right that the other sorts of "worsening" mentioned in this paragraph should not be included in such a principle?

Discussion Questions

1. The historical practice of human slavery in the American South prior to the Civil War is a good example of a past injustice that might require rectification under Nozick's envisaged principle of rectification. Part of the injustice associated with slavery is that the results of the slave's labor were appropriated by the owner (under threat of force). Discuss what, if anything, should be done now to rectify this injustice, being careful to specify clearly who should receive the benefits of such rectification and who should pay the cost. What if the relevant groups cannot be reliably identified?

2. Is Wilt Chamberlain (or any star athlete) entitled to receive all that people are freely willing to pay (out of their just allotments) to watch him play? Is he entitled to bequeath as much of it as he likes to his heirs? What if the amount is so large in relation to the resources of others that Chamberlain (or his heir) is able to exert a much larger influence than anyone else on such things as the results of political elections?

3. Does taxation for redistribution of income and wealth amount to forced labor or ownership of the taxed person by those who are (allegedly) entitled to the results of such redistribution according to some patterned theory of justice? If not, why not? Is there any difference between taxation for this purpose and taxation for the support of other government services (such as police and fire protection, highway maintenance, etc.)?

4. Why should there by *any* limitation, even the one Nozick proposes, on the acquisition of unowned items? If they are unowned, why isn't anyone who comes upon them free to take possession? Try to think here of examples of unowned things, perhaps in earlier times (land in unexplored places, undiscovered mineral resources, fish in the open sea, etc.).

$$\boxed{\textit{John Rawls}}$$

John Rawls (1921–2002), like Nozick a professor at Harvard, was one of the best known and most influential figures in recent political and social philosophy. Unlike Hobbes, Locke, and Nozick, Rawls's basic concern is less with the issue of whether and why any sort of governmental power is legitimate than with the issue of which sorts of governmental and societal structures and institutions satisfy the demands of *justice*. In his book *A Theory of Justice* (1971), Rawls offers a complicated and nuanced account of justice, focusing on what he calls "the basic structure of society" and especially on the issue of how income, wealth, and other results of social cooperation should be distributed among the members of a particular society.

Rawls sometimes describes his view of justice as a version of a social contract theory. For him, however, the contractual situation is a purely hypothetical one ("the original position") in which members of society, denied the knowledge of their own situation that would allow them to bias the results in favor of themselves, reach an agreement as to the basic principles of justice by pursuing their own self-interest (insofar as they can discern it). The most distinctive result that Rawls claims would be agreed upon in this hypothetical situation is the principle ("the difference principle") that while social benefits need not be distributed equally, an unequal distribution can only be justified by the fact that even the worst-off member of society is thereby better off (because of the increased production that results from giving more to others).

There are three aspects of Rawls's discussion that need to be carefully sorted out. First, there is the account of how the reasoning of people in the original position would actually go; this comes at the very end of the present selection. Second, there is Rawls's argument that the way in which the original position is specified is the right one to yield the correct conception of justice—with the crucial issue being whether Rawls is right about just what knowledge should be excluded there; this occurs both at the beginning of the selection and toward the end, just prior to the account of the actual reasoning in the original position. Third, there is independent argument defending the alleged results of the original position as being in fact the right conception of justice; this begins with the account of the two principles (p. 786) and continues through the discussion of equality and meritocracy (ending on p. 791).

Justice as Fairness, From *A Theory of Justice*

THE ROLE OF JUSTICE

Justice is the first virtue of social institutions, as truth is of systems of thought. A theory however elegant and economical must be rejected or revised if it is untrue; likewise laws and institutions no matter how efficient and well-arranged must be reformed or abolished if they are unjust. Each person possesses an inviolability founded on justice that even the welfare

From A Theory of Justice *(Cambridge Mass.; Harvard University Press, 1971)*

of society as a whole cannot override. For this reason justice denies that the loss of freedom for some is made right by a greater good shared by others. It does not allow that the sacrifices imposed on a few are outweighed by the larger sum of advantages enjoyed by many. Therefore in a just society the liberties of equal citizenship are taken as settled; the rights secured by justice are not subject to political bargaining or to the calculus of social interests. . . . analogously, an injustice is tolerable only when it is necessary to avoid an even greater injustice. Being first virtues of human activities, truth and justice are uncompromising.

These propositions seem to express our intuitive conviction of the primacy of justice. No doubt they are expressed too strongly. In any event I wish to inquire whether these contentions or others similar to them are sound, and if so how they can be accounted for. To this end it is necessary to work out a theory of justice in the light of which these assertions can be interpreted and assessed. I shall begin by considering the role of the principles of justice. Let us assume, to fix ideas, that a society is a more or less self-sufficient association of persons who in their relations to one another recognize certain rules of conduct as binding and who for the most part act in accordance with them. Suppose further that these rules specify a system of cooperation designed to advance the good of those taking part in it. Then, although a society is a cooperative venture for mutual advantage, it is typically marked by a conflict as well as by an identity of interests. There is an identity of interests since social cooperation makes possible a better life for all than any would have if each were to live solely by his own efforts. There is a conflict of interests since persons are not indifferent as to how the greater benefits produced by their collaboration are distributed, for in order to pursue their ends they each prefer a larger to a lesser share. A set of principles is required for choosing among the various social arrangements which determine this division of advantages and for underwriting an agreement on the proper distributive shares. These principles are the principles of social justice: they provide a way of assigning rights and duties in the basic institutions of society and they define the appropriate distribution of the benefits and burdens of social cooperation.①

Now let us say that a society is well-ordered when it is not only designed to advance the good of its members but when it is also effectively regulated by a public conception of justice. That is, it is a society in which (1) everyone accepts and knows that the others accept the same principles of justice, and (2) the basic social institutions generally satisfy and are generally known to satisfy these principles. In this case while men may put forth excessive demands on one another, they nevertheless acknowledge a common point of view from which their claims may be adjudicated. . . .②

① So the account of justice to be developed is concerned primarily with the basic institutions of society and with specifying the way in which the "benefits and burdens" of social cooperation should be distributed—and not with issues of justice that arise in more limited contexts (such as criminal justice). This is a very abstract specification, and you should try to identify for yourself some of the aspects of society that such a conception will be concerned with.

② Thus a society that satisfied even optimum principles of justice but was not believed by its members to do so would not be "well-ordered."

THE SUBJECT OF JUSTICE

Many different kinds of things are said to be just and unjust: not only laws, institutions, and social systems, but also particular actions of many kinds, including decisions, judgments, and imputations. We also call the attitudes and dispositions of persons, and persons themselves, just and unjust. Our topic, however, is that of social justice. For us the primary subject of justice is the basic structure of society, or more exactly, the way in which the major social institutions distribute fundamental rights and duties and determine the division of advantages from social cooperation. By major institutions I understand the political constitution and the principal economic and social arrangements. Thus the legal protection of freedom of thought and liberty of conscience, competitive markets, private property in the means of production, and the monogamous family are examples of major social institutions.③ Taken together as one scheme, the major institutions define men's rights and duties and

③ Here is a little more help in picking out which social institutions are "basic."

influence their life prospects, what they can expect to be and how well they can hope to do. The basic structure is the primary subject of justice because its effects are so profound and present from the start. . . .

THE MAIN IDEA OF THE THEORY OF JUSTICE

My aim is to present a conception of justice which generalizes and carries to a higher level of abstraction the familiar theory of the social contract as found, say, in Locke, Rousseau, and Kant. In order to do this we are not to think of the original contract as one to enter a particular society or to set up a particular form of government. Rather, the guiding idea is that the principles of justice for the basic structure of society are the object of the original agreement. They are the principles that free and rational persons concerned to further their own interests would accept in an initial position of equality as defining the fundamental terms of their association. These principles are to regulate all further agreements; they specify the kinds of social cooperation that can be entered into and the forms of government that can be established. This way of regarding the principles of justice I shall call justice as fairness.

. . .

In justice as fairness the original position of equality corresponds to the state of nature in the traditional theory of the social contract. This original position is not, of course, thought of as an actual historical state of affairs, much less as a primitive condition of culture. It is understood as a purely hypothetical situation characterized so as to lead to a certain conception of justice. Among the essential features of this situation is that no one knows his place in society, his class position or social status, nor does any one know his fortune in the distribution of natural assets and abilities, his intelligence, strength, and the like. I shall even assume that the parties do not know their conceptions of the good or their special psychological propensities. The principles of justice are chosen behind a veil of ignorance.④ This ensures that no one is advantaged or disadvantaged in the choice of principles by the outcome of natural chance or the contingency of social circumstances. Since all are similarly situated and no one is able to design principles to favor his particular

condition, the principles of justice are the result of a fair agreement or bargain. . . .

One feature of justice as fairness is to think of the parties in the initial situation as rational and mutually disinterested. This does not mean that the parties are egoists, that is, individuals with only certain kinds of interests, say in wealth, prestige, and domination. But they are conceived as not taking an interest in one another's interests. . . .⑤

. . . once the principles of justice are thought of as arising from an original agreement in a situation of equality, it is an open question whether the principle of utility would be acknowledged. Offhand it hardly seems likely that persons who view themselves as equals, entitled to press their claims upon one another, would agree to a principle which may require lesser life prospects for some simply for the sake of a greater sum of advantages enjoyed by others. Since each desires to protect his interests, his capacity to advance his conception of the good, no one has a reason to acquiesce in an enduring loss for himself in order to bring about a greater net balance of satisfaction.⑥ In the absence of strong and lasting benevolent impulses, a rational man would not accept a basic structure merely because it maximized the algebraic sum of advantages irrespective of its permanent effects on his own basic rights and interests. Thus it seems that the principle of utility is incompatible with the conception of social cooperation among equals for mutual advantage. It appears to be inconsistent with the idea

④ The original position is thus not a real situation that could actually occur: probably no actual person could be as ignorant of his own characteristics as the "veil of ignorance" requires. Rather it is a hypothetical thought experiment that is supposed to reflect fairness and equality among citizens in a way that leads them to choose the correct principles of justice.

⑤ The concern of the parties in the original position is their own rational self-interest. They are not concerned altruistically with the welfare of others, nor are they supposed to be moved by moral values, not even by any antecedent idea of justice itself. The whole point is that the correct principles of justice are those that rationally self-interested individuals would choose in a situation in which they are unable (because of the veil of ignorance) to unfairly favor their own actual situation or characteristics.

of reciprocity implicit in the notion of a well-ordered society. Or, at any rate, so I shall argue.

I shall maintain instead that the persons in the initial situation would choose two rather different principles: the first requires equality in the assignment of basic rights and duties, while the second holds that social and economic inequalities, for example inequalities of wealth and authority, are just only if they result in compensating benefits for everyone, and in particular for the least advantaged members of society.⑦ These principles rule out justifying institutions on the grounds that the hardships of some are offset by a greater good in the aggregate. It may be expedient but it is not just that some should have less in order that others may prosper. But there is no injustice in the greater benefits earned by a few provided that the situation of persons not so fortunate is thereby improved. The intuitive idea is that since everyone's well-being depends upon a scheme of cooperation without which no one could have a satisfactory life, the division of advantages should be such as to draw forth the willing cooperation of everyone taking part in it, including those less well situated. The two principles mentioned seem to be a fair basis on which those better endowed, or more fortunate in their social position, neither of which we can be said to deserve, could expect the willing cooperation of others when some workable scheme is a necessary condition of the welfare of all. Once we decide to look for a conception of justice that prevents the use of the accidents of natural endowment and the contingencies of social circumstance as counters in a quest for political and economic advantage, we are led to these principles.⑧ They express the result of leaving aside those aspects of the social world that seem arbitrary from a moral point of view.

. . .

THE ORIGINAL POSITION AND JUSTIFICATION

I have said that the original position is the appropriate initial status quo which insures that the fundamental agreements reached in it are fair. This fact yields the name "justice as fairness." It is clear, then, that I want to say that one conception of justice is more reasonable than another, or justifiable with respect to it, if rational persons in the initial situation would choose its principles over those of the other for the role of justice. Conceptions of justice are to be ranked by their acceptability to persons so circumstanced. Understood in this way the question of justification is settled by working out a problem of deliberation: we have to ascertain which principles it would be rational to adopt given the contractual situation. . . .

One should not be misled, then, by the somewhat unusual conditions which characterize the original position. The idea here is simply to make vivid to ourselves the restrictions that it seems reasonable to impose on arguments for principles of justice, and therefore on these principles themselves. Thus it seems reasonable and generally acceptable that no one should be advantaged or disadvantaged by natural fortune or social circumstances in the choice of principles. It also

⑥ Here is a good initial example of reasoning based on the original position. The principle of utility (discussed further in Chapter 6) holds roughly that the morally right action in a set of choices is the one that produces the best overall consequences for everyone taken together. Self-interested people in the original position would reject such a principle, Rawls argues, because it says nothing about how these good consequences are distributed among people, leaving the possibility open that any given person might do very poorly.

⑦ Here is the initial statement of Rawls's two basic principles of justice. The main idea behind the second principle ("the difference principle") is that inequalities that give talented or productive people an incentive to develop and utilize their talents may lead to enough of an increase in production to make everyone, even those who receive the smallest relative shares, better off in absolute terms than they would have been in a situation of equality.

⑧ Here are two important things that would be hidden behind the veil of ignorance in the original position and so cannot be used to seek advantages in a just system. By "contingencies of social circumstance," Rawls means things like social class. This is one of the clearest examples of the point of the veil of ignorance: people in the original position cannot choose a principle that gives advantages to their social class, because they do not know which one that is. One of the main questions about Rawls's view is whether he is right that "accidents of natural endowment" (natural talents and abilities) should be treated in the same way.

seems widely agreed that it should be impossible to tailor principles to the circumstances of one's own case. We should insure further that particular inclinations and aspirations, and persons' conceptions of their good do not affect the principles adopted. The aim is to rule out those principles that it would be rational to propose for acceptance, however little the chance of success, only if one knew certain things that are irrelevant from the standpoint of justice. For example, if a man knew that he was wealthy, he might find it rational to advance the principle that various taxes for welfare measures be counted unjust; if he knew that he was poor, he would most likely propose the contrary principle. To represent the desired restrictions one imagines a situation in which everyone is deprived of this sort of information. One excludes the knowledge of those contingencies which sets men at odds and allows them to be guided by their prejudices. In this manner the veil of ignorance is arrived at in a natural way. This concept should cause no difficulty if we keep in mind the constraints on arguments that it is meant to express. At any time we can enter the original position, so to speak, simply by following a certain procedure, namely, by arguing for principles of justice in accordance with these restrictions.⑨

⑨ Here are some further, more specific examples of things that would be excluded from the knowledge of the hypothetical persons in the original position. Rawls seems here to suggest that the specification of what should be thus excluded is fairly obvious, but not all would agree—thus you should think carefully about the issue.

. . .

TWO PRINCIPLES OF JUSTICE

I shall now state in a provisional form the two principles of justice that I believe would be agreed to in the original position. The first formulation of these principles is tentative. As we go on I shall consider several formulations and approximate step by step the final statement to be given much later. I believe that doing this allows the exposition to proceed in a natural way.

The first statement of the two principles reads as follows.

First: each person is to have an equal right to the most extensive scheme of equal basic liberties compatible with a similar scheme of liberties for others.

Second: social and economic inequalities are to be arranged so that they are both (a) reasonably expected to be to everyone's advantage, and (b) attached to positions and offices open to all.

There are two ambiguous phrases in the second principle, namely "everyone's advantage" and "open to all." Determining their sense more exactly will lead to a second formulation of the principle. . . .

These principles primarily apply, as I have said, to the basic structure of society and govern the assignment of rights and duties and regulate the distribution of social and economic advantages. Their formulation presupposes that, for the purposes of a theory of justice, the social structure may be viewed as having two more or less distinct parts, the first principle applying to the one, the second principle to the other. Thus we distinguish between the aspects of the social system that define and secure the equal basic liberties and the aspects that specify and establish social and economic inequalities. Now it is essential to observe that the basic liberties are given by a list of such liberties. Important among these are political liberty (the right to vote and to hold public office) and freedom of speech and assembly; liberty of conscience and freedom of thought; freedom of the person, which includes freedom from psychological oppression and physical assault and dismemberment (integrity of the person); the right to hold personal property and freedom from arbitrary arrest and seizure as defined by the concept of the rule of law. These liberties are to be equal by the first principle.

The second principle applies, in the first approximation, to the distribution of income and wealth and to the design of organizations that make use of differences in authority and responsibility. While the distribution of wealth and income need not be equal, it must be to everyone's advantage, and at the same time, positions of authority and responsibility must be accessible to all. One applies the second principle by holding positions open, and then, subject to this constraint, arranges social and economic inequalities so that everyone benefits.

These principles are to be arranged in a serial order with the first principle prior to the second. This ordering means that infringements of the basic equal liberties protected by the first principle cannot be justified, or compensated for, by greater social and economic advantages. ⑩ These liberties have a central range of application within which they can be limited and compromised only when they conflict with other basic liberties. Since they may be limited when they clash with one another, none of these liberties is absolute; but however they are adjusted to form one system, this system is to be the same for all. . . .

The two principles are rather specific in their content, and their acceptance rests on certain assumptions that I must eventually try to explain and justify. For the present, it should be observed that these principles are a special case of a more general conception of justice that can be expressed as follows.

> All social values—liberty and opportunity, income and wealth, and the social bases of self-respect— are to be distributed equally unless an unequal distribution of any, or all, of these values is to everyone's advantage.

Injustice, then, is simply inequalities that are not to the benefit of all. Of course, this conception is extremely vague and requires interpretation.⑪

As a first step, suppose that the basic structure of society distributes certain primary goods, that is, things that every rational man is presumed to want. These goods normally have a use whatever a person's rational plan of life. For simplicity, assume that the chief primary goods at the disposition of society are rights, liberties, and opportunities, and income and wealth. . . .These are the social primary goods. . . .

⑩ Does it seem obvious that self-interested people in the original position would be unwilling to sacrifice basic liberties to *any* extent in return for greater social and especially economic advantages? What might be an example of this sort of sacrifice? (See the further discussion of this point at Annotation 27.)

⑪ Here we see a kind of presumption in favor of egalitarianism: inequalities need to be justified, and can only be justified by being shown to be in everyone's interests. (Pretty clearly our actual society does not satisfy this requirement.) What might the justification be for this presumption?

INTERPRETATIONS OF THE SECOND PRINCIPLE

I have already mentioned that since the phrases "everyone's advantage" and "equally open to all" are ambiguous, both parts of the second principle have two natural senses. Because these senses are independent of one another, the principle has four possible meanings. Assuming that the first principle of equal liberty has the same sense throughout, we then have four interpretations of the two principles. These are indicated in the table below.

"Equally open"	"Everyone's advantage"	
	Principle of efficiency	Difference principle
Equality as careers open to talents	System of Natural Liberty	Natural Aristocracy
Equality as equality of fair opportunity	Liberal Equality	Democratic Equality

. . .

In the system of natural liberty the initial distribution is regulated by the arrangements implicit in the conception of careers open to talents. . . . These arrangements presuppose a background of equal liberty (as specified by the first principle) and a free market economy. They require a formal equality of opportunity in that all have at least the same legal rights of access to all advantaged social positions. But since there is no effort to preserve an equality, or similarity, of social conditions, except insofar as this is necessary to preserve the requisite background institutions, the initial distribution of assets for any period of time is strongly influenced by natural and social contingencies. The existing distribution of income and wealth, say, is the cumulative effect of prior distributions of natural assets—that is, natural talents and abilities—as these have been developed or left unrealized, and their use favored or disfavored over time by social circumstances and such chance contingencies as accident and good fortune. Intuitively, the most obvious injustice of the system of natural liberty is that it permits distributive shares to be improperly influenced by these factors so arbitrary from a moral point of view.⑫

The liberal interpretation, as I shall refer to it, tries to correct for this by adding to the requirement of careers open to talents the further condition of the principle of fair equality of opportunity. The thought here is that positions are to be not only open in a formal sense, but that all should have a fair chance to attain them. Offhand it is not clear what is meant, but we might say that those with similar abilities and skills should have similar life chances. More specifically, assuming that there is a distribution of natural assets, those who are at the same level of talent and ability, and have the same willingness to use them, should have the same prospects of success regardless of their initial place in the social system. In all sectors of society there should be roughly equal prospects of culture and achievement for everyone similarly motivated and endowed. The expectations of those with the same abilities and aspirations should not be affected by their social class. [13]

The liberal interpretation of the two principles seeks, then, to mitigate the influence of social contingencies and natural fortune on distributive shares. To accomplish this end it is necessary to impose further basic structural conditions on the social system. Free market arrangements must be set within a framework of political and legal institutions which regulates the overall trends of economic events and preserves the social conditions necessary for fair equality of opportunity. The elements of this framework are familiar enough, though it may be worthwhile to recall the importance of preventing excessive accumulations of property and wealth and of maintaining equal opportunities of education for all. Chances to acquire cultural knowledge and skills should not depend upon one's class position, and so the school system, whether public or private, should be designed to even out class barriers.

While the liberal conception seems clearly preferable to the system of natural liberty, intuitively it still appears defective. For one thing, even if it works to perfection in eliminating the influence of social contingencies, it still permits the distribution of wealth and income to be determined by the natural distribution of abilities and talents. Within the limits allowed by the background arrangements, distributive shares are decided by the outcome of the natural lottery; and this outcome is arbitrary from a moral perspective. There is no more reason to permit the distribution of income and wealth to be settled by the distribution of natural assets than by historical and social fortune. . . . [14]

Before turning to the conception of democratic equality, we should note that of natural aristocracy. On this view no attempt is made to regulate social contingencies beyond what is required by formal equality of opportunity, but the advantages of persons with greater natural endowments are to be limited to those that further the good of the poorer sectors of society. The aristocratic ideal is applied to a system that is open, at least from a legal point of view, and the better situation of those favored by it is regarded as just only when less would be had by those below, if less were given to those above. [15] In this way the idea of *noblesse oblige* is carried over to the conception of natural aristocracy.

Now both the liberal conception and that of natural aristocracy are unstable. For once we are troubled by the influence of either social contingencies or natural chance on the determination of distributive shares, we are bound, on reflection, to be bothered by the influence of the other. From a moral standpoint the two seem equally arbitrary. So however we move

---

[12] The "system of natural liberty" is at least approximately the system defined by Nozick's entitlement theory. Rawls's claim is that the distribution of wealth and other advantages in such a system is unjust because it reflects the long-term results of distributions of natural talents and abilities, all of this being "arbitrary from a moral point of view" in that there is no *moral* reason why one person should have such a talent while another does not. Is he right that such a result is an "obvious injustice"? (Consider what Nozick might say.)

[13] The main difference between "liberal equality" and the "system of natural liberty" is that in "liberal equality," people with the same natural assets should have the same chance of success, the same chance for desirable careers and positions. Think of how this might not be so under natural liberty (different opportunities for education is one obvious consideration) and what would have to be done under liberal equality to change this result.

[14] Even if the influence of "social contingencies" (such things as family status and wealth) are eliminated under liberal equality, the "life chances" of different persons will still be influenced by their natural abilities and talents. Is Rawls right that this is clearly unjust?

[15] The idea of "natural aristocracy" is perhaps the least clear of Rawls's four alternatives. In this system there is only "formal" and not "fair" equality of opportunity: those from better family backgrounds will have a better chance to succeed, but their rewards will be only as great as is required to yield the best result (in absolute, not relative terms) for those who are worst off.

away from the system of natural liberty, we cannot be satisfied short of the democratic conception. . . .

DEMOCRATIC EQUALITY AND THE DIFFERENCE PRINCIPLE

The democratic interpretation, as the table suggests, is arrived at by combining the principle of fair equality of opportunity with the difference principle. This principle removes the indeterminateness of the principle of efficiency by singling out a particular position from which the social and economic inequalities of the basic structure are to be judged. [16] Assuming the framework of institutions required by equal liberty and fair equality of opportunity, the higher expectations of those better situated are just if and only if they work as part of a scheme which improves the expectations of the least advantaged members of society. The intuitive idea is that the social order is not to establish and secure the more attractive prospects of those better off unless doing so is to the advantage of those less fortunate. . . .

[16] If the different ways in which liberal equality and natural aristocracy are (allegedly) improvements over natural liberty are combined, we have the difference principle: inequalities are justified only if they make the least advantaged members of society better off (again, in absolute terms).

THE TENDENCY TO EQUALITY

I wish to conclude this discussion of the two principles by explaining the sense in which they express an egalitarian conception of justice. Also I should like to forestall the objection to the principle of fair opportunity that it leads to a meritocratic society. In order to prepare the way for doing this, I note several aspects of the conception of justice that I have set out.

First we may observe that the difference principle gives some weight to the considerations singled out by the principle of redress. This is the principle that undeserved inequalities call for redress; and since inequalities of birth and natural endowment are undeserved, these inequalities are to be somehow compensated for. Thus the principle holds that in order to treat all persons equally, to provide genuine equality of opportunity, society must give more attention to those with fewer native assets and to those born into the less favorable social positions. The idea is to redress the bias of contingencies in the direction of equality. In pursuit of this principle greater resources might be spent on the education of the less rather than the more intelligent, at least over a certain time of life, say the earlier years of school. [17]

Now the principle of redress has not to my knowledge been proposed as the sole criterion of justice, as the single aim of the social order. It is plausible as most such principles are only as a prima facie principle, one that is to be weighed in the balance with others. For example, we are to weigh it against the principle to improve the average standard of life, or to advance the common good. But whatever other principles we hold, the claims of redress are to be taken into account. It is thought to represent one of the elements in our conception of justice. Now the difference principle is not of course the principle of redress. It does not require society to try to even out handicaps as if all were expected to compete on a fair basis in the same race. But the difference principle would allocate resources in education, say, so as to improve the long-term expectation of the least favored. If this end is attained by giving more attention to the better endowed, it is permissible; otherwise not. And in making this decision, the value of education should not be assessed solely in terms of economic efficiency and social welfare. Equally if not more important is the role of education in enabling a person to enjoy the culture of his society and to take part in its affairs, and in this way to provide for each individual a secure sense of his own worth.

Thus although the difference principle is not the same as that of redress, it does achieve some of the intent of the latter principle. It transforms the aims of the basic structure so that the total scheme of institutions no longer emphasizes social efficiency and technocratic values. The difference principle represents, in effect, an agreement to regard the distribution of natural talents as in some respects a common asset [18] and to share in the greater social and economic benefits made

[17] The "principle of redress" says that society should *compensate* those who are less well off in terms of family status or natural endowment, thereby coming closer to genuine equality of opportunity. Does this seem right? For example, does a person with less natural intelligence than others deserve to be compensated by society for this situation?

possible by the complementarities of this distribution. Those who have been favored by nature, whoever they are, may gain from their good fortune only on terms that improve the situation of those who have lost out. The naturally advantaged are not to gain merely because they are more gifted, but only to cover the costs of training and education and for using their endowments in ways that help the less fortunate as well. No one deserves his greater natural capacity nor merits a more favorable starting place in society. But, of course, this is no reason to ignore, much less to eliminate these distinctions. Instead, the basic structure can be arranged so that these contingencies work for the good of the least fortunate. Thus we are led to the difference principle if we wish to set up the social system so that no one gains or loses from his arbitrary place in the distribution of natural assets or his initial position in society without giving or receiving compensating advantages in return.

---

18 Rawls elsewhere says that this means only that the *distribution* of talents, the fact that different people have different and often complementary abilities, is to be treated as a "common asset," not the talents themselves (which would seemingly amount to saying that other people have a claim on a given person's talents). But it is hard to avoid thinking that the difference principle involves both of these ideas—why else are people allowed to profit from their own talents only if everyone else benefits too?

In view of these remarks we may reject the contention that the ordering of institutions is always defective because the distribution of natural talents and the contingencies of social circumstance are unjust, and this injustice must inevitably carry over to human arrangements. Occasionally this reflection is offered as an excuse for ignoring injustice, as if the refusal to acquiesce in injustice is on a par with being unable to accept death. The natural distribution is neither just nor unjust; nor is it unjust that persons are born into society at some particular position. These are simply natural facts. What is just and unjust is the way that institutions deal with these facts.**19** Aristocratic and caste societies are unjust because they make these contingencies the ascriptive basis for belonging to more or less enclosed and privileged social classes. The basic structure of these societies incorporates the arbitrariness found in nature. But there is no necessity for men to resign themselves to these contingencies.

The social system is not an unchangeable order beyond human control but a pattern of human action. In justice as fairness men agree to avail themselves of the accidents of nature and social circumstance only when doing so is for the common benefit. The two principles are a fair way of meeting the arbitrariness of fortune; and while no doubt imperfect in other ways, the institutions which satisfy these principles are just.

A further point is that the difference principle expresses a conception of reciprocity. It is a principle of mutual benefit. At first sight, however, it may appear unfairly biased towards the least favored. To consider this question in an intuitive way, suppose for simplicity that there are only two groups in society, one noticeably more fortunate than the other. Subject to the usual constraints (defined by the priority of the first principle and fair equality of opportunity), society could maximize the expectations of either group but not both, since we can maximize with respect to only one aim at a time. It seems clear that society should not do the best it can for those initially more advantaged; so if we reject the difference principle, we must prefer maximizing some weighted mean of the two expectations. But if we give any weight to the more fortunate, we are valuing for their own sake the gains to those already more favored by natural and social contingencies. No one had an antecedent claim to be benefited in this way, and so to maximize a weighted mean is, so to speak, to favor the more fortunate twice over. Thus the more advantaged, when they view the matter from a general perspective, recognize that the well-being of each depends on a scheme of social cooperation without which no one could have a satisfactory life; they recognize also that they can expect the willing cooperation of all only if the terms of the scheme are reasonable. So they regard themselves as already compensated, as it were, by the advantages to which no one (including themselves) had a prior claim. They forego the idea of maximizing a weighted mean and regard the differ-

---

19 Think again about this basic comparison: It is unjust for society to reward people because they happen to be born in "better" families. Is it in the same way unjust to allow those with greater abilities to benefit from them in ways that do not also benefit everyone else? (Think here of a talented writer or inventor.) Why does everyone else have a just claim to benefit from their talents?

---

ence principle as a fair basis for regulating the basic structure.[20]

[20] Here is Rawls's answer (somewhat altered from the first edition of the book, as we will see in the following selection) to the question of why the terms of cooperation between people with more talents and those with less should be such as to yield the maximum advantage for the less talented, rather than some compromise between the interests of the two groups.

. . .

Thus it is incorrect that individuals with greater natural endowments and the superior character that has made their development possible have a right to a cooperative scheme that enables them to obtain even further benefits in ways that do not contribute to the advantages of others. We do not deserve our place in the distribution of native endowments, any more than we deserve our initial starting place in society. That we deserve the superior character that enables us to make the effort to cultivate our abilities is also problematic; for such character depends in good part upon fortunate family and social circumstances in early life for which we can claim no credit. The notion of desert does not apply here. To be sure, the more advantaged have a right to their natural assets, as does everyone else; this right is covered by the first principle under the basic liberty protecting the integrity of the person. And so the more advantaged are entitled to whatever they can acquire in accordance with the rules of a fair system of social cooperation. Our problem is how this scheme, the basic structure of society, is to be designed. From a suitably general standpoint, the difference principle appears acceptable to both the more advantaged and the less advantaged individual.[21] Of course, none of this is strictly speaking an argument for the principle, since in a contract theory arguments are made from the point of view of the original position. But these intuitive considerations help to clarify the principle and the sense in which it is egalitarian.

[21] Should people with greater talents be satisfied with the different principle? (They will agree to it in the original position, Rawls is claiming, because they don't know their own situation in this respect. But this *might* show only that the original position is wrongly conceived, that this bit of knowledge should not be excluded.)

. . .

Now it seems evident in the light of these observations that the democratic interpretation of the two principles will not lead to a meritocratic society. This form of social order follows the principle of careers open to talents and uses equality of opportunity as a way of releasing men's energies in the pursuit of economic prosperity and political dominion. There exists a marked disparity between the upper and lower classes in both means of life and the rights and privileges of organizational authority. The culture of the poorer strata is impoverished while that of the governing and technocratic elite is securely based on the service of the national ends of power and wealth. Equality of opportunity means an equal chance to leave the less fortunate behind in the personal quest for influence and social position. Thus a meritocratic society is a danger for the other interpretations of the principles of justice but not for the democratic conception. For, as we have just seen, the difference principle transforms the aims of society in fundamental respects. . . .

THE CIRCUMSTANCES OF JUSTICE

The circumstances of justice may be described as the normal conditions under which human cooperation is both possible and necessary. Thus, as I noted at the outset, although a society is a cooperative venture for mutual advantage, it is typically marked by a conflict as well as an identity of interests. There is an identity of interests since social cooperation makes possible a better life for all than any would have if each were to try to live solely by his own efforts.[22] There is a conflict of interests since men are not indifferent as to how the greater benefits produced by their collaboration are distributed, for in order to pursue their ends they each prefer a larger to a lesser share. Thus principles are needed for choosing among the various social arrangements which determine this division of advantages and for underwriting an agreement on the proper distributive shares. These requirements define the role of justice. The background conditions that

[22] This is clearly true even of the more talented, which is one of Rawls's reasons for thinking that they should be satisfied with the distribution of benefits that results from the difference principle. But does this really speak to the issue raised in Annotation 21?

give rise to these necessities are the circumstances of justice.

These conditions may be divided into two kinds. First, there are the objective circumstances which make human cooperation both possible and necessary. Thus, many individuals coexist together at the same time on a definite geographical territory. These individuals are roughly similar in physical and mental powers; or at any rate, their capacities are comparable in that no one among them can dominate the rest. They are vulnerable to attack, and all are subject to having their plans blocked by the united force of others. Finally, there is the condition of moderate scarcity understood to cover a wide range of situations. Natural and other resources are not so abundant that schemes of cooperation become superfluous, nor are conditions so harsh that fruitful ventures must inevitably break down. While mutually advantageous arrangements are feasible, the benefits they yield fall short of the demands men put forward. 23

> 23 It is only in situations where these general conditions are satisfied that justice becomes both an important social value and one capable of being reasonably achieved. Fundamental differences in these respects would make justice either of little importance or virtually impossible to achieve.

The subjective circumstances are the relevant aspects of the subjects of cooperation, that is, of the persons working together. Thus while the parties have roughly similar needs and interests, or needs and interests in various ways complementary, so that mutually advantageous cooperation among them is possible, they nevertheless have their own plans of life. These plans, or conceptions of the good, lead them to have different ends and purposes, and to make conflicting claims on the natural and social resources available. Moreover, although the interests advanced by these plans are not assumed to be interests in the self, they are the interests of a self that regards its conception of the good as worthy of recognition and that advances claims in its behalf as deserving satisfaction. I also suppose that men suffer from various shortcomings of knowledge, thought, and judgment. Their knowledge is necessarily incomplete, their powers of reasoning, memory, and attention are always limited, and their judgment is likely to be distorted by anxiety, bias, and a preoccupation with their own affairs. Some of these defects spring from moral faults, from selfishness and negligence; but to a large degree, they are simply part of men's natural situation. As a consequence individuals not only have different plans of life but there exists a diversity of philosophical and religious belief, and of political and social doctrines.

. . .

THE VEIL OF IGNORANCE

The idea of the original position is to set up a fair procedure so that any principles agreed to will be just. . . . Somehow we must nullify the effects of specific contingencies which put men at odds and tempt them to exploit social and natural circumstances to their own advantage. Now in order to do this I assume that the parties are situated behind a veil of ignorance. They do not know how the various alternatives will affect their own particular case and they are obliged to evaluate principles solely on the basis of general considerations.

It is assumed, then, that the parties do not know certain kinds of particular facts. First of all, no one knows his place in society, his class position or social status; nor does he know his fortune in the distribution of natural assets and abilities, his intelligence and strength, and the like. Nor, again, does anyone know his conception of the good, the particulars of his rational plan of life, or even the special features of his psychology such as his aversion to risk or liability to optimism or pessimism. . . .

As far as possible, then, the only particular facts which the parties know is that their society is subject to the circumstances of justice and whatever this implies. It is taken for granted, however, that they know the general facts about human society. They understand political affairs and the principles of economic theory; they know the basis of social organization and the laws of human psychology. Indeed, the parties are presumed to know whatever general facts affect the choice of the principles of justice. . . . 24

> 24 Because such general knowledge will not allow them to bias the choice of principles in their own favor.

THE RATIONALITY OF THE PARTIES

I have assumed thoughout that the persons in the original position are rational. But I have also assumed that they do not know their conception of the good. This means that while they know that they have some rational plan of life, they do not know the details of this plan, the particular ends and interests which it is calculated to promote. How, then, can they decide which conceptions of justice are most to their advantage? Or must we suppose that they are reduced to mere guessing? To meet this difficulty, I postulate that they accept . . . that they normally prefer more primary social goods rather than less.[25] Of course, it may turn out, once the veil of ignorance is removed, that some of them for religious or other reasons may not, in fact, want more of these goods. But from the standpoint of the original position, it is rational for the parties to suppose that they do want a larger share, since in any case they are not compelled to accept more if they do not wish to. Thus even though the parties are deprived of information about their particular ends, they have enough knowledge to rank the alternatives. They know that in general they must try to protect their liberties, widen their opportunities, and enlarge their means for promoting their aims whatever these are. Guided by the theory of the good and the general facts of moral psychology, their deliberations are no longer guesswork. They can make a rational decision in the ordinary sense.

[25] "Primary social goods" are those that will be of value to almost anyone, no matter what their conception of the good or rational plan of life might be.

. . .

The assumption of mutually disinterested rationality, then, comes to this: the persons in the original position try to acknowledge principles which advance their system of ends as far as possible. They do this by attempting to win for themselves the highest index of primary social goods, since this enables them to promote their conception of the good most effectively whatever it turns out to be. The parties do not seek to confer benefits or to impose injuries on one another; they are not moved by affection or rancor. Nor do they try to gain relative to each other; they are not envious or vain. . . .

THE REASONING LEADING TO THE TWO PRINCIPLES OF JUSTICE

. . .

Now consider the point of view of anyone in the original position. There is no way for him to win special advantages for himself. Nor, on the other hand, are there grounds for his acquiescing in special disadvantages. Since it is not reasonable for him to expect more than an equal share in the division of social primary goods, and since it is not rational for him to agree to less, the sensible thing is to acknowledge as the first step a principle of justice requiring an equal distribution. Indeed, this principle is so obvious given the symmetry of the parties that it would occur to everyone immediately. Thus the parties start with a principle requiring equal basic liberties for all, as well as fair equality of opportunity and equal division of income and wealth.

But even holding firm to the priority of the basic liberties and fair equality of opportunity, there is no reason why this initial acknowledgment should be final. Society should take into account economic efficiency and the requirements of organization and technology. If there are inequalities in income and wealth, and differences in authority and degrees of responsibility, that work to make everyone better off in comparison with the benchmark of equality, why not permit them?[26] One might think that ideally individuals should want to serve one another. But since the parties are assumed to be mutually disinterested, their acceptance of these economic and institutional inequalities is only the recognition of the relations of opposition in which men stand in the circumstances of justice. They have no grounds for complaining of one another's motives. Thus the parties would [refuse to] agree to these differences only if they would be dejected by the bare knowledge or

[26] Such inequalities might be necessary to give those with special talents the incentive to develop and employ them, thereby increasing the total social production and making everyone, even the least advantaged, better off.

perception that others are better situated; but I suppose that they decide as if they are not moved by envy. Thus the basic structure should allow these inequalities so long as these improve everyone's situation, including that of the least advantaged, provided that they are consistent with equal liberty and fair opportunity. Because the parties start from an equal division of all social primary goods, those who benefit least have, so to speak, a veto. Thus we arrive at the difference principle. Taking equality as the basis of comparison, those who have gained more must do so on terms that are justifiable to those who have gained the least.

By some such reasoning, then, the parties might arrive at the two principles of justice in serial order. I shall not try to justify this ordering here, but the following remarks may convey the intuitive idea. . . .

The priority of liberty means that whenever the basic liberties can be effectively established, a lesser or an unequal liberty cannot be exchanged for an improvement in economic well-being. It is only when social circumstances do not allow the effective establishment of these basic rights that one can concede their limitation; and even then these restrictions can be granted only to the extent that they are necessary to prepare the way for the time when they are no longer justified. The denial of the equal liberties can be defended only when it is essential to change the conditions of civilization so that in due course these liberties can be enjoyed. [27] Thus in adopting the serial order of the two principles, the parties are assuming that the conditions of their society, whatever they are, admit the effective realization of the equal liberties. Or that if they do not, circumstances are nevertheless sufficiently favorable so that the priority of the first principle points out the most urgent changes and identifies the preferred path to the social state in which all the basic liberties can be fully instituted. The complete realization of the two principles in serial order is the long-run tendency of this ordering, at least under reasonably fortunate conditions.

It seems from these remarks that the two principles are at least a plausible conception of justice. The question, though, is how one is to argue for them more

[27] Here is an exception to the idea that the first principle (equal liberty) has complete priority over the second principle (the difference principle). Try to think of possible cases or conditions in which this exception would apply.

systematically. . . .In order to see how this might be done, it is useful as a heuristic device to think of the two principles as the maximin solution to the problem of social justice. There is a relation between the two principles and the maximin rule for choice under uncertainty. This is evident from the fact that the two principles are those a person would choose for the design of a society in which his enemy is to assign him his place. The maximin rule tells us to rank alternatives by their worst possible outcomes: we are to adopt the alternative the worst outcome of which is superior to the worst outcomes of the others. [28] The persons in the original position do not, of course, assume that their initial place in society is decided by a malevolent opponent.

[28] Maximin is a very conservative, risk-aversive principle of decision. Rawls's claim is that this principle, though not generally the best principle of rational choice, is the right one to follow in the very special case of the original position.

As I note below, they should not reason from false premises. The veil of ignorance does not violate this idea, since an absence of information is not misinformation. But that the two principles of justice would be chosen if the parties were forced to protect themselves against such a contingency explains the sense in which this conception is the maximin solution. And this analogy suggests that if the original position has been described so that it is rational for the parties to adopt the conservative attitude expressed by this rule, a conclusive argument can indeed be constructed for these principles. Clearly the maximin rule is not, in general, a suitable guide for choices under uncertainty. But it holds only in situations marked by certain special features. My aim, then, is to show that a good case can be made for the two principles based on the fact that the original position has these features to a very high degree.

Now there appear to be three chief features of situations that give plausibility to this unusual rule. First, since the rule takes no account of the likelihoods of the possible circumstances, there must be some reason for sharply discounting estimates of these probabilities. . . .Thus it must be, for example, that the situation is one in which a knowledge of likelihoods is impossible, or at best extremely insecure. In this case it is unreasonable not to be skeptical of probabilistic calculations unless there is no other way out, particularly if the decision is a fundamental one that needs to be justified to others.

The second feature that suggests the maximin rule is the following: the person choosing has a conception of the good such that he cares very little, if anything, for what he might gain above the minimum stipend that he can, in fact, be sure of by following the maximin rule. It is not worthwhile for him to take a chance for the sake of a further advantage, especially when it may turn out that he loses much that is important to him. This last provision brings in the third feature, namely, that the rejected alternatives have outcomes that one can hardly accept. The situation involves grave risks. Of course these features work most effectively in combination. The paradigm situation for following the maximin rule is when all three features are realized to the highest degree.

Let us review briefly the nature of the original position with these three special features in mind. To begin with, the veil of ignorance excludes all knowledge of likelihoods. The parties have no basis for determining the probable nature of their society, or their place in it. Thus they have no basis for probability calculations. They must also take into account the fact that their choice of principles should seem reasonable to others, in particular their descendants, whose rights will be deeply affected by it. These considerations are strengthened by the fact that the parties know very little about the possible states of society. Not only are they unable to conjecture the likelihoods of the various possible circumstances, they cannot say much about what the possible circumstances are, much less enumerate them and foresee the outcome of each alternative available. . . .

Several kinds of arguments for the two principles of justice illustrate the second feature. Thus, if we can maintain that these principles provide a workable theory of social justice, and that they are compatible with reasonable demands of efficiency, then this conception guarantees a satisfactory minimum. There may be, on reflection, little reason for trying to do better. . . . ㉙

Finally, the third feature holds if we can assume that other conceptions of justice may lead to institutions that the parties would find intolerable. For example, it has sometimes been held that under some conditions the utility principle (in either form) justifies, if not slavery or serfdom, at any rate serious infractions of liberty for the sake of greater social benefits. We need not consider here the truth of this claim. For the moment, this contention is only to illustrate the way in which conceptions of justice may allow for outcomes which the parties may not be able to accept. And having the ready alternative of the two principles of justice which secure a satisfactory minimum, it seems unwise, if not irrational, for them to take a chance that these conditions are not realized. ㉚

. . .

㉙ Is this second feature clearly satisfied in the situation of the original position? Relative to the choice of the difference principle, it amounts to saying that the possible gains that might result by departing from that principle (being extremely well off, more than could be justified by the difference principle) are not very important to any reasonable person.

㉚ Much of this is concerned with departures from the first principle (of liberty). But departures from the difference principle could also lead to dire outcomes such as starvation or extreme poverty. These are obviously undesirable, but is it clear that no rational person would risk them in pursuit of the sorts of possible gains indicated in the previous Annotation?

Discussion Questions

1. Consider two people, one from an upper-class family and one from a lower-class family. Describe what sort of principle of "justice" each of them would favor out of self-interest if they were not behind the "veil of ignorance," and why neither of these principles seems intuitively to be the right account of justice. How does the veil of ignorance prevent them from favoring these principles out of self-interest? What sort of a principle pertaining to how people should be treated according to their social class might they end up adopting under the veil of ignorance? Does the principle they would choose in this situation seem to you to be the most clearly just one? Why or why not?

2. Now consider the comparable situation of two people with different degrees of natural talent or ability, for example, one more intelligent

and one less intelligent. Describe what principles pertaining to the allocation of gains resulting from intelligence each of these people would choose out of self-interest if not behind the veil of ignorance. Is it clear in this case that neither of these principles is an acceptable principle of justice? What principle governing the allocation of gains resulting from intelligence does Rawls think they would adopt in the original position and why? Is this principle clearly preferable, from the standpoint of justice, to the principles that each would choose outside the original position?

3. Rawls claims that the *maximin* principle is the right principle of decision to follow in the original position. Contrast this with the *maximax* principle, which says that choices should be ranked according to their *best* possible outcome. This is an extremely optimistic, risk-taking principle. Consider different situations in which you have to make a choice in which each alternative could lead to more than one possible outcome, and explain what each of these principles would tell you to do in such cases.

One way to formulate such issues is with a decision-theoretic matrix, like the following one for a schematic choice (where you have

no knowledge of which condition actually obtains):

	Choice 1	Choice 2	Choice 3
Condition 1	100	5	90
Condition 2	−100	10	85
Condition 3	−100	5	0

In this case, maximin would select choice 2 and maximax would select choice 1. Is either decision-making principle clearly the right one in all such cases—or even any such cases? Can you think of any other principles for making such decisions that seem better? Would any of these be applicable in the original position?

4. The basic idea of Rawls's argument for the choice of the difference principle (reflected in the maximin principle) is that the rational thing to do when faced with such a fundamental choice (one that has major effects on your whole life) is to play it safe, rather than gambling that you will do much better at the risk of doing much worse. Do you think it is obvious that this is the right choice, that no rational person would be willing to gamble? Might it be that this is a matter of temperament—that some people would be willing to gamble and some would not? What effect would this have in the original position?

Robert Nozick

In this selection, also from *Anarchy, State, and Utopia,* Nozick offers his objections to Rawls's account of justice. He challenges whether the difference principle is really fair to those who have better natural assets, and questions whether Rawls has any good argument that such assets should be treated in the way his principle requires. Nozick also suggests that the Rawlsian view would yield dubious results in the more limited situation of fairly assigning grades (though Rawls does say that his view is not intended to apply to such situations).

A Critique of Rawls, from *Anarchy, State, and Utopia*

TERMS OF COOPERATION AND THE DIFFERENCE PRINCIPLE

... Rawls imagines rational, mutually disinterested individuals meeting in a certain situation, or abstracted from their other features not provided for in this situation. In this hypothetical situation of choice, which Rawls calls "the original position," they choose the first principles of a conception

From Anarchy, State, and Utopia *(New York: Basic Books, 1974).*

of justice that is to regulate all subsequent criticism and reform of their institutions. While making this choice, no one knows his place in society, his class position or social status, or his natural assets and abilities, his strength, intelligence, and so forth.

. . .

What would persons in the original position agree to?

> Persons in the initial situation would choose two . . . principles: the first requires equality in the assignment of basic rights and duties, while the second holds that social and economic inequalities, for example, inequalities of wealth and authority are just only if they result in compensating benefits for everyone, and in particular for the least advantaged members of society.* . . .

This second principle, which Rawls specifies as the difference principle, holds that the institutional structure is to be so designed that the worst-off group under it is at least as well off as the worst-off group (not necessarily the same group) would be under any alternative institutional structure. If persons in the original position follow the minimax policy in making the significant choice of principles of justice, Rawls argues, they will choose the difference principle. . . .

Rawls holds . . . that

> since everyone's well-being depends upon a scheme of cooperation without which no one could have a satisfactory life, the division of advantages should be such as to draw forth the willing cooperation of everyone taking part in it, including those less well situated. Yet this can be expected only if reasonable terms are proposed. The two principles mentioned seem to be a fair agreement on the basis of which those better endowed or more fortunate in their social position . . . could expect the willing cooperation of others when some workable scheme is a necessary condition of the welfare of all.*

No doubt, the difference principle presents terms on the basis of which those less well endowed would be willing to cooperate. (What *better* terms could they propose for themselves?) But is this a fair agreement on the basis of which those *worse* endowed could expect the *willing* cooperation of others? With regard to the existence of gains from social cooperation, the situation is symmetrical. The better endowed gain by cooperating with the worse endowed, *and* the worse endowed gain by cooperating with the better endowed. Yet the difference principle is not neutral between the better and the worse endowed. Whence the asymmetry?[1]

Perhaps the symmetry is upset if one asks *how much* each gains from the social cooperation. This question might be understood in two ways. How much do people benefit from social cooperation, as compared to their individual holdings in a *non*cooperative scheme? . . . Or, alternatively, how much does each individual gain from general social cooperation, as compared, not with *no* cooperation, but with more limited cooperation? The latter is the more appropriate question with regard to general social cooperation. For failing general agreement on the principles to govern how the benefits of general social cooperation are to be held, not everyone will remain in a noncooperative situation if there is some other beneficial cooperative arrangement involving some, but not all, people, whose participants *can* agree. These people will participate in this more narrow cooperative arrangement. To focus upon the benefits of the better and the worse endowed cooperating together, we must try to imagine less extensive schemes of partitioned social cooperation in which the better endowed cooperate only among themselves and the worse endowed cooperate only among themselves, with no cross-cooperation.[2]

> [1] Under the difference principle, the less well endowed are getting the *most* they could possibly get: any attempt to give them more would end up giving them less. But the better endowed are getting the *least* they could possibly get without hurting the position of the less well endowed. (Think about this carefully.)

> [2] Rawls considers only the situation where everyone cooperates with everyone. But more limited sorts of cooperation are also possible. Nozick argues that these must also be considered in deciding how much each group benefits from everyone cooperating together.

---

*Rawls, *Theory of Justice,* 1st ed. pp. 14–15. [Page 785 in this book.]
*Rawls, *Theory of Justice,* 1st ed. p. 15. [Page 785 in this book.]

The members of both groups gain from the internal cooperation within their respective groups and have larger shares than they would if there were no social cooperation at all. An individual benefits from the wider system of extensive cooperation between the better and the worse endowed to the extent of his incremental gain from this wider cooperation; namely, the amount by which his share under a scheme of general cooperation is greater than it would be under one of limited intragroup (but not cross-group) cooperation. *General* cooperation will be of more benefit to the better or to the worse endowed if (to pick a simple criterion) the mean incremental gain from general cooperation (when compared with limited intragroup cooperation) is greater in one group than it is in the other.

One might speculate about whether there is an inequality between the groups' mean incremental gains and, if so, which way it goes. If the better-endowed group includes those who manage to accomplish something of great economic advantage to others, such as new inventions, new ideas about production or ways of doing things, skill at economic tasks, and so on, it is difficult to avoid concluding that the *less* well endowed gain *more* than the better endowed do from the scheme of general cooperation.③ What follows from this conclusion? I do *not* mean to imply that the better endowed should get even more than they get under the entitlement system of general social cooperation. What *does* follow from the conclusion is a deep suspicion of imposing, in the name of fairness, constraints upon voluntary social cooperation (and the set of holdings that arises from it) so that those already benefiting most from this general cooperation benefit even more!

Rawls would have us imagine the worse-endowed persons say something like the following: "Look, better endowed: you gain by cooperating with us. If you want our cooperation you'll have to accept reasonable terms. We suggest these terms: We'll cooperate with you only if we get *as much as possible.* That is, the terms of our cooperation should give us that maximal share such that, if it was tried to give us more, we'd end up with less." How generous these proposed terms are might be seen by imagining that the better endowed make the almost symmetrical opposite proposal: "Look, worse endowed: you gain by cooperating with *us.* If you want our cooperation you'll have to accept reasonable terms. We propose these terms: We'll cooperate with you so long as *we* get as much as possible. That is, the terms of our cooperation should give us the maximal share such that, if it was tried to give us more, we'd end up with less." If these terms seem outrageous, as they are, why don't the terms proposed by those worse endowed seem the same?④ Why shouldn't the better endowed treat this latter proposal as beneath consideration, supposing someone to have the nerve explicitly to state it?

> ③ Nozick *speculates* that it is the less endowed who gain the most from general cooperation, as opposed to more limited cooperation among themselves, because the more endowed group will contribute more in the way of productive ideas and skills. Does this seem reasonable or not?

> ④ Nozick imagines the two groups making what he describes as "almost symmetrical" proposals. Is he right about this? Or is there some way in which the proposal of the less well endowed (which is more or less identical to what is required by the difference principle) is more reasonable or more just?

Rawls devotes much attention to explaining why those less well favored should not complain at receiving less. His explanation, simply put, is that because the inequality works for his advantage, someone less well favored shouldn't complain about it; he receives *more* in the unequal system than he would in an equal one. (Though he might receive still more in another unequal system that placed someone else below him.) But Rawls discusses the question of whether those *more* favored will or should find the terms satisfactory *only* in the following passage, where A and B are any two representative men with A being the more favored:

> The difficulty is to show that A has no grounds for complaint. Perhaps he is required to have less than he might since his having more would result in some loss to B. Now what can be said to the more favored man? To begin with, it is clear that the well-being of each depends on a scheme of social cooperation without which no one could have a satisfactory life. Secondly, we can ask for the willing cooperation of everyone only if the terms of the scheme are reasonable. The difference principle, then, seems to be a fair basis on which those better endowed, or more fortunate in their social circumstance, could expect others to collaborate

with them when some workable arrangement is a necessary condition of the good of all.*

What Rawls imagines being said to the more favored men does *not* show that these men have no grounds for complaint, nor does it at all diminish the weight of whatever complaints they have. That the well-being of all depends on social cooperation without which no one could have a satisfactory life could also be said to the less well endowed by someone proposing any other principle, including that of maximizing the position of the best endowed. Similarly for the fact that we can ask for the willing cooperation of everyone only if the terms of the scheme are reasonable. The question is: What terms *would be* reasonable? What Rawls imagines being said thus far merely sets up his problem; it doesn't distinguish his proposed difference principle from the almost symmetrical counterproposal that we imagined the better endowed making, or from any other proposal. Thus, when Rawls continues, "The difference principle, then, seems to be a fair basis on which those best endowed, or more fortunate in their social circumstances, could expect others to collaborate with them when some workable arrangment is a necessary condition of the good of all," the presence of the "then" in his sentence is puzzling. Since the sentences which precede it are neutral between his proposal and any other proposal, the conclusion that the difference principle presents a fair basis for cooperation *cannot* follow from what precedes it in this passage. Rawls is merely repeating that it seems reasonable; hardly a convincing reply to anyone to whom it doesn't seem reasonable. Rawls has not shown that the more favored man *A* has no grounds for complaint at being required to have less in order that another *B* might have more than he otherwise would. And he can't show this, since *A does* have grounds for complaint. Doesn't he?[5]

[5] The passage Nozick quotes is from the first edition of *A Theory of Justice.* In the revised edition, from which the selection from Rawls in this book is taken, this passage is replaced by the paragraph continued from p. 780 to p. 791 (to which Annotation 20 is attached). Does the later version provide a better answer to the challenge Nozick is raising here?

THE ORIGINAL POSITION AND END-RESULT PRINCIPLES

. . .

Suppose there were a group of students who have studied during a year, taken examinations, and received grades between 0 and 100 which they have not yet learned of. They are now gathered together, having no idea of the grade any one of them has received, and they are asked to allocate grades among themselves so that the grades total to a given sum (which is determined by the sum of the grades they actually have received from the teacher). First, let us suppose they are to decide jointly upon a particular distribution of grades; they are to give a particular grade to each identifiable one of them present at the meeting. Here, given sufficient restrictions on their ability to threaten each other, they probably would agree to each person receiving the same grade, to each person's grade being equal to the total divided by the number of people to be graded. Surely they would *not* chance upon the particular set of grades they already have received. Suppose next that there is posted on a bulletin board at their meeting a paper headed ENTITLEMENTS, which lists each person's name with a grade next to it, the listing being identical to the instructor's gradings. Still, this particular distribution will not be agreed to by those having done poorly. Even if they know what "entitlement" means (which perhaps we must suppose they don't, in order to match the absence of moral factors in the calculations of persons in Rawls' original position), why should they agree to the instructor's distribution? What self-interested reason to agree to it would they have?[6]

Next suppose that they are unanimously to agree not to a *particular* distribution of grades, but rather to general principles to govern the distribution of grades. What principle would be selected? The equality principle, which gives each person the same grade, would have a prominent chance. And if it

[6] The students who receive better grades under the "Entitlements" distribution would have self-interested reasons for accepting that distribution, but why would the others be willing to agree?

*Rawls, *Theory of Justice,* 1st ed., p. 103. [See pp. 790–91 in this book for the revised edition version of this passage.]

turned out that the total was variable depending upon how they divided it, depending on which of them got what grade,⑦ and a higher grade was desirable though they were not competing among each other (for example, each of them was competing for some position with the members of separate distinct groups), then the principle of distributing grades so as to maximize the lowest grades *might* seem a plausible one. Would these people agree to the non-end-state *historical* principle of distribution: give people grades according to how their examinations were evaluated by a qualified and impartial observer? If all the people deciding knew the particular distribution that would be yielded by this historical principle, they wouldn't agree to it. For the situation then would be equivalent to the earlier one of their deciding upon a particular distribution, in which we already have seen they would not agree to the entitlement distribution. Suppose then that the people do not know the particular distribution actually yielded by this historical principle. They cannot be led to select this historical principle because it looks just, or fair, to them; for no such notions are allowed to be at work in the original position. (Otherwise people would argue there, like here, about what justice requires.) Each person engages in a calculation to decide whether it will be in his own interests to accept this historical principle of distribution. Grades, under the historical principle, depend upon nature and developed intelligence, how hard the people have worked, accident, and so on, factors about which people in the original position know almost nothing. . . . Each person in the original position will do something like assigning probability distributions to his place along these various dimensions. It seems unlikely that each person's probability calculations would lead to the historical-entitlement principle, in preference to every other principle. Consider the principle we may call the reverse-entitlement principle. It recommends drawing up a list of the historical entitlements in order of magnitude, and giving the most anyone is entitled to, to the person entitled to the least; the second most to the person entitled to the second least, and so on. Any probability calculations of self-interested persons in Rawls' original position, or any

> ⑦ This is Nozick's attempt to make this case somewhat parallel to the situation where giving incentives to some people results in greater overall production.

probability calculations of the students we have considered, will lead them to view the entitlement and the reverse-entitlement principles as ranked equally insofar as their own self-interest is concerned! (What calculations could lead them to view one of the principles as superior to the other?) Their calculations will not lead them to select the entitlement principle.

. . .

Rawls' construction is incapable of yielding an entitlement or historical conception of distributive justice. . . . The whole procedure of persons choosing principles in Rawls' original position presupposes that no historical-entitlement conception of justice is correct.⑧

It might be objected to our argument that Rawls' procedure is designed to *establish* all facts about justice; there is no independent notion of entitlement, not provided by his theory, to stand on in criticizing his theory. But we do not need any *particular* developed historical-entitlement theory as a basis from which to criticize Rawls' construction. If *any* such fundamental historical-entitlement view is correct, then Rawls' theory is not. We are thus able to make this structural criticism of the type of theory Rawls presents and the type of principles it must yield, without first having formulated fully a particular historical-entitlement theory as an alternative to his. We would be ill advised to accept Rawls' theory and his construal of the problem as one of which principles would be chosen by rational self-interested individuals behind a veil of ignorance, unless we were sure that no adequate historical-entitlement theory was to be gotten.

> ⑧ Nozick's claim is that the way that Rawls sets up the issue and defines the original position guarantees that no historical-entitlement theory could be chosen and thus presupposes that no such theory is correct. Does this mean that Rawls's approach is unreasonably biased against Nozick's view or does he have good reasons for ruling out views of this kind?

. . .

NATURAL ASSETS AND ARBITRARINESS

Rawls comes closest to considering the entitlement system in his discussion of what he terms the system of natural liberty. . . .

. . . *Rawls'* reason for rejecting a system of natural liberty [is that] it "permits" distributive shares to be improperly influenced by factors that are . . . arbitrary from a moral point of view. These factors are: "prior distribution . . . of natural talents and abilities as these have been developed over time by social circumstances and such chance contingencies as accident and good fortune." . . .

Rawls has explicitly *designed* the original position and its choice situation so as to embody and realize his negative reflective evaluation of allowing shares in holdings to be affected by natural assets: "Once we decide to look for a conception of justice that nullifies the accidents of natural endowment and the contingencies of social circumstance . . . ."*⑨ . . . This quest crucially shapes Rawls' theory, and it underlies his delineation of the original position. . . .

⑨ This passage is also altered in the revised edition of *A Theory of Justice*—and in the selection in this volume. Compare the quotation here with the passage at Annotation 8 to the Rawls section, in which Rawls no longer speaks of *nullifying* the accidents of natural endowment. How important is this difference?

Why shouldn't holdings partially depend upon natural endowments? (They will also depend on how these are developed and on the uses to which they are put.) Rawls' reply is that these natural endowments and assets, being undeserved, are "arbitrary from a moral point of view." . . .

. . . How might the point that differences in natural endowments are arbitrary from a moral point of view function in an argument meant to establish that differences in holdings stemming from differences in natural assets ought to be nullified? We shall consider [two] possible arguments; the first, the following argument A:

1. Any person should morally deserve the holdings he has; it shouldn't be that persons have holdings they don't deserve.

2. People do not morally deserve their natural assets.

3. If a person's *X* partially determines his *Y,* and his *X* is undeserved then so is his *Y.*

Therefore,

4. People's holdings shouldn't be partially determined by their natural assets.

. . . But Rawls explicitly and emphatically *rejects* distribution according to moral desert.

> There is a tendency for common sense to suppose that income and wealth, and the good things in life generally, should be distributed according to moral desert. Justice is happiness according to virtue. While it is recognized that this ideal can never be fully carried out, it is the appropriate conception (according to common sense) of distributive justice, at least as a *prima facie* principle, and society should try to realize it as circumstances permit. Now justice as fairness rejects this conception. Such a principle would not be chosen in the original position.*⑩

Rawls could not, therefore, accept any premiss like the first premiss in argument *A,* and so no variant of this argument underlies his rejection of differences in distributive shares stemming from undeserved differences in natural assets. . . .

⑩ Think carefully about *why* such a principle would not be chosen in the original position.

I turn now to our [second] positive argument which purports to derive the conclusion that distributive shares shouldn't depend upon natural assets from the statement that the distribution of natural assets is morally arbitrary. This argument focuses on the notion of equality. Since a large part of Rawls' argument serves to justify or show acceptable a particular deviation from equal shares (some may have more if this serves to improve the position of those worst off), perhaps a reconstruction of his underlying argument that places equality at its center will be illuminating. Differences between persons (the argument runs) are arbitrary from a moral point of view if there is no moral argument for the conclusion that there ought to be the differences. . . .

Thus we have argument D:

1. Holdings ought to be equal, unless there is a (weighty) moral reason why they ought to be unequal.

---

*Rawls, *Theory of Justice,* 1st ed. p. 15. [See page 785 in this book.]
*Rawls, *Theory of Justice,* 1st ed. p. 310. [Not included in the selection in this book.]

2. People do not deserve the ways in which they differ from other persons in natural assets; there is no moral reason why people ought to differ in natural assets.
3. If there is no moral reason why people differ in certain traits, then their actually differing in these traits does not provide, and cannot give rise to, a moral reason why they should differ in other traits (for example, in holdings).

Therefore,

4. People's differing in natural assets is not a reason why holding ought to be unequal.
5. People's holdings ought to be equal unless there is some other moral reason (such as, for example, raising the position of those worst off) why their holdings ought to be unequal.

. . . Here let us focus on the first premiss, the equality premiss. Why ought people's holdings to be equal, in the absence of special moral reason to deviate from equality? (Why think there *ought* to be *any* particular pattern in holdings?) Why is equality the rest (or rectilinear motion) position of the system, deviation from which may be caused only by moral forces? Many "arguments" for equality merely *assert* that differences between persons are arbitrary and must be justified. Often writers state a presumption in favor of equality in a form such as the following: "Differences in treatment of persons need to be justi-

fied." . . . That differences in treatment need to be justified *does* fit contemporary *governments*. Here there is a centralized process treating all, with no entitlement to bestow treatment according to whim. The major portion of distribution in a free society does not, however, come through the actions of the government, nor does failure to overturn the results of the localized individual exchanges constitute "state action." When there is no *one* doing the treating, and all are entitled to bestow their holdings as they wish, it is not clear why the maxim that differences in treatment must be justified should be thought to have extensive application. Why must differences between persons be justified? Why think that we must change, or remedy, or compensate for any inequality which can be changed, remedied, or compensated for?⑪ . . . Here we need only note that the connection argument D forges between not deserving natural assets and some conclusion about distributive shares *assumes* equality as a norm (that can be deviated from with, and only with, moral reason); and hence argument D itself cannot be used to establish any such conclusion about equality.

⑪ Nozick grants that holdings and other benefits derived from government ought to be equal unless there is a "weighty moral reason" to the contrary, but denies that this is true of holdings whose distribution does not result from governmental action but instead from free choices by individuals. How do you think Rawls would respond to this point?

. . .

Discussion Questions

1. How might Rawls justify the asymmetrical treatment that the difference principle gives to the less and more endowed? Is such treatment compatible with justice? (Notice carefully that this question cannot be settled by appeal to the original position, since it in effect challenges whether the way Rawls conceives the original position is itself compatible with the demands of justice.)
2. Nozick is offering the grade distribution case as an analogy to challenge whether something like the original position is a good way to decide what justice requires. In this case, it seems fairly clear that a procedure analogous

to that suggested by Rawls is neither required by justice nor in fact yields just results. In fact, Rawls says explicitly that his view is not intended to determine what is just in more limited situations of this kind. But is there any good explanation he can give of why the demands of justice with regard to the basic structure of society are apparently so different from those in more limited cases?

3. If Rawls's view is supposed to determine what justice requires, how can he be justified in appealing to a procedure that apparently excludes a view like Nozick's as even a possibility? Is Nozick right that it does this? If so, is

there any way that Rawls can justify approaching the issue in this way?

4. Does justice require that differences in natural endowments be *nullified,* as Rawls says in the first edition of *A Theory of Justice?* (See Annotation 9 and the corresponding passage.) Is this what adherence to the difference principle in effect does? Might there be differences that cannot be nullified in this way? (Think here of something like physical attractiveness and the benefits that it leads to.) Is there any other way you can think of to *nullify* such differences? Does justice really require that this be done in this sort of case?

Thomas M. Scanlon

Thomas Scanlon (1940–) is an American moral and political philosopher who taught at Princeton and now teaches at Harvard. In the following selection, he offers an extended critique of Nozick's account of justice and, in passing, a defense of Rawls against some of Nozick's criticisms.

Nozick on Rights, Liberty, and Property

In *Anarchy, State and Utopia** Robert Nozick approaches political philosophy within a framework . . . which emphasizes individual rights and the derivation of political obligation from consent. . . . Nozick holds that the only legitimate state is the minimal state, whose activities are confined to the protection of individuals and their property and to the enforcement of contracts. This state is unique among social organizations in having the right to force residents to pay for its services whether or not they have consented to do so. Citizens may band together for whatever other purposes they may desire—to provide education, to aid the needy, to organize social insurance schemes—but such schemes must be purely voluntary, and the state must enforce anyone's right not to be compelled to contribute to them.

Nozick reaches these conclusions by adhering as closely as possible to the idea that, in economic life as in politics, all valid obligations derive from consent.① Of course, . . . the obligations and entitlements one person acquires through voluntary agreements can affect the alternatives open to others who have not been parties to these agreements. Something must determine when such side effects make an agreement void. In Nozick's theory these conditions and limits are set by a skeletal framework of rights derived from Locke. The minimal role allowed to the state and the great scope left to voluntary agreement and consent in his theory are direct consequences of the particular character of these rights. This system of rights is not argued for directly in the book, however, and Nozick does not claim to have given these rights a foundation. . . .

The central theoretical device of the book is the classification of principles of justice as "historical," "end-state," and "patterned." Nozick classifies a principle of justice as historical if that principle makes the justice of a distribution depend on how it came about

① This is, of course, a view that would have been accepted by both Hobbes and Locke as well. As Scanlon points out later, Rawls's view can also be seen as a kind of consent theory, though with the very important difference that the consent is hypothetical (in relation to the "original position") rather than actual.

From Philosophy and Public Affairs *(Fall 1976).*

---

*(New York, 1974). Page numbers in the text refer to the excerpts in this book.

(p. 775). It will follow from a historical principle of justice that "past circumstances or actions of people can create differential entitlements or differential deserts to things" (p. 775). By contrast, under what Nozick calls an end-state principle, the justice of a distribution will depend only on certain structural features of the situation it represents, for example, on the amount of utility produced or on the degree of equality obtaining. Of course, the structural features of a distribution that are deemed relevant by a principle of justice might make reference to historical events. A principle might require, for example, that people's holdings should be proportional to their moral worth as determined by their past actions. Such a principle is historical in Nozick's sense, but it clearly has a great deal in common with end-state principles. Nozick calls such a principle, one which specifies that holdings are to "vary along with some natural dimension" or some combination of such dimensions, a patterned principle. Nozick's own theory of justice is based on unpatterned historical principles. This theory is an entitlement conception of justice. Such a conception is specified by three components: a principle of (initial) acquisition, a principle of transfer, and a principle of rectification. Its central tenet is that any configuration of holdings that results from the legitimate transfer of legitimately acquired holdings is itself just. There is no reason to expect (or to require) that such holdings conform to any natural pattern. (The principle of rectification comes into play to explain how, if holdings are affected by violations of the principles of just acquisition and transfer, this situation is to be remedied.)

Many theories of justice, almost any theory perhaps, will give some role to considerations of entitlement; that is, they will recognize some processes as conferring legitimacy on their outcomes. What is special about Nozick's view is that it makes entitlement principles the beginning and end of distributive justice. While his principles are not described in detail, it appears that his theory differs from other pure entitlement conceptions chiefly in admitting fewer restrictions on the acquisition and exchange of property. He mentions only one such restriction, called "the Lockean Proviso," which provides that any acquisition,

transfer, or combination of transfers is void if it leaves third parties worse off then they were in the state of nature.* Such a worsening might occur, for example, if someone were to buy, in simultaneous secret transactions, rights to all the available sources of water. This restriction could be substantial were it not for the fact that the baseline for its application is set by conditions in the state of nature. According to Nozick the productivity of the capitalist system in improving our material condition makes it unlikely that (in a competitive economy) anyone could acquire holdings that would leave others below this standard.

Nozick clearly feels that the distinction between historical (unpatterned) principles of justice and patterned or end-state principles is of fundamental importance. He emphasizes that almost all of the principles of justice commonly offered are end-state or patterned principles and, as such, are clearly mistaken. If this were correct it would indeed be important. Certainly Nozick's distinction does capture something intuitively appealing. It has often been said as a criticism of utilitarianism that it ignores morally significant relations resulting from past actions.[2] Nozick's distinction is of great interest if it gives this criticism a more abstract form and shows it to apply not only to utilitarianism but also to Rawls' theory and to virtually every other theory commonly offered. But I do not think that the distinction has the importance claimed for it. To see why, let me consider the reasons Nozick offers for holding that all patterned principles are clearly wrong.

> [2] Thus, for example, the fact that one has made a promise to someone has little or no moral weight for the utilitarian, since the right action is determined entirely by future consequences. (See Chapter 6 for more discussion of utilitarianism.)

These reasons can be quickly seen in Nozick's frequent remark that, since gift giving can upset a pattern of distribution, supporters of patterned principles of justice would have to forbid this form of "loving behavior" (p. 777). More generally, let D_1 be the distribution of goods obtaining in a given society and suppose that this distribution is in accord with our favorite pattern (for example, strict equality). This dis-

---

*Worse off, that is, in what they are able to use; it is not enough that they be worse off with respect to what remains available for initial appropriation. See p. 780.

tribution can be changed into another distribution D_2, not in accord with this pattern, by any one of a variety of means: by gifts, by someone's starting a very successful business in his spare time using only resources to which he was already entitled under D_1, or, as Nozick suggests, by all one million of us willingly paying Wilt Chamberlain 25¢ apiece for the privilege of watching him play basketball. To maintain D_1 one would have to restrict these activities. Such "continuous interference" is, Nozick says, obviously unacceptable. Therefore one must conclude that no patterned conception of justice can be correct.

One immediate response to this argument is to doubt whether anyone ever held a "patterned" conception of justice in the sense that is here refuted. A person who objects to the inequality in the world is unlikely to be concerned with those who have less as a result of their giving away or trading part of what was once an equal share. What offends an egalitarian primarily is the great inequality in the initial resources people have as a result of the social positions in to which they are born. But here Nozick can respond that this does not escape his point. Arbitrarily great inequalities in the starting places of members of one generation can result from gifts and voluntary exchanges by members of previous generations. Thus, maintaining even this looser kind of equality can require restricting these activities.

So put, this is not such a startling conclusion; certainly it does not make egalitarianism look as foolish as first appeared. This is so, first, because there is no longer the appearance of unanimous consent. It is no longer plausible to respond, "Well, if the fans are all happy to pay [everyone now living in the society is a fan] and Wilt is willing to play at that price, how can a meddling egalitarian object?" ③ Second, this way of looking at the example changes our picture of the liberties that are likely to be infringed. The liberties involved in the example seem to be these: the liberty of the fans to pay an extra quarter to see Wilt play, his liberty to keep any amount he may receive through such transactions, his liberty to decide whether or not he wants to play for the amount remaining after taxes from what the fans and promoters

③ That everyone is a fan of Chamberlain is not part of the example as Nozick presents it. Does the plausibility of the example require adding this additional stipulation?

offer him, and, finally, the liberty of his heirs to keep any amount of money he wishes to pass on to them. It does not seem likely that egalitarians, if their objectives are as I have described them, will want to keep watch over everyone's quarters or to conscript basketball stars. What is at issue, then, is the right of a person to keep as much as others are willing to pay him for his services and the right of heirs to receive unlimited bequests. But there is no strong intuitive ground for thinking that these rights are absolute, and little ground for surprise at the suggestion that the pursuit of equality might call for their infringement. ④

Nozick tries to make such measures seem more alarming to us by tying them to more extreme forms of intervention. Thus he says that "Taxation of earnings from labor is on a par with forced labor" (p. 778), and elsewhere he asks why, if we are going to set a limit on how long a person can control goods and transfer them to others, we do not have immediate confiscation. But there seems to be no reason to disregard such obvious differences in the degree of regulation of a person's life. It may be true, as Nozick claims, that there is a continuum of interferences extending from taxation to forced labor, each foreclosing a few more options than the preceeding. But the fact that there is such a continuum is no reason why we must be indifferent between any two points along it. ⑤ Even if Nozick does not convince us that restrictions on earnings or inheritance in order to maintain equality are unacceptable, however, his examples do raise the question why any interference at all should be justified in order to preserve a pattern. As he says, what is so great about a pattern?

④ Think about the liberties that Scanlon lists here. Nozick would probably say that the example supports all four of them equally, while Scanlon is suggesting that two of them are less obviously immune to legitimate infringement than the other two. Who is right?

⑤ This seems to be a substantially weaker claim than Nozick actually makes. When he says that taxation of earnings is "on a par with forced labor," he seems to mean that they amount to the same thing from a moral standpoint. Is Nozick's stronger claim plausible?

There are many different concerns which lead people to call for greater equality, and not all of these involve a pattern in a fundamental way. For example, a person's primary political goal may be to alleviate the terrible conditions under which many are forced to live. The fact that others are at the same time much better off shows that it would be possible to eliminate this suffering and, one might add, to do so without reducing anyone else to this low a level. The resources are there; they just need to be redistributed. For a person taking this position, a humanitarian, equalization is merely a means to the improvement of the lot of those currently worst off. It is possible that a person who is intensely concerned with this cause today might be quite satisfied if the living standard of everyone in the world were significantly improved, even if the gap between rich and poor was left unchanged.⑥

⑥ Rawls, of course, does not hold such a view. (What might Nozick say about the remark that "The resources are there; they just need to be redistributed"?)

A second position would take pattern more seriously but still assign it a purely instrumental role. A person taking this position is concerned by the fact that where there are great differences between rich and poor, especially where wealth is concentrated in a few hands, the wealthy come to have an unacceptable degree of control over what jobs there are, over what is to be produced and over political processes as well. For this reason, the growth of inequality can turn acceptable institutions into unacceptable ones even when this inequality is generated through what otherwise appear to be innocent means.⑦ These considerations seem to me powerful where they apply, but they argue only for the elimination of the more extreme forms of inequality. A more rigorously egalitarian position might hold that even where neither of the preceding evils arises (no one is in want, and there is no threat of domination), inequalities are still objectionable because they are incompatible with healthy social relations and the development of genuine community. Putting the matter in terms of the

⑦ Scanlon seems right that some of the effects of great differences of wealth are seriously undesirable. Is this enough to make them "unacceptable," so that corrective measures are thereby morally justified—even if they involve restricting the "innocent means" (free choices that people seemingly have a right to make) that led to this situation? See Discussion Question 1.

pursuit of a social ideal seems to rob the demand for equality of some of its force. It needs to be explained why this particular ideal is morally important.

This explanation might be sought in a fourth egalitarian position. A person holding this position would object to inequalities in life-prospects flowing from differences in family wealth by arguing that all differences in treatment require justification, and these differences are undeserved and arbitrary. It is worth noting that Nozick, while being generally hard on egalitarian claims, allows that the demand for a justification of inequalities in initial resources would be valid if these were the result of some centralized mechanism of distribution (p. 802). He rejects this demand on the ground that such inequalities do not result from "state action" but instead flow from the independent actions of many individuals all acting within their rights. The results of such a process, he claims, need no independent justification. I shall return to this point later.

A supporter of this fourth position needs to say something about why unequal distributions, and not equal ones, require special justification. One reason might be that we recognize it is a distinct kind of bad thing for a person to be made worse off than others in his society are. The evil in question here is essentially comparative. It is not just that it is a bad thing to be at a low level of well-being, nor is it just that anyone would prefer to be at a certain higher level (the one where, as it happens, others are). What is bad is being at a lower level *when others around are much better off.* (It is worst when the level others have attained is the norm in your society.)⑧ If this kind of relative disadvantage is a bad thing, then institutions which inflict it on people require a defense. Such a defense can be given. The better circumstances of others may be somehow earned, or it may be impossible to eliminate such differences or too expensive in terms of other benefits to do so. What is special about equal distributions is just that they require no defense of this particular kind.

⑧ Scanlon seems correct in saying that this is in some way a bad thing. Is it a *morally* bad thing, so that it automatically constitutes a *moral* objection to any sort of institution that leads to such a result?

If the evil of being relatively disadvantaged justifies eliminating inequalities by redistribution, however, it may be asked whether it does not provide an equally strong reason for simply worsening the position of the better off when redistribution is not possible. This may sound irrational, but in the case of many social inequalities, for example, distinctions of rank or social caste, egalitarian demands for the elimination of nonredistributable advantages are not implausible. In other cases, where we think that nonredistributable advantages should not be eliminated, this is not because these advantages are consistent with pure egalitarianism but because we temper the demands of equality with other considerations. Equality is not our only concern.⑨

> ⑨ In the cases of rank or social caste, of course, the advantage one person has seems to depend essentially on disadvantages imposed on others (one cannot have a higher rank unless others have a lower rank). The more difficult cases are ones where this is not so: cases involving things like intelligence, physical strength, etc. (See Discussion Question 2.)

Similarly, it is open to the supporters of any of these egalitarian positions to recognize that powers to dispose of one's possessions—to give them away, to exchange them for others, to determine what will happen to them after one's death—are very important. Indeed in speaking of "distribution" they have always assumed that to distribute a good to a person is to give him some powers of this kind over it. Nozick's examples show that the interests served by these powers are among those things which must be weighed against the various considerations supporting equality. This is something that a realistic egalitarian can accept.⑩

> ⑩ On this view, a morally acceptable system of property will require striking a balance among many different sorts of considerations, with the value of a person's control over their "possessions" being only one of them. There will be no absolute property rights of the sort that Nozick recognizes.

Certainly a theory cannot talk sensibly of patterns of holdings without considering how these patterns are to be produced and maintained. If this were all he was claiming in saying that no purely end-state or patterned theory is tenable, then Nozick would certainly be right. This would not do much to clear the field, however. As Nozick rightly points out, philosophical theories of distributive justice have often neglected the problems of how patterns of distribution can be established and preserved, but a theory can incorporate such considerations, and so avoid being an end-state theory in this narrow sense of the term without coming close to the position Nozick favors.

It seems, however, that Nozick's rejection of end-state theories encompasses more than the claims I have just endorsed. For he wishes to reject Rawls' theory as an unacceptable end-state theory, despite the fact that it incorporates considerations of entitlement through the notion of pure procedural justice. If the basic institutions of a society are just, according to Rawls, then the holdings people acquire through the operation of those institutions are legitimate, whatever these holdings may be, and people have rights over these holdings as the rules of the institution provide.⑪ The basic structure itself is just, according to Rawls, if it conforms to his Two Principles, namely the principle of maximum equal basic liberties and

> ⑪ This is the sort of entitlement that Scanlon said earlier that almost any theory of justice would recognize. It differs from the sort Nozick advocates in that both the scope of such entitlements and the rights that they confer are set by the account of justice on other grounds (such as whether the institutions in question satisfy the difference principle).

the principle that institutions generating unequal holdings are just only insofar as these inequalities are to the benefit of the worse off, and only if the positions of greater reward are open to all under conditions of fair equality of opportunity. Nozick objects to this theory on the ground that the entitlements it supports have only a derived status; its fundamental principles, he says, are end-state, and it is therefore to be rejected. This rejection would also apply to the modified egalitarian positions I have described.

What is the basis for this strong claim, that any acceptable theory must make entitlements fundamental? In arguing against Rawls, Nozick maintains that a theory which brings in entitlement principles as derived principles to be defended by appeal to more fundamental moral notions together with empirical facts will strike us as wrong for the same reason that act-utilitarian attempts to account for rights seem so obviously mistaken. What is derived in such theories will be only approximations of the principles we intuitively want, and even where they support the same conclusions as these principles do, they do so for what seem to be the wrong reasons.⑫

Whether this objection is persuasive against an end-state theory will depend on the character of the end-states with which that theory is concerned. Consider, for example, a theory concerned solely with the production of certain valued states of consciousness, or one concerned with securing equality in what people physically possess. It might be claimed within such a theory that certain rights to dispose of one's holdings are justified because they are a good means for producing an end-state of the required kind. Such an argument would indeed strike us as mistaken for reasons of the kind Nozick mentions, reasons strictly analogous to those that plague an act-utilitarian account of the obligation to keep one's promises or of the prohibition against paternalism. But a modified egalitarian theory of the kind I suggested above would not have this problem. In such a theory, control over various aspects of one's life is something which has an independent value. This provides a direct basis for arguments in support of the personal rights that secure and protect such control, removing any need to appeal to whatever tendency these rights may have to promote other, intuitively unrelated effects. It is on such a basis that Rawls' theory recognizes powers and liberties, including the right to hold personal property, as primary social goods.

[12] Thus a utilitarian might try to argue that keeping promises will in general lead to more utility (see Annotation 2), but this is virtually certain to be true only for the most part at best. And even if it were somehow true in every case, the reason thereby offered for keeping promises would not be the intuitively correct one that one has a moral duty to do this simply because of having made the promise.

The value attached to the ability to exercise control over a certain aspect of one's life is not the same thing as a right assigning a person a particular form of such control. . . . But this value is the natural reason for having such a right, and it is, I think, the element often missing from utilitarian accounts that seek the value of a right in its tendency to promote some further unrelated effects. To recognize a particular interest as meriting protection in rights is not to say that it is to have absolute protection. It may be a difficult question how a right can be designed to protect that interest and how much protection can be given at tolerable cost. . . . [13]

[13] "Tolerable cost" in terms of other, competing values.

This general point about the relation between workable rights and the human interests that make them important has a further relevance to Nozick's argument. In defending his particular system of rights, Nozick often seems to assume that any alternative rights would be wholesale in character. One such right which he considers is "the right to have a say over what affects you." Nozick properly points out that a right literally to have a say in all decisions that affect you, or even in all those that affect you deeply and intimately, would be impossibly broad. It is essential to distinguish between different ways in which something can affect a person. As Nozick puts it, what decision affects me more deeply than the decision the person I love makes in deciding whom to marry? But this does not mean that I should have a right to a role in making that decision. Nozick's conclusion is that it is my "Lockean" rights that determine which things, among all those that affect me, I have the right to a say over.

I would agree that, while the importance of rights largely flows from the importance of having control over things that affect one, the function of a system of rights is to distinguish between the various ways that things can affect people and to apportion out particular forms of control. It follows that if we are agreed how this is to be done, then we will refer to people's rights in order to determine what they are entitled to a say over. But it does not follow that Nozick's "Lockean" rights are the correct ones, and this is just what is at issue.

If a supposed right turns out to give the person holding it an obviously unacceptable degree of control over other people's lives then that is ground for saying that there is no such right. The proposed "right to have say over what affects you" fails this test. But what the objection formulated in terms of this right is really claiming is that unrestricted property rights of the sort favored by Nozick must also be rejected on the same grounds. [14]

[14] Because unrestricted property rights will give some people the sort of control over the lives of others reflected in the passage at Annotation 7.

. . .

The contrast between Nozick's and Rawls' views on political obligation illustrates the important difference between two types of consent theory. In theories of the first type, actual consent has a fundamental role as the source of legitimacy of social institutions. Theories of the second type start from the assumption that the institutions with which political philosophy is concerned are fundamentally nonvoluntary. These institutions are held to be legitimate if they satisfy appropriate conditions, and the idea of hypothetical consent enters as a metaphorical device used in the formulation and defense of these conditions. [15] . . . The difference between these two theories is magnified by the fact that the idea of consent involves choice against some background of alternatives. If what is at issue is initial consent to institutions from without, then the relevant background is that of this pre-institutional condition. It is only this viewpoint that makes the "baseline" of conditions in the state of nature seem relevant. By contrast, since the questions raised through the device of the hypothetical contract are questions about the justifiability of social institutions to people who find themselves living under them, the relevant background is given by the alternatives actually available to people in societies and the values that such people attach to these alternatives. . . . there is no temptation, on this view, to take the standards of some earlier (for example, pretechnological) age as relevant to the acceptability of contemporary institutions. [16]

The idea that respect for individual liberty requires that consent be a necessary condition for all obligations beyond the requirements of a minimal framework of rights arises in the same way as the idea that makes subjective preference seem the only acceptable basis for ethically significant judgments of relative well being. Further, the two views involve similar mistakes. Welfare economists and those who support subjective versions of utilitarianism are moved by the belief that the interests of the affected parties are the bases on which social policies should be appraised and by the belief that it is unacceptable to "impose" on these parties, as the relevant account of their interests, a system of values that they do not share. The response to these beliefs is generally to bring individual preferences into a theory at the foun-

dational level, making them the basis for all judgments of relative value. A few restrictions on what can count as admissible preferences may be allowed in the form of requirements of consistency, transitivity, and so on, but anything beyond such purely formal restrictions is seen as a threat. When a theory is constructed in this way, so that it treats almost all preferences at face value regardless of their origins or content, its conclusions can be substantially affected by the social conditions which influence prevailing preferences and their relative strengths. This robs the theory of an important kind of critical power and, in addition, makes it an uncertain guardian of even those values of individual autonomy which it set out to protect. Many different conditions are important for the development of autonomous preferences, and the ability of individuals to give effect to their preferences in their own lives and in the determination of social policy depends on a variety of powers and liberties. To give appropriate recognition to the value of individual autonomy a theory must assign appropriate weights to all these factors in balancing them against each other and against other competing considerations. Autonomy is not adequately recognized simply by letting these weights and all others be determined by whatever constellation of individual preferences happens to prevail at the point at which the theory is applied. [17]

Similar problems arise for a view which, acting out of a desire to safeguard individual liberty, brings consent in at the foundational level as the basis of almost all obligations, and allows it to be restricted by only a minimum of "imposed" moral requirements. The consequences such a theory can endorse are unacceptably open to determination by factors affecting the relative bargaining strength of various individuals, for example, variations in the demand for and scarcity of particular talents and resources. In particular, the ability of individuals to exercise the kind of control over

---

[15] Hypothetical consent is something like Rawls's original position. Rawls's view is that this is the only sort of consent that is realistically applicable to social and political institutions.

---

[16] The suggestion is that a state of nature is too remote from actual conditions to make what people might consent to there "relevant to the acceptability of contemporary institutions."

---

[17] The problem Scanlon is pointing to is that people's preferences may be warped by existing institutions in ways that make those institutions seem more acceptable than they genuinely are. (An extreme example would be slaves who are influenced by the very institution of slavery to prefer remaining enslaved. A view that relied on actual preferences would then be unable to find any basis for rejecting slavery—and the same thing would be true of one that appealed to consent.)

their lives that freedom from imposed obligations is supposed to secure will be to an unacceptable degree merely a function of their bargaining strength.⟨18⟩ As in the previous case, the conclusion to be drawn here is that individual liberty is not adequately protected simply by bringing consent in as the foundation of obligation. An adequate theory must take into account the various ways— other than merely by being morally free to withhold one's services—in which individuals may be enabled to exercise control over their own lives and their common institutions (or disabled from doing so.)

⟨18⟩ A different problem for the appeal to actual consent (though Scanlon says it is "similar") is that what people consent to is a function of their individual bargaining power, which in turn depends on their resources and natural talents. He is saying, first, that differences in these things will give some people much less control than others over what sorts of institutions result from consent (which is very plausible); and, second, that this difference in degree of control is morally unacceptable (something that Nozick, at least, would question).

. . .

The two forms of consent theory correspond to two differing views of rights. Either view may recognize rights as a basis for individual claims against social institutions. Thus both see some rights as "natural" in the sense of having validity that does not derive from positive law or social institutions. On the first view, however, the rights that are the basis for moral criticism and defense of social institutions are seen as "natural rights" in the stronger sense that they are the very same rights which individuals possess and can claim against one another in a state of nature. On the second view, rights represent general judgments about the conditions of legitimacy of social institutions, for example, judgments of the form "Any institutions granting *that* power are morally unacceptable." Exactly which such generalizations seem true and important—what things are rights and what these rights encompass—are matters that will change as social conditions change. Some of these rights concern things that would be of no relevance, or only a very different and more limited kind of relevance, in a state of nature. (Rights to freedom of expression, due process of law and political participation seem to have this character.)⟨19⟩

It is central to Nozick's argument that the rights with which he is concerned are claimed to be natural rights in the stronger sense. The objections I have raised to his examples almost all demand that he consider the consequences of enforcement of absolute property and contract rights and that he explain why the loss of liberty this involves for some people is not worse than that which is involved in the alternative systems which he deplores. Such objections suppose that the property rights enforced by the minimal state and those embodied in socialist institutions are two alternative social systems open to the same kind of objections and needing the same kind of defense. Nozick rejects this symmetrical picture. In his view, the particular property rights protected by the minimal state are not licensed or created by it and consequently do not need to be defended as part of its justification. These rights are ones that individuals have quite independently of the social institutions in which they live. In enforcing these rights the minimal state is only doing for them what they were already entitled to do for themselves. Consequently it is not doing anything that could be held to infringe anyone's liberty.⟨20⟩

How plausible is the claim that the rights appealed to in Nozick's examples are ones that individuals would have in a state of nature? This claim has greatest initial plausibility with respect to the right of nonaggression. An unprovoked attack occurring today on the streets of New York seems to be wrong for the same reasons that would apply to a similar attack in the state of nature. But the right of nonaggression as Nozick interprets it covers more than this. It prohibits generally "sacrificing one person to benefit another" I take it that what Nozick wants to rule out here is any use of force or the threat of force to make one person contribute to the welfare of another who

⟨19⟩ Thus on the second view, there are no definite natural rights (or at least very few of them). As already noted, what rights people have and exactly how far they extend will depend on a complicated weighing of different morally relevant considerations.

⟨20⟩ Thus in Nozick's view, rights (at least the most fundamental ones) do not derive from society or from the state, and even the right of the state to enforce such rights is derivative from the antecedent right of individuals to enforce their own rights (in roughly the same way advocated by Locke).

has no right to this contribution. This last qualification reduces the right considerably, but without it the right would be absurd.[21] This shows that the right of non-aggression cannot be interpreted in isolation from other rights. Its invariance between the state of nature and other conditions will consequently depend on that of these other rights.

> [21] Nozick's view is essentially that another person's right to such a contribution must derive from a voluntary arrangement of some kind.

Chief among these is the right to one's property. A system of property is a set of rules defining the conditions under which a person owns an object and specifying the extent and character of the rights of owners. What a person's property rights are will normally depend not only on what systems of property could be validly enforced under the conditions in which he lives but also on what system is actually in use. To the extent that this system is morally legitimate, its provisions determine his rights. But the provisions of this system may also be wrong. They may claim for him rights that no one could really have or they may fail to protect claims that any valid system would have to recognize. Surely we can imagine an incident, occurring in a state of nature, which strikes us intuitively as a violation of property rights. Imagine that a family is living in the wilderness when a group of strangers comes along and drives them off part of their land and takes their crops. This strikes us as a clear wrong. I take it that the point of saying that this happens "in a state of nature" is just that the wrongness involved does not seem to depend on any system of law or social convention. But it is open to question whether what we feel to be violated in such examples is really a natural right to property. For these cases strikes us as clear wrongs only if we suppose, first, that what is taken is of use to the person who loses it (that is, that the taking actually constitutes an interference with his life and activities) and, second, that his appropriation and use of the thing did not already constitute an interference with others. . . .When these conditions are satisfied, the taking infringes upon what might be called the natural right of noninterference. A system of property rights goes beyond this primitive right by specifying formal criteria of ownership.[22] If a person is deprived of something to which he has acquired title in the specified way, then his property right has been violated whether the taking makes any difference

to his life at all. Different systems of property carry out this extension in different ways, each specifying its own criteria of ownership and defining and limiting the rights of owners in its own way. . . .

To support the claim that some property rights are natural rights we need to think of a state of nature example involving a clear wrong which seems to violate one of these rights without violating the primitive right of noninterference. But if we imagine such a case we may be open to the question of why we should imagine a state of nature containing *that* particular system of property, rather than some other system which would not be violated by the act in question.

> [22] Scanlon's claim is that there is no natural right to property that is definite enough to yield a specific account of who owns what, and that Nozick's claim to the contrary results from confusing such a specific system of property rights with the "natural right of noninterference"—which, Scanlon would say, does not really involve property as such at all. (See Discussion Question 3.)

This objection could be avoided if we could show that the primitive right of noninterference does not exhaust the common core of systems of property rights. Perhaps there are certain provisions falling outside this right which would be incorporated in any system of property rights that could plausibly be held to be valid in a state of nature. It could then be argued that the provisions which Nozick's examples turn on fall in this class, for example, that an unrestricted right of inheritance does so. But this is far from clear. Suppose the grandfather of the family we previously imagined lived on land a short distance away and that when he died he said, "Now this is yours." But they had all they could do to take care of their own place, and one day they noticed that someone else had moved onto their grandfather's old farm. Are they entitled (in the state of nature) to throw the people off or to demand payment? It is not obvious to me that they are.[23] Even if there is "as much land and as good" not far off, their claim to demand that the new people

> [23] This example is supposed to support the claim that there is no natural system of property rights beyond the right of noninterference. If there were, then the family in question would have a right to repossess the grandfather's farm or at least demand payment, which Scanlon says is not obviously the case. (What might Nozick say about this case?)

move to it is quite debatable. Furthermore, even if we were to be convinced by such examples that any system of property valid in a state of nature would have to include unrestricted inheritance, there would remain the question of how much this judgment is dependent upon our assessment of the consequences that this provision would have in a "natural state." These consequences are apt to be quite different from those that would result from the same provision under other social conditions.

. . .

Nozick . . . faces the problem, then, of deriving an extended system of property rights involving money, commerce, and extensive holdings from something like Locke's original "natural" foundation. This derivation faces two problems. The first is that the lack of natural bounds on acquisition means that others are likely to be threatened—there may not be enough and as good left for them. . . . Nozick's re-

sponse here is that the increase in the stock of goods due to increasing productivity will keep pace with increased acquisition, making it unlikely that anyone will be made worse off relative to the baseline of expectations in the state of nature. The second problem is that, with holdings extending far beyond "the conveniences of life" (certainly far beyond what these included in the state of nature), the case for absolute protection of these holdings becomes weaker. This makes even more controversial the choice of an extremely low baseline for determining whether the condition of others is worsened.(24)

(24) The suggestion is that as holdings become greater, the claim that they should be absolutely protected becomes weaker; and also that large property holdings make it more doubtful that what would exist in the state of nature is the right "baseline" for determining whether the condition of others has been worsened by acquisition.

. . .

Discussion Questions

1. Scanlon says that any departure from equality requires a special defense simply because it is a bad thing for someone to be worse off than others and especially to be worse off than the norm in his or her society. This suggests that equality is a kind of "default" position: it needs no special justification, but any departure from it—even one that results from such things as natural endowments—does. How plausible is this view?

2. Consider the issue of what, if anything, egalitarianism says or should say about natural assets, such as intelligence or physical strength. These have the following two features: first, they cannot be redistributed to others in the interest of equality; and, second, unlike such things as a social class or caste system, the advantages they yield for the people who have them do not derive in any obvious way from disadvantages imposed on others. A closer approximation to equality could, however, be achieved by *worsening* the situation of those who have such assets in various ways (such as through surgery). Scanlon says (see the passage at Annotation 9) that other consider-

ations may "temper" the demands of equality in this area. But a thoroughgoing egalitarian might still say that worsening the situation of favored people in such respects is in *one* way a moral improvement, even if one that is outweighed by these other considerations. Does even this seem right?

3. Nozick claims that there is a natural right to property, while Scanlon suggests that superficially plausible cases (like that at Annotation 22) involve only a right of noninterference, so that any definite system of property is a social creation. Scanlon's view would mean that any system of property rights would have to be judged by weighing all the relevant kinds of value, so that a system of private property might or might not turn out to be the best. Is he right about this? Or are there at least some principles (whether or not Nozick has them exactly right) that any acceptable societal system of property rights must conform to, principles that cannot properly be abandoned in pursuit of other sorts of values (such as equality)?

Philosophy and
the Good Life

The reading selections in this chapter concern the timeless question: what is a—or *the*—good life? Many different answers have been given to this question. On one extreme, there are views according to which only certain definite kinds of lives or in the most extreme versions only a single kind of life is best (as suggested by the version of the question using "the"). On the other extreme, there are views according to which there is no objective answer at all as to what sort of life is good, so that the only relevant consideration is the person's own subjective judgment: if people think that they are living good or satisfactory lives, then they are, and there is nothing more to be said. Between those two extremes are views claiming that while what counts as a good life varies from person to person and perhaps on other dimensions as well, there are some objective conditions or requirements that must be satisfied for a life to be good.

Many people are at least tempted by the idea that whether a life is a good one depends only on the character of the subjective experiences that it contains, with the most obvious version of this idea being the view (a version of **hedonism**) that a good life is one that contains lots of pleasurable experiences and few if any painful ones. Consider then the option of plugging into the "experience machine" described in the selection by Robert Nozick: a computer that will give you whatever set of experiences you choose. If all that matters to a good life is the character of your subjective experience, then the prospect of plugging into such a machine should be highly attractive. But does a life that is in this way divorced from real life really constitute a good life? Nozick suggests that it does not—that a truly good life involves actually doing and accomplishing things and not just having the artificially created experience of doing so. And if this is right, then the character of your subjective experience is not the only thing that matters in determining whether your life is a good one.

Epictetus offers a somewhat different conception of the good life, though one that still reflects the idea that the only thing that really matters to each of us—or at least the only thing that really should matter to us—is our own subjective experiences, including importantly our reactions to things in the world. For him, what matters most is not pleasures of various sorts but an absence of painful and distressing emotional reactions. And the way to achieve this in a necessarily messy and unpredictable world is to control your own thoughts and desires, so that external events beyond your control cease to matter. A person who cares about nothing beyond the inner reactions that are (he thinks) within one's control will achieve peace of mind, whereas one who attaches significance to external occurrences (including what happens to his own physical body) is doomed to unhappiness and frustration.

The selections by Thomas Nagel and Susan Wolf raise a different sort of issue about a good life: must a good life, in addition to whatever else it may require, be *meaningful?* And what does a meaningful life require—indeed, is it even possible for a human life to be genuinely meaningful? According to Nagel, our lives are in an important way *absurd,* where this means that they both lack meaning and can be seen by us to do so. Nagel argues that it is simply part of the human condition to have available a perspective from which everything that might seem to give meaning to our lives can be called into question. Wolf's more optimistic view is that a meaningful life is possible and that meaning is a fundamental aspect of a good life. According to her conception, a life is meaningful when it involves active engagement in activities that are objectively worthwhile.

$$\boxed{\textit{Robert Nozick}}$$

Robert Nozick (1938–2002), for many years a professor at Harvard, was a major figure in twentieth-century philosophy, making contributions to many areas but most importantly to political philosophy and epistemology. The thought experiment elaborated in this selection is a rich example, raising issues about what things matter to us, what kinds of things we most fundamentally desire, what motivates us, and what constitutes a good life. For our purposes in this chapter, the last of these issues is most germane.

The Experience Machine

There are . . . substantial puzzles when we ask what matters other than how *people's* experiences feel "from the inside." Suppose there were an experience machine that would give you any experience you desired. Superduper neuropsychologists could stimulate your brain so that you would think and feel you were writing a great novel, or making a friend, or reading an interesting book. All the time you would be floating in a tank, with electrodes attached to your brain. Should you plug into this machine for life, preprogramming your life's experiences? If you are worried about missing out on desirable experiences, we can suppose that business enterprises have researched thoroughly the lives of many others.① You can pick

From Anarchy, State, and Utopia *(New York: Basic Books, 1974).*

and choose from their large library or smorgasbord of such experiences, selecting your life's experiences for, say, the next two years. After two years have passed, you will have ten minutes or ten hours out of the tank, to select the experiences of your *next* two years. Of course, while in the tank you won't know that you're there; you'll think it's all actually happening. Others can also plug in to have the experiences they want, so there's no need to stay unplugged to serve them. (Ignore problems such as who will service the machines if everyone plugs in.)②

① Suppose that this research has resulted in a rich catalog of lives, an effective personality test that you can take, and some reliable general principles about which personality types match which types of lives to produce the best results. You need not worry, therefore, about whether or not you know enough about the options or yourself to pick the best life for yourself.

② Also ignore the possibility that the people you leave behind will miss you. Suppose, for example, that the programmers create a robotic duplicate of you, indiscernible to others, who will take your place in your relationships. And, of course, your friends and family might choose to take advantage of the experience machine themselves, programming your presence into their experience.

③ Focusing just on what you care about, about what would be good *for you,* would you plug into this machine?

Would you plug in? *What else can matter to us, other than how our lives feel from the inside?* Nor should you refrain because of the few moments of distress between the moment you've decided and the moment you're plugged. What's a few moments of distress compared to a lifetime of bliss (if that's what you choose), and why feel any distress at all if your decision *is* the best one?③

What does matter to us in addition to our experiences? First, we want to *do* certain things, and not just have the experience of doing them. In the case of certain experiences, it is only because first we want to do the actions that we want the experiences of doing them or thinking we've done them. (But *why* do we want to do the activities rather than merely to experience them?) A second reason for not plugging in is that we want to *be* a certain way, to be a certain sort of person. Someone floating in a tank is an indeterminate blob. There is no answer to the question of what a person is like who has long been in the tank. Is he courageous, kind, intelligent, witty, loving? It's not merely that it's difficult to tell; there's no way he is. Plugging into the machine is a kind of suicide. It will seem to some, trapped by a picture, that nothing about what we are like can matter except as it gets reflected in our experiences. But should it be surprising that what *we are* is important to us?④ Why should we be concerned only with how our time is filled, but not with what we are?

④ Someone might object to Nozick that *what we are* is entirely constituted by *what we experience.* Are you tempted by such a view?

Thirdly, plugging into an experience machine limits us to a man-made reality, to a world no deeper or more important than that which people can construct. There is no *actual* contact with any deeper reality, though the experience of it can be simulated. Many persons desire to leave themselves open to such contact and to a plumbing of deeper significance.*⑤ This clarifies the intensity of the conflict over psychoactive drugs, which some view as mere local experience machines, and others view as avenues to a deeper reality; what some view as equivalent to surrender to the experience machine, others view as following one of the reasons *not* to surrender!

⑤ Would this consideration be a reason for an atheist to refuse to plug into the machine? (See Discussion Question 2.)

We learn that something matters to us in addition to experience by imagining an experience machine and then realizing that we would not use it. We can continue to imagine a sequence of machines each designed to fill lacks suggested for the earlier machines. For example, since the experience machine doesn't meet

---

*Traditional religious views differ on the *point* of contact with a transcendent reality. Some say that contact yields eternal bliss or Nirvana, but they have not distinguished this sufficiently from merely a *very* long run on the experience machine. Others think it is intrinsically desirable to do the will of a higher being which created us all, though presumably no one would think this if we discovered we had been created as an object of amusement by some superpowerful child from another galaxy or dimension. Still others imagine an eventual merging with a higher reality, leaving unclear its desirability, or where that merging leaves *us.*

our desire to *be* a certain way, imagine a transformation machine which transforms us into whatever sort of person we'd like to be (compatible with our staying us).⑥ Surely one would not use the transformation machine to become as one would wish, and thereupon plug into the experience machine!* So something matters in addition to one's experiences *and* what one is like. Nor is the reason merely that one's experiences are unconnected with what one is like. For the experience machine might be limited to provide only experiences possible to the sort of person plugged in. Is it that we want to make a difference in the world?

⑥ Would you use the transformation machine to learn French? Would you use it to become a kind person?

Consider then the result machine, which produces in the world any result you would produce and injects your vector input into any joint activity.⑦ We shall not pursue here the fascinating details of these or other machines. What is most disturbing about them is their living of our lives for us. Is it misguided to search for *particular* additional functions beyond the competence of machines to do for us? Perhaps what we desire is to live (an active verb) ourselves, in contact with reality. (And this, machines cannot do *for* us.) . . .

⑦ Suppose that someone refused to plug into the experience machine because she wanted to help unfortunate people in the world. Should she use the results machine if what she cares about is those people being helped?

Discussion Questions

1. Suppose that Grace is a young woman from a very wealthy family who falls in love with Bob, a common young man. Grace's family disapproves of Bob, suspecting that he is only after Grace's money. Grace listens carefully to their concerns, but insists that Bob genuinely loves her. Grace and Bob marry and seem blissfully happy for several years, but Grace's family remains vigilant, hoping to be proven wrong, but still very suspicious of Bob's real feelings and motives. Eventually the members of Grace's family hire a detective to follow Bob, finally obtaining definitive proof that Bob has been seeing many other women. When they confront him, he laughs, saying that he can't believe that it took them so long, and brags that Grace has no idea of his deception. He suggests that they think about the pain that revealing his betrayal would cause Grace, but though the family members are concerned about this, they decide to tell Grace anyway. Before they can do so, however, they learn that Grace has been diagnosed with pancreatic cancer, which will lead to her death within six months. As she sobs in her mother's arms,

Grace thanks her lucky stars that she has such a wonderful husband who can see her through these last few difficult months. After agonizing further about the decision, Grace's family decides to offer Bob a substantial financial settlement to keep up the lie, thus making sure that her last few months are spent with what seems to be a loving husband. He agrees, and Grace lives another five months, dying in the firm belief that her husband loves her dearly and will miss her enormously. Did her family do the right thing, if all that matters to Grace is her experiences? Did her family do the right thing?

2. Nozick's third reason for refusing to plug into the experience machine appeals to our desire to connect to a "deeper reality," and he suggests that the transcendent reality of some religions might count as such a reality. Does it seem then that this third reason will appeal to only religious people? But Nozick contrasts the deeper reality with man-made reality, and so one might think that even an atheist could appeal to this reason, if nature could count as a deeper reality. How might someone develop

---

*Some wouldn't use the transformation machine at all; it seems like *cheating.* But the one-time use of the transformation machine would not remove all challenges; there would still be obstacles for the new us to overcome, a new plateau from which to strive even higher. And is this plateau any the less earned or deserved than that provided by genetic endowment and early childhood environment? But if the transformation machine could be used indefinitely often, so that we could accomplish anything by pushing a button to transform ourselves into someone who could do it easily, there would remain no limits we *need* to strain against or try to transcend. Would there be anything left *to do?* Do some theological views place God outside of time because an omniscient omnipotent being couldn't fill up his days?

such an atheistic interpretation of his third reason for refusing to plug into the experience machine?

3. Nozick offers the transformation machine as a response to the objection that one might resist going into the experience machine because really being someone who is, for example, kind was more important than merely experiencing oneself as being kind. (While the experience machine seems at least remotely possible, it is not as clear that the transformation machine makes sense. Think about the difference between the two machines.) But when you step out of the transformation machine, you are kind. How successful is this response to that objection? It has been argued that you would still be "cheating" if you used the transformation machine for some things but not for others. For example, if you needed to learn to speak French for a trip, then it would be acceptable to use the transformation machine, but if you wanted to be kind, you should do that "the hard way." How might someone argue for such a view?

Epictetus

Epictetus (55 A.D.–135 A.D.), a Greek-born Roman slave, was a famous Stoic philosopher. Although Epictetus was born into slavery, he was freed while still a young man and was sent to study Stoicism with a master. After years of study, he eventually founded a school, which taught the elements of Stoicism to students from many lands. While he never published any of his ideas, one of his students, Flavius Arrianus, published notes from Epictetus's lectures. The *Manual* was extracted from a longer work called the *Discourses*.

This reading has a different form than most of the other readings in this book. Instead of a sustained line of reasoning, there are many independent instructions for how to live a good life. But those instructions make sense only if certain assumptions about what makes us happy are true. If you are tempted to plug into Nozick's experience machine, then you value your own states of mind more than anything else. If you value a peaceful state of mind over everything else, then the recommendations of Epictetus will be very attractive to you.

From the *Manual*

1

Of all existing things some are in our power, and others are not in our power. In our power are thought, impulse, will to get and will to avoid, and, in a word, everything which is our own doing. Things not in our power include the body, property, reputation, office, and, in a word, everything which is not our own doing.① Things in our power are by nature free, unhindered, untrammelled; things not in our power are weak, servile, subject to hindrance, dependent on others. Remember then that if you imagine that what is naturally slavish is free, and what is naturally another's is your own, you will be hampered, you will mourn, you will be put to confusion, you will blame gods and men; but if you think that only your own belongs to you, and that what is another's is indeed another's, no one will ever put compulsion or hindrance on you, you will blame none, you will accuse none,

From The Stoic and Epicurean Philosophers, *edited by Whitney J. Oates (New York: Random House, 1940).*

you will do nothing against your will, no one will harm you, you will have no enemy, for no harm can touch you.②

① To what extent, if any, are our thoughts and our desires in our control? There may be some thoughts and some desires that one has no control over (see Discussion Question 2), but suppose for now that Epictetus is right that each person has some degree of control, perhaps only indirectly, over many of his or her thoughts an d desires.

② What does Epictetus mean by things that are "your own"? What things are "another's"? (Are there things that are neither your own or another's?) Why will you escape harm as long as you have true beliefs about what is truly your own?

③ The state of freedom and happiness, according to Epictetus, consists in being concerned with only those things within your power.

④ Every thought and every desire must be tested. If you find yourself wanting something outside your power (money, prestige, grades, cars, and so forth), then you must stop wanting it. You should want only that which is in your power. (Has any clear reason been given for this view?)

Aiming then at these high matters, you must remember that to attain them requires more than ordinary effort; you will have to give up some things entirely, and put off others for the moment. And if you would have these also— office and wealth—it may be that you will fail to get them, just because your desire is set on the former, and you will certainly fail to attain those things which alone bring freedom and happiness.③

Make it your study then to confront every harsh impression with the words, 'You are but an impression, and not at all what you seem to be'. Then test it by those rules that you possess; and first by this—the chief test of all—'Is it concerned with what is in our power or with what is not in our power?' And if it is concerned with what is not in our power, be ready with the answer that it is nothing to you.④

2

Remember that the will to get promises attainment of what you will, and the will to avoid promises escape from what you avoid; and he who fails to get what he wills is unfortunate, and he who does not escape what he wills to avoid is miserable. If then you try to avoid only what is unnatural in the region within your control, you will escape from all that you avoid; but if you

try to avoid disease or death or poverty you will be miserable.⑤

Therefore let your will to avoid have no concern with what is not in man's power; direct it only to things in man's power that are contrary to nature. But for the moment you must utterly remove the will to get; for if you will to get something not in man's power you are bound to be unfortunate; while none of the things in man's power that you could honourably will to get is yet within your reach. Impulse to act and not to act, these are your concern; yet exercise them gently and without strain, and provisionally.

3

When anything, from the meanest thing upwards, is attractive or serviceable or an object of affection, remember always to say to yourself, 'What is its nature?' If you are fond of a jug, say you are fond of a jug; then you will not be disturbed if it be broken. If you kiss your child or your wife, say to yourself that you are kissing a human being, for then if death strikes it you will not be disturbed.

4

When you are about to take something in hand, remind yourself what manner of thing it is. If you are going to bathe put before your mind what happens in the bath—water pouring over some, others being jostled, some reviling, others stealing; and you will set to work more securely if you say to yourself at once: 'I want to bathe, and I want to keep my will in harmony with nature,' and so in each thing you do; for in this way, if anything turns up to hinder you in your bathing, you will be ready to say, 'I did not want only to bathe, but to keep my will in harmony with nature, and I shall not so keep it, if I lose my temper at what happens'.⑥

⑤ Even if you sometimes succeed when you try to get or avoid things outside your power, you will not always succeed, and so you will at least sometimes be unfortunate and miserable. Epictetus's recommendation seems to assume that it is better to *never* be disappointed. Does that seem right? (See Discussion Question 3.)

⑥ During the Roman Empire, public baths were commonplace. They provided ample opportunity to practice "acceptance."

5

What disturbs men's minds is not events but their judgements on events. For instance, death is nothing dreadful, or else Socrates would have thought it so. No, the only dreadful thing about it is men's judgement that it is dreadful.⑦ And so when we are hindered, or disturbed, or distressed, let us never lay the blame on others, but on ourselves, that is, on our own judgements. To accuse others for one's own misfortunes is a sign of want of education; to accuse oneself shows that one's education has begun; to accuse neither oneself nor others shows that one's education is complete.

⑦ Epictetus's claim is that it is not events themselves—things such as death—that are dreadful. The only thing that is dreadful is *the judgment* that some particular occurrence is dreadful. How plausible is this view?

. . .

8

Ask not that events should happen as you will, but let your will be that events should happen as they do, and you shall have peace.

9

Sickness is a hindrance to the body, but not to the will, unless the will consent. Lameness is a hindrance to the leg, but not to the will. Say this to yourself at each event that happens, for you shall find that though it hinders something else it will not hinder you.

. . .

11

Never say of anything, 'I lost it', but say, 'I gave it back'. Has your child died? It was given back. Has your wife died? She was given back. Has your estate been taken from you? Was not this also given back? But you say, 'He who took it from me is wicked'. What does it matter to you through whom the Giver asked it back? As long as He gives it you, take care of it, but not as your own; treat it as passers-by treat an inn.⑧

12

If you wish to make progress, abandon reasonings of this sort: 'If I neglect my affairs I shall have nothing to live on'; 'If I do not punish my son, he will be wicked.' For it is better to die of hunger, so that you be free from pain and free from fear, than to live in plenty and be troubled in mind. It is better for your son to be wicked than for you to be miserable.⑨ Wherefore begin with little things. Is your drop of oil spilt? Is your sup of wine stolen? Say to yourself, 'This is the price paid for freedom from passion, this is the price of a quiet mind.' Nothing can be had without a price. When you call your slave-boy, reflect that he may not be able to hear you, and if he hears you, he may not be able to do anything you want. But he is not so well off that it rests with him to give you peace of mind.

⑧ By "the Giver," Epictetus seems to mean more reality at large than a personal deity. Think about the inn analogy: what would your attitude be toward a pleasant, well-furnished room that you stayed in for a limited period of time? Can this be plausibly extended to things like children and spouses?

⑨ This claim vividly expresses the supreme value Epictetus places on one's own peaceful state of mind. It is surely not better *for your son* that he be wicked, but if all you care about is your own peace of mind, then it is better *for you.*

13

If you wish to make progress, you must be content in external matters to seem a fool and a simpleton; do not wish men to think you know anything, and if any should think you to be somebody, distrust yourself. For know that it is not easy to keep your will in accord with nature and at the same time keep outward things; if you attend to one you must needs neglect the other.

14

It is silly to want your children and your wife and your friends to live for ever, for that means that you want what is not in your control to be in your control, and what is not your own to be yours. In the same way if you want your servant to make no mistakes, you are a fool, for you want vice not to be vice but something different. But if you want not to be disappointed in your will to get, you can attain to that.

Exercise yourself then in what lies in your power. Each man's master is the man who has authority over what he wishes or does not wish, to secure the one or to take away the other. Let him then who wishes to be free not wish for anything or avoid anything that depends on others; or else he is bound to be a slave. ⑩

> ⑩ Imagine someone who has mastered this advice: he cares only about his own thoughts and desires; he neither wants to have or to avoid anything that pertains to anyone but himself. Does this sound like an admirable person?

15

Remember that you must behave in life as you would at a banquet. A dish is handed round and comes to you; put out your hand and take it politely. It passes you; do not stop it. It has not reached you; do not be impatient to get it, but wait till your turn comes. Bear yourself thus towards children, wife, office, wealth, and one day you will be worthy to banquet with the gods. But if when they are set before you, you do not take them but despise them, then you shall not only share the gods' banquet, but shall share their rule. ⑪ For by so doing Diogenes and Heraclitus and men like them were called divine and deserved the name.

> ⑪ Here is an even more extreme claim: you should *despise* all things not within your control. Why is this supposed to be better than the attitude described earlier in this paragraph?

16

When you see a man shedding tears in sorrow for a child abroad or dead, or for loss of property, beware that you are not carried away by the impression that it is outward ills that make him miserable. Keep this thought by you: 'What distresses him is not the event, for that does not distress another, but his judgement on the event.' Therefore do not hesitate to sympathize with him so far as words go, and if it so chance, even to groan with him; but take heed that you do not also groan in your inner being.

. . .

19

You can be invincible, if you never enter on a contest where victory is not in your power. ⑫ Beware then that when you see a man raised to honour or great power or high repute you do not let your impression carry you away. For if the reality of good lies in what is in our power, there is no room for envy or jealousy. And you will not wish to be praetor, or prefect or consul, but to be free; and there is but one way to freedom—to despise what is not in our power.

> ⑫ If you are hurt only by not getting what you want, and if you want only what you have in your power, then you will always get what you want and you will never be hurt. You will be "invincible" in a sense, but is this sort of "invincibility" worth the cost of not caring about anything outside your own mind?

20

Remember that foul words or blows in themselves are no outrage, but your judgement that they are so. So when any one makes you angry, know that it is your own thought that has angered you. Wherefore make it your first endeavour not to let your impressions carry you away. For if once you gain time and delay, you will find it easier to control yourself.

21

Keep before your eyes from day to day death and exile and all things that seem terrible, but death most of all, and then you will never set your thoughts on what is low and will never desire anything beyond measure.

. . .

28

If any one trusted your body to the first man he met, you would be indignant, but yet you trust your mind to the chance comer, and allow it to be disturbed and confounded if he revile you; are you not ashamed to do so?

. . .

30

Appropriate acts are in general measured by the relations they are concerned with. 'He is your father.' This means you are called on to take care of him, give way to him in all things, bear with him if he reviles or strikes you.

'But he is a bad father.'

Well, have you any natural claim to a good father? No, only to a father.

'My brother wrongs me.'

Be careful then to maintain the relation you hold to him, and do not consider what he does, but what you must do if your purpose is to keep in accord with nature. For no one shall harm you, without your consent; you will only be harmed, when you think you are harmed.[13] You will only discover what is proper to expect from neighbour, citizen, or praetor, if you get into the habit of looking at the relations implied by each.

[13] Here we begin to get recommendations that go beyond the idea of confining one's concern to things within one's control, to one's own states of mind. Part of the idea is that one should not allow oneself to be harmed by the actions and nature of others, even members of one's own family. But there is also an idea of doing one's *duty* toward, for example, one's father.

. . .

33

Lay down for yourself from the first a definite stamp and style of conduct, which you will maintain when you are alone and also in the society of men. Be silent for the most part, or, if you speak, say only what is necessary and in a few words. Talk, but rarely, if occasion calls you, but do not talk of ordinary things—of gladiators, or horse-races, or athletes, or of meats or drinks—these are topics that arise everywhere—but above all do not talk about men in blame or compliment or comparison. If you can, turn the conversation of your company by your talk to some fitting subject; but if you should chance to be isolated among strangers, be silent. Do not laugh much, nor at many things, nor without restraint.[14]

Refuse to take oaths, altogether if that be possible, but if not, as far as circumstances allow.

Refuse the entertainments of strangers and the vulgar. But if occasion arise to accept them, then strain every nerve to avoid lapsing into the state of the vulgar. For know that, if your comrade have a stain on him, he that associates with him must needs share the stain, even though he be clean in himself.

For your body take just so much as your bare need requires, such as food, drink, clothing, house, servants, but cut down all that tends to luxury and outward show.[15]

Avoid impurity to the utmost of your power before marriage, and if you indulge your passion, let it be done lawfully. But do not be offensive or censorious to those who indulge it, and do not be always bringing up your own chastity. If some one tells you that so and so speaks ill of you, do not defend yourself against what he says, but answer, 'He did not know my other faults, or he would not have mentioned these alone.'

It is not necessary for the most part to go to the games; but if you should have occasion to go, show that your first concern is for yourself; that is, wish that only to happen which does happen, and him only to win who does win, for so you will suffer no hindrance. But refrain entirely from applause, or ridicule, or prolonged excitement. And when you go away do not talk much of what happened there, except so far as it tends to your improvement. For to talk about it implies that the spectacle excited your wonder.[16]

Do not go lightly or casually to hear lectures;

[14] Here are more recommendations whose connection with the views expressed earlier is simply not clear. Epictetus is recommending a kind of restrained, modest style of conduct. Such a style clearly does not follow from the recommendation to desire only that which is in one's control.

[15] Suppose that Epictetus is right that we can control our desires. Why couldn't you take as much as you had available for your body, knowing that you could always control your desires if later you no longer had access to as much? Why not enjoy it while you can with no expectation of having it in the future?

[16] Surely we are not supposed to care what others think about us or about what they do. But then it is not clear why one should cultivate such a modest style of conduct.

but if you do go, maintain your gravity and dignity and do not make yourself offensive. When you are going to meet any one, and particularly some man of reputed eminence, set before your mind the thought, 'What would Socrates or Zeno have done?' and you will not fail to make proper use of the occasion.

When you go to visit some great man, prepare your mind by thinking that you will not find him in, that you will be shut out, that the doors will be slammed in your face, that he will pay no heed to you. And if in spite of all this you find it fitting for you to go, go and bear what happens and never say to yourself, 'It was not worth all this'; for that shows a vulgar mind and one at odds with outward things.

In your conversation avoid frequent and disproportionate mention of your own doings or adventures; for other people do not take the same pleasure in hearing what has happened to you as you take in recounting your adventures.

Avoid raising men's laughter; for it is a habit that easily slips into vulgarity, and it may well suffice to lessen your neighbour's respect.

It is dangerous too to lapse into foul language; when anything of the kind occurs, rebuke the offender, if the occasion allow, and if not, make it plain to him by your silence, or a blush or a frown, that you are angry at his words. [17]

[17] But we are not supposed to care about what others are interested in or what others respect or whether others are vulgar.

34

When you imagine some pleasure, beware that it does not carry you away, like other imaginations. Wait a while, and give yourself pause. Next remember two things: how long you will enjoy the pleasure, and also how long you will afterwards repent and revile yourself. And set on the other side the joy and self-satisfaction you will feel if you refrain. And if the moment seems come to realize it, take heed that you be not overcome by the winning sweetness and attraction of it; set in the other scale the thought how much better is the consciousness of having vanquished it.

35

When you do a thing because you have determined that it ought to be done, never avoid being seen doing it, even if the opinion of the multitude is going to con-

demn you. For if your action is wrong, then avoid doing it altogether, but if it is right, why do you fear those who will rebuke you wrongly?

. . .

37

If you try to act a part beyond your powers, you not only disgrace yourself in it, but you neglect the part which you could have filled with success.

. . .

41

It is a sign of a dull mind to dwell upon the cares of the body, to prolong exercise, eating, drinking, and other bodily functions. These things are to be done by the way; all your attention must be given to the mind.

42

When a man speaks evil or does evil to you, remember that he does or says it because he thinks it is fitting for him. It is not possible for him to follow what seems good to you, but only what seems good to him, so that, if his opinion is wrong, he suffers, in that he is the victim of deception. In the same way, if a composite judgement which is true is thought to be false, it is not the judgement that suffers, but the man who is deluded about it. If you act on this principle you will be gentle to him who reviles you, saying to yourself on each occasion, 'He thought it right.' [18]

[18] The suggestion is that you will not be angry (and thus disrupted) by someone's actions if you assume that the other person thought he had a good reason for what he did.

43

Everything has two handles, one by which you can carry it, the other by which you cannot. If your brother wrongs you, do not take it by that handle, the handle of his wrong, for you cannot carry it by that, but rather by the other handle—that he is a brother, brought up with you, and then you will take it by the handle that you can carry by. [19]

. . .

45

If a man wash quickly, do not say that he washes badly, but that he washes quickly. If a man drink much wine, do not say that he drinks badly, but that he drinks much. For till you have decided what judgement prompts him, how do you know that he acts badly? If you do as I say, you will assent to your apprehensive impressions and to none other.[20]

46

[19] The suggestion here is that while any event can be judged in such a way that you cannot accept the event, it can also be judged in such a way that you can accept the event. If your own peace of mind is the most important thing to you, then you should judge any event in such a way that you can accept it. Does it seem right that *any* event can be judged in such a way that you can accept it?

[20] A more contemporary version of this recommendation is: make no value judgments, but only describe events. Does it seem right that one is not usually in an appropriate position to evaluate someone else's actions?

[21] How is this supposed to be a danger, according to Epictetus? If all I care about are my own thoughts and desires, what does it matter that someone else might think that I'm a fool?

On no occasion call yourself a philosopher, nor talk at large of your principles among the multitude, but act on your principles. For instance, at a banquet do not say how one ought to eat, but eat as you ought. Remember that Socrates had so completely got rid of the thought of display that when men came and wanted an introduction to philosophers he took them to be introduced; so patient of neglect was he. And if a discussion arise among the multitude on some principle, keep silent for the most part; for you are in great danger of blurting out some undigested thought.[21] And when some one says to you, 'You know nothing', and you do not let it provoke you, then know that you are really on the right road. For sheep do not bring grass to their shepherds and show them how much they have eaten, but they digest their fodder and then produce it in the form of wool and milk. Do the same yourself; instead of displaying your principles to the multitude, show them the results of the principles you have digested.

47

When you have adopted the simple life, do not pride yourself upon it, and if you are a water-drinker do not say on every occasion, 'I am a water-drinker.' And if you ever want to train laboriously, keep it to yourself and do not make a show of it.[22] Do not embrace statues. If you are very thirsty take a good draught of cold water, and rinse your mouth and tell no one.

[22] Again, it is not clear what the recommendation of a modest, simple life has to do with the earlier recommendation to care only about one's own thoughts and desires.

48

The ignorant man's position and character is this: he never looks to himself for benefit or harm, but to the world outside him. The philosopher's position and character is that he always look to himself for benefit and harm.

The signs of one who is making progress are: he blames none, praises none, complains of none, accuses none, never speaks of himself as if he were somebody, or as if he knew anything.[23] And if any one compliments him he laughs in himself at his compliment; and if one blames him, he makes no defence. He goes about like a convalescent, careful not to disturb his constitution on its road to recovery, until it has got firm hold. He has got rid of the will to get, and his will to avoid is directed no longer to what is beyond our power but only to what is in our power and contrary to nature. In all things he exercises his will without strain. If men regard him as foolish or ignorant he pays no heed. In one word, he keeps watch and guard on himself as his own enemy, lying in wait for him.

[23] Here is another aspect of the style of conduct recommended by Epictetus: take responsibility for yourself—don't blame others. Obviously you could accept that recommendation while still rejecting the view that you ought to care only about what is in your direct control.

. . .

50

Whatever principles you put before you, hold fast to them as laws which it will be impious to transgress.

But pay no heed to what any one says of you; for this is something beyond your own control.

51

How long will you wait to think yourself worthy of the highest and transgress in nothing the clear pronouncement of reason? You have received the precepts which you ought to accept, and you have accepted them. Why then do you still wait for a master, that you may delay the amendment of yourself till he comes? You are a youth no longer, you are now a full-grown man. If now you are careless and indolent and are always putting off, fixing one day after another as the limit when you mean to begin attending to yourself, then, living or dying, you will make no progress but will continue unawares in ignorance. Therefore make up your mind before it is too late to live as one who is mature and proficient, and let all that seems best to you be a law that you cannot transgress. And if you encounter anything troublesome or pleasant or glorious or inglorious, remember that the hour of struggle is come, the Olympic contest is here and you may put off no longer, and that one day and one action determines whether the progress you have achieved is lost or maintained.

This was how Socrates attained perfection, paying heed to nothing but reason, in all that he encountered. And if you are not yet Socrates, yet ought you to live as one who would wish to be a Socrates.

. . .

Discussion Questions

1. One of the main tenets of Epictetus's thought is that one ought to limit one's desires to what is in one's power, and thus that one ought to accept or submit to all that is outside of one's power. And since all that is really in one's power is how one responds, one should care *only* about how one responds. Remember that Epictetus spent his early life as a slave. Would his view be a plausible recommendation for someone in that specific position? Is its plausibility limited to that situation or one closely similar to it?

2. Do you find the picture recommended by Epictetus attractive? Supposing that you do, is it within your power to do what he recommends? One might argue that Epictetus's thought is an important antidote to the unhealthy obsession with outward things. But can one really control what judgment one makes about an event or how one feels about it?

3. Suppose you could choose between the following three possibilities: in the first case, you want only that which is in your control (according to Epictetus), and thus you get everything that you want; in the second case, you limit your desires to reasonable ones—things that you would expect to be able to achieve, given who you are—and you get most of what you want, but are occasionally disappointed; and in the third case, your wants are uncontrolled and extravagant, and while some few of them are satisfied, you are disappointed about most of them. According to Epictetus, the first case is clearly the best one for human beings: happiness consists in avoiding disappointment as completely as possible. Does that seem right?

4. Epictetus's most fundamental recommendation is to care only about one's own states of mind. Think about the main aspects of the kind of life recommended by Epictetus: one ought to take responsibility for oneself, resisting the temptation to blame others; one ought to live modestly, abstaining from worldly desires; one ought to accept reality, rejecting the futile attempt to control outside events. How, if at all, are these further recommendations related to the fundamental one?

5. What would Epictetus think about Nozick's experience machine? Would he choose to plug in if it were available?

Thomas Nagel

Thomas Nagel (1937–) is an American philosopher who has taught at Princeton and presently at New York University. He has made important contributions to a wide range of areas, including the philosophy of mind, ethics, metaphysics, epistemology, and social philosophy.

It is natural to think that philosophers should have something to say about the meaning of life. For the vast majority of philosophers in the English-speaking world in recent times, however, this question has seemed to be outside the bounds of sober philosophical discussion. Nagel is one of the few recent philosophers who has made any attempt to engage this issue. (Susan Wolf, in the following selection, is another.) Nagel argues that our lives are absurd, though his reasons for this view are more complicated and subtle than those usually given.

The Absurd

Most people feel on occasion that life is absurd, and some feel it vividly and continually.① Yet the reasons usually offered in defense of this conviction are patently inadequate: they *could* not really explain why life is absurd. Why then do they provide a natural expression for the sense that it is?

I

① According to Nagel, most people sometimes find life to be absurd. Have you (or perhaps someone you know well) ever had this experience? If so, what was the content of it? In what way or in what sense did life seem absurd? Try, if you can, to spell out this idea as clearly as you can, before seeing what Nagel has to say about it.

Consider some examples. It is often remarked that nothing we do now will matter in a million years. But if that is true, then by the same token, nothing that will be the case in a million years matters now. In particular, it does not matter now that in a million years nothing we do now will matter. Moreover, even if what we did now *were* going to matter in a million years, how could that keep our present concerns from being absurd? If their mattering now is not enough to accomplish that, how would it help if they mattered a million years from now?

Whether what we do now will matter in a million years could make the crucial difference only if its mattering in a million years depended on its mattering, period. But then to deny that whatever happens now will matter in a million years is to beg the question against its mattering, period; for in that sense one cannot know that it will not matter in a million years whether (for example) someone now is happy or miserable, without knowing that it does not matter, period.②

② For something to "matter, period" is for it to matter *in itself,* apart from any relation to other things that might not have existed—to matter, as Nagel later puts it, *sub specie aeternitatis* (from the perspective of eternity). Most things matter because of their relation to other things—for example, money matters because of what money can get you, but does not "matter, period."

What we say to convey the absurdity of our lives often has to do with space or time: we are tiny specks in the infinite vastness of the universe; our lives are mere instants even on a geological time scale, let alone a cosmic one; we will all be dead any minute. But of course none of these evident facts can be what *makes* life absurd, if it is absurd. For suppose we lived for ever; would not a life that is absurd if it lasts seventy

From Mortal Questions *(Cambridge, Mass.: Cambridge University Press, 1979).*

years be infinitely absurd if it lasted through eternity? And if our lives are absurd given our present size, why

3 Is there, as Nagel suggests, a connection between our "finiteness and brevity" and the sense that our lives are meaningless—and if so, what might that connection be? (As Nagel will make clear later, to say that life is meaningless is not the same thing as to say that it is absurd, though the two claims are connected.)

would they be any less absurd if we filled the universe (either because we were larger or because the universe was smaller)? Reflection on our minuteness and brevity appears to be intimately connected with the sense that life is meaningless; but it is not clear what the connection is.**3**

Another inadequate argument is that because we are going to die, all chains of justification must leave off in mid-air: one studies and works to earn money to pay for clothing, housing, entertainment, food, to sustain oneself from year to year, perhaps to support a family and pursue a career—but to what final end? All of it is an elaborate journey leading nowhere. (One will also have some effect on other people's lives, but that simply reproduces the problem, for they will die too.)

There are several replies to this argument. First, life does not consist of a sequence of activities each of which has as its purpose some later member of the sequence. Chains of justification come repeatedly to

4 It is a fairly common mistake to think that the point or purpose of every act must lie in some further end or goal, so that if the chain of acts terminates (at a person's death or the death of those they affect), then everything he did was without point. But in fact, many acts have a point or meaning in themselves, without this depending on any further ends.

an end within life, and whether the process as a whole can be justified has no bearing on the finality of these end-points. No further justification is needed to make it reasonable to take aspirin for a headache, attend an exhibition of the work of a painter one admires, or stop a child from putting his hand on a hot stove. No larger context or further purpose is needed to prevent these acts from being pointless.**4**

Even if someone wished to supply a further justification for pursuing all the things in life that are commonly regarded as self-justifying, that justification would have to end somewhere too. If *nothing* can justify unless it is justified in terms of something

outside itself, which is also justified, then an infinite regress results, and no chain of justification can be complete. Moreover, if a finite chain of reasons cannot justify anything, what could be accomplished by an infinite chain, each link of which must be justified by something outside itself?**5**

5 Suppose, for example, that we were put on this earth by some powerful being. Our existence, then, is justified by satisfying his purposes, but then what, outside of him, justifies his purposes (which is required if it is true that "*nothing* can justify unless it is justified in terms of something outside itself")?

Since justifications must come to an end somewhere, nothing is gained by denying that they end where they appear to, within life—or by trying to subsume the multiple, often trivial ordinary justifications of action under a single, controlling life scheme. We can be satisfied more easily than that. In fact, through

its misrepresentation of the process of justification, the argument makes a vacuous demand. It insists that the reasons available within life are incomplete, but suggests thereby that all reasons that come to an end are incomplete. This makes it impossible to supply any reasons at all.**6**

6 Nagel is suggesting that this argument for the absurdity of life in effect **begs the question,** by assuming for no good reason that the only way to insure that life is not absurd is to provide a chain of justifications that goes on forever (which is obviously impossible).

The standard arguments for absurdity appear therefore to fail as arguments. Yet I believe they attempt to express something that is difficult to state, but fundamentally correct.

II

In ordinary life a situation is absurd when it includes a conspicuous discrepancy between pretension or aspiration and reality: someone gives a complicated speech in support of a motion that has already been passed; a notorious criminal is made president of a major philanthropic foundation; you declare your love over the telephone to a recorded announcement; as you are being knighted, your pants fall down.**7**

When a person finds himself in an absurd situation, he will usually attempt to change it, by modifying his aspirations, or by trying to bring reality into better accord with them, or by removing himself from the situation entirely. We are not always willing or able to extricate ourselves from a position whose absurdity has become clear to us. Nevertheless, it is usually possible to imagine some change that would remove the absurdity—whether or not we can or will implement it. The sense that life as a whole is absurd arises when we perceive, perhaps dimly, an inflated pretension or aspiration which is inseparable from the continuation of human life and which makes its absurdity inescapable, short of escape from life itself.

Many people's lives are absurd, temporarily or permanently, for conventional reasons having to do with their particular ambitions, circumstances, and personal relations. If there is a philosophical sense of absurdity, however, it must arise from the perception of something universal—some respect in which pretension and reality inevitably clash for us all. This condition is supplied, I shall argue, by the collision between the seriousness with which we take our lives and the perpetual possibility of regarding everything about which we are serious as arbitrary, or open to doubt.

We cannot live human lives without energy and attention, nor without making choices which show that we take some things more seriously than others. Yet we have always available a point of view outside the particular form of our lives, from which the seriousness appears gratuitous. These two inescapable viewpoints collide in us, and that is what makes life absurd. It is absurd because we ignore the doubts that we know cannot be settled, continuing to live with nearly undiminished seriousness in spite of them. [8]

This analysis requires defense in two respects: first as regards the unavoidability of seriousness; second as regards the inescapability of doubt.

We take ourselves seriously whether we lead serious lives or not and whether we are concerned primarily with fame, pleasure, virtues, luxury, triumph, beauty, justice, knowledge, salvation, or mere survival. If we take other people seriously and devote ourselves to them, that only multiplies the problem. Human life is full of effort, plans, calculation, success and failure: we *pursue* our lives, with varying degrees of sloth and energy. [9]

It would be different if we could not step back and reflect on the process, but were merely led from impulse to impulse without self-consciousness. But human beings do not act solely on impulse. They are prudent, they reflect, they weigh consequences, they ask whether what they are doing is worth while. Not only are their lives full of particular choices that hang together in larger activities with temporal structure: they also decide in the broadest terms what to pursue and what to avoid, what the priorities among their various aims should be, and what kind of people they want to be or become. Some men are faced with such choices by the large decisions they make from time to time; some merely by reflection on the course their lives are taking as the product of countless small decisions. They decide whom to marry, what profession to follow, whether to join the Country Club, or the Resistance; or they may just wonder why they go on being salesmen or academics or taxi drivers, and then stop thinking about it after a certain period of inconclusive reflection.

Although they may be motivated from act to act by those immediate needs with which life presents them, they allow the process to continue by adhering to the general system of habits and the form of life in which such motives have their place—or perhaps only by clinging to life itself. They spend enormous quantities of energy, risk, and calculation on the details. Think of how an ordinary individual sweats over his appearance, his health, his sex life, his emotional honesty, his social utility, his self-knowledge, the quality of his ties with family, colleagues, and friends, how well he does his job, whether he understands the world and what is going on in it. Leading a human life is a full-time occupation, to which everyone devotes decades of intense concern. ⑩

> ⑩ Again, more evidence that we take our lives very seriously.

This fact is so obvious that it is hard to find it extraordinary and important. Each of us lives his own life—lives with himself twenty-four hours a day. What else is he supposed to do—live someone else's life? Yet humans have the special capacity to step back and survey themselves, and the lives to which they are committed, with that detached amazement which comes from watching an ant struggle up a heap of sand. Without developing the illusion that they are able to escape from their highly specific and idiosyncratic position, they can view it *sub specie aeternitatis*—and the view is at once sobering and comical.

The crucial backward step is not taken by asking for still another justification in the chain, and failing to get it. The objections to that line of attack have already been stated; justifications come to an end. But this is precisely what provides universal doubt with its object.

> ⑪ According to Nagel, every person has the capacity to "step back" and view his life from "the perspective of eternity," a perspective that transcends the interests and concerns of his life or even of human life generally. From this perspective, he claims, all of our justifications for all of our actions are open to doubt.

We step back to find that the whole system of justification and criticism, which controls our choices and supports our claims to rationality, rests on responses and habits that we never question, that we should not know how to defend without circularity, and to which we shall continue to adhere even after they are called into question. ⑪

The things we do or want without reasons, and without requiring reasons—the things that define what is a reason for us and what is not—are the starting points of our skepticism. We see ourselves from outside, and all the contingency and specificity of our aims and pursuits become clear. Yet when we take this view and recognize what we do as arbitrary, it does not disengage us from life, and there lies our absurdity: not in the fact that such an external view can be taken of us, but in the fact that we ourselves can take it, without ceasing to be the persons whose ultimate concerns are so coolly regarded. ⑫

III

One may try to escape the position by seeking broader ultimate concerns, from which it is impossible to step back—the idea being that absurdity results because what we take seriously is something small and insignificant and individual. Those seeking to supply their lives with meaning usually envision a role or function in something larger than themselves. They therefore seek fulfillment in service to society, the state, the revolution, the progress of history, the advance of science, or religion and the glory of God.

But a role in some larger enterprise cannot confer significance unless that enterprise is itself significant. And its significance must come back to what we can understand, or it will not even appear to give us what we are seeking. If we learned that we were being raised to provide food for other creatures fond of human flesh, who planned to turn us into cutlets before we got too stringy—even if we learned that the human race had been developed by animal breeders precisely for this purpose—that would still not give our lives meaning, for two reasons. First, we would still be in the dark as to the significance of the lives of those other beings; second, although we might acknowledge that this culinary role would make our lives meaningful to them, it is not clear how it would make them meaningful to us. ⑬

> ⑫ Thus we can allegedly take a point of view from which we can recognize that all our actions and purposes are arbitrary. And yet we continue to care about them seriously—and therein, according to Nagel, lies the absurdity. (Do we really *recognize* that the things we care about really are arbitrary—or do they merely *seem* arbitrary from that standpoint? Nagel is unclear on this pretty critical point.)

> ⑬ Nagel's claim is that making a contribution to a larger project cannot *by itself* confer meaning on your life. If we were being raised for food, we would be making a contribution to a larger project. But Nagel is surely right that such a contribution would fail to confer meaning on our lives.

Admittedly, the usual form of service to a higher being is different from this. One is supposed to behold and partake of the glory of God, for example, in a way in which chickens do not share in the glory of coq au vin. The same is true of service to a state, a movement, or a revolution. People can come to feel, when they are part of something bigger, that it is part of them too. They worry less about what is peculiar to themselves, but identify enough with the larger enterprise to find their role in it fulfilling.

However, any such larger purpose can be put in doubt in the same way that the aims of an individual life can be, and for the same reasons. It is as legitimate to find ultimate justification there as to find it earlier, among the details of individual life. But this does not alter the fact that justifications come to an end when we are content to have them end—when we do not find it necessary to look any further. If we can step back from the purposes of individual life and doubt their point, we can step back also from the progress of human history, or of science, or the success of a society, or the kingdom, power, and glory of God, and put all these things into question in the same way.⑭ What seems to us to confer meaning, justification, significance, does so in virtue of the fact that we need no more reasons after a certain point.

What makes doubt inescapable with regard to the limited aims of individual life also makes it inescapable with regard to any larger purpose that encourages the sense that life is meaningful. Once the fundamental doubt has begun, it cannot be laid to rest.

Camus maintains in *The Myth of Sisyphus* that the absurd arises because the world fails to meet our demands for meaning. This suggests that the world might satisfy those demands if it were different. But now we can see that this is not the case. There does not appear to be any conceivable world (containing us) about which unsettlable doubts could not arise. Consequently the absurdity of our situation derives not from a collison between our expectations and the world, but from a collision within ourselves.⑮

IV

It may be objected that the standpoint from which these doubts are supposed to be felt does not exist—that if we take the recommended backward step we will land on thin air, without any basis for judgment about the natural responses we are supposed to be surveying. If we retain our usual standards of what is important, then questions about the significance of what we are doing with our lives will be answerable in the usual way. But if we do not, then those questions can mean nothing to us, since there is no longer any content to the idea of what matters, and hence no content to the idea that nothing does. ⑯

But this objection misconceives the nature of the backward step. It is not supposed to give us an understanding of what is *really* important, so that we see by contrast that our lives are insignificant. We never, in the course of these reflections, abandon the ordinary standards that guide our lives. We merely observe them in operation, and recognize that if they are called into question we can justify them only by reference to themselves, uselessly. We adhere to them because of the way we are put together; what seems to us important or serious or valuable would not seem so if we were differently constituted.⑰

⑭ Is it clear, as Nagel claims, that the significance or justification of any larger purpose (or the source of that purpose) can always be called into question in the same way, by "stepping back"? Many people have thought that the significance of God or God's purposes cannot be doubted in this way, but is there any clear reason why this is supposed to be so? Does Nagel have any clear reason for his opposite claim?

⑮ So it is not just that we *may not* be able to find unchallengeable meaning or significance in our lives, depending on exactly what reality is like, but rather that we are doomed to try forever to find a way to escape such doubts while at the same time seeing clearly that this cannot be done. (Do we in fact see this as clearly as Nagel claims?)

⑯ This is the most serious objection to Nagel's view. It claims that the supposed perspective from which we can legitimately question the standards of significance by which we ordinarily assess our lives does not really exist, because there are no alternative standards of significance to which we can appeal.

⑰ Nagel's first response is that the supposed perspective does not involve alternative standards, but instead lets us see that our standards depend on the sorts of creatures we are and would not apply if we were creatures of a different sort. (Is this really something we see clearly—or is it merely a possibility that cannot be ruled out?)

In ordinary life, to be sure, we do not judge a situation absurd unless we have in mind some standards of seriousness, significance, or harmony with which the absurd can be contrasted. This contrast is not implied by the philosophical judgment of absurdity, and that might be thought to make the concept unsuitable for the expression of such judgments. This is not so, however, for the philosophical judgment depends on another contrast which makes it a natural extension from more ordinary cases. It departs from them only in contrasting the pretensions of life with a larger context in which *no* standards can be discovered, rather than with a context from which alternative, overriding standards may be applied. ⟨18⟩

⟨18⟩ Here is what seems like a different answer: from the larger perspective, there are no standards of significance to be discerned—thereby allegedly showing the arbitrariness of the ordinary standards of significance that we employ in our more limited perspective. (But why should we assume that the larger perspective provides the more accurate view, rather than just making it hard to see something that is still perfectly genuine?)

V

⟨19⟩ What Nagel is calling epistemological skepticism is the doubt that we know anything at all, the doubt that we even know anything about ordinary aspects of our world, ordinary things like tables and chairs and trees and cars.

In this respect, as in others, philosophical perception of the absurd resembles epistemological skepticism. ⟨19⟩ In both cases the final, philosophical doubt is not contrasted with any unchallenged certainties, though it is arrived at by extrapolation from examples of doubt within the system of evidence or justification, where a contrast with other certainties *is* implied. In both cases our limitedness joins with a capacity to transcend those limitations in thought (thus seeing them as limitations, and as inescapable).

Skepticism begins when we include ourselves in the world about which we claim knowledge. We notice that certain types of evidence convince us, that we are content to allow justifications of belief to come to an end at certain points, that we feel we know many things even without knowing or having grounds for believing the denial of others which, if true, would make what we claim to know false.

For example, I know that I am looking at a piece of paper, although I have no adequate grounds for claiming I know that I am not dreaming; and if I am dreaming then I am not looking at a piece of paper. Here an ordinary conception of how appearance may diverge from reality is employed to show that we take our world largely for granted; the certainty that we are not dreaming cannot be justified except circularly, in terms of those very appearances which are being put in doubt. ⟨20⟩ It is somewhat far-fetched to suggest I may be dreaming; but the possibility is only illustrative. It reveals that our claims to knowledge depend on our not feeling it necessary to exclude certain incompatible alternatives, and the dreaming possibility or the total-hallucination possibility are just representatives for limitless possibilities most of which we cannot even conceive. ⟨21⟩

⟨20⟩ Here is a different example. On Nagel's view, I am confident that I'm not in an experience machine (see the Nozick selection in this chapter) only because of my sense experience, but that would be the same whether I was in the experience machine or not. Thus my sense experience cannot justify the claim that I am *not* in an experience machine. (For more on this issue, including some views that disagree with Nagel on this point, see Chapter 3.)

⟨21⟩ So, on Nagel's view, I am confident that I'm not now in an experience machine, while at the same time seeing clearly that I have no justification for my confidence. This is supposed to be parallel to the situation in which I continue to take my goals and purposes seriously while recognizing at the same time that I have no good reason to do so (or at least that there is a perspective from which there *seems* to be no good reason).

Once we have taken the backward step to an abstract view of our whole system of beliefs, evidence, and justification, and seen that it works only, despite its pretensions, by taking the world largely for granted, we are *not* in a position to contrast all these appearances with an alternative reality. We cannot shed our ordinary responses, and if we could it would leave us with no means of conceiving a reality of any kind.

It is the same in the practical domain. We do not step outside our lives to a new vantage point from which we see what is really, objectively significant.

We continue to take life largely for granted while seeing that all our decisions and certainties are possible only because there is a great deal we do not bother to rule out.

Both epistemological skepticism and a sense of the absurd can be reached via initial doubts posed within systems of evidence and justification that we accept, and can be stated without violence to our ordinary concepts. We can ask not only why we should believe there is a floor under us, but also why we should believe the evidence of our senses at all—and at some point the framable questions will have outlasted the answers. [22] Similarly, we can ask not only why we should take aspirin, but why we should take trouble over our own comfort at all. The fact that we shall take the aspirin without waiting for an answer to this last question does not show that it is an unreal question. We shall also continue to believe there is a floor under us without waiting for an answer to the other question. In both cases it is this unsupported natural confidence that generates skeptical doubts; so it cannot be used to settle them.

Philosophical skepticism does not cause us to abandon our ordinary beliefs, but it lends them a peculiar flavor. After acknowledging that their truth is incompatible with possibilities that we have no grounds for believing do not obtain—apart from grounds in those very beliefs which we have called into question—we return to our familiar convictions with a certain irony and resignation. Unable to abandon the natural responses on which they depend, we take them back, like a spouse who has run off with someone else and then decided to return; but we regard them differently (not that the new attitude is necessarily inferior to the old, in either case). [23]

[22] Nagel's claim is that we are left with skepticism and a sense of the absurdity of life because there are questions that seem to make sense but have no answers.

[23] Even if I become convinced that I have no good reasons to trust my senses, that I have no good reason for believing that there is a table in front of me, I'll still believe that there is a table in front of me, if it seems that way to me. But the realization that there is in the end no good reason for this belief is supposed to give a "peculiar flavor" to this belief—a sense of its insecure status even as we accept it.

The same situation obtains after we have put in question the seriousness with which we take our lives and human life in general and have looked at ourselves without presuppositions. We then return to our lives, as we must, but our seriousness is laced with irony. Not that irony enables us to escape the absurd. It is useless to mutter: 'Life is meaningless; life is meaningless . . .' as an accompaniment to everything we do. In continuing to live and work and strive, we take ourselves seriously in action no matter what we say. [24]

What sustains us, in belief as in action, is not reason or justification, but something more basic than these—for we go on in the same way even after we are convinced that the reasons have given out. If we tried to rely entirely on reason, and pressed it hard, our lives and beliefs would collapse—a form of madness that may actually occur if the inertial force of taking the world and life for granted is somehow lost. If we lose our grip on that, reason will not give it back to us.

[24] Similarly, after realizing the absurdity that Nagel is arguing for, we continue to take our lives seriously, but with the ironic realization that the significance we attach to them cannot ultimately be justified (or ultimately does not exist?—again, it is not clear which of these things Nagel is saying).

VI

In viewing ourselves from a perspective broader than we can occupy in the flesh, we become spectators of our own lives. We cannot do very much as pure spectators of our own lives, so we continue to lead them, and devote ourselves to what we are able at the same time to view as no more than a curiosity, like the ritual of an alien religion.

This explains why the sense of absurdity finds its natural expression in those bad arguments with which the discussion began. Reference to our small size and short lifespan and to the fact that all of mankind will eventually vanish without a trace are metaphors for the backward step which permits us to regard ourselves from without and to find the particular form of our lives curious and slightly surprising. By feigning a nebula's-eye view, we illustrate the capacity to see ourselves without presuppositions, as arbitrary, idiosyncratic, highly specific occupants of the world, one of countless possible forms of life.(25)

Before turning to the question whether the absurdity of our lives is something to be regretted and if possible escaped, let me consider what would have to be given up in order to avoid it.

Why is the life of a mouse not absurd? The orbit of the moon is not absurd either, but that involves no strivings or aims at all. A mouse, however, has to work to stay alive. Yet he is not absurd, because he lacks the capacities for self-consciousness and self-transcendence that would enable him to see that he is only a mouse. If that *did* happen, his life would become absurd, since self-awareness would not make him cease to be a mouse and would not enable him to rise above his mousely strivings. Bringing his new-found self-consciousness with him, he would have to return to his meager yet frantic life, full of doubts that he was unable to answer, but also full of purposes that he was unable to abandon.(26)

Given that the transcendental step is natural to us humans, can we avoid absurdity by refusing to take that step and remaining entirely within our sublunar lives? Well, we cannot refuse consciously, for to do that we would have to be aware of the viewpoint we were refusing to adopt. The only way to avoid the relevant self-consciousness would be either never to attain it or to forget it—neither of which can be achieved by the will.

On the other hand, it is possible to expend effort on an attempt to destroy the other component of the absurd—abandoning one's earthly, individual, human life in order to identify as completely as possible with that universal viewpoint from which human life seems arbitrary and trivial. (This appears to be the ideal of certain Oriental religions.) If one succeeds, then one will not have to drag the superior awareness through a strenuous mundane life, and absurdity will be diminished.

However, insofar as this self-etiolation is the result of effort, will-power, asceticism, and so forth, it requires that one take oneself seriously as an individual—that one be willing to take considerable trouble to avoid being creaturely and absurd. Thus one may undermine the aim of unworldliness by pursuing it too vigorously.(27) Still, if someone simply allowed his individual, animal nature to drift and respond to impulse, without making the pursuit of its needs a central conscious aim, then he might, at considerable dissociative cost, achieve a life that was less absurd than most. It would not be a meaningful life either, of course; but it would not involve the engagement of a transcendent awareness in the assiduous pursuit of mundane goals. And that is the main condition of absurdity—the dragooning of an unconvinced transcendent consciousness into the service of an immanent, limited enterprise like a human life.(28)

The final escape is suicide; but before adopting any hasty solutions, it would be wise to consider carefully whether the absurdity of our existence truly presents us with a *problem,* to which some solution must be found—a way of dealing with *prima facie* disaster. That is certainly the attitude with which Camus approaches the issue, and it gains support from the fact that we are all eager to escape from absurd situations on a smaller scale.(29)

Camus—not on uniformly good grounds—rejects suicide and the other solutions he regards as escapist. What he recommends is defiance or scorn. We can salvage our dignity, he appears to believe, by shaking a fist at the world which is deaf to our pleas, and continuing to live in spite of it. This will not make

---

(25) Nagel returns to the suggestion, made briefly earlier, that there could be very different kinds of creatures, creatures who care about very different kinds of things. But why is the fact, even if it is a fact, that there could be creatures who care about very different kinds of things *relevant to* whether or not I should take the things I care about seriously?

(26) The mouse would now have grave doubts about those purposes he cannot abandon. Before he had those doubts, his life was not absurd, but once he has the doubts, his life becomes absurd, given that he nonetheless cannot avoid seriously pursuing those purposes.

(27) The other way to eliminate the absurdity of one's life is to stop taking life so seriously. But to pursue this course too vigorously would defeat itself by being a way of taking life seriously after all.

(28) Notice that our lives are *not* absurd merely because they are meaningless. What leads to absurdity is the double apprehension (a) that the seriousness with which we take our lives is not justified, and (b) that we can't seem to stop taking our lives seriously.

(29) Is the absurdity that Nagel claims to have explained even a serious problem at all, let alone one that might reasonably motivate suicide?

our lives un-absurd, but it will lend them a certain nobility.*

This seems to me romantic and slightly self-pitying. Our absurdity warrants neither that much distress nor that much defiance. At the risk of falling into romanticism by a different route, I would argue that absurdity is one of the most human things about us: a manifestation of our most advanced and interesting characteristics. Like skepticism in epistemology, it is possible only because we possess a certain kind of insight—the capacity to transcend ourselves in thought.

If a sense of the absurd is a way of perceiving our true situation (even though the situation is not absurd until the perception arises), then what reason can we have to resent or escape it? Like the capacity for epistemological skepticism, it results from the ability to understand our human limitations. It need not be a matter for agony unless we make it so.㉚ Nor need it evoke a defiant contempt of fate that allows us to feel brave or proud. Such dramatics, even if carried on in private, betray a failure to appreciate the cosmic unimportance of the situation. If *sub specie aeternitatis* there is no reason to believe that anything matters, then that does not matter either, and we can approach our absurd lives with irony instead of heroism or despair.㉛

㉚ Epictetus would approve of Nagel's attitude here.

㉛ Suppose that Nagel is right about the absurdity of our lives. Does *irony* seem like an appropriate response to that fact? (See Discussion Question 3.)

Discussion Questions

1. In *The Myth of Sisyphus,* Albert Camus writes: "The gods had condemned Sisyphus to ceaselessly rolling a rock to the top of a mountain, whence the stone would fall back of its own weight. They had thought with some reason that there is no more dreadful punishment than futile and hopeless labor." What do you think about Sisyphus's life—is it meaningless? Does it matter whether he enjoys the task or not? If Sisyphus fully realizes how futile his task is and thus does not take his efforts seriously, then his life is not absurd (in the very specific sense that Nagel specifies). Suppose that Sisyphus takes his task very seriously, as we take our lives. What else would have to be true of him in order to keep his life from being absurd?

2. It is the paradoxical character of our lives that makes them absurd, according to Nagel, where the paradox consists in our being unable to stop taking our lives seriously even though we can see, from the broader perspective, that there is no reason (or at least seems to be no reason) to take them seriously. Consider his reasons for the claim that from the broader perspective there is no reason to take our lives seriously. One crucial reason, one he seems to think is sufficient for the claim, is that there could be lives very different from ours, lives led by creatures who take very different things seriously. It is surely true, that *from their perspective,* there is no reason to take seriously the things we take seriously. But the broader perspective is not their particular perspective. What exactly is the broader perspective?

3. Suppose that Nagel is right about the paradoxical nature of the human condition: that we are unable to stop taking our lives seriously even though we can see, from the broader perspective, that there is no reason to take them seriously. Does that seem like a problem that needs a solution? Camus thinks so and recommends defiance. Nagel thinks not and seems to endorse the ironic response to the absurdity of our lives. What seems to you to be the right response, given the assumption that Nagel is right about the nature of the human condition?

4. Suppose that someone were to respond to Nagel in the following way: "All this talk of the

---

*'Sisyphus, proletarian of the gods, powerless and rebellious, knows the whole extent of his wretched condition: it is what he thinks of during his descent. The lucidity that was to constitute his torture at the same time crowns his victory. There is no fate that cannot be surmounted by scorn' (*The Myth of Sisyphus,* trans. Justin O'Brien (New York: Vintage, 1959), p. 90; first published, Paris: Gallimard, 1942).

perspective of eternity or the larger perspective makes little real sense. Perhaps we can have some faint idea of such a perspective, but not enough of one to give us any clear idea of what things would look like from there. And even if we were sure (which we cannot ever be), that from the larger perspective our actions or our standards of significance would not *seem* justified, that isn't enough to show that they really are unjustified or arbitrary. The most we would ever have is a conflict between that perspective and our ordinary one, and what seems true from our ordinary perspective is both much clearer and has a far greater claim to be correct (because of its clarity and apparent cogency) than anything about this elusive and murky alternative perspective. Thus Nagel has offered no real reason for thinking that our lives are absurd, or even for taking the possibility of absurdity seriously." Which view seems to you more defensible, Nagel's or that of the imagined critic? How would you argue further for one side or the other?

Susan Wolf

Susan Wolf (1952–) teaches philosophy at the University of North Carolina-Chapel Hill (and previously at the University of Maryland and Johns Hopkins University). Her work focuses on ethics, with special attention to issues concerning free will and moral responsibility. Wolf is another one of the very few philosophers who are willing to articulate and defend a view about the meaning of life. In this selection, she argues that one who is actively engaged in projects that are objectively worthwhile is living a meaningful life.

Happiness and Meaning: Two Aspects of the Good Life

The topic of self-interest raises large and intractable philosophical questions—most obviously, the question "In what does self-interest consist?" The concept, as opposed to the content of self-interest, however, seems clear enough. Self-interest is interest in one's own good. To act self-interestedly is to act on the motive of advancing one's own good. Whether what one does actually is in one's self interest depends on whether it actually does advance, or at least, minimize the decline of, one's own good. Though it may be difficult to tell whether a person is motivated by self-interest in a particular instance, and difficult also to determine whether a given act or decision really is in one's self interest, the meaning of the claims in question seems unproblematic.①

My main concern in this essay is to make a point about the content of self-interest.* Specifically I shall put forward the view that meaningfulness, in a sense I shall elaborate, is an important element of a good life. It follows, then, that it is part of an enlightened self-interest that one wants to secure meaning in one's life, or, at any rate, to

> ① It is not always easy to tell what truly motivates someone, and it is not always easy to tell what is truly good for someone, but if one's act *is* motivated by what one thinks is in one's own good, then it is a self-interested act.

From Social Philosophy & Policy, *Vol. 14, No. 1 (Winter 1997).*

---

*The view described and defended here shows the influence of and my sympathy with the views of Aristotle and John Stuart Mill throughout. I cannot individuate my debts to them; they are pervasive.

allow and promote meaningful activity within it. Accepting this substantial conception of self-interest, however, carries with it a curious consequence: the concept of self-interest which formerly seemed so clear begins to grow fuzzy. Fortunately, it comes to seem less important as well.②

THEORIES OF SELF-INTEREST

② Though Wolf's ultimate concern (which emerges mainly at the end of the paper) is with issues pertaining to self-interest, the bulk of the paper argues for a particular conception of the good life (a view that plays a crucial role in her argument about self-interest).

③ Nozick's experience machine should be very attractive to a hedonist, since one would thereby have great control over one's own subjective experiences, enhancing one's own good.

In *Reasons and Persons,** Derek Parfit distinguishes three sorts of theories about self-interest — hedonistic theories, preference theories, and what he calls "objective-list theories." *Hedonistic theories* hold that one's good is a matter of the felt quality of one's experiences. The most popular theory of self-interest, which identifies self-interest with happiness, and happiness with pleasure and the absence of pain, is a prime example of a hedonistic theory.③ Noting that some people do not care that much about their own happiness, however—and, importantly, that they do not even regard their own happiness as the exclusive element in their own good—has led some to propose a *preference theory* of self-interest, which would identify a person's good with what the person most wants for herself. Thus, for example, if a person cares more about being famous, even posthumously famous, than about being happy, then a preference theory would accord fame a proportionate weight in the identification of her self-interest. If a person cares more about knowing the truth than about believing what is pleasant or comfortable to believe, then it in her self-interest to have the truth, unpleasant as it may be.④

A person's preferences regarding herself, however may be self-destructive or otherwise bizarre, and it may be that some things (including pleasure) are good for a person whether the person prefers them or not. It is not absurd to think that being deceived is bad for a person (and thus that not being deceived is good for a person) whether or not the person in question consciously values this state. Friendship and love may also seem to be things whose goodness explains, rather than results from, people's preferences for them. The plausibility of these last thoughts explains the appeal of *objective-list theories,* according to which a person's good includes at least some elements that are independent of or prior to her preferences and to their effect on the felt quality of her experience. On this view, there are some items, ideally specifiable on an "objective list," whose relevance to a fully successful life are not conditional on the subject's choice.⑤

④ There are no constraints on what you might prefer, according to this type of theory about self-interest. Your good has been enhanced as long as your preferences are satisfied.

⑤ Only according to this third kind of theory does self-interest involve requirements that are objective in the sense that they go beyond the individual person's happiness or preferences. What exactly these objective requirements are depends on what is on the "objective list."

The view that I shall be advancing, that meaningfulness is an ingredient of the good life, commits one to a version of this last kind of theory, for my claim is that meaningfulness is a nonderivative aspect of a good life—its goodness does not result from its making us happy or its satisfying the preferences of the person whose life it is. Thus, it follows that any theory that takes self-interest to be a wholly subjective matter, either in a sense that identifies self-interest with the subjective quality of a person's subjective experiences or in a sense that allows the standards of self-interest to be set by a person's subjective preferences, must be inadequate. At the same time, it would be a mistake to think that the objective good for a person to live a meaningful life is one that is wholly independent of the subject's experience or preferences, as if it could be good for a person to live a meaningful life whether or not it makes her happy or satisfies her preferences. Indeed, as we will see, the very idea that activities can make a life

*Derek Parfit, *Reasons and Persons* (Oxford: Oxford University Press, 1984).

meaningful without the subject's endorsement is a dubious one.

MEANING IN LIFE

What is a meaningful life? Spelling it out will constitute the bulk of my essay, for my hope is that once the idea is spelled out, it will be readily agreed that it is an element of a fully successful life.

A meaningful life is, first of all, one that has within it the basis for an affirmative answer to the needs or longings that are characteristically described as needs for meaning. I have in mind, for example, the sort of questions people ask on their deathbeds, or simply in contemplation of their eventual deaths, about whether their lives have been (or are) worth living, whether they have had any point, and the sort of questions one asks when considering suicide and wondering whether one has any reason to go on.[6] These questions are familiar from Russian novels and existentialist philosophy, if not from personal experience. Though they arise most poignantly in times of crisis and intense emotion, they also have their place in moments of calm reflection, when considering important life choices. Moreover, paradigms of what are taken to be meaningful and meaningless lives in our culture are readily available. Lives of great moral or intellectual accomplishment—Gandhi, Mother Teresa, Albert Einstein—come to mind as unquestionably meaningful lives (if any are); lives of waste and isolation—Thoreau's "lives of quiet desperation," typically anonymous to the rest of us, and the mythical figure of Sisyphus—represent meaninglessness.[7]

To what general characteristics of meaningfulness do these images lead us and how do they provide an answer to the longings mentioned above? Roughly, I would say that meaningful lives are lives of active engagement in projects of worth. Of course, a good deal needs to be said in elaboration of this statement. Let me begin by discussing the two key phrases, "active engagement" and "projects of worth."

A person is actively engaged by something if she is gripped, excited, involved by it. Most obviously, we are actively engaged by the things and people about which and whom we are passionate. Opposites of active engagement are boredom and alienation. To be actively engaged in something is not always pleasant in the ordinary sense of the word. Activities in which people are actively engaged frequently involve stress, danger, exertion, or sorrow (consider, for example: writing a book, climbing a mountain, training for a marathon, caring for an ailing friend). However, there is something good about the feeling of engagement: one feels (typically without thinking about it) especially alive.[8]

That a meaningful life must involve "projects of worth" will, I expect, be more controversial, for the phrase hints of a commitment to some sort of objective value. This is not accidental, for I believe that the idea of meaningfulness, and the concern that our lives possess it, are conceptually linked to such a commitment. Indeed, it is this linkage that I want to defend, for I have neither a philosophical theory of what objective value is nor a substantive theory about what has this sort of value. What is clear to me is that there can be no sense to the idea of meaningfulness without a distinction between more and less worthwhile ways to spend one's time, where the test of worth is at least partly independent of a subject's ungrounded preferences or enjoyment.[9]

Consider first the longings or concerns about meaning that people have, their wondering whether their lives are meaningful, their vows to add more meaning to their lives. The sense of these concerns and resolves cannot fully be captured by an account in which what one does

---

[6] Suppose that Wolf is right that many people want more out of life than pleasant experiences, that when they look back on their life, they want it to be something more than a life full of pleasant experiences. Is "meaning" that extra something that people want—or can you think of another way to articulate that something extra?

---

[7] Sisyphus was condemned by the gods to roll a rock up a mountain, just to have it roll back down, over and over again, for the rest of his life.

---

[8] Even Mother Theresa's life (assume that it is obviously worthwhile) is not *meaningful*, according to Wolf, if she is bored with it or apathetic.

---

[9] Suppose, for example, that you really enjoyed counting blades of grass in your yard. Wolf's claim is that such an activity must have some independent value (in addition to the fact that you enjoy it) in order for it to have objective worth. (See Discussion Question 2.)

with one's life doesn't matter, as long as one enjoys or prefers it. Sometimes people have concerns about meaning despite their knowledge that their lives to date have been satisfying. Indeed, their enjoyment and "active engagement" with activities and values they now see as shallow seems only to heighten the sense of meaninglessness that comes to afflict them. Their sense that their lives so far have been meaningless cannot be a sense that their activities have not been chosen or fun. When they look for sources of meaning or ways to add meaning to their lives, they are searching for projects whose justifications lie elsewhere.

Second, we need an explanation for why certain sorts of activities and involvements come to mind as contributors to meaningfulness while others seem intuitively inappropriate. Think about what gives meaning to your own life and the lives of your friends and acquaintances. Among the things that tend to come up on such lists, I have already mentioned moral and intellectual accomplishments and the ongoing activities that lead to them. Relationships with friends and relatives are perhaps even more important for most of us. Aesthetic enterprises (both creative and appreciative), the cultivation of personal virtues, and religious practices frequently loom large. By contrast, it would be odd, if not bizarre, to think of crossword puzzles, sitcoms, or the kind of computer games to which I am fighting off addiction as providing meaning in our lives, though there is no question that they afford a sort of satisfaction and that they are the objects of choice. Some things, such as chocolate and aerobics class, I choose even at considerable cost to myself (it is irrelevant that these particular choices may be related), so I must find them worthwhile in a sense. But they are not the sorts of things that make life worth living.

"Active engagement in projects of worth," I suggest, answers to the needs an account of meaningfulness in life must meet. If a person is or has been thus actively engaged, then she does have an answer to the question of whether her life is or has been worthwhile, whether it has or has had a point. When someone looks for ways to add meaning to her life, she is looking (though perhaps not under this description) for worthwhile projects about which she can get enthused. [10] The account also explains why some activities and projects but not others come to mind as contributors to meaning in life. Some projects, or at

any rate, particular acts, are worthwhile but too boring or mechanical to be sources of meaning. People do not get meaning from recycling or from writing checks to Oxfam and the ACLU. Other acts and activities, though highly pleasurable and deeply involving, like riding a roller coaster or meeting a movie star, do not seem to have the right kind of value to contribute to meaning.

> [10] Notice that you have to be able to be *enthusiastic* about the project. If you are not enthused, then you won't be actively engaged, according to Wolf's view.

Bernard Williams once distinguished categorical desires from the rest. Categorical desires give us reasons for living—they are not premised on the assumption that we will live. The sorts of things that give meaning to life tend to be objects of categorical desire. We desire them, at least so I would suggest, because we think them worthwhile. They are not worthwhile simply because we desire them or simply because they make our lives more pleasant. [11]

Roughly, then, according to my proposal, a meaningful life must satisfy two criteria, suitably linked. First, there must be active engagement, and second, it must be engagement in (or with) projects of worth. A life is meaningless if it lacks active engagement with anything. A person who is bored or alienated from most of what she spends her life doing is one whose life can be said to lack meaning. Note that she may in fact be performing functions of worth. A housewife and mother, a doctor, or a busdriver may be competently doing a socially valuable job, but because she is not engaged by her work (or, as we are assuming, by anything else in her life), she has no categorical desires that give her a reason to live. At the same time, someone who *is* actively engaged may also live a meaningless life, if the objects of her involvement are utterly worthless. It is difficult to come up with examples of such lives that will be uncontroversial without being bizarre. But both bizarre and controversial examples have their place. In the bizarre category, we

> [11] According to Wolf's view, the order of dependence here is very important. If you are attracted to something because you judge that it is worthwhile, then it may provide meaning to your life. But if you judge that it is worthwhile merely because you are attracted to it, and you have no reason beyond your own pleasure for being attracted to it, then it is not capable of providing meaning to your life.

might consider pathological cases: someone whose sole passion in life is collecting rubber bands, or memorizing the dictionary, or making handwritten copies of *War and Peace*. Controversial cases will include the corporate lawyer who sacrifices her private life and health for success along the professional ladder, the devotee of a religious cult, or . . . the pig farmer who buys more land to grow more corn to feed more pigs to buy more land to grow more corn to feed more pigs.

We may summarize my proposal in terms of a slogan: "Meaning arises when subjective attraction meets objective attractiveness." The idea is that in a world in which some things are more worthwhile than others, meaning arises when a subject discovers or develops an affinity for one or typically several of the more worthwhile things and has and makes use of the opportunity to engage with it or them in a positive way.

An advantage of the slogan is that it avoids the somewhat misleading reference to "projects." That term is less than ideal in its suggestion of well-defined and goal-oriented tasks. To be sure, many projects do add meaning to life—mastering a field of study, building a house, turning a swamp into a garden, curing cancer—but much of what gives meaning to life consists in ongoing relationships and involvements—with friends, family, the scientific community, with church or ballet or chess. These ongoing strands of life give rise to and are partly constituted by projects—you plan a surprise party for your spouse, coach a little league team, review an article for a journal—but the meaning comes less from the individuated projects than from the larger involvements of which they are parts. The slogan, moreover, is intentionally vague, for if pretheoretical judgments about meaning even approximate the truth, then not only the objects of worth but also the sorts of interaction with them that are capable of contributing to meaning are immensely variable. One can get meaning from creating, promoting, protecting (worthwhile) things, from helping people one loves and people in need, from achieving levels of skill and excellence, from overcoming obstacles, from gaining understanding, and even from just communing with or actively appreciating what is there to be appreciated. ⑫

It is part of our job, if not our natural bent, as philosophers to be skeptical—about the correctness of these pretheoretical judgments, about our ability reliably to distinguish meaningful from meaningless activities, and about the very coherence of the distinction. About the first two worries I am not very concerned. Assuming that the distinctions are coherent and that some activities are more worthwhile than others, our culture-bound, contemporary judgments of which activities are worthwhile are bound to be partly erroneous. History is full of unappreciated geniuses, of artists, inventors, explorers whose activities at their time were scorned, as it is full of models of behavior and accomplishment that later seem to have been overrated. Though we may improve our judgments, both particular and general, by an open-minded, concentrated, and communal effort to examine and articulate the basis for them (a project that strikes me as both worthwhile and intrinsically interesting), the hope or expectation that such scrutiny will yield a reliable method for generally distinguishing worthwhile from worthless activities seems overly optimistic. Why do we respect people who devote themselves to chess more than those who become champions at pinball? Why do we admire basketball stars more than jump-rope champions? What is more worthwhile about writing a book on the philosophy of language than writing one on Nicole Brown Simpson's sex life? It is useful to ask and to answer such questions, so far as we can, both to widen and correct our horizons and to increase our understanding. But our inability to give complete and adequate answers, or to be confident in the details of our assessments, need not be a serious problem. The point of recognizing the distinction, after all, is not to give rankings of meaningful lives. There is no need, in general, to pass judgment on individuals or even on activities in which people want to engage. The point is rather at a more general level to understand the ingredients of our own and others' good, and to get a better idea of the sorts of considerations that provide reasons for living our lives one way rather than another. ⑬

The point, which I am in the midst of developing, is that meaningfulness is a nonderivative part of an in-

⑫ It is so easy to see how activities that contribute to well-defined projects or goals count toward a meaningful life that one might fail to appreciate the importance of more ordinary activities—ones that do not contribute to a specific project, but are still important to a meaningful life because of the relationships and involvements they reflect.

dividual's good, and that meaningfulness consists in active engagement in projects or activities of worth.

[13] To accept the distinction between meaningful and meaningless activities does not require that that it is easy to distinguish the two in practice or that there cannot be debatable cases. Nor does it require that you be concerned with ranking the lives of your friends and family (and yourself) in this respect.

Though it seems to me that the point and most of its usefulness can stand despite acknowledged difficulties with identifying precisely which projects or activities these are, it would be utterly destroyed if it turned out that there were no such things as projects or activities of worth at all—if it turned out, in other words, as Bentham thought, that pushpin were as good as poetry, not because of some heretofore undiscovered excellences in the game of pushpin, but because the very idea of distinctions in worth is bankrupt or incoherent. If there are no projects of worth (in contrast to other projects), then there are no such things as what I have in mind by more and less meaningful lives, and so it cannot be a part of one's good to live a more meaningful rather than a less meaningful life. If the idea of a worthwhile project is just a fraud or a hoax, then my account of self-interest is undone by it.

Since I have no *theory* of worth by which to prove the coherence of the concept or refute all skeptical challenges, I can only acknowledge the vulnerability of my account of self-interest in this regard. That we do, most of us, believe that some activities and projects are more worthwhile than others, that we regard certain activities as wastes of time (or near wastes of time) and others as inherently valuable, seems undeniable. These beliefs lie behind dispositions to feel proud or disgusted with ourselves for time spent well or badly, and they account for at least some of our efforts to steer our children and our friends toward some activities and away from others. When I try to take up a point of view that denies the distinction between worthwhile and worthless activity, I cannot find it convincing. Still, it is an article of faith that these untheoretical judgments, or some core of them, are philosophically defensible. It is on the assumption that they are defensible that my views about meaningfulness and self-interest are built. [14]

TWO CHALLENGES

My proposal so far has been that meaningfulness in life arises from engagement in worthwhile activity. I have argued for the plausibility of this account on the grounds that it fits well both with the needs that are typically referred

[14] Does it seem right to you that we all believe that there is a distinction between worthwhile and worthless activities? To what extent could people agree about which activities are worthwhile and which are worthless?

to as needs for meaning and with the concrete judgments of meaningful and meaningless activity that are most commonly made. Before proceeding with an examination of the relation between meaning and self-interest, two challenges to this account of meaning should be answered.

The first objects that, contrary to my claims, my account of meaning fails to meet the requirements I have set up for it. It fails, more particularly, to answer to the needs of at least one type of longing for meaning that members of our species tend to have. Traditional worries about the meaning of life, often set off by reflections on our own mortality and on the indifference of the cosmos in which we occupy so tiny a place, are rarely appeased by the reflection that one can actively engage in projects of worth. At least, they are not appeased by reflection on the availability of the kind of projects I have been talking about, like taking up the cello, writing a novel, volunteering at a child's day-care center or a nursing home. Tolstoy, the publicly acclaimed author of some of the greatest works of literature ever written, the father and spouse of what he described (perhaps inaccurately) as a loving and successful family, could have had no doubt that, relatively speaking, his life was spent in projects as worthwhile as any. Yet he was plagued by the thought that it was all for naught.* Nothing he did seemed to save his life from meaninglessness. Like Tolstoy, such philosophers as Albert Camus† and Thomas Nagel‡ see the meaning or meaninglessness

---

*See Leo Tolstoy, "My Confession," in E. D. Klemke, ed., *The Meaning of Life* (New York: Oxford University Press, 1981).

†Albert Camus, *The Myth of Sisyphus and Other Essays* (New York: Vintage Books, 1955).

‡Thomas Nagel, "The Absurd," in Nagel, *Mortal Questions* (Cambridge: Cambridge University Press 1979).

of life as an issue relating to the human condition. The difference between a person who wastes her time in frivolous or shallow pursuits and one who makes something of herself and serves humanity cannot, on their views, make the difference between a meaningful and a meaningless life. 15

> 15 According to this first objection, Wolf is wrong that actively engaging in objectively worthwhile activities provides meaning to one's life. Genuine meaning requires something more than this, perhaps something unobtainable for human beings.

To try to give a wholly adequate answer to this challenge would take us too far afield from the purposes of this essay. The issue of The Meaning of Life is too obscure and complex, and the differences among the philosophers whose views seem to pose a challenge to the one I am offering call for different responses. Some brief remarks, however, will at least indicate what a more detailed answer might look like and will give some reason for thinking that the challenge can be met.

Among those who think that meaning in life, or the lack of it, is primarily concerned with facts about the human condition, some disagree not with my general account of meaning but with, if you will, its application. Their position, in other words, shares my view that meaning comes from engagement in projects of worth, but assigns certain facts about the human condition a crucial role in settling whether there are any such projects. If God does not exist, they think, then nothing is any more worthwhile than anything else. Within this group, some believe that God is the only possible standard for judgments of nonsubjective value. If God does not exist, they think, then neither does moral or aesthetic value or any other sort of value that could distinguish some projects as better than others. Others believe that though there may be a difference between great literature and junk, and between virtue and vice, there is no point in bothering about which you occupy yourself with. Nothing lasts forever; the human race will be destroyed; the earth will crash into the sun. Only God, and the promise of an eternal life either for ourselves or for the universe in which our accomplishments have a place, can give a point to our living lives one way rather than another. Only God can make meaningful life so much as a possibility. 16

My own view about this position is that it expresses an irrational obsession with permanence; but

it is enough for the purposes of this essay to note that it does not really challenge the account of meaning I have offered. I have already acknowledged that the usefulness of my account rests on the assumption that the distinction between worthwhile and worthless projects is defensible, and on the assumption that at least a core of our beliefs about what is worthwhile and what is worthless is roughly correct. Those who think that God is a necessary grounding for these assumptions and who believe in Him may still find my account of meaning acceptable. Those who think that God is a necessary grounding that unfortunately does not exist will reject my substantive claims about meaning for reasons we have already admitted.

Others, including Nagel and arguably Camus, think that there are differences between better and worse ways to live our lives. Evidently, they think that projects and activities can be more and less worthwhile, and that we have some sort of reason to favor the more worthwhile. They do not, however, see these facts as supplying a basis for meaning. Like the group just discussed, they link meaning inextricably to facts about our place in space-time and in the order of the cosmos. In an indifferent universe, they think, our lives are unavoidably meaningless no matter what we do with them. 17 On the other hand, there may be some other point to choosing to do something good or worthwhile. This view disagrees explicitly with my own proposal—indeed, it appears to be in outright contradiction to it. However, it seems to me to be largely a disagreement in the use of words. *The* issue of meaning, which these philosophers tie essentially to issues about our significance (or lack of it) in the

> 16 What role do you think God plays in determining the value of things? Consider a version of the question asked in Plato's *Euthyphro* (p. 19): does God value things because they are valuable or are they valuable because God values them? Is God a reliable indicator of *preexisting* value or does he *make* something valuable by valuing it?

> 17 See the previous selection by Nagel for the view that there is a broader perspective from which it is very doubtful that Wolf's conditions for meaningfulness are even relevant, let alone sufficient—in spite of the fact that from a narrower perspective, the satisfaction of those conditions clearly seems to support the claim that our lives are meaningful.

universe, seems to me to be really a tangle of issues with overlapping strands. Though talk about meaning sometimes expresses a concern about our relation to the cosmos, the use of the term and its cognates to refer to differences among human lives and activities is no less common. I believe that there are relations between these different uses that have not been fully appreciated, and that philosophers like Nagel and Camus have insufficiently recognized the degree to which anthropocentric values can serve as a basis for addressing worries about our place in the universe. However, this issue is not relevant to my present purpose. My purpose here is to advance the view that it is in our interest to live lives of a certain sort, and to explore some of that view's implications. Whether we should describe these lives as more meaningful than others, or describe the desire to live them as a desire for meaning, is relatively superficial and may in any case be left to another day. I shall continue to use my terminology, however, and hope that no one will be confused by it. [18]

[18] Do you think Nagel would disagree that it is in one's interest to live a life of active engagement in worthwhile activities?

The second challenge to my account of meaningfulness is more directly relevant to the issue of the nature of self-interest. It consists of an alternative subjective account of meaning that is forcefully suggested, although not in quite the terms I shall use, by Richard Taylor's discussion of the meaning of life in his book *Good and Evil.** According to this position, meaning is not a matter of one's projects in life being worthwhile from some objective point of view. (Taylor himself seems to think that no projects could meet this standard.) Rather, a person's life is meaningful, one might say, if it is meaningful *to her,* and it is meaningful to her if she thinks or feels it is.

The suggestion that something is meaningful to someone as long as she thinks it is can be of no help to us in developing an account of meaningfulness, for we cannot understand what it would be for someone to think her life meaningful until we have an account of what meaningfulness is. The view I want to discuss, however, is, strictly speaking, more concerned with a feeling or, better, a sense or qualitative character that some of our experiences have. We may use the term "fulfillment" to refer to it. It is pleasant to be or to feel fulfilled or to find an activity or a relationship fulfilling, but it is a pleasure of a specific sort, one that seems closely associated with the thought that our lives or certain activities within them are meaningful. Recognizing this, it may be suggested, gives us all the basis we need for an account of meaning that meets my requirements. We may understand people's longing for meaning as a longing for this particular feeling, a longing which other sorts of pleasure cannot satisfy. We can also explain why some activities characteristically answer the call of meaning better than others. Some yield the feeling of fulfillment while others do not. Chocolate is filling but not fulfilling; it gives pleasure but not of this particular kind. When a person steps back, wondering whether her life has had meaning, or searching for a way to give it more meaning, she may simply be surveying her life for its quotient of fulfillment or looking for ways to increase it.

The very close ties between meaningfulness and fulfillment on which this account of meaning relies are important for understanding both the concept of meaning and its value. That meaningful activity or a meaningful life is at least partly fulfilling is, as this account suggests, a conceptual truth. To *identify* meaningfulness with fulfillment, however, neglects aspects of our use of the terms, and aspects of the experiences that are described by them, that my more objective account of meaningfulness better accommodates. [19]

[19] According to Wolf's analysis, a meaningful life will include these *feelings* of fulfillment, but such feelings are not enough for genuine meaning, since what seems fulfilling to someone might be a life with no objective worth at all.

For one thing, fulfillment is not a brute feeling but one with some cognitive content or concomitant. That certain activities tend to be fulfilling and others not seems connected to features of the relevant activities that make this fact intelligible. There is a fittingness between certain kinds of activities and the potential for fulfillment. When a relationship or a job is fulfilling, there is something about it that makes it so. One feels appreciated or loved, or has the sense of doing good, or

*Richard Taylor, *Good and Evil* (New York: Macmillian, 1970).

finds the challenge of the work rewarding. It is not just that the activities in question meet our expectations, though that is a part of it. Some things are fine but not fulfilling—my relationship with my hairdresser, for example, or my weekly trips to the supermarket.

These considerations suggest that we find things fulfilling only if we can think about them in a certain way. It is difficult precisely to identify a single belief that is always associated with the experience of fulfillment. Still, I propose that there is some association between finding an activity fulfilling and believing, or at least dimly, inarticulately perceiving, there to be something independently worthwhile or good about it. [20]

In his discussion of the meaning of life, Richard Taylor considers the case of Sisyphus and imagines that the gods, by inserting some substance in Sisyphus's veins, give Sisyphus a love for stone-rolling. Sisyphus's life is thereby transformed from one of miserable bondage to one of ecstatic fulfillment. Taylor himself recognizes that the thought experiment is an odd one, and that the passion for stone-rolling will strike his readers as bizarre. Taylor, however, seems to think that the strangeness of the example comes simply from its being unusual. People do not characteristically get passionate about mindless, futile, never-ending tasks; nor is this the sort of disposition that drugs typically induce. To many, however, the example is not just surprising but somewhat horrifying. The state of being fulfilled by perpetual stone-rolling is not unreservedly enviable. Of course, for Sisyphus, who is condemned to roll stones in any case, there is a great benefit in being able to be happy with his lot. In general, however, I suspect that most people would think that stone-rolling (mere stone-rolling, that is, without any purpose or development of skill) is not the sort of thing by which one ought to be fulfilled. That Sisyphus is fulfilled by stone-rolling suggests an understanding of Sisyphus as a victim (albeit a happy one) of a kind of drug-induced illusion. He finds something in stone-rolling that isn't really there. [21]

If we accept the idea that the feeling of fulfillment is necessarily connected with beliefs about its objects—if we accept that an activity or relationship can be fulfilling only if one believes it to be somehow independently good—then we can distinguish two hypotheses about the relationship between meaning and fulfillment. Does meaning come from the experience of fulfillment, no matter what its cause, or is a meaningful life one in which a subject is fulfilled by activities suitable to the experience? The subjective account suggested by Taylor opts for the former; but the latter seems to square better with our ordinary use of the concept.

One test case is Taylor's version of Sisyphus itself. That Sisyphus finds his life fulfilling is built in by assumption. But should we describe his life as meaningful? This seems to me a misuse of the word. "It is meaningful to him," someone will say, and we understand what this means. It means that he finds his life fulfilling, and, perhaps, that he thinks it is meaningful (or would think it, if asked). But, for those who find the example horrifying, that is part of the problem: he thinks his life gets meaning from mindless, futile stone-rolling, but it does not. [22]

We can construct a second test case by considering someone whose judgment of an aspect of her life has changed. A woman previously blissfully in love discovers that the man she loved has been using her. She had found the relationship fulfilling before she learned of his deceits. She would have said, had you asked her earlier, that the relationship contributed to the meaningfulness of her life. What would she say now, however, and what should we say about her? No one can take away the feelings of fulfillment she expe-

[20] Fulfillment, according to Wolf, is clearly different from mere pleasure, since one cannot experience fulfillment from an activity without first finding the activity objectively worthwhile. Fulfillment thus involves "cognitive content": believing or perceiving something about the activity in question. (And if this cognitive content is false, then the feeling is misguided in an important way.)

[21] If this new Sisyphus experiences fulfillment from his activity, then he must see it (mistakenly) as objectively worthwhile. If the gods injected something that merely made Sisyphus feel pleasure as a result of his activity but not fulfilled, then this cognitive dimension would not be required.

[22] What judgment should be made of the new Sisyphus? Is his life genuinely meaningful or does it only seem meaningful? (How would he feel if the drug wore off and his life-long activity no longer seemed worthwhile? Would the previous part of his life still be meaningful because he found it meaningful at the time?)

rienced during the period she was deceived; but it seems unlikely that she would say, after the fact, that the relationship truly had given meaning to her life. Indeed, part of what makes this sort of event so sad is that, in addition to the pain that is caused when the deception is discovered, it undermines the value of all the pleasure that came before.

Less fanciful than Sisyphus are cases of addicts or inductees of religious cults whose feelings of contentment are caused, but not justified, by the things that bring them about.⟨23⟩ Though we should be cautious about passing judgment on the activities that others take to be worthwhile, this is no reason to rule out the possibility that people are sometimes mistaken, that their finding something fulfilling can be wrongly induced, either through the establishment of false factual beliefs (such as belief in a loved one's fidelity or in the divine status of a charismatic leader) or by drugs or electrodes. If, moreover, they are led by such mind-altering means to spend their lives occupied by some equivalent of stone-rolling—watching endless reruns of *Leave It to Beaver* or counting and recounting the number of tiles on the bathroom floor—then it seems to me most in line with ordinary language to describe them as leading meaningless lives, however fulfilled they may feel themselves to be. If, further, such people wake up or snap out of it—if they come to occupy a point of view that devalues their former lives—then their later descriptions would not, I think, grant meaning to the things in which they had found contentment before.

⟨23⟩ Think about the idea that feelings can be caused but not justified by something. The deceived woman's feelings of fulfillment were caused by what she perceived as the loving actions of her husband. When she comes to see that those actions weren't loving at all, then those feelings no longer seem appropriate. His actions no longer give her good reasons for her feelings of fulfillment. Had her husband been as faithful as he pretended to be, then her feelings would have been both caused *and* justified by his actions.

MEANINGFULNESS AND SELF-INTEREST

So far I have been occupied with spelling out a conception of what meaningfulness in life is. My point in doing so, in the present context, is to bring it to bear on the idea of self-interest. Meaningfulness seems to me an important ingredient of a good life, and one that is too often either neglected or distorted by contemporary accounts of individual well-being.

I do not know what an argument for this claim would look like. My hope, as I mentioned before, is that the mere spelling out of the claim will be enough to incline most people to assent to it.⟨24⟩ Still, I think that without attending explicitly to our interest in meaning, we tend to misunderstand and misdescribe it, with the eventual result that the shapes our lives take have less meaning than may be good for us.

⟨24⟩ Wolf is very forthright about what she has *not* argued for. She has not given us reasons for her claim that there is a distinction between meaningful and meaningless activities, and she has not given us reasons for her claim that meaningfulness (as she has defined it) is an important ingredient of a good life. (The suggestion is that these claims will seem intuitively reasonable, even without a developed argument.)

Most people—at least most people within a certain group, bounded perhaps by class or education as well as by culture and history—behave in ways that suggest that they are looking for worthwhile things to do with their lives. They actively seek projects or, more typically, happily seize upon activities, from among those to which they are attracted, that they believe to be worthwhile. Explicit thoughts about worth and meaning often occur in connection with major life decisions, in addition to those moments of crisis to which I referred before. Some people decide to have children because they think it will give meaning to their lives. Others decide not to have children because they fear that the attendant responsibilities will deprive them of the time and resources and peace of mind that they need for other things in which they do find meaning. Deliberations about whether to pursue a particular career, or any career, may similarly involve concerns about whether the job is worthwhile, or whether it would demand time and energy that would distract one from what is worthwhile. Even many who do not talk explicitly in terms of meaning or worth make choices that are best explained by reference to them. In other words, our behavior, including some of our speech, seems to reveal a preference for a meaningful life.

We are, however, more apt to explain our choices in terms of fulfillment than meaning. A man opts for the more challenging of two possible careers, even at the cost of stress and insecurity. A woman chooses to work for less pay at a job she believes is morally valuable. People arrange their lives so as to give a few hours a week to Meals on Wheels, or to practicing piano, or to keeping up with their book group, even though it means going with a little less sleep, less flexibility, less straightforward fun. Why? Because, they will say, they find these things fulfilling. They choose to live this way because they regard it as, in some sense, best for them.

To defend these choices in terms of fulfillment establishes them as choices made out of self-interest. Talk of fulfillment may, however, suggest a more hedonistic interpretation of what is going on than the one I have offered.[25] To choose something because it is fulfilling is, after all, to choose it because of a qualitative character of one's experience—and though fulfilling activities are not always as much fun or as intensely pleasurable as some of the alternatives, it may be that in the long run, or the wide run (taking into account Mill's differences in the quality as well as the quantity of pleasure, as it were), a fulfilling life is qualitatively better, and thus happier in the truest sense, than a life with as many or more pleasures but no fulfillment. So at least must the people described in the paragraph above believe, and so must we believe if we think their choices are rational, and are rational for the reason they give.[26]

> [25] On a hedonist view, only one's own felt experiences of pleasure (and the avoidance of pain) are relevant to one's own good. The hedonistic interpretation of fulfillment takes it to be just a specific sort of pleasurable experience.

> [26] Wolf is raising a further objection to her view. If people's choices are aimed merely at the subjective experience of fulfillment (rather than at achieving meaning)—as their own descriptions of them seem to indicate—then Wolf's emphasis on objective worth seems to be mistaken as an account of what people actually care about.

It is no part of my aim to deny this suggestion. On the contrary, that fulfillment is a great qualitative good, and that it deserves an important place in an adequate theory of happiness, are important contributing factors to my claim that meaning is a component of our good. We have already seen that the links between meaningfulness and fulfillment are very tight. Since a meaningful life is necessarily at least partly fulfilling, and since fulfillment is a major component of happiness, a very important reason for taking meaningfulness to be in our interest is that it brings fulfillment with it. It would be misleading, however, to draw from this the conclusion that meaningfulness is an instrumental good for us. To think of meaning as good because it is a means to an independent good of fulfillment would be a mistake.

It is doubtful that fulfillment is an independent good, although feeling fulfilled is pleasant and feeling unfulfilled unpleasant. If fulfillment were an independent good, it would follow that the feeling of fulfillment would be desirable no matter what its cause. It would have to be better to be Sisyphus happy (or, more precisely, Sisyphus fulfilled) than Sisyphus unhappy (unfulfilled), even if this required that Sisyphus was perpetually stoned out of his normal mind. Opinion, however, divides on this matter. Many value fulfillment only on the condition that it be based on appropriate thoughts or perceptions. Moreover, even among those who believe that feeling fulfilled is unconditionally better than the alternative, many would still prefer that these feelings were suitably caused. Better to be Sisyphus happy than Sisyphus unhappy, they may say, but better still not to be Sisyphus at all.[27]

> [27] Wolf's response to the objection is to appeal again to the case of Sisyphus experiencing fulfillment in a way that depends on a drug-induced illusion. That most people would find his situation unsatisfactory suggests that they care about more than the subjective experience of fulfillment. (See Discussion Question 3.)

A proponent of a purely hedonistic theory of self-interest may point out that reports of such intuitions prove nothing. People's thinking that justified or appropriate fulfillment is better than unjustified inappropriate fulfillment doesn't make it so. To those who have these intuitions, however, the burden of proof seems to lie with the hedonist. Unless one is committed to a purely hedonistic account of value ahead of time, there seems no reason to doubt that what is principally desirable is getting fulfillment from genuinely fulfilling activities, from activities, that is, whose accompanying feeling of fulfillment comes from the correct perception of their value. There seems no reason to doubt, in other words, that what is principally desirable is living a meaningful life and not living a life that seems or feels meaningful. Insofar as we prefer a truly meaningful life to one that merely seems or feels meaningful, a purely hedonistic theory of self-interest will not account for it.[28]

A preference theory of self-interest, however, would not have to account for it—preference theorists simply accept our preferences and go on to compute our self-interest from there. This suggests an alternative account of the relation between meaning and self-interest. According to preference theories, meaning is important to our well-being if and only if meaning matters to us. Since many of us do want to live meaningful lives—since we think it is better for us if we do—preference theorists will agree that it is in our interest that our lives are meaningful. From their point of view, there is no need to make any more objective claims than that.

From a practical perspective, it matters little whether we accept this theory or a more objective one, particularly if you think, as I do, that the preference for a meaningful life is widespread and deep. If it is accepted as a fact of human nature (even a statistical fact, and even of a culturally created human nature) that people just do care about meaning in their lives, then this gives us reason enough to shape our lives in ways that will encourage not just fulfillment but meaningfulness, and it gives us reason enough to shape our social and political institutions in ways that will increase the opportunities for everyone to live not just happily and comfortably but meaningfully as well.[29]

A preference theory does not, however, seem accurately to reflect the status a meaningful life has for most of us. Most of us, it seems, do not regard our preference for a meaningful life as an ungrounded preference we just happen to have. If we did think so, then we would judge it a matter of indifference whether anyone else had or lacked this preference, and indeed, we would

[28] Think again about Nozick's experience machine: if your machine-induced experiences include a satisfactory proportion of experiences of fulfillment, would you plug into the machine? According to a purely hedonistic theory of self-interest, it would be in your self-interest to do so.

[29] The preference view of self-interest is different from the hedonistic view. According to a preference view, self-interest consists in fulfilling one's preferences, whatever those preferences may happen to be. If people happen to prefer meaningful lives, then achieving such lives will be part of their self-interest; but if not, then it won't be.

have no reason to want to keep this preference ourselves if we were convinced that we would be better off without it. For most people, however, at least so it seems to me, having a meaningful life is a value and not just a preference. We do not just want our lives to be meaningful, we think it good that we want it. Indeed, our interest and concern for meaning is sometimes mentioned as a mark of our humanity, as an aspect of what raises us above brutes. We think that we would be diminished as a species if we lost the aspiration, or the interest, in living meaningful lives and not just happy ones. Individuals who lack the desire that their lives be meaningful we regard with regret or even pity.[30]

Again it may be noted that our believing something is no proof of its being true, and again I must acknowledge that I have no proof of the value or objective desirability of meaningfulness. At the same time, the claim that a meaningful life is preferable (and not just brutely preferred) to a meaningless one may seem so nearly self-evident as to require no proof. Once one is willing to apply the terms of meaningfulness and meaninglessness at all, it may seem unstable to believe that a life that lacks meaning is no worse than one that possesses it. Even if we can logically distinguish the position that some lives are more meaningful than others from the position which adds that (some) meaningfulness is a good, this latter position seems more natural than one which denies it. Though we may be unable to argue for caring about meaning in a way that would convince someone who doesn't care to begin with, the concern or the desire for meaningful activity is, for those who have it, more rationally coherent with other values and dispositions than its absence would be.

In response to the question "Why care about living a meaningful life rather than a meaningless one?" the answer that I believe best expresses reflective common sense will begin with the connection between meaning and happiness: Nine times out of ten, perhaps ninety-nine times out of a hundred, a meaningful life will be happier than a meaningless one. The feelings of fulfillment one gets from interacting positively and supportively with things or creatures (or "realms")

[30] Wolf argues, in contrast, that we think it is good to have this preference, in which case, meaning is a value and not merely a preference—so that people *ought* to prefer it and are to be pitied if they don't.

whose love seems deserved are wonderful feelings, worth more, on qualitative grounds alone, than many other sorts of pleasure, and worth the cost of putting up with considerable quantities of pain. Moreover, the awareness, even dim and inarticulate, of a lack of anything that can constitute a source of pride or a source of connection to anything valuable outside of oneself can be awful, making one irritable, restless, and contemptuous of oneself. [31]

31 Is she right that a life without connections to things that are objectively worthwhile will include these feelings of irritability, restlessness, and self-contempt?

Except in an academic philosophical context such as this, it is perhaps unnatural to press further. If we do press further, however, it seems to me that the strength and character of these feelings of pleasure and pain are not best explained as mere quirks of our natural or culturally conditioned psyches. Rather, that we feel so good or so bad in accordance with our sense of connection to value outside ourselves seems to me best explained in terms of an underlying belief that a life is better when it possesses such connections. What precisely is better about it is difficult to say. But perhaps it has to do with our place in the universe: since we are, each of us, occupants in a world full of value independent of our individual selves, living in such a way as to connect positively and supportively with some nonsubjective value harmonizes better with our objective situation than would a life whose chief occupations can be only subjectively defended.

THE DECONSTRUCTION OF SELF-INTEREST

I have in this essay been concerned to defend, or rather to elaborate, what I take to be a deeply and widely held view about individual human good, namely, that a fully successful life is, among other things, a meaningful one. Further I have urged that this claim is distorted if it is understood as an element of either a hedonistic or a preference theory of self-interest. Properly understood, it requires a rejection of both these sort of theories.

As a substantive claim, I do not expect that the point that a good life must be meaningful will be surprising. We are not used to thinking very explicitly or very analytically about it, however; and in popular unreflective consciousness, a substantive interest in a meaningful life often sits side by side with assumptions that are incompatible with it. How often have you heard someone say, "What is the point of doing something if it isn't fun, or if you don't enjoy it?" I hear this sentiment expressed quite frequently, despite living on the East Coast. [32] To be fair, such expressions tend to be limited to contexts of self-interest. They are not intended as rejections of rational authority of moral or legal obligation. Moreover, there is often a point behind such remarks that I would strongly endorse. Against a kind of workaholism and related neurotic obsessions with some forms of success and achievement, it can be useful to step back and reflect in the way these remarks would invoke. Still, the suggestion that there can be no point to things if they are neither duties or fun is, strictly speaking, both false and dangerous. [33]

32 This is an odd remark. Do you think people in some parts of the country are more interested in fun than people in other parts of the country?

33 That something is fun is a reason for doing it, but one might have a reason for doing something even if it is not fun.

Much of what we do would be inexplicable, or at least indefensible, if its justification depended either on its being a duty or, even in the long run, on its maximally contributing to our net fun. Relationships with friends and family, nonobligatory aspects of professional roles, and long-term commitments to artistic, scholarly, or athletic endeavors typically lead us to devote time and energy to things that are difficult and unpleasant, and to forgo opportunities for relaxation and enjoyment. It is arguable that many of these choices advance our happiness (in the broadest sense, our fun) in the long run, but such arguments are best uncertain, and the thought that they are necessary for the defense of these choices puts a regrettable kind of pressure on the commitments that give rise to them. There is, however, a point—even a self-interested point—to doing things that fall outside the categories both of duty and fun. One can find a reason, or at least a justifying explanation, for doing something in the fact that the act or activity in question contributes to the meaningfulness of one's life. [34]

34 As Wolf has argued before, there could easily be activities that contribute to the meaningfulness of one's life that are not themselves fun. On her view, one still has a reason to do such things.

Once we have ceased to identify self-interest with happiness, however, other assumptions are also undermined. The concept of self-interest becomes more difficult to work with. Specifically, a conception of self-interest that recognizes the importance of meaning to a good life admits of much greater indeterminacy than the more traditional conceptions. This is partly a function of indeterminacy within the category of meaningfulness itself. Though meaningfulness is not an all-or-nothing concept—some lives are more meaningful than others, a person's life may not have *enough* meaning in it to be satisfactory—there is no well-formed system for making comparative judgments. The meaningfulness of a life may vary depending on how much of it is spent in meaningful activity, on how worthwhile the activities in question are, or on how fully engaged (or attracted) the individual is. In many instances, however, it seems absurd to think there is a correct comparison to be made. Is the life of a great but lonely philosopher more or less meaningful than that of a beloved housekeeper? There seems to be no reason to assume that there is a fact of the matter about this. Moreover, from a self-interested point of view, it is unclear whether, beyond a certain point, it matters whether one's life is more meaningful. A meaningful life is better than a meaningless one, but once it is meaningful enough, there may be no self-interested reason to want, as it were, to squeeze more meaning into it. Finally, the mix between meaning and felt happiness may have no determinate ideal. A person often has to choose between taking a path that would strengthen or expand part of his or her life that contributes to its meaningfulness (going to graduate school, adopting a child, getting politically involved) and taking an easier or more pleasant role. Once one has accepted a conception of self-interest that recognizes meaningfulness as an independent aspect of one's personal good, one may have to admit that in such cases there may be no answer to the question of what is most in one's self-interest.[35]

Fortunately, as the concept of self-interest becomes more difficult to apply, it becomes less important to be able to apply it. In accepting the value of meaningfulness as an ingredient of our own interest, we necessarily also accept that meaningful activity has a value that is partly independent of our own interest. We accept, in other words, the availability of a kind of reason for doing things that can compete with self-interest, a kind that will, at any rate, draw us away from the concern for our self-interest. What I have in mind is the sort of reason given by the worthiness of the meaningful activity (or its object) itself.

Meaningful activity, remember, involves engagement in projects of worth. It occurs where subjective attraction meets objective attractiveness. To acknowledge that an activity or a project is worthwhile, however, is to acknowledge, among other things, that there is a reason for doing it—a reason, at least, for doing it if you are attracted to doing it. A reason for writing a book on free will is to stimulate thought in a fruitful direction. A reason to plant bulbs and weed the garden is to maintain a place of natural beauty. A reason to sew a groundhog costume for an eight-year-old is to make her happy.

To those who get meaning from the activities just mentioned, these sorts of reasons will dominate. Being suitably engaged in these activities in the same way which people get meaning from them *are* engaged involves being drawn by their specific good or value. One so engaged is not likely to step back from the activity and ask, "Is this the best thing I can be doing *for me?*"

The point here is not just the one with which we are familiar from the paradox of hedonism. It is not just that, by not caring too much about whether her activities will be best for her, the agent is more likely to be living a life that is best for her. Rather, it is that she has a reason for her activities that is not conditional on their being best for her. Accepting a conception of self-interest that incorporates meaningfulness, then, involves rejecting too dominant a place for self-interest.[36] Yet meaningful activity and self-interest cannot psychologically stretch too far

[35] Recognizing that meaningfulness is a part of self-interest makes self-interest less clearly defined than it would be on the hedonistic and preference views. There are many kinds of worthwhile things and so many potential sources of meaning. And there is also no clear answer as to how much meaning a satisfactory life must have.

[36] But once we see that meaningfulness is important for self-interest, we see that people have reasons for action that are *independent* of their own self-interest. Meaningfulness involves a recognition of things that are objectively worthwhile, whether they serve a person's self-interest or not. (For a related discussion, see the selection by Feinberg in Chapter 6.)

apart. Activity is meaningful only if one can engage in it, be attracted to it, be in love with it or the object around which it revolves. Such activity will always be somewhat fulfilling, and therefore will always make one somewhat happy. And as the fulfillment and happiness will be appropriate or deserved, that is all to one's good.

Discussion Questions

1. When Wolf articulates the concerns about meaning that people have (p. 858), she says that people can come to see activities that they used to enjoy as "shallow," that even though they've had fun in their lives, they sense that something is lacking. Do you recognize this phenomenon? Do you think that most people do have concerns about meaning?

2. Wolf insists that the activities of a meaningful life must be objectively worthwhile. Consider the following example: suppose a woman named Katie counts the blades of grass in the central quad at the University of Washington. She is there every morning at 8 a.m., takes an hour break at lunch time, and stops counting around 5 p.m. She takes the weekends off, but rarely takes any other time off. She is independently wealthy, and so she doesn't need to work for a living. When you ask her why she is counting the blades of grass, she responds that she finds it fascinating. She is very systematic, leaving a mark (nothing permanent) where she stops for the day so that she'll know where to begin the next day. When students stop to talk, she'll take a few minutes to show them what she is doing, explaining about the different kinds of grass or her method of counting, but if they take too much time, she gently tells them that she must get back to work. The grounds crew was very suspicious of her activity at first, but they have come to appreciate her, since she has warned them of infestations that they might have otherwise missed. Her family was very upset when she started this activity, insisting that she see a therapist. She humored them, but the therapist could find nothing wrong with her. She has been doing this for 10 years now and can't imagine doing anything else. She has her own family now, and her children tell their friends that mommy works at the university. While Katie is not paid for what she does, she takes it very seriously and enjoys the activity enormously. She sometimes wishes that it didn't rain quite so much in Seattle, but every job has its drawbacks. Does Katie lead a meaningful life, according to Wolf? Is there any way to argue that her activity is objectively worthwhile?

3. Suppose that Sisyphus is controlled by the gods in such a way that he will continue to roll the stone up the hill again and again whether or not he finds it fulfilling or meaningful. On Wolf's view, it would clearly be better for Sisyphus to be allowed instead to do something with more objective worth. But given that this is impossible, is he ultimately better off finding his activity fulfilling even though this involves believing mistakenly that it has objective worth, or would he be better off (even if not happier) if he did not have such an illusion? If you were Sisyphus, would you want to know the truth or not?

A P P E N D I X

Writing a Philosophical Essay

Most students will have written many essays of other kinds before they write their first philosophical essay. While this previous experience is invaluable because of the essential writing skills that it should have produced, it is inadequate as a basis for understanding what a good philosophical essay requires. Philosophy is very different from most other subjects, and good philosophical writing reflects this difference. Students often say if they had known *before* they wrote their first essay just what the professor was looking for, how their essay would be evaluated, they could have done a much better job to begin with. Here is your opportunity to find out before you start writing what you should be aiming for.

By the time you are asked to write a philosophical essay, you will have read some philosophy, heard some lectures, and participated in some discussions. You will have begun to practice "doing philosophy" with all that involves: drawing distinctions, clarifying both terms or concepts and whole claims, arguing for and against these claims, considering objections to those arguments, replying to these objections, etc. A good philosophical essay involves the written expression of all of these things. Return to the introductory essay about philosophical thinking in Chapter 1 (p. 3) to remind yourself of the basic structure of a philosophical issue and the various sorts of claims, arguments, and other elements that pertain to it.

FIRST, WHAT IS DISTINCTIVE ABOUT A PHILOSOPHICAL ESSAY?

A philosophical essay is most fundamentally an argumentative defense of some philosophical claim. The defense will consist of, first, giving a main line of argument for the claim (which will typically involve some subsidiary arguments in defense of intermediate claims) and, second, considering and responding to objections to either your main claim or your argument. A consequence of this is that if you haven't clearly understood what an argument is, you will have a very hard time writing a good philosophical essay. A good philosophical essay is a rich piece of philosophical **dialectic.**

A good philosophical essay is not a mere report of someone else's argument, even if the someone else is René Descartes, Immanuel Kant, or some other famous philosopher, but is instead an argument that *you* (the author of the essay) are defending for some particular philosophical claim. Think carefully about the difference between reporting someone else's argument and presenting an argument of your own.

Your philosophical essay should reflect the fundamental categories essential to the philosophical habits of mind you've been learning as you read this book:

- clearly stated claims;
- cogent lines of argument (including well-developed points relevant to either defending or illustrating the premises of the argument);
- clear, carefully developed objections pointing out possibly serious flaws in the arguments; and
- responses that show why the objections, while initially compelling, are not ultimately convincing (and may in fact show even more clearly how persuasive the main argument of the essay really is).

Good philosophical essays have a very distinctive character, a specific shape to them. While they share many features with essays from other disciplines, there are some aspects to a good philosophical essay that no other kind of essay has. For example, while all good essays need to be well-written, writing that is both clear and careful is especially important in a philosophical essay because of the subtle and abstract character of the thought involved. Moreover, while essays in many other disciplines involve arguments along the way, philosophical essays are almost exclusively argumentative: the main point, the very essence, of a philosophical essay is to argue for a claim. Think about the claim in the introductory essay that studying philosophy is valuable. We *argued* for that claim by presenting and defending reasons for the claim, where the truth of the reasons allegedly made the truth of the claim more likely. Someone could instead talk in a very different way about studying philosophy, a way that is not at all argumentative, that does not even try to give reasons for thinking that the claim is true, but instead has a different point altogether.

Second, How Does One Go About Producing a Good Philosophical Essay?

The simple answer: read, think, write, revise, perhaps reread or read further, think, write, revise, ad infinitum (or until it is due!). What follows is the more complicated answer.

Preassignment Writing Practice

Writing philosophy is an especially valuable form of philosophical thinking and provides you with writing practice even before you work on a formal essay. Writing of any sort forces you—more than any other intellectual activity—to become clearer about your ideas. In particular, writing philosophy is the most active, demanding way to engage in philosophy. You'll notice that when you listen to a philosophy lecture, you will normally be able to follow it; and if you've done the reading, you may even be able to anticipate some of the ideas and transitions of thought. You'll sometimes leave the lecture hall thinking that you really understand a particular issue or view or line of thought. One good test of your understanding is to try to explain it orally to someone else: sometimes you won't even be able to do that (suggesting that you didn't understand it as well as you thought); but sometimes even if you are able to explain it orally, you would be unable to write it down in a fully clear and accurate way. Formulating an idea well in writing requires a higher degree of understanding and clarity than any other form of thought or expression. So it is valuable to attempt to formulate the various ideas and arguments you encounter in writing, whether this takes the form of an extended passage or just brief notes and jottings. This will also give you valuable practice in philosophical writing even before you are assigned to write an essay.

Think and Make Notes About the Assignment

Once you are assigned to write an essay, you will often be given a specific assignment that is intended to guide your thought process in creating your essay—and perhaps also a specific topic or choice of topics. If your assignment includes questions to be answered by your essay, then be sure to answer them. This may sound obvious, but it has been our experience that many students just start writing and often end up going out on tangents of their own, rather than following the assignment guidelines.

Having chosen or arrived at a topic, you should think as hard as you can about it, trying out different lines of thought until you find one that strikes you as one that you may be able to defend. (You can't possibly be sure at this point.) At this stage, you should be taking notes, sketching the arguments and objections you might include in your essay. The clearer you can make your thoughts, the better your essay will be: murky thoughts can turn good writers into bad writers. As you think about your topic, taking notes, you may need to return to the reading with more specific questions in mind. Philosophical texts have a kind of depth that continues to reward a reader: you'll understand more and more as you read the second and third time, and even more when you approach the reading with specific questions you want to answer. This process should produce a line of argument that you can defend in your essay, including possible objections and responses.

Outline the Essay

Once you have your overall line of argument pretty clearly in mind, you should create an outline for your essay. This can take many different forms, but the main idea is that it should lay out the *structure* of your essay: this includes listing its main ingredients, specifying the order in which they will occur, and making clear how they are related to each other. The outline will include a statement of your main claim or thesis, a specification of your main argument, and a listing of further problems and objections to be considered. (Remember that considering objections is an essential part of any philosophical essay.) You obviously need to see the whole shape of the paper before you can start writing the first draft.

One reason that an outline is important is that it can help you avoid a potential pitfall that students writing philosophical essays for the first time often fall into: failing to anticipate a problem or objection that forces them to substantially alter their main argument or even to change their main claim. It is a most unfortunate student who comes to talk to his professor the day before the essay is due, in a state of panic because he has written most of the paper but has now encountered an objection that he didn't anticipate and can't figure out how to answer. Had this student created a more complete outline before writing his first draft, he might have seen that he didn't have a response to this objection—and so might have chosen a different main argument or even a different main claim.

Creating a good outline is much of the work of writing a philosophical essay. There is still important work to be done, but most of it is refinement.

Write the First Draft

Now you are ready to write the first draft. Working from your outline, write a complete draft of your essay. It is important to do this early enough to allow plenty of time for revision: the first draft of a philosophical essay rarely says exactly what you are trying to say and often has lots of problems and deficiencies of various sorts that need to be corrected.

Especially in your first draft, be sure to include lots of "signposts" to help you keep clearly in mind the ways in which the points being made are relevant to the overall argument; some (but not all) of these may be deleted as you revise and polish the essay. For example, early in the essay (probably on the first page) you should have a sentence stating the main claim of the essay: "in this essay, I will argue that Descartes's argument in *Meditation I* that we can doubt any belief based on experience fails"; or "in this essay, I argue that mental states are distinct from physical states"; or "in this essay, I will defend Hume's objection to the social contract theory." (It is permissible—and even, we think, often recommended—to write in the first person.) A clear statement of the main claim of the essay is a very important signpost (probably the single most important one). You'll mention many other philosophical claims in the paper that you won't be arguing for (background assumptions, illustrations of particular points, contrasting claims that you aren't arguing for, etc.), and you don't want to create the expectation in your reader that you will defend all of those.

Another kind of signpost, again often most clearly expressed in the first person, is a word or phrase that indicates to the reader the role that one claim or passage plays in relation to the overall argument of the paper. For example, "I will explain Descartes's argument in *Mediation I,* before criticizing the crucial premise" or "while this passage is initially plausible, I will show that by distinguishing between two different senses of 'mental,' it becomes clear that the argument equivocates" or "before I defend Hume's objection, I will explain the importance of the idea of consent to the social contract theory."

Sometimes signposts are needed to alert the reader to a shift in perspective: for example, "I've argued that introspective beliefs are not subject to doubt on the basis of the dreaming hypothesis, but one might wonder what Descartes would say about such a claim" or "Fodor's claims that the account of how one physical state causally affects another physical state is the paradigm clear case of causality, but I will argue that such a presumption has serious problems."

For some reason, students are often tempted when first writing philosophical essays to use the most sophisticated language possible. That is a serious mistake. You should try to use language that is as clear and straightforward as possible, given what you are trying to say. Do not search through a thesaurus looking for words that sound important. Just try to state as clearly and as simply as possible the points you need to make in order to defend your argument.

You should also avoid philosophical terminology that is unclear or unnecessary—which is *not* to say that all philosophical terminology can be avoided. Some instructors make this point by directing the student to write in a way that would be accessible to a particular audience: for example, a bright but philosophically ignorant undergraduate. The idea behind this advice is that if you think of the audience of your paper as your professor, then there is a great temptation to assume too much prior understanding—both of terminology and of background issues—and so not to explain your ideas and arguments adequately.

Revise

Once you have a first draft, put it aside and give yourself a day or two before you look at it again. You need to read the draft with "fresh eyes," as if you were reading something that someone else wrote. One of the typical problems for beginning writers is to think that you've said something that you haven't in fact succeeded in saying—at least not clearly. Many students unfortunately end up explaining to their professor, after the paper has already been turned in and graded, what they meant to say, coming to see in the process that what they actually wrote did not capture what they intended. You need to review what you have actually written and not what is in your mind, since your professor will of course not be able to read your mind, but will have access only to the paper itself.

Now read the draft of your paper all the way through, focusing as carefully as possible on what it actually says. Assuming that your outline is sound, the first thing you should look for in this first stage of the revision process is whether you've accurately expressed the content of your outline. Sometimes in the process of writing the first draft, you can be tempted to explore a line of thought that turns out to be a tangent that is not closely relevant to the main claim you are defending. You should ask yourself at each paragraph: what is the point that I'm making with this paragraph and how does this point fit into the overall argument of my essay?

Once you are convinced that your intended line of argument has been clearly expressed and that you have no extraneous material, you can then attempt to refine your prose. Looking again at each paragraph, ask yourself whether the point is clear and whether each of the sentences clearly and succinctly expresses exactly what you want to say. At this stage of revision, it is often helpful to read the essay out loud, either to a friend or roommate or just to yourself, listening carefully for awkward constructions or unclear formulations. This only works if you focus on your specific words and phrases and sentences as you read them, thinking again about just what the essay as written actually says, as opposed to what you meant it to say.

Good philosophical essays are often revised three or four times. To repeat, it is very rare for the first draft of an essay to say what you really want it to say or to be even approximately as good as you can make it—or as your professor will want it to be.

THIRD, HOW WILL YOUR ESSAY BE EVALUATED?

As we have said, the most important feature that a philosophical essay must have is that it must be *a reasoned defense of a philosophical claim:* you must have defended an argument for some specific, reasonably clear claim. Your professor won't be able to tell that you've done that unless the structure of the paper is clear. (Indeed you don't count as having done that unless the structure is clear.) So clear structures and good arguments enhance the quality of the paper substantially and murky structures and weak arguments detract from it.

As we argued in the introductory essay in Chapter 1, a strong defense of a philosophical claim is one that considers objections and alternative points of view. So the essays that consider and respond to good objections will be substantially stronger than those that don't.

And it is obviously very hard to see whether you've given a good argument or considered objections if your essay is unclear or poorly written.

SOME FREQUENTLY ASKED QUESTIONS

Should I write about my own opinions?   If "write about" means argue for instead of ramble on about, and if "opinion" means a well-thought-out, defended belief instead of whatever you happen to think at the moment, then yes. You should be arguing for a carefully chosen belief for which you can mount a cogent defense. You should make a case for a claim whose point you can see. Maybe a better way to express this concern is the next question.

Should I argue only for claims that I truly believe?   Sometimes students are warned away from arguing for a deeply held cherished belief because they sometimes have a hard time seeing the need for any reasons, and they certainly cannot imagine any possible objections to the belief itself or to any argument for the belief. Obviously one ought not to try to write a philosophical essay defending such a belief. On the other hand, if the claim is something that you can't imagine that someone could seriously believe, then you will similarly have a hard time arguing for it. So defend claims that you either believe on the basis of reasons or that you can imagine believing. Sometimes the worry behind this question is really the worry expressed by the next question.

Should I avoid disagreeing with the views of my professor?   You certainly do not need to argue only for claims that your professor accepts in order to write a good paper. Sometimes professors disagree about what the right answer is to some philosophical question (some, for example, are dualists and others materialists about the nature of the mind), but they will usually agree about whether or not a philosophical essay is good or not. You need to cogently defend a clearly structured argument and consider and respond to objections in order to write a good philosophical essay, and your work will be evaluated accordingly. The assessment of your paper will not depend on whether your professor agrees with the claim that you have defended.

Do I have to make up my own arguments? Or, how much originality is required for introductory philosophical essays?   You surely are not expected to make up your own arguments without any help from the many philosophers that you've read so far. Presumably you've learned a great deal from the readings, and your philosophical essays will be based on some of that knowledge. There is still some room for originality, however, in the way you put the ideas together, in the way you defend your premises, and in the examples you give. Often students exercise originality in their choice of objections or responses. There are many ways to exercise a degree of originality in writing a philosophical essay without inventing a wholly new argument for a philosophical claim.

Should I quote the philosopher I'm talking about?   You may quote the philosopher in question, but you must explain every quotation. You can't show that you understand a philosopher by quoting the relevant passage without explanation—after all, it would be entirely possible to know which passage is the right one and still not understand clearly what it says! Usually introductory philosophical essays are sufficiently short that there is not enough space to quote and also explain to make a point, and many excellent introductory essays do not use quotations at all. Sometimes this question is asked because the student has not yet quite absorbed the real nature of a philosophical essay. Students are sometimes tempted to argue in the following way: Descartes accepted some particular claim, therefore that claim is true, with the defense for the premise that Descartes accepted the claim consisting in some quotation from Descartes's *Meditations*. But remember that your essay is supposed to be a defense of a philosophical claim, and the fact that Descartes (or anyone else) thought something is not in itself a reason to think that it is true. (Such an attempted argument commits the fallacy in reasoning called appeal to authority.)

Should I use ordinary dictionaries to clarify philosophical terms or cite them in my essay?   No. Ordinary dictionaries do not contain reliable definitions of most philosophical terms. (There are specialized dictionaries that are much more dependable.) You may need to use an ordinary dictionary to understand other terms in some of the readings.

What if my first draft is too short?   This is a very common question. Some students have yet to learn how to develop a point. They try to state a complicated, subtle idea in too few words. Sometimes you need to work up to an idea gradually, and sometimes you need to distinguish your point from other points that a reader might think you are making. One way to see how and where you need to elaborate your claims is to put your draft aside for a day or two, so that you can read it as if someone else wrote it, and thereby see more clearly what else needs to be said to make the content clearer and more explicit.

What if my first draft is too long?   Go back to your outline, and make sure that all the points you make in your draft are necessary for your argument. Scrutinize every paragraph or even every sentence, asking yourself how it fits into your argument and whether it is really necessary.

Glossary

Many of the concepts expressed by terms in this glossary are ones about which many philosophers have doubts or misgivings: as to their ultimate intelligibility, their application to the world, or both; we have not, for the most part, attempted to take note of such doubts and misgivings here.

abduction   See **explanatory argument.**

abstract/concrete   A metaphysical distinction between modes of being. Concrete things are things that exist in space and time and causally interact with other such entities, or things that exist in the same general way. Thus an ordinary material object is a paradigm of a concrete thing, but the mind or spirit of a particular individual person (according to **dualism**) resembles a material object in that it exists in time and on most views stands in causal relations the person's body (a material thing), and thereby also counts as concrete. God, though on some views existing outside of both space and time, is still concrete by virtue of his causal relation to the world. Abstract things or entities, in contrast, do not exist in space and time, and do not causally interact with concrete entities. The paradigm of an abstract entity would be an abstract property such as redness or triangularity or justice. But things like numbers and sets of objects are also standardly regarded as abstract in the same way.

act utilitarianism   See **utilitarianism.**

ad hoc   Responses or qualifications given merely for the purpose of meeting some objection or problem without having any independent merit (the Latin phrase literally means "for this specific purpose").

agnosticism   See **theism.**

altruism   See **ethical egoism.**

analogy, argument by   Arguing from the similarity between things in one respect to the conclusion that they are thereby (probably) similar in another respect.

analytic/synthetic   This is a distinction concerning the structure of a proposition, claim, or statement. The fact that a proposition is analytic is often offered (especially by proponents of **moderate empiricism**) as an explanation of how it can be justified or known **a priori.** As Kant defines the distinction, an analytic proposition is one of subject-predicate form whose predicate is included in its subject, either explicitly (*all tall men are tall*) or implicitly (*all bachelors are unmarried*); while a synthetic proposition is one that does *not* have this sort of form, one in which the predicate is not contained in the subject. Other accounts of analyticity have been offered in an attempt to account for the apparent a priori status of propositions that do not clearly fit Kant's definition. Of these, the two most common are (a) that a proposition is analytic if it is a truth of logic or transformable into a truth of logic by substituting correct definitions for some of its terms; and (b) that a proposition is analytic if it is true just by virtue of its meaning (and, in both cases, otherwise synthetic). Here definition (a) is a fairly obvious generalization of Kant's definition, which would include the propositions that fit his definition, but also propositions like *either it is raining or not raining.* Definition (b), on the other hand, is more vague: just *how* does meaning account for truth? (If it means only that anyone who understands the proposition can see or grasp immediately that it is true, then it is not clearly distinct from the definition of **a priori,** making it **circular** to attempt to explain a priori justification or knowledge by appeal to analyticity.)

antecedent   Literally that which comes before: in a **conditional** claim, one of the form *if A, then B,* the *A* part is the antecedent of the conditional.

a posteriori   See **a priori/a posteriori.**

a priori/a posteriori   This is a distinction concerning the reasons or justification offered for a claim. *A posteriori* reasons are reasons based on or derived from experience; thus "*a posteriori*" means the same thing as "**empirical.**" A priori reasons are independent of experience. According to a **rationalist,** these reasons derive from rational insight or rational intuition, operating independently of experience, while a **moderate empiricist** has to say that these reasons are in some way available independently of experience but do not depend on rational insight. The claim that all bachelors are unhappy is *a posteriori* (or empirical) because it can be justified only by reasons derived from sense experience, but the claim that all bachelors are unmarried is a priori because sense experience is not required for its justification; as long as you understand the claim, you can see clearly that it is true.

argument   A set of claims, some of which are *premises,* advanced with the purpose of establishing the truth of one of the other claims, the *conclusion.* (Arguments may also include intermediate conclusions or lemmas, arrived at in the process of reasoning to the main conclusion.) The truth of the premises must at least appear to make the conclusion more likely to be true (than it would seem to be if the premises were false), but this need not actually be so: a fallacious argument is still an argument.

argument from illusion   (sometimes called the argument from hallucination) An argument for the view that what we are directly aware of in normal cases of perception is not an externally existing material object, but instead something mental like an **idea** or a **sense datum.** The crucial premise of the argument is the claim that the character of our experience does not in itself indicate whether we are having a veridical (true) experience or not; in other words, our experience of illusions or hallucinations can seem as veridical, as genuine, as an experience of an external object.

The external object is clearly not the object of direct awareness in the case of hallucination (since there is no object at all) or in the case of illusion (since the real object is very different from the experienced object). But if the external object is not what we are directly aware of in these cases, and there is no experiential difference between the veridical and nonveridical experiences, then, it is argued, the immediate object of experience must be the same in all of these cases—and so cannot be an external material object. The argument from illusion is thus an argument against **direct realism.**

artificial intelligence (*AI*)   Intelligence that has been constructed artificially (as opposed to the natural intelligence of humans). Many scientists (engineers and computer scientists) believe that it is possible in principle to build a computer that is genuinely intelligent (this is the program of *Strong AI*). A quite different view (*Weak AI*) holds only that computer simulations can be useful in understanding intelligence, making no claim that the computer that runs the simulation is itself intelligent.

atheism   See **theism.**

attribute dualism   See **dualism.**

autonomy   The ability to freely determine one's own action.

axiology   The general study of the nature of *value,* including moral value, aesthetic value, and values of other kinds.

begging the question   The mistake in reasoning consisting of assuming in the premises the very thing the argument is supposed to be proving. Also called a **circular** argument. (In recent times, this phrase has come to be mistakenly used in the media and elsewhere to mean simply raising the question.)

behaviorism   The view that bodily behavior is in some way fundamental to understanding mental states. Logical behaviorism is the view (a version of **materialism**) that mental states are reducible to (nothing more than) behavior and dispositions to behavior. Methodological behaviorism in psychology is the view that the proper way to study mental states is to study behavior (as opposed to appealing to introspective reports). These are distinct views, and it is possible to accept methodological behaviorism without accepting logical behaviorism.

belief The mental state of accepting or assenting to a particular proposition that is the content of the belief. If this acceptance or assent is actually present in consciousness at a particular moment of time, the belief is *occurrent;* if it takes the form of a standing disposition to assent if the issue is raised, the belief is *dispositional.* (Obviously most of the beliefs that a person has are merely dispositional at any particular moment.)

categorical imperative A moral requirement derived from reason that is binding on any rational being, that obligates one no matter what else is the case. (Contrasting term: **hypothetical imperative.**)

cause and effect The relation between two events whereby one, the cause, precedes and brings about the other, the effect. According to the *regularity (or Humean) theory of causation,* the "bringing about" is nothing more than the two events regularly occurring in that sequence. On other views, causation requires a stronger relation of *necessary connection* between the cause and the effect.

causal determinism The view that every event and every state of affairs is caused in every detail by prior events or states of affairs according to laws of nature; according to this view, given any particular state of the universe and given the actual laws of nature, there is only one genuinely possible future and only one genuinely possible past. A being (sometimes referred to as Laplace's demon, after the French mathematician Pierre Laplace) who knew all the laws of nature and everything true at one moment could thus infer the entire history of the universe. The term is also used in such a way that it can be said to be true of some events (those for which there is a determining cause) and false for others.

circular A term used to describe an argument or explanation that illegitimately presupposes the very

thing it is supposed to establish or account for. A circular **argument** is one where one of the premises is either the conclusion allegedly arrived at or something so close to that conclusion as to amount to the same thing in different words. The problem with such an argument (one that is also said to **beg the question**) is that anyone who does not already accept the conclusion will also (unless he is confused) not accept the premise in question, so that the argument could not give anyone a good reason to accept its conclusion. Analogously, a circular definition is one where the term being defined (or something so close to it as to amount to the same thing) is used in giving the definition. In such a case, a person who does not already understand the term being defined will be unable to understand the proposed definition, so that the definition could not help anyone to come to understand the defined term.

claim An asserted proposition, declared with the intention of stating a truth.

compatibilism The position on the free will problem (also called soft determinism) that holds that **causal determinism** is compatible with free will, with an action being free when it is caused in the right way (roughly by the agent's own desires or wants, and without external constraint). Compatibilists also normally hold that this condition is satisfied for most human actions, so that human beings are in fact genuinely free. (Contrasting terms: **hard determinism, libertarianism.**)

concept A mental entity or element that gives a person the ability to think about a certain kind of thing. For example, to have the concept of electricity is to be able to think specifically about electricity. Both the nature of concepts and how the mind comes to have them are matters of controversy. (On the latter question, see **empiricism** and **innate.**)

concept empiricism See **empiricism.**

concrete See **abstract/concrete.**

conditional proposition (or just a conditional) A complex proposition (or claim) having the form *if A, then B,* and expressing a kind of dependence between the two component propositions *A* and

B. The first part of the conditional (the *A* part) is called the antecedent, while the second part (the *B* part) is called the consequent. Philosophers often use conditionals to express their views and arguments, making it important to be able to decide when a conditional is true and when it is false. Unfortunately, this is a matter of some difficulty. The one clear fact is that a conditional whose antecedent is true and whose consequent is false is itself false, since that is the one case that the conditional clearly guarantees will not happen. Logicians and philosophers have introduced an interpretation of the conditional (sometimes referred to as the *material conditional*), under which a conditional is true in the other three possible cases (both antecedent and consequent true, both false, and false antecedent with true consequent), and it is this construal of the conditional that is employed in symbolic logic. But it is clear that conditionals in ordinary language are sometimes true and sometimes false in these three cases, with the reason being that their truth depends (not at all surprisingly) on the relations (such as, especially, causation) between the events described by the antecedent and consequent and not just on the truth or falsity of these claims. (Consider, for example, the conditional claim "if George Washington had been an elephant, then he could have barked like a dog." It is a silly claim to be sure, but according to a natural interpretation of it, the claim is false, since elephants cannot bark like dogs. But according to the material conditional interpretation, the claim is true, because the antecedent is false.)

consequent Literally, that which follows: in a **conditional** claim, one of the form *if A, then B,* the *B* part is the consequent of the conditional.

consequentialism The view that whether an action is right or wrong is entirely determined by the value (good or bad) of the results or consequences of the action. **Utilitarianism** is the main variety of consequentialism. (Contrasting term: **deontological.**)

contingent See **necessary/contingent.**

contradiction, contradictory A contradiction is a proposition that is **necessarily** false just because of the logical properties of the proposition itself,

with the clearest case being a proposition that explicitly asserts and denies the very same thing (*today is Tuesday and today is not Tuesday*), often referred to as an *explicit contradiction.* (An *implicit contradiction* is a proposition that can be turned into an explicit proposition by providing correct definitions for some of its component terms (*John is a bachelor and John is married*).) Sometimes the term "contradiction" is used loosely to refer to any necessarily false proposition (in which case being contradictory could not *explain* necessary falsehood). Two individually noncontradictory propositions contradict each other if and only if the conjunction of the two is contradictory (in which case the truth of either one is sufficient to prove the falsity of the other). The *principle of contradiction* (sometimes also referred to as the *principle of noncontradiction*) is the logical principle that a contradiction can never be true.

corporeal Made entirely of bodily or physical or material components.

counter-example An example or particular case which shows that some particular claim is false; if the claim in question is, for example, that all bachelors are unhappy, then coming up with a specific example of a happy bachelor would show that the claim is false, and thus would be a counter-example.

deductive argument An argument whose premises purport to *guarantee* the truth of the conclusion (see **argument**).

deontological A view which holds that the rightness or wrongness of an action depends on something other than the value of the consequences of the action. Deontological views may say, for example, that rightness or wrongness depends on the *form* of the action or the *principle* that it conforms to. Such views often stress duties or rights as the source of rightness or wrongness.

determinism See **causal determinism, hard determinism, compatibilism.**

dialectic A term used to describe the characteristic structure of philosophical reasoning and argument, involving problems or questions, views or positions on those problems, arguments for those views, responses to those arguments, replies to those responses, etc.; and also arguments against those views, responses to those arguments, replies to the responses, etc. Philosophical progress or discovery may sometimes consist of finding a definitive solution to a philosophical problem, but more often in adding new ingredients to this dialectical structure: a new argument or objection, a new response to an old argument or objection, a further reply, etc.; or (more rarely) a new position on an old problem; or (rarest of all) a genuinely new problem or issue.

direct realism (also called naïve realism) The view that the direct or immediate objects of sense perception are common-sense physical objects (and that these objects have at least largely the features they are perceived to have). (Contrasting term: **representative realism.**)

distributive justice Justice as it pertains to the distribution of valuable commodities among people.

double effect, law (or principle) of The view that there is a morally relevant difference between actions whose bad consequences are intended and other actions whose bad consequences are unintended either as an end or as a means to an end, though still foreseen. Compare, for example, the following two actions: (1) a doctor performs an operation on a pregnant woman to remove a cancerous tumor, killing the fetus as a foreseen but unintended side effect; and (2) a doctor performs an abortion on a pregnant woman whose life is threatened by the pregnancy. According to the standard version of the principle, (1) is permissible (because the death of the fetus is not intended), but (2) is not (because the death of the fetus is a means to an end and so intended). And this is so even in the version of case (2) where both mother and fetus will die if nothing is done and where the fetus is too immature to survive if surgically delivered.

dualism The metaphysical view that mind and body (or mental states and bodily states) are in some way fundamentally different and distinct from each. (Contrasting term: **materialism.**) According to *substance dualism,* the mind and the physical body (including the brain) are two different entities or substances, each having their own distinctive properties. Bodies have physical properties like size, weight, spatial position, etc.; whereas minds have none of these features, but are instead immaterial and spiritual in character. A second, importantly different version of dualism is *attribute* or *property dualism,* according to which there are two irreducibly different kinds of properties or attributes or features, physical features (like the ones listed earlier) and mental or spiritual features (consciousness and more specific conscious properties), but both belonging to the same thing or substance. This thing or substance that has both kinds of properties is what we refer to as the body (or perhaps the brain); but since it has both kinds of properties, it is in itself neither purely physical nor purely mental or spiritual in nature. (A further issue for both versions of dualism is what causal relations, if any, there are between the two kinds of substance or the two kinds of properties, with **interactionism, epiphenomenalism,** and **parallelism** being the main alternatives.)

duty A duty is an obligation, something that a person is required to do. If something is a legal duty, then the person is required by law to do it; if something is a moral duty, then the person is required by morality to do it. Kant distinguished between *imperfect duties,* requirements that have some flexibility about how to satisfy them; and perfect duties, requirements that have no such leeway. So, for example, if I have an imperfect duty to help others, then just exactly how I satisfy that duty (who I help and when I do so) is to some extent at least up to me; while if I have a perfect duty to keep my promises, then I must always keep all my promises.

egalitarianism The general view that all people should be treated equally. More specifically, the view with regard to **distributive justice** is that every person should have an equal share of income, wealth, property, and the like.

eliminativism The view that minds or mental states simply do not exist, in spite of the fact that we think they do (as, for example, one could have said that witches did not exist, even though people involved in the Salem witch trials surely thought they did). The usual eliminativist view is that mental states and properties are postulated by a plausible but ultimately unsatisfactory theory of human behavior: *folk psychology.*

entail   Premises entail a conclusion when the truth of the premises guarantees the truth of the conclusion; or equivalently, where it is not **possible** in the logical or metaphysical sense for the premises to be true and the conclusion false.

empirical   Depending on sense experience; if a claim or statement is empirical, then the justification of the claim depends on sense experience; if a question is empirical, then the correct answer to the question is determined by sense experience. (See **a priori**/*a posteriori*.)

empiricism   A view that emphasizes the cognitive role of sense experience. Concept empiricism is the view that all concepts (or ideas) are acquired by abstraction from sense experience. (Contrasting term: **innate.**) Justificatory empiricism, on the other hand, is the view that all claims (or, in some versions, all claims that are not **analytic** or mere definitional **tautologies**) must be justified by appeal to sense experience. (Contrasting term: **rationalism.**)

empiricism, concept   See **empiricism.**

empiricism, justificatory   See **empiricism.**

empiricism, moderate   The version of justificatory empiricism which holds that while there is both **a priori** and *a posteriori* (or **empirical**) justification for claims, a priori justification pertains only to claims that are **analytic** (or are **tautologies**)—so that there is no synthetic a priori justification or knowledge. (Contrasting term: **rationalism, radical empiricism.**)

empiricism, radical   The version of justificatory empiricism which holds that there is no **a priori** justification for claims of any sort—so that all justification is empirical. (Contrasting terms: **rationalism, moderate empiricism.**)

epiphenomenalism   The version of **dualism** in the philosophy of mind which holds that the body (or bodily properties) causally affects the mind (or mental properties), but that the mind does not causally affect the body. (Contrasting terms: **interactionism, parallelism.**)

epistemology   The philosophical study of the nature of knowledge and of how it is acquired and justified.

equivocation   A mistake in reasoning where a word or term has one meaning at one point in an argument and a different meaning at another point in the argument, so that the argument appears to be cogent but really is not. A simple example: all banks are next to bodies of water; the First National Bank is a bank; therefore, the First National Bank is next to some body of water.

ethical egoism   The view that morality requires only that people act so as to promote their own self-interest, instead of requiring people to act so as to promote the interest of someone else (which would be an altruistic act). (Contrasting term: **psychological egoism.**)

ethics   The philosophical study of morality: of right and wrong behavior, and especially of how people ought to behave in relation to each other.

eudaimonia   The Greek term for the most desirable state for an individual person. It is sometimes translated as "happiness" and sometimes instead as "flourishing."

evil, problem of   The objection to the existence of God (conceived as omnipotent and morally perfect) that appeals to the existence of evil and suffering in the world, and especially to the large amount of evil and suffering the world contains. As conceived, God would apparently be both able and willing to prevent evil, so why then does evil exist? (See **theodicy.**)

explanatory argument (or inference)   Sometimes called an *inference to the best explanation* or an *abductive* argument, this is a form of argument in which one concludes that something is (probably) the case because it is the *best explanation* of something else that one believes to be true. Astronomers used this kind of argument when they argued that there was a ninth planet beyond Neptune: the reasoning appealed to the fact that there are perturbations in Neptune's orbit, claimed that the best explanation for such disturbances in Neptune's orbit was the existence of another planet, and so concluded that such a planet probably exists (the one we now know as Pluto).

first cause argument An argument for the existence of God based on the claim that everything must have a cause, but that the chain of causes cannot go backward to infinity, and so there must be some first cause (which is claimed to be God).

formal Devoid of specific content, pertaining only to the form or structure of something. If the input to a computer system is formal, then the system operates only on the aspects of the input that are independent of its meaning or content (for example the shape or structure of the symbols employed).

functionalism A recent view in the philosophy of mind which identifies mental states by their causal role in relation to inputs, outputs, and other mental states. Such a definition does not require that the specific state that occupies such a causal role be material in character, or that it be immaterial, but allows it to be either. Functionalists standardly believe, however, that the states that actually occupy the causal roles in normal humans are states of the brain and so material.

hard determinism The position on the free will problem that denies the existence of free will on the grounds that freedom is incompatible with the causal determination of human actions. The most straightforward version of hard determinism asserts the truth of **causal determinism** and then concludes on this basis that freedom, being incompatible with causal determinism, does not exist. But there is a second view that is also sometimes referred to as hard determinism: this view accepts the possibility of random or chance events, but argues that randomness is also incompatible with freedom; since causal determination and randomness are the only two possibilities, this second view claims, freedom still does not exist. (Contrasting terms: **compatibilism, libertarianism.**)

hedonism The view that pleasure or happiness is the only thing that is **intrinsically good.** As this suggests, hedonists tend to regard pleasure and happiness as the same thing, but this is in fact quite dubious: pleasure is usually thought of as a kind of sensation, while happiness is a more complicated and demanding state of mind in which pleasant sensations play only a minor role at best.

hedonistic utilitarianism The version of **utilitarianism** that holds that utility is to be understood entirely in a hedonistic way, and thus in terms of pleasure or happiness. Both Jeremy Bentham and John Stuart Mill are hedonistic utilitarians. (Contrasting terms: **ideal utilitarianism, preference utilitarianism.**)

hypothetical imperative A rational requirement that derives from a want or desire that a person happens to have. For example, if you want to become a first-rate pianist, then you have a rational requirement to practice. (Contrasting term: **categorical imperative.**)

idealism The metaphysical view that that reality consists only of minds or spirits and mental contents. This means that there are no independently existing material things (so the view could also be called *immaterialism*). Instead, what common sense refers to as material objects of various kinds are nothing more than patterns of ideas or experience. See also **phenomenalism.**

ideal utilitarianism The version of **utilitarianism** that holds that utility involves many different kinds of **intrinsically good** things (and correlative bad things), not just pleasure or happiness. Knowledge is a good example of something that would be regarded as an intrinsic good by many ideal utilitarians, but that is clearly distinct from pleasure or happiness. (A further issue is whether intrinsic goods are all states of mind of one sort or another.) (Contrasting terms: **hedonistic utilitarianism, preference utilitarianism.**)

idea For Locke, whatever one is immediately aware of when one thinks. This seems to include both specific sensations or **sense-data** and general concepts.

identity theory, the The view in the philosophy of mind (one version of **materialism**) according to which any given sort of mental state is identical to exactly one kind of brain state. In contrast to **logical behaviorism,** this identity is claimed to be **contingent** and discovered by **empirical** investigation, rather than being a consequence of the meaning of mental state concepts. The identity theory is sometimes described as "type-type materialism" (or physicalism) because each type of mental state is identical with a specific type of physical state; in contrast, according to **functionalism,** a given type of mental state might be realized by different physical states in different kinds of creatures or even in different human beings ("token-token materialism," because each specific instance of a mental state is identical with some specific instance of a physical state).

ignoratio elenchi   A mistake in reasoning that involves arguing for a conclusion that is irrelevant to the original issue—also missing the point.

illusion, argument from   See **argument from illusion.**

immaterialism   See **idealism.**

imperfect duty   See **duty.**

inductive argument   The sort of argument (also called *enumerative* or *instantial* induction) that infers from many specific cases (many cases of A that are also cases of B, and perhaps also some cases of A that are not cases of B) to a general claim formulated in the same terms (where there are no exceptions, that all As are Bs; or, where there are exceptions, that some specific percentage of As are Bs). More generally, any sort of reasoning where the premises provide good but not conclusive support for the truth of the conclusion. (In this more general sense but not in the narrower one, an **explanatory argument** would be an instance of inductive reasoning.)

inference   The transition from a set of premises to a conclusion.

innate   Implanted at birth, rather than acquired through subsequent experience. An innate idea (or concept) would be one that is somehow present in a person's cognitive abilities at birth, rather than being acquired via abstraction from experience. (The contrasting view is **concept empiricism.**) Such an idea might be one that infants are actually conscious of or, more plausibly, one that needs to be activated or "triggered" by experience before emerging into consciousness—with the difference from concept of empiricism being that the triggering experience would not need to be one from which the idea in question could be derived by abstraction. Earlier proponents of innate-

ness (such as René Descartes) tended to think of innate ideas as being implanted by God, but some more recent philosophers have appealed instead to evolution.

insight, rational   See **rational insight.**

instrumental good   See **intrinsic good/instrumental good.**

intentional content   See **intentionality.**

intentionality   The general property of being *about* something that is possessed by some but not all mental states and also by language. A thought concerning polar bears is an intentional state (because it is about polar bears), whereas neither a free-floating state of anxiety nor a sensation of redness or pain is about anything. (A sensation of redness is a sensation of a certain distinctive kind, but is not in itself about anything.)

interactionism   The version of **dualism** in the philosophy of mind that holds that there is causal interaction between immaterial minds or mental states and material bodies or bodily states: that each can and does causally affect the other. (Contrasting terms: **epiphenomenalism, parallelism.**)

intrinsic good/instrumental good   Something is an intrinsic good (or has intrinsic value) if it is good in itself, good for its own sake, independently of anything else or of any further purpose; whereas something is an instrumental good if it is good as a *means* to something else. Happiness is the most obvious example of something that is intrinsically good; whereas, for all but misers, money is merely an instrumental good: it is good only for what it can get you, not for its own sake. It is possible for something to be good in both ways: knowledge is an example of something that has often claimed to be intrinsically good, but which is instrumentally good as well.

intuition, rational   See **rational insight.**

invalid   See **valid.**

justification   In epistemology, a reason or basis for thinking that some claim or view is true; in ethics, a reason to think that an action is right.

justificatory empiricism   See **empiricism, justificatory.**

knowledge The proper definition or analysis of knowledge has been a matter of ongoing controversy in recent philosophy. According to what is often referred to as "the traditional conception of knowledge," knowledge is **belief** that is both adequately **justified** and **true.** (Thus a lucky guess, even if true, does not count as knowledge.) The problem with this definition, raised by Edmund Gettier, is that there seem to be cases where all three of these conditions are satisfied, but which do not seem to be genuine cases of knowledge. Intuitively, these are cases where the belief is true, not in the way that the justification would suggest, but in some accidental or unexpected way. In perhaps the most widely discussed example, you have excellent reasons for thinking that a specific one of your coworkers (Mr. Nogot) owns a Ford automobile, and come to believe on that basis the more general claim that one of your coworkers owns a Ford. In fact, however, Nogot does not own a Ford (your evidence is somehow mistaken or misleading), but another one of your coworkers (Mr. Havit) does own a Ford—though you have no reason at all for thinking this is so. In this situation, your general belief that one of your coworkers owns a Ford seems to be both justified (by your evidence about Nogot) and true (because of Havit), but still intuitively not to be an instance of knowledge. Many solutions have been offered for this "Gettier problem," involving modifications of one of the three original conditions or else the addition of a fourth condition, but none has received general acceptance. (One thing worth noting is that the possibility of "Gettier cases" depends on the assumption that it is possible for a belief to be justified to the degree that is adequate for knowledge and still be false—this is what allows it to also be true in an accidental or unexpected way.)

libertarianism (1) In metaphysics, the position on the free will problem which holds both (a) that free will is incompatible with causal determination and (b) that free will genuinely exists (and thus that **causal determinism** is false for at least some human actions). Thus characterized, the general libertarian view is compatible with the idea that a free action is simply a random or

chance occurrence, but virtually all recent libertarians have also held that freedom is incompatible with randomness. Thus a libertarian is committed to there being a third alternative with regard to the production of human actions, one that is distinct from both causal determination and randomness. (Contrasting terms: **hard determinism, compatibilism.**) (2) In political philosophy, the view that emphasizes the importance of individual liberty and individual rights, and on this basis advocates severely limited government.

logical behaviorism See **behaviorism.**

logical positivism A philosophical movement of the early to mid-twentieth century dominated by a scientific outlook, which advocated both **moderate empiricism** and the view that only claims that can be verified by sense experience or else reduced to logical **tautologies** are meaningful.

materialism The metaphysical view (also referred to as *physicalism*) that all that exists is material, that every event, object, property, or state is entirely material, that there are no immaterial entities, aspects, or properties; in the philosophy of mind, the view that minds and mental states can be somehow reduced to or entirely accounted for in material or physical terms (so that **dualism** is false).

metaphysics The philosophical study of the ultimate nature and fundamental constituents of reality; there are metaphysical questions about, for example, the nature of space and time, the nature of causation, whether everything is material, whether human actions are free or causally determined, whether **universals** exist, and so on.

moderate empiricism See **empiricism, moderate.**

moral evil The evil caused by human actions (or, possibly, by the actions of other rational creatures such as demons or angels) instead of by natural events such as hurricanes or tornadoes (see **natural evil**).

moral nihilism The view that there are no true moral claims of any sort (and so that no action is ever morally right or morally wrong). Moral nihilism does not, of course, deny that people often make moral claims and have moral opinions; it just says that none of these claims or opinions is ever genuinely true or correct. (Contrasting terms: **moral objectivism, moral relativism.**)

moral objectivism   The view that there are at least some moral claims that are objectively true, true independently of any limited perspective or point of view (also referred to, somewhat misleadingly, as *moral absolutism*). Two possible sorts of misconception about this view are worth noting: (a) The objective moral truths need not be simple (never tell a lie), but may instead refer to circumstances in complicated ways (never tell a lie unless telling the truth will do more harm than good, and it is impossible to avoid saying something). (b) Moral objectivism does not claim that there are objective moral truths on every subject about which moral opinions have been offered; in particular, it is possible that even though moral objectivism is true, there are no objective moral truths pertaining to some or all aspects of sexual morality. (Contrasting terms: **moral nihilism, moral relativism.**)

moral relativism   The view that there are moral truths, but that moral truth is not objective, but instead is relative to the individual (different moral truths for different individuals), to the community (different moral truths for different communities), or to something else (cultures, historical epochs, etc.). (Contrasting terms: **moral nihilism, moral objectivism.**)

moral virtue   A morally valuable character trait. Examples would include such things as courage, temperance, kindness, and honesty.

naïve realism   See **direct realism.**

natural (or physical) evil   The evil caused by natural events (such as hurricanes or tornadoes), rather than by human actions (see **moral evil**). The evil resulting from diseases, birth defects, and the like also counts as natural evil as long as it is not deliberately produced by human beings.

necessary/contingent   In the strongest and most common sense (*logical* or *metaphysical* necessity), a necessary truth is a proposition that could not have been false, that is true no matter what the actual course of events in the world happens to be, that is true in any possible world or situation (and a necessary falsehood is a proposition that could not have been true); while a contingent truth is a proposition that is true but might have been false, one whose truth or falsity depends on the actual course of events in the world, one that is true in some possible worlds or situations and false in others (and a contingent falsehood is a proposition that is false but might have been true). For example, true mathematical claims (such as $2 + 2 = 4$) are necessary truths, as are the various truths of logic (such as *either today is Tuesday or today is not Tuesday*); while claims like *George W. Bush is president in 2004* or *the population of the United States is larger than the population of France* are contingent, as are most other ordinary claims about the world. Contingent *events* are events described by contingent propositions, and so events that might or might not occur. (For a related but weaker use of these terms, see **necessity, causal or nomological.**)

necessary condition/sufficient condition   If X is a necessary condition for Y, then Y cannot happen or obtain unless X happens or obtains; whereas if X is a sufficient condition of Y, then Y cannot fail to happen or obtain if X happens or obtains. For example, oxygen is a necessary condition for fire (because there can be no fire unless there is oxygen), but oxygen is not a sufficient condition for fire (because there isn't fire every time and every place where there is oxygen). Whereas having a knife driven through one's heart is a sufficient condition for death (anyone to whom this is done dies), but not a necessary condition (there are lots of other ways to die). Some conditions may be both necessary and sufficient: being an unmarried adult male is both necessary and sufficient for being a bachelor: necessary, because any bachelor must have these properties; sufficient, because these three properties are all that it takes to be a bachelor.

necessity, causal or nomological   A grade of necessity (and contingency), weaker than logical or metaphysical necessity (see **necessary/contingent**), that results from laws of nature rather than laws of logic and metaphysics. A proposition is causally or nomologically necessary if it could not have failed to be true without altering the actual laws of nature that govern the world, and thus is true in any possible world obeying those same laws of nature; while a proposition is causally or nomologically contingent if both its truth and its falsity is compatible with the actual laws of nature (and thus if it is true in some possible worlds obeying those laws of nature and false in others). The same terms are also applied to the events described by such propositions. For example, *the gravitational attraction between two bodies varies with the square of the distance between them* is causally or nomologically necessary (but not logically or metaphysically necessary, since there are possible worlds with different laws of gravitation). Whereas many ordinary claims about the world (*it is not raining today, there are pine trees in Washington state, gold is more expensive than lead,* and so on, and so on) are contingent in both the causal or nomological sense and the logical or metaphysical sense. (Anything that is logically or metaphysically necessary is also causally or nomologically necessary: if there is no possible world in which it is false, then it follows trivially that there is no possible world with the same laws of nature in which it is false.)

normative Having to do with norms or rules or standards specifying the way that something properly ought to be.

objection A reason to reject a claim or view or argument.

objectivism The view that the subject matter in question is what it is independently of what anyone believes; for example, ethical objectivism is the view that there are facts about what is morally required that don't depend on what humans happen to believe.

Ockham's (or Occam's) razor An intellectual presumption in favor of simplicity or theoretical economy (sometimes called the principle of parsimony), by which one is advised to accept only those entities genuinely required to explain or account for something. Named after William of Ockham (c. 1285–1347 A.D.), a medieval philosopher.

occasionalism See **parallelism.**

original position In John Rawls's account of justice, this is the hypothetical starting point in which people, operating behind a "veil of ignorance" with respect to their own position in society, natural talents, and other features, choose the correct principles of justice.

panpsychism The view that all of reality is in some sense made up of mental stuff, but not necessarily of human mentality, since human mentality might be just an instance of a more general type of thing. This is different from **idealism:** whereas the idealist reduces material things to patterns of experience, the panpsychist grants them an independent existence, but holds that they are in some way still ultimately psychical in character.

parallelism The version of **dualism** in the philosophy of mind which holds that there is no causal relation between immaterial minds or mental states and material bodies or bodily states in either direction, that the mental and physical realms have no causal influence at all on each other, despite seeming to interact. The main versions of parallelism explain the appearance of interaction by appeal to divine intervention, either a *preestablished harmony* established at the beginning of creation (so that mind and body are like two perfect clocks, running side by side but neither influencing the other) or constant divine intervention to keep the two realms in agreement with each other (*occasionalism*).

perfect duty See **duty.**

person For philosophers, this is not a biological category but a moral one: a person is a being (of any sort or species) that by virtue of its nature and characteristics should be accorded the sort of respect and rights ordinarily ascribed to normal adult human beings. Thus some animals might turn out to be persons, some aliens or extraterrestrials might also be persons, and some humans (for example, those in a permanent coma) may not in fact be persons.

phenomenalism A version of **idealism** which holds that the common-sense material objects of our experience (things such as tables, trees, and mountains) are really nothing more than systematic patterns of sensory experience—what John Stuart Mill calls "permanent possibilities of sensation."

phenomenal properties Those properties of mental states that have to do with the way the mental state seems or feels from the inside, determining "what it is like" to experience that mental state; the experience of a headache, for example, has a very different phenomenal property (or *quale,* plural *qualia*) from the experience of tasting a lemon, and both of these are very different from the experience of a patch of red color.

physical evil See **natural evil.**

physicalism See **materialism.**

possible A proposition is possibly true, in either the strong logical or metaphysical sense or the weaker nomological sense, if it is not **necessarily** false in the correlative sense. A situation or event is possible in one of these senses if the proposition describing it is possible in that same sense. A *possible world* is a world whose complete description is possible in one or the other of these senses (thus there are logically or metaphysically possible worlds and causally or nomologically possible worlds, with the latter being included in the former).

preestablished harmony See **parallelism.**

preference utilitarianism The version of utilitarianism which holds that utility consists in the satisfaction of preferences (so that in the act utilitarian version, the morally right action would be the one that led to the maximal amount of preference satisfaction, measured by both the number and the strength of the preferences satisfied).

premise See **argument.**

primary quality/secondary quality Primary qualities are those qualities that any object must have, no matter how much change it endures or whether it is being perceived or not: for example (according to John Locke), size (extension), shape (figure), motion, number, and solidity. A further claim is that our ideas or perceptions of primary qualities accurately depict their nature as they exist in objects. Secondary qualities, on the other hand, are mere powers (causal capacities) of the object to systematically produce ideas in us, ideas, for example of colors, sounds, tastes, and smells, so that there is no quality actually in the object like the one that is represented in our experience. Thus, for example, a ripe apple genuinely has the distinctive shape and size that we experience it to have, but it does not have any property like the red color we experience (though it does have some property—presumably some combination of the primary qualities of its surface—in virtue of which it systematically causes experiences of red in creatures like us.)

principle of sufficient reason (PSR) The metaphysical principle that for everything that happens and for everything that exists, there must be a reason or explanation or cause for it being the way that it is, instead of some other way or no way at all.

property dualism See **dualism.**

proposition An abstract object capable, in virtue of its meaning or content, of being true or false. A proposition is what is expressed by a declarative sentence, and on the most standard view, can be expressed by many different sentences from different languages; for example, the sentences "Snow is white," "Das Schnee ist weiss," and "La neige est blanche" all express the same proposition. Propositions can also be entertained in thought in various ways: believed, doubted, desired to be true, feared to be true, etc. Any act of thought that has a proposition as its object or content is called a *propositional attitude.*

psychological egoism The view that as a matter of psychological fact, a human being is capable of being motivated only by his or her own selfish interests, that humans are incapable of genuine acts of altruism (acts whose goal is to further the interest of someone else).

psychophysical laws Laws describing regular relations between mental or psychological events and material or physical events.

quale (plural qualia) See **phenomenal property.**

question-begging See **begging the question.**

radical empiricism See **empiricism, radical.**

rational insight The alleged direct or immediate grasp, without any appeal to experience, of the truth or necessity of a proposition. (Also referred to as *rational intuition.*) According to **rationalism,** such insight is the basic source of **a priori** justification and knowledge.

rational intuition See **rational insight.**

rationalism Broadly, the epistemological view that reason is a significant source or basis for knowledge (in the most extreme versions, now rarely if ever held, that it is the *only* such source or basis). As with **empiricism,** there are two main versions, one pertaining to the source of concepts and the other to the source of **justification.** A rationalist view of concept possession says that some or all concepts are **innate.** A rationalist view of justification says that some (a moderate version of rationalism) or all (an extreme version of rationalism) justification derives from **rational insight,** rather than sensory experience. Since the a priori justification of **analytic** claims does not require rational insight, this means that, in opposition to **moderate empiricism,** justificatory rationalists hold that some **synthetic** claims can be justified **a priori.**

realism A metaphysical view holding that things of some specified sort exist on their own, independently of human perceivers or knowers. Versions of realism have been held with respect to material objects, **universals,** moral properties or truths, theoretical entities in science (such as electrons), and many other categories of things. (Contrasting term, as regards material objects: **idealism.**)

reductio ad absurdum Sometimes philosophers argue against a claim by showing that it leads to a **contradiction.** For example, consider the claim that some bachelors are married; replace "bachelor" with its definition: "unmarried adult male." Now you have a contradiction: some unmarried adult male is married; or, slightly more explicitly, some individual is both unmarried and married. If you can infer a contradiction from a claim, then you have an excellent reason for rejecting that claim and affirming its denial.

reduction Sometimes philosophers will claim that entities of one kind (for example, material objects) are really nothing more than entities of some other, seemingly different kind, or some pattern or assemblage thereof (for example, sensory experiences). Where such a claim can be successfully defended as true, the entities of the first kind have been reduced to, shown to be nothing more than, the entities of the second kind. This can be valuable for reasons of simplicity or economy (see **Ockham's razor**) and also because it may avoid problems or puzzles pertaining to the entities that are reduced. Though it is very doubtful whether many of them have succeeded, many attempts at reduction have been made: material objects to sense experiences (by George Berkeley and by **phenomenalists**), **universals** to features of language use, theoretical entities in science (such as electrons) to patterns of observation, mental states to material states or processes of various kinds (by the various versions of **materialism**), and others. (Contrasting term: **realism.**)

representative realism (also called indirect realism) The view (held by René Descartes, John Locke, and others) that external material objects are not directly or immediately perceived, but instead that our experience of such objects is mediated by an experience of mental entities or states (called "ideas" by earlier philosophers and "sense-data" by more recent ones) which (a) are caused by material objects and (b) represent or depict or resemble them. Our knowledge of the external material world is then the result of an inference starting from the character of our ideas or sense-data and concluding with beliefs about external objects.

rights In the most important sense, for a person to have a right is for there to be *claim* of some sort that some or all others have a correlative moral or legal **duty** to honor (depending on whether the right is a moral right or a legal right). Thus to have a legal right to payment for goods of some sort that have been delivered is to have a claim for payment that someone else (presumably the receiver of the goods) has a legal duty to honor. And to have a moral right not to be killed is to have a claim that one not be killed that others (in this case, normally all others) have a moral duty to honor.

rule utilitarianism   See **utilitarianism.**

secondary quality   See **primary quality/secondary quality.**

self-evident   The property a **proposition** has when its very content provides a compelling reason to think that it is true. Once one understands a self-evident proposition, one can see clearly that it must be true, and that seeing constitutes a good reason for believing it. Self-evident propositions are the alleged objects of **rational insight.**

semantics   The meaning or reference of words and also of larger linguistic structures like sentences or whole theories; also sometimes applied to concepts and to acts of thought. Semantical theory is the systematic study of such meaning and the principles that govern it. (Contrasting term: **syntax.**)

sense-data   (singular: sense-datum) The direct or immediate objects of awareness in sense experience, according to those who reject **direct realism** on the basis of arguments like the **argument from illusion.** John Locke and George Berkeley speak instead of **ideas,** or more specifically of ideas of perception. Sense-data are usually viewed as mental entities, but some philosophers have regarded them as in themselves neither mental nor material (though the objects of mental acts of awareness or apprehension)

skepticism   The view that knowledge is unattainable. One can be a skeptic about knowledge generally or only with respect to knowledge in some limited domain (for example, a skeptic about God's existence or about morality).

soft determinism   See **compatibilism.**

solipsism   The view that the only things that exist are the mind and the experiences of a single person, the one from whose point of view the claim is formulated. Solipsism is not really a view that anyone advocates (to whom would they advocate it?), but instead a pitfall into which philosophers sometimes fall by advocating other, more general views that lead to it.

substance   Something capable of independent existence, as contrasted with properties or relations, which exist only in substances. Thus, for example, a material object like a table would be a substance, while properties (like its color) or relations in which it stands to other substances (like being next to several chairs) would not be. The term is also used to refer to the supposed ingredient in a substance that is distinct from all its properties (and relations) and in some way underlies or supports them (*substratum* is another term for this latter notion).

sufficient condition   See **necessary condition/ sufficient condition.**

syntax   The formal structural relations among words and larger linguistic structures; also the rules (such as rules of grammar) that govern such relations. A person who knew all the rules of French grammar (and so could construct and identify grammatically correct French sentences), but did not understand the meanings of any French words (and so could not understand or translate any of those sentences) would know the syntax of French but not its **semantics.** (Contrasting term: **semantics.**)

synthetic   See **analytic/synthetic.**

tabula rasa   Literally, blank tablet; John Locke held the view that our minds are like blank tablets when we are born, and that experience provides the content or ideas that we subsequently use to think.

tautology   Originally a proposition that is true by virtue of trivial repetition (such as *tall men are tall*). More generally, a sentence that is true in this trivial way or whose denial is either contradictory or leads immediately to a contradiction (such as *either it is raining or it is not raining*). Sometimes the term is construed so broadly as to include all **analytic** truths, but more commonly it is limited to those that are especially obvious and/or trivial.

theism/atheism/agnosticism   Theism is the view that God does exist, while atheism is the view that God does not exist. Agnosticism is the view that it is *seriously* uncertain whether or not God exists— that the reasons or evidence on each side are quite closely balanced, so that we cannot know whether or not such a being exists and don't have enough evidence one way or the other to hold either belief responsibly. (In earlier times, the term "agnostic" was sometimes used to describe anyone who has any doubt at all that God exists, whether or not such a person thinks that the evidence is closely balanced—thus many who were so described are better regarded as atheists.)

theodicy An attempt to explain how and why the existence of evil in the world is compatible with the existence of an all-powerful and morally perfect God.

truth The metaphysical relation in which a proposition or claim that is accurate or correct stands to reality. This is most naturally taken to involve a relation of correspondence or agreement or accordance between the content of the proposition or claim and the corresponding part of reality (the *correspondence theory of truth*). But alleged problems with the correspondence theory have led some philosophers to propose various other accounts of truth, such as the *coherence theory of truth* (for a proposition to be true is for it to fit together with other propositions in such a way as to make up a tightly unified and cohesive system), various *pragmatic theories of truth* (for a proposition to be true is for it to lead to practical success of some specified sort when believed or applied), and others.

Turing machine Not a physical machine, but instead an abstract specification of a machine (invented by A.M. Turing). Such a machine has the capacity to scan a tape divided into squares, erase what is in a given square, print something in an empty square, move left or right on the tape, and change its own inner "logical state," with what it actually does at a given point being determined, according to a machine table or program, by what is on the square it is scanning and the logical state it is in. The idea of a Turing machine is in effect the most general specification of a computer and can do anything that any computer can do, if given enough time and enough memory (that is, a large enough tape).

universal An **abstract** property or feature, such as redness or triangularity or justice. Philosophers have disputed whether universals (a) exist independently of the **concrete** things (particulars) that are instances of such properties (*Platonic realism,* the view held by Plato), (b) exist only in their instances (*Aristotelian realism,* the view held by Aristotle), (c) exist only in the minds of people who conceive of them (*conceptualism*), or (d) do not really exist at all, but are merely an illusion created by the use of words (*nominalism*).

utilitarianism The moral theory that the rightness of an action depends only on the goodness or badness of its consequences (this is its *utility*). According to *act utilitarianism,* the morally right action is the one out of the available alternatives that leads to the greatest overall utility, computed by adding up the good consequences and subtracting the bad ones. According to *rule utilitarianism,* the right action is the one prescribed by the set of moral rules whose adoption would lead to greater utility than that which would result from the adoption of any other set of rules. Different versions of utilitarianism construe the goodness or badness of consequences in different ways: see **hedonistic utilitarianism, ideal utilitarianism,** and **preference utilitarianism.**)

valid An argument is valid if it is impossible for the premises of the argument to be true while the conclusion of the argument is false. Any argument whose conclusion could be false even though its premises are true is *invalid.*

veil of ignorance See **original position.**

Credits

Page 134: "The Will to Believe," William James, 1896. This essay was originally an address delivered before the Philosophical Clubs of Yale and Brown Universities.

Page 149: René Descartes, *Meditations on First Philosophy*, trans. by Donald Cress, 3rd ed., Hackett Publishing Company, Inc. © 1993 Hackett Publishing Company, Inc. Reprinted by permission of Hackett Publishing Company, Inc. All rights reserved.

Page 174: John Locke, *An Essay Concerning Human Understanding*, 1689.

Page 192: George Berkeley, *Three Dialogues Between Hylas and Philonous In Opposition to Sceptics and Atheists*, 1713.

Page 222: Thomas Reid, *Essays on the Intellectual Powers of Man*, 1814 and 1815.

Page 239: Laurence BonJour, "Knowledge of the External World," from *Epistemology: Classic Problems and Contemporary Responses*, Rowman & Littlefield, 2002, pp. 129–161. Reprinted by permission.

Page 258: Immanuel Kant, *Introduction to The Critique of Pure Reason*, translated by Norman Kemp Smith, (London: Macmillan Press Ltd., 1933), pp. 41–58. Reproduced with permission of Palgrave MacMillan.

Page 267: "The A Priori," A.J. Ayer, from *Language, Truth and Logic*, 2nd ed., Dover, 1952; originally published by Gollantz, 1946. Reprinted by permission of Dover Publications, Inc.

Page 275: "The 'A Priori' and the Empirical," A.C. Ewing, from *The Fundamental Questions of Philosophy*, 1962, Routledge. Reprinted by permission of the publisher.

Page 284: "Sceptical Doubts Concerning The Operations of the Understanding," David Hume, *An Enquiry Concerning Human Understanding*, 1748.

Page 291: From *The Foundations of Scientific Inference*, by Wesley Salmon, © 1967 by University of Pittsburgh Press. Reprinted by permission of the University of Pittsburgh Press.

Page 315: From *Body and Mind* by Keith Campbell, copyright © 1970, 1984 by Keith Campbell. Used by permission of Doubleday, a division of Random House, Inc.

Page 327: John Foster, "A Defense of Dualism," from *The Case of Dualism*, John R. Smylines and John Beloff (eds.), University Press of Virginia, 1989. Reprinted by permission of the publisher.

Page 334: J.J.C. Smart, "Sensations and Brain Processes," from *The Philosophy of Mind*, V.C. Chappell, ed., Englewood Cliffs: Prentice-Hall, Inc., 1962. This article originally appeared in the April 1959 issue of *Philosophical Review*.

Page 341: Jerry Fodor, "The Mind-Body Problem," *Scientific American*, (Jan. 1981), pp. 114–120, 122, 123. Reprinted with permission. Copyright © 1981 by Scientific American, Inc. All rights reserved.

Page 354: A.M. Turing, "Computing Machinery and Intelligence," *Mind*, Vol. LIX, No. 236, 1950, pp. 433–460. Used by permission of Oxford University Press.

Page 366: John Searle, "Is the Brain's Mind a Computer Program?" *Scientific American*, Vol. 262, Jan. 1990, pp. 26–31. Reprinted with permission. Copyright © 1990 by Scientific American, Inc. All rights reserved.

Page 375: "Searle on What Only Brains Can Do," J.A. Fodor, from *Behavioral and Brain Sciences* III, 3 (September 1980): 431–432 and "Author's Response," John R. Searle, from *Behavioral and Brain Sciences* III, 3 (September 1980): 450–456. Reprinted with the permission of Cambridge University Press.

Page 381: Thomas Nagel, "What Is It Like to Be a Bat?" *Philosophical Review*, vol. 83, (1974), pp. 435–449.

Page 391: "What Mary Didn't Know," Frank Jackson, from *The Journal of Philosophy* LXXX111, 5 (May 1986):291–95. Reprinted by permission of The Journal of Philosophy and Frank Jackson.

Page 405: David Lewis, "Knowing What It's Like," from *Philosophical Papers* Vol. 1, Oxford University Press, where it appears as a Postscript to "Mad Pain and Martian Pain," Oxford University Press, 1983, pp. 394–395. Reprinted by permission.

Page 407: David Chalmers, "The Puzzle of Conscious Experience," *Scientific American*, December 1985, pp. 80–86. Reprinted by permission of David Chalmers.